CRIMINAL LAW:
TEXT AND MATERIALS

AUSTRALIA
The Law Book Company
Sydney

CANADA
The Carswell Company Ltd
Toronto, Ontario

INDIA
N. M. Tripathi (Private) Ltd
Bombay

Eastern Law House (Private) Ltd
Calcutta

M.P.P. House
Bangalore

Universal Book Traders
New Dehli

ISRAEL
Steimatzky's Agency Ltd
Tel Aviv

PAKISTAN
Pakistan Law House
Karachi

CRIMINAL LAW:
TEXT AND MATERIALS

Second Edition

by

C. M. V. CLARKSON, B.A., LL.B., LL.M.
Lecturer in Law, University of Bristol

H. M. KEATING, LL.M.
Lecturer in Law, University of Sussex
Former Senior Lecturer in Law, Kingston Polytechnic

LONDON
SWEET & MAXWELL
1990

Published in 1990 by
Sweet & Maxwell Limited of
South Quay Plaza,
183 Marsh Wall, London E14 9FT
Computerset by
Promenade Graphics Ltd., Cheltenham
Printed and bound in Great Britain by
BPCC Hazell Books
Aylesbury, Bucks, England
Member of BPCC Ltd.

First Edition 1984
Reprinted 1986
Reprinted 1988
Second Edition 1990
Reprinted 1991

British Library Catologuing in Publication Data
Clarkson, C. M. V. (Christopher, M.).
    Criminal Law: text and materials.—2nd. ed.
    1. England. Criminal Law
    I. Title   II. Keating, H. M. (Heather M.).
    344.205

ISBN 0–421–39270–3

PREFACE

The aim of this book is to examine the main principles and rules of the criminal law and to expose the theoretical bases upon which they are founded.

The criminal law is inextricably linked to issues of moral philosophy, criminology and the punishment of offenders. Fletcher has stated that "the criminal law should express the way we live." It is a reflection of community values aimed at isolating the blameworthy who are deserving of punishment. Equally, it is a means of social control; it attempts to uphold, as well as reflect, these community values; it sets a standard, albeit at times a minimal one, of necessary compliance. In short, it is a set of moral commandments that are backed up by the legal threat of punishment. It thus follows that whether sanctions are imposed on the basis of desert or on utilitarian grounds, the rules of the criminal law and the punishment of offenders are the two sides of the same coin. A whole range of substantive issues—such as, whether "recklessness" should include "inadvertence," whether one can justify the existence of offences of "strict liability," how the boundaries of the law of "attempt" and "accessorial" crime should be drawn, and so on—are, in reality, issues relating to the justification of punishment in such cases. A true appreciation of the substantive criminal law must thus involve some understanding of the rationale of punishment and why conduct is criminalised—and it is in this context that we have sought to present the main rules of the law.

Like most other works in this field, this is a book on the actual rules of the criminal law. We have attempted to provide a full analysis of these main rules on the topics covered. But, in doing this, we have attempted the more ambitious task of using the law to extract, and develop, some fundamental ideas underlying the law. We have tried to explore, in the context of punishment, such issues as: the relationship between blame and harm, the criteria for identifying the blameworthy, the structure of offences in relation to each other and the role of the general defences. In short, we have attempted to subject the criminal law to the beginnings of a philosophical analysis that can throw some light on the substantive rules. We have also attempted to unite some of the common themes and, in our concluding chapter, have formulated some tentative proposals for a general theory of criminal liability.

The criminal law changes with great rapidity and therefore this book has been substantially rewritten and updated for the second edition. This is particularly the case for those sections of the book dealing with intention, murder, manslaughter, causing death by reckless driving, the *mens rea* of attempt, aiding and abetting, self-defence, duress and necessity.

However, it is in two other respects that this book differs mostly from the first edition. First, the amount of sociological or criminological material has been significantly increased. All the major offences have now been introduced in their social context. This has not been done at the expense of the substantive rules—but in the hope of rendering those rules more easily explicable. Secondly, this second edition includes a chapter on the major property offences. The omission of such offences from the first edition was the major criticism in the reviews of that edition—and persuaded us that, having clearly established in that first edition what the object of the book was and how it differed from other books in the field, such property offences should be included in this edition. Also, our publishers were generously prepared to be more indulgent with their word limit in this second edition—meaning that property offences could be included but without any sacrifice to the basic discursive, "in context" style adopted throughout. Indeed, this chapter has now become central to the coherence of the book and we now readily and happily concede that an examination of the underlying rationale and purposes of this area of law is crucial for an understanding of the criminal law as a whole.

We have been anxious to ensure that this book be accessible to, and easily digestible by, undergraduate and other students concerned with criminal law. We have approached our task, and included appropriate materials, with this concern very much in mind. We have tried to cover the range of competing views and present them in a discursive manner allowing the reader to make choices—while not being afraid to state our own preferences.

A brief word about the format of this book is necessary. It is neither a straight "textbook," nor a "cases and materials" book. Instead, we have tried to combine what we regard as the best features of both such styles—a book with the flow and coherence of a textbook thus providing the reader with guidance and direction, but one that also enables a substantial amount of original material from a diversity of sources to be absorbed.

We are very grateful to our publishers for their kindness, help and patience during the preparation of this book. We are also especially grateful to Mark Entwisle for agreeing to paint the picture appearing on the cover of this book.

Chris Clarkson would like to thank David Smith and Malik Ali for their help with research. But most of all, his thanks go to his wife, Barbara, for all her help with proof-reading and for the love, support and understanding shown throughout this project. His share of this book is dedicated to her and to his children, Cathy and Nicky.

Heather Keating would like to thank Sarah Geering and Anne-Marie Price for their assistance in proof-reading. She would also like to express her gratitude to all her colleagues at Kingston Polytechnic who have supported her during her time at the Law School there. But, more than ever, she would like to say how very much she appreciates the help given and love and understanding shown by her husband, Barry. Her share of the book is dedicated to him and to her children, Matthew, Alice and Elizabeth.

C. M. V. CLARKSON
H. M. KEATING

June 1990

CONTENTS

ACKNOWLEDGMENTS

Grateful acknowledgment is made to the following authors and publishers for permission to quote from their works:

ADLER, Z.: "Rape—the Intention of Parliament and the Practice of the Courts" (1982) 45 M.L.R. 664

ALEXANDER, F. and STAUB, H.: *The Criminal, The Judge and the Public* (1956) pp. 212, 213. Reprinted with permission of the Free Press, a Division of Macmillan, Inc. Copyright© 1957 by the Free Press, copyright renewed 1985 by Anita Alexander

AMIR, M.: "Patterns in Forcible Rape". Federal Probation (1967) 51

ANDENAES, J.: "General Prevention" (1952) 43 J. Crim. L., C. & P.S. 176. Reprinted by special permission of Northwestern University, School of Law, Vol. 43, Journal of Criminal Law and Criminology 1952.

——: *The Morality of Deterrence*© 1970 by the University of Chicago. Reprinted by permission from 37 U. Chi. L. Rev. 649 (1970)

——: "The General Preventive Effects of Punishment" (1966) 114 U. Pa. L. Rev. 949, 960–970

ASHWORTH, A.: *Sentencing and Penal Policy* (1983 Weidenfeld & Nicolson)

——: "Criminal Attempts and the Role of Resulting Harm under the Code, and in the Common Law" (1988) Rutgers Law Journal© Rutgers University Press

——: "Belief, Intent and Criminal Liability" in J. Eekelaar and J. Bell *Oxford Essays in Jurisprudence* (1987) Oxford University Press

——: "Intoxication and General Defences" [1980] Crim.L.R. 556

——: *Custody Reconsidered* (1989) (Centre for Policy Studies, Study No. 104) Policy Studies Institute

BENTHAM, J.: "An Introduction to the Principles of Morals and Legislation" in Bentham and Mill, *The Utilitarians* (1961)© Oxford University Press

BLOM-COOPER, L.: "Criminal Law that leaves Children at Risk" *The Independent*, August 7, 1989

BOTTOMS, A.E.: "An Introduction to 'The Coming Crisis' " in A. E. Bottoms and R. H. Preston, *The Coming Penal Crisis* (1980) Reprinted by permission of Scottish Academic Press Ltd.

BOX, S.: *Power, Crime and Mystification* 1983 Routledge

BRADY, J.B.: "Recklessness, Negligence, Indifference and Awareness" (1980) 43 M.L.R. 381

——: "Punishing Attempts" 1980 63 *The Monist*, 246, 247–250, 255. © 1979 *The Monist*, La Salle, Illinois 61301. Reprinted by permission.

——: "Strict Liability Offenses: A Justification". Reprinted by permission from the Criminal Law Bulletin, Volume 8, Number 3

April, 1972. Copyright© 1972, Warren Gorham & Lamont Inc., 210 South Street, Boston, Mass. All Rights Reserved

BUTTERWORTH LAW PUBLISHERS LTD.: All England Law Reports; extracts from various other publications

CARDOZO, B.N.: "What Medicine Can Do For Law" (from *Law and Literature*) Publishers, Harcourt Brace Jovanovich, Inc., New York

CLARKSON, C.M.V.: *Understanding Criminal Law* (1987). Reprinted by permission of Collins

COHEN, MORRIS R.: "Moral Aspects of the Criminal Law". Reprinted by permission of the Yale Law Journal Company and Fred B. Rothman & Company from the Yale Law Journal, (1940) Vol. 49, pp. 987, 1012–1014

CONKLIN, J.E.: *Criminology*. Reprinted with permission of Macmillan. Copyright© 1981 by John E. Conklin

DAVIS, M.: "Why Attempts Deserve less Punishment than Complete Crimes" 5 Law and Philosophy 1986. Reprinted by permission of Kluwer Academic Publishers

DESSIAN, G.H.: "Justice After Conviction" (1951) 25 Connecticut Bar Journal, Copyright© Connecticut Bar Association

DEVLIN, Patrick: *The Enforcement of Morals*© (1968, Oxford University Press) pp. 7–8, 14–17. Reprinted by permission of Oxford University Press

DOMINION LAW REPORTS: Extract from *R* v. *City of Sault Ste. Marie* (1978) 85 D.L.R. (3d) 161. Reproduced with the permission of Canada Law Book Inc., 240 Edward St., Aurora Ontario, Canada L4G 3S9

DUFF, R.A.: "Intentions, Legal and Philosophical" (1989) 9 Oxford Journal of Legal Studies. Oxford University Press

EDWARDS, J.: "Automatism and Criminal Responsibility" (1958) 21 M.L.R. 375

EWING, A.C.: "A Study of Punishment II: Punishment as Viewed by the Philosopher" (1943) 21 Canadian Bar Review

FARRIER, M.D.: "The Distinction between Murder and Manslaughter in its Procedural Context" (1976) 39 M.L.R. 414

FEINBERG, Joel: "The Expressive Function of Punishment" (1965) Vol. 49, No. 3, *The Monist*, 397–423© 1965. *The Monist*, La Salle, Illinois 61301. Reprinted by permission
Harmless Wrongdoing (The Moral Limits of the Criminal Law Vol. 4) (1988)

FINE, R.P. and COHEN, G.M.: "Is Criminal Negligence a Defensible Basis for Penal Liability" (1967) 16 Buffalo L. Rev. 749. Copyright© by Buffalo Law Review

FINNIS, J.: "The Restoration of Retribution" (1971) Analysis. Basil Blackwell

FLETCHER, G.P.: *Rethinking Criminal Law* (1978, Reprinted by permission of Little, Brown & Co., Boston)
——: "The Theory of Criminal Negligence: A Comparative Analysis" (1971) 119 U. Pa. L. Rev. 401, 415–418

FLOUD, J.: "Dangerousness and Criminal Justice" (1982) 22 Brit. J. Criminol. 213 Oxford University Press

FRANKLIN, R.L.: *Freewill and Determinism* (1968, Routledge & Kegan Paul Ltd. Published by Humanities Press Inc. in the U.S.A.)

GARDINER, G.: "The Purposes of Criminal Punishment" (1958) 21 M.L.R. 117

GERBER, R.J. and MCANANY, P.D.: "Punishment: Current Survey of Philosophy and Law" (1967) 11 St. Louis U.L.J. 491

GOLDSTEIN, A.: *The Insanity Defense* (1967) Published by the Yale University Press© Yale University Press

——: "Conspiracy to Defraud the United States". Reprinted by permission of The Yale Law Journal Company and Fred B. Rothman & Company from The Yale Law Journal, Vol. 68, pp. 405–463

GOLDSTEIN, J.J. and KATZ, J.: "Abolish the Insanity Defense—Why Not?" Reprinted by permission of the Yale Law Journal Company and Fred B. Rothman & Company from The Yale Law Journal (1963) Vol. 72, pp. 853–876

GROSS, HYMAN: *A Theory of Criminal Justice* (1979)

HART, H.L.A. "Immorality and Treason", 62 *Listener* 162–163 (July 30, 1959)

——: *Punishment and Responsibility, Essays in the Philosophy of Law* (1968,© Oxford University Press) pp. 11–13, 21–24, 101–102, 119–122, 131, 152–156, 183. Reprinted by permission of Oxford University Press

HART, H.L.A. and HONORÉ, A.M.: *Causation in the Law* (2nd ed. 1985) © Oxford University Press 1959. Reprinted with permission by Oxford University Press

HENDERSON, D. and GILLESPIE, R.D.: *Textbook of Psychiatry for Students and Practitioners* revised by Ivor R. C. Batchelor (17th ed., 1950 pp. 125, 191. Reprinted by permission of Oxford University Press

HER MAJESTY'S STATIONERY OFFICE: Various extracts reprinted with permission of the Controller, HMSO

——: M. Hough and P. Mayhew Taking Account of Crime: Key Findings from the 1984 British Crime Survey 1985 H.O.R.S. No. 85

von HIRSCH, A.: *Doing Justice—The Choice of Punishments (Report of the Committee for the Study of Incarceration)* Copyright© 1976 by Andrew von Hirsch. Reprinted by permission of Hill and Wang, a division of Farrar, Strauss and Giroux, Inc.

——: *Past or Future Crimes: Deservedness and Dangerousness in the Sentencing of Criminals* (Crime, Law and Deviance Series)© 1985, Rutgers, The State University, reprinted by permission of Rutgers University Press

HONORÉ, A.M.: "Responsibility and Luck" (1988) 104 L.Q.R. 530

HUGHES, G.: "Criminal Omissions". Reprinted by permission of The Yale Law Journal Company and Fred B. Rothman & Company from The Yale Law Journal (1958) Vol. 67, pp. 590, 626, 634

———: "Morals and the Criminal Law". Reprinted by permission of The
    Yale Law Journal Company and Fred B. Rothman and Company
    from The Yale Law Journal (1962) Vol. 71, pp. 662 at pp. 676–678
THE INCORPORATED COUNCIL OF LAW REPORTING FOR ENGLAND AND
    WALES: Weekly Law Reports
———: The Independent: Extract from Law Report January 31, 1990
JACOBS, F.: Criminal Responsibility (1971) George Weidenfeld and
    Nicholson Ltd.
JOHNSON, P.: "The Unnecessary Crime of Conspiracy", 61 Cal. L.R. 1137
    at 1157 (1973). Copyright© 1973, California Law Review, Inc.,
    Reprinted by permission
KADISH, S H.: "The Crisis of Over-criminalization, (1967) Vol. 374 of
    The Annals.© 1967 The American Academy of Political and Social
    Science
KATZ, L.: *Bad Acts and Guilty Minds* (1987) The University of Chicago Press
KADISH, S.H. and PAULSEN, M.G.: *Criminal Law and Its Processes* (1969,
    Little, Brown & Co., Boston)
KAPLAN, J.: "The Role of the Law in Drug Control" (1971) Duke Law
    Journal Copyright© (1971) J. Kaplan. Published by Duke University
    School of Law
KENNY, A.: *Freewill and Responsibility* (1978) Routledge
LACEY, N.: State Punishment: Political Principles and Community
    Values (1988) Routledge
LaFAVE and SCOTT Jnr.: *Criminal Law* (2nd ed. 1986) with permission of
    the West Publishing Company
LANHAM, D.: "Accomplices, Principals and Causation" (1980) 12
    Melbourne University Law Review 490
———: "Accomplices and Transferred Malice" (1980) 96 L.Q.R. 110
———: "Larsonneur Revisited" [1976] Crim.L.R. 276
LAWSON, F.H. and Rudden, B.: The Law of Property (1982) Clarendon
    Law Series. Reprinted by permission of Oxford University Press
LEAVENS, A.: "A Causation Approach to Criminal Omissions" (1988) 76
    Cal. L.R. 547, California Law Review Inc. Reprinted by permission
LEIGH, L.H.: (With assistance of Susannah Brown) "Crimes in Bank-
    ruptcy" in L.H. Leigh ed. *Economic Crime in Europe* (1980).
    Reprinted with permission of Macmillan
LEWIS, C.S.: "The Humanitarian Theory of Punishment". Res Judicatae
    VI (1953), 224 Melbourne University Law Review
LLOYD-BOSTOCK, S.: "The Ordinary Man, and the Psychology of Attri-
    buting Causes and Responsibility" (1979) 42 M.L.R. 143
MANDIL, D.M.: "Chance, Freedom, and Criminal Liability". Copyright
    © 1987 by the Directors of the Columbia Law Review Association
    Inc. the rights reserved. This article originally appeared at 87
    Colum. L. Rev. 125. Reprinted by permission.
MODEL PENAL CODE: Extracts from Tentative Drafts Nos. 1 (1953), 4
    (1955), 8 (1958), 9 (1959) and Model Penal Code (1962). © American

Law Institute. Reprinted with permission of the American Law Institute

MORAWETZ, T.H.: *The Philosophy of Law: An Introduction.* Reprinted with permission of Macmillan. Copyright© 1980 by Thomas H. Morawetz

MORRIS, A.: *Women, Crime and Criminal Justice* (1987) Basil Blackwell

MORRIS, N.: "Somnambulistic Homicide, Ghosts, Spiders and North Koreans". Res Judicatae (1951) p. 29. Pub. University of Chicago. © Copyright 1951 by the Melbourne University Law Review Association and each author with respect to his or her contribution. All rights by all media reserved

——: *Madness and the Criminal Law*©1982 by The University of Chicago pp. 31–32, 61–64, All rights reserved

MORRIS, N. and HOWARD, C.: *Studies in Criminal Law©* Oxford University Press 1964, pp. 175–176, 199. Reprinted with permission by Oxford University Press

MORRIS, N. and BLOM-COOPER: *A Calender of Murder.* Published by Michael Joseph Ltd.© Dr. Terence Morris and Louis Blom-Cooper 1964

MORSE, S.J.: "Retaining a Modified Insanity Defense" (1985) The Annals.© 1985. The American Academy of Political and Social Science

MURPHY, D.J.I.: *Customers and Thieves—An Ethnography of Shoplifting* (1986). Reprinted by permission of Gower Publishing Co.

NEMERSON, S.: "Criminal Liability without Fault: A Philosophical Perspective". The Columbia Law Review Association. Reprinted by permission

NEW ZEALAND COUNCIL OF LAW REPORTING: Extract from New Zealand Law Reports

NOTE: "The Conspiracy Dilemma: Prosecution of Group Crimes or Protection of Individual Defendants" 62 Harv. L.R. 276. Copyright© 1948 by the Harvard Law Review Association

NOTE: "Why do Criminal Attempts Fail? A New Defense". The Yale Law Journal Company and Fred B. Rothman and Company from The Yale Law Journal (1960) Vol. 70 p. 160 at pp. 166–167

PACKER, H.: "Mens Rea and the Supreme Court" (1962) Supreme Court Rev. 107 at 109

—— H.L.: *The Limits of The Criminal Sanction.* Reprinted with the permission of the publishers, Stanford University Press, © 1968 by Herbert L. Packer

PEASE, K.: "Sentencing and Measurement: Some Analogies from Psychology" in *Sentencing Reforms* (1987) eds. K. Pease and M. Wasik. Reprinted by permission of Manchester University Press

PEASE, K. and FITZMAURICE, C.: *The Psychology of Judicial Sentencing* (1986). Reprinted by permission of Manchester University Press

PICKARD, T.: "Culpable Mistakes and Rape", 30 University of Toronto Law Journal 75

ROBINSON, P.: "Criminal Law Defences: A Systematic Analysis".

ROSENHAN, D.L.: "On Being Sane in Insane Places". *Science* (1973) Vol. 199, pp. 250–258. Copyright (1973) by the American Association for the Advancement of Science

SELLERS, J.: "Mens Rea and the Judicial Approach to 'Bad Excuses' in the Criminal Law" (1978) 41 M.L.R. 245

SELLIN, T.: "The Law and Some Aspects of Criminal Conduct." *Aims and Methods of Legal Research* (1955) pp. 113, 119–120

SILBER, J.R.: "Being and Doing" 35 Univ. of Chicago L.R. 47 at 61, 62, 90

SIMPSON, A.W.B.: "The Butler Committee's Report: The Legal Aspects" (1976) 16 Brit. J. Criminol. Oxford University Press

STEVENS & SONS LTD.: Extracts from Law Quarterly Review

SULLIVAN, G.R.: "Aiding and Abetting the Commission of a Non-Existent Offence" (1976) 39 M.L.R. 350

SWEET & MAXWELL LTD.: Extracts from Criminal Law Review and various other publications

SZASZ, T.: "The Myth of Mental Illness" (1960) 15 American Psychologist. Copyright 1960 by the American Psychological Association. Adapted by permission of the author and publisher

——: "Psychiatry, Ethics and the Criminal Law". Copyright© 1983 by the Directors of the Columbia Law Review Association Inc. All rights reserved. This Article originally appeared at (1958) 58 Col.L.R. 183 at 190. Reprinted by permission

TARLING, R. and WEATHERITT, M.: Home Office Research Study No. 56, Sentencing Practice in Magistrates' Courts (1979), H.M.S.O. Reproduced with the permission of the Controller of Her Majesty's Stationery Office

TEMPKIN, J.: "Impossible Attempts—Another View" (1976) 39 M.L.R. 55

THOMAS, D.A.: *The Justice Model of Sentencing—Its Implications for the English Sentencing System* (from the University of Cambridge, Institute of Criminology (Occasional Papers No. 8), The Future of Sentencing (1982)

——: The Times, Extract from Law Report. October 10, 1987. Copyright© Times Newspapers Ltd. 1987

VELTFORD, H. and LEE, G.: "The Coconut Grove," American Psychological Association

WALKER, N.: *Sentencing In a Rational Society* (1972, Penguin Books) p. 117. Copyright© Nigel Walker 1969, 1972. Reprinted by permission of Penguin Books Ltd.

WASIK, M.: "Partial Excuses in The Criminal Law" (1982) 45 M.L.R. 516

WECHSLER, Prof. H.: "The Challenge of the Model Penal Code". 65 Harv. L.R. 1097, pp. 1106–1107 Copyright© 1951–1952 by the Harvard Law Review Association

WECHSLER, H. and MICHAEL, J.: "A Rationale of the Law of Homicide". Copyright© 1983 by the Directors of the Columbia Law Review Association, Inc. All rights reserved. This Article originally appeared at 37 (1937) Col. L.R. 701. Reprinted by permission

WECHSLER, H., JONES, W. and KAHN, H.: "The Treatment of Inchoate Crime". Copyright© 1983 by the Directors of the Columbia Law Review Association, Inc. All rights reserved. This Article originally appeared at 61 Col. L.R. 571 1961. Reprinted by permission

WEIHOFEN, H.: National Probation and Parole Association News. Vol. 39 (1960) pp. 1 and 4. Copyright 1960 by Sage Publications. Reprinted by permission of Sage Publications, Inc.

WHITE, R.W.: *The Abnormal Personality* Ed. pp. 203–205, 288. Copyright© 1948 Ronald Press Co. Reprinted by permission of John Wiley and Sons, Inc.

WILLIAMS, Glanville: "Recklessness Redefined" (1982) C.L.J. 252 (Publishers Cambridge Law Journal, Cambridge University Press)

——: "Finis for Novus Actus"? 1989 C.L.J. 391 (Publishers Cambridge Law Journal, Cambridge University Press)

——: *Textbook of Criminal Law* (2nd ed., 1983, Stevens & Sons)

——: "Divergent Interpretations of Recklessness" (1982) 132 New L.J. 289© Glanville Williams (Butterworths)

WOLFGANG, M.E.: "Victim—Precipitated Homicide" 1957 48 J. Crim. L., C. & P.S. 2–3. Reprinted by special permission of Northwestern University, School of Law, Vol. 48, Journal of Criminal Law and Criminology, 1957

WOOTTON, Lady B.: *Crime and Penal Policy, Reflections on Fifty Years Experience* (2nd ed., 1981 George Allen & Unwin (Publishers) Ltd.)

——: *Crime and The Criminal Law* (2nd ed. 1981 Stevens and Sons Ltd.)

ZEITLIN L.: "A Little Larceny can do a lot for Employee Morale". Reprinted with permission from Psychology Today Magazine. Copyright© 1971 (PT Partners, L.P.)

TABLE OF CASES

TABLE OF STATUTES

xlii

TABLE OF STATUTORY INSTRUMENTS

CHAPTER 1

CRIME AND PUNISHMENT

I Punishment

A. Introduction

Any attempt to understand the rules of criminal law must involve some understanding of the function of those rules. It would of course be possible simply to list the rules relating to various offences, *e.g.* murder, rape, and attempt, but such a stark analysis would not be particularly helpful or illuminating. The student of criminal law must be in a position to evaluate such rules and answer questions such as: Why do we regard murder as more serious than manslaughter, when after all in both cases the victim has been killed? What difference does it make how or by whom he was killed? In rape does/should it make any difference whether the "rapist" believed his victim was consenting? Why do we hold someone liable for attempted murder if he has not caused any harm to his victim, because, say, his gun was defective and could never have injured anyone? Should such a person be held liable? These and numerous other fundamental questions that will be posed in the course of this book cannot be answered and the present rules and reform proposals cannot be evaluated, without understanding the objective of these rules.

What, then, is the function of the criminal law? Most definitions of crime or the criminal law emphasise that the one crucial and distinguishing characteristic of a crime is that it may be followed by punishment.[1] The criminal law is not simply a series of moral commandments: thou shalt not steal, etc. It is a series of legal commandments backed up with the threat of punishment: you must not steal and if you do you can be sent to prison for a maximum of 10 years.[2] Thus an understanding of the function of the criminal law involves understanding the concept of punishment. Why do we punish? What do we hope to achieve thereby? Once the answers to these questions have been discovered, one can understand why we have a body of rules called the

---

[1] Glanville Williams, *Textbook of Criminal Law* (2nd ed., 1983), p. 27 (hereafter cited as Glanville Williams, *Textbook*. All references are to the second edition unless otherwise stated).
[2] Theft Act 1968, s.7.

1

criminal law and what the purpose of those rules is. And further, one will be in a position then not only to understand the relationship of the various rules to each other, but also to evaluate, criticise and, if necessary, try and reform these rules.

B. "Theories" of Punishment

Hart has pointed out that much confusion has been caused by the numerous writers who have put forward various "theories" of punishment.[3] This is because those who have put forward their various "theories," or attempted to counter opposite "theories," have generally not been arguing on common ground. They have been arguing as though they were all trying to answer the same question (Why do we punish?), when in reality they have failed to appreciate that there are several quite distinct questions that need answering such as: What is the *purpose* of punishment? What is the *justification* of a punishment? *To whom* may punishment be applied? *How severely* may we punish? Until one has agreed upon the question it is difficult to have a meaningful discussion as to the answer.

Nevertheless in the interests of clarity of exposition it is necessary to state the various competing theories of punishment. We will then be in a position to return to the series of distinct questions posed by Hart to answer each in turn.

There are four main theories of punishment:

1. retribution
2. deterrence
3. incapacitation
4. rehabilitation

The retributive theory looks back to the crime, and punishes *because* of the crime. The remaining three theories all look forward to the consequences of punishment and hope to achieve something thereby, namely, crime reduction. They are thus often termed consequentialist or *utilitarian* theories. (A consequentialist seeks to achieve a consequence at any price; a utilitarian sets a price on the achievement of that goal—in this context, only the minimum amount of punishment thought necessary to achieve the consequence can be justified.) The boundaries between these theories are far from clear with several of them containing sub-categories, many of which are perceived quite differently by different writers.

1. Retribution

Discussion of the principle of retribution tends to be confused because the word is used in various senses. It is generally used to indi-

---

[3] Hart, "Prolegomenon to the Principles of Punishment" in H.L.A. Hart, *Punishment and Responsibility—Essays in the Philosophy of Law* (1968), p. 3.

cate one of the following: vengeance, denunciation or reprobation, atonement, or "just desert."

(i) *Vengeance*

2 Stephen, A History of the Criminal Law of England (1883), 81–82:

" . . . [T]he infliction of punishment by law gives definite expression and a solemn ratification and justification to the hatred which is excited by the commission of the offence, and which constitutes the moral or popular as distinguished from the conscientious sanction of that part of morality which is also sanctioned by the criminal law. The criminal law thus proceeds upon the principle that it is morally right to hate criminals, and it confirms and justifies that sentiment by inflicting upon criminals, punishments which express it . . . I am also of opinion that this close alliance between criminal law and moral sentiment is in all ways healthy and advantageous to the community. I think it highly desirable that criminals should be hated, that the punishments inflicted upon them should be so contrived as to give expression to that hatred, and to justify it so far as the public provision of means for expressing and gratifying a healthy natural sentiment can justify and encourage it."

This desire for vengeance supposedly operates at two levels. First, it is asserted that punishment satisfies the victim's (or his relatives' and friends') desire for vengeance and the state is merely exacting vengeance on their behalf to prevent private retaliation. Thus during the *Sutcliffe* (so-called Yorkshire Ripper) trial, parents of some of Sutcliffe's victims and a girl who survived one of his assaults were interviewed on television and claimed that only the maximum penalty would satisfy them. But what if a particular victim (or his relatives) did not want vengeance? Would the state nevertheless be justified in exacting punishment? Should one ascertain whether victims "in general" desire vengeance, or should each prosecution be dependent on the feelings of the particular victim? Should such an onerous responsibility be placed upon the victim? Indeed, even if victims did desire vengeance, and this fact could be realistically ascertained, should the state pander to such "primitive conceptions?"[4]

Secondly, it is asserted, that quite apart from any societal response on behalf of the victim, there is a public need for vengeance. It is argued that there is an instinctive demand which is active in every human being to retaliate—just as an animal strikes back with hate at those who attack it. This reaction is not only understandable but desirable as a socially acceptable outlet for our aggressions. If there were no punishment our aggressions would become repressed to the point when they might break out in an anti-social manner.[5] But, on the other hand, even if there were such an "instinctive demand" for vengeance, should we be institutionalising it through formal punishment? If humans suffered

[4] Royal Commission on Capital Punishment, Cmd. 8932, (1953) para. 52, citing Sir John Anderson (House of Commons, Official Report, April 14, 1948, cols. 998–999).
[5] See Puttkammer, *Administration of Criminal Justice* 9 (1953) for a discussion and criticism of such a view.

from an "instinctive demand" to rape, ought we then to organise ritual and public rapes for the release of our repressions? It has been suggested that punishment based on vengeance "represents the breakdown of human intelligence, as well as good will. It shows perhaps the ugliest phase of our human nature."[6] It seems difficult to dispute this or to mount any serious defence of vengeance-based punishment.

(ii) *Denunciation or reprobation*

In 1934 a German court in Leipzig found one Marinus van der Lubbe guilty of arson and high treason. He was sentenced to death and duly decapitated. After years of legal wrangling, a ruling in 1967 cleared van der Lubbe of high treason, but upheld his conviction of arson. His sentence was reduced from death to eight years' imprisonment.[7] Why did the German court sentence a dead man to eight years' imprisonment?

In the *Sutcliffe* trial the defendant pleaded guilty to manslaughter and the prosecution were content to accept this plea. However, the judge refused to accept the plea and insisted on a trial with the result that he was convicted of murder and sentenced to life imprisonment.[8] Why did the judge insist upon a costly public trial when he could have accepted the original plea and would almost certainly have sentenced the defendant to the same sentence, namely life imprisonment?

Joel Feinberg, "The Expressive Function of Punishment," (1965) Vol. 49, No. 3, The Monist, 397–423:

" . . . [P]unishment is a conventional device for the expression of attitudes of resentment and indignation, and of judgments of disapproval and reprobation, on the part either of the punishing authority himself or of those 'in whose name' the punishment is inflicted. Punishment, in short, has a *symbolic significance* largely missing from other kinds of penalties.

That the expression of the community's condemnation is an essential ingredient in legal punishment is widely acknowledged by legal writers. Henry M. Hart, for example, gives eloquent emphasis to the point:

'What distinguishes a criminal from a civil sanction and all that distinguishes it, it is ventured, is the judgment of community condemnation which accompanies . . . its imposition. As Professor Gardner wrote not long ago, in a distinct but cognate connection:

"The essence of punishment for moral delinquency lies in the criminal conviction itself. One may lose more money on the stock market than in a court-room; a prisoner of war camp may well provide a harsher environment than a state prison; death on the field of battle has the same physical characteristics as death by sentence of law. It is the expression of the community's hatred, fear, or contempt for the convict which alone characterises physical hardship as punishment."

---

[6] Morris R. Cohen, "Moral Aspects of the Criminal Law," (1940) 49 Yale L.J. 987 at p. 1025.
[7] "Raking the Reichstaf Ashes," *The Sunday Times,* January 4, 1981, 13.
[8] *The Times,* April 30, 1981; *The Times,* May 23, 1981.

If this is what a 'criminal' penalty is, then we can say readily enough what a 'crime' is . . . It is conduct which, if duly shown to have taken place, will incur a formal and solemn pronouncement of the moral condemnation of the community . . . Indeed the condemnation plus the added [unpleasant physical] consequences may well be considered, compendiously, as constituting the punishment.' ("The Aims of the Criminal Law," *Law and Contemporary Problems*, 23 (1958), II, A, 4.) . . .

Consider the standard international practice of demanding that a nation whose agent has unlawfully violated the complaining nation's rights should punish the offending agent. For example, suppose that an airplane of nation A fires on an airplane of nation B while the latter is flying over international waters. Very likely high authorities in nation B will send a note of protest to their counterparts in nation A demanding, among other things, that the transgressive pilot be punished. Punishing the pilot is an emphatic, dramatic, and well-understood way of *condemning* and thereby *disavowing* his act. It tells the world that the pilot had no right to do what he did, that he was on his own in doing it, that his government does not condone that sort of thing. It testifies thereby to government A's recognition of the violated rights of government B in the affected area and, therefore, to the wrongfulness of the pilot's act. Failure to punish the pilot tells the world that government A does not consider him to have been personally at fault. That in turn is to claim responsibility for the act, which in effect labels that act as an 'instrument of deliberate national policy' and hence an act of war. In that case either formal hostilities or humiliating loss of face by one side or the other almost certainly will follow. None of this scenario makes any sense without the clearly understood reprobative symbolism of punishment. In quite parallel ways punishment enables employers to disavow the acts of their employees (though not civil liability for those acts), and fathers the destructive acts of their sons . . .

This symbolic function of punishment was given great emphasis by Kant, who, characteristically, proceeded to exaggerate its importance. Even if a desert island community were to disband, Kant argued, its members should first execute the last murderer left in its jails, 'for otherwise they might all be regarded as participators in the [unpunished] murder . . . ' (*The Philosophy of Law*, tr. W. Hastie [Edinburgh: T. & T. Clark, 1887], 198). This Kantian idea that in failing to punish wicked acts society endorses them and thus becomes *particeps criminis* does seem to reflect, however dimly, something embedded in common sense."

Royal Commission on Capital Punishment, Minutes of Evidence, Ninth Day, December 1, 1949, Memorandum Submitted by the Rt. Hon. Lord Justice Denning, 207:

"Whilst everyone agrees that crimes must be punished, there is profound disagreement as to the form which punishment should take. Many are inclined to test the efficacy of punishment, solely by its value as a deterrent: but this is too narrow a view. Punishment is the way in which society expresses its denunciation of wrong doing: and, in order to maintain respect for law, it is essential that the punishment inflicted for grave crimes should adequately reflect the revulsion felt by the great majority of citizens for them. It is a mistake to consider the objects of punishment as being deterrent or reformative or preventive and nothing else. If that were so, we should not send to prison a man who was guilty of motor manslaughter, but only disqualify him from driving; but would public opinion be content with this? The truth is that some crimes are so outrageous that society insists on adequate punishment, because the wrong-doer deserves it, irrespective of whether it is a deterrent or not . . . Some cases are so outrageous that, irrespective of the value of the death penalty as a deterrent, the great bulk of the community consider that the only fitting penalty is death. In my view the ultimate justification of any punishment is, not that it is a deterrent, but that it is the emphatic denunciation by the community of a crime."

(iii) *Expiation*

According to this view the offender must be made to work off his guilt; he must be purified through suffering: "The essence of the expiatory view is that in suffering his punishment, the offender has purged his guilt, has 'paid for' his crime, and that his account with society is therefore clear."[9] This is regarded as a species of retribution in that the offender is "paying his debt" owed to society, and, in so doing, becomes reconciled with that society. The focus is on the past crime; the attempt is to wipe the slate clean.

However, unlike other retributive theories, the emphasis here can be on the offender's perspective. It is thought that he *wants* to expiate his sins; he needs, and perhaps even has a right to, punishment so that he can be cleansed and have his reputation restored.

These ideas stem largely from the religious influences on our culture; but some would argue that there is a deeper psychological explanation underlying an offender's need for expiation. From the time we are children we are conditioned to expect punishment when we have done wrong. Guilt is a state of tension which gives rise to a need for the removal of this tension. We are conditioned to expect this relief through punishment. The most famous illustration of this form of punishment comes from Dostoyevsky's *Crime and Punishment* in which Raskolnikov, after committing a brutal murder, becomes obsessed with feelings of guilt and eventually gives himself up as the only means of coming to terms with himself and achieving peace of mind. Some of these ideas are illustrated by the following case. The defendant was to be punished so that he could expiate his sins, and thereafter become an accepted member of society again.

R. v. Williams [1974] Crim.L.R. 558 (Court of Appeal, Criminal Division)

"*Facts*: Pleaded guilty to attempting to bugger a sheep and aiding and abetting another to do so. The offence was committed about midnight after the defendants had been drinking heavily. They were seen by a man taking his dog for a walk. Sentenced to twelve months' imprisonment: *Previous convictions*: eight for dishonesty and road traffic offences: probation, fined, six months' imprisonment. *Special considerations*: they lived in a small community and the judge said: 'I fully appreciate that it is going to be a matter of comment about

---

[9] H. Jones, *Crime and the Penal System* (3rd ed., 1965), p. 134.

you for years to come and I think the kindest thing I can do is to visit upon you the outrage which I think anybody with any decent feelings would feel about it so that nobody can say, in your village, that you haven't paid for it.' *Decision*: it had been submitted that, the remarks indicated that the judge included a deterrent factor in the sentence. The court did not so regard them. The judge was giving the defendants an opportunity to expiate their offences and there was nothing wrong in his approach. However, having regard to the circumstances, and the remorse they had shown and the fact that they had been in custody for six weeks, and in the hope that they had learned their lesson, the sentence would be suspended for two years."

While society might offer an offender the opportunity of expiation, it clearly cannot insist or demand it as the will or desire for *true* expiation must proceed from the defendant himself. But, of course, as *Williams* makes clear, one is not necessarily dealing with true expiation of sin. Society simply deems the offender to have purged his guilt by punishment.

(iv) *Desert*

Over the last two decades "theories" of punishment such as deterrence and rehabilitation have come under increasing attack both by academics and lawmakers.[10] The view that has fast gained ascendency is that we punish criminals primarily because they deserve it.[11] For instance, the latest Government White Paper proclaims that the aim of their proposals is "better justice through a more consistent approach to sentencing, so that convicted criminals get their 'just deserts'."[12] To gain such a wide acceptance it has been necessary for proponents of this view to shun psychological notions of retribution concerning revenge, and to rest their case on the more acceptable philosophical ideas of Kant that a man deserves to be punished if he has broken the law. In this way we are according a man respect as an autonomous and responsible human being who has chosen to commit a crime. ("To be punished for reform reasons is to be treated like a dog"[13]). Under a general theory of political obligation all persons owe duties to others not to infringe their rights. Justice and fairness insist that all persons must bear the sacrifice of obeying the law equally. By committing a crime the offender has gained an unfair advantage over all the others who have "toed the line" and restrained themselves from committing crime. Social equilibrium in society must be restored. The offender deserves and must receive punishment in order to destroy his unfair advantage.

[10] Andrew Von Hirsch, *Doing Justice—The Choice of Punishments* (Report of the Committee for the Study of Incarceration), (1976); Marvin E. Frankel, *Criminal Sentences—Law without Order* (1973); Norval Morris, *The Future of Imprisonment* (1975); E. van der Haag, *Punishing Criminals* (1975).

[11] This is (and probably always has been) the view of the public: N. Walker and M. Hough, *Public Attitudes to Sentencing* (1988) pp. 185–186.

[12] Home Office White Paper, *Crime, Justice and Protecting the Public*, (1990) Cm. 965, para. 1.6.

[13] J. Mabbott, "Freewill and Punishment," in *Contemporary British Philosophy* (1956), pp. 289, 303.

Andrew von Hirsch, Doing Justice—The Choice of Punishments (Report of the Committee for the Study of Incarceration), (1976) pp. 45–49:

"In everyday thinking about punishment, the idea of desert figures prominently. Ask the person on the street why a wrongdoer should be punished, and he is likely to say that he 'deserves' it . . .

To say someone 'deserves' to be rewarded or punished is to refer to his *past* conduct, and assert that its merit or demerit is reason for according him pleasant or unpleasant treatment. The focus on the past is critical. That a student has written an outstanding paper is grounds for asserting that he deserves an award; but that the award will yield him or others future benefits (however desirable those might be) cannot be grounds for claiming he deserves it. The same holds for punishment: to assert that someone deserves to be punished is to look at his past wrongdoing as reason for having him penalized. This orientation to the past distinguishes desert from the other purported aims of punishment—deterrence, incapacitation, rehabilitation—which seek to justify the criminal sanction by its prospective usefulness in preventing crime . . .

A useful place to begin is with Kant's explanation of deserved punishment, which he based on the idea of fair dealing among free individuals. To realise their own freedom, he contended, members of society have the reciprocal obligation to limit their behaviour so as not to interfere with the freedom of others. When someone infringes another's rights, he gains an unfair advantage over all others in the society—since he has failed to constrain his own behaviour while benefitting from other persons' forbearance from interfering with his rights. The punishment—by imposing a counterbalancing disadvantage on the violator—restores the equilibrium: after having undergone the punishment, the violator ceases to be at advantage over his non-violating fellows. (This righting-of-the-balance is not a matter of preventing future crimes. Aside from any concern with prospective criminality, it is the violator's *past* crime that placed him in a position of advantage over others, and it is that advantage which the punishment would eliminate.) As Herbert Morris puts it in a recent restatement of the Kantian argument:

> 'A person who violates the rules has something others have—the benefits of the system [of mutual non-interference with others' rights]—but by renouncing what others have assumed, the burdens of self-restraint, he has acquired an unfair advantage. Matters are not even until this advantage is in some way erased . . . Justice—that is punishing such individuals—restores the equilibrium of benefits and burdens . . . ' ("Persons and Punishment", 52 *The Monist* 475, 478 (1968).)

Kant's theory, however, accounts only for the imposition of *some* kind of deprivation on the offender to offset the 'advantage' he obtained in violating others' rights. It does not explain why that deprivation should take the peculiar form of punishment. Punishment differs from other purposefully inflicted deprivations in the moral disapproval it expresses: punishing someone conveys in dramatic fashion that his conduct was wrong and that he is blameworthy for having committed it. Why, then, does the violator deserve to be *punished*, instead of being made to suffer another kind of deprivation that connotes no special moral stigma?

To answer this question it becomes necessary, we think, to focus specifically on the reprobation implicit in punishment and argue that *it* is deserved. Someone who infringes the rights of others, the argument runs, does wrong and deserves blame for his conduct. It is because he deserves blame that the sanctioning authority is entitled to choose a response that expresses moral disapproval; namely, punishment. In other words, the sanction ought not only to deprive the offender of the 'advantage' obtained by his disregard of the rules (the Kantian explanation); but do so in a manner that ascribes blame (the reprobative explanation).

This raises the question of what purpose the reprobation itself serves. Blaming persons who commit wrongful acts is, arguably, a way of reaffirming the moral values that were infringed. But to speak of reaffirming such values prompts the further question: Why should the violator be singled out for blame to achieve that end? The answer must ultimately be that the censure is itself deserved: that someone who is responsible for wrongdoing is blame*worthy* and hence may justly be blamed."

John Finnis, "The Restoration of Retribution" (1971) Analysis, 32.4, 131:

"These obscurities about the nature and occasion of the criminal's profiting can be cleared up if we . . . say that

(1) what the criminal gains in the act of committing crime (whatever the size and nature of the loot, if any, and indeed quite apart from the success or failure of his overall purpose) is the advantage of indulging a (wrongful) self-preference, of permitting himself an excessive freedom in choosing—this advantage (of exercising a wider freedom and of acting according to one's tastes . . .) being something that his law-abiding fellow citizens have denied themselves insofar as they have chosen to conform their will (habits and choices) to the law even when they would "prefer" not to;

(2) this advantage is gained at the time of the crime, because and insofar as the crime is . . . a free and "responsible" exercise of self-will; the wrongfulness of gaining this advantage is the specifically relevant moral turpitude adverted to in the retributivist's talk of criminal "guilt"; and the advantage is one that cannot be lost, unless and until . . .

(3) the criminal has the disadvantage of having his wayward will restricted in its freedom by being subjected to the representative "will of society" (the "will" which he disregarded in disregarding the law) through the process of punishment; a punishment is thus to be defined not, formally speaking, in terms of the infliction of pain (nor as incarceration), but rather in terms of the subjection of will (normally, but not necessarily, effected through the denial of benefits and advantages of social living: compulsory employment on some useful work which the criminal would not of himself have chosen to do would satisfy the definition) . . . .

It is not just the victim and the wrondoer who should be put back on a footing of equality: the "satisfaction" which the wrondoer gains is an advantage not only as against the victim but also as against all those who might have been wrongdoers but restrained themselves . . . .

Aquinas . . . [said,] "anyone who has indulged his will more than he ought [*plus voluntati suae indulsit quam debuit*], by transgressing the law, should either of his own accord or without his consent undergo something opposed to what he wills—so that the quality of justice may thus be restored [*reintegretur*].

On this view . . . we can say . . . that the restoration of a fair distribution of advantages and disadvantages as between citizens is *an aim* of punishment . . .

At the end of a period one should be able to look back over the *whole* period and say that, because of the adjustments that were made in response to criminal disruption of that order, no one has (overall and taking the period as a whole) been disadvantaged unfairly by attempting to live in strict accordance with that basic order of fairness . . . ."

Nicola Lacey, State Punishment: Political Principles and Community Values (1988) pp. 24–26:

"[Desert theories do not give] very clear practical guidance about the fair measure of punishment in particular cases. What actual punishment would forfeit a set of rights equivalent to those violated by a rapist, a petty thief, a reckless driver? . . . As in the case of the law of the talion and the culpability principle, resort to arguments from conventionally agreed, customary or consequence-based penalty scales seem hard to avoid. Secondly, real difficulties have been raised about the social contract tradition itself; in what sense can a *fictitious* agreement generate obligations for real people? . . . Furthermore, these views are dependent for their force, as we have already noted, on the existence of a fair set of rules. This is not fatal in itself, but the criteria which dictate that there is indeed a just equilibrium which can be restored are not generated by the forfeiture of rights or unfair advantage principles alone. The views do presuppose an independent account of what counts as an unfair advantage and a just equilibrium.

Finally, it seems legitimate to ask whether the metaphorical ideas of restoring relationships of justice or moral equilibria outweigh the obvious disvalues attached to the suffering and other costs of punishment. Do these theories really ignore such costs completely? If not, what weight do they accord to them? In what real sense does punisment 'restore the right'? Do these theories really remove the mystery attaching to the original, simple desert principle, or are they, too, a form of moral alchemy? Or, in trying to avoid the mystery, do they not collapse into versions of utilitarian or other consequentialist justification? . . . Even the more sophisticated versions barely rise above the level of metaphor, and leave us with the suspicion that the idea of desert cannot be distinguished from a principle of vengeance or the unappealing assertion that two wrongs somehow make a right."

C. S. Lewis, "The Humanitarian Theory of Punishment," Res Judicatae VI (1953), 224:

" . . . My subject is . . . that theory of punishment . . . (that) . . . may be called the Humanitarian theory. Those who hold it think that it is mild and merciful. In this I believe that they are seriously mistaken. I believe that the 'Humanity' which it claims is a dangerous illusion and disguises the possibility of cruelty and injustice without end. I urge a return to the traditional or Retributive theory not solely, not even primarily, in the interests of society, but in the interests of the criminal.

According to the Humanitarian theory, to punish a man because he deserves it, and as much as he deserves, is mere revenge, and therefore barbarous and immoral. It is maintained that the only legitimate motives for punishing are the desire to deter others by example or to mend the criminal. When this theory is combined, as frequently happens, with the belief that all crime is more or less pathological, the idea of mending tails off into that of healing or curing and punishment becomes therapeutic. Thus it appears at first sight that we have passed from the harsh and self righteous notion of giving the wicked their deserts to the charitable and enlightened one of tending the psychologically sick. What could be more amiable? One little point which is taken for granted in this theory needs, however, to be made explicit. The things done to the criminal, even if they are called cures, will be just as compulsory as they were in the old days when we called them punishments. If a tendency to steal can be cured by psychotherapy, the thief will no doubt be forced to undergo the treatment. Otherwise, society cannot continue.

My contention is that this doctrine, merciful though it appears, really means that each one of us, from the moment he breaks the law, is deprived of the rights of a human being.

The reason is this. The Humanitarian theory removes from Punishment the concept of Desert. But the concept of Desert is the only connecting link between punishment and justice. It is only as deserved or undeserved that a sentence can be just or unjust. I do not here contend that the question 'Is it deserved?' is the only one we can reasonably ask about a punishment. We may very properly ask whether it is likely to deter others and to reform the criminal. But neither of these two last questions is a question about justice. There is no sense in talking about a 'just deterrent' or a 'just cure.' We demand of a deterrent not whether it is just but whether it will deter. We demand of a cure not whether it is just but whether it succeeds. Thus when we cease to consider what the criminal deserves and consider only what will cure him or deter others, we have tacitly removed him from the sphere of justice altogether: instead of a person, a subject of rights, we now have a mere object, a patient, a 'case.'

The distinction will become clearer if we ask who will be qualified to determine sentences when sentences are no longer held to derive their propriety from the criminal's deservings. On the old view the problem of fixing the right sentence was a moral problem. Accordingly, the judge who did it was a person trained in jurisprudence: trained, that is, in a science which deals with rights and duties, and which in origin at least, was consciously accepting guidance from the Law of Nature, and from Scripture. We must admit that in the actual penal code of most countries at most times these high originals were so much modified by local custom, class interests and utilitarian concessions, as to be very imperfectly recognisable. But the code was never in principle and not always in fact, beyond the control of the conscience of the society. And when (say, in eighteenth century England) actual punishments conflicted too violently with the moral sense of the community, juries refused to convict and reform was finally brought about. This was possible because, so long as we are thinking in terms of Desert, the propriety of the penal code, being a moral question, is a question on which every man has the right to an opinion, not because he follows this or that profession, but because he is simply a man, a rational animal enjoying the Natural Light. But all this is changed when we drop the concept of Desert. The only two questions we may now ask about a punishment are whether it deters and whether it cures. But these are not questions on which anyone is entitled to have an opinion simply because he is a man. He is not entitled to an opinion even if, in addition to being a man, he should happen also to be a jurist, a Christian and a moral theologian. For they are not questions about principle but about matter of fact and for such *cuiquam in sua arte credendum*. Only the expert 'penologist' (let barbarous things have barbarous names), in the light of previous experiment can tell us what is likely to deter: only the psychotherapist can tell us what is likely to cure. It will be in vain for the rest of us, speaking simply as men, to say, 'but this punishment is hideously unjust, hideously disproportionate to the criminal's deserts.' The experts with perfect logic will reply 'but nobody was talking about deserts. No one was talking about *punishment* in your archaic vindictive sense of the word. Here are the statistics proving that this treatment deters. Here are the statistics proving that this other treatment cures. What is your trouble?'

The Humanitarian theory, then, removes sentences from the hands of jurists whom the public conscience is entitled to criticize and places them in the hands of technical experts whose special sciences do not even employ such categories as rights or justice. . . .

If we turn from the curative to the deterrent justification of punishment we shall find the new theory even more alarming. When you punish a man *in terrorem*, make of him an 'example' to others, you are admittedly using him as a means to an end: someone else's end. This, in itself, would be a very wicked thing to do. On the classical theory of Punishment it was of course justified on the ground that the man deserved it. That was assumed to be established before any question of 'making him an example' arose. You then, as the saying is, killed two birds with one stone; in the process of giving him what he deserved you set an example to others. But take away desert and the whole morality of the punishment disappears. Why, in Heaven's name, am I to be sacrificed to the good of society in this way?—unless, of course, I deserve it . . .

To be 'cured' against one's will and cured of states which we may not regard as a disease is to be put on a level with those who have not yet reached the age of reason or those who never will: to be classed with infants, imbeciles, and domestic animals. But to be punished however severely, because we have deserved it, because we 'ought to have known better,' is to be treated as a human person . . .

[T]he Humanitarian theory wants simply to abolish Justice and substitute Mercy for it. This means that you start being 'kind' to people before you have considered their rights, and then force upon them supposed kindnesses which they in fact had a right to refuse, and finally kindnesses which no one but you will recognise as kindnesses and which the recipient will feel as abominable cruelties. You have overshot the mark. Mercy detached from Justice, grows unmerciful. That is the important paradox. As there are plants which will flourish only in mountain soil, so it appears that Mercy will flower only when it grows in the crannies of the rock of Justice: transplanted to the marshlands of mere Humanitarianism, it becomes a man-eating weed, all the more dangerous because it is still called by the same name as the mountain variety. But we ought long ago to have learned our lesson. We should be too old now to be deceived by those humane pretensions which have served to usher in every cruelty of the revolutionary period in which we live. These are the 'precious balms' which will 'break our heads.' "

What are the consequences of acceptance of the above views? Does justice demand that all offenders who have committed the same crime receive the same sentence? The answer here must be in the negative. The extent to which punishment is deserved can depend on factors other than the offence committed in at least two situations. First, an offender with many previous convictions might *deserve* more punishment than a first-time offender committing the same offence. Secondly, there is the problem of the differential impact of sentences. A fine of £200 might have little impact on a wealthy offender but could have a devastating effect on an impoverished one. Would it be just to subject both to the same fine?

Magistrates' Courts Act 1980, s.35.

"In fixing the amount of a fine, a magistrates' court shall take into consideration among other things the means of the person on whom the fine is imposed so far as they appear or are known to the court."

Andrew Ashworth, Sentencing and Penal Policy (1983) p. 290:

"A sentencer who fines a poor man £20 should be quite prepared to fine a wealthy offender £500 for the same offence, if his means are so great that this is the level of fine necessary to make the equivalent impact upon him. If he is not prepared to fine him £500, then he should equally not be prepared to fine the poor man £20, because £20 may mean a great sacrifice to a person who relies entirely on State assistance."

Home Office White Paper, Crime, Justice and Protecting the Public, (1990) Cm 965, para. 5.3:

"[T]he Government proposes to provide a legislative framework for unit fines. This would include a requirement for defendants to provide information about their means and for the courts to reduce or increase fine levels according to the means of convicted offenders. The simplest way to do this would be to assess the fine level in units, according to the seriousness of the offence. The court's penalty would be given in units, which would then be translated into monetary values according to each offender's means. In the recent experiments, the unit used for assessment was a week's disposable income, after deducting tax and necessary living expenses. So, for example, an offence would be judged serious enough to warrant a fine of 10 units; an offender with £20 disposable income a week would pay £200, but an offender with only £5 a week would pay £50."

R. v. Fairbairn (1980) 2 Cr. App. R. (S) 315 (Court of Appeal, Criminal Division)

A relatively wealthy defendant was convicted of theft of goods valued at some £700. He was sentenced to nine months imprisonment and fined £7,500. He appealed against his sentence.
Glidewell J.:
"[I]n the view of this Court, the fine of £7,500 was excessive. In principle, the amount of the fine should be determined in relation to the gravity of the offence, and then—and only then—should the offender's means be considered to decide whether he has the capacity to pay such an amount.
In this case the amount of the fine was over 10 times the value of the goods stolen, and in this court's view that amount is out of scale in relation to the gravity of the offence of which he was convicted . . . "

Fine reduced to £1,000.

Andrew von Hirsch, Doing Justice—The Choice of Punishments (Report of the Committee for the Study of Incarceration), (1976), pp. 89–90:

"The assessment of severity (of punishment), as the assessment of the harmfulness of the offense, should be standardised: the focus should be on how unpleasant the punishment *characteristically* is. Such standardisation is necessary . . . as a safeguard against class justice. Judges sometimes impose different penalties on persons convicted of similar crimes, in the hope of producing equivalent amounts of discomfort: the middle-class person is put on probation and the ghetto youth jailed for the same infraction on the theory that the former's sensitivities are greater . . .

The principle of commensurate deserts calls for maintenance of a 'proportion' between the seriousness of the crime and the severity of the penalty.''

2. Deterrence

Unlike retributive theories, deterrent theories are forward looking in that they are concerned with the consequences of punishment; their aim is to reduce further crime by the threat or example of punishment. Deterrence supposedly operates at three levels:

(i) *Individual deterrence*

The deterrent theories seek to discourage crime. In the case of individual or specific deterrence it is hoped that the experience of punishment will be so unpleasant that the offender will not reoffend. The task of the sentencer is, therefore, to look to the future and select the sentence which is likely to have most impact on the individual. In the case of some offenders, no punishment at all may be necessary—the risk of the convicted person reoffending may be minimal. In other cases the required sentence may be so severe as to be inhumane.

It is often said that every time a crime is committed the theory of deterrence is weakened; it is an argument that has some force when applied to the reoffender. One can argue that his reconviction reveals the failure of the previous sentence.

Nigel Walker, Sentencing in a Rational Society (1969), p. 117:

"There are of course practical issues, such as the minimum acceptable length for a follow-up period, or the number of further convictions which should be regarded as the criterion for 'failure' (most investigators classify offenders with one subsequent conviction as failures, but some prefer two, especially where young offenders are concerned). These, however, are merely matters which affect the reliance placed by penologists on the results of this or that investigation.

There is, however, one fundamental difficulty which has not yet been overcome. Suppose that our information about the subsequent records of a sample of ex-prisoners is comprehensive, accurate and in every way satisfactory: and suppose that by the strictest criteria 80% have 'gone straight.' It would be fallacious to attribute this to the effects of imprisonment unless we had good grounds for saying that none of them would have gone straight if not imprisoned. Some would probably have gone straight if fined or put on probation. . . . Some might even have gone straight if they had not been detected at all . . . ''

Thus, the average reconviction rate of 45 per cent. is of limited usefulness.[14] Research tends, as a result, to be of a comparative rather than absolute nature. The efficacy of one type of sentence in preventing reconviction is tested against others.

---

[14] R. Hood and R. Sparks, *Key Issues in Criminology* (1970), p. 177. Walker, Farrington and Tucker, "Reconviction Rates of Adult Males after Different Sentences" (1981) 21 Brit. J. Criminol., 357, 359 revealed a reconviction rate as high as 88 per cent. for men with five or more previous convictions.

Andrew Ashworth, Sentencing and Penal Policy (1983) p. 29:

"At face value, [the research of Walker, Farrington and Tucker ('Reconviction Rates of Adult Males after Different Sentences' (1981) 21 Brit. J. Criminol. 357)] . . . suggests that those with 5 or more convictions are extremely likely to be reconvicted, no matter which sentence they are given. First offenders are much more likely to be reconvicted if given a suspended sentence or probation order than if fined or imprisoned. Those with between 1 and 4 previous convictions are likely to do better when fined or put on probation than when conditionally discharged, given a suspended sentence or imprisoned. Financial measures performed better than expected throughout. [Ashworth then noted that as the numbers for certain categories of sentence were small, reservations would have to exist about some results, and furthermore, that at the time of the study, 1971, community service, deferment of sentence and 6 month probation orders were not available]. It is not, however, the sentence imposed which has the strongest association with reconviction but the number of previous convictions an offender has . . . "

The deterrent effect of sentences thus becomes weaker with each subsequent reconviction; it is possible to argue from this that what is needed is a more severe sentence than that merited by the present offence, at an early stage in the defendant's criminal career to have a strong deterrent effect. Indeed, this kind of approach was encapsulated in the much discussed "short, sharp shock" that imposed detention centre orders on young offenders under the Criminal Justice Act 1982.[15] Even if research established (and all indications are to the contrary)[16] that such measures would prove more effective in preventing recidivism, there would be problems of whether it was just to impose a more severe punishment than that merited by the offence. Indeed, there is a further problem at another level: "If a criminal does what he must do in the light of his background and his hereditary equipment, it is obviously both futile and unjust to punish him as if he could go straight and had deliberately chosen to do otherwise. It would be as foolish to punish him for having contracted tuberculosis."[17]

(ii) *General deterrence*

Under this theory it is the threat of punishment that deters people from committing crimes. At the legislative level, Parliament lays down penalties to threaten those who might contemplate crime. At the sentencing level, offenders are punished in order that others will be discouraged from committing crimes; this punishment is held up as an example of what will happen if others engage in similar activities.

There are two aspects to this theory. Firstly, punishment "at the normal rate"[18] must be imposed in most cases to keep the threat of punish-

---

[15] Now abolished by the Criminal Justice Act 1988, s.123.
[16] This was the main reason for the abolition of detention centre orders (C.J. Emmins and G. Scanlan, *Criminal Justice Act 1988* (1988), p. 101.
[17] H. Barnes and N. Teeters, *New Horizons in Criminology* (2nd ed., 1954), pp. 817–8. See further, *post*, pp. 238–246.
[18] *Post*, pp. 51–55.

ment alive. But secondly, when a specific type of crime is on the increase or has attracted much publicity, then excessively severe penalties (known as "exemplary sentences") may be imposed to try and prevent that particular crime. For example, exemplary sentences were imposed to suppress attacks on ethnic minority groups in Notting Hill in 1958,[19] to prevent the sudden increase of muggings on elderly people in the early 1970s,[20] to contain football hooliganism in the late 1970s[21] and to try and put a halt to the wave of rioting and looting in Brixton and Toxteth.[22] In 1985 concern over the rise of football hooliganism led to an exemplary sentence of life imprisonment for riotous assembly outside a football ground.[23]

The theory of general deterrence rests upon one crucial assumption—that people are deterred from committing crime by the threat of punishment. Is this assumption justifiable?

J. Andenaes, "The General Preventive Effects of Punishment," (1966) 114 U.Pa.L.Rev. 949, at 960–970:

"Reports on conditions of disorganisation following wars, revolution or mutinies provide ample documentation as to how lawlessness may flourish when the probability of detection, apprehension and conviction is low. In these situations, however, many factors work together. The most clear cut examples of the importance of the risk of detection itself are provided by cases in which society functions normally but all policing activity is paralyzed by a police strike or a similar condition. For example, the following official report was made on lawlessness during a 1919 police strike, starting at midnight on July 31st, during which nearly half of the Liverpool policemen were out of service: 'In this district the strike was accompanied by threats, violence and intimidation on the part of lawless persons. Many assaults on the constables who remained on duty were committed. Owing to the sudden nature of the strike the authorities were afforded no opportunity to make adequate provision to cope with the position. Looting of shops commenced about 10 p.m. on August 1st, and continued for some days. In all about 400 shops were looted. Military were requisitioned, special constables sworn in, and police brought from other centers.' (Mannheim, Social Aspects of Crime in England Between the Wars, 156–57 (1940).)

A somewhat similar situation occurred in Denmark when the German occupation forces arrested the entire police force in September, 1944. During the remainder of the occupation period all policing was performed by an improvised unarmed watch corps, who were ineffective except in those instances when they were able to capture the criminal red handed. The general crime rate rose immediately, but there was a great discrepancy between the various types of crime. The number of cases of robbery increased generally in Copenhagen during the war, rising from ten per year in 1939 to ten per month in 1943. But after the Germans arrested the police in 1944, the figure rose to over a hundred

---

[19] *E.g.* Hurst, *The Times*, November 26, 1958; see [1958] Crim. L.R. 709.

[20] *E.g. Storey* (1973) 57 Cr.App.R. 840.

[21] *E.g. Motley* (1978) 66 Cr.App.R. 274; *Bruce* (1977) 65 Cr.App.R. 148.

[22] See *The Times*, November 23, 1981; LAG Bulletin, August, 1981, 174; *The Guardian,* July 14, 1981.

[23] *Whitton, The Times*, November 9, 1985. This sentence was reduced to three years' imprisonment on appeal (*Whitton, The Times*, May 20, 1986).

per month and continued to rise. Larcenies reported to the insurance companies quickly increased tenfold or more. The fact that penalties were greatly increased for criminals who were caught and brought before the courts did not offset the fact that most crimes were going undetected. On the other hand, crimes like embezzlement and fraud, where the criminal is usually known if the crime itself is discovered, do not seem to have increased notably . . .

The involuntary experiments in Liverpool and Copenhagen showed a reduction in law obedience following a reduction of risks. Examples of the opposite are also reported—the number of crimes decreases as the hazards rise. Tarde mentions that the number of cases of poisoning decreased when research in chemistry and toxicology made it possible to discover with greater certainty the causes as well as the perpetrator of this type of crime. (Tarde, Penal Philosophy 476 (1912)). A decline in bank robberies and kidnappings in the United States is reported to have followed the enactment of federal legislation which increased the likelihood of punishment (Taft, Criminology 322, 361 (rev. ed. 1950)) . . .

The decisive factor in creating the deterrent effect is, of course, not the objective risk of detection but the risk as it is calculated by the potential criminal. We know little about how realistic these calculations are. It is often said that criminals tend to be overly optimistic—they are confident that all will work out well. It is possible that the reverse occurs among many law abiding people; they are deterred because of an over-estimation of the risks. A faulty estimate in one direction or the other may consequently play an important part in determining whether an individual is to become a criminal. If fluctuations in the risks of detection do not reach the potential offender, they can be of no consequence to deterrence. If on the other hand, it were possible to convince people that crime does not pay, this assumption might act as a deterrent even if the risks, viewed objectively, remained unchanged . . .

Interesting lessons may be drawn from an experiment launched in some of the Scandinavian countries to fight drunken driving. In Norway, for example, the motor vehicle code prohibits driving of motor vehicles when the alcohol percentage in the driver's blood exceeds 0·05. . . . [T]he consistent policy of the courts has been to give prison sentences for violations, except in cases involving very exceptional circumstances. The prison terms are short, usually not much more than the minimum jail period of twenty-one days, but the penalty is exacted on anyone who is detected, whether or not the driving was dangerous or caused damage.

A person moving between Norway and the United States can hardly avoid noticing the radical difference in the attitudes towards automobile driving and alcohol. There is no reason to doubt that the difference in legal provisions plays a substantial role in this difference in attitudes. The awareness of hazards of imprisonment for intoxicated driving is in our country a living reality to every driver, and for most people the risk seems too great. When a man goes to a party where alcoholic drinks are likely to be served, and if he is not fortunate enough to have a wife who drives but does not drink, he will leave his car at home or he will limit his consumption to a minimum. It is also my feeling—although I am here on uncertain grounds—that the legislation has been instrumental in forming or sustaining the widespread conviction that it is wrong, or irresponsible, to place oneself behind the wheel when intoxicated. 'Alcohol and motor car driving do not belong together' is a slogan commonly accepted. Statistics on traffic accidents show a very small number of accidents due to intoxication. . . .

It seems reasonable to conclude that as a general rule, though not without exceptions, the general preventive effect of the criminal law increases with the growing severity of penalties. Contemporary dictatorships display with almost frightening clarity the conformity that can be produced by a ruthlessly severe justice."

T. Sellin, "The Law and Some Aspects of Criminal Conduct," in Aims and Methods of Legal Research (1955) 113 at 119–120:

"Our statistics suggest the imperative need for paying more legislative attention to law enforcement, since it is law enforcement in the broad sense, which
gives the law any intimidating effect it may be assumed to possess. In this connection reference might be made to the extremely interesting experiment performed in New York City last year. It was prompted by the felt need for
increasing the personnel of the police department of the city. The 25th pre-
cinct . . . was chosen, an area with high crime rates . . . . The experiment began
on September 1, 1954, and lasted four months. Essentially, it consisted of
increasing the number of police in the area. The foot and motor patrol was
increased from 25 to 99 men, plus a special squad of sixteen patrolmen for the
evening and early morning hours. The detective squad was increased from 33 to
54, thirteen of whom were formed into a special narcotics squad. A special unit
of the Juvenile Aid Bureau was set up, consisting of seventeen officers.

The effect of the experiment was interesting indeed, when the data covering
the period are compared with those of the last four months of the year before.
Eight persons were murdered in the area compared with six in 1953, adding
further proof of the absence of any specially deterrent effect in the law so far as
this crime is concerned. The number of rapes declined from 12 to 9, of which
five were statutory, and felonious assaults fell from 185 to 132. Robberies
declined from 166 to 50, burglary from 425 to 148, grand larceny from 153 to 46,
and auto thefts from 78 to 24. On the other hand, cases of possessing dangerous
weapons rose from 13 to 27, cases of sale or possession of narcotics from 78 to
186, and disorderly conduct cases from 77 to 177. Prostitution cases dropped
slightly, while gambling cases rose from 125 to 170, mostly in connection with
the policy racket and card playing, while arrests for dice games declined
sharply. The number of juvenile delinquency referrals rose from 135 to 372.
Summonses, mostly in connection with parking violations, increased 140%."

D. Cressey and D. Ward, Delinquency, Crime and Social Process (1969), p. 210 (citing Mr. Spirack, a high-ranking official of the Antitrust Division of the United States Justice Department):

"No one in direct contact with the living reality of business conduct in the
United States is unaware of the effect of the imprisonment of seven high
officials in the electrical machinery Industry in 1960 had on the conspiratorial
price fixing in many areas of our economy; similar sentences in a few cases each
decade would almost completely cleanse our economy of the cancer of collusive
price fixing and the mere prospect of such sentences is itself the strongest available deterrent to such activities."

Gerald Gardiner, "The Purposes of Criminal Punishment" (1958) 21 M.L.R. 117, 122–125:

"The belief in the value of deterrence rests on the assumption that we are
rational beings who always think before we act, and then base our actions on a
careful calculation of the gains and losses involved. These assumptions, dear to
many lawyers, have long since been abandoned in the social sciences. No econ-
omist would seriously maintain them today, and even to the uninformed the
movements of shares on the stock exchange—where one might expect to see
Bentham's principle of 'enlightened self-interest' vindicated most clearly—

demonstrate that men's actions are governed quite as much by fear or greed as by reason; and that the ability to ignore hard facts and to see only what you want to see, is shared by a surprisingly large and influential section of the community.

Amongst criminals, foresight and prudent calculation is even more conspicious by its absence. . . . Even though there is no consensus amongst doctors about the exact description of the so-called 'psychopaths,' experienced Prison Medical Officers, and for that matter, Prison Governors, are agreed that there is a type of prisoner who is quite incapable of foresight, who cannot learn even from the experience of punishment, much less from the threat of it. Yet other offenders, notably some sex-offenders (but also others subject to compulsive behaviour) are sometimes at the mercy of their impulses, and unable, without proper help and treatment, to control themselves adequately. Such persons are frequently in conflict, not only with society, but also with themselves.

Another factor on which the effectiveness of deterrence depends is the certainty of conviction. But according to the latest official Criminal Statistics, only 48 per cent. of the offences known to the police are 'cleared up.' Offences cleared up include those for which a person is arrested or summoned, or for which he is cautioned, those taken into consideration by a court when the offender is found guilty on another charge, and even some which are strongly suspected but which cannot be definitely cleared up; for instance, where the suspect dies or commits suicide before the case has been tried. Even so, this still leaves an unknown quantity of offences which remain undetected altogether, so that the chances of your *not* being caught are distinctly better than those of your being apprehended and brought to trial. Add to this the fact that by no means all those who come before the courts are found guilty, and it is clear that the threat of punishment loses something of its persuasive force."

George H. Dessian, "Justice after Conviction" (1951) 25 Connecticut Bar Journal 215:

"I suppose that it is evident that the deterrent effect of any particular sentence imposed must depend on two things: the way in which the convict sentenced is capable and has been conditioned to respond to such a prescription; and the way in which others of comparable personality and similar inclination in the general population are capable and have been conditioned to respond to the example of the sentence inflicted on the convict. If deterrence is to work the latter must presumably identify with the convict, must be averse to suffering a similar sentence themselves, and must be made aware that there is a high probability of the latter eventuality.

For these reasons it seems to me that we must rule out as promising subjects for the deterrence approach those who will consider any expected sentence a martyrdom preferable to conformity with the law (the political fanatic who identifies with an alien hostile culture, the religious fanatic, the patriot who engages in espionage on behalf of his own country abroad), those in whom the conscious awarenesses involved in the process of being deterred will not be controlling (the mental defective in a complicated situation, the psychotic in many situations, the intoxicated or drug-influenced, the extremely neurotic offender who 'does not know why he did it' in the sense that he was driven by subconscious or not altogether conscious impulses, and the 'temporarily insane' offender who happened to be confronted by a situation with which he could not otherwise emotionally cope), and those who will not identify with the convict and hence not take him as an example (members of elite groups in the community who may consider themselves, rightly or wrongly, as exempt from the law or regulation in question, persons who feel that in any event they have adequate protection, and persons who feel that they are sufficiently smarter than the convict to avoid getting caught)."

J. Andenaes, "The Morality of Deterrence," (1970) 37 University of Chicago Law Review, 649 at 652:

"Such criticism [of the theory of deterrence] could be based on a deterministic view of human life. If every act is the product of heredity and environment, the choice between conforming to the law and breaking it is somewhat illusory. To say that a person *could* have acted differently is merely to state in another way that *if* he had possessed a different personality, or *if* the external situation had been different, the action too, would have been different. The person makes a choice, to be sure, but with this given personality in this given situation, the choice could only be what it was. The Swedish law professor Vilhelm Lundstedt, one of the best known proponents of general prevention, considered punishment a necessary means to inculcate moral standards in the populace; but recognising the force of the deterministic position, he characterised the convicted offender as a kind of martyr to the maintenance of the social order. (As quoted in 31 Svensk Juristtidning 373 (1946))."[24]

The problem of whether we are justified in punishing one person in order to deter another is considered below,[25] as is the question of how severely we may punish one in order to deter another.[26]

(iii) *Education*

Under the theory of general deterrence a person who is contemplating committing a crime is deterred therefrom by the positive threat that he will suffer the same punishment as others have suffered. But punishment can have a more profound subconscious effect on society. Punishment of criminals builds up in the community over a period of time the habit of not breaking the law. It creates unconscious inhibitions against committing crimes and thus serves to educate the public as to the proper distinctions between good conduct and bad. Every time someone is punished for theft the public morality that theft is wrong is strengthened and our habit of not stealing is reinforced. If suddenly nobody were to be punished for theft and this state of affairs were to endure for a considerable period of time, our inhibitions against stealing and our moral view that theft was wrong would start breaking down. The habit would be broken; we might start stealing. This theory goes a long way towards explaining the prevalence of petty white-collar crime in our offices and factories. Take for example, the use of the office telephone for private phone calls beyond those permitted by the employer. This is a criminal offence carrying a maximum penalty of five years' imprisonment.[27] The fact that prosecutions in this context are so rare has resulted in a lack of public morality on the subject; the public

---

[24] For a discussion of determinism see *post*, pp. 241–246.
[25] *Post*, p. 43.
[26] *Post*, p. 51.
[27] Theft Act 1968, s.13.

have not been educated to accept the gravity of the conduct. There is no subconscious inhibition against committing the crime. For most people the only inhibition is that the employer "might disapprove." This does not have the same powerful impact on the subconscious that punishment for this offence would have. If we were to cease punishing for other offences, *e.g.* theft, they could, in time, come to be regarded as no more serious than using the office telephone for unpermitted private calls.

Hyman Gross, A Theory of Criminal Justice, (1979), pp. 400–401:

"There is a third version of deterrence, one that places no stock in considerations of intimidation and makes no claim that the law has a general tendency to scare off would-be wrongdoers by its threat. In this version stress is still placed on the threats made by the law, and for that reason it can be called a deterrence theory . . .

According to this theory, punishment for violating the rules of conduct laid down by the law is necessary if the law is to remain a sufficiently strong influence to keep the community on the whole law-abiding and so to make possible a peaceable society. Without punishment for violating these rules the law becomes merely a guide and an exhortation to right conduct. No doubt even without liability to punishment an appreciation of the consequences of crime would itself encourage many to forbear in the face of temptation. But most of us would sometimes succumb on occasions when the urge was particularly strong if getting away with it was a certainty because liability for crime was something unknown in the community. Only saints and martyrs could be constantly law-abiding in a community that had no system of criminal liability, for at the very least in acts of retaliation and of self-preservation everyone else would occasionally do what the law prohibited. The threats of the criminal law are necessary, then, only as part of a system of liability ensuring that those who commit crimes do not get away with them. The threats are not laid down to deter those tempted to break the rules, but rather to maintain the rules as a set of standards that compel allegiance in spite of violations by those who commit crimes. In short, the rules of conduct laid down in the criminal law are a powerful social force upon which society is dependent for its very existence, and there is punishment for violation of these rules in order to prevent the dissipation of their power that would result if they were violated with impunity."

J. Andenaes, "General Prevention," (1952) 43 J.Crim.L., C. & P.S. 176 at 179–181:

"Later theory puts much stress on the ability of penal law to arouse or strengthen inhibitions of another sort. In Swedish discussion the *moralising*—in other words the *educational*—function has been greatly stressed. The idea is that punishment as a concrete expression of socety's disapproval of an act helps to form and to strengthen the public's moral code and thereby creates conscious and unconscious inhibitions against committing crime. Unconscious inhibitions against committing forbidden acts can also be aroused without apealing to the individual's concepts of morality. Purely as a matter of habit, with fear, respect for authority or social imitation as connecting links, it is possible to induce favourable attitudes toward this or that action and unfavourable attitudes toward another action. We find the clearest example of this in the military, where extended inculcation of discipline and stern reaction against breach thereof can induce a purely automatic, habitual response—not only where obeying specific orders is concerned, but also with regard to general orders and regulations. We have another example in the relationship between an occupying power and an occupied population. The regulations set down by the occupier are not regarded by the people as morally binding; but by a combination of terror and habit formation a great measure of obedience can be elicited—at any rate in response to commands which do not conflict too greatly with national feelings . . . .

. . . To the lawmaker, the achievement of inhibition and habit is of greater value than mere deterrence. For these apply in cases, where a person need not fear detection and punishment, and they can apply without the person even having knowledge of the legal prohibition.''

Franz Alexander and Hugo Staub, The Criminal, the Judge and the Public, (1956), p. 213:

''We can state now that the power of the Super-ego over our instinctive life is undermined, not only when some one is punished unjustly and too severely, but also when the offender escaped punishment and thus fails to pay for his offence. Unwarranted acquittal means simply that the court permits the defendant to do things which we prohibit to ourselves. Under such circumstances, the righteous member of the community finds himself facing the following dilemma: he must either give up his own inhibitions and give in to his own anti-social tendencies, or he must demand that the offender be punished without fail. 'What I do not allow myself must not be allowed others; if others are not called upon to pay for their violations of the law, then I shall not abide by my self-imposed restrictions.'

We may say, then, that what creates the public demand for atonement is one's anxiety lest his own Superego be overturned and that one's own impulses, which have been curbed with so much difficulty, might break through to expression. This anxiety is quite justified, because before our Superego was set up, our unbridled impulses kept us always in a state of painful conflict with the outside world. Was not the Superego set up for the purpose of ridding ourselves of or escaping from such painful situations? Moreover, the original pressure of our instinctual drives remains so strong that man's Superego, if it is to preserve its power of repression, always needs the support of outside authorities. Hence, in the case of every violation of the law, our Ego makes an appeal for the atonement of the transgression; it does this in order to enforce the opposition of the Superego against the pressure of its instincts. The example of a criminal has a stimulating effect on our own repressed impulses, and increases the pressure coming from them. That is why our Ego needs the constant reinforcement of our Superego; it can obtain this reinforcement only from those in authority, who are the prototype of our Superego. If the Ego can show that the secular authorities agree with the Superego, then it is able to keep the instinctual impulses in check: if, however, these secular authorities happen to disavow the Superego by setting a guilty man free, then the individual feels that no support is given him to counteract a pending breaking through of his own anti-social tendencies. The demand that every crime should be expiated represents, then, a defence reaction on the part of the Ego against one's own instinctual drives; the Ego puts itself at the service of the inner repressing forces, in order to retain the state of equilibrium, which must always exist between the repressed and the repressing forces of the personality. The demand that the lawbreaker be punished is thus a demonstration against one's own inner drives, a demonstration which tends to keep these drives amenable to control: 'I forbid the law-breaker what I forbid myself.'

[T]he greater the pressure coming from repressed impulses, the more aware becomes the Ego that it needs the institution of punishment as an intimidating example, acting against one's own primitive world of repressed instinctual drives. In other words, the louder man calls for the punishment of the law-breaker, the less he has to fight against his own repressed impulses. It is, as a matter of fact, a definite sign that the given individual failed to assimilate his own anti-social tendencies, if he becomes too zealous in his demands for the punishment of transgressions of the law. These psychological considerations explain, perhaps, the fact that *the underworld and its official prosecutors show not infrequently a sort of subterranean affinity.* The unconscious, impulsive part of every man's psyche, particularly that of the too zealous prosecutor of crime, takes the side of the violator of the law. This unconscious sympathetic under-standing of the criminal is prevented from appearing in our consciousness by the repressive agencies; it becomes over-compensated and expresses itself in the form of a protest against the criminal. If and when, however, the criminal is duly punished, our demand for atonement is thoroughly satisfied and we feel that we have proved to ourselves that we are good and loyal to society; under such circumstances, we can afford, as we do, to express sympathy with and kindliness towards the very same criminal. What happened is this: through the gratification of our demand for expiation of the crime, we won a victory over the evil within ourselves: we may well be grateful to the criminal, for *he* paid for what *we* unconsciously wished to do. That is why our forefathers preferred a penitent sinner to a hundred righteous men, for the repenting sinner is much more helpful to us in our struggle against our own repressed impulses."

This theory should be contrasted with the retributive theory of denunciation.[28] The theories are similar in that punishment, under both theories, is performing a symbolic, expressive function—but there is an important difference between them. The idea of denunciation, as with all retributive theories, is not concerned with the effects of punishment. It is not a forward looking theory aimed at preventing crime. Rather, it is concerned with the relation of the punishment to the past event, the crime. It is concerned that there be a relationship between the gravity of the offence and the degree of reprobation or denunciation. The educative theory, on the other hand, is exclusively forward-looking, as are all deterrent theories. Punishment is used as a means of preventing crime and maintaining obedience to the law.

The educative theory rests upon an important premise, namely, that public morality and inhibitions against committing crimes are created and/or preserved by the regular punishment of others. This is a difficult premise to test although some research suggests a clear link between criminality and moral assessments of behaviour. For instance, Kaufmann asked a group of subjects to evaluate the morality of certain behaviour (failing to rescue a drowning man). Some subjects were told that this behaviour was criminal; others were told that there was no duty to rescue. The former group judged the inaction more harshly than

---

[28] *Ante*, p. 4.

the latter group.[29] Similarly, Walker and Marsh discovered that subjects stated that their disapproval of not wearing a seat-belt would increase when this became an offence.[30] Clearly most laws are designed to have some symbolic or expressive function. The point asserted here (and so difficult to validate—although one's intuitions do indicate some plausibility to the claim) is that *punishment* (or at least the real possibility thereof) pursuant to criminal liability is what gives the law its sting. For instance, we have civil laws against race and sex discrimination whose function is not merely to provide a remedy but to underline the important message that such discrimination is *wrong*. The argument here is that if such discrimination had been made *criminal*, the message would have been stronger. This of course raises many questions, including the critical one of determining when conduct is sufficiently "wrong" for criminalisation to be justifiable—an issue to be addressed at the end of this chapter.

3. Incapacitation

The aim of incapacitation or protective sentencing acknowledges the limitations of the other aims of penal policy in practice. It requires a decision on the part of the sentencer that the defendant is a persistent danger or nuisance to others and that the most suitable course of action is "cold-storage"—formerly the death penalty, severance of limbs, deportation to penal colonies and now long-term incarceration in prison or hospital. We are to protect society by preventing the re-emergence of the offender for as long a period as is deemed necessary or acceptable given the severity of the defendant's present offence.

R. v. Sargent (1975) 60 Cr.App. R.74 (Court of Appeal, Criminal Division)

Lawton L.J.:
"We come now to the element of prevention. Unfortunately it is one of the facts of life that there are some offenders for whom neither deterrence nor rehabilitation works. They will go on committing crimes as long as they are able to do so. In those cases the only protection which the public has is that such persons should be locked up for a long period."

It may, additionally, be argued that such longer periods of imprisonment imposed on the persistent offender, are *deserved* on a retributive basis, for what has *already* been done.

Andrew Ashworth, Sentencing and Penal Policy, (1983), p. 211:

"In general, . . . persistent offenders are more blameworthy because they have lost all trace of mitigating circumstances—they know the law only too well,

---

[29] Kaufmann, "Legality and Harmfulness of a Bystander's Failure to Intervene as Determinants of Moral Judgement" in J. Macaulay and L. Berkowitz (eds.) *Altruism and Helping Behaviour: Social Psychological Studies of Some Antecedents and Consequences* (1970).

[30] N. Walker and C. Marsh, "Do Sentences Affect Public Disapproval?" (1984) 24 Brit. J. Criminol. 27.

they know what they can expect if caught offending, and it is no isolated lapse . . . . It is not that to flout the law three times is necessarily more than three times as harmful to society—indeed, from the point of view of society and of the victims the damage is the same whether the offences are committed by one person or by three separate persons. It is that the individual offender is generally more blameworthy on the third occasion than he was on the first."

K. L. Koh, C. M. V. Clarkson and N. A. Morgan, Criminal Law in Singapore and Malaysia: Text and Materials, (1989), p. 19:

"It need not be a question of (the offender's) dangerousness justifying extra punishment . . . , but rather, because of his failure to learn lessons from previous convictions and punishment, he deserves more punishment. Such a person has persisted in criminal behaviour after being specifically warned and already punished. Perhaps such repeated defiance of the law could even be viewed as an additional harm. Alternatively, viewed negatively, a first offender deserves *less* punishment because of the following reason:
'We wish to condemn the person for his act but accord him some respect for the fact that his inhibitions against wrongdoing have functioned on previous occasions, and show some sympathy for the all-too-human frailty that can lead someone to such a lapse. This we do by showing a reduced disapproval of him for his first misdeed' (Von Hirsch, *Past and Future Crimes*, 1985,)."

The problem of the persistent offender is thus sought to be answered in many ways: in terms of the protection of society when there seems no other avenue of approach, in terms of a higher degree of blameworthiness, or even, possibly, that the longer sentence may at long last have a deterrent effect upon the defendant. This latter justification seems particularly wistful given the well-known deleterious effects on criminality of long-term imprisonment. But are the other justifications any better? Is it enough in justification of longer periods of imprisonment than that normally given for the defendant's present offence to say that nothing else has worked, or do we need the retributive argument as well? And how convincing is the argument that the persistent offender is more blameworthy? He is supposed to have "paid the pice" and redressed the balance for previous offences.

Even if one tentatively concludes that justification can be found for the more severe punishment of persistent offenders, points of difficulty do remain.

First, should the longer sentences given to persistent offenders be without any limitation whatsoever? And secondly, should longer sentences of imprisonment be available to deal with all kinds of persistent offenders or only to some?

In both these respects the English experience is illuminating. The Criminal Justice Act of 1948 introduced preventive detention; the sentence was expressly intended to be for the protection of society. By virtue of section 21(2), if conditions as to age and previous convictions were satisfied, a court could impose a sentence of preventive detention of not less than five and not more than fourteen years' imprisonment. It was envisaged that this measure would be used against dangerous offenders—instead it was widely employed against minor, inadequate recidivists. In 1967 preventive detention was replaced by the extended sentence; this, too, is couched in terms of protecting society and is subject to a ceiling.[31] It has also tended to suffer the same fate in the degree of abuse that has taken place. Nevertheless cases do arise in which the need for some kind of protective sentence is sharply focussed.

R. v. Nicholls (1970) 55 Cr.App.R. 150 (Court of Appeal, Criminal Division)

Sachs L.J :
"On March 14, 1970, at Greenwich Magistrates' Court the appellant, who is forty-three years of age, pleaded Guilty to an indecent assault on a girl of the age of seven. Having been committed to quarter sessions under section 29 of the 1952 Act, he was on April 23, 1970 sentenced by the Chairman of Inner London Quarter Sessions to an extended sentence of ten years' imprisonment.

The facts of the case are as follows. On March 1, 1970, a little girl aged seven was playing in a park with her elder sister aged nine and a younger brother. The boy hurt his knee and that resulted in the elder sister having to take him home. However, she had lost a mitten and was looking for it with the girl. At this stage the appellant came up and ingeniously suggested that if the elder sister took her brother away, he and the girl could continue to search for the mitten. Then he went on to invite the girl to go for a drive in his van and they went to another park. The time duly came when he sat on the grass, pulled down the girl's knickers and inserted his finger into her private parts. That was a very serious interference with this little girl, and a bus conductor noticed her distressed condition later on and got in touch with the police. Then followed a series of events that led to the appellant being questioned by the police and eventually admitting his guilt.

This is one of those very unfortunate cases in which the appellant has a record that can justly be described as horrifying. From 1952 when he was aged twenty-five there commenced the series of offences to which this Court must refer. In 1952 there was an indecent assault on a girl aged seven and one taken into consideration; in 1954 attempted rape of a girl aged four; 1961 indecent assault on a girl aged eight and again in 1961 indecent assault on a girl aged seven; in 1962 a common assault on a girl aged eight; and in 1963 indecent assault on a girl aged five. Then in 1964 attempted rape on a girl aged seven with other counts for indecent assaults on a girl aged seven and on one aged nine, as a result of which the appellant received sentences totalling seven years' imprisonment in all. From this term he was released on May 18, 1969, and, as already indicated, within the year comes the offence with which this Court is now concerned.

The appellant in his grounds of appeal rightly states that as regards this last offence the maximum sentence prescribed by statute was (subject to the provisions of an extended sentence in the Criminal Justice Act 1967), five years. He also rightly points out that the ten-year prison sentence is twice the five-year

---

[31] Criminal Justice Act 1967, ss.37–38; Powers of the Criminal Courts Act 1973, s.28; subject to fulfilling certain conditions, an extended sentence may exceed the maximum term authorised for the offence; it may not, however, exceed five years if the normal maximum is less than five years, and ten years if the normal maximum is less than ten years. See further, *post*, pp. 32, 34.

maximum and that he has thus been given the maximum extended sentence available in this particular case. What is said on his behalf is that it should be reduced because there is a possibility of certain treatment. . . .

Now this court has before it a report of September 15 from Dr. Scott. From this and from other reports before the Court it is quite clear that, in the present state of medical knowledge, at best, and I advisedly use the words 'at best,' the only thing that can be done for this man is to give certain six-monthly treatments which may result, and indeed on some occasions have resulted in, a useful damping down of the characteristics which cause these offences. It is absolutely clear that at best this is something that has to be repeated six-monthly and that there is no such thing at present as an absolute cure. It is also patently clear from Dr. Scott's report that this appellant, whatever he may say, is unlikely to co-operate by coming for six-monthly treatments if he is free to do exactly what he likes, and that the only real chance of his submitting himself to such treatment at the requisite intervals is if he is under some sort of pressure such as would result if he was sentenced to an extended sentence and then given parole on terms that he submitted to treatment.

In cases such as the present there is one factor which the Court has to regard as paramount, and that is the protection of these wretched little girls from a man such as the appellant. The Court appreciates it may be a tragedy in the individual case for a person who cannot restrain himself from actions which make him a menace to have a characteristic that necessitates his being treated as a danger to the public, but a danger he is and in those circumstances the only proper course which a court can take is to see that he is not a danger that is allowed to roam about. There is no hope in these cases, as experience has shown, from courses such as probation or allowing the man to be under the care of relatives and so forth. They can only be visited by the maximum custodial sentence, appreciating those prospects which may be of help to the man should the time come for parole. In those circumstances this Court has come, without any hesitation, to the conclusion that this sentence was entirely correct and the appeal must be dismissed."

Appeal dismissed

It is within the context of dangerous offenders such as Nicholls that most debates about persistent offenders have taken place, and it is submitted that this—with the possible extension to the professional criminal (who although defying accurate definition and, indeed, complete separation from other types of criminal, may be described as the criminal who makes a calculated living out of crime)—is where the debate properly belongs. The inadequate recidivist of petty crimes ought not to be brought within the framework of protective sentencing. An example from the United States shows all too clearly how abuses of protective sentencing can take place. In 1979 a state court sentenced a defendant to life imprisonment with no possibility of parole for passing a bad cheque for $100. The normal maximum for the offence was five years' imprisonment but because of the defendant's prior criminal record (for theft, obtaining by deception, burglary and drunk driving) the maximum was raised to life. The trial judge in sentencing said:

"I think you certainly earned this sentence and certainly proved that you're an habitual criminal and the record would indicate that you're beyond rehabilitation and that the only prudent thing to do is to lock you up for the rest of your natural life, so you won't have further victims of your crimes. . . . You'll have plenty of time to think this one over."[32]

This decision was eventually reversed on appeal by the U.S. Supreme Court on the basis that the sentence was disproportionate (and therefore in breach of the Eighth Amendment) and thus a crucial concept is introduced—that of proportionality. Some offences are so minor, that not only should the recidivist not be subject to *longer* periods of imprisonment, he ought not to be subject to imprisonment at all. In other words, as Ashworth suggests, for the persistent petty offender, a ceiling of liability must exist which is drawn by the "normal range of sentences for the kind of offence of which he now stands convicted."[33] Furthermore, this principle of a ceiling, or of proportionality, should apply to other types of persistent offenders. Even though they qualify for longer periods of imprisonment, their present offence must play a large part in determining the length of their sentence. Protective sentencing cannot be without limit; it cannot ignore the dictates of just deserts—of justice.

So according to this view of punishment with which the public have much sympathy,[34] there can be cases where society needs protection; it is thus permissible to incarcerate dangerous offenders who pose a threat to society for longer than non-dangerous offenders committing the same offence. In other words, a penal policy of bifurcation is adopted. On the one hand are "ordinary" offenders (for whom, if anything, the sentences should be shorter) and on the other, dangerous offenders for whom very long sentences might be appropriate. This view has been endorsed in the recent Government White Paper which, while endorsing the principle that punishment ought to be proportionate to the seriousness of the harm done, asserts that longer sentences (*i.e.* up to the maximum available) are justified if necessary to protect the public from serious harm.[35]

Because of the dramatic effect of being categorised a dangerous offender, it becomes crucial to have a satisfactory definition of dangerous. One immediately confronts a problem: "dangerousness" is a matter of degree rather than absolutes. It requires an assessment not only about the *nature* of the risk but the likelihood of its occurrence.

Numerous attempts[36] have been made to define a more satisfactory and workable concept of dangerousness than preventive detention or the extended sentence. The latest and most important attempt was initiated by the Howard League for Penal Reform and has become

---

[32] *Solem* v. *Helm* 463 U.S. 277; 77 L.Ed.2d. 637 (1983).

[33] A. Ashworth, *Sentencing and Penal Policy*, (1983), p. 227. For further discussion of petty and professional persistent offenders, see pp. 235–241. See also *R.* v. *McGarvie* [1989] Crim.L.R. 516.

[34] See N. Walker and M. Hough, *Public Attitudes to Sentencing* (1988) pp. 178–9.

[35] Home Office White Paper, *Crime, Justice and Protecting the Public* (1990) Cm. 965 para. 3.13.

[36] The Report of the Committee on Mentally Abnormal Offenders, (Butler Report) Cmnd. 6244 (1975); Report of the Advisory Council on the Penal System, Sentences of Imprisonment (A Review of Maximum Penalties) (1978), H.M.S.O.; F. Floud and W. Young, *Dangerousness and Criminal Justice*; (The Floud Report,) 1981.

known as the Floud Report on Dangerous Offenders.[37] Three initial
points need to be made in relation to it; first, it concerns itself with
those offenders who are legally sane and thus will bear legal responsibility for their actions; secondly, much emphasis is placed upon the
requirement of *fault* (in terms of intentionality and lack of mitigating
factors), and, thirdly, it is based upon a premise in sentencing policy
that has not yet materialised. The Report of the Advisory Council on the
Penal System[38] recommended in 1978 that the legal maxima for offences
ought to be reduced to such a level that they would have a realistic
impact on actual sentences given by the courts and thus present a realistic ceiling. Presently, because the maxima are so high courts have
resorted to informal sentencing guidelines known as the tariff, or to so-
called "guideline judgments,"[39] to determine normal standards of punishment for different classes of crimes. For example, the offence of
wounding or causing grievous bodily harm with intent contrary to section 18 of the Offences Against the Person Act 1861 carries a maximum
of life imprisonment, yet 90 per cent. of those convicted under section
18 get sentences of five years or less. The Report accordingly recommended that the new maximum ought to be placed at the 90 per cent.
level; five years would thus become the maximum for an offence under
section 18. This procedure was carried out for all offences; in virtually
all cases (except where the maximum was already low) it was recommended that the maximum be reduced to the 90 per cent. level. Such a
process is in itself open to criticism[40] but most attacks have centred on
the provisions designed to deal with the lacuna left by such low maxima. How were the remaining 10 per cent., who presently receive
heavier sentences, to be dealt with? The exceptional sentence that they
advocated has been criticised at length elsewhere[41]; what is of interest
now is that the recommendations from the Floud Report have taken the
lacuna as their starting point. They accept that there is no special case
for a preventive form of detention whilst the legal maxima are so high;
their recommendations are thus dependent upon a substantial change
first being wrought in sentencing guidelines.

Jean Floud, "Dangerousness and Criminal Justice" (1982) 22 Brit. J. Criminol. 213 at 215–218, 220–222:

" . . . [T]he shorter sentences become, the more difficult it seems to be to
argue that there should not be a special protective sentence for the small
number of exceptional offenders judged to present an unacceptable risk of
further serious harm. Indeed, the provision of such a special sentence may well
be a condition of securing shorter sentences overall.

[37] *Ibid.* n. 36.
[38] *Ibid.* n. 36.
[39] *Post* p. 61.
[40] H. M. Keating, "Sentencing Reform: Has the Time Come for New Maxima?" (1979) 9 Kingston
Law Review 55; Cross and Ashworth, *The English Sentencing System* (3rd ed., 1981) pp. 204–217.
[41] Sir L. Radzinowicz and R. Hood, "Dangerousness and Criminal Justice" [1981] Crim.L.R. 756.

This was recognised by the Advisory Council on the Penal System which proposed that legislation to effect a drastic reduction of maximum penalties should include provision for a special discretionary sentence, of unrestricted but determinate length, for a minority of exceptional, 'dangerous' offenders. The proposed two-tier system was itself the target of objections of a practical kind; but the suggestion that the distinction recognised in practice by the courts between the 'ordinary' and the 'dangerous' offender should be formalised and given statutory recognition aroused fierce opposition grounded in fundamental objections of principle. Our own proposals are attracting the same opposition.

It is worth noting that no-one dismisses the practical problem. That is, no-one denies the existence of a minority of serious offenders who present a continuing risk. The argument is all about degrees of risk, perceptions of danger and justifiable public alarm, the difficulty of deciding whether or not someone is 'dangerous' and the legitimacy of confining people for what they *might* do as well as for what they have actually done.

The question of the legitimacy of protective sentencing goes to the root of the matter and we considered it carefully. We took seriously the fundamental objections raised by those who argue that it is never permissible to detain a legally responsible offender in anticipation of the harm he may cause, and that restraint must be justified in some other way (for example, as retributive punishment). We do not claim to have said the last word on a difficult ethical problem; but, for the reasons set out in our Report, we found these arguments unconvincing.

We found ourselves less resistant to the argument of other critics who object that it is impossible to define and identify dangerous offenders satisfactorily for legal purposes and rest their case on the ambiguousness of the concept of dangerousness itself and the inherent unpredictability of human behaviour . . .

To reject protective sentencing, as morally unacceptable in principle and incapable of just administration in practice, completely avoids all the difficulties and dilemmas inherent in the practice—but it is the only way of doing so. Since we could not follow the critics to the end of the road, we were left with no alternative but to review the practical ethics of protective sentencing and to try to formulate the problems raised by the practice, in terms which would permit us to propose solutions that seemed to be both just and workable . . .

We paid a great deal of attention to the practical difficulty of identifying, with any degree of confidence, serious offenders against whom protection is needed because they present a continuing risk of serious harm. As will be evident from our Report, we sifted a considerable quantity of theoretical argument and empirical evidence bearing directly or indirectly on the state of the art of assessing 'dangerousness.' We reached a conclusion which is not surprising, in so far as it amounts to saying that, since it is impossible to be sure how people will behave in the future, if only because of the working of chance, any attempt to apply precautions selectively against some persons for the sake of others is bound to be more or less wide of the mark. What *is* surprising—and very alarming—is to discover just how wide of the mark it turns out to be, whenever it is possible to put predictive judgments to the test by following the post–release careers of 'dangerous' offenders. Statisticians have calculated the probabilities: so many judgments of *dangerous* falsified by the offender's subsequent behaviour (that is to say, by his failure to cause further grave harm) and so many judgments of *safe* falsified by the further serious offences he commits. Not surprisingly, it tends to be the critics of protective sentencing who worry about the former and members of the general public who worry about the latter. But the former figure, the proportion of falsified judgments of *dangerous*, even at its lowest, is so uncomfortably high that no-one engaged in making predictive judgments in the administration of justice can fail to be impressed—or, more likely, depressed. As matters now stand, parole boards and similar bodies, to say nothing of courts, are, on average, at best likely to be wrong as right in thinking that the offenders they decide to detain as dangerous will actually do further serious harm if left at large. Whatever be the prospects of improvement—and it must be admitted that, though they exist, they are not rosy and are forever constrained by a large factor of chance, it is likely that at least two persons are detained for every one person who is prevented from doing serious harm. This is to say that each offender in protective custody probably suffers, in addition to the usual hardships of imprisonment, at least a 50 per cent. risk of being unnecessarily detained. On what grounds are we justified in doing him this grave harm—for grave harm it undoubtedly is, on any reckoning?

The justification can only be that we are thereby relieving someone else of a substantial risk of grave harm—that we are justly redistributing a burden of risk that we cannot immediately reduce. This formulation of the answer, in terms of redistributing risk, seems to us to be more appropriate to the jurisprudence of protective sentencing than the one that is frequently given in terms of social utility . . .

. . . The general objective of our proposals is to bring protective sentencing under statutory control, while leaving ample scope for the necessary exercise of judicial discretion in the sentencing of a very heterogeneous group of exceptional offenders. To this end, we have formulated categories of grave harm, against which the public, in certain circumstances, may claim the protection of a special sentence outside the permitted maximum for a relevant serious offence; and we have defined a severely restricted class of offenders who might be eligible for such a sentence and mandatory evidential and procedural requirements within which judicial and executive discretion would be exercised in the administration of the proposed sentence.

I want to say something about three features of these proposals which are likely to attract criticism: our attempt to say what the public should be protected against (i.e. our definition of 'grave harm'); our decision not to place a statutory upper limit on the proposed protective sentence; and not to give statutory expression to tests of 'dangerousness.'

We took it as axiomatic that the public is entitled to the protection of a special sentence only against grave harm; and that no offender should be eligible for a protective sentence unless grave harm is manifested in his criminal conduct. Our first thought was, naturally, that the interpretation of grave harm in this context should be as specific as possible . . .

[But] we are forced to the conclusion that the problem of distinguishing between 'serious' and other harm, cannot be wholly objectified; that harms to the person are sui generis and enjoy special moral status, whatever their degree; but that a protective sentence, which carries the risk to the offender that he will be unnecessarily deprived of his liberty, should be used only where the victims of the anticipated harm are themselves exposed to the risk of unusual hardship (pain and suffering, shock and fear, injury to health or beggary). We therefore propose that grave harm for the purposes of protective sentencing should be interpreted as comprising the following categories: death, serious bodily injury, serious sexual assault, severe or prolonged pain or mental stress, loss of or damage to property which causes severe personal hardship, damage to the environment which has a severely adverse effect on public health or safety, serious damage to the security of the state. This classification is similar in intended scope to that proposed by the Advisory Council on the Penal System, though it is formulated in somewhat more precise and concrete terms. Thus, we propose that the elements of grave physical and psychological harm should be specified and that serious sexual asaults, which we take to be harmful sui generis, should be given separate mention. We have added to the category of indirect, generalised harm, which is represented in their classification by serious damage to the security of the state, another, *viz.* damage to the environment resulting in serious damage to public health or safety. We rejected the category 'damage to the general fabric of society' as being either redundant or too inclusive in its vagueness . . . "

The Report then goes on to recommend that the length of the protective sentence should be a matter for judicial discretion; they agreed, therefore, with earlier recommendations of the Advisory Council that such sentences could be of any determinate length. For this group of offenders then, no ceiling was thought appropriate. In theory, therefore, the idea of proportionality could be completely ignored. Further they felt unable to formulate restrictive criteria of dangerousness for the court to apply; this too would be left to judicial discretion.

This Report, like the others that preceded it, has been subject to much discussion. Despite the infrequency with which the present extended sentence is imposed,[42] the issue of protective sentencing is highly controversial. The discussion falls into two main camps.

Firstly, there is what Floud called "the difficult ethical question." Instead of punishing the offender on the basis of what he has already done (and perhaps punishing him more severely because he has *already* committed several crimes), punishment is sought to be based on past *and future* predictions of criminality. How, as an issue of morality, can punishment be based on something the offender has yet to (and may never) do?

Andrew von Hirsch, Past or Future Crimes, (1985), p. 11:

"Advocates of the desert model opposed the use of individual prediction in sentencing as a matter of principle, not merely because of such forecasts' tendency to error. Their objection to predictive sentencing was simply that it led to undeserved punishments and would do so even if the false-positive rate could be reduced. The use of predictions, accurate or not, meant that those identified as future recidivists would be treated more severely than those not so identified, not because of differences in the blameworthiness of their past conduct, but because of crimes they supposedly would commit in future. It was felt that punishment, as a blaming institution, was warranted only for past culpable choices and could not justly be levied for future conduct. Unless the person actually made the wrongful choice he was predicted to make, he ought not to be condemned for that choice—and hence should not suffer punishment for it."

The Floud Report resolves this normative debate by reference to two principles: that of just redistribution of risk (in other words, the risk of grave harm to potential victims must be considered against the grave harm of unnecessary protective sentences) and that citizens of a free society have the right to be presumed free of harmful intentions. This second principle means that the State should not be able to act (by

---

[42] An extended sentence was imposed in thirteen cases in 1987; this represents typical usage of the provision. The government accordingly proposes to abolish such extended sentences. See *post*, p. 74.

means of preventive detention) against those who have not yet committed any act; they are to be presumed to be free of whatever harmful intentions they have. These principles have been judged by others to be deficient[43] but even if a satisfactory answer is provided, the second group of objections remain.

For these anti-protectionists it is objectionable in terms of justice to confine people in the name of public safety for longer periods than would otherwise be justified, given the unreliability of predictions of dangerous behaviour, with the preponderance of so-called "false positives"[44] and the danger of abuse of special sentencing provisions by the judiciary.[45]

Nigel Walker, Punishment, Danger and Stigma (1980), pp. 98–99:

"(In challenging the anti-protectionist's view) . . . let us accept that in our present state of partial ignorance any labelling of the individual as a future perpetrator of violence is going to be mistaken in the majority of cases. Does it follow that it is wrong to apply this label? Only if we swallow two assumptions. One is that it is *morally wrong* to make mistakes of this kind. Everyone would agree that it is *regrettable*; but if the decision is taken with good intentions, and one has done one's best, with the available information, to minimise the percentage of mistaken detentions, is it *morally wrong*? Only if we swallow the second assumption—namely the anti-protectionist's insistence that our overriding objective must be to minimise the total number of mistaken decisions, treating a mistaken decision to detain as exactly equal to a mistaken decision to release. The anti-protectionist is using two neat rhetorical tricks at once. By referring to mistaken detentions and mistaken releases simply as 'mistakes,' he is implying that they all count the same; and by glossing over the difference between 'regrettable' and 'morally wrong,' he is implying that it is our moral duty to go for the smallest number of mistakes irrespective of their nature.

To put this point in concrete terms, suppose that you have in custody three men who have done serious violence to more or less innocent victims. Suppose too that the best actuarial information you can get tells you that one of them— but not *which* one—will do more violence if released. The anti-protectionist is saying that it is your moral duty to release all three instead of continuing to detain all three because release will involve only one mistaken decision instead of two mistaken decisions. Yet the one mistaken release would mean injury or death to someone, while the two mistaken detentions would mean something quite different: the continued deprivation of freedom for three men of whom an unidentifiable two would not do anybody injury if released."[46]

There clearly is difficulty in reconciling the principle of desert with

[43] See, *e.g.*, A. E. Bottoms and R. Brownsword, "The Dangerousness Debate after the Floud Report," (1982) 22 Brit. J. Criminol. 229.
[44] Those wrongly predicted as being dangerous. See, *e.g.*, N. Morris, *The Future of Imprisonment*, (1974), although Morris's views seem to have undergone some change since then.
[45] *Ante* pp. 26–27. See further, L. Radzinowicz and R. Hood, "Dangerousness and Criminal Justice: A few Reflections," (1981) Crim. L. R. 756.
[46] For a critique of Walker's views, see D. Wood, "Dangerous Offenders and the Morality of Protective Sentencing," (1988) Crim.L.R. 424 at pp. 425–429. The conclusion drawn by Wood is that there is no need to distinguish between dangerous offenders and dangerous non-offenders. He likens their civil committment to the quarantining of carriers of deadly diseases. It should be obvious from what has been said in the course of this chapter that such a view is entirely repugnant to us.

that of incapacitation and as we have seen this has caused some to turn against any form of protective sentencing. There are others, however, who argue for its retention for reasons other than so far canvassed.

David A. Thomas, "The Justice Model of Sentencing—Its Implications for the English Sentencing System" in the University of Cambridge, Institute of Criminology (Occasional Papers No. 8), The Future of Sentencing, (1982), pp. 66–67:

"The extended sentence . . . appears to be dying a natural death . . . . [It] has fallen out of favour with the sentencers, probably on the grounds both of the principle on which it is founded and the complexity of its provisions. The number of extended sentences passed annually has now declined to less than thirty, and many of these are probably not disproportionate to the offences for which they are imposed . . . . I would not advocate the resuscitation of the extended sentence, but I see at least one advantage in retaining the extended sentence legislation on the statute book. This is that its existence constitutes a statutory reminder of the proportionality principle which applies to ordinary sentences of imprisonment. The existence of a special legislative provision creating a limited exception to a major principle which is not itself defined in legislation serves indirectly to reinforce that principle while avoiding the difficulties which might arise from an attempt to pin the major principle down in precise legislative form. The danger of abolishing provisions authorising the detention of habitual offenders for periods of time disproportionate to their most recent offence is that it might lead to the adoption of the practice of imposing disproportionate sentences to recidivists generally, and the weakening of the central principle of proportionality in relation to ordinary terms of imprisonment."

More ambitiously, von Hirsch has argued recently that it may be possible to construct a form of protective sentencing *within* a framework of desert.[47] First, he reviews that form of protective sentencing known as "selective incapacitation" based around the work of Greenwood[48] and Wilson[49] which involves the construction of a prediction index based on factors such as prior record, employment status and drug use to identify those offenders most likely to commit the most serious offences. Studies based upon this index have apparently impressive results but von Hirsch dismisses this as the way forward for a number of reasons. All of the studies are based on imprisoned offenders only which is likened to "trying to learn about the smoking habits of smokers generally by studying the smoking activity of residents of a lung cancer ward."[50] More importantly even than this however, selective incapacitation, despite claims by some of its adherents, does not take us any closer to resolving the conflict between desert and protective sentencing. To do this von Hirsch goes on to suggest that we have to consider the implementation of "categorical incapacitation." "The focus is no longer on individual offender characteristics associated with

---

[47] *Past or Future Crimes*, (1985).
[48] *Selective Incapacitation*, (1982).
[49] *Thinking about Crime*, (1983).
[50] "Deservedness and Dangerousness in Sentencing Policy" (1986) Crim.L.R. 79 at p. 81.

recidivism but, rather, on *categories* of crimes. Conviction for some crimes may be predictive of an increased average likelihood of convicts offending again. One tries to identify which crime categories are thus linked with higher recidivism rates."[51] This research is still in its infancy but it may, in the light of the following extract, enable those of us who would currently feel that protective sentencing is unjust because of the lack of ceiling and proportionality, to reassess its worth. As Floud has stated,[52] no-one doubts that there are dangerous offenders who remain a threat to society.

Andrew von Hirsch, Past or Future Crimes, (1985), p. 159:

"Let me emphasise how a categorical incapacitation strategy comporting with desert would differ from the individual prediction strategies to which I have objected. First, those convicted of equally reprehensible conduct would have to be treated similarly. Categorical incapacitation concentrates on offence categories, not on the selection of a subclass of dangerous persons within an offence category. The emphasis would be neither on the offender's prior record nor on status factors, as is the case with selective incapacitation. Second and equally important, the other requirements of desert need to be complied with: the requirements of rank ordering and cardinal proportionality. Thus it would not be permissible to give convicted car thieves substantial prison sentences, even if researchers were to find that these thieves were high risks."

4. Rehabilitation

To punish with the aim of reforming or rehabilitating the offender has constituted one of the most ambitious developments in penal theory. One aims to secure conformity, not through fear (which is the more limited object of deterrence) but through some inner positive motivation on the part of the individual. The process has been described as "improving [the offender's] . . . character so that he is less often inclined to commit offences again even when he can do so without fear of the penalty."[53] The source of the change in motivation or improvement in behaviour has been variously described but remains one of the ambiguities of the concept of reform.

The origins of the rehabilitative ideal are inextricably linked with the humanitarian movement for prison reform; as the institutions were to be reformed so too were the inmates. The great penal reformers of the eighteenth century, Beccaria, Bentham, Eden and Romilly, all advocated a system of punishment which combined deterrent with reformative features. It was their belief, however, that reform could come of punishment itself—by, for example, a period of solitude which would induce remorse, repentance and reform. Indeed, the first penitentiary in the United States was created by the Quakers in Philadelphia in 1793 in order that prisoners could pay "penance" for their sins and thereby

---

[51] *Past or Future Crimes* (1985), p. 150.
[52] *Ante* p. 29.
[53] N. Walker "Punishing, Denouncing or Reducing Crime" from *Reshaping the Criminal Law* (1978), p. 393.

become "cleansed."[54] The object here was to make offenders "better persons" capable of being reintegrated into society (rather than simply "cleansed" by having purged their sins and thereby repaying their debt to society, which is the more limited object of expiation). When, towards the end of the nineteenth century the aim of reform became (with deterrence) part of official penal policy in this country, there was more than an element of this thinking present in the measures taken.

This view of reform has since been thoroughly discredited but in its place grew the belief that reform could and should be a concomitant of punishment. Proponents argued that herein lay the best way of reducing crime; indeed so much of an obvious truth did the rehabilitative ideal become that one searches almost in vain for a reasoned statement of its merits. What does become clear is the disenchantment with moral or religious exhortations. In their place came the developing behavioural sciences and medicine; as more was learnt about the antecedents of human behaviour it was hoped that therapeutic measures could be designed which would "improve"[55] the offender's behaviour. In the 1960s and early 1970s a variety of measures were introduced in this country[56] but although claims were made concerning their reformative potential, only community service can truly be seen in this light.[57] Prison was also seen as having a role to play in the process of rehabilitation.

Gladstone Committee (1895) C. 7702, para. 25:

" . . . [P]rison treatment should be effectually designed to maintain, stimulate, or awaken the higer susceptibilities of prisoners . . . whenever possible and turn them out of prison better men and women, both physically and morally, than when they came in."

Prison Rules 1964 (S.I. 1964 No. 1):

" . . . [T]he purpose of the training and treatment of convicted prisoners shall be to encourage and assist them to lead a good and useful life."

Judges, with this in mind, have sometimes passed longer sentences to allow time for retraining.[58]

It is with steps such as these that the full implications of the rehabili-

---

[54] For further discussion see N. Walker, *Crime and Punishment in Great Britain* (1968), pp. 134–138, and Morris, *ante*, n. 44.

[55] Advocates of reform consistently employ such vague terms, yet their reference and reliance upon studies of recidivism rates leads one to conclude that most writers mean that the offender would be less likely to reoffend.

[56] Parole and the suspended sentence were introduced by the Criminal Justice Act 1967, ss.60 and 22. Both measures were much more concerned with reducing the prison population; in that respect they were of only limited and temporary success.

[57] Criminal Justice Act 1972, Powers of Criminal Courts Act 1973, s.14. The effect of an order of community service is to require the offender to perform unpaid work under supervision of a probation officer for the number of hours (more than 40 and less than 240) laid down in the order. See *post*, p. 75.

[58] R. Cross, *Punishment, Prison and the Public* (1971).

tative ideal becomes clear. Instead of looking to the past—to the offence committed—the sentencer must concern himself with the future needs of the offender. The sentence should then be chosen which has the best chance of bringing about the desired change; thus the principle of treating like cases in a like manner has no part to play. This latter concept is based on the offence whereas with reform there are no like cases. Each case has to be determined on its own merits. There ought, in theory at least, to be complete individualisation of sentences—the sentence should depend, not on the offence, but on the offender.[59]

H. Weihofen, "Retribution is Obsolete," National Probation and Parole Association News, XXXIX (1960) 1, 4:

"Crime and criminal responsibility are not mere interesting abstractions for the amusement of philosophers dreaming up metaphysical constructs. Crime is a reality, an ever present danger which in some cases is literally a matter of life and death.

The voices of ignorance and hate are loud enough now to shout down almost every effort to improve criminal administration by substituting rational for irrational solutions, a rehabilitative for a punitive approach. The rationale of these programs calls for understanding the sociological, economic and cultural sources of criminality, the psychology of criminals and our reactions to criminality. This is too sophisticated for the single-minded devotees of punishment . . .

I resent the apostles of punishment-for-its-own-sake arrogating to themselves words like 'moral' and 'justice' and implying in consequence that those who scorn their metaphysics are amoral or at least unconcerned with moral values. Surely the feeling of concern for the offender as a human being; the desire to save him from a criminal career and to help him redeem himself as a member of the human family; the even wider concern to prevent others from falling into criminality by searching out the influences and conditions that produce those frustrating and embittering defeats, degradations and humiliations of the human spirit that turn a man against his fellow men; the effort, therefore, to give men those advantages that will help them to keep their feet on the right path—better education, more healthful dwellings, readier aid for casualties of sickness, accident and failures of employment—surely all of this is not a less moral ideal than that which knows only one measure of morality, an eye for an eye and a tooth for a tooth.

Half a century ago, Winston Churchill said, in the House of Commons:

'The mood and temper of the public with regard to the treatment of crime and criminals is one of the most unfailing tests of the civilisation of any country. A calm, dispassionate recognition of the rights of the accused, and even of the convicted criminal against the State—a constant heart searching by all charged with the duty of punishment—a desire and eagerness to rehabilitate in the world of industry those who have paid their due in the hard coinage of punishment: tireless efforts towards the discovery of curative and regenerative processes: unfailing faith and there is a treasure, if you can only find it, in the heart of every man. These are the symbols which, in the treatment of crime and criminals mark and measure the stored-up strength of a nation.'

Yes; and I would add, these are the sign and proof of its morality."

[59] The judge is not, therefore, necessarily the person best suited to carry out the task of sentencing. The rehabilitative ideal is often coupled with an acceptance of the need for an "expert" bench.

Von Hirsch suggests that much of the true appeal of rehabilitative ideology lies in the fact that its advocates were both able to have their cake and eat it. "(I)t offered both therapy and restraint. One did not have to assume that all criminals were redeemable but could merely hope that some might be. Therapy could be tried on apparently amenable defendants, but always with a fail-safe: the offender who seemed unsuitable for, or unresponsive to, treatment could be separated from the community."[60]

Despite the attractiveness of the idea of rehabilitated offenders who would not wish to re-offend, the rehabilitative ideal has declined sharply in popularity. As can be seen from the following extracts, criticisms have come from almost every possible quarter. Initially such attacks were deflected by the argument that the criminal justice system was not truly committed to rehabilitation; often it was sacrificed completely to other competing ideals (such as deterrence), or that appropriate means had yet to be found to have the desired impact upon the defendant. However, rehabilitation has been a feature of the criminal justice system for long enough now for some judgments to be made. Studies of recidivism rates do not lend any support to the rehabilitative ideal. As it has become apparent that reform is not working, so has come the demand (met in some of the states of the U.S.A.) that punishment ought once again to concentrate on what the offender has done.

A. E. Bottoms, "An Introduction to 'The Coming Crisis' "in A. E. Bottoms and R. H. Preston, The Coming Penal Crisis, (1980), pp. 1–3:

"First, and the dominant factor in much current penal consideration, comes *the collapse of the rehabilitative ideal.* . . . A succession of negative research reports has—with a few exceptions which do not seriously disturb the conclusion—suggested that different types of treatment make little or no difference to the subsequent reconviction rates of offenders. . . . As the Serota Report (ACPS 1977) succinctly put it:

'A steadily accumulating volume of research has shown that, if reconviction rates are used to measure the success or failure of sentencing policy, there is virtually nothing to choose between different lengths of custodial sentence, different types of institutional regime, and even between custodial and non-custodial treatment; (para. 8).'

Very recently, the Home Office's *Review* has endorsed this view. . . .

But the objections to the treatment (or rehabilitation) ethic have not been solely based on empirical demonstratons of lack of efficacy. Strong theoretical objections have also been raised, perhaps most influentially in the American Friends Service Committee's (1971) *Struggle for Justice,* which argued that there was:

'compelling evidence that the individualised-treatment model, the ideal

---

[60] *Past or Future Crimes,* (1985), p. 5.

towards which reformers have been urging us for at least a century, is theoretically faulty, systematically discriminatory in application, and inconsistent with some of our most basic concepts of justice (p. 12).'

What lies behind these claims?

(i) *'Theoretically faulty'*—because, it can be claimed, the treatment model implies that criminal behaviour has its roots in the deficiencies of the individual and his upbringing, and that if these are remedied, the crime rate will be cut; but this medical analogy is inappropriate, and crime is far more a result of the overall organization of society than of the deficiencies of the individual.

(ii) *'Systematically discriminatory'*—because the treatment model typically takes more severe coercive action in cases of 'unsatisfactory' home circumstances or 'dubious' moral background; but these judgments are made by middle-class workers who unwittingly but systematically discriminate against the poor and the disadvantaged, and in favour of the 'good' homes of the privileged.

(iii) *'Inconsistent with justice'*—because judgments involving the liberty of the individual are made (in the name of 'casework' or whatever) on the basis of extremely impressionistic evidence which is usually not revealed to the offender, and which he cannot therefore challenge; and the result may be, for example, that some will serve long sentences for trivial crimes because their 'attitudes have not improved,' while others convicted of serious crime but who have allegedly 'responded' are let out.

Underneath criticisms like these, it will be noted, lies a fundamental conviction by the critics as to the essentially *coercive* nature of the rehabilitative ideal . . . . Many adherents of the ideal blinded themselves as to this coerciveness, in the false belief that benevolent intentions preclude a coercive result . . . ."

M. Cohen, "Moral Aspects of the Criminal Law" (1940) 49 Yale L.J. 987 at 1012–1014:

"The most popular theory today is that the proper aim of criminal procedure is to reform the criminal so that he may become adjusted to the social order. A mixture of sentimental and utilitarian motives gives this view its great vogue. With the spread of humane feeling and the waning of faith in the old conception of the necessity for inflicting pain in the treatment of children and those suffering from mental disease, there has come a revulsion at the hardheartedness of the old retributive theory. The growing belief in education and in the healing powers of medicine encourages people to suppose that the delinquent may be re-educated to become a useful member of society. Even from the strictest economic point of view, individual men and women are the most valuable assets of any society. Is it not better to save them for a life of usefulness rather than punish them by imprisonment which generally makes them worse after they leave than before they entered?

There are, however, a number of highly questionable assumptions back of this theory which need to be critically examined.

We have already had occasion to question the assumption that crime is a physical or mental disease. We may now raise the question whether it is curable and if so at what cost to society? Benevolent social reformers are apt to ignore the amount of cold calculating business shrewdness among criminals. Some hot-blooded ones may respond to emotional appeal; but they are also likely to back-slide when opportunity or temptation comes along. Human beings are not putty that can be remolded at will by benevolent intentions. The overwhelming majority of our criminals have been exposed to the influence of our school system which we have at great cost tried to make as efficient as possible. Most criminals are also religious, as prison chaplains can testify. Yet with all our efforts school education and religion do not eliminate crime. It has not even been demonstrated that they are progressively minimising it . . . . The analogy of the criminal law to medicine breaks down. The surgeon can determine with a fair degree of accuracy when there is an inflamed appendix or cancerous growth, so that by cutting it out he can remove a definite cause of distress. Is there in the complex of our social system any one cause of crime which any social physician can as readily remove on the basis of similarly verifiable knowledge?

Let us abandon the light-hearted pretension that any of us know how all cases of criminality can be readily cured, and ask the more modest and serious question: to what can criminals be re-educated or re-conditioned so that they can live useful lives? It would indeed be illiberal dogmatism to deny all possibility and desirability of effort along this line. Yet we must keep in mind our human limitations.

If the causes of crime are determined by the life of certain groups, it is foolish to deal with the individual as if he were a self-sufficient and self-determining system. We must deal with the whole group to which he naturally belongs or gravitates and which determines his morale. Otherwise we have to adapt him completely to some other group or social condition, which is indeed a very difficult problem in social engineering.

And here we must not neglect the question of cost. When we refer to any measure as impracticable, we generally mean that the cost is too great. There is doubtless a tremendous expense in maintaining our present system of punishment. But this expense is not unlimited. Suppose that fiendish perpetrators of horrible crimes on children could be reformed by being sent first for several years to a special hospital. Will people vote large funds for such purposes when honest law-abiding citizens so often cannot get adequate hospital facilities? . . . We certainly should not give even the appearance of reward for criminality. Let us not forget that there is always a natural resentment in any society against those who have attacked it. Will people be satisfied to see one who is guilty of horrible crimes simply reformed, and not give vent to the social horror and resentment against the miscreant? It is difficult to believe that any such course would not result in a return to personal vengeance on the part of the relatives or friends of the victim."

R. J. Gerber & P. D. McAnany, "Punishment: Current Survey of Philosophy and Law," (1967) 11 Saint Louis University L.J., 491 at 502–535:

"To begin with rehabilitation, it is clear that its image has been tarnished by a series of exposés. The initial discovery has shown that rehabilitation has frequently been a cover for neglect. Persons put into penal incarceration in the name of social reform have been left there interminably because they are being 'cured.' The ugly truth is that few states have facilities to implement a rehabilitation program at the level at which their policy insists on treatment under terms of confinement. The result is far worse than an entirely punitive system whose sanctions are carefully measured by law.

A second serious charge made against the treatment-minded is that their approach is an invitation to personal tyranny and denial of human rights. Once a prisoner is placed in the hands of the doctor to be cured before he is released, there is no one who can predict how long the cure will take, nor control the autonomy of the doctor's judgment. The real impact of [the] C. S. Lewis . . .

article[61] comes in the fact that all of 'treatment' is done in the name of a benevolent, but uncontrolled, humanitarianism. It is not Lewis' point, nor any other of its critics, that rehabilitation is not a valid goal of society, but they all insist that some other more fundamental justification must be present to provide support for what must be conceived as only ancillary to the essential nature of punishment. Nor only must we seek justification for punishment elsewhere, but a clear limit must be placed on what criminals can be forced to undergo for their own benefit . . . .

Finally, an argument is made that all the science in the world cannot really rehabilitate a person whose attitudes are anti-social. The only way to change a man is from the inside out, beginning with the heart. While this may sound a bit revivalistic, behind it is couched a theory as to the real nature of the 'cure'. Do criminals need psychotherapy, job-training, education, or do they have a more basic need to draw them from criminal ways, a need for 'repentance' and forgiveness? To put the issue at a practical level, what possible motivations can a social scientist give a prisoner when he is not interested in the prisoner as a person? Can we really expect to have a good program without a proper understanding of motivations in the personal sense? Further, can a rehabilitation expert give proper motivation when he himself has no commitment to the motives he insists on, or can he insist on the goals of 'normal' society when these are at best morally ambiguous? . . . Society at large has not been overly successful in offering a pattern for living except to the already successful."

Andrew Von Hirsch, Doing Justice—The Choice of Punishments (Report of the Committee for the Study of Incarceration), (1976), pp. 11–18:

"Rehabilitation, according to the conventional assumptions, is the pre-eminent goal. The sentence itself is seen as an instrument for treatment: when deciding between imprisonment and probation, for example, the sentencer is supposed to take into account which disposition will best promote the offender's rehabilitation. Thus, the American Law Institute's Model Penal Code, completed in 1962, recommends that a sentencing court may choose prison rather than probation if, among other reasons, the offender is 'in need of correctional treatment that can be provided most effectively by his commitment to an institution.'

Since this theory looks to offenders' need for treatment rather than to the character of their crimes, it allows different sentences for similar offences. If one of two convicted burglars is thought likely to respond to community-based treatment while the other seems more amenable to a prison-based program, that would be reason for putting one on probation and imprisoning the other. The difference in the two sentences is rationalised as necessary for the protection of the public: the two burglars will be less likely to return to crime if each is given treatment suited to his particular need. That explanation holds, however, only if the programs work. Unless the programs can demonstrably prevent recidivism, the discrepancy in the two dispositions remains unaccounted for. It is therefore essential to ask: How effective are treatment programs?

Proponents of correctional treatment once had reason to complain that their methods had never really been given a chance to work. Prison administrators, while long on talk about rehabilitation, were short on programs: the available 'treatments' did little more than train convicts in skills for which there existed no market in the outside world, such as making license plates. But during recent decades—especially in California—seriously thought-out and well-financed

[61] *Ante*, p. 10.

experimental programs have been tried. The results have not been encouraging. . . . To judge the effectiveness of a program, one must evaluate it comparatively: how much better do offenders placed in the program perform than those with similar characteristics who did not ·participate? No program is proven effective unless those enrolled in it show a consistently lower rate of return to crime than comparable offenders not enrolled.

A wide variety of rehabilitation programs have now been studied. A few successes have been reported, but the overall results are disappointing. Thus, for example:

> The character of the institution seems to have little or no influence on recidivism. It was hoped that prisoners in smaller and less regimented institutions would return to crime less often on release, but that hope has not been borne out.
>
> Although probation has long been acclaimed for its rehabilitative usefulness, the recidivism rate among otherwise like offenders fails to show a clear difference whether they are placed on probation or confined. While those on probation perform no worse, the claim that they perform better has not been sustained.
>
> More intensive supervision on the streets, a recurring theme in rehabilitation literature, has not been shown to curb recidivism. Probationers or parolees assigned to small caseloads with intense supervision appear to return to crime about as often as those assigned to large caseloads with minimal supervision.
>
> Vocational training has been widely advocated, on the theory that people turn to crime because they lack the skills enabling them to earn a lawful living. The quality of many programs has been poor. But where well-staffed and well-equipped programs of vocational training for marketable skills have been tried in institutions, studies fail to show a lower rate of return to crime. In California, where this technique has most extensively been used, authorities have all but given up hope . . .
>
> In the late 1960s, 'community-based' treatment received increased emphasis. It was thought that offenders' chances for being rehabilitated would be enhanced if the treatment were undertaken in their home neighborhoods. Some of these 'community-based' programs consisted of intensive counselling or other therapy conducted in small, residential facilities located in low-income neighbourhoods; others consisted of daytime treatment programs that allowed the participants to live at home. Results thus far have not been encouraging . . .

Some advocates of rehabilitation attribute the current failures to inadequate screening. Programs are applied indiscriminately to heterogeneous groups of offenders, some of whom may be responsive while others are not . . . It is, they say, like using insulin to treat all diseases: . . . Arguably, outcomes could begin to improve were one able in rehabilitation as in medicine, to identify with greater precision the particular subgroups of offenders who are amenable to different types of treatment. However, ignorance of the causes of crime remains a serious barrier to successful screening . . .

It would be an exaggeration to say that no treatment methods work, for some positive results have been reported, which further follow-up may confirm. But, certainly, few programs seem to succeed; and it is still uncertain to what extent the claimed success would survive replication or close analysis.

In those special instances where it might be possible to find treatment that works, the more difficult question has to be confronted: aside from effectiveness, what other limitations should there be on the rehabilitative disposition? Is it just, for example, to impose dissimilar sentences for treatment purposes upon offenders convicted of similar crimes? We shall argue later that there are limitations of justice on the rehabilitative disposition, even if the treatment were known to be effective.

But in the more commonplace instances where no successful treatments are known, the rehabilitative disposition is plainly untenable. It cannot be rational or fair to sentence for treatment, without a reasonable expectation that the treatment works."

N. Morris and C. Howard, Studies in Criminal Law (1964), pp. 175–176:

"We have reached the stage in penal theory and practice where it is necessary to incorporate into our sentencing and correctional methods some of the techniques stressed by the Positivists and their acolytes of Social Defence, and in doing so to provide a system of punishment in which power over men's lives will not be taken on unproven assumptions of knowledge of therapeutic skills. Principles will now be suggested by which we may keep the advantages of these utilitarian, reformative, socially protective approaches to punishment and yet avoid the dangers to human rights implicit in them . . .

There are, in our submission, two steps to this result. First, *power over a criminal's life should not be taken in excess of that which would be taken were his reform not considered as one of our purposes.* Let the maximum of his punishment be never greater than that which would be justified by the other aims of our system of criminal justice. Within the term of that sentence, let us utilise our reformative skills to assist him towards social readjustment, but never put forward the possibility of reforming him to justify an extension of power over him. The jailer in a white coat with a degree in a behavioural science remains a jailer. . . .

The second essential step is this: *correctional practices must cease to rest on surmise and good intentions: they must be based on facts.* We are under a moral obligation to use our best intelligence to discover whether and to what extent our various penal sanctions do deter or reform."

C. Distinguishing Justification of Punishment from Purpose of Punishment

It is difficult to make any sense of the above competing "theories" until one knows precisely what question it is that they are trying to answer—as in reality there are several quite distinct questions that need answering. Hart has clearly distinguished two separate questions[62]:

1. What is the purpose or justification of the entire social institution of criminal punishment?
2. What is the justification of punishment in particular cases?[63]

That these are separate questions that might require different answers can be illustrated by the following example:

[62] "Prolegomenon to the Principles of Punishment" in *Punishment and Responsibility* (1969), p. 1.
[63] Hart subdivides this second question under the general heading of "Distribution" into:
(a) Who may be punished?, and
(b) how much punishment may be imposed in the particular case?
This latter question is dealt with in the following section (pp. 51–55).

Suppose that there was only one question—Why do we punish?—
and suppose that it was agreed that the purpose of punishment was
general deterrence. On this basis it might be perfectly permissible to
punish the children of offenders if that were thought to be the most
effective deterrent. Yet most people would recoil in horror at the notion
of punishing an innocent person to achieve the purpose of deterring
others. But why is there this recoil if such a form of punishment was an
effective deterrent? The answer is simply that while the aim of the institution of punishment might be general deterrence, we are still not justified in punishing an innocent person to achieve that end. We need
some further justification before we actually impose a punishment in a
particular case. There are two questions involved; they need to be distinguished and they might need separate answers. This distinction is
illustrated by Fletcher:

> "The analogy that comes to mind is the distinction between justifying the
> income tax as a whole and justifying the imposition of burdens on particu-
> lar taxpayers. The justification of the system as a whole is raising revenue
> for the government; the justification of burdens on particular taxpayers is
> (roughly) the taxpayer's relative ability to pay. It would obviously be
> improper to interweave these two levels of justification and justify the
> denial of claim for a charitable deduction on the ground of the claimant's
> relative ability to pay. Similarly, if the justification for the criminal law as a
> whole is the isolation of dangerous offenders, it is improper to decide par-
> ticular cases by appealing to the alleged offender's relative dangerous-
> ness."[64]

The most common way of answering these separate questions is as
follows:

(1) The purpose of the institution of punishment, (*i.e.* the "general jus-
     tifying aim") is a utilitarian one. It is concerned with deterrence,
     incapacitation and rehabilitation.
(2) The justification of punishment in a particular case, (*i.e.* "distribu-
     tion" of punishment) is a retributive one. Only the actual offender
     deserves to be punished.

Let us now look at each of these questions in a little more detail.

(1) *Purpose of institution of punishment*
All the above "theories" of punishment can be seen as attempts to
answer this question with commentators and judges each having their
own "favourite theory."[65] It used to be widely accepted that the
purpose of the institution of punishment was the utilitarian one of
reducing crime (whether through deterrence, incapacitation or

---

[64] *Rethinking Criminal Law* (1978), p. 419.
[65] See first edition of this book, p. 45.

rehabilitation). However, in the United States there has been an increasing view that the purpose of the whole institution of punishment is to give offenders their just deserts. The rehabilitative model, in particular, has been thoroughly discredited on the grounds of injustice and inefficiency.[66] For instance, California, once the fore-runner of the rehabilitation movement, in 1976 abolished its Adult Authority (in which "experts" imposed the sentence most appropriate for the rehabilitation of the offender) and proclaimed:

> "The Legislature finds and declares that the purpose of imprisonment for crime is punishment. This purpose is best served by terms proportionate to the seriousness of the offence with provision for uniformity in the sentences of offenders committing the same offence under similar circumstances".[67]

It is submitted that there must surely be some greater purpose to the whole institution of the criminal law and punishment than the somewhat metaphysical justifications of just desert.[68] It must be permissible at least to strive for some concrete benefit such as crime reduction and to allow such utilitarian considerations to inform the development and reform of the criminal law and the institution of punishment. Such a wholesale embrace of the concept of just desert could lead to mechanistic sentencing and limit humane improvement to the facilities available to those sentenced for committing crimes.

This movement towards just desert has been largely inspired by concern over injustice, inequality and disparity in sentencing.[69] The concept of just desert has been heralded as the only means of ensuring justice in sentencing. It is however submitted that concerns of justice are matters affecting the second question of "distribution"—and are not as important to this first question. Indeed, much of the confusion generated in the just deserts debate (both by proponents and critics) has been the result of a failure to distinguish between justifying the entire social institution of criminal punishment and justifying a particular punishment.

(2) *Justification of particular punishment*

While the purpose of the institution of punishment might be utilitarian, we have seen that it is difficult to justify a particular punishment in

---

[66] R. Martinson, "What Works—Questions and Answers about Prison Reform," 22 The Public Interest (Spring 1974). See also Robinson and Smith, "The Effectiveness of Correctional Programs," (1971) 17 Crime and Delinquency 67; D. Lipton, R. Martinson and J. Wilks, *Effectiveness of Correctional Treatment: A Survey of Treatment Evaluation Studies* (1975); Von Hirsch, *Doing Justice, the Choice of Punishments, ante,* n. 10; M. Frankel, *Criminal Sentences—Law Without Order* (1973); N. Morris, *The Future of Imprisonment* (1975); American Friends Service Committee, *Struggle for Justice* (1971); Report of the Twentieth Century Fund Task Force on Criminal Sentencing, *Fair and Certain Punishment* (1976). For an extensive reading list, see Gross and von Hirsch, *Sentencing* (1981), pp. 300–301.
[67] Cal. Penal Code, s.1170(a)(i).
[68] *Ante,* pp. 7–14.
[69] *Post,* pp. 55–73.

such terms and it is here that the concept of just desert is rightly introduced. Justice demands that it is the offender, and only the offender,
who deserves to be punished.

H. L. A. Hart, "Prolegomenon to the Principles of Punishment," in Punishment and Responsibility (1968), pp. 11–13, 21–24:

" . . . First, though we may be clear as to what value the practice of punishment is to promote, we have still to answer as a question of Distribution 'Who
may be punished?'. Secondly, if in answer to this question we say 'only an
offender for an offence' this admission of retribution in Distribution is not a
principle from which anything follows as to the severity or amount of punishment: in particular it neither licenses nor requires, as Retribution in General
Aim does, more severe punishments than deterrence or other utilitarian criteria
would require.

The root question to be considered is, however, why we attach the moral
importance which we do to retribution in Distribution. . . .

The standard example used by philosophers to bring out the importance of
retribution in Distribution is that of a wholly innocent person who has not even
unintentionally done anything which the law punishes if done intentionally. It
is supposed that in order to avert some social catastrophe officials of the system
fabricate evidence on which he is charged, tried, convicted and sent to prison or
death. Or it is supposed that without resort to any fraud more persons may be
deterred from crime if wives and children of offenders were punished vicar-
iously for their crimes. In some forms, this kind of thing may be ruled out by a
consistent sufficiently comprehensive utilitarianism. Certainly expedients
involving fraud or faked charges might be very difficult to justify on utilitarian
grounds. We can of course imagine that a negro might be sent to prison or
executed on a false charge of rape in order to avoid widespread lynching of
many others; but a *system* which openly empowered authorities to do this kind
of thing, even if it succeeded in averting specific evils like lynching would
awaken such apprehension and insecurity that any gain from the exercise of
these powers would by any utilitarian calculation be offset by the misery caused
by their existence. But official resort to this kind of fraud on a particular
occasion in breach of the rules and the subsequent indemnification of the
officials responsible might save many lives and so be thought to yield a clear
surplus of value. Certainly vicarious punishment of an offender's family might
do so and legal systems have occasionally resorted to this. An example of it is
the Roman *Lex Quisquis* providing for the punishment of the children of those
guilty of *majestas*. In extreme cases many might still think it right to resort to
these expedients but we should do so with the sense of sacrificing an important
principle. We should be conscious of choosing the lesser of two evils, and this
would be inexplicable if the principle sacrificed to utility were itself only a
requirement of utility.

Similarly the moral importance of the restriction of punishment to the
offender cannot be explained as merely a consequence of the principle that
the General Justifying Aim is Retribution for immorality involved in breaking
the law. Retribution in the Distribution of punishment has a value quite independent of Retribution as Justifying Aim. This is shown by the fact that we
attach importance to the restrictive principle that only offenders may be
punished, even where breach of this law might not be thought immoral. Indeed
even where the laws themselves are hideously immoral as in Nazi Germany, *e.g.*
forbidding activities (helping the sick or destitute of some racial group) which

might be thought morally obligatory, the absence of the principle restricting punishment to the offender would be a further *special* iniquity: whereas admission of this principle would represent some residual respect for justice shown in the administration of morally bad laws. . . .

It is clear that like all principles of Justice it (punishment) is concerned with the adjustment of claims between a multiplicity of persons. It incorporates the idea that each individual person is to be protected against the claim of the rest for the highest possible measure of security, happiness or welfare which could be got at his expense by condemning him for a breach of the rules and punishing him. For this a moral licence is required in the form of proof that the person punished broke the law by an action which was the outcome of his free choice, and the recognition of excuses is the most we can do to ensure that the terms of the licence are observed. Here perhaps, the elucidation of this restrictive principle should stop. Perhaps we (or I) ought simply to say that it is a requirement of Justice, and Justice simply consists of principles to be observed in adjusting the competing claims of human beings which (i) treat all alike as persons by attaching special significance to human voluntary action and (ii) forbid the use of one human being for the benefit of others except in return for his voluntary actions against them. I confess however to an itch to go further; though what I have to say may not add to these principles of Justice. There are, however, three points which even if they are restatements from different points of view of the principles already stated, may help us to identify what we now think of as values in the practice of punishment and what we may have to reconsider in the light of modern scepticism.

(a) We may look upon the principle that punishment must be reserved for voluntary offences from two different points of view. The first is that of the rest of society considered as *harmed* by the offence (either because one of its members has been injured or because the authority of the law essential to its existence has been challenged or both). The principle then appears as one securing that the suffering involved in punishment falls upon those who have voluntarily harmed others: this is valued, not as the Aim of punishment, but as the only fair terms on which the General Aim (protection of society, maintenance of respect for law, etc.) may be pursued.

(b) The second point of view is that of society concerned not as harmed by the crime but as *offering* individuals including the criminal the protection of the laws on terms which are fair, because they not only consist of a framework of reciprocal rights and duties, but because within this framework each individual is given a *fair* opportunity to choose between keeping the law required for society's protection or paying the penalty. From the first point of view the actual punishment of a criminal appears not merely as something useful to society (General Aim) but as justly extracted from the criminal who has voluntarily done harm; from the second it appears as a price justly extracted because the criminal had a fair opportunity beforehand to avoid liability to pay.

(c) Criminal punishment as an attempt to secure desired behaviour differs from the manipulative techniques of the Brave New World (conditioning, propaganda, etc.) or the simple incapacitation of those with anti-social tendencies, by taking a risk. It defers action till harm has been done; its primary operation consists simply in announcing certain standards of behaviour and attaching penalties for deviation, making it less eligible, and then leaving individuals to choose. This is a method of social control which maximises individual freedom within the coercive framework of law in a number of different ways, or perhaps, different senses. First, the individual has an option between obeying or paying. The worse the laws are, the more valuable the possibility of exercising this choice becomes in enabling an individual to decide how he shall live. Secondly, this system not only enables individuals to exercise this choice but increases the power of individuals to identify beforehand periods when the law's punishments will not interfere with them and to plan their lives accordingly."

Hyman Gross, A Theory of Criminal Justice (1979), pp. 382–385:

"First the Kantian objection is to *mere use* of a person for some social (or even personal) benefit so that he is not treated as an end in himself. But this is not an objection to making use of persons when the use does not constitute such moral degradation. Each person being regarded as an end in himself does not require that each of us treat one another as an island unto himself not to be used for the benefit of others. If it did, many commonplace and uncontroversial acts of social intercourse would be forbidden simply because use was made of a person without his permission. On the Kantian view, when the guilty are punished and they receive their just desert, their moral autonomy is accorded full respect. Indeed, only then is full moral respect shown to the guilty. Having given moral autonomy its due, however, there is no reason why a guilty person may not serve a socially desirable end either as an example or in some other way that contributes to maintaining a less dangerous community than there might otherwise be.

A second argument is this. Since the benefits of laws backed by effective sanctions are in theory conferred on everyone, and since in theory these laws impose on everyone the same restraints, it seems reasonable to view the legal system as the continuing performance of a contract which all members of society enter into and renew by continuing to live under its provisions. Punishment of the guilty is one provision of this social contract, and those who live under and are parties to it are bound by their contractual assent to submit to punishment according to their guilt. Since this obligation is consensual, it is not in derogation of a right of autonomy but on the contrary represents an exercise of that very right.

The third argument places less stress on the give-and-take of mutual agreement, and instead sees greater overall benefit to each individual when certain collective interests are served at the expense of more immediate individual interests. On this view, individual autonomy is to be accorded ample respect. Indeed, it may even be more important than anything else, and for this very reason it is subject to certain curtailments that are necessary for its enjoyment. If collective as well as individual well-being depends upon an effective system of laws, and if an effective legal system requires punishment of those who break the law, then punishment is necessary for both collective and individual well-being. True, punishing a person in order to benefit him individually is a violation of his moral autonomy no less than if the benefit were collective. But part of the individual benefit (and a most important part) is the preservation of those conditions of life that are necessary if personal autonomy is to be worth anything. In a world without law in which human life is lived in a state of nature, the value of free personal choice would be extremely small, since urgent matters of survival in the face of constant peril would dictate the activities that one chose, and to a great extent one's fate would be determined by forces beyond one's control. The possibility of an environment allowing autonomy to be valuable in the first place depends upon effective laws, and they in turn depend upon the punishment of lawbreakers.

These arguments furnish solid grounds for punishment of the guilty with full respect for personal autonomy, even though punishment is for some common good: and since these arguments are in no way inconsistent with one another it is not necessary to choose between them. None of these arguments, furthermore, is consistent with a view much feared by defenders of moral autonomy—namely, the view that a person who is not *responsible* for what he has done may be punished for it nevertheless. If persons who are not responsible were punished, there would in those cases be a use of individuals for the collective good without regard to their powers of choice."

This whole approach has been criticised.

Nicola Lacey, State Punishment: Political Principles and Community Values (1988), pp. 51–52:

"All these hybrid theories proceed on the assumption that there are genuinely separate questions to be answered: . . . It seems to be true . . . that rules themselves contain their own conditions of application. No sensible system has rules and then fails to apply them: prima facie, the reasons for having the rules generate the reasons for applying them in individual cases. This seems to indicate that the principle of distribution, if one is (as it seems to be) needed, must come in at the first stage: *a* principle of distribution is inevitably contained within or at least envisaged by the general justifying aim of the rules. And if the general justifying aim is straighforwardly utilitarian, the project of grafting on a separate distributive principle, begins to look deeply problematic, for utilitarianism does *not*, as its critics sometimes claim, lack such a principle. It rather embodies criteria of distribution which are vulnerable to serious objection. It is necessary, then, to identify an alternative general justifying aim which incorporates or is consistent with an acceptable distributive principle, rather than to separate different questions and give different answers to them. Conversely, I think it can be argued, that a justification for institutions of punishment must include a justification for their actual use in individual cases, and that the individual question is in some ways primary: can any single infliction of punishment ever be justified? The mere fact that such an inflication is according to rules does not seem to generate any additional justification in itself. In justifyng a system of rules, we generally assume that those rules will be applied: therefore the justification which we seek must also justify the application of the rules. For these reasons it is my belief that the . . . Hartian distinction does not really withstand close analysis."

Lacey's approach is however dependent on the "general justifying aim" itself embodying *effective* criteria of "distribution." To assess this let us briefly consider the utilitarian response to the problem of punishing the innocent. Why not punish an innocent person if, say, it would be an effective deterrent? The answer here is that such punishment could never in fact be an effective deterrent as punishment would become a lottery and there would be no special disincentive to would-be offenders. To be an effective deterrent only actual offenders can be punished. Jeremy Bentham, the father of utilitarianism, adduced further reasons for not punishing the innocent.

Nicola Lacey, State Punishment: Political Principles and Community Values (1988), p. 39:

"In characteristically single-minded style, he [Bentham] lists a number of disutilities peculiar to punishment of the innocent as opposed to the guilty, which aim to show that such an act would never, or only exceptionally (and of course, we cannot always rely on our intuitions in exceptional cases, but must be willing to be guided by our considered principles) maximise utility. The list includes the extra suffering caused to the victim by reason of her innocence— her additional frustration and feeling of insecurity, as well as those to her family: the risk of very serious damage to general respect for the legal system should the fraud ever be discovered, plus increased insecurity, apprehension and alarm flowing from the knowledge that one might be punished despite conforming one's behaviour to the law, that a guilty person is still at large, free to re-offend, and that the law is incapable of protecting the law-abiding. We could also mention the pain of sympathy which would be felt for the innocent victim, and, paradoxically, the comfort to the guilty person—which presumably cannot be an evil in itself on utilitarian terms, but may count as one in encouraging her to offend again with impunity."

There are problems with this utilitarian approach. Punishment of the innocent *could* be an effective deterrent if the public were deceived into thinking that the victim actually committed the crime.[70] This would not alter the manifest injustice of so doing. Further, even if this approach were to tell us *who* to punish, it tells us little about *how much* to punish—or, at least, tells us far less than the just deserts principle. And, finally, even if the "general justifying aim" did embody criteria of distribution, *why would they be any better* than those yielded by the concept of just desert, which, as demonstrated in the Hart and Gross extracts above, provides fair, consistent and just results?

One final problem remains. Having established that one is justified in punishing the actual offender (as the only one who deserves punishment), and that the purpose of the institution of punishment is utilitarian, must one actually impose that punishment? Or does one have an option whether to go ahead and punish—and if one has an option, on what basis would one exercise one's choice?

Some writers such as Kant maintain that there is no option in the matter. One *has* to punish the criminal. Failure to do so would involve society endorsing the criminal's acts and thus becoming participants in it. It would further involve failing to treat the criminal as a responsible human being who deserves the consequences of his actions.

On the other hand, it can be argued that after establishing that one is justified in punishing an offender, one does have an *option* whether to go ahead and actually impose that punishment. One needs sound reasons for inflicting the "pain of punishment."[71] Such reasons lie in the utilitarian soil of the "general justifying aim." Thus, when a defendant has committed a crime we are *entitled* to punish that person. However, if there is nothing to be gained in utilitarian terms by such punishment, it should be avoided.[72]

---

[70] An unreported instance brought to the author's attention occurred in the United States where a judge sentenced his clerk (who was innocent and had agreed to the exercise) to six months imprisonment for a speeding violation. It had been privately agreed that the clerk would not actually serve the sentence. The object of the exercise was to deter speeding motorists. Discovery of the truth of this exercise caused much public indignation.

[71] *Post*, p. 52.

[72] This view was put forward in the first edition of this book (pp. 44–45). See also A. H. Goldman, "The Paradox of Punishment," Philosophy and Public Affairs, Vol. 9, 1979, p. 42.

Nicola Lacey, State Punishment: Political Principles and Community Values (1988) pp. 54–55:

"The idea that desert furnishes the state with a non-conclusive reason to punish raises the question of what types of extra reasons must be adduced in order to produce a justification of particular acts of punishment. On some accounts, apparently non-utilitarian factors are appealed to—factors such as fairness and justice. But it is clear that the most obvious candidates are utilitarian reasons such as prevention, deterrence, avoidance of private vengeance and so on. It is important to note that on most weak retributivist views desert operates not only as the central justification but also as a limit on the amount of punishment: the only function of the consequentialist considerations is to add an element which provides the sufficient reason for some punitive action. On this view, consequentialism cannot tell us whom to punish or how much to punish; it merely defeats the argument from the pointlessness of purely retributive punishment. The difficulty here is that these utilitarian arguments do purport to provide not just an explanation of when we may exercise our right or power of punishment, but actually to make it right for us to punish. According to utilitariansim, it is right to punish wherever such an action maximises the aggregate of pleasure over pain. It is thus hard to see how it is that the weak retributive principle fails to become redundant. In addition, it is not clear whether the desert argument is intended to apply to the design of institutions and the utilitarian one to individual acts of punishment, ... If this were so, we would be invited to endorse the unattractive vision of a legal system based on a principle of desert, in which individual acts of punishment were left to judicial discretion which should be exercised on the basis of consequentialist reasoning, or else of a system in which the legislator made utilitarian generalisations in framing the rules which were nevertheless primarily based on considerations of desert."

It is quite clear that it cannot be left to unfettered judicial discretion whether an individual defendant should be punished or not. However, if some mechanism for controlling judicial discretion were to be developed[73] it could well be that the "sound reasons" for choosing punishment or a particular punishment could be informed by utilitarian considerations. This would not alter the basic point that no punishment could be justified unless it was deserved.

Separating these questions in this way is not simply an intellectual exercise; it is of great practical importance—both for the structure and content of the substantive criminal law (the theme of much of this book), and in terms of limiting the severity of any punishment for a particular offender and/or offence. It is to this latter question that we now turn.

D. How Severely do we Punish?

Having considered the various aims of punishment we may now turn to the question: How severely should we punish? The answer may well be very different in a system which aims to reform or deter from one in which retributive thinking dominates. And the ease with which the

[73] See *post*, pp. 55–73.

question may be answered will depend on whether one seeks to achieve one or a multiplicity of aims.

Let us start with the utilitarian view of punishment. How would a utilitarian determine the amount of punishment to be imposed for a particular offence? If it were thought necessary, for example, for reasons of deterrence, could extreme sentences be imposed that bore no relationship to the seriousness of the crime? Could one give life sentences for parking on double yellow lines if this were thought to be an effective deterrent? Could one give life sentences to persons who repeatedly stole milk bottles from doorsteps if this would prevent the recurrence of the crime?

The classic answer to this question is still that provided by Jeremy Bentham, that all punishment is evil and ought only to be imposed to achieve some greater good—and accordingly one should only impose the minimum punishment necessary to achieve that objective.

Jeremy Bentham, An Introduction to the Principles of Morals and Legislation, Chap. 13, in Bentham and Mill, The Utilitarians, (1961), pp. 162, 166:

"The general object which all laws have, or ought to have, in common, is to augment the total happiness of the community; and therefore, in the first place, to exclude, as far as may be, every thing that tends to subtract from that happiness: in other words, to exclude mischief.

But all punishment is mischief: all punishment in itself is evil. Upon the principle of utility, if it ought at all to be admitted, it ought only to be admitted in as far as it promises to exclude some greater evil.

It is plain, therefore, that in the following cases punishment ought not to be inflicted.

1. Where it is *groundless:* where there is no mischief for it to prevent, the act not being mischievous upon the whole.
2. Where it must be *inefficacious:* where it cannot act so as to prevent the mischief.
3. Where it is *unprofitable;* or too *expensive:* where the mischief it would produce would be greater than what it prevented.
4. Where it is *needless:* where the mischief may be prevented, or cease of itself, without it: that is, at a cheaper rate . . . .

Now the evil of the punishment divides itself into four branches, by which so many different sets of persons are affected. 1. The evil of *coercoin* or *restraint:* or the pain which it gives a man not to be able to do the act, whatever it be, which by the apprehension of the punishment he is deterred from doing. This is felt by those by whom the law is *observed.* 2. The evil of *apprehension:* or the pain which a man, who has exposed himself to punishment, feels at the thought of undergoing it. This is felt by those by whom the law has been *broken,* and so feel themselves in *danger* of its being executed upon them. 3. The evil of *sufferance:* or the pain which a man feels, in virtue of the punishment itself, from the time when he begins to undergo it. This is felt by those by whom the law is broken, and upon whom it comes actually to be executed. 4. The pain of sympathy, and the other *derivative* evils resulting to the persons who are in *connection* with the several classes of original sufferers just mentioned."

Accordingly, the utilitarian reason why we do not punish parking on a double yellow line with life imprisonment is that it is thought that the aim of deterrence can be effectively achieved at a lower cost—and crime must be prevented as economically in terms of the suffering of the offender as possible. Further, such an extreme sentence would undoubtedly attract public sympathy for the offender and thus "instead of reaffirming the law and intensifying men's consciousness that the kind of act punished is wrong, will have the opposite effect of casting discredit on the law and making the action of the law-breaker appear excusable or even almost heroic."[74]

It must not however be thought that this principle of parsimony or frugality of punishment will in any way lead to lesser punishments.

K. Pease and C. Fitzmaurice, The Psychology of Judicial Sentencing (1986), p. 49:

"Let us first assume that, the more serious a crime is, the more we disapprove of it and the more we would like to reduce its incidence. How would a judge operating according to each of the sentencing purposes set out above relate offence seriousness to sentence severity? When incapacitation is the informing principle, the more serious the offence the longer the time for which the offender would properly be incapacitated, thereby preventing more of the serious crime. When deterrence is the informing principle, the more serious the offence the more severe the sentence, on the ground that the more serious the offence, the more the offender and other citizens should be provided with disincentives against committing it. When rehabilitation is the sentencing purpose, the more serious the offence, the more damaged must be the personality of the offender, and hence the longer he must be detained by the state in order to repair the damage."

With a retributive system of punishment one is looking back to the crime and punishing *because* of that crime. The crime itself provides the necessary guidance as to the amount of punishment necessary. The punishment must be proportionate to the crime; it must "fit" the crime. At its crudest this is encapsulated by the phrase "an eye for an eye and a tooth for a tooth"—of course, this is no longer meant literally. A better explanation is as follows.

A. C. Ewing, "A Study of Punishment II: Punishment as Viewed by the Philosopher," (1943) 21 Can.B.Rev. 102 at 115–116:

"[W]hy [is] a graver offence . . . punished more than a lighter one[?] . . . To punish a lesser crime more severely than a greater would be either to suggest to men's minds that the former was worse when it was not, or, if they could not accept this, to bring the penal law in some degree into discredit or ridicule. One of the requirements of a good moral code is that there should be a right proportion between values, and, in so far as penal laws affect popular morality, they ought to help and not hinder right judgment in this matter."

[74] A. C. Ewing, "A Study of Punishment II: Punishment as viewed by the Philosopher" (1943) 21 Can.B.Rev. 102, 116.

The more sophisticated version is that the offender *deserves* punishment *to the extent* of the crime he has committed. In Kantian terms, he has gained an unfair advantage by committing the crime; punishment is necessary to eliminate that advantage and restore social equilibrium.[75] But how is one to decide what punishment is proportionate to the crime? *How much* punishment is deserved? The Kantian answer is that the offender must be punished to that extent, *no more* and *no less*, which is necessary to destroy the unfair advantage. Thus society must place a value on the interests being infringed by a particular crime and then strive for some equivalent in terms of punishment—some level of punishment that can be *deemed* appropriate to eliminate the offender's unfair advantage.

A variation of this Kantian philosophy, and one more in tune with current sentencing practices in England, is that Kant's notion of just desert need not indicate the *exact extent* of the punishment; instead, it specifies the *maximum* possible penalty beyond which punishment would be undeserved. Within the permissible range, punishment is deserved; one is justified in punishing; but one has a choice as to the severity of the punishment—that choice being informed by all the circumstances of the offence—and by utilitarian considerations.

But how are we to place a relative scale of values on the interests being infringed by the commission of various crimes? And how are we to decide what their equivalents are in terms of punishment? For example, how are we to decide on the relative seriousness of robbery, burglary and kidnapping and what should be the appropriate level of punishment for each?

Two approaches, both of which operate in the criminal justice system, are possible. We may say that punishment is related to the harm done. By such a criterion the person who takes a life is rightfully punished more severely than the person who causes minor injury, and the burglar who steals the contents of a safe more severely than a minor pick-pocket. But what of the person whose attempted crime fails miserably? He ought to receive a much less severe sentence because the harm he has caused (which may amount to no more than a threat to society's feelings of security) is substantially less. And yet, the crime of attempt is, as we shall see, punishable to the same extent as the completed crime. In practice, however, such crimes do tend to be punished more lightly. The judges, tacitly, if not openly, adhere in such cases to the criterion of harm done.

The other approach relates punishment to moral blameworthiness and is epitomised by the concept of *mens rea*—regarded by some as almost an index of the degree of sophistication that a criminal justice system has achieved. Culpability is assessed in accordance with the state of mind of the offender. A criminal act done intentionally is regarded as more blameworthy and more deserving of punishment

---

[75] See *ante*, p. 8. *Cf.* H. Gross: "A person deserves to be punished according to the culpability of his criminal conduct because that measures exactly the extent to which his innocence has been lost. To the extent his innocence is lost, he deserves punishment. To the extent his innocence remains intact, he deserves impunity." ("Culpability and Desert," p. 12—Paper delivered to Association for Legal and Social Philosophy, 1983 Conference, at the University of Manchester, April 8–10.)

than, say, one done negligently (indeed, crimes of negligence are rare in the criminal justice system). Murder has traditionally been a crime of intentional killing—this label has been reserved for the "worst" of killings—yet as has been pointed out,[76] the harm is still the same whether the act is deliberate or a complete mischance. Here, it would seem, one approach has been preferred to the other. It is one of our main purposes in this book to examine closely the relationship between these two approaches.

Using a combination of these two approaches, the courts gradually developed a "tariff system" of sentencing that enables them to pass a "normal" sentence for a particular crime.

Alverstone, Memorandum on Normal Punishments in Certain Kinds of Crime, 1901:

"The Judges of the King's Bench Division are agreed that it would be convenient and of public advantage in regard to certain classes of crime to come to an agreement, or, at least, an approximate agreement, as to what may be called a 'normal' standard of punishment: a standard of punishment, that is to say, which should be assumed to be properly applicable, unless the particular case under consideration presented some special feature of aggravation or extenuation. . . ."[77]

Such a tariff is still in operation today although many attempts have (and are) being made to "tighten up" the tariffs in an effort to ensure greater consistency in sentencing. It is to these efforts that we now turn.

E. Sentencing Disparity

A matter of grave concern to those involved in study of the criminal justice process is the problem of sentencing disparity. This occurs where there are large discrepancies in the sentences being imposed for similar crimes. Case A, which looks on all fours with Case B attracts a longish custodial sentence whilst case B is dealt with, for example, by way of a fine.

As we shall see, most of the extreme examples of disparity come from the United States, but, nevertheless, there is sufficient evidence of its taking place here to warrant a very close examination of the sentencing process and the decisions thereby reached. For example, the 1979 study by Tarling on sentencing practice in the Magistrates' Courts revealed sometimes quite wide discrepancies in the use of fines and imprisonment:

"Almost all clerks and chairmen emphasised the necessity for the establishment and maintenance of a consistent policy in their own individual courts but this concern did not extend to maintaining consistency with their neighbours. It was more important, they believed, that the decision taken

---

[76] B. Wootton, *Crime and the Criminal Law* (2nd ed., 1981), pp. 46–48.
[77] Set out in full in Appendix E of Sentences of Imprisonment, A Review of Maximum Penalties, Report of the Advisory Council on the Penal System (H.M.S.O. 1978).

by the courts should be determined by the particular characteristics of the offenders coming before it and of the district it served than that wider consistency be achieved at the expense of sensitivity."[78]

Other studies have followed this lead. Ashworth conducted a pilot study in 1984 into the sentencing practices of Crown Courts but was unable to obtain permission to undertake a full-scale study on the basis that it was unlikely to reveal anything of any use to judges![79] Nevertheless, it revealed enough to reinforce the view that there is cause for concern as did the more recent studies by N.A.C.R.O.[80] and Corbett.

C. Corbett, Magistrates' Court Clerks' Sentencing Behaviour: an Experimental Study, in The Psychology of Sentencing, eds. S. Lloyd-Bostock and D. Pennington, (1987), pp. 205, 210–211.

"Seven magistrates' courts agreed to take part in the study. They were, as far as possible, geographically representative of England, comprising a mixture of rural and urban courts, and were of roughly similar size. The sampling procedure used ensured the participation of a random selection of approximately 23 justices from each court. In addition, all but a few court clerks out of a possible total of 53 at the seven courts completed the exercises.

Seven case vignettes were presented, each in a similar written format. This gave details of the age of the defendant, the plea, a statement of offence facts, police antecedents, a social inquiry report and a short statement of the mitigation given by the defence. Participants first studied each case on their own and evaluated it on several dimensions, such as the relative seriousness of the case and the blameworthiness of the offender. A few weeks later, the magistrates in the sample came to court and assessed three of the same cases in 'benches,' to which justices' clerks has assigned the most senior magistrates to act as chairmen. Free choice of sentence was allowed, provided it was legally appopriate to both the case and the court. No clerks were present to advise. Among several other tasks, respondents were asked to give reasons for their sentence choices, including any sentencing aims they hoped would be achieved. . . .

Considering all responses together shows that again a broad selection of sentence choices was made both by clerks and magistrates, ranging from conditional discharges to immediate imprisonment (indeed one JP preferred committal). Nevertheless, although the presence of some main preference was strongest in this case (about half the magistrates at each court chose a fine, as had happened in the original case), the selections of all the remaining JPs and of the clerks at courts A and G showed sentences of quite different seriousness.

In sum, it appears that benches achieved little more internal agreement than individual magistrates. Should this result be generalisable to overall pratice, it would seem that the influence of senior justices acting as chairmen would not have the effect of promoting internal consistency. Nor did it appear that clerks would provide much of a steadying influence on bench decisions.

As a group, clerks were more likely than JPs to select a custodial sentence in each of these three cases (and indeed in the other four). It is therefore possible

---

[78] R. Tarling and M. Weatheritt, Home Office Research Study No. 56, *Sentencing Practice in Magistrates' Courts*, (1979), p. 45.

[79] A. Ashworth, E. Genders, G. Mansfield, J. Peay and E. Player, *Sentencing in the Crown Court: Report of an Exploratory Study*, (1984), (Centre for Criminological Research Occasional Paper No. 10).

[80] This Report describes sentencing as "highly inconsistent" with differences that cannot be explained by local variations in crime: *The Real Alternative* (1989), pp. 10–17.

that clerks in real life may have an influence in the direction of steering benches towards heavier penalties. Of course, these simulated sentences may not mirror people's real thoughts about cases in general, and in practice clerks may have little effect on the final bench decision. However, clerks in this sample believed they did have an effect on sentencing. Only 8 per cent. said they had 'no influence at all,' and at the other extreme 21 per cent. believed they had a 'considerable' 'or a great deal' of influence.''

Even more startling evidence of sentencing disparity was found very early on in research conducted in the United States. Some examples will illustrate this:

(a) In 1974 the average sentence for bank robbery in the Northern District of Georgia was 17 years imprisonment, but in the Northern District of Illinois it was $5\frac{1}{2}$ years imprisonment.[81]

(b) In a sentencing study, 50 federal district judges from the 2nd Circuit were given 20 identical files drawn from actual cases and asked what sentence they would impose. In one case of extortion, the sentences ranged from 20 years imprisonment plus a $65,000 fine to 3 years imprisonment with no fine. In a bank robbery case the sentences ranged from 18 years imprisonment with a $5,000 fine to 5 years imprisonment with no fine. In a case relating to the sale of heroin the sentences ranged from 10 years imprisonment plus 5 years probation to 1 year's imprisonment plus 5 years probation. In a case of theft and possession of stolen goods the sentences ranged from $7\frac{1}{2}$ years imprisonment to 4 years probation.[82]

(c) Marvin E. Frankel: "Criminal Sentences—Law Without Order (1973) 21–22:

"Take, for instance, the case of two men we received last spring. The first man had been convicted of cashing a cheque for $58.40. He was out of work at the time of his offence, and when his wife became ill and he needed money for rent, food and doctor's bills, he became the victim of temptation. He had no prior criminal record. The other man cashed a cheque for $35·20. He was also out of work and his wife had left him for another man. His prior record consisted of a drunk charge and a non-support charge. Our examination of these two cases indicated no significant differences for sentencing purposes but they appeared before different judges and the first man received 15 years in prison and the second man 30 days. . . .
In one of our institutions a middle-aged credit union treasurer is serving 117 days for embezzling $24,000 in order to cover his gambling debts. On the other hand, another middle-aged embezzler with a fine past record and a fine family is serving 20 years, with 5 years probation to follow. (Citing 'Countdown for Judicial Sentencing' in *Of Prisons and Justice* S.Doc. No. 70, 88th Cong., 2nd sess., p. 331 (1964))."

(d) Numerous other studies are to the same effect. A sentencing study

[81] Kramer, "Different Judges, Different Justice," *Washington Post*, November 14, 1975, p. 19, col. 3.
[82] A. Partridge and W. Eldridge, *The Second Circuit Sentencing Study*, A Report of the Judges of the Second Circuit (1974). See also *Crime and Punishment in New York: An Inquiry into Sentencing and the Criminal Justice System*, Report to Gov. Hugh L. Carey, prepared by the Executive Advisory Committee on Sentencing (1979).

in Montgomery County, Ohio, disclosed that certain judges imprison defendants twice as often as other judges for the same offence. In cases of robbery, for example, one judge imposed prison sentences in 77 per cent. of his cases, whereas another judge imprisoned in only 17 per cent. of his cases.[83] A 1971 sentencing survey in South Carolina disclosed similar disparity. A female who pleaded guilty to voluntary manslaughter was sentenced to two years incarceration and four years probation by one judge; another judge sentenced a male defendant, in similar circumstances, to 21 years imprisonment—both were first offenders. A plea of guilty to assault and battery with intent to kill brought a 7 day sentence of imprisonment and 5 years probation, while a grand-larceny defendant who had stolen two suits received 7 years imprisonment.[84]

All of these examples, old and new, help to set the scene for our discussion. All of them are alarming but they have to be considered in the light of a fuller examination of what is meant by disparity. If, as suggested, it means that inconsistent decisions are being reached, then the question must be inconsistent with what? As Von Hirsch says "(s)entencing offenders invariably according to their height or weight would be consistent, but nevertheless irrational"[85] and unjust. The same point is made by Pease in the following extract.

K. Pease, "Sentencing and Measurement: Some Analogies from Psychology," in Sentencing Reform, (1987), eds. K. Pease and M. Wasik, pp. 127–128:

"Imagine a naive psychologist (called Psyche) who wishes to do her doctoral thesis on judicial sentencing. She has the advantage over psychologists already working in the field of a complete ignorance of criminal justice, and an utter disregard for the conventional accounts by judges of what they are doing when they sentence. The first thing Psyche notices about sentencing is what an extraordinary activity it is, even when it is not accompanied by strange custom and ritual and eighteenth-century dress. People listen to accounts of the actions of other people, and proceed to match these actions to punishment choice. The aspects of the action which are relevant to punishment choice are not made explicit. The punishments are expressed in units (usually of time or money) which bear no obvious relation to the actions. The way in which the response is arrived at is ineffable. There is no debate about the mechanisms of scaling, simply the observation that the occasional response is 'wrong', or that there are wide differences in punishments awarded to overtly similar acts. A rhetoric of 'principles of sentencing' exists. These principles are only evident from the words which accompany sentence. There is seldom any way of inferring sentencing principles from sentencing practice.

---

[83] L. Cargan and M. Coates, "The indeterminate Sentence and Judicial Bias" in *Crimes and Delinquency* 19 (1974) 144.

[84] L.J. Toliver, *Sentencing and the Law and Order Syndrome in South Carolina* (1974).

[85] "Guidance by Numbers or Words?" in *Sentencing Reform* (1987), eds. K. Pease and M. Wasik, p. 49.

Faced with a situation of this kind, Psyche seeks clarification by applying concepts familiar from other parts of her discipline. She seeks insight in the field of psychological testing. The classic concepts of test theory are those of reliability and validity. Validity concerns the capacity of an instrument to measure what it sets out to measure. Reliability refers to the capacity of an instrument to measure whatever it is measuring consistently. An instrument can be reliable without being valid. The converse is not true. For instance, tape-measures provide a reliable measure of something. That is to say, almost all tape-measures will come up with the same measures of difference between people, and will keep on doing so. The tape-measure is reliable. If, however, what it is measuring is described as intelligence, the test is not valid. If it is described as height, it is. While the issue seems ludicrous in the example, it is not so when one has to deal with the measurement of personality traits like aggression or professional aptitude—nor with sentencing.

Looking over research on sentencing, Psyche remarks that there has been more concern with the *reliability* of sentencing than with the *validity* of sentencing. Studies of sentencing disparity and attempts to reduce that disparity, she opines, are rather like attempts to produce a set of judges who behave as consistently as tape-measures. The trouble seems to be a relative indifference as to whether what is measured is height or intelligence!"

Talk, therefore, of sentencing disparity is unhelpful unless one has a criterion or criteria against which the sentence can be judged. This fact has enabled some of the judiciary to pretend that sentencing disparity cannot, therefore, exist. The sentencing task is *so* complex, with *so* many factors to be taken into account that no two cases are alike. This will be maintained particularly when the purpose of the sentence has been described as rehabilitative and tailored to suit the defendant's needs.

C. M. V. Clarkson, "Sentencing—U.S.A. Style," (1982) 12 Kingston Law Review 32 at 39–41:

"Even if rehabilitation were still the generally accepted goal, such sentencing disparity cannot be attributed to individualisation of sentences. The reality is that different judges impose punishment for different purposes. Even the same judge is not always consistent in his sentencing. There is no agreement among judges as to what criteria ought to be taken into account in the sentencing decision and what weight ought to be given to factors such as prior record, age, good family, perceived future dangerousness, whether the accused pleaded guilty and other such matters. One of the most vehement (and influential) criticisms of judicial discretion in sentencing has come from a member of the judiciary, Judge Marvin E. Frankel. Responding to the argument that judges in general are calm and dispassionate in their sentencing role, Judge Frankel writes:

'But nobody has the experience of being sentenced by "judges in general." The particular defendant on some existential day confronts a specific judge. The occupant of the bench on that day may be punitive, patriotic, self-righteous, guilt-ridden, and more than customarily dyspeptic. The vice in our system is that all such qualities have free rein as well as potentially fatal impact upon the defendant's finite life.' (*Criminal Sentences—Law Without Order*, (1972), p. 23.)

Other studies are to the same effect:

> 'That some judges are arbitrary and even sadistic in their sentencing prac-
> tices is notoriously a matter of record. By reason of senility or a virtually
> pathological emotional complex some judges summarily impose the maxi-
> mum on defendants convicted of certain types of crimes or all types of
> crimes . . . I know of one judge who continued to sit on the bench and sen-
> tence defendants to prison while he was undergoing shock treatment for a
> mental illness.' ('The Sentence—Its Relation to Crime and Rehabilitation' in
> *Of Prisons and Justice*, 5. Doc. No: 70, 88th Cong., 2nd SCSS, p. 311 (1964).)

The idea that most sentences have been 'individualised' to the particular
offender appears to be a fiction. Judge Frankel concludes that most judges spend
a minimal amount of time in determining the appropriate sentence in a given
case:

> 'The judge is likely to read thick briefs, hear oral argument, and then take
> days or weeks to decide who breached a contract for delivery of onions. The
> same judge will read a pre-sentence report, perhaps talk to a probation offi-
> cer, hear a few minutes of pleas for mercy—invest, in sum, less than an
> hour in all—before imposing a sentence of ten years in prison.' (Frankel, p.
> 15.)"

Additionally, despite claims about the multiplicity of factors having
to be taken into account, research consistently points to the pre-
eminence of offence seriousness in determinations of sentence.[86] This
finding has an important bearing, as we shall see, on attempts that have
been made in the United States and in this country to deal with sentencing disparity, but one other related issue needs to be considered
first. Judges are not currently obliged, except in a few specified situations,[87] to give reasons for their chosen sentence. In most cases no
reasons at all are given and even when they are, stock and almost meaningless phrases may be employed. This obviously makes the task of
judging whether the sentence is disparate or truly individualised rather
difficult! Would the sentencing process be improved by a requirement
that reasons always be given for the imposition of a particular sentence?[88]

C. Fitzmaurice and K. Pease, The Psychology of Judicial Sentencing, (1986), pp. 40, 45:

"(V)erbal expressions of reasons for behaving in a particular way, whether
that behaviour is judicial sentencing or any other complex behaviour, cannot
confidently be accepted as accurate. This is evident both from psychological
study and from honest introspection. It is true whether reasons seem bizarre or

---

[86] C. Fitzmaurice and K. Pease, *The Psychology of Judicial Sentencing*, (1986), pp. 52–59.

[87] *E.g.*, section 123(5) of the Criminal Justice Act 1988 requires the court to explain why detention in a
young offender institution is being ordered and s.20 of the Powers of Criminal Courts Act 1973
requires that reasons be given for the imposition of the first sentence of imprisonment to offenders
aged 21 and over.

[88] See, *e.g.*, D. A. Thomas, "Sentencing—The Case for Reasoned Decisions," (1963) Crim.L.R. 243.
See also C. Corbett, "Magistrates' and Court Clerks' Sentencing Behaviour: An Experimental Study,"
in *The Psychology of Sentencing* (1987), pp. 204–215.

bland. For instance, we would not now regard confessions of witchcraft as credible accounts by people of their own actions, even in those cultural settings where witchcraft is still a socially favoured explanation. Similarly, it seems to us that offenders' accounts of crime on television and radio owe much to fashionable theories of crime. To be consistent, one should be as sceptical of such reasons as much as of judges' reasons for sentence. Such reasons are *post hoc* justifications of what was actually done rather than accurate representations of why it was done . . . (We) suggest that a proper understanding of principles of sentencing should not be based on judicially expressed reasons for passing particular sentences, or on judges' general pronouncements about sentencing policy. An understanding of sentencing practice and policy must be based on empirical examination of the variables with which sentence choice co-varies, and how it co-varies. For example, although unemployment is . . . a major source of criminal justice excuses, it is reliably associated with more, not with less, severe sentencing. . . . So in the case of employment, at least, sentencing practice and an excuse for crime co-vary in the way opposite to that which one might expect.

Disparaging the reliability of reasons given as indicators of real reasons should set up in the reader an attitude of scepticism about reasons, not one of rejection of reasons as worthless in the court context. If reasons have a place in court, it is because they are defensible, not because they are true. When available for challenge, reasons invite people in the court to behave as if they were true, to test, challenge and appeal against. Even spurious reasons (and, it is contended, no reason is known not to be spurious) may, when challenged, enforce patterns of sentencing which correspond with what the practice would be if the reason were the real one. In fact, in informing court practice, it may become the real one."

Given the overwhelming evidence of sentencing disparity, moves have been made both in the United States and in this country to deal with the problem. In this country, in addition to the tariff already discussed,[89] has come the development of so-called guideline judgments. These are generally when a number of appeals are heard at the same time and the Court of Appeal takes the opportunity to make generalised statements about sentencing for that type of offence.

R. v. Billam (1986) 82 Cr.App.R. 347 (Court of Appeal, Criminal Division).

The Lord Chief Justice:
"We have had listed before us today a number of cases where there has been a conviction for rape or attempted rape, in order to give us an opportunity to restate principles which in our judgment should guide judges on sentencing in this difficult and sensitive area of the criminal law.

In the unhappy experience of this Court, whether or not the number of convictions for rape has increased over the years, the nastiness of the cases has certainly increased, and what would ten years ago have been considered incredible perversions have now become commonplace. This is no occasion to explore the reasons for that phenomenon, however obvious they may be.

We would like, if we may, to cite a passage from the Criminal Law Revision Committee's 15th Report on Sexual Offences, Command Paper 9213 of 1984,

[89] *Ante* p. 55.

which reflects accurately the views of this Court. It is as follows: 'Rape is generally regarded as the most grave of all the sexual offences. In a paper put before us for our consideration by the Policy Advisory Committee on Sexual Offences the reasons for this are set out as follows—"Rape involves a severe degree of emotional and psychological trauma; it may be described as a violation which in effect obliterates the personality of the victim. Its physical consequences equally are severe: the actual physical harm occasioned by the act of intercourse; associated violence or force and in some cases degradation; after the event, quite apart from the woman's continuing insecurity, the fear of venereal disease or pregnancy. We do not believe this latter fear should be underestimated because abortion would usually be available. This is not a choice open to all women and it is not a welcome consequence for any. Rape is also particularly unpleasant because it involves such intimate proximity between the offender and victim. We also attach importance to the point that the crime of rape involves abuse of an act which can be a fundamental means of expressing love for another; and to which as a society we attach considerable value." '

This Court emphasised in *Roberts* (1982) 4 Cr.App.R.(S.) 8, that rape is always a serious crime which calls for an immediate custodial sentence other than in wholly exceptional circumstances. The sort of exceptional circumstances in which a non-custodial sentence may be appropriate are illustrated by the decision in *Taylor* (1983) 5 Cr.App.R.(S.) 241. Although on the facts that offence amounted to rape in the legal sense, the Court observed that it did not do so in ordinary understanding.

Judges of the Crown Court need no reminder of the necessity for custodial sentences in cases of rape. The criminal statistics for 1984 show that 95 per cent. of all defendants who were sentenced in the Crown Court for offences of rape received immediate custodial sentences in one form or another. But the same statistics also suggest that judges may need reminding about what length of sentence is appropriate.

Of the 95 per cent. who received custodial sentences in 1984, 28 per cent. received sentences of two years or less; 23 per cent. over two and up to three years; 18 per cent. over three and up to four years; 18 per cent. over four and up to five years and 8 per cent. over five years (including 2 per cent. life). These included partly suspended sentences and sentences to detention centre or detention under section 53(2) of the Children and Young Persons Act 1933, as well as imprisonment or youth custody. Although it is important to preserve a sense of proportion in relation to other grave offences such as some forms of manslaughter, these statistics show an approach to sentences for rape which in the judgment of this Court are too low.

The variable factors in cases of rape are so numerous that it is difficult to lay down guidelines as to the proper length of sentence in terms of years. That aspect of the problem was not considered in *Roberts* (cited above). There are however many reported decisions of the Court which give an indication of what current practice ought to be and it may be useful to summarise their general effect.

For rape committed by an adult without any aggravating or mitigating features, a figure of five years should be taken as the starting point in a contested case. Where a rape is committed by two or more men acting together, or by a man who has broken into or otherwise gained access to a place where the victim is living, or by a person who is in a position of responsibility towards the victim, or by a person who abducts the victim and holds her captive, the starting point should be eight years.

At the top of the scale comes the defendant who has carried out what might be described as a campaign of rape, committing the crime upon a number of different women or girls. He represents a more than ordinary danger and a sentence of fifteen years or more may be appropriate.

Where the defendant's behaviour has manifested perverted or psychopathic tendencies or gross personality disorder, and where he is likely, if at large, to remain a danger to women for an indefinite time, a life sentence will not be inappropriate.

The crime should in any event be treated as aggravated by any of the following factors: (1) violence is used over and above the force necessary to commit the rape; (2) a weapon is used to frighten or wound the victim; (3) the rape is repeated; (4) the rape has been carefully planned; (5) the defendant has previous convictions for rape or other serious offences of a violent or sexual kind; (6) the victim is subjected to further sexual indignities or perversions; (7) the victim is either very old or very young; (8) the effect upon the victim, whether physical or mental, is of special seriousness. Where any one or more of these aggravating features are present, the sentence should be substantially higher than the figure suggested as the starting point.

The extra distress which giving evidence can cause to a victim means that a plea of guilty, perhaps more so than in other cases, should normally result in some reduction from what would otherwise be the appropriate sentence. The amount of such reduction will of course depend on all the circumstances, including the likelihood of a finding of not guilty had the matter been contested.

The fact that the victim may be considered to have exposed herself to danger by acting imprudently (as for instance by accepting a lift in a car from a stranger) is not a mitigating factor; and the victim's previous sexual experience is equally irrelevant. But if the victim has behaved in a manner which was calculated to lead the defendant to believe that she would consent to sexual intercourse, then there should be some mitigation of the sentence. Previous good character is of only minor relevance.

The starting point for attempted rape should normally be less than for the completed offence, especially if it is desisted at a comparatively early stage. But, as is illustrated by one of the cases now before the Court, attempted rape may be made by aggravating features into an offence even more serious than some examples of the full offence.

About one-third of those convicted of rape are under the age of 21 and thus fall within the scope of the Criminal Justice Act 1982, s.1. Although the criteria to which the Court is required to have regard by section 1(4) of that Act must be interpreted in relation to the facts of the individual case rather than simply by reference to the legal category of the offence, most offences of rape are "so serious that a non-custodial sentence cannot be justified" for the purposes of that provision. In the ordinary case the appropriate sentence would be one of youth custody, following the term suggested as terms of imprisonment for adults, but making some reduction to reflect the youth of the offender. A man of 20 will accordingly not receive much less than a man of 22, but a youth of 17 or 18 may well receive less.

In the case of a juvenile, the Court will in most cases exercise the power to order detention under the Children and Young Persons Act 1933, s.53(2). In view of the procedural limitations to which the power is subject, it is important that a Magistrates' Court dealing with a juvenile charged with rape should *never* accept jurisdiction to deal with the case itself, but should invariably commit the case to the Crown Court for trial to ensure that the power is available."

There are now guideline decisions on a variety of issues; for example, for drug offences,[90] for incest,[91] for breach of trust,[92] for social security frauds,[93] on the factors to be taken into account in causing death by reckless driving cases,[94] on the sentencing of young offenders,[95] on when to defer sentence,[96] and when to impose a partially suspended sentence.[97] There is evidence that many of these decisions have resulted in sharp increases in sentencing levels. For example, in 1984 30% of those convicted of rape received sentences of at least five years imprisonment. In 1987, the year following *Billam*, the figure had risen to 80%.[98] But are these guideline judgments effective in removing disparity?

Andrew Ashworth, Custody Reconsidered, (1989), (Centre for Policy Studies study no. 104), p. 22:

"The real problem with calling upon the judiciary to provide a complete network of sentencing guidelines is that they would be fashioned solely from a judicial perspective, and informed only by the judicial outlook on the aims and effectiveness of sentencing. But I have argued that many of the assumptions underlying sentencing practice in recent years are badly mistaken. Whilst the senior judges have developed the guideline judgment into an important vehicle, and in doing so have shown that the common law can still be adapted to perform new functions, it is a vehicle which is at present being driven in the wrong direction.

A mechanism is needed which allows the judicial expertise in formulating guidelines to be harnessed to the experience of other professionals such as probation officers, prison governors and magistrates. This is particularly important because there is no indication that the senior judiciary can successfully develop guidelines for use in the magistrates' courts: they lack the necessary practical experience to do so. Yet the magistrates' courts are the source of some 55 per cent. of receptions into prison each year, and make a large number of other sentencing decisions which have great consequences for people's lives. The present structure of sentencing guidance does not and cannot cope with sentencing in the magistrates' courts."

K. Pease, "Sentencing and Measurement: Some Analogies from Psychology," in Sentencing Reform, (1987), eds. K. Pease and M. Wasik, p. 134:

"It was asserted that guideline judgments in an appellate system do not offer the same advantages for retributive sentence validation as do sentencing guidelines themselves. This assertion should be justified. Guideline judgments do

---

[90] *R.* v. *Aramah* (1983) 76 Cr.App.R. 190. *R.* v. *Bilinski* (1988) 86 Cr.App.R. 146. But see also the Controlled Drugs (Penalties) Act 1985.

[91] *Att.-Gen.'s Reference (No. 1 of 1989)*, The Times, August 1, 1989.

[92] *R.* v. *Barrick* (1985) 149 J.P. 705.

[93] *R.* v. *Stewart* [1987] 1 W.L.R. 559.

[94] *R.* v. *Boswell* [1984] 1 W.L.R. 1047.

[95] *R.* v. *Fairhurst* [1986] 1 W.L.R. 1374.

[96] *R.* v. *George* [1984] 1 W.L.R. 1082.

[97] *R.* v. *Clarke* [1982] 1 W.L.R. 1090. For further examples of guideline decisions, see *R.* v. *Keys* (1986) 84 Cr.App.R. 204, *R.* v. *Howard* (1985) 82 Cr.App.R. 262; *R.* v. *King* (1985) 82 Cr.App.R. 120 and *R.* v. *Al-Mograbi* (1979) 70 Cr.App.R. 24.

[98] Home Office White Paper, *Crime, Justice and Protecting the Public* (1990) Cm. 965, para. 2.14.

not assume, nor do they attempt to reflect, consensus judicial assessments of culpability. A guideline judgment may cut across agreed judgments of relative severity or suggest differentials which bear no relationship to judicial thought or action. Critically, guideline judgments do no 'calibrate' judges by specifying the range of normal variation. Ashworth ('Techniques of Guidance on Sentencing' (1984) Crim.L.R. 661) has extrapolated a scale of punishments from a guideline judgment of Lord Chief Justice Lane. It relates street value of a drug consignment to the 'proper' sentence. It runs as follows: £100,000: 7 years; £250,000: 8 years; £400,000: 9 years; £550,000: 10 years; £700,000: 11 years; £850,000: 12 years; £1,000,000: 13 years.

It is interesting that the scaling of sentence against value does not correspond with most judgments on the matter. . . . For example, does this really mean that a consignment worth £2,500,000 gets you twenty-three years and a consignment worth £1.00 gets you six years and a bit?

Crucially, the judgment does not offer the range within which the normal sentence for a particular street value may vary. Can prior record take the proper sentence for a crime worth £700,000 below 10·5 years or above 11·5 years? Unless information of this kind can be given, *no real guidance is being given*. To the writer's knowledge, no guideline judgment has provided information about the range of acceptable dispersion around the guideline judgment. The most troubling aspect of this is that the Lord Chief Justice seems unaware of what guidance is necessary for valid retributive sentencing to be possible. . . .

Even were guideline judgments to include information about dispersion, guidelines themselves afford other advantages. Reliable judgments of relative culpability are more likely to be found among a group of judges than in individual judges, however distinguished. Assuming general social consensus about culpability, there are likely to remain individual differences. *General* judgments, enshrined in guidelines, are more likely to coincide with more general views of culpability than are the judgments of one or three Court of Appeal judges. Because guidelines derive from the collective views of brother judges, individual judges may feel more constrained to take them seriously."

Given that doubts exist about the effectiveness of guideline judgments in giving guidance and in reducing disparity, therefore, it is helpful to turn to reforms attempted elsewhere.

C. M. V. Clarkson, "Sentencing—U.S.A. Style," (1982) 12 Kingston Law Review 32 at pp. 42–52:

"With the plethora of evidence and studies emerging over the last decade revealing such widespread sentencing disparity, it is understandable that a strong movement should have developed (in the United States) aimed at achieving uniformity of sentencing. Those who still cling to the rehabilitive ideal greatly wish to reduce the sentencing disparity, while still retaining some discretion for the 'individualisation' of sentences. Those (the majority of commentators) who favour a return to 'just desert' as the basis of punishment, favour elimination of all discretion and have been advocating fixed or presumptive sentences, or guideline models of sentencing.

. . . These proposals aimed at eliminating, minimising or structuring sentencing discretion fall broadly into three categories:

1. *Fixed penalties*
A fixed, specific penalty should be attached to each statutory offence. Thus, for example, first degree robbery would be punished by imprisonment for four

years. No individual circumstances of the offence or offender could be taken
into account. Release on parole would be abolished—thus four years would
mean four years. (However most proponents of such a scheme concede that in
the interests of prison discipline some allowance for "good time" would need to
be retained.) A popular variant of this proposal is that the prior record of the
defendant could be taken into account. Thus, for example, first degree robbery
would be punished by imprisonment for four years; if the defendant had a previous felony conviction he would be punished for five years; if he had two previous felony convictions he would be punished for six years, and so on.

2. *Presumptive penalties*

The legislature would provide a presumptive sentence for each statutory
offence, *e.g.* four years imprisonment for first degree robbery. This would be the
penalty normally imposed. However if there were special aggravating or mitigating circumstances this presumptive penalty could be varied but such variations could not depart from the presumptive sentence by more than a
prescribed amount and the judge would have to justify, in writing, his departure from the presumptive penalty. General principles governing the aggravating and mitigating circumstances that could be taken into account, would be set
forth in legislative standards. Thus, for example, if aggravating or mitigating
circumstances were found, the four year presumptive penalty for first degree
robbery would be increased or decreased but under no circumstances could a
penalty of more than five years or less than three years be imposed.

In 1976 California adopted such a sentencing scheme. California Penal Code,
s.1170(*a*)(1) declares that 'the elimination of disparity and the provision of uniformity of sentences can best be achieved by determinate sentences fixed by
statute in proportion to the seriousness of the offence as determined by the
Legislature to be imposed by the court with certified discretion.' The same statute has fixed the penalty for most offences at three levels. Thus, for example,
voluntary manslaughter is punishable by imprisonment for two, four or six
years and involuntary manslaughter by imprisonment for two, three or four
years. Section 1170(*b*) directs that normally the court must impose the middle
term. [Assuming he is to be sentenced to imprisonment. Provision is made for
fines, probation or suspended sentences to be imposed.] However, if aggravating circumstances are found to exist the judge may impose the upper term; and
if mitigating circumstances are established, he may impose the lower term. The
sentence may, in addition, be enhanced within specified limits, based on prior
criminal record, use of weapons, infliction of great bodily harm or large property loss. Judges retain the discretion to sentence concurrently or consecutively
and, for most crimes, to grant probation.[99] A Judicial Council has been created
to establish mandatory guidelines to control the court's decision, *inter alia*, as to
whether to grant or deny probation, impose the lower or upper prison term and
whether to impose concurrent or consecutive sentences.

Thus the move towards presumptive sentences has started to become a
reality. As it did with individualised sentences, California is once again setting
the trend, but already other states are following suit.

3. *Guideline model*

Such a model represents a compromise between the inflexibility of fixed or
presumptive sentences and the unfettered judicial discretion presently under

[99] All sentences of imprisonment are subject to appellate review; the aim of this review is *exclusively*
to eliminate sentencing disparity (Cal. Penal Code, s.1170(f)). See generally M.L. Fenili, "California's
Disparate Sentence Review Process" in M.L. Forst (ed.), *Sentencing Reform: Experiments in Reducing
Disparity* (1982), and R. Puglia, "Determinate Sentencing in California" in the University of Cambridge, Institute of Criminology (Occasional Papers No: 8), *The Future of Sentencing*, (1982).

attack. Judicial discretion is retained, but specific criteria and guidelines are developed to structure and control the exercise of that discretion. The legislature continues to set maximum terms. A specialised body, usually referred to as a Sentencing Commission, is created to establish sentencing guidelines within these broad statutory boundaries. These guidelines are generally based on two factors: the severity of the offence and the offender's prior criminal history. Offences are ranked in order of their seriousness and the Commission specifies a limited number of aggravating and mitigating circumstances which increase or decrease the severity of the offence. Factors relating to the offender's prior criminal history include his prior convictions, prior incarcerations and whether he was on parole or probation at the time the offence was committed. For each combination of offence and offender, including a consideration of aggravating or mitigating circumstances, the guidelines provide a narrow sentencing range. The sentencing judge is expected to impose a sentence within this range, but if there are special circumstances not adequately taken into account by the guidelines, he may depart from the guidelines; reasons for the departure must be given and the sentence then becomes automatically subject to appellate review.

Under such schemes the sentence imposed on an offender is the sentence he will actually serve (except for 'good time' reductions). Accordingly there is no necessity for a Parole Board.

The role of the Sentencing Commission is viewed as crucial to the guideline model. Unlike the legislature, such a body would have the time and 'expertise' to establish guidelines on the basis of careful study of existing sentencing practices; they could periodically alter these guidelines on the basis of on-going experience; it would be removed from partisan politics; it would be a publicly accountable body; its rule-making would be on the record and open to public scrutiny."

The table on p. 68 is an example of such sentencing guidelines.

Minnesota Sentencing Guidelines Grid, Revised, 1988.

Presumptive Sentence Lengths in Months

Italicised numbers within the grid denote the range within which a judge may sentence without the sentence being deemed a departure.

All felony offences are assigned an appropriate level of severity. The offences listed on the grid are simply the most frequently occurring offences within each severity level.

The offender's criminal history score is computed by assigning points (or units, equal to a quarter of a point each) to the following:

(a) prior felony convictions (one point each unless 15 years has elapsed since expiration of the last sentence);

(b) custody status at the time of the offence (one point if the offender was on parole or probation or confined in jail or released pending sentencing);

(c) prior misdemeanor and gross misdemeanor record (one and two units respectively, unless 10 years has elapsed since expiration of the last sentence);

(d) prior juvenile adjudications for offences that would have been felonies if committed by an adult (one point for every two adjudications).

		CRIMINAL HISTORY SCORE						
SEVERITY LEVELS OF CONVICTION OFFENSE		0	1	2	3	4	5	6 or more
Unauthorized Use of Motor Vehicle Possession of Marijuana	I	12*	12*	12*	13	15	17	19 18–20
Theft Related Crimes ($2500 or less) Check Forgery ($200–$2500)	II	12*	12*	13	15	17	19	21 20–22
Theft Crimes ($2500 or less)	III	12*	13	15	17	19 18–20	22 21–23	25 24–26
Nonresidential Burglary Theft Crimes (over $2500)	IV	12*	15	18	21	25 24–26	32 30–34	41 37–45
Residential Burglary Simple Robbery	V	18	23	27	30 29–31	38 36–40	46 43–49	54 50–58
Criminal Sexual Conduct, 2nd Degree (a) & (b)	VI	21	26	30	34 33–35	44 42–46	54 50–58	65 60–70
Aggravated Robbery	VII	24 23–25	32 30–34	41 38–44	49 45–53	65 60–70	81 75–87	97 90–104
Criminal Sexual Conduct 1st Degree Assault, 1st Degree	VIII	43 41–45	54 50–58	65 60–70	76 71–81	95 89–101	113 106–120	132 124–140
Murder, 3rd Degree Murder, 2nd Degree (felony murder)	IX	105 102–108	119 116–122	127 124–130	149 143–155	176 168–184	205 195–215	230 218–242
Murder, 2nd Degree (with intent)	X	216 212–220	236 231–241	256 250–262	276 269–283	296 288–304	316 307–325	336 326–346

1st Degree Murder is excluded from the guidelines by law and continues to have a mandatory life sentence.

*one year and one day

The presumptive sentence for cases contained in cells above and to the left of the solid line should be "stayed," (*i.e.* delayed until some future date; if the offender complies with imposed conditions until that date, the case is discharged). The presumptive sentence for cases contained in cells below and to the right of the solid line should be "executed," (*i.e.* served immediately).

Minnesota Sentencing Commission: Sentencing Guidelines (Revised, 1988):

"Statement of Purpose and Principles

The purpose of the sentencing guidelines is to establish rational and consistent sentencing standards which reduce sentencing disparity and ensure that sanctions following conviction of a felony are proportional to the severity of the offence of conviction and the extent of the offender's criminal history . . .

The sentences provided in the Sentencing Guidelines Grid are presumed to be appropriate for every case. The judge shall utilize the presumptive sentence . . . unless the individual case involves substantial and compelling circumstances . . . When departing from the presumptive sentence, the court should pronounce a sentence which is proportional to the severity of the offense of conviction and the extent of the offender's prior criminal history . . . When departing from the presumptive sentence, a judge must provide written reasons which specify the substantial and compelling nature of the circumstances, and which demonstrate why the sentence selected in the departure is more appropriate, reasonable or equitable than the presumptive sentence. . . .

[The commentary goes on to emphasise that the presumptive sentences are to be 'applied with a high degree of regularity. Sentencing disparity cannot be reduced if judges depart from the guidelines frequently.']

A. Factors that should not be used as reasons for departure: . . .

(1) Race
(2) Sex
(3) Employment factors . . .
(4) Social factors . . .
(5) The exercise of constitutional rights by the defendant . . .

B. Factors that may be used as reasons for departure:
The following is a nonexclusive list of factors . . .
(1) Mitigating Factors

(a) The victim was an aggressor in the incident.
(b) The offender played a minor or passive role in the crime or participated under circumstances of coercion or duress.
(c) The offender, because of physical or mental impairment, lacked substantial capacity for judgment. . . .
(d) Other substantial grounds exist which tend to excuse or mitigate the offender's culpability, although not amounting to a defense.

(2) Aggravating Factors:

(a) The victim was particularly vulnerable due to age, infirmity, or reduced physical or mental capacity . . .
(b) The victim was treated with particular cruelty.
(c) [If the victim was injured and there is a similar prior felony conviction].
(d) The offense was a major economic offense . . . [if two or more of the following circumstances exist]:
    (i) The offense involved multiple victims or multiple incidents per victim
    (ii) the offense involved an attempted or actual monetary loss substantially greater than the usual offense . . .
    (iii) the offense involved a high degree of sophistication or planning . . .
    (iv) the defendant used his or her position or status to facilitate the commission of the offense, including positions of trust, confidence or fiduciary relationships; or
    (v) the defendant has been involved in other conduct similar to the current offense. . . .
(e) The offense was a major controlled substance offense, identified as an offense or series of offenses related to trafficking in controlled substances . . . [if two or more aggravating factors (omitted) exist.]
(f) The offender committed, for hire, a crime, against the person.
(g) The offender committed a crime against the person in furtherance of criminal activity by an organised gang. . . . "

Sentencing guidelines have been implemented in many other states of America but none have been in operation for as long as the Minnesota guidelines and thus provide less fuel for assessment. Even a preliminary evaluation, however, would have to conclude that they have suffered mixed fortunes, much depending on the underlying rationale of the system and the quality of staff both designing and operating it.[1] The Minnesota guidelines thus still hold a special place in reform discussions because it is only here that a common law of sentencing has emerged. So important are they that one commentator has concluded, "(t)he work of the Minnesota Sentencing Guidelines Commission is probably the most significant development in sentencing policy and practice in the English-speaking world since the establishment of parole boards half a century ago."[2] It is inappropriate here to go into a detailed evaluation of the Minnesota guidelines[3] but the implications for any movement in this direction in England have to be explored.

One of the most significant findings has been the adaptive behaviour of the sentencing judges; after initial adherence to the guidelines there has been a tendency to revert to old sentencing habits. For example, the guidelines were designed to reduce the rate of imprisonment of minor recidivist property offenders, yet three years after the introduction of the guidelines "the imprisonment rate . . . was almost at the same level as the pre-guidelines imprisonment rate."[4] So in one sense, at least, the guidelines are still giving the judiciary too much discretion. Paradoxically, it may be that the English judiciary would regard them as not flexible enough because offence categories are too broad to allow what are really different cases to be dealt with differently.

Furthermore, the guidelines deal with the control of discretion at one stage of the criminal justice process only—that of sentencing. There are many other stages at which discretion operates, and it is interesting to note in this context that there has been a marked decline in sentence-bargaining since the introduction of the guidelines in Minnesota but a sharp increase in charge negotiations. If, as it seems, prosecutors are deliberately manipulating the guidelines (by insisting that offenders plead guilty to a number of charges so that their offender score is raised[5]), then injustice may just be removed to an earlier, less visible stage of the process.

What are the lessons that can be learnt from this? Certainly, it will not do in the face of less than perfect results elsewhere to lean back metaphorically on our own Court of Appeal as being a sufficient filter of dis-

---

[1] For further discussion of other U.S. guideline systems see, M. Tonry, "Sentencing Guidelines and Sentencing Commissions—the Second Generation," in *Sentencing Reform*, (1987) eds. K. Pease and M. Wasik, pp. 22–45.

[2] *Ibid.* p. 44.

[3] Reference should be made to the article by Tonry *ante* n. 1, to M. Wasik, "Sentencing guidelines in America—are they working?" (1985) Justice of the Peace 149 and to von Hirsch, Knapp and Tonry, *The Sentencing Commission and its Guidelines*, (1987).

[4] K. Knapp, *The Impact of the Minnesota Sentencing Guidelines Commission*, (1984), p. 31.

[5] Tonry, *ante* n. 1, p. 39.

parity and injustice. The Court of Appeal may now be able to hear appeals by the prosecution against too lenient a sentence[6] but leave is still required and it hears too few cases. Moreover, it is too far removed from the main place of sentencing business—the magistrates' courts, for us to be that sanguine. There are two ways in which it may be appropriate to proceed. Firstly, there are the newly issued guidelines for magistrates' courts drawn up by the Magistrates' Association in an attempt "to establish consistency and not to introduce a system of uniform sentencing."[7]

Magistrates' Association, A Sentencing Guide for Criminal Offences (Other than Road Traffic), (1989), pp. i–ii, 20:

"The Offence
Each page deals with a separate offence. This process is:
    – how serious is this case compared with other offences of this type?
    – consider the various "Seriousness Indicators" (listed in alphabetical order, not order of importance) and
    – remember that these lists are not comprehensive, and that other factors may be important in individual cases
Form a view about the relative seriousness of this case
If the offence is triable either way, the Seriousness Indicators are relevant to the mode of trial decision.

The Offender
In considering the sentence the court should
    – consider any mitigating factors (e.g. offender's age or health, assistance to the police or victim, guilty plea)
    – consider the offender's criminal record. Where there are recent and non-minor convictions, the court may use a higher starting point than the guidelines suggest
    – however, the sentence should be kept in proportion to the offence(s) now being dealt with.
The guidelines fines are set on the assumption of a guilty plea.

Guideline Fines
The fine is the penalty most frequently imposed by magistrates' courts, and any attempt to improve consistency of approach must therefore concentrate on fines even though
    – a compensation order now has priority over a fine
    – other measures (e.g. absolute and conditional discharges, probation, attendance centre, etc) should be considered for use in appropriate cases.
Where the court decides a fine *is* appropriate, it should bear in mind that the guideline fine represents the relative gravity of an average offence of this type
    – the court should move upwards or downwards from the guideline, according to whether this case is more or less serious than the average
    – the court should then consider the offender's means.

---

[6] Criminal Justice Act 1988 s.36. The first appeal heard on this basis was *Att.-Gen.'s Reference (No. 1 of 1989)* [1989] 3 W.L.R. 1117 where the Court of Appeal raised a sentence of imprisonment for incest from three to six years. It has to be remembered that a disparate sentence may be an unduly light one as well as one that is too heavy.

[7] Magistrates' Association, *The Times*, July 29, 1989.

The guidelines are based on an offender taking home £150 a week, and the court must consider the means of the individual offender, and local conditions.

– if local rates of pay are higher or lower than the suggested level, the guideline fine may be adjusted accordingly. . . . . [The following table is an example of offences dealt with by the Guide]

Class C Drug Offences

Misuse of Drugs Act 1971
Triable Either Way

Offence	Penalty	Guideline
i) Production	£500 and / or 3 months	- consider committal for trial if large scale operation - if serious, consider custody/substitutes - guideline fine is £200 for simplest cases
ii) Supply	£500 and / or 3 months	- consider committal for trial if large scale operation - if serious, consider custody/substitutes - guideline fine is £150 for simplest cases
iii) Possession with intent to supply	£500 and / or 3 months	- guideline fine is £100 for simplest cases
iv) Possession	£200 and / or 3 months	- guideline fine is £50 for simplest cases

Cultivation of Cannabis

Triable Either Way	
Penalty	**Guideline**
£2000 and / or 6 months	- personal use £100 - commercial cultivation consider committing to Crown Court for trial

Consider forfeiture of all drugs and equipment.''

The second proposal does not rest on numerical guidelines. Perhaps the English criminal justice system is more suited to the setting up of a sentencing commission that lays down statements of principle such as those favoured in Canada and in parts of Scandanavia.[8] As von Hirsch says, this has the advantage "of having the rationale and overall policy direction articulated through explicitly stated principles, and then allowing the appellate courts to implement that rationale and policy in a case-law jurisprudence."[9] Ashworth, too, believes that this is the way forward.

Andrew Ashworth, Custody Reconsidered, (1989), (Centre for Policy Studies, study No. 104), p. 23.

"What, then, is needed is the creation of an independent Sentencing Council or Commission to carry out the work of developing practical guidance and guidelines. This body should be composed of a senior judge together with a circuit judge and a recorder, who have greater and more recent experience of Crown Court sentencing; a lay magistrate; a stipendiary magistrate; a justices' clerk; a prison governor; a chief probation officer; a senior civil servant; and an academic. This suggests a complement of ten, of whom five would be sentencers. The body should be supported by a secretariat which could provide the support needed.

The first task of the Council would be to establish the sentencing aims and policies to be pursued. This should not prove as controversial a task as might be thought. There has been a succession of official reports in this country all pointing towards less use of custody and less reliance on deterrent reasons for sentencing. And these have now been joined by a number of well-argued and detailed papers from other Commonwealth countries. Close study of the report of the Canadian Sentencing Commission (1987) would make an excellent foundation for the work of such a Sentencing Council as I propose.

The second task would be to review the sentencing levels for the crimes with which the courts most frequently deal. Existing practice should be assessed, using both official statistics and recent research into Crown Court sentencing. Levels of custodial sentence would then be lowered, in accordance with the principle of restraint, but the whole sentence would have meaning. . . . The Council would discuss and weigh the factors relevant to sentencing for each type of offence; here the expertise already gained from the construction of guideline judgments would be most helpful. The objective would be to construct a set of guidelines for each of the crimes which frequently come before the courts. Whether the guidelines should be in the narrative form pioneered by the Court of Appeal . . . , or in a more summary form, would be for the Council to decide."

---

[8] See, *e.g.* A. von Hirsch and N. Jareborg "Sweden's Sentencing Statute Enacted" [1989] Crim. L.R. 275, the Finnish Criminal Code, Chap. 6 and the Report of the Canadian Sentencing Commission, *Sentencing Reform—A Canadian Approach*, (1987).

[9] "Guidance by Numbers or Words," in *Sentencing Reform*, (1987), *ante* n. 1, p. 67.

F. Sentences

For the sake of completeness this section will conclude with a list of the sentences available to the sentencing judge. No more than the briefest of outlines can be given in a book such as this.

There is an enormous variety of sentences now available. When dealing with adults, the sentencing judge has the following different types of sentence at his disposal.[10]

1. *Imprisonment:*

This is normally a "determinate" sentence, that is, for a fixed number of years. (A prisoner is entitled to remission of one third of the sentence subject to good behaviour in prison and after serving a third of the sentence can apply for parole, the granting of which is discretionary).

For murder and in some other extreme circumstances, an "indeterminate" sentence of life imprisonment can be imposed. Persons serving life imprisonment can be released at any time on licence—but remain on licence for life and may be recalled to prison at any time.

Courts also have power to impose an "extended sentence." This is where a sentence (up to 10 years) may be imposed upon dangerous and persistent offenders despite that sentence being in excess of the maximum prescribed for the offence.[11]

2. *Suspended sentence:*

The whole of a sentence of imprisonment may be suspended for between one and two years. If the defendant commits a further offence during this period his first sentence of imprisonment usually becomes activated—and of course he is liable to be sentenced for the new offence as well.

3. *Partly suspended sentence:*

The offender serves a portion of his sentence in prison; the remainder is suspended and can only be activated if a further offence is committed during the specified period.[12]

4. *Suspended sentence supervision order:*

When a sentence is suspended an offender can be placed under the supervision of a probation officer for a specified period of time.

---

[10] For details of the legislative provisions governing these sentences, see Christopher Harding and Lawrence Koffman, *Sentencing and the Penal System* (1988) and *The Sentence of the Court* (*A Handbook for Courts on the Treatment of Offenders*) (1988).

[11] The Government is proposing to abolish such extended sentences on the grounds that they are only used very infrequently; many maximum penalties have been increased since 1967 making extended sentences unnecessary. Home Office White Paper, *Crime, Justice and Protecting the Public,* (1990) Cm. 965, para. 3.17. See also *ante,* p. 26.

[12] The Government is proposing to alter the rules on parole so that all released prisoners remain at risk of being returned to custody if they commit a further imprisonable offence before the end of their sentences. Partly suspended sentences would accordingly become redundant and the Government has recommended their abolition. (Home Office White Paper, *Crime, Justice and Protecting the Public* (1990) Cm. 965, para. 3.18.

5. *Community service order:*

The offender is made to perform unpaid community work such as gardening, decorating or repairing the homes of the elderly or the handicapped. Such orders are for a specified period of time of between 40 and 240 hours and the consent of the offender is needed. In the words of the Home Office:

> "A community service order represents a substantial deprivation of time . . . The order also involves reparation to the community and a demanding regular commitment. When Parliament accepted the proposal for the introduction of a community service order, it was seen as a penal sanction that made serious demands on the offender and could thus be regarded as a realistic alternative for a custodial sentence."[13]

6. *Probation order:*

The offender is placed under the supervision of a probation officer for a specified period of between six months and three years. The order may include various requirements such as that the offender reside at an approved probation hostel, or that he attend a specified "day centre," or that he undertake psychiatric treatment, and so on. The official view of probation is expressed in the words of the Home Office again: "The fundamental aim of probation is to uphold the law and protect society by the probation service working with the offender to improve his behaviour."[14]

7. *Deportation order:*

A court may recommend to the Home Secretary that a foreigner be deported. There must be another country able to accept such a person.

8. *Disqualification from driving:*

Such disqualification is sometimes obligatory (for example, driving with an excess concentration of alcohol in the breath, blood or urine) and sometimes discretionary (for example, exceeding speed limits).

9. *Fine:*

An offender may be fined for any offence (except murder or treason). For indictable offences (the more serious ones) the court may impose any fine unless the statute prescribes a special maximum. Summary offences (the less serious ones) are grouped into five categories, each carrying its own maximum penalty which can be increased by an order of the Home Secretary to take account of inflation. "The fine is a purely punitive measure, which enables the court to demonstrate society's disapproval of the offence in a case where punishment (short of custody) is the appropriate response."[15] "The fine has great advantages for the public as well as the offender. It involves the offender actually paying

---

[13] *The Sentence of the Court (A Handbook for Courts on the Treatment of Offenders)* (1988), p. 41.
[14] *Idem* p. 31.
[15] *Idem* p. 23.

back to the community something in return for the damage he has done, rather than requiring society to spend even more money upon him so that he can repay the debt."[16]

10. *Compensation orders:*

With a compensation order the offender is ordered to pay money to his victim who has suffered personal or proprietary harm.[17]

These orders were introduced as part of a reawakening of interest in the victims of crime "as a convenient and rapid means of avoiding the expense of resort to civil litigation when the criminal clearly has the means which would enable compensation to be paid."[18] Since 1982 a compensation order can be made "instead of or in addition to" any other sentence.[19] This highlights the uneasy place such orders currently occupy within the penal system Are they or are they not a punishment? They may be seen as a way of making amends for the harm that has occurred—of reparation. Whether one views this in terms of retribution—of making the defendant pay for his crimes, or whether one argues from a more utilitarian premise, there would appear to be a sound basis upon which compensation orders can be fitted into the legal system. However, it is conceded that the Court of Appeal has generally[20] preferred the view that the primary focus rests upon the victim's needs and that a compensation order is not a punishment.[21]

11. *Other ancillary orders:*

There are various other ancillary orders available to a court when passing sentence. These orders cannot be made on their own but must be issued in conjunction with another sentence. The orders here are restitution (ordering stolen goods to be returned to the person entitled to them), forfeiture of property used in the offence (for example, a gun or a motor car), exclusion orders (excluding persons from certain licensed premises) and the new confiscation orders introduced in 1988[22] allowing courts to confiscate profits made by offenders from crime.

12. *Binding over:*

The offender is "bound over" when he is required to furnish a recognisance that he will keep the peace or be of good behaviour. If he fails to do this, the money he has furnished as the recognisance may be forfeited and he may be brought before the court and dealt with for the original offence.

---

[16] Home Office White Paper, *Crime, Justice and Protecting the Public*, (1990) Cm. 965, para. 5.1.

[17] This sentencing provision should not be confused with the wholly separate criminal injuries compensation scheme, which is a state-funded scheme for victims of violent crime.

[18] *Per* Lord Scarman in *Inwood* (1974) 60 Cr.App.R. 70 at p. 73.

[19] S.67, Criminal Justice Act 1982.

[20] There are exceptional cases where compensation orders may be made "to remind the defendant of the evil he has done" (*Miller* [1976] Crim.L.R. 694).

[21] *Inwood* (1974) 60 Cr.App.R. 70. See further, Martin Wasik "The Place of Compensation in the Penal System" [1978] Crim.L.R. 599.

[22] Criminal Justice Act 1988, ss.71–103.

13. *Absolute discharge:*
The offender is convicted of the offence but no further action is taken. There is no punishment as such. This occurs where the offence is trivial or where the conviction is only regarded as "technical."

14. *Conditional discharge:*
The offender is discharged but this is conditional upon not offending again within three years. If the condition is broken and another offence committed within that period the offender is liable to be sentenced for the original offence as well as the subsequent one.

II WHAT CONDUCT OUGHT TO BE CRIMINAL?

A. Introduction

We have been concerned so far to identify the basis upon which punishment can be justified, but that assumes that a logically anterior question has already been answered: what conduct does one want to punish by means of the *criminal law*?

The criminal law "is merely one amongst several methods of social control in society. Morality, religion and custom, amongst others provide alternative and often complementary normative systems for the control of behaviour and indeed attitudes with their own distinctive type of sanction."[23] It is to the crucial question of how decisions to criminalise are and should be made that we will now turn. How, for example, did the legislature decide recently that insider dealing (using privileged information to buy and sell shares) on the stock exchange ought to be a criminal offence[24]? On what basis was the decision made to make simple possession of indecent photographs of children a criminal offence as well as the taking of them[25]? Why should incest be a criminal offence? Why is it a criminal offence in English law to bugger an animal or one's consenting wife,[26] but no crime to bugger another consenting male over the age of 21 in private?[27] Why is it a crime to publish an obscene article,[28] but no crime to masturbate while reading the same article in private? Similar questions can be addressed to many areas of human conduct, but in an attempt to sharpen the focus on this section, we shall lay particular emphasis on the laws relating to insider dealing, incest, homosexuality between consenting adults and obscenity.

[23] Nicola Lacey, *State Punishment: Political Principles and Community Values*, (1988), p. 100.
[24] Company Securities (Insider Dealing) Act 1985 s.8(1)(*a*).
[25] Possession of indecent photos of children was made a criminal offence by virtue of s.160 of the Criminal Justice Act 1988; the taking of such photos was made a criminal offence under the Protection of Children Act 1978 s.1(1)(*a*).
[26] Sexual Offences Act 1956, s.12(1).
[27] Sexual Offences Act 1967, s.1.
[28] Obscene Publications Act 1959, s.2.

In attempting to answer such questions as these we will, in part at least, be rehearsing a debate that has been continually fuelled by academic exchanges—that of the relationship of the criminal law to morality.

B. Immorality as a Necessary Condition

Few would deny that the criminal law has a moral content[29]; many actions prohibited by the criminal law, such as murder, theft and violence to the person, are undoubted moral wrongs as well. By this one means that even in the absence of a prohibitory law, a large majority would still feel that the actions were wrong. Something that is immoral, is something, therefore, that offends against the community spirit. In a secular age, such as ours, it need have no special religious connotations at all; immorality is thus not necessarily the same thing as sin, which is a transgression of "the laws of God."[30] In adopting, for the sake of discussion, this view of immorality, one would not wish to deny the existence of the problem of actually ascertaining moral opinion.

> "To assume a common culture or a normative consensus in American society (for example) as in most modern societies, is to ignore the deep and divisive role of class, ethnic, religious, status, and regional culture conflicts which often produce widely opposing definitions of goodness, truth, and moral virtue."[31]

But if, for the moment, such a simple definition of immorality is accepted, we may then question the nature of its relationship to the criminal law. Is it just historical coincidence that both should operate so often in the same fields of activity or is it possible to state some more definite relationship?

Hyman Gross, A Theory of Criminal Justice, (1979) pp. 13–15:

> "It seems obvious that those crimes of violence, theft and destruction that stand as paradigms of crime and comprise the core of any penal code are also moral wrongs. Everyone has a right to be free of such harm inflicted by others, and when murder, rape, arson, assault or larceny is committed there is also a moral wrong since a moral duty to refrain from doing harm to others has been breached. The right to be free of such harm does not have its origin in law but in a general consensus on the rights enjoyed by any member of society, or even by any person, no matter how he lives. This consensus is a more fundamental element of society even than the law, and for that reason the violation of such a right is a moral wrong and not simply a legal wrong.
> But beyond the most obvious crimes, legions of others are on the books for

---

[29] Some theorists, adopting a conflict view of society, would argue that the criminal law represents nothing more than the vested interests of the powerful, *e.g.* Richard Quinney, *The Social Reality of Crime* (1970).

[30] In the Wolfenden Committee on homosexual offences (Homosexual Offences and Prostitution (1957), p. 13) it is disquieting to find sin and immorality used synonymously. Their usage is adopted by Devlin in *The Enforcement of Morals* (1959) and criticised by G. Hughes in "Morals and the Criminal Law" (1962) 71 Yale L.J. 662 at 666–669.

[31] Gussfield, "On Legislating Morals; The Symbolic Process of Designating Deviancy" (1968) 56 Calif. L.R. 54 at 55–56.

the reason that doing what is prohibited (or failing to do what is required) makes life hazardous or unpleasant. Members of the public are entitled to live and to work in safety and to enjoy life in public places without fear, disquiet or embarrassment . . . these rights are also moral rights and not simply legal rights, since entitlement to the security and freedom that they represent is a matter of fundamental social consensus and not a matter simply of legal enactment.

Other crimes that are not common crimes are morally wrong for a different reason. Income tax fraud or draft evasion seem to place an unfair burden on others or deprive others of what is due to them . . . "[32]

H. Packer, The Limits of the Criminal Sanction (1968), pp. 262–264:

"Can we . . . assert that there is any kind of connection between the immorality of a category of conduct and the appropriate use of the criminal sanction? I think we can, but only on a prudential basis. Leaving aside for the moment what we mean by immoral, we may discern an analogy between the requirement of culpability in the individual case and a limiting criterion for the legislative invocation of the criminal sanction: only conduct generally considered 'immoral' should be treated as criminal. Several reasons support this prudential limitation. To begin with, the principles of selection we use in determining what kinds of undesirable conduct to treat as criminal should surely include at least one that is responsible to the basic character of the criminal sanction, *i.e.* its quality of moral condemnation. To put it another way, we should use the strengths of the sanction rather than ignore or undermine them. If the conduct with which the original sanction deals is already regarded as being morally wrong, the processes of the criminal law have, so to speak, a 'leg up' on the job. This is a matter partly of public attitude and partly of the morale maintained by those who operate the criminal process. The way to keep those processes running at peak efficiency is to ensure that those who operate them are convinced that what they are doing is right. The surest way to persuade them that what they are doing is right is to have them act only against what they think is wrong. If the criminal sanction is widely used to deal with morally neutral behaviour, law enforcement officials are likely to be at least subconsciously defensive about their work, and the public will find the criminal law a confusing guide to moral, or even acceptable, behaviour. [Packer then dismisses the argument that the criminal law can be used to shape people's views on immorality, and continues]: . . . The question remains: whose morality are we talking about? It is easy to slide into the assumption that somewhere in society there is an authoritative body of moral sentiment to which the law should look. That assumption becomes particularly dangerous . . . when it is used to buttress the assertion that the immorality of a given form of conduct is a *sufficient* condition for declaring the conduct to be criminal. But when one is talking about immorality as a *necessary* condition for invocation of the criminal sanction, the inquiry should simply be whether there exists any significant body of dissent from the proposition that the conduct in question is immoral. Is there a social group that will be alienated or offended by making (or keeping) the conduct in question criminal? If there is, then prudence dictates caution in employing the criminal sanction.

We can sum up this prudential limitation as follows: the criminal sanction should ordinarily be limited to conduct that is viewed, without significant

---

[32] Gross argues further that committing a crime is necessarily a moral wrong because it involves violating a "solemn promise to live according to the rules" of society. However, we are here concerned with the *content* of these rules and their relationship to morality.

social dissent, as immoral. The calendar of crimes should not be enlarged beyond that point and, as views about morality shift, should be contracted."

Is incest immoral? Is homosexual behaviour or the publication of "obscene" material about homosexual practices immoral? Insider dealing may have gone through the transition from accepted practice to something "gentlemen" in the city do not do, but has it become a moral wrong? If any of these examples fail to satisfy that test, ought they, nevertheless, to be criminal? The answer would generally have to be a negative one for the reasons given by Packer.

C. Immorality as a Sufficient Condition

Some commentators have argued that it is possible to pinpoint more precisely the relationship between the criminal law and morality: they believe that not only is immorality a necessary condition for invocation of the criminal sanction, but that it is a sufficient one. It is not necessary to search for further justification (harm, enforceability, etc.) before the criminal law can be brought into action; the fact that the conduct is morally wrong is enough. This view is epitomised by such statements by James Fitzjames Stephen as "How can the state or the public be competent to determine any question whatever if it is not competent to decide that gross vice is a bad thing? I do not think that the State ought to stand bandying compliments with pimps."[33]

Graphic though this picture is, the view that immorality is a sufficient condition is now more likely to be couched in more qualified terms.

Lord Devlin, Morals and the Criminal Law (reprinted in The Enforcement of Morals), (1965), pp. 7–8, 14–17:

"I think it is clear that the criminal law as we know it is based upon moral principle. In a number of crimes its function is simply to enforce a moral principle and nothing else. The law, both criminal and civil, claims to be able to speak about morality and immorality generally. Where does it get its authority to do this and how does it settle the moral principles which it enforces? Undoubtedly, as a matter of history, it derived from Christian teaching. But I think that the strict logician is right when he says that the law can no longer rely on doctrines in which citizens are entitled to disbelieve. It is necessary therefore to look for some other source . . . I have framed three interrogatories addressed to myself to answer.

(1) Has society the right to pass judgment at all on matters of morals? Ought there, in other words, to be a public morality, or are morals always a matter for private judgment?[34]

---

[33] *Liberty, Equality, Fraternity* (1873).

[34] Feinberg argues that this question is extremely badly phrased: that the issue is not whether morality is *always* a matter of private judgment but whether it is *ever* a matter of private judgment. Accepting that a common morality is required in order for there to be a society does not necessitate that there be consensus about anything more than the moral minimum. "We cannot live together without agreement, but it is not the sole alternative to no agreement that there be total agreement." *Harmless Wrongdoing* (1988), p. 136.

(2) If society has the right to pass judgment, has it also the right to use the weapon of the law to enforce it?

(3) If so, ought it to use that weapon in all cases or only in some: and if only in some on what principles should it distinguish? . . .

[Lord Devlin then explained that a public morality is one of the vital ingredients of a society, and that the State has the right to safeguard anything that is essential to its existence. In other words, he answered the first two questions affirmatively.]

In what circumstances the State should exercise its power is the third of the interrogatories I have framed. But before I get to it I must raise a point which might have been brought up in any one of the three. How are the moral judgments of society to be ascertained . . . It is surely not enough that they should be reached by the opinion of the majority; it would be too much to require the individual assent of every citizen. English law has evolved and regularly uses a standard which does not depend on the counting of heads. It is that of the reasonable man. He is not to be confused with the rational man. He is not expected to reason about anything and his judgment may be largely a matter of feeling . . . for my purpose I should like to call him the man in the jury box . . .

Immorality then, for the purpose of the law, is what every right-minded person is presumed to consider immoral. Any immorality is capable of affecting society injuriously and in effect to a greater or lesser extent it usually does: this is what gives the law *locus standi*. It cannot be shut out. But—and this brings me to the third question—the individual has a *locus standi* too; he cannot be expected to surrender to the judgment of society the whole conduct of his life. It is the old familiar question of striking a balance between the rights and interests of society and those of the individual . . . there must be toleration of the maximum individual freedom that is consistent with the integrity of society.[35] Nothing should be punished by the law that does not lie beyond the limit of tolerance. It is not nearly enough to say that a majority dislike a practice: there must be a real feeling of reprobation . . . I do not think one can ignore disgust if it is deeply felt and not manufactured. Its presence is a good indication that the bounds of toleration are being reached . . .

[B]efore a society can put a practice beyond the limits of tolerance there must be a deliberate judgement that the practice is injurious to society . . . We should ask ourselves in the first instance whether, looking at it calmly and dispassionately, we regard it as a vice so abominable that its mere presence is an offence. If that is the genuine feeling of the society in which we live, I do not see how society can be denied the right to eradicate it . . . "

Criminal sanctions, according to Lord Devlin therefore, should be determined by the deep disgust (dispassionately felt!) of the right-minded man, or more accurately, they should depend upon the law-maker's interpretation of the likelihood of the right-minded man being deeply disgusted!

We may apply Lord Devlin's criteria to a number of past and present crimes. Theft, for example, is undoubtedly immoral and one could certainly argue that society is not prepared to tolerate it, but does it produce deep disgust? Is there not another factor involved in the decision to criminalise, that is, harm?

Lord Devlin himself uses the example of homosexuality; it was only

[35] Lord Devlin goes on to say that privacy, for example, should be protected so far as it is consistent with society's integrity.

natural that he should—since his thesis was a direct response to the
Wolfenden Report, which had recommended decriminalising homosexual acts between consenting males in private. According to Lord Devlin,
although "some people sincerely believe that homosexuality is neither
immoral nor unnatural,"[36] there is nevertheless a collective judgment
against it, and a deep feeling of disgust towards it. But as Hughes
states:

> "One cannot help suspecting that the morality of an established caste is
> being too uninquiringly proferred here as the morality of the right-think-
> ing majority. For is it not a strange society that is disgusted at private, con-
> sensual, homosexual behaviour, but can look with equanimity upon fox
> and stag hunting?
>   . . . It is not beyond the bounds of possibility that proper inquiry might
> reveal that, while the ordinary man contemplates homosexual behaviour
> with adversion and distaste, the knowledge of this practice by others does
> not disgust him so deeply as Lord Devlin suspects . . .
>   There is no suggestion of an inquiry into the harm such homosexual
> behaviour does to society, into the effectiveness of criminal prohibition as
> a check, or into the evils which may attend criminal prohibition. The only
> yardstick is the depth of disgust."[37]

Whatever the reasons were for the introduction of the offence of
insider dealing (and these will be examined later), it does seem most
unlikely that Lord Devlin's criteria figured prominently amongst them.
Even in relation to the new offences of possession and taking of
indecent photographs of children, arguments favouring criminalisation
are by no means based solely on the disgust felt by right-minded thinking people. Incest was not criminalised until 1908 (by a private members bill)[38]; whilst this must figure as an example where a large number
of people would feel exactly the sort of emotions described by Lord
Devlin, here too other reasons can be adduced for the removal of this
behaviour from the ecclesiastical courts to the criminal sphere. What
these reasons are and whether they are persuasive is something that
must be returned to later.

The Obscene Publications Act 1959 makes it a criminal offence to
publish an obscene article and section 1 states that "an article shall be
deemed to be obscene if its effect . . . is . . . such as to tend to deprave
and corrupt . . . [its likely readers]."[39] In *Anderson*[40] the conviction was
quashed because the jury had been left with the impression that
obscenity meant "repulsive, filthy, loathesome, indecent or lewd." An
article might be all of these, yet not have a tendency to deprave or corrupt. But the courts have made it clear that a tendency to deprave and
corrupt does *not* mean a tendency to make a reader behave any worse

[36] At p. 10.
[37] G. Hughes, "Morals and the Criminal Law," (1962) 71 Yale L.J. 662 at 676–678.
[38] Punishment of Incest Act 1908. The offence is now governed by sections 10 and 11 of the Sexual
Offences Act 1956. For a discussion of the historical background to this offence see, J. Morton "The
Incest Act 1908—Was it Ever Relevant?" (1988) New L.J. 59.
[39] Or those likely to see or hear the matter contained in the "article."
[40] [1972] 1 Q.B. 304

than he would otherwise have done; his character does not need to be changed in any demonstrable sense. All that is required is a tendency to moral or spiritual corruption.[41] The law is aimed at protecting the minds of people. An article could thus be obscene if it enabled readers to engage in private fantasies of their own (and relieve themselves by masturbation in the privacy of their own homes). Perhaps these developments bear witness to a judicial acceptance of Lord Devlin's views in this context at least.

Finally, do the deliberately non-rationalist arguments of Lord Devlin really qualify the position adopted a century earlier by Stephen?[42] Does the deep disgust of the right-minded man mean anything more than the criminalisation of immorality *simpliciter*?

It is submitted that the criminalisation of conduct cannot be based on such limited criteria. One cannot, as Lord Devlin has done, throw rationality completely to the winds in order to replace it with the reasonable man's disgust—which, as Hart points out, may be based on "ignorance, superstition or misunderstanding."[43] Instead,

> "the examination of existing law and the debate about proposed laws should be conducted by making as explicit a statement as is possible of the values that the law is designed to protect, by a careful investigation of the harm done to those values by the conduct prohibited or which it is sought to prohibit, and by a careful consideration of the probable efficacy of legal prohibition. In this debate the prevalence of feelings of disgust or revulsion in the community is one factor to be considered and no more than that."[44]

In other words, whilst immorality (with all its attendant difficulties of identification) may be a necessary condition for the imposition of the criminal law, it ought not to be a sufficient one.

D. Harm

H.L.A. Hart, "Immorality and Treason," 62 Listener 162–163 (July 30, 1959):

"The Wolfenden Committee on Homosexual Offences and Prostitution recommended by a majority of 12 to 1 that homosexual behaviour between consenting adults in private should no longer be a criminal offence. One of the Committee's principal grounds for this recommendation was expressed in its report in this way: 'There must remain a realm of private morality and immorality which in brief and crude terms is not the law's business.' I shall call this the liberal point of view: for it is a special application of those wider principles of liberal thought which John Stuart Mill formulated in his essay on Liberty. Mill's

---

[41] *D.P.P.* v. *Whyte* [1972] A.C. 849 (H.L.); *Calder & Boyars Ltd.* [1969] 1 Q.B. 151.

[42] For a defence of Lord Devlin, see E. Rostow, "The Enforcement of Morals" [1960] C.L.J. 174 where he suggests that Lord Devlin so qualifies his central conditions with cries for tolerance, etc., that the gap between him and his critics is very small.

[43] H. L. A. Hart, in for example "Immorality and Treason" 62 Listener 163 (July 30, 1959).

[44] G. Hughes, (*ante*, n. 37, at p. 682). He points out that this approach will still contain elements of irrationality but that it is better than the "throwing the baby out with the bath water" (Hart, "Immorality and Treason," p. 163) approach of Devlin.

most famous words, less cautious perhaps than the Wolfenden Committee's were:

> 'The only purpose for which power can be rightfully exercised over any member of a civilized community against his will is to prevent harm to others. His own good, either physical or moral, is not a sufficient warrant. He cannot rightfully be compelled to do or forbear . . . because in the opinion of others to do so would be wise or even right.'

The liberal point of view has often been attacked, both before and after Mill. I shall discuss here the repudiation of it made by Sir Patrick Devlin . . .

Mill's formulation of the liberal point of view may well be too simple. The grounds for interfering with human liberty are more various than the single criterion of 'harm to others' suggests: cruelty to animals or organizing prostitution for gain do not, as Mill himself saw, fall easily under the description of harm to others. Conversely, even where there is harm to others in the most literal sense, there may well be other principles limiting the extent to which harmful activities should be repressed by law. So there are multiple criteria, not a single criterion, determining when human liberty may be restricted. Perhaps this is what Sir Patrick means by a curious distinction which he often stresses between theoretical and practical limits. But with all its simplicities the liberal point of view is a better guide than Sir Patrick to clear thought in the proper relation of morality to the criminal law: for it stresses what he obscures—namely, the points at which thought is needed before we turn popular morality into criminal law.

No doubt we would all agree that consensus of moral opinion on certain matters is essential if society is to be worth living in. Laws against murder, theft, and much else would be of little use if they were not supported by a widely diffused conviction that what these laws forbid is also immoral. So much is obvious. But it does not follow that everything to which the moral vetoes of accepted morality attach is of equal importance to society; nor is there the slightest reason for thinking of morality as a seamless web: one which will fall to pieces carrying society with it, unless all its emphatic vetoes are enforced by law. Surely even in the face of the moral feeling that is up to concert pitch—the trio of intolerance, indignation, and disgust—we must pause to think. We must ask a question at two different levels which Sir Patrick never clearly enough identifies or separates. First, we must ask whether a practice which offends moral feeling is harmful, independently of its repercussion on the general moral code? Secondly, what about repercussion on the moral code? Is it really true that failure to translate this item of general morality into criminal law will jeopardize the whole fabric of morality and so society?

We cannot escape thinking about these two different questions merely by repeating to ourselves the vague nostrum: 'This is part of public morality and public morality must be preserved if society is to exist.' Sometimes Sir Patrick seems to admit this, for he says in words which both Mill and the Wolfenden Report might have used, that there must be the maximum respect for individual liberty consistent with the integrity of society. Yet this, as his contrasting examples of fornication and homosexuality show, turns out to mean only that the immorality which the law may punish must be generally felt to be intolerable. This plainly is no adequate substitute for a reasoned estimate of the damage to the fabric of society likely to ensue if it is not suppressed.

Nothing perhaps shows more clearly the inadequacy of Sir Patrick's approach to this problem than his comparison between the suppression of sexual immorality and the suppression of treason or subversive activity. Private subversive activity is, of course, a contradiction in terms because 'subversion' means overthrowing government, which is a public thing. But it is grotesque, even where moral feeling against homosexuality is up to concert pitch, to think of the homosexual behaviour of two adults in private as in any way like treason or sedition either in intention or effect. We can make it *seem* like treason only if we assume that deviation from a general moral code is bound to affect that code, and to lead not merely to its modification but to its destruction. The analogy could begin to be plausible only if it was clear that offending against this item of morality was likely to jeopardize the whole structure. But we have ample evidence for believing that people will not abandon morality, will not think any better of murder, cruelty, and dishonesty, merely because some private sexual practice which they abominate is not punished by the law . . . "

Before continuing, we need to consider more closely this concept of harm.

A useful starting point is the definition of harm proposed by Gross: harm is any violation of an interest of a person. "All natural persons have interests, but so do those social creations of persons that are collective bearers of personal interests: humanity, the State, the community, the family, corporations and many other varieties of human associations."[45] From this Gross goes on to identify four main groups of harms that are the concern of the criminal law. They can be summarised thus:

1. Harms that consist of violations of interest in retaining or maintaining what one is entitled to have, for example, interests regarding life, liberty and property.
2. Offences to sensibility. "Such concern is reflected in penal provisions that deal with punishing pornography, publicly uttering an obscenity, . . . prostitution . . . and the like."[46]
3. Harms that consist of some impairment of collective welfare; modern society creates inter-dependancy that has to be protected by penal provisions concerned with, for example, health, safety and security from foreign enemies.
4. Violations of some governmental interest. Crimes such as "filing a fraudulent tax return; failing to register as an alien; or for military service . . . bribing a government official . . . "[47] are examples resulting from this harm.

According to Gross, any penal provision in a modern legal system will be addressed to one (or more) of these four groups of harms. Under a definition as wide as this, it is possible to argue that anything which is immoral constitutes a "harm" to society (and vice versa). But this still leaves the central question unanswered. How do we identify those harms that ought to be punished by the criminal law? The mere fact that an activity causes some "harm" (as defined by Gross) cannot be *in itself* a sufficient warrant for the intervention of the criminal law. Picking one's nose in public might be an "offence to sensibility" but that can-

---

[45] H. Gross, *A Theory of Criminal Justice* (1979), pp. 115–116.
[46] *Ibid.* p. 120.
[47] *Ibid.* p. 121.

not, alone, be sufficient grounds for declaring the activity criminal. Thus, although we might now be able to identify a "harm" in the publication or possession of obscene material, or indecent photographs of children, homosexual behaviour, and insider dealing, we still do not know whether these activities ought to be criminal.

Insider dealing may, indeed, make transactions on the stock exchange more hazardous (by the spread of rumours about dealing, for example) and amount to an abuse of trust, but it is still not clear why that form of social control that is the criminal law should be chosen rather than, for example, a self-regulatory mechanism.

The concept of "harm," therefore, requires yet further elaboration. Of initial attractiveness, at least, is the commonly drawn distinction between primary and secondary harms.

J. Kaplan, "The Role of the Law in Drug Control" [1971] Duke L.J. 1065 at 1065–1068:

"Typically the use of the law to prevent conduct which harms only the actor himself is distinguished from the use of the law as a means of preventing the individual from harming others, including society at large. In practice, however, this is not an easy distinction to draw, for there are few actions in which one can engage that threaten harm only to himself.

The purest example of laws aimed at such conduct are the statutes which require the driver of a motorcycle to wear a protective helmet. It is true that one can argue that the helmet really protects others, since it shields the motorcyclist from thrown pebbles which might make him lose control and injure innocent pedestrians or automobile drivers. Though this approach makes the problem easier, it is disingenuous. As a result, many courts and commentators have refused to take it and have assumed that the helmet protects only the cyclist himself.

Though the helmetless cyclist does not expose others to any appreciable physical danger, he does drive in a society that is committed to preventing people from dying of their injuries. Thus, rather than allowing the cyclist to die unnecessarily, society is prepared to undertake the enormous expense of treating him until he either expires or recovers. In Professor Robert Bartel's apt phrase, the helmetless cyclist exposes others to 'public ward' harm—the danger of having to treat him should he not be killed outright. It is on this theory that society feels it has the right to demand that he do his share to protect himself.

The expense and inconvenience that the helmetless driver may cause does not, however, stop at public ward harm. Insofar as his failure to wear a helmet results in his own injury, he may force society to assume the cost of his neglected responsibilities to others. Here the issue cannot be avoided by saying that it is all society's fault for not letting him die in the street at minimal cost, because his responsibilities must still be fulfilled. As an emotional matter, moreover, non-support justifications for laws which attempt to prevent self-harming conduct often command considerably more power than do public ward justifications. Thus, despite the enormous public ward justifications for halting alcohol abuse, one of the most powerful Prohibitionist posters contained a drawing of a saloon with a father drinking at the bar while his clean, but poorly dressed little daughter stood in the doorway saying, 'Father, Father, please come home. Mother needs you.' The same public interest which underlies non-support laws, then, can also justify helmetless cyclist laws—at least in the case of those who owe someone a support obligation.

In addition to the public ward and non-support justifications for forbidding conduct which on first glance would appear to harm only the actor, a further justification exists which might be called the 'modelling' justification. Modelling is the psychological term for the process by which one repeats a type of behaviour one sees in others. Modelling of behaviour may thus occur where the watcher first learns that the behaviour which he had thought impossible can indeed be performed; where the watcher, by observing, learns how to do it; where he simply gets the idea from watching; or where he, for any one of many reasons, imitates the action. It is true, of course, that the same values which underlie the freedom of communication may interfere with preventing the harm caused by modelling. The individual who models the helmetless cyclist does so without coercion, and, apart from the indirect harms discussed, he harms only himself. Nevertheless, where those persons society tries to protect from modelling are children, the fact that the helmetless cyclist in a causal sense may have caused the modelling, which in turn might lead to injury, may be very significant. Children are regarded as much more likely than adults to model dangerous conduct, and we certainly acknowledge a greater responsibility to protect them from harm.

The final justification by which some may find social harm in conduct which appears to harm only the actor might be called the 'categorical imperative' justification. This relies on the fact that although an act might harm only the actor if performed by relatively few people, it could cause harm to everyone if it were performed by almost all. This justification is not heard in the helmetless cyclist case, but it is heard with respect to some sexual and drug laws . . . "

If one were to apply the distinction made by Kaplan between harms which may be referred to as primary (involving direct harm to others) and secondary (involving indirect harm to others) to the examples we have employed before, theft would clearly belong to the former category; it causes harm to others and can be criminalised on that basis. Clearly also, incest involving a non-consenting child can be criminalised on this basis (although that still leaves unresolved the issue of whether one needs a law of *incest* to secure the necessary protection). But what of consensual incest between a brother and sister who have both attained their majority and what of homosexuality? *Prima facie*, they appear to belong more naturally to the second category; there is no direct harm to others. But as Kaplan shows with the use of the protective helmet legislation[48] example, a case *can* be made out on the basis of indirect harm done to others for the criminalisation of both homosexuality and consensual incest. The "public ward" and "non-support" justifications would be inapplicable, and one would have to rely, therefore, solely on the "modelling" and "categorical imperative" justifications: "The picture which is called to mind is that of a nation where most of the population is homosexual—in which case there would be an enormous population implosion with consequent economic catastrophe"[49]

---

[48] In the first edition an analogy was drawn between this example of Kaplan's and the then recent introduction of legislation making it an offence to fail to wear a seat-belt in the front of cars (p. 70).
[49] Kaplan, p. 1068.

How compelling a reason do you find this for the criminalisation of homosexual behaviour?

Finally, by way of example, we may return to the obscenity laws and laws concerning the taking and possession of indecent photographs of children. We might conclude in relation to all of them, that they represent examples that are potentially both primary and secondary harms; but on the way some difficult questions might have to be asked about the nature of the harm to the child if, for example, he is unaware that he is being photographed or if he consents because his parents had allowed some photos to be taken in their presence,[50] and much would depend, in relation to obscenity, on the age of those involved.

Crudely distinguishing, therefore, between primary and secondary harms does not provide us with the information that we need. Not only may they be a front for the criminalisation of immorality *simpliciter* (as would be the case with homosexuality) but it does not enable us to answer which (if any)[51] secondary harms should be prohibited by the criminal law. Just as no one today argues that all immoral acts ought to be criminal,[52] so no one argues that all secondary harms ought to be criminal. "The obvious secondary harm resulting from such almost universally performed acts as over-eating or poor nutrition is the *reductio ad absurdum* of such arguments."[53]

We return, therefore, to the central question: how are we to distinguish between that behaviour which should be dealt with by means of the criminal law and that which should be dealt with, if necessary, in some other way?'

Joel Feinberg, Harmless Wrongdoing, (The Moral Limits of the Criminal Law, Vol. 4) (1988), pp. ix–x:

"What sorts of conduct may the state rightly make criminal? Philosophers have attempted to answer this question by proposing what I call 'liberty-limiting principles' . . . which state that a given type of consideration is always a morally relevant reason in support of penal legislation even if other reasons may in the circumstances outweigh it. . . . The principle that the need to prevent harm to persons other than the actor is always a morally relevant reason in support of proposed state coercion I call *the harm to others principle* . . . At least in its vague formulation it is accepted as valid by nearly all writers. Controversy arises when we consider whether it is the *only* valid liberty-limiting principle, as John Stuart Mill declared.

Three other coercion-legitimising principles, in particular, have won widespread support. It has been held (but not always by the same person) that it is always a good and relevant reason in support of penal legislation that (1) it is necessary to prevent hurt or offense (as opposed to injury or harm) to others (*the*

---

[50] As in the recent case of *Graham-Kerr* (1989) 88 Cr.App.R. 302 where the parents of a boy had allowed the defendant to take photos of the child in the swimming pool but were unaware of later photos of the boy taken in the changing room, although the boy was.

[51] J. S. Mill would accept the criminalisation of primary harms only. *Ante* p. 84.

[52] The argument that was put forward was that all criminal law ought to be based ordinarily on moral wrongs.

[53] Kaplan, p. 1068.

offense principle); (2) it is necessary to prevent harm to the very person it prohibits from acting, as opposed to 'others' (*legal paternalism*); (3) it is necessary to
prevent inherently immoral conduct whether or not such conduct is harmful or
offensive to anyone (*legal moralism*). I defined 'liberalism' . . . as the view that
the harm and offense principles, duly clarified and qualified, between them
exhaust the class of morally relevant reasons for criminal prohibitions. . . . I
then candidly expressed my own liberal predilections. . . .
    What are we to mean by the key terms 'harm' and 'offense' . . .
    I distinguish at the outset a non-normative sense of 'harm' as setback to inter-
est, and a normative sense of 'harm' as a *wrong*, that is a violation of a person's
rights."

Feinberg discusses the harm principle in detail in an earlier volume,
Harm to Others.[54] A combination of both the senses in which harm is
described leads him to conclude that "the term 'harm' . . . refers to
those states of set-back interest that are the consequence of wrongful
acts or omissions by others. This interpretation, based on primarily
moral judgments, thus excludes set-back interests produced by justified
or excused conduct. . . . " So if, for example, the victim consents to the
risk of injuries then he has not been wronged and not, therefore,
harmed. Similarly, the legitimate businessman has not wronged his
competitor and thus has not harmed him.
    In addition to the harm principle itself, Feinberg argues for various
supplementary guides or "mediating maxims" to govern the application of the harm principle. Some of these flow from the harm principle itself and others are provided by independent moral principles.
Without any of these mediating maxims being satisfied, criminalisation
would not be justified. For example, Feinberg suggests that where harm
may (but is not certain to) result from a given kind of conduct, that a
suitable test would be that the greater the gravity of a possible harm,
the less probable its occurrence need be to justify prohibition of the
conduct and that the more valuable the dangerous conduct, the more
reasonable it is to take the risk of harmful consequences.[55]
    Other writers have suggested different limiting criteria.[56]

H. Packer, The Limits of the Criminal Sanction (1969), pp. 266–272:

"The question is not one of whether or not there will be harm done; it is one
of the remoteness and probability of the harm. Some things are more harmful
than others. Homicide is more harmful than muttering voodoo incantations;
rape is more harmful than reading dirty books. And in a world of limited
resources, we need to draw discriminations about the gravity and remoteness of
harms. Seen in this light, 'harm to others' is a prudential criterion rather than a
hard and fast distinction of principle.
    'Harm to others' does not, of course, mean identifiable others. It has become

[54] Joel Feinberg, *Harm to Others—The Moral Limits of the Criminal Law* (1984)
[55] *Harm To Others*, (1984) p. 216. Reference should also be made to pp. 214–217, 243–245.
[56] See also Nicola Lacey, *State Punishment: Political Principles and Community Values*, (1988), pp.
100–120.

fashionable to talk about 'victimless crimes,' meaning those in which there is no immediately identifiable victim to lodge a complaint. The absence of an identifiable victim can make enforcement difficult, and can encourage undesirable enforcement practices. But the prospect of these difficulties should not end the inquiry into the wisdom of any given use of the criminal sanction. Many offenses against the administration of government are 'victimless crimes' in the sense that there is nobody to complain. Consensual transactions like bribery and espionage are admittedly difficult to detect because of the absence of an identifiable victim; yet they do not necessarily cause so little 'harm to others' that we can forget about subjecting them to the criminal sanction.

The 'harm to others' formula seems to me to have two uses that justify its inclusion in a list of limiting criteria for invocation of the criminal sanction. First, it is a way to make sure that a given form of conduct is not being subjected to the criminal sanction purely or even primarily because it is thought to be immoral. It forces an inquiry into precisely what bad effects are feared if the conduct in question is not suppressed by the criminal law. Second, it immediately brings into play a host of secular inquiries about the effects of subjecting the conduct in question to the criminal sanction. One cannot meaningfully deal with the question of 'harm to others' without weighing benefits against detriments. In that sense, it is a kind of threshold question, important not so much in itself as in focusing attention on further considerations relevant to the ultimate decision. It is for these two instrumental reasons rather than for either its intrinsic rightness or its ease of application that it deserves inclusion . . . [Packer then considers the further conditions]

Goals of Punishment:

To begin with, there is the obvious point that unless at least *one* utilitarian mode of prevention is likely to be served by employing the criminal sanction against a particular form of conduct, we had better forget about it. Sneezing in church is a relatively uncontroversial example . . .

[A] utilitarian case for defining conduct as criminal can best be made in situations where both deterrence and incapacitation are effective: where people are relatively likely to be deflected by the possibility of being caught *and* where punishment is likely to prevent the commission of further crimes. There are many situations in which the two are not correlated and . . . very few in which they are . . .

Remoteness and Triviality:

The conduct proscribed by any criminal code can be ranked in a hierarchy of remoteness from the ultimate harm that the law seeks to prevent. We prohibit the sale of liquor to an intoxicated person to lessen the likelihood that he will drive while drunk (an offense), crash into another car (an offense), injure an occupant of the other car (an offense), or cause the death of someone in the other car (an offense). There we have a spectrum of remoteness ranging from the illegal sale of liquor to manslaughter. Similarly, we make it an offense to possess tools specially adapted for burglary so that we may reduce the incidence of burglary (an offense), and thereby reduce the incidence of further offenses, such as larceny, robbery, rape, and even murder, that can ensue from burglary. Mayhem or murder might not be intended by most burglars, but they are nonetheless possible results of the confrontation between burglar and victim.

One of the most delicate problems in framing criminal proscriptions is to locate the point farthest removed from the ultimate harm apprehended at which meaningful preventive intervention can take place. If dangerous conduct can be deterred and dangerous persons identified well short of the point at which the danger becomes acute, so much the better. Or so it seems. Actually, increasing the radius of the criminal law in the interest of early intervention is a very risky business. The first question in every case is, or should be: how high is the probability that the preparatory conduct, if not inhibited by the threat of criminal punishment, will result in an ultimate harm of the sort that the law should try to prevent? A related consideration is whether the preparatory conduct is itself socially useful, or at least neutral, so that its proscription or curtailment might unduly inhibit people from doing what they should otherwise be free to do. To put the issue in terms that are familiar in the law, is the risk substantial and is it justifiable? . . .

Still another consideration relates to the problem of enforcement. By and large, the further removed the conduct in question is from the ultimate harm apprehended, the more difficult it is going to be to detect the occurrence of the conduct and to apprehend people who engage in it. Considerations of maximizing personal freedom and of minimizing the strain on law enforcement combine, then, to suggest considerable caution in the progression towards the remote end of the spectrum.

An example that is amusing because it is so extreme is a recent action of the New York City Council. At the urgent request of the Fire Commissioner, the Council voted to make it a criminal offense, punishable by a hundred-dollar fine, a thirty-day jail term or both, to smoke in bed in a hotel, motel, or other place of public abode. A subsidiary provision required that a notice to that effect be displayed by the proprietor of every place covered by the ban. Now, nobody doubts that a great many serious and sometimes fatal accidents are caused by people's smoking in bed and that it would be a far better thing if people did not smoke in bed. But consider the impossibility of enforcing such a prohibition without the most detailed kind of surveillance. Consider the invasions of privacy that such surveillance would entail. And, enforcement problems aside, consider the effect of announcing that such commonly engaged in conduct has now become criminal. One wonders what was accomplished by the criminal prohibition that would not equally well be accomplished by requiring hotels to display in each room a notice warning about the danger. Alternatively, the solution might have been to make it criminal to cause a fire by smoking in bed, regardless of the amount of harm done. That kind of prohibition would at least have been enforceable, whether or not it was enforced. As it is, given the well-known relationship between intoxication and fires resulting from smoking in bed, I suppose travellers should be grateful that the City Council did not go one step further and make it a crime to go to bed drunk in a New York hotel.

The idea of a criminal conviction no longer inspires the awe that it once did, because of the tendency of legislative bodies (like the New York City Council in this example) to prescribe criminal penalties simply as a means of expressing their disapproval of conduct. This tendency results in two kinds of triviality: triviality of object and triviality of intention. By triviality of object I mean the selection of behaviour for which the regular imposition of criminal punishment is disproportionate. By triviality of intention I mean an attitude of indifference or cynicism on the part of legislators toward the actual enforcement of the proscriptions they vote for. Both forms of triviality should be carefully avoided. A rational legislator should not vote to subject previously legal conduct to criminal proscription unless he is prepared to say, first, that the conduct being proscribed is so threatening to important social interests that he is willing to see people who engage in it subjected to criminal punishment and, second, that he expects law enforcement to devote adequate resources to detecting, apprehending, and convicting violators. The two will tend in most cases to be complementary . . . [Such trivial offences should be decriminalised and made 'civil offences' or 'infractions.']"

Packer then identifies further conditions that need to be taken into account when making the "ultimate decision" about criminalisation. In addition to what has been said so far, we need to avoid the possibility of creating a "crime tariff"[57]; by this he means that the demand for the illegalised activity or product may be so inelastic that rather than reducing the incidence of the activity, it merely drives it underground and forces the price up. The provision of illegal abortions and the sale of narcotics are cases in point. The same may well be said of activities prohibited by obscenity laws.

We may finally consider dangers pointed to by both Packer[58] and Kadish (in the context of a discussion of sexual crimes) which are all too likely to materialise if conduct is criminalised (or not decriminalised) without careful investigation:

S. Kadish, "The Crisis of Overcriminalisation," (1967) 374 Annals 157 at 159–162:

"But law enforcement pays a price for using the criminal law . . . [to enforce morality]. First, the moral message communicated by the law is contradicted by the total absence of enforcement; for while the public sees the conduct condemned in words, it also sees in the dramatic absence of prosecutions that it is not condemned in deed. Moral adjurations vulnerable to a charge of hypocrisy are self-defeating no less in law than elsewhere. Second, the spectacle of nullification of the legislature's solemn commands is an unhealthy influence on law enforcement generally. It tends to breed a cynicism and an indifference to the criminal-law processes which augment tendencies towards disrespect for those who make and enforce the law, a disrespect which is already widely in evidence. In addition: 'Dead letter laws, far from promoting a sense of security, which is the main function of the penal law, actually impair that security by holding the threat of prosecution over the heads of people whom we have no intention to punish.' (Model Penal Code §.307.11,—comments at p. 111).

Finally, these laws invite discriminatory enforcement against persons selected for prosecution on grounds unrelated to the evil against which these laws are purportedly addressed, whether those grounds be 'the prodding of some reform group, a newspaper-generated hysteria over some local sex crime, a vice drive which is put on by the local authorities to distract attention from defects in their administration of the city government.' . . .

Despite the fact that homosexual practices are condemned as criminal in virtually all states, usually as a felony with substantial punishment, and despite sporadic efforts at enforcement in certain situations, there is little evidence that the criminal law has discouraged the practice to any substantial degree. The Kinsey Report as well as other studies suggest a wide incidence of homosexuality throughout the country. One major reason for the ineffectiveness of these laws is that the private and consensual nature of the conduct precludes the attainment of any substantial deterrent efficacy through law enforcement. There are no complainants, and only the indiscreet have reasons for fear. Another reason is the irrelevance of the threat of punishment. Homosexuality involves not so much a choice to act wickedly as the seeking of normal sexual fulfillment in abnormal ways (though not abnormal to the individual) preferred by the individual for reasons deeply rooted in his development as a personality. Moreover, in view of the character of prison environments, putting the homosexual

[57] Packer, pp. 277–282.
[58] Packer, pp. 282–295.

defendant into the prison system is, as observed recently by a United States District Court Judge, 'a little like throwing Br'er Rabbit into the briarpatch.' (*Perkins* v. *North Carolina* 234 F. Supp. 333 *per* Chief Judge Craven).

On the other hand, the use of the criminal law has been attended by grave consequences. A commonly noted consequence is the enhanced opportunities created for extortionary threats of exposure and prosecution . . . But, of more significance for the administration of justice, enforcement efforts by police have created problems both for them and for the community. Opportunities for enforcement are limited by the private and consensual character of the behaviour . . . To obtain evidence, police are obliged to resort to behaviour which tends to degrade and demean both themselves personally and law enforcement as an institution. However one may deplore homosexual conduct, no one can lightly accept a criminal law which requires for its enforcement that officers of the law sit concealed in ceilings, their eyes fixed to 'peepholes,' searching for criminal sexuality in the lavatories below; or that they loiter suggestively around public toilets or in corridors hopefully awaiting a sexual advance. Such conduct corrupts both citizenry and police and reduces the moral authority of the criminal law, especially among those portions of the citizenry—the poor and subcultural—who are particularly liable to be treated in an arbitrary fashion. The complaint of the critical [is] that the police have more important things to do with their time . . . "

In returning to the examples of insider dealing, incest, homosexuality and obscene publications it may be useful at this point to summarise Packer's criteria:

H. Packer, The Limits of the Criminal Sanction (1969), p. 296:

"These criteria can be used in making up a kind of priority list of conduct for which the legislature might consider invoking the criminal sanction . . .

(1) The conduct is prominent in most people's view of socially threatening behaviour, and is not condoned by any significant segment of society.
(2) Subjecting it to the criminal sanction is not inconsistent with the goals of punishment.
(3) Suppressing it will not inhibit socially desirable conduct.
(4) It may be dealt with through even-handed and nondiscriminatory enforcement.
(5) Controlling it through the criminal process will not expose that process to severe qualitative or quantitative strains.
(6) There are no reasonable alternatives to the criminal sanction for dealing with it."

What conclusions are to be drawn, therefore, about the examples used throughout this section?

Insider dealing does undoubtedly cause a harm; our interest in a sound economy is threatened by behaviour which makes the stock market even more volatile than it naturally is and legitimate business is harmed by the unfair dealing that constitutes insider dealing. But even if the threshold of harm has been passed, are the limiting criteria of Packer or Feinberg satisfied? Is the behaviour *so* harmful that no other form of social control is appropriate? Perhaps it really is the case that the City is incapable of monitoring its own affairs effectively.

The crime of incest covers a wide variety of situations—from consensual adult relationships between siblings to forced sexual intercourse by a father with his young daughter. Given the change in the law in relation to homosexuality, is it really possible to distinguish that from incest between consenting adults?[59] But there is an argument that even this reform would not go far enough.

L. Blom-Cooper, "Criminal Law That Leaves Children at Risk," The Independent, August 7, 1989:

"The real question is how to deal with incestuous relationships. Is there any need for a criminal offence of incest? It is axiomatic that children need to be protected against incestuous adults. But how? Protection, so far as it is possible for it to be provided through legal measures, is already provided by statutes dealing with child cruelty and neglect. Incest is only one manifestation of child abuse, and by no means the worst. . . .
The 1908 legislation could be justified as an attempt to protect children at a time when legal protection was minimal . . . the essence of any prohibition on incest must be the protection of dependants unable to protect themselves.
The experience of 80 years of law enforcement against incestuous adults does not encourage one to believe that the criminal process has done much to control incestuous conduct. The Lord Chief Justice himself confessed that incestuous relationships might well be "a situation which arose more often than was generally realised." There are about 100 prosecutions each year. Incest surfaces to public knowledge only when there has been a rupture in the family. . . . The gross inequity in the application of the law cannot command public respect. And the infliction of imprisonment on the few who are caught does little to help society with the problem of child abuse. . . .
Something more subtle than the heavy hand of the criminal law needs to be deployed in order to provide optimum protection for abused children . . . "[60]

Finally, we turn to the offences of taking and possession of indecent photographs of children and law relating to obscene publications. The arguments for and against criminalisation are broadly similar. Do you think that their current status is justified despite obvious difficulties, for example, of law enforcement? The feminist answer in relation to pornographic depictions of women is one that deserves serious consideration. The view put forward would be that such depictions not only cause offence but that they constitute a harm as well, even if the participants are acting entirely voluntarily. They defame women (by degrading them) and they constitute an incitement to rape. These arguments would apply with only slight modification to the laws prohibiting indecent photographs of children.[61] But again it must be stressed

[59] See, in this context the recommendations of the Criminal Law Revision Committee, Fifteenth Report, *Sexual Offences* (Cmnd. 9213), paras. 8.15–8.36, where it is proposed that brother-sister incest over the age of 21 should not be a criminal offence.
[60] For an expression of similar views, see J. Morton "The Incest Act 1908—Was it Ever Relevant?" (1988) New L.J. 59.
[61] But see J. Feinberg, *Offence To Others* (1985), pp. 143–164, where he eventually rejects the feminist argument. He does, however, leave the door open to criminal prohibition of pornography legitimated on liberal grounds, should better empirical evidence accumulate about the relationship between pornography and rape.

that even if one accepts that there is a harm (and immorality) it has to be determined that the "heavy hand" of the criminal law is the most appropriate mechanism of social control for dealing with the conduct.

E. Conclusion

The question which we have attempted to answer in this chapter is startling in its apparent simplicity: what sort of conduct ought to be prohibited by the criminal law? That the answer is by no means clear-cut should by now be obvious, but it is submitted that in assessing the relationship between immorality and the criminal law, and the concept of harm and the criminal law, that a framework has been provided by which specific activities can be adjudged. It is not enough in our submission that a practice is widely regarded as immoral. Nor is it enough that it should cause harm. Both of these are minimal conditions for action by means of the criminal law but they are not sufficient. Whenever, throughout this book, we refer to the necessity for "harm done," it is assumed that the harm has been subjected to rigorous scrutiny by use of criteria such as those suggested by Feinberg and Packer. Only if a case has been made out under such criteria, ought the legislature to take the step of criminalising a certain species of conduct.

III The Principle of Legality

The Universal Declaration of Human Rights 1948, Art. 11(2):

"No one shall be held guilty of any penal offence on account of any act or omission which did not constitute a penal offence at the time when it was committed. Nor shall a heavier penalty be imposed than the one that was applicable at the time the penal offence was committed."

The principle of legality enshrined in the Universal Declaration, the Latin maxim for which is *Nullum Crimen Sine Lege, Nulla Poena Sine Lege*, has been regarded as a major element of justice for over two hundred years.[62] The premise upon which the principle rests is that men are ruled by the law and by nothing else. Dicey, for example, stated: "A man may with us be punished for a breach of the law, but he can be punished for nothing else."[63] If no law appropriate to the man's actions is already in existence, then he cannot be punished, no matter "how harmful" his actions may have been. The effect, then, of such a principle is to prohibit *ex post facto* or retroactive law-making, either legislative or judicial, and means that, in theory at least, citizens have advance notice of the limitations on their freedom of action. Not to allow the citizen to know how he stands with regard to the criminal law

---

[62] Its appearance was traced back to the French Revolution.
[63] *Law of the Constitution* (10th ed.) p. 202.

and then to punish him for what he does, would, as Glanville Williams points out, be "arbitrary violence."[64] How persuasive do you find the argument of advance notice when generally, at least, ignorance of the law is not a defence?[65]

Further justification, if required, is available:

D. Cressey, The Functions and Structure of Criminal Syndicate (President's Commission on Law Enforcement and the Administration of Justice, Task Force Report: Organised Crime (1967)), pp. 45–46:

"A 'posture of silent awe and unthinking acceptance' is, after all, what inspires conformity to the criminal law in most members of democratic societies. A 'sense of morality,' or a 'sense of duty,' or a 'sense of decency' keep the crime rate low. It is this kind of 'sense' which constitutes 'consent to be governed' in a democracy . . .

Yet even a democratic government must constantly be seeking to maintain among its members the consent to be governed. Further, even in a democracy, government must constantly be seeking measures for the control of those members whose 'sense of morality' and 'decency' does not stop them from violating the criminal law. . . . Maintaining 'consent of the governed' then, requires that punishments for deviation be accepted as legitimate by those being governed.

This is the basic meaning of 'justice' in criminal cases. One who believes that criminals should be dealt with 'justly' believes, among other things, that punishments can be inflicted on criminals without great danger of revolt or rebellion, providing sufficient *advance notice* is given in the form of rules. Especially in the Western societies with long traditions of barring ex post facto legislation, elaborate systems for *warning* citizens that nonconformity of certain kinds will have punishment as its consequence stimulate rather docile acceptance of official punishments when they are in fact ordered by the courts and executed by prison officials and others. In other words, democratic states operate on the basic assumption that conformity can be maximized only if the punitive system has a rational base. If punishments were imposed irrationally or capriciously, the citizen would be unable to determine to which rules he should conform. Moreover, the infliction of punishments in an apparently arbitrary way would be viewed as 'unjust' and would then contribute to divisiveness in the society.

An important function of the criminal law, so far as maintaining consent of the governed is concerned, is providing the 'advance notice' necessary for justice. The carefully-stated and precisely-stated prohibitions stipulated in criminal laws give advance notice that wrongdoers will be punished, thus contributing to the maintenance of the consent of the governed even when the latter are punished . . . "

In other words, "the true rationale of the non-retroactivity doctrine is revulsion against the use of unfettered power by public officials."[66] Despite the obvious and strong case that can be made for the maintenance of a principle such as this, it has not always been consistently upheld. Indeed, the principle of legality has in the past (and one could not categorically dismiss any present threat) been severely eroded by one or the other of two prongs of attack.

---

[64] *Criminal Law: The General Part* (1961), p. 575.
[65] For rebuttal of this and other criticisms see *ibid.* pp. 601–606; see generally, *post*, p. 268.
[66] LaFave and Scott, *Criminal Law* (1972), p. 90 (hereafter referred to as LaFave and Scott).

The first, which has sometimes appeared in dramatic form, is the so-called analogy principle.

The Nazi law of 1935 stated that "Whoever commits an action which the law declares to be punishable or which is deserving of punishment according to the fundamental idea of a penal law and the sound perception of the people, shall be punished. If no determinate penal law is directly applicable to the action, it shall be punished according to the law, the basic idea of which fits it best." In other words, any law could be *made* to apply to actions of people who were deemed anti-Nazi.

The second prong of the attack builds upon what one can think of as a soft form of the analogy principle and also defends, as part of the judicial role, the task of guarding society's morals:

Shaw v. Director of Public Prosecutions [1962] A.C. 220 (House of Lords)

The defendant published a magazine which was called the Ladies Directory in which names, addresses, telephone numbers, photographs and salient details of prostitutes appeared. He was convicted of conspiracy to corrupt public morals (and two other counts) and appealed.

Viscount Simonds:

"My Lords, as I have already said, the first count in the indictment is 'Conspiracy to corrupt public morals,' and the particulars of offence will have sufficiently appeared. I am concerned only to assert what was vigorously denied by counsel for the appellant, that such an offence is known to the common law, and that it was open to the jury on the facts of this case that the appellant was guilty of such an offence. I must say categorically that, if it were not so, Her Majesty's courts would strangely have failed in their duty as servants and guardians of the common law. Need I say, My Lords, that I am no advocate of the right of the judges to create new criminal offences? . . . But I am at a loss to understand how it can be said either that the law does not recognise a conspiracy to corrupt public morals or that, though there may not be an exact precedent for such a conspiracy as this case reveals, it does not fall fairly within the general words by which it is described. . . . The fallacy in the argument that was addressed to us lay in the attempt to exclude from the scope of general words acts well calculated to corrupt public morals just because they had not been committed or had not been brought to the notice of the court before. It is not thus that the common law has developed. We are perhaps more accustomed to hear this matter discussed upon the question whether such a transaction is contrary to public policy. At once the controversy arises. On the one hand it is said that it is not possible in the twentieth century for the court to create a new head of public policy, on the other it is said that this is but a new example of a well-established head. In the sphere of criminal law I entertain no doubt that there remains in the courts of law a residual power to enforce the supreme and fundamental purpose of the law, to conserve not only the safety and order but also the moral welfare of the State, and that it is their duty to guard it against attacks which may be the more insidious because they are novel and unprepared for. That is the broad head (call it public policy if you wish) within which the present indictment falls. It matters little what label is given to the offending act. To one of your Lordships it may appear an affront to public decency, to another considering that it may succeed in its obvious intention of provoking libidinous desires it will seem a corruption of public morals. Yet others may deem it aptly described as the creation of a public mischief or the undermining of moral conduct. The same act will not in all ages be regarded in the same way. The law must be related to the changing standards of life, not yielding to every shifting impulse of the popular will but having regard to fundamental assessments of human values and the purpose of society. Today a denial of the fundamental Christian doctrine, which in past centuries would have been regarded by the ecclesiastical courts as heresy and by the common law as blasphemy, will no longer be an offence if the decencies of controversy are observed. When Lord Mansfield, speaking long after the Star Chamber had been abolished, said that the Court of King's Bench was the *custos morum* of the people and had the superintendency of offences *contra bonos mores*, he was asserting, as I now assert, that there is in that court a residual power, where no statute has yet intervened to supersede the common law, to superintend those offences which are prejudicial to the public welfare. Such occasions will be rare, for Parliament has not been slow to legislate when attention has been sufficiently aroused. But gaps remain and will always remain since no one can foresee every way in which the wickedness of man may disrupt the order of society. Let me take a single instance . . . Let it be supposed that at some future, perhaps early, date homosexual practices between adult consenting males are no longer a crime. Would it not be an offence if even without obscenity, such practices were publicly advocated and encouraged by pamphlet and advertisement? Or must we wait until Parliament finds time to deal with such conduct? I say, my Lords, that if the common law is powerless in such an event, then we should no longer do her reverence. But I say that her hand is still powerful and that it is for Her Majesty's judges to play the part which Lord Mansfield pointed out to them. . . . "

Appeal dismissed.

The residual power to make law in analogous cases where morality made it appropriate to do so, which the majority in *Shaw* upheld, was firmly disapproved in subsequent cases. In *Knuller*[67] Lord Reid, for example, stated that "in upholding the decision in *Shaw's* case we are, in my view, in no way affirming or lending any support to the doctrine that the courts still have some general or residual power either to create new offences or so as to widen existing offences as to make punishable conduct of a type hitherto not subject to punishment."[68] The argument against such judicial discretion has been most forcibly put:

D.P.P. v. Lynch [1975] A.C. 653 (House of Lords)

(For facts of case see p. 323.)
Lord Kilbrandon:
"It is my misfortune that while I agree with those of your Lordships who consider that the law is in a very unsatisfactory state, and is in urgent need of restatement, I remain convinced that the grounds on which the majority propose that the conviction of the appellant be set aside involve changes in the law which are outside the proper functions of your Lordships in your judicial capacity. If duress per minas has never been admitted as a defence to a charge of murder, and if the proposal that it should now be so admitted be approved, it seems to me that your Lordships, in countenancing a defence for many years

---

[67] *R. v. Knuller* [1973] A.C. 435.
[68] *Ibid.* at pp. 457–458. According to this view, every time judges interpret the law so as to widen the ambit of existing offences they thereby in strict terms infringe the principle of legality. But see *Tan* [1983] Q.B. 1053 and *Badry* v. *D.P.P. of Mauritius* [1983] 2 A.C. 397.

authoritatively (though not in your Lordship's House) denied, would be doing what, in the converse, was firmly and properly disapproved in *R. v. Knuller* . . . Instead of, for reasons of public policy, declaring criminal for the first time conduct until then not so described, your Lordships would be for the first time declaring the existence of a defence to a criminal charge which had up to now by judges, text writers, and law teachers throughout the common law world, been emphatically repudiated . . .

An alteration in a fundamental doctrine of law, such as this appeal proposes, could not properly be given effect to save after the widest reference to interests, both social and intellectual, far transcending those available in the judicial committee of your Lordship's House. Indeed general public opinion is deeply and properly concerned. It will not do to claim that judges have the duty—call it the privilege—of seeing to it that the common law expands and contracts to meet what the judges conceive to be the requirement of modern society. Modern society rightly prefers to exercise that function for itself, and this it conveniently does through those who represent it in Parliament. And its representatives nowadays demand, or should demand, that they be briefed by all those who can qualify an interest to advise them. The fascinating discussions of policy which adorn the speeches of your Lordships—and to which I intend to make a short and undistinguished addition—are themselves highly illustrative of what I mean. They may perhaps be taken as the ultimate in the distillation of legal policy-opinion, but that is not enough. I will not take time to enumerate the various other disciplines and interests whose views are of equal value in deciding what policy should inform the legislation, necessary if reform of the law is really called for, giving effect to the defence of duress per minas in all crimes including murder. In the absence of such consultations I do not think it would be right to decide an appeal in such a way as to set aside the common understanding of the law . . . "

Whilst few would deny the force of this argument when applied to the creation of criminal laws prohibiting conduct, Lord Kilbrandon applies the same arguments to the creation of new defences. Do you think that the creation of new offences and defences ought to be judged on similar bases? Is there not a case for allowing judges to create or extend defences as this necessarily operates to the defendant's advantage?

Chapter 2

THE GENERAL PRINCIPLES OF CRIMINAL LIABILITY

I Introduction

The criminal law is an institution of blame and punishment. Blame is attached to the defendant's conduct and if that conduct violates the law he is punished for it (whether for retributive or deterrent, etc., reasons). But in what circumstances are we to blame someone for his conduct— and blame him to a degree sufficient to justify the imposition of punishment? And in what circumstances can someone's actions be said to have violated the law?

Generally, the law is concerned with punishing harmful actions that are committed in circumstances or in conditions in which we can fairly blame the perpetrator of the actions. This, of course, is only a general proposition. Not all acts that are criminal cause an obvious harm. With the crime of attempt, for instance, no actual harm has been caused.[1] Similarly, criminal liability is often imposed in circumstances where many feel that no blame can be attached to the actor. Thus, in crimes of strict liability a person who has acted to the best of his ability can be punished if, albeit inadvertently, he violates a statute making certain conduct criminal. The question whether such conduct, which either involves no obvious harm, or is generally perceived to involve no blameworthiness, should be punishable, will be considered later in this book.[2]

But let us return to the general proposition which can be broken down into two limbs.

1. Harmful conduct: Sometimes "conduct" can in itself be forbidden on the basis that it constitutes or threatens a harm. Alternatively, it is conduct that causes a harmful result that is forbidden by the criminal law. The word "conduct" is here used in its broadest sense to encompass an omission to act or even a state of affairs. The law has developed a short-hand term, *actus reus*, to describe this.

---

[1] No injury has been sustained, no property lost etc. It is of course possible to define "harm" expansively, enabling one to conclude that there is indeed a "harm" (a "secondary harm") in all such cases. See *ante* pp. 83–88 and *post* p. 434.

[2] *Post*, pp. 216–223.

2. Committed in conditions in which we can fairly blame the actor:
The problem here is to determine the indicia of blame. It is widely accepted that two such indicia exist:

(a) *Mental element.* Some would only blame those who acted with a subjective mental element. Others would blame those whose actions objectively failed to conform to a set standard. Either way, the law has developed a short-hand term, *mens rea*, to describe this.

(b) *Absence of defence.* A defendant might have committed an *actus reus* and have *mens rea*, but because of the circumstances we might not wish to hold him liable and punish him. He might have a valid defence in that he acted, say, in self-defence or under duress. (There might be further indicators of blame. For the sake of simplicity, a discussion of these will be reserved until later in the book.[3])

Viewed in this way, the constituent ingredients of a crime are three-fold, *actus reus, mens rea* and the absence of a valid defence.[4]

There are, however, other modes of analysing the constituent elements of a crime. Glanville Williams, for instance, has argued that all elements of a crime are divisible into either *actus reus* or *mens rea* and that the *actus reus* requirement includes absence of defence.[5] Others argue that *mens rea* means blameworthiness in the sense of mental element plus absence of defence.[6]

This divergence of views can be illustrated simply. The crime of murder is defined as the "unlawful killing of a human being with malice aforethought."[7] The constituent elements of this crime can be analysed in three ways:

(1) There are three elements—the *actus reus* of killing a human being, the *mens rea* of malice aforethought, and the requirement of unlawfulness indicating the absence of any defence.

(2) The *actus reus* is unlawfully killing a human being; the requirement of unlawfulness (absence of defence) is part of the *actus reus*. The *mens rea* requirement is malice aforethought.

(3) The *actus reus* is killing a human being. The *mens rea* is the element of blameworthiness which encompasses both the malice aforethought and the unlawfulness (absence of defence) requirement.

The possible importance of these different modes of analysis will be discussed in due course,[8] but for the moment the fact that there are

---

[3] *Post*, pp. 558–562, 665–673, 797–798.

[4] D. Lanham, "Larsonneur Revisited," [1976] Crim.L.R. 276.

[5] C.L.G.P. p. 20; (1976) N.L.J. 1032, 1034; see also *Williams (Gladstone)* (1984) 78 Cr.App.R. 276 and *post*, pp. 259–262, for a discussion thereof.

[6] *Post*, p. 151.

[7] *Post*, pp. 584.

[8] *Post*, pp. 259–262.

these very different modes of analysis must serve to emphasise an important point. The terms *actus reus* and *mens rea* are no more than tools that are useful in the exposition of the criminal law. Dividing crime into its constituent elements in this way should be no more than an exercise of analytical convenience.[9] Whether defendants are to be convicted should depend on important principles aimed at deciding whether their conduct deserves condemnation as criminal; such questions should not be answered by reference only to definitions of *actus reus* and *mens rea*. Questions of policy should not be determined by reference to definition and terminology.[10]

In *Miller*, Lord Diplock disapproved of such terminology:

> "My Lords, it would I think be conducive to clarity of analysis of the ingredients of a crime that is created by statute, as are the greater majority of criminal offences today, if we were to avoid bad Latin and instead to think and speak . . . about the conduct of the accused and his state of mind at the time of that conduct, instead of speaking of actus reus and mens rea."[11]

In this chapter we have chosen to disregard Lord Diplock's command. We shall analyse crimes in terms of *actus reus*, *mens rea* and absence of defence.[12] We do this for the simple reason that as long as one appreciates that these terms are no more than tools, they are tools that *can* usefully aid the clear exposition of the rules of criminal law. Further, they have been so much part of the criminal law vocabulary for hundreds of years that many of the cases to be discussed in this book would be highly confusing, if not totally meaningless, without some understanding of the orthodox meaning of these terms. In later chapters, however, we shall be suggesting that it is the concept of "blame" that ought to provide one of the fundamental bases upon which criminal liability is imposed.[13] *Mens rea* is always an important indicator of blame, but by no means the exclusive one. But such proposals and ideas can make no sense until the concept, *mens rea* (as commonly understood) has been closely examined.

In this chapter then we shall consider the primary basis of criminal liability in terms of *actus reus* and *mens rea*. For the sake of clarity the discussion of the general defences has been reserved for a separate chapter.

[9] See, however, *post*, pp. 254–263 where recent decisions have lost sight of this simple point and actually made criminal liability dependent upon a particular mode of analysing the constituent elements of a crime.

[10] A. T. H. Smith, "On Actus Reus and Mens Rea" in P. R. Glazebrook, *Reshaping the Criminal Law* (1978), 95, 96, 102.

[11] [1983] A.C. 161, 175.

[12] Except for certain so-called "defences" such as automatism or mistake which we shall deal with in this chapter. The arguments that they negate the *actus reus* and *mens rea* of a crime are particularly powerful. Further, it is convenient to deal with them in this way because of the light they help throw on our understanding of these concepts.

[13] See particularly, *post*, pp. 209–211, 277–279, 795–798.

II Actus Reus

A. *Introduction*

To many people evil thoughts, desires and intentions are as reprehensible as evil deeds and if we had the means to detect such criminal propensities we would be justified in punishing such persons. The law, however, is not concerned with punishing people for thinking evil thoughts or having evil intentions. The law will not interfere unless there has been some conduct, some physical manifestation of the evil intention. Some crimes only require the slightest manifestation—in conspiracy, for example, all that is needed is an agreement; but minimal as it might be, this agreement is nevertheless a physical manifestation of the evil intention; it is conduct and can form the basis of an *actus reus*.

Why does the law insist upon an *actus reus* as a prerequisite of criminal liability?

Powell v. State of Texas 392 U.S. 514, 88 S. Ct. 2145 (Supreme Court of the United States) (1968)

Black J.:
"The reasons for this refusal to permit conviction without proof of an act are difficult to spell out, but they are nonetheless perceived and universally expressed in our criminal law. Evidence of propensity can be considered relatively unreliable and more difficult for a defendant to rebut: the requirement of a specific act thus provides some protection against false charges. Perhaps more fundamental is the difficult of distinguishing, in the absence of any conduct, between desires of the day-dream variety and fixed intentions that may pose a real threat to society; extending the criminal law to cover both types of desire would be unthinkable, since '[t]here can hardly be anyone who has never thought evil. When a desire is inhibited it may find expression in fantasy; but it would be absurd to condemn this natural psychological mechanism as illegal' (Glanville Williams, (1961), p. 2.)"

A. Goldstein, "Conspiracy to Defraud the United States," (1959) 68 Yale L.J. 405–406:

"[The notion of not punishing evil intentions alone] expresses today, as it did three centuries ago, the feeling that the individual thinking evil thoughts must be protected from a state which may class him as a threat to its security. Rooted in scepticism about the ability either to know what passes through the minds of men or to predict whether antisocial behaviour will follow from antisocial thoughts, the act requirement serves a number of closely-related objectives: it seeks to assure that the evil intent of the man branded a criminal has been *expressed in a manner signifying harm to society*; that there is no longer any substantial likelihood that he will be deterred by the threat of sanction; and that there has been an identifiable occurrence so that multiple prosecution and punishment may be minimized."

As seen above, a mere agreement to commit a crime is regarded as a sufficient manifestation of evil intentions to constitute the *actus reus* of conspiracy; similarly mere words of instruction or encouragement are sufficient to render one liable for aiding and abetting a crime. Whether these are a sufficient manifestation of evil intentions to justify the imposition of criminal liability is a question to be considered later.[14]

B. *Constituent Elements of Actus Reus*

What exactly is an *actus reus*?

The *actus reus* of every crime is different. The *actus reus* of theft is "the appropriation of property belonging to another"[15] and the *actus reus* of rape is "unlawful sexual intercourse with a woman who at the time of the intercourse does not consent to it."[16] With all crimes the *actus reus* is the external element of the crime—the objective requirements necessary to constitute the offence. Crimes can be divided into two categories and the essential elements of an *actus reus* depend on which of these two species of crime one is dealing with. First, there are crimes known as conduct crimes where the only external elements required are the prohibited conduct itself. Thus the *actus reus* of the offence of reckless driving is simply "driving a motor vehicle on a road."[17] No harm, no consequence of that reckless driving need be established. The second species of crime is known as result crime where the external elements of the offence require proof that the conduct caused a prohibited result or consequence. Thus the *actus reus* of the offence of causing death by reckless driving is "causing the death of another person by driving a motor vehicle on a road."[18] Here it is necessary to establish that the same reckless driving caused the forbidden consequence specified in the *actus reus*, namely the death of another person.

Conduct crimes provide a good illustration of the criminal law punishing offenders who have caused no obvious harm. Is such an approach justifiable? Or can it be argued that in the above example there is a harm, namely causing danger to other road users? If this is indeed a harm, it is clearly a lesser harm than actually killing another road-user. Should this difference be reflected by differing penalties for the two offences?[19] Or should one proceed on the basis that as the forbidden conduct is the same in both offences and the *mens rea* (recklessness) is constant, the result (death) could be entirely fortuitous, thus not reflecting upon the driver's responsibility and consequently the two offences should carry the same penalty?

From the above it can be seen that both conduct crimes and result crimes have two elements in common:

---

[14] *Post*, pp. 481, 505.
[15] Theft Act 1968, s.1.
[16] Sexual Offences (Amendment) Act 1976, s.1(1).
[17] Road Traffic Act 1988, s.2.
[18] *Ibid.*, s.1.
[19] *Post*, pp. 634–638.

(1) Both require an "act" or conduct, *i.e.* driving.
(2) Both require that the act be carried out in defined *legally relevant circumstances*,[20] *i.e.* on a road. If the same act of driving the car occurred in a field, the *actus reus* of the offence would not be made out. It is only reckless driving *on a road* that is prohibited. Similarly, the *actus reus* of theft requires that the property "belong to another." In the absence of this circumstance, if, for example, the property is owned by the would-be thief, the *actus reus* of the crime is not made out. Just as *mens rea* may or may not be required for the act and for the consequences in result crimes, we shall see that liability may similarly depend upon whether the accused had the required mental state in relation to the legally defined relevant circumstances. The *actus reus* of rape, for example, requires the act of intercourse to be committed in the circumstance of the woman not consenting. In *Morgan*[21] the House of Lords ruled that if the defendant honestly believes that the woman is consenting to the act of intercourse, he cannot be liable. In such a case there would be no *mens rea* in relation to a vital element of the *actus reus*.

With result crimes it is necessary to establish an additional third element, namely, that the act committed, *caused* the prohibited consequence, for example, *caused* the death of another person. If poison is put into the drink of another person with intent to kill that person who subsequently dies with the drink found beside them, liability for murder cannot exist unless it was the poison that caused the death. If the deceased had died of a heart attack, the only possible charge would be attempted murder.[22]

Putting these elements together it is common to find an *actus reus* described as

(1) an "act,"
(2) committed in legally relevant circumstances, and
(3) (for result crimes) causing the prohibited result.[23]

The issue of causation is thus treated as part of the *actus reus* requirement.

One final point needs to be made by way of introduction. Whilst there are numerous instances of crimes so defined that the defendant may be convicted on the basis of the *actus reus* alone (crimes of so-called strict liability where no *mens rea* need be proved as to one or more elements of the *actus reus*[24] the reverse is not true. As we have seen, there must always be an *actus reus* for liability to be at issue at all. If, for example, in an alleged case of theft, the property already belongs to the

[20] Smith and Hogan p. 39.
[21] [1976] A.C. 182. See *post*, pp. 254.
[22] *White* [1910] 2 KB 124; See also *Hensler* (1870) 11 Cox CC 570. Causation is discussed, *post*, Chap. 4.
[23] Smith and Hogan, p. 39.
[24] *Post*, pp. 215–233.

person taking it, then despite any intention he may have to steal, his actions cannot amount to the crime of theft. Similarly, where a defendant persuades another to purchase his car by representing that it is free from encumbrances, believing he is lying, he cannot be found guilty of obtaining by false pretences if it turns out that it was in fact free from encumbrances.[25] The defendant has unwittingly told the truth; the car was his to sell and his dishonest state of mind counts for nothing. The fact that a defendant believes he has committed an *actus reus* is not enough. The *actus reus* must be proved objectively to exist.

We are now in a position to examine in greater detail the requirement of an act.

C. *The Act must be Voluntary*

J. LI. J. Edwards, "Automatism and Criminal Responsibility" (1958) 21 M.L.R. 375 at 379–380:

"[It is] the fundamental requirement of all criminal liability, whether the offence is one of absolute prohibition or one involving proof of a guilty mind and whether statutory or common law in origin. This requirement stated in its simplest form, is that the 'act' of the accused, in the sense of a muscular movement, must be willed. It must be a voluntary expression of the accused's will."

Without this minimum degree of accountability, punishment, it is claimed, is unjust. We will examine the extent to which human conduct can and should be described in this way and the effect of a finding that the defendant's conduct is involuntary or autonomic.

The law traditionally distinguishes between an act and its accompanying mental state: thus, when someone is shot and killed "by accident" by a defendant who thought he possessed only a toy, he has committed the act of killing but lacks the degree of foresight that enables a court to find him guilty of murder. But what of the man who shoots another as a result of having stumbled on some steps? Again the death is "accidental"; it was not "meant" to happen by the defendant. But one feels that the accident is more fundamental in this second case. Just as we would not wish to describe a person whose fist is jammed into another's face as having struck the victim, so we feel disquiet at holding the stumbling man answerable for his behaviour. What is missing is not only some mental state; the act itself is defective. Even had we been describing situations where no accompanying mental state was required for liability (so-called crimes of strict liability), we would question a decision to punish such a man. The act is not his own. The

---

[25] *Deller* (1952) 36 Cr.App.R. 184. This case is commonly discussed in relation to *Dadson* (1850) 2 Den 35.

difficulty lies in trying to pinpoint the defect. As we shall see, the law has generally shied away from identifying the missing component, but has singled out examples only by means of the device of automatism. The precise meaning of "voluntary act" is one that has been explored instead by academic lawyers and philosophers. Traditionally, the view taken has been that opined in the opening quotation, a direct legacy of Austinian philosophy.

Austin, Lectures on Jurisprudence (5th ed.) (XVIII–XIX) Vol. I, 411–415:

"Certain movements of our bodies follow invariably and immediately our wishes and desires for those same movements. Provided, that is, that the bodily organ be sane, and the desired movement be not prevented by any outward obstacle. . . . These antecedent wishes and those consequent movements, are human volitions and acts (strictly and properly so-called). . . . And as these are the only volition; so are the bodily movements by which they are immediately followed the only acts or actions (properly so-called). It will be admitted on the mere statement, that the only objects which can be called acts are consequences of volitions. A voluntary movement of my body, or a movement which follows a volition, is an act. The involuntary movements which (for example) are the consequences of certain diseases, are not acts. . . . "

We are asked, therefore, to divide the human act into two elements: the desire for the muscular movement and the movement itself. In our example, there would be no accountability for the harm done because of the absence of the willed or desired muscular movement. *A fortiori*, the person who is unconscious throughout the "conduct" because of, say, sleep, could not be held accountable.

This breakdown of human behaviour has been fiercely criticised. Hart rightly points out that described in these terms it cannot apply to omissions (where to speak instead of the necessity for a willed failure to move one's muscles is not only clumsy but an inaccurate reflection of the law).[26] Furthermore, such an analysis does not reflect the reality of our movements.

H. L. A. Hart, Punishment and Responsibility (1968), pp. 101–102:

" . . . a desire to contract our muscles is a very rare occurrence: there are no doubt *some* special occasions when it would be quite right to say that what we are doing is contracting our muscles, and that we have a desire to do this. An

---

[26] H.L.A. Hart, *Punishment and Responsibility* (1968), p. 100: "It is surely absurd even to attempt to fit omissions into such a picture of voluntary or involuntary conduct . . . [because] in the case of omissions no muscular movement or contraction need occur . . . [Such a theory] would have very unwelcome consequences for legal responsibility: for the only omissions which would then be culpable would be deliberate omissions. We could then only punish those who failed to stop at traffic lights if they deliberately shot the lights."

example of this is what we may do under instruction in a gymnasium. The instructor says 'lift your right hand and contract the muscles of the upper arm.' If we succeed in doing this (and it is not so easy) it would be quite appropriate to say we desired to and did contract our muscles. . . . [But] when we shut a door, or when we hit someone, or when we fire a gun at a bird, these things are done without any previous thought of the muscular movements involved and without any desire to contract the muscles. . . . The simple but important truth is that when we deliberate and think about actions, we do so not in terms of muscular movements but in the ordinary terminology of actions."

Glanville Williams, The Mental Element in Crime (1965), pp. 17–18:

" . . . one cannot by introspection, identify a conscious exercise of will previous to movement. Indeed, one cannot always find an exercise of will at all. Many acts are performed unthinkingly; not only a reflex like dropping a hot poker but much of the routine of life, such as shaving, eating, walking. We seem to switch on an 'automatic pilot' for many of the familiar tasks we perform; yet we are undoubtedly acting. Even when we make a conscious decision and act to carry it out, the act is something different from the preceding deliberation."

In this final statement Glanville Williams, in accordance with other English commentators, tacitly upholds the distinction drawn in English law between *mens rea* and *actus reus*. But other critics of the willed movement principle do not. Welzel,[27] a German philosopher, is convinced that the causal theory upon which this principle, and much of the rest of the criminal law rests, is misconceived. He does not accept that there are a set of desires which *cause* the movements to occur. Instead, he favours a view of acting that looks to the actor's goal. The distinction between a bodily movement and an "act" lies not in any preceding will but in the purpose of the actor—what he was seeking to achieve. According to this philosophical stance, not only is it wrong to divide up the act, as Austin and supporters do, but to divide any mental state from its act would be equally invalid. The two, he would claim, are inextricably linked and are incapable of separate analysis. We will return to this view later in our discussion of *mens rea*.[28]

More representative of the standard approach is the view of Glanville Williams that:

"Notwithstanding these difficulties of definition everyone understands the proposition that an act is something more than bodily movement—for bodily movement might occur in tripping and falling, which would not be described as an act."[29]

And, we could add, ought not to render the "actor" answerable for his

---

[27] For a discussion of Welzel's view, see George P. Fletcher, *Rethinking Criminal Law* (1978), pp. 434–439.

[28] So, according to Welzel there are bodily movements (non-acts) and purposive/intentional acts. This overlooks a third possibility—that of unintentional acts. Yet as the opening passage to this section shows, these clearly exist. See also the discussion of dualism, *post*, p. 238.

[29] *The Mental Element in Crime*, p. 18.

movements. Broad consensus does seem to exist that it would be unjust to punish in the sort of situations outlined earlier, despite the harm done. What is felt to be missing is an ability to control one's actions— some sort of choice as to whether one acts or not.[30] Perhaps this is a more helpful description than that couched in terms of willed movements.

Herbert L. Packer, The Limits of the Criminal Sanction (1969), pp. 76–77:

"Conduct must be, as the law's confusing term has it, 'voluntary.' The term is one that will immediately raise the hackles of the determinist, of whatever persuasion. But . . . the law's language should not be read as plunging into the deep waters of free will vs. determinism, Cartesian dualism, or any of a half-dozen other philosophic controversies that might appear to be invoked by the use of the term 'voluntary' in relation to conduct. The law is not affirming that some conduct is the product of the free exercise of conscious volition; it is excluding, in a crude kind of way, conduct that in any view is not. And it does so primarily in response to the simple intuition that nothing would more surely undermine the individual's sense of autonomy and security than to hold him to account for conduct that he does not think he can control. He may be deluded, if the determinists are right, in his belief that such conduct differs significantly from any other conduct in which he engages. But that is beside the point. He thinks there is a difference, and that is what the law acts upon."

The law, therefore, continues to uphold the view that incorporated somehow into the *actus reus* is a mental element of volition or control or purposiveness. Where this mental element is missing, the mechanism of automatism may be brought into play by the courts to protect the defendant from the consequences of his actions.[31]

Bratty v. A.-G. for Northern Ireland [1963] A.C. 386, 409 (House of Lords)

Lord Denning:
"No act is punishable if it is done involuntarily and an involuntary act in this context—some people nowadays prefer to speak of it as 'automatism'—means an act which is done by the muscles without any control by the mind such as a spasm, a reflex action or a convulsion; or an act done by a person who is not conscious of what he is doing, such as an act done whilst suffering from concussion or whilst sleep-walking. . . .
[However] to prevent confusion it is to be observed that in the criminal law

---

[30] The lack of control may arise through classical automatism, such as unconsciousness or in other ways. In *Burns* v. *Bidder* [1966] 3 All E.R. 29, the defendant was acquitted of failing to accord precedence to a pedestrian when his brakes failed. In *Neal* v. *Reynolds* [1966] Crim.L.R. 393, the defendant was convicted of the same crime which had occurred as a result of a pedestrian unforeseeably stepping out into the road. Can the control test reconcile these two different results?

[31] For a discussion of the defence of automatism in the context of strict liability, see, *post*, pp. 229–230.

an act is not to be regarded as an involuntary act simply because the actor does not remember it. . . . Nor is an act to be regarded as an involuntary act simply because the doer could not control his impulse to do it."

King v. Cogdon, Supreme Court of Victoria, (1950) (Unreported) (From N. Morris, "Somnambulistic Homicide: Ghosts, Spiders and North Koreans," Res Judicatae V (1951), 29)

"Mrs. Cogdon was charged with the murder of her only child, a daughter called Pat, aged nineteen. Pat had for some time been receiving psychiatric treatment for a relatively minor neurotic condition of which, in her psychiatrist's opinion, she was now cured. Despite this, Mrs Cogdon continued to worry unduly about her. Describing the relationship between Pat and her mother, Mr. Cogdon testified: 'I don't think a mother could have thought any more of her daughter. I think she absolutely adored her.' On the conscious level, at least, there was no reason to doubt Mrs. Cogdon's deep attachment to her daughter.

To the charge of murdering Pat, Mrs. Cogdon pleaded not guilty. Her story, though somewhat bizarre, was not seriously challenged by the Crown, and led to her acquittal. She told how, on the night before her daughter's death she had dreamt that their house was full of spiders and that these spiders were crawling all over Pat. In her sleep, Mrs. Cogdon left the bed she shared with her husband, went into Pat's room and awakened to find herself violently brushing at Pat's face, presumably to remove the spiders. This woke Pat. Mrs. Cogdon told her she was just tucking her in. At the trial she testified that she still believed, as she had been told, that the occupants of a nearby house bred spiders as a hobby, preparing nests for them behind the pictures on their walls. It was these spiders which in her dreams had invaded their home and attacked Pat. There had also been a previous dream in which ghosts had sat at the end of Mrs. Cogdon's bed and she had said to them, 'Well, you have come to take Pattie.' It does not seem fanciful to accept the psychological explanation of these spiders and ghosts as the projections of Mrs. Cogdon's subconscious hostility towards her daughter; a hostility which was itself rooted in Mrs. Cogdon's own early life and marital relationship.

The morning after the spider dream she told her doctor of it. He gave her a sedative and, because of the dream and certain previous difficulties she had reported, discussed the possibility of psychiatric treatment. That evening Mrs. Cogdon suggested to her husband that he attend his lodge meeting, and asked Pat to come with her to the cinema. After he had gone Pat looked through the paper, not unusually found no tolerable programme, and said as she was going out the next evening she thought she would rather go to bed early. Later while Pat was having a bath preparatory to retiring, Mrs. Cogdon went into her room, put a hot water bottle in the bed, turned back the bedclothes and placed a glass of hot milk beside the bed ready for Pat. She then went to bed herself. There was some desultory conversation between them about the war in Korea and just before she put out her light, Pat called out to her mother, 'Mum, don't be so silly worrying about the war, it's not on our front door step yet.'

Mrs. Cogdon went to sleep. She dreamt that 'the war was all around the house,' that the soldiers were in Pat's room, and that one soldier was on the bed attacking Pat. This was all of the dream that she could later recapture. Her first 'waking' memory was of running from Pat's room, out of the house to the home of her sister who lived next door. When her sister opened the front door Mrs. Cogdon fell into her arms crying, 'I think I've hurt Pattie.' In fact Mrs. Cogdon had, in her somnambulistic state, left her bed, fetched an axe from the wood-heap, entered Pat's room, and struck her two accurate forceful blows on the head with the blade of the axe, thus killing her.

Mrs. Cogdon's story was supported by the evidence of her physician, a psychiatrist and a psychologist. The burden of the evidence of all three, which was not contested by the prosecution, was that Mrs. Cogdon was suffering from a form of hysteria with an overlay of depression, and that she was of a personality in which such dissociated states as fugues, amnesias and somnambulistic acts are to be expected. They agreed that she was not psychotic and that if she had been awake at the time of the killing no defence could have been spelt out under the *M'Naughten Rules*. They hazarded no statement as to her motives, the idea of defence of the daughter being transparently insufficient. However, the psychologist and the psychiatrist concurred in hinting that the emotional motivation lay in an acute conflict situation in her relations with her own parents; that during marital life she suffered very great sexual frustration; and that she overcompensated for her own frustration by over-protection of her daughter. Her exaggerated solicitude for her daughter was a conscious expression of her subconscious emotional hostility to her, and the dream ghosts, spiders and Korean soldiers were projections of that aggression. . . .

At all events the jury believed Mrs. Cogdon's story, and regarded the presumption that the natural consequences of her acts were intended as being completely rebutted by her account of her mental state at the time of the killing and by the unanimous support given to it by the medical and psychological evidence. . . . She was acquitted because the act of killing itself was not, in law, regarded as her act at all."

Mrs. Cogdon was not held accountable for her actions because they were held to be involuntary. But it has to be stressed that such a result—and one that leads to a complete acquittal, will be a fairly rare occurrence. The courts have consistently limited the protection they offer to defendants in such circumstances by two means. Firstly, the ambit of "involuntariness" is kept very narrow. Secondly, (although a full discussion of this defence will take place later[32]), the definition of insanity has been extended to embrace many cases that could otherwise have been dealt with as automatism. So inter-related are the two concepts of automatism and insanity, that it has become common to refer to the former as sane automatism and the latter as insane automatism. What is common to both is a finding that the defendant acted involuntarily. However, for insane automatism (insanity), the defendant must be suffering from a "disease of the mind."[33] Such an insane defendant, while escaping formal criminal liability, nevertheless receives a special verdict "not guilty by reason of insanity" and is subjected to mandatory commitment, *i.e.* indefinite detention "at Her Majesty's pleasure." Mrs. Cogdon was found not to be suffering from a disease of the mind; she thus escaped all liability. The distinction between insane automatism and sane automatism is, therefore, crucial; if the defendant's actions are deemed involuntary but sane, he gets a complete acquittal; if involun-

---

[32] *Post*, p. 345.
[33] This is required under the legal test of insanity—the M'Naghten Rules, *post*, pp. 349–354.

tary but insane, mandatory commitment results. Generally, since *Bratty*,[34] acts have been regarded as involuntary but sane if they have resulted from some external factor, such as where the victim has received a blow to the head or, has been suggested in the recent Crown Court decision *R* v. *T.*,[34a] where the victim had been raped (causing post-traumatic stress disorder). They will be regarded as insane, on the other hand, if the acts arise from some internal factor or disease. Such a distinction seeks to identify those who can safely be acquitted and those who are dangerous and thus need restraint. Whilst this must be a major concern for the courts, the implications of the external/internal factor distinction are revealed by the case of *Sullivan*.[35] The House of Lords decided that epilepsy, because it is a disease of the mind and an internal condition, is to be regarded as insane automatism.

On this basis arteriosclerosis, because it results from an internal factor, would be similarly regarded. The same would be true, one would have thought, of sleep-walking; yet, in the case of *Lillienfield*,[36] a Crown court refused to accept this view and regarded as sane automatism the actions of a sleep-walker who stabbed a friend twenty times. Where would hyperglycaemia (excessively high blood sugar) and hypoglycaemia (a deficiency in blood sugar) fit into this form of categorisation? In the case of *Quick*[37] the court drew a distinction between a transitory malfunctioning of the mind caused by *hypoglycaemia* due to external factors (for example, the taking of insulin), and *hyperglycaemia* caused by an inherent defect (a disease which is under normal circumstances controlled by taking insulin). In the former case, the diabetic offender would be entitled as a consequence to be acquitted. In the latter, the diabetic offender would be raising the defence of insanity by pleading that his actions were involuntary. Both the recent cases of *Broome* v. *Perkins*[38] and *Hennessy*[39] concerned diabetic defendants raising the defence of automatism. In *Broome* v. *Perkins* the defendant claimed to be in a hypoglycaemic condition in answer to a charge of driving without due care and attention. He was acquitted at first instance on the basis that his actions were involuntary. However, an appeal by case stated resulted in a direction to the magistrates to convict. It was held that his actions were only at intervals automatic; at times "the respondent's mind must have been controlling his limbs

---

[34] [1963] A.C. 386, *ante* p. 109.

[34a] In this case the defendant alleged to have been violently raped (and there was medical evidence that could support this). Three days later she robbed two girls and assaulted another. She claimed to have been suffering from post-traumatic stress disorder which meant that although conscious, she was in a state of psychogenic fugue and thus automatic. There was no evidence of any history of psychiatric illness. The trial judge decided that she was entitled to have this defence raised as non-insane automatism and it was put to the jury in that form; the jury, nevertheless, convicted her.

[35] [1984] A.C. 156.

[36] *The Times*, October 17, 1985. See also the unreported case of *Dennehy* discussed in B. McConnell, "Sleep, perchance to dream" (1989) 139 New L.J. 1772.

[37] [1973] 1 Q.B. 910.

[38] [1987] Crim.L.R. 271.

[39] [1989] 1 W.L.R. 287.

(from the evidence) and thus he was driving." In *Hennessy* the defendant was charged with taking a conveyance and with driving whilst disqualified. His defence was that at the relevant time he had failed to take
his proper dose of insulin due to stress, anxiety and depression, and
was thus in a state of hyperglycaemia and automatic. The Court of
Appeal accepted the *Quick* distinction between hyper- and hypoglycaemia and rejected the defence argument that stress, anxiety and
depression were the sort of factors that could count as external for the
purposes of sane automatism. They constituted a state of mind that was
prone to recur and lacked the feature of novelty or accident. Thus, the
defendant was raising the defence of insanity.

A number of comments flow from these cases, all of them pointing to
the highly unsatisfactory state of the law in relation to both sane and
insane automatism. As a consequence of finding that their defences
were being dealt with on the basis of insanity, both *Sullivan* and *Hennessy* changed their pleas from not-guilty to guilty. The fact that they
should have to do so to avoid mandatory committment makes a mockery of the law; the court in *Sullivan* itself expressed its sympathy for the
defendant's plight! Moreover, the decision of *Broome* v. *Perkins* reveals
how very narrow the defence of sane automatism has become.

J. C. Smith, Commentary to Broome v. Perkins [1987] Crim.L.R. 272:

The defendant was held not to be in a state of automatism thoughout his journey because, from time to time, he apparently exercised conscious control over
his car, veering away from other vehicles so as to avoid a collision, braking violently when approaching the back of another vehicle and so on. This is a very
harsh decision, resulting in the conviction of a person who appears to have suffered a misfortune, not to have been at fault in any real sense and to have
behaved most responsibly by going to the police and saying that he believed he
must have been involved in a road accident. More important, if generally
applied, the decision would confine the defence of automatism within very narrow limits. If it is right, surely Barry J. was wrong in *Charlson* (*post* p. 118) (even
on the assumption which he made that the evidence of the defect resulting from
the brain tumour was evidence of non-insane automatism) to leave the defence
of automatism to the jury. Charlson's acts of striking his son with a mallet and
throwing him out of the window were certainly no less purposeful that the acts
of the present respondent. Charlson's acts were no mere spasm or convulsion.
Common sense suggests that the limbs cannot pick up a mallet and strike a
blow, still less pick up a child and throw him out of a window, without some
direction of the mind. If Charlson, on the assumption made above, should have
been acquitted at all, it was on the grounds of lack of *mens rea*, not on the
ground that he did no voluntary act. In the present case, no mental element
beyond that necessarily involved in the act of driving need be proved. The
defendant is then guilty if he failed to observe 'an objective standard, impersonal and universal, fixed in relation to the safety of other users of the highway:'
(*McCrone* v. *Riding* [1938] 1 All E.R. 157)"

One can understand and accept the reason for the distinction between internal and external factors: if the law is trying to protect society by isolating the dangerous then the risk of recurrence of harm is something they are bound to consider. However, the current law leads us to the absurd and offensive conclusion that somehow epileptics are more dangerous than diabetics, who at least in hypoglycaemic states are able to raise the defence of sane automatism. Not only is the label wholly out of place but, in addition, there is the very real problem of what to do with epileptics, sleep-walkers (if our analysis is correct) etc. who have been or may be deemed to be legally insane. Indefinite detention hardly seems appropriate as the form of treatment here.[40] At the end of this section we will examine whether there are any other ways in which this problem could be resolved.

One final problem remains to be considered at this stage. Even if the defendant can show that his automation is the result of an external factor, and is, therefore, not insanity, is he to be acquitted if it transpires that he brought about his own involuntariness?

What would have been the position, for example, if Mrs. Cogdon had drunk herself into an intoxicated stupor, or if she had been a diabetic who failed to take food after a dose of insulin, this resulting in a hypoglycaemic episode?

In *Quick* the defendant, a diabetic, was charged with an assault that occurred during a hypoglycaemic episode. This arose from eating too little and drinking too much alcohol after having taken his insulin. It led to an aggressive outburst and eventually to an impairment of consciousness. Lawton L.J. stated that: "A self-induced incapacity will not excuse . . . nor will one which could have been reasonably foreseen as a result of either doing, or omitting to do something, as, for example, taking alcohol against medical advice after using certain prescribed drugs, or failing to have regular meals while taking insulin."[41]

So while "accidental" hypoglycaemia would have secured an acquittal for the defendant, Quick's abuse of his body changed the position fundamentally. Although the conviction was actually reversed on appeal (on the basis that the issue of automatism should have been left to the jury), it was made very clear that self-induced automatism will not provide a defence[42] to crimes of basic intent.[43]

It could be argued that some doubt has been cast on the correctness of this view by the more recent decision of *Bailey*.[44] In this case it was accepted that self-induced automatism due to drink or drugs is no defence to crimes of basic intent because such persons should realise

---

[40] It has to be acknowledged, of course, that indefinite detention means just that—the release of defendants actually dealt with by means of the insanity defence rather than pleading guilty, *could* be speedily secured.

[41] [1973] 1 Q.B. 910.

[42] This reasoning has been employed in some cases on driving and automatism. See *Kay* v. *Butterworth* (1947) 173 L.T. 191; *contra Hill* v. *Baxter* [1958] 1 Q.B. 277.

[43] For the meaning of this term, see *post* pp. 378–386.

[44] [1983] 1 W.L.R. 760.

the risk they are running. The same would not necessarily be true, however, in other situations. In *Bailey* itself, the defendant was a diabetic who had not taken sufficient food after his dose of insulin to combat its effects. But the court held (somewhat controversially) that it was not common knowledge amongst diabetics that such failure could lead to aggressive, dangerous or unpredictable behaviour. The defendant could not be *expected* to know of these risks and should not be penalised for his lack of knowledge. A conviction would only be possible if the defendant knew of the risk and nevertheless took it.[45] In other cases, "self-induced automatism, other than that due to intoxication from alcohol or drugs, may provide a defence to crimes of basic intent."[46]

Despite the sweeping nature of this dictum, it is submitted that this decision does not constitute a major inroad on the *Quick* principle that self-induced automatism is no defence. The essence of *Quick* is that where a person, through his own actions, induces a state of automatism, he can be blamed for that resultant state. It was his own fault. He should have been aware of the risks he was taking. When such fault is established, the requirement of voluntariness for an *actus reus* is dispensed with (largely because that requirement is only there to protect the faultless)—and this same fault can be used to attribute *mens rea* to the actor (in the form of recklessness[47]). *Bailey* is following this reasoning by holding that one cannot blame a diabetic who fails to take food after a dose of insulin as the risks involved are not "common knowledge, even among diabetics." If such risks were common knowledge or known to the defendant, liability would ensue.

The courts have, therefore, adopted three solutions to the problem of automatism:

(1) It may lead to a complete acquittal.

(2) It may be evidence of a disease of the mind and thus the starting point for a special verdict of not guilty by reason of insanity.

(3) It may be the basis of liability for crimes of basic intent if it can be shown to be self-induced in circumstances where the risks should have been appreciated.

The first solution is the general rule based on the doctrine of voluntariness; arguably, the other solutions are exceptions based on policy rather than principle.

These three categories of response would be broadly retained (with modification to the insanity defence) under the provisions in the Draft Criminal Code Bill. (This is a Bill published by the Law Commission which, if enacted, would result in a codification of most important areas of English criminal law.)

---

[45] The appeal was in fact dismissed because of insufficient evidence that the defendant had been autonomic.

[46] P. 765. For the meaning of basic intent, see p. 381.

[47] See *post* pp. 390–394.

Draft Criminal Code Bill 1989 (Law Com. No. 177), clause 33:

(1) A person is not guilty of an offence if—
(a) he acts in a state of automatism, that is, his act—
   (i) is a reflex, spasm, or convulsion; or
   (ii) occurs while he is in a condition (whether of sleep, unconsciousness, impaired consciousness or otherwise) depriving him of effective control of the act; and
(b) the act or condition is the result neither of anything done or omitted with the fault required for the offence nor of voluntary intoxication."

As the examples in the Draft Criminal Code make clear, this provision would still be denied to the epileptic and hyperglycaemic diabetic who would be dealt with under the mental disorder provisions. The diabetic in a hypoglycaemic state would, however, be protected, as would the sleep-walker *if* the sleep-walking episode was not a feature of an underlying condition and, therefore, not prone to recur.[48]

We need finally to examine whether this whole approach is sound. Should automatism provide a complete defence?

The result may be open to doubt at two levels.

1. Psychiatry's view of the automaton's true state of mind
Remember, for example, Mrs Cogdon,[49] who was acquitted of killing her daughter because her act was held to be involuntary. It had been committed during sleep.

David Henderson and R. D. Gillespie, A Textbook of Psychiatry (7th ed., 1950) pp. 125, 191:

"A *somnambulism* is a general automatism occurring in the course of, and interrupting, normal sleep. In this condition the patient rises from sleep, disregards the ordinary significance of his environment and those in it, and behaves as if he were living in an environment conjured up by himself. If spoken to, not brusquely, he may reply in terms of the phantasy which he is enacting. If roughly stimulated, he may regain full consciousness, or pass into a trance state of immobility, muscular flaccidity and total lack of response of any kind. Patients in somnambulic states have sometimes met with unfortunate accidents, *e.g.* scalding, or even death from drowning. . . .

During the somnambulism the patient commonly lives through a vivid experience, little or not at all related to his surroundings, and therefore hallucinatory in character. By talking to him, not insistently, but in a persuasive attempt to enter into his experience, the patient may be got to describe the nature of the experience while he is still in the somnambulistic state. Although such patients appear to be 'walking in their sleep' they are not really asleep. Their perceptions are often acute."

---

[48] *Draft Criminal Code, (Law Com. No. 143), (1985), illustration 38(v).* See also the comments on the proposed code by R. D. Mackay in "Craziness and Codification—Revising the Automatism and Insanity Defences" from *Criminal Law and Justice* (1987), ed. Ian Dennis, pp. 112–118.
[49] *Ante* p. 110.

Robert W. White, The Abnormal Personality (1948), pp. 203–205, 288:

"A colour-sergeant was carrying a message, riding his motorcycle through a dangerous section of the front. All at once it was several hours later and he was pushing his motorcycle along the streets of a costal town nearly a hundred miles away. In utter bewilderment he gave himself up to the military police, but he could tell absolutely nothing of his long trip. The amnesia was ultimately broken by the use of hypnosis. The man then remembered that he was thrown down by a shell explosion, that he picked up himself and his machine, that he started straight for the coastal town, that he studied signs and asked for directions in order to reach this destination.

It is clear, in this case, that the amnesia entailed no loss of competence. The patient's actions were purposive, rational, and intelligent. The amnesia rested only on his sense of personal identity. The conflict was between fear, suddenly intensified by his narrow escape and duty to complete the dangerous mission. The forgetting of personal identity made it possible to give way to his impulse toward flight, now irresistible, without exposing himself to the almost equally unbearable anxiety associated with being a coward, failing his mission, and undergoing arrest as a deserter. When he achieved physical safety the two sides of the conflict resumed their normal proportions and his sense of personal identity suddenly returned. . . .

Hypnotism makes a very strong appeal to a man's delight in the marvellous and his desire for omnipotence. So strong is this appeal that many people would rather not be told that hypnotic phenomena are measurable and that they can be explained by straightforward psychological principles. It is more fun to believe that every vestige of the response to pain can be wiped out, or that suggested blindness produces the equivalent of real blindness, than to regard these as limited, measurable changes in the usual organisation of behaviour. As a result of this secret joy in magic and omnipotence, there has tended to be a large and important constant error in all thinking about the nature of hypnotism. This error is the belief that the *hypnotist, rather than the subject produces the phenomena*. The trouble began with Mesmer, who believed that he possessed a peculiar magnetic force which could be directed into his patient's bodies. It continued in those theories which represented the subject as a helpless automaton whose will, body and muscles were given over completely to the operator's whims and wishes. It continues today in the minds of those hypnotists who believe that the subject does not know what is going on, that you can fool him with statements which do not in the least fool an onlooker, that you can divide him up into dissociated pockets and hold private conversation with different parts of him. We should always bear in mind that the subject is still a person, even though he is participating in an unusual experiment and entering an unusual state. He has not become a fool, and it is he who produces the hypnotic behaviour.

. . . [There have been] various experimental investigations in which hypnotized persons were given suggestions to perform criminal acts. These experiments laboured under one great disadvantage. As it was not known whether the subjects would carry out the suggestions, the 'criminal acts' had to be arranged so that a really dangerous outcome was impossible. Rubber daggers and wooden pistols were used, the subjects being assured that they were real weapons. The outcome of all these earlier experiments can be condensed in a single illustration, amusingly described by Janet:

'A number of persons of importance, magistrates and professors, had assembled in the main hall of the Salpetriere museum to witness a great seance of criminal suggestions. Witt, the principal subject, thrown into the somnambulist state, had under the influence of suggestion displayed the most saguinary instincts. At a word or sign, she had stabbed, shot and poisoned; the room was littered with corpses. The notables had withdrawn, greatly impressed, leaving only a few students with the subject, who was still in the somnambulist state. The students, having a fancy to bring the seance to a close by a less blood-curdling experiment, made a very simple suggestion to Witt. They told her that she was now quite alone in the hall. She was to strip and take a bath. Witt, who had murdered all the magistrates without turning a hair was seized with shame at the thought of undressing. Rather than accede to the suggestion, she had a violent fit of hysteria.' (P. Janet, *Psychological Healing* (1925), Vol. 1, p. 184).

This example exposes the fallacy that has ruined so much experimental work with hypnotism: the notion that the subject is a helpless fool who has no idea that he is being deceived. It points unmistakably to the conclusion that hypnotized persons will not carry out suggested acts which are repugnant to them— not when they think the consequences are real.''

If one accepts the above psychiatric evidence, what should be the law's response to a defendant who, while under a hypnotic influence, commits a crime? Do you agree that such persons should have a complete defence as "the dependency and helplessness of the hypnotised subject are too pronounced,"[50] and that many persons are saved from being criminals by the force of their inhibitions which hypnotism removes? Should Mrs. Cogdon have had a complete defence?

2. *That even if insanity is not an issue, the public interest may not be served by a complete acquittal.*

Even those who would not go so far as to accept psychiatry's view of autonomic acts have sometimes expressed concern that certain automatons have been given absolute acquittals.

R. Cross, "Reflections on Bratty's Case" (1962) 78 L.Q.R. 236 at 238–239:

"Although they are still comparatively rare, pleas of non-insane automatism are becoming increasingly frequent, and questions may be legitimately raised concerning the sufficiency of the courts' powers. Is it right that someone who has been acquitted on the ground of non-insane automatism should inevitably go free? In *R* v. *Charlson* (1955) 29 Cr.App.R. 37 the accused was acquitted on various charges of causing grievous bodily harm to his son because he acted in a state of automatism which may have been due to a cerebral tumour. It is only natural to feel the deepest sympathy for the accused in such a case, but it is equally natural to question the propriety of an unqualified acquittal. One way of dealing with such problems would be to give the judge powers in all cases of a successful plea of automatism, insane or non-insane, to order the detention of the accused pending a medical inquiry, after which the appropriate order could be made."[51]

A similar approach to that preferred by Cross is to be found in the Scottish case of *H.M. Advocate* v. *Fraser*.[52] In this sleepwalking case it

---

[50] A.L.I. Model Penal Code, Tent. Draft. No. 4 (1955) Comments to s.2.01 at p. 122.

[51] *Cf.* N. Morris and C. Howard, *Studies in Criminal Law* (1964), p. 67.

[52] (1878) 4 Couper 70. But see now *Carmichael* v. *Boyle* [1985] S.L.T. 399.

was made a condition of discharge that the defendant should not sleep in the same room with anyone else. If medical evidence suggested that Mrs. Cogdon might behave similarly again during sleepwalking, what would an order have to stipulate in her case? Would the requirement of justice, as well as protection of the public, be served by ordering her, for example, to live alone? We have seen that as a result of *Sullivan*, epileptics, sleepwalkers, those suffering from arteriosclerosis and diabetics during hyperglycaemic episodes, all may be regarded as insane. It has been argued that this is inappropriate for two main reasons. Firstly, there is the requirement of mandatory commitment thereafter and, secondly, there is an undeniable stigma attached to a finding of insanity. Any changes to the status quo would, therefore, have to tackle both issues. The Draft Criminal Code does attempt to do so by providing for flexible disposal powers after a special verdict[53] and by renaming the special verdict itself. However, it is doubtful whether the proposed term "mental disorder" is neutral enough to have the desired effect.[54] Two options, therefore, fall to be discussed. One could continue to include some automatons within the "special verdict" but demedicalise the test and label,[55] or one could deal with all automatons outside the special verdict but qualify the acquittal as and when necessary by appropriate orders. Clearly there would be problems in empowering courts to make appropriate orders in these cases—but such an approach might well be preferable to including such automatons within the definition of insanity.

D. *Status Offences*

The requirement that there must be an act and that this involves voluntary human conduct has caused particular problems in the context of what are known as "status offences."

A crime can be defined in such a manner that no conduct is required, but the crime is committed when a certain state of affairs exists or the defendant is in a certain condition or is of a particular status. The following notorious case is a classic example of this.

R. v. Larsonneur (1933) 24 Cr.App.R 74 (Court of Criminal Appeal)

A French subject was permitted to land in the United Kingdom subject to certain conditions endorsed on her passport. These conditions were subsequently varied by a condition requiring her to depart from the United Kingdom not later than a certain date. On that date she went to the Irish Free State. An order for her deportation from the Irish Free State was made by the executive auth-

---

[53] In this context, see G. N. Eastman, "Defending the Mentally Ill" in *Psychiatry and the Criminal Law* (1986), eds. R. D. Mackay and K. Russell.

[54] Griew argues that a job of public education would be necessary. "Let's Implement Butler on Mental Disorder and Crime." [1984] C.L.P. 47 at p. 52. We would tend to agree with Mackay that this is unlikely to be successful: *ante* n. 48 at p. 115.

[55] See R. D. Mackay, *ante* n. 48 and *post* pp. 355–370.

orities of that country, and she was subsequently brought back to Holyhead in the custody of the Irish Free State police, who there handed her over to the police of the United Kingdom, by whom she was detained. She was convicted on a charge that she "being an alien to whom leave to land in the United Kingdom has been refused was found in the United Kingdom," contrary to Articles 1(3)(*g*) and (18)(1)(*b*) of the Aliens Order, 1920, as amended. She appealed against her conviction.

Marston Garsia, for the appellant:
"Under the Aliens Order, 1920, Art, 1(3)(*g*), read in conjunction with Art. 1(4), the mere fact of the appellent being found in the United Kingdom after the expiration of the time limited for her departure therefrom automatically made her an alien to whom leave to land had been refused. This in itself, however, is not an offence under the Aliens Order, 1920. For an alien to whom leave to land has been refused to commit an offence under Art. 18(1)(*b*) of the Order three elements are necessary:
  i. the alien must land in the United Kingdom;
  ii. such landing must be contrary to Art. 1 of the Order;
  iii. the alien, having so landed in the United Kingdom, must be found therein.
Therefore the mere fact of being found in the United Kingdom after the time limited for her departure therefrom had expired was not in itself an offence, unless it could be proved in addition that she landed in the United Kingdom in contravention of Art 1. Here the evidence showed that she had not landed at all, but that she had been landed by a superior force over which she had no control. Having thus come to be found in the United Kingdom, she was not guilty of any offence under Art. 18(1)(b)."

J. F. Eastwood, for the Crown:
"The whole point is whether the appellant was found within the United Kingdom; how she got here makes no difference at all. The word 'found' was used deliberately in the section so that if any alien who had no right to be here is here an offence is committed. By reason of Art 1(4) of the Order she falls within the same category as one who had originally been prohibited from landing."

Hewart, L.C.J.:
"The fact is, as the evidence shows, that the appellant is an alien. She has a French passport, which bears this statement under the date March 14, 1933, 'Leave to land granted at Folkstone this day on condition that the holder does not enter any employment, paid or unpaid, while in the United Kingdom,' but on March 22 that condition was varied and one finds these words: 'The condition attached to the grant of leave to land is hereby varied so as to require departure from the United Kingdom not later than March 22, 1933.' Then follows the signature of an Under-Secretary of State. In fact, the appellant went to the Irish Free State and afterwards, in circumstances which are perfectly immaterial, so far as this appeal is concerned, came back to Holyhead. She was at Holyhead on April 21, 1933, a date after the day limited by the condition on her passport.
    In these circumstances, it seems to be quite clear that Art. 1(4) of the Aliens Order, 1920 (as amended by the Orders of March 12, 1923, and August 11, 1931), applies. The article is in the following terms: 'An immigration officer, in accordance with general or special directions of the Secretary of State, may, by general order or notice or otherwise, attach such conditions as he may think fit to the grant of leave to land, and the Secretary of State may at any time vary such con-

ditions in such manner as he thinks fit, and the alien shall comply with the conditions so attached or varied. An alien who fails to comply with any conditions so attached or varied, and an alien who is found in the United Kingdom at any time after the expiration of the period limited by any such conditions, shall for the purposes of this Order be deemed to be an alien to whom leave to land has been refused.'

The appellant was, therefore, on April 21, 1933, in the position in which she would have been if she had been prohibited from landing by the Secretary of State and, that being so, there is no reason to interfere with the finding of the jury. She was found here and was, therefore, deemed to be in the class of persons whose landing had been prohibited by the Secretary of State, by reason of the fact that she had violated the condition on her passport. The appeal, therefore, is dismissed and the recommendation for deportation remains.''

Appeal dismissed

What is objectionable about convictions for status offences such as that in *Larsonneur* is that the defendant's actions are involuntary. There is nothing objectionable about the offence *per se* in *Larsonneur* and had Larsonneur brought herself voluntarily into the U.K. her conviction would have aroused no comment. It was the involuntary nature of her forced entry that aroused the controversy. In short, status offences are not objectionable if the defendant has control over the status. It would be wrong to have an offence of having a common cold but as Husak argues[56] it could be justifiable to have an offence of having a beard, as this is a process over which one has control. Under section 1(1)(*a*) of the Prevention of Terrorism (Temporary Provisions) Act 1976 it is a criminal offence to belong to a proscribed organisation such as the I.R.A. This provision is not aimed merely at prohibiting the "act" of joining the I.R.A.; it applies equally to those who joined before the date of commencement of the Act. This looks as though it is punishing persons for the mere status of being members of the I.R.A. However, section 1(6) provides a defence if one became a member before the organisation was proscribed and if one has not taken part in any of its activities while the organisation is proscribed. Thus, what is being punished in reality is a status over which there is control—evidenced by action (*i.e.* either joining the I.R.A. after the date of commencement of the Act or, if one joined before then, taking part in its activities).[57]

It follows from such reasoning that these "status offences" should simply be dealt with as another species of involuntary conduct to be dealt with on the same basis as the automatism cases already discussed.[58] If this is so, it follows that the requirement of voluntariness can be dispensed with if it was the defendant's own fault that he got into that status. It has even been argued that the decision in *Larsonneur*

[56] Douglas N. Husak, *Philosophy of Criminal Law*, (1987), p. 102.
[57] This is not to be read as a defence of section 1(1)(*a*) or of an offence of growing beards! All that is being claimed here is that such offences are not necessarily inconsistent with the general principles of criminal liability. Whether such a status should ever be criminalised in the first place must be assessed by the principles considered earlier at pp. 77–95.
[58] *Ante*, pp. 106–119.

was justifiable because it was her own fault that she was in the situation of being an illegal immigrant.

David Lanham, "Larsonneur Revisited" [1976] Crim.L.R. 276 at 278–280:

"[The defence of physical compulsion is] not an absolute defence. It may, at least with regard to certain types of crime, be defeated if the defendant has been at fault in bringing about the situation which has exposed him to compulsion. . . . It is the thesis of this paper that Miss Larsonneur was probably the author of her own misfortune and that the fact that at the last moment she was acting under compulsion was properly regarded as affording her no defence. . . . Miss Larsonneur's recorded confession is worth quoting: . . .

'A short time ago my sister Mrs. McCorry came to see me in France and invited me to visit her in London. On my arrival my sister introduced me to a Frenchman named René, who was living with her, and also introduced me to an Englishman named Harold Brown. René and Brown said they would arrange a marriage for me with an Englishman and they later introduced me to a man named George Drayton. We tried to get married at Guildford but the police stopped the marriage. They took my French passport from me but returned it the same day, telling me that the Home Office had ordered me to leave the country at once. Brown and René told me not to worry as they were going to get legal advice.

Next day I went to Ireland with Brown. We travelled as Mr. & Mrs. Wiggins. Brown said he had seen a solicitor, and that if I went to Ireland I would be in order. I naturally believed him. René and Drayton also travelled to Ireland, but not with us. There were difficulties in Ireland about marrying and eventually the police told me to leave Ireland by April 17. I wanted to leave Ireland at once, but René and Brown told me that everything would be alright, and that they were trying to find an Irish priest willing to marry us. I think it terrible that I should be the only one to suffer.' "

It is difficult to see that this justifies the decision in *Larsonneur*. What is meant by the defendant being "at fault"? Must this "fault" be related in some way to the offence charged? Was it in this case?

Winzar v. Chief Constable of Kent, The Times, March 28, 1983, Co/ 1111/82 (Lexis), (Queen's Bench Divisional Court)

The defendant was brought on a stretcher to hospital. The doctor discovered that he was merely drunk and asked him to leave. He was later seen slumped on a seat in the corridor and so the police were called. They removed him to the roadway, "formed the opinion he was drunk," and placed him in their car parked nearby. He was charged with being found drunk in a highway and convicted.

Robert Goff L.J.:
"Does the fact that the Appellant was only momentarily on the highway and not there of his own volition, prevent his conviction of the offence of being found drunk in a highway? . . .

In my judgment, looking at the purpose of this particular offence, it is designed . . . to deal with the nuisance which can be caused by persons who are drunk in a public place. This kind of offence is caused quite simply when a person is found drunk in a public place or in a highway. . . . [A]n example . . . illustrates how sensible that conclusion is. Suppose a person was found as being drunk in a restaurant or a place of that kind and was asked to leave. If he was asked to leave, he would walk out of the door of the restaurant and would be in a public place or in a highway of his own volition. He would be there of his own volition because he had responded to a request. However, if a man in a restaurant made a thorough nuisance of himself, was asked to leave, objected and was ejected, in those circumstances, he would not be in a public place of his own volition because he would have been put there either by a gentleman on the door of the restaurant, or by a police officer, who might have been called to deal with the man in question. It would be nonsense if one were to say that the man who responded to the plea to leave could be said to be found drunk in a public place or in a highway, whereas the man who had been compelled to leave could not.

This leads me to the conclusion that a person is 'found to be drunk in a public place or in a highway,' within the meaning of those words as used in the section, when he is perceived to be drunk in a public place. It is enough for the commission of the offence if (1) a person is in a public place or a highway, (2) he is drunk, and (3) in those circumstances he is perceived to be there and to be drunk. Once those criteria have been fulfilled, he is liable to be convicted of the offence of being found drunk in a highway. Finally, I turn to the question: Does it matter if the Appellant was only momentarily in the highway? In my judgment, it makes no difference. A man may be perceived to be drunk in the highway for five minutes, for one minute or for ten seconds. However short the period of time, if a man is perceived to be drunk in a highway, he is guilty of the offence under the section. Of course, if the period of time is very short, the penalty imposed may be minimal; indeed in such circumstances a police officer, using his discretion, may think it unnecessary to charge the man. The point is simply that the offence is committed if a person is perceived to be drunk in a public place or in the highway. Once that criterion is fulfilled, then the offence is committed."

Conviction affirmed

Again it could be argued that it was Winzar's "fault" he was in that situation. The report does not make it clear how he got to be taken to the hospital. Presumably he must have been found in some public place, or have summoned medical assistance when he was only drunk and not in need of such attention.

A different approach to a similar problem was adopted by the Supreme Court of Alabama.

Martin v. State, 31 Ala. App. 334, 17 So. 2d 427 (1944) (Alabama Court of Appeals)

Simpson J.:
"Appellant was convicted of being drunk on a public highway, and appeals. Officers of the law arrested him at his home and took him onto the highway where he allegedly committed the proscribed acts, viz. manifested a drunken condition by using loud and profane language. The pertinent provisions of our statute are:
'Any person who, while intoxicated or drunk, appears in any public place where one or more persons are present, . . . and manifests a drunken con-

dition by boisterous or indecent conduct, or loud and profane discourse, shall, on conviction be fined.' (Code 1940, Title 14, Section 120.)

Under the plain terms of this statute a voluntary appearance is presupposed. The rule has been declared, and we think it sound, that an accusation of drunkeness in a designated public place cannot be established by proof that the accused, while in an intoxicated condition, was involuntarily and forcibly carried to that place by the arresting officer.

Conviction of appellant was contrary to this announced principle and in our view, erroneous. It appears that no legal conviction can be sustained under the evidence, so, consonant with the prevailing rule, the judgment of the trial court is reversed and one here rendered discharging appellant.'[59]

Can this case be reconciled with *Larsonneur* and *Winzar* on the basis that Martin was arrested in his own home and therefore could not in any way be blamed for his resultant situation?

Herbert L. Packer, The Limits of the Criminal Sanction, (1969), pp. 78–79:

"There is a strong tradition in Anglo-American law of treating certain kinds of status, such as vagrancy, as criminal. To be a person 'without visible means of living who has the physical ability to work, and who does not seek employment, nor labor when employment is offered him' (in the words of a now-repealed California statute) may perhaps be characterized as engaging in a kind of omissive conduct: but common sense rebels at the use of the word 'conduct' to describe a condition that does not 'take place' but rather exists without reference to discrete points in time. It must be acknowledged that when the law makes the status of vagrancy or the status of 'being a common drunkard' (that phrase redolent of Elizabethan England) a criminal offense, it is departing from the restriction to conduct. Laws of this sort are in fact very much on the way out. Courts are giving them a helpful push on the road to oblivion. . . .

Offenses of status can best be understood as embodiments of the preventive ideal at a time when the criminal law offered no alternatives. Their demise is the result whatever the rubric under which it is accomplished of the development of alternatives that have permitted us the previously unavailable luxury of recognizing that such offenses are anomalies in the criminal law. There has always been pressure to rid the community of people who are perceived as dangerous, threatening or merely odd. That pressure until fairly recently, has had to find its outlet almost entirely in the criminal law. But the extraordinary expansion of the concept of illness, and especially of mental illness, that has taken place during the last century has furnished us another set of outlets. Now we can afford to insist on the doctrinal purity from which crimes of status represents so marked a lapse."

Powell v. State of Texas, (1968), 292 U.S. 514, 88 S.Ct. 2145, 20 L.Ed. 2d 1254 (Supreme Court of the United States)

Marshall J. announced the judgment of the Court and delivered an opinion in which the Chief Justice, Black J. and Harlan J. joined:

"[The appellant was convicted in a Texas court of 'being found in a state of intoxication in any public place' and fined $20. His defence was that he was a chronic alcoholic, and that his public drunkenness was therefore involuntary. The trial court ruled that chronic alcoholism was no defence.]

[59] See also *O'Sullivan* v. *Fisher* [1954] S.A.S.R. 33 (S. Aust.); *Achterdam* (1911) E.D.L. 336 (S.A.).

However, facilities for the attempted treatment of indigent alcoholics are woefully lacking throughout the country. It would be tragic to return large numbers of helpless, sometimes dangerous and frequently unsanitary inebriates to the streets of our cities without even the opportunity to sober up adequately which a brief jail term provides. Presumably no State or city will tolerate such a state of affairs. Yet the medical profession cannot, and does not, tell us with any assurance that, even if the buildings, equipment and trained personnel were made available, it could provide anything more than slightly higher-class jails for our indigent habitual inebriates. Thus we run the grave risk that nothing will be accomplished beyond the hanging of a new sign— reading 'hospital'—over one wing of the jail-house.

One virtue of the criminal process is, at least, that the duration of penal incarceration typically has some outside statutory limit; this is universally true in the case of petty offenses, such as public drunkenness, where jail terms are quite short on the whole. 'Therapeutic civil commitment' lacks this feature; one is typically committed until one is 'cured.' Thus, to do otherwise than affirm might subject indigent alcoholics to the risk that they may be locked up for an indefinite period of time under the same conditions as before, with no more hope than before of receiving effective treatment and no prospect of periodic 'freedom.' . . .

Obviously, chronic alcoholics have not been deterred from drinking to excess by the existence of criminal sanctions against public drunkenness. But all those who violate penal laws of any kind are by definition undeterred. The longstanding and still raging debate over the validity of the deterrence justification for penal sanctions has not reached any sufficiently clear conditions to permit it to be said that such sanctions are ineffective in any particular context or for any particular group of people who are able to appreciate the consequences of their acts. Certainly no effort was made at the trial of this case, beyond a monosyllabic answer to a perfunctory one-line question, to determine the effectiveness of penal sanctions in deterring Leroy Powell in particular or chronic alcoholics in general from drinking at all or from getting drunk in particular places or at particular times. . . . Appellant, however, seeks to come within the application of the Cruel and Unusual Punishment Clause announced in *Robinson* v. *State of California*, 370 U.S. 660, 82 S. Ct. 1417, 8 L.Ed. 2d 758 (1962), which involved a state statute making it a crime to 'be addicted to the use of narcotics.' This Court held there that 'a state law which imprisons a person thus afflicted [with narcotic addiction] as a criminal, even though he has never touched any narcotic drug within the State or been guilty of any irregular behaviour there, inflicts a cruel and unusual punishment . . .' *ibid*. at 667, and 82 S. Ct., at 1420–1421.

On its face the present case does not fall within that holding, since appellant was convicted, not for being a chronic alcoholic but for being in public while drunk on a particular occasion. The State of Texas thus has not sought to punish a mere status as California did in *Robinson*; nor has it attempted to regulate appellant's behaviour in the privacy of his own home. Rather, it has imposed upon appellant a criminal sanction for public behaviour which may create substantial health and safety hazards, both for appellant and for members of the general public, and which offends the moral and esthetic sensibilities of a large segment of the community. This seems a far cry from convicting one for being an addict, being a chronic alcoholic, being 'mentally ill, or a leper. . . . ' *ibid*. at 666, and 82 S.Ct., at 1420.''

Fortas J. (with whom Douglas J., Brennan J. and Stewart J. joined) dissenting:

''*Robinson* stands upon a principle which, despite its sublety, must be simply stated and respectfully applied because it is the foundation of individual liberty and the cornerstone of the relations between a civilized state and its citizens:

Criminal penalties may not be inflicted upon a person for being in a condition he is powerless to change. In all probability, Robinson at some time before his conviction elected to take narcotics. But the crime as defined did not punish this conduct. The statute imposed a penalty for the offense of 'addiction'—a condition which Robinson could not control. Once Robinson had become an addict, he was utterly powerless to avoid criminal guilt. He was powerless to choose not to violate the law.

In the present case, appellant is charged with a crime composed of two elements—being intoxicated and being found in a public place while in that condition. The crime, so defined, differs from that in *Robinson*. The statute covers more than a mere status. But the essential constitutional defect here is the same as in *Robinson*, for in both cases the particular defendant was accused of being in a condition which he had no capacity to change or avoid. The trial judge sitting as trier of fact found upon the medical and other relevant testimony, that Powell is a 'chronic alcoholic.' He defined appellant's 'chronic alcoholism' as 'a disease which destroys the afflicted person's will power to resist the constant, excessive consumption of alcohol.' He also found that 'a chronic alcoholic does not appear in public by his own volition but under a compulsion symptomatic of the disease of chronic alcoholism.' I read these findings to mean that appellant was powerless to avoid drinking; that having taken his first drink, he had 'an uncontrollable compulsion to drink' to the point of intoxication; and that, once intoxicated, he could not prevent himself from appearing in public places."

Affirmed

In the United States the Eighth Amendment to the United States Constitution prohibits the infliction of cruel and unusual punishment and on this basis it was held to be unconstitutional in *Robinson* to punish for the mere status of being addicted to narcotics. In England, on the other hand, it is generally assumed that Parliament could, in theory, punish for any mere status. It could, as did the criminal code of Stalinist Russia, make it an offence to be a relative of an enemy of the people.

The majority in *Powell* are drawing a distinction between punishment for a status and punishment for the manifestations of that status. Presumably they would hold it to be wrong to punish someone for having a common cold, but permissible to punish him for sneezing. Is this a valid distinction? This seems extraordinary and quite inconsistent with the view expressed above that it is the question of control and voluntariness that ought to be decisive in these cases. The dissenting judgement on the other hand does recognise this and focuses on the voluntariness of the defendant's actions. On this basis the question becomes simply whether Larsonneur, Winzar, Martin and Powell had control over their status or, which is deemed to be the equivalent, it was their own fault that they allowed themselves to get into that status.

E. *Omissions*

Most crimes are committed by positive action and thus the requirement of an "act" will usually be met by a positive act. But in certain circumstances a passive failure to act may be deemed to constitute the requisite "act." A failure to act may result in the imposition of criminal liability in two situations.

1. In conduct crimes the failure to act may itself, without more, constitute the crime. This usually occurs in statutory crimes which are specifically defined in terms of an omission to act, for example, failing to provide for a child in one's care,[60] failing to provide a specimen of breath under the breathaliser legislation,[61] and failure to accord precedence to a pedestrian on a pedestrian crossing.[62]

2. In result crimes the failure to act may contribute towards the harm specified in the offence and may thus, in certain circumstances, be deemed the requisite "act" for the purposes of the offence. This will only be so if the actor is under a duty to act—thus a father would be under a duty to rescue his child drowning in a shallow pool; his failure to act would constitute the requisite "act" of the crime of homicide. However, a stranger could with impunity watch the same child drowning; there is no general duty to act in English law. As Lord Diplock stated in *Miller*.

"The conduct of the parabolical priest and Levite on the road to Jericho may have been indeed deplorable, but English law has not so far developed to the stage of treating it as criminal."[63]

Thus criminal liability in these cases is completely dependent upon the existence of a duty to act.[64] It is to this, and other related problems, that we now turn.

1. Form of Duty to Act

It is not entirely certain when a duty to act will arise[65] but it is generally thought that the following situations cover the present English law:

(i) *Where there is a special relationship*:

The most commonly cited example of a duty to act is where there is a close personal relationship. Parents are under a duty to aid their small children; husbands and wives are under a duty to aid each other.[66]

In *Downes*[67] a parent, being a member of a religious sect called the Peculiar People, who believed in prayer rather than in medicine, failed

---

[60] Children and Young Persons Act 1933, s.1(2)(*a*).
[61] Road Traffic Act 1988, s.6(4).
[62] 'Zebra' Pedestrian Crossings Regulations 1971 (S.I. 1971 No. 1524), reg. 8.
[63] [1983] 2 A.C. 161, 175.
[64] In *Miller* (*ibid.*) Lord Diplock preferred the use of the word "responsibility" to "duty" (p. 179).
[65] The first draft of the Criminal Code Bill specified the circumstances in which one would be under a duty to act. (cl. 20(2)). These detailed proposals were dropped from the revised Draft Criminal Code; they are matters that must remain for the development of the common law. (Law Com. No. 77, vol. 2, para. 7.12.)
[66] *Smith* [1979] Crim.L.R. 251.
[67] (1875) 13 Cox C.C. 111.

to call a doctor for his sick child who died; he was convicted of manslaughter.[68]

It used to be asserted that the reason for the imposition of a duty of care in such cases was that the blood or marriage relationship was so strong as to generate a legal duty to preserve life. In *People* v. *Beardsley*,[69] for instance, it was held that a man owes no duty to act to aid his "week-end" mistress, as distinguished from his wife. However, such a rationale can no longer be accepted. The true reason for the existence of a duty in such cases must be the interdependence that springs from shared family life or close communal living.[70] In such a situation one comes to rely on the other members of the family and it is this expectation of assistance if necessary that generates the duty to act, rather than any blood tie. Thus in *Shepherd*,[71] it was held that no duty to act is owed by a parent to her 18 year old "entirely emancipated" daughter. In such a case there could not be the same expectation of assistance as with a minor child. Thus it is suggested that separated spouses owe no duty to each other, and with other relatives it is not a question of blood relationship but the assumption of responsibility[72] that generates the expectation of assistance and hence the legal duty to act. In *Stone and Dobinson* Lane L.J. did allude to the fact that the victim "was a blood relation of the appellant" but it is clear from his ensuing comments that the true basis of the duty to act was the fact that the appellant had taken the victim into his home and assumed responsibility for her.[73]

(ii) *Where responsibility has been assumed*:

If the defendant assumes responsibility towards another or voluntarily assumes a duty towards another, then he becomes under a legal duty to act.

R. v. Instan [1893] 1 Q.B. 450 (Court for Crown Cases Reserved)

The defendant lived with her 73 year old aunt. The aunt who had been healthy until shortly before her death developed gangrene in her leg. During the last twelve days of her life she could not fend for herself, move about or summon help. Only the defendant knew of her state and gave her aunt no food and did not seek medical assistance. The defendant was charged with manslaughter and convicted.

[68] In this case and in *Shepherd* (*post* n. 71) it was indicated that the duty was imposed by statute (Poor Law Amendment Act 1868, s.37—making it an offence if any parent wilfully neglected to provide (*inter alia*) medical aid for his child, being in his custody under the age of 14 years, whereby the health of such child had been or was likely to be seriously injured). In *Downes*, Coleridge C.J. deliberately left open the question whether there would be a duty to act in the absence of such a statutory duty. While many of the earlier cases were decided on this basis, it is now generally accepted that there is a *common law* duty to act in such cases but there is little express authority on this point.

[69] 150 Mich. 206; 113 N.W. 1128; 13 L.R.A.(N.S.) 1020; 121 Am.St.Rep. 617; 13 Ann.Cas. 39 (1907).

[70] Fletcher, p. 613.

[71] (1862) 9 Cox C.C. 123.

[72] See *post*, pp. 128–130.

[73] [1977] 1 Q.B. 354, *post*, p. 140.

Lord Coleridge C.J.:

"We are all of the opinion that this conviction must be affirmed. It would not be correct to say that every moral obligation involves a legal duty; but every legal duty is founded on a moral obligation. A legal common law duty is nothing else than the enforcing by law of that which is a moral obligation without legal enforcement. There can be no question in this case that it was the clear duty of the prisoner to impart to the deceased so much as was necessary to sustain life of the food which she from time to time took in, and which was paid for by the deceased's own money for the purpose of the maintenance of herself and the prisoner; it was only through the instrumentality of the prisoner that the deceased could get the food. There was, therefore, a common law duty imposed upon the prisoner which she did not discharge.

Nor can there be any question that the failure of the prisoner to discharge her legal duty at least accelerated the death of the deceased, if it did not actually cause it. There is no case directly in point; but it would be a slur upon and a discredit to the administration of justice in this country if there were any doubt as to the legal principle, or as to the present case being within it. The prisoner was under a moral obligation to the deceased from which arose a legal duty towards her; that legal duty the prisoner has wilfully and deliberately left unperformed, with the consequence that there has been an acceleration of the death of the deceased owing to the non-performance of that legal duty. It is unnecessary to say more than that upon the evidence this conviction was most properly arrived at."[74]

The real problem in these cases is one of determining the circumstances in which a person can be said to have undertaken a duty towards another. A ship captain would be liable for failing to pick up a seaman, or a passenger who had fallen overboard.[75] Depending on the circumstances of employment, an employer could be liable for failing to aid his endangered employee. And as LaFave and Scott assert:

"If two mountain climbers, climbing together, are off by themselves on a mountainside, and one falls into a crevass, it would seem that the nature of their joint enterprise, involving a relationship of mutual reliance, ought to impose a duty upon the one mountaineer to extricate his imperilled colleague. So also if two people, though not closely related, live together under one roof, one may have a duty to act to aid the other who becomes helpless."[76]

Thus in *Beardsley*[77] if the parties had lived together or embarked on a dangerous joint enterprise together, as opposed to an adulterous weekend, the defendant would probably have been held to have assumed a duty to act. Again, as suggested before, it is a question of whether, because of the relationship or the circumstances or both together, the parties have an expectation of assistance from each other. On this basis it is submitted that even a "week-end" mistress has a reasonable expec-

---

[74] *Stone and Dobinson, post,* p. 140 provides another good example of an assumption of responsibility generating a duty to act.

[75] *U.S.* v. *Knowles,* 26 Fed.Cas. 800 (N.D. Cal. 1864).

[76] *Criminal Law* 2nd ed., (1986), p. 204.

[77] *Ante,* n. 69.

tation of assistance from her lover who ought, accordingly, to be held to have been under a duty to act.

(iii) *Where a duty has been assumed by contract*:

A duty to assist others may arise out of a contract. Thus a lifeguard employed at a swimming pool to ensure the safety of swimmers cannot sit idly by while a swimmer is drowning.

In *Pittwood*[78] a railway gate-keeper who was employed to keep a gate shut whenever a train was passing was held liable for manslaughter when he forgot to shut the gate with the result that a train hit a hay cart crossing the railway line and killed a man.

Again, the basis of the duty in these cases is not so much the contract itself, but rather the fact that the contract is evidence of the assumption of responsibility creating an expectation in the mind of others that the defendant will act. The public expect railway gate-keepers to act and close the gates of railway crossings when trains are approaching. It is their reliance on this fact that creates the duty to act. The fact that the railway gate-keeper has contracted to perform these duties is merely strong evidence that he has assumed these responsibilities. It is submitted that the position would be no different if, during a strike, a volunteer offered (without any contract) to perform these duties. The fact that he had undertaken this responsibility would cause the public to rely upon his performing these tasks. On this basis, this whole category (along with the first category above) simply becomes a species of the second category, namely the assumption of responsibility.

(iv) *Where a duty is imposed by statute*:

As indicated, a failure to act may in itself, without more, constitute a criminal offence. Thus failing to provide for a child in one's care is a criminal offence contrary to section 1(2)(*a*) of the Children and Young Persons Act 1933, even if this failure to act causes no ulterior harm. But this same statutory duty to act may, if breached, constitute the necessary "act" for the purpose of an ulterior offence if further harm results from the breach of duty.

R. v. Lowe [1973] 1 Q.B. 702 (Court of Appeal, Criminal Division)

The appellant, a man of low intelligence, was alleged to have neglected his daughter, a baby of nine weeks old, by failing to call a doctor when she became ill. The child died some ten days later of dehydration and gross emaciation. The woman with whom the appellant had been living had four other children and was of subnormal intelligence. The appellant stated that he had told her to take the child to the doctor, but she had not done so because she was afraid that the child would be taken into care by the local authority. The appellant was charged

[78] (1902) 19 T.L.R. 37.

with manslaughter and cruelty by wilfully neglecting the child so as to cause her unnecessary suffering or injury to health, contrary to s.1(1) of the Children and Young Persons Act 1933.

On appeal the conviction for manslaughter was quashed on the ground that while the failure to act could constitute the requisite "act" for the crime of manslaughter, the requisite mental element for that crime had not been established.

Phillimore L.J.:
"This court feels that there is something inherently unattractive in a theory of constructive manslaughter. It seems strange that an omission which is wilful solely in the sense that it is not inadvertent, the consequences of which are not in fact foreseen by the person who is neglectful should, if death results, automatically give rise to an indeterminate sentence instead of the maximum of two years which would otherwise be the limit imposed.

We think there is a clear distinction between an act of omission and an act of commission likely to cause harm. Whatever may be the position in regard to the latter it does not follow that the same is true of the former. In other words if I strike a child in a manner likely to cause harm it is right that if the child dies I may be charged with manslaughter. If, however, I omit to do something with the result that it suffers injury to health which results in its death, we think that a charge of manslaughter should not be an inevitable consequence, even if the omission is deliberate."

This case provides an interesting illustration of the reluctance of the English courts to impose criminal liability for omissions to act. In the quoted passage Phillimore L.J. appears to be suggesting that there needs to be a higher degree of blameworthiness for crimes committed through omission, than for crimes where there has been a positive act of commission. This approach is only justifiable if positive acts are regarded as "worse" than omissions.[79]

(v) *Where the defendant has created a dangerous situation*:

R. v. Miller [1983] 2 A.C. 161 (House of Lords)

One night while squatting in someone else's house, the appellant lit a cigarette and then lay down on a mattress in one of the rooms. He fell asleep before he had finished smoking the cigarette and it dropped onto the mattress. Later he woke up and saw that the mattress was smouldering. He did nothing about it; he merely moved to another room and went to sleep again. The house caught fire. The appellant was rescued and subsequently charged with arson, contrary to s.1(1) and (3) of the Criminal Damage Act 1971. At this trial he submitted that there was no case to go to the jury because his omission to put out the fire, which he had started accidentally, could not in the circumstances amount to a sufficient *actus reus*. The judge ruled that once he had discovered the mattress was smouldering the appellant had been under a duty to act. The appellant was convicted. The Court of Appeal upheld his conviction on the ground that his

[79] See *post*, p. 137.

whole course of conduct constituted a continuous *actus reus*. On appeal, to the House of Lords:

Lord Diplock:
"The first question is a pure question of causation. . . . If . . . the question . . . to: 'Did a physical act of the accused start the fire which spread and damaged property belonging to another?,' is answered 'Yes,' as it was by the jury in the instant case, then for the purpose of the further questions the answers to which are determinative of his guilt of the offence of arson, the conduct of the accused, throughout the period from immediately before the moment of ignition to the completion of the damage to the property by the fire, is relevant; so is his state of mind throughout the period.

Since arson is a result-crime the period may be considerable, and during it the conduct of the accused that is causative of the result may consist not only of his doing physical acts which cause the fire to start or spread but also of his failing to take measures that lie within his power to counteract the danger that he has himself created. And if his conduct, active or passive, varies in the course of the period, so may his state of mind at the time of each piece of conduct. If at the time of any particular piece of conduct by the accused that is causative of the result, the state of mind that actuates his conduct falls within the description of one or other of the states of mind that are made a necessary ingredient of the offence of arson by s.1(1) of the Criminal Damage Act 1971 (*i.e.* intending to damage property belonging to another or being reckless whether such property would be damaged) I know of no principle of English criminal law that would prevent his being guilty of the offence created by that subsection. Likewise I see no rational ground for excluding from conduct capable of giving rise to criminal liability, conduct which consists of failing to take measures that lie within one's power to counteract a danger that one has oneself created, if at the time of such conduct one's state of mind is such as constitutes a necessary ingredient of the offence. . . .

I cannot see any good reason why, so far as liability under criminal law is concerned, it should matter at what point of time before the resultant damage is complete a person becomes aware that he has done a physical act which, whether or not he appreciated that it would at the time when he did it, does in fact create a risk that property of another will be damaged; provided that, at the moment of awareness, it lies within his power to take steps, either himself or by calling for the assistance of the fire brigade if this be necessary, to prevent or minimise the damage to the property at risk.

Let me take first the case of the person who has thrown away a lighted cigarette expecting it to go out harmlessly, but later becomes aware that, although he did not intend it to do so, it has, in the event, caused some inflammable material to smoulder and that unless the smouldering is extinguished promptly, an act that the person who dropped the cigarette could perform without danger to himself or difficulty, the inflammable material will be likely to burst into flames and damage some other person's property. The person who dropped the cigarette deliberately refrains from doing anything to extinguish the smouldering. His reason for so refraining is that he intends that the risk which his own act had originally created, though it was only subsequently that he became aware of this, should fructify in actual damage to that other person's property; and what he so intends, in fact occurs. There can be no sensible reason why he should not be guilty of arson. If he would be guilty of arson, having appreciated the risk of damage at the very moment of dropping the lighted cigarette, it would be quite irrational that he should *not* be guilty if he first appreciated the risk at some later point in time but when it was still possible for him to take steps to prevent or minimise the damage. . . .

The recorder, in his lucid summing up to the jury . . . told them that the accused having by his own act started a fire in the mattress which, when he became aware of its existence, presented an obvious risk of damaging the house, became under a duty to take some action to put it out. The Court of Appeal upheld the conviction, but its ratio decidendi appears to be somewhat different from that of the recorder. As I understand the judgment, in effect it treats the whole course of conduct of the accused, from the moment at which he fell asleep and dropped the cigarette on to the mattress until the time the damage to the house by fire was complete, as a continuous act of the accused, and holds that it is sufficient to constitute the statutory offence of arson if at any stage in that course of conduct the state of mind of the accused, when he fails to try to prevent or minimise the damage which will result from his initial act, although it lies within his power to do so, is that of being reckless whether property belonging to another would be damaged.

My Lords, these alternative ways of analysing the legal theory that justifies [the] decision. . . . provoked academic controversy. Each theory has distinguished support. Professor J. C. Smith espouses the 'duty theory' (see [1982] Crim.L.R. 526 at 528); Professor Glanville Williams . . . now prefers that of the continuous act (see [1982] Crim.L.R. 773). When applied to cases where a person has unknowingly done an act which sets in train events that, when he becomes aware of them, present an obvious risk that property belonging to another will be damaged, both theories lead to an identical result; and since what your Lordships are concerned with is to give guidance to trial judges in their task of summing up to juries, I would for this purpose adopt the duty theory as being the easier to explain to a jury; though I would commend the use of the word 'responsibility,' rather that 'duty' which is more appropriate to civil than to criminal law, since it suggests an obligation owed to another person, *i.e.* the person to whom the endangered property belongs, whereas a criminal statute defines combinations of conduct and state of mind which render a person liable to punishment by the state itself. . . .

[A] suitable direction to the jury would be: that the accused is guilty of the offence under s.1(1) of the Criminal Damage Act 1971 if, when he does become aware that the events in question have happened as a result of his own act, he does not try to prevent to reduce the risk of damage by his own efforts or if necessary by sendng for help from the fire brigade, and the reason why he does not is either because he has not given any thought to the possibility of there being any such risk or because, having recognised that there was some risk involved, he has decided not to try to prevent or reduce it."

Appeal dismissed

Lord Diplock's reasoning is, with respect, to be welcomed. We all bear a responsibility for our actions, even if those actions are unintentional. They are *our* actions. Where others are placed in danger from these actions, they expect us to "do something." There is an expectation of reasonable assistance, even if that only amounts to summoning help. Therefore, consistent with the general principle, we should be under a duty to act when we become aware of the danger. On this basis it is irrelevant whether the defendant's initial actions involved any fault. Thus if, as in *Fagan* v. *M.P.C.*[80] the defendant accidentally parks his car with a wheel resting on a policeman's foot, we would surely be justified

[80] [1969] 1 Q.B. 439.

in saying that the defendant had assumed a responsibility (namely to get off the foot); his initial action would raise an expectation on the part of the police officer that he would act. He is under a duty to act.

2. Performance of Duty

Assuming the defendant is under a duty to act, how much danger, inconvenience or expense must he undergo in order to fulfil his duty and avoid criminal liability?

United States v. Knowles, 26 Fed.Cas. 801 (No. 15, 540) (N.D. Cal. 1864) (District Court, Northern District California)

The defendant was captain of the American ship *Charger* when a seaman, Swainson, accidentally fell into the sea, and drowned. The defendant was charged with manslaughter on the ground that death had been caused by his wilful omission to rescue Swainson when it was his duty to do so.

Field, Circuit Justice (charging jury):
"Now, in the case of a person falling overboard from a ship at sea, whether the passenger or seamen, when he is not killed by the fall, there is no question as to the duty of the commander. He is bound, both by law and by contract, to do everything consistent with the safety of the ship and of the passengers and crew, necessary to rescue the person overboard, and for that purpose to stop the vessel, lower the boats, and throw to him such buoys or other articles which can be readily obtained, that may serve to support him in the water until he is reached by the boats and saved. No matter what delay in the voyage may be occasioned, or what expense to the owners may be incurred, nothing will excuse the commander for any omission to take these steps to save the person overboard, provided they can be taken with a due regard to the safety of the ship and others remaining on board. Subject to this condition, every person at sea, whether passenger or seaman, has a right to all reasonable efforts of the commander of the vessel for his rescue, in case he should by accident fall or be thrown overboard. Any neglect to make such efforts would be criminal, and if followed by the loss of the person overboard, when by them he might have been saved, the commander would be guilty of manslaughter, and might be indicted and punished for that offense.

In the present case it is not pretended that any efforts were made by the defendant to save Swainson nor is the law as to the duty of the commander, and his liability for omitting to perform it under the conditions stated, controverted by counsel. The positions taken in the defense of the accused are: (1) That Swainson was killed by his fall from the yard; (2) that if not killed, it would have been impossible to save him in the existing condition of the sea and weather; (3) that to have attempted to save him would have endangered the safety of the ship and the lives of the crew. If in your judgment either of these positions is sustained by the evidence the defendant is entitled to an acquittal. . . .

If you are satisfied that the fall was not immediately fatal, the next inquiry will be whether Swainson could have been saved by any reasonable efforts of the captain, in the then condition of the sea and weather. That the wind was high there can be no doubt. The vessel was going at the time, at the rate of twelve knots an hour; it had averaged, for several hours, ten knots an hour. A wind capable of propelling a vessel at that speed would, in a few hours, create a strong sea. To stop the ship, change its course, go back to the position where the seaman fell overboard, and lower the boats, would have required a good deal of time, according to the testimony of several witnesses. In the meanwhile, the man overboard must have drifted a good way from the spot where he fell. To these considerations, you will add the probable shock and consequent exhaustion which Swainson must have experienced from the fall, even supposing that he was not immediately killed.

It is not sufficient for you to believe that possibly he might have been saved. To find the defendant guilty, you must come to the conclusion that he would, beyond a reasonable doubt, have been saved if proper efforts to save him had been resonably made, and that his death was the consequence of the defendant's negligence in this respect. Beside the condition of the weather and sea, you must also take into consideration the character of the boats attached to the ship. According to testimony of the mate, they were small and unfit for a rough sea.

During the trial, much evidence was offered as to the character of the defendant as a skillful and able officer and as a humane man. The act charged is one of gross inhumanity; it is that of allowing a sailor falling overboard, whilst at work upon the ship, to perish, without an effort to save him, when by proper efforts, promptly made, he could have been saved. If there be any doubt as to the conduct of the defendant, his past life and character should have some consideration with you.

With these views, I leave the case with you. It is one of much interest, but I do not think that, under the instruction given, you will have any difficulty in arriving at a just conclusion."

The jury returned a verdict of acquittal

3. Distinguishing Positive Acts from Omissions

The distinction between positive acts and omission is crucial as criminal liability will only be imposed for the latter if a duty to act can be established. But it is not always clear whether one is dealing with a positive act or an omission. Consider, for instance, the following case:

R. v. Speck (1977) 65 Cr.App.R. 161 (Court of Appeal, Criminal Division)

Widgery L.C.J.:
"The offence was charged under section 1 of the Indecency with Children Act 1960, and that, so far as material, reads: 'Any person who commits an act of gross indecency with or towards a child under the age of fourteen . . . shall be liable on conviction on indictment to imprisonment. . . . ' The essential features of the offence therefore are that the person must commit an act of gross indecency with or towards a child.

. . . [T]he essence of the case was simply this. The appellant had been sitting down in a chair. A small girl of the age of eight, who was with other girls, came up to him and put her hand on his penis outside his trousers as he sat in the chair. She had left her hand there for a period variously estimated, but probably of the order of five minutes. By reason of the pressure of her hand the appellant had an erection. He said that he did absolutely nothing to encourage the child. He did not move. He stayed there placid. . . .

The . . . point of course was whether, having regard to the inactivity of the appellant himself, it could fairly be said that what has passed between him and the child constituted an act of gross indecency with or towards the child.

In considering whether that was or was not so the learned recorder had regard to the well-known principle that in general mere inactivity, mere absence of movement or action, does not amount to a criminal offence. . . .

In supporting this appeal today it has been said that this inactivity which I have described was not something prohibited by the section, and that in view of the sheer inactivity there was no proof of the essentials of an offence. . . .

Getting to the essential features of this problem, and accepting that for present purposes there was inactivity on the part of the appellant at all material times, we think that such inactivity can nevertheless amount to an invitation to the child to undertake the act. If a fair view of the facts be that the appellant has in any sense invited the child to do what she did, then the mere fact that the appellant himself remained inactive is no defence to it. . . .

Since in our opinion the element of invitation is important, and that is an element which the jury ultimately would have to consider, the ruling in law should have been that the conduct described by the learned recorder could be an offence if the jury took the view that it amounted to an invitation from the male to the child, either to start, to stop, or to continue this activity."

Do you agree that there was "inactivity on the part of the appellant at all material times"? Could it be argued that his allowing the girl to keep her hand on his penis was "an act"? Or that his erection was "an act"? If the latter, could it be described as "voluntary conduct"? Widgery L.C.J. held that "such inactivity can nevertheless amount to an invitation to the child to undertake the act" and that this would be sufficient to constitute the offence. But section 1(1) requires an *act* of gross indecency. Can an invitation to commit an act amount to the act itself? Is this simply an example of a distortion of a legal principle in order to uphold a conviction?

Katz has suggested that the test for distinguishing an act from an omission should be as follows: "if the defendant did not exist, would the harmful outcome in question still have occurred in the way it did?"[81] There is an omission when the stranger fails to rescue the child because the child would still have died even if the stranger had not existed. On the other hand, the defendant in *Speck* was clearly acting, as his existence was critical to the performance of the crime.

4. A General Duty to Act?

It is often asserted that liability for omissions ought not to be restricted to those areas where there is a legal duty to act. The man who sees a strange child drowning in a shallow pool of water and neglects to rescue him when he could have easily done so with no danger to himself, has killed that child as surely as if he had held the child's head under the water and ought to be punished to the same extent. If one of the objects of the criminal law and punishment is to stimulate socially approved conduct then the imposition of criminal liability in such cases would encourage people to act in cases such as these.

There are many arguments as to why English law has not introduced a general duty to act. The central argument relates to individual liberty

[81] Leo Katz, *Bad Acts and Guilty Minds* (1987), p. 143.

and autonomy. Our freedom should only be restricted insofar as it is necessary to prevent persons causing harm to others. Further, "the criminal law should recognise an individual's choices rather than allowing liability to be governed by chance, and the obligation to assist someone in peril may be thrust upon a chance passer-by, who may well prefer not to become involved at all."[82] It is further argued that the imperilled stranger has no *right* to be rescued and therefore the defendant is under no *duty* to rescue.[83]

These arguments are fortified by the claim that it is basic to our morality that it is worse to, say, shoot or strangle a victim than merely to look the other way when he is drowning. As Fletcher puts it: "The difference between killing and letting die, between creating a risk, and tolerating a risk, is one of the principles that sets the framework for assessing moral responsibility."[84]

Leo Katz, Bad Acts and Guilty Minds (1987), p. 145:

"[T]he consequences of an omission are generally less certain that those of an act. Holding somebody's head under water is more likely to kill him than not throwing him a life vest.

But there is a deeper, moral, reason why killing-by-omission offends us less than killing-by-commission. Compare these two situations. (1) Bert will die unless Berta gives him one of her kidneys. Berta is ailing and doesn't want to risk an operation. So she lets Bert die. (2) Berta will die unless Bert gives her his only kidney. She kills Bert and takes his kidney. In both 1 and 2 Berta brings about Bert's death to assure her own survival; in 1 she does it by an omission, in 2 by an act. Why are we less offended by her conduct in 1 than 2? Because in 1 she simply holds on to her own kidney, whereas in 2 she appropriates somebody else's kidney. We value personal autonomy and Berta's conduct in 2 offends against that value, while her conduct in 1 doesn't. Our sentiments about every other case of omission can be understood by analogizing it to these two cases. The person who fails to prevent harm that would occur even if he didn't exist simply fails to give away something he owns. The person who brings about harm that wouldn't occur if he didn't exist takes away something owned by someone else. Both persons may be callous, but only the latter offends our sense of personal autonomy."

Husak suggests the reason why it is worse to kill than to let die is because the defendant has more control in the former than in the latter situation: "persons generally exercise far less control over what happens as a result of their omission than as a result of their positive

---

[82] Andrew Ashworth, "The Scope of Criminal Liability for Omissions" (1989) 105 L.Q.R. 424, 425–426.

[83] Jeffrie G. Murphy. "Blackmail: A Preliminary Inquiry" The Monist 63, No. 2, (1980) n. 6; Lance K. Stell "Dueling and the Right to Life" 90 (1979) Ethics, 12 cites John Stuart Mill's distinction between perfect and imperfect obligations: "Duties of perfect obligation are those duties in virtue of which a correlative right resides in some person or persons; duties of imperfect obligation are those moral obligations which do not give birth to any right." (*Utilitarianism* (1957), p. 61).

[84] *Rethinking Criminal Law* (1978), p. 601.

actions. Control over a consequence is typically exercised by positive action."[85]

In addition to these arguments of principle there are many objections of a more practical nature to any idea of introducing a general duty to act. If a large crowd watch someone drown, would they all be liable? How much help would need be given? After dragging a drowning person from the sea, would one be under a duty to provide mouth-to-mouth resuscitation (irrespective of risk of disease) and then drive the rescued person to the nearest hospital if necessary? How much danger would the rescuer be expected to risk? What if the rescuer's efforts exacerbated the situation and worsened the plight of the imperilled person? Might not such a law be counterproductive in that fear of being forced to intervene might keep people away from places where they might be called upon to help?

On the other hand there is a strong case for the introduction of a general duty—or, at least, an extension of the present circumstances in which one is under a duty to act.

Andrew Ashworth, "The Scope of Liability for Omissions" (1989) 105 L.Q.R. 424, pp. 430–432:

"Individuals tend to place a high value on interpersonal contacts, relationships, mutual support and the fulfilment of obligations, and a society which values collective goals and collective goods may therefore provide a wider range of worthwhile oppportunities for individual development . . . The counter-argument to the conventional view is thus that a duty to co-operate with or to assist others should not be ruled out ab initio by an asocial and falsely restricted view of individual autonomy . . .

Individuals need others, or the actions of others, for a wide variety of tasks which assist each one of us to maximise the pursuit of our personal goals. A community or society may be regarded as a network of relationships which support one another by direct and indirect mean . . .

It follows that there is good case for encouraging co-operation at the minimal level of the duty to assist persons in peril, so long as the assistance does not endanger the person rendering it . . .

The foundation of the argument is that a level of social co-operation and social responsibility is both good and necessary for the realisation of individual autonomy. Each member of society is valued intrinsically, and the value of one citizen's life is generally greater than the value of another citizen's temporary freedom. Thus it is the element of emergency which heightens the social responsibility in 'rescue' cases, and which focusses other people's vital interests into a 'deliberative priority,' and it is immediacy to me that generates my obligation. The concepts of immediacy and the opportunity of help (usually because of physical nearness) can thus be used to generate, and to limit the scope of, the duty of assistance to those in peril."

Joel Feinberg argues that any person in peril becomes one's neigh-

---

[85] *Philosophy of Criminal Law* (1987), p. 100. Husak advocates replacing the *actus reus* requirement in criminal law generally with a "control principle."

bour for the purposes of the moral exhortation "love thy neighbour" and is therefore owed a duty.

Joel Feinberg, Harm to Others (1984) p. 133:

"[I]n certain basic respects the 'special relationship duties' of neighbors in the strict sense find parallels in the moral relationships that exist between any pair of human beings whose life paths happen to cross in a time of crisis for one. When it comes to *aiding the imperiled*, all people who happen to find themselves in a position to help—all who have by chance wandered into the vicinity, or 'portable neighborhood,' of the imperiled party—are his 'neighbors,' with reciprocal dependencies, expectations, duties, and claims."

Graham Hughes, "Criminal Omissions" (1958) 67 Yale L.J. 590 at 626, 634:

"But a view of moral responsibility is surely outmoded which imposes liability on the father who does not warn his child of the precipice before him, but not on a stranger who neglects to warn the child. . . . The law often lags a half century or so behind public mores, but the spectacle cannot be lightly entertained in a field of this importance. The duty to take active steps to save others, and a liability for homicide in the absence of such action, could well be based on the defendant's clear recognition of the victim's peril plus his failure to take steps which might reasonably be taken without risk to himself to warn or protect the victim. . . .

Conventional criticisms of the imposition of a duty to rescue are usually based on objections to compelling one man to serve another, to creating a fear of prosecution which might cause citizens to interfere officiously in the affairs of others, and to the feasibility of imposing liability on a crowd of spectators all of whom had knowledge of the peril but were too selfish to intervene. These objections, however, do not seem to have much merit. To the first, the reply may be made that the evil of interfering with individual liberty by compelling assistance is much outweighed by the good of preserving human life. The second is a speculation which would be difficult to support. The third point appears to pose a real difficulty, but it is no different from a situation which commonly occurs in offenses of commission. In a riot, for example, it is difficult if not impossible to bring all the participants to book, but this has never been considered an obstacle to trial and punishment of those who can be reached. If a crowd of spectators stands by and watches a child drown in shallow water, nothing seems objectionable in trying and punishing all who can be tracked down and cannot show a reasonable excuse. To think that such an example of selfish group inertia could exist in our society is distressing, but, if it did, there would be every reason for invoking the criminal law against it.

The time is ripe for Anglo-American systems to translate into legislative fact the modern consciousness of interdependence. Surely, it is not in socialist countries alone that the duty of a citizen to help his fellows in these situations of extreme peril can be recognized."

But quite apart from objections of principle there are very real problems involved in attempting to impose a general duty to act. In all cases of omissions there are problems in establishing the requisite causal link between the inactivity of the defendant and the harm that results.

Brian Hogan "Omissions and the Duty Myth" in P. Smith (ed)
Criminal Law: Essays in Honour of J. C. Smith (1986) pp. 85–86:

"[T]here is no way you can *cause* an event by doing nothing . . . to prevent it.
If grandma's skirts are ignited by her careless proximity to the gas oven, the
delinquent grandson cannot be said to have killed her by his failure to dowse
her. . . . To say to the child, 'You have killed your grandmother' would simply
be untrue."

The failure to rescue the drowning child does not "cause" death in
the same sense that holding his head under the water does. The causal
link is more remote. When we examine causation we will see that many
actions could potentially be classified as "causes" of consequences.
Thus if I invite you for dinner at my house and you are run over and
killed while on your way to me, then, in a sense, I have caused your
death. You would not have died but for my invitation. However, while
there might be causation "in fact" in such a case, the law employs various devices to limit such an endless chain of causation and to ensure a
much closer link between act and event before being satisfied that there
is *legal* causation. With omissions the device employed to limit causation is the requirement of a legal duty to act as in the circumstances
ennumerated above.

R. v. Stone and Dobinson [1977] 1 Q.B. 354 (Court of Appeal, Criminal
Division)

The facts appear from the judgment of Geoffrey Lane L.J.

Geoffrey Lane L.J.:
"[The two appellants were convicted of manslaughter and now appeal against
conviction. Stone and his housekeeper/mistress, Dobinson, admitted Stone's
younger sister, Fanny, aged 61, to their household].
[Fanny] was eccentric in many ways. She was morbidly and unnecessarily
anxious about putting on weight and so denied herself proper meals. She would
take to her room for days. She would often stay in her room all day until the two
appellants went to the public house in the evening when she would creep down
and make herself a meal.
In early Spring 1975 the police called at the house. Fanny had been found
wandering about in the street by herself without apparently knowing where
she was. This caused the appellants to try to find Fanny's doctor. They tried to
trace him through Rosy, [a sister of Fanny's with whom she had previously
lived] but having walked a very considerable distance in their search they
failed. It transpired that they had walked to the wrong village. Fanny herself
refused to tell them the doctor's name. She thought she would be 'put away' if
she did. Nothing more was done to enlist outside professional aid.
In the light of what happened subsequently there can be no doubt that
Fanny's condition over the succeeding weeks and months must have deterior-
ated rapidly. By July 1975 she was, it seems, unable or unwilling to leave her
bed and, on July 19, the next-door neighbour, Mrs. Wilson, gallantly volunteered to help the female appellant to wash Fanny. She states:
'On July 19 Mrs. Dobinson and I went to Fanny's room in order to clean her

up. When I went into the room there was not a strong smell until I moved her. Her nightdress was wet and messed with her own excreta and the dress had to be cut off. I saw her back was sore; I hadn't seen anything like that before. I took the bedclothes off the bed. They were all wet through and messed. And so was the mattress. I was there for about two hours and Mrs. Dobinson helped. She was raw, her back, shoulders, bottom and down below between her legs. Mrs. Dobinson appeared to me to be upset because Fanny had never let her attend to her before. I advised Mrs. Dobinson to go to the social services.'

Emily West, the licensee of the local public house, the Crossed Daggers, gave evidence to the effect that during the whole of the period, from July 19 onwards, the appellants came to the public house every night at about 7 p.m. The appellant Dobinson was worried and told Emily West that Fanny would not wash, go to the toilet or eat or drink. As a result Emily West immediately advised Dobinson to get a doctor and when told that Fanny's doctor lived at Doncaster, Emily West suggested getting a local one. It seems that some efforts were made to get a local doctor, but the neighbour who volunteered to do the telephoning (the appellants being incapable of managing the instrument themselves) was unsuccessful.

On August 2, 1975 Fanny was found by Dobinson to be dead in her bed. The police were called. On arrival they found there was no ventilation in the bedroom, the window had to be hammered open and the bed was so sited that it was impossible to get the door fully open. At one side of the bed on a chair was an empty mineral bottle and on the other chair a cup. Under the bed was an empty polythene bucket. Otherwise there was no food, washing or toilet facilities in the room. There was excrement on the bed and floor. It was a scene of dreadful degradation.

The pathologist, Dr. Usher, gave evidence that the deceased was naked, emaciated, weighing five stone and five pounds, her body ingrained with dirt, lying in a pool of excrement. On the bed on which she was lying were various filthy and crumpled bed-clothes, some of which were soaked in urine. There was excrement on the floor and wrapped in newspapers alongside the bed. There was a tidemark of excreta corresponding with the position in which her body was lying. At the mortuary, Dr. Usher found the deceased's body to be ulcerated over the right hip joint and on the underside of the left knee; in each case the ulceration went down to the bone. There were maggots in the ulcers. . . . Such ulcers could not have been produced in less than two or three weeks. The ulcers were due to the general poor condition of the skin and the protruding bones which would have had a greater effect upon her than a normal person. She was soaked in urine and excreta. Her stomach contained no food products but a lot of bile stained fluid. She had not eaten recently. He found no natural disease. The disinclination to eat was a condition of anorexia nervosa which was not a physical condition but a condition of the brain or mind. She had been requiring urgent medical attention for some days or even weeks. He said:

'If two weeks prior to my seeing the body she had gone into hospital there is a distinct possibility that they may have saved her; and three weeks earlier the chances would have been good. If her condition on July 19 was no worse than that described by Mrs. Wilson, then her survival would have been probable.' . . .

The prosecution alleged that in the circumstances the appellants had undertaken the duty of caring for Fanny who was incapable of looking after herself, that they had, with gross negligence, failed in that duty, that such failure caused her death and that they were guilty of manslaughter. . . .

[Counsel for the appellant] suggests that the situation here is unlike any reported case. Fanny came to this house as a lodger. Largely, if not entirely due to her own eccentricity and failure to look after herself or feed herself properly, she became increasingly infirm and immobile and eventually unable to look after herself. Is it to be said, asks [counsel for the appellant] rhetorically, that by the mere fact of becoming infirm and helpless in these circumstances she casts a duty on her brother and the appellant Dobinson to take steps to have her looked after or taken into hospital? The suggestion is that, heartless though it may seem, this is one of those situations where the appellants were entitled to do nothing; where no duty was cast upon them to help, any more than it is cast upon a man to rescue a stranger from drowning, however easy such a rescue might be.

This court rejects that proposition. Whether Fanny was a lodger or not she was a blood relation of the appellant Stone; she was occupying a room in his house; the appellant Dobinson had undertaken the duty of trying to wash her, of taking such food to her as she required. There was ample evidence that each appellant was aware of the poor condition she was in by mid-July. It was not disputed that no effort was made to summon an ambulance or the social services or the police despite the entreaties of Mrs. Wilson and Mrs. West. A social worker used to visit Cyril. No word was spoken to him. All these were matters which the jury were entitled to take into account when considering whether the necessary assumption of a duty to care for Fanny had been proved.

This was not a situation analogous to the drowning stranger. They did make efforts to care. They tried to get a doctor; they tried to discover the previous doctor. The appellant Dobinson helped with the washing and the provision of food. All these matters were put before the jury in terms which we find it impossible to fault. The jury were entitled to find that the duty had been assumed. They were entitled to conclude that once Fanny became helplessly infirm, as she had by July 19, the appellants were, in the circumstances, obliged either to summon help or else to care for Fanny themselves."

Appeal dismissed

This case (along with most cases where criminal liability is imposed for omissions) presents problems in relation to causation.[86] To be liable for manslaughter it had to be established that the "acts" (including their omissions) of the appellants *caused* the death of the victim. Obviously, in one sense, their failure to act did cause her death as the medical testimony established that Fanny's life might have been saved if she received medical attention. But in this sense the failure to act on the part of Mrs. Wilson (whose daughter was a nurse) and possibly even Emily West, was also a cause of Fanny's death. If either of them had summoned medical assistance Fanny's life might have been saved. If there was a general duty to act in English law could they too have been charged with manslaughter? This would surely be extending the notion of legal causation too far. The law generally attempts to limit the potentially infinite chain of causation by insisting that only operative or *substantial* causes will suffice. With omissions, similar results are achieved by limiting liability to the existing categories of duty of care. Because they had taken Fanny into their house and attempted to care for her, the

---

[86] Glanville Williams has gone so far as to say: "It revolts me to have to say that Mrs. Dobinson 'killed' Fanny." ("What should the Code do about Omissions?" (1987) 7 Legal Studies 92, 107.)

appellants had made themselves responsible for her. Because of this position of responsbility, their failure to provide her with the necessary care did become a substantial cause of Fanny's death. But because Mrs. Wilson and Emily West had not assumed this responsibility, they were further removed in terms of causation from the consequence; their failure to act was not a *substantial* cause of Fanny's death. Thus even if there were a general duty to act they could not be convicted of manslaughter as causation would not be established.

Thus, to summarise, it would be pointless to impose a general duty to act as the only people who could be held responsible in terms of causation would be those who owed duties to their victims under one of the recognised heads. It is only *because of* the special relationship, the assumption of duty etc. that causation is established. Without this pre-existing duty the causative link between the inactivity and the ensuing consequence would be too remote.[87]

Does this thesis, which would be fatal to any argument in favour of a general duty to act, apply in all cases? Would it apply, for example, to cases where, unlike *Stone and Dobinson*, there is only one person available to come to the rescue of the imperilled victim? Take the classic example of the father who fails to rescue his child from a shallow pool of water, and compare it with the stranger who fails to rescue a child from the same pool. It has been argued[88] that there is no difficulty in establishing a causal link in both these cases. Again, in one sense, the actions of both men did cause the death of the child. But for their failure to act, the child would have survived. But, again, the father's failure to act is a far more immediate and operative cause of death than the stranger's. Like the appellants in *Stone and Dobinson* the father has a special responsibility to his child. It is the failure to exercise this responsibility that is the substantial cause of the death. It is the existence of this duty that converts a mere cause into a legally sufficient cause. The stranger has no special responsibility towards the child and therefore no particular interest in the child. His inactivity is "a cause" of the child's death but because of his distance (metaphorically speaking) from the child his mere inactivity cannot become a legally attributable cause.

Arthur Leavens, "A Causation Approach to Criminal Omissions" (1988) 76 Cal. L.R. 547, 572–575:

"[I]t seems at first inappropriate to apply commonsense causation analysis to an individual's failure to engage in particular conduct. If one focuses solely on the circumstances of an omission at the time directly preceding the harm, the omission often appears not to have affected the at rest state of affairs. For

[87]; This point was recognised in *Miller* [1983] A.C. 161, when Lord Diplock indicated that a "passive bystander" could not be said to have caused a fire, or presumably any injuries sustained in the fire.
[88] Graham Hughes, "Criminal Omissions" (1958) 67 Yale L.J. 590 at 627; Hall, *General Principles of Criminal Law*, (1947), pp. 256–266.

example, a person sitting in the park while a nearby flower dies from lack of water is usually not considered to have caused the plant's demise, even if a full watercan sits nearby . . .

The difficulty in conceptualizing an omission as a casual force is that omissions do not seem to fit within the parameters of the physical cause and effect model. In the physical paradigm, there is a direct and identifiable chain of events through which the actor can readily be seen as intervening and changing what existed before. In cases of omission, however, the actor does not physically alter the status quo, but rather appears simply to permit the preexisting state of affairs to continue. Without direct physical involvement in the causal process leading to a particular result, an omitter seems no more causally responsible for the result than anyone else . . .

Such a view of causation is flawed because its inquiry is too limited. It depends on a definition of the status quo as the existing physical state of affairs at the precise time of the omission, much as if we took a picture of the scene at the moment before the omission and then compared it to a similar picture taken immediately thereafter, searching for a change in circumstances physically attributable to the omissive conduct. Our everyday notions of causation, however, are not so limited because we understand that the status quo encompasses more than the physical state of affairs at a given time. Indeed, in everyday usage the status quo is taken to include expected patterns of conduct, including actions designed to avert certain unwanted results. When, for example, a driver parks a car on a steep hill, it is normal to set the parking brake and put the car in gear. If the driver forgets to do so and the car subsequently rolls down the hill, smashing into another car, we would say that the failure to park properly was a departure from the status quo. This failure, not the visibly steep hill or the predicate act of pulling the car to the curb, was the cause of the collision.

Once we realize that a particular undesirable state of affairs can be avoided by taking certain precautions, we usually incorporate these precautions into what we see as the normal or at rest state of affairs. A failure to engage in the preventive conduct in these cases can thus be seen as an intervention that disturbs the status quo. When such a failure to act is a necessary condition (a 'but for' cause) of a particular harm, then that failure fairly can be said to cause that harm. In the above example, the driver's failure to park the car in a proper manner caused the accident as surely as if he had actually driven his car into the other . . .

[W]e do expect certain persons to engage in particular types of preventive conduct as a matter of routine. Because of this expectation, we perceive any failure of those persons to take prescribed actions as a departure from normality. While we do not see the bystander's failure to water the flower as the cause of its withering away, we take a different view of such a failure by the park's gardener. We expect that the gardener will take reasonable steps to prevent the flower's demise, that is, his preventive conduct represents normality. A departure from that status quo—his failure to water—is thus more than a necessary condition of the flower's death: it causes that result every bit as much as the act of an intruder pulling the plant from its soil.

Of course, society's expectation of particular preventive conduct could be described as merely another formulation of 'duty.'

A 'duty' sufficient to support criminal sanctions must be founded on both an empirically valid expectation that persons in similar circumstances will act to prevent a harm—the probability aspect of normality—and also a deeply ingrained common understanding that society relies on that individual to prevent the harm—the normative aspect of normality. Thus parents have a "duty" to prevent harm to their children because empirically, almost all parents act this way, and normatively, our society would consider it reprehensible if they did not. It is this combination of deviance—departing from a pattern of regular performance—and reprehensibility—being blameworthy—that makes us conclude that failure to act caused the harm."

There is a further problem with this attempt to create a general duty to act, a problem relating to *mens rea*. The concept of *mens rea* was developed within the context of positive acts of commission.

George P. Fletcher, Rethinking Criminal Law (1978), p. 626:

"Yet when we turn to the case of failing to avert harm, our concepts of intention and negligence no longer appear to be at home. If a nurse sits idly by and knowingly lets her patient die, can we say that the nurse intends the death of the patient? Does it matter whether the nurse fervently wishes the death of her patient? Regardless of the nurse's mental attitude, there is something odd about saying that in not rendering care she 'intends' the death of her patient. If two people are fighting and a bystander wishes that one of them would win and the other lose, it could hardly be said that by failing to intervene, the bystander 'intends' the favoured party to win. It is even more inappropriate to say that by standing by and failing to intervene, he 'carries out' or 'executes' his intentions. The most we can say in these cases is that the nurse or the bystander wants or wishes death to occur. But wanting something to happen is not the same thing as intending it to happen. The distinction between wanting and intending is that the latter is executed in an intervention causing harm. . . . This explains, I believe, the intuitive oddity of 'intending' a particular result by failing to intervene. By contrast, there is nothing linguistically amiss in 'intentionally' or 'negligently' breaching a duty where the duty consists in acting a particular way."

Why does Fletcher assert that the nurse does not intend the death of the patient? If her mental state is one of deliberately abstaining from action in order to cause the death of the patient, surely this can be described as "intending death"? In the same way were not the inactivities of Stone and Dobinson grossly negligent *with regard to the death of Fanny*, and not merely a grossly negligent breach of their duty?

Fletcher concludes the above passage by suggesting that while the nurse has not intended death or been negligent as to the death, if she was under a duty to act, she has intentionally or negligently breached her duty. In this way only those who are under a legal duty to act can be described as having *mens rea*. In *Morgan*[89] the House of Lords held that *mens rea* must exist with regard to the whole of the *actus reus* of a crime. The *actus reus* of homicide is "an act (or omission if under a duty to act) causing the death of a human being." If the accused has no *mens rea* in relation to causing death, but only has *mens rea* in relation to breaching his duty, how can he be said to have the requisite *mens rea* in relation to the *whole* of the *actus reus*?

In discussing whether there ought to be a general duty to act we have, until now, assumed that the purpose of such a general duty is that a breach thereof constitutes the requisite "act" for the purposes of some ulterior offence—for example, a failure to rescue becomes the requisite

[89] [1976] A.C. 182.

act for the purposes of the crime of homicide. It is, however, not necessary to go as far as this. The law could still issue its moral directive that people must render assistance to others, but avoid all problems of causation and *mens rea*, by the creation of separate offences imposing limited and complete liability for a failure to act. A failure to act would render one liable for this separate offence. In the United States the state of Vermont has such a provision.

12 Vt. Stat. Ann., s.519. (Emergency Medical Care):

"(a) A person who knows that another is exposed to grave physical harm shall, to the extent that the same can be rendered without danger or peril to himself or without interference with important duties owed to others, give reasonable assistance to the exposed person unless that assistance or care is being provided by others.

(b) A person who provides reasonable assistance in compliance with subsection (a) of this section shall not be liable in civil damages unless his acts constitute gross negligence or unless he will receive or expects to receive remuneration. Nothing contained in this subsection shall alter existing law with respect to tort liability of a practitioner of the healing arts for acts committed in the ordinary course of his practice.

(c) A person who wilfully violates subsection (a) of this section shall be fined not more than \$100.00."[90]

If such a provision were part of English law then defendants such as Stone and Dobinson could have been charged with this offence instead of manslaughter. Some might argue that this would have been preferable: in moral terms one can condemn Stone and Dobinson for neglecting Fanny; but can we really condemn them morally for *killing* Fanny? Of course if such a provision were introduced in England, without more, Stone and Dobinson would have been guilty of both this offence *and* manslaughter, their duty to act being now statutory in addition to the other grounds giving rise to their duty. Thus in England, section 1(2)(*a*) of the Children and Young Persons Act 1933 creates a separate criminal offence of neglecting a child for whom one is responsible. As the case of *Lowe*[91] demonstrates, the existence of such an offence does not preclude the possibility of liability for manslaughter if the child dies. If the new provision were to *replace* the possibility of any criminal liability for an ulterior offence, this would need to be made explicit. On the other hand, where there is a duty under one of the already established heads, we would generally want to continue imposing criminal liability for the ulterior offence. Thus the father who watches his young child drown in the shallow pool *ought* arguably to be liable for manslaughter (at least) and not merely liable for a lesser offence of failing to act. Such a result could easily be achieved by maintaining the present law and introducing the new provision with a proviso that it, by itself,

[90] Many continental Criminal Codes contain similar and even broader provisions. See, Hughes at n. 88, at pp. 631–634.
[91] *Ante*, p. 130.

will not give rise to a statutory duty to act for the purposes of any ulterior offence. This would still leave the problem of defendants like Stone and Dobinson unresolved. Should they be simply charged with the new statutory offence? Or should they be charged with manslaughter on the basis that they have breached one of the existing categories of duty? Should such a decision be left to prosecutorial discretion?

5. Punishment of Omissions

Under English law, once liability for an offence has been established, one is liable to any punishment up to the maximum, regardless of whether one's "act" consisted of positive action or an omission to act. This approach can be defended: the harm is the same in both cases and as the case of *Speck*[92] demonstrates, it is often difficult to distinguish between acts of commission and omissions to act.

On the other hand, it can be argued that omissions ought on principle to be punished less severely than positive acts and that this lesser level of punishment should be clearly articulated. One of the views considered earlier was that it was worse to "kill" than to "let die." If that view were accepted, such values, if they were not reflected at the substantive level, should be reflected at the punishment level. The lesser punishment should be imposed when the harm has occurred through a failure to act when action is required. Such an approach might also have the advantage of encouraging our courts to be less inflexible in their attitude towards the imposition of criminal liability based on omissions.

III Mens Rea

A. *Introduction*

1. Historical Development

A young child learns very early in life that to plead "I didn't mean to . . . " may evoke at the least a sympathetic response or possibly even complete exoneration from blame. We do, it seems, draw distinctions in everyday life between deliberate destruction of property or harm to another and that which is accidental. This distinction has become firmly established in the criminal law through the development of the concept of *mens rea*.

F. Jacobs, Criminal Responsibility (1971), pp. 13–14:

"Early law knew no distinction between civil and criminal wrongs. In the absence of a legal remedy the person injured, or his kin might avenge the wrong; and the act of vengeance might itself in turn be avenged. The law's main

---

[92] *Ante*, p. 135.

function was to preserve the peace by providing an alternative to self-help and private vengeance. To this end it reserved to itself the right of avenging wrongs.

No distinction was necessary at this stage between compensation and punishment. It is generally said that most wrongs were treated by early law primarily as matters for compensation. But to say this may be to read into the law more refined notions of justice than were current. The distinction between compensation as the principal object of the civil law and punishment as the object of the criminal law is a product of a system which attaches some importance to fault. But fault, at any rate as now understood, was immaterial if the wrong which had been done was likely to be avenged whether it had been done intentionally or unintentionally. In a society with rougher notions of justice than our own, the danger to the peace was the same whether the wrong was deliberate or accidental. If fault was disregarded, there was no reason for the law to make any distinction between compensation and punishment. To make the wrongdoer 'pay for' his wrong was simultaneously, as the ambiguity of the expression still suggests, to compensate the injured and to punish the wrongdoer. The measure of guilt was identical with the amount of harm done.

Implicit in this doctrine is a conception of man as an instrument of harm, rather than as a moral agent. Accordingly, some systems of primitive law punished not only the man who inflicted harm, but also the weapon with which he did it; and a beast, as well as a man, might be executed for homicide.

Slowly these attitudes were replaced with a different conception of man, a view of man as a moral agent, possessed of reason and free will, capable of understanding the social norms to which he is subject, and of choosing whether to conform to them. . . .

Before Bracton, attempts seem to have been made, especially by the clergy, to mitigate the rigours of the laws of the Saxon Kings by attaching importance to the actor's intention; but the absence of a voluntary or intentional act was regarded as a mitigating circumstance rather than exempting him from liability. The doctrine of *mens rea* makes its first recorded appearance in the laws of Henry I, compiled about the year 1118. . . .

[But] alongside the references to *mens rea*, we find more than once . . . the ominous phrase 'Qui inscienter peccat, scienter emendat.' 'He who does wrong unknowingly, must pay knowingly.' There runs through the whole of legal history, from the earliest times to the present day, this dichotomy between the principle of *mens rea* and the principle of absolute liability, or liability independent of fault."

P. Brett, An Inquiry into Criminal Guilt, (1963), pp. 37–38:

"There has been some dispute as to how long [the] association [between criminal guilt and mental fault in the lay understanding] has existed. Some authorities have regarded it as derived from Christianity, and have suggested that in the early collection of laws, dating from a period when Christian doctrine and ethics had not begun to influence the legal norms, no trace of insistence on moral fault is to be found. . . . My own inclination is to doubt [such] evidence of absolute liability. It must be remembered that it is based on the interpretation of old texts, and that we know little or nothing about the practice of those who were concerned with the everyday application of those texts to actual cases. We do know, however, that the printed word is not always followed in practice."

The origins of the concept of *mens rea* may have been obscure and tentative but it has since gone from strength to strength.

Morrissette v. United States, 342 U.S. 246 (1951)

Jackson J.:
"The contention that an injury can amount to a crime only when inflicted by intention is no provincial or transient notion. It is as universal and persistent in mature systems of law as belief in freedom of human will and a consequent ability and duty of the normal individual to choose between good and evil."

2. The Concept of Responsibility

The criminal law thus uses the device of *mens rea* to identify those who may fairly be blamed and, therefore, punished for their actions. Underpinning this is a fundamental premise:

United States v. Currens 290, F.2d 751 (3rd Cir. 1961), (United States Court of Appeals)

Biggs, Chief Judge:
"The concept of *mens rea*, guilty mind, is based on the assumption that a person has the capacity to control his behaviour and to choose between alternative courses of conduct. This assumption, though not unquestioned by theologians, philosophers, and scientists, is necessary to maintenance and administration of social controls. It is only through this assumption that society has found it possible to impose duties and create liabilities designed to safeguard persons and property . . . Essentially these duties and liabilities are intended to operate upon the human capacity for choice and control of conduct so as to inhibit and deter socially harmful conduct. When a person possessing capacity for choice and control, nevertheless breaches a duty of this type he is subjected to the sanctions of the criminal law."

Nicola Lacey, State Punishment: Political Principles and Community Values (1988) p. 63:

"This conception of responsibility [from H. L. A. Hart's *Punishment and Responsibility* (1968)] consists in both a cognitive and a volitional element: a person must both understand the nature of her actions, knowing the relevant circumstances and being aware of possible consequences, and have a genuine opportunity to do otherwise than she does—to exercise control over her actions, by means of choice. If she has not a real opportunity to do otherwise, if she has not genuinely chosen to act as she does, she cannot be said to be truly responsible, and it would be unfair to blame, yet alone to punish her for her actions."

According to this traditional view, because the defendant could choose to do otherwise we are entitled to hold him morally blameworthy and to punish him. Similarly, because it is difficult to say that the mentally disordered defendant could have done otherwise he is exonerated from blame and punishment.[93] Yet, as we shall see,[94] this approach is not without major difficulties in relation to, for example, the

---

[93] Because of the danger of repetition of harm in such circumstances, it might be necessary to retain control over the defendant. See *post* p. 345.
[94] *Post* p. 206.

punishment of reckless and negligent offenders. This conception, adopted in full, would also be a bar to the imposition of strict liability.[95]

An alternative conception of responsibility has been developed based upon the character of the defendant. "(A)ctions for which we hold a person fully responsible are those in which her usual character is centrally expressed. . . . The finding of a mental element such as intention or recklessness on the character model provides an important piece of evidence from which the existence of character responsibility may be inferred, given that single acts do not always indicate settled dispositions."[96] This approach does have certain attractions; not least it accords with our tendency to regard as significant the fact that someone acts "out of character" and may be more in keeping with the function of the criminal law as a form of social control. Nevertheless, it is unlikely to replace the capacity conception of responsibility because it looks too much like punishing people for what they are rather than what they do.[97] We will return to a discussion of the premises upon which *mens rea* is based at the end of this chapter.

B. *What is Mens Rea?*

J. F. Stephen, History of the Criminal Law of England, Vol. II (1883), pp. 94–95:

"The maxim, '*Actus non facit reum nisi mens sit rea*, is sometimes said to be the fundamental maxim of the whole criminal law; but I think that, like many other Latin sentences supposed to form part of the Roman law, the maxim not only looks more instructive than it really is, but suggests fallacies which it does not precisely state.

It is frequently though ignorantly supposed to mean that there cannot be such a thing as legal guilt where there is no moral guilt, which is obviously untrue, as there is always a possibility of a conflict between law and morals.

It also suggests the notion that there is some state of mind called a '*mens rea*,' the absence of which, on any particular occasion, deprives what would otherwise be a crime of its criminal character. This also is untrue. There is no one such state of mind, as any one may convince himself by considering the definitions of dissimilar crimes. A pointsman falls asleep, and thereby causes a railway accident and the death of a passenger; he is guilty of manslaughter. He deliberately and by elaborate devices produces the same result: he is guilty of murder. If in each case there is a *mens rea*, as the maxim seems to imply, *mens rea* must be a name for two states of mind, not merely differing from but opposed to each other, for what two states of mind can resemble each other less than indolence and an active desire to kill?

The truth is that the maxim about *mens rea* means no more than that the definition of all or nearly all crimes contains not only an outward and visible element, but a mental element, varying according to the different nature of different crimes. Thus, in reference to murder, the *mens rea* is any state of mind

---

[95] For a discussion of responsibility and strict liability see *post* p. 215. See also T. Honoré, "Responsibility and Luck" (1988) 104 L.Q.R. 531.

[96] Nicola Lacey, *State Punishment: Policital Principles and Community Values*, (1988), p. 66.

[97] It is recognised that this is a gross over-simplification of this approach; for a full discussion of the merits and demerits of the character conception of responsibility, see, Nicola Lacey, *ibid.*, pp. 65–78.

which comes within the description of malice aforethought. In reference to theft the *mens rea* is an intention to deprive the owner of his property permanently, fraudulently, and without claim of right. In reference to forgery the *mens rea* is anything which can be described as an intent to defraud. Hence the only means of arriving at a full comprehension of the expression *mens rea* is by a detailed examination of the definitions of particular crimes, and therefore the expression itself is unmeaning."

One could say, therefore, that the term *mens rea* is a technical form of shorthand for a number of conditions that need to be met in order for criminal liability to follow. Whilst correct, this does leave unresolved some difficulties.

What sort of conditions are to be included within the umbrella of the term *mens rea*?

Two approaches are possible:

(1) The term may encompass a very large number of conditions—the only linking factor being the presence of blameworthiness on the part of the accused. Thus, in addition to any particular mental state required, one would include amongst the conditions an absence of duress, or insanity or other excuse or justification. There could be no culpability if either the mental state required was absent or the defendant had some further legally recognised excuse or justification for his actions.[98]

(2) The term may, on the other hand, bear a more specialist meaning—the meaning that Stephen imputed to it. It may refer to the particular state of mind required for the definition of the crime to be satisfied. This has been further interpreted to mean that there should be a positive requirement of culpability (as opposed to an absence of excuse) in every case.[99] Excuses, such as insanity, infancy, mistake are dealt with separately—they are extrinsic to the concept of *mens rea*. There are, however, difficulties with this interpretation.

P. Brett, An Inquiry into Criminal Guilt (1963), pp. 41–42:

"If one regards the principle of *mens rea* as no more than a phrase for collecting together a number of excuses, the problem, in each case raising the matter, will be that of determining whether there is any reason for holding the accused to be free from blame. On the other hand, if one regards the principle as involving the enumeration of the conditions of imputability, one is forced to ask in each case whether those conditions are present. This in its turn, presupposes that we are capable of enumerating in advance the conditions of imputability,

---

[98] S. Kadish: "The Decline of Innocence," (1968) 26 Camb. L.J. 273, at 273–275; H. Packer, *The Limits of the Criminal Sanction* (1969), pp. 107–118 and H. L. A. Hart, "The Ascription of Responsibility and Rights," (1949) 49 Proc. Arist. Soc. 171 at 179–180, all adopt this negative approach to *mens rea*. See *ante* p. 101. Recent English decisions appear to reject this approach—see *post*, pp. 254–263.

[99] Glanville Williams adopts this interpretation: *Criminal Law: The General Part* pp. 30–31.

and I doubt whether this can be effectively done. . . . [I]n that analysis something always is left out.

My argument is not an unfamiliar one. We can recognise freedom from blame when we can see it, even though we may not be able to enumerate the conditions of blameworthiness. In much the same way we can recognise cases of injustice when we see them even though philosophers and jurists have for thousands of years, attempted to define the nature of justice without any evident success."

Despite the difficulties inherent in this approach, for the purposes of explanation in this chapter, the term *mens rea* will be used in its narrower sense of the mental state required by the definition of the crime. This accords with what is probably the majority viewpoint; a feeling that *mens rea* has developed into a requirement of positive culpability on the part of the defendant.

There is a further reason for the adoption of this approach. Later in this book we shall be developing a thesis that criminal liability ought to be based, in part, on the notion of blame. This blame element approximates more closely (but not entirely) to the broader idea of *mens rea* discussed above. It is useful to have the terminology to distinguish between this broad notion of blame, and one of its components—the mental attitude of the defendant. We shall reserve the term *mens rea* for this latter use.

What exactly is this mental element or *mens rea* that is required for so many crimes in English law? One thing is clear. *Mens rea* does not represent any single standard. There are degrees of *mens rea*. But what are these degrees? There are three candidates for inclusion:

   (a) intention
   (b) recklessness
   (c) negligence.

While there is great controversy as to whether negligence can rightly be classed as a species of *mens rea*,[1] there is wide agreement that both intention and recklessness are correctly classified as degrees of *mens rea*, and for many crimes it is unnecessary to distinguish between these two as the crime may be committed either intentionally or recklessly. For example, section 1(1) of the Criminal Damage Act 1971 provides that it is an offence to destroy or damage any property belonging to another "intending to destroy or damage any such property or being reckless as to whether any such property would be destroyed or damaged." But there are some crimes that can only be committed intentionally—for example, section 18 of the Offences Against the Person Act 1861 makes it an offence to wound or cause grievous bodily harm "with intent to cause grievous bodily harm." For these crimes it is essential to define intention with some precision in order to distinguish it from recklessness.

---

[1] *Post*, pp. 201–212.

1. Intention

(i) *The Law*

There is no agreement in English law as to the meaning of the word "intention." There are four main views.

(1) A consequence is intended when it is the aim or the objective of the actor. This is often called "direct" intent.

(2) A consequence is intended when it is the aim or objective of the actor or is foreseen as certain to result.

(3) A consequence is intended when it is the aim or objective of the actor, or is foreseen as a *virtual, practical* or *moral certainty*, or as the Criminal Code Bill defines it, "being aware that it will occur in the ordinary course of events."[2] (If this state of mind is classed as intention, it is sometimes called "oblique intention.")[3]

(4) A consequence is intended when it is the aim or objective of the actor, or is foreseen as a *probable* or *likely consequence* of his actions.

Until recently the courts adopted the broadest possible view, holding that all the above states of mind could be embraced within the term "intention."[4] Thus in *Hyam*,[5] for instance, Mrs. Hyam poured petrol through the letterbox of the house of her lover's new mistress and then ignited it knowing people were asleep in the house. She claimed that she had not meant to kill but had foreseen death or grievous bodily harm as a highly probable result of her actions. Her conviction was upheld with the House of Lords arguably ruling that her state of mind amounted to an *intention* to kill or cause grievous bodily harm.

As a result of the following decisions this view no longer represents the law. Foresight of a consequence as probable, likely or even highly probable (the fourth possible view expressed above) does *not* amount to intention. However, it remains somewhat unclear which of the remaining three views does constitute an accurate definition of the concept.

R. v. Moloney [1985] A.C. 905 (House of Lords)

The appellant and his stepfather, both of whom had been drinking heavily, engaged in a contest to ascertain who was quicker on the draw with a shotgun. The appellant's version of the facts was that: "I didn't aim the gun. I just pulled the trigger and he was dead." The trial judge directed the jury that the appellant

---

[2] Cl. 18(*b*)(ii) (Law Com. No. 177).

[3] See, for example, Glanville Williams, "Oblique Intention" [1987] C.L.J. 417. In the last edition of this book the phrase "oblique intent" was used (correctly) to describe the fourth view of intention in the text. This was correct in that it followed Bentham's original usage of the word. However, as this fourth view has been rejected by English law and as leading commentators are starting to use the phrase "oblique intention" to describe this third state of mind, this edition will follow the current practice.

[4] This was the view (*obiter*) of the House of Lords in *Lemon* [1979] A.C. 617 and was *arguably* the view adopted in *Hyam* [1975] A.C. 55. The alternative interpretation of *Hyam* is that the House of Lords was there defining "malice aforethought," the *mens rea* of murder—and not defining "intention." See generally, Buzzard, " 'Intent' " [1978] Crim.L.R. 5 and Smith, " 'Intent': A Reply" [1978] Crim.L.R. 14.

[5] *Ibid.*

would have the necessary intention to kill or cause grievous bodily harm "when he foresees that it will probably happen, whether he desires it or not." The appellant was convicted of murder and his appeal was dismissed by the Court of Appeal. He appealed to the House of Lords.

Lord Bridge of Harwich:
"The definition of intent . . . in . . . *Archbold Criminal Pleading Evidence & Practice* published in 1982 is . . .

'In law a man intends the consequence of his voluntary act, (a) when he desires it to happen, whether or not he foresees that it probably will happen, or (b) when he foresees that it will probably happen, whether he desires it or not.' . . .

But looking on their facts at the decided cases where a crime of specific intent was under consideration, including *Reg.* v. *Hyam* [1975] A.C. 55 itself, they suggest to me that the probability of the consequence taken to have been foreseen must be little short of overwhelming before it will suffice to establish the necessary intent. Thus, I regard the *Archbold* definition of intent as unsatisfactory and potentially misleading and one which should no longer be used in directing juries.

The golden rule should be that, when directing a jury on the mental element necessary in a crime of specific intent, the judge should avoid any elaboration or paraphrase of what is meant by intent, and leave it to the jury's good sense to decide whether the accused acted with the necessary intent, unless the judge is convinced that, on the facts and having regard to the way the case has been presented to the jury in evidence and argument, some further explanation or elaboration is strictly necessary to avoid misunderstanding. In trials for murder or wounding with intent, I find it very difficult to visualise a case where any such explanation or elaboration could be required, if the offence consisted of a direct attack on the victim with a weapon, except possibly the case where the accused shot at A and killed B, which any first year law student could explain to a jury in the simplest of terms. Even where the death results indirectly from the act of the accused, I believe the cases that will call for a direction by reference to foresight of consequences will be of extremely rare occurrence. . . .

I do not, of course, by what I have said in the foregoing paragraph, mean to question the necessity, which frequently arises, to explain to a jury that intention is something quite distinct from motive or desire. But this can normally be quite simply explained by reference to the case before the court or, if necessary, by some homely example. A man who, at London Airport, boards a plane which he knows to be bound for Manchester, clearly intends to travel to Manchester, even though Manchester is the last place he wants to be and his motive for boarding the plane is simply to escape pursuit. The possibility that the plane may have engine trouble and be diverted to Luton does not affect the matter. By boarding the Manchester plane, the man conclusively demonstrates his intention to go there, because it is a moral certainty that that is where he will arrive . . .

Starting from the proposition . . . that the mental element in murder requires proof of a intention to kill or cause really serious injury, the first fundamental question to be answered is whether there is any rule of substantive law that foresight by the accused of one of those eventualities as a probable consequence of his voluntary act, where the probability can be defined as exceeding a certain degree, is equivalent or alternative to the necessary intention. I would answer this question in the negative . . .

The irrationality of any such rule of substantive law stems from the fact that it is impossible to define degrees of probability, in any of the infinite variety of situations arising in human affairs, in precise or scientific terms. . . .

I am firmly of opinion that foresight of consequences, as an element bearing on the issue of intention in murder, or indeed any other crime of specific intent, belongs, not to the substantive law, but to the law of evidence. Here again I am happy to find myself aligned with my noble and learned friend, Lord Hailsham of St. Marylebone L.C., in *Reg.* v. *Hyam* [1975] A.C. 55, where he said, at p. 65: 'Knowledge or foresight is at the best material which entitles or compels a jury to draw the necessary inference as to intention.' . . .

I think we should now no longer speak of presumptions in this context but rather of inferences. In the old presumption that a man intends the natural and probable consequences of his acts the important word is 'natural.' This word conveys the idea that in the ordinary course of events a certain act will lead to a certain consequence unless something unexpected supervenes to prevent it. One might almost say that, if a consequence is natural, it is really otiose to speak of it as also being probable . . .

In the rare cases in which it is necessary to direct a jury by reference to foresight of consequences, I do not believe it is necessary for the judge to do more than invite the jury to consider two questions. First, was death or really serious injury in a murder case (or whatever relevant consequence must be proved to have been intended in any other case) a natural consequence of the defendant's voluntary act? Secondly, did the defendant foresee that consequence as being a natural consequence of his act? The jury should then be told that if they answer yes to both questions it is a proper inference for them to draw that he intended that consequence."

Appeal allowed

R. v. Hancock and Shankland [1986] A.C. 455 (House of Lords)

The defendants, two striking miners, pushed a large lump of concrete from a bridge on to a convoy of cars below carrying a miner to work. The concrete struck a taxi's windscreen and killed the driver. The defendants claimed they had not meant to kill or cause serious injury. Their plan was to drop the concrete in the middle lane of the carriageway while the convoy was in the nearside lane. Their aim was to frighten the miner or block the road in order to prevent him from getting to work. The defendants were convicted of murder. The Court of Appeal allowed their appeals and substituted verdicts of manslaughter. The Crown appealed to the House of Lords.

Lord Scarman:
"[T]he cases to which the guidance was expressly limited by the House in *Moloney*, *i.e.* the 'rare cases' in which it is necessary to direct a jury by reference to foresight of consequences, are unlikely to be so rare or so exceptional as the House believed. As the House then recognised, the guidelines as formulated are applicable to cases of any crime of specific intent, and not merely murder. But further and disturbingly crimes of violence where the purpose is by open violence to protest, demonstrate, obstruct, or frighten are on the increase. Violence is used by some as a means of public communication. Inevitably there will be casualties: and inevitably death will on occasions result. If death results, is the perpetrator of the violent act guilty of murder? It will depend on his intent. . . .

The question for the House is, therefore, whether the *Moloney* guidelines are sound. . . .

[T]he House [in *Moloney*] made it absolutely clear that foresight of consequences is no more than evidence of the existence of the intent; it must be considered, and its weight assessed, together with all the evidence in the case.

Foresight does not necessarily imply the existence of intention, though it may be a fact from which when considered with all the other evidence a jury may think it right to infer the necessary intent. . . .

[T]he House [in *Moloney*] emphasised that the probability of the result of an act is an important matter for the jury to consider and can be critical in their determining whether the result was intended . . .

[Lord Bridge of Harwich in *Moloney*] omitted any reference in his guidelines to probability. He did so because he included probability in the meaning which he attributed to 'natural.' My Lords, I very much doubt whether a jury without further explanation would think that 'probable' added nothing to 'natural.' I agree with the Court of Appeal that the probability of a consequence is a factor of sufficient importance to be drawn specifically to the attention of the jury and to be explained. In a murder case where it is necessary to direct a jury on the issue of intent by reference to foresight of consequences the probability of death or serious injury resulting from the act done may be critically important. Its importance will depend on the degree of probability: if the likelihood that death or serious injury will result is high, the probability of that result may, as Lord Bridge of Harwich noted and the Lord Chief Justice emphasised, be seen as overwhelming evidence of the existence of the intent to kill or injure. Failure to explain the relevance of probability may, therefore, mislead a jury into thinking that it is of little or no importance and into concentrating exclusively on the causal link between the act and its consequence. In framing his guidelines Lord Bridge of Harwich emphasised that he did not believe it necessary to do more than to invite the jury to consider his two questions. Neither question makes any reference (beyond the use of the word 'natural') to probability. I am not surprised that when in this case the judge faithfully followed this guidance the jury found themselves perplexed and unsure. In my judgment, therefore, the *Moloney* guidelines as they stand are unsafe and misleading. They require a reference to probability. They also require an explanation that the greater the probability of a consequence the more likely it is that the consequence was foreseen and that if that consequence was foreseen the greater the probability is that that consequence was also intended. But juries also require to be reminded that the decision is theirs to be reached upon a consideration of all the evidence.

Accordingly, I accept the view of the Court of Appeal that the *Moloney* guidelines are defective. I am, however, not persuaded that guidelines of general application, albeit within a limited class of case, are wise or desirable . . .

I fear that their elaborate structure may well create difficulty. Juries are not chosen for their understanding of a logical and phased process leading by question and answer to a conclusion but are expected to exercise practical common sense. . . .

In a case where foresight of a consequence is part of the evidence supporting a prosecution submission that the accused intended the consequence, the judge, if he thinks some general observations would help the jury, could well, having in mind section 8 of the Criminal Justice Act 1967, emphasise that the probability, however high, of a consequence is only a factor, though it may in some cases be a very significant factor, to be considered with all the other evidence in determining whether the accused intended to bring it about. The distinction between the offence and the evidence relied on to prove it is vital. Lord Bridge's speech in *Moloney* made the distinction crystal clear: it would be a disservice to the law to allow his guidelines to mislead a jury into overlooking it.

For these reasons I would hold that the *Moloney* guidelines are defective and should not be used as they stand without further explanation."

Appeal dismissed

R. v. Nedrick [1986] 1 W.L.R. 1025 (Court of Appeal, Criminal Division)

The appellant poured paraffin through the letterbox of a house and set light to it. The house caught fire and a child died. The appellant claimed that he did not want anyone to die. He was convicted of murder and appealed.

Lord Lane C.J.:
"What then does a jury have to decide so far as the mental element in murder is concerned? It simply has to decide whether the defendant intended to kill or do serious bodily harm. In order to reach that decision the jury must pay regard to all the relevant circumstances, including what the defendant himself said and did.

In the great majority of cases a direction to that effect will be enough, particularly where the defendant's actions amounted to a direct attack upon his victim, because in such cases the evidence relating to the defendant's desire or motive will be clear and his intent will have been the same as his desire or motive. But in some cases, of which this is one, the defendant does an act which is manifestly dangerous and as a result someone dies. The primary desire or motive of the defendant may not have been to harm that person, or indeed anyone. In that situation what further directions should a jury be given as to the mental state which they must find to exist in the defendant if murder is to be proved?

We have endeavoured to crystallise the effect of their Lordships' speeches in *Reg.* v. *Moloney* and *Reg.* v. *Hancock* in a way which we hope may be helpful to judges who have to handle this type of case.

It may be advisable first of all to explain to the jury that a man may intend to achieve a certain result whilst at the same time not desiring it to come about . . .

When determining whether the defendant had the necessary intent, it may therefore be helpful for a jury to ask themselves two questions. (1) How probable was the consequence which resulted from the defendant's voluntary act? (2) Did he foresee that consequence?

If he did not appreciate that death or serious harm was likely to result from his act, he cannot have intended to bring it about. If he did, but thought that the risk to which he was exposing the person killed was only slight, then it may be easy for the jury to conclude that he did not intend to bring about that result. On the other hand, if the jury are satisfied that at the material time the defendant recognised that death or serious harm would be virtually certain (barring some unforeseen intervention) to result from his voluntary act, then that is a fact from which they may find it easy to infer that he intended to kill or do serious bodily harm, even though he may not have had any desire to achieve that result.

As Lord Bridge of Harwich said in *Reg.* v. *Moloney* [1985] A.C. 905, 925: 'the probability of the consequence taken to have been foreseen must be little short of overwhelming before it will suffice to establish the necessary intent.' At p. 926 he uses the expression 'moral certainty'; he said, at p. 929 'will lead to a certain consequence unless something unexpected supervenes to prevent it.'

Where the charge is murder and in the rare cases where the simple direction is not enough, the jury should be directed that they are not entitled to infer the necessary intention, unless they feel sure that death or serious bodily harm was a virtual certainty (barring some unforeseen intervention) as a result of the defendant's actions and that the defendant appreciated that such was the case.

Where a man realises that it is for all practical purposes inevitable that his actions will result in death or serious harm, the inference may be irresistible that he intended that result, however little he may have desired or wished it to happen. The decision is one for the jury to be reached upon a consideration of all the evidence."

Appeal allowed
Conviction of manslaughter substituted

R. v. Walker and Hayles (1990) 90 Cr.App.R. 226 (Court of Appeal, Criminal Division)

The appellants threw their victim from a third floor balcony. At their trial for attempted murder the trial judge directed the jury that they could infer intention if there was a high degree of probability that the victim would be killed and if the defendants knew "quite well that in doing that there was a high degree of probability" that the victim would be killed. The appellants appealed on the ground that the trial judge was confusing foresight of death with an intention to kill and should have directed the jury in the *Nedrick* terms of "virtual certainty".

Lloyd L.J.:
"By the use of the word 'entitled' [the recorder] was making it sufficiently clear to the jury that the question whether they drew the inference or not was a question for them . . . So we reject the submission that the recorder was equating foresight with intent, or that he may have given that impression to the jury. He was perfectly properly saying that foresight was something from which the jury could infer intent. He was treating the question as part of the law of evidence, not as part of the substantive law of attempted murder . . .

Counsel submitted that virtual certainty is the correct test in all cases where the simple direction is not enough, and that to substitute high degree of probability is to water down that test. . . .

[W]e do not accept that the reference to 'very high degree of probability' was a misdirection. The truth is, as Messrs. Smith and Hogan point out in *Criminal Law*, 6th ed., at p. 59, that once one departs from absolute certainty, there is bound to be a question of degree. We do not regard the difference of degree, if there is one, between very high degree of probability on the one hand and virtual certainty on the other as being sufficient to render what the recorder said a misdirection . . . Reading Lord Scarman's speech in *Hancock* and [reading] *Nedrick* we are not persuaded that it is only when death is a virtual certainty that the jury can infer intention to kill. Providing the dividing line between intention and recklessness is never blurred, and provided it is made clear, as it was here, that it is a question for the jury to infer from the degree of probability in the particular case whether the defendant intended to kill, we would not regard the use of the words 'very high degree of probability' as a misdirection.

To avoid any misunderstanding, we repeat that in the great majority of cases of attempted murder, as in murder, the simple direction will suffice, without any reference to foresight. In the rare case where an expanded direction is required in terms of foresight, courts should continue to use virtual certainty as the test, rather than high probability."

Appeals dismissed

The following propositions would seem to appear from these cases:

1. Wanting Result

A defendant who wants a result to happen—when it is his aim or objective ("direct" intention in the first view above)—clearly intends that result. This is so even if the chances of the result occurring are slim: if the defendant shoots at his victim half a mile away knowing he could easily miss, he still intends to kill because that is what he is trying to do. Lord Reid has expressed this point in terms of a golfing analogy:

"If I say I intend to reach the green, people will believe me although we all know that the odds are ten to one against my succeeding."[6] However, no matter how much a person may want to achieve a result, he can only be said to intend it if he recognises that there is a chance of achieving it. If one does not believe that the consequence is a possible result of one's actions one can hardly be said to be trying to achieve it.[7]

2. Dual purposes

A defendant can have two or more purposes in acting. Both purposes are intended. This simple point has not always been recognised as the following well known case demonstrates.

R. v. Steane [1947] K.B. 997 (Court of Criminal Appeal)

The appellant, a British film actor was resident and working in Germany before World War II. When war broke out he was arrested. As a result of threats to place his wife and children in a concentration camp and physical threats to himself, the appellant reluctantly agreed to broadcast on the radio for the Germans. For four months he read the news three times a day. After the war he was convicted of doing acts likely to assist the enemy, with intent to assist the enemy, contrary to Regulation 2A of the Defence (General) Regulations 1939 and was sentenced to three years' imprisonment. He appealed against conviction.

Goddard L.C.J.:
"The appellant also asserted . . . that he never had the slightest idea or intention of assisting the enemy and what he did was done to save his wife and children. . . .
The . . . difficult question that arises, however, is in connection with the direction to the jury with regard to whether these acts were done with the intention of assisting the enemy. . . . While no doubt the motive of a man's act and his intention in doing the act are in law different things, it is none the less true that in many offences a specific intention is a necessary ingredient, and the jury have to be satisfied that a particular act was done with that specific intent. . . .
An illustration . . . would be if a person deliberately took down his blackout curtains or shutters with the result that light appeared on the outside of his house, perhaps during an air raid; it might well be that if no evidence or explanation were given and if all that was proved was that during that raid the prisoner exposed lights by a deliberate act, a jury could infer that he intended to signal or assist the enemy. But if the evidence in the case showed, for instance, that he or someone was overcome by heat and that he tore down the blackout to ventilate the room, the jury would certainly have to consider whether his act was done with intent to assist the enemy or with some other intent, so that while he would be guilty of an offence against the Blackout Regulations, he would not be guilty of the offence of attempting to assist the enemy. . . .
British soldiers who were set to work on the Burma road, or if invasion had unhappily taken place, British subjects who might have been set to work by the enemy digging trenches would undoubtedly be doing acts likely to assist the enemy. It would be unnecessary surely in their cases to consider any of the niceties of the law relating to duress because no jury would find that merely by

---

[6] *Gollins* v. *Gollins* [1964] A.C. 644 at p. 664.
[7] R. A. Duff, "The Obscure Intentions of the House of Lords" [1986] Crim.L.R. 771, 779.

doing this work they were intending to assist the enemy. In our opinion it is impossible to say that where an act was done by a person in subjection to the power of others, especially if that other be a brutal enemy, an inference that he intended the natural consequences of his acts must be drawn merely from the fact that he did them. The guilty intent cannot be presumed and must be proved. The proper direction to the jury in this case would have been that it was for the prosecution to prove the criminal intent, and that while the jury would be entitled to presume that intent if they thought that the act was done as the result of the free uncontrolled action of the accused, they would not be entitled to presume it if the circumstances showed that the act was done in subjection to the power of the enemy or was as equally consistent with an innocent intent as with a criminal intent, for example, a desire to save his wife and children from a concentration camp. They should only convict if satisfied by the evidence that the act complained of was in fact done to assist the enemy and if there was doubt about the matter the prisoner was entitled to be acquitted."

Conviction quashed

In this case the appellant, Steane, clearly foresaw that his actions would almost certainly assist the enemy, yet because it was not his aim or purpose to assist the enemy, it was held he had no intent to assist the enemy. Lord Denning has written of this case:

"This man Steane had no desire or purpose to assist the enemy. The Gestapo had said to him: 'If you don't obey, your wife and children will be put in a concentration camp.' So he obeyed their commands. It would be very hard to convict him of an 'intent to assist the enemy' if it was the last thing he desired to do."[8]

But could one not say that Steane did intend to assist the enemy *in order to save his family*? His motive might have been to save his family, but that does not alter the proposition that he intentionally assisted the enemy. On this basis *Steane* appears inconsistent with a general rule of criminal law that motive usually has no effect on criminal liability. Motive is an emotion which gives rise to an intention and causes one to act. Thus my desire (motive) to help the poor might cause me to steal in order to feed them: this motive would be ignored by the law; I would clearly have an intention to steal and would be convicted of theft. Similarly, it was Steane's desire (motive) to save his family that caused him to broadcast. This motive should have been ignored except insofar as it might be relevant to any defence of duress that he would then raise.

In *Chandler* v. *Director of Public Prosecutions*[9] the appellants were deeply opposed to nuclear weapons. In order to demonstrate their opposition they planned non-violent action to immobilise an aircraft at an RAF station for a period of six hours. They were convicted of conspiracy to commit a breach of section 1 of the Official Secrets Act 1911, namely to enter a prohibited place for "a purpose prejudicial to the safety or interests of the state." The trial judge ruled that they were not entitled to call evidence to show that it would be for the benefit of the

[8] Denning, *Responsibility before the Law*, (1961), p. 27.
[9] [1964] A.C. 763.

country to give up nuclear armament. He directed the jury to convict if they were satisfied that the immediate purpose of the appellants was the obstruction of an aircraft. The Court of Criminal Appeal dismissed their appeals against conviction. Radcliffe L.J. stated:

> "The trial judge . . . directed the jury that they should not be influenced by what, he said, was the undisputed fact that the views as to the wrongness and, indeed, unwisdom of nuclear weapons held by the appellants were deeply and passionately held and that they were honest and sincere views. In effect, he put it to the jury that they should look on the appellants as having made their entry for two separate purposes, an immediate purpose of obstructing the airfield, and a further or long-term purpose of inducing or compelling the government to abandon nuclear weapons in the true interests of the state. His ruling was that, if they found the immediate purpose proved, that of obstruction, they ought to find the appellants guilty of offences under section 1 of the Act, regardless of whether they might think the long-term purpose in itself beneficial or, at any rate, non-prejudicial to the interests and safety of the state. In my opinion there was nothing defective in law in this ruling."

Should not *Steane* have been resolved in a similar manner? Did he not broadcast for two separate purposes, an immediate purpose of assisting the enemy and a long-term purpose of saving his family?[10] It is not disputed that on the facts Steane should have been acquitted, but his acquittal should have been by reason of the defence of duress (that he was forced to broadcast) rather than the somewhat tortuous reasoning that he had no intent to assist the enemy. Perhaps this case is a good illustration that the concept "intention" can be expanded or restricted to meet the demands of justice in any particular case.

3. Question of fact for jury

In the normal, average case the term "intention" should not be given a legal definition. Judges should refrain from telling juries what it means. Whether a defendant intended a result is a question of fact which only the jury, applying their common sense to an ordinary English word, can answer. It is thus impossible to define intention or to know precisely what it means. It could well mean different things to different juries. Presumably, but one is only guessing, most juries will opt for the ordinary, common-sense meaning, namely, "as 'a decision to bring about a certain consequence' or as the aim.' "[11]

4. "Exceptional" cases

However, there may be other cases where a defendant has a purpose other than causing the prohibited harm—but where that result was an

---

[10] See Glanville Williams, "Oblique Intention" [1987] C.L.J. 417.
[11] *Mohan* [1976] 1 Q.B. 1.

inevitable or likely consequence. For example, the defendant's main aim in *Nedrick* was to burn down the house in order to frighten the occupant thereof. But in so doing, causing death was a likely result. Lord Bridge in *Moloney* thought such guidance would only be necessary in "rare" and "exceptional" cases. However, Lord Scarman in *Hancock* recognised that such cases would not be at all rare or exceptional—and accordingly guidance to the jury will be necessary in most cases where the defendant has a primary aim in acting other than causing the prohibited harm.[12]

In these cases it is permissible to give juries some guidance. Juries are still *not* to be told what intention is, but they can be told what it is not—and the can be given guidance as to how to infer its existence.

(a) *What it is not*:

[i] intention is not the same as desire;
[ii] foresight of a consequence as likely, probable or highly probable is not intention. The old *Hyam* formulation is thus no longer good law.

(b) *Permissible inferences*:

[i] when a result *is* (objectively) a virtually certain consequence of one's actions, *and*
[ii] the defendant foresees it as virtually certain,

then

the jury *may* infer that the result is intended.

This last point is from the *Nedrick* synthesis. This was approved in *Walker and Hayles* although it was made clear that directions in terms of lesser degree of foresight would not necessarily amount to a misdirection. The two House of Lords decisions also do not go quite as far and allow inferences of intention to be drawn where the result is less certain—but the important point is that the greater the probability of the consequence occurring, the more likely that it was intended.

5. Conclusion on Moloney/Hancock/Nedrick

The central objection to these cases is that the law is left in as uncertain a state as ever. Intention is not defined. *Perhaps* that could be accepted if the learned judges in the above cases had stopped at that. After all, many key concepts in the criminal law, for example "dishonesty" under the Theft Acts,[13] are left undefined for jury determination. But such restraint has not been shown. Unable to resist the temptation, various titbits have been thrown to those scavenging for the meaning of intention. We are told what is not intention. We are told how it is to be established in evidential terms. We are *nearly* told that

---

[12] In *Walker and Hayles* [1990] Crim. L.R. 44, it was held that a mere request from a jury for a further direction did not make the case a rare and exceptional one requiring a direction on foresight.

[13] *Post*, p. 725.

the meaning of intention is foresight of a consequence as a virtually certain result of one's actions. Such an inference "might be irresistible." (*Nedrick*) Indeed, in *Moloney* we are told that if a consequence is foreseen as "little short of overwhelming" that this will suffice to *establish* intention, (*i.e.* that this amounts in law to intention).[14] And we are further told that the reluctant Manchester-bound air traveller "*conclusively* demonstrates his *intention* to go there, because it is a *moral certainty* that that is where he will arrive" (italics added). But at the last moment the carrot is snatched away and it is made clear that intention is something else which *may* be inferred from foresight of a virtual certainty. What it is is a mystery. There is always a "logical gap"[15] between such foresight and intention. We are not told what further needs to be established to bridge the gap. Or, looking at the matter negatively, when and in what circumstances could the inference ever be resisted?

A second objection relates to the guidelines for cases where guidance can be given as to the drawing of inferences. It seems strange that there be a precondition that a result *be* (objectively) a virtually certain consequence. We are dealing here with person's intentions, his state of mind. It is now clear law that this is a subjective matter. A defendant may foresee a result as virtually certain (from which there may be an inference of intention) even though objectively it was not likely to occur at all. The proposition becomes less objectionable of course if it is recognised that there is no such "necessary condition"[16] but that, as in most cases where inferences have to be drawn from objective facts, the objective likelihood of a consequence occurring does raise an inference of the defendant himself foreseeing it as such.

6. A variable meaning?

In *Moloney* and *Hancock* it was stressed that the court was not merely dealing with murder, but with all crimes of "intention." This would clearly suggest that "intention" bears the same meaning throughout the criminal law.[17]

However, it is possible that the concept "intention" has a chameleon-like character and changes its meaning according to its context. For example, Glanville Williams has argued that "intent" should bear its broader third meaning above of including foresight of a virtual certainty—but that there are three exceptions where it should bear its narrowest, purposive meaning of "direct" intent: namely, offences of causing mental stress or annoyance; certain instances of complicity; and treason.[18] Duff, on the other hand, also argues for a concept of "oblique" intention but with three different exceptions where only "direct"

[14] Glanville Williams, "Oblique Intention" [1987] C.L.J. 417, 431.
[15] Duff, *ante*, n. 7, 771.
[16] Smith & Hogan, p. 56.
[17] This seems to have been the view adopted in *Purcell* (1986) 83 Cr.App.R. 45; *A.M.K. Property Management Ltd.* [1985] Crim.L.R. 600; *Bryson* [1985] Crim.L.R. 669; *Burke* [1988] Crim.L.R. 839.
[18] *Ante*, n. 14, pp. 435–437.

intention will suffice. His exceptions are attempted crimes, other "with intent" crimes where there has to be an intention to cause a result not specified in the *actus reus* of the crime and finally, the doctrine of implied malice.[19]

It is however submitted that such an approach is unacceptable. As can be seen from the divergent views of the above writers, agreement as to which crimes should require which type of intention would be impossible to secure and would only increase the uncertainty in this area of law. Further, it is difficult to see that there is any sound justifiable legal policy insisting on a variable meaning for "intention." It is submitted that the concept "intention" should have a fixed meaning. If it were felt that for certain crimes this fixed meaning was inappropriate, then an additional or alternative species of *mens rea* should be stipulated—without the concept of "intention" having to shrink or expand to meet the exigencies of all situations.

This approach was accepted in *Walker and Hayles* where it was held that the *Moloney/Hancock* meaning of intention applied to attempts to commit a crime.

(ii) *Evaluation*

On what basis is one to evaluate the above decisions in deciding what meaning the law ought to attribute to the word and concept "intention"? It is suggested that a meaning can only be ascribed to "intention" after the following three matters have been considered.

1. There ought to be some semantic precision about the law's use of the word "intention" so that it correlates with the layman's perceptions of the word.

Intention is an ordinary word in everyday usage. The criminal law ought to reflect the values of society and thus if the word "intention" is to have any useful function, it ought to bear this ordinary meaning. As Duff states:

"[T]he 'appeal to ordinary language' should not be despised: not just because it may cause confusion if the law uses terms whose legal and extra-legal meanings differ radically; but because the term's ordinary usage reflects our moral understanding of its relevance to ascriptions of responsibility, and of those distinctions which we regard as morally significant. Thus if it is any part of the law's purpose to assign legal liability in accordance with moral responsibility, there must be a presumption in favour of preserving the ordinary meanings of the concepts through which responsibility is assigned."[20]

Further, the task of the jury is made easier when legal terms are given

---

[19] R. A. Duff, "Intention, Mens Rea and the Law Commission Report" [1980] Crim.L.R. 147; R. A. Duff, "Intentions Legal and Philosophical" (1989) 9 Oxford J. of L.S. 76. See *post*, p. 170. A similar argument for a variable meaning was put forward by Judge Buzzard before *Moloney* ("Intent" [1978] Crim.L.R. 5).

[20] Duff, "Intention, Mens Rea and the Law Commission Report" [1980] Crim.L.R. 147. See also, Glanville Williams, *Textbook of Criminal Law*, p. 83.

their ordinary meanings. It was this desire to avoid confusing juries that led the Court of Appeal in *Belfon* to reject the broad view of intention:

"There has never been any need to explain what 'intent' means since the specific intent is defined in the section. Juries do not seem to have experienced any difficulty in understanding the word 'intent' without further explanation." . . . [21]

It was this reasoning that led Lord Bridge in *Moloney* to his view that generally juries needed no guidance as to the meaning of "intention." It was a matter of fact to be decided by them according to the ordinary usage of the word.

It is not however always easy to ascertain the "ordinary, everyday" meaning of words. Most commentators are agreed that in its ordinary, common usage, the term "intend" means "aiming at," or "meaning to achieve." The consequence must be one's purpose, objective or goal. The Oxford English Dictionary defines "intend" as purpose or design. Yet in the now discredited House of Lords decision of *Hyam*[22] Lord Cross considered that the "ordinary man" would equate foresight of injury with intentionally causing injury. Lord Cross was here probably falling into the common trap of confusing the issue of how ordinary people would describe the concept of intention with the issue of whom ordinary people would want to hold responsible for their actions. Further, now that the fourth view of intention above has been rejected, one is left with three views that are not far removed from each other and it is by no means certain that there would be a clear view as to which of these three is the ordinary meaning.

Should intention be defined or simply left to the jury? It is becoming increasingly common in criminal law to leave crucial issues such as this to the jury. For instance, one of the critical concepts in theft, "dishonesty," is largely left to jury determination.[23] However, a concept such as "dishonesty" involves value judgments; ethical stances have to be taken. In short, a judgment has to be taken as to the morality of the defendant's actions. The jury, as the mouthpiece of community values, is probably the most appropriate body to express such judgments. The meaning to be attributed to "intention" does of course involve moral judgments but these are less various, and perhaps more capable of reduction to a single formula, than the never-ending range of factors affecting ethical judgments as to the meaning of a concept such as dishonesty.[24] Accordingly, it would be preferable for "intention" to be given a legal definition—but the point being made here is that that definition should largely reflect the ordinary meaning of the word.

[21] (1976) 63 Cr.App.R. 59 at 60, 65.
[22] [1975] A.C. 55; see *ante*, p. 153.
[23] *Post*, p. 725.
[24] C. M. V. Clarkson & H. M. Keating, "Codification: Offences against the Person under the Draft Criminal Code" (1986) 50 J.C.L. 405, 410.

2. The law ought to define intention in such a manner that it can be clearly distinguished from recklessness. One of the main problems with the old *Hyam* formulation that foresight of a probable or highly consequence amounted to intention was that no principle could be discerned to establish the cut-off point when recklessness became intention. Foreseeing a consequence as probable or likely was intention but foreseeing it as less than probable was recklessness! Such a test involved having to define "probable" and "likely."

Glanville Williams, The Mental Element in Crime (1965), pp. 29–30:

"[L]ikelihood . . . is a word to which it is difficult to attach a fixed meaning. The word 'possible' is meaningful; it covers the whole range of possibility, including certainty. . . . The word 'probable' is generally taken to include something beyond bare possibility and less than certainty; I think that most people would say that it implies at least a 50 per cent. chance. What does 'likely' imply? Some may feel that it is a stronger word than 'probable,' implying, say a 66 per cent. chance. Others may feel that it is not so strong, and that it would be satisfied by a 33 per cent. chance. If the word is used in a legal rule to refer to the degree of possibility, then surely we need to have some agreement upon the degree, at least upon its order of magnitude."

Glanville Williams, Textbook of Criminal Law (1st ed., 1978), pp. 215–216:

"There is no agreed mathematical translation of 'probable,' and all we can say about 'likely' is that it may cover a lower degree of probability than 'probable' (though dictionaries make them both the same). In statistics, probability means the whole range of possibility between impossibility and certainty (in mathematical terms, between nought and one). 'Chance' is a non-technical synonym for probability, as also is 'risk' (the chance of an untoward fact or event). The degree of probability is expressed either as a vulgar fraction or as a decimal fraction. So one can speak of a probability of $\frac{1}{100}$ or ·01, meaning that it is a chance of one in a hundred, or that the odds are 99 to one against. Popular 'probability' means a substantial chance, but no one knows whether this means a probability of at least ·34, ·51 (more likely than not), ·67, ·80 or what. It *could* mean something much less than those figures. Even if there were an Act of Parliament saying that probability in law means a probability of (say) ·51 or more, the jury would have great difficulty in adjudicating the issue unless evidence were presented of elaborate experiments to determine the probability."

It is interesting to contrast two recent Antipodean decisions on this subject. In the Australian High Court decision of *Crabbe*[25] it was held that if one knows a consequence is probable one expects that consequence will be the likely result "for the word 'probable' means likely to happen." However, in the New Zealand Court of Appeal decision of *Piri*[26] it was held that "likely" did not mean "probable" in the sense of more probable than not. A consequence is "likely" where there is "a

---

[25] (1984–1985) 58 A.L.R. 417.
[26] (1987) 1 N.Z.L.R. 66.

real or substantial risk. It need not be more probable than not but it should be more than a bare possibility."

It was this kind of interpretive nightmare that led the House of Lords in *Moloney* and *Hancock* to jettison the *Hyam* reasoning and the Law Commission to reject this old view of intention: it made it impossible to distinguish intention from recklessness.[27]

3. The final factor to be taken into account in ascribing a meaning to the concept, intention is the most important, but also the most elusive. Is there a moral difference between the four states of mind described at the beginning of this section—and, if so, where is this "moral line" to be drawn?

The first question for consideration is whether the House of Lords in *Moloney* and *Hancock* was justified in rejecting the *Hyam* test of intention (the fourth state of mind above). *If* there is no significant moral difference between the person who aims to achieve a consequence and the person who merely foresees that a consequence is probable, then one *might* be justified in describing both as intention; but if there is a moral distinction between the two, this distinction will need to be reflected by the law in order that different levels of liability and punishment can be imposed. So is there a moral distinction between the two?

H. L. A. Hart, "Intention and Punishment" in Punishment and Responsibility, (1968), pp. 119–122:

"[Hart cites the case of *R. v. Desmond, Barrett and Others* (*The Times*, April 28, 1868) where the defendant, Barrett, dynamited a prison wall in order to effect the escape of two Irish Fenians imprisoned therein. Though the plot failed, the explosion killed some persons living nearby].

[F]or the law, a foreseen outcome is enough, even if it was unwanted by the agent, even if he thought of it as an undesirable by-product of his activities, and in Desmond's case this is what the death of those killed by the explosion was. It was no part of Barrett's purpose or aim to kill or injure anyone; the victims' deaths were not a means to his end; to bring them about was not his reason or part of his reason for igniting the fuse, but he was convicted on the ground that he foresaw their death or serious injury. . . .

The reason [that the law should neglect the difference between direct intention and foreseeing the consequence] is, I suggest, that both the case of direct intention and that of oblique intention share one feature which any system of assigning responsibility for conduct must always regard as of crucial importance. This can be seen if we compare the actual facts of the Desmond case with a case of direct intention. Suppose Barrett shot the prison guard in order to obtain from them the keys to release the prisoners. Both in the actual Desmond case and in this imaginary variant, so far as Barrett had control over the alternative between the victims' dying or living, his choice tipped the balance; in both these cases he had control over and may be considered to have chosen the outcome, since he consciously opted for the course leading to the victims' deaths. Whether he sought to achieve this as an end or a means to his end, or merely foresaw it as an unwelcome consequence of his intervention, is irrelevant at the stage of conviction where the question of control is crucial. However, when it

[27] Law Com. No. 89, Report on the Mental Element in Crime, (1978), para. 43.

comes to the question of sentence and the determination of the severity of punishment it may be (though I am not at all sure that this is in fact the case) that on both a retributive and a utilitarian theory of punishment the distinction between direct and oblique intention is relevant."

This "control" test of intention is similar to the views of Lord Diplock in *Hyam* when he equated desiring to produce a consequence with foreseeing that consequence as likely because "what is common to both these states of mind is willingness to produce the particular evil consequence."

Even if one accepts Hart's premise that the actor has "control" in both situations, does that necessarily mean that both states of mind must be defined as "intention," and that both deserve the same level of criminal liability? The actor who acts recklessly in merely foreseeing a remote possibility of a consequence occurring, is also "in control," but if one were to designate his actions as being intentional,[28] one would have eliminated much of the concept of recklessness, and surely there is, or could be, a significant moral difference between such a reckless actor and the actor who aims at achieving a consequence.

Hart goes on to discuss the distinction (or lack of it) between these two states of mind in relation to the crime of attempt.

H. L. A. Hart, "Intention and Punishment" in Punishment and Responsibility, (1968) pp. 126–127:

"For this notion, too, involves the idea of doing something with the direct intention that some consequence should come about, as distinct from merely doing it with the belief that it would come about. A hypothetical case has been used by Professor Glanville Williams to illustrate the absurdity that the application of this distinction might have in the case of attempted murder. Suppose one man is walking with another along the edge of a cliff and sees a diamond ring on the path before him. Knowing that his companion also wishes to get the ring, he pushes him over the cliff, believing that this will in all probability lead to his death, but, in fact, a bush breaks his fall a short distance down the cliff, and he is unharmed. This, according to the usual interpretation of the notion of an attempt, probably does not constitute an attempt to murder, for A did not push his companion over in order to kill him, though he believed it would cause his death; whereas if, in order to get the ring, instead of pushing the victim over the cliff, A had shot at him to kill him but missed, this would have been attempted murder. Yet the ultimate aim is the same in both cases.

Can one formulate any intelligible theory of punishment which would make sense of this distinction? No calculation of the efficacy of deterrence or reforming measures, and nothing that would ordinarily be called retribution, seems to justify this distinction. In the attempt case, for example, the variant where the direct intention to kill is present and the variant where the intention is indirect seem equally wicked, equally harmful, and equally in need of discouragement by the law. The distinction seems to make its appeal to a feeling that to *use* a man's death as a means to some further end is a defilement of the agent: his will is thus identified with an evil aim and it is somehow morally worse than the

---

[28] *Cf.*, Lord Diplock in *Miller* [1983] 2 A.C. 161.

will of one who in the pursuit of the same further end does something which, as the agent realizes, renders the man's death inevitable as a second effect. If this is the basis of the distinction we may well ask whether the law should in such cases give recognition to it, especially where, as in the attempt case, recognition will lead to an acquittal, except on a relatively trivial charge of assault."

Many commentators feel that there is a significant moral difference between wanting a result to occur and merely foreseeing its occurrence as probable,[29] as a man's objectives or aims influence our perceptions of his character as a moral agent. His actions become more reprehensible if they are deliberate and purposeful. The boy, throwing a ball dangerously near a window and realising that there is a better than even chance that in the course of his game he could break the window, will instinctively cry out: "I didn't mean to break it," when the window is duly shattered. Our characterisation of the boy as a moral agent would be different if he had deliberately aimed at the window and thrown the ball, trying to break the window. As Duff says:

"To do what I believe will help the enemy, or cause injury, may be counted criminal even when I do it for reasons which have nothing to do with helping the enemy or causing injury: but to act with the *intention* of helping the enemy, or causing injury, gives a quite different moral character to the action, which we may wish to mark by making only that an offence, or by making it a more serious offence."[30]

A combination of these three factors has led the majority of commentators[31] to reject the view that foreseeing a consequence as probable amounts to intending that consequence. But which of the remaining three views[32] on the meaning of intention is to be accepted, and why? The prevailing view appears to support the idea that a consequence is intended when it is the aim or objective of the actor or is foreseen as a virtual, practical or moral certainty ("oblique" intent).

Glanville Williams, Textbook of Criminal Law (2nd ed., 1983), pp. 84–85:

"Clearly, a person can be taken to intend a consequence that follows under his nose from what he continues to do, and the law should be the same where he is aware that a consequence in the future is the certain or practically certain result of what he does. As Lord Hailsham said in *Hyam*, 'intention' includes 'the means as well as the end and the inseparable consequences of the end as well as the means.' (What he evidently meant was the consequences known to the defendant to be inseparable.) . . .

To take a hypothetical case: suppose that a villain of the deepest dye sends an insured parcel on an aircraft, and includes in it a time-bomb by which he

---

[29] See, for example, Glanville Williams, *The Mental Element in Crime*, p. 29, and *Textbook on Criminal Law*, p. 83.
[30] "Intention, Mens Rea and The Law Commission Report" [1980] Crim.L.R. 147.
[31] Glanville Williams, *ante*. n. 29; Smith, " 'Intent': A Reply," [1978] Crim.L.R. 14.
[32] See, *ante*, p. 153.

intends to bring down the plane and consequently to destroy the parcel. His immediate intention is merely to collect on the insurance. He does not care whether the people on board live or die, but he knows that success in his scheme will inevitably involve their deaths as a side-effect. On the theoretical point, common sense suggests that the notion of intention should be extended to this situation; it should not merely be regarded as a case of recklessness. A consequence should normally be taken as intended although it was not desired, if it was foreseen by the actor as the *virtually certain* accompaniment of what he intended. This is not the same as saying that any consequence foreseen as *probable* is intended. . . .

Clearly, one cannot confine the notion of foresight of certainty to certainty in the most absolute sense. It is a question of human certainty, or virtual certainty, or practical certainty. This is still not the same as speaking in terms of probability."

Duff has suggested that there are two approaches to the concept of responsibility in the criminal law: a consequentialist and a non-consequentialist perspective on human action. He argues that both these views lead to acceptance of oblique intent *generally* sufficing—but that in certain (very important) exceptional cases intention should be given its narrow direct meaning. One's list of exceptions depends on whether one adopts a consequentialist or a non-consequentialist view.

R. A. Duff, "Intentions, Legal and Philosophical" (1989) 9 Oxford Journal of Legal Studies 76, 87–88, 91:

"To a consequentialist, actions are right or wrong only in so far as their consequences are good or bad. Her primary focus is thus not on actions themselves, but on *outcomes*; on the state of affairs which actions bring about. The logical basis for judging an action to be right or wrong is a judgment of a state of affairs as being good or bad. . . .

If actions thus matter as ways of causing significant outcomes, an agent's culpability will be a function of his responsibility for an actual or likely outcome of his action, and of the badness of that outcome; and he will be responsible for an outcome in so far as he has effective control over it. He controls an outcome in so far as, first, he knows that it will or might be caused by his action; and, second, he has the power to act either so that it occurs or so that it does not occur. The basic conditions of moral responsibility (and thus, ideally, of criminal liability) are therefore voluntary conduct and foresight of the relevant outcomes of my actions: the paradigm of moral culpability involves the certainty that my voluntary act will bring about an evil outcome; and lesser degrees of culpability are generated by foresight falling short of certainty. . . . It follows from this that oblique intention, intentional agency, provides the consequentialist paradigm of criminal fault. . . .

[O]n . . . [a] non-consequentialist view, the paradigm of crime is an *attack* on another person (on his life, on his rights); and the idea of an attack is essentially that of an act which is (directly) *intended* to injure or to harm. The paradigm of murder is thus not the *occurrence* of a foreseen and avoidable death (as it is for a consequentialist), but the wilful *killing* of a human being; and the paradigm of wilful killing is a directly, not an obliquely, intended killing. Such a non-consequentialist will also count as a murderer one who intentionally kills; one who does, without justification or excuse, what he knows will cause death: though he does not directly attack his victim, he exhibits such an utter disregard for, or indifference to, her life an rights that we hold him to be, without qualification or mitigation, culpably responsible for the death which he knowingly causes. More generally, when what is at issue is culpability as to a harm which actually occurs (as with crimes of basic intent), she will usually hold one who intentionally causes such harm to be as culpably responsible as one who directly intends it. . . . [S]he will not take the difference between direct and oblique intent to mark a significant difference in *degree* of responsibility or culpability. The two types of intention manifest different *kinds* or paradigms of culpable responsibility; one paradigm is that of a direct attack on another person, the other is that of an utter indifference to their rights and interests (oblique intention thus marks the perfection of recklessness; they exhibit to different degrees the same kind of fault)."

The view that foresight of a virtual certainty amounts to intention has been embraced by the Criminal Law Revision Committee[33] and is essentially the test adopted by the Law Commission in their Draft Criminal Code.[34]

Draft Criminal Code Bill 1989 (Law Com. No. 177), clause 18:

" . . . a person acts—
(b) 'intentionally' with respect to— . . .
(ii) a result when he acts either in order to bring it about or being aware that it will occur in the ordinary course of events."

The Law Commission (Law Com. No. 177), A Criminal Code for England and Wales, Commentary on Draft Criminal Code Bill, 8.14–8.16:

"Acting in order to bring about a result is, as it were, the standard case of 'intending' to cause a result. But we are satisfied that a definition of 'intention' for criminal law purposes must refer, as Lord Hailsham of St. Marylebone L.C. expressed it in *Hyam* to 'the means as well as the end and the inseparable consequences of the end as well as the means.' Where a person acts in order to achieve a particular purpose, knowing that this cannot be done without causing another result, he must be held to intend to cause that other result. The other result may be a pre-condition—as where D, in order to injure P, throws a brick through the window behind which he knows P to be standing; or it may be a necessary concomitant of the first result—as (to use a much quoted example) where D blows up an aeroplane in flight in order to recover on the insurance covering its cargo, knowing that the crew will inevitably be killed. D intends to break the window and he intends to kill the crew. But there is no absolute certainty in human affairs. P *might* fling up the window while the brick is in flight.

---

[33] 14th Report, Offences against the Person, Cmnd. 7844 (1980), para. 10.

[34] It also represents the common law position in the United States where Burger C.J. in *United States* v. *United States Gypsum* (438 U.S. 422) held that a person intended a result "when he knows that the result is practically certain to follow from his conduct, whatever his desire may be as to that result." The Canadian Law Reform Commission has produced an even stricter definition that the defendant must act "in order to effect: (a) that consequence; or (b) another consequence which he knows involves that consequence" (Report 31, Recodifying Criminal Law (1987); see J.C. Smith "A Note on 'Intention' " [1990] Crim.L.R. 85.

The crew *might* make a miraculous escape by parachute. D's purpose *might* be achieved without causing the second result—but these are only remote possibilities and D, if he contemplates them at all (which may be unlikely), must know that they are only remote possibilities. The result will occur, and D knows that it will occur, 'in the ordinary course of events . . . unless something supervenes to prevent it.' It is, and he knows it is, 'a virtual certainty.' We have adopted the phrase, 'in the ordinary course of events' to ensure that 'intention' covers the case of a person who knows that the achievement of his purpose will necessarily cause the result in question, in the absence of some wholly improbable supervening event.

A person's awareness of any degree of probability (short of virtual certainty) that a particular result will follow from his acts ought not, we believe, to be classed as an 'intention' to cause that result for criminal law purposes. This accords with the general tendency of modern decisions on offences defined in terms of intention. Liability based on the awareness of a probable result can be provided for by casting the offence in terms of recklessness.

'*Intention*' *as a term of art*. The proposal to define 'intention' involves a departure from recent statements of the House of Lords on the law of murder."

(iii) *The preferred solution*

However, in spite of such weighty authority, it is suggested that it would be incorrect to adopt such a view, and that a consequence ought only to be regarded as intended when it is the aim or objective of the actor, or is foreseen as *certain* to result (view 2 above). The reasons for this suggestion are two-fold. The first reason relates to the meaning of the word "intention" itself. As suggested earlier, the term "intend" means "aiming at," "meaning to achieve." The consequence must be one's purpose, objective or goal. Even the Law Commission in an earlier draft Bill accept that they are attributing an artificial meaning to the word intention when they define their "standard test of intention" as being to "*either* intend . . . *or* have no substantial doubt."[35] Having no substantial doubt is clearly accepted as being something different from "intend."[36] As suggested earlier, there are strong reasons for assigning to words their ordinary, normal meanings.

But from this it does not follow that the meaning of intention must be limited to view 1.[37] It must also include cases where a consequence is foreseen as *certain*, even though it was not the actor's primary aim or objective. In such a situation the foreseen consequence is foreseen as something that *must* happen; it is a condition precedent to the occurrence of the primary consequence. To take the classic example where I intend to shoot you; you are standing behind a window. Do I intend to break the window? In this case I foresee it as certain that I will break the

---

[35] Law Com. No. 89, Report on the Mental Element in Crime, (1978), p. 56.

[36] See Duff, "Intention, Mens Rea and The Law Commission Report" [1980] Crim.L.R. 147, 151–155 who argues that the Law Commission have produced a definition of "intentional action," rather than intention: "if I know that my action will cause death, I surely cause that death *intentionally*, even if I do not act with the *intention* of causing it: for I voluntarily make myself its agent. The category of 'intentional action' is wider than that of 'intended action': but it does not include *all* the foreseen results of an action. For we count as parts of an agent's intentional action only such results as are in some way *significant* and for which he is *responsible*."

[37] *Ante*, p. 153.

glass; I cannot shoot you without doing so. Thus breaking the glass is my aim or objective, albeit only a secondary aim or objective to my main one of killing you. It is a necessary and "wanted" means to my end. I clearly intend to break the window. Lord Hailsham in *Hyam* endorsed this when he spoke of "intention, which embraces, in addition to the end, all the necessary consequences of an action including the means to the end and any consequences intended along with the end."[38]

But where an undesired consequence is only foreseen as "virtually certain" or "morally certain" it ceases to be an inescapable consequence or a necessary means to an end. It thus ceases to be a secondary aim and can no longer be described as intention. In the celebrated example where I blow up an aircraft in flight in order to obtain the insurance money and the passengers are killed, I would foresee the death of these passengers as virtually certain. But, if it is not my objective to kill them, the fact that there is a chance (albeit one in a million) that they could parachute to safety, means that their death was not a necessary means to an end. It is simply a by-product which will almost certainly occur; it is not a secondary aim or objective and thus cannot be described as intention. The line of demarcation is a thin one, but it is conceptually clear. Only if a consequence can be described as an aim or objective, whether primary or secondary, can the state of mind of the actor be described as intentional.

The same point can be explained differently. Duff has suggested that intention can be defined in terms of "the test of failure": "an effect is directly intended only if its non-occurrence would mark the (partial) failure of the agent's action."[39] If one blew up the aeroplane without killing its occupants this would not mark the failure of the enterprise. On the contrary, it would represent the ultimate in success. On the other hand, failing to break the window (when the poposed victim is standing behind it) will represent a failure of the agent's action because not breaking the glass necessarily involves not killing the person behind it. Perhaps a clearer way of approaching the problem is to ask whether it is *possible* for the main objective to be achieved without the secondary consequence. It is empirically possible[40] (albeit extraordinarily unlikely) to blow up an aeroplane in flight without killing anyone; it is empirically impossible to shoot a person standing behind a sheet of glass without the bullet penetrating the glass. Accordingly, there is no intention to kill the passengers on the aeroplane, but there is an intention to break the glass.

This leads to the second reason for the submitted limitation of inten-

---

[38] [1975] A.C. 55 at 73.
[39] *Ante*, n. 19, 77. See also Duff, "Intention, Mens Rea and the Law Commission Report" [1980] Crim.L.R. 147, 150–151.
[40] This idea of empirical possibility is suggested by Duff, *ante*, n. 19, but he develops the idea somewhat differently.

tion to consequences foreseen as certain. If one were to adopt the prevailing view that foresight of a practical or substantial certainty constituted intention, it would be impossible to distinguish intention from gross recklessness. How could one differentiate between a consequence that was foreseen as virtually certain and one that was foreseen as very highly probable? Neither consequence is an objective of the actor. They are both simply by-products of the actor's actions foreseen as having varying chances of occurring. No principle can be discerned to establish the cut-off point when recklessness becomes intention. If a consequence is foreseen as 98 per cent. certain to occur, is this foresight of a virtual certainty or merely foresight of a high probability? On the other hand, if intention were limited to foresight of a certainty on the basis that such consequences must be secondary objectives, as opposed to mere by-products, then no blurring between the concepts of intention and recklessness is necessary. A clear distinction between the two concepts is apparent.

It could be asserted that while there is a linguistic justification for drawing this distinction, there is little moral justification for distinguishing between an actor who foresees a result as certain and one who foresees it as substantially certain. After all, the willingness to kill in both cases is almost equal. But surely if there is a distinction between the two, one must avoid the hypocrisy of pretending one is punishing intentional wrong-doing if one is not. If one wishes to punish for something less than intention, then one should name that "something" and be explicit that it is rendering the defendant liable to the same extent as if he had the requisite intention.

This is the approach recommended in the United States by the American Law Institute's Model Penal Code and which has been widely adopted in state code revisions throughout the United States. The Code does not adopt the view of intention favoured by the Law Commission and leading commentators in England. It adopts the narrower view argued for above, that a person acts intentionally "when . . . it is his conscious object to engage in conduct of that nature or to cause such a result."[41] What of foresight of a virtual certainty? The Model Penal Code does not assimilate this with intention, nor does it relegate it to the realms of recklessness. Instead, it has created a special category of *mens rea* between intention and recklessness, namely, knowledge. Section 202(2)(*b*) defines "knowingly" in the following terms:

"A person acts knowingly with respect to a material element of an offense when: . . . (ii) if the element involves a result of his conduct, he is aware that it is practically certain that his conduct will cause such a result."

The commentary to this sub-section recognises that the distinction

---

[41] American Law Institute, Model Penal Code, s.202(2)(*a*) prefers the term "purposely." However most code revisions have used this same definition for the term "intention." The Canadian Law Reform Commission (*ante*, n. 34) also prefer the term "purposely".

drawn is a narrow one and is "no doubt inconsequential for most purposes of liability." But apart from being conceptually necessary and helping to promote clarity of definition, the distinction does have some practical utility as

"there are areas where the discrimination is required. . . . This is true in treason, for example, in so far as a purpose to aid the enemy is an ingredient of the offense . . . and in attempts and conspiracy, where a true purpose to effect the criminal result is requisite for liability. . . . The distinction also has utility in differentiating among grades of an offense for purposes of sentence, *e.g.* in the case of homicide."[42]

Thus, according to this view, not only is there a linguistic, but also a moral, justification for drawing this fine distinction. Indeed there are two states in the United States that have employed this Model Penal Code terminology and have felt the distinction to be sufficiently material to warrant using it as the basis for a grading of homicide offences. Alaska provides that it is murder in the first degree to kill "with intent to cause the death of another person," but only murder in the second degree to kill "knowing that his conduct is substantially certain to cause death."[43] And New Hampshire provides that it is first degree murder to kill "purposely" and second degree murder to kill "knowingly."[44] Louisiana, while not following the Model Penal Code formulation, has adopted a similar distinction. For murder it is necessary to prove a "specific intent" which requires that the offender "actively desired the prescribed criminal consequences to follow his act"; it is only manslaughter if he has a "general intent" which includes "advert[ing] to the prescribed criminal consequences as reasonably certain to result from his act."[45]

If there are indeed linguistic, practical and moral justifications for distinguishing between intention (including the condition precedent cases) and foresight of the substantially certain, English law would surely not be justified in following the Draft Criminal Code's proposal to treat both as acting "intentionally."

2. Recklessness

(i) *The background*

Some crimes, such as attempt, can only be committed intentionally and it is thus crucial to be able to distinguish intention from recklessness. This line of demarcation depends, as we have just seen, on how broadly one chooses to define "intention." Any degree of foresight less than that specified in the definition of intention will constitute recklessness. But a vast numer of crimes in English law today can be committed

[42] American Law Institute, Model Penal Code, Tent. Draft No. 4 (1955) Art. 2, pp. 124, 125.
[43] Alaska Stat. tit. 11, ss.11.41.100, 110.
[44] N.H. Rev.Stat.Ann. ss.630: 1–a, b.
[45] La.Rev.Stat. s.14: 30, 30.1, s.14–10.

"intentionally or recklessly." Indeed, the Draft Criminal Code 1989 proposes that recklessness should be the basic fault element for *all* offences (unless otherwise stated).[46] For all these crimes the distinction between intention and recklessness is unimportant—what matters is the definition of recklessness and the parameters drawn around recklessness at its lowest levels in distinguishing it from negligence or other forms of conduct not regarded as equally blameworthy. This demarcation is vital as it has been the general policy of English law to punish reckless wrongdoing, but, with notable exceptions,[47] to exempt negligent wrongdoing from criminal liability.

The concept "recklessness" has had a chequered and uncertain history with judges vacillating as to whether it meant "gross negligence"[48] (an objective *major* deviation from the standards of the reasonable man) or whether it should be limited to cases where the defendant subjectively realised that there was a possibility of the consequence occurring (or the circumstance existing) but carried on regardless. By the late 1970s it appeared that the law had at last settled down and had clearly approved this latter subjective meaning of recklessness, that it was the conscious running of an unjustifiable risk.[49] The following was one of the leading cases illustrating this subjective approach.

R. v. Stephenson [1979] 1 Q.B. 695, (Court of Appeal, Criminal Division)

The appellant, who had crept into a hollow in the side of a large straw stack to sleep, felt cold and lit a fire of twigs and straw inside the hollow. The stack caught fire and was damaged. The appellant admitted that he had lit the fire but said the damage was an accident. He was charged with arson contrary to section 1(1) of the Criminal Damage Act 1971. Evidence on his behalf was given by a consultant psychiatrist that the appellant suffered from schizophrenia, and that the schizophrenia could have the effect of depriving him of the ability of a normal person to foresee or appreciate the risk of damage from the act of lighting the fire. The judge directed the jury that a person who without lawful excuse destroyed or damaged another's property was "reckless as to whether any such property would be destroyed or damaged," within section 1(1) of the 1971 Act, if he closed his mind to the obvious fact of risk from his act, and that schizophrenia might be a reason which made a person close his mind to the obvious fact of risk. The jury returned a verdict of guilty and the appellant was convicted. He appealed against the conviction on the ground, inter alia, of misdirection by the judge on what constituted recklessness.

Geoffrey Lane L.J.:
"The problem is not difficult to state. Does the word 'reckless' require that the defendant must be proved actually to have foreseen the risk of some damage resulting from his actions and nevertheless to have run the risk (the subjective

---

[46] Clause 20(1), Law Com. No. 177 (1989).
[47] For example, manslaughter, and careless driving contrary to the Road Traffic Act 1988, s.3.
[48] *Andrews* v. *D.P.P.* [1937] A.C. 576.
[49] *Cunningham* [1957] 2 Q.B. 396; *Briggs* [1977] 1 W.L.R. 605; *Parker* [1977] 1 W.L.R. 600; Law Commission, Report on the Mental Element in Crime (Law Com. No. 89), 1978, paras. 20, 21.

test), or is it sufficient to prove that the risk of damage resulting would have been obvious to any reasonable person in the defendant's position (the objective test)? In our view it is the subjective test which is correct.

What then must the prosecution prove in order to bring home the charge of arson in circumstances such as the present? They must prove that (1) the defendant deliberately committed some act which caused the damage to property alleged or part of such damage; (2) the defendant had no lawful excuse for causing the damage; these two requirements will in the ordinary case not be in issue; (3) the defendant either (a) intended to cause the damage to the property, or (b) was reckless as to whether the property was damaged or not. A man is reckless when he carries out the deliberate act appreciating that there is a risk that damage to property may result from his act. It is however not the taking of every risk which could properly be classed as reckless. The risk must be one which it is in all the circumstances unreasonable for him to take.

Proof of the requisite knowledge in the mind of the defendant will in most cases present little difficulty. The fact that the risk of some damage would have been obvious to anyone in his right mind in the position of the defendant is not conclusive proof of the defendant's knowledge, but it may well be and in many cases doubtless will be a matter which will drive the jury to the conclusion that the defendant himself must have appreciated the risk. The fact that he may have been in a temper at the time would not normally deprive him of knowledge or foresight of the risk. If he had the necessary knowledge or foresight and his bad temper merely caused him to disregard it or put it to the back of his mind not caring whether the risk materialised, or if it merely deprived him of the self-control necessary to prevent him from taking the risk of which he was aware, then his bad temper will not avail him. This was the concept which the court in *Reg.* v. *Parker (Daryl)* [1977] 1 WLR 600, 604 was trying to express when it used the words 'or closing his mind to the obvious fact that there is some risk of damage resulting from that act. . . . ' We wish to make it clear that the test remains subjective, that the knowledge or appreciation of risk of some damage must have entered the defendant's mind even though he may have suppressed it or driven it out. . . .

How do these pronouncements affect the present appeal? The appellant, through no fault of his own, was in a mental condition which might have prevented him from appreciating the risk which would have been obvious to any normal person. When the judge said to the jury 'there may be . . . all kinds of reasons which make a man close his mind to the obvious fact—among them may be schizophrenia'—we think he was guilty of a misapprehension, albeit possibly an understandable misapprehension. The schizophrenia was on the evidence something which might have prevented the idea of danger entering the appellant's mind at all. If that was the truth of the matter, then the appellant was entitled to be acquitted. That was something which was never left clearly to the jury to decide."

Appeal allowed

Under this subjective approach the definition of recklessness, both as to consequences and circumstances,[50] imposes a double test:

    (1) whether the defendant foresaw the possibility of the consequence occurring; and

---

[50] For the sake of simplicity the remainder of this section will refer only to consequences, but this should be taken to include circumstances.

(2) whether it was unjustifiable or unreasonable for him to take the risk.

Whether a risk is justifiable or not depends on the social importance of the acts and on the chances of the forbidden consequence occurring. As the Law Commission have stated:

> "The operation of public transport, for example, is inevitably accompanied by risks of accident beyond the control of the operator, yet it is socially necessary that these risks be taken. Dangerous surgical operations must be carried out in the interests of the life and health of the patient, yet the taking of these risks is socially justifiable."[51]

Thus if there was a perceived one in a thousand chance of high speed trains being involved in an accident, the social value of high-speed public transport would be such as to render the taking of such a remote risk justifiable, but if it was realised that there was a one in twenty chance of these trains being involved in an accident, then the chances of an accident occurring would outweigh the social importance of the activity and it would become unjustifiable to take such a risk. On the other hand, if there was the same (subjectively perceived) one in a thousand chance of killing a friend while playing Russian roulette, the complete absence of any social value to the activity would render the taking of the risk unjustifiable. Thus the test of whether the taking of a risk is justifiable or not involves a subtle balancing operation between the following questions: how socially useful is the activity? What are the perceived chances of the harm occurring? How serious is the harm that could occur?

In line with this approach the Law Commission in their Draft Criminal Code Bill 1989 have proposed the following:

> "cl. 18 . . . a person acts—
>   (c) 'recklessly' with respect to—
>   (i) a circumstance when he is aware of a risk that it exists or will exist:
>   (ii) a result when he is aware of a risk that it will occur;
>   and it is, in the circumstances known to him, unreasonable to take the risk."[52]

(ii) *Caldwell and Lawrence*

In 1981 however, English law changed direction radically when the House of Lords handed down two judgments on the same day, both concerned with the meaning of the concept of recklessness.

R. v. Caldwell [1982] A.C. 341 (House of Lords)

The respondent had done some work for the owner of a hotel as the result of which he had a quarrel with the owner, got drunk and set fire to the hotel in

---

[51] Law Com. No. 31, Working Paper on the Mental Element in Crime, p. 53.
[52] Law Com. No. 177, *A Criminal Code for England and Wales* (1989).

revenge. The fire was discovered and put out before any serious damage was caused and none of the ten guests in the hotel at the time was injured. The respondent was indicted on two counts of arson under section 1(1) and (2) of the Criminal Damage Act 1971. At his trial he pleaded guilty to the lesser charge of intentionally or recklessly destroying or damaging the property of another, contrary to section 1(1) but pleaded not guilty to the more serious charge under section 1(2) of damaging property with intent to endanger life or being reckless whether life would be endangered. He claimed that he was so drunk at the time that the thought that he might be endangering the lives of the people in the hotel had never crossed his mind. The trial judge directed the jury that drunkenness was not a defence to a charge under section 1(2) and he was convicted.

The Court of Appeal allowed his appeal. The Crown appealed to the House of Lords, where, in order to decide whether drunkenness was a defence to a charge under section 1(2), the House ruled that it was necessary to decide upon the precise meaning of the term recklessness as employed in section 1(2).

Lord Diplock (with whom Lord Keith and Lord Roskill concurred):
"My Lords, the Criminal Damage Act 1971 replaced almost in their entirety the many and detailed provisions of the Malicious Damage Act 1861. Its purpose, as stated in its long title, was to revise the law of England and Wales as to offences of damage to property. As the brevity of the Act suggests, it must have been hoped that it would also simplify the law.

In the Act of 1861, the word consistently used to describe the mens rea that was a necessary element in the multifarious offences that the Act created was 'maliciously'—a technical expression, not readily intelligible to juries, which became the subject of considerable judicial exegesis. This culminated in a judgment of the Court of Criminal Appeal in *Reg.* v. *Cunningham* [1957] 2 Q.B. 396, 399 which approved, as an accurate statement of the law, what had been said by Professor Kenny in the first edition of his *Outlines of Criminal Law* published in 1902:

> 'In any statutory definition of a crime, malice must be taken . . . as requiring either (1) an actual intention to do the particular kind of harm that in fact was done; or (2) recklessness as to whether such harm should occur or not (*i.e.* the accused has foreseen that the particular kind of harm might be done and yet has gone on to take the risk of it).'

My Lords, in this passage Professor Kenny was engaged in defining for the benefit of students the meaning of 'malice' as a term of art in criminal law. To do so he used ordinary English words in their popular meaning. Among the words he used was 'recklessness,' the noun derived from the adjective 'reckless,' of which the popular or dictionary meaning is careless, regardless, or heedless, of the possible harmful consequences of one's acts. It presupposes that if thought were given to the matter by the doer before the act was done, it would have been apparent to him that there was a real risk of its having the relevant harmful consequences; but, granted this, recklessness covers a whole range of states of mind from failing to give any thought at all to whether or not there is any risk of those harmful consequences, to recognising the existence of the risk and nevertheless deciding to ignore it. Conscious of this imprecision in the popular meaning of recklessness as descriptive of a state of mind, Professor Kenny, in the passage quoted, was, as it seems to me, at pains to indicate by the words in brackets the particular species within the genus reckless states of mind that constituted 'malice' in criminal law. This parenthetical restriction on the natural meaning of recklessness was necessary to an explanation of the meaning of the adverb 'maliciously' when used as a term of art in the description of an offence under the Malicious Damage Act 1861 (which was the matter in point in *Reg.* v.

Cunningham [1957] 2 Q.B. 396); but it was not directed to and consequently has no bearing on the meaning of the adjective 'reckless' in section 1 of the Criminal Damage Act 1971. To use it for that purpose can, in my view, only be misleading.

My Lords, the restricted meaning that the Court of Appeal in *Reg.* v. *Cunningham* had placed upon the adverb 'maliciously' in the Malicious Damage Act 1861 in cases where the prosecution did not rely upon an actual intention of the accused to cause the damage that was in fact done, called for a meticulous analysis by the jury of the thoughts that passed through the mind of the accused at or before the time he did the act that caused the damage, in order to see on which side of a narrow dividing line they fell. If it had crossed his mind that there was a risk that someone's property might be damaged but, because his mind was affected by rage or excitement or confused by drink, he did not appreciate the seriousness of the risk or trusted that good luck would prevent its happening, this state of mind would amount to malice in the restricted meaning placed upon that term by the Court of Appeal; whereas if, for any of these reasons, he did not even trouble to give his mind to the question whether there was any risk of damaging the property, this state of mind would not suffice to make him guilty of an offence under the Malicious Damage Act 1861.

Neither state of mind seems to me to be less blameworthy than the other; but if the difference between the two constituted the distinction between what does and what does not in legal theory amount to a guilty state of mind for the purposes of a statutory offence of damage to property, it would not be a practicable distinction for use in a trial by jury. The only person who knows what the accused's mental processes were is the accused himself—and probably not even he can recall them accurately when the rage or excitement under which he acted has passed, or he has sobered up if he were under the influence of drink at the relevant time. If the accused gives evidence that because of his rage, excitement or drunkenness the risk of particular harmful consequences of his acts simply did not occur to him, a jury would find it hard to be satisfied beyond reasonable doubt that his true mental process was not that, but was the slightly different mental process required if one applies the restricted meaning of 'being reckless as to whether' something would happen, adopted by the Court of Appeal in *Reg.* v. *Cunningham*.

My Lords, I can see no reason why Parliament when it decided to revise the law as to offences of damage to property should go out of its way to perpetuate fine and impracticable distinctions such as these, between one mental state and another. One would think that the sooner they were got rid of, the better.

When cases under section 1(1) of the new Act, in which the prosecution's case was based upon the accused having been 'reckless as to whether . . . property would be destroyed or damaged,' first came before the Court of Appeal, the question as to the meaning of the expression 'reckless' in the context of that subsection appears to have been treated as soluble simply by posing and answering what had by then, unfortunately, become an obsessive question among English lawyers: Is the test of recklessness 'subjective' or 'objective'? The first two reported cases, in both of which judgments were given off the cuff, are first *Reg.* v. *Briggs* (*Note*) [1977] 1 W.L.R. 605 which is reported in a footnote to the second, *Reg.* v. *Daryl Parker* [1977] 1 W.L.R. 600. Both classified the test of recklessness as 'subjective.' This led the court in *Reg.* v. *Briggs* (*Note*) [1977] 1 W.L.R. 605, 608 to say: 'A man is reckless in the sense required when he carries out a deliberate act knowing that there is some risk of damage resulting from that act but nevertheless continues in the performance of that act.' This leaves over the question whether the risk of damage may not be so slight that even the most prudent of men would feel justified in taking it, but it excludes that kind of recklessness that consists of acting without giving any thought at all to whether or not there is any risk of harmful consequences of one's act; even though the risk is great and would be obvious if any thought were given to the matter by the doer of the act. *Reg.* v. *Daryl Parker* [1977] 1 W.L.R. 600, 604, however, opened the door a chink by adding as an alternative to the actual knowledge of the accused that there is some risk of damage resulting from his act and his going on to take it, a mental state described as 'closing his mind to the obvious fact' that there is such a risk.

Reg. v. *Stephenson* [1979] 1 Q.B. 695, the first case in which there was full argument, though only on one side, and a reserved judgment, slammed the foor again upon any less restricted interpretation of 'reckless' as to whether particular consequences will occur than that originally approved in *Briggs* . . . [His Lordship then recited the facts of *Stephenson* and continued.] The court [in *Stephenson*] however, reached its final conclusion by a different route. It made the assumption that although Parliament in replacing the Act of 1861 by the Act of 1971 had discarded the word 'maliciously' as descriptive of the mens rea of the offences of which the actus reus is damaging property, in favour of the more explicit phrase 'intending to destroy or damage any such property or being reckless as to whether any such property would be destroyed,' it nevertheless intended the words to be interpreted in precisely the same sense as that in which the single adverb 'maliciously' had been construed by Professor Kenny in the passage that received the subsequent approval of the Court of Appeal in *Reg.* v. *Cunningham* [1957] 2 Q.B. 396.

My Lords, I see no warrant for making any such assumption in an Act whose declared purpose is to revise the then existing law as to offences of damage to property, not to perpetuate it. 'Reckless' as used in the new statutory definition of the mens rea of these offences is an ordinary English word. It had not by 1971 become a term of legal art with some more limited esoteric meaning than that which it bore in ordinary speech—a meaning which surely includes not only deciding to ignore a risk of harmful consequences resulting from one's acts that one has recognised as existing, but also failing to give any thought to whether or not there is any such risk in circumstances where, if any thought were given to the matter it would be obvious that there was.

If one is attaching labels, the latter state of mind is neither more nor less 'subjective' than the first. But the label solves nothing. It is a statement of the obvious; mens rea is by definition, a state of mind of the accused himself at the time he did the physical act that constitutes the actus reus of the offence; it cannot be the mental state of some non-existent, hypothetical person.

Nevertheless, to decide whether someone has been 'reckless' as to whether harmful consequences of a particular kind will result from his act, as distinguished from his actually intending such harmful consequences to follow, does call for some consideration of how the mind of the ordinary prudent individual would have reacted to a similar situation. If there were nothing in the circumstances that ought to have drawn the attention of an ordinary prudent individual to the possibility of that kind of harmful consequence, the accused would not be described as 'reckless' in the natural meaning of that word for failing to address his mind to the possibility; nor, if the risk of the harmful consequences was so slight that the ordinary prudent individual upon due consideration of the risk would not be deterred from treating it as negligible, could the accused be described as 'reckless' in its ordinary sense if, having considered the risk, he decided to ignore it. (In this connection the gravity of the possible harmful consequences would be an important factor. To endanger life must be one of the most grave.) So to this extent, even if one ascribes to 'reckless' only the restricted meaning, adopted by the Court of Appeal in *Reg.* v. *Stephenson* [1979] Q.B. 695 and *Reg.* v. *Briggs (Note)* [1977] W.L.R. 605, of foreseeing that a particular kind of harm might happen and yet going on to take the risk of it, it involves a test that would be described in part as 'objective' in current legal jargon. Questions of criminal liability are seldom solved by simply asking whether the test is subjective or objective.

In my opinion, a person charged with an offence under section 1(1) of the Criminal Damage Act 1971 is 'reckless as to whether any such property would be destroyed or damaged' if (1) he does an act which in fact creates an obvious risk that property will be destroyed or damaged and (2) when he does the act he either has not given any thought to the possibility of there being any such risk or has recognised that there was some risk involved and has nonetheless gone on to do it. That would be a proper direction to the jury; cases in the Court of Appeal which held otherwise should be regarded as overruled. [His Lordship then went on to consider the defence of drunkenness.]"

Appeal dismissed

Lord Edmund-Davies (with whom Lord Wilberforce concurred) dissenting:

"[His Lordship considered Lord Diplock's views on Professor Kenny's statement of the law, approved in *Cunningham*, and Lord Diplock's views on 'recklessness' bearing its popular or dictionary meaning].

I have to say that I am in respectful, but profound, disagreement. The law in action compiles its own dictionary. In time, what was originally the common coinage of speech acquires a different value in the pocket of the lawyer than when in the layman's purse. Professor Kenny used lawyers' words in a lawyer's sense to express his distillation of an important part of the established law relating to mens rea, and did so in a manner accurate not only in respect of the law as it stood in 1902 but also as it has been applied in countless cases ever since, both in the United Kingdom and in other countries where the common law prevails: see, for example, in Western Australia, *Lederer* v. *Hutchins* [1961] W.A.R. 99, and, in the United States of America, Jethro Brown's *General Principles of Criminal Law*, (2nd ed. 1960) p. 115. And it is well known that the Criminal Damage Act 1971 was in the main the work of the Law Commission, who, in their Working Paper No. 31, Codification of the Criminal Law, General Principles, The Mental Element in Crime (issued in June, 1970) defined recklessness by saying, at p. 52:

> 'A person is reckless if, (a) knowing that there is a risk that an event may result from his conduct or that a circumstance may exist, he takes that risk, and (b) it is unreasonable for him to take it, having regard to the degree and nature of the risk which he knows to be present.'

It was surely with this contemporaneous definition and the much respected decision of *Reg.* v. *Cunningham* [1957] 2 Q.B. 396 in mind that the draftsman proceeded to his task of drafing the Criminal Damage Act 1971.

It has therefore to be said that, unlike negligence, which has to be judged objectively, recklessness involves foresight of consequences, combined with an objective judgment of the reasonableness of the risk taken. And recklessness in vacuo is an incomprehensible notion. It *must* relate to foresight of risk of the particular kind relevant to the charge preferred, which, for the purpose of section 1(2), is the risk of endangering life and nothing other than that.

So if a defendant says of a particular risk, 'it never crossed my mind,' a jury could not on those words alone properly convict him of recklessness simply because they considered that the risk ought to have crossed his mind, though his words might well lead to a finding of negligence. But a defendant's admission that he 'closed his mind' to a particular risk could prove fatal, for, 'A person cannot, in any intelligible meaning of the words, close his mind to a risk unless he first realises that there is a risk; and if he realises that there is a risk, that is the end of the matter.': See Glanville Williams, *Textbook of Criminal Law* (1978) p. 79.

In the absence of exculpatory factors, the defendant's state of mind is therefore all-important where recklessness is an element in the offence charged and section 8 of the Criminal Justice Act 1967 has laid down that:
'A court or jury, in determining whether a person has committed an offence—(a) shall not be bound by law to infer that he intended or foresaw a result of his actions by reason only of its being a natural and probable consequence of those actions; but (b) shall decide whether he did intend or foresee that result by reference to all the evidence, drawing such inferences from the evidence as appear proper in the circumstances.'
My Lords, it is unnecessary to examine at length the proposition that ascertainment of the state of mind known as 'recklessness' is a *subjective* exercise for the task was expansively performed by Geoffrey Lane L.J. in *Reg.* v. *Stephenson* [1977] Q.B. 695. . . . [His Lordship then went on to consider the defence of drunkenness]."

Appeal dismissed

R. v. Lawrence [1982] A.C. 510 (House of Lords)

The facts appear from the judgment of Lord Diplock.

Lord Diplock (with whom Lord Fraser, Lord Roskill and Lord Bridge agreed):
"The respondent ('the driver') was riding his motor cycle along an urban street in Lowestoft. The street was subject to a 30 m.p.h. speed limit and there was a good deal of other traffic using it at the time. The driver ran into and killed a pedestrian who was crossing the road to return from an off-licence shop to her car which was parked on the opposite side of the street. The driver was in due course tried on indictment for the offence of causing her death by driving a motor vehicle on a road recklessly, contrary to section 1 of the Road Traffic Act 1972. . . . The prosecution's case was that the motor cycle was being driven at between 60 and 80 m.p.h. and probably much nearer to the latter. The case for the defence was that the speed of the motor cycle was no more than 30 or, at most 40 m.p.h. and probably near to the former. . . .
[His Lordship cited sections 1 and 2 of the Road Traffic Act 1972, as amended by section 50(1) of the Criminal Law Act 1977:
'1. A person who causes the death of another person by driving a motor vehicle on a road recklessly shall be guilty of an offence.
2. A person who drives a motor vehicle on a road recklessly shall be guilty of an offence.'
He then contrasted these with the 'lesser offence' of section 3 of the Road Traffic Act 1972:
'If a person drives a motor vehicle on a road without due care and attention, or without reasonable consideration for other persons using the road, he shall be guilty of an offence.']
Section 3 creates an absolute offence in the sense in which that term is commonly used to denote an offence for which the only mens rea needed is simply that the prohibited physical act (actus reus) done by the accused was directed by a mind that was conscious of what his body was doing, it being unnecessary to show that his mind was also conscious of the possible consequences of his doing it. So section 3 takes care of the kind of inattention or misjudgment to which the ordinarily careful motorist is occasionally subject without its necessarily involving any moral turpitude, although it causes inconvenience and annoyance to other users of the road. So there is no reason why your Lordships

should go out of your way to give to the new section 2 a wide ambit that would recreate the former overlap with section 3.

My Lords, this House has very recently had occasion in *Reg.* v. *Caldwell* [1982] A.C. 341 to give close consideration to the concept of recklessness as constituting mens rea in criminal law. The conclusion reached by the majority was that the adjective 'reckless' when used in a criminal statute, *i.e.* the Criminal Damage Act 1971, had not acquired a special meaning as a term of legal art, but bore its popular or dictionary meaning of careless, regardless, or heedless of the possible harmful consequences of one's acts. The same must be true of the adverbial derivative 'recklessly.'

The context in which the word 'reckless' appears in section 1 of the Criminal Damage Act 1971 differs in two respects from the context in which the word 'recklessly' appears in sections 1 and 2 of the Road Traffic Act 1972, as now amended. In the Criminal Damage Act 1971 the actus reus, the physical act of destroying or damaging property belonging to another, is in itself a tort. It is not something that one does regularly as part of the ordinary routine of daily life, such as driving a car or a motor cycle. So there is something out of the ordinary to call the doer's attention to what he is doing and its possible consequences, which is absent in road traffic offences. The other difference in context is that in section 1 of the Criminal Damage Act 1971 the mens rea of the offences is defined as being reckless as to whether particular harmful consequences would occur, whereas in sections 1 and 2 of the Road Traffic Act 1972, as now amended, the possible harmful consequences of which the driver must be shown to have been heedless are left to be implied from the use of the word 'recklessly' itself. In ordinary usage 'recklessly' as descriptive of a physical act such as driving a motor vehicle which can be performed in a variety of different ways, some of them entailing danger and some of them not, refers not only to the state of mind of the doer of the act when he decides to do it but also qualifies the manner in which the act itself is performed. One does not speak of a person acting 'recklessly,' even though he has given no thought at all to the consequences of his act, unless the act is one that presents a real risk of harmful consequences which anyone acting with reasonable prudence would recognise and give heed to. So the actus reus of the offence under sections 1 and 2 is not simply driving a motor vehicle on a road, but driving it in a manner which in fact creates a real risk of harmful consequences resulting from it. Since driving in such a manner as to do no worse than create a risk of causing inconvenience or annoyance to other road users constitutes the lesser offence under section 3, the manner of driving that constitutes the actus reus of an offence under sections 1 and 2 must be worse than that; it must be such as to create a real risk of causing physical injury to someone else who happens to be using the road or damage to property more substantial than the kind of minor damage that may be caused by an error of judgment in the course of parking one's car. . . .

I turn now to the mens rea. My task is greatly simplified by what has already been said about the concept of recklessness in criminal law in *Reg.* v. *Caldwell* [1982] A.C. 341. Warning was there given against adopting the simplistic approach of treating all problems of criminal liability as soluble by classifying the test of liability as being either 'subjective' or 'objective.' Recklessness on the part of the doer of an act does pre-suppose that there is something in the circumstances that would have drawn the attention of an ordinary prudent individual to the possibility that his act was capable of causing the kind of serious harmful consequences that the section which creates the offence was intended to prevent, and that the risk of those harmful consequences occurring was not so slight that an ordinary prudent individual would feel justified in treating them as negligible. It is only when this is so that the doer of the act is acting 'recklessly' if before doing the act, he either fails to give any thought to the possibility of there being any such risk or, having recognised that there was such risk, he nevertheless goes on to do it.

In my view, an appropriate instruction to the jury on what is meant by driving recklessly would be that they must be satisfied of two things:

First, that the defendant was in fact driving the vehicle in such a manner as to create an obvious and serious risk of causing physical injury to some other person who might happen to be using the road or of doing substantial damage to property; and

Second, that in driving in that manner the defendant did so without having given any thought to the possibility of there being any such risk or, having recognised that there was some risk involved, had nonetheless gone on to take it.

It is for the jury to decide whether the risk created by the manner in which the vehicle was being driven was both obvious and serious and, in deciding this, they may apply the standard of the ordinary prudent motorist as represented by themselves.

If satisfied that an obvious and serious risk was created by the manner of the defendant's driving, the jury are entitled to infer that he was in one or other of the states of mind required to constitute the offence and will probably do so; but regard must be given to any explanation he gives as to his state of mind which may displace the inference."

Lord Hailsham (in a concurring judgment):

"I share the distaste for the obsessive use of the expressions 'objective' and 'subjective' in crime. In all indictable crime it is a general rule that there are objective factors of conduct which constitute the so-called 'actus reus,' and a further guilty state of mind which constitutes the so-called 'mens rea.' The necessity for this guilty state of mind has been increasingly emphasised of recent years (see *Reg.* v. *Sheppard* [1981] A.C. 394) and this I regard as a thoroughly praiseworthy development. It only surprises me that there should have been any question regarding the existence of mens rea in relation to the words 'reckless,' 'recklessly' or 'recklessness.' Unlike most English words reckless has been in the English language as a word in general use at least since the 8th century A.D. almost always with the same meaning, applied to a person or conduct evincing a state of mind stopping short of deliberate intention, and going beyond mere inadvertence, or in its modern, though not its etymological and original sense, mere carelessness. . . . There is no separate legal meaning to the word. This retains its dictionary sense, adequately, I believe, expounded by my noble and learned friend Lord Diplock. It is, of course, true that in a legal context, the state of mind described as 'reckless' is discussed in connection with conduct objectively blameworthy as well as dangerous, while in common speech it is possible to conceive (for instance in the context of the winner of a military decoration in circumstances in which he is reckless of his own safety) of the use of the word without a blameworthy connotation. Now that my noble and learned friend has given it a lucid legal interpretation I trust that it will cause no more trouble to the profession, academics or juries. . . . [T]here is nothing I can usefully add, except that I respectfully accept the view of the majority in [*Caldwell*]."

Appeal dismissed

(iii) *Effect of Caldwell and Lawrence*

The effect of these two decisions upon English criminal law is profound. Their impact upon the substantive rules will be assessed at appropriate points throughout this book. Also the crucial question of whether the law *ought* to distinguish between subjective advertence and objective inadvertence will be delayed until later when negligence has been discussed. But, at this stage, several important questions need to be raised.

(a) **The meaning of recklessness:** It is of course important that legal language does not stray too far from ordinary language, but does that mean that the legal meaning of the term "recklessness" is to be fixed exclusively on a semantic basis? Surely not. What is important, concerning levels of culpability leading to differential criminal liability, is for the law not to miss any distinctions that it perceives as relevant. Lord Diplock clearly felt that it was unnecessary for the law to distinguish between the man who realises that a consequence could occur and the man who failed to appreciate this possibility in circumstances when he ought to have, when he stated: "Neither state of mind seems to me to be less blameworthy than the other."[53]

In the context of the two cases before him, one can have some sympathy for such an approach.

In *Caldwell* he was intent upon defining recklessness in such a manner as to prevent every drunk claiming: "But I was so drunk it never occurred to me that harm could result." Lord Diplock has now developed a quick and rational (in the context of his definition of recklessness) response to such a plea, namely, "That is irrelevant. The risks were obvious; you ought to have foreseen them; you were reckless." So in the context of drunkenness one can at least put forward an argument in terms of policy, that one does not wish to distinguish between subjective advertence and objective inadvertence. Similarly in *Lawrence*, Lord Diplock was concerned "to ensure that young tearaways and others who drive cars or motor cycles disgracefully will not get off a charge of reckless driving by saying that they were perfectly convinced that their manner of driving presented no danger, because they were so clever that they could always avoid a mishap . . . The object of the offence of reckless driving is to catch the driver who flagrantly disregards rules of prudence, whatever he may think about the safety of his behaviour."[54] Lord Diplock's new test has provided him with the same ready response: "The risks were obvious; you ought to have foreseen them; you were reckless."

But does this mean we will *never* want to distinguish advertence from inadvertence in assessing appropriate levels of criminal liability? Might we not conceivably want to draw a distinction between the man who flings open his car door when he knows there is a cyclist approaching who could be knocked over, but he really couldn't care less (case 1), and the man who, through sheer forgetfulness, throws open his car door

---

[53] *Caldwell, ante*, pp. 178–183.
[54] Glanville Williams, "Recklessness Redefined," [1981] C.L.J. 252 at 272.

without any knowledge of the approaching cyclist and without the possibility of harm to another ever entering his mind (case 2)?[55] Whether the law *should* distinguish between these two will be discussed more fully later,[56] but surely there is at least some argument for distinguishing between them in terms of culpability. Every leading law reform body both in England[57] and the United States[58] and most academic writers[59] feel that the two cases are distinguishable, the former being "worse" and deserving of punishment, or at any rate, greater punishment. We shall argue later[60] that Lord Diplock has in reality equated recklessness with *gross* negligence. In doing this, he has deprived us of the terminology to distinguish between advertence and gross inadvertence. Further, as the distinction between gross inadvertence and inadvertence *simpliciter* is extremely difficult to draw, (it is by no means certain into which category case 2 falls), he has in reality blurred the distinction between recklessness and negligence. Surely it would have been better to have maintained the distinction in terminology between recklessness (case 1), gross negligence and negligence (case 2 falling into one of the latter categories), and *then, if one wanted to*, argue that one ought to punish for negligence or gross negligence. It is widely felt that the law needs to provide sharp distinctions between various states of mind in order to attach different levels of criminal liability. *If* ordinary language is incapable of providing sufficiently sharp distinctions to reflect moral distinctions, then, of necessity, the law must develop its own terminology to achieve this task.[61] This terminology, in terms of recklessness, gross negligence and negligence, was already clearly developed in law, and widely approved. It has now been savagely jettisoned.

(b) Creating an obvious risk. Lord Diplock defined recklessness as (i) doing an act "which in fact creates an obvious risk" of the relevant harm occurring and (ii) "when he does the act he either has not given any thought to the possibility of there being any such risk or has recognised that there was some risk involved and has nonetheless gone on to do it."[62]

A major problem is to ascertain what is meant by the phrase "creates an obvious risk." Obvious to whom? To the reasonable man? Or, to the defendant himself? A strong argument has been put forward that the risk must have been obvious to the defendant himself had he bothered

---

[55] See Glanville Williams, *ibid.* at 260.
[56] *Post*, p. 206.
[57] Law Com. No. 89 (1978); C.L.R.C., 14th Report, Offences Against the Person, Cmnd. No. 7844, para. 11.
[58] Model Penal Code, s.2.02.
[59] Glanville Williams, *ante*, n. 54; Smith & Hogan, pp. 67–68.
[60] *Post*, pp. 200–201.
[61] See Glanville Williams (1962) 25 M.L.R. 56, who suggests the terms "conchneg" or "conscious negligence."
[62] *Caldwell, ante*, p. 178.

to think about the matter.[63] This argument is largely based on two passages by Lord Diplock in *Caldwell* when he said of "recklessness":

"It presupposes that, if thought were given to the matter *by the doer* before the act was done, it would have been apparent *to him* that there was a real risk of its having the relevant harmful consequences."[64]

Later he criticised the *Briggs* (old subjective) test of recklessness as "it excludes that kind of recklessness that consists of acting without giving any thought at all to whether or not there is any risk of harmful consequences of one's act, even though the risk is great and would be obvious if any thought were given to the matter *by the doer* of the act."[65]

Glanville Williams, "Divergent Interpretations of Recklessness" (1982) 132 New L.J. 289, 313, 336 at 289–290:

"The main problem is the theory of subjective recklessness concerns the person who knew of a particular risk in a general way but did not think of it at the moment when he was acting . . . Just as we may be said to 'know' a thing because we can instantly recall it, even though it is not at the moment present in our minds, so it is not unreasonable to say that a person knows of a risk for the purpose of the law of recklessness if he would be aware of it the moment he attended to it, even though, being intent upon something else, he does not consciously attend to it. What is required is not present awareness but general knowledge, given the will and ability to recall the knowledge. It does not matter whether we say the defendant 'really' knew of the risk but paid no attention to it, or that he would have known of it if he had paid attention; the difference between these two modes of statement is only verbal. . . .

[I]f the courts are prepared to read the opinion [Lord Diplock in *Caldwell*] as a whole, without concentrating on the model direction, it can be understood to refer to the proposition already advanced, that a person who knows of a risk is to be regarded as aware of it although, being intent upon something else, he does not consciously advert to it. This is how Mr. George Syrota explains the decision in an able article. He says:

'Their Lordships were merely seeking to ensure that juries would not in future become "bogged down" in a particular intractable and fruitless inquiry: was D's knowledge of the risk at the forefront or the back of his mind at the moment he committed the *actus reus*.' [1982] Crim.L.R. 102).

If this is what the rule in *Caldwell* means it can be fully accepted."

On this view the schizophrenic *Stephenson*[66] would presumably still have to be acquitted as even if he had stopped and thought, he still might not have appreciated the risks involved in his activities as knowledge of the risks would not even be at the back of his mind. If this view is correct, why then did Lord Diplock expressly overrule *Stephenson*?

[63] Glanville Williams, "Recklessness Redefined," [1981] C.L.J. 252; G. Syrota, "A Radical Change in the Law of Recklessness" [1982] Crim.L.R. 97; J. S. Fisher, " 'Driving Recklessly' Defined" (1981) 131 New L.J. 694. Some support for this view is to be found in *Bashir* [1982] Crim.L.R. 687 and commentary thereto.

[64] *Ante*, p. 179 (emphasis added).

[65] *Ante*, p. 180 (emphasis added).

[66] *Ante*, p. 176.

Indeed, this whole interpretation seems somewhat tenuous.[67] In *Lawrence* Lord Diplock clearly held that the risk must have been obvious to the reasonable man: "Recklessness on the part of the doer of an act does presuppose that there is something in the circumstances that would have drawn the attention *of an ordinary prudent individual* to the possibility that his act was capable of causing the kind of serious harmful consequences."[68] Similar passages are to be found in *Caldwell* where Lord Diplock states that recklessness "does call for some consideration of how the mind of the ordinary prudent individual would have reacted to a similar situation,"[69] and it is a question whether that "ordinary prudent individual" would foresee the possibility of the harm occurring. Further, it is clear from Lord Diplock's model direction in *Caldwell* that it is only necessary that the risk be obvious to this "ordinary prudent individual." This interpretation has been endorsed by the courts.

Elliott v. C. (A Minor) (1983) 77 Cr.App.R. 103 (Queen's Bench Divisional Court)

The defendant, a 14 year old schoolgirl, was in a remedial class at school. After staying out all night without sleep she poured white spirit on the carpet of a garden shed and then threw two lighted matches on the spirit. The shed was destroyed by fire. She was charged with criminal damage contrary to section 1(1) of the Criminal Damage Act 1971, it being alleged that she had been reckless as to whether the shed be destroyed. The justices concluded that because of her age, lack of understanding, lack of experience and exhaustion, the risk of destroying the shed would not have been obvious to her if she had given any thought to the matter. Accordingly they found she was not reckless and dismissed the information. The prosecutor appealed by way of case stated.

Glidewell J:
"Mr. Moses [counsel for the prosecution] . . . submits that the phrase 'creates an obvious risk' means that the risk is one which must have been obvious to a reasonably prudent man, not necessarily to the particular defendant if he or she had given thought to it. It follows, says Mr. Moses, that if the risk is one which would have been obvious to a reasonably prudent person, once it has also been proved that the particular defendant gave no thought to the possibility of there being such a risk, it is not a defence that because of limited intelligence or exhaustion she would not have appreciated the risk even if she had thought about it.
It is right to say, as Mr. Moses pointed out to us, that there are passages in the speech of Lord Diplock in R. v. *Caldwell* (*supra*) which suggest that his Lordship was indeed using the phrase 'creates an obvious risk' as meaning, 'creates a risk which was obvious to the particular defendant.' . . .
In the light of [the authorities, viz. *Caldwell, Lawrence* and *Miller*] . . . , we are in my judgment bound to hold that the word 'reckless' in section 1 of the Criminal Damage Act 1971 has the meaning ascribed to it by Mr. Moses.
The questions posed by the case were: '1. The justices were correct in their

---

[67] See J. C. Smith [1981] Crim.L.R. 660; E. Griew, "Reckless Damage and Reckless Driving: Living with Caldwell and Lawrence" [1981] Crim.L.R. 743 at 748. The problems associated with this approach are well exposed in R. A. Duff, "Professor Williams and Conditional Subjectivism" [1982] C.L.J. 273.
[68] *Ante*, p. 184 (emphasis added).
[69] *Ante*, p. 181.

interpretation of the meaning of reckless, namely, that a defendant should only be held to have acted recklessly by virtue of his failure to give any thought to an obvious risk that property would be destroyed or damaged, where such risk would have been obvious to him if he had given any thought to the matter? 2. Whether properly directing themselves on the evidence the justices could properly have come to their decision that the defendant had acted neither intentionally nor recklessly in destroying by fire the shed and its contents?'
I would answer 'No' to both questions, and allow the appeal.''

ROBERT GOFF L.J.
"I agree with the conclusion reached by Glidewell J. but I do so simply because I believe myself constrained to do so by authority. I feel moreover that I would be lacking in candour if I were to conceal my unhappiness about the conclusion which I feel compelled to reach . . .

This is not a case where there was a deliberate disregard of a known risk of damage or injury of a certain type or degree; nor is it a case where there was mindless indifference to a risk of such damage or injury, as is expressed in common speech in the context of motoring offences (though not, I think, of arson) as 'blazing on regardless'; nor is it even a case where failure to give thought to the possibility of the risk was due to some blameworthy cause, such as intoxication. This is a case where it appears that the only basis upon which the accused might be held to have been reckless would be if the appropriate test to be applied was purely objective—a test which might in some circumstances be thought justifiable in relation to certain conduct, (*e.g.* reckless driving), particularly where the word 'reckless' is used simply to characterise the relevant conduct. But such a test does not appear at first sight to be appropriate to a crime such as that under consideration in the present case, especially as recklessness in that crime has to be related to a particular consequence.''
(His Lordship however felt himself bound to follow *Caldwell*)

Appeal allowed

This approach has been followed. In R,[70] it was held that the risk had to be obvious to an ordinary prudent person and it was *not* appropriate to endow such an ordinary prudent person with the characteristics of the defendant—say, age, sex etc.[71] In *Bell*,[72] the defendant, with a history of mental illness, suffered a schizophrenic attack and feeling he was being driven on by an outside force which he thought was God, used his car as a "weapon to attack various targets which he regarded as evil"—namely, a Butlins holiday camp. He was held to be acting recklessly in that he had failed to foresee obvious risks. The fact that he might have been unable to foresee those risks was irrelevant—they were obvious to ordinary prudent people.[73]

It is thus clear that the test is a purely objective one. The schizophrenic Stephenson would now clearly be regarded as having acted recklessly.

---

[70] (1984) 79 Cr.App.R. 334.
[71] This approach has been employed with regard to the partial defence of provocation. See, *post*, pp. 643–651.
[72] [1984] 3 All E.R. 842.
[73] The mental illness was only relevant insofar as a verdict of not guilty by reason of insanity was possible.

This is quite remarkable. The *Caldwell* and *Lawrence* tests of reckless-ness have been largely disapproved by academic commentators—but were defended in the first edition of this book. That defence is still maintained[74]—but on the assumption that one is dealing with an actor who is *capable* of improving his behaviour. We have seen that the notion of responsibility, upon which the doctrine of *mens rea* is premised, is based on choice. We can blame a defendant for making the wrong choice. But how can we realistically blame the schizophrenics in *Stevenson* or *Bell* or the young backward girl in *Elliott* v. *C.*? They were not able to assume the responsibility we expect most people to shoulder. They "chose" to act as they did only in the most meaningless sense of the word "choice." And, crucially, their actions did not demon-strate lack of concern—they were simply the inevitable product of their inadequacy. No civilised society can blame people for inadequacies over which they have no control (as opposed to self-induced inadequa-cies such as drunkenness as in *Caldwell*).[75]

It follows that not only does the ordinary prudent person have no inadequacies, but also possesses no particular expertise.

R. v. Sangha [1988] 2 All E.R. 385 (Court of Apeal, Criminal Division)

The defendant set fire to a mattress and two armchairs in a flat with the result that the premises were burnt out. The defendant was charged with causing criminal damage by fire, being reckless whether the life of another would be thereby endangered, contrary to section 1(2)(*b*) of the Criminal Damage Act 1971. In fact, but unknown to the defendant, because of the construction of the flat there was no danger of the fire spreading to adjoining properties. As there was no-one in the flat in which he started the fire he claimed he had not created a risk of danger to the lives of others. He was convicted and appealed to the Court of Appeal.

Tucker J:
"In our judgment, when consideration is given whether an act of setting fire to something creates an obvious and serious risk of damaging property and thereby endangering the life of another, the test to be applied is this: is it proved that an ordinary prudent bystander would have perceived an obvious risk that property would be damaged and that life would thereby be endan-gered? The ordinary prudent bystander is not deemed to be invested with expert knowledge relating to the construction of the property, nor to have the benefit of hindsight. The time at which his perception is material is the time when the fire is started.

Section 1(2) of the 1971 Act uses the word 'would' in the context of reckless-ness whether property would be destroyed or damaged, and whether the life of another would be thereby endangered. We interpret this word 'would' as going to the expectations of the normal prudent bystander.

Applying this test to the facts of the case before us, it is clear that in setting fire to these armchairs as the jury found the appellant did, he created a risk which was obvious and serious that property would be damaged and that the

---

[74] *Post*, pp. 203–212.
[75] C. M. V. Clarkson, *Understanding Criminal Law*, (1987), p. 67.

life of another would thereby be endangered. The fact that there were special features here which prevented that risk from materialising is irrelevant."

Appeal dismissed

(c) **Ruling out the risk.** The new formulation of recklessness, particularly as articulated in Lord Diplock's model direction appears to exclude from its ambit the defendant who stops to think whether there is a risk, concludes there is no risk and consequently acts. Such a person does not come within the test which requires that he must have either "not given any thought to the possibility of there being any such risk" (he *has* given thought to such a possibility), or that he must have "recognised that there was some risk involved" (he has *not* recognised that there is any risk involved).[76] Thus if Stephenson could have established that he had contemplated the possibility of his straw stack catching fire but had dismissed the possibility (say, because of his schizophrenia) then he could not be held reckless under Lord Diplock's test. Such an actor would of course be negligent. This supports the view, that will be later argued, that there is a distinction between negligence and the new recklessness test.[77]

Chief Constable of Avon v. Shimmen (1987) 84 Cr.App.R. 7 (Queen's Bench Divisional Court)

The defendant who held a green belt and yellow belt in the Korean art of self-defence was showing off his skills to some friends. He aimed a kick at a plate-glass window contending that he believed he had the necessary muscular control and skill to avoid breaking the window. He did however break it and was charged with criminal damage contrary to section 1(1) of the Criminal Damage Act 1971. The justices concluded that the defendant "after considering such risk concluded that no damage would result" and so dismissed the charge. The prosecutor appealed by way of case stated.

Taylor J.:
"[A] number of the writers have expressed the view that between the two possible states of mind constituting recklessness as defined in *R. v. Caldwell*, there exists or could exist a lacuna, that is a state of mind which fell into neither of the two alternative categories posed by Lord Diplock . . . Professor Griew ("Reckless Damage and Reckless Driving: Living with Caldwell and Lawrence" [1981] Crim.L.R. 743, 748) cited two hypothetical cases. . . .

'The following cases are outside the terms of the model direction in *Caldwell*. (a) M. does give thought to whether there is a risk of damage to another's property attending his proposed act. He mistakenly concludes that there is no risk; or he perceives only a risk such as would in the circumstances be treated as negligible by the ordinary prudent individual. He missed the obvious and substantial risk. (b) N.'s case is a more likely one. He is indeed aware of the kind of risk that will attend his act if he does not take adequate precautions. He takes pre-

---

[76] Glanville Williams, "Recklessness Redefined" [1981] C.L.J. 252, 278–281; Glanville Williams, "Divergent Interpretations of Recklessness," 132 (1982) New L.J. 289, 313, 336 at 313–314, 336; J. C. Smith [1981] Crim.L.R. 393, 394; E. Griew, "Reckless Damage and Reckless Driving: Living with Caldwell and Lawrence," [1981] Crim.L.R. 743 at 748–9; Smith and Hogan, p. 55.

[77] See *post*, pp. 200–201.

cautions that are intended and expected to eliminate the risk (or to reduce it to negligible proportions). But the precautions are plainly, though not plainly to him, inadequate for this purpose. These appear not to be cases of recklessness. Evidence of conscientiousness displaces what would otherwise be an available inference of recklessness, (to use the language of Lord Diplock in *Lawrence,* . . .)' . . .

Those two examples which were given by Professor Griew seem to me not to be "on all fours." In the first example, it may well be arguable that the lacuna exists because it is not a case where M. failed to give any consideration to the possibility of a risk. It is a case where he did give consideration to the possibility of the risk and concluded, albeit mistakenly, that there was no risk. In terms, therefore, of Lord Diplock's definition, he has not recognised that there was some risk involved. He therefore is outside the second possible state of mind referred to in *R. v. Caldwell.*

A different situation, however, seems to me to apply in the case of N. posed by Professor Griew. He was aware of the kind of risk which would attend his act if he did not take adequate precautions. He seeks to rely upon the fact that he did take precautions which were intended, and by him expected, to eliminate the risk. He was wrong, but the fact that he was conscientious to the degree of trying to minimize the risk does not mean that he falls outside the second limb of Lord Diplock's test. Lord Diplock's second limb is simply whether or not he has recognised that there was some risk. It seems clear to me that in the case of N., as posed by Professor Griew, N. certainly did recognise that there was some risk and went on to do the act.

In my judgment, therefore, the second example given by Professor Griew does not constitute any lacuna in the definition given by Lord Diplock. Applying those examples to the present case, it seems to me that on the findings of the justices and more particularly, as I shall indicate in a moment, on the evidence which they exhibited to their case, this defendant did recognise the risk. It was not a case of his considering the possibility and coming to the conclusion that there was no risk. What he said to the justices in cross-examination should be quoted. He said: 'I thought I might break the window but then I thought I will not break the window . . . I thought to myself, the window is not going to break.' A little later on he said: 'I weighed up the odds and thought I had eliminated as much risk as possible by missing by two inches instead of two millimetres.'

The specific finding of the justices, at para. 5(c) of the case, was as follows: ' . . . the defendant perceived there could be a risk of damage but after considering such risk concluded that no damage would result.' It seems to me that what this case amounts to is as follows; that this defendant did perceive, which is the same as Lord Diplock's word 'recognise,' that there could be a risk, but by aiming off rather more than he normally would in this sort of display, he thought he had minimised it and therefore no damage would result. In my judgment, that is far from saying that he falls outside the state of mind described by Lord Diplock in these terms, ' . . . has recognised that there was some risk involved, and has nonetheless gone on to do it.'

In my judgment, therefore, whatever may be the situation in a hypothetical case such as that of M. as detailed by Professor Griew, which may need to be considered on another occasion, so far as this case is concerned, the justices were wrong in coming to the conclusion that this was not recklessness."

Appeal allowed
Case remitted with direction to convict

There can be no doubt that the defendant in this case had not truly ruled out the risk. Professor Glanville Williams commenting on this case has written:

"This was a case where the defendant needed to be cross-examined. 'Would you have kicked with such force towards your girl friend's or wife's or your baby's head, relying on your ability to stop within an inch of it? No? Then you knew that there was some risk of your boot travelling further than you intended.' A person may be convinced of his own skill, and yet know that on rare (perhaps very rare) occasions it may fail him."[78]

This judgment is unsatisfactory in many respects. The Divisional Court is drawing an impossibly fine distinction. A defendant who rules out a risk by mistakenly concluding that there is no risk is not reckless. On the other hand, the defendant who thinks there is no risk because he is taking all steps to eliminate the risk, is reckless. Such hair-splitting distinctions, apart from lacking any solid moral foundations, can only give rise to numerous interpretive problems. A different objection can be levelled at the Court's apparent acceptance that there is no recklessness where the defendant "perceives only a risk such as would in the circumstances be treated as negligible by the ordinary prudent individual." This cannot be correct. If a defendant perceives *any* risk of the harmful consequence occurring he has not "ruled out the risk" and will be reckless provided the remaining components of the *Caldwell* test have been satisfied.

It is uncertain how far the courts will go in accepting the view that there is no recklessness in such cases. Any other interpretation would run counter to two other House of Lords' decisions, *Derry* v. *Peek*[79] and *Morgan*.[80] Lord Diplock in the House of Lords did hold that recklessness was a state of mind. It seems odd to assert that one who positively believes that something will not happen is reckless as to that thing happening. There would appear to be a clear moral difference between a person who is *convinced* that no harm will occur and one who does not bother to think of the risks involved in his conduct. If there is a moral difference the law ought to provide the vocabulary (negligence and recklessness respectively) to make the necessary discriminations.

On the other hand, there are problems with such an approach. Surely we do not want to acquit appalling drivers "whose unshakeable faith in their ability to avoid danger displays an arrogance bordering on lunacy."[81] Further, it is possible to argue that *everyone* who does not subjectively foresee a risk must believe his act is safe, which is another way of saying that the risk has been ruled out.[82] Acceptance of such a view would destroy the rule in *Caldwell* and is unlikely to be accepted.

[78] "The Unresolved Problem of Recklessness" (1988) 8 Legal Studies 74, 75.
[79] (1889) 14 App.Cas. 337.
[80] [1976] A.C. 182.
[81] D. J. Birch, "The Foresight Saga: The Biggest Mistake of All?" [1988] Crim. L.R. 4, 5.
[82] Glanville Williams, "The Unresolved Problem of Recklessness" (1988) 8 Legal Studies 74.

Indeed, it is going to be difficult in any case to convince a jury that the defendant actually did contemplate an obvious risk but ruled it out. Such a contention may simply not be believed in many cases. Further, such an argument would necessitate "a meticulous analysis by the jury of the thoughts that passed through the mind of the accused."[83] It was such fine distinctions that Lord Diplock was rejecting, yet he appears, albeit by omission, to have perpetuated it in this one sphere—in theory at any rate.

(d) To which crimes does the new test of recklessness apply? The position is still somewhat confused and it is necessary to distinguish between three types of crime:

(i) *Statutory offences that can be committed recklessly.* It was widely assumed that the new definition of recklessness was clearly applicable to all statutes expressly using the concept. In *Pigg*[84] it was applied to section 1(1) of the Sexual Offences (Amendment) Act 1976, and in *Seymour*[85] the House of Lords clearly indicated that recklessness should bear its new meaning in *all* statutory offences. However, in *Satnam and Kewal*, Bristow J. held that the *Caldwell/Lawrence* test of recklessness did *not* apply to section 1(1) of the Sexual Offences (Amendment) Act 1976 (despite the ruling in *Pigg*):

"[*Caldwell* and *Lawrence*] were concerned with recklessness in a different context and under a different statute. The word 'reckless' in relation to rape involves a different concept to its use in relation to malicious damage or, indeed, in relation to offences against the person. In the latter cases the forseeability, or possible forseeability, is as to the consequences of the criminal act. In the case of rape the forseeability is as to the state of mind of the victim."[86]

It will be argued later[87] that it is not feasible to distinguish recklessness as to a result from recklessness as to a circumstance (as Bristow J. appears to do). Nevertheless, there might be grounds for distinguishing "recklessness" as employed in the Sexual Offences (Amendment) Act 1976—this is because section 1(2) of this Act expressly endorses a subjective test.[88]

If this reasoning is accepted, it would appear that the *Caldwell/Lawrence* test of recklessness applies to all statutory offences employing the term, unless that statute makes it plain that the term is being used in a subjective sense.

However, in *Large* v. *Mainprize*[89] the Divisional Court surprisingly adopted the old subjective meaning of recklessness when interpreting

[83] *Caldwell, ante,* p. 178.
[84] (1982) 74 Cr.App.R. 352.
[85] [1983] 2 A.C. 493.
[86] (1984) 78 Cr.App.R. 149.
[87] *Post,* pp. 263–264.
[88] *Post,* pp. 575–577.
[89] [1989] Crim.L.R. 213.

an E.E.C. Regulation.[90] Such an approach is unacceptable. If the *Caldwell* test of recklessness is not liked, it must be abolished. Until then for the sake of certainty and consistency the command of *Seymour* should be followed and the *Caldwell* test applied to all statutory offences of recklessness.

(ii) *Common law offences that can be committed recklessly.* Many common law offences can be committed recklessly. For instance, in *Venna*[91] the Court of Appeal held that the crime of assault can be committed either intentionally or recklessly. Will the new definition of recklessness apply to such offences? Strictly speaking, the ratio of *Caldwell* and *Lawrence* does not extend to such crimes. In *Kimber*[92] the Court of Appeal, dealing with the common law offence of indecent assault,[93] stated that the defendant's "attitude to . . . [the victim] was one of indifference to her feelings and wishes. This state of mind is aptly described in the colloquial expression 'couldn't care less.' In law this is recklessness."[94] No mention was made of *Caldwell* or *Lawrence*.[95] However, with regard to offences of recklessness at common law, it is submitted that the *Caldwell* test ought to be applied. Lord Diplock clearly felt that his new test of recklessness was applicable to *Majewski*[96] which had approved *Venna* in holding that recklessness sufficed in assault cases—this is common law recklessness.

This view is supported by the House of Lords decision of *Seymour* where Lord Roskill stated:

> "it would be quite wrong to give the adjective 'reckless' or the adverb 'recklessly' a different meaning according to whether the statutory or the common law offence is charged. 'Reckless' should today be given the same meaning in relation to all offences which involve 'recklessness' as one of the elements unless Parliament has otherwise ordained."[97]

Following this dictum the Divisional court in *D.P.P.* v. *K (a Minor)*[98] held that "in the light of the authorities" the *Caldwell* test of reckless-

---

[90] Recklessly furnishing false information as to a fishing catch, contrary to reg. 3(2) of the Sea Fishing (Enforcement of Community Control Measures) Regulations 1985.

[91] [1976] Q.B. 421.

[92] [1983] 1 W.L.R. 1118.

[93] The Sexual Offences Act 1956, s.14 makes it a statutory offence to commit an indecent assault on a woman but the meaning of indecent assault is not provided by the statute; the common law meaning applies.

[94] In *Pigg* (1982) 74 Cr.App.R. 352 at 362 the Court again referred to this requirement of "indifference." For a criticism of this additional requirement, see Smith and Hogan, p. 55.

[95] Arguably reference to *Caldwell* and *Lawrence* was unnecessary as any jury would have concluded, on the facts of the case, that the defendant *must* have subjectively realised there was a possibility that the woman was not consenting, or was incapable of consenting. Nevertheless this failure even to mention the two House of Lords authorities on recklessness is somewhat remarkable.

[96] [1977] A.C. 443. See *Caldwell* at 355.

[97] *Ante*, n. 85.

[98] [1990] 1 All E.R. 331. While the offence charged in this case was the statutory offence of section 47 of the Offences against the Person Act 1861, an essential component of the offence is an "assault" which is a common law offence.

ness did apply to the common law offence of assault. In *Spratt*,[98a] however, the Court of Appeal disapproved this view holding that the old *Cunningham* subjective test of recklessness applied to the offence of assault.

(iii) *Offences that can be committed "maliciously."* Several statutes, such as the Offences against the Person Act 1861, s.20, employ the concept "maliciously" which has in the past been interpreted as meaning "intentionally or recklessly."[99] While Lord Diplock's dislike of *Cunningham*, and its subjective interpretation of recklessness for statutory offences employing the term "maliciously," was plain, he was nevertheless careful to distinguish such offences: "maliciously" was a "term of art" whereas "recklessness" was not and should bear its ordinary meaning.[1]

W (a Minor) v. Dolbey (1989) 88 Cr.App.R. 1 (Queen's Bench Divisional Court)

The defendant, aged 15, had been shooting at bottles with an air rifle. He met R and fired the gun at him saying 'there is nothing in the gun; I have got no pellets.' There was a pellet in the gun which hit R between the eyes, wounding him. The defendant was charged with unlawfully and maliciously wounding R contrary to section 20 of the Offences against the Person Act 1861. The justices found as facts (i) that the defendant believed the gun to have been unloaded, because he thought he had used the last pellet whilst shooting at the bottles; (ii) that he had not opened the gun before aiming it at R; and (iii) that he had ignored the risk that the gun might be loaded. The justices concluded that the defendant had been reckless, and that that was sufficient to constitute the malicious state of mind required by the 1861 Act. They convicted the defendant, who appealed by case stated to the Queen's Bench Divisional Court.

Robert Goff L.J.:
"Lord Diplock was concerned to distinguish the meaning of the word 'maliciously' as used in the Offences against the Person Act 1861 from the meaning of the word 'reckless' as used in section 1 of the Criminal Damage Act 1971. No guidance can be derived from the definition of the latter word in Lord Diplock's speech in the consideration of the problem in the present case. It also follows that it was the view of Lord Diplock that *Cunningham* was still good law so far as the subject matter of that case was concerned, and that what he was saying in *Caldwell* was not considered by him to have any impact on either the decision or the reasoning in that case. So we can put on one side the definition of 'reckless' in *Caldwell* and it follows from what Lord Diplock said that we are simply concerned with the meaning of the word 'maliciously' used as a term of art, as he put it, in the criminal law . . .
[T]he word 'maliciously' postulates foresight of consequence. That means, in the ordinary sense of the words, that the accused person must have actually foreseen that a particular kind of harm might be done. . . .
In my judgment, on the findings of fact in this case the defendant did not foresee that any physical harm might come to Rimmer at all, however foolhardy

[98a] [1990] *The Times*, May 14.
[99] *Cunningham* [1975] 2 Q.B. 396; *Flack* v. *Hunt* (1979) 70 Cr.App.R. 51.
[1] See also *Grimshaw* [1984] Crim.L.R. 108; *Rainbird* [1989] Crim.L.R. 505.

he **was** in pointing the gun at Rimmer and pulling the trigger without checking to see if the gun was loaded."

Appeal allowed
Conviction quashed

The overall effect of the above would appear to be as follows: recklessness bears its new *Caldwell/Lawrence* meaning throughout the criminal law, unless it is clear from its context that some other meaning is intended. Malice is a quite separate concept and not synonomous with recklessness; its meaning is quite unaffected by *Caldwell* and *Lawrence*.

(e) General criticism. These two decisions and Lord Diplock's reasoning have been described as "pathetically inadequate,"[2] "slap-happy," and "profoundly regrettable."[3] They have provoked Professors Smith and Glanville Williams, the two most prominent academic criminal lawyers in this country, to suggest that the House of Lords should be abolished as the ultimate appellate criminal court.[4]

Two points can be made with confidence. First, Lord Diplock was purporting to give effect to Parliament's intentions in using the concept "recklessness" in the Criminal Damage Act 1971. There can be no doubt that Parliament intended the word to bear its subjective meaning[5]— that much is almost beyond dispute. Lord Diplock must have been aware of this—yet he deliberately chose to ignore the obvious. But Lord Diplock is not the first judge to resort to such devices to achieve his objectives. Is this really a sufficient justification for such an onslaught by commentators? Secondly, there are many ambiguities and inconsistencies in his two judgments as the above pages reveal. But again, when subjected to such close scrutiny, it would be rare for any judgment handed down by the courts to escape such a charge.

The true reason for the ferocity of the attack upon *Caldwell* and *Lawrence* is neither of the above. It is simply that many commentators do not like the result achieved by these decisions, and of course, it is right that ultimately they should be judged on this basis, rather than on lawyerly nit-picking grounds. *Caldwell* and *Lawrence* have effectively expanded the category of *mens rea* beyond subjective advertence to include certain categories of negligence. To some, this has sounded the death-knoll of subjective *mens rea* as we have known it. The crucial question is of course: was it right to do this? The answer to this all important question must be delayed until the concept of negligence has been explored.

---

[2] J. C. Smith [1981] Crim.L.R. 393, 394.

[3] Glanville Williams, "Recklessness Redefined," [1981] C.L.J. 252.

[4] J. C. Smith [1981] Crim.L.R. 393; Glanville Williams [1981] Crim.L.R. 580, 581–2. Commonwealth courts have shown resistance to following the new test. (*R.* v. *Harney* [1987] 2 N.Z.L.R. 577).

[5] See Lord Edmund-Davies' dissenting judgment; Glanville Williams, *ante*, n. 3.

3. Negligence

(i) *Introduction*

"A person is negligent if he fails to exercise such care, skill or foresight as a reasonable man in his situation would exercise"[6]

"A person acts negligently with respect to a material element of an offence when he should be aware of a substantial and unjustifiable risk that the material element exists or will result from his conduct. The risk must be of such a nature and degree that the actor's failure to perceive it, considering the nature and purpose of his conduct and the circumstances known to him, involves a gross deviation from the standard of care that a reasonable person would observe in the actor's situation."[7]

The introduction to this chapter opened with the example of a child claiming that the injury, caused by him had not been "meant." A contrast was drawn between intentional and accidental harms. That does not, of course, tell the whole story. The accident may have been one which could not possibly have been avoided—the child would get the sympathy and relief from blame and punishment that he desired. The accident may, however, have been one which with some simple precautions and care could have been avoided. Is our response the same as in the first case? Do we now want to blame the child for his lack of care? In every-day life might we not respond to his denial of responsibility with "Well, you should have known what could happen." Might we not find his actions blameworthy? If so, the law might be justified in translating this moral condemnation into legal blame.

The legal concept of negligence has developed to reflect the responsibility that is attributed in everyday life. Legal liability for negligent conduct has been, however, much more limited than one might have expected given society's attitude.[8] Instead it has been restricted to some statutory offences, such as driving without due care and attention.[9] But for more serious crimes the law has clung to the notion that punishment of ordinary negligence would be wrong and unjust. Here the law has developed the idea that there can be degrees of negligence. In other words, in some cases the defendant has shown such a total lack of care that his conduct transcends mere negligence; it can be described as gross negligence and can be regarded as blameworthy and deserving of punishment. Even here, however, there has been great reluctance to punish such conduct, the most notable exception being manslaughter

---

[6] Law Commission, Working Paper No. 31, p. 57.
[7] American Law Institute, Model Penal Code, Proposed Official Draft, 1962, s.202(2)(*d*).
[8] The reluctance to punish negligent conduct has arguably left the way open for the more stringent concept of strict liability to develop.
[9] Road Traffic Act 1988, s.3.

by gross negligence.[10] This was clearly the position until 1981. But what is the effect of *Caldwell* and *Lawrence*?

(ii) *Is recklessness now synonymous with negligence?*

If the effect of *Caldwell* and *Lawrence* has been to equate recklessness with negligence, then it follows that a very large number of crimes, both common law and statutory, can, in effect, be committed negligently. But do *Caldwell* and *Lawrence* go that far?

It will be recalled that the most likely interpretation of *Caldwell* and *Lawrence*, and the one approved in *Elliott* v. *C (a Minor)*,[11] was that it was only necessary to establish that the risks involved in the defendant's acts were obvious to an "ordinary prudent individual." This looks at first glance like a definition of negligence. However, it is submitted that closer inspection reveals that there is still a distinction between recklessness and negligence *simpliciter*. There are three reasons for this submission.

First, it would appear from *Caldwell*, *Lawrence* and *Shimmen* that a defendant who considers a risk, but rules it out, is not acting recklessly.[12] Such a defendant may, however, be acting negligently if the reasonable man in his position would not have so dismissed the risk.

Secondly, Lord Diplock's judgment in *Lawrence* indicates that something more than negligence *simpliciter* is required for a finding of recklessness. He refers to the necessity of establishing an "obvious and serious risk." As has been commented:

" 'Serious risk' refers to the degree of the risk, not to the degree of the injury. It is expressed as a requirement additional to the requirement that the risk must be 'obvious,' *i.e.* obvious to a reasonable and prudent man. The reasonable man must see as obvious a *serious* risk. The jury have to distinguish between an obvious serious risk and an obvious lesser risk."[13]

This clearly indicates that foresight of a *merely* obvious risk (negligence *simpliciter*) will not suffice; there must be foresight (albeit objective) of something more serious.

Thirdly, Lord Diplock, in *Lawrence*, indicated that there must be "moral turpitude" for a finding of recklessness, while such "moral turpitude" was not necessary for a finding of negligence. He stated that an offence under section 3 of the Road Traffic Act 1972 (now the Road Traffic Act 1988) did not involve any "moral turpitude"; it was a "lesser offence" than the offences under sections 1 and 2 of the Road Traffic Act 1972 which require recklessness and where the "manner of driving . . . must be worse than [s.3]." Now section 3 is a crime of negligence.[14] So

---

[10] Now replaced by the new terminology of "reckless manslaughter." See *post*, pp. 607–611.
[11] *Ante*, p. 189.
[12] *Ante*, p. 192.
[13] Glanville Williams, "Recklessness Redefined" [1981] C.L.J. 252 at 276.
[14] *Simpson* v. *Peat* [1952] 2 Q.B. 24.

this crime of negligence, involving no moral turpitude,[15] is something less than crimes of recklessness which by implication do involve such moral turpitude. Crimes of recklessness are "worse" than crimes of negligence. How much "worse" and how this is to be established are matters on which Lord Diplock chose to remain silent. Perhaps he has done no more than take us back to the pre-subjective days earlier this century when recklessness was equated with gross negligence, typified by Lord Atkin's famous comment in *Andrews* v. *D.P.P.*:

"Simple lack of care such as will constitute civil liability is not enough. For the purposes of the criminal law there are degrees of negligence, and a very high degree of negligence is required to be proved before the felony is established. Probably of all the epithets that can be applied 'reckless' most nearly covers the case."[16]

Support for this approach is now to be found in the House of Lords judgment in *Seymour*[17] and subsequent manslaughter cases.[18] Previously there had been a species of manslaughter known as "gross negligence manslaughter." These cases, with virtually no discussion, have proceeded on the assumption that the *Lawrence* test of recklessness now applies in such cases.

(iii) *Is negligence a state of mind or an objective failure to comply with a set standard of behaviour?*

One view of negligence is that it is a *blank* state of mind; it is inadvertence. The argument is usually expressed in the form: if negligence is a failure to think about the possible consequences of one's actions, it is, therefore, not thinking. Not thinking equals a blank state of mind. This approach has important implications for the commonly accepted view that there can be degrees of negligence. If the mind is empty how can one possibly talk about degrees of negligence or emptiness? How, for example, could negligence have been "gross" for the purposes of manslaughter? One cannot have degrees of nothingness. However, as the following extract demonstrates, it is possible to assert that negligence is a state of mind and that there can be degrees of such negligence.

P. Brett, An Inquiry into Criminal Guilt (1963), pp. 98–100:

"Yet however strong may be the traditional arguments which apparently demonstrate that the careless person neither can nor should be blamed, there are two brute facts which cannot be ignored. The first is that people who cause harm by their carelessness feel guilt. The second is that the threat of punishment can deter people from acting carelessly. It is common knowledge that as soon as traffic police appear on the roads drivers begin to pay great attention to what they are doing, and the standard of driving care rises sharply. If the theory

---

[15] Is it true to say that crimes of negligence involve no moral turpitude? See *post*, pp. 206–212.
[16] [1937] A.C. 576 at p. 583.
[17] (1983) 76 Cr.App.R. 211.
[18] *Post*, pp. 608–611.

that a careless person has a 'blank mind' on the matter is correct, it is difficult to understand why this should happen. . . .

Faced with these problems, let us see whether the philosophers can help us. The account given by Ryle (The Concept of Mind (1949)) of recklessness and negligence, or carelessness, is useful. He points out that both these concepts are what he terms heed concepts. When we say that a person has been careless, we are stating that he was not minding what he was doing. And 'minding, in all its sorts, can vary in degree. A driver can drive a car with great care, reasonable care, or slight care, and a student can concentrate hard or not very hard' (at p. 136). Ryle goes on to point out that there is no unique ingredient common to all the different concepts of heed which we use in everyday speech. And he stresses that doing something with care or heed does not involve 'coupling an executive performance wih a piece of theorising, investigating, scrutinising or "cognising" ' (at p. 137) . . . [Ryle] continues:

'To describe someone as now doing something with some degree of some sort of heed is to say not merely that he has had some such preparation, but that he is actually meeting a concrete call and so meeting it that he would have met, or will meet, some of whatever other calls of that range might have cropped up, or may crop up. He is in a "ready" frame of mind, for he both does what he does with readiness to do just that in just this situation and is ready to do some of whatever else he may be called on to do. To describe a driver as taking care does not entail that it has occurred to him that a donkey may bolt out of that side street. He can be ready for such contingencies without having anticipated them. Indeed, he might have aticipated them without being ready for them' (p. 147).

This is surely in accord with the ordinary usage of the terms under discussion, and also with our own personal experience of how we behave when we are either being careful or being careless. And just as there can be varying degrees of readiness, so there can be varying degrees of unreadiness. It thus makes sense to talk of gross negligence, or of recklessness as a very high degree of carelessness, and to distinguish such forms of carelessness for legal purposes from 'mere inadvertence.' In all these cases we are stating that the person concerned was not minding what he was doing; and that although he possessed the capacity to react in a proper way to the situation, he failed to react properly because he was not at the time ready to react.

Recognising, as we surely must, that we do in fact blame people for being unready in a situation which demands readiness, we may enquire whether we are justified in blaming them. To this I suggest that the answer is plainly yes, provided that the person concerned was endowed with the capacity to recognise that the situation demanded a degree of readiness."

Brett, therefore, accepts that negligence is being in an unready "frame" of mind and finds no difficulties in distinguishing between degrees of unreadiness. The criminal law can make the same distinctions and decide at which level negligence becomes blameworthy. Without the same philosophical support Lord Diplock took a broadly similar stance in *Caldwell*, where he made several references to his new test of recklessness (which is basically a type of negligence) as a "state of mind."[19]

However the more common approach is to assert that negligence is not merely inadvertence to the consequence of one's actions; it is not a

---

[19] Lord Hailsham echoed these views in *Lawrence, ante,* p. 183.

blank state of mind. It is the failure to comply with a standard of behaviour objectively assessed.

Glanville Williams, "Recklessness Redefined" [1982] C.L.J. 252 at 256:

"But failing to think can be called a state of mind only in the sense that unconsciousness is a state of mind; that is to say, it is an absence of a relevant state of mind. To say that absence of a state of mind is a state of mind is an abuse of language. Not to think about risks is, of corse, legal fault if a reasonable man would have thought about them; but that does not make not-thinking a state of mind . . . [it] is negligence, and properly punishable as such (in order to impress upon people that this is a dangerous situation in which they are required to stop and think)."

It is this view of negligence that has been accepted by law reform bodies in both England and the United States.[20]

(iv) *Hart's concept of negligence*

Hart, although accepting that negligence is an objective standard of liability (as opposed to a state of mind), has suggested a test of negligence that does allow the characteristics and capacities of the defendant to be taken into account.

H. L. A. Hart, "Negligence, Mens Rea and the Elimination of Responsibility" in Punishment and Responsibility (Essays in the Philosophy of Law) (1968), pp. 152–157:

"Excessive distrust of negligence and excessive confidence in the respectability of 'foresight of harm' or 'having the thought of harm in mind' as a ground of responsibility have their roots in a common misunderstanding. Both over-simplify the character of the subjective element required in those whom we punish, if it is to be morally tolerable, according to common notions of justice, to punish them. . . . What is crucial is that those whom we punish should have had, when they acted, the normal capacities, physical and mental, for doing what the law requires and abstaining from what it forbids, and a fair opportunity to exercise these capacities. Where these capacities and opportunities are absent, as they are in different ways in the varied cases of accident, mistake, paralysis, reflex action, coercion, insanity, etc., the moral protest is that it is morally wrong to punish because 'he could not have helped it' or 'he could not have done otherwise' or 'he had no real choice.' But, as we have seen, there is no reason (unless we are to reject the whole business of responsibility and punishment) *always* to make this protest when someone who 'just didn't think' is punished for carelessness. For in some cases at least we may say 'he could have thought about what he was doing' with just as much rational confidence as one can say of any intentional wrong-doing 'he could have done otherwise.'

Of course, the law compromises with competing values over this matter of the subjective element in responsibility . . .

---

[20] Law Com. Working Paper No. 31, p. 51—the final Report however did not think it necessary to define negligence; The Mental Element in Crime (Law Com. No. 89) para. 68; Model Penal Code, Proposed Official Draft, 1962, s.3.02(2)(*d*). The Draft Criminal Code Bill 1989 (Law Com. No. 177) also does not utilise the concept of negligence at all.

The most important compromise which legal systems make over the subjective element consists in its adoption of what has been unhappily termed the 'objective standard.' This may lead to an individual being treated for the purposes of conviction and punishment as if he possessed capacities for control of his conduct which he did not possess, but which an ordinary or reasonable man possesses and would have exercised. The expression 'objective' and its partner 'subjective' are unhappy because, as far as negligence is concerned, they obscure the real issue. We may be tempted to say with Dr. Turner that just because the negligent man does not have 'the thought of harm in his mind,' to hold him responsible for negligence is *necessarily* to adopt an objective standard and to abandon the 'subjective' element in responsibility. It then becomes vital to distinguish this (mistaken) thesis from the position brought about by the use of objective standards in the application of laws which make negligence criminally punishable. For, when negligence is made criminally punishable, this itself leaves open the question: whether, before we punish, both or only the first of the following two questions must be answered affirmatively:

(i) Did the accused fail to take those precautions which any reasonable man with normal capacities would in the circumstances have taken?

(ii) Could the accused, given his mental and physical capacities, have taken those precautions?

One use of the dangerous expressions 'objective' and 'subjective' is to make the distinction between these two questions; given the ambiguities of those expressions, this distinction would have been more happily expressed by the expressions 'invariant' standard of care, and 'individualised conditions of liability.' It may well be that, even if the 'standard of care' is pitched very low so that individuals are held liable only if they fail to take very elementary precautions against harm, there will still be some unfortunate individuals who, through lack of intelligence, powers of concentration or memory, or through clumsiness, could not attain even this low standard. If our conditions of liability are invariant and not flexible, *i.e.* if they are not adjusted to the capacities of the accused, then some individuals will be held liable for negligence though they could not have helped their failure to comply with the standard. In *such* cases, indeed, criminal responsibility will be made independent of any 'subjective element,' since the accused could not have conformed to the required standard. But this result is nothing to do with negligence being taken as a basis for criminal liability; precisely the same result will be reached if, in considering whether a person acted intentionally, we were to attribute to him foresight of consequences which a reasonable man would have foreseen but which he did not. 'Absolute liability' results, not from the admission of the principle that one who has been grossly negligent is criminally responsible for the consequent harm even if 'he had no idea in his mind of harm to anyone,' but from the refusal in the application of this principle to consider the capacities of an individual who has fallen below the standard of care.

It is of course quite arguable that no legal system could afford to individualise the conditions of liability so far as to discover and excuse all those who could not attain the average or reasonable man's standard. It may, in practice, be impossible to do more than excuse those who suffer from gross forms of incapacity, *viz.* infants, or the insane, or those afflicted with recognisably inadequate powers of control over their movements, or who are clearly unable to detect, or extricate themselves, from situations in which their disability may work harm. Some confusion is, however, engendered by certain inappropriate ways of describing these excusable cases, which we are tempted to use in a system which, like our own, defines negligence in terms of what the reasonable man would do. We may find ourselves asking whether the infant, the insane, or those suffering from paralysis did all that a reasonable man would *in the circumstances* do, taking 'circumstances' (most queerly) to include personal qualities like being an infant, insane or paralysed.[21] This paradoxical approach leads to many difficulties. To avoid them we need to hold apart the primary question (1) What *would* the reasonable man with ordinary capacities have done in these circumstances? from the second question (2), *Could* the accused with *his* capacities have done that? Reference to such factors as lunacy or disease should be made in answering only the second of these questions. This simple, and surely realistic, approach avoids difficulties which the notion of individualising the standard of care has presented for certain writers; for these difficulties are usually created by the mistaken assumption that the only way of allowing for individual incapacities is to treat them as part of the 'circumstances' in which the reasonable man is supposed to be acting. Thus Dr. Glanville Williams said that if 'regard must be had to the make-up and circumstances of the particular offender, one would seem on a determinist view of conduct to be pushed to the conclusion that there is no standard of conduct at all. For if every characteristic of the individual is taken into account, including his heredity the conclusion is that he could not help doing as he did.' (The General Part (1st Ed.) p. 82.)

But 'determinism' presents no special difficulty here. The question is whether the individual had the capacity (inherited or not) to act otherwise than he did, and 'determinism' has no relevance to the case of one who is accused of negligence which it does not have to one accused of intentionally killing."

Punishment for negligent conduct can, therefore, be justified if a combination of objective (the reasonable man) and subjective (could the particular man) factors are taken into account.

Some support for Hart's approach is to be found in the case of *Hudson*[22] where the appellant was convicted of having sexual intercourse with a defective, contrary to section 7 of the Sexual Offences Act 1956 and sentenced to eighteen months' imprisonment. He raised a defence under section 7(2) of the Sexual Offences Act 1956 which reads: "A man is not guilty of an offence under this section because he has unlawful sexual intercourse with a woman if he does not know and has no reason to suspect her to be a defective." In considering whether the appellant had "reason to suspect her to be a defective," Ashworth J. stated:

"Equally, in considering his state of mind, in the view of this court a jury is entitled and indeed bound to take into account the accused himself. There may be cases, of which this is not one, where there is evidence before the jury to show that the accused himself is a person of limited intelligence, or possibly suffering from some handicap which would prevent him from appreciating the state of affairs which an ordinary man might realise. That is a matter again which in the appropriate case would no doubt receive consideration in the summing-up."[23]

We have seen that in assessing recklessness the courts (for example, in *Elliott* v. *C (a Minor)*[24]) have refused to take any account of personal weaknesses or idiosyncracies of the defendant. If capacity to appreciate

[21] Cf. *Camplin* [1978] A.C. 705, *post* p. 645.
[22] [1966] 1 Q.B. 448.
[23] At p. 455.
[24] [1983] 2 All E.R. 1005. See *ante*, p. 189.

the consequences of one's actions is to be ignored for the purposes of recklessness, it is most unlikely to be considered relevant in assessing negligence. This is extremely unfortunate. Most of the hostility, both academic and judicial, to *Caldwell* and *Lawrence* is based on this point: monstrous injustice can result in the punishment of a person who could not have acted otherwise.

(v) *Should negligence be a basis for imposing criminal liability?*

As already seen, there are mixed views as to whether negligence ought to be a basis for the imposition of criminal liability. Much of that debate has been limited to the question whether the then existing, (*i.e.* pre-*Caldwell*) crimes of negligence were justifiable. Since *Caldwell*, the issue is clearly broader. Should negligence (or gross negligence) be the basis upon which *all* or *most* criminal liability is imposed. Such an approach would of course mean the end of *mens rea* in its traditional English sense of intention and subjective recklessness. The Draft Criminal Code Bill 1989, has firmly rejected such a proposal, stating that "every offence requires a fault element of recklessness with respect to each of its elements other than fault elements, unless otherwise provided."[25] Recklessness under the Bill is given its old subjective meaning involving awareness of risks. There is no room in the Bill for *Caldwell*-recklessness, let alone negligence. The question is whether this approach is justifiable.

R. v. Lamb [1967] 2 Q.B. 981 (Court of Appeal, Criminal Division)

The facts appear in the judgment.

Sachs L.J.:
"The defendant, aged twenty-five, had become possessed of a Smith & Wesson revolver. It was a revolver in the literal old-fashioned sense, having a five-chambered cylinder which rotated clockwise each time the trigger was pulled. The defendant, in jest, with no intention to do any harm, pointed the revolver at the deceased, his best friend, when it had two bullets in the chambers, but neither bullet was in the chamber opposite the barrel. His friend was similarly treating the incident as a joke. The defendant then pulled the trigger and thus killed his friend, still having no intention to fire the revolver. The reason why the pulling of the trigger produced that fatal result was that its pulling rotated the cylinder and so placed a bullet opposite the barrel so that it was struck by the striking pin or hammer.

The defendant's defence was that, as neither bullet was opposite the barrel he thought they were in such cylinders that the striking pin could not hit them; that he was unaware that the pulling of the trigger would bring one bullet into the firing position opposite the barrel; and that the killing was thus an accident. There was not only no dispute that this was what he in fact thought, but the mistake he made was one which three experts agreed was natural for somebody who was not aware of the way the revolver mechanism worked."

Lamb was convicted of manslaughter and sentenced to three years'

---

[25] Law Com. No. 177, clause 20(1).

imprisonment. On appeal this conviction was quashed because of a misdirection as to the law of manslaughter. However the Court of Appeal clearly stated that with a proper direction, Lamb would have been convicted and no criticism was made of the sentence he had received.

Getsie v. State, 193 So. 2d. 679 (1966) (District Court of Appeal of Florida, Fourth District)

The defendant, a happily married man who "loved his wife very much," was showing her his new gun that he had received for Christmas. The defendant was experienced with guns. He started releasing the hammer of his gun slowly with his index finger, seeing how it worked, when 1½ feet away from his wife. He then started to sit on her lap. The gun, which he knew was loaded, went off killing his wife. On appeal his conviction for manslaughter was quashed on the ground that there was insufficient evidence of criminal negligence.

People v. Johnson, 33 Ill. App. 3d 168, N.E. 2d 240 (1975) (District Court of Appeal of Illinois, Fourth District)

The defendant, in order to play out a sexual fantasy, frequently tied young boys up, "hypnotised" them and engaged in a smothering ritual with pillows which often induced unconsciousness. He would then revive the boys. On one occasion, however, the victim, a boy aged 13, suffocated to death. The defendant's conviction for murder (and sentence of 20–30 years' imprisonment) was upheld on appeal on the ground that he (a 20 year old college student) must have known that such acts created "a strong probability of death or grievous bodily harm." However the court clearly stated: "If the defendant was unaware of the risk involved, he could not be guilty of involuntary manslaughter"—*i.e.* without subjective awareness of the risk of death or grievous bodily harm, he would be guilty of *no* homicide offence.[26]

What are we to make of these three cases? In relation to *Lamb*, Glanville Williams writes:

"I do not hesitate to say that I regard the sentence as outrageous, a wholly mistaken exercise of judicial discretion. Lamb was a fool, but there is no need to punish fools to that degree. There is no need to punish Lamb at all. He had killed his friend, and that was punishment enough."[27]

Presumably then Williams would agree with the decision that Getsie be guilty of no criminal offence; and if Johnson had been unaware of the risks involved in his strange activities, he too should escape all criminal liability for homicide. They were all "fools" and fools do not deserve punishment.

Lord Diplock in *Caldwell* and *Lawrence* on the other hand, would presumably have disagreed with Williams. In *Caldwell* he compared the state of mind of a man who foresaw a risk with that of a man who "did

---

[26] For an English case with similar facts, see *Pike* [1961] Crim.L.R. 114, 547.
[27] Glanville Williams, "Recklessness Redefined" at 281–282.

not even trouble to give his mind to the question whether there was any risk" and concluded: "Neither state of mind seems to me to be less blameworthy than the other."[28] So to Lord Diplock it would not matter whether Lamb, Getsie and Johnson were aware of the risks they were running. Their failure to consider such obvious risks renders their actions and state of mind just as worthy of punishment; morally they are just as culpable and therefore legally their liability should be the same.

Robert P. Fine and Gary M. Cohen, "Is Criminal Negligence a Defensible Basis for Penal Liability," (1967) 16 Buffalo L.Rev. 749 at 750–752:

"Since negligence involves no *mens rea*, the question is raised as to the advisability of punishing negligent conduct with criminal sanctions. Professor Edwin Keedy responded to this question as follows: 'If the defendant, being mistaken as to the material facts, is to be punished because his mistake is one an average man would not make, punishment will sometimes be inflicted *when the criminal mind does not exist*. Such a result is contrary to fundamental principles, and is plainly unjust, for a man should not be held criminal because of lack of intelligence.' (Keedy, "Ignorance and Mistake in the Criminal Law," 22 Harv.L.Rev. 75, 84 (1908) (Emphasis added.)). This argument is persuasive, especially when considered in conjunction with the traditional concepts and goals of criminal punishment.

The concept of criminal punishment is based on one, or a combination, of four theories: deterrence, retribution, rehabilitation and incapacitation.

The deterrence theory of criminal law is based on the hypothesis that the prospective offender knows that he will be punished for any criminal activity, and, therefore, will adjust his behaviour to avoid committing a criminal act. This theory rests on the idea of 'rational utility,' *i.e.* prospective offenders will weigh the evil of the sanction against the gain of the contemplated crime. However, punishment of a negligent offender in no way implements this theory, since the negligent harm-doer is, by definition, unaware of the risk he imposes on society. It is questionable whether holding an individual criminally liable for acts the risks of which he has failed to perceive will deter him from failing to perceive in the future.

The often-criticised retributive theory of criminal law presupposes a 'moral guilt,' which justifies society in seeking its revenge against the offender. This 'moral guilt' is ascribed to those forms of conduct which society deems threatening to its very existence, such as murder and larceny. However, the negligent harm-doer has not actually committed this type of morally reprehensible act, but has merely made an error in judgment. This type of error is an everyday occurrence, although it may deviate from a normal standard of care. Nevertheless, such conduct does not approach the moral turpitude against which the criminal law should seek revenge. It is difficult to comprehend how retribution requires such mistakes to be criminally punished.

It is also doubtful whether the negligent offender can be rehabilitated in any way by criminal punishment. Rehabilitation presupposes a 'warped sense of values' which can be corrected. Since inadvertence, and not a deficient sense of values, has caused the 'crime,' there appears to be nothing to rehabilitate.

---

[28] *Ante*, p. 178. See also G. Gordon "Subjective and Objective *Mens Rea*" 17 Crim.L.Q. (1975) 355 at 384–385.

The underlying goal of the incapacitation theory is to protect society by isolating an individual so as to prevent him from perpetrating a similar crime in the future. However, this approach is only justifiable if less stringent methods will not further the same goal of protecting society. For example, an insane individual would not be criminally incarcerated, if the less stringent means of medical treatment would afford the same societal protection. Likewise, with a criminally negligent individual, the appropriate remedy is not incarceration, but 'to exclude him from the activity in which he is a danger.'

The conclusion drawn from this analysis is that there appears to be no reasonable justification for punishing negligence as a criminal act under any of these four theories. It does not further the purposes of deterrence, retribution, rehabilitation or incapacitation; hence, there is no rational basis for the imposition of criminal liability on negligent conduct . . .

In addition, Hall ("Negligent Behaviour Should be Excluded from Penal Liability," 36 Colum.L. Rev. (1963)), suggests scientific arguments for the exclusion of negligence from penal liability. One contention is that the incorporation of negligence into the penal law imposes an impossible function on judges, namely, to determine whether a person, about whom very little is known, had the competence and sensitivity to appreciate certain dangers in a particular situation when the facts plainly indicate that he did not exhibit that competence."[29]

In relation to one of the arguments above, that punishment for negligence does not have the desired deterrent effect, consider the view that "punishment supplies men with an additional motive to take care before acting, to use their faculties and to draw upon their experience."[30] Does the argument here not depend on whether one is discussing individual deterrence, general deterrence or deterrence in its educative sense? If the latter, might not punishment for negligence help instil a subconscious belief that it is necessary to be careful in one's actions?

The above passage opens with the widely-held view that negligence involves no *mens rea* because "the criminal mind does not exist." Originally *mens rea*, literally "evil mind" was associated with moral wickedness; it signified the mental state of a person who had chosen to break ethico-legal rules; it was thus an evil intent.[31] The meaning of *mens rea* has however shifted over the years. It no longer has connotations of an "evil" mind, but has embraced notions of "moral blameworthiness," "culpability," "responsibility." But what do these terms mean? Surely behind the verbose and misleading nomenclature, these terms raise one simple question: can the actor be fairly blamed for his actions? The issue then becomes one of determining the basis upon which blame is to be attributed. One could assert that there is no blame to be laid at the doors of Lamb, Getsie or Johnson if they did not realise the risks they were running. Or one could assert that these three gentlemen should be

---

[29] See also Glanville Williams, *Criminal Law: The General Part* (2nd ed., 1961), pp. 122–124; Note, "Negligence and the General Problem of Criminal Liability," 81 Yale L.J. (1972).

[30] A.L.I., Draft Model Penal Code, Tentative Draft No. 4, pp. 126–127.

[31] S. Nemerson, "Criminal Liability without Fault: A Philosophical Perspective" (1975) 75 Col.L.Rev., 1517, 1521.

blamed because of their total disregard for such obvious and serious risks.

George P. Fletcher, "The Theory of Criminal Negligence: A Comparative Analysis," (1971) 119 U.Pa.L.Rev. 401 at 415–418:

"At first blush it seems odd that anyone would argue that negligence is not an appropriate ground for censuring the conduct of another . . . In daily conduct, we all confidently blame others who fail to advert to significant risks. If we confront a motorist driving without his lights on and thereby endangering the lives of many others, we would hardly condition our condemnation of his conduct on whether he knew his lights were off. His failure to find out whether his lights were on or off would itself be a basis for condemning him.[32] Yet theorists have repeatedly argued that this judicual practice is primitive and that, as a matter of principle, an actor must *choose* to do harm in order to be culpable and fairly subject to penal sanctions. Jerome Hall has vigorously advanced this view . . . [T]he proponents of punishing negligence have relied upon the same reply: the culpability of negligence is not the culpability of choice, but rather of failing to bring to bear one's faculties to perceive the risks that one is taking . . . The battleground of one segment of the literature is the role of culpability in justifying criminal sanctions. Jerome Hall argues, for example, that 'in the long history of ethics . . . *voluntary* harm-doing is the essence of (culpability).' From this premise he reasons that negligence is involuntary, and that therefore it is unjust to punish negligent risk-taking. The question Hall raises is the right one. We do wish to know whether it is just to punish the negligent actor. It is not enough to show that punishing negligence has a deterrent impact on other potential risk-creators, for the goal of deterrence, however sound, does not speak to the fairness of forcing the specific defendant to be the object of exemplary sanctioning. Yet the issue of fairness to the defendant is not resolved by positing that negligence is not voluntary and therefore not culpable. Surely, the negligent actor, like the intentional actor, has the capacity of doing otherwise; he could have brought to bear his faculties to perceive and to avoid the risk he created. That is all we typically require to label conduct as voluntary . . .

With the idea of forfeiture in the foreground, culpability functions as the touchstone of the question whether by virtue of his illegal conduct, the violator has lost his moral standing to complain of being subjected to sanctions. If his illegal conduct is unexcused, if he had a fair chance of avoiding the violation and did not, we are inclined to regard the state's imposing a sanction as justified. The defendant's failure to exercise a responsibility shared by all, be it a responsibility to avoid intentional violations or to avoid creating substantial and unjustified risks, provides a warrant for the state's intrusion upon his autonomy as an individual. From the viewpoint of culpability as a standard of moral forfeiture, it seems fair and consistent to regard negligence as culpable and to subject the negligent offender to criminal sanctions."

Fletcher suggests that we ought largely to exclude deterrent considerations in deciding whether to punish for negligence. Surely an argument for punishing negligence is strengthened if supported by *two* propositions, namely:

[32] Compare Glanville Williams, *ante*, n. 3, p. 261: "can it possibly be said, with justice, that a driver who opens his door being momentarily forgetful of risk is 'no less blameworthy' than the driver who realises the possibility of causing injury to a cyclist whom he sees approaching but flings open his door regardless?"

(1) that negligence is culpable or blameworthy; *and*
(2) that it does deter.

R. A. Duff, "Recklessness" [1980] Crim.L.R. 282 at 289–292:

"[There is a] view that inadvertence, however negligent, cannot constitute *mens rea* since we cannot blame a man for what he does not know. That view has been convincingly demolished: whether I notice some aspect of my action or its context may depend on the attention I pay to what I am doing, and be thus within my control; failures of attention may be as 'voluntary' and culpable as other omissions . . .

Some failures of attention or realisation may manifest, not mere stupidity or 'thoughtlessness,' but the same indifference or disregard which characterises the conscious risk-taker as reckless. If I intend to injure someone seriously, I may not realise that this might kill them: not because I am *mistaken* about the likely effects of my assault, but because it 'just doesn't occur to me'—I am blind to that aspect of my action. But such blindness to such an essential and integral aspect of a serious assault, though possible, itself manifests a 'reckless disregard' for my victim's life no different from that of an assailant who knows he is endangering life . . .

[M]y failure to realise this aspect of my action expresses a certain attitude to it: I do not realise it because I regard it as unimportant; my failure expresses my complete lack of concern about it. In general, the extent to which I notice or realise the various aspects of my action, its context, and its results, is a function as much of my attitudes and values as of my powers of observation and attention: to say that I forgot or did not realise something is to admit that I thought it unimportant, and thus to convict myself of a serious lack of concern for it (which is why a bridegroom would hardly mitigate his offence of missing his wedding by the plea that he forgot it). If, as I have suggested, an agent is reckless to the extent that his actions manifest a serious kind of 'practical indifference,' a 'willingness' to bring about some harm, then such recklessness, indifference, and willingness can be exhibited as much in his failure to notice obvious and important aspects of his action as in his conscious risk-taking. A man may be reckless even though, and even partly *because*, he does not realise the risk which is in fact an essential and significant aspect of his action."

In the light of the above extracts, do you think that Lamb, Getsie and Johnson (assuming Johnson did not have foresight) can all be fairly *blamed* for their conduct? Could Stone and Dobinson be fairly blamed? Does this mean they therefore deserve punishment?

The last two extracts above have argued that liability should be imposed for some kind of negligence. If this argument were accepted as a general proposition, three specific issues would need to be resolved:

(1) whether negligence should be given a "purely objective" meaning. It is our submission that it should not and that Hart's concept of negligence, taking into account any incapacities of the defendant should be employed.
(2) whether negligence *simpliciter*, or some higher degree of negligence, such as gross negligence, should be the basis for the imposition of criminal liability. It is our submission that at least for serious crimes only gross negligence should suffice.

(3) whether, on a technical point of nomenclature, this negligence should be classed as a species of *mens rea*. Although little turns on the point as the term "*mens rea*" is purely a term of art employed for convenience sake,[33] it is submitted that such "negligence" should be so included. This approach seems to be one that is now accepted in England. Recklessness (synonymous at least with gross negligence) is widely regarded as a species of *mens rea*.[34]

(vi) *Levels of culpability*

A final important point needs consideration. *Assuming* that Lamb, Getsie and Johnson (with no foresight) are to be blamed for their actions, are they *as* blameworthy as their hypothetical counterparts who might have committed these same actions intentionally or with subjective foresight of the risks they were running? If not, should the law reflect such differences by imposing different levels of liability and/or punishment? Should the law, for example, reflect the view that "to break your Ming china, deliberately or intentionally, is worse than to knock it over while waltzing wildly round the room and not thinking of what might get knocked over?"[35]

A. Kenny, Freewill and Responsibility (1978), pp. 85–92:

"In the same way as the justification of the general requirement of *mens rea* flows from the nature of punishment and the nature of practical reasoning, so the justification of distinguishing between different degrees of *mens rea* arises from the different degrees of proximity to the actuality or possibility of practical reasoning in particular criminal behaviour. The same act, when performed negligently, may be punished less severely than when performed knowingly, and the same act when performed recklessly may be punished less severely than when performed intentionally. We must ask why this is so, and whether it should be so . . .

No doubt almost everyone would regard a reckless killer as more wicked than an inadvertent killer; but the law's principal concern is the prevention of harm, and the harm done by either killer is identical. Should not the penalty too be identical? No: for the point at which the threat of punishment is intended to be brought to bear upon practical reasoning is different in the two cases. The threat of punishment for negligence is meant to enforce at all times a standard of care to ensure that one's actions do not endanger life: the threat of punishment for recklessness is meant to operate at the secific points at which one is contemplating a course of action known to be life-endangering. The actions, therefore, on which the threat of punishment for negligence is brought to bear are less dangerous than those on which the threat of punishment for recklessness is brought to bear: for in general actions which, for all one knows, may be dangerous are less dangerous than actions which one positively knows to be a risk to

---

[33] *Ante*, p. 150.
[34] See Lord Diplock in *Lawrence* (*ante*, p. 183) and the manslaughter cases decided in the wake of *Seymour* (*post*, p. 608). This view is also supported by H. L. A. Hart. *Punishment and Responsibility—Essays in the Philosophy of Law* (1968) at pp. 139–140.
[35] Hart, *ibid.* p. 136.

life. Hence the more severe threat of punishment is held out to the citizen contemplating the more dangerous action.

Just as actions known to be likely to cause death are in general more dangerous than those not known to be so likely, so actions done with the intention of causing death are in general more dangerous than those merely foreseen as likely to cause death. (The latter, for instance, unlike the former, are compatible with the taking of precautions against the causing of death.) This perhaps offers a reason for punishing intentional homicide more severely than reckless homicide, just as reckless homicide is punished more severely than negligent homicide . . .

Thus we have seen the rationale, on the deterrent theory of punishment, for the discriminations made in law between the different forms of *mens rea* from negligence, recklessness and basic intent up to specific intent. It may well be thought that the theory behind such discriminations presupposes a coolness in calculation and a competence in the theory of games which it is unrealistic to impute to the average citizen tempted to commit a crime. On the other hand, it is surely not a mere accident that the gradations of severity in punishment which a comparatively recondite application of the theory of deterrence suggests should correspond in such large measure with the intuitions of moral common sense about the comparative wickedness of frames of mind.

In practice, of course, the deterrent effect of the law operates unevenly and erratically. The elaborate efforts of lawyers and academics to sort offences into precise categories and to fit crimes to punishment on impeccable theoretical grounds may well strike a layman as resembling an attempt to make a town clock accurate to a millisecond in a community most of whom are too short-sighted to see the clock-face, too deaf to hear the hours ring, and many of whom set no great store on punctuality in any case.''

Do such utilitarian arguments adequately explain why we distinguish between different levels of culpability and reflect this by different punishments for each?

James B. Brady, "Recklessness, Negligence, Indifference and Awareness" (1980) 43 M.L.R. 381 at 396–399:

"What is the justification for the decreasing culpability attaching to intentional, reckless and negligent couduct? . . . First of all, I do not believe that an utilitarian rationale concerning the purpose of punishment will suffice. For example, it has been argued that the culpability distinction between intentional action and recklessness may be justified since there is a greater likelihood that an intentional action will result in harm. If the purpose of punishment is the prevention of harm, the argument goes, the degree of seriousness of the offence should be proportionate to the degree of dangerousness. On this theory we punish the intentional offender more because (a) a more severe penalty may be necessary to deter a person from accomplishing a result that is his aim or purpose than to deter one who acts knowing that there is a risk but whose purpose is not to bring about that result, and (b) the intentional offender may require a longer sentence, for purpose of reform or special deterrence, than the reckless or negligent offender. Although there may be particular cases where the difference in degree between reckless and intentional action may be explained on grounds of deterrence, these arguments from an utilitarian rationale are not persuasive in general. For example, considering the class of negligent or reckless offenders as contrasted with the class of intentional offenders there seems to be no reason to believe that the former pose less of a continuing threat of harm than the latter.

If the degree of seriousness of the offence were only dictated by utilitarian reasons, negligence might well be viewed as more serious, in light of the greater number of negligent harms in comparison to intentional harms, and might in special cases require more punishment for purposes of general or special deterrence than intentional offences require.

These distinctions between different modes are to be viewed as distinctions of culpability in the strict sense. If they are justified at all, they are justified because they mark moral distinctions. The strongest argument is that unless the law is to treat morally disparate cases alike the law should reflect these distinctions . . .

What more can be said concerning culpability? At several places in this article I have drawn attention to different modes of culpability; for example, to the fact that negligent conduct is less culpable than reckless conduct, which is less culpable than intentional action. Further, that there are degrees of culpability in recklessness and also mixed modes of recklessness and negligence. Perhaps one has to stop with these intuitions and say, for example, that there often just appears to be 'clear moral distinctions between intention and foresight' (Kenny, *Essays in Legal Philosophy* (1971), p. 160) or that the distinction between recklessness and intention rests on 'unarticulated moral assumptions' (Howard and Elliott, *Law and Crime* (1972), p. 50). But why are these distinctions justified? The question here is not whether the law should reflect moral distinctions, but what is the basis for these distinctions in morality? The following comments are addressed, in a tentative way, to this question . . .

There does not seem to be any single criterion which fully captures our intuitions concerning degrees of culpability. One might argue, for example, that the distinctions could be maintained on the basis of the degree of voluntariness of the action. The reason that negligence, where the agent is unaware of the risk, is less blameworthy than recklessness is that negligent conduct is less voluntary than reckless conduct. But this will not explain the distinction between intentional and reckless conduct. Since in reckless conduct the agent is aware of the risk, it would seem that in both reckless and intentional action the agent has the choice of forbearing from his action. From a consideration of control of conduct, therefore, reckless conduct seems to be as voluntary as intentional conduct.

Suppose that we consider another theory, that it is the factor of likeliness to cause harm which is the criterion of blame. This is a different theory than the one discussed earlier which attempts to explain these distinctions on utilitarian grounds relating to a greater degree of likelihood of harm. The argument here is that the greater likelihood of harm marks a moral distinction and that one who engages in conduct which is more likely to cause harm is more *culpable* than one who engages in conduct with a lesser chance of harm. Under this theory the reason that intentional conduct is more culpable than recklessness causing the same harm is that harm is judged more likely to occur if that is the purpose of one's action than if it is the merely foreseen consequence of one's action.

To a certain extent this factor might explain some of the distinctions in culpability. It seems to be part of the reason, for example, for one who hopes that the harm will not occur, is more blameworthy than one who 'doesn't care one way or the other' in regard to a less likely risk. In this case 'hoping not' is not a mitigating factor because of the greater likelihood of the harm occurring.

But while the likelihood of harm is an important factor, it cannot explain other distinctions. For example, a person who causes harm with the desire of bringing about that harm is thought more culpable, even where the chance of his succeeding was slight, than a person who causes harm by recklessly taking a substantial risk. This cannot, of course, be explained on the grounds of likelihood of harm since the likelihood where the person intentionally takes a 'long shot' is less than where the person acts recklessly in regard to a likely risk. And in cases regarding the same risk, the person's hopes that the harm will not occur does reduce culpability in comparison with one who does not care at all. Again, the difference in degree cannot be explained on the basis of greater likelihood of harm since the risk is the same. Similarly, this theory evidently cannot explain the distinctions between negligent and reckless conduct involving the same risk of harm since, of course, the likelihood of harm is the same. Why then do we blame the reckless agent more? Here the answer seems to be that recklessness manifests a trait of the person that is not present to the same degree in negligence. The person who realises the risk would not have acted unless he was indifferent, in the broad sense, to the interests of others. We properly blame him more, since he is more indifferent. And the person who hopes that harm will not occur is less indifferent, in regard to the same risk, than one who does not care at all. Though again in some cases involving different degrees of risk 'hoping not' does not show a lesser degree of indifference."

It is interesting to compare this with the earlier extract from Duff[36] and speculate on what Lord Diplock's response would have been. One of the most serious aspects of Lord Diplock's judgments is that he has deprived us of the terminology with which to distinguish, should we want to, between subjective recklessness and objective negligence (or, at least, gross negligence).

Assuming again that we wish to maintain these distinctions between intention, subjective recklessness and negligence, there are further problems to be considered. In particular, we would need to decide whether these distinctions should be reflected at a substantive level (*i.e.* different criminal offences for the different states of mind) or at the sentencing stage (*i.e.* same crime, but differing punishments depending on state of mind). If the latter, should this be left to judicial discretion or be prescribed by law in some way (say, in a guideline model of sentencing)?[37]

There is a further question that has not yet been posed. Returning to our three moot defendants, Lamb, Getsie and Johnson—should we take the further, more radical, step of punishing them because they killed their victims, irrespective of whether they were negligent or not? Should we punish them in the absence of blame simply because they caused the harm? They were the cause of the death of their victims who are "just as dead" as if they had been killed intentionally, (subjective) recklessly or negligently. The answer to this question involves a consideration of what are known as crimes of "strict liability."

C. *Strict Liability*

1. Introduction

Running alongside the development of *mens rea*, has been the continuing theme of strict liability. Liability is "strict" because the prosecution are relieved of the necessity of proving *mens rea* as to one or

---

[36] *Ante*, p. 211.
[37] These issues are addressed later at pp. 807–810.

more of the elements of the *actus reus*.[38] In the first "modern" case of strict liability,[39] for example, the defendant was accused of selling adulterated milk. It was sufficient for liability to prove that the milk was adulterated and that he was selling it; his mistake that he had thought the milk was pure was irrelevant. Similarly in the much later case of *Alphacell* v. *Woodward*[40] liability was established under section 2(1)(*a*) of the Rivers (Prevention of Pollution) Act 1951 by the defendants causing polluted water to enter a river. The fact that they had not known that the pollution was taking place and that they had mistakenly thought that their filtering system was operating efficiently did not exonerate them.[41]

How can punishment in such cases be justified? How can *mens rea*, supposedly the central vehicle by which the blameworthy are identified, be sacrificed?

2. Should strict liability be a basis for liability?

In considering possible justifications for the imposition of strict liability, it is crucial that one relates these to the general purposes of punishment.

H. Packer, "Mens Rea and the Supreme Court," (1962) Sup.Ct.Rev. 107 at 109:

"To punish conduct without reference to the actor's state of mind is both inefficacious and unjust. It is inefficacious because conduct unaccompanied by an awareness of the factors making it criminal does not mark the actor as one who needs to be subjected to punishment in order to deter him or others from behaving similarly in the future, nor does it single him out as a socially dangerous individual who needs to be incapacitated or reformed. It is unjust because the actor is subjected to the stigma of a criminal conviction without being morally blameworthy."

This attack by Packer requires careful consideration; two major questions are involved:

  (i) Can strict liability be justified on deterrent or other utilitarian grounds?
  (ii) Is it a morally justifiable doctrine?

---

[38] Modern crimes of strict liability are almost always statutory in origin. It is debateable, however, in many cases whether Parliament intended to create a crime of strict liability; the omission of a requirement of *mens rea* may be deliberate; it may on the other hand be an oversight. While the courts engage in the game of trying to discern Parliament's intention the reality is that it is often they who create crimes of strict liability. See *Sweet* v. *Parsley*, *post*, p. 225.

[39] *Woodrow* (1846) 153 E.R. 907 (Exch.).

[40] [1972] A.C. 824.

[41] Most discussions of strict liability centre around some mistake of fact being made by the defendant which means that he lacks *mens rea*. For example, in the case of *F. J. H. Wrothwell Ltd.* v. *Yorkshire Water Authority* [1984] Crim.L.R. 43 the defendant, in a prosecution under the same Act as *Alphacell*, mistakenly thought that the drains from his factory led into the public sewer system (and on the basis of that poured concentrated herbicide down them). In fact the drains led to a nearby stream. His lack of *mens rea* was not seen as fatal to the prosecution—liability is "strict."

(i) *The utilitarian arguments*

(a) In favour of strict liability, it is claimed that the interests of the public require that the highest possible standards of care be exercised by people engaged in certain forms of conduct.[42] This, in utilitarian terms, is the greater good to be achieved by occasionally convicting someone who may have taken all reasonable care to abide by the law; this greater good could not be achieved to the same extent, if, for example, the defence of reasonable mistake were available.

United States v. Dotterweich, 320 U.S. (1943) 277 at 284–285 (Supreme Court of the United States)

Dotterweich, the president of a pharmaceutical company, was convicted of introducing into interstate commerce drugs that were misbranded. Despite his lack of knowledge of this, his conviction was upheld on appeal.

Frankfurter J.:
"The Food and Drugs Act of 1906 was an exertion by Congress of its power to keep impure and adulterated food and drugs out of the channels of commerce. By the Act of 1938, Congress extended the range of its control over illicit and noxious articles and stiffened the penalties for disobedience. The purposes of this legislation thus touch phases of the lives and health of people which, in the circumstances of modern industrialism, are largely beyond self-protection. Regard for these purposes should infuse construction of the legislation if it is to be treated as a working instrument of government and not merely as a collection of English words. The prosecution to which Dotterweich was subjected is based on a now familiar type of legislation whereby penalties serve as effective means of regulation. Such legislation dispenses with the conventional requirement for criminal conduct—awareness of some wrongdoing. In the interest of the larger good it puts the burden of acting at hazard upon a person otherwise innocent but standing in responsible relation to a public danger. . . . And so it is clear that shipments like those now in issue are 'punished by the statute if the article is misbranded (or adulterated), and that the article may be misbranded (or adulterated), without any conscious fraud at all. It was natural enough to throw this risk on shippers with regard to identity of their wares. . . . ' (*United States* v. *Johnson*, 221 U.S. 488, 497–98.)
Hardship there doubtless may be under a statute which thus penalizes the transaction though consciousness of wrongdoing be totally wanting. Balancing relative hardships, Congress has preferred to place it upon those who have at least the opportunity of informing themselves of the existence of conditions imposed for the protection of consumers before sharing in illicit commerce, rather than to throw the hazard on the innocent public who are wholly helpless."

A. Kenny, Freewill and Responsibility (1978), p. 93:

"The application of strict liability can be justified in special cases: particularly with regard to the conduct of a business. In such a case, even a strict liability

---

[42] Commentators vary in the range of activities they would be prepared to include; some limit it to ultra-hazardous activities, others to "trader offences." For example, S. Nemerson, "Criminal Liability without Fault: A Philosophical Perspective" (1975) Col. L.R. 1517; J. Brady, "Strict Liability Offences: A Justification" (1972) 8 Crim.L.Bull. 217.

statute makes an appeal to the practical reasoning of the citizens: in this case, when the decision is taken whether to enter the business the strictness of the liability is a cost to be weighed. Strict liability is most in place when it is brought to bear on corporations. In such cases there may not be, in advance, any individual on whom an obligation of care rests which would ground a charge of negligence for the causing of the harm which the statute wishes to prevent: the effect of the legislation may be to lead corporations to take the decision to appoint a person with the task of finding out how to prevent the harm in question."

Countering this view, two arguments are usually presented:

(1) R. v. City of Sault Ste Marie, (1978) 85 D.L.R. (3d) 161 (Supreme Court of Canada)

Dickson J.:
"There is no evidence that a higher standard of care results from absolute liability. If a person is already taking every reasonable precautionary measure, is he likely to take additional measures, knowing that however much care he takes, it will not serve as a defence in the event of breach? If he has exercised care and skill, will conviction have a deterrent effect upon him or others?"

(2) It is further argued that instead of increasing the standard of care by deterrence, it may actually be worsened. The defendant may as well be "hanged for a sheep as for a lamb"[43]; why should he take any precautions at all? Such an attitude scarcely increases respect for the law. There may be further disutile effects; the innocent may be made to feel insecure not only in general psychological terms but to the extent that they may be deterred from entering into socially beneficial enterprises governed by strict liability.[44]

J. Brady, "Strict Liability Offences: A Justification," (1972) 8 Crim.L. Bulletin 217 at 224:

"There are two replies to this argument. First, there is little evidence to show that the effect of strict liability offences has been to make these socially beneficial enterprises less attractive. The second, and more important point is that a person who does not have the capacity to run (for example) a dairy in such a manner as to prevent the adulteration of milk is not to be protected on the sole ground that he is engaged in a 'socially beneficial' enterprise. An incompetent carrying on an enterprise in which there is the danger of widespread harm actually is *not* engaged in a 'socially beneficial' enterprise. There can be no objection, therefore, to his choosing not to enter the business."

(b) In addition to the arguments above, one more broadly utilitarian (in the sense that the greater good sought is based on expediency) argument may be adduced. Because of the sheer volume of criminal offences, particularly those of a regulatory nature, it is argued that it

---

[43] P. Brett, *An Inquiry into Criminal Guilt* (1963), p. 8.
[44] R. Brandt: *Ethical Theory* (1959), p. 493. *Contra* S. Nemerson, *ante* n. 42.

would be too time-consuming to require the prosecution to prove a mental element. There is, instead, a presumption of culpability on the part of "responsible" members of a concern that need not be proved.

N. Morris and C. Howard, Studies in Criminal Law (1964), p. 199:

"[It is often alleged that there is] an administrative problem. Prosecutions are numerous: if P were required to prove a wrongful intention, in itself impossible in most regulatory offence cases, the speed at which these charges can at present be dealt with would be much diminished and overwhelming arrears of work would accumulate. . . . There is no evidence of an administrative problem. Proof of absence of fault is admissible in mitigation of punishment. If such proof is admissible for one purpose, no loss of time is involved in admitting it for another. Prosecutions for regulatory offences may be numerous but so are prosecutions for many other offences, particularly the various forms of larceny. No one suggests that the pressure of work should be relieved by removing the requiremnt of *mens rea* from larceny. Indeed, it is arguable that, far from saving time, strict liability often wastes time by necessitating legal argument as to whether it applies to the case in hand."

Supporters of the expediency argument sometimes temper their support by claiming that prosecutorial discretion will prevent the obviously blameless being charged. In this way, the presumption of culpability could be rebutted in extreme cases. There are great difficulties with this approach however. Prosecutorial discretion is notoriously unreliable; there is no guidance as to how extreme the cases must be to justify a prosecution.[45] And, most importantly, it amounts to a negation of strict liability. To some extent at least, liability is being made to depend upon fault. We will return to this point later.[46]

(ii) *The moral arguments*:

S. Nemerson, "Criminal Liability Without Fault: A Philosophical Perspective" (1975) 75 Col.L.Rev. 1517 at 1557:

"It seems, however, that unless we are prepared to abandon a fundamental and common-sense moral belief we must reject utilitarianism as the *ultimate* standard by reference to which . . . [strict liability is] . . . to be decided. It must be rejected because it fails to account for our duty to require desert.
    As Mill wrote:
        '(I)t is universally considered just that each person should obtain that (whether good or evil) which he deserves, and unjust that he should obtain a good or be made to undergo an evil which he does not deserve. This is, perhaps, the clearest and most emphatic form in which the idea of justice is conceived by the general mind' (*Utilitarianism* p. 55)."

According to this view, the man who has taken reasonable precautions does not *deserve* to be punished. He is blameless and it is unjust to subject him to the stigma of a criminal conviction and penalty.

---

[45] Or how to judge who is a "responsible" member of the community.
[46] *Post*, p. 231.

This argument has been answered at two levels,[47] both of which have been subjected to much criticism.
  (a) That crimes of strict liability are not crimes at all in the real sense, and
  (b) That the question of moral blameworthiness is a misconceived one. We ought instead to concentrate on the harm done.

(a) That strict liability offences are not "real" crimes

P. Brett, "An Inquiry into Criminal Guilt" (1963), pp. 114–116:

"Let us now consider what ought to be the future of the doctrine of strict liability. There are those who believe that there is no great objection to it, and even that it serves a useful and proper social purpose. Sayre's general conclusion ('Public Welfare Offences,' 33 Col. L. Rev. 55 (1933)) was that the doctrine was applicable only to the minor public welfare offences, despite his recognition of its applicability in some other fields, which he attempted to distinguish on special grounds. In his view there is no objection to applying strict liability so long as only a light penalty is involved; but it ought not to be applied to 'true crimes.' This seems rather like saying that it is all right to be unjust so long as you are not too unjust. My own posiion is that any doctrine which permits the infliction of punishment on a morally innocent man is reprehensible.

If my view is accepted, we are then faced with the question whether it can be implemented without imperilling the social fabric. There seems to be a strong belief that it cannot. The argument is that the regulation of public welfare has been successfully accomplished under a regime of strict liability, and that it is thus proved that 'strict liability regulation works.' This is doubtless true, but it does not take us one step further to the proposition that effective public welfare regulation will not work without strict liability. That proposition must for most countries remain empirically unverified, for the simple reason that it has never been tried out in practice.

A school of thought has sprung up in recent years which attempts to resolve the question by attaching new labels to strict liability offences. Thus it has been argued that the strict liability offences should be termed 'civil offences,' and that to such offences mistake of fact should not be a defence. They would be punishable only by a fine, and not by any form of imprisonment.[48] . . . The *Model Penal Code* appears to accept this basic position save that it proposes to treat the strict liability offences as still being criminal in nature, but classes them as violations: as such the punishment which may be imposed when they are committed without fault is strictly limited, and the determination whether to class an offence as a violation is left to the lesiglature.

The difficulty which I have with proposals of this kind is that their proponents seem to regard the injustice of punishing innocent conduct as a matter which may be disregarded if it takes place under a different label. My own view is that the injustice remains unaffected despite the semantic change. A fine continues to be a punishment whether it is labelled civil or criminal. I do not deny that the change of label may accomplish a removal of part, if not the whole, of the stigma which results from the mere fact of conviction for a crime; nor would

---

[47] J. Brady, *ante,* n. 42 at pp. 224–227 has added a third answer—in relation to trader offences. There can be no moral objection, he feels, to punishing someone in such cases if he failed to meet the high standard of care if he had the capacity to do so.

[48] This view is, of course, relevant also to the deterrent argument. Some commentators have argued (*e.g.* Brady and Nemerson, *ante,* n. 42) that higher penalties might increase the deterrent effect.

I wish to diminish the importance of such a step. But when this step has been taken, there still remains the brute fact that a man is being *punished* for innocent behaviour. I cannot reconcile this with any theory of justice with which I am acquainted."

The distinction drawn between "real" and "regulatory" crimes (sometimes known as crimes *mala in se* and *mala prohibita*), although one employed by many judges, is open to further criticism. Leigh has pointed out that regulatory crimes may cause as much, if not more, harm than real crimes. "Murder can, no doubt, be contrasted with illegal parking, but is it clear that theft necessarily poses a graver violation of a basic rule than does the pollution of a beach in a resort which depends upon its summer trade for prosperity? . . . Is assault necessarily worse than reckless driving?"[49] Baroness Wootton also entered into the debate by asserting that the distinction being drawn between crimes *mala in se* and *mala prohobita* does not rest on any inherent characteristics of the former category other than the antiquity of such crimes.[50] The complexities of this debate are added to by the argument that, by imposing strict liability for regulatory offences, they are thereby "marginalised"; nobody, least of all the perpetrator, has to take them seriously.

(b) The justifiability of strict liability on the basis of harm done

R. v. Lemon [1979] A.C. 617 (House of Lords)

A magazine aimed at homosexual readers, Gay News, published a poem and accompanying drawings describing and depicting in detail various acts of sodomy and fellatio upon the crucified body of Christ. A prosecution for blasphemous libel was brought. The editor, Lemon, claimed *inter alia*, that while he had knowingly published the poem and drawings, he had no *mens rea* as to its blasphemous nature.

Lord Russell:
"Why then should this House, faced with a deliberate publication of that which a jury with every justification has held to be a blasphemous libel, consider that it should be for the prosecution to prove, presumably beyond reasonable doubt, that the accused recognised and intended it to be such or regarded it as immaterial whether it was? I see no ground for that. It does not to my mind make sense: and I consider that sense should retain a function in our criminal law. The reason why the law considers that the publication of a blasphemous libel is an offence is that the law considers that such publications should not take place. And if it takes place, and the publication is deliberate, I see no justification for holding that there is no offence when the publisher is incapable for some reason particular to himself of agreeing with a jury on the true nature of the publication."

Baronness Wootton was almost the only commentator who called for

[49] L. Leigh, *Strict and Vicarious Liability*, p. 104.
[50] *Crime and the Criminal Law*, (2nd ed., 1981), pp. 42–44.

an increase in crimes of strict liability. She believed that punishment ought to be based on harm done rather than on some perceived wickedness involved in certain states of mind.[51]

Baroness Wootton, Crime and the Criminal Law (2nd ed., 1981), pp. 43, 46–48:

"[The] alternative theory [is] that the wickedness of an action is inherent not in the action itself, but in the state of mind of the person who performs it. To punish people merely for what they have done, it is argued, would be unjust, for the forbidden act might have been an accident, for which the person who did it cannot be held to blame. Hence the requirement to which traditionally the law attaches so much importance, that a crime is not, so to speak, a crime in the absence of *mens rea*. . . .

[Baroness Wootton continues by claiming that the attack on strict liability by most commentators is based upon this pemise: that those with *mens rea* are the wicked who deserve punishment. The function of the criminal law is, therefore, punitive.]

If, however, the primary function of the courts is conceived as the prevention of forbidden acts, there is little cause to be disturbed by the multiplication of offences of strict liability. If the law says that certain things are not to be done, it is illogical to confine this prohibition to occasions on which they are done from malice aforethought; for at least the material consequences of an action, and the reasons for prohibiting it, are the same whether it is the result of sinister malicious plotting, of negligence or of sheer accident. A man is equally dead and his relatives equally bereaved whether he was stabbed or run over by a drunken motorist or by an incompetent one; and the inconvenience caused by the loss of your bicycle is unaffected by the question whether or no the youth who removed it had the intention of putting it back, if in fact he had not done so at the time of his arrest. It is true, of course, as Professor Hart has argued, that the material consequences of an action by no means exhaust its effects. 'If one person hits another, the person struck does not think of the other as *just* a cause of pain to him. . . . If the blow was light but deliberate, it has a significance for the person struck quite different from an accidental much heavier blow.' To ignore this difference, he argues, is to outrage 'distinctions which not only underlie morality but pervade the whole of our social life.' That these distinctions are widely appreciated and keenly felt no one would deny. Often perhaps they derive their force from a purely punitive or retributive attitude; but alternatively they may be held to be relevant to an assessment of the social damage that results from a criminal act. Just as a heavy blow does more damage than a light one, so also perhaps does a blow which involves psychological injury do more damage than one in which the hurt is purely physical.

The conclusion to which this argument leads is, I think, not that the presence or absence of the guilty mind is unimportant, but that *mens rea* has, so to speak—and this is the crux of the matter—*got into the wrong place*. Traditionally, the requirement of the guilty mind is written into the actual definition of a crime. No guilty intention, no crime, is the rule. Obviously this makes sense if the law's concern is with wickedness: where there is no guilty intention, there can be no wickedness. But it is equally obvious, on the other hand, that an action does not become innocuous merely because whoever performed it meant no harm. If the object of the criminal law is to prevent the occurrence of socially

---

[51] This would avoid what Baroness Wootton believed to be an impossible search; man's responsibility (in the sense of capacity to conform to the law's requirements) cannot be ascertained by any rational means. See further *post*, p. 239.

damaging actions, it would be absurd to turn a blind eye to those which were due to carelessness, negligence or even accident. The question of motivation is *in the first instance* irrelevant.

But only in the first instance. At a later stage, that is to say, after what is now known as a conviction, the presence or absence of guilty intention is all-important for its effect on the appropriate measures to be taken to prevent a recurrence of the forbidden act. The prevention of accidental deaths presents different problems from those involved in the prevention of wilful murders. The result of the actions of the careless, the mistaken, the wicked and the merely unfortunate may be indistinguishable from one another, but each case calls for a different treatment. Tradition, however, is very strong, and the notion that these differences are relevant only after the fact has been established that the accused committed the forbidden act seems still to be deeply abhorrent to the legal mind."

Hart has taken issue with these claims of Baroness Wootton by putting forward what has become the classic justification of the doctrine of *mens rea*.[52] He clearly believes in man's ability to determine his own actions and he rests his defence of *mens rea* upon that belief. His view is that even if one accepts man as "responsible," it does not mean that the notion of "wickedness" need automatically be accepted as well, nor that one, therefore, punishes retributively on the basis of it. Instead, as we have seen, the value of punishment rests on the "simple idea that unless a man has the capacity and a fair opportunity or chance to adjust his behaviour to the law its penalties ought not to be applied to him."[53] By punishing when there is some mental element one acknowledges his capacity and has given him the chance not to overstep the legal boundaries of action. It gives man the maximum power to determine his own future. The person who has exercised self-restraint and who has made the right choices is not made to suffer for mistakes or accidents.

Hart then adds a more general justification:

H. L. A. Hart, Punishment and Responsibility (1968), p. 183:

"If you strike me, the judgment that the blow was deliberate will elicit fear, indignation, anger, resentment: these are not voluntary responses; but the same judgment will enter into deliberations about my future voluntary conduct towards you and will colour all my social relations with you. Shall I be your friend or enemy? Offer soothing words? Or return the blow? All this will be different if the blow is not voluntary. This is how human nature in society actually is and as yet we have no power to alter it. The bearing of this fundamental fact on the law is this. If as our legal moralists maintain it is important for the law to reflect common judgments of morality, it is surely even more important that it should in general reflect in its judgments on human conduct distinctions which not only underlie morality, but pervade the whole of our social life. This it would fail to do if it treated men merely as alterable, predictable, curable or manipulative things."

[52] *Punishment and Responsibility* (1968), Chapter 3. *Ante*, p. 149.
[53] Hart, *ibid.* p. 181.

3. The Law

Given the controversy that surrounds strict liability it is not surprising that the law should represent an uneasy compromise between the demands of full *mens rea* and the desire to protect society; sometimes *mens rea* appears to become dominant, at others it is sacrificed entirely—with the legislature continually vacillating between one approach and the other.

How, then, are the courts to determine whether an offence is one of strict liability? At first sight, at least, the issue resolves itself into a problem of statutory interpretation. Where the legislature has done its job efficiently, there is no difficulty. It may indicate, by the inclusion of terms such as "knowingly" or "recklessly," that the offence being created is one requiring *mens rea*. It may, alternatively, make it clear that an offence of strict liability is being created. However, the mere absence of *mens rea* terms is not conclusive evidence that Parliament intended the offence to be one of strict liability. The wording of the provision and its statutory context then have to be examined closely to determine Parliament's intentions.

Pharmaceutical Society of Great Britain v. Storkwein Ltd. (1986) 83 Cr.App.R. 359 (House of Lords)

The appellants, retail chemists, supplied prescription-only drugs in accordance with a forged prescription. They were charged with an offence contrary to section 58(2)(*a*) of the Medicines Act 1968 which provides that "no person shall sell by retail, or supply in circumstances corresponding to retail sale, a medicinal product of a description, or falling within a class, specified in an order under this section except in accordance with a prescription given by an appropriate practitioner. . . . " As the appellants were in no way to blame for what happened, it had to be determined whether section 58(2)(*a*) was an offence of strict liability.

Lord Goff of Chieveley:
"It is, in my opinion, clear from the Act of 1968 that Parliament must have intended that the presumption of *mens rea* should be inapplicable to s.58(2)(*a*). First of all, it appears from the Act of 1968 that, where Parliament wished to recognize that *mens rea* should be an ingredient of an offence created by the Act, it has expressly so provided. Thus, taking first of all offences created under provisions of Part II of the Act of 1968, express requirements of *mens rea* are to be found both in s.45(2) and in s.46(1), (2) and (3) of the Act. More particularly, in relation to offences created by Part III and Parts V and VI of the Act of 1968, section 121 makes detailed provision for a requirement of *mens rea* in respect of certain specified sections of the Act, including ss.63 to 65 (which are contained in Part III), but significantly not s.58, nor indeed ss.52 and 53. . . . It is very difficult to avoid the conclusion that, by omitting s.58 from those sections to which s.121 is expressly made applicable, Parliament intended that there should be no implication of a requirement of *mens rea* in s.58(2)(*a*)."

In addition to the normal principles of statutory interpretation, the courts have developed particular principles in relation to the issue of strict liability. Ostensibly, these are just further rules of interpretation—

enabling them to identify Parliament's intention. It is at least arguable that Parliament in many cases gave no real thought to the matter at all, and that the courts are, in reality, deciding *for themselves* whether an offence is one of strict liability or not. In either case, it is important to consider the principles governing the "decision."

(i) *The presumption of mens rea*

Sweet v. Parsley [1970] A.C. 132 (House of Lords)

The defendant, a teacher, let rooms to students in a farmhouse in which she did not reside although she occasionally stayed overnight in the one room retained for her use. She exercised no control over the students beyond collecting rent from them and occasionally shouting at them to be quiet if on her vists there was excessive noise late at night.

Nevertheless she was convicted of being concerned in the management of premises which were used for the purpose of smoking cannabis contrary to section 5(b) of the Dangerous Drugs Act 1965, when such substances were found during a police search. The Divisional Court upheld her conviction on the basis that she was not only in a position of being able to choose her tenants but could make it a term of the letting that the smoking of cannabis was prohibited.[54] She appealed to the House of Lords.

Lord Reid:
"How has it come about that the Divisional Court has felt bound to reach such an obviously unjust result? It has in effect held that it was carrying out the will of Parliament because Parliament has chosen to make this an absolute offence. And, of course, if Parliament has so chosen the courts must carry out its will, and they cannot be blamed for any unjust consequences. But has Parliament so chosen? . . . Our first duty is to consider the words of the Act: if they show a clear intention to create an absolute offence that is an end of the matter. But such cases are very rare. Sometimes the words of the section which creates a particular offence make it clear that mens rea is required in one form or another. Such cases are quite frequent. But in a very large number of cases there is no clear indication either way. In such cases there has for centuries been a presumption that Parliament did not intend to make criminals of persons who were in no way blameworthy in what they did. That means that whenever a section is silent as to *mens rea* there is a presumption that, in order to give effect to the will of Parliament, we must read in words appropriate to require *mens rea.* . . .

In the absence of a clear indication in the Act that an offence is intended to be an absolute offence, it is necessary to go outside the Act and examine all relevant circumstances in order to establish that this must have been the intention of Parliament. I say 'must have been' because it is a universal principle that if a penal provision is reasonably capable of two interpretations, that interpretation which is most favourable to the accused must be adopted."

[54] *cf.* J. C. Smith [1968] Crim.L.R. 328 who identifies the emptiness of such reasoning. Even had such a term appeared in the letting agreement it would not have absolved the defendant from liability if the crime was, as was stated by the court, one of strict liability. She could, therefore, have done everything reasonable—and more—and still have been found guilty. Her crime was, in effect, "being concerned in the management of premises."

Lord Pearce:

"My Lords, the prosecution contend that any person who is concerned in the management of premises where cannabis is in fact smoked even once, is liable, though he had no knowledge and no guilty mind. This is, they argue, a practical act intended to prevent a practical evil. Only by convicting some innocents along with the guilty can sufficient pressure be put upon those who make their living by being concerned in the management of premises. Only thus can they be made alert to prevent cannabis being smoked there. And if the prosecution have to prove knowledge or mens rea, many prosecutions will fail and many of the guilty will escape. I find that argument wholly unacceptable.

The notion that some guilty mind is a constituent part of crime and punishment goes back far beyond our common law. And at common law mens rea is a necessary element in a crime. Since the Industrial Revolution the increasing complexity of life called into being new duties and crimes which took no account of intent. Those who undertake various industrial and other activities, especially where these affect the life and health of the citizen, may find themselves liable to statutory punishment regardless of knowledge or intent, both in respect of their own acts or neglect and those of their servants. But one must remember that normally mens rea is still an ingredient of any offence. Before the court will dispense with the necessity for mens rea it has to be satisfied that Parliament so intended. The mere absence of the word 'knowingly' is not enough. But the nature of the crime, the punishment, the absence of social obloquy, the particular mischief and the field of activity in which it occurs, and the wording of the particular section and its context,[55] may show that Parliament intended that the act should be prevented by punishment regardless of intent or knowledge."

Appeal allowed

(ii) *Rebutting the presumption*

Gammon Ltd. v. Att.-Gen. of Hong Kong [1985] 1 A.C. 1 (Privy Council)

Lord Scarman:

"In their Lordships' opinion, the law . . . may be stated in the following propositions . . . : (1) there is a presumption of law that *mens rea* is required before a person can be held guilty of a criminal offence; (2) the presumption is particularly strong where the offence is 'truly criminal' in character; (3) the presumption applies to statutory offences, and can be displaced only if this is clearly or by necessary implication the effect of the statute; (4) the only situation in which the presumption can be displaced is where the statute is concerned with an issue of social concern, and public safety is an issue; (5) even where a statute is concerned with such an issue, the presumption of *mens rea* stands unless it can also be shown that the creation of strict liability will be effective to promote the objects of the statute by encouraging greater vigilance to prevent the commission of the prohibited act."

As the above extracts make clear, the presumption in favour of *mens rea* is only a starting point for deliberations. Guiding criteria have gradually emerged as to when the presumption is rebuttable.

[55] See, for example, *Sherras* v. *De Rutzen* [1895] 1 Q.B. 918 and *Neville* v. *Mavroghenis* [1984] Crim.L.R. 42.

(1) *Regulatory offences*

Strict liability is more likely to be imposed in relation to this type of offence. Such an offence is one that:

— pertains to matters of social regulation and public welfare such as health and safety or road traffic.

— is regarded generally as only "quasi-criminal"; that is, there is little or no stigma attached to its violation,[56] and

— carries a light punishment, typically a fine.

Lim Chin Aik v. The Queen [1963] A.C. 160 (Privy Council)

(For facts see *post* p. 228.)

Lord Evershed:
"Where the subject matter of the statute is the regulation for the public welfare of a particular activity—statutes regulating the sale of food and drink are to be found among the earliest examples—it can be and frequently has been inferred that the legislature intended that such activities could be carried out under conditions of strict liability. The presumption is that the statute or statutory instrument can be effectively enforced only if those in charge of the relevant activities are made responsible for seeing that they are complied with. When such a presumption is to be inferred, it displaces the ordinary presumption of *mens rea*. Thus sellers of meat may be made responsible for seeing that meat is fit for human consumption and it is no answer for them to say that they were not aware that it was polluted. If that were a satisfactory answer, then . . . the distribution of bad meat (and its far-reaching consequences) would not be effectively prevented. . . . "

However, these guiding principles are not by any means universally applied. There are glaring examples of cases where strict liability has been imposed where the crime has the stamp of traditional criminality. *Lemon*[57] is an obvious example. So too is *Warner*.[58] Moreover, the courts do create offences of strict liability even where the penalty may be imprisonment. In *Hussain*,[59] the defendant was convicted of unlawful possession of a firearm contrary to section 1 of the Firearms Act even though he believed it was a toy used by his son. Despite the fact that this offence carried a maximum penalty of three years imprisonment, it was held to be one of strict liability.[60]

Gammon Ltd. v. Att.-Gen. of Hong Kong [1985] 1 A.C. 1 (Privy Council)

The appellants were charged under Hong Kong Building Ordinances with deviating in a material way from work shown on an approved plan. It had to be

---

[56] See the speech of Lord Pearce in *Sweet* v. *Parsley, ante*, p. 226.
[57] *Ante*, p. 221.
[58] [1969] A.C. 256. In this case strict liability was imposed for the serious crime of possession of dangerous drugs contrary to s.1 of the Drugs (Prevention of Misuse) Act 1964.
[59] (1981) 47 Cr.App.R. 143.
[60] See also R. v. *Wells Street Magistrates' Court and Martin, ex p. Westminster City Council* [1986] Crim.L.R. 695 and commentary thereto.

determined whether they had to know that their deviation was *material* or whether liability was strict in relation to that element of the offence, the maximum penalty for which was a fine of $250,000 and imprisonment for three years.

Lord Scarman:
"The severity of the penalties is a more formidable point. But it has to be considered in the light of the Ordinance read as a whole. . . . [T]here is nothing inconsistent with the purpose of the Ordinance in imposing severe penalties for offences of strict liability. The legislature could reasonably have intended severity to be a significant deterrent, bearing in mind the risks to public safety arising from some contraventions of the Ordinance. . . . It must be crucially important that those who participate in or bear responsibility for the carrying out of works in a manner which complies with the requirements of the Ordinance should know that severe penalties await them in the event of any contravention or non-compliance with the Ordinance. . . . "

Appeal dismissed

(2) *Effectiveness in promoting the objectives of the statute*

Lim Chin Aik v. The Queen [1963] A.C. 160 (Privy Council)

The defendant was convicted of contravening an immigration ordinance by remaining in Singapore after he had been declared a prohibited immigrant. There was no evidence that the prohibition order had been brought to his attention or that any effort had been made to do so. He appealed.

Lord Evershed:
"But it is not enough in their Lordships' opinion merely to label the statute as one dealing with a grave social evil and from that to infer that strict liability was intended. It is pertinent also to inquire whether putting the defendant under strict liability will assist in the enforcement of the regulations. That means there must be something he can do, directly or indirectly, by supervision or inspection, by improvement of his business methods or by exhorting those whom he may be expected to influence or control, which will promote the observance of the regulations. Unless this is so, there is no reason in penalising him, and it cannot be inferred that the legislature imposed strict liability merely in order to find a luckless victim. . . . Their Lordships prefer . . . [this] to the alternative view that strict liability follows simply from the nature of the subject matter and that persons whose conduct is beyond any sort of criticism can be dealt with by the imposition of a nominal penalty. . . . [61]

Where it can be shown that the imposition of strict liability would result in the prosecution and conviction of a class of persons whose conduct could not in any way affect the observance of the law, their Lordships consider that, even where the statute is dealing with a grave social evil, strict liability is not likely to be intended. . . . The subject-matter, the control of immigration, is not one in which the presumption of strict liability has generally been made. Nevertheless, if the courts of Singapore were of the view that unrestricted immigration is a social evil which it is the object of the Ordinance to control most rigorously, their Lordships would hesitate to disagree. That is a matter peculiarly within the cognisance of the local courts. But Mr. Le Quesne [counsel for the respondent] was unable to point to anything that the appellant could possibly have

[61] As happened indeed in the case of *Hussain* (*ante*, n. 59) where the defendant was only fined £100.

done so as to ensure that he complied with the regulations. It was not, for example, suggested that it would be practicable for him to make continuous inquiry to see whether an order had been made against him. Clearly one of the objects of the Ordinance is the expulsion of prohibited persons from Singapore, but there is nothing that a man can do about it if, before the commission of the offence, there is no practical or sensible way in which he can ascertain whether he is a prohibited person or not."

Appeal allowed

4. Defences to strict liability

(1) *General defences*

The accepted definition of strict liability, as we have seen, is an offence where *mens rea* is not required in relation to one or more elements of the *actus reus*. Liability is thus strict and not absolute, although courts often misleadingly use this latter term. The importance of this point is only fully realised when one comes to consider what, if any, defences are available to the defendant charged with a strict liability offence. Had the offence been "absolute" then no defences would save the defendant from the consequences of his actions. But, given that this is not the case, one has to consider whether, for example, the defendant may plead duress or self-defence or even automatism in answer to a charge.

One possible line of argument would be that whether a defence was available should depend upon the nature of the defence being raised. As we will see, it is possible to distinguish between defences that are justificatory in nature (and result in a determination that there was no wrongful act at all) and those which are excusatory (and relieve the defendant from blame whilst acknowledging the wrongfulness of the conduct).[62] It would be logical to allow the defendant to plead defences that are justifications for his conduct (such as self-defence) but deny defences that are excuses to him (because the defendant is really claiming absence of blame—which is not required anyway to convict). If this argument were adopted, the defences of insanity, infancy, intoxication and automatism (usually regarded as an excuse) would be denied to the defendant.

There might be a certain logic to this but one would have to doubt whether such a result would be either fair or serve any useful purpose. If the underlying rationale of strict liability is to promote higher standards of care, then it seems unlikely to be served by the punishment of, say, infants.

It would appear that the law has not, so far, followed this approach. In *Hill* v. *Baxter*,[63] the defendant successfully pleaded automatism in answer to a charge of dangerous driving (now abolished). The general

---

[62] *Post* p. 274.
[63] [1958] 1 Q.B. 277.

consensus appears to be that other general defences would also be available to the defendant charged with a strict liability offence.

(2) *No-negligence defences*

In addition to any general defences that may be available to the defendant, there is the possibility that the offence with which he is charged may contain within it a specific defence. This will be based upon showing absence of fault or "due diligence." If he can show that he was not negligent, then he will be acquitted. A good example of this is to be found in the Misuse of Drugs Act 1971. Until the passing of this Act possession of drugs was regarded as an offence of strict liability.

Misuse of Drugs Act 1971, s.28(3):

"(3) Where in any proceedings for an offence to which this section applies it is necessary if the accused is to be convicted of the offence charged to prove that some substance or product involved in the alleged offence was the controlled drug which the prosecution alleges it to have been and it is proved that the substance or product in question was that controlled drug, the accused—
   (a) shall not be acquitted of the offence charged by reason only of proving that he neither knew nor suspected nor had reason to suspect that the substance or product in question was the particular controlled drug alleged but
   (b) shall be acquitted thereof—
      (i) if he proves that he neither believed nor suspected nor had reason to suspect that the substance or product in question was a controlled drug; or
      (ii) if he proves that he believed the substance or product in question to be a controlled drug, or controlled drug of a description, such that, if it had in fact been that controlled drug or controlled drug of that description, he would not at the material time have been committing any offence to which this section applies."[64]

C. Howard, "Strict Responsibility in the High Court of Australia" (1960) 76 L.Q.R. 547 at 547–548:

"A court faced with the task of deciding into which class a new minor statutory offence falls, may find itself in a difficulty. If it decides that the offence requires full mens rea, it may put an impossible burden upon P and thereby virtually nullify the legislation. But if it decides that P. need prove no mental element at all, it runs the risk of penalising innocent and guilty alike, to the detriment of justice and respect for the law. Yet this difficulty is often illusory. 'There is a half-way house between mens rea and strict responsibility which has not yet been properly utilised and that is responsibility for negligence.' (Williams, *Criminal Law: The General Part* (1953), p. 21.) The object of most of those offences for which one is now strictly responsible is to impose a high standard of care. Nothing is to be gained by convicting D if he proves that he took reasonable care, or, if this be desired, all possible care. To impose strict responsibility in such circumstances is to punish a useful member of society for a con-

---

[64] See also Trade Descriptions Act 1968, s.24 and *Denard* v. *Abbas* (1987) 151 J.P. 421.

sequence which he has done his utmost to avoid, which is a pointless exercise. If the danger to society from any error at all is so great, then the activity itself should be prohibited; yet no one seriously suggests that the sale of milk should be abolished. If in the cases where strict responsibility is now the rule, responsibility for negligence had been imposed instead, there would have been nothing to prevent the standard of care being set very high, if the court thought this desirable in the public interest; and if the burden upon P were still too great, D could have been required to prove any ground of exculpation on the balance of probability."

L. H. Leigh, Strict and Vicarious Liability (1983), pp. 79, 115:

"In respect of many activities, particularly in relation to public health and consumer safety and standards such [due-diligence] defences do exist. They tend to follow roughly standardised forms, are particular in their address, and enable persons and companies who show that they have complied with their exacting requirements to avoid conviction. Generally speaking, the courts have applied them strictly but sensibly, certain exceptions apart.[65] Much, therefore, of the debate concerning the supposed rigour of the law and the absence of any recognition of a fault principle is beside the point. To a marked extent Parliament has supplied the omission of the courts. . . . [Such defences] coupled with a wide measure of discretion on the part of enforcement authorities, do much to minimise injustice in the operation of the law. Plainly, they do not cover the whole ground. If we have not as yet avoided subjecting the 'blameless harm-doer' to the risk of criminal conviction, we have at least gone a long way towards reconciling his interest in individual justice with the need to protect the public against a variety of evils associated primarily with carrying on particular trades and industries."

5. Enforcement

In the above extract Leigh refers to much of the debate about the principle of fault being beside the point. Given the patchy development of due-diligence defences, that may be over-stating his case, but there is another context in which it is also partly true. As we have seen, one of the classic arguments against strict liability is that it results in the charging and conviction of people who were not at fault (who, indeed, may have done everything they possibly could to avoid bringing about the harm which is the cause of the charge). However, empirical studies of the enforcement of many strict liability offences do not always support this conclusion. Instead, they point to the prime role that fault may play in the decision to prosecute.[66]

Where enforcement agencies such as the factory inspectorate or the Health and Safety Executive are involved, the process of securing compliance with the law is seen much more in terms of co-operation than in coercion. The primary task of the agencies is defined as the prevention of harm and not in the punishment of miscreants. This shapes their prosecuting policies which are thus highly structured. Advice, repeat

---

[65] *e.g. Smedleys Ltd.* v. *Breed* [1974] A.C. 839.

[66] See, *e.g.*, W. G. Carson "White-collar Crime and the Enforcement of Factory Legislation" (1970) 10 B.J. Criminol. 383, I. Paulus, *The Search for Pure Food: A Sociology of Legislation in Britain* (1974) and J. McLoughlin, *The Law and Practice Relating to Pollution Control in the United Kingdom*, (1976).

visits, warnings, improvement notices and the like, are all much more likely to be employed than prosecution. It is only when these fail to secure compliance and the failure to do so thus becomes deliberate that a prosecution will be sought. "[T]he use of the criminal sanction is a last resort; it is a buttress, but it is not a primary tool of enforcement. In effect, there has been a change in formal emphasis from a stress upon the criminal law to a stress upon administrative procedures."[67]

Genevra Richardson, "Strict Liability for Regulatory Crime: The Empirical Research" [1987] Crim.L.R. 295 at p. 303:

"[T]he existing research also indicates that despite their effective rejection of strict liability in practice the majority of enforcement officers regard it with favour and urge its retention. Although prosecution and its direct threat are seldom used, routine enforcement is conducted against a background of the criminal law and the implicit threat of its invocation. The fewer the uncertainties which attach to the law, therefore, the stronger is the agencies' bargaining position."[68]

One final point must be made here, however. There are a large number of strict liability offences that fall outside the schemes discussed above and where liability tends, indeed, to be strict. Many of the summary motoring offences, such as exceeding a speed limit, driving whilst disqualified, etc., would be cases in point. In this particular context, with prosecuting policies varying considerably from one area to another, it is much harder to ascertain what role, if any, is played by fault.

6. Conclusion

There is a plethora of statutory offences that are regarded as imposing strict liablity and despite the weight of the arguments against them it would be naive to imagine that they can all be transposed into offences requiring full *mens rea* or that they could all be decriminalised. It seems clear that strict liability for the most minor of offences is a necessary evil. However, for the rest a number of possibilities exist.

First, it is open to the courts to extend the presumption in favour of *mens rea*.[69] One important enhancement, copied from Canada, would be to state that if the penalty for the offence involves imprisonment, then strict liability is precluded.[70]

---

[67] L. H. Leigh, *Strict and Vicarious Liability* (1982), p. 92. On the same page Leigh gives the example of the enforcement techniques of the Health and Safety Executive that resulted in 1977 in 6,233 improvement notices and 2,666 prohibition notices being issued, but only 1,600 prosecutions being brought.

[68] See also David Nelkin's study of landlords and harrassment: *The Limits of the Legal Process*, (1983).

[69] Under the Draft Criminal Code, clause 20 there is a presumption in favour of *mens rea* "unless otherwise provided."

[70] See [1987] Crim.L.R. pp. 721–723.

Secondly, again following the lead set elsewhere,[71] existing offences of strict liability could be converted into what would amount to offences of negligence by the general, rather than as current, selective, use of due-diligence defences. This would not have the effect of making the prosecutor's task too difficult because it would be up to the defendant to show that he was not negligent.

Lastly, increased use could be made of administrative procedures to secure compliance. Whether actual decriminalisation is the appropriate way forward, is, however, a moot point. As we have seen, those enforcement agencies already involved in such procedures rely upon the stick of the criminal sanction as their last resort. It might be, however, that the threat of, for example, closure of a business, might be as potent a weapon. In any event, using the criteria discussed in chapter one it would have to be decided that these offences were better dealt with outside the criminal law and that the loss of procedural safeguards thereby occasioned was not likely to lead to administrative malpractice.

Clearly, it is desirable that the approach taken to strict liability becomes more structured. What is needed is a reappraisal of strict liability offences and their future role at legislative level. It has been left to the courts to make what best they can out of the mass of modern legislation for far too long.

D. *Dispensing with Mens Rea*

Whether we should dispense with *mens rea* depends of course on what we mean by the phrase "*mens rea*." For present purposes this phrase will be given its traditional meaning[72] of a blameworthy state of mind in the sense of intention or subjective recklessness. If one were to conclude that *mens rea* in this sense should be dispensed with, one would then need to decide on what basis liability should be imposed. Should liability be generally imposed on the ground of gross negligence, negligence, or should liability be generally strict as advocated by Baroness Wootton? Many of these questions and arguments have already been raised in the preceding sections of this chapter, and the discussion in this section pre-supposes some familiarity with those arguments.

The case for dispensing with *mens rea* in its purely subjective sense falls broadly into four categories:

(1) There is no difference in moral terms between intention, recklessness and negligence; the law ought not to reflect distinctions devoid of moral content. Some go further and assert that there is no difference between these and simply causing the harm; pun-

[71] *e.g.*, see the American Law Institute, Model Penal Code, Tent. Draft No. 4, 1985, s.2.05 and comment at p. 140. In Australia, statutes that in other jurisdictions have been held to impose strict liability are held by the High Court to impose liability for negligence instead. See, for example, *Master Butchers* v. *Laughton* [1915] S.A.L.R. 3; *Maher* v. *Musson* (1954) 52 C.L.R. 100. *Cf.* Morris and Howard, *Studies in Criminal Law* (1964). To impose strict liability the legislature must expressly exclude the defence of reasonable mistake.

[72] Smith & Hogan, *Criminal Law*, p. 70; Glanville Williams, *Textbook* p. 71.

ishment is equally necessary. These arguments have been fully canvassed in the preceding sections on negligence and strict liability and will not be repeated here.

(2) It is impossible to prove what a man's state of mind was when he committed a crime. It is an illusion, and perhaps even a deception, for the law to pretend that this is what it is doing.

(3) The idea of subjective *mens rea* is based on outmoded philosophical and psychological ideas. If modern philosophy and psychology has rejected such a concept, the law ought to follow suit.

(4) *Mens rea* is based on notions of responsibility and free will. But these notions have been strongly challenged by the proponents of "determinism"; the law ought not to ignore this challenge.

1. The Problem of Proof

The subjective theory of criminal liability assumes that there is such a thing as a state of mind and that this is ascertainable. But is it possible to inquire into a man's mind to ascertain what his intentions were when he committed the crime (maybe many months or even years previously)? As Ackner J. said in his summing-up to the jury in *Hyam*[73]:

"There is no scientific measurement or yardstick for gauging a person's intention. Unfortunately, there is no form of meter which one can fix to an accused person, like an amp meter or something of that kind, in order to ascertain what the intention is, no X-ray machine which will produce a useful picture."

This immense difficulty in proving a man's state of mind was an important reason behind Lord Diplock's conclusion in *Caldwell* that recklessness should be given an objective meaning. He described the distinction between consciously running a risk and failing to appreciate a risk as "not being a practicable distinction for use in a trial by jury." He stated that "[t]he only person who knows what the accused's mental processes were is the accused himself, and probably not even he can recall them accurately when the rage or excitement under which he acted has passed."[74] He was not prepared to perpetuate such "fine and impracticable distinctions."

This, taken to its logical conclusion, is the argument that because it is unrealistic to believe that one can reliably determine the state of a man's mind, the criminal law should not attempt to make criminal liability turn on states of mind.

In order to assess the strength of this claim, it is first necessary to inquire how courts (at least try to) prove intention or other subjective states of mind.

Without direct evidence of a man's state of mind such as a confession (but even this might not be reliable), *mens rea* has to be established by drawing inferences from facts; the jury must consider all the circum-

---

[73] No. 6530, C. 72, Warwick Crown Court; tried November 22 to 24, 1972.
[74] *Ante*, p. 180.

stantial evidence—the conduct of the defendant before, during and after the crime, motive, statements by the defendant, type of weapon used etc.,—and from that infer what the defendant must have intended. The jury can only perform this task by trying to ascertain what any normal or reasonable person would have intended or foreseen in those circumstances. From this developed the important maxim that a man must be taken to intend the natural and probable consequences of his actions. This maxim, which of course went a long way towards destroying any subjective notion of *mens rea*, was interpreted rigidly by the House of Lords in the following decision.

Director of Public Prosecutions v. Smith [1961] A.C. 290 (House of Lords)

The respondent was driving a car in which there was stolen property. While he was stopped by a police officer on point duty, another officer came to the driver's window and spoke to the respondent. As a result of what he saw in the back of the car, this constable told the respondent to draw into the near side. The respondent began to do so and the constable walked beside the car. Then the respondent suddenly accelerated and made off down an adjoining road. The constable succeeded in hanging on to the car which pursued an erratic course until the constable was thrown off in the path of a vehicle which ran over him, causing him fatal injuries.

At his trial for capital murder, the respondent maintained that he had no intention of killing or causing serious injury to the constable. Donovan J. directed the jury: "if you are satisfied that . . . he must, as a reasonable man, have contemplated that grievous bodily harm was likely to result to that officer . . . and that such harm did happen and the officer died in consequence, then the accused is guilty of capital murder."

The jury returned a verdict of guilty. The Court of Criminal Appeal quashed his conviction on the ground of misdirection. The crown appealed to the House of Lords.

Viscount Kilmuir:
"The jury must, of course, in such a case as the present make up their minds on the evidence whether the accused was unlawfully and voluntarily doing something to someone. The unlawful and voluntary act must clearly be aimed at someone in order to eliminate cases of negligence or of careless or dangerous driving. Once, however, the jury are satisfied as to that, it matters not what the accused in fact contemplated as the probable result or whether he ever contemplated at all, provided he was in law responsible and accountable for his actions, that is, was a man capable of forming an intent, not insane within the M'Naghten Rules and not suffering from diminished responsibility. On the assumption that he is so accountable for his actions, the sole question is whether the unlawful and voluntary act was of such a kind that grievous bodily harm was the natural and probable result. The only test available for this is what the ordinary responsible man would, in all the circumstances of the case, have contemplated as the natural and probable result. That, indeed, has always been the law. . . .

My Lords, the law being as I have endeavoured to define it, there seems to be no ground upon which the approach by the trial judge in the present case can be criticised. Having excluded the suggestion of accident, he asked the jury to consider what were the exact circumstances at the time as known to the respondent and what were the unlawful and voluntary acts which he did towards the police officer. The learned judge then prefaced the passages of which complaint is made by saying, in effect, that if in doing what he did he must as a reasonable man have contemplated that serious harm was likely to occur then he was guilty of murder.

My only doubt concerns the use of the expression 'a reasonable man,' since this to lawyers connotes the man on the Clapham omnibus by reference to whom a standard of care in civil cases is ascertained. In judging of intent, however, it really denotes an ordinary man capable of reasoning who is responsible and accountable for his actions, and this would be the sense in which it would be understood by a jury.

Another criticism of the summing-up and one which found favour in the Court of Criminal Appeal concerned the manner in which the trial judge dealt with the presumption that a man intends the natural and probable consequences of his acts. I will cite the passage again: 'The intention with which a man did something can usually be determined by a jury only by inference from the surrounding circumstances including the presumption of law that a man intends the natural and probable consequences of his acts.' It is said that the reference to this being a presumption of law without explaining that it was rebuttable amounted to a misdirection. Whether the presumption is one of law or of fact or, as has been said, of common sense, matters not for this purpose. The real question is whether the jury should have been told that it was rebuttable. In truth, however, as I see it, this is merely another way of applying the test of the reasonable man. Provided that the presumption is applied, once the accused's knowledge of the circumstances and the nature of his acts have been ascertained, the only thing that could rebut the presumption would be proof of incapacity to form an intent, insanity or diminished responsibility. In the present case, therefore, there was no need to explain to the jury that the presumption was rebuttable."

Appeal allowed

This decision was greeted with howls of derision by most English commentators.[75] The exact effect of the decision was never settled: did it lay down an irrebuttable evidential presumption of intention—that intention was to be ascertained objectively for all crimes? Or did it lay down a new *mens rea* for murder—a completely objective test where it was only necessary to establish that death or grievous bodily harm was objectively foreseeable?[76] Either way its effect was profound. Murder (and possibly all crimes) had been transformed into a crime of negligence: if the reasonable man would have foreseen the harm, the defendant was liable. It is interesting to note that Viscount Kilmuir emphasised that the defendant must be capable of forming the intent—this is, in essence, Hart's test of negligence.[77]

Intense criticism of this decision[78] led to the passing of the Criminal Justice Act 1967, s.8:

---

[75] Fletcher regards the reaction to this case as "even more unfortunate" than the decision itself in that English judges and commentators have "gone to the opposite extreme" in eschewing "any reliance on the projected behaviour of a reasonable person" (p. 704).

[76] Smith & Hogan, (4th ed.) p. 295.

[77] *Ante*, p. 203, *cf. Eliot* v. C (*a Minor*), *ante*, p. 189.

[78] *e.g.*, Law Commission Imputed Criminal Intent (*Director of Public Prosecutions* v. *Smith*) 1965.

"A court or jury, in determining whether a person has committed an offence—

(a) shall not be bound in law to infer that he intended or foresaw a result of his actions by reason only of its being a natural and probable consequence of these actions; but

(b) shall decide whether he did intend or foresee that result by reference to all the evidence, drawing such inferences from the evidence as appear proper in the circumstances."

So the legislature has here clearly endorsed the idea that intention is to be subjectively ascertained—as must foresight.[79] But what is this foresight? It was generally assumed that this was synonymous with recklessness[80] (a view that was clearly correct); this is now equally clearly an incorrect view in the light of *Caldwell* which states that recklessness is objectively determined. Does this mean we now have a new category of *mens rea*, foresight, somewhere between intention and recklessness? This would be an extraordinary conclusion. Again, *Caldwell* has thrown up the question; no answer is yet apparent. One further, unfortunate implication of the section would appear to be that by laying emphasis upon *mens rea*, the police have to exert more pressure to get confessions from defendants to strengthen their case.[81]

But section 8 does not actually solve the practical problem of proving *mens rea* at all; it merely states what *ought* to be done in theory. It is true that if there is clear evidence that the defendant did not intend a result, the jury can so find. But in what circumstances would a jury conclude that while a reasonable man would have foreseen a result, the defendant did not? Surely this would generally only occur where there was clear evidence that the defendant's state of mind was in some material way different from that of the reasonable man—say, because he was a schizophrenic, or mentally retarded etc. But Viscount Kilmuir in *D.P.P. v. Smith* was careful to exclude those persons not capable of conforming to the standards of the reasonable man—just as Hart excluded such persons from his test of negligence.

In most other cases, however, it is doubtful if juries can do otherwise than draw inferences from conduct and apply their own standards, the standards of ordinary people: "If I had been in that situation, what would I have foreseen?" Perhaps this is what was meant by this startling extract from a recent training manual for magistrates: "It is sometimes said on the defendant's behalf that he did not intend to inflict the particular injury which the victim suffered. This is always a weak point because any sane person who commits an act of violence must expect injury to result. The fact that it happens to be greater than anticipated

---

[79] See also, *Frankland* [1987] A.C. 576 where the Privy Council reiterated the point that the test is a subjective one.

[80] Glanville Williams, *Textbook*, (1st ed.) p. 63; Lord Edmund-Davies' dissenting judgment in *Caldwell*.

[81] A. Sanders, "Some Dangers of Policy Oriented Research—The Case of Prosecutions," in *Criminal Law and Justice* (1987) ed. I. Dennis, p. 208.

provides no excuse whatsoever."[82] The Court of Appeal can sometimes pay lip-service to section 8 and quash convictions because the jury were not clearly directed that the test of intention is subjective.[83] Critics of *Caldwell* can maintain that "no evidence is quoted to show that the distinction (between subjective foresight and failing to foresee) has not worked perfectly well in practice,"[84] and can claim "the truth is that arguments based upon the jury system are worthless."[85] But if the reality is that section 8 is impracticable and juries in fact have to apply objective tests in most cases, then surely the time has come for a drastic rethinking of the concept *mens rea* in its subjective form. The law of the books should correlate with the law in action. If our whole system of criminal law is based upon an impracticable premise, might not the time have come to rethink the premise?

2. Philosophical objections

In addition to the above objections to the concept of *mens rea*, several important philosophical questions need to be raised.

At the start of this chapter the view was expressed that the criminal law sees man as generally responsible for his actions—one can attribute blame and praise to him for his actions. He could, if he had wished to, have done otherwise and we, therefore, punish the "deliberate" actor who has made the wrong choice and caused harm.

Two premises are involved in this conclusion about the nature of man's conduct:

(i) That there is a distinction between what a man does and what he thinks about his actions: he *decides* to *act*. The twin concepts *actus reus* and *mens rea* explored in this chapter thus accept a "dualist" viewpoint. The implications of dualism may, however, not be as supportive to the legal theory of *mens rea* as might at first sight appear.

(ii) That there is freedom of will. Man is distinguishable from inanimate plants and animal life because of this feature. It is the ability to choose that provides the "humanness" of man. The opposing view states that man's actions are instead governed by preceding events and conditions. They are thus "determined" and freedom of will a myth.

(i) *Dualism*

The modern concept of dualism draws a distinction between mind and body and owes its formulation to the work of René Descartes.[86] Its roots, however, are much deeper and can be traced back, through the

---

[82] R. Bartle, *Crime and the New Magistrate* (1985), quoted from David Nelken, "Criminal Law and Criminal Justice" in *Criminal Law and Justice* (1987), ed. Ian Dennis, p. 149.
[83] *Ingram* [1975] Crim.L.R. 457.
[84] J. C. Smith [1981] Crim.L.R. 393, 394.
[85] Glanville Williams "Divergent Interpretations of Recklessness," 132 (1982) N.L.J. 313 at p. 314.
[86] Hence the term "Cartesian" dualism.

link of the Christian immortal soul, to the ideas of Plato. It was he who postulated the existence of two elements in man—the soul (which entered the body at birth and left at death) and the body.[87] This view was modified and defended by Descartes as a result of the onslaught of scientific investigation.

P. Brett, An Inquiry into Criminal Guilt (1963), p. 46:

"Descartes was both scientifically inclined and religiously devout. He perceived strong implications of the broadening scientific research, and in response to the change developed the doctrine of the dual existence of mind and body in its modern form. . . . In Descartes' view, every human being possesses a mind and a body. The mind corresponds to what had been termed by older writers the soul; it was responsible for directing the actions of the body. Taken by itself, the body could be seen to work on more or less well-defined mechanical principles. But if human action is merely the result of a series of causes and effects operating in accordance with mechanical laws, there is no longer any place for a belief in the freedom of human choice, or for the attribution of praise or blame to human conduct. Such a view was quite incompatible with Descartes' religious views, and he accordingly sharply distinguished from the material body the non-material mind, which directed and governed the actions of the body. The body was like a clock, which goes when wound up; the winder was the mind."

We could simplistically refer then to the *actus reus* of a crime as the watch, and the *mens rea* as the result of the winder operating. We find from dualism, therefore, support for these concepts. However, the ground is not as safe as might appear. It is all very well to refer to the analogy of the clock and the winder; we know precisely how the one operates the other through a mechanical process. But is the same true of the workings of the body and the mind? Is there such a straightforward causal link between mind and body?

Descartes never comes anywhere near finding a solution to this which satisfies his religious and scientific learnings (he does attempt to locate the point of contact between the mind and the body in the pineal gland and asserts that a volition of the mind causes a bodily reaction in the gland and hence through to the body). And there are certainly commentators who feel that if there are two separate entities related in some way,[88] that the relationship is of so tortuous a shape that any action of the body says little, if anything, meaningful about the workings of the mind.[89]

Two strands of thought may be identified in such a conclusion. First,

---

[87] Plato considered the soul to be tripartite. The immortal soul resided in the mind and governed the activities of the two elements of the mortal soul. They in turn were responsible for emotions and feelings of the body. One was reponsible for emotions of courage and love, the other for feelings like hunger and thirst. It was Plato's view of the soul, of an entity separable from the body (rather than Aristotle's concept of inseparable aspects of the body) that became an integral part of western religious doctrine.

[88] This is not uncontested. Some philosophers refute the idea of dualism and believe instead that the mind and the body are the same thing. *Post* n. 92

[89] *e.g.* Baroness Wootton, *Crime and the Criminal Law*, (2nd ed., 1981).

although another person's actions are open to investigation, we lack direct means of access to the workings of the mind. We work instead by inference from the actions[90] combined with an interpretation of the workings of our own minds given a similar scenario. The impression gained may be totally false.[91] Dualism may, therefore, lead one to the conclusion that because the mental world is private it ought not to be investigated at all. Legal liability ought to be based on the actions of the body which can be examined. Liability ought therefore to be strict.

Secondly, the mind itself is extremely complex and operates on a number of levels. The law has confined its inquiry to the reasoning processes of the mind only. Modern psychology has presented a strong case for many other mental processes being involved as well. Feelings, desires and subconscious motivations also need to be included if we are to come near understanding the relationship between action and mind.

John R. Silber, "Being and Doing" (1967) 35 Univ. of Chicago L.R. 47 at 61, 62, 90:

"I urge . . . that there are relevant facts about human action which are denied when one insists that a person has to be conscious of what he intends in order to have an intention. . . .

[C]onsider the Christmas dinner at which the spinster aunt, . . . delivers a temperance lecture while the father is opening a bottle of wine saved for the occasion. Are we to deny that the aunt's dislike of the father for having destroyed her only immediate family by marrying her sister, and the aunt's envy of her sister for being the mother in another family, are expressed in her action? Are we to believe that she does not desire and intend to hurt this family, to dampen the pleasures of its Christmas feast? Yet who would call the aunt a liar when later, in tears, she apologises for having spoiled the celebration while she continues to insist that her only concern was for the welfare of the father and mother and children who are going to destroy their health by drinking. . . . [S]ince her actions are *hers*, it is not surprising that they should reveal much more of herself than she consciously intends to express: what she *does* is a function of *all* that she *is*, all her loves, hates, and wants, and not merely the expression of what she consciously intends when she acts. In this case all of her action, including its disruptive consequences and its good and bad will, was intended and was done intentionally, despite the fact that her conscious intention was merely to save the family she loved from alcoholism. The most accurate account of this situation is one which simply accepts *as fact* the presence of unconscious and often ambivalent intentions. . . .

We have neither understanding of man nor a basis for moral and legal judgment of him, unless we recognise the human person as a unity of being and doing."

Acceptance of such reasoning would mean that sharp distinctions presently drawn between mental states such as intention and recklessness would almost certainly have to be abandoned. Indeed, the whole concept of *mens rea*, as presently understood, is incompatible with such

---

[90] We seek to explain the action by reference to a state of mind which is in itself evidenced by the action: a circular investigation.

[91] See also the discussion on difficulties of proof (*ante*, p. 234).

reasoning. Yet most lawyers do not even pause to consider such ideas. Has the time not come when such issues ought at least to be faced?

(ii) *Freedom of Will* v. *Determinism*

The concept of freedom of will rests on a dualist framework. The freely choosing will or mind decides between one course of action and another. Descartes was thus able to have his cake and eat it. The will chooses freely (satisfying religious feelings) but governs the operations of the body (dealing with scientific objections). The difficulty he experienced in identifying the nature of the relationship between mind and body has already been introduced. We may now examine an alternative version of the relationship—that the operations of the mind are themselves *caused*. We thus encounter the philosophical confrontation between those who accept freedom of will and those who assert determinism in a variety of forms.[92] The confrontation rests on the acceptance or rejection of choice in man's make-up.

Thomas Morawetz, The Philosophy of Law (1980), p. 183:

"The debate over free will and determinism is one of the oldest in philosophy. It begins with the observation that the habit of thinking of oneself as having free will is deeply ingrained in human nature. All thoughts about choice, decision, and responsibility are based on the assumption of free will. At the same time (it is said), the more we find out about human nature through science, the more the assumption that there is such a thing as free will conflicts with other closely held and well-based beliefs.

This incompatibility is explained in the following way. The progress of scientific knowledge is progress in being able to give causal explanations; we come to understand events better as we come to know their causes. In the world of everyday experience all events are caused and the idea of an uncaused or free event is an absurdity. (Philosophers have made this point in various ways. Hume said that persons inevitably form the habit of thinking in causal terms. Kant said that causation was one of the categories through which the understanding operates.)

As we learn to explain events causally, we learn to predict and control them. To know that certain conditions are sufficient to cause an event is to be able to predict with certainty that the event will occur. If one can manipulate the antecedent conditions, one can bring about the event. Prediction and control will obviously be easier in some fields than others, easier in chemistry than in history because chemical events can be isolated and duplicated by experiment. But in all fields the principle of explanation is the same: to understand events is to understand them as parts of determinate causal chains.

It is clear why someone who holds this general view of causal explanation and of the explainability of all events would reject the notion of free will. He sees the doctrine of free will as the doctrine that when persons choose or decide to act, and do so freely, their actions are not in turn caused by anything else. Persons

---

[92] Whilst the most influential work on determinism has come from dualists, another branch of determinism—"monism"—does exist. "Monists" believe that the mind is merely one of the many functions of the body, in the same way that the heartbeat is merely one function of the body. The mind is nothing more than a series of electrochemical impulses inside the brain just as, for instance, a computer programme is nothing more than a series of electronic blips inside a computer. We would not (or should not!) praise or blame a computer, so we cannot praise or blame man. *Cf.* Brett, pp. 63–65.

are uncaused causers. The determinist points out, in opposing this conclusion, that there is no reason to think that human action is exempt from causal explanation. In fact, it is explainable from several different perspectives; biochemistry, physiology, psychology, and sociology are only some of the sciences that involve the prediction and/or the control of human behaviour.

. . . [T]o say that an action is free is to say that the actor could have done otherwise; to say it is caused is to say that the actor could not have done otherwise."

R. L. Franklin, Freewill and Determinism (1968), pp. 4–5:

"The central issue may be put in terms of a contrast between two notions, which may be called self-determinism and indeterminism. No one other than an absurd fatalist would suggest that a man is in normal circumstances at the mercy of his environment, as a rudderless boat is driven by the waves. It is we who decide how to act, and act as we decide. We respond to situations with more or less intelligence and integrity. Another person, or we in a different mood, might respond to the same situation quite differently. No account of a man's environment and external stimuli would usually enable us to know what he will do; the answer will depend on his own deliberation and choice. We might express this manifest ability of human beings to transcend a mere immediate reaction to stimuli by saying that they are *self-determined*. But this is quite compatible with saying that there are causal or scientific laws (for example, psychological ones about thought-processes, or physiological ones about brain-processes) which govern an agent's decision. The fact that a full causal account would have to be enormously complicated, that it would have to include statements about the agent as well as about his environment, and that it cannot in practice be achieved, does not show that it is in principle unobtainable. So self-determinism is compatible with determinism; indeed it is the only intelligent form of determinism. The determinist says that this self-determinism is the only sense (if any) in which a man is free, and . . . that it is in fact all we mean when we speak of human freedom. The libertarian, however, denies this. He insists that such laws, if they existed, would be incompatible with our most basic conception of freedom. His view may be put by saying that man's freedom is *undetermined*."[93]

Three propositions are thus identifiable:
  (1) That man is an uncaused causer; he possesses the freedom to do otherwise—"the libertarian."
  (2) That man possesses the freedom to do otherwise but is influenced in his choice by a variety of factors—"self-determinism."[94]
  (3) That man could not have done otherwise; his actions are the net sum of antecedent conditions and events—"determinism."

It becomes clear that propositions one or two are inherent in the legal concept of responsibility. One must accept that man could have done

---

[93] Both extracts (and many other commentators do the same) speak of determinism in terms of a (complicated) cause and effect relationship. This has been criticised as adopting a view long since abandoned by the physical sciences which look instead for invariable relationships. Night always follows day, but it does not mean that day causes night. Even if human behaviour is invariably predictable it may be unwise to transform this into a causal relationship.

[94] Much difficulty has been experienced with this "compatibility" approach. *Cf.* A. Kenny, *Freewill and Responsibility* (1978), pp. 22–34.

otherwise, that he could choose to obey, in order to find him morally blameworthy. *Mens rea*, the means by which the blameworthy are traditionally and primarily identified, is thus dependent upon this philosophical stance.

If, on the other hand, one accepts that all actions are the result of complex mental processes and antecedent environmental, biological conditions or even chemical conditions of the body, one loses the basis for blame and praise. How can a person be brought to account, be held responsible for something that he was inevitably going to do? *Mens rea* would be redundant and some other basis would have to be found for dealing with those whose actions constitute a menace to the community—perhaps the aim of protection of society.[95]

State v. Sikora 44 N.J. 453 210 A. 2d. 193 (1965) (Supreme Court of New Jersey)

The defendant, Sikora, was charged with murder (in the first degree). In a detailed statement Sikora had given a large number of details about the events leading up to the shooting, but claimed to have "lost his head" when he shot a man who had beaten him up earlier in the same evening. All the psychiatrists agreed that he was sane; the defence of insanity was not in issue.

Francis J.:

"[The evidence of Dr. Galen who] . . . had three years training as a psychoanalyst . . . taught him that people are a product of their own life history, their own genetic patterns, and that they all feel differently under the stresses of their daily lives. As a result of his study and experience, he believes that mental disturbance and disorder, as distinguished from objective disease, are merely gradients, that people range from being essentially normal, perceiving the world substantially in its normal appearance, all the way to marked distortion of the thinking mechanism, and between the two extremes is a rather jagged line which is prone to and open to many variations. In short, all human behaviour is distributed upon an infinite spectrum of fine gradations, there being no all or none in human dynamics. It is his view that mental disorder is one degree of an indeterminate line between gross disorganization and normal functioning, and it is often impossible to say at what point on the line a particular person is functioning at a given time. Mental illness or disorder in this context is a relative term as he sees it; it is a disorganization of the personality which causes a person to react in a specific way to a specific kind of stress in a way characteristic for him.

Psychodynamics is the study of what makes a man 'tick.' In effect the doctor said its purpose is to seek an explanation of an individual's mental condition at a given time in terms of his lifelong emotional development; to relate his questioned conduct and its accompanying emotional symptoms to their long antecedent, predetermining factors. In appearing as a witness, Dr. Galen indicated his function was to help the court understand 'the dynamics of what happened to this man with his particular history at this particular time in his life.' It was not his place as a psychiatrist to consider the premeditation aspect of murder in terms of right or wrong or good or evil. Evil is a philosophical concept. In his

---

[95] Harno, "Rationale of a Criminal Code" (1937) 85 U. of P.L. Rev. 549; Baroness Wootton: *Crime and the Criminal Law* (1981).

view the psychodynamic psychiatrist cannot consider the aspect of first degree murder which in law requires the conceiving of a design to kill in terms of evil, or evil intent. These moral judgments are best left to the courts to decide. Such a physician deals with the problem in a scientific way by applying his knowledge of the 'way people operate,' his knowledge of stress and 'the way people react to particular kinds of stress, based on their personality disorganization.' He feels 'somewhat medieval in talking about evil.' Basically Dr. Galen's thesis is that man is a helpless victim of his genes and his lifelong environment; that unconscious forces from within dictate the individual's behaviour without his being able to alter it. . . .

[W]hen Dr. Galen made his examination about four months after the homicide for about one and three-quarter hours, he obtained substantially the history detailed above. Sikora had a clear recollection of his previous life and of the events of the fatal night, and he was able to give the doctor a step-by-step account of the circumstances of the shooting. On the basis of the history, it was his opinion that at the time of the crime (and perhaps all his adult life) Sikora was suffering from a personality disorder of a passive-dependent type, with aggressive features. This kind of disorder is a function of his personality 'which is his way of dealing with himself and with life and with people and with stress.' He found no evidence of any overt hallucinations, delusions or ideas of reference; nor any evidence of organic mental disease. The accused's insight and judgment were consonant with his education, emotional status and intellect; he was 'estimated' to have a normal to dull-normal level of intelligence. . . .

According to Dr. Galen, tensions had been building up in Sikora, particularly since his female friend rejected him. When he was humiliated in the tavern by the remarks about her availability for other men because she had broken with him, and then physically beaten by Hooey and his companions, the tensions mounted to the point where they represented a situation in life with which he felt unable to cope. So he began to act in an automatic way; the manner in which a person with his personality inadequacy would characteristically act. He responded to the stress in the way which inevitably would be his way of dealing with that kind of stress. . . .

The beating administered by Hooey in the tavern precipitated the disorganisation of his personality to the extent that from then on he probably 'acted in at least a semi-automatic way, and probably an automatic way.' . . .

In short the doctor opined that the circumstances to which Sikora had been subjected imposed on his personality disorder a stress that impaired or removed his ability consciously to premeditate or weigh a design to kill. The tension was so great that he could handle it only by an automatic reaction motivated by the predetermined influence of his unconscious. Plainly the doctor meant that Sikora's response was not a voluntary exercise of his free will. The stress was such as to distort his mechanisms. During the various actions Sikora took leading up to the killing, which so clearly indicate conception, deliberation and execution of a plan to kill, he was thinking but the thinking was automatic; it was simply subconscious thinking or reaction; it was not conscious thinking. The doctor said Sikora's anxieties at the time were of such a nature that conceivably, his reaction in that automatic way and the commission of the homicide, actually prevented a further disorganisation of his personality. The killing, said the doctor, was 'a rational murder' but 'everything this man did was irrational,' and engaged in when he could not conceive the design to kill. . . .

The question now presented is whether psychiatric evidence of the nature described is admissible in first degree murder cases on the issue of premeditation. Defendant argues that it should have been received at the trial on that issue. . . .

For protection of society the law accepts the thesis that all men are invested with free will and capable of choosing between right and wrong. In the present state of scientific knowledge that thesis cannot be put aside in the administration of the criminal law. Criminal blameworthiness cannot be judged on a basis that negates free will and excuses the offence, wholly or partially, on opinion evidence that the offender's psychological processes or mechanisms were such that even though he knew right from wrong he was predetermined to act the way he did at that time because of unconscious influences set in motion by the emotional stresses then confronting him. In a world of reality such persons must be held responsible for their behaviour. . . .

Criminal responsibility must be judged at the level of the conscious. If a person thinks, plans and executes the plan at that level, the criminality of his act cannot be denied, wholly or partially, because although he did not realise it, his conscious was influenced to think, to plan and to execute the plan by unconscious influences which were the product of his genes and his lifelong environment. So in the present case criminal guilt cannot be denied or confined to second degree murder (when the killing was a 'rational murder' and the product of thought and action), because Sikora was unaware that his decisions and conduct were mechanistically directed by unconscious influences bound to result from the tensions to which he was subjected at the time. If the law were to accept such a medical doctrine as a basis for a finding of second rather than first degree murder, the legal doctrine of *mens rea* would all but disappear from the law. Applying Dr. Galen's theory to crimes requiring specific intent to commit, such as robbery, larceny, rape, etc., it is difficult to imagine an individual who perpetrated the deed as having the mental capacity in the criminal law sense to conceive the intent to commit it. Criminal responsibility, as society now knows it, would vanish from the scene, and some other basis for dealing with the offender would have to be found. At bottom, this would appear to be the ultimate aim of the psychodynamic psychiatrist. . . .

[F]or purposes of administration of the criminal law in this State, we cannot accept a thesis that responsibility in law for a criminal act perpetrated by a legally sane defendant, can be considered non-existent or measured by the punishment established for a crime of lower degree, because his act was motivated by subconscious influences of which he was not aware, and which stemmed inevitably from his individual personality structure. A criminal act of that nature is nothing more than the consequence of an impulse that was not resisted.

In first degree murder cases psychiatric testimony of the type adduced here should be admitted but its probative function limited to the area of sentence or punishment."

Conviction Affirmed

George P. Fletcher, Rethinking Criminal Law (1978), pp. 801–802:

"It is difficult to resolve [the issue of determinism and responsibility] except by noting that we all blame and criticise others, and in turn subject ourselves to blame and criticism, on the assumption of responsibility for our conduct. In order to defend the criminal law against the determinist critique, we need not introduce freighted terms like 'freedom of the will.' Nor need we 'posit' freedom as though we were developing a geometric system on the basis of axioms. The point is simply that the criminal law should express the way we live. Our culture is built on the assumption that, absent valid claims of excuse, we are accountable for what we do. If that cultural presupposition should someday prove to be empirically false, there will be far more radical changes in our way of life than those expressed in the criminal law."

Glanville Williams, Textbook of Criminal Law (2nd ed., 1983), p. 92:

"Sufficient to say that the determinist philosophy, though it may be true, is of little interest either to the lawyer or to the moralist. The question in law and morals is whether the offender could have acted otherwise *if he had willed*. If he could, he is morally and legally responsible. The further question 'Was he able to will?' may be speculated on by philosophers, but is eschewed in law and morals for a pragmatic reason. The object of the law and of a moral system is to influence our wills in a socially desired direction. Once this simple point is grasped, the apparent difficulty of reconciling the philosophy of determinism with ordinary moral attitudes disappears."

IV Relationship of Mens Rea to Actus Reus

A. *Introduction*

A general rule of the criminal law[96] is that *mens rea* must exist in relation to the *actus reus*. Bearing in mind that an *actus reus* can consist of:

(1) an act;

(2) committed in certain specified circumstances; and

(3) leading to the prohibited consequence,

mens rea must exist in relation to each of these separate elements. But it does not necessarily follow that the same degree of *mens rea* is required in relation to each. Thus the crime of attempt, for example, could require (1) an intentional act, (2) recklessness as to surrounding circumstances, and (3) an intention to bring about the forbidden consequences. But whatever the level of *mens rea*, it must exist "in relation to" the *actus reus*, or to put it another way, the *actus reus* must be attributable to the *mens rea*. In order to understand this rule it is necessary to investigate two principles that are well established in criminal law, and to consider the problem of mistake.

B. *Coincidence of Actus Reus and Mens Rea*

1. The Problem

In *Shorty*[97] the defendant violently assaulted the deceased with intent to kill him. The defendant, genuinely believing the victim to be dead, attempted to dispose of the "body" by putting it down a sewer. The deceased was in fact still alive at the time but died of drowning in the sewer. The court ruled that these actions must be divided into:

(1) The assault which did not cause death—this was accompanied by an intent to kill, and

---

[96] Crimes of strict liability form an exception to this rule.

[97] (1950) S.R. 280.

(2) The *actus reus* of murder (placing the "body" in a sewer with resultant drowning)—but this was not accompanied by *mens rea* at this stage.

Because the *actus reus* of murder did not coincide with the *mens rea* thereof, the defendant could not be convicted of murder. He was convicted only of attempted murder (stage 1), the *actus reus* of which did coincide with the requisite *mens rea*.

Is such a result realistic? The defendant intended to kill his victim; he did kill him. Should his mistake as to the method and time of death affect his liability?

2. The Solution

Thabo Meli v. R. [1954] 1 All E.R. 373 (Privy Council)

The appellants, in accordance with a pre-arranged plan, took a man to a hut, gave him beer so that he was partially intoxicated and then struck him over the head. Believing him to be dead, they took his body and rolled it over a low cliff, dressing the scene to look like an accident. In fact the man was not dead, but died of exposure when unconscious at the foot of the cliff.

Lord Reid:
"The point of law which was raised in this case can be simply stated. It is said that two acts were done:—first, the attack in the hut; and, secondly, the placing of the body outside afterwards—and that they were separate acts. It is said that, while the first act was accompanied by mens rea, it was not the cause of death; but that the second act, while it was the cause of death, was not accompanied by mens rea; and on that ground, it is said that the accused are not guilty of murder, though they may have been guilty of culpable homicide. It is said that the mens rea necessary to establish murder is an intention to kill, and that there could be no intention to kill when the accused thought that the man was already dead, so their original intention to kill had ceased before they did the act which caused the man's death. It appears to their Lordships impossible to divide up what was really one series of acts in this way. There is no doubt that the accused set out to do all these acts in order to achieve their plan, and as parts of their plan; and it is much too refined a ground of judgment to say that, because they were under a misapprehension at one stage and thought that their guilty purpose had been achieved before, in fact, it was achieved, therefore they are to escape the penalties of the law. . . . Their crime is not reduced from murder to a lesser crime merely because the accused were under some misapprehension for a time during the completion of their criminal plot."

Appeal dismissed

Dealing with a basically similar situation in *Church*,[98] it was stated that the jury should have been told they could convict of murder "if they regarded the appellant's behaviour from the moment he first struck

[98] (1965) Cr.App.R. 206.

her to the moment when he threw her into the river as a series of acts designed to cause death or grievous bodily harm."[99]

Fagan v. Metropolitan Police Commissioner [1969] 1 Q.B. 439 (Queen's Bench Divisional Court)

The appellant was told by a police officer to park his car in an exact position against the kerb. He drove the vehicle forward and stopped with its front off-side wheel on the constable's left foot. When told to reverse off, the appellant replied, 'Fuck you, you can wait,' and turned off the ignition. After several further requests, the appellant reversed the vehicle off the constable's foot. He was convicted of assaulting a police officer in the execution of his duty. On appeal he claimed that the initial driving on to the foot was unintentional and therefore not an assault, and that his refusal to drive off was not an 'act' capable of amounting to an assault.

James J.:
"We think that the crucial question is whether, in this case, the act of the appellant can be said to be complete and spent at the moment of time when the car wheel came to rest on the foot, or whether his act is to be regarded as a continuing act operating until the wheel was removed. In our judgment, a distinction is to be drawn between acts which are complete—though results may continue to flow—and those acts which are continuing. . . . For an assault to be committed, both the elements of actus reus and mens rea must be present at the same time. . . . It is not necessary that mens rea should be present at the inception of the actus reus, it can be superimposed on an existing act. On the other hand, the subsequent inception of mens rea cannot convert an act which has been completed without mens rea into an assault. . . .
There was an act constituting a battery which at its inception was not criminal because there was no element of intention, but which became criminal from the moment the intention was formed to produce the apprehension which was flowing from the continuing act. The fallacy of the appellant's argument is that it seeks to equate the facts of this case with such a case as where a motorist has accidentally run over a person and, that action having been completed, fails to assist the victim with the intent that the victim should suffer."

Appeal dismissed

This notion of a "continuing *actus reus*" with a *mens rea* being superimposed on it at any stage is not without problems. It is difficult to determine when the continuing *actus reus* starts and when it finishes.

How would the above cases (and the problem cited by James J. in *Fagan* of the motorist accidentally running over a person and then failing to assist him intending he should suffer) be decided now in the light of *Miller*?

R. v. Miller [1983] A.C. 161 (House of Lords)

The facts and further extracts are provided *ante*, p. 131.

---

[99] See also *Moore* and *Dorn* [1975] Crim.L.R. 229. In *A.G.'s Reference (No. 4 of 1980)* [1981] 1 W.L.R. 705 the Court of Appeal left open the question whether this "series of acts" test was a correct extension of the *Thabo Meli* principle.

Lord Diplock:

"[T]he conduct of the accused, throughout the period from immediately before the moment of ignition to the completion of the damage to the property by the fire, is relevant; so is his state of mind throughout that period.

Since arson is a result-crime the period may be considerable, and during it the conduct of the accused that is causative of the result may consist not only of his doing physical acts which cause the fire to start or spread but also of his failing to take measures that lie within his power to counteract the danger that he himself created. And if his conduct, active or passive, varies in the course of the period, so may his state of mind at the time of each piece of conduct. If at the time of any particular piece of conduct by the accused that is causative of the result, the state of mind that actuates his conduct falls within the description of one or other of the states of mind that are made a necessary ingredient of the offence of arson by section 1(1) of the Criminal Damage Act 1971. . . . I know of no principle of English criminal law that would prevent his being guilty of the offence created by that subsection. . . . [The ratio decidendi of the Court of Appeal] treats the whole course of conduct of the accused, from the moment at which he fell asleep and dropped the cigarette on to the mattress until the time the damage to the house by fire was complete, as a continuous act of the accused, and holds that it is sufficient to constitute the statutory offence of arson if at any stage in that course of conduct the state of mind of the accused, when he fails to try to prevent or minimise the damage which will result from his initial act, although it lies within his power to do so, is that of being reckless as to whether property belonging to another would be damaged.

My Lords . . . the judgment of the Court of Appeal in the instant case [has] provoked academic controversy. [There are two theories.] Each theory has distinguished support. Professor J.C. Smith espouses the 'duty theory'; Professor Glanville Williams, who, after the decision of the Divisional Court in *Fagan* v. *Metropolitan Police Commissioner* [1969] 1 Q.B. 439 appears to have been attracted by the duty theory, now prefers that of the continuous act. When applied to cases where a person has unknowingly done an act which sets in train events that, when he becomes aware of them, present an obvious risk that property belonging to another will be damaged, both theories lead to an identical result; and since what your Lordships are concerned with is to give guidance to trial judges in their task of summing up to juries, I would for this purpose adopt the duty theory as being the easier to explain to a jury."

C. *Transferred Malice*

1. Background

There are two well-established and accepted rules of criminal law:

(a) If a defendant causes the *actus reus* by a different method than he intended he is nevertheless liable. Thus if the defendant intended to kill his victim by stabbing him but after the first stab the victim fell and struck his head on a kerb, the blow killing him, the defendant is clearly guilty of murder and cannot claim the death is accidental. He intended to kill his victim; by his actions he has killed the victim; he has *mens rea* in relation to his *actus reus*; he is liable.

(b) If the defendant is mistaken as to the identity of his victim, he is nevertheless liable. Thus if the defendant shoots at his victim thinking he is Smith but in fact it is Jones and Jones dies, the defendant is clearly guilty of murder. Again he committed the *actus reus* of murder; he had the requisite *mens rea*; he is liable.

2. The Problem

(a) What if the defendant fires his gun at Smith, but misses and hits a passing stranger, Jones, and kills him? If the defendant was unaware of the existence of Jones, can he nevertheless be liable for murder?

(b) What if the defendant throws a brick at Smith, but misses and breaks a window near Smith? If the defendant was unaware of the existence of the window, can he be liable for criminal damage?

3. The Solution

The response of English law to these two situations is clear:

(a) The defendant will be liable for murder. He intended to cause the *actus reus* of murder; he did cause the *actus reus* of murder. His malice against Smith is transferred to Jones. The *actus reus* of murder is killing *a* human being. This he has done, intentionally; the identity of his victim is irrelevant. The leading illustration of this principle is *Latimer*[1] where the defendant swung his belt at a man with whom he was quarrelling but the belt hit the face of a woman to whom he was talking. Lord Coleridge C.J. held:

"if a person has a malicious intent towards one person, and in carrying into effect that malicious intent he injures another man, he is guilty of what the law considers malice against the person so injured."

(b) The defendant will *not* be liable for criminal damage because the doctrine of transferred malice does not apply where the *actus reus* (criminal damage) is different from the *mens rea* (of an offence against the person). Only if the *actus reus* intended and the *actus reus* caused are the same can the malice be transferred from the one to the other.[2]

A. J. Ashworth, "Transferred Malice and Punishment for Unforeseen Consequences" in Ed. P. R. Glazebrook, Reshaping the Criminal Law (1978), pp. 77, 84–89:

"The principle that a person should not be convicted of an offence unless he brought about the proscribed harm either intentionally or recklessly is frequently urged. . . . The doctrine known as transferred malice seems to stand out as an exception to this principle, for it results in criminal liability for conse-

---

[1] (1886) 17 Q.B.D. 369. For a more recent illustration of transferred malice (and where the doctrine was expressly approved), see *Mitchell* (1983) 75 Cr.App.R. 293. In *Jones (Peter)* [1987] Crim.L.R. 701 the doctrine was applied in a provocation case.

[2] See *Pembliton* (1874) 12 Cox 607, where the facts were similar to our hypothetical example and the defendant was acquitted (on appeal) of malicious damage to a window.

quences which would in ordinary language be described as accidental. The doctrine applies 'when an injury intended for one falls on another by accident.' . . .

But if the indictment charges D with wounding P with intent to do grievous bodily harm to P, contrary to section 18 of the Offences Against the Person Act 1861, is it not an affront to common sense to convict him in the knowledge that his intent was to harm O and not P? . . . The apparent illogicality can of course be ignored in the belief that transferred malice represents a higher principle of criminal liability which must be applied even where the particular words of a statute do not sit happily with it. . . .

What, if anything, would be lost if the doctrine were abolished here? Does our criminal law offer any acceptable alternative methods of dealing with these cases? There are two obvious possibilities—liability for the crime attempted (thus ignoring the accidental result), and liability for the actual result based on recklessness—and these will be examined in turn. . . .

A conviction for attempt is possible in virtually all cases which fall within the doctrine of transferred liability . . . In *Latimer*, for example, D could quite simply have been convicted of the attempted unlawful wounding of O; and likewise in *Pembliton* there were strong grounds for convicting D of attempted unlawful wounding of persons in the crowd . . .

In many of the cases to which transferred malice applies, the harm to P was quite unforeseen. But in some of them D could be held liable for harm to P without invoking transferred malice—on the basis that, in attempting to harm O, he was reckless as to harming P. . . . It is often said that in *Pembliton* the jury should have found D reckless as to damaging the window, and that this would have spared counsel and the courts much fruitless argument . . .

The doctrine could, then, be abolished without material loss to criminal justice; and it is desirable that it should be. For, quite apart from any problems over the consistency of the doctrine with general principles of criminal liability, it attributes significance to matters of chance and results in a mischaracterisation of D's criminality which could simply and effectively be avoided by charging an attempt. What, then, are the objections to using the law of attempts?

The first is that it would be wrong for a person who intended to cause harm of a certain kind and did cause such a harm to escape with a lighter sentence merely because he was charged with an attempt . . .

A second objection . . . is that even if the punishment were the same, it is more appropriate to convict of the completed crime in the 'transferred malice' situation. Where D set out to cause harm of a certain kind and did cause harm of that kind, it seems empty and insufficient to convict him of a mere attempt. He has actually caused a loss to the community of the kind he intended to cause, and that fact should be recorded. Once again, however, this reasoning leans too heavily on results which may be entirely a matter of chance. In a system based on subjective liability, the legal label attached to D's offence should generally reflect his intentional act and not the chance result."

Where the defendant intends to kill another human being and does kill another human being, albeit a different one from the one intended, is it fair to describe that result as a "matter of chance," exempting the defendant from liability for murder? Is this mistake as to the identity of his victim relevant in any *material* way?[3]

In the light of *Caldwell* it is doubtful whether it will be necessary to resort to the doctrine of transferred malice much in the future. Using the

[3] See Smith & Hogan, p. 75; Stroud, *Mens Rea* (1914) p. 184; Glanville Williams, "Convictions and Fair Labelling" [1983] C.L.J. 85 at 86–88.

pre-*Caldwell* subjective test of recklessness, it might be difficult to establish that the defendant was reckless as to the precise harm caused. But under the new test, recklessness would be easily established—in most cases the reasonable man would have been aware that there was an obvious risk of the actual harm ensuing—or the defendant himself would have been so aware if he had stopped to think.

The expressly stated premise underlying the Ashworth extract above is that our system of criminal law should be based upon a purely subjective notion of *mens rea*. Even accepting this premise, one can still justify the doctrine of transferred malice in the manner already suggested. But rejection of the premise involves a rejection of many of the arguments in the extract. It was this premise that was firmly rejected in *Caldwell*.

D. *Mistake*

A defendant may make many different types of mistake. Sometimes he will think he is committing no crime at all. At other times he will think he is committing a different crime from the one that transpires. What is the law's response to such pleas?

To have any claim to consideration a mistake must relate in a relevant way to the elements of the crime. Thus, it is no defence to make a mistake as to a completely extraneous fact. For example, to use the popular Boomtown Rats song, when killing members of one's family because one doesn't like Mondays, it is irrelevant that the defendant has made a mistake and it is in fact Tuesday! Such a mistake has no bearing on the fact that the defendant had full *mens rea* in relation to all elements of the crime.

A mistake might have relevance in the following three situations:
1. mistake as to one of the elements of the *actus reus*; or
2. mistake as to a defence element; or
3. mistake as to law.

As we shall see, it is impossible to distinguish rigidly between these three, but such a classification is useful for purposes of exposition.

1. Mistake as to element of actus reus

For most crimes the defendant must have *mens rea* in relation to the *actus reus*. This means he must have *mens rea* in relation to every element of the *actus reus*—often referred to as the "definitional elements." However, the mistake must not simply be one as to *some quality* of the definitional element. It must be as to the *existence* of the definitional element. For example, the *actus reus* of criminal damage is *destroying or damaging any property belonging to another*.[4] If the defendant thinks the property belongs to Smith when in fact it belongs to Jones his mistake is irrelevant because he nevertheless knows that the

---

[4] Criminal Damage Act 1971, s.1(1).

property *belongs to another.* On the other hand, if the defendant thinks the property belongs to *himself* this mistake now negates his *mens rea.* He does not have *mens rea* in relation to a definitional element and could thus escape liability.[5]

Section 170(2) of the Customs and Excise Management Act 1979 makes it an offence to be knowingly concerned in the fraudulent evasion of the prohibition on the importation of prohibited goods. In *Ellis*[6] the defendants believed they were importing prohibited pornographic goods but in fact it was prohibited drugs. Their convictions were upheld. They had *mens rea* in relation to the definitional element "prohibited goods." The precise nature and quality of such prohibited goods was of no more relevance than whether the property belonged to Smith or Jones in the earlier example.[7]

Where the mistake is as to the existence of a definitional element the position used to be that the defendant would only escape liability if the mistake was a reasonable one.

R. v. Tolson (1889) 23 Q.B. 168 (Court of Crown Cases Reserved)

The defendant's husband deserted her in 1881. Inquiries revealed that the vessel he had taken to America had been lost at sea. Believing herself to be a widow, in 1887 she went through a ceremony of marriage with another man. Later in the same year, Tolson returned from America.

Stephen J.:
"The full definition of every crime contains expressly or by implication a proposition as to a state of mind. Therefore, if the mental element of any conduct alleged to be a crime is proved to have been absent in any given case, the crime so defined is not committed; or, again, if a crime is fully defined, nothing amounts to that crime which does not satisfy that definition. Crimes are in the present day much more accurately defined by statute or otherwise than they formerly were. The mental element of most crimes is marked by one of the words 'maliciously,' 'fraudulently,' 'negligently,' or 'knowingly,' but it is the general— I might, I think, say, the invariable—practice, of the legislature to leave unexpressed some of the mental elements of crime . . .

With regard to knowledge of fact, the law, perhaps, is not quite so clear, but it may, I think, be maintained that in every case knowledge of fact is to some extent an element of criminality as much as competent age and sanity . . .

I think it may be laid down as a general rule that an alleged offender is deemed to have acted under that state of facts which he in good faith and on reasonable grounds believed to exist when he did the act alleged to be an offence . . .

---

[5] *Smith (David)* [1974] Q.B. 354.
[6] [1987] Crim.L.R. 44.
[7] Professor J. C. Smith has pointed out that this decision might have been unexceptional when the importation of prohibited drugs and pornographic material were both punishable with two years imprisonment—but it becomes questionable now that the penalties in relation to drugs have been increased. ([1987] Crim.L.R. 46)

[On the basis of the earlier case of *Prince*[8] Stephen J. distinguished the case where Parliament had intended that the wrongdoer should act at his peril (so that no mistake, however reasonable, would avail him) from that presently before him. The distinction he thus makes is between a crime of strict liability and one where some fault is implied by general principles although not explicit in the statute.]

The general principle is clearly in favour of the prisoner, but how does the intention of the legislature appear to have been against them? It could not be the object of Parliament to treat the marriage of widows as an act to be, if possible, prevented as presumably immoral. The conduct of the women convicted was not in the smallest degree immoral, it was perfectly natural and legitimate. Assuming the fact to be as she supposed, the infliction of more than a nominal punishment on her would have been a scandal. Why then should the legislature be held to have wished to subject her to punishment at all? . . . It appears to me that every argument which showed, in the opinion of the judges in *Prince* (Law Rep. 2 C.C.R. 154), that the legislature meant seducers and abductors to act at their peril, shows that the legislature did not mean to hamper what is not only intended, but naturally and reasonably supposed by the parties, to be a valid and honourable marriage, with a liability to seven years' penal servitude."

Conviction quashed

A radical change of direction was however adopted by the House of Lords in the following leading case.

D.P.P. v. Morgan [1976] A.C. 182 (House of Lords)

A husband invited a number of companions to have sexual intercourse with his wife, apparently in order to be avenged for her real or imagined infidelity. He suggested that she might put up a struggle but that they were not to take it seriously; it was her way of increasing her sexual satisfaction. The men, so urged, had intercourse in turn without her consent. They were tried and convicted of rape; the husband was convicted of aiding and abetting rape. The judge directed the jury that the men were guilty of rape even if they in fact believed that Mrs. Morgan consented if such belief was not based on reasonable grounds.

The question certified to the House of Lords was whether the defendants belief in her consent had to be based on reasonable grounds.

Lord Cross:
"In fact, however, I can see no objection to the inclusion of the element of reasonableness in what I may call a 'Tolson' case. If the words defining an offence provide either expressly or impliedly that a man is not to be guilty of it if he believes something to be true, then he cannot be found guilty if the jury think that he may have believed it to be true, however inadequate were his reasons for doing so. But, if the definition of the offence is on the face of it 'absolute' and the defendant is seeking to escape his prima facie liability by a defence of mistaken belief, I can see no hardship to him in requiring the mistake—if it is to afford him a defence—to be based on reasonable grounds. As

---

[8] (1875) Law Rep. 2 C.C.R. 154. The defendant abducted a girl under the age of 16, believing on good grounds that she was above that age. He was convicted under what is now section 5, Offences Against the Person Act 1861, of taking a girl under the age of 16 out of the possession of her parents without their consent: Lord Bramwell stated that had his mistake been to the question of the father's consent his conviction would have been quashed (p. 175).

Lord Diplock said in *Sweet* v. *Parsley* [1970] A.C. 132, there is nothing unreasonable in the law requiring a citizen to take reasonable care to ascertain the facts relevant to his avoiding doing a prohibited act. To have intercourse with a woman who is not your wife is, even today, not generally considered to be a course of conduct which the law ought positively to encourage and it can be argued with force that it is only fair to the woman and not in the least unfair to the man that he should be under a duty to take reasonable care to ascertain that she is consenting to the intercourse and be at the risk of prosecution if he fails to take such care. So if the Sexual Offences Act 1956 had made it an offence to have intercourse with a woman who was not consenting to it, so that the defendant could only escape liability by the application of the 'Tolson' principle, I would not have thought the law unjust.

But, as I have said, section 1 of the Act of 1956, does not say that a man who has sexual intercourse with a woman who does not consent to it commits an offence; it says that a man who rapes a woman commits an offence. Rape is not a word in the use of which lawyers have a monopoly and the question to be answered in this case, as I see it, is whether according to the ordinary use of the English language a man can be said to have committed rape if he believed that the woman was consenting to the intercourse and would not have attempted to have it but for his belief, whatever his grounds for so believing. I do not think that he can. Rape, to my mind imports at least indifference as to the woman's consent. I think, moreover, that in this connection the ordinary man would distinguish between rape and bigamy. To the question whether a man who goes through a ceremony of marriage with a woman believing his wife to be dead, though she is not, commits bigamy, I think that he would reply 'Yes,—but I suppose that the law contains an escape clause for bigamists who are not really to blame.' On the other hand, to the question whether a man, who has intercourse with a woman believing on inadequate grounds that she is consenting to it, though she is not, commits rape, I think that he would reply 'No. If he was grossly careless then he may deserve to be punished but not for rape.' That being my view as to the meaning of the word 'rape' in ordinary parlance, I next ask myself whether the law gives it a different meaning. There is very little English authority on the point but what there is—namely, the reported directions of several common law judges in the early and the middle years of the last century—accords with what I take to be the proper meaning of the word . . . For these reasons, I think that the summing up contained a misdirection.

The question which then arises as to the application of the proviso [to section 2(1) of the Criminal Appeal Act 1968] is far easier of solution . . . The jury obviously considered that the appellants' evidence as to the part played by Mrs. Morgan was a pack of lies and one must assume that any other jury would take the same view as to the relative culpability of the parties. . . . So I would apply the proviso and dismiss the appeal."

Lord Hailsham:

"If it be true, as the learned judge says [in his summing up at the trial] 'in the first place,' that the prosecution have to prove that 'each defendant intended to have sexual intercourse without her consent, not merely that he intended to have intercourse with her but that he intended to have intercourse without her consent,' the defendant must be entitled to an acquittal if the prosecution fail to prove just that. The necessary mental ingredient will be lacking and the only possible verdict is 'not guilty.' If, on the other hand, as is asserted in the passage beginning 'secondly,' it is necessary for any belief in the woman's consent to be 'a reasonable belief' before the defendant is entitled to an acquittal, it must either be because the mental ingredient in rape is not 'to have intercourse and to have it without her consent' but simply 'to have intercourse' subject to a special defence of 'honest and reasonable belief,' or alternatively to have intercourse without a reasonable belief in her consent. Counsel for the Crown argued for each of these alternatives, but in my view each is open to insuperable objections of principle. No doubt it would be possible, by statute, to devise a law by which intercourse, voluntarily entered into, was an absolute offence subject to a 'defence' of belief whether honest or honest and reasonable, of which the 'evidential' burden is primarily on the defence and the 'probative' burden on the prosecution. But in my opinion such is not the crime of rape as it has hitherto been understood. The prohibited act in rape is to have intercourse without the victim's consent. The minimum mens rea or guilty mind in most common law offences, including rape, is the intention to do the prohibited act, and that is correctly stated in the proposition stated 'in the first place' of the judge's direction. In murder the situation is different, because the murder is only complete when the victim dies, and an intention to do really serious bodily harm has been held to be enough if such be the case.

The only qualification I would make to the direction of the learned judge's 'in the first place' is the refinement for which, . . . there is both Australian and English authority, that if the intention of the accused is to have intercourse nolens volens, that is recklessly and not caring whether the victim be a consenting party or not, that is equivalent on ordinary principles to an intent to do the prohibited act without the consent of the victim. . . .

Once one has accepted, what seems to me abundantly clear, that the prohibited act in rape is non-consensual sexual intercourse, and that the guilty state of mind is an intention to commit it, it seems to me to follow as a matter of inexorable logic that there is no room either for a 'defence' of honest belief or mistake, or of a defence of honest and reasonable belief or mistake. Either the prosecution proves that the accused had the requisite intent, or it does not. In the former case it succeeds, and in the latter it fails. Since honest belief clearly negatives intent, the reasonableness or otherwise of that belief can only be evidence for or against the view that the belief and therefore the intent was actually held, and it matters not whether, to quote Bridge J. . . . 'the definition of a crime includes no specific element beyond the prohibited act.' . . . Any other view, as for insertion of the word 'reasonable' can only have the effect of saying that a man intends something which he does not.

By contrast, the appellants invited us to overrule the bigamy cases from *Reg.* v. *Tolson*, 23 Q.B.D. 168 onwards and perhaps also *Reg.* v. *Prince*, L.R. 2 C.C.R. 154 (the abduction case) as wrongly decided at least in so far as they purport to insist that a mistaken belief must be reasonable. The arguments for this view are assembled, and enthusiastically argued, by Professor Glanville Williams in his treatise on Criminal Law, 2nd ed. (1961) between pages 176 and 205, and by Smith and Hogan. . . .

Although it is undoubtedly open to this House to reconsider *Reg.* v. *Tolson* and the bigamy cases, and perhaps *Reg.* v. *Prince* which may stand or fall with them, I must respectfully decline to do so in the present case. Nor is it necessary that I should. I am not prepared to assume that the statutory offences of bigamy or abduction are necessarily on all fours with rape, and before I was prepared to undermine a whole line of cases which have been accepted as law for so long, I would need argument in the context of a case expressly relating to the relevant offences. I am content to rest my view of the instant case on the crime of rape by saying that it is my opinion that the prohibited act is and always has been intercourse without consent of the victim and the mental element is and always has been the intention to commit that act, or the equivalent intention of having intercourse willy-nilly not caring whether the victim consents or no. A failure to prove this involves an acquittal because the intent, an essential ingredient, is lacking. It matters not why it is lacking if only it is not there, and in particular it matters not that the intention is lacking only because of a belief not based on reasonable grounds. . . .

For the above reasons I would answer the question certified in the negative, but would apply the proviso to the Criminal Appeal Act on the ground that no miscarriage of justice has or conceivably could have occurred. In my view, therefore, these appeals should be dismissed."

Lord Simon:
"The problem which faces your Lordships arises when the accused raises a case fit for the jury's consideration that he believed that the woman was consenting to sexual intercourse, though in fact she was not doing so. Does an honest but unreasonable belief that the woman is consenting to sexual intercourse suffice to negative the charge of rape? . . .

It remains to consider why the law requires, in such circumstances, that the belief in a state of affairs whereby the actus would not be reus must be held on reasonable grounds. One reason was given by Bridge J. in the Court of Appeal . . . :

'The rationale of requiring reasonable grounds for the mistaken belief must lie in the law's consideration that a bald assertion of belief for which the accused can indicate no reasonable ground is evidence of insufficient substance to raise any issue requiring the jury's consideration.'

I agree; but I think there is also another reason. The policy of the law in this regard could well derive from its concern to hold a fair balance between victim and accused. It would hardly seem just to fob off a victim of a savage assault with such comfort as he could derive from knowing that his injury was caused by a belief, however absurd, that he was about to attack the accused. A respectable woman who has been ravished would hardly feel that she was vindicated by being told that her assailant must go unpunished because he believed, quite unreasonably, that she was consenting to sexual intercourse with him. The policy behind s.6 of the Sexual Offences Act is presumably that Parliament considered that a girl under sixteen is generally unlikely to be sufficiently mature to realise the full implications of sexual intercourse; so that her protection demands that a belief by a man under the age of twenty-four that she herself was over the age of sixteen should not be only an honest but also a reasonable belief . . .

I would therefore answer the question certified for your Lordships' consideration, Yes. But, even did I consider that it should be answered No, I would, for the reasons given by my noble and learned friends, think this a suitable case to apply the proviso.

I would therefore dismiss the appeal."

(Lord Fraser held that the defendant's belief in the woman's consent did not have to be based on reasonable grounds; Lord Edmund-Davies, however, felt that only the legislature could effect such a reform in the law.)

Appeal dismissed

Despite suggestions that *Morgan* should be confined to the crime of rape,[9] it is now clear that it applies throughout English law—at least to all those offences requiring proof of intention or recklessness as to each of the definitional elements.[10]

---

[9] *Phekoo* [1981] 1 W.L.R. 1117. See also *Brown* [1984] 1 W.L.R. 1211.
[10] *Jones* [1987] Crim.L.R. 123; *Brown* (1985) 80 Cr.App.R. 36.

R. v. Kimber [1983] 1 W.L.R. 1118 (Court of Appeal, Criminal Division)

The appellant was charged with indecent assault, contrary to section 14(1) of the Sexual Offences Act 1956. He had sexual contact with a mentally disordered female patient in a mental hospital but claimed he thought she was consenting.

Lawton L.J.:
"The appeal raises these points. First, can a defendant charged with an indecent assault on a woman raise the defence that he believed she had consented to what he did? The trial judge, Mr. Recorder Smyth Q.C., ruled that he could not. Secondly, if he could, did the jury have to consider merely whether his belief was honestly held or, if it was, did they have to go on to consider whether it was based on reasonable grounds? Another way of putting these points is to ask whether the principles upon which the House of Lords decided *Reg.* v. *Morgan* [1976] A.C. 182, should be applied to a charge of indecent assault on a woman . . .

The burden of proving lack of consent rests upon the prosecution . . . The consequence is that the prosecution has to prove that the defendant intended to lay hands on his victim without her consent. If he did not intend to do this, he is entitled to be found not guilty; and if he did not so intend because he believed she was consenting, the prosecution will have failed to prove the charge. It is the defendant's belief, not the grounds on which it was based, which goes to negative the intent.

In analysing the issue in this way we have followed what was said by the majority in *Reg.* v. *Morgan* . . . If, as we adjudge, the prohibited act in indecent assault is the use of personal violence to a woman without her consent, then the guilty state of mind is the intent to do it without her consent. Then, as in rape at common law, the inexorable logic, to which Lord Hailsham referred in *Reg.* v. *Morgan*, takes over and there is no room either for a 'defence' of honest belief or mistake, or of a 'defence' of honest and reasonable belief or mistake . . . The application of the *Morgan* principle to offences other than indecent assault on a woman will have to be considered when such offences come before the courts. We do, however, think it necessary to consider two of them because of what was said in the judgments. The first is a decision of the Divisional Court in *Albert* v. *Lavin* [1982] A.C. 546. The offence charged was assaulting a police officer in the execution of his duty, contrary to section 51 of the Police Act 1964. The defendant in his defence contended, inter alia, that he had not believed the police offer to be such and in consequence had resisted arrest. His counsel analysed the offence in the same way as we have done and referred to the reasoning in *Morgan*. Hodgson J., delivering the leading judgment, rejected this argument and in so doing said, at pp. 561–562:

'But in my judgment Mr. Walker's ingenious argument fails at an earlier stage. It does not seem to me that the element of unlawfulness can properly be regarded as part of the definitional elements of the offence. In defining a criminal offence the word "unlawful" is surely tautologous and can add nothing to its essential ingredients . . . And no matter how strange it may seem that a defendant charged with assault can escape conviction if he shows that he mistakenly but unreasonably thought his victim was consenting but not if he was in the same state of mind as to whether his victim had a right to detain him, that in my judgment is the law.'

We have found difficulty in agreeing with this reasoning, even though the judge seems to be accepting that belief in consent does entitle a defendant to an acquittal on a charge of assault. We cannot accept that the word 'unlawful' when used in a definition of an offence is to be regarded as 'tautologous.' In our judgment the word 'unlawful' does import an essential element into the offence. If it were not there social life would be unbearable, because every touching would amount to a battery unless there was an evidential basis for a defence . . .

In *Reg.* v. *Phekoo* . . . Hollings J. . . . [confined *Morgan*] to the offence of rape. We do not accept that this was the intention of their Lordships in *Morgan's* case. Lord Hailsham of St. Marylebone started his speech by saying that the issue as to belief was a question of great academic importance in the theory of English criminal law.

In our judgment the recorder should have directed the jury that the prosecution had to make them sure that the appellant never had believed that [the woman] was consenting. [Lawton L.J., however, concluded that no reasonable jury would have accepted the appellant's version of the facts. He was, at least, reckless as to whether she was consenting. Accordingly, there had been no miscarriage of justice.]"

Appeal dismissed

We shall be turning shortly to the second type of mistake a defendant can make, namely a mistake as to a defence element. The law there has long been, and was confirmed in *Albert* v. *Lavin* discussed in the above case, that the defendant must establish that his mistaken belief was a reasonable one to have made in the circumstances. But if the mistake can be classified as one relating to a definitional element, the requiremet for reasonableness now disappears.

R. v. Williams (Gladstone) (1984) 78 Cr.App.R. 276 (Court of Appeal, Criminal Division)

The appellant saw a man, Mason, dragging a youth along a street and striking him; the youth was calling for help. Mason claimed he was a police officer and was arresting the youth for mugging a lady. When he was unable to produce a warrant card, a struggle ensued during which the appellant punched Mason, who sustained injuries to his face. The appellant, who was charged with assault occasioning actual bodily harm, claimed that he honestly believed Mason was unlawfully assaulting the youth and that he was trying to rescue the youth. (One is entitled to use reasonable force to prevent an unlawful assault on another.[11]) However, the appellant had made a mistake. While Mason was not a police officer, he had nevertheless seen the youth seize the woman's handbag and was acting lawfully in restraining the youth with a view to taking him to a police station. At his trial, the jury were directed that the appellant's mistake would only be relevant if it were a reasonable one. He was convicted and appealed on the ground of a misdirection.

Lane L.C.J.:
" 'Assault' . . . is an act by which the defendant, intentionally or recklessly, applies unlawful force to the complainant. There are circumstances in which force may be applied to another lawfully. Taking a few examples: first, where the victim consents, as in lawful sports, the application of force to another will, generally speaking, not be unlawful. Secondly, where the defendant is acting in self-defence: the exercise of any necessary and reasonable force to protect himself from unlawful violence is not unlawful. Thirdly, by virtue of section 3 of the

[11] *Post*, p. 292.

Criminal Law Act 1967, a person may use such force as is reasonable in the circumstances in the prevention of crime or in effecting or assisting in the lawful arrest of an offender or suspected offender or persons unlawfully at large. In each of those cases the defendant will be guilty if the jury are sure that first of all he applied force to the person of another, and secondly that he had the necessary mental element to constitute guilt.

The mental element necessary to constitute guilt is the intent to apply unlawful force to the victim. We do not believe that the mental element can be substantiated by simply showing an intent to apply force and no more.

What then is the situation if the defendant is labouring under a mistake of fact as to the circumstances? What if he believes, but believes mistakenly, that the victim is consenting, or that it is necessary to defend himself, or that a crime is being committed which he intends to prevent? He must then be judged against the mistaken facts as he believes them to be. If judged against those facts or circumstances the prosecution fail to establish his guilt, then he is entitled to be acquitted.

The next question is, does it make any difference if the mistake of the defendant was one which, viewed objectively by a reasonable onlooker, was an unreasonable mistake? . . .

[I]n our judgment the answer is provided by the judgment of this Court in *Kimber* . . . by which . . . we are bound . . .

We respectfully agree with what Lord Justice Lawton said there [in *Kimber* when disapproving *Albert* v. *Lavin*] with regard both to the way in which defence should have been put and also with regard to his remarks as to the nature of the defence. The reasonableness or unreasonableness of the defendant's belief is material to the question of whether the belief was held by the defendant at all. If the belief was in fact held, its unreasonableness, so far as guilt or innocence is concerned, is neither here nor there. It is irrelevant. Were it otherwise, the defendant would be convicted because he was negligent in failing to recognise that the victim was not consenting or that a crime was not being committed and so on. In other words the jury should be directed first of all that the prosecution have the burden or duty of proving the unlawfulness of the defendant's actions; secondly, if the defendant may have been labouring under a mistake as to the facts, he must be judged according to his mistaken view of the facts; thirdly, that is so whether the mistake was, on an objective view, a reasonable mistake or not. . . .

We have read the recommendations of the Criminal Law Revision Committee, Part IX, paragraph 72(a), in which the following passage appears: 'The common law defence of self-defence should be replaced by a statutory defence providing that a person may use such force as is reasonable in the circumstances as he believes them to be in the defence of himself or any other person.' In the view of his Court that represents the law as expressed in *Morgan* and in *Kimber* and we do not think that the decision of the Divisional Court in *Albert* v. *Lavin* from which we have cited can be supported."

Appeal allowed

Beckford v. R. [1988] A.C. 130 (Privy Council)

The appellant was a police officer who was a member of an armed posse which chased, shot and killed a fleeing man. The appellant claimed he had killed in self defence. The trial judge directed the jury that the belief that life was in danger had to be a reasonable belief. The Court of Appeal of Jamaica confirmed this. The appellant appealed to the Privy Council.

Lord Griffiths:

"There can be no doubt that prior to the decision of the House of Lords in *Reg.* v. *Morgan* [1976] A.C. 182 the whole weight of authority supported the view that it was an essential element of self-defence not only that the accused believed that he was being attacked or in imminent danger of being attacked but also that such belief was based on reasonable grounds . . .

The question then is whether the present Lord Chief Justice, Lord Lane, in *Reg.* v. *Williams* (*Gladstone*), 78 Cr.App.R. 276, was right to depart from the law as declared by his predecessors in the light of the decision of the House of Lords in *Reg.* v. *Morgan*. . . .

It is because it is an essential element of all crimes of violence that the violence or the threat of violence should be unlawful that self-defence, if raised as an issue in a criminal trial, must be disproved by the prosecution. If the prosecution fail to do so the accused is entitled to be acquitted because the prosecution will have failed to prove an essential element of the crime namely that the violence used by the accused was unlawful.

If then a genuine belief, albeit without reasonable grounds, is a defence to rape because it negatives the necessary intention, so also must a genuine belief in facts which if true would justify self-defence be a defence to a crime of personal violence because the belief negatives the intent to act unlawfully. Their Lordships therefore approve the following passage from the judgment of Lord Lane C.J. in *Reg.* v. *Williams* (*Gladstone*), 78 Cr.App.R. 276, 281, as correctly stating the law of self-defence . . .

(His Lordship then cited the penultimate paragraph from the above extract from *Williams* (*Gladstone*) (*ante*, p. 260).)

There may be a fear that the abandonment of the objective standard demanded by the existence of reasonable grounds for belief will result in the success of too many spurious claims of self-defence. The English experience has not shown this to be the case. The Judicial Studies Board with the approval of the Lord Chief Justice has produced a model direction on self-defence which is now widely used by judges when summing up to juries. The direction contains the following guidance:

'Whether the plea is self-defence or defence of another, if the defendant may have been labouring under a mistake as to the facts, he must be judged according to his mistaken belief of the facts: that is so whether the mistake was, on an objective view, a reasonable mistake or not.' "

Appeal allowed

So, according to this approach it is necessary to draw a sharp distinction between:

(a) mistakes which affect a definitional element of the crime: mistake need only be genuine, and;

(b) mistakes as a result of which the defendant claims he is entitled to a defence: mistake must be reasonable.

The problem with this approach is that such distinctions are not always easily drawn. We saw in the introduction to this chapter,[12] it is possible to construe most defences as actually being definitional elements, as opposed to being elements extrinsic to the *actus reus* or *mens rea*. Thus, murder is "unlawfully killing a human being with malice aforethought." We saw that it was possible to analyse this in several ways. In

[12] *Ante*, p. 101.

particular, the *actus reus* could be regarded as "killing a human being," and the requirement of "unlawful" as relating to the absence of a defence, for example, self-defence or duress. Following this analysis, a defendant who mistakenly thought he was under attack, would have to establish that his mistake was a reasonable one. Alternatively, the *actus reus* could equally be regarded as "unlawfully killing a human being." Under this analysis, a mistaken belief that a defendant was acting in self-defence now relates to an element in the definition of the *actus reus*. Following *Morgan* the mistake need only be genuine to exempt the defendant from liability.

This was the approach adopted in *Williams* (*Gladstone*) and *Beckford*.

Glanville Williams, Textbook of Criminal Law (2nd ed., 1983), p. 138:

"No other rule of the substantive criminal law distinguishes between the definitional and defence elements of a crime, and it is a distinction that is impossible to draw satisfactorily. (Our notion of what issue is a 'defence,' in so far as we have any clear notion, seems to depend largely on whether we think that the defendant should be required to take the initiative in introducing it, *i.e.* on whether he should bear an evidential burden in respect of it. But there is no reason why the distribution of evidential burdens should affect the rules of liability. See 2 Leg. Stud. 255). A rule creating a *defence* merely supplies additional details of the scope of the *offence*. To regard the offence as subsisting independently of its limitations and qualifications is unrealistic. The defence is a negative condition of the offence, and is therefore an integral part of it. What we regard as part of the offence and what as part of a defence depends only on traditional habits of thought or accidents of legal drafting; it should have no bearing on the important question of criminal liability. For example, it is purely a matter of convenient drafting whether a statute says, on the one hand, that damaging the property of another without his consent is a crime, or, on the other hand, that damaging the property of another is a crime but that his consent is a defence. In fact we regard the non-consent of the owner as a definitional element, but there is no particular reason why this should be so, and the question of guilt or innocence should not depend on it."

Up to this point we have been dealing with crimes requiring intention or recklessness as the requisite *mens rea* and the view has been adopted by the courts that a mistake as to a definitional element negates *mens rea*. However, if the crime is one that is satisfied by proof of negligence, the approach must be different. An unreasonable mistake is a negligent mistake thus providing the requisite *mens rea*. It follows that in such offences the defendant must establish that the mistake was a reasonable one if liability is to be escaped. This approach provides a ready explanation for the decision in *Tolson* and a means of reconciling that decision with *Morgan*. While the crime of rape requires nothing less than intention or recklessness (*Morgan*), the crime of bigamy is satisfied by negligence (*Tolson*).

It follows that for offences of strict liability it is irrelevant whether the defendant has made a mistake, whether reasonable or not. Liability is strict; the blameworthiness of the accused is irrelevant. However, if the offence is only one of prima facie strict liability with the defendant being afforded a defence (a view expressed in *Morgan* in relation to *Tolson*), then, as will be seen in the next section, the mistake must be based on reasonable grounds (rendering the offence, in effect, one of negligence).

At this point it becomes necessary to consider the potential impact of *Caldwell* and *Lawrence* on the law relating to mistake. The defendants in both *Kimber* and *Williams* (*Gladstone*) were charged with offences that could be committed recklessly. In both cases this was common law recklessness which ought now to be interpreted in the light of *Caldwell* and *Lawrence*. According to this test, a defendant who fails to consider an obvious risk is reckless. Thus, if a defendant makes a mistake, but there is an obvious risk that he might be wrong in his assessment of the facts, he might be accounted reckless. However, it is difficult to see how this applies to genuine mistakes in most cases. A defendant who makes such a mistake is not one who has failed to consider the possible risks. He has addressed his mind to the matter in question; he has "ruled out any risks"; he has reached a clear view (albeit a mitaken one) as to the relevant facts. As seen earlier,[13] even under *Caldwell* and *Lawrence*, such a defendant is not reckless. This view has now been endorsed in several recent cases on reckless rape.[14] These cases indicate that if a defendant genuinely believes that the woman is consenting to intercourse he cannot be liable. He is only reckless if he "could not care less" or was "indifferent" as to whether she was consenting—such a defendant has clearly *not* made a genuine mistake.

However, there must remain some cases where a defendant makes a genuine mistake because he has failed to consider a circumstance that would be obvious to any ordinary observer. The circumstance (risk) never enters his head; he, therefore, never "rules it out"; he simply *assumes* (mistakenly) that the facts are as he believes them to be. The defendant in *Williams* (*Gladstone*) clearly considered the possibility that Mason was restraining a mugger, but when Mason was unable to produce a warrant card, he dismissed from his mind any possibility that Mason's story was true (a generous interpretation of the facts, but one upon which the Court of Appeal seemed to proceed). But what if the defendant had *never considered the possibility* that Mason might be acting lawfully, but simply rushed in and assaulted him? Surely such a defendant could fall within the *Caldwell* test in that he has failed to consider an obvious risk (if, in the circumstances, the risk was obvious). In *Satnam and Kewal*[15] the Court of Appeal distinguished *Caldwell* and *Lawrence* on the ground that the House of Lords had been concerned in those cases with foresight of the *consequences* of criminal acts, *i.e.* reck-

---

[13] *Ante*, p. 192.
[14] *Satnam and Kewal* (1984) 78 Cr.App.R. 149; *Breckenridge* (1984) 79 Cr.App.R. 244; *Bashir* (1983) 77 Cr.App.R. 59; *Thomas* (1983) 77 Cr.App.R. 63. See *post*, pp. 576–577.
[15] *Ibid.*

lessness as to some result, while in the resent case they were concerned with reckless rape, *i.e.* recklessness as to a circumstance—the consent of the woman. While there might be grounds for distinguishing reckless rape on the basis that this involves the construction of a particular statute, namely, section 1 of the Sexual Offences (Amendment) Act 1976, it nevertheless remains difficult to see why, in general terms, it should make any difference whether recklessness relates to a result or to a circumstance. The underlying basis of *Kimber* and *Williams* (*Gladstone*) is that a defendant must possess *mens rea* in relation to the whole of the *actus reus*. If the crime can be committed recklessly and is one to which the *Caldwell* and *Lawrence* test applies, then any mistake ought to be subjected to the rigours of that test. If the mistake is genuine, most defendants would still escape liability—for the reasons already given. But others might not be so fortunate. It is important that the criminal law operates as a cohesive body of rules if it is to be perceived as fair and just. If *Caldwell* is not liked, its effect can be altered by Parliament.[16] But pending this, the above arguments ought to be seriously canvassed by the courts—rather than being brazenly swept aside on the totally inadequate basis that *Caldwell* and *Lawrence* were only dealing with result-crimes.

2. Mistake as to a defence element

We have already seen that there is strong authority that where a defendant claims to have made a mistake and thus thought he was entitled to a defence, the burden is on him to establish that his mistake was reasonable. However, we also saw in cases such as (*Gladstone Williams*) and *Beckford* where the defendant mistakenly thought he was entitled to use self-defence (previously thought of as a defence) the court remoulded the offence and held self-defensive action rendered conduct "lawful" and therefore there was no *mens rea* in relation to the "definitional element" of unlawfulness.

This, however, creates a problem. Why can this approach not be adopted across the board? If a defendant honestly believes he is being subjected to duress, could one not say that he lacks *mens rea* in relation to the same definitional element of "unlawfulness." And what if he is drunk? Do the same principles apply? If a defendant makes a drunken mistake and does not know that property belongs to another, must we simply exculpate him on the ground of lack of *mens rea* in relation to the *actus reus*?

In *Graham*[17] and *Howe*[18] it was held that the defence of duress would only be available to one who *reasonably* believed that he was being subjected to the requisite threats for a defence of duress. The same test was

---

[16] Draft Criminal Code Bill 1989, cl. 18(c), 20(1). The effect of this is to "subjectivise" recklessness. See *ante*, p. 206.

[17] [1982] 1 W.L.R. 294. See *post*, p. 316.

[18] [1987] A.C. 417. See *post*, p. 325.

applied in *Martin*[19] to "duress of circumstances" (necessity). In *O'Grady*[20] it was held that a person who made a drunken mistake in thinking he was being attacked was not entitled to a defence. In *Fotheringham*[21] the defendant made a drunken mistake when having non-consensual intercourse with his 14 year-old baby-sitter: he thought it was his wife.[22] It was held that such a drunken mistake was no defence. While it was held in both these cases that a drunken mistake was no defence, there can be little doubt that if, in fact, despite the defendant's drunkenness, the mistake made was a perfectly reasonable mistake that an ordinary sober person would have made, it would be a defence. In this latter situation the drunken defendant would not in any way be profiting from his drunkenness. The drunkenness would in short be irrelevant as the same mistake would probably have been made if he had been sober.

It is interesting to note that the main group of cases where the requirement of reasonableness has been dispensed with are cases concerning consent and self-defence. These are both "justificatory" defences. On the other hand, the areas where a mistake will only exculpate if it is reasonable, namely duress and intoxication, raise "excusatory" defences.[23] The distinction between justifications and excuses is an important one to be considered later[24] but at its very simplest boils down to this:

[i] when conduct is "justified" it is in effect "approved of"—or, at least, tolerated as acceptable conduct. Thus a person acting in self-defence is effectively doing "right"; he is doing what we expect him to do; he is restricting unprovoked aggression and ensuring that the law is enforced by the wrongdoer being subjected to restraint. The argument appears to be that if someone thinks he is doing a socially and legally approved act there is little point in punishing him.

[ii] when conduct is excused, the conduct of the defendant remains wrong and unacceptable but because he has an excuse, we punish him less or not at all. If thinking he is being subjected to duress a defendant robs a bank, this is "wrong and disapproved of" conduct—but we might wish to exempt the defendant from liability if he had been subjected to terrible threats. But because the conduct remains wrong we will only excuse those who have a plausible excuse—and a plausible excuse is surely a reasonable one.

---

[19] [1989] 1 All E.R. 652.

[20] [1987] Q.B. 995.

[21] (1989) 88 Cr.App.R. 207.

[22] A husband cannot rape his wife, therefore her consent is irrelevant. For discussion and criticism of this rule, see *post*, pp. 567–571, 579–580.

[23] It is uncertain how "duress of circumstances" is to be classified. The approach in *Martin* (*ante*, n. 19) suggests it is an excuse. See *post*, p. 276.

[24] *Post*, p. 274.

Finally, how are we to evaluate the law's response to the problem of mistake? Are we to approve of *Morgan* and its progeny and the view that, generally, genuine mistakes should exempt defendants from criminal liability, irrespective of the reasonableness or otherwise of that mistake?

D. Cowley, "The Retreat from Morgan" [1982] Crim.L.R. 198 at 206–208:

"What is particularly remarkable about the apparent eagerness to retreat from *Morgan* is the lack of any really convincing justification for requiring reasonableness in mistake cases. . . .

One theory suggests that whether the objective test of mistake applies depends upon where in respect of the relevant issue the evidential burden lies, and that where an evidential burden lies on the accused to show that he believed in facts inconsistent with the offence, 'a bald assertion of belief for which the accused can indicate no reasonable ground is evidence of insufficient substance to raise any issue requiring the jury's consideration.' (*per* Lord Simon in *Morgan* at 367). It is respectfully submitted that this theory is unsound and that there is no connection between the incidence of the evidential burden and the question whether the mistake must be reasonable, the main reason being that an evidential burden on the defendant merely requires him to give some *reasonable evidence of belief* as opposed to *evidence of reasonable belief*. It may well be the case that his assertion of belief is not 'bald' but is fully corroborated by independent evidence leading the jury to accept that the unreasonable belief was in fact held and, in such circumstances, the defendant will have discharged the burden cast upon him.

An alternative reason for requiring the belief to be reasonable put forward by Lord Simon is the fact that the victim must be 'vindicated' by punishing *e.g.* an assailant who has made an unreasonable mistake: 'the policy of the law in this regard could well derive from its concern to hold a fair balance between the victim and the accused. It would hardly seem just to fob off a victim of a savage assault with such comfort as he could derive from knowing that his injury was caused by a belief, however absurd, that he was about to attack the accused.' One cannot but agree with Professor Williams' opinion ((1975) N.L.J. p. 968) that this is not only a somewhat old-fashioned view of the criminal law but also fails to explain who is vindicated when a bigamist is punished. The lawful spouse, in particular, may not care a jot about the bigamy.

Perhaps the current judicial insistence on there being reasonable grounds for mistaken belief can, rather, be put down to a simple lack of confidence in the jury as the final arbiter of fact. If so, such judicial mistrust is very reminiscent of the somewhat misconceived and blinkered popular reaction to the decision in *Morgan*. What was apparently overlooked by those whose passions were aroused by *Morgan's* effect on the law of rape, and those whose railing against the case implied a serious lack of faith in the tribunal of fact in criminal cases, was not only the total lack of gullibility of that particular jury who decided that the defendants' tale as to Mrs. Morgan's consent to their intercourse with her was a 'pack of lies,' but also the ultimate result of the case—the dismissal of the defendants' appeals against conviction. There is little evidence there to support the often heard claim that a requirement of mere honest belief facilitates bogus defences, and before seeking to impose any kind of restriction upon the freedom of the jury to determine issues of fact the judiciary might reflect upon the oft-quoted words of Dixon J. that 'a lack of confidence in the ability of a tribunal correctly to estimate evidence of states of mind and the like can never be sufficient ground for excluding from inquiry the most fundamental element in a rational and humane criminal code.' *Thomas* v. *R.* (1937) 59 C.L.R. 278 at 309."

Celia Wells, "Swatting the Subjectivist Bug," [1982] Crim.L.R. 209, 212–213:

"If there is sufficient evidence to satisfy a jury that consent was absent, can it not be argued that this is sufficient to distinguish in terms of culpability, the mistaken defendant from those men who have never had sexual intercourse with a woman who was not consenting? If the defendant is so out of touch with the reality of the situation, is there not a suggestion that he should take more care to ensure that his sexual partner is willing? Social protection might be better served by the punishment of a defendant who failed to acquaint himself with this (seemingly) elementary fact. But would the pillar of personal guilt be demolished in the process? Is a system of criminal law only 'just' if it confines itself to punishing those who 'feel' culpable? 'The state of the actor's mind or conscience is a factual claim. Guilt, fault and culpability are normative judgments, based on an evaluation of the actor's conduct and state of mind.' (Fletcher: at p. 509.) Fletcher goes on to suggest that an alternative method of answering culpability would combine both objective and subjective elements. 'The assessment of attribution and accountability obviously requires the application of standards to the particular situation of the actor . . . the standard has a variety of forms, but it always recurs to the same normative question. Could the actor have been fairly expected to avoid the act of wrongdoing? Did he or she have a fair opportunity to perceive the risk, to avoid the mistake, to resist the external pressure . . . ' (at 510) It could be argued, that although the mistaken rapist is culpable, he is not as culpable as the deliberate rapist and that his crime should not be rape but some lesser offence such as 'negligent sexual invasion.' "

George P. Fletcher, Rethinking Criminal Law (1978), pp. 696–697, 707, 709–710, 712:

"[W]e would be naive to think we had a definitive, unassailable solution to the enduring problem of determining when mistakes must be reasonable in order to have an exculpatory effect. The thesis is tentative, and to aid those who might wish to carry the effort further, we should restate the critical premises for recognising that some mistakes have a categorical exculpatory effect.
1. The definition of an offence is the violation of a prohibitory norm.
2. The prohibitory norm identifies the minimal set of objective circumstances necessary, in the given cultural context, to state a coherent moral or social imperative.
3. There is no violation of a prohibitory norm unless the actor acts intentionally or knowingly with respect to the elements of the definition (the prohibitory norm). . . .
A mistake as to one of these elements . . . has the same effect in barring liability for an intentional offence as the absence of one of the objective elements. . . . Of course, if the offense is one that can be committed negligently, then the mistake only bars conviction for the intentional offence. The premises supporting the alternative track requiring mistakes to be reasonable are the following:
4. Relevant mistakes about elements extrinsic to the definition are excuses.
5. Elements of justification are extrinsic to the definition.
6. Excuses are not valid unless they negate the actor's culpability.

7. A mistake does not negate culpability unless the making of the mistake was blameless. . . .
[Fletcher admits that this distinction is as yet fragile. For example, he finds the issue of consent in *Morgan* to be justificatory, rather than definitional.] . . . [I]n the field of putative self-defense and other imagined circumstances of justified conduct, it is generally assumed that the mistake must be reasonable. We could interpret this requirement as a concern about whether the actor's mistake is free from fault. But the doctrine could also be read as a theory about the justifying effect of appearances. If the circumstances warrant a reasonable belief, the actor is entited to rely upon appearances, whatever the facts may actually be. . . .
[C]ommon-law courts are reluctant to reveal to the jury the extent to which a conviction rests on a moral assessment of the actor's wrongful conduct. . . . As a step toward overcoming these inhibitions about moral discourse, we should try to state precisely how individuals can be fairly blamed for making mistakes or for remaining inadvertent to the risks implicit in their conduct. The inquiry encompasses not only mistakes in the narrow sense, but the culpability of inadvertent negligence. . . .
The normative theory of attribution takes the interaction of the actor with his surroundings to lie at the core of assessing personal culpability. Culpability for intentional wrongdoing turns on the degree of self-actuation, independent of surrounding influences. Culpability for inadvertence turns on the actor's failure to respond to circumstances that signal danger."

Fletcher must surely be correct when he argues that the central issue is one of moral blame: who can fairly be blamed for having made a mistake? And, as he points out, and as was accepted in *Williams* (*Gladstone*), this often reduces itself to the simple issue: can we fairly blame the negligent wrongdoer?[25] A sharper focus on this central issue would hopefully introduce more coherence into this confused, indecisive area of law.

3. Mistake as to law

Traditionally, mistakes of law have been generally regarded as irrelevant. The citizen is presumed to know the law of the land—his ignorance or mistake cannot avail him.[26]

However, this proposition that mistakes of law are irrelevant is somewhat misleading. Some mistakes of law can be highly relevant. In this context it is necessary to distinguish between:
  (i) mistake as to civil law, and
  (ii) mistake as to criminal law.[27]

(i) *Mistake as to civil law*

Some mistakes of civil law may negate the *mens rea* required for a crime. So if a defendant takes a bicycle thinking that the bicycle is his own because, say, he mistakenly thinks that a legal sale had taken place,

---

[25] This question is considered, *ante*, pp. 206–212.

[26] The reason often given being that the law sets an objective standard; a citizen should not be able to make it subjective by his mistaken view of it—(J. Hall, *General Principles of Criminal Law* (2nd ed. 1960)), or that it might encourage ignorance (O. W. Holmes, *The Common Law*, (1881) p. 45).

[27] See A. Ashworth, "Excusable Mistake of Law" [1974] Crim.L.R. 652; Smith & Hogan, p. 71; Glanville Williams, *Textbook*, p. 256.

he has made a mistake of the civil law relating to sale of goods; as a result of this mistake he would lack the intention to appropriate property *belonging to another*[28]; he would escape all liability.

In essence, a mistake of civil law is (or results in) a mistake of *fact*—*e.g.* thinking one was appropriating a bicycle belonging to oneself. So whether a mistake as to civil law needs to be based on reasonable grounds or not, will be determined by the principles already discussed in relation to mistakes of fact. Thus where a defendant mistakenly believes his first marriage has been dissolved by a divorce entitled to recognition in Englnd, he will, following *Tolson*,[29] only escape liability if his mistake as to the civil law on recognition of foreign divorces is based on reasonable grounds. This is because the law of bigamy does not require intention or recklessness as to the definitional element of "being married"—for policy reasons negligence suffices, and thus the mistake must be based on reasonable grounds.

(ii) *Mistake as to criminal law*

Here the maxim "ignorance of the law is no defence" comes into operation. A mistake as to whether one's actions are criminal will generally be irrelevant. So if a defendant thinks it is legal to have more than one wife, the *actus reus* and *mens rea* of the crime of bigamy are present; he is merely alleging that he did not know bigamy was a crime—such a mistaken belief is irrelevant.

There are many problems in distinguishing between mistakes of civil law and criminal law, and much turns on the wording of particular statutory provisions. Two cases demonstrate this. In *Grant v. Borg*[30] the offence charged was under section 24(1)(*b*)(i) of the Immigration Act 1971, which makes it an offence if a non-patrial "having only limited leave to . . . remain . . . knowingly . . . remains beyond the time limited by the leave."

The House of Lords held that a mistake as to whether "leave" had expired was a mistake of law and thus irrelevant. Lord Bridge went so far as to state that:

"The principle that ignorance of the law is no defence in crime is so fundamental that to construe the word 'knowingly' in a criminal statute as requiring not merely knowledge of the facts material to the offender's guilt, but also knowledge of the relevant law, would be revolutionary and, to my mind, wholly unacceptable."[31]

But in this case there was no dispute that the defendant knew it was a crime to overstay his leave. The question was whether he might have

---

[28] The Theft Act 1968, s.2(1) specifically provides that there is no dishonesty for the purposes of the Theft Act if the defendant has a "belief that he has in law the right to deprive the other of (the property)."

[29] *Ante*, p. 253.

[30] [1982] 1 W.L.R. 638.

[31] At p. 646. See to similar effect, *Millward* [1985] Q.B. 519.

been mistaken as to when his leave had expired—surely a question of civil law.

In *Secretary of State for Trade and Industry* v. *Hart*[32] a somewhat different approach was adopted. In this case the defendant acted as the auditor of two companies while being disqualified from so acting because he was a director of the companies. He was charged with an offence under section 13(5) of the Companies Act 1976 which prohibits a person acting as auditor of a company "at a time when he knows that he is disqualified for appointment to that office." The defendant admitted he knew all the facts or circumstances disqualifying him, but did not know that he was disqualified in law—in other words, he was unaware of the disqualification and its criminal sanctions—surely a mistake or ignorance of the criminal law. Yet the Divisional Court held the defendant must know he was disqualified; an awareness of the statutory restrictions was a prerequisite of liability. As Ormrod L.J. said:

"If that means that he is entitled to rely on ignorance of the law as a defence, in contrast to the usual rule, the answer is that the section gives him that right."[33]

A final question remains for consideration. Is it right that mistake or ignorance of the law should have no bearing on the imposition of criminal liability?

Paul H. Robinson, Criminal Law Defences (Vol. 2) (1984), 375–376:

"Austin argues that to permit mistakes as to criminality as an excuse for criminal conduct would be to present insoluble problems of proof (Austin on Jurisprudence: 13th ed. 1920). Everyone could claim such ignorance and it could be disproved only with considerable difficulty.

An examination of the structure of a general mistake excuse gives this concern considerable support. It is the one excuse that has no disability, no observable and verifiable abnormality, to lend support to the actor's claim of an excusing condition. The mistaken actor, except for his mistake, is indistinguishable from all other 'normal' persons. Evidence of the defendant's excusing condition, of his ignorance of criminality, must come solely from circumstantial evidence of his state of mind.

The absence of a distinguishing abnormality not only makes it difficult to distinguish the defendant and to establish his excusing condition, but also makes it more difficult to maintain the integrity of the prohibition violated while excusing the actor for his violation. '[O]nce the conduct has been so defined [as criminal], one cannot usurp the lawmaking function by pleading that his ignorance must mean that the conduct is not criminal as to him.' (Packer, "The Model Penal Code and Beyond" 63 Colum. L. Rev. 594, 596–97, 1963). In light of the heightened need for clear proof and the simultaneous increased difficulty in reliably determining mistake of law claims, one may reasonably concur with Holmes that 'to admit [such an] excuse at all would be to encourage ignorance where the lawmaker has determined to make men know and obey . . . ' (O. W. Holmes, The Common Law 48, 1881) It is on the basis of these arguments that 'ignorance of the law is no excuse' is a maxim of long standing."

[32] [1982] 1 W.L.R. 481.
[33] At p. 487.

A. T. H. Smith, "Error and Mistake of Law in Anglo-American Criminal Law" (1985) 14 Anglo-Am. L.R. 3, pp. 16–18:

"1. Problems of proof.

. . . [I]t may be argued that mistakes of fact and law and mistakes of law are not essentially different in kind, and since the inquiry is manifestly not impossible in the case of the former, it is equally not impossible in the latter. This response does not directly confront the brutal utilitarianism that lies behind the objection; it is not so much that proof is impossible but that the pursuit of absolute justice must be curtailed by considerations of social utility and the distribution of resources . . .

2. To admit the defence would be to encourage ignorance. . . .

Even the utilitarian should allow that where a particular individual can show that he has taken all the steps that he conceivably can to conform his conduct to what he reasonably believes to be the dictates of the law, he has done all that can be asked of him.

3. The argument from legality. According to Jerome Hall, (1976) 24 Am. Jo. Comp. Law 680) if the law were to assess a defendant's culpability on the footing of the law as he believed it to be, then for those purposes the law would be thus and so. This could undercut the rule of law, which relies on an objective law impartially administered by officials who declare what the law is. But this, as has been most persuasively argued, is to fail to distinguish between wrongdoing and attribution, justification and excuse. The mere fact that an individual is not held to be legally accountable for a wrong act does not mean that the act is not condemned; it means only that the actor is not to be blamed for what he did."

The present approach of English law is perhaps justifiable in relation to the major offences where there is a close correlation between law and morality, for instance, crimes of murder and rape and so on. It can also be defended in relation to specialist activities in which the actor may be engaged.[34] However, when turning to the plethora of legislation surrounding twentieth century life, one is forced to question whether this approach is either just or efficacious.

In relation to mistake of fact it was argued that the central issue was one of moral blame: could the defendant be fairly blamed for having made such a mistake? Surely when dealing with ignorance of the law this is still the fundamental issue. With the vast array of regulatory offences, with constantly changing and varying standards of permissible conduct, for example, in relation to obscenity, with the law often being unclear and uncertain even to lawyers, do we necessarily blame all defendants who have made mistakes as to the criminal law? The paradigmatic blameworthy defendant is one who has culpably brought about the prohibited result or state of affairs **and has acted in open defiance of the law**. With mistake of law there is no such flouting of the rules. Bearing in mind that one is not **justifying** the wrong done, but

---

[34] Some countries provide a defence of mistake of law but exclude it in such situations. *e.g.* Norway, (Penal Code of 1902, § 57, added 1939). See also A.L.I. Model Penal Code, Proposed Official Draft 1962, s.2.04(3), Fletcher, pp. 713–6, 736.

merely **excusing**[35] the actor—and, therefore, an excuse will only be available if the mistake were a *reasonable* one—there must surely be a strong case for exempting such an actor from criminal liability.

It is however conceded that such a proposal would only have a limited impact, as a reasonable mistake of law could only be a defence to crimes requiring some degree of *mens rea.* Neither mistake of fact nor mistake of law could be defences to crimes of strict liability without those offences ceasing to be "strict." Yet, ironically, it is in the field of "regulatory offences" where liability is so often strict that there is the greatest likelihood of persons being ignorant of the law. However, the fact that a proposal would only have a limited impact is no argument for not proceeding with it. For those crimes requiring some degree of blameworthiness a reasonable mistake of law should exempt from liability.[36]

---

[35] *Ante*, p. 265 and *post*, pp. 274–283.

[36] The Draft Criminal Code Bill 1989 (Law Com. No. 177, 1989) does not accept this and states: "Ignorance or mistake as to a matter of law does not affect liability to conviction of an offence except— (a) where it is so provided; or (b) where it negatives a fault element of the offence." (clause 21).

CHAPTER 3

GENERAL DEFENCES

I JUSTIFICATION AND EXCUSE

A. Introduction

A defendant may commit the *actus reus* of an offence with the requisite *mens rea* and yet escape liability because he has a "general defence." For example, he may have intentionally killed his victim—but have been acting in self-defence: the victim was trying to kill him. In such a case, assuming the requirements of self-defence are made out, he escapes all liability.

We have already seen that there are different ways of analysing criminal liability.[1] It could be, continuing the above example, that the defendant is regarded as having committed the *actus reus* with an appropriate *mens rea* but the existence of a defence is a superimposed, external third element. This mode of analysis could be useful in describing the shifting burdens of proof in a criminal trial in those jurisdictions[2] where it is for the prosecution to prove beyond reasonable doubt that the defendant committed the *actus reus* with appropriate *mens rea*, but the burden then shifts to the defendant to establish on a balance of probabilities that he had a defence. This "procedural analysis" is employed in England with the defences of insanity[3] and diminished responsibility.[4] Such an approach is however not accurate in describing the burden of proof in other cases in England where, in relation to common law defences, the burden remains on the prosecution throughout.[5] Nor is this "procedural analysis" helpful in understanding the true bases of criminal liability: who, why and when persons should be adjudged blameworthy and held criminally responsible for their actions. Accordingly, a "substantive interpretation" tends to focus on the requirement of blameworthiness. Criminal liability is imposed on a blameworthy actor who causes a prohibited harm. If a defendant has a

---

[1] *Ante*, p. 101.
[2] *e.g.*, Singapore and Malaysia: see K. L. Koh, C. M. V. Clarkson and N. A. Morgan, *Criminal Law in Singapore and Malaysia: Text and Materials* (1989), p. 103.
[3] M'Naghten Rules, *post*, p. 349; *Bratty* v. *A. G. for Northern Ireland* [1963] A.C. 386.
[4] Homicide Act 1957, s.2(2).
[5] *Woolmington* v. *D.P.P.* [1935] A.C. 462; see Smith and Hogan, p. 31.

"general defence" he is not blameworthy and, therefore, deserves to escape criminal liability.

The term "general defences" is used to convey that such defences are available to all crimes. There are some defences that are not "general" but specific to particular offences: for example, provocation is a defence only to murder, reducing liability to manslaughter. Such specific defences are dealt with later in relation to their particular offences.[6] We have however chosen to deal with one specific defence, diminished responsibility, in this chapter. This is because of its close affinity to the "general defence" of insanity and is best understood being examined in that context.

Further, it must be stressed that the title "general defences" is adopted purely for expository convenience. It is patently untrue that all these defences are available to all offences. For example, duress is not available for murder and intoxiation is not available for most offences. Another problematic area is the extent to which the "general defences" are available to offences of strict liability.

These general defences used to be listed as isolated sets of identifiable conditions or circumstances which prevented a defendant being convicted. However, over the last decade it has become more usual to try and synthesise them into some sort of coherent theoretical scheme enabling more careful and rational analysis.[7]

Defences can be broadly classed into two groups: those that provide a *justification* for the defendant's conduct, and those that *excuse* his conduct.

Paul Robinson, "Criminal Law Defences: A Systematic Analysis" (1982) 82 Col.L.R. 199 at 213, 221, 229:

"[J]ustification defences are not alterations of the statutory definition of the harm sought to be prevented or punished by an offense. The harm caused by the justified behaviour remains a legally recognised harm which is to be avoided whenever possible. Under the special justifying circumstances, however, that harm is outweighed by the need to avoid an even greater harm or to further a greater societal interest. . . .

Excuses admit that the need may be wrong, but excuse the actor because conditions suggest that the actor is not responsible for his deed. For instance, suppose that the actor knocks the mailman over the head with a baseball bat because she believes he is coming to surgically implant a radio receiver which will take control of her body. The defendant has satisfied all elements of the offense of aggravated assault—she struck the mailman with a deadly weapon with the purpose of causing him bodily injury. This is precisely the harm sought to be prevented by the statute, and it is not outweighed by any greater societal harm avoided or greater societal interest furthered. It is conduct that

---

[6] *Post*, p. 638.

[7] The distinction was important before 1828 as, under the common law, a killer's goods were forfeited if the killing was excusable but not if it was justifiable. In 1828 forfeiture was abolished. See further, J. C. Smith, *Justification and Excuse in the Criminal Law* (1989) p. 7. The revived interest in the distinction can largely be traced back to the publication in 1978 of George P. Fletcher, *Rethinking Criminal Law* (1978).

society would in fact condemn and seek to prevent. The defendant is exculpated only because her condition at the time of the offense—her paranoid delusion—suggests that she has not acted through a meaningful exercise of free will and therefore is not an appropriate subject for criminal liability. . . .

Justifications and excuses may seem similar in that both are general defenses which exculpate an actor because of his blamelessness. . . . The conceptual distinction remains an important one, however. Justified conduct is correct behaviour which is encouraged or at least tolerated. In determing whether conduct is justified, the focus is on the *act*, not the actor. An excuse represents a legal conclusion that the conduct is wrong, undesirable, but that criminal liability is inappropriate because some characteristic of the actor vitiates society's desire to punish him. Excuses do not destroy blame . . . rather, they shift it from the actor to the excusing conditions. The focus in excuses is on the *actor*. Acts are justified; actors are excused."

How does one determine whether a particular defence is justificatory or excusatory in nature?

B. Justification

The best approach is that "all justificatory arguments can be reduced to a balancing of competing interests and a judgment in favour of the superior interest."[8] Or as Glanville Williams has expressed it, "a defence is justificatory (for the purpose of the criminal law) whenever it denies the objective wrongness of the act (that is, wrongness apart from matters of excuse) . . . Normally a justification is any defence affirming that the act, state of affairs or consequences are, on balance, to be socially approved, or are matters about which society is neutral."[9]

On this basis the following defences can be classified as justificatory in nature:

(a) *Self-defence.* The interests of the person attacked are greater than those of the attacker. The aggressor's culpability in starting the fight tips the scales in favour of the defendant.[10] Further "a rule allowing defensive action tends to inhibit aggression, or at least to restrain its continuance, as a rule forbidding defensive action would tend to promote it."[11]

(b) *Necessity (Where the Harm Threatened is Greater than the Harm Caused).* Where a lesser evil is committed in order to prevent a greater evil (*e.g.* killing one person to save the lives of 20 people), the interests of the latter outweigh the interests of the former. In the United States necessity is widely regarded as a paradigmatic example of justification.[12] As we shall see, there is enormous doubt in England as to whether this defence exists at all—although recent cases do appear to

[8] Fletcher, p. 769; and see Eser, "Justification and Excuse," (1976) 24 Am.J.Comp.L. 621 at 629–631.
[9] "The Theory of Excuses" [1982] Crim.L.R. 732 at 735.
[10] Fletcher, p. 858.
[11] Glanville Williams, *ante*, n. 9 p. 739.
[12] Model Penal Code, s.3.02; N.Y. Penal Law, s.35.05.

accept it under the nomenclature "duress of circumstances." As will be argued later, it is because of this classification of necessity as a justification that our judges have shown reluctance to admit the defence at all. Perhaps if necessity had been viewed as an *excuse* only, there might have been a greater willingness to accept the defence into English law as it would have been seen as posing less threat to the established prohibitions of the criminal law. The closely related defence of duress is widely regarded as an excuse and in the leading case of *Howe*[13] the House of Lords seemed to think that the same principles applied to both. The recent "duress of circumstances" cases have a distinct excusatory flavour to them. Perhaps, then, if a fully-blown defence of necessity were to be admitted into English law it will be in an excusatory format. However, given the current uncertainty, we have chosen to follow the position suggested in the United States and adopted in the first edition of this book, to distinguish two situations. First, where the threatened harm is greater than the harm inflicted, the defence bears all the hall-marks of a justification. On the other hand, where the harm inflicted is roughly equal to that threatened, it could be classified as an excuse.

(c) *Public authority.* The use of force by the police, for example, in effecting an arrest is justified, the superior interest being the enforcement of the law.

(d) *Discipline.* Parents are justified in using reasonable force against their children, the superior interest being to "promote the welfare of the minor" and to prevent or punish misconduct.

(e) *Consent.* Force against a person who has consented is justified,[14] the superior interest being the value of human autonomy. Individuals are free and responsible agents and respect must be given to their right to consent to the infliction of force against them. However in certain cases the interests of society prevail over any value attached to human autonomy and thus consent may not be given to certain types of force (mainly serious force such as death or grievous bodily harm, or disapproved-of-force such as sado-masochistic beatings inflicting injury).

(f) *Superior orders.* Again, the existence of such a defence in this country is in doubt. To the extent that obeying the orders of superiors is a defence in the United States, the harm done is justified on the basis that the superior interest protected is military discipline and effectiveness. The superiority of this interest is only overturned when the unlawfulness of the order is transparently obvious. Although following

---

[13] [1987] A.C. 417.
[14] Model Penal Code, Proposed Official Draft 1962, s.308(1)(*a*). That this is a "superior interest" is not always accepted. (*Tyrer* Eur.Ct. Series A. Vol. 26; *Campbell and Cosans* v. *U.K.* (1980) 3 E.H.R.R. 531).

this reasoning, superior orders is tenatively classified here as a justification, a better view could be that like duress, it constitutes an *excuse*. Such an approach could make the defence more "politically acceptable" and lead to its acceptance into English law. Whether this would be desirable is discussed later.

C. Excuses

With excusatory defences there is a wrong to be excused, but the actor because of an excusing condition is not accountable or culpable for the wrong act.

Glanville Williams, "The Theory of Excuses" [1982] Crim.L.R. 732, 735:

"What, then, is an excuse? The answer seems to be that a defence is an excuse when (1) it amounts to a denial of the proscribed state of mind or negligence, or when (2) it affirms that the defendant was not a fully free and responsible agent so as to be fairly held accountable (*e.g.* when he was under the age of responsibility, or subject to duress . . .)

. . . Injuring people is socially deplored, and it remains deplored, or at least regretted, even though the actor has the defence of duress, provocation, infancy, insanity, lack of *mens rea*, or lack of negligence, as the case may be; consequently, these defences are only excuses.[15]

Sanford H. Kadish, "Excusing Crime" (1987) 75 Cal.L.R. 257 at p. 264:

"To blame a person is to express a moral criticism, and if the person's action does not deserve criticism, blaming him is a kind of falsehood and is, to the extent the person is injured by being blamed, unjust to him. It is this feature of our everyday moral practices that lies behind the law's excuses. Excuses, then, . . . represent no sentimental compromise with the demands of a moral code; they are, on the contrary, of the essence of a moral code."

Thus according to this view an excuse destroys blame.[16] We do not blame an actor who has an excuse for his actions. We do not blame someone for being insane or for being only seven years old. Because we cannot blame them punishment is impermissible: the criminal law *is* an institution of blame and punishment; the latter is generally dependant upon a finding of the former. Blame is thus a cornerstone of criminal liability—which ought only to be imposed when a blameworthy actor causes harm. Or to put this in equation form: blame plus harm[17] equals criminal liability.

What is meant by "blame?" Blaming someone or regarding their

[15] Fletcher (pp. 575, 577) and Robinson (*ante*, p. 274 at 222) both deny that *mens rea* (including negligence) raises issues of excuse; it relates solely to the definition of the offence. See, further, Glanville Williams, "Offences and Defences" (1982) 2 Legal Studies 233.

[16] Robinson, (*ante*, p. 274) accepts that the *actor* is free from blame but that blame is transferred (rather than being destroyed) to the *excusing condition* itself. Such a view is only possible because Robinson excludes from excuse (*ante*, n. 15) lack of *mens rea*: it would be absurd to shift the blame onto this. We, however, have adopted the view of Glanville Williams that excuses not only include lack of *mens rea*, but also have the effect of destroying blame.

[17] The notion of harm is discussed (*ante*, p. 83 and *post*, pp. 434–435, 798–799, 801–805).

conduct as blameworthy involves a moral assessment of that conduct as committed by that actor. Such an assessment involves a consideration of the defendant's state of mind or failure to take precautions. Thus, for reasons already explained,[18] we blame the actor who intentionally, recklessly or negligently (assuming he had the requisite capacity) produces the harmful consequence. In more familiar language, *mens rea* is an important indicator of blame. But a moral assessment of blame can also involve factors beyond the particular conduct and accompanying mental state of the defendant. Some of these factors will be considered in subsequent chapters,[19] but in the present context we can say that part of our moral assessment will be a consideration of *how* and *why* the defendant got himself into the situation wherein he caused the harmful consequence. Thus, using duress as an example, if an "innocent" man is subjected to such dire threats that his subsequent actions are morally involuntary, and if we are satisfied that most ordinary people would have responded in the same way, then we do not blame him if he commits a crime. But if that same man had joined a terrorist organisation knowing that he might be compelled to commit crimes, then we do blame him for being in that situation (and deny him a defence of duress). This is the approach adopted by English law.

Blame, of course, is not an "all or nothing" concept. We might blame certain actors more or less than others. Thus we might wish to blame the intentional killer more than the negligent killer, and we might wish to blame the provoked killer less than the unprovoked killer. We shall be arguing later[20] that it is the conjunction of these different degrees of blame and the different levels of seriousness of harm that provides the key to the structuring of all criminal offences. The implication of having degrees of blameworthiness is, of course, that excuses can also differ in degree.

Martin Wasik, "Partial Excuses in the Criminal Law" (1982) 45 M.L.R. 516 at 524–525:

"A more helpful model of the operation of excuses in the criminal law would involve the recognition of a 'scale of excuse,' running downwards from excusing conditions, through partial excuses to mitigating excuses. Excuses towards the higher end of the scale are those where maximum moral pressure for exculpation outweighs reasons of policy and practicality for not permitting the excuse. Automatism is an example. Those towards the lower end of the scale, while they may be morally significant, are out-weighed by practical and policy considerations. A general excusing condition of good motive is an example. Partial excuses fall into the centre of this range, and exhibit a fine balance between rival considerations. The partial excuse of provocation, for example, has been said to be ' . . . an extremely strong exculpatory claim . . . ' (Gross,

---

[18] *Ante*, pp. 147–150, 206–212, 216–223.
[19] *Post*, pp. 561–562, 665–668.
[20] *Post*, p. 795.

p. 158) . . . On the other hand this excusatory power should surely be weighed against the law's requirement of self-control. . . .

All 'middle range' excuses may be regarded as potential partial excuses, but it is clearly not inevitable that they will turn out to be so. At a given stage in the history of criminal law, policy claims against admitting a particular excuse as an excusing condition will be seen as more or less compelling."

It must be emphasised at this stage that the concept of blame is not necessarily synonymous with "lack of excuse,"[21] but as should be clear by now, the overlap between the two is substantial.

In the light of the above, the following may be presented as excuses:

(a) *Insanity.*

(b) *Automatism.*

(c) *Lack of age.*
In these three cases the abnormal condition of the actor is an excusing condition. Because a defendant, for example, cannot accurately perceive the physical nature or consequences of his actions through, say insanity, it is no longer proper to hold him accountable for those actions.

(d) *Lack of mens rea (including lack of negligence).*

(e) *Mistake.*

Sanford H. Kadish, "Excusing Crime" (1987) 75 Cal.L.R. 257 at p. 261:

"Other mens rea requirements, on the other hand, are excuses in mens rea clothing. They are excusing conditions because they serve to deny blame for a harm done. That they are cast in the form of mens rea requirements does not change their character. . . . This is why accident and mistake are excuses, despite their formal character as definitional mens rea requirements."

We have seen that there is fierce controversy over whether mistake negates a definitional element of the crime (and therefore is simply lack of *mens rea*), or whether it is a defence that previously had to be based on reasonable grounds.[22] This problem could easily be solved within the existing framework by asserting that *no* blame attaches to a person who makes a reasonable mistake (*i.e.* complete excuse), but that *some* blame attaches to the person who makes an unreasonable mistake, and he should be liable to *that* extent (*i.e.* a partial excuse).

(f) *Duress.* In the United States duress is generally treated as an excuse rather than a justification[23] on the basis that while the disability might

---

[21] See *post*, pp. 795–798.
[22] *Ante*, pp. 252–268.
[23] Model Penal Code, Art. 2; N.Y. Penal Law, s.40.00.

have an external cause, the "excusing condition" is the morally involuntary response of the actor. The approach adopted by English law to this problem is discussed later.[24]

(g) *Provocation.*

(h) *Diminished responsibility.*
These two are partial excuses to murder only. The defendant in both these cases is claiming he is not *fully* responsible.[25]

(i) *Intoxication.* Again, this is generally only a partial excuse. The defendant lacks *mens rea* but because he is blamed for being so intoxicated, he is only partially excused (or for certain, generally lesser crimes, not excused at all).

(j) *Necessity (Where the harm threatened is equal to the harm caused).*
This cannot be regarded as justificatory as the harm being caused is not less than the harm being threatened, but such a defence must be regarded as an excuse. We can understand the predicament of an actor faced with such a choice. In the context of homicide one might wish to treat this as only a partial excuse, *i.e.* an excuse to murder but not to manslaughter, which is the approach adopted to provocation.[26]

D. Significance of distinction between justification and excuse
What is the point of this theoretical distinction?
The distinction between justification and excuse is the key to defining the parameters of each of the general defences. For example, approaching duress as an excuse and not as a justification, informs one as to what the detailed rules on the defence should be. Its importance as a theoretical guide cannot therefore be overestimated. But there is a practical utility as well. The distinction between justification and excuse has the following important consequences:

(a) Whether one is entitled to resist conduct for which the aggressor has a defence, or entitled to assist the aggressor, depends upon whether the aggressor's defence is justificatory or excusatory in nature.

Paul Robinson, "Criminal Law Defenses: A Systematic Analysis" (1982) 82 Col.L.R. 199 at 274–275:

"Where an aggressor has a justification defense, the proper rule is clear: justified aggression should never be lawfully subject to resistance or interference.

---

[24] *Post*, pp. 311–313.
[25] See Peter Alldridge, "The Coherence of Defences" [1983] Crim.L.R. 665 who argues that the effect of section 3 of the Homicide Act 1957 has been to transmute provocation from a partial justification to a partial excuse.
[26] See Commentary to Model Penal Code, Tent. Draft No. 8, 1958, pp. 8–9; the defence of provocation is discussed, *post*, pp. 638–655.

When conduct is deemed justified, it creates, by definition, a net benefit to society. The owner of a field should not be allowed to resist one who would burn it to stop a spreading fire, and others should be encouraged to assist, and not permitted to interfere.

An excused aggressor, on the other hand, should be subject to lawful resistance. That is, the victim of the psychotic attacker should be able lawfully to defend himself and to have others lawfully assist him in such defense. While the aggressor may be ultimately blameless, the conduct is clearly harmful. All required elements of the offense are satisfied and no justification exists."

Similar principles apply to accessories to crime. Thus in *Quick and Paddison*[27] the principal offender had a defence of automatism—an "excuse" under the above analysis. Paddison assisted him in his aggression and was held liable as an accessory. Had Quick's defence been justificatory in nature, say, acting reasonably to defend himself, then Paddison would have been quite entitled to assist him.

(b) When conduct is justified, it is in effect "approved" of; there is no need to try and prevent such conduct re-occurring, but where conduct is merely excused, society might wish to protect itself from repetition of such conduct and thus might wish to resort to coercive remedies against the defendant despite his acquittal. Thus a successful defence of insanity leads nevertheless to commitment in a secure mental hospital. Lack of age is a defence to a criminal charge, but civil "care proceedings" may be resorted to. Diminished responsibility is an excuse for murder, but not for manslaughter, enabling the court to take appropiate steps in relation to the defendant. So too, intoxication is only an excuse to certain crimes—generally where there is a lesser included offence available to which it is no defence. Automatism, on the other hand, enables a defendant to escape all coercive measures, but as we have seen, even here, there are suggestions that some new form of special verdict should be returned to such cases enabling a court to exercise some supervision over such a person to prevent recurrence of the involuntary action. The remaining excuses such as duress present little threat of repetition of the conduct and therefore there is no need to resort to coercive measures in relation to such a defendant, but a finding of an excuse (as opposed to a justification) alerts one to the possibility at least of considering some form of restriction, whether criminal or civil, over the defendant.[28]

The next two consequences of the distinction are admittedly somewhat speculative:

(c) Whether a defence is justificatory or excusatory may affect the law's response to defendants who make a mistake in relation thereto. Thus the law's response at present seems to be that those who make a mistake in relation to a *justification*, for example, self-defence, need only

---

[27] [1973] Q.B. 910; see also discussion of *Cogan and Leek, post*, pp. 521–524.
[28] See generally, Robinson pp. 285–291.

have made a genuine mistake. On the other hand, those who make mistakes in relation to an *excuse*, for example, duress, must have made a reasonable mistake to escape liability.[29]

(d) It has been suggested that the justification/excuse distinction provides the key to determining which of the general defences are available to crimes of strict liability. Justificatory defences are, but excusatory defences are not, available in such cases.[30] According to this view one could successfully plead self-defence to a strict liability offence, but could not plead intoxication or mistake to such an offence.

This view has some merit. The effect of an excusatory defence is that it destroys *blame*: the whole point of strict liability is that it is not concerned with blame. It would therefore be contradictory to allow excusatory defences to strict liability offences.[31] However, it is submitted that this argument is unacceptable. Duress is generally regarded as an excuse. It would surely be absurd to deny the defence of duress when an actor, with a gun pointed at his head, commits a minor traffic offence. Automatism is also an excuse and it is true that it was denied as a defence to the involuntary conduct in committing strict liability offences in *Larsonneur*[32] and *Winzar* v. *Chief Constable of Kent*.[33] These two cases have, however, been widely condemned and, it is submitted, ought not to be followed.[34] Perhaps the best way to determine what defences are available to strict liability offences is to examine each defence in turn and explore its rationale. This would then need to be contrasted with the rationale of strict liability and a decision made on a defence by defence basis as to whether each was available to offences of strict liability.[35]

A fuller recognition of the distinction could have further implications:

(e) Where conduct is justified, the law, for conduct in those circumstances, is effectively amended. A precedent is generated that others, in similar circumstances, may act in the same manner. Excuses on the other hand do not constitute exceptions or modifications to the law— they simply involve an assessment that in the particular circumstances it would be unjust to hold a particular actor accountable for his actions. As we have seen, had this distinction between appreciated, different results might have been achieved in *Dudley and Stevens*, *Abbott* and *Green*.

---

[29] *Ante*, pp. 264–265.

[30] M. Sornarajah, "Defences to Strict Liability Offences in Singapore and Malaysia" (1985) 27 Mal.L.R. 1.

[31] K. L. Koh, C. M. V. Clarkson and N. A. Morgan, *Criminal Law in Singapore and Malaysia: Text and Materials* (1989), p. 96.

[32] (1933) 24 Cr.App.R. 74.

[33] *The Times*, March 28, 1983.

[34] Unless preceding fault could be established. See *ante*, p. 121.

[35] See K. L. Koh, C. M. V. Clarkson and N. A. Morgan (*ante*, n. 31 at pp. 97–98) for an illustration as to how this would work.

**Paul Robinson, "Criminal Law Defenses: A Systematic Analysis"
(1982) 82 Col. L.R. 199 at 245–247:**

"When conduct is justified there is again nothing to condemn or punish. The defendant's conduct did not, under the circumstances, violate the prohibition of the law, and indeed may be desired and encouraged. Yet a harm or evil was inflicted, and such conduct should remain generally prohibited and condemned. Arson, for example, remains a crime even though the law may permit the burning of a field if it creates a fire break that saves an entire town, but when an actor is acquitted under a justification defense, the message to the public may be unclear, especially since the verdict of 'not guilty' gives no hint that justification defense is at work. Thus, the condemnation and general deterrence of arson may be undercut. It might be desirable to alter the jury verdict to 'justified,' thereby acquitting the actor because his conduct caused no net harm, yet noting the continuing prohibition of arson . . .

Excuses have a great potential for undercutting the condemnation and general deterrence of the harmful conduct. Even taking the objective circumstances into account, the conduct in an excuse case *does* constitute a net harm or evil that is condemned by the criminal law. Society will continue to condemn and seek to deter such conduct even in identical circumstances. It is the *actor*, not the act, which causes us to excuse. Furthermore, the explanation for acquittal of the offender is much less apparent than in cases of justification. Excuses, for the most part, rely on subjective criteria like mental illness, mistake, or subnormality. Often only a person who is aware of the evidence adduced at trial will understand that acquittal is based upon these special characteristics of the actor, not an approval or tolerance of the act.

The limited value of a simple 'not guilty' verdict to convey the proper message accounts for some of the difficulties which have arisen in cases of excuse [such as *Dudley and Stevens*] . . .

It may be because of this potential for misapprehension that an acquittal based on insanity is reported as a verdict of 'not guilty by reason of insanity' . . .

The only sound approach is to recognize excuse defenses, but to minimize the danger of misperception of the acquittal by relying upon special verdicts—not guilty by reason of excuse—and assuring that the public understands that special message. Civil commitment and similar procedures outside the criminal justice system are available to further the goals of special deterrence and rehabilitation in the absence of condemnable culpability."

II THE DEFENCES

A. Consent

1. Introduction

Certain crimes are defined in such a manner that they can only be committed without the victim's consent. Rape, for instance is "unlawful sexual intercourse with a woman who . . . does not consent to it."[36] In such cases a defendant who claims that a woman was consenting to sexual intercourse is not pleading consent as a defence, but is claiming that one of the definitional elements of the offence is missing—that the *actus*

---

[36] Sexual Offences (Amendment) Act 1976, s.1(1).

reus of the crime has not been committed.[37] Most crimes are however not expressly defined in such a manner, but the consent of the "victim" might exempt the defendant from liability. It is implicit in *Kimber*[38] that even for such crimes, consent is not truly a "defence." The requirement of "lack of consent" is a definitional element or part of the *actus reus* of the crime. If there is consent, there is no *actus reus*. If the defendant believes his victim is consenting, there is no *mens rea*.

The better view however is that in this latter type of crime consent is truly a defence.[39] The defendant admits that he has committed the full *actus reus* of the offence, but claims that the consent of the "victim" justifies the wrong he would otherwise be committing. As we have seen, a defence that is justificatory in nature is one that necessitates a superior interest being upheld. In relation to consent, the superior interest being upheld is human autonomy: the foundation of the criminal law is the concept of responsibility—here it finds expression in the freedom of people to consent to what would otherwise be criminal offences against themselves. However, consent is not a defence to all crimes. This may be because the "victim" is held not to be sufficiently responsible to give consent, but it may also be because other interests, such as "public policy," are held to be superior.

R. v. Donovan [1934] 2 K.B. 498 (Court of Criminal Appeal)

Swift J.:
"The appellant was convicted . . . upon an indictment charging him with indecent assault and common assault on Norah Eileen Harrison . . . It appeared that the appellant was addicted to a form of sexual perversion, and . . . there was talk between the appellant and the prosecutrix [Harrison] which left no doubt that she had expressed her willingness to submit herself to the kind of conduct to which he was addicted. . . . They met by appointment . . . [and] his first remark was 'Where would you like to have your spanking, in Hyde Park, or in my garage?' . . . She went with him . . . to a garage . . . [and] [t]here the alleged offences were committed.

. . . A doctor, who . . . [later] examined her . . . said that there were seven or eight red marks upon her body, and expressed the opinion that the marks indicated that she had suffered a 'fairly severe beating.' He found no sign of any other injury . . .

The appellant gave evidence on his own behalf, asserting that the prosecutrix had so acted throughout as to make it plain that she consented to all that he did.''

Here the defendant was clearly admitting that he had committed the harm complained of, but was claiming consent as a defence.[40] In this

---

[37] *D.P.P.* v. *Morgan* [1976] A.C. 182.

[38] (1983) 77 Cr.App.R. 225.

[39] The only practical difference between these two modes of analysis relates to cases where the defendant mistakenly believes his victim has consented. See *ante*, pp. 261–268. As to whether there is a difference in the burden of proof, see *ante*, p. 273.

[40] The analysis under *Kimber* (*ante*, n. 38) would be different. According to this view "the prohibited act in indecent assault is the use of personal violence to a woman without her consent." If she consented, there would be no "prohibited act" or *actus reus*.

section we shall consider the extent to which pleas such as this exculpate a defendant. In assessing this, three issues need to be examined:
(1) the "reality" of consent;
(2) the nature and degree of the harm to which consent may be given; and
(3) the rationale of consent as a defence.

2. The reality of consent

Consent must not be induced by duress or by certain kinds of fraud. The woman, who, for example, submits to anal intercourse (buggery)[41] rather than suffer serious physical injury is not deemed to have given real consent. Further, the person alleged to have consented must be capable of giving consent; their consent may be regarded as invalid by reason of lack of age or infirmity. In *Howard*,[42] for example, the alleged consent of a six year old to attempted sexual intercourse with the defendant was deemed invalid. It was judged that she was incapable of giving real consent. Whilst transparently the right decision in that particular case, the principle that there must be informed consent by minors may not always operate so simply. A six year old may truthfully be said not to have attained the "age of discretion" but can the same thing be said of 12 and 13 year olds? The reality is that the "age of discretion" rests not only upon the mental and physical age of the child but also depends upon the harm to which they have allegedly given their consent.

Gillick v. West Norfolk A.H.A. [1986] 1 A.C. 112 (House of Lords)

(For facts see page 511).

Lord Scarman:
"Mrs. Gillick relies on both the statute law and the case law to establish her proposition that parental consent is in all . . . circumstances necessary [other than in emergency or where a court order exists]. The only statutory provision directly in point is section 8 of the Family Law Reform Act 1969. Subsection (1) of the section provides that the consent of a minor who has attained the age of 16 to any surgical, mental or dental treatment which in the absence of consent would constitute a trespass to his person shall be effective as if he were of full age and that the consent of his parent or guardian need not be obtained. Subsection (3) of the section provides:
"Nothing in this section shall be construed as making ineffective any consent which would have been effective if this section had not been enacted."
[Lord Scarman goes on to argue that nothing in this provision nor in previous case-law precludes the consent of minors less than 16 being valid.]
Parental rights clearly do exist, and they do not wholly disappear until the age of majority. Parental rights relate to both the person and the property of the child—custody, care and control of the person and guardianship of the property of the child. But the common law has never treated such rights as sovereign or

---

[41] Sexual Offences Act 1956, s.12(1).
[42] [1966] 1 W.L.R. 13.

beyond review or control. Nor has our law ever treated the child as other than a person with capacities and rights recognised by law. The principle of the law, as I shall endeavour to show is that parental rights are derived from parental duty and exist only so long as they are needed for the protection of the person and the property of the child. The principle has been subjected to certain age limits set by statute for certain purposes: and in some cases the courts have declared an age of discretion at which the child acquires before the age of majority the right to make his (or her) own decision. But these limitations in no way undermine the principle of the law, and should not be allowed to obscure it. . . .

[N]either statute nor the case-law has ruled on the extent and duration of parental right in respect of children under the age of 16. More specifically, there is no rule yet applied to contraceptive treatment, which has special problems of its own and is a late-comer in medical practice. It is open, therefore, to the House to formulate a rule. The Court of Appeal favoured a fixed age limit of 16 . . . [but] the law relating to parent and child is concerned with the problems of the growth and development of the human personality. If the law should impose upon the process of 'growing up' fixed limits where nature knows only a continuous process, the price would be artificiality and a lack of realism in an area where the law must be sensitive to human development and social change. . . .

In the light of the foregoing I would hold that as a matter of law the parental right to determine whether or not their minor child below the age of 16 will have medical treatment terminates if and when the child achieves a sufficient understanding and intelligence to enable him or her to understand fully what is proposed. It will be a question of fact whether a child seeking advice has sufficient understanding of what is involved to give a consent valid in law. . . .

When applying these conclusions to contraceptive advice and treatment it has to be borne in mind that there is much that has to be understood by a girl under the age of 16 if she is to have legal capacity to consent to such treatment. It is not enough that she should understand the nature of the advice which she has been given: she must also have a sufficient maturity to understand what is involved. There are moral and family questions, especially her relationship with her parents; long-term problems associated with the emotional impact of pregnancy and its termination; and there are risks to health of sexual intercourse at her age, risks which contraception may diminish but cannot eliminate. It follows that a doctor will have to satisfy himself that she is able to appraise these factors before he can safely proceed upon the basis that she has at law capacity to consent to contraceptive treatment. And it further follows that ordinarily the proper course will be for him, as the guidance lays down, first to seek to persuade the girl to bring her parents into consultation, and if she refuses, not to prescribe contraceptive treatment unless he is satisfied that her circumstances are such that he ought to proceed without parental knowledge and consent."

Appeal allowed

This flexible, and it is submitted, entirely appropriate, approach was also taken in *R.* v. *D.*[43] in assessing whether a child could give consent to what would otherwise be a kidnapping by one parent. In the case of *Sutton*[44] it was held that boys of 10, 11 and 12 could consent to their naked bodies being touched in order to indicate the pose the photographer required. However, had the touching been held to be indecent, the

---

[43] [1984] A.C. 778.
[44] [1977] 1 W.L.R. 1086. But see now the Protection of Children Act 1978, s.1(1)(*a*) which prohibits the taking of indecent photographs of children.

same consent would have been held to be invalid and the photographer convicted of indecent assault.[45]

Similarly, in *Re D (A Minor)*,[46] Heilbron J. suggested that any purported consent by an 11 year old girl (who suffered from sobos syndrome and was of "dull, normal" intelligence) to a sterilisation operation desired for her by her mother and doctor would have been valueless. The reasoning behind this decision cannot simply be on the basis of the retardation of the child alone, for subnormal and mentally disordered people commonly give consent that is regarded as valid (and is not subject to veto by relatives) if they possess certain basic powers of comprehension.[47] If the decision is based upon not only the extreme youth of the child but also a finding that the operation would not be of any medical or social benefit to the child, is it likely that there would be a different judicial response after *Gillick*? Finally, is it possible that courts might allow a girl under the age of 16 to give valid consent to an abortion? In one case a local authority, who had in their care a pregnant girl of 15 (already mother of one child), applied to court after objections by the girl's parents to an abortion. The judge overruled the parents objections stating: "I am satisfied that she wants this abortion. She understands the implications of it."[48] However this was a case of *the court consenting* to the abortion, while exercising its prerogative powers as *parens patriae*[49] and taking the child's views into consideration. The question whether a girl can *by herself* consent to an abortion remains an open one.

3. The nature and degree of the harm

Harm has been defined for the purposes of this book as any violation of an interest[50] and as we have already begun to see there are violations of some interests to which courts will not allow consent to be given.

Whether consent will constitute a defence is ultimately a question of public policy that involves balancing the seriousness of the harm inflicted against the social utility or acceptability of the defendant's conduct. The greater the injury inflicted, the more the defendant must have some justification (in terms of social utility). Stephen J. in *Coney* held:

"The principle as to consent seems to me to be this: When one person is

[45] By virtue of s.14(2) of the Sexual Offences Act 1956 the consent of a boy under the age of 16 is regarded as irrelevant for the purposes of determining whether there has been an indecent assault.
[46] [1976] 2 W.L.R. 279.
[47] Severely subnormal women ("defectives"), however, cannot consent to sexual intercourse or indecent assault—nor in the latter case can severely subnormal men (Sexual Offences Act 1956, ss.7, 14(4), 15(3), 45, as amended by Mental Health Act 1959). The degree of subnormality required here is extreme. In *Kimber (ante*, n. 38) a woman suffering from a severe degree of mental disorder so "that it was highly unlikely that she would be capable of giving comprehending consent to sexual advances" was held not to be a defective within the meaning of section 7.
[48] In *Re P (A minor)* (1982) 80 L.G.R. 301.
[49] *Re Baker (Infants)* [1962] Ch. 201. See generally, on this point Stephen M. Cretney, *Principles of Family Law* (4th ed., 1984), pp. 563–569.
[50] *Ante*, p. 85, although of course, not all harms ought to be subject to the criminal sanction.

indicted for inflicting personal injury upon another, the consent of the person who sustains the injury is no defence to the person who inflicts the injury, if the injury is of such a nature, or is inflicted under such circumstances, that its infliction is injurious to the public as well as to the person injured."[51]

Thus consent by persons over the age of 16 is a defence to most surgical operations because of the social value placed upon such operations. This is so even though very serious bodily harm may be caused by the operation. However where the operation has little or no social value the position is less clear. Sterilization operations are now carried out regularly for birth control purposes.[52] The castration of males involved in sex change operations has come to be regarded as lawful,[53] but grave doubts have been expressed about the practice of so-called female circumcision performed for religious reasons by some doctors at the request of parents of young girls. Indeed, a Parliamentary bill to make this practice an offence, except where "necessary for the health of that person" was passed by the House of Lords in 1983 although it was withdrawn before the House of Commons second reading.[54]

Consent is similarly a defence to sports participants who injure one another in the course of their sporting activities. Lawful sports are socially approved of; they are "manly diversions, they tend to give strength, skill and activity, and may fit people for defence, public as well as personal, in time of need."[55] In *Billinghurst*[56] the jury were directed that rugby players consent to such force as can reasonably be expected during the game. If the force was used in the course of play then consent could be a defence even to a serious injury, such as a fractured jaw. However, the attitude taken by courts to off the ball incidents is very different; not only are players not deemed to have consented to such violence but the offender will almost always receive a custodial sentence.[57]

Further, social necessity is such that we are all deemed to have consented to a certain degree of minor bodily contact in everyday activities—on buses, trains, etc. However, consent is only deemed to have been given to a reasonable use of force in such situations. Consent

---

[51] (1882) 8 Q.B.D. 549.

[52] *Cf.* Glanville Williams, *Textbook*, p. 590. The National Health Service (Family Planning) Amendment Act 1972 authorises the provision of voluntary vasectomy services.

[53] D. W. Meyers, *The Human Body and the Law* (1970), Chap. 3.

[54] The Prohibition of Female Circumcision (No. 2) Bill, No. 42, 1983; *cf.* R. D. Mackay, "Is Female Circumcision Unlawful?" [1983] Crim.L.R. 717. See generally, Glanville Williams, "Consent and Public Policy" [1962] Crim.L.R. 74, 154; Glanville Williams, *The Sanctity of Life and the Criminal Law*, 1958, Ch. 3; P. D. G. Skegg, "Medical Procedures and the Crime of Battery" [1974] Crim.L.R. 694.

[55] Sir M. Foster, *Crown Cases*, (3rd ed.) p. 260.

[56] [1978] Crim.L.R. 553.

[57] See, *e.g. R.* v. *Birkin* [1988] Crim.L.R. 855 where the defendant was sentenced to six months imprisonment by the Court of Appeal for a blow that fractured the jaw of a member of the opposing team in two places. The court stressed that such incidents would not be tolerated. See further, Edward Grayson, "The Day Sport Dies" [1988] New L.J. 9 and *Sport and the Law* (1988), where the author suggests that team managers, coaches etc. who persistently select and encourage known violent field offenders ought also to be criminally liable as aiders and abettors.

would be no defence to an aggressive, excessive use of force—even in a bus queue.

However despite any "social utility" arguments over euthanasia and mercy-killing, it is clear that a "victim" cannot consent to his own death. It is murder to kill another deliberately, even if he is consenting. This is so despite the fact that self-murder (suicide) is no longer a crime.[58] The Criminal Law Revision Committee emphatically rejected the view that such a killing "should be a special offence removed from the law of murder and should carry a reduced sentence, the reason being that such a killing did not present a threat to public security as did murder in general."[59]

But what about injuries short of death? In the absence of any social utility it seems clear that consent will be no defence to really serious injuries, such as maiming or endangering life.[60] In *Leach*[61] the "victim" organised his own crucifixion on Hampstead Heath. The defendants nailed him to a wooden cross; his hands had been pierced by 6 inch nails. The defendants were liable for unlawful wounding; the consent of the victim was disregarded. It had no social utility. With lesser injuries the extent to which consent is a defence depends upon the actual seriousness of the injury when weighed against the reprehensibility of the defendant's conduct and motivation.

R. v. Donovan [1934] 2 K.B. 498 (Court of Criminal Appeal)

(The facts are given above, *ante*, p. 284)

Swift, J.:
"No person can licence another to commit a crime. So far as the criminal law is concerned, therefore, where the act charged is in itself unlawful, it can never be necessary to prove absence of consent on the part of the person wronged in order to obtain the conviction of the wrongdoer. There are, however, many acts in themselves lawful which become unlawful only if they are done without the consent of the person affected. What is, in the one case, an innocent act of familiarity or affection, may, in another, be an assault, for no other reason than that, in the one case there is consent, and in the other consent is absent. As a general rule, although it is a rule to which there are well-established exceptions, it is an unlawful act to beat another person with such a degree of violence that the infliction of bodily harm is a probable consequence, and, when such an act is proved, consent is immaterial . . .

In the present case it was not in dispute that the motive of the appellant was to gratify his own perverted desires. If, in the course of so doing, he acted so as to cause bodily harm, he cannot plead his corrupt motive as an excuse. . . . Nothing could be more absurd or more repellant to the ordinary intelligence

---

[58] Suicide Act 1961, s.1.

[59] 14th Report, Offences against the Person, Cmnd. 7844 (1980), para. 128. The German Penal Code St.G.B. Art. 216 creates a special lesser offence of "killing on request" on the basis that the victim's consent reduces the wrongfulness of the killing. See Fletcher, pp. 332–334, where he distinguishes between voluntary, involuntary, passive and active euthanasia.

[60] *Wright* (1603) Co.Lit.f. 127 a–b; this principle is still clearly valid today. See also *Cato* [1976] 1 All E.R. 260 where consent to the administration of a noxious thing likely to endanger life was no defence.

[61] *The Times*, January 15, 1969.

than to regard his conduct as comparable with that of a participant in one of those 'manly diversions' (lawful sporting activities). . . . For this purpose we think that 'bodily harm' has its ordinary meaning and includes any hurt or injury calculated to interfere with the health or comfort of the prosecutor. Such hurt or injury need not be permanent, but must, no doubt, be more than merely transient and trifling.

. . . There are many gradations between a slight tap and a severe blow, and the question whether particular blows were likely or intended to cause bodily harm is one eminently fitted for the decision of a jury."

Appeal allowed

However, in the following case, Lord Lane C.J. described the reasoning in *Donovan* as "tautologous," for it starts "with the proposition that consent is irrelevant if the act complained of is 'unlawful. . . . in itself,' which it will be if it involves the infliction of bodily harm."[62]

Attorney-General's Reference (No. 6 of 1980) [1981] Q.B. 715 (Court of Appeal, Criminal Division)

Two youths who had been arguing in a street decided to settle their quarrel by means of a fight. Blows were exchanged and the respondent caused the other bruising and a bleeding nose. The respondent claimed that the other had consented; he was subsequently acquitted and the principle of consent fell to be determined by reference.

Lord Lane C.J.:

"Bearing in mind the various cases and the views of the textbook writers cited to us, and starting with the proposition that ordinarily an act consented to will not constitute an assault, the question is: at what point does the public interest require the court to hold otherwise?. . . . The answer to this question, in our judgment, is that it is not in the public interest that people should try to cause or should cause each other actual bodily harm for no good reason. Minor struggles are another matter. So, in our judgment, it is immaterial whether the act occurs in private or in public; it is an assault if actual bodily harm is intended and/or caused. This means that most fights will be unlawful regardless of consent. . . . "

Determination accordingly

In the course of his judgment, Lord Lane C.J. went on to say that he was not precluding consent to sporting contact, lawful correction or reasonable surgical interference because these either involved the exercise of a legal right or could be justified by public policy. This list has recently been extended to include "rough and undisciplined play" even

---

[62] At p. 718.

where it results in one boy receiving a broken arm and another rupturing his spleen.[63] As Smith makes clear in his commentary to this decision[64] neither of the justifications offered by Lord Lane "seems to apply to horseplay. But the decision recognises that boys always have indulged in rough and undisciplined play among themselves, and probably always will, and that it is not appropriate for the criminal law to intervene when there is consent." One wonders whether the behaviour involved in the case of *Donovan* could be justified on a similar basis!

4. The rationale of consent as a defence

All of the issues raised in this section have been shaped to a greater or lesser extent by "public policy," but stating this gets us no closer to understanding the basis upon which decisions to exclude the issue of consent are or ought to be made. We may return to the questions posed in the earlier sections. Why is it that consent is irrelevant to a charge of murder if suicide itself is not a crime? Why cannot someone who enjoys being beaten submit themselves to the experience without the other party committing an assault? To answer these questions we need briefly to reconsider in this context those arguments which were addressed to the question of determining the sort of conduct that ought to be criminal.[65] True liberatarians, such as Mill, for example, would argue that conduct ought to be criminal on the basis that it causes harm to another and that where the other consents to it, no harm has been caused; there has been no violation of their interests. How then can the response of the law to the issue of consent be justified?

S. Kadish and M. Paulson, Criminal Law and its Processes (1969), p. 16:

"Devlin argued that the function of disallowing the defence is 'to enforce a moral principle and nothing else'—the moral principle being the sanctity of human life and physical integrity of the person. Hart disagrees, stating that the 'rules excluding the victim's consent as a defense to charges of murder or assault may perfectly well be explained as a piece of paternalism, designed to protect individuals against themselves. Mill no doubt might have protested against a paternalistic policy of using the law to protect even a consenting victim from bodily harm nearly as much as he protested against laws used merely to enforce positive morality; but this does not mean that those two policies are identical.' (*Law, Liberty and Morality*, p. 31). To what extent can the distinctions which courts have made as to when to recognise consent as a defence . . . be explained on grounds of paternalism rather than legal moralism? Is it physical injury to persons, even consenting persons, that the courts are protecting against, or physical harm in the course of immoral behaviour?"

[63] *R. v. Jones and others* [1987] Crim.L.R. 123.
[64] [1987] Crim.L.R. 124.
[65] *Ante*, pp. 77–95.

George P. Fletcher, Rethinking Criminal Law (1978), pp. 770–771:

"The principle that individuals are free and responsible agents informs the analysis of consent, . . . Once accepted, the value of autonomy does not lend itself to being offset by competing social interests. So far as the rationale of consent is that individuals should be free to waive their rights, this capacity of waiver is not a contingent value, subject to repeated balancing against the opposing array of interests.

There is some evidence that at the fringes, however, the principle of autonomy gives way to competing social values. The prevailing view in Western legal systems is that the individual has the right to take his own life or to torture himself, but he does not have the right to authorise others to do the killing or to perform a sado-masochistic beating. That there is a personal right to suffer in these cases indicates that the rationale for limiting personal autonomy is not a paternalistic governmental posture toward the victim's injuring himself. If the issue were paternalism, the government should employ sanctions as well against suicide and other forms of self-destruction.

A more convincing account of the distinction between self-injury and consenting to injury by others derives from the danger of implicating other persons in dangerous forms of conduct. The individual who kills or mutilates himself might affect the well-being of family and friends, but this result depends upon the actor's relationships with other people. In contrast, the self-destructive individual who induces another person to kill or to mutilate him implicates the latter in the violation of a significant social taboo. The person carrying out the killing or the mutilation crosses the threshold into a realm of conduct that, the second time, might be more easily carried out. And the second time, it might not be particularly significant whether the victim consents or not. Similarly, if someone is encouraged to inflict a sado-masochistic beating on a consenting victim, the experience of inflicting the beating might loosen the actor's inhibitions against sadism in general."

In those areas where consent is no defence, such as murder and sado-masochistic beatings, is the law really trying to protect society from the consequences of secondary harms? Or is it simply condemning immoral behaviour? Is such a harm (threatening established morality) one that deserves the sanctions of the criminal law?

Even if one concedes that in certain cases, consent ought not to provide a complete defence, do we blame such defendants *as much* as those who commit similar harms against their victims who are *not* consenting? Is there an argument in such cases that even if consent does not provide a complete justification, it is nevertheless a partial excuse which ought, at least, to reduce the defendant's level of criminal liability?

B. Necessary Defence

1. Introduction
Almost as long as the criminal law has been in existence it has consistently restricted the right of the individual to self-help; it is the function of the law to preserve law and order and protect the weak. There are, however, inevitably occasions when to depend upon the arrival of

official help would be to court disaster and it would be extremely unjust if the remedy of self-help were altogether denied. The law recognises this and in certain situations deems the use of force to be lawful. "The source of [this] right is a comparison of the competing interests of the aggressor and the defender, as modified by the important fact that the aggressor is the one party responsible for the fight. . . . As the party morally at fault for threatening the defender's interests, the aggressor is entitled to lesser consideration in the balancing process."[66]

Again, as with consent, it is possible to assert that necessary defence is not truly a "defence." A defendant acting in self-defence is acting lawfully—an element of the *actus reus* is thus not established.[67] As we have seen, this method of characterisation has important implications in cases where the defendant has made a mistake, *i.e.* mistakenly thinks he needs to defend himself or others.[68] But apart from such cases, the parameters of necessary defence are constant—irrespective of whether it is regarded as a defence, or a denial of a definitional element.

2. The triggering conditions

The triggering conditions for a successful claim of necessary defence "are the circumstances which must exist before an actor will be eligible to act under a justification. In defensive force justifications an aggressor must present a threat of unjustified harm to the protected interest."[69] The "protected interests" currently recognised by the law are protection of self, protection of others, and property.[70] Overlapping these interests to a considerable extent is the further protected interest of acting in the prevention of crime.[71]

It seems only just that an innocent person who is attacked ought to be able to defend himself and should also be able to go to the aid of his immediate family. But what if his friends or even strangers are in need of help; should he be blamed or protected if he chooses to step in? Some authorities, including *Devlin* v. *Armstrong*[72] suggest that there must be "some special nexus or relationship between the person relying on the doctrine to justify what he did in aid of another, and that other."[73] However, it is now clear that no such limitation exists and it makes no difference whether one is defending oneself or a complete stranger.[74]

---

[66] Fletcher, pp. 857–858.

[67] *Abraham* [1973] 1 W.L.R. 1270; *Williams (Gladstone)* (1984) 78 Cr.App.R. 276.

[68] *Ante,* p. 261.

[69] P. Robinson, "Criminal Law Defences: A Systematic Analysis" (1982) 82 Col.L.R. 216.

[70] It seems, therefore, too restrictive to refer to this defence as "self-defence," as it is commonly called.

[71] The overlap is not complete, *e.g.* if one defends oneself against an infant's attack there is no crime. For discussion of acting in prevention of crime, see *post,* p. 296.

[72] [1972] N.I. 13. The relationship between Bernadette Devlin M.P., and her Londonderry constituents was held not to be a sufficient relationship.

[73] At pp. 35–36.

[74] *Williams (Gladstone)* (1984) 78 Cr.App.R. 276; *Tooley* (1709) 11 Mod at 250, 88 E.R. at 1020; *Prince* (1875) 2 C.C.R. at 178; *People* v. *Keatley* [1954] I.R. 12. See Glanville Williams, *Textbook,* p. 501.

One may also use physical force to protect one's property.[75] As we shall see, however, one of the real dilemmas here is in defining how much defensive physical force one may use to protect one's property.

3. The permitted response

The law recognises the right to protect both personal and proprietary interests. One can use violence to repel an attack. It is clear, however, that there are severe restrictions as to the circumstances in which one is justified in using such force. One does not have *carte blanche* simply to defend oneself entirely as one chooses. The law will simply not accept that it is justifiable to kill a human being in order to protect a much-loved pet guinea-pig. In order for conduct to be justified the defender must only have adopted *such force as is necessary* to avert the attack.

But what is meant by "such force as is necessary?" This involves a consideration of the following issues:

 (i) the necessity for *any* defensive action
 (ii) the amount of responsive force that may be used
 (iii) the duty to retreat
 (iv) the imminence of the threatened attack.

It is important to emphasise that with each of these one is ultimately balancing the competing interests of the initial aggressor and the defender—but as the aggressor was the culpable one responsible for starting the violence, the law has tended to tip the scales in favour of the defender.

(i) *The necessity for any defensive action*

It is quite clear that the person seeking to rely upon the defence must believe his action to be necessary; if he is, in reality, the aggressor seeking to disguise his status behind a smoke-screen of self-defence, the defence will not apply to him.

What is the position if the response is not in fact necessary, but the defendant genuinely believes it is (because, say, he mistakenly believes he is about to be attacked)? Until recently it was thought that such a defendant would only escape liability if his mistake was a reasonable one.[76] In *Williams (Gladstone)*,[77] however, it was held by the Court of Appeal that the defendant's mistake need not be reasonable. If he had made a genuine mistake he must be judged according to his mistaken view of the facts.[78]

The Draft Criminal Code Bill 1989 also adopts this view. The amount of force the defendant may use depends on the circumstances "which exist or which he believes to exist."[79]

---

[75] *Hussey* (1924) 18 Cr.App.R. 160. See further, J. C. Smith, *Justification and Excuse in the Criminal Law* (The Hamlyn Lectures, 40th Series), 1989, pp. 109–112.

[76] *E.g. Rose* (1884) 15 Cox 540 where the defendant shot and killed his father whom he mistakenly thought was killing his mother by cutting her throat; *Albert* v. *Lavin* [1982] A.C. 546, *ante*, p. 258.

[77] *Ante*, n. 259.

[78] This was confirmed in *Beckford* [1988] 1 A.C. 130. See *ante*, pp. 260 *et seq.*

[79] Clause 44(1) (Law Com. No. 177, 1989).

Self-defence is regarded as a *justificatory* defence. This, however, can only be the case where the defendant is actually acting in self-defence. Where he has made a mistake and is therefore attacking the interests of an innocent party, his actions cannot be *justified* as not involving any wrongdoing. But in such a case the law has decided that such a mistake negates blameworthiness and *excuses* the defendant from blame. This whole approach of excusing all honest mistakes, even if unreasonable, is highly questionable.

Suppose two police officers see a man in a car. They think he is a dangerous, wanted criminal. They stop the car to arrest the man. Genuinely believing him to be a violent criminal who would shoot them to effect an escape, they beat him nearly to death with their guns. It transpires that the victim is a completely innocent man. According to *Williams (Gladstone)* the actions of the police officers must be judged according to their view of the facts. On that basis, assuming their response was not excessive, they will escape all liability.[80] They thought force was necessary; that is all that is required. Now, if their mistake was a reasonable one—if the facts were such that all reasonable police officers would similarly have thought that the man in the car was the wanted criminal and that it was necessary to use force against him—we would all have sympathy with the police officers' actions and wish to exempt them from blame and criminal liability (leaving aside, for the moment, the issue of whether their response might have been excessive). But if their mistake was an unreasonable one—if there were no reasonable grounds for thinking the man was the wanted criminal or that he would attack them—then, surely, our response is entirely different. We are now appalled at the enormity of their error. We blame the police officers for making such an unreasonable mistake—and blame them to an extent that we feel they should be made criminally accountable for their actions. In other words, the former requirement that the defendant's mistake had to be based on reasonable grounds not only mitigated the practical difficulty of proving whether the defendant actually held the belief or not, but also reflected a more fundamental attitude towards the determination of culpability. The objective requirement of reasonableness brought to account those whom, when consideration had been taken of the anguish of the moment, were still considered blameworthy. As a result of *Williams (Gladstone)* such reasoning has been firmly rejected by the courts.

(ii) *The amount of responsive force that may be used*

It has long been accepted that the defender may only use such force as is reasonable in the circumstances. The general rule is that the response must be proportionate to the attack.

A person acting to repel an unlawful attack is, at the same time as try-

[80] This is broadly what occurred in *Finch and Jardine* (Unreported, Central Criminal Court, October 12–19, 1982); see *post*, pp. 295–308.

ing to protect himself or others, also acting to prevent a crime. This latter situation has been put on a statutory basis.

(a) Criminal Law Act 1967, s.3

"3.—(1) A person may use such force as is reasonable in the circumstances in the prevention of crime, or in effecting or assisting in the lawful arrest of offenders or suspected offenders or of persons unlawfully at large.

(2) Subsection (1) above shall replace the rules of the common law on the question when force used for a purpose mentioned in the subsection is justified by that purpose."

It could be argued that section 3 applies to all cases of necessary defence. A person acting in self-defence is always engaged in preventing a crime—even if that is not his primary motivation in acting. However, the general view is that the common law rules of defensive force have not been effectively put on a statutory footing by virtue of section 3.[81] Not only are the express terms of section 3 restricted to prevention of crime (there was nothing in the preceding Criminal Law Revision Committee report about private defence), but also, the overlap between the two is incomplete.[82] Edmund-Davies L.J. in *McInnes*[83] endorsed this view when he stated that the law of self-defence was "similarly limited as in section 3." In other words, whilst operating along similar lines it is still perfectly proper to regard as authoritative common-law decisions on necessary force.

What is meant by "reasonable" and "proportionate" force here? This has always posed problems—especially in relation to the use of physical force in the defence of property. It would seem clear, for instance, that despite a common belief to the contrary, one is not at liberty to shoot dead a burglar wandering around one's house if one does not fear for one's own life. This causes difficulties because for many persons, such a degree of force is the only method by which they can protect their property. If they are not permitted to use such force, they are in effect condemned to forfeiting their property and having to rely on subsequent legal remedies for redress—remedies that will often be useless. However, the alternative is even worse. One cannot allow persons to go round inflicting death or severe personal injuries on others merely in defence of property.

English law used to insist on a fairly rigorous and objective test of reasonableness. Such an approach can be supported when one recalls that necessary defence amounts to a *justification*:

"[C]haracterizing self-defence as justification . . . involves finding that the attacker's life has become of less value *to society* than the life

---

[81] See A. Ashworth, "Self-Defence and the Right to Life" (1975) C.L.J. 282; C. Harlow, "Self-Defence, Public Right or Private Privilege" [1974] Crim.L.R. 528; Glanville Williams, *Textbook* (1st ed.), p. 455.
[82] *Ante*, n. 71.
[83] (1971) 55 Cr.App.R. 551.

of the person attacked. To reach this difficult conclusion, the law must make the self-defence elements strict enough to ensure that the attacker was really the more culpable party and that there was really no reasonable alternative to killing him."[84]

However, more recent English cases have tended to favour the interests of the defender more heavily.

Attorney-General for Northern Ireland's Reference [1977] A.C. 105 (House of Lords)

The reference arose out of concern over a case in which a soldier had been charged with murder for shooting and killing someone whom he had mistakenly thought to be a member of the I.R.A.

Lord Diplock:
"What amount of force is 'reasonable in the circumstances' for the purpose of preventing crime is, in my view, always a question for the jury in a jury trial, never a 'point of law' for the judge . . .

The jury would also have to consider how the circumstances in which the accused had to make his decision whether or not to use force and the shortness of the time available to him for reflection, might affect the judgment of a reasonable man . . . [The jury] should remind themselves that the postulated balancing of risk against risk, harm against harm, by the reasonable man is not undertaken in the calm analytical atmosphere of the court-room after counsel with the benefit of hindsight have expounded at length the reasons for and against the kind of degree of force that was used by the accused; but in the brief second or two which the accused had to decide whether to shoot or not and under all the stresses to which he was exposed . . .

On the facts that are to be assumed for the purposes of the reference the only options open to the accused were either to let the deceased escape or to shoot at him with a service rifle. A reasonable man would know that a bullet from a self-loading rifle if it hit a human being, at any rate at the range at which the accused fired, would be likely to kill him or injure him seriously. So in one scale of the balance the harm to which the deceased would be exposed if the accused aimed to hit him was predictable and grave and the risk of its occurrence high. In the other scale of the balance it would be open to the jury to take the view that it would not be unreasonable to assess the level of harm to be averted by preventing the accused's escape as even graver—the killing or wounding of members of the patrol by terrorists in ambush and the effect of this success by members of the Provisional I.R.A. in encouraging the continuance of the armed insurrection and all the misery and destruction of life and property that terrorist activity in Northern Ireland has entailed. The jury would have to consider too what was the highest degree at which a reasonable man could have assessed the likelihood that such consequences might follow the escape of the deceased if the facts had been as the accused knew or believed them reasonably to be."[85]

Decision of the Court of Criminal Appeal of Northern Ireland varied

---

[84] Donald L. Creach, "Partially Determined Imperfect Self-Defense: The Battered Wife Kills and Tells Why" (1982) Stan.L.R. 616, 632.

[85] But see, *post*, pp. 298–300 for a discussion of *Shannon* (1980) 71 Cr.App.R. 192.

Palmer v. The Queen [1971] A.C. 814 (Privy Council)

The appellant, who carried a gun, went with other men to buy ganga. During a dispute they left with the ganga without paying; during the following chase one of the pursuers was shot by the appellant, who was charged and convicted of murder, although he had claimed self-defence.

Lord Morris:
"In their Lordships' view the defence of self-defence is one which can be and will be readily understood by any jury. It is a straightforward conception. It involves no obstruse legal thought . . . only common sense is needed for its understanding. It is both good law and good sense that a man who is attacked may defend himself. It is both good law and good sense that he may do, but may only do what is reasonably necessary. But everything will depend upon the particular facts and circumstances. Of these a jury can decide. It may in some cases be only sensible and clearly possible to take some simple avoiding action. Some attacks may be serious and dangerous. Others may not be. If there is some relatively minor attack it would not be common sense to permit some action of retaliation which was wholly out of proportion to the necessities of the situation. If an attack is serious so that it puts someone in immediate peril then immediate defensive action may be necessary. . . . If the attack is all over and no sort of peril remains then the employment of force may be by way of revenge or punishment or by way of paying off an old score or may be pure aggression. There may no longer be any link with a necessity of defence. Of all these matters the good sense of the jury will be the arbiter . . . If there has been an attack so that defence is reasonably necessary, it will be recognised that a person defending himself cannot weigh to a nicety the exact measure of his necessary defensive action. If a jury thought that in a moment of unexpected anguish a person attacked had only done what he honestly and instinctively thought was necessary that would be most potent evidence that only reasonable defensive action had been taken. A jury will be told that the defence of self-defence, where the evidence makes the raising possible, will only fail if the prosecution show beyond doubt that what the accused did was not by way of self-defence."

R. v. Shannon (1980) 71 Cr.App.R. 192 (Court of Appeal, Criminal Division)

The defendant was charged with murder by stabbing with a pair of scissors while being attacked. The case alleged against him was that he stabbed in revenge, punishment or pure aggression. He first claimed that he lacked an intention to inflict grievous bodily harm and, secondly, that he acted in self-defence. On the issue of self-defence the instruction to the jury was simply "Did the defendant use more force than was necessary in the circumstances?" He was convicted of *manslaughter* and appealed.

Ormrod L.J.:
"The learned judge, in the course of his summing up, used verbatim several extracts from Lord Morris's statement of the law in *Palmer* v. *R.* [ante], but throughout the summing up, and at the end he left the jury with the bald question, 'Are you satisfied that the appellant used more force than was necessary in the circumstances?' without Lord Morris's qualification that if they came to the conclusion that the appellant honestly thought, without having to weigh things to a nicety, that what he did was necessary to defend himself, they should regard that as 'most potent evidence' that it was actually reasonably necessary.

In other words, if the jury came to the conclusion that the stabbing was the act of a desperate man in extreme difficulties, with his assailant dragging him down by the hair, they should consider very carefully before concluding that the stabbing was an offensive and not a defensive act, albeit it went beyond what an onlooker would regard as reasonably necessary. . . .

In the judgment of this Court the evidence of the appellant, if accepted by the jury, raised the questions (a) whether the stabbing was in fact the act of a desperate man trying to defend himself and to force his assailant to let go of his hair and (b) whether, although not reasonably necessary by an objective standard, nonetheless, to use Lord Morris's words, the appellant honestly and instinctively thought that it was; in which case his honest belief would be 'most potent evidence' that he had only taken defensive action; in other words, in the circumstances the stabbing was essentially defensive in character. The case for the prosecution, on the other hand, if accepted by the jury, was a perfect illustration of a man going over to the offensive and stabbing by way of revenge, punishment, retaliation or pure aggression.

The learned judge touched on this aspect of the matter when he was directing the jury on the issue of intent in relation to the charge of murder. At the end of the summing up he said this: 'If you think that he lashed out because he lost his temper, having been treated in this painful, humiliating, frightening way, then you may think—it is a matter for you—that because he lost his temper in those circumstances he gave little or no thought to what might be the consequences of his lashing out and in the circumstances he did not form the intent suggested. This is the matter which you must consider, clearly. The more a man loses his temper, the less likely he may be to consider what are likely to be the consequences of his acts even though when he is in a balanced state of mind he realises that if you lash out with scissors and it lands and you do it with force then it is going to do a lot of personal injury.'

But on the issue of self-defence he, effectively, excluded the state of the accused's mind. In other words, by leaving that issue to the jury on the bald basis of 'Did the appellant use more force than was necessary in the circumstances?' the learned judge may have precluded the jury from considering the real issue, which to paraphrase Lord Morris in *Palmer* was 'Was this stabbing within the conception of necessary self-defence judged by the standards of common sense, bearing in mind the position of the appellant at the moment of the stabbing, or was it a case of angry retaliation or pure aggression on his part.'[86]

It is, we think, significant that in relation to intent, that is applying the test of what was in the accused's mind, the jury concluded that it was not murder but only manslaughter on the basis of no intent to cause really serious bodily harm, but seems to have excluded the appellant's state of mind in considering self-defence.

In those circumstances the Court came to the conclusion, not without considerable hesitation and anxiety, that the verdict of manslaughter was unsafe and unsatisfactory and ought to be quashed."

Appeal allowed

Palmer and *Shannon* were cited with approval in *Whyte* with Lane C.J. adding:

"In most cases, where the issue is one of self-defence, it is necessary and desirable that the jury should be reminded that the defendant's state of mind, that is his view of the danger threatening him at the

---

[86] Our emphasis.

time of the incident, is material. The test of reasonableness is not, to put it at its lowest, a purely objective test."[87]

Glanville Williams has written that *Shannon* represents "a radical change in the law"[88] in that any requirement of proportionality of response is thrown out by the approved dictum, at least where the defender fears death or serious injury. Self-defence in such cases is either necessary or pure aggression; anything that was previously considered "unnecessary but putative self-defence"[89] is now subsumed in the first category. Some support for this view comes from *Attorney-General's Reference (No. 2 of 1983)* that a defender may adopt those means "which *he believed* were no more than reasonably necessary to meet the force used by the attackers."[90]

It now seems clear that these decisions are not jettisoning the requirement of reasonableness—but rather reinterpreting it so that the defendant's *belief* that his actions are necessary becomes "the most potent evidence" that the defensive action was reasonable in the circumstances.

However, the effect of this amelioration of the rule is that a person can be held *justified* in using excessive defensive force provided he acted in a moment of "unexpected anguish" and "honestly thought" that what he was doing was necessary—even though objectively the response was unreasonable. This is surely going too far. Even the Draft Criminal Code Bill 1989 which so largely endorses a subjectivist philosophy requires that after the circumstances have been adjudged according to the defendant's assessment of them, the defender only use "such force as . . . is immediately necessary and reasonable."[91] The initial aggressor, in initiating the attack, is culpable and deserves to forfeit some of his rights (to the extent of the defender's reasonable retaliation)—but surely he does not sacrifice every right. Allowing unreasonable retaliatory force to constitute a justification is in effect to endorse it; it is to approve whatever degree of force the defender thinks is necessary.

It is submitted that the real basis of the law's response here to excessive self-defence, is that the person acting in self-defence in a moment of crisis, who honestly believes his degree of retaliatory force is necessary, is less blameworthy in that he has an excuse for acting as he does. He has still done wrong, (*i.e.* the actions were not justified) but we can excuse him (wholly or partially) from blame.

The Australian courts used to adopt an approach that a person who killed using excessive force was not guilty of murder, but only of manslaughter.[92] He was partially excused: "the moral culpability of a person

---

[87] [1987] 3 All E.R. 416.
[88] Glanville Williams, *Textbook*, p. 507.
[89] *Ibid.*, p. 507.
[90] [1984] 2 W.L.R. 465 at 478.
[91] Clause 44(1), (Law Com. No. 177, 1989).
[92] *McKay* [1957] V.R. 560; *Howe* [1958] 100 C.L.R. 448. Such an approach has recently been proposed in this country. (Report of the Select Committee on Murder and Life Imprisonment, H.L. Paper 78–1, 1989, para. 89).

who kills another in defending himself but who fails in a plea of self-defence only because the force which he believed to be necessary exceeded that which was reasonably necessary falls short of the moral culpability ordinarily associated with murder."[93] This approach recognises excessive self-defence as a partial excuse—a view which would be more acceptable than the present English approach of trying to squeeze what is really an excuse into the straight-jacket of justification. It is accordingly a matter of extreme regret that the High Court of Australia in *Zecevic*[94] has now turned its back on this approach and for largely pragmatic reasons (the complexity and difficulty of applying the partial defence) has now brought its law in line with *Palmer*.

(iii) *The duty to retreat*

It can be argued that if it is possible to escape from the attack by retreating then it is unnecessary and unreasonable to use defensive force.

Joseph H. Beale, "Retreat from a Murderous Assault" (1903) 16 Harv.L.Rev. 567, at pp. 580–582:

"The conclusion of the courts which deny the duty to retreat is, as we have seen, more commonly rested upon two arguments: that no one can be compelled by a wrongdoer to yield his rights, and that no one should be forced by a wrongdoer to the ignominy, dishonor, and disgrace of a cowardly retreat.

As to the argument of right, the . . . law does not ordinarily secure the enjoyment of rights; it grants redress for a violation of rights. . . .

The argument based upon the honor of the assailed is more elusive and more difficult to answer. . . . The feeling at the bottom of the argument is one beyond all law; it is the feeling which is responsible for the duel, for war, for lynching; the feeling which leads a jury to acquit the slayer of his wife's paramour; the feeling which would compel a true man to kill the ravisher of his daughter. We have outlived dueling, and we deprecate war and lynching; but it is only because the advance of civilization and culture has led us to control our feelings by our will. And yet in all these cases sober reflection would lead us to realize that the remedy is really worse than the disease. So it is in the case of killing to avoid a stain on one's honor. A really honorable man, a man of truly refined and elevated feeling, would perhaps always regret the apparent cowardice of a retreat, but he would regret ten times more, after the excitement of the contest was past, the thought that he had the blood of a fellow-being on his hands. It is undoubtedly distasteful to retreat; but it is ten times more distasteful to kill. . . . "

Glanville Williams, Textbook of Criminal Law (1st ed., 1978), p. 461:

"[I]t seems unreasonable to require a token retreat by one who has not been involved in any kind of aggression. There is no point in requiring a token yielding away from one who is wholly to blame. The only value of a token yielding is to show a disinclination to fight on the part of a person who has previously shown that inclination."

---

[93] *Viro* (1976–1978) 141 C.L.R. 88 at 139, *per* Mason J.
[94] (1987) 71 A.L.R. 641. See David Lanham, "Death of a Qualified Defence?" (1988) 104 L.Q.R. 239.

English law used to adopted a strict approach that a "retreat to the wall" was required before extreme force could be justified.[95] Since then, however, there has been considerable amelioration of the rule. In *Julien* the law was stated thus:

"It is not, as we understand it, the law that a person threatened must take to his heels and run in the dramatic way suggested . . . but what is necessary is that he should demonstrate by his actions that he does not want to fight. He must demonstrate that he is prepared to temporise and disengage and perhaps to make some physical withdrawal; and to the extent that that is necessary as a feature of the justification of self-defence, it is true, in our opinion, whether the charge is a homicide charge or something less serious."[96]

In *McInnes*[97] this was accepted as an accurate statement of the law but Edmund-Davies L.J. added that a failure to retreat is only one of the factors to be taken into account in determining the reasonableness of the defendant's conduct. This approach has now been confirmed.

R v. Bird [1985] 1 W.L.R. 816 (Court of Appeal, Criminal Division)

Lord Lane C.J.:
"The matter is dealt with accurately and helpfully in Smith and Hogan, *Criminal Law* (5th ed., 1983) at p. 327 as follows: 'There were formerly technical rules about the duty to retreat before using force, or at least fatal force. This is now simply a factor to be taken into account in deciding whether it was necessary to use force, and whether the force was reasonable. If the only reasonable course is to retreat, then it would appear that to stand and fight must be to use unreasonable force. There is however, no rule of law that a person attacked is bound to run away if he can; but it has been said that— . . . "what is necessary is that he should demonstrate by his actions that he does not want to fight. He must demonstrate that he is prepared to temporise and disengage and perhaps to make some physical withdrawal." It is submitted that it goes too far to say that action of this kind is *necessary*. It is scarcely consistent with the rule that it is permissible to use force, not merely to counter an actual attack, but to ward off an attack honestly and reasonably believed to be imminent. A demonstration by D [defendant] at the time that he did not want to fight is, no doubt, the best evidence that he was acting reasonably and in good faith in self-defence; but it is no more than that. A person may in some circumstances so act without temporising, disengaging or withdrawing; and he should have a good defence.'
We respectfully agree with that passage. If the defendant is proved to have been attacking or retaliating or revenging himself, then he was not truly acting in self-defence. Evidence that the defendant tried to retreat or tried to call off the fight may be a cast-iron method of casting doubt on the suggestion that he was the attacker or retaliator or the person trying to revenge himself. But it is not by any means the only method of doing that."

[95] Subject to certain exceptions: a man was not under a duty to retreat if he were in his own home or if it would leave his family or friends in danger.
[96] (1969) 53 Cr.App.R. 407 at 411.
[97] (1971) 55 Cr.App.R. 551.

This approach has been adopted by the Draft Criminal Code Bill 1989, clause 44(7):

"The fact that a person had an opportunity to retreat before using force shall be taken into account, in conjunction with other relevant evidence, in determining whether the use of force was immediately necessary and reasonable."[98]

(iv) *The imminence of the threatened attack*

In Western films the two protagonists tend to stand at opposite ends of a dusty street, each with their fingers hovering near their holsters ready to draw and fire. In such films (apart from the occasional good one) the "baddie" will draw first; the "goodie" will then follow suit; he will inevitably be the quicker on the draw and the "baddie" will be killed. The film will then end with the "goodie," surrounded by what might today be called "cowboy groupies," looking brave and honourable. The "baddie" drew first. The "goodie" was thus fully justified in acting in self-defence. However, had the "goodie" been the one to draw first, all would have changed. A plea of anticipatory self-defence would be meaningless in a Hollywood Western. By reaching for his gun first he would have become the aggressor.

Life however is not lived on a Hollywood film-set and the criminal law has to reflect life as it is and mirror everyday values. Restricting rights of self-defence to pure defensive retaliation could effectively condemn some innocent persons to death or other injury. In certain limited circumstances the law must permit the right to strike first. As Lord Griffiths said in *Beckford*:

"A man about to be attacked does not have to wait for his assailant to strike the first blow or fire the first shot; circumstances may justify a pre-emptive strike."[99]

The problem however is in defining the parameters of such a right. Allowing too much anticipatory defensive action could become a charter for vigilantism.

Devlin v. Armstrong [1971] N.I. 13 (Court of Appeal for Northern Ireland)

The defendant, during a riot in Londonderry, urged others to build barricades and throw petrol bombs at the police. She was convicted of riotous behaviour and incitement to riotous behaviour. She appealed on the basis that she thought her action necessary to prevent people being assaulted and property damaged by the police.

[98] Law Com. No. 177, 1989.
[99] [1988] 1 A.C. 130, 144.

MacDermott L.J.:

"The plea of self-defence may afford a defence where the party raising it uses force, not merely to counter an actual attack, but to ward off or prevent an attack which he has honestly and reasonably anticipated. In that case, however, the anticipated attack must be imminent: see *R.* v. *Chisam* (1963) 47 Cr.App.R. 130 . . . and the excerpt from Lord Normand's judgment in *Owens* v. *H.M. Advocate* (1946) S C (J) 119 which is there quoted and which runs:

'In our opinion self-defence is made out when it is established to the satisfaction of the jury that the panel believed that he was in imminent danger and that he held that belief on reasonable grounds. Grounds for such belief may exist though they are founded on a genuine mistake of fact' . . .

However reasonable and convinced the appellant's apprehensions may have been, I find it impossible to hold that the danger she anticipated was sufficiently specific or imminent to justify the actions she took as measures of self-defence."

Appeal dismissed

Attorney-General's Reference (No. 2 of 1983) [1984] 2 W.L.R. 465 (Court of Appeal, Criminal Division)

During the rioting in Toxteth in 1981 the defendant's shop was damaged and looted. Fearing further attacks he made ten petrol bombs "to use purely as a last resort to keep them away from my shop." The expected attack never materialised. The defendant was charged with an offence under section 4 of the Explosive Substances Act 1883 which provides that: "Any person who makes or knowingly has in his possession or under his control any explosive substance, under such circumstances as to give rise to a reasonable suspicion that he is not making it or does not have it in his possession or under his control for a lawful object, shall, unless he can show that he made it or had it in his possession or under his control for a lawful object, be guilty of a felony."

At his trial the judge ruled that it was "open to a defendant to say 'my lawful object is self-defence.' " The defendant was acquitted and the Attorney–General referred the following question for consideration: "Whether the defence of self-defence is available to a defendant charged with [an] offence under section 4 of the Explosive Substances Act 1883."

Lane L.C.J.:

"[Counsel for the Attorney–General] contends that . . . [self-defence] does not exist as a justification for preliminary and premeditated acts anticipatory of an act of violence by the defendant . . .

[He] submits that to allow a man to justify in advance his own act of violence for which he has prepared runs wholly contrary to the principle and thinking behind legitimate self-defence and legitimate defence of property. Both are defences which the law allows to actual violence by a defendant, and both are based on the principle that a man may be justified *in extremis* in taking spontaneous steps to defend himself, others of his family and his property against actual or mistakenly perceived violent attack.

It was argued that if a plea of self-defence is allowed to section 4 of the Act of 1883, the effect would be that a man could write his own immunity for unlawful acts done in preparation for violence to be used by him in the future. Rather than that, goes on the argument, in these circumstances a man should protect himself by calling on the police or by barricading his premises or by guarding them alone or with others, but not with petrol bombs. . . .

In *R* v. *Fegan* (1972) N.I.L.R. 80 . . . [it was held that]: 'Possession of a firearm for the purpose of protecting the possessor or his wife or family from acts of violence, *may* be possession for a lawful object. But the lawfulness of such a purpose cannot be founded on a mere fancy, or on some aggressive motive. The threatened danger must be reasonably and genuinely anticipated, must appear reasonably imminent, and must be of a nature which could not reasonably be met by more pacific means.' . . .

In our judgment, approaching *a priori* the words 'lawful object,' it might well seem open to a defendant to say, 'My lawful object is self-defence.' The defendant in this case said that his intentions were to use the petrol bombs purely to protect his premises should any rioters come to his shop. It was accordingly open to the jury to find that the defendant had made them for the reasonable protection of himself and his property against this danger. The fact that in manufacturing and storing the petrol bombs the defendant committed offences under the Act of 1875 did not necessarily involve that when he made them his object in doing so was not lawful. . . . The object or purpose or end for which the petrol bombs were made was not itself rendered unlawful by the fact that it could not be fulfilled except by unlawful means. . . .

In the Judge's summing up the threatened danger was assumed, as was the defendant's anticipation of it. Also assumed, no doubt upon the basis of the evidence led, was the imminence of the danger. What the learned Judge upon the facts of the case before him left to the jury was the reasonableness of the means adopted for the repulsion of raiders. . . .

In our judgment a defendant is not left in the paradoxical position of being able to justify acts carried out in self-defence but not acts immediately preparatory to it. There is no warrant for the submission on behalf of the Attorney–General that acts of self-defence will only avail a defendant when they have been done spontaneously. There is no question of a person in danger of attack 'writing his own immunity' for violent future acts of his. He is not confined for his remedy to calling in the police or boarding up his premises.

He may still arm himself for his own protection, if the exigency arises, although in so doing he may commit other offences. That he may be guilty of other offences will avoid the risk of anarchy contemplated by the Reference. It is also to be noted that although a person may 'make' a petrol bomb with a lawful object, nevertheless, if he remains in possession of it after the threat has passed which made his object lawful, it may cease to be so. It will only be very rarely that circumstances will exist where the manufacture or possession of petrol bombs can be for a lawful object.

For these reasons the point of law referred by Her Majesty's Attorney General for the consideration of this Court is answered by saying: The defence of lawful object is available to a defendant against whom a charge under section 4 of the Act of 1883 has been preferred, if he can satisfy the jury on balance of probabilities that his object was to protect himself or his family or his property against imminent apprehended attack and to do so by means which he believed were no more than reasonably necessary to meet the force used by the attackers."

Determination accordingly

In *Georgiades*[1] the defendant was charged with possession of a firearm with intent to endanger life contrary to section 16 of the Firearms Act 1968. Police visited his flat. He came on to the balcony with a loaded shotgun and raised it to waist level before being arrested. He believed

---

[1] [1989] 1 W.L.R. 759.

he was in danger of being attacked and had not realised his visitors were police officers. On appeal it was held that self-defence should have been put to the jury. Accordingly, his conviction was set aside and a conviction for possessing a shortened firearm without a licence contrary to sections 1 and 4 of the Firearms Act 1968 was substituted.

In *Butler*[2] the defendant was travelling on London underground carrying his Malacca sword-stick. (He used this as a walking stick as he had a "gammy leg.") A drunken youth assaulted and kicked him whereupon he defended himself stabbing the youth with his sword causing serious injuries. The defendant was not charged with any offence against the youth, presumably as it was felt that that was justifiable self-defence. He was however convicted of carrying an offensive weapon in a public place contrary to the Prevention of Crime Act 1953.

Malnik v. D.P.P. [1989] Crim.L.R. 451 (Queen's Bench Divisional Court)

The appellant, acting as an "advisor" to X went to "visit" one J who was thought to have taken two of X's valuable cars without authority. As J was known to have a tendency to violent and irresponsible behaviour the appellant (who was accompanied by three others) armed himself with a rice flail (two pieces of wood joined by a chain which the appellant was capable of using in connection with the martial arts). He was arrested approaching J's house. He was charged with having an offensive weapon in a public place without lawful authority or reasonable excuse contrary to section 1 of the Prevention of Crime Act 1953. The appellant argued that he had a reasonable excuse for having the flail with him, namely, that he had reasonable cause to believe that he was in imminent danger of being subjected to a violent attack. The appellant was convicted and appealed.

Held, "dismissing the appeal, the magistrate had correctly concluded that as a matter of law the defence of reasonable excuse was not available to the appellant. The case of *Evans* v. *Hughes* [defence to charge of carrying an offensive weapon if there was 'an imminent particular threat affecting the particular circumstances in which the weapon was carried' [1972] 3 All E.R. 412] and *R.* v. *Field* [one cannot drive people off the streets and compel them not to go to places where they might lawfully be because they might be subjected to an attack there—[1972] Crim.L.R. 435] were distinguishable. Ordinarily, individuals could not legitimately arm themselves with an offensive weapon in order to repel unlawful violence which such individual had knowingly and deliberately brought about by creating a situation in which violence was liable to be inflicted. It was quite different where those concerned with security and law enforcement were concerned. If private citizens set out on expeditions such as this, armed with offensive weapons, the risk of unlawful violence and serious injury was great, and obvious. The policy of the law must therefore be against such conduct, which conclusion was consistent with the very narrow limits which previous decisions had imposed on the freedom of the citizen to arm himself against attack. It had been rightly concluded that the risk of violence could have been avoided and thus the need to carry weapons, by inviting the appropriate agency to repossess the cars by the usual means."

[2] Appeal No. 5853/C1/87, June 10, 1988, discussed by J. C. Smith, *Justification and Excuse in the Criminal Law* (The Hamlyn Lectures, 40th series), 1989, pp. 117–119.

The Criminal Law Revision Committee have recommended that "it is desirable to make it clear that a man is not allowed to take the law into his own hands by striking before self-defence becomes necessary. We therefore recommend that the defence of self-defence should be confined to cases where the defendant feared an imminent attack."[3] The Draft Criminal Code Bill 1989 follows this by providing that a defender may do "an act immediately preparatory to the use of" self-defensive force. We have seen that, assuming defensive force is necessary and justified the *degree of that force* must be reasonably proportionate to the gravity of the attack. How is this rule of proportionate defensive action to be applied in cases of anticipatory defence? Suppose a jealous husband, armed with a gun, informs his wife that he is about to drive to the other side of town to kill her lover. The wife would presumably be entitled to use some force to disarm her husband at this stage. But she would surely not be entitled to use that degree of force that would be acceptable at the scene of the crime when the husband was about to pull the trigger. In other words, where the crime is less imminent, *less* defensive force is necessary at that stage to avert the situation.[4] Thus while the defendant in *Attorney-General's Reference (No. 2 of 1983)* was justified in *making and possessing* his petrol bombs, he would not have been justified in *using them* until his shop was actually under attack. But as Glanville Williams has pointed out: "there is a distinction between the immediacy of the necessity for acting and the immediacy of the threatened violence. The use of force may be immediately necessary to prevent an attack in the future."[5]

Following *Williams (Gladstone)* it is only necessary that the defendant *believe* that he is in imminent danger or that it is immediately necessary to take steps to avert a threatened attack; the belief need not be based on reasonable grounds. This again demonstrates the potential width of the present defence. A defendant who uses an excessive amount to anticipatory force when no force at all was actually necessary can escape all liability if he believed all those things to be necessary. The result of this can be seen in the case of *Finch and Jardine* discussed above,[6] where two police officers dragged an innocent man from a car and nearly beat him to death. They were acquitted of attempted murder and wounding with intent to cause grievous bodily harm because (1) they thought (mistakenly) that the victim was a dangerous wanted criminal; (2) they believed anticipatory force was necessary; if he were the dangerous criminal they would need to strike first in order to disarm him; and (3) acting in the heat of the moment as they were, they believed the amount

---

[3] 14th Report, para. 286.
[4] *Cousins* [1982] Q.B. 526. The conviction of the defendant under section 16, Offences Against the Person Act 1861 of *threatening* to kill was quashed on the basis that even in this situation the trial judge should have left the question of imminence to the jury as part of the question of reasonableness.
[5] *Textbook*, p. 503.
[6] *Ante*, n. 80.

of force they were using was reasonable—and this became "the most potent evidence" that it was a reasonable use of defensive force.

C. Discipline

Parents are entitled to take reasonable disciplinary measures against their children, including the use of moderate physical punishment. The parent will not, however be protected from criminal proceedings for assault or more serious offences, if the force used is excessive in nature, degree or duration.[7] School teachers used have similar powers of discipline whilst the child was in their care provided that they acted reasonably. In *Taylor*[8] it was held that reasonable chastisement involved "a controlled, if not entirely cool response"—this did not encompass throwing an exercise book at a pupil. Section 47 of the Education Act 1986, however, abolished corporal punishment in all maintained schools (including those independent schools which receive pupils on assisted places schemes etc). Since then schools have had to develop alternative strategies to deal with disruptive behaviour.[9]

As far as parents are concerned the defence of discipline undoubtedly still exists and has even received statutory recognition.[10] It is however, open to serious criticism. It has been argued that it unleashes a dangerous power, that much child abuse is simply discipline that has gone too far, and that it perpetuates the cycle of violence: children who have been abused tend in turn to become abusers.[11]

In view of these and other criticisms do you think that the European Convention on Human Rights with its prohibition of inhuman and degrading treatment[12] provides sufficient protection of the personal integrity of children? Should the defence of the discipline of children[13] be abolished?

D. Duress

1. Introduction

The defence of duress arises where a defendant is threatened with serious violence if he does not commit a crime. Thus in *Hudson and Taylor*[14] two girls committed perjury in an unlawful wounding case in which they were the principal prosecution witnesses. When charged

---

[7] *Hopley* (1860) 2 F. & F. 202; *Smith* [1985] Crim.L.R. 42.

[8] *The Times*, December 28, 1983.

[9] cf. *Discipline in Schools* (Report of the Committee of Enquiry chaired by Lord Elton), (1989) (D.E.S.).

[10] *E.g.* Children and Young Persons Act 1933, s.1.

[11] M. Crawford, "The Defense of Discipline: The Case for Abolition," (1982) 1 Med. Law 113. On child abuse generally, see H. Keating, "Child Abuse: The Law's Response" (1979) 9 Kingston Law Review 333; M.D.A. Freeman, *Violence in the Home* 1979; J. Eekelaar and S. Katz, *Family Violence* (1978).

[12] Article 3. See *Campbell and Cosans* v. *United Kingdom* [1982] 4 E.H.R.R. (Eur.Ct. H.R.) where it was held that corporal punishment can, depending on the circumstances, be regarded as a breach of the European Convention on Human Rights.

[13] The right to discipline exists in other contexts, for example, in the armed forces although corporal punishment may be prohibited.

[14] [1971] 2 Q.B. 202.

with perjury they claimed that they had been threatened that they would be "cut up" unless they committed perjury; they were so frightened that they had duly told lies in court. On appeal it was held that their defence of duress should have been put to the jury.

2. Should duress be a defence?

J. F. Stephen, History of the Criminal Law of England, Vol. 2 (1883), pp. 107–108:

"Criminal law is itself a system of compulsion on the widest scale. It is a collection of threats of injury to life, liberty and property if people do commit crimes. Are such threats to be withdrawn as soon as they are encountered by opposing threats? The law says to a man intending to commit murder, If you do it I will hang you. Is the law to withdraw its threat if someone else says, If you do not do it I will shoot you? Surely it is the moment when temptation to crime is strongest that the law should speak most clearly and emphatically to the contrary. It is, of course, a misfortune for a man that he should be placed between two fires, but it would be a much greater misfortune for society at large if criminals could confer impunity upon their agents by threatening them with death or violence if they refused to execute their commands. If impunity could be so secured a wide door would be opened to collusion, and encouragement would be given to associations of malefactors, secret or otherwise. No doubt the moral guilt of a person who commits a crime under compulsion is less than that of a person who commits it freely, but any effect which is thought proper may be given to this circumstance by a proportional mitigation of the offender's punishment. These reasons lead me to think that compulsion by threats ought in no case whatever to be admitted as an excuse for crime, though it may and ought to operate in mitigation of punishment in most though not in all cases."

The Law Commission (Law Com. No. 83), Report on Defences of General Application (1977) para. 2.14:

"Those who favour the conclusion that duress should not afford a defence which absolves criminal liability contend that it can never be justifiable for a person to do wrong, in particular to do serious harm to another merely to avoid some harm to himself; that it is not for the individual to balance the doing of wrong against the avoidance of harm to himself. They argue that duress does not destroy the will or negative intention in the legal sense, but that it merely deflects the will so that intention conflicts with the wish; in short that it provides a motive for the wrongful act and that motive is, on general principle, irrelevant to whether a crime has been committed."

Abbott v. The Queen [1977] A.C. 755 (Privy Council)

Lord Salmon (delivering the majority judgment of their Lordships):
"It seems incredible to their Lordships that in any civilised society, acts such as the appellant's, whatever threats may have been made to him, could be regarded as excusable or within the law. We are not living in a dream world in which the mounting wave of violence and terrorism can be contained by strict logic and intellectual niceties alone. Common sense surely reveals the added dangers to which in this modern world the public would be exposed, if the

change in the law proposed on behalf of the appellant were affected. It might well . . . prove to be a charter for terrorists, gang leaders and kidnappers . . . [If the accused were allowed to go free he would now have] gained some real experience and expertise, he might again be approached by the terrorist who would make the same threats . . . [the accused] would then give a repeat performance, killing even more men, women and children. Is there any limit to the number of people you may kill to save your own life and that of your family?"

Those who oppose a defence of duress generally concede that it is a relevant matter to take into consideration in mitigation of sentence. The courts have wide discretionary powers when sentencing and in extreme cases of duress only a minimal sentence need be imposed.[15]

Thus the arguments against a general defence of duress fall broadly into two groups:

  (i) The law would lose some of its deterrent effect if duress were allowed as a defence;

  (ii) The defendant is morally blameworthy and accordingly deserves punishment (because of the duress his blameworthiness might be *less* and accordingly he can receive a mitigated sentence—but he is still, to some extent, morally blameworthy).

We shall now examine these arguments in turn:

(i) Deterrence[16]

Was Stephen correct in asserting that "it is the moment when temptation to crime is strongest that the law should speak most clearly and emphatically to the contrary"?[17] Are the law's threats likely to serve any useful purpose to a man placed in such a perilous situation?

Ian Dennis, "Duress, Murder and Criminal Responsibility," (1980) 96 L.Q.R. 208, 234, 236:

"The deterrent argument is clear. If we assume that the accused acted as a reasonable man in not resisting the threat, and that both he and the reasonable man would act in the same way again whatever the attitude of the law, then the imposition of punishment cannot act as either an individual or a general deterrent. It will amount only to the useless infliction of a penalty and, on a utilitarian hypothesis, will therefore be unjustifiable . . .

[A] man under pressure to kill or be killed may well reason correctly that he does, at least, gain time by ignoring the law's prohibition; the alternative of heeding the prohibition and resisting the threat simply leads more quickly to unpleasant consequences. Secondly, if duress is to be taken into account anyway when sentence is passed, then the law's sanction for ignoring its threat is uncertain and may well not be heavy . . . An appeal to the deterrent value of a law disallowing duress as a defence is thus an empty gesture; the deterrent is

---

[15] M. Wasik, "Duress and Criminal Responsibility" [1977] Crim.L.R. 453; I. Dennis, "Duress, Murder and Criminal Responsibility" (1980) 96 L.Q.R. 208, 235–237.

[16] The other utilitarian arguments hardly seem applicable here. A person who has committed a crime because of duress does not need rehabilitation. He is also not a danger to society needing incapacitation (unless, as Lord Salmon suggested in *Abbott*, he was to be continually subjected to threats to induce him to commit crimes; this is highly unlikely—a terrorist or gang leader would be extremely foolish to use the same "agent," to whom the police were now alerted, more than once).

[17] *Ante*, p. 309.

ineffective because it is not immediate and because it is subverted by admitting duress through the back door as evidence in mitigation."

On the other hand, "[w]e do not and we cannot know what choices may be different if the actor thinks he has a chance of exculpation on the ground of his peculiar disabilities than if he knows that he does not,"[18] and thus "[t]here is an argument for saying that we should nourish the hope, however faint, that the threat of punishment may be enough to tip the balance of decision by those who have only doubtfully sufficient fortitude to undergo martyrdom for the sake of a moral principle."[19]

And quite apart from general deterrence, there is the more realistic "educative" species of deterrence that "legal norms and sanctions operate not only at the moment of climactic choice but also in the fashioning of values and of character."[20] The denial of a defence of duress would strengthen values so that persons in situations of duress would be less likely to submit to the threats.

(ii) *Moral blameworthiness*

Is the actor who submits to duress morally blameworthy or morally responsible for his actions so that he deserves punishment for them?

We saw in Chapter 2 that moral responsibility has been traditionally confined to those who *choose* to break the law and thus choose to become subject to criminal liability.

H. L. A. Hart, Punishment and Responsibility (1968), pp. 22–23:

"The . . . view is that of society . . . *offering* individuals including the criminal the protection of the laws on terms which are fair . . . because . . . each individual is given a *fair* opportunity to choose between keeping the law required for society's protection or paying the penalty . . .

Criminal punishment . . . consists simply in announcing certain standards of behaviour and attaching penalties for deviation, making it less eligible, and then leaving individuals to choose. This is a method of social control which maximises individual freedom within the coercive framework of law in a number of different ways. . . . First, the individual has an option between obeying or paying. . . . Secondly, this system not only enables individuals to exercise this choice but increases the power of individuals to identify beforehand periods when the law's punishments will not interfere with them and to plan their lives accordingly."

The question in duress is whether the actor had this "fair opportunity" to choose between conforming to the law or breaking it. Where the circumstances have overwhelmed his capacity for choice, where his freedom of choice is too restricted, we do not account him blameworthy or responsible. This is what was meant by Lord Widgery C.J. in *Kray*[21]

[18] A.L.I., Model Penal Code, Comments (To Tent. Draft No. 10 (1960)).
[19] Glanville Williams, *Textbook*, p. 628.
[20] *Ante*, n. 18.
[21] [1970] 1 Q.B. 125.

when he spoke of the accused being "so terrified that he ceased to be an independent actor" and what he meant in *Hudson and Taylor*[22] when he required that the defendant's "will" must have been "overborne"; the threats had to "neutralise the will." This does not mean that the defendant had no *mens rea*.[23] Ms. Hudson and Ms. Taylor both told their lies deliberately and intentionally. As was emphasised in the House of Lords in the leading case of *Howe*:

> "[An] unacceptable view is that . . . duress as a defence affects only the existence or absence of mens rea. The true view is stated by Lord Kilbrandon (of the minority) in *Lynch* [1975] A.C. 653 . . . at p. 703:
>
>> 'the decision of the threatened man whose constancy is overborne so that he yields to the threat, is a calculated decision to do what he knows to be wrong, and is therefore that of a man with, perhaps to some exceptionally limited extent, a 'guilty mind.' But he is at the same time a man whose mind is less guilty than is his who acts as he does but under no such constraint.' "[24]

So the basis of the defence of duress is that the defendant did not have an effective opportunity to make a choice as to whether to commit the crime. Of course, in a physical sense the defendant has made a choice; he is not an involuntary actor in the same sense as a sleepwalker.[25] However, because the external pressure is so great, it has, in a moral sense, "forced" the actor to commit the crime, Fletcher describes such conduct as "morally involuntary."[26] Morally involuntary conduct is not blameworthy; the defendant does not deserve punishment.

In England this view has been largely[27] accepted—primarily on the ground that it would be unjust or unfair to punish in such circumstances.

D.P.P. v. Lynch [1975] A.C. 653 (House of Lords)

Lord Morris:
"[I]t is proper that any rational system of law should take fully into account the standards of honest and reasonable men. By those standards it is fair that actions and reactions may be tested. If then someone is really threatened with death or serious injury unless he does what he is told to do is the law to pay no heed to the miserable, agonising plight of such a person? For the law to understand not only how the timid but also the stalwart may in a moment of crisis behave is not to make the law weak but to make it just. In the calm of the courtroom measures of fortitude or of heroic behaviour are surely not to be demanded when they could not in moments for decision reasonably have been expected even of the resolute and the well disposed . . .

The law must, I think, take a common sense view. If someone is forced at gunpoint either to be inactive or to do something positive—must the law not remember that the instinct and perhaps the duty of self-preservation is power-

---

[22] *Ante*, n. 14.
[23] As was suggested by Lord Goddard C.J. in *Bourne* (1952) 36 Cr.App.R. 125.
[24] [1987] 1 A.C. 417; see also Lord Bridge's similar comments in *Howe* at p. 436.
[25] See *ante*, p. 106.
[26] Fletcher, p. 803.
[27] With the exception of murder. See *post*, p. 323.

ful and natural? I think it must. A man who is attacked is allowed within reason to take necessary steps to defend himself. The law would be censorious and inhumane which did not recognise the appalling plight of a person who perhaps suddenly finds his life in jeopardy unless he submits and obeys."

Duress is a "concession to human frailty."[28] It is thus best viewed as an excuse—and not as a justification. The defendant has done wrong; he has violated the interests of an innocent person, but because of his appalling predicament, he is excused from blame.[29]

3. Parameters of the defence

In what circumstances may a defendant break the law but escape liability because of duress? Or to put it another way, when will conduct be regarded as "morally involuntary"? When will the circumstances be such that we will not account the defendant blameworthy for his actions?

Hyman Gross, A Theory of Criminal Justice (1979), p. 276:

"Sometimes people are forced to do what they do. When what they are forced to do is wrong it seems that the compulsion ought to count in their favor. After all, we say, such a person wasn't free to do otherwise—he couldn't help himself, not really. No claim to avoid blame appeals more urgently to our moral intuitions, yet none presents more problems of detail. There are times, after all, when we ought to stand firm and run the risk of harm to ourselves instead of taking a way out that means harm for others. In such a situation we must expect to pay the price if we cause harm when we prefer ourselves, for then the harm is our fault even though we did not mean it and deeply regret it. But how shall the line be drawn to separate cases in which the constraint is sufficiently powerful to make blame inappropriate from cases in which constraint is simply a challenge to avoid harm to oneself as best one can while doing no harm to others? A line too far in either direction means injustice, for it is not right to allow with impunity harming that should have been avoided, nor is it right to punish for harm whose avoidance cannot reasonably be expected."

Essentially the attribution of blame involves a moral judgment relating, *inter alia*, to our expectations of how people should act in certain situations.[30] This inevitably involves a comparison between the defendant's response and how we imagine *we*, or other "ordinary people," would respond in that situation. If we perceive that ordinary people would have responded as the defendant did, then we do not blame the defendant for his actions. But if we perceive that ordinary people would have withstood the threats, then we legitimately blame the defendant for his failure to do so.

---

[28] *Howe, ibid.; Shepherd* (1988) 86 Cr.App.R. 47.

[29] Sanford H. Kadish, "Excusing Crime" (1987) 75 Cal.L.R. 257; *cf.* K. J. M. Smith, "Must Heroes Behave Heroically?" [1989] Crim.L.R. 622.

[30] For a fuller account of the notion of "blame," see *post*, pp. 795–798.

This test provides us with the key to answering the following questions concerning the parameters of the defence of duress.

(i) *What type of threat will be sufficient to afford a defence?*

In making our moral judgment as to whether to blame the defendant, one would surely wish to compare the crime committed with the nature of the threats to which the defendant was exposed. Suppose a defendant had been threatened that his house would be burnt to the ground if he did not steal a tin of beans from the local supermarket. We would surely not blame a defendant who committed such a crime. Suppose the defendant who had access to the water supply of London was threatened with death or serious bodily harm if he did not place a deadly poison in the water supply. If he poisons the water and 10,000 people die (as he knows they must), surely we would blame him for his actions because the harm he has caused is so much greater than the harm threatened. This "balancing of harms" approach ought not to operate in a rigid mechanistic manner, but it is a useful aid to our moral judgment as to whether to blame the defendant.[31] This is broadly the approach of the Model Penal Code which states that any "use of, or a threat to use, unlawful force against his person[32] or the person of another, which a person of reasonable firmness in his situation would have been unable to resist"[33] will afford a defence of duress. Lord Wilberforce flirted with this notion in *Lynch* when he said that "[n]obody would dispute that the greater the degree of heinousness of the crime, the greater and less resistable must be the degree of pressure, if pressure is to excuse."[34] In *Howe* Lord Hailsham said he "believe[d] that some degree of proportionality between the threat and the offence must, at least to some extent, be a prerequisite of the defence under the existing law."[35]

English law, however appears committed to the view that only threats of death or serious bodily harm will suffice for a defence of duress.[36] If the threats were less terrible they should be matters of mitigation only.[37] Thus a threat to reveal the defendant's homosexuality cannot suffice for duress—but if there was also a threat of death or grievous bodily harm the jury can take into account the cumulative effects of the various threats.[38] It is thus clear that under English law the only people to escape blame for their actions, *regardless of the crimes they commit*, are those who were exposed to the worst threats.

---

[31] Fletcher, p. 804.

[32] Threats to property are surprisingly not included. The commentary (to Tent. Draft No. 8 (1958)) points out that threats to property are covered by the necessity defence in s.3.02.

[33] A.L.I., Model Penal Code, Proposed Official Draft (1962), s.2.09(1).

[34] At p. 681.

[35] [1987] 1 A.C. 417 at pp. 432–433.

[36] *Hudson and Taylor* [1971] 2 Q.B. 202; *D.P.P.* v. *Lynch* [1975] A.C. 653; *Conway* [1988] 3 W.L.R. 1238; *Martin* [1989] 1 All E.R. 652.

[37] Law Com. No. 83, Criminal Law: Report on Defences of General Application, para. 2.18.

[38] *Valderrama-Vega* [1985] Crim.L.R. 220; see also *Ortiz* (1986) 83 Cr.App.R. 173.

The Law Commission, Working Paper No. 55, Defences of General Application (1974) paras. 16, 17:

"16 . . . We have considered whether a defence of duress could be framed in terms of the balancing of one harm against another, permitting it to be raised only when the harm to be inflicted upon the defendant is greater than the harm which he is obliged to do. For various reasons, however, we regard this as impracticable. In the first place, if the defence were so framed it would follow that where the defendant, to save his own life, imperilled the lives of more than one other person, the defence would be unavailable. . . .

Secondly, a test involving the concept of balance of harms cannot, it seems to us, operate satisfactorily where the offences involved are of an entirely different character. There is, for example, no sensible means of weighing a threat of severe injury to the person against an enforced disclosure of information contrary to the Official Secrets Act which might lead to a danger to national security. Our provisional conclusion is, therefore, that in defining the kind of threats which are the subject of duress, it must be borne in mind that the basic justification of the defence is that it is a concession to human infirmity in situations of extreme peril.

17. This conclusion leads us to take the provisional view that duress ought for the future to be available only in cases where the threat is a threat of death or of serious injury."[39]

(ii) *Is the threat subjective or objective in character?*

What is the position if the defendant thinks he has been threatened with death or serious injury but a reasonable man in his situation would not have interpreted the threat thus? Further, what is the position if the defendant is terrified by the threats and duly commits a crime, but the reasonable man would have "stood his ground" and not committed the crime?

The Law Commission (No. 83), Defences of General Application (1977), paras. 2.27, 2.28:

"2.27. The defence of duress is essentially a concession to human weakness in the face of an overwhelming threat of harm by another, and it is therefore right that so far as possible the criteria to be applied should be subjective. It should be sufficient, provided always that there is a threat of harm, that the defendant believes that the threat is of death or serious personal injury and believes that there is no way of avoiding or preventing the threatened harm other than by committing the offence. That a reasonable person would not have so believed may be relevant in testing the defendant's evidence as to his own belief but it should not of itself disentitle the defendant to the defence.

2.28. It may be said that the whole test as to whether the requirements of duress exist should be subjective, but we feel that this would create too wide a defence. Serious personal injury can cover a wide range of threatened harm, and if the defence is to be available even in respect of the most serious offences, it would be unsatisfactory in the final event to dispense with some objective

[39] These provisional views were confirmed in Law Com. No. 83, para. 2.25. In *Graham* [1982] 1 W.L.R. 294 the question whether fear of physical injury (rather than of death) could ever amount to duress was expressly left open. The Draft Criminal Code Bill 1989 requires that the threat be of "death or serious personal harm" (cl. 42(3)) (Law Com. No. 177, 1989).

assessment of whether the defendant could reasonably have been expected to resist the threat. The solution which is adopted by section 2.09(1) of the American Law Institute's Model Penal Code is to provide that the threat of unlawful force (which is left undefined) must be that 'which a person of reasonable firmness in his situation would have been unable to resist.' Whether the words 'in his situation' comprehend more than the surrounding circumstances, and extend to characteristics of the defendant himself, it is difficult to say, and for that reason we would not recommend without qualification the adoption of that solution. We think that there should be an objective element in the requirements of the defence so that in the final event it will be for the jury to determine whether the threat was one which the defendant in question could not reasonably have been expected to resist. This will allow the jury to take into account the nature of the offence committed, its relationship to the threats which the defendant believed to exist, the threats themselves and the circumstances in which they were made, and the personal characteristics of the defendant. The last consideration is, we feel, a most important one. Threats directed against a weak, immature or disabled person may well be much more compelling than the same threats directed against a normal healthy person."

R. v. Graham (1982) 74 Cr.App.R. 235 (Court of Appeal, Criminal Division)

The appellant, a practising homosexual, lived in a flat with his wife and another homosexual man, K, in a ménage à trois. The appellant was taking drugs for anxiety which made him more susceptible to bullying. K was a violent man and was jealous of his wife. One night after the appellant and K had been drinking heavily K put a flex round the wife's neck, pulled it tight and then told the appellant to take hold of the other end of the flex and pull on it. The appellant did so for about a minute. The wife was killed as a result of the pressure of the flex on her neck. The appellant was charged with murder, as was K, who pleaded guilty. The appellant pleaded not guilty and in evidence said that he had complied with K's demand to pull on the flex only because of his fear of K. The Crown conceded that it was open to the appellant to raise the defence of duress and did not seek to contend that the defence was not available to a principal to murder. In directing the jury on the defence, the judge posed two questions for the jury: (i) the subjective question of whether the appellant took part in the killing because he feared for his life or personal safety as a result of K's words or conduct, and (ii) if so, the objective question of whether, taking into account all the circumstances, including the appellant's age, sex, sexual propensities and other personal characteristics, and his state of mind and the drink and drugs he had taken, it was reasonable for the appellant, because of fear of K, to take part in killing his wife. The judge further stated that the test of reasonableness in that context was whether, having regard to those circumstances, the appellant's behaviour reflected the degree of self-control and firmness of purpose to be expected from a person in today's society. The appellant was convicted of murder. He appealed on the ground that the judge had misdirected the jury in posing the second, objective question, because the availability of the defence of duress depended solely on the subjective test of whether the appellant's will was overborne by threats by another. The Crown submitted that the judge had been right to impose the second, objective test in addition to the subjective test, but that he had formulated it too favourably to the appellant.

Lord Lane C.J.:
"[T]he direction appropriate . . . [to the first question] should have been in these words: 'Was this man at the time of the killing taking part because he held

a well-grounded fear of death [or serious physical injury] as a result of the words or conduct on the part of King?' The bracketed words may be too favourable to the defendant. The point was not argued before us.

. . . [Counsel for the appellant] contends that no second question arises at all; the test is purely subjective. He argues that if the appellant's will was in fact overborne by threats of the requisite cogency, he is entitled to be acquitted and no question arises as to whether a reasonable man, with or without his characteristics, would have reacted similarly . . .

[Counsel for the Crown], on the other hand, submits that such dicta as can be found on the point are in favour of a second test; this time an objective test. . . .

As a matter of public policy, it seems to us essential to limit the defence of duress by means of an objective criterion formulated in terms of reasonableness. Consistency of approach in defences to criminal liability is obviously desirable. Provocation and duress are analogous. In provocation the words or actions of one person break the self-control of another. In duress the words or actions of one person break the will of another. The law requires a defendant to have the self-control reasonably to be expected of the ordinary citizen in his situation. It should likewise require him to have the steadfastness reasonably to be expected of the ordinary citizen in his situation. So too with self-defence, in which the law permits the use of no more force than is reasonable in the circumstances. And, in general, if a mistake is to excuse what would otherwise be criminal, the mistake must be a reasonable one.

It follows that we accept [counsel for the Crown's] submission that the direction in this case was too favourable to the appellant. The Crown having conceded that the issue of duress was open to the appellant and was raised on the evidence, the correct approach on the facts of this case would have been as follows: (1) Was the defendant, or may he have been, impelled to act as he did because, as a result of what he reasonably believed King had said or done, he had good cause to fear that if he did not so act King would kill him or (if this is to be added) cause him serious physical injury? (2) If so, have the prosecution made the jury sure that a sober person of reasonable firmness, sharing the characteristics of the defendant, would not have responded to whatever he reasonably believed King said or did by taking part in the killing? The fact that a defendant's will to resist has been eroded by the voluntary consumption of drink or drugs or both is not relevant to this test.

We doubt whether the Crown were right to concede that the question of duress ever arose on the facts of this case. The words and deeds of King relied on by the defence were far short of those needed to raise a threat of the requisite gravity. However, the Crown having made the concession, the judge was right to pose the second objective question to the jury. His only error lay in putting it too favourably to the appellant."

Appeal dismissed

If, as Lord Lane C.J. asserts, "consistency of approach in defences to criminal liability is obviously desirable," why did he choose to adopt a different approach in the self-defence case of *Williams (Gladstone)*?[40] In that case he ruled that the defendant must be judged according to the facts as he believed them to be, yet in relation to the "first question" in *Graham* he held that this would only be so if the defendant's belief was

---

[40] (1984) 78 Cr.App.R. 276; see also Peter Alldridge, "Developing the Defence of Duress" [1986] Crim.L.R. 433.

reasonably held. (The "second question" is unaffected by the decision of *Williams* (*Gladstone*)). It was suggested earlier that a possible explanation for this divergence of approach is that mistakes as to justifications (such as self-defence) only have to be honest, while mistakes as to excuses (such as duress) have to be reasonable as well.[41]

Graham has now received the unanimous endorsement of the House of Lords in *Howe*.[42] Their Lordships added the important qualification that what was required was that the threats be such that a person of reasonable firmness *sharing the characteristics of the defendant* would have given way to the threats.[43] Following the analogous provocation cases where a similar test is used[44] this means that one can take into account "characteristics" such as age and sex, but not qualities affecting temperament. In particular, this means that the defendant's personal level of courage or fortitude is something that may not be taken into account.[45] The fact that someone is physically frail and old is relevant in assessing their reaction, but the fact that someone is nervous and cowardly must be discounted.

This approach can be supported. If an ordinary person (sharing the same characteristics as the appellant such as age, sex, intelligence) would have thought he was being threatened with death or serious injury and would have complied with K's orders, then we cannot blame the appellant for doing so. But if an ordinary person (sharing the appellant's characteristics) would not have had such a belief or would not have responded in such a manner, then we can rightly blame the appellant for failing to match the standards we expect of people. (Because of the duress which explains his behaviour, we would however blame him *less* and would wish to mitigate his sentence.) It is right that the appellant's characteristics such as age, sex, intelligence, etc., be taken into account, as he cannot be blamed for any of these. It is equally right that his consumption of drink and drugs (which might have made him more susceptible to the threats) be disregarded as we *can* blame him for allowing himself to get into such a state.[46]

The Draft Criminal Code Bill 1989 answers the first question subjectively (in line with *Williams* (*Gladstone*)) and the second objectively (in line with *Graham* and *Howe*). A person acts under duress if "he knows or believes" that a threat of the requisite gravity has been made (clause 42(3)(a)). Secondly, the threat must be "one which in all the circumstances (including any of his personal circumstances that affect its gravity) he cannot reasonably be expected to resist" (clause 42(3)(b)).[47]

---

[41] *Ante*, p. 265.
[42] [1987] 1 A.C. 417.
[43] Lord Hailsham at p. 426; Lord Mackay at p. 459; the certified question which was answered in the affirmative by the House of Lords was framed in this same manner (p. 423).
[44] *Post*, p. 643.
[45] K. J. M. Smith, "Must Heroes Behave Heroically?" [1989] Crim.L.R. 622, 626.
[46] See *post*, pp. 390–394.
[47] Law Com. No. 177, 1989.

(iii) *How imminent must the threat be?*

It is generally stated that the defence of duress is only available if there is a threat of *immediate* harm. Thus in *Gill*[48] the defendant was threatened with personal violence if he did not steal his employer's lorry. It was held *obiter* that he probably could not have pleaded duress because there had been a period of time during which he could have raised the alarm and wrecked the whole enterprise. As Lord Morris said in *Lynch*:

"[The question is whether] a person the subject of duress could reasonably have extricated himself or could have sought protection or had what has been called a 'safe avenue of escape.' "[49]

Again this can be supported. We would blame someone who had a reasonable opportunity to raise the alarm and wreck the criminal enterprise,[50] but we could not blame someone who had no such opportunity. What is the position if the defendant has an opportunity to seek help but fears that police protection will be ineffective?

R. v. Hudson and Taylor [1971] 2 Q.B. 202 (Court of Appeal, Criminal Division)

(The facts are set out, *ante*, p. 308)

Widgery L.J.:
"In the present case the threats . . . were likely to be no less compelling, because their execution could not be effected in the court room, if they could be carried out in the streets of Salford the same night . . .

[Counsel for the Crown] . . . submits on grounds of public policy that an accused should not be able to plead duress if he had the opportunity to ask for protection from the police before committing the offence and failed to do so. The argument does not distinguish cases in which the police would be able to provide effective protection, from those when they would not, and it would, in effect, restrict the defence of duress to cases where the person threatened had been kept in custody by the maker of the threats, or where the time interval between the making of the threats and the commission of the offence had made recourse to the police impossible . . .

In the opinion of this court it is always open to the Crown to prove that the accused failed to avail himself of some opportunity which was reasonably open to him to render the threat ineffective, and that upon this being established the threat in question can no longer be relied on by the defence. In deciding whether such an opportunity was reasonably open to the accused the jury should have regard to his age and circumstances, and to any risks to him which may be involved in the course of action relied upon."

The Law Commission, Working Paper No. 55, Defences of General Application (1974) para. 20:

"20 . . . We recognise that effective protection may not be continuously available; yet it seems to us that a defendant subject to this kind of threat must

---

[48] (1963) 47 Cr.App.R. 166.
[49] [1975] A.C. 653 at 668.
[50] A. J. Ashworth, "Reason, Logic and Criminal Liability" (1975) 91 L.Q.R. 102 at 104.

always be under a duty at least to seek that protection in order to reduce the possibility of its execution and failure to do so through fear of the consequences ought properly to be a factor in mitigation rather than a complete defence."[51]

In *Hudson and Taylor* the threats could have been reported to the police, but the two young girls, aged 17 and 19 were convinced that the police protection would be ineffective. Are we to blame them for their failure to seek official protection? It would appear that their response was typical of the response of most ordinary girls of that age faced with such a predicament. It would surely be ludicrous to assert that the defence of duress would only be available to them if there had been a sniper sitting in court ready to execute his threats immediately. These views were echoed by Lord Griffiths in *Howe*:

"if duress is introduced as a merciful concession to human frailty it seems hard to deny it to a man who knows full well that any official protection he may seek will not be effective to save him from the threat of death under which he has acted."[52]

The Draft Criminal Code 1989 has, however, not responded to these calls and provides that duress will only be available if the defendant believes "that the threat will be carried out immediately if he does not do the act or, if not immediately, before he or that other can obtain official protection" (clause 42(3)(a)(ii)). It further provides: "It is immaterial that the person doing the act believes, or that it is the case, that any official protection available in the circumstances will or may be ineffective" (clause 42(4)).[53]

(iv) *Against whom must the threat be directed?*

The Law Commission, Working Paper No. 55, Defences of General Application (1974) para. 18:

"[W]e consider that no limitation should be placed upon the persons against whom the threat may be made. Obviously, a threat of imminent death, for example, to the defendant's wife or children ought to suffice for the defence[54]; but it is not, in our view, possible to maintain with confidence that it should not apply also in the case of threats to a friend of the defendant nor, indeed, to someone he does not know. No rational dividing line is discernible in this context."

Recent "duress of circumstances" cases have indicated that the threat can be to the defendant or "some other person,"[55] and the Draft Crimi-

---

[51] See also Law Com. No. 83, paras. 2.29–2.31.
[52] At p. 443.
[53] Law Com. No. 177, 1989.
[54] In "*K*" ((1984) 148 J.P. 410) the defendant's conviction for contempt of court was quashed on grounds of duress. Although the defendant did fear personal violence to himself, the court also regarded it as important that his mother's address had been obtained by the threatener who "was in a position to wreak vengeance on her if K gave evidence."
[55] *Conway* [1988] 3 All E.R. 1025; *Martin* [1989] 1 All E.R. 652.

nal Code Bill 1989 provides that the threat must be to the defendant "or another."[56]

Where the threat is directed against the defendant, his family or others to whom a responsibility is owed, one can legitimately describe the defendant's conduct as being "morally involuntary" and excusable.[57] But where strangers are involved, it is questionable whether a defendant should be permitted to, say, cause grievous bodily harm to one stranger in order to save another stranger from grievous bodily harm (especially as there must always be a chance, however small, that the threat will not be carried out). This is in effect allowing the defendant to choose between the two strangers. How is he to assess their relative "worth"? Of course, in many cases the harm to be inflicted by the defendant will be much less than that threatened against the stranger and in such situations it ought certainly to be an excuse that the defendant committed his crime to save the third party from at least serious injury.

(v) *Is the defence available where the defendant has placed himself in a position where he might be open to threats?*

A defendant who joins a criminal association (whether terrorist, gangster or otherwise) which could force him to commit crimes can be blamed for his actions. In joining such an organisation fault can be laid at his door and his subsequent actions described as blameworthy. This is the approach adopted by English law which denies the defence of duress to such a person.

R. v. Sharp [1987] 1 Q.B. 853 (Court of Appeal, Criminal Division)

The appellant joined a gang of robbers, knowing they used firearms. He participated in a robbery upon a sub-post office but claimed he had been forced to as one of the other robbers had threatened to kill him if he did not carry through the plan. He was convicted of manslaughter and appealed.

Lord Lane C.J.:
"No one could question that if a person can avoid the effects of duress by escaping from the threats, without damage to himself, he must do so. In other words if there is a moment at which he is able to escape, so to speak, from the gun being held at his head by Hussey, or the equivalent of Hussey, he must do so. It seems to us to be part of the same argument, or at least to be so close to the same argument as to be practically indistinguishable from it, to say that a man must not voluntarily put himself in a position where he is likely to be subjected to such compulsion . . .

[In] our judgment, where a person has voluntarily, and with knowledge of its nature, joined a criminal organisation or gang which he knew might bring

---

[56] Clause 42(3)(a)(i) (Law Com. No. 177, 1989).
[57] In *Ortiz* (1986) 83 Cr.App.R. 173 it was assumed that threats to the defendant's wife and child would suffice for duress.

pressure on him to commit an offence and was an active member when he was put under such pressure, he cannot avail himself of the defence of duress."

Appeal dismissed

R. v. Shepherd (1988) 86 Cr.App.R. 47 (Court of Appeal, Criminal Division)

The appellant joined a group of thieves. They would enter retail premises and while one of them distracted the shopkeeper, others would carry away boxes of goods, usually cigarettes. The appellant claimed that after the first burglary he wanted to give up, but had been threatened with violence to himself and his family if he did not carry on with the thefts. He was convicted of five offences of burglary and appealed against conviction.

Mustill L.J.:

"It was (and still is) accepted on behalf of the appellant that this defence is not available when the defendant has, to put the matter neutrally, voluntarily brought himself into the situation from which the duress has arisen. The problem concerns the breadth of this exception . . .

At the conclusion of the argument we had arrived at the following opinion:

(1) Although it is not easy to rationalise the existence of duress as a defence rather than a ground of mitigation, it must in some way be founded on a concession to human frailty in cases where the defendant has been faced with a choice between two evils.

(2) The exception which exists where the defendant has voluntarily allied himself with the person who exercises the duress must be founded on the assumption that, just as he cannot complain if he had the opportunity to escape the duress and failed to take it, equally no concession to frailty is required if the risk of duress is freely undertaken.

(3) Thus, in some instances it will follow inevitably that the defendant has no excuse: for example, if he has joined a group of people dedicated to violence as a political end, or one which is overtly ready to use violence for other criminal ends. Members of so called paramilitary illegal groups, or gangs of armed robbers, must be taken to anticipate what may happen to them if their nerve fails, and cannot be heard to complain if violence is indeed threatened.

(4) Other cases will be difficult. There is no need for recourse to extravagant examples. Common sense must recognise that there are certain kinds of criminal enterprises the joining of which, in the absence of any knowledge of propensity to violence on the part of one member, would not lead another to suspect that a decision to think better of the whole affair might lead him into serious trouble. The logic which appears to underlie the law of duress would suggest that if trouble did unexpectedly materialise, and if it put the defendant into a dilemma in which a reasonable man might have chosen to act as he did, the concession to human frailty should not be denied to him. . . .

The members of the jury have had to ask themselves whether the appellant could be said to have taken the risk of P's violence simply by joining a shoplifting gang of which he was a member. . . .

That was the position at the conclusion of the argument. Since then we have been able to study a transript of the ruling of the trial judge in *Sharp* (Kenneth Jones J.), a ruling which was approved on appeal:

'It is not merely a matter of joining in a criminal enterprise; it is a matter of joining in a criminal enterprise of such a nature that the defendant appreciated the nature of the enterprise itself and the attitudes of those in charge of it, so that when he was in fact subjected to compulsion he could fairly be said by a jury to have voluntarily exposed himself and submitted himself to such compulsion.'

This ruling, if we may say so, corresponds exactly with the view which we had independently formed."

Appeal allowed

It appears from these cases that the defendant must know of the risks when joining the violent organisation. But what of the person who *ought* to know he was likely to be exposed to threats? If the basis of this exemption is that the defendant is blameworthy in joining such an organisation, then if there was an obvious risk of violence to which he gave no thought, there is clearly a strong case for denying the defence of duress.

(vi) *Is duress a defence to all crimes?*

If the defendant's conduct can be described as being "morally involuntary," and if we are satisfied that we do not blame the defendant for his actions, because ordinary people would have responded in the same way, it clearly follows that he ought to have a defence to any crime. However, English law adopts the view that duress is a defence to all crimes *except* murder, and possibly attempted murder[58] and treason.[59] In *Lynch* the House of Lords decided that duress was a defence to an accessory to murder but in *Abbott* the Privy Council ruled that it was not a defence to the principal offender (the one who actually does the killing) of murder. In *Howe*[60] the House of Lords held that duress was not a defence to murder, irrespective of the degree of participation.

D.P.P. v. Lynch [1975] A.C. 653 (House of Lords)

The appellant was ordered to drive members of the IRA in Northern Ireland to a place where they intended to kill, and did kill a policeman. The appellant claimed that he was convinced that he would be shot if he did not obey. He was convicted of murder, the trial judge holding that the defence of duress was not available to an accessory to murder. The Court of Criminal Appeal in Northern Ireland dismissed his appeal.

Lord Morris:
"It may be that the law must deny such a defence to an actual killer, and that the law will not be irrational if it does so.

Though it is not possible for the law always to be worked out on coldly logical lines there may be manifest factual differences and contrasts between the situation of an aider and abettor to a killing and that of the actual killer. Let two situations be supposed. In each let it be supposed that there is a real and effec-

[58] See *Howe, post*, p. 325.
[59] "Prosecutions for treason are virtually confined to the circumstances of war. Perhaps in war even the private citizen is expected to cast himself in a heroic mould." (Glanville Williams, *Textbook*, p. 627). There are however dicta in *Lynch* to the effect that duress could in some circumstances be a defence to treason. See, for example, Lord Morris at 672.
[60] [1987] 1 A.C. 417.

tive threat of death. In one a person is required under such duress to drive a car to a place or to carry a gun to a place with knowledge that at such place it is planned that X is to be killed by those who are imposing their will. In the other situation let it be supposed that a person under such duress is told that he himself must there and then kill X. In either situation there is a terrible agonising choice of evils. In the former, to save his life, the person drives the car or carries the gun. He may cling to the hope that perhaps X will not be found at the place or that there will be a change of intention before the purpose is carried out or that in some unforeseen way the dire event of a killing will be averted. The final and fatal moment of decision has not arrived. He saves his own life at a time when the loss of another life is not a certainty. In the second (if indeed it is a situation likely to arise) the person is told that to save his life he himself must personally there and then take an innocent life. It is for him to pull the trigger or otherwise personally to do the act of killing. There, I think, before allowing duress as a defence it may be that the law will have to call a halt. May there still be force in what long ago was said by Hale?

'Again, if a man be desperately assaulted, and in peril of death, and cannot otherwise escape, unless to satisfy his assailant's fury he will kill an innocent person then present, the fear and actual force will not acquit him of the crime and punishment of murder, if he commit the fact; for he ought rather to die himself, than kill an innocent.' (*Hale's Pleas of the Crown*, Vol. 1., p. 51).

[Lord Wilberforce and Lord Edmund-Davies agreed that duress was a defence to an accessory to murder. However, they both indicated that they might be prepared to allow duress as a defence to the principal offender of murder. Lord Simon and Lord Kilbrandon dissented on the ground that no distinction could be drawn between a principal offender and an accessory and as a defence of duress could not, in their opinion, be afforded the former, it had to be denied the latter.]"

Appeal allowed: new trial ordered

Abbott v. The Queen [1977] A.C. 755 (Privy Council)

The appellant was ordered by one Malik to kill a girl. He claimed he was afraid that if he did not obey he and his mother would be killed. He dug a hole for the body and held the girl while she was stabbed by another man. She was left dying in the hole while the appellant and others filled in the hole. Both the trial judge and the Court of Appeal of Trinidad and Tobago held that duress was not available as a defence.

Lord Salmon (delivering the majority judgment of their Lordships):
"Whilst their Lordships feel bound to accept the decision of the House of Lords in *Lynch's* case they find themselves constrained to say that had they considered (which they do not) that that decision is an authority which requires the extension of the doctrine to cover cases like the present they would not have accepted it . . .

Counsel for the appellant has argued that the law now presupposes a degree of heroism of which the ordinary man is incapable and which therefore should not be expected of him and that modern conditions and concepts of humanity have rendered obsolete the rule that the actual killer cannot rely on duress as a defence. Their Lordships do not agree. In the trials of those responsible for wartime atrocities such as mass killings of men, women or children, inhuman experiments on human beings, often resulting in death, and like crimes, it was invariably argued for the defence that these atrocities should be excused on the ground that they resulted from superior orders and duress: if the accused had refused to do these dreadful things, they would have been shot and therefore they should be acquitted and allowed to go free. This argument has always been universally rejected. Their Lordships would be sorry indeed to see it accepted by the common law of England."

Lord Wilberforce and Lord Edmund-Davies dissenting:
"If the Crown is right, there is no let-out for any principal in the first degree, even if the duress be so dreadful as would be likely to wreck the morale of most men of reasonable courage, and even were the duress directed not against the person threatened but against other innocent people (in the present case, the appellant's mother) so that considerations of mere self-preservation are not operative. That is indeed 'a blueprint for heroism': *S. v. Goliath*, 1972 (3) S.A. 1 . . .
The question that immediately arises is whether any acceptable distinction can invariably be drawn between a principal in the first degree to murder and one in the second degree, with the result that the latter *may* in certain circumstances be absolved by his plea of duress, while the former may never even advance such a plea.
The simple fact is that *no* acceptable basis of distinction has even now been advanced. In *Lynch* Lord Simon of Glaisdale and Lord Kilbrandon, who dissented, adverted to the absence of any valid distinction as a ground for holding that duress should be available to *neither*. . . .
Lynch having been decided as it was, the most striking feature of the present appeal is the lack of any indication, in the judgment of the majority, *why* a flat declaration that in no circumstances whatsoever may the actual killer be absolved by a plea of duress makes for sounder law and better ethics. In truth, the contrary is the case. For example D attempts to kill P but, though injuring him, fails. When charged with attempted murder he may plead duress (*Reg.* v. *Fagan* (unreported), September 20 1974, and several times referred to in *Lynch*). Later P dies and D is charged with his murder; if the majority of their Lordships are right, he now has no such plea available. Again, no one can doubt that our law would today allow duress to be pleaded in answer to a charge, under section 18 of the Offences against the Person Act 1861, of wounding with intent. Yet, here again, should the victim die after the conclusion of the first trial, the accused when faced with a murder charge would be bereft of any such defence. It is not the mere lack of logic that troubles one. It is when one stops to consider why duress is *ever* permitted as a defence even to charges of great gravity that the lack of any moral reason justifying its *automatic* exclusion in such cases as the present becomes so baffling—and so important. . . .
To hold that a principal in the first degree in murder is never in any circumstances to be entitled to plead duress, whereas a principal in the second degree may, is to import the possibility of grave injustice into the common law."

Appeal dismissed

R. v. Howe and Others [1987] 1 A.C. 417 (House of Lords)

Two appellants, Howe and Bannister, participated with others in torturing, kicking, punching and sexually abusing a man. The man was then strangled to death by one of the others. These events were repeated on a second occasion but this time it was Howe and Bannister who themselves killed the victim by strangling him with a shoelace. The appellants claimed that they had acted under duress at the orders of and through fear of one Murray. "Murray was the dominant figure. He was dishonest, powerful, violent and sadistic. Through acts of actual violence or threats of violence, Murray gained control of each of the appellants, who became fearful of him." (Lord Mackay). At their trial the judge, following *Lynch* and *Abbott* directed the jury that duress could be a defence to the first killing where the appllants were only accessories, but not to the second killing where the appellants were the principal offenders. The Court of Appeal held this was correct. They appealed to the House of Lords.

Lord Hailsham of St. Marylebone L.C.:
"In general, I must say that I do not at all accept in relation to the defence of murder it is either good morals, good policy or good law to suggest, as did the majority in *Lynch* and the minority in *Abbott* that the ordinary man of reasonable fortitude is not to be supposed to be capable of heroism if he is asked to take an innocent life rather than sacrifice his own. Doubtless in actual practice many will succumb to temptation, as they did in *Dudley and Stephens*. But many will not, and I do not believe that as a 'concession to human frailty' the former should be exempt from liability to criminal sanctions if they do. I have known in my own lifetime of too many acts of heroism by ordinary human beings of no more than ordinary fortitude to regard a law as either 'just or humane' which withdraws the protection of the criminal law from the innocent victim and casts the cloak of its protection upon the coward and the poltroon in the name of a 'concession to human frailty.'

I must not, however, underestimate the force of the arguments on the other side. . . .

A long line of cases . . . establish duress as an available defence in a wide range of crimes, some at least, like wounding with intent to commit grievous bodily harm, carrying the heaviest penalties commensurate with their gravity. To cap this, it is pointed out that at least in theory, a defendant accused of this crime under section 18 of the Offences against the Person Act 1861, but acquitted on the grounds of duress, will still be liable to a charge of murder if the victim dies within the traditional period of one year and a day. I am not, perhaps, persuaded of this last point as much as I should. It is not simply an anomaly based on the defence of duress. It is a product of the peculiar mens rea allowed on a charge of murder which is not confined to an intent to kill. More persuasive, perhaps, is the point based on the availability of the defence of duress on a charge of attempted murder, where the actual intent to kill is an essential prerequisite. It may be that we must meet this casus omissus in your Lordships' House when we come to it. It may require reconsideration of the availability of the defence in that case too. . . .

I . . . believe that some degree of poportionality between the threat and the offence must, at least to some extent, be a prerequisite of the defence under existing law. Few would resist threats to the life of a loved one if the alternative were driving across the red lights or in excess of 70 m.p.h. on the motorway. But, . . . , it would take rather more than the threat of a slap on the wrist or even moderate pain or injury to discharge the evidential burden even in the case of a fairly serious assault. In such a case the 'concession to human frailty' is no more than to say that in such circumstances a reasonable man of average courage is entitled to embrace as a matter of choice the alternative which a reasonable man could regard as the lesser of two evils. Other considerations necessarily arise where the choice is between the threat of death or a fortiori of serious injury and deliberately taking an innocent life. In such a case a reasonable man might reflect that one innocent human life is at least as valuable as his own or that of his loved one. In such case a man cannot claim that he is choosing the lesser of two evils. Instead he is embracing the cognate but morally disreputable principle that the end justifies the means. . . .

During the course of argument it was suggested that there was available to the

House some sort of half way house between allowing these appeals and dismissing them. The argument ran that we might treat duress in murder as analogous to provocation, or perhaps diminished responsibility, and say that, in
indictments for murder, duress might reduce the crime to one of manslaughter.
I find myself quite unable to accept this. The cases show that duress, if available
and made out, entitles the accused to a clean acquittal, without, it has been said,
the 'stigma' of a conviction. . . . [The suggestion] is also contrary to principle.
Unlike the doctrine of provocation, which is based on emotional loss of control,
the defence of duress, as I have already shown, is put forward as a 'concession
to human frailty' whereby a conscious decision, it may be coolly undertaken, to
sacrifice an innocent human life is made as an evil lesser than a wrong which
might otherwise be suffered by the accused or his loved ones at the hands of a
wrong doer."

Lord Griffiths:
"It is therefore neither rational nor fair to make the defence dependent upon
whether the accused is the actual killer or took some other part in the murder. . . .
I am not troubled by some of the extreme examples cited in favour of allowing
the defence to those who are not the killer such as a woman motorist being
highjacked and forced to act as getaway driver or a pedestrian being forced to
give misleading information to the police to protect robbery and murder in a
shop. The short, practical answer is that it is inconceivable that such persons
would be prosecuted; they would be called as the principal witnesses for the
prosecution.
As I can find no fair and certain basis upon which to differentiate between
participants to a murder and as I am firmly convinced that the law should not be
extended to the killer, I would depart from the decision of this House in *Director
of Public Prosecutions for Northern Ireland* v. *Lynch* [1975] A.C. 653 and declare
the law to be that duress is not available as a defence to a charge of murder, or to
attempted murder. I add attempted murder because it is to be remembered that
the prosecution have to prove an even more evil intent to convict of attempted
murder than in actual murder. Attempted murder requires proof of an intent to
kill, whereas in murder it is sufficient to prove an intent to cause really serious
injury.
It cannot be right to allow the defence to one who may be more intent upon
taking a life than the murderer. This leaves, of course, the anomaly that duress
is available for the offence of wounding with intent but not to murder if the victim dies subsequently. But this flows from the special regard that the law has for
human life, it may not be logical but it is real and has to be accepted.
I do not think that your Lordships should adopt the compromise solution of
declaring that duress reduces murder to manslaughter. Where the defence of
duress is available it is a complete excuse. This solution would put the law back
to lines upon which Stephen suggested it should develop by regarding duress
as a form of mitigation. English law has rejected this solution and it would be
yet another anomaly to introduce it for the crime of murder alone. I would have
been more tempted to go down this road if the death penalty had remained for
murder. But the sentence for murder although mandatory and expressed as
imprisonment for life, is in fact an indefinite sentence, which is kept constantly
under review by the parole board and the Home Secretary with the assistance of
the Lord Chief Justice and the trial judge. I have confidence that through this
machinery the respective culpability of those involved in a murder case can be
fairly weighed and reflected in the time they are required to serve in custody."
[Lords Bridge, Brandon and Mackay agreed that duress should never be a
defence to murder irrespective of the defendant's degree of participation. In

addition to the above concerns over the special value accorded human life and the difficulty in drawing moral and legal distinctions between perpetrators and accomplices, the House felt there were three further reasons justifying their approach:

(1) if duress were to be made a defence to the perpetrator of murder, that should be done by Parliament, not the courts; the Law Commission (Law Com. No. 83) recommended ten years previously that duress should be a defence to the principal offender of murder; Parliament's failure to enact this recommendation is an indication that they have rejected the proposal.

(2) The defence of duress is imprecisely defined and extending it to murder would cause too much uncertainty;

(3) administrative remedies such as not prosecuting, use of parole and the royal prerogative would ensure that no injustice was perpetrated.]

Appeals dismissed

This decision has been roundly condemned as requiring unrealistic heroism.[61] Heroism might be a desirable quality but it is unduly harsh to sentence someone to life imprisonment for failing to achieve such heights. The criminal law should rest content if its exhortations induce persons to act reasonably. It seems an odd and an unjust law that can proclaim that the defendant has acted perfectly reasonably but is to be guilty of murder. And it is simply no answer to assert that injustice will be avoided by the use of administrative discretion, whether by the prosecution or the Parole Board. The whole thrust in recent criminal law thinking is against granting too much discretion to those administering the criminal justice system. Further, these platitudes have been heard before in other areas of criminal law—and been blatantly ignored.[62]

It is unfortunate that the House of Lords did not address the underlying theoretical basis on which the defence of duress rests. The better view is that duress is an *excuse*. What the defendant has done remains wrong but we can understand his predicament and excuse him. Given the severe threats his actions are in effect morally involuntary. Perhaps if the majority in *Abbott* had realised this they might have produced a different result. Instead they seemed to think they were dealing with a justificatory defence when they spoke of duress bringing the defendant's act "within the law."[63] Lord Mackay in *Howe* spoke of a defendant subject to duress having a "right" to commit a crime.[64] This is simply not so. With excusatory defences one has no "right" to commit crimes. One is simply excused from blame: "To acquit him on grounds of dur-

---

[61] Smith and Hogan, p. 233; Peter Alldridge, "Duress, Murder and the House of Lords" (1988) 52 J.C.L. 186; H. P. Milgate, "Duress and the Criminal Law: Another About Turn by the House of Lords" [1988] C.L.J. 61; Ian Dennis, "Developments in Duress" (1987) 51 J.C.L. 463; Lynden Walters, "Murder under Duress and Judicial Decision-making in the House of Lords" (1988) 8 Legal Studies 61.

[62] See the prosecution that was brought in *Anderton* v. *Ryan* [1985] A.C. 560—exactly the sort of case in which The Law Commission (Law Com. Working Paper No. 102) had predicted that a prosecution would never be brought.

[63] At p. 766; see Fletcher, p. 832.

[64] At p. 456; see Walters, *ante*, no. 61 at p. 72.

ess is merely to sympathise, understand, commiserate with what he did."[65]

E. Necessity

1. Introduction

The defence of necessity is similar to that of duress in many respects—so much so that it is being increasingly referred to as "duress of circumstances" for reasons which will be explored shortly. The defendant claims that he was "forced" to commit a crime, not because *someone* was threatening him, but because *something* (in the shape of surrounding circumstances which may or may not have been caused by a human being) deprived him of any real choice. Two examples will illustrate the situations in which a defence of necessity might be claimed.

   (i) Ten people are climbing a ladder to safety from a vessel that is sinking. One of these "freezes" on the ladder, so petrified by fear that despite every effort being made to persuade him to move, he does not respond. Eventually he is pushed from the ladder and falls to his death.[66] If charged with murder the survivors would claim that their actions were *necessary* and that it had to be better for one to die so that nine should live.

  (ii) A fifteen year old boy is alone with his mother on their remote farm. The mother suffers a heart attack and is critically ill. If she is not rushed to a hospital she will almost certainly die. The boy drives his mother to the hospital. If charged with an offence, contrary to section 101 of the Road Traffic Act 1988, of "driving whilst being under the specified age" he would claim that it was *necessary* for him to break the law in order to prevent his mother dying.

Are such defendants pleading that their actions are justified by necessity—made lawful, in fact by the "greater good" that can be achieved by their "breaking the law"? Or are they recognising the wrong that has been done but asking to be excused from punishment because of the acute dilemma in which they found themselves? We saw in relation to duress how the courts' interpretation of that defence as a justification has led them to a reluctance to extend the defence; the same point applies even more forcefully as we shall see in relation to the birth pangs of the defence of necessity.

2. Should necessity be a defence?

The answer to this question involves a consideration of largely the same issues as those explored in the preceding section on duress and

---

[65] Leo Katz, *Bad Acts and Guilty Minds* (1987), p. 65.
[66] As seems to have happened during the sinking of the *Herald of Free Enterprise*; *The Times*, June 13, 1988.

reference should be made to the discussion there.[67] Applying the same questions to the area of necessity we must ask:

(1) Are there any utilitarian reasons for denying the defence of necessity? The answer here must surely be negative. The defendants in the above two examples would clearly not have been deterred from their actions by the knowledge that they could be held criminally responsible. As to the other utilitarian aims of punishment, Packer has written that "it seems foolish to make rules . . . that discourage people from behaving as we would like them to behave . . . punishment would serve no useful purpose . . . these people are not in need of either restraint or reform."[68]

(2) Are defendants who commit crimes in such situations morally blameworthy? Have they been afforded a fair opportunity to choose between breaking or keeping the law?[69] Do they come within Fletcher's test that "[e]xcuses apply on behalf of morally involuntary responses to danger; they acknowledge that when individuals merely react rather than choose to do wrong, they cannot fairly be held accountable"?[70]

State v. Green 470 S.W. 2d 565 (1971) (Supreme Court of Missouri)

The defendant was charged with the offence of escaping from prison. While confined in prison he had been homosexually raped several times. He had reported the matter to the Prison authorities who on one occasion had told him to "go back and fight it out" and on another to "fight it out, submit to the assaults, or go over the fence." On the day in question he was told by five inmates that he would have to submit to their homosexual desires that night or they would kill or seriously harm him. He did not report this threat to anyone but escaped at 6.00 p.m. that evening. He was convicted of escaping from a state institution and sentenced to three years imprisonment. He appealed.

Henley J:
"[For the defence of necessity] [t]he compulsion from the harm or evil which the actor seeks to avoid, should be present and impending . . .

This is not a case where the defendant escaped while being closely pursued by those who sought by threat of death or bodily harm to have him submit to sodomy. Moreover, the threatened consequences of his refusal to submit could have been avoided that day by reporting the threats and the names of those making the threats to the authorities in charge of the Center. Defendant had several hours in which to consider and report these threats. . . . The judgment is affirmed."

Seiler J. (dissenting):
"It is a fundamental legal principle that criminal punishment should not be visited upon the blameless. See Holmes, *The Common Law*, (1948), p. 50; 'It is not intended to deny that criminal liability . . . is founded on blameworthiness . . .

---

[67] *Ante*, pp. 309–313.
[68] H. Packer, *The Limits of The Criminal Sanction*, p. 114.
[69] See *ante*, p. 311.
[70] Fletcher, p. 811.

[A] law which punished conduct which would not be blameworthy in the average member of the community would be too severe for that community to bear . . . ' Juries in criminal cases are instinctively aware of this. One illustration of this principle is the right to present to the jury the defence of self-defence . . . where defendant was resisting attempted sodomy. The affirmative defenses of coercion and necessity are based upon the same principle. 'If a person commits an act under compulsion, responsibility for the act cannot be ascribed to him since in effect, it was not his own desire, or motivation, or will, which led to the act.' Newman and Weitzer, 'Duress, Free Will and the Criminal Law' 30 So.Cal.L.Rev. 313. There appear to be no Missouri cases considering the defense of necessity, but it is well established that coercion is a defense to all crimes except murder. . . .

I interpret the majority opinion to decide that the proposed defense is not available because (1) defendant did not delay his escape until his would-be assailants had him in close pursuit and (2) because he could have avoided his predicament had he only turned in their names earlier in the day.

As to the first, defendant knew from prior experience that if he waited until the band was close at hand, it would be too late. If escape were to save him, it had to be made earlier than the last minute. Five against one is hopeless odds. As to the second, this overlooks the evidence that to turn in the names to the prison authorities meant defendant was risking his life by being a 'snitch.'

Defendant had already been told by a high prison official that he had three alternatives; submit, defend himself, or escape. The majority opinion does not recommend submission, and as a practical matter, self defense was impossible. All that was left was escape, and under these circumstances, the coercion and necessity were not remote in time, but present and impending. Escape or submission (and I do not believe defendant was unreasonable in not being willing to submit to five-fold sodomy) were literally all this defendant had left.

There are a number of cases in which the defense of coercion has been offered to justify an escape. . . .

This case differs much from the usual escape case. Defendant should have been permitted to submit to the jury the defense of coercion as justification for the escape, and I, therefore, respectfully dissent. The evidence shows defendant was confronted with a horrific dilemma, not of his making. No one, I am sure, wants to force a prisoner to live under conditions where he must either become a 'punk' and debase himself, or a 'snitch' at the risk of his life, but nevertheless this is the effect of our decision, until and unless the state improves the conditions in the prisons. I am not advocating that we should permit each prisoner to determine whether the conditions of his imprisonment justify an escape. What I am saying is that when the facts presented, if believed, would establish the defense of coercion, then this defense should be available to a charge of escape."

Judgment affirmed

Note that Seiler J. is using the word "coercion" as a synonym for duress. Is the concept of duress appropriate to cover situations such as these? Contrast this decision with that of *Hudson and Taylor*[71] where the defence of duress was available. If Hudson and Taylor were not blameworthy, was Green?

Contrast the views expressed in the dissenting judgment in *Green* with Lord Coleridge's statements in the following English case on the defence of necessity:

[71] *Ante*, p. 319.

R. v. Dudley and Stephens (1884) 14 Q.B.D. 273 (Queen's Bench Division)

The two defendants, with a third man and a 17 year old boy, were cast away on the high seas in an open boat, 1,600 miles from land. They drifted in the boat for twenty days. When they had been eight days without food and six days without water, and fearing they would all die soon without some sustenance, the defendants killed the boy, who was likely to die first. The men ate his flesh and drank his blood for four days. They were then rescued by a passing vessel and were subsequently charged with murder. The jury found the facts of the case in a special verdict and the case was referred to the Queen's Bench Division for its decision.

Lord Coleridge C.J.:
"[T]he prisoners put to death a weak and unoffending boy upon the chance of preserving their own lives by feeding upon his flesh and blood after he was killed, and with a certainty of depriving *him* of any possible chance of survival. The verdict finds in terms that: 'if the men had not fed upon the body of the boy, they would *probably* have not survived . . . ' and that 'the boy, being in a much weaker condition, was *likely* to have died before them.' They might possibly have been picked up next day by a passing ship; they might not have been picked up at all; in either case it is obvious that the killing of the boy would have been an unnecessary and profitless act. It is found by the verdict that the boy was incapable of resistance, and, in fact, made none; and it is not even suggested that his death was due to any violence on his part attempted against, or even so much as feared by, those who killed him . . .

[I]t is admitted that the deliberate killing of this unoffending and unresisting boy was clearly murder, unless the killing can be justified by some well-recognised excuse admitted by the law. It is further admitted that there was in this case no such excuse, unless the killing was justified by what has been called 'necessity.' But the temptation to the act which existed here was not what the law has ever called necessity. Nor is this to be regretted. Though law and morality are not the same, and though many things may be immoral which are not necessarily illegal, yet the absolute divorce of law from morality would be of fatal consequence, and such divorce would follow if the temptation to murder in this case were to be held by law an absolute defence of it. It is not so. To preserve one's life is generally speaking, a duty, but it may be the plainest and the highest duty to sacrifice it. War is full of instances in which it is a man's duty not to live, but to die. . . .

It is not needful to point out the awful danger of admitting the principle which has been contended for. Who is to be the judge of this sort of necessity? By what measure is the comparative value of lives to be measured? Is it to be strength, or intellect, or what? It is plain that the principle leaves to him who is to profit by it to determine the necessity which will justify him in deliberately taking another's life to save his own. In this case the weakest, the youngest, the most unresisting was chosen. Was it more necessary to kill *him* than one of the grown men? The answer be, No . . .

It must not be supposed that, in refusing to admit temptation to be an excuse for crime, it is forgotten how terrible the temptation was; how awful the suffering; how hard in such trials to keep the judgment straight and the conduct pure. We are often compelled to set up standards we cannot reach ourselves, and to lay down rules which we could not ourselves satisfy. But a man has no right to declare temptation to be an excuse, though he might himself have yielded to it, nor allow compassion for the criminal to change or weaken in any manner the legal definition of the crime. It is therefore our duty to declare that the prisoners' act in this case was wilful murder."

Judgment for the Crown. Sentence of death, later commuted to six month's imprisonment

United States v. Holmes 26 Fed. Cas. 360 (1842) (Circuit Court, Eastern District, Pennsylvania)

The defendant along with eight other seamen and 32 passengers were in an overcrowded lifeboat. Fearing that the boat would sink he threw 16 passengers overboard. The crew were directed " 'not to part man and wife, and not to throw over any women.' There was no other principle of selection." The next morning the survivors in the boat were all rescued.

Baldwin C.J. directing jury:
"[M]an, in taking away the life of a fellow being, assumes an awful responsibility to God, and to society; and that the administrators of public justice do themselves assume that responsibility if, when called on to pass judicially upon the act, they yield to the indulgence of misapplied humanity. It is one thing to give a favourable interpretation to evidence in order to mitigate an offence. It is a different thing, when we are asked, not to extenuate, but to justify, the act . . . [T]he case does not become 'a case of necessity,' unless all ordinary means of self-preservation have been exhausted. The peril must be instant, over-whelming, leaving no alternative but to lose our own life, or to take the life of another person . . .
[He then held that the seamen should have been sacrificed first as they were not in an equal position with the passengers as 'the sailor is bound . . . to undergo whatever hazard is necessary to preserve the boat and the passengers.' As between equals the decision as to who should be sacrificed should be made by drawing lots].
When the solution has been made by lots, the victim yields of course to his fate, or, if he resists, force may be employed to coerce submission. Whether or not 'a case of necessity' has arisen, or whether the law under which death has been inflicted have been so exercised as to hold the executioner harmless, cannot depend on his own opinion; for no man may pass upon his own conduct when it concerns the rights and especially, when it affects the lives, of others. . . . [H]omicide is sometimes justifiable; and the law defines the occasions in which it is so. The transaction must, therefore, be justified to the law . . .
[The jury returned a verdict of guilty. The defendant who had already been confined in jail for several months was sentenced to six months imprisonment with hard labour and fined $20. The penalty was subsequently remitted.]"

These cases illustrate the implications of treating necessity as a justification rather than an excuse. In the United States this defence is widely regarded as a paradigmatic example of justification: the superior interest at stake is the greater harm that can be avoided.

American Law Institute, Model Penal Code, Tent. Draft No. 8 (1958), Comments to Art. 3, pp. 8–9:

"It would be particularly unfortunate to exclude homicidal conduct from the scope of the defense . . . For recognising that the sanctity of life has a supreme place in the hierarchy of values, it is nonetheless true that conduct which results in taking life may promote the very value sought to be protected by the law of homicide. Suppose, for example, that the actor has made a breach in a dike, knowing that this will inundate a farm, but taking the only course available to save a whole town. If he is charged with homicide of the inhabitants of the farm house, he can rightly point out that the object of the law of homicide is to save life, and that by his conduct he has effected a net saving of innocent lives. The life of every individual must be assumed in such a case to be of equal value and the numerical preponderance in the lives saved compared to those sacrificed surely establishes an ethical and legal justification for the act. So too a mountaineer, roped to a companion who has fallen over a precipice who holds on as long as possible but eventually cuts the rope, must certainly be granted the defense that he accelerated one death slightly but avoided the only alternative, the certain death of both.

. . . [T]he evil sought to be avoided [must] be a greater evil than that sought to be protected by the law defining the offense. For the result is that the defense would not be available to a defendant who killed A to save B, in circumstances where had he done nothing B would have been killed and A saved, assuming, of course, that there was not . . . aggression on either's part . . . Nor would the defense be available to one who acted to save himself at the expense of another, as by seizing a raft when men are shipwrecked . . . In all ordinary circumstances lives in being must be assumed, as we have said, to be of equal value, equally deserving the protection of the law."

It is reasonable to infer that it was because the majority in *Green* assumed that they were dealing with a justificatory defence that they refused to admit it. In *Dudley*, Lord Coleridge expressed the view that a defence of necessity would alter "the legal definition of the crime"[72] which would only be the case if it acted as a justificatory defence. Yet Seilor J., the dissenting judge in *Green* regarded it as an excuse and thus less threatening to the established prohibitions of the criminal law. So too the defendants in *Dudley* could have been seen as pleading an excuse: it was not a case of the lives of the three men being a superior interest to that of the cabin-boy but that given that their lives were of equal value, due consideration had to be given to the awfulness of the situation they were in. The fact that their sentences were so rapidly commuted gives further strength to this argument. Indeed, it has been said that the pardon had been arranged well in advance of the sentences being passed![73]

Finally, in relation to the issue of whether necessity ought to be a defence, two more points of contrast may be considered.

B. N. Cardozo, "Law and Literature" from Selected Writings (1947), p. 390:

"Where two or more are overtaken by a common disaster, there is no right on the part of one to save the lives of some by the killing of another. There is no

---

[72] *Ante*, p. 332.
[73] Leo Katz, *Bad Acts and Guilty Minds* (1987), p. 27.

rule of human jettison. Men there will often be who, when told that their going will be the salvation of the remnant, will choose the nobler part and make the plunge into the waters. In that supreme moment the darkness for them will be illuminated by the thought that those behind will ride to safety. If none of such mould are found aboard the boat, or too few to save the others, the human freight must be left to meet the chances of the waters. Who shall choose in such an hour between the victims and the saved? Who shall know when masts and sails of rescue may emerge out of the fog?"

Hyman Gross, A Theory of Criminal Justice (1979), pp. 26–27:

"But [conduct] may also be morally wrong without being culpable under standards of culpability that suit the administration of criminal justice in a community of ordinary people. In cases like those we are considering, the act may be morally wrong, and yet an alternative course of action that avoids doing what is morally wrong can be expected only from a hero, a martyr, a paragon of self-restraint, or perhaps a prodigy of insight, inventiveness, and daring who devises on the spot still a third course of action that avoids any harm and so bypasses the moral dilemma. Since the law is designed to regulate affairs in a community of ordinary men and not on Olympus, it should regard the morally unworthy course as not deserving blame and therefore not criminally wrong. If the law does not regard such acts as legally justifiable but chooses instead to condemn them from a higher moral plateau where ordinary human limitations do not count, the law will itself outrage a common sense of justice at the more mundane level at which life is normally lived. This will weaken the ties of allegiance to the law that are found in a community of ordinary men, for ordinary men would rightly regard the law then as assuming an arrogant and unbending posture of moral superiority."

3. The law's response

Until recently it was commonly thought that a general defence of necessity did not exist in English Law.[74] Thus in *Buckoke* v. *Greater London Council* Lord Denning indicated *obiter* that the driver of a fire engine was compelled to stop at a red traffic light, even though "he sees 200 yards down the road a blazing house with a man at an upstairs window in extreme peril . . . [and if he] waits for that time, the man's life will be lost."[75] In *O'Toole*[76] and *Wood* v. *Richards*[77] an ambulance driver and a police officer respectively were involved in car accidents while rushing to answer emergency calls. Both were convicted of road traffic offences,[78] necessity being no defence.[79] In *Kitson*[80] a passenger woke up drunk in a car to find it running downhill; he steered the car on to a

---

[74] Smith and Hogan, 5th ed., pp. 201–209; *Dudley and Stephens* is usually cited to support this proposition. It has been argued that the facts of that case did not disclose a true case of necessity: Smith and Hogan, p. 227; Glanville Williams, *Textbook*, p. 606, but it is submitted that the overall tenor of the judgment indicates that Lord Coleridge was simply not prepared to accept necessity as a defence to murder.
[75] [1971] Ch. 655 at 668.
[76] (1971) 55 Cr.App.R. 206.
[77] [1977] Crim.L.R. 295.
[78] Dangerous driving, contrary to the Road Traffic Act 1960, s.2 and driving without due care and attention, contrary to Road Traffic Act 1972, s.3, respectively. See now Road Traffic Act 1988, ss.2 and 3.
[79] Cf. *Johnson* v. *Phillips* [1976] 1 W.L.R. 65 where necessity was accepted as a basis for *convicting* a defendant.
[80] (1955) 39 Cr.App.R. 66.

grass verge to avoid a possible accident; he was convicted of driving while under the influence of drink—the defence of necessity was not even raised. And in *Southwark L.B.C.* v. *Williams* where defendants in dire need of housing accommodation entered empty houses owned by the local authority, it was held that the defence of necessity did not apply. Lord Denning M.R. stated:

"If homelessness were once admitted as a defence to trespass, no one's house could be safe. Necessity would open a door which no man could shut. It would not only be those in extreme need who would enter. There would be others who would imagine that they were in need, or would invent a need, so as to gain entry."[81]

And Edmund-Davies L.J. held:

"[T]he law regards with the deepest suspicion any remedies of self-help, and permits those remedies to be resorted to only in very special circumstances. The reason for such circumspection is clear—necessity can very easily become simply a mask for anarchy . . . [I]t appears that all the cases where a plea of necessity has succeeded are cases which deal with an urgent situation of imminent peril: for example, the forcible feeding of an obdurate suffragette, . . . or performing an abortion to avert a grave threat to the life, or . . . health of a pregnant young girl who had been ravished in circumstances of great brutality"[82]

However, there has never been a blanket prohibition against the defence of necessity in all guises and in all situations and the following situations require separate consideration.

(i) *Statutory defences that are in substance necessity*

Some statutes expressly provide defences that are in substance defences of necessity, for example, fire-engines, police and ambulances are exempted from observing the speed limit in certain circumstances,[83] and in specified circumstances they may treat a red traffic light as a warning to give way[84]; in order to protect property that is in immediate need of protection, it is permissible to destroy the property of another person.[85] Further, many statutes contain phrases such as "unlawful," "without unlawful excuse" or "without reasonable excuse" which may be construed to cover situations in which a defence of necessity might be appropriate—for example, sections 8–10 of the old Forgery Act 1913 prohibited the possession of forged bank notes "without lawful authority or excuse."[86] In *Wuyts*[87] it was held that if the defendant's sole

---

[81] [1971] Ch. 734, 744.
[82] *Ibid.* pp. 745–746. Is Edmund-Davies L.J. conceding that in extreme cases, a defence of necessity does exist in English law?
[83] Road Traffic Regulation Act 1984, s.87.
[84] Traffic Signs Regulations and General Directions (S.I. 1981 No. 859), reg. 34(1)(b).
[85] Criminal Damage Act 1971, s.5(2)(b).
[86] See now Forgery and Counterfeiting Act 1981, s.16(2).
[87] [1969] 2 Q.B. 474.

purpose in retaining possession of the notes was to hand them to the police, it would have been a "lawful excuse."[88]

(ii) *Hidden defences of necessity*

It has been argued that although judges may be reluctant to admit a general defence of necessity through the front door, they may be happy to achieve the same result by rather artificial means. Smith has argued that the case of *Gillick*[89] is really only explicable as one which provides the doctor who prescribes contraceptive advice and treatment to a girl under the age of sixteen with a defence of necessity to any charge of aiding and abetting the crime of underage sexual intercourse that may then be committed.[90]

(iii) *Necessity in relation to homicide*

It is undoubtedly the case that one of the greatest handicaps to the development of a general defence of necessity has been that discussion takes place so often within the context of a homicide case, where as Alldridge states "there is always a corpse, casting a shadow across the proceedings."[91] Now, not only is there the shadow of the hapless cabinboy, Richard Parker and the conviction of those who killed him in the way, but there is the judicial reconsideration of *Dudley* in the recent case of *Howe*.

R. v. Howe [1987] 1 A.C. 417 (House of Lords)

(For facts see p. 325).

Lord Hailsham L.C.:
"[I]f we were to allow this appeal [against a conviction for murder on the basis of duress], we should, I think, also have to say that *Dudley and Stephens* was bad law. There is, of course, an obvious distinction between duress and necessity as potential defences; duress arises from the wrongful threats of violence of another human being and necessity arises from any other objective dangers threatening the accused. This, however, is in my view a distinction without a relevant difference, since on this view duress is only that species of the genus of necessity which is caused by wrongful threats. I cannot see that there is any way in which a person of ordinary fortitude can be excused from the one type of pressure on his will rather than the other."

This is a highly significant passage. Lord Hailsham is saying that because the defences are so similar both have to be denied to the person

---

[88] For a full discussion of the circumstances when a statute can be construed to cover situations of necessity, see P. R. Glazebrook "The Necessity Plea in English Criminal Law" [1972] C.L.J. 87.
[89] [1986] A.C. 112.
[90] J. C. Smith, *Justification and Excuse in the Criminal Law*, (1989), pp. 64–68. Prof. Smith argues that there are many other "concealed defences" in the criminal law (pp. 61–72).
[91] Peter Alldridge, "Duress, duress of circumstances and necessity" (1989) N.L.J. 911.

who kills.[92] We have already discussed the merits and demerits of such an approach. But is he not also impliedly acknowledging the existence of the defence of necessity in other non-homicidal contexts? In other words, just as *Dudley* can be interpreted as relating to homicide only, so too can the ratio of *Howe*. The door is open for the development of the defence to all other offences.

(iv) *Duress of circumstances*

Lord Hailsham in *Howe* referred to duress as a form of necessity, but other recent cases have chosen instead to refer to what is transparently necessity as "duress of circumstances." Quite who they think is fooled by this is unclear, but if it enables judges to overcome their reluctance to accept necessity then it is a tolerable fiction. In *Willer*[93] the defendant was charged with driving recklessly to which he pleaded necessity—he had had to do so (although the Court of Appeal was not even convinced his actions were reckless) in order to escape from a gang of youths. The Court of Appeal held *inter alia* that regardless of whether necessity had been established or was available, the defence of "duress of circumstances" was applicable.[94] "Duress of circumstances" was also considered in the case of *Conway*.[95] The defendant pleaded that he had to make off in his car when approached by two men (who were in fact police officers) because his passenger was fearful of an attack. In saying that the defence of duress of circumstances should have been put to the jury, the Court of Appeal indicated that it was immaterial whether the defence was called necessity or duress. This move away from the use of the fiction has been followed in the case of *Martin*.

R. v. Martin (1989) 88 Cr.App.R. 343

(The defendant was charged with driving whilst disqualified under section 99(*b*) of the Road Traffic Act 1972. The facts appear from the judgment.)

Simon Brown J.:
. . . "The circumstances which the appellant desired to advance by way of defence of necessity were essentially these. His wife has suicidal tendencies. On a number of occasions before the day in question she had attempted to take her own life. On the day in question her son, the appellant's stepson, had overslept. He had done so to the extent that he was bound to be late for work and at risk of losing his job unless, so it was asserted, the appellant drove him to work. The appellant's wife was distraught. She was shouting, screaming, banging her head against a wall. More particularly, it is said she was threatening suicide unless the appellant drove the boy to work.

The defence had a statement from a doctor which expressed the opinion that 'in view of her mental condition it is likely that Mrs. Martin would have attempted suicide if her husband did not drive her son to work.'

---

[92] Further, according to his logic, both should receive the same classification as being either justificatory or excusatory. See *ante*, p. 274.
[93] (1986) 83 Cr.App.R. 225.
[94] See also *Denton* (1987) 131 S.J. 476.
[95] (1989) 88 Cr.App.R. 159. See Peter Alldridge, "Duress, duress of circumstances and necessity" (1989) New L.J. 911.

The appellant's case on the facts was that he genuinely, and he would suggest reasonably, believed that his wife would carry out that threat unless he did as she demanded. Despite his disqualification he therefore drove the boy. He was in fact apprehended by the police within about a quarter of a mile of the house.

Sceptically though one may regard that defence on the facts—and there were, we would observe, striking difficulties about the detailed evidence when it came finally to be given before the judge in mitigation—the sole question before this court is whether those facts, had the jury accepted they were or might be true, amounted in law to a defence. If they did, then the appellant was entitled to a trial of the issue before the jury. The jury would of course have had to be directed properly on the precise scope and nature of the defence, but the decision on the facts would have been for them. As it was, such a defence was pre-empted by the ruling. Should it have been?

In our judgment the answer is plainly not. The authorities are now clear. Their effect is perhaps most conveniently to be found in the judgment of this court in *R. v. Conway* (1988) 88 Cr.App.R. 159. The decision reviews earlier relevant authorities.

The principles may be summarised thus. First, English law does, in extreme circumstances, recognise a defence of necessity. Most commonly this defence arises as duress, that is pressure on the accused's will from the wrongful threats or violence of another. Equally however it can arise from other objective dangers threatening the accused or others. Arising thus it is conveniently called 'duress of circumstances.'

Secondly, the defence is available only if, from an objective standpoint, the accused can be said to be acting reasonably and proportionately in order to avoid a threat of death or serious injury.

Thirdly, assuming the defence to be open to the accused on his account of the facts, the issue should be left to the jury, who should be directed to determine these two questions: first, was the accused, or may he have been, impelled to act as he did because as a result of what he reasonably believed to be the situation he had good cause to fear that otherwise death or serious physical injury would result? Second, if so, would a sober person of reasonable firmness, sharing the characteristics of the accused, have responded to that situation by acting as the accused acted? If the answer to both those questions was Yes, then the jury would acquit; the defence of necessity would have been established. . . .

We see no material distinction between offences of reckless driving and driving whilst disqualified so far as the application and scope of this defence is concerned. Equally we can see no distinction in principle between various threats of death; it matters not whether the risk of death is by murder or by suicide or indeed by accident. One can illustrate the latter by considering a disqualified driver being driven by his wife, she suffering a heart attack in remote countryside and he needing instantly to get her to hospital.

It follows from this that the judge quite clearly did come to a wrong decision on the question of law, and the appellant should have been permitted to raise this defence for what it was worth before the jury.

It is in our judgment a great pity that that course was not taken. It is difficult to believe that any jury would have swallowed the improbable story which this appellant desired to advance. There was, it emerged when evidence was given in mitigation, in the house at the time a brother of the boy who was late for work, who was licensed to drive, and available to do so; the suggestion was that he would not take his brother because of 'a lot of aggravation in the house between them.' It is a further striking fact that when apprehended by the police this appellant was wholly silent as to why on this occasion he had felt constrained to drive. But those considerations, in our judgment, were essentially for the jury, and we have concluded, although not without hesitation, that it would be inappropriate here to apply the proviso.

In the result this appeal must be allowed and the conviction quashed."

Appeal allowed. Conviction quashed

Elliot has said that the development of the law in this area "can be likened to the overnight growth of a mushroom"[96] and Smith in his commentary to *Martin* states that "we seem to be witnessing the development of a general, if limited, defence of necessity under which there is no need to distinguish between one type of duress and another because they are all governed by the same principles."[97] In this respect, the Court of Appeal in this succession of driving cases is making exactly the same point as Lord Hailsham—although it took them a few cases to "come clean" about what they were doing.

It is a development of law that is very welcome, but it has the odd effect of actually over taking the law reform proposals. In 1974 the Law Commission proposed that a general defence of necessity be introduced into English law.[98] However, three years later they rejected the idea, going so far as to say that if it already existed at common law, it should be abolished. They felt that allowing such a defence to a charge of murder could effectively legalise euthanasia in England. For "human rights" reasons they were not prepared to see necessity covering a situation where "an immediate blood transfusion must be made in order to save an injured person: the only one who has the same blood type as the injured refuses to give blood. Can he be overpowered and the blood taken from him?"[99] They felt that specific statutory provisions already covered those areas where the defence might be most needed. For minor offences they argued that prosecutions were unlikely and, in any event, the sentencing policy of the English courts was such that people convicted in these situations would probably receive a minimal sentence, say an absolute or conditional discharge.

It should be remembered that at the same time as making these "totally negative"[1] proposals, the Law Commission were recommending that duress be extended to *all* crimes. Not only was the absurdity of this position exposed by the drafters of the Criminal Code Bill but it was said that it would not do to rely on prosecutorial discretion. As a result the team proposed firstly that to the extent that necessity was a defence at common law, it should be unaffected by the Code, and

---

[96] D. W. Elliot, "Necessity, Duress and Self-Defence" [1989] Crim.L.R. 611 at p. 612.

[97] [1989] Crim.L.R. 285.

[98] Working Paper No. 55 (1974), para. 57.

[99] Law Com. No. 83. (1977). Para. 4.27. Glanville Williams, *Textbook*, p. 602 states: "The doctrine of necessity is an expression of the philosophy of utilitarianism; but utilitarianism does not exercise undisputed sway over our minds. Many people give allegiance to a notion of human rights or fundamental values; and sometimes, at least, these interests do not merely enter into the utilitarian calculus but supersede it."

[1] Law Com. No. 143 (1985), para. 119.

secondly they proposed a defence of necessity called "duress of circumstances."[2]

Draft Criminal Code Bill, 1989, (Law Com. No. 177), clause 43:

"(1) A person is not guilty of an offence [to which this section applies] when he does an act under duress of circumstances.
(2) A person does an act under duress of circumstances if—
  (a) he does it because he knows or believes that it is immediately necessary to avoid death or serious personal harm to himself or another; and
  (b) the danger that he knows or believes to exist is such that in all the circumstances (including any of his personal characteristics that effect its gravity) he cannot reasonably be expected to act otherwise.
(3) This section—
[(a) applies to any offence other than murder or attempt to murder;]"

It is submitted that this terminology "duress of circumstances" is unfortunate. Perhaps it was introduced in *Willer*[3] and *Conway*[4] because the threats there came from *other persons* rather than from objective circumstances. However, *Martin*[5] was a classic case of necessity and it is unfortunate that it chose to perpetuate this terminology.

However, more significant than the nomenclature is the development itself. In *Buckoke* Lord Denning said that a fire-engine driver is "guilty of an offence" but "such a man should not be prosecuted. He should be congratulated."[6] We at long last appear to be moving towards a law that will reflect more realistically society's lack of condemnation of such actions.

F. Superior Orders

In discussing duress it was recognised that that defence could be rationalised on the basis that the defendant lacked effective and real choice in committing the crime; he was forced by someone else to do something he was loathe to do. In the same way, a subordinate may assert that he was forced by duty and loyalty to a superior to obey an order which leads him into conflict with the criminal law. Following this analogy it would seem that superior orders constitutes an *excuse*. The inferior has done wrong but is excused from blame. However, in the United States the view that is adopted is that superior orders constitutes a *justification*. The defendant is seeking to justify his actions by reference to a superior interest—the requirement that those who give orders must be able to rely on their being obeyed.

[2] *Ibid.*
[3] *Ante*, n. 93.
[4] *Ante*, p. 338.
[5] *Ante*, p. 338.
[6] *Ante*, p. 335.

English authority is scant[7] but tends to confirm a feeling that in neither civil nor military situations ought there to be a defence of superior orders. Lord Salmon, for example in the duress case of *Abbott* v. *The Queen*,[8] said that the idea of such a defence "has always been universally rejected" and Lord Hailsham takes a similar position in the case of *Howe*.[9] While such an approach might be uncontroversial in relation to civil situations, the matter is not free from dispute in relation to military situations where it may be argued that the claims of duty, especially in war-time, are so strong as to warrant some kind of defence of superior orders.[10]

McCall v. McDowell, 1 Abb 212 Fed Cas. No. 8673 (1867) (Circuit Court of California)

Deaty J.:
"I cannot but think that the law should excuse the military subordinate when acting in obedience to the orders of his commander. Otherwise he is placed in the dangerous dilemma of being liable in damages to a third party[11] for obedience of an order or to the loss of his commission and disgrace for disobedience thereto[12] . . . The first duty of a soldier is obedience, and without this there can be neither discipline nor efficiency in an army. If every subordinate officer and soldier were at liberty to question the legality of the orders of the commander . . . the camp would be turned into a debating school, where the precious moment for action would be wasted in wordy conflicts between the advocates of conflicting opinions."

This apparent *carte blanche* to obey orders whatever their nature, is, in fact, made subject to an important qualification, but we must first consider the implications of such a solution.

After the Second World War, the Nuremberg trials sought to bring to account Nazis who had participated in crimes of war and crimes against humanity, including the extermination or enslavement of civilian or prison populations and torture, rape or experimentation with human beings.[13] Should the officers and soldiers involved in such atrocities be able to claim that they were obeying orders? If there is indeed an authorised "shoot-to-kill" policy operating in relation to terrorist members

---

[7] *Thomas* (1816) 4 M. & S. 441, C.C.R. (Russell 12th Ed. Vol. 1 p. 87): A naval sentinel was convicted of murder having killed a man while firing at a boat, despite having been ordered to keep boats away and feeling that it was his duty to do so. The Manual of Military Law states that if the order is in fact unlawful a serviceman has no defence. In *Lewis* v. *Dickson* [1976] R.T.R. 431 a security officer who had been ordered to check vehicles entering his employer's premises had no defence to a charge of obstructing the highway which had resulted from his actions.

[8] [1976] 3 W.L.R. 462 at p. 469.

[9] [1987] A.C. 417 at p. 427.

[10] As no similar justification exists in civil situations it is not proposed to discuss superior orders further in that context.

[11] Or subject to a criminal charge.

[12] The soldier may claim further that he would have been shot himself for disobedience (Nazi war criminals included this in their defence), therefore, pleading duress.

[13] Including experiments with the quickest method of sterilising millions of people, experiments with poison, with bone transplants on deliberately created injuries, with freezing, with high altitudes etc. *United States* v. *Karl Brandt*, Nuremberg War Trials 1 & 2.

of the I.R.A., should soldiers be able to rely upon this in defence of their actions?

United States v. Goering; Trial of the major war criminals before the International Military Tribunal, Vol. XXII.

Lieutenant Colonel Volkchov:
"Many of these men have made a mockery of the soldier's oath of obedience to military orders. When it suits their defense they say they had to obey; when confronted with Hitler's brutal crimes, which are shown to have been within their general knowledge, they say they disobeyed. The truth is that they actively participated in all these duties, or sat silent and acquiescent, witnessing the commission of crimes on a scale larger and more shocking than the world has ever had the misfortune to know."

Jackson J.:
"The Charter[14] recognises that one who has committed criminal acts may not take refuge in superior orders nor in the doctrine that his crimes were acts of State. These twin principles, working together, have heretofore resulted in immunity for practically everyone concerned in the really great crimes against peace and mankind. Those in lower ranks were protected against liability by the orders of their superiors. The superiors were protected because their orders were called acts of State. Under the Charter, no defense based on either of these doctrines can be entertained. Modern civilization puts unlimited weapons of destruction in the hands of men. It cannot tolerate so vast an area of legal irres-ponsibility. . . . Of course, we do not argue that the circumstances under which one commits an act should be disregarded in judging the legal effect. . . . The Charter implies common sense limits to liability, just as it places common sense limits upon immunity."

Despite the Charter being described as an "accurate statement of the common law both in England and the United States"[15] at the time of the trials, there have been numerous cases[16] since then in the United States which have attempted to recognise the "practical dilemma" of the soldier[17] by striking a balance between total immunity and total liab-ility. The following case is now regarded as decisive.

United States v. Calley 22 U.S.M.C.A. 534 (1973) (U.S. Court of Military Appeals)

Lieutenant Calley was a platoon leader engaged in sweeping out the enemy in part of Vietnam. He was charged with the premeditated murder of 22 infants, children, women and old men. His defence was that he was acting under the direct orders of his commanding officer; he had been told that under no circum-

---

[14] Charter of the International Military Tribunal, Cmnd. 6903 (1946) *United States* v. *Goering* at 42.
[15] *Per* Lord Hailsham in *Howe* [1987] A.C. 417 at p. 427. This view has not gone without challenge. See Glanville Williams, *Criminal Law, the General Part*, (1961), pp. 296–301 and Ian D. Brownlie, "Super-ior Orders—Time for a New Realism?" [1989] Crim.L.R. 395.
[16] *United States* v. *Kinder* (1953) A.C.M. 7321, 14 C.M.R. 742, *United States* v. *Quarles* 350 U.S. II (1955). Both cases arose from incidents in the Korean War.
[17] Ian D. Brownlie, *ante*, n. 15 at p. 396.

stances were they to leave Vietnamese alive as they passed through the villages. He was to "waste them."[18]

Quinn J.:

"[There is] ample evidence from which to find that Lieutenant Calley directed and personally participated in the intentional killing of men, women and children who were unarmed and in the custody of soldiers . . . [T]he uncontradicted evidence is that . . . they were offering no resistance. In his testimony, Calley admitted he was aware of the requirement that prisoners be treated with respect . . . he knew that the normal practice was to interrogate villagers, release those who could satisfactorily account for themselves and evacuate the suspect among them for further examination. . . .

We turn to the contention that the [trial] judge erred in his submission of the defense of superior orders to the court [by framing the instructions thus]: '[I]f you find that Lieutenant Calley received an order directing him to kill unresisting Vietnamese within his control . . . that order (as a matter of law) would be an illegal order. A determination that an order is illegal does not, of itself, assign criminal responsibility to the person following the order for acts done in compliance with it. . . . [such] acts of a subordinate . . . are excused and impose no criminal liability upon him unless the superior's order is one which a man of ordinary sense and understanding would, under the circumstances, know to be unlawful, or if the order in question is actually known to the accused to be unlawful.' . . .

[Defence counsel urged that this was too high a standard for soldiers who may not be persons of ordinary sense and understanding; they argued for a lower test of 'commonest understanding'] . . . [W]hether Lieutenant Calley was the most ignorant person in the United States Army in Vietnam or the most intelligent, he must be presumed to know that he could not kill the people involved here . . . [the order was] so palpably illegal that whatever conceptual difference there may be between a person of 'commonest understanding' and a person of 'common understanding,' that difference could not have had any impact on a court."

Decision of the Court of Military Review affirmed[19]

This approach of "manifest illegality" has been adopted in some parts of Australia as well as in the United States.[20] It has been argued that given the lack of decisive authority on the point and given the very special circumstances that exist in relation to the civil emergency in Northern Ireland where "military personnel are brought into closer contact with the civilian population and with the civilian law than is usual" and soldiers "are asked to play a role for which they are prepared neither by outlook nor (on the whole) by training"[21] that "the stringent

---

[18] The commanding officer claimed that no such order had been given.

[19] In the *New York Times*, April 10, 1971, Marshall Burke argued that to hold Calley personally accountable was unjust; rather that the whole nation was accountable and ought to push for the end of the war. In "The Meaning of Calley" The New Republic, Vol. 194, No. 19, pp. 13–14 Goldstein argued against this view: "if future wars must be fought, there [must] be some expectation that each participant will abide by minimum standards of conduct which a law of crimes is designed to maintain."

[20] In Queensland and Western Australia; Criminal Code, s.31(2).

[21] Ian D. Brownlie, [1989] Crim.L.R. 396 at p. 407.

denial of a superior orders defence . . . is inappropriate and unrealistic."[22]

Ian D. Brownlie, "Superior Orders—Time For a New Realism?" [1989] Crim.L.R. 396, at p. 411:

"It is inappropriate because the harm it is aimed at remedying, namely the abuse of executive fiat, is being perpetrated, if at all, by the superiors at various levels who have committed him to that situation. It is unrealistic because it requires the individual soldier to make decisions on legal niceties in situations where sometimes his or her military competence and perhaps even instinct for physical survival will compel instant obedience. The strict "no-defence" position is predicated upon assumptions about constitutional law and the possible consequences of allowing such a defence which cannot be demonstrated in practice. . . . On the contrary, therefore, it is submitted that courts should be allowed to decide the bona fides of such a defence on the basis that military orders which are not manifestly illegal may give rise to a mistake of law . . . [which should be relevant]. It is in this way that the interests of justice both for the individual soldier and for the wider civil society in which increasingly, the soldier is becoming involved, will best be served."

Given recent judicial pronouncements against both duress and necessity as defences to murder[23] it seems most unlikely that any change will take place in relation to superior orders. Moreover, there must remain grave doubts as to the wisdom of introducing a defence that would allow soldiers to kill innocent persons deliberately and claim that their actions were excused—or even justified!

G. Insanity

1. Introduction

(i) *The problem*

The defence of insanity brings into sharp focus many of the issues discussed in the previous chapters and has thus been the source of more debate and heart-searching than almost any other area of criminal law.[24]

Requiring a jury to decide whether a person accused of a crime is to be punished as criminal or "treated" as insane forces two major ques-

---

[22] *Ibid.*, at p. 411.
[23] *Ante*, pp. 323–328, 337–338.
[24] The importance the subject has attained is out of all proportion to its statistical importance; there are only about four successful pleas of insanity in any given year in this country. Rather it is the question of principle that has taxed the minds of academics. However, recent reseach by MacKay shows that the verdict is not quite as uncommon as the official statistics suggest, because they give figures for insanity verdicts in relation to murder only—*e.g* between 1975–88 there were 23 special verdicts in relation to non-fatal offences of violence: R. D. MacKay, "Fact and Fiction about the Insanity Defence "[1990] Crim.L.R. 247 at p. 248.

tions to the surface. The first addresses itself to the premise upon which the sane man is punished. We have seen[25] that inherent in the criminal justice system is a view of man as a responsible agent. He possesses freedom of will and can choose one course of action rather than another. If he steps outside the limits of legal action we are, therefore, justified in blaming and punishing him. By the same argument we cannot blame the person who did not have this ability to choose or control his actions.[26] The insanity defence thus seeks to distinguish the responsible from those lacking responsibility.[27] The difficulty lies, as we shall see, in determining where the line between sanity and responsibility on the one hand, and insanity and irresponsibility on the other, is to be drawn. It has been increasingly argued that absolute states of sanity and insanity rarely (if ever) exist; instead there are shades of sanity. This attitude towards sanity and responsibility has expressed itself in a number of forms. For some commentators it has necessitated a more rigorous approach to the search for the crucial dividing line. For them the question of ascertaining who is responsible has been made more important, not less. The same doubt in others has, however, led to demands that the insanity defence (or the concept of responsibility itself) be abolished.[28] As we shall see, however, where the insanity defence has been abolished or amended in some of the states in the United States, it has clearly been in response to criticisms other than those concerning the principle of responsibility.[29]

Secondly, and closely related to the first question, if the premise upon which we punish is responsibility, what are the objectives of the criminal law when it punishes the sane man?[30] How are these objectives affected when it comes to the punishment of the insane?

Stephen J. Morse, "Retaining a Modified Insanity Defense" (1985) The Annals 137 at p. 138:

"The basic moral issue is whether it is just to hold responsible and punish a person who was terribly crazy at the time of the offense. . . .

There is virtually unanimous agreement today that desert is a necessary prerequisite for criminal punishment. Although many advocate a mixed theory of the criminal sanction that blends desert and utilitarian justifications, virtually none advocates a purely utilitarian theory. Consequently, only morally responsible actors may fairly be convicted and punished. Any condition or circum-

---

[25] *Ante*, p. 149.

[26] H. Gross, *A Theory of Criminal Justice*, pp. 298–305, points out that three contentions may be involved. It may, first, be thought that it is wrong in these situations to punish the accused *for being sick*, or secondly that it is wrong to punish someone for what he does *as a result of being sick*, or lastly that it is cruel to add to the suffering of someone who is sick; in other words that it is wrong to punish someone *when he is sick*.

[27] Baroness Wootton distinguishes between "the criminally responsible goats and the medically irresponsible sheep." *Crime and Penal Policy* (1978) p. 228.

[28] *Post*, p. 366.

[29] *Post*, p. 367.

[30] *Ante*, Chap. 1.

stance that sufficiently compromises responsibility will negate desert and must be incorporated in a just criminal law's doctrines of excuse."

Abraham Goldstein, The Insanity Defense (1967), pp. 11–15:

"At the present time, the objectives of the criminal law are ordinarily said to be retribution, deterrence and rehabilitation. . . . The *retributive* function building on the widely held feeling that the criminal owes the community a measure of suffering comparable to that which he has inflicted . . . channelled the anger of victims (and of their friends) lest they . . . [sought] revenge. But to do so, it was necessary to make a criminal conviction sufficiently consequential to satisfy those who were inclined to feel retributive . . . A corollary of this, however, was the feeling that so serious a sanction ought not to be imposed in situations in which the initial impulse to anger was likely to give way, even among victims, to feelings of compassion. These were situations in which the offender seemed so obviously different from most men that he could not be blamed for what he had done. Even under a retributive theory, therefore, an insanity defense was needed to trace in outline those who could not be regarded as blameworthy. . . .

Under the *deterrent* theory—which is probably the dominant one—the primary function of criminal law is to move men to conform to social norms, particularly those which cannot be left entirely to informal processes of social control or to those of the civil law. This is accomplished by announcing in a criminal code what conduct is prohibited and how much of a sanction of imprisonment or fine will be visited upon those who ignore the prohibition. Such a system can be effective only with men who can understand the signals directed at them by the code, who can respond to the warnings, and who feel the significance of the sanctions imposed upon violators. . . . If a man cannot make the calculations or muster the feelings demanded of him by the theory, he is classed as insane. He lacks the requisite degree of intelligence, reasoning power and foresight of consequence. If he were held criminally responsible he would be made to suffer harsh sanction without serving the purpose of individual deterrence.

It would still be possible, however, to conceive that such a man might serve the ends of general deterrence . . . [but]the examples are likely to deter only if the person who is not involved in the criminal process regards the lessons as applicable to him. He is likely to do so only if he identifies with the offender and with the offending situation. This feat of identification is difficult enough to achieve under ordinary circumstances . . . it is probably hopeless if the deterrent example is so different from most men that the crime can be attributed to the difference. Yet it is difficult to avoid the suspicion that the 'public' is not watching all that closely whose punishment is held up to it by way of example and that talk of 'identification' masks a fundamental limit upon how far one may use law as an instrument of terror. . . .

The third view of the insanity . . . tends to view deviant behaviour as psychological maladjustment, the product of forces beyond the individual's control; he is less to be blamed than to be helped to restore the balance between him and his background or his environment. The tacit assumption is that a paternal state can put him right by psychotherapy or by judicious social planning, if only the 'helping' professions are provided with the resources to do the job. . . . This 'mental health' image has unquestionably captured the imagination of the reformers and has been propagated almost as a faith. . . .

Because it is widely assumed that 'blame' plays a critical role in maintaining individual responsibility and social order, the insanity defense continues to be regarded as exceptional. It becomes the occasional device through which an offender is found to be inappropriate for the social purposes served by the criminal law. He is too much unlike the man in the street to permit his example to be useful for the purposes of deterrence. He is too far removed from normality to make us angry with him. But because he is sick rather than evil, society is cast as specially responsible for him and obligated to make him better."

(ii) *Is the insanity defence really a "defence" at all?*

The issue of insanity is invariably included in discussions of defences to crime, yet this classification is not without its difficulties. To make the statement that a defendant has a defence to crime has connotations that may or may not prove to be applicable to the case of insanity. Three matters, in particular, require consideration.

(a) Is insanity regarded as a general condition or as a specific excuse to a particular wrongful act? If the former is accepted then insanity is akin to the condition of infancy which makes children unaccountable for their actions; it prevents the courts having *criminal* jurisdiction over them. One could certainly accept the logic of the case for regarding insanity in such a light.[31] This, however, seems not to be so; as we shall see, the wording of the test of insanity (the M'Naghten Rules) links the mental condition of the accused causally to the prohibited *act*. Insanity thus operates as an excuse for a particular crime and is more akin to a defence like duress than infancy. What the defence conveys is that although grievous wrong may have been done, the actor has to be excused from blame because of his mental condition at the time of the act.

(b) Is insanity a true defence or does it negate a definitional element? We may properly raise the question here in a preliminary form, although full consideration must be deferred until the various tests of insanity have been explored. We may then examine the validity of the claim that to raise the "defence" of insanity is in reality to plead lack of *mens rea*.

(c) Is insanity a "defence" in name only—in view of the effects of a finding of insanity?

Abraham Goldstein, The Insanity Defence (1967), pp. 19–20:

"In virtually every state,[32] a successful insanity defense does not bring freedom with it. Instead, it has become the occasion for either mandatory commitment to a mental hospital or for an exercise of discretion by the court regarding the advisability of such commitment. And because the commitment is for treatment, it continues until such time as the hospital authorities conclude the patient is ready for release. The defense has become, therefore, a way of avoiding one species of state control and of substituting another for it. It fuses criminal law with a species of administrative law, shifting the defendant from a criminal process to a civil-medical one which explicitly incorporates elements of

---

[31] See H. Packer, *The Limits of the Criminal Sanction*, p. 134.
[32] Including England. See P. Robinson: "Criminal Law Defences: A Systematic Analysis" (1982) 82 Col.L.R. 247, note 182 for a detailed analysis of United States provisions on mandatory commitment.

preventive detention. In substance, defendant may make out his defense only if he authorizes the court to protect the community from him.

The man who is insane, therefore, may not fare differently from the man who is sane and guilty, except in capital cases where the insanity defense may save his life. For the rest, the advantage he enjoys is that he suffers no formal judgment of condemnation . . . and the institution to which he is sent is ostensibly dedicated to the ideal of treating his illness and making him better. But he must weigh those advantages against the fact that his detention is for an entirely indeterminate period; that he may be kept in a hospital as long or longer than he would have remained in prison; and that being regarded as mentally ill may bring him as much stigma, economic deprivation, family dislocation, and often as little treatment or physical comfort as being a criminal."[33]

In England, the result of a successful plea of insanity is the special verdict of not guilty by reason of insanity.[34] The court is then obliged to make an order of commitment whereby the defendant is detained at the Queen's Pleasure in a hospital to be selected by the Home Secretary[35]— usually one of the secure hospitals of Mosside, Rampton, Broadmoor and Park Lane. He is detained there until the Home Secretary directs release.[36]

2. The law

Our discussion of insanity relates to insanity as a "defence" in a criminal trial only. In other words, it proceeds on the basis that the defendant has sufficient powers of comprehension to be tried at all—he has been found "fit to plead."[37] Some offenders are so fundamentally disordered that such an initial finding is not possible. The effect of this is that the *most* extreme cases rarely fall to be determined under the insanity defence which is reserved instead for problematic and borderline cases.

(i) *The M'Naghten Rules*

M'Naghten's Case (1843) 10 C & F, 200, 8 Eng. Rep. 718

The defendant was indicted for the murder of Edward Drummond, Secretary to the Prime Minister, Sir Robert Peel. The defence introduced evidence of the defendant's insanity, particularly his obsession with certain morbid delusions. The presiding judge, Lord Tindal C.J., directed the jury in the following terms: "The question to be asked is whether . . . the prisoner had or had not the use of his understanding, so as to know that he was doing a wrong and wicked act." The jury returned a verdict of not guilty by reason of insanity. The furore occasioned by the verdict led to the whole issue of insanity being debated in the

---

[33] See H. Packer, *The Limits of the Criminal Sanction*, p. 134.
[34] Criminal Procedure (Insanity) Act 1964, s.1.
[35] *Ibid.*, s.5(1).
[36] *Ibid.*, Sched. 1, para. 2.
[37] He must be able to understand the charge, realise the difference between the pleas of guilty and not guilty, able to challenge jurors, instruct counsel and to follow the evidence. If found unfit under the Criminal Procedure (Insanity) Act 1964, s.4, the court will order admission to such hospital as specified by the Home Secretary without limitation of time. See Smith and Hogan, pp. 182–185.

House of Lords. As a result, five questions were put to the judges of the day; the answers to questions two and three form the basis of the "M'Naghten Rules" by which lack of criminal responsibility is tested.

> Lord Tindal C.J.:
> "Your lordships are pleased to inquire of us, secondly, 'What are the proper questions to be submitted to the jury, where a person alleged to be afflicted with insane delusion respecting one or more particular subjects or persons, is charged with the commission of a crime (murder, for example), and insanity is set up as a defence?' And, thirdly, 'In what terms ought the question to be left to the jury as to the prisoner's state of mind at the time when the act was committed?' And as these two questions appear to us to be more conveniently answered together, we have to submit our opinion to be, that the jurors ought to be told in all cases that every man is to be presumed to be sane, and to possess a sufficient degree of reason to be responsible for his crimes, until the contrary be proved to their satisfaction; and that *to establish a defence on the ground of insanity, it must be clearly proved that, at the time of the committing of the act, the party accused was labouring under such a defect of reason, from disease of the mind, as not to know the nature and quality of the act he was doing; or, if he did know it, that he did not know he was doing what was wrong.* The mode of putting the latter part of the question to the jury on these occasions has generally been, whether the accused at the time of doing the act knew the difference between right and wrong: which mode, though rarely, if ever, leading to any mistake with the jury, is not, as we conceive, so accurate when put generally and in the abstract, as when put with reference to the party's knowledge of right and wrong in respect to the very act with which he is charged. If the question were to be put as to the knowledge of the accused solely and exclusively with reference to the law of the land, it might tend to confound the jury, by inducing them to believe that an actual knowledge of the law of the land was essential in order to lead to a conviction; whereas the law is administered upon the principle that every one must be taken conclusively to know it, without proof that he does know it. If the accused was conscious that the act was one which he ought not to do, and if the act was at the same time contrary to the law of the land, he is punishable; and the usual course therefore has been to leave the question to the jury, whether the party accused had a sufficient degree of reason to know that he was doing an act that was wrong: and this course we think is correct, accompanied with such observations and explanations as the circumstances of each particular case may require." (Emphasis added)

Although the essence of the M'Naghten Rules may be simply stated—it asks whether the defendant knew what he was doing at the time the crime was committed—certain of the phrases used in the formulation of the rules have been subject to much judicial (and academic) interpretation. It is not our purpose to enter into a detailed analysis[38] of such phrases but some indication of the flavour of the interpretations is useful.

One can envisage the M'Naghten Rules as a series of hurdles over which the defendant must jump in order to be excused liability.

He must, first, be suffering from a *"disease of the mind."* The case of *Kemp*[39] (where the defendant suffered from arteriosclerosis which

---

[38] Which has been thoroughly done elsewhere: See Smith and Hogan, pp. 185–197.
[39] [1975] 1 Q.B. 399.

induced a state of unconsciousness in which he attacked his wife with a hammer) makes it clear that the condition of the brain may be irrelevant. The test is not necessarily whether there is some damage to that physical entity (although the mental disease may have a physical origin) but, more widely, whether the mental faculties of reason, understanding and memory are impaired or absent. This approach has recently been affirmed by the House of Lords.

R. v Sullivan [1984] A.C. 156 (House of Lords)

The defendant was charged with inflicting grievous bodily harm, contrary to section 20 of the Offences Against the Person Act 1861, after he had attacked Payne, his friend, during the post-ictal stage of an epileptic seizure. The trial judge ruled that this amounted to insanity rather than automatism; consequently the defendant changed his plea to guilty to the lesser offence of assault occasioning actual bodily harm. He then appealed against conviction on the basis that he should have been allowed to raise the issue of automatism.[40]

Lord Diplock:
"The M'Naghten Rules have been used as a comprehensive definition for this purpose by the courts for the last 140 years. Most importantly, they were so used by this House in *Bratty* v. *Attorney-General for Northern Ireland* [1963] A.C. 386. That case was in some respects the converse of the instant case. Bratty was charged with murdering a girl by strangulation. He claimed to have been unconscious of what he was doing at the time he strangled the girl and he sought to run as alternative defences non-insane automatism and insanity. The only evidential foundation that he laid for either of these pleas was medical evidence that he might have been suffering from psychomotor epilepsy which, if he were, would account for his having been unconscious of what he was doing. No other pathological explanation of his actions having been carried out in a state of automatism was supported by evidence. The trial judge first put the defence of insanity to the jury. The jury rejected it; they declined to bring in the special verdict. Thereupon, the judge refused to put to the jury the alternative defence of automatism. His refusal was upheld by the Court of Criminal Appeal of Norther Ireland and subsequently by this House.

The question before this House was whether, the jury having rejected the plea of insanity, there was any evidence on non-insane automatism fit to be left to the jury. The ratio decidendi of its dismissal of the appeal was that the jury having negatived the explanation that Bratty might have been acting unconsciously in the course of an attack of psychomotor epilepsy, there was no evidential foundation for the suggestion that he was acting unconsciously from any other cause.

In the instant case, as in *Bratty*, the only evidential foundation that was laid for any finding by the jury that Mr. Sullivan was acting unconsciously and involuntarily when he was kicking Mr. Payne, was that when he did so he was in the post-ictal stage of a seizure of psychomotor epilepsy. The evidential foundation in the case of Bratty, that he was suffering from psychomotor epilepsy at the time he did the act with which he was charged, was very weak and was rejected by the jury; the evidence in Mr. Sullivan's case, that he was so suffering when he was kicking Mr. Payne, was very strong and would almost inevitably be accepted by a properly directed jury. It would be the duty of the judge to

---

[40] For an informative discussion of the medical background to this case, see G. N. Eastman, "Defending the Mentally Ill" in *Psychiatry and the Criminal Law*, (1986), eds. R. MacKay and K. Russell.

direct the jury that if they did accept that evidence the law required them to bring in a special verdict and none other. The governing statutory provision is to be found in section 2 of the Trial of Lunatics Act 1883. This says 'the jury *shall* return a special verdict . . . '

My Lords, I can deal briefly with the various grounds on which it has been submitted that the instant case can be distinguished from what constituted the ratio decidendi in *Bratty* v. *Attorney-General for Northern Ireland* [1963] A.C. 386, and that it falls outside the ambit of the M'Naghten Rules.

First, it is submitted the medical evidence in the instant case shows that psychomotor epilepsy is not a disease of the mind, whereas in *Bratty* it was accepted by all the doctors that it was. The only evidential basis for this submission is that Dr. Fenwick said that in medical terms to constitute a 'disease of the mind' or 'mental illness,' which he appeared to regard as interchangeable descriptions, a disorder of brain functions (which undoubtedly occurs during a seizure in psychomotor epilepsy) must be prolonged for a period of time usually more than a day; while Dr. Taylor would have it that the disorder must continue for a minimum of a month to qualify for the description 'a disease of the mind.'

The nomenclature adopted by the medical profession may change from time to time; Bratty was tried in 1961. But the meaning of the expression 'disease of the mind' as the cause of 'a defect of reason' remains unchanged for the purposes of the application of the M'Naghten Rules. I agree with what was said by Devlin J. in *Reg.* v. *Kemp* [1957] 1 Q.B. 399, 407, that 'mind' in the M'Naghten Rules is used in the ordinary sense of the mental faculties of reason, memory and understanding. If the effect of a disease is to impair these faculties so severely as to have either of the consequences referred to in the latter part of the rules, it matters not whether the aetiology of the impairment is organic, as in epilepsy, or functional, or whether the impairment itself is permanent or is transient and intermittent, provided that it subsisted at the time of commission of the act. The purpose of the legislation relating to the defence of insanity, ever since its origin in 1800, has been to protect society against recurrence of the dangerous conduct. The duration of a temporary suspension of the mental faculties, of reason, memory and understanding, particularly if, as in Mr. Sullivan's case, it is recurrent, cannot on any rational ground be relevant to the application by the courts of the M'Naghten Rules, though it may be relevant to the course adopted by the Secretary of State, to whom the responsibility for how the defendant is to be dealt with passes after the return of the special verdict 'not guilty by reason of insanity.'

To avoid misunderstanding I ought perhaps to add that in expressing my agreement with what was said by Devlin J. in *Kemp*, where the disease that caused the temporary and intermittent impairment of the mental faculties was arteriosclerosis, I do not regard that learned judge as excluding the possibility of non-insane automatism (for which the proper verdict would be a verdict of 'not guilty') in cases where temporary impairment (not being self-induced by consuming drink or drugs) results from some external physical factor such as a blow on the head causing concussion or the administration of an anaesthetic for therapeutic purposes. I mention this because in *Reg.* v. *Quick* [1973] Q.B. 910, Lawton L.J. appears to have regarded the ruling in *Kemp* as going as far as this. If it had done, it would have been inconsistent with the speeches in this House in *Bratty*, [1963] A.C. 386, where *Kemp* was alluded to without disapproval by Viscount Kilmuir L.C., at p. 403, and received the express approval of Lord Denning, at p. 411. The instant case, however, does not in my view afford an appropriate occasion for exploring possible casues of non-insane automatism.

The only other submission in support of Mr. Sullivan's appeal which I think it necessary to mention is that, because the expert evidence was to the effect that

Mr. Sullivan's acts in kicking Mr. Payne were unconscious and thus 'involuntary' in the legal sense of that term, his state of mind was not one dealt with by the M'Naghten Rules at all, since it was not covered by the phrase 'as not to know the nature and quality of the act he was doing.' Quite apart from being contrary to all three speeches in this House in *Bratty* v. *Attorney-General for Northern Ireland* [1963] A.C. 386, this submission appears to me, with all respect to counsel, to be quite unarguable. Dr. Fenwick himself accepted it as an accurate description of Mr. Sullivan's mental state in the post-ictal stage of a seizure. The audience to whom the phrase in the M'Naghten Rules was addressed consisted of peers of the realm in the 1840's when a certain orotundity of diction had not yet fallen out of fashion. Addressed to an audience of jurors in the 1980's it might more aptly be expressed as 'He did not know what he was doing.'

My Lords, it is natural to feel reluctant to attach the label of insanity to a sufferer from psychomotor epilepsy of the kind to which Mr. Sullivan was subject, even though the expression in the context of a special verdict of 'not guilty by reason of insanity' is a technical one which includes a purely temporary and intermittent suspension of the mental faculties of reason, memory and understanding resulting from the occurrence of an epileptic fit. But the label is contained in the current statute, it has appeared in this statute's predecessors ever since 1800. It does not lie within the power of the courts to alter it. Only Parliament can do that. It has done so twice; it could do so once again.

Sympathise though I do with Mr. Sullivan, I see no other course open to your Lordships than to dismiss this appeal."

Appeal dismissed

Whilst at one level this case merely "confirm(s) the status quo,"[41] in the sense that it has long been recognised that psychomotor epilepsy is a "disease of the mind," and judges before Lord Diplock have referred to the test of dangerousness that is thought to be able to illuminate the "grey area between insanity and automation,"[42] this case is, nevertheless, highly significant.

It reveals not only that a *temporary* absence of reasoning powers of *very* limited duration may amount to a "disease of the mind," but that the distinction drawn between external and internal factors is of crucial importance. Epileptic fits are regarded as arising from an internal condition, as are hyperglycaemic states.[43] Hypoglycaemic states, on the other hand, arising from the combination of diabetes, insulin, food (or lack of it) and possibly alcohol, are not so regarded.[44] Sleep-walking, which has been described as a "near cousin" of epilepsy,[45] may well occur because of an internal factor—there is some evidence of a link between it and abnormal E.E.G. readings.

Does this mean that all epileptics (0·5 per cent. of the population) and

---

[41] Celia Wells, "Whither Insanity?" [1983] Crim.L.R. 787.
[42] *Isitt* [1978] 67 Cr.App.R. 44 at 49, *per* Lawton L.J.; *Bratty* v. *Att-Gen for N.I.* [1963] A.C. 386.
[43] *Hennessey* (1989) 89 Cr.App.R. 10, *ante*, p. 112.
[44] *Quick* [1973] Q.B. 910; *Bailey* [1983] 1 W.L.R. 760. *Ante* p. 114.
[45] G. N. Eastman, "Defending the Mentally Ill" in *Psychiatry and the Criminal Law*, (1986), eds. R. MacKay and K. Russell.

all sleepwalkers are now at risk of an insanity verdict?[46] Lord Diplock cannot circumvent his reluctance in attaching the label of insanity to defendants such as Sullivan by saying that the label is merely a "technical" one. What his misgivings demonstrate is a two-fold problem.

First, if Lord Diplock is right in saying that the purpose of the insanity test is, and always has been, to identify the dangerous from the non-dangerous (who may safely be acquitted on the basis of sane automatism), then is it the case that epileptics are any more dangerous than diabetics?[47] Or even more problematically, are diabetics in a hyperglycaemic state any more dangerous than diabetics in a hypoglycaemic state? The internal/external factor distinction does not seem well-designed to constitute a test of dangerousness.

Secondly, faced with the prospect of an insanity verdict, defendants will change their pleas, just as Sullivan did, to guilty.[48] Not only does this place unacceptable pressure upon them, but, if the isolation of the dangerous is our main concern, it is questionable whether they should be allowed to do so—conviction for some lesser offence may not lead to a sentence of imprisonment.[49]

Both of these flaws highlight not only the failure of the internal/external factor distinction, but also what many commentators have perceived to be a more fundamental failure of the insanity test (and perhaps, any insanity test) to come to terms with the issue of the responsibility of the individual defendant on the one hand, and the protection of the public (and the defendant himself) against harm on the other. We shall return to this question later, once the remaining elements of the test of insanity, and proposed reform thereof, have been considered.[50]

Assuming that the defendant is suffering from a disease of the mind, the next hurdle to be overcome is that this disease of the mind must induce a "defect of reason." The reasoning ability of the defendant must be affected; it is not enough that he simply failed to use powers of reasoning which he had.[51] This aspect of the insanity test is classically illustrative of one of the basic premise's of responsibility in law; guilt cannot be adduced in the absence of the *capacity* to reason.

Having passed over the initial hurdles the defendant may be brought within the ambit of the special verdict if he can satisfy either of two

[46] But see *ante*, p. 112 the case of *Lilienfield* where a sleep-walker was found not guilty on the basis of non-insane automatism.

[47] See Celia Wells, "Whither Insanity?" [1983] Crim.L.R. 787 at 791–792.

[48] The defendant in *Hennessey* also changed his plea to guilty; *ante*, p. 112. Mackay, however, suggests that the fear of indefinite (and prolonged) detention that makes defendants change their pleas may be exaggerated—that there is a realistic prospect of quick release for a substantial number: R. D. Mackay, "Fact and Fiction about the Insanity Defence" [1990] Crim. L.R. 247 at pp. 251–255.

[49] However, under the Mental Health Act 1983, s.37, the court does have power to make a hospital order if the defendant is convicted of an imprisonable offence, if certain further conditions are satisfied. *Cf.* A. Ashworth and L. Gostin, "Mentally Disordered Offenders and the Sentencing Process" [1984] Crim.L.R. 195 and J. Hamilton, "Sentencing the Mentally Disordered" in *Psychiatry and the Criminal Law* (1986) eds. R. MacKay and K. Russell.

[50] *Post*, p. 362.

[51] *Clarke* [1972] 1 All E.R. 219.

further conditions. The first is vividly described by Kenny's example: "The madman who cuts a woman's throat under the idea that he is cutting a loaf of bread"[52] does not know the "nature and quality of his act." The second, and alternative, hurdle causes more difficulty. The defendant will not be found responsible for his actions if he does not know them to be wrong. This has been held to mean that he does not know them to be legally and not morally wrong.[53]

The courts have made it plain from *M'Naghten* onwards that they regard all these questions as legal ones for their determination with the aid of a jury.[54] Medical evidence is, in theory, just that—evidence from which decisions can be made. However, there can be little doubt that a large part of the burden of decision-making rests with the medical expert. He may not be asked baldly, "Do you think this man insane?" (the word would be of no medical significance to him anyway) but he could well be asked, "Do you think this man has a disease of the mind?" The intermingling of medical and legal concepts is fraught with danger. Not only may medical experts fundamentally disagree amongst themselves about a particular diagnosis but they may, if their sympathies are engaged with their "patient," distort their evidence to fit the "manifest absurdity of the M'Naghten test."[55] Further, neither judiciary nor medical experts seem wholly convinced about their role in the adjudication process. Even if they are clear in their own minds the juries may ignore their representations and ask themselves simply "Is this man mad, or not?"[56]

Two much publicised cases highlight the battle between judge, expert and jury. In *Sutcliffe*,[57] despite substantial evidence that the defendant lacked mental responsibility for his actions, the jury rejected a plea of diminished responsibility, preferring to believe either that the "Yorkshire Ripper" had invented his stories of hallucinations and delusions of God-given missions to kill prostitutes, or that despite some truth in them, his responsibility was not radically impaired. In the United States, just as much concern was expressed from different quarters about the finding of insanity on John Hinckley,[58] the man who attempted to murder President Reagan. Critics took the view that Hinckley's story of an obsession with a film star, his plan to have a

---

[52] Kenny, *Outlines of Criminal Law*, (17th ed.), p. 76.

[53] *Windle* [1952] 2 Q.B. 826. It is commonly thought that this hurdle adds very little to the test, but recent research suggests that it is this hurdle that is most commonly used to secure a special verdict: R. D. Mackay, "Fact and Fiction about the Insanity Defence" [1990] Crim. L.R. 247 at p. 250.

[54] The burden of proof rests on the defence, in contrast to the general rule, who have to prove their case on a balance of probabilities.

[55] Royal Commission on Capital Punishment, Cmnd. 8932 (1953), p. 104.

[56] Cooper L.J. in testimony to the Royal Commission on Capital Punishment. *Ibid.* p. 113.

[57] *The Times*, May 23, 1983. The case actually concerned diminished responsibility (*post*, p. 370); both prosecution and defence had agreed to this plea, but the trial judge, Boreham J., refused to accept it and insisted that it go to the jury. For a discussion of this case, see H. Prins, "Diminished Responsibility and the Sutcliffe case: Legal, Psychiatric and Social Aspects," (1983) 23 Med. Sci. Law 17.

[58] *U.S.A.* v. *Hinckley* Criminal No. 81, 306 U.S. Dt. Ct. for the District of Columbia, 525 F. Supp. 1342, Nov. 17, 1981.

"love-in-death unification" with her and his delusion of acting out a movie script, was a cloak of confusion; he was a sane, "rich kid" aided by an expensive psychiatrist. The cases of *Hinckley* and *Sutcliffe* added momentum to the movement for reform in both countries; in the United States President Reagan threw his support behind those who wanted restriction or even abolition of the insanity defence[59]; in England the M'Naghten Rules have been subjected to yet further criticism.

Report of the Committee on Mentally Abnormal Offenders (Butler Committee), Cmnd. 6244 (1975) pp. 217–219:

"18.5 Almost throughout their existence the M'Naghten Rules have been criticised, generally as being based on too limited a concept of the nature of mental disorder. The Royal Commission on Capital Punishment in 1953 noted that the interpretation of the rules by the courts had been broadened and stretched to make them fit particular cases, to the point where 'the gap between the natural meaning of the law and the sense in which it is commonly applied has for so long been so wide, it is impossible to escape the conclusion that an amendment of the law, to bring it into closer conformity with the current practice, is long overdue.' The Royal Commission pointed out that many offenders who know what they are doing and that it is wrong are nevertheless undoubtedly insane and should not be held responsible for their actions. Another serious difficulty lies in the outmoded language of the rules which gives rise to problems of interpretation. It is unclear, for example, whether the reference to the knowledge of the accused of the nature and quality of his act should be taken to cover the whole mental element in crime or some narrower concept. Similarly the nineteenth century term 'disease of the mind' raises the question whether the rules are intended to cover severe subnormality, neurosis or psychopathy.

18.6 But the main defect of the M'Naghten test is that it was based on the now obsolete belief in the pre-eminent role of reason in controlling social behaviour. It therefore requires evidence of the cognitive capacity, in particular the knowledge and understanding of the defendant at the time of the act or omission charged. Contemporary psychiatry and psychology emphasise that man's social behaviour is determined more by how he has learned to behave than by what he knows or understands. For many years a number of mental disorders differing in their clinical characteristics have been recognised and distinguished from one another. In some disorders the patient's beliefs are so bizarre or his change of mood is so profound and inexplicable, or he is so changed in manner and conduct, that his condition can only be described as alien, or mad. In such cases it is accepted opinion in civilised countries that he should not be held responsible for his actions.

18.7 Strictly interpreted the M'Naghten Rules would provide that mentally disordered defendant with very limited protection. Just as a person must generally be very mad indeed not to know what he is doing (the nature and quality of his act) when he is killing a man or setting fire to a building, so he must be very mad not to know that these acts attract the unfavourable notice of the police (his knowledge of wrong). For example, if a psychotic patient kills a person whom he believes to be putting thoughts into his mind, or kills him and gives as a reason that the victim is spying on him, or simply kills him because he has an overpowering urge to do so, the M'Naghten Rules, strictly interpreted, will not

[59] *Post*, p. 367.

give him a defence if he admits that he knew that he was killing a man and that murder was a crime.

18.8 The M'Naghten Rules are in part linked with the *mens rea* doctrine, in recognising that evidence of disease of the mind may have the effect of negativing a mental element of the crime. The 'knowledge of wrong' test is not an application of the ordinary rules of *mens rea*, however. 'Wrong' has been held to mean 'legally wrong' and a sane defendant cannot set up a defence of ignorance of the criminal law. Knowledge of the law is hardly an appropriate test on which to base ascription of criminal responsibility to the mentally disordered. It is a very narrow ground of exemption since even persons who are grossly disturbed generally know that murder and arson, for instance, are crimes. It might seem at first sight more attractive to have regard to the defendant's appreciation of what is morally wrong, but the problems in applying such a test to the mentally disordered would be very great. 'Knowledge of wrong,' as included in M'Naghten, is not therefore a satisfactory test of criminal responsibility."

The Rules do still, however, have their defenders.

American Law Institute, Model Penal Code Tent. Draft. No. 4 (1955), comments to § 4.01 pp. 156–157:

"The traditional M'Naghten rule resolves the problem solely in regard to the capacity of the individual to know what he was doing and to know that it was wrong. Absent these minimal elements of rationality, condemnation and punishment are obviously both unjust and futile. They are unjust because the individual could not, by hypothesis, have employed reason to restrain the act; he did not and he could not know the facts essential to bring reason into play. On the same ground, they are futile. A madman who believes that he is squeezing lemons when he chokes his wife or thinks that homicide is the command of God is plainly beyond reach of the restraining influence of law; he needs restraint but condemnation is entirely meaningless and ineffective. Thus the attacks on the M'Naghten rule as an inept definition of insanity or as an arbitrary definition in terms of special symptoms are entirely misconceived. The rationale of the position is that these are cases in which reason can not operate and in which it is totally impossible for individuals to be deterred. Moreover, the category defined by the rule is so extreme that to the ordinary man the exculpation of the person it encompasses bespeaks no weakness in the law. He does not identify such persons and himself; they are a world apart."[60]

Does this satisfactorily answer the criticisms?

(ii) *Durham formula*

In the United States dissatisfaction with the M'Naghten Rules expressed itself in the 1950s with an alternative test of insanity: the so-called Durham Formula[61] under which the defendant is not criminally responsible if his unlawful act was the product of mental disease or

---

[60] See also Devlin, "Mental Abnormality and the Criminal Law" in *Changing Legal Objectives*, ed. R. St. J. MacDonald (1963).
[61] Propounded in *Durham* v. *United States* (1954) 214 F 2d 862.

mental defect. This apparently straight-forward test was adopted in many states of the United States: it was hoped that it would greatly facilitate the identification of the person not deserving of blame and answer the defects in the M'Naghten Rules. In one respect it probably did; the "Durham" formula was wider than the M'Naghten test which has always been thought to be too restrictive a defence.

In *Durham*, the defendant was suffering from a psychosis with a psychopathic personality.[62] He heard voices, had hallucinations, and felt that he was being watched by his fellow employees. The psychiatrist agreed that he had a "disease of the mind" and it was found that his acts were a "product" of his illness. He was, therefore, found insane. Had Durham been tried in England he would not have been able to rely upon the insanity defence for he would have failed to satisfy the further conditions necessary. The psychiatrist had testified: "If the question of right and wrong were propounded to him he could give you the right answer."

Whilst removing one of the objections to the M'Naghten Rules, however, the Durham formula failed to achieve its other main purpose. The Durham formula had been designed to reduce the role of the medical expert. It failed to do so. By leaving the crucial terms "mental disease or mental defect" undefined, the Durham formula was doomed from the start, for psychiatrists were required to interpret these words in every case. Despite judicial attempts[63] after *Durham* to clarify and minimise the role of the expert, Judge Bazelon, the judge responsible for the formulation of the Durham approach, concluded:

"In the end, after 18 years, I favoured the abandonment of the Durham approach because in practice it had failed to take the issue of criminal responsibility away from the experts. Psychiatrists continued to testify to the naked conclusion instead of providing information about the accused so that the jury could render the ultimate moral judgment about blameworthiness. Durham had secured little improvement over M'Naghten."[64]

We might add that in one respect the Durham formula might actually have made things worse than under M'Naghten. The Durham formula is sometimes aptly referred to as the "product" rule, aptly, because the question of a causal connection between the mental disease and prohibited act is made far more important under Durham than under M'Naghten (where the condition has to be so extreme that a causal requirement adds little). It is, however, very difficult to assert that a specific act is the "product" of a certain mental disease or defect.

---

[62] The term psychopath or sociopath (sometimes referred to as a personality disorder) has been the subject of fierce controversy; some claim that it is a valid medical diagnosis (corresponding to the layman's idea of an aggressive, habitual, indifferent criminal), others that it is nothing more than a "waste-paper basket" category. See the Butler Committee on Mentally Abnormal Offenders, Cmnd. 6244 pp. 81–87.

[63] *E.g. Blocker* v. *United States* 274 F 2d 572 D.C. (1959).

[64] "Psychiatrists and the Adversary Process" 230 *Scientific American* (1974), 18 at 21.

American Law Institute, Model Penal Code, Tent. Draft. No. 4, (1955), comments to § 4.01, p. 159:

"The difficulty with [the Durham] formulation inheres in the ambiguity of 'product.' If interpreted to lead to irresponsibility unless the defendant would have engaged in the criminal conduct even if he had not suffered from the disease or defect, it is too broad: an answer that he would have done can be given very rarely; this is intrinsic to the concept of the singleness of personality and unity of mental processes that psychiatry regards as fundamental."

An even more fundamental attack on the principle of a causal relationship is possible.

T. S. Szasz, "Psychiatry, Ethics and the Criminal Law," (1958) 58 Col.L.R. 183, 191–192:

"Suppose a man 'goes berserk,' pulls out a gun in broad daylight, and shoots down several people who are sightseeing in front of the White House. When arrested and questioned about his deed, he explains that he was protecting the President from communist assassins who were about to throw an atomic bomb on the White House lawn. . . .

The very occurrence of the crime—of almost any crime today—functions as a powerful impetus for the creation of a theory to explain it. Everyone wants to know what happened, and, indeed, everyone forms his own theory, on the basis of his own level of educational and technical sophistication. The psychiatrist, in this sense, is equipped to formulate a more sophisticated and necessarily more complicated theory than the layman. Similarly, the theoretical physicist has a more sophisticated theory of how electricity flows in a wire than does the layman. Indeed, the former may express his theory in mathematical equations whereas the latter pictures the process as consisting of electrons, visualized as little balls rolling along on little copper rails. In any case, does the theory of electric flow in a wire *cause* the light bulb to glow and the radio to play? Clearly, this question itself is improper. Similarly, I maintain that it is utter nonsense to ask, much less to answer, whether in the hypothetical case cited the murderer's 'schizophrenia' was the cause of his criminal act. An explanation or theory can never be a cause.

What, then, it may be asked, did cause the killer to shoot these people whom he did not even know? This question can be answered, more or less satisfactorily, and psychiatry can contribute much to providing such answers. But such answers, I hasten to add, are of no use to a jury. In general, the 'causes,' as I would conceive of them, of such a 'schizophrenic murder' may be arranged in a temporal hierarchy ranging from the way the patient's parents treated him when he was a child to his experiences five minutes before the shooting. The waitress in the cafeteria where he had breakfast might have been gruff and unfriendly, and this might have been the proverbial 'last straw' that broke his precariously weakened self-concept and self-esteem—thus the paranoid-megalomanic 'crime.' But, provided this sort of theory is psychologically meaningful and correct, this is not the sort of 'cause' that would assist a jury in assigning blame to anyone. Surely, the waitress could not be blamed, nor could the patient.

In this way we discover what we should have known all along—that genuine scientific 'causal' theories render the assignment of moral 'blame' to persons unnecessary and, in fact, impossible."

(iii) *Proposals for reform*

In both England and the United States reforms have been proposed to alter the present tests. The proposals in the United States have already been implemented in numerous states[65] but the English proposals (put forward by the Butler Committee on Mentally Abnormal Offenders)[66] have fared less well; in fact, they have been ignored by Parliament despite no government having ever stated the objections to them.

American Law Institute, Model Penal Code, Proposed Official Draft, 1962, § 4.01:

"1. A person is not responsible for criminal conduct if at the time of such conduct as a result of mental disease or defect he lacks substantial capacity either to appreciate the criminality (wrongfulness) of his conduct or to conform his conduct to the requirements of law.

2. As used in this article the terms 'mental disease or defect' do not include an abnormality manifested only by repeated criminal or otherwise anti-social conduct"[67]

Hyman Gross, A Theory of Criminal Justice (1979), p. 297:

"[This] version of the insanity defence consists of some form of M'Naghten to which is added an excuse based on grossly deficient inhibitory capacity. This addition is usually referred to as the irresistible impulse rule—though any suggestion that the act need be impulsive would be seriously misleading. Under this provision, if the accused was incapable of restraining himself from doing what he knew he was doing and knew that he ought not to be doing, he may invoke as an excuse his inability to exercise self-control. The gravamen of this excuse is . . . the actor's helplessness in being unable to avoid doing the proscribed acts."

Does this constitute a significant improvement to the M'Naghten Rules?[68]

Draft Criminal Code Bill (1989) (Law Com. No. 177), clauses 35–36:

"35.—(1) A mental disorder verdict shall be returned if the defendant is proved to have committed an offence but it is proved on the balance of probabilities (whether by the prosecution or the defence) that he was at the time suffering from severe mental illness or severe mental handicap.

(2) Subsection (1) does not apply if the court or jury is satisfied beyond reasonable doubt that the offence was not attributable to the severe mental illness or severe mental handicap.

36. A mental disorder verdict shall be returned if—

(a) the defendant is acquitted of an offence only because, by reason of evidence of mental disorder or a combination of mental disorder and intoxication,

---

[65] *E.g.* by statute in Illinois, Utah, Montana, and Maryland; in addition, the courts of other states have approved a test along the lines of the Model Penal Code's proposal. *Post*, p. 367.

[66] Cmnd. 6244 (1975).

[67] The psychopath is hereby excluded from the operation of the defence.

[68] See the Butler Committee on Mentally Abnormal Offenders, Cmnd. 6244, pp. 221–222 where the test of capacity to conform is criticised.

it is found that he acted or may have acted in a state of automatism, or without the fault required for the offence, or believing that an exempting circumstance existed; and

(b) it is proved on the balance of probabilities (whether by the prosecution or by the defendant) that he was suffering from mental disorder at the time of the act."

If the Code, which is predominantly based upon the recommendations of the Butler Committee,[69] is enacted then a substantial improvement will have been made.[70] The new verdict of guilty by reason of mental disorder would not lead to mandatory commitment, thus answering the criticisms of those such as Eastman who have taken the view that "(i)t is only the mandatory commitment to hospital which results from insanity which has, teleologically, given rise to the judicial need to construct artificial mental definitions which go towards the verdict."[71] Not only does this give the court much more flexibility to resolve the problem of the appropriate form of disposal for, say, epileptics who commit violent acts during the course of an epileptic fit, but the new label avoids the offensiveness involved at present in having to describe such defendants as insane or forcing them to change their pleas to guilty. Because of these changes the draft team have so defined mental disorder[72] that it will no longer be possible to distinguish between the epileptic defendant or the diabetic defendant or the defendant with a brain tumour: "(i)f any of these conditions causes a state of automatism in which the sufferer commits what would otherwise be an offence of violence, his acquittal should be on evidence of 'mental disorder.' "[73]

Finally, we may consider some of the proposals made by academics for reform of the test of insanity. Duff[74] and Fingarette,[75] for example, take broadly similar views. Duff begins by explaining *why* someone who is insane ought not to be held responsible. He cites as example the hypothetical case of a husband Mr. Green who kills his wife because he believes that she is unfaithful to him whilst in bed with him with an invisible lover. It is, he says, "senseless" to punish him "because his understanding of his relationship to his wife and to those around him is so distorted that he can in this context understand neither the law's demands nor the criminality of his actions. We can no longer appeal to him as a member of the moral community which the law presupposes—

---

[69] *Ante* p. 356.
[70] See, *e.g.* M. Wasik, "Codification: Mental Disorder and Intoxication under the Draft Criminal Code" [1986] 50 J.C.L. 393. For an earlier defence of the Butler proposals see S. Dell, "Wanted; An Insanity Defence that can be Used" [1983] Crim L.R. 431.
[71] G. N. Eastman, "Defending the Mentally Ill" in *Psychiatry and the Criminal Law* (1986) eds. R. MacKay and K. Russell at p. 24.
[72] In clause 34.
[73] Draft Criminal Code (1989), Law Com. No. 177, p. 224.
[74] R. A. Duff, "Mental Disorder and Criminal Responsibility," Paper given at the 10th Annual Conference of the Association for Legal and Social Philosophy, 1983.
[75] H. Fingarette, "Diminished Mental Capacity as a Criminal Law Defence," (1974) 37 M.L.R. 264. and "The Disability of Mind Doctrine" [1985] 477 Annals 104.

not because he rejects that community or sees it to be a myth, but because his grasp of the ideas and values which inform it is radically impaired. We should not excuse him for breaking a law which is binding on him . . . we should rather say that the law is not, and cannot be, binding on him since he can no longer understand it."[76] On the basis of this reasoning Duff defines insanity as "labouring under such a defect of reason as not to understand the nature and quality of the act he was doing, or of the law which prohibits such acts."

The key to Duff's (and Fingarette's) proposals is non-rationality rather than irrationality (for we are all sometimes irrational). A belief could be regarded as non-rational if the evidence does not exist to support it and the belief persists despite all the evidence and argument against it. Such a concept, as has been pointed out,[77] is not without difficulties. Psychiatrists, for example, seem to succeed in getting through this barrier; non-rationality is not absolute, and insanity is not incurable. There are also problems in distinguishing the person whose views cannot be changed, from those whose views will not be changed. Above all, do you think that mental disorder must always evidence itself in non-rationality, and if so, is it sufficient that the sufferer is non-rational in respect to one specific area of activity rather than the entire spectrum?

3. Should the insanity defence be retained?

There are critics who would still be profoundly dissatisfied even if reforms of the type indicated above were to take place. It is their belief that the insanity defence ought to be completely abolished. Most, although not all, of these attacks have been taking place in the United States but the reasoning behind them ranges from one of principle about the concept of responsibility to mistaken assessments of the danger to which the public are exposed by abuse of the insanity defence.

(i) *Procedural criticisms*

There are doubtless very real problems of procedure in this area; expert evidence often conflicts, trials may be long, the difficulty of sifting through the evidence to assess accountability is immense but as Fletcher points out "it is curious to argue from these problems to the conclusion that the defence ought to be abolished. Would anyone wish to abolish the defence of duress because it might be difficult to establish whether the accused was fairly capable of resisting pressure exerted against him?"[78]

---

[76] At pp. 14–15.
[77] M. Wasik, "Mental Disorder and Criminal Responsibility—A Reply," Paper given at 10th Annual Conference of the Association for Legal and Social Philosophy, 1983.
[78] *Rethinking Criminal Law* at p. 845.

(ii) *Therapeutic criticisms*

A. W. B. Simpson, "The Butler Committee's Report: The Legal Aspects" (1976) 16 Brit.J.Criminol. 175 at 176:

"If one takes the central recommendation of the Butler Committee on the disposal of mentally disordered 'offenders'[79]—'the guiding principle in disposal of mentally disordered offenders by the courts is that they should be sent wherever they can best be given the treatment they need: generally treatment by the health services is appropriate'—one cannot but be struck by the incongruity of involving criminal courts in the matter at all. What are red judges doing performing functions which, in the case of measles or mumps, we assign to general practitioners and supporting medical staff? It is as if a doctor, lighting on a case where a patient contracted a chill whilst stealing, took to prescribing aspirins and six months in the local prison.

This fundamental incongruity makes it extremely difficult, and perhaps impossible, to produce a set of recommendations designed to adapt a penal system to a task utterly out of character with the nature of such a system."

(iii) *Criminal Law v. Mental Health Powers*

Commentators have increasingly voiced their doubts about the uneasy mixture of the criminal law and its objectives with the power of courts under Mental Health legislation to confine dangerous people to hospitals. Some critics of the insanity defence have argued (as was pointed out earlier[80]) that discussion of mental disorder should be limited to the issue of *mens rea*. If the mental condition of the defendant negated the *mens rea* required for the offence, then no further criminal questions could arise—the defendant would be entitled to an acquittal. There would, however, remain the separate issue of civil commitment.

J. Goldstein and J. Katz, "Abolish the 'Insanity Defense'—Why Not?" (1963) 72 Yale L.J. 853 at 854–855, 862–864, 865:

" 'Insanity,' however formulated, has been considered a defense. An evaluation of such a defense rests on first identifying a need for an exception to criminal liability. Unless a conflict can be discovered between some basic objective of the criminal law and its application to an 'insane' person, there can be no purpose for 'insanity' as a defense. Until a purpose is uncovered, debates about the appropriateness of any insanity defense formula as well as efforts to evaluate various formulae with respect to the present state of psychiatric knowledge are destined to continue to be frustrating and fruitless. . . .

In enunciating yet another formula for insanity, the Court of Appeals for the Third Circuit in *United States* v. *Currens* (1961) (290 F.2d 751, 773, (3d Cir. 1961)) contaminates its thinking by confusing and merging the inherently incompatible concepts of 'insanity' as a defense to a crime with 'insanity' as evidence to cast doubt on a material element of an offense. It suggests, as did the court in *Durham*, that some relationship exists between the insanity defense and *mens rea*, a material element of every major crime. . . .

And the court criticized the *Durham* and *M'Naghten* formulae because:

'They do not take account of the fact that an "insane" defendant commits the

---

[79] Adopted in the Draft Criminal Code, *ante*, n. 73.
[80] *Ante*, pp. 348–349.

crime not because his mental illness causes him to do a certain prohibited act but because the totality of his personality is such, because of mental illness, that he has lost the capacity to control his acts in the way that the normal individual can and does control them. If this effect has taken place he must be found not to possess the guilty mind, the *mens rea*, necessary to constitute his prohibited act *a crime.*' (at p. 774).

At this point the court by the force of its own reasoning *should* have been led to say:

> 'Without the essential element of *mens rea*, there is no crime from which to relieve the defendant of liability and consequently, since no crime has been committed, there is no need for formulating an insanity defense.'

But instead the court actually concludes:

> 'We are of the opinion that the following (insanity) formula most nearly fulfills the objectives just discussed. . . . '

The court uses the word 'crime' first to mean 'dangerous conduct' and then, without alerting itself to the shift, to mean technically the establishment beyond doubt of each material element of an offense. With this sleight of thought the court shifts focus from 'insanity' as a *defense* to conduct 'otherwise criminal' to insanity as *evidence* to negate an element essential to categorizing the accused's conduct 'criminal.'

In announcing a new formula for the insanity defense, the court fails to recognize that there is no need for such a defense to remove criminal liability since it has concluded that no crime is established once mental illness (however defined) has cast doubt on *mens rea* (however defined). Conceptually, at least, outright acquittal would result and instructions to the jury would reflect a time, pre-*M'Naghten*, when evidence of mental condition, like any other relevant evidence, was used to cast doubt on a material element of the crime. . . .

In our efforts to understand the suggested relationship between 'insanity' and '*mens rea*' there emerges a purpose for the 'insanity defense' which, though there to be seen, has remained of extremely low visibility. That purpose seems to be obscured because thinking about such a relationship has generally been blocked by unquestioning and disarming references to our collective conscience and our religious and moral traditions. Assuming the existence of the suggested relationship between 'insanity' and '*mens rea*,' the defense is not to absolve of criminal responsibility 'sick' persons who would otherwise be subject to criminal sanction. Rather, its real function is to authorize the state to hold those 'who must be found not to possess the guilty mind *mens rea*,' even though the criminal law demands that no person be held criminally responsible if doubt is cast on any material element of the offense charged. . . .

What this discussion indicates, then, is that the insanity defense is not designed, as is the defense of self-defense, to define an exception to criminal liability, but rather to define for sanction an exception from among those who would be free of liability. It is as if the insanity defense were prompted by an affirmative answer to the silently posed question: 'Does *mens rea* or any essential element of an offense exclude from liability a group of persons whom the community wishes to restrain?' If the suggested relationship between *mens rea* and 'insanity' means that 'insanity' precludes proof beyond doubt of *mens rea* then the 'defense' is designed to authorize the holding of persons who have committed no crime. So conceived, the problem really facing the criminal process has been how to obtain authority to sanction the 'insane' who would be excluded from liability by an overall application of the general principles of the criminal law.

Furthermore, even if the relationship between insanity and '*mens rea*' is rejected, this same purpose re-emerges when we try to understand why the consequence of this defense, unlike other defenses, is restraint, not release.''

Norval Morris, Madness and the Criminal Law (1982) pp. 31–32, 61–64:

"It is the overarching theme of this book that injustice and inefficiency invariably flow from any blending of the criminal-law and mental health powers of the state. Each is sufficient unto itself to achieve a just balance between freedom and authority; each has its own interested constituency; when they are mixed together, only the likelihood of injustice is added. . . .

My belief is that practice and scholarship have been led astray by the following ambivalent and corruptive reaction: though he has done a criminal act, being mentally abnormal he is less guilty in moral terms; St. Peter may indeed hold him morally faultless or at least less blameworthy and so should we; but also he is different from the rest of us, strange and probably more dangerous, and therefore, since he has committed a crime, we had better for his sake and ours separate him from the community or prolong his separation, for his treatment and our protection. We are at the same time more forgiving and more fearful, less punitive and more self-protective; we wish to have it both ways. . . .

[From this position Morris goes on to attack the notion that we seek to identify the truly responsible by means of an insanity defence]. [The central issue is]—the question of fairness, the sense that it is unjust and unfair to stigmatize the mentally ill as criminals and to punish them for their crimes. The criminal law exists to deter and to punish those who would or who would choose to do wrong. If they cannot exercise choice, they cannot be deterred and it is a moral outrage to punish them. The argument sounds powerful but its premise is weak.

Choice is neither present nor absent in the typical case where the insanity defense is currently pleaded; what is at issue is the degree of freedom of choice on a continuum from the hypothetically entirely rational to the hypothetically pathologically determined—in states of consciousness neither polar condition exists.

The moral issue sinks into the sands of reality. Certainly it is true that in a situation of total absence of choice it is outrageous to inflict punishment; but the frequency of such situations to the problems of criminal responsibility becomes an issue of fact in which tradition and clinical knowledge and practice are in conflict. The traditions of being possessed of evil spirits, of being bewitched, confront the practices of mental health system which increasingly fashions therapeutic practices to hold patients responsible for their conduct. And suppose we took the moral argument seriously and eliminated responsibility in those situations where we thought there had been a substantial impairment of the capacity to choose between crime and no crime (I set aside problems of strict liability and of negligence for the time being). Would we not have to, as a matter of moral fairness, fashion a special defense of gross social adversity? The matter might be tested by asking which is the more criminogenic, psychosis or serious social deprivation? . . .

[A]t first blush, it seems a perfectly legitimate correlational and, I submit, causal inquiry, whether psychosis, or any particular type of psychosis, is more closely related to criminal behavior than, say, being born to a one-parent family living on welfare in a black inner-city area. And there is no doubt of the empirical answer. Social adversity is grossly more potent in its pressure toward criminality, certainly toward all forms of violence and street crime as distinct from white-collar crime, than is any psychotic condition. As a factual matter, the exogenous pressures are very much stronger than the endogenous.

But the argument feels wrong. Surely there is more to it than the simple calculation of criminogenic impact. Is this unease rationally based? I think not, though the question certainly merits further consideration. As a rational matter it is hard to see why one should be more responsible for what is done to one than for what one is. Yet major contributions to jurisprudence and criminal-law theory insist that it necessary to maintain the denial of responsibility on grounds of mental illness to preserve the moral infrastructure of the criminal law. For many years I have struggled with this opinion by those whose work I deeply respect, yet I remain unpersuaded. Indeed, they really don't try to persuade, but rather affirm and reaffirm with vehemence and almost mystical sincerity the necessity of retaining the special defense of insanity as a moral prop to the entire criminal law.[81]

And indeed I think that much of the discussion of the defense of insanity is the discussion of a myth rather than of a reality. It is no minor debating point that in fact we lack a defense of insanity as an operating tool of the criminal law other than in relation to a very few particularly heinous and heavily punished offenses. There is not an operating defense of insanity in relation to burglary or theft, or the broad sweep of index crimes generally; the plea of not guilty on the ground of insanity is rarely to be heard in city courts of first instance which handle the grist of the mill of the criminal law—though a great deal of pathology is to be seen in the parade of accused and convicted persons before these courts. As a practical matter we reserve this defence for a few sensational cases where it may be in the interest of the accused either to escape the possibility of capital punishment (though in cases where serious mental illness is present, the risk of execution is slight) or where the likely punishment is of a sufficient severity to make the indeterminate commitment of the accused a preferable alternative to a criminal conviction. Operationally the defense of insanity is a tribute, it seems to me, to our hypocrisy rather than to our morality.

To be less aggressive about the matter and to put aside anthropomorphic allegations of hypocrisy, the special defense of insanity may properly be indicted as producing a morally unsatisfactory classification on the continuum between guilt and innocence. It applies in practice to only a few mentally ill criminals, thus omitting many others with guilt-reducing relationships between their mental illness and their crimes; it excludes other powerful pressures on human behavior, thus giving excessive weight to the psychological over the social. It is a false classification in the sense that if a team of the world's most sensitive and trained psychiatrists and moralists were to select from all those found guilty of felonies and those found not guilty by reason of insanity any given number who should not be stigmatized as criminals, very few of those found not guilty by reason of insanity would be selected.

[Morris concludes that the mentally disordered are entitled to be held responsible for their actions; their condition may, however, be relevant in sentencing when it might result in mitigation on grounds of less moral blameworthiness, or aggravation because of constituting a danger to the public.]"

How do these views differ from those expressed by Baroness Wootton below?

(iv) *Denial of responsibility*

Baroness Wootton, Crime and the Criminal Law (2nd ed., 1981) pp. 90–91:

"At a more fundamental level, acceptance of mental disorder as diminishing

---

[81] Stephen J. Morse in "Retaining a Modified Insanity Defense" (1985) 477 The Annals 137 at pp. 139–140 argues that the argument for a defence of 'social adversity or disadvantage' is misconceived. It may well be a powerful cause of *criminal* behaviour but has nothing to do with rationality.

or *eliminating* criminal responsibility demands an ability to get inside someone else's mind so completely as to be certain whether he has acted wilfully or knowingly, and also to experience the strength of the temptations to which he is exposed. This, I submit, is beyond the competence of even the most highly qualified expert. Psychiatrists may uncover factors in patients' backgrounds (often in terms of childhood experience) by which they profess to 'explain' why one individual has an urge to strangle young girls and another to rape elderly women: but these 'explanations' are merely predictive of the *likelihood* of such behaviour occurring. . . .

I submit, therefore, that the present law, under which offenders must be classified as either mentally disordered or criminally responsible for their actions not only produces anomalies but attempts the impossible. . . . In the end it would seem that for practical purposes we are brought to the paradoxical conclusion that, if a person's crimes are by ordinary standards only moderately objectionable, he should be regarded as wicked and liable to appropriate punishment, but if his wickedness goes beyond a certain point (when we cannot comprehend how anyone could commit such a crime) it ceases to be wickedness at all and becomes a medical condition.''[82]

At least some of Baroness Wootton's arguments would be supported by a movement that has gained an enormous amount of ground over a very short period of time in the United States. This anti-crime and pro-victim lobby received a major boost with the acquittal of John Hinckley on the ground of insanity.[83] The insanity defence was thought to have been blatantly misused with expensive defence lawyers hoodwinking juries into false acquittals. It was also said that dangerous persons were being given early release from psychiatric detention after having been "cured," only to commit further terrible crimes.[84]

In fact, evidence fails to support either of these criticisms of the operation of the defence[85] but the perception of their validity has prompted reconsideration of the insanity defence in more than half of the states of America.[86] In some states reform has done nothing more than shift the burden of proof from the prosecution to the defence to prove that the defendant was insane; the fact that in the District of Columbia, unlike in England, the prosecution had to prove that Hinckley was sane was thought to be one of the main reasons he was acquitted. Sometimes, in addition to this change, the standard of proof has also been raised.[87] Other states have opted to make the test of insanity more rigorous in a remarkable move away from the test in the Model Penal Code back to M'Naghten. Still other states have introduced new verdicts of "guilty

---

[82] Although said in the context of a discussion of diminished responsibility, (*post*, p. 370) Baroness Wootton clearly does not limit her disapproval to partial responsibility. The jury in *Sutcliffe* (*ante*, p. 355) however did not display this attitude. See also Hart, *Punishment and Responsibility*. Chap. 8.

[83] *Ante*, p. 355.

[84] Alexander Brooks, "The Merits of Abolishing the Insanity Defense" (1985) 477 The Annals 125 at p. 126.

[85] Henry Steadman "Empirical Research on the Insanity Defense" (1985) 477 The Annals 58.

[86] R. D. Mackay, "Post-Hinckley Insanity in the U.S.A." [1988] Crim.L.R. 88.

[87] For example, in Arizona the defendant must prove his insanity by "clear and convincing evidence" (Ariz.Rev.Stat.An. s.13–502(*b*) (1984)); Mackay, p. 93.

but mentally ill"[88] and some have completely abolished the insanity defence.[89] Where this reform has taken place, the trend is for restriction of discussion of insanity to the issue of whether the defendant lacked the necessary mental state for the definition of the crime. If for this reason the defendant cannot be convicted of an offence, then automatic civil commitment follows.

The effect of this is, of course to make *mens rea* even more important and this aspect of reform of the insanity defence would have found no favour at all with Baroness Wootton. Her view, explored earlier (in connection with the desirability of strict liability[90]), was that the entire assessment of responsibility was a futile one and that questions relating to the mental state of the defendant ought to be reserved for the post-conviction, sentencing stage.

In complete contrast to Baroness Wootton we may examine the views of Szasz, a psychologist who embraces so whole-heartedly the concept of responsibility that he feels everyone ought to be regarded as sane and accountable for their actions.

T. S. Szasz, "The Myth of Mental Illness," (1960) 15 American Psychologist p. 115–118:

"[A] currently prevalent claim [is that] . . . mental illness is just as 'real' and 'objective' as bodily illness. . . . This is a confusing claim since it is never known exactly what is meant by such words as 'real' and 'objective.' I suspect, however, that what is intended by the proponents of this view is to create the idea in the popular mind that mental illness is some sort of disease entity, like an infection or a malignancy. If this were true, one could *catch* or *get* a 'mental illness,' one might *have* or harbour it, one might transmit it to others, and finally one could get rid of it. In my opinion there is not a shred of evidence to support this view. To the contrary, all the evidence is the other way and supports the view that what people now call mental illnesses are for the most part communications expressing unacceptable ideas, often framed, moreover in an unusual idiom. . . .
[T]he diversity of human values and the methods by means of which they may be realized is so vast . . . that they cannot fail but lead to conflicts in human relations. Indeed, to say that human relations at all levels from mother to child, through husband and wife, to nation and nation—are fraught with stress, strain and disharmony is, once again, making the obvious explicit. . . . I submit that the idea of mental illness is now being put to work to obscure certain difficulties which at present may be inherent—not that they need be unmodifiable—in the social intercourse of persons. If this is true, the concept functions as a disguise; for instead of calling attention to conflicting human needs, aspirations and

---

[88] In the 12 states where this reform has taken place (as in Michigan and Illinois, for example) the new verdict became available as an alternative to the orthodox one and did not replace it. The reason for its introduction was clearly to reduce the number of acquittals on the basis of insanity. Research suggests that it has made very little impact upon the already small number of such verdicts: Henry Steadman, "Empirical Resarch on the Insanity Defense" (1985) 477 The Annals 58 at pp. 67–68 and R. D. Mackay, "Post-Hinckley Insanity in the U.S.A." [1988] Crim.L.R. 88.

[89] As in Montana (Mont. Code s.46–14–102 (1985)), Idaho (Idaho Code 18–207 (1986 Supp.)) and Utah (Utah Code Ann. ss.77–35–21 (1986 Supp.)). For discussion of the provisions of these states see, R. D. Mackay, *ante*, n. 86.

[90] *Ante*, p. 222.

values, the notion of mental illness provides an amoral and impersonal 'thing' (an illness) as an explanation for *problems in living*. We may recall in this connection that not so long ago it was devils and witches who were held responsible for men's problems in social living. The belief in mental illness, as something other than man's trouble in getting along with his fellow man, is the proper heir to the belief in demonology and witchcraft. Mental illness exists or is 'real' in exactly the same sense in which witches existed or were 'real.'

. . . The myth of mental illness encourages us, moreover, to believe in its logical corollary: that social intercourse would be harmonious, satisfying and the secure basis of a good life were it not for the disrupting influences of mental illness. The potentiality for universal human happiness, in this form at least, seems to me but another example of the I-wish-it-were-true type of fantasy. I do believe that human happiness or well-being on a hitherto unimaginably large scale, and not for a select few, is possible. This goal could be achieved, however, only at the cost of many men, and not just a few being willing and able to tackle their personal, social and ethical conflicts. This means having the courage and integrity to forgo waging battles on false fronts, finding solutions for substitute problems—for instance, fighting the battle of stomach acid and chronic fatigue instead of facing up to a marital conflict. . . .

My argument [is] . . . limited to the proposition that mental illness is a myth, whose function it is to disguise and thus render more palatable the bitter pill of moral conflicts in human relations."

One final insight might be considered.

D. L. Rosenhan, "On being Sane in Insane Places," Science 1973, Vol. 199, 250–258:

"If sanity and insanity exist, how shall we know them?

The question is neither capricious nor itself insane. However much we may be personally convinced that we can tell the normal from the abnormal, the evidence is simply not compelling. It is commonplace, for example, to read about murder trials wherein eminent psychiatrists for the defense are contradicted by equally eminent psychiatrists for the prosecution on the matter of the defendant's sanity. More generally, there are a great deal of conflicting data on the reliability, utility and meaning of such terms as 'sanity,' 'insanity,' 'mental illness' and 'schizophrenia' . . . what is viewed as normal in one culture may be seen as quite aberrant in another. Thus, notions of normality and abnormality may not be quite so accurate as people believe they are . . . [this] in no way questions the fact that some behaviours are deviant or odd.

[Rosenhan then goes on to describe the nature of the research he had undertaken; 8 sane people gained secret admission to 12 different hospitals, all complained that they had heard voices, saying in particular, 'thud,' 'hollow and empty.' In all other respects (save their name and if necessary their profession) the pseudo-patients told the truth about their feelings, their background, and their present lives. The aim of the research was to ascertain whether and how the sane people would be detected. If they were, it would be some support at least for the view that sanity and insanity are distinct enough to be recognised wherever they occur. *All* the pseudo-patients were admitted to hospital, whereupon they ceased simulating any symptoms of abnormality but behaved as they 'normally' behaved.]

Despite their public 'show' of sanity, the pseudo-patients were never detected. Admitted, except in one case, with a diagnosis of schizophrenia each was discharged after hospitalization of between 7 to 52 days, with a diagnosis of schizophrenia 'in remission.' The label 'in remission' should in no way be dismissed as a mere formality, for at no time during any hospitalization had any question been raised about any pseudo-patients' simulation. Nor are there any indications in hospital records that the pseudo-patients status was suspect. Rather, the evidence was strong that once labelled schizophrenic, the pseudo-patient was stuck with that label. If the pseudo-patient was to be discharged, he must naturally be 'in remission'; but he was not sane, nor in the institutions' view, had he ever been sane. . . .

The facts of the matter are that we have known for a long time that diagnoses are often not useful or reliable, but we have nevertheless continued to use them. We now know that we cannot distinguish insanity from sanity. It is depressing to consider how that information will be used.

Not merely depressing but frightening. How many people, one wonders are sane but not recognised as such by our psychiatric institutions? How many have been needlessly stripped of their privileges of citizenship, from the right to vote and drive to that of handling their own accounts? How many have feigned insanity in order to avoid the criminal consequences of their behaviour, and conversely, how many would rather stand trial than live interminably in a psychiatric hospital—but are wrongly thought to be mentally ill? . . . The label sticks, a mark of inadequacy forever.

Finally, how many patients might be 'sane' outside psychiatric hospital but seem insane in it—not because craziness resides in them, as it were, but because they are responding to a bizarre setting."[91]

How are we to respond to arguments such as these? Do they constitute a persuasive case for abolition that "trumps" the arguments addressed in the introductory discussion of this defence? Fletcher, for example, remains unconvinced.

George P. Fletcher, Rethinking the Criminal Law (1978), p. 846:

"The criminal law expresses respect for the autonomy of the sane as much as it shows compassion for the insane. The line between the two may shift over time. Our theories of sanity may change, but one remains. If the criminal law is to be an institution expressing respect as well as compassion, its institutions must be able both to punish the guilty and excuse the weak. These two sentiments depend on each other. Punishing wrongdoing is possible only so far as we have a concept of accountability for wrongdoing. Respect for autonomy and compassion for the weak are too important to our culture to be easily shaken by the skeptics!"

H. Diminished Responsibility

1. Introduction

The "defence" of diminished responsibility is not a general defence and ought strictly to be discussed elsewhere in this book, since, like provocation, it operates only as a defence to murder, reducing liability

---

[91] Rosenhan, himself one of the researchers, describes the depersonalisation that took place in the wards, "At times, depersonalisation reached such proportions that pseudo-patients had the sense that they were invisible, or at least unworthy of account . . . . . . A nurse unbuttoned her uniform to adjust her brassiere in the presence of an entire ward of viewing men. One did not have the sense that she was being seductive. Rather, she didn't notice us . . . " The pseudo-patients found themselves trying to assert some individuality, some link with their "real" lives to fight off the depersonalisation. The implication is that the other patients might respond similarly with outbreaks of personality which will then be seen as indicative of their need for treatment.

to manslaughter. However, it will be discussed at this stage, rather than in the context of homicide, for two important reasons.

First, the partial defence raises further problems of responsibility to those encountered in the discussion of the insanity defence, and secondly, the practical effect of the availability of the defence of diminished responsibility has been to decrease resort to the insanity plea.[92]

2. The problem

Royal Commission on Capital Punishment, Cmnd. 8932, (1949–1953) para. 411:

"It must be accepted that there is no sharp dividing line between sanity and insanity, but that the two extremes of 'sanity' and 'insanity' shade into one another by imperceptible gradations. The degree of individual responsibility varies equally widely; no clear boundary can be drawn between responsibility and irresponsibility. The existence of degrees of responsibility has been recognised in . . . [other] legal systems. . . . The acceptance of the doctrine of diminished responsibility would undoubtedly bring the law into closer harmony with the facts."

Thus the doubts that have led many to argue for the abolition of the insanity defence[93] have here been used to justify a half-way house; some device, it was felt, was needed to reflect the view that where there was less responsibility there ought to be less punishment. Such acceptance of partial responsibility would enable the courts to do what, after all discussion of responsibility was ended, they really desired: to avoid the fixed penalty for murder by convicting the killer of manslaughter instead. For all other crimes which do not carry a fixed penalty, a partial defence was unnecessary. The lesser degree of responsibility could be reflected at the sentencing stage by "less punishment."

3. The solution

Homicide Act 1957, s.2.

"(1) Where a person kills or is party to the killing of another, he shall not be convicted of murder if he was suffering from such abnormality of mind (whether arising from a condition of arrested or retarded development of

---

[92] According to official statistics, in 1988 diminished responsibility was successfully pleaded in 50 cases (in proceedings for which the outcome is already known); there were no special verdicts. In 1987, the equivalent figures were 73 and 0. (But see *ante* n.24). Diminished responsibility is certainly easier to prove than insanity; indeed, 80 per cent. of cases proceed on the basis of acceptance of a plea of guilty to manslaughter. Where the plea is successful, the defendant has a good chance of a determinate sentence or more lenient treatment; *post*, p. 374. However, where the case does go before a jury, chances of success are low, with a 64 per cent. chance of a murder conviction: Suzanne Dell, *Murder into Manslaughter* (1984).

[93] *Ante*, p. 366.

mind or any inherent causes or induced by disease or injury) as substantially impaired his mental responsibility for his acts and omissions in doing or being a party to the killing. . . .

(3) . . . [he] shall be liable instead to be convicted of manslaughter."[94]

What is the effect of the provision?

In evidence to the Butler Committee[95] members of the judiciary suggested that section 2 of the Homicide Act embodies a concept which is easier to grasp than define and that normally it requires the defendant to show "recognisably abnormal mental symptoms."[96] More particularly, the requirements of the section may be broken down thus: There must be an *abnormality of mind* arising from arrested development, or inherent causes[97] or disease or injury, and it must result in *substantial impairment of mental responsibility*.

Both of the key phrases have caused considerable problems. "Abnormality of mind" is extremely vague; the concept has only been slightly clarified by the case of *Byrne*.[98] The appellent strangled and then horribly mutilated a girl. It was alleged that he suffered from violent perverted sexual desires which he found difficult or impossible to control. (He was in fact described as a sexual psychopath). In the course of his judgment (allowing the appeal) Lord Parker C.J. defined "abnormality of mind" thus:

"[it is] . . . a state of mind so different from that of ordinary human beings that the reasonable man . . . would term it abnormal. It appears to us wide enough to cover the mind's activities in all its aspects, not only the perception of physical acts and matters, and the ability to form a rational judgment as to whether the act was right or wrong, but also the ability to exercise will-power to control physical acts in accordance with that rational judgment."[99]

As the evidence to the Butler Committee suggested, this interpretation still leaves the meaning of "abnormality of mind" somewhat imprecise. It is a quasi-legal, quasi-medical formula that can satisfy no-one.

The second key phrase "substantial impairment of mental responsibility" has also given rise to interpretative difficulties.

---

[94] The issue of diminished responsibility is raised by the defence (on whom the burden of proof also rests); however, the prosecution may do so if the defendant is pleading insanity: *Campbell* (1987) 84 Cr.App.R. 255.

[95] Report of the Committee on Mentally Abnormal Offenders, Cmnd. 6244 (1975).

[96] *Ibid.* p. 242, para. 19.4.

[97] It is within this limb that the vexed problem of the psychopathic offender (*ante*, n. 62) arises; some psychiatrists are prepared to state that psychopathy may be due to inherent causes; others, feeling that it may be due to mishandling in childhood, will not. If the former view is held then psychopathic offenders who fall outside the M'Naghten Rules may have a partial defence to a charge of murder. Another problem arises with reactive depression—as the name implies it arises from outside influences and so can hardly be described as an "inherent cause."

[98] (1960) 44 Cr.App.R. 246.

[99] In *Seers* (1985) 149 J.P. 124, the Court of Appeal held that the jury should have been directed in these terms, without the "unhelpful" addition of the description of diminished responsibility as "partial or borderline insanity."

Report of the Committee on Mentally Abnormal Offenders (Butler Committee) Cmnd. 6244 (1975) p. 242, para. 19.5:

" 'Mental responsibility,' a phrase not to be found elsewhere in any statute, has created difficulties both for doctors and jurors. It is either a concept of law or a concept of morality; it is not a clinical fact relating to the defendant. 'Legal responsibility' means liability to conviction (and success in a defence of diminished responsibility does not save the defendant from conviction of manslaughter); 'moral responsibility' means liability to moral censure (but moral questions do not normally enter into the definition of a crime). It seems odd that psychiatrists should be asked and agree to testify as to legal and moral responsibility. It is even more surprising that courts are prepared to hear that testimony. Yet psychiatrists commonly testify to impaired 'mental responsibility' under section 2. Several medical witnesses pointed out to us that the difficulty is made worse by the use of the word substantial.[1] The idea that ability to conform to the law can be measured is particularly puzzling."

The difficulty unfolded in the preceding passage is illustrative of the central problem with section 2: the compromise it achieves between medical and legal issues leaves neither side on safe ground. Neither medical experts nor jury can satisfactorily answer the questions demanded of them. This does not mean, however, that the defence of diminished responsibility has not worked—after a fashion. What has happened is the familiar story of medical experts being made to determine the issue of responsibility.[2] They have done so by interpreting section 2 very widely. Not only has the psychopath and the person acting under "irresistible impulse"[3] been brought within the framework of the defence but reactive depressions,[4] and alcoholism[5] and disassociated states have likewise been included. Protection has recently been extended to women suffering from "pre-menstrual syndrome" by means of this provision in what may be a very significant development.[6] The main examples of use of this defence have occurred in relation to killing through compassion (mercy-killing) or jealousy. In *Miller*[7] a woman of 67 stabbed her aged husband to death in a fit of jealousy (on

---

[1] The intention of the Act was that juries would undertake the task of assessing the substantiality of the impairment. *Cf. Gittens* [1984] Q.B. 698, and *Atkinson* [1985] Crim.L.R. 314. As this latter case shows, this task can be a very difficult one.

[2] Although juries can reject medical evidence (*Walton* v. *The Queen* [1977] 3 W.L.R. 902) there must be evidence justifying their refusal: *Matheson* [1958] 1 W.L.R. 474 and *Vernege* [1982] 1 W.L.R. 293. If there is no such evidence the conviction for murder may be quashed and one of manslaughter substituted.

[3] Traditionally excluded from the M'Naghten Rules, because of the difficulty of distinguishing the unresistable from the unresisted impulse. Such a person will have a partial defence here if he was either unable to conform or experienced substantially more difficulty in conforming to the law than an ordinary man; the jury should approach this question in "a broad common-sense way" because it is not one, given the present state of medical knowledge, that can be solved scientifically: (*Byrne* (*ante*, n. 98)).

[4] As was argued in *Seers* (1985) 149 J.P. 124.

[5] *Tandy* [1988] Crim.L.R. 308, although the partial defence was denied to the defendant on the facts of the case because the taking of "the first drink" was not involuntary.

[6] *Reynolds* 23 April, 1988 (C.A.). For discussion of this and other cases of P.M.T. (including that of *Smith* (*Sandie*) [1982] Crim.L.R. 531), see Susan Edwards, "Mad, bad or pre-menstrual?" (1988) New L.J. 456.

[7] *The Times*, May 16, 1972.

mistaken grounds) and then tried to kill herself; her plea of diminished responsibility was accepted. In *Price*[8] a father placed his severely handicapped son on a river and watched him float away; he was convicted of manslaughter on the basis of diminished responsibility. However, whilst the courts are prepared to accept almost any medical evidence as sufficient in the case of mercy-killing, they do have some reservations in the case of killing through jealousy.

R. v. Vinagre (1979) 69 Cr.App.R. 104 (Court of Appeal, Criminal Division)

The appellant stabbed his wife to death thinking she had been unfaithful.

Lawton L.J.:
"We are sure that it was never intended that pleas should be accepted on flimsy grounds. As Scarman L.J. pointed out two or three years ago in *R. v. Ford* (1976, unreported) cases are tried by the courts and not by psychiatrists. It seems to us that pleas to manslaughter on grounds of diminished responsibility should only be accepted where there is clear evidence of mental imbalance. We do not consider that in this case there was clear evidence of mental imbalance. There was clear evidence of a killing by a jealous husband which, until modern times, no one would have thought was anything else but murder."[9]

What becomes clear, despite the courts' demand for real evidence of mental imbalance, is that psychiatrists will stretch the medical diagnosis to provide evidence in deserving cases and that juries (in those rare cases where the defendant pleads not guilty and the case actually goes to them) will accept it if their sympathies are engaged.[10] The fact is that section 2 operates less on clear psychiatric grounds than on the gut-reaction[11] of those who have the final say—the judge and jury.

What is the outcome of a successful plea of diminished responsibility if widely divergent cases are going to be brought within its protection? Simply because the conviction is for manslaughter rather than murder does not ensure lenient treatment. Neither does a finding of mental imbalance automatically entail a hospital order under section 37 of the Mental Health Act 1983 (formerly section 60 of the Mental Health Act 1959) although this is now imposed in approximately one-third of diminished responsibility cases.[12] In slightly less than one third of cases imprisonment is imposed—although it is increasingly rare for this to be

---

[8] *The Times*, December 22, 1971.

[9] The court, however, felt bound by the finding of the trial judge and the finding of diminished responsibility stood; sentence was varied. See also *Dix* (1982) 44 Cr.App.R. 306, where the judges similarly insisted on medical evidence.

[10] There is some evidence that the defendant may have a better chance of acquittal if he pleads diminished responsibility and provocation together. *Post*, p. 648.

[11] One paradoxical example of this is provided by the case of *Sutcliffe* (*The Times*, May 23, 1982) where there was the clearest of medical evidence to suggest that Sutcliffe was a paranoid schizophrenic, yet the judge left the issue to the jury who found him guilty of murder. See H. Prins, "Diminished Responsibility and the *Sutcliffe* Case: Legal, Psychiatric and Social Aspects" (1983) 23 Med. Sci. Law 17.

[12] Normally with what was a section 65 restriction order (Mental Health Act 1959). In more limited circumstances it may now be possible to make a restriction order under s.41 of the Mental Health Act 1983. (Gibson: Homicide in England and Wales 1967–1971 (H.O.R.S. No. 31 1975)).

a life term.[13] The Court of Appeal in *Chambers*[14] felt that a life sentence of imprisonment could only be imposed where the defendant constituted a danger to the public for an unpredictable length of time (and where a hospital order was not deemed appropriate). Determinate sentences of imprisonment could be imposed where there was no proper basis for a hospital order, but where the defendant's degree of responsibility was not minimal. The residue of cases "which have been felt to merit sympathetic consideration have resulted in more lenient disposal."[15] The case of *Price*[16] is typical. In passing sentence the judge told the father that he would be required to "undergo treatment as a doctor may prescribe for the next few weeks or so"; in such cases a psychiatric probation order is felt the most appropriate form of sentence.

4. Should the partial defence of diminished responsibility be retained?

Those who attack the diminished responsibility defence often do so on the same grounds as the insanity defence has been criticised.[17] However the concept of diminished responsibility has also been subject to more specific criticism. As we have seen, this defence operates on the premises of a half-way house of responsibility. It is this that has caused other commentators some misgivings.

Sparks[18] feels that the concept of diminished responsibility rests on a mistaken view of the relationship of mental disorder to criminal liability. In any discussion of this relationship, two questions are involved:

(1) Was he mentally abnormal, and

(2) Could the accused in that condition help committing his crime?

One cannot deduce the answer to the second question merely by reference to the first; the illness may be completely unrelated to the conduct. If that is the case it is not at all unfair to punish: "to say that we are less willing to blame such a man if he does something wrong, surely does not mean: we are willing to blame him less, if he does something wrong."[19] Moreover, if there is a connection between the mental abnormality and the crime committed because he could not help committing the crime in that condition, he ought to be excused all punishment. He is not responsible at all; the concept of a half-way house is, therefore, devoid of substance.

Contrast this reasoning with that of the Royal Commission on Capital Punishment. Which do you find more persuasive? If the latter and dimi-

---

[13] Between 1983–1987, *e.g.* an average of 6 of the defendants convicted under s.2 got life sentences in comparison with an average of 20 for the period 1977–1982; *Official Statistics for England and Wales* (1988) Law Com. No. 847.

[14] [1983] Crim.L.R. 688. The court also laid down guidelines as to when hospital orders or supervision orders would be appropriate.

[15] Butler Committee on Mentally Abnormal Offenders, Cmnd. 6244, p. 243, para. 19.7.

[16] *Ante*, n. 8.

[17] *Ante*, p. 362; H. L. A. Hart, *Punishment and Responsibility, Essays in the Philosophy of Law* (1968), pp. 202–209.

[18] R. Sparks, "Diminished Responsibility in Theory and Practice" (1964) 27 M.L.R. 9 disagreeing fundamentally with the reasoning in the Royal Commission on Capital Punishment, *ante*, p. 371.

[19] *Ibid.* at p. 16.

nished responsibility is to be seen as more than "a device for circumventing the embarrassments that flow from a mandatory sentence"[20] is there any justification for restricting the operation of the defence to murder only?[21] The force of this argument, however, was not accepted by the Criminal Law Revision Committee in its 14th Report and has not been incorporated into the Draft Code. Instead diminished responsibility is to continue to be a partial defence to murder only.

Draft Criminal Code Bill 1989 (Law Com. No. 177) clause 56:

"(1) A person who but for this section, would be guilty of murder is not guilty of murder if, at the time of his act, he is suffering from such mental abnormality as is a substantial enough reason to reduce his offence to manslaughter.

(2) In this section 'mental abnormality' means mental illness, arrested or incomplete development of mind, psychopathic disorder, and any other disorder or disability of mind, except intoxication."[22]

I Intoxication

1. Introduction

What is the position where a person consumes such large quantities of alcohol and/or drugs that he becomes unaware of what he is doing, and while in this state commits a crime requiring *mens rea*? For example, in *Lipman*[23] the defendant, a drug addict, while on an L.S.D. "trip" had the illusion of descending to the centre of the earth and being attacked by snakes. In his attempt to fight off these reptiles he struck the victim (also a drug addict on an L.S.D. "trip") two blows on the head causing haemorrhage of the brain and crammed some eight inches of sheet into her mouth causing her to die of asphyxia. He claimed to have had "no knowledge of what he was doing and no intention to harm her." In *Brennan* v. *H.M. Advocate*[24] the defendant consumed between 20 and 25 pints of beer, a glass of sherry and then a quantity of the drug L.S.D. He then stabbed his father to death with a knife. Does such a person have *mens rea*? Can he even be said to be "acting" (which requires conscious willed movement)?

As these cases make clear, the law is *not* concerned with a defendant who has several (or many) drinks that merely "loosen him up" and remove his inhibitions. If at the time of the crime he knows what he is

---

[20] S. Dell, "Diminished Responsibility Reconsidered" [1982] Crim.L.R. 809 at 814, and *Murder into Manslaughter* (1984).

[21] In several European countries (France, Italy and Belgium) the defence operates more widely. The Butler Committee's preference was for the abolition of the mandatory life sentence for murder and with it the device of diminished responsibility. Failing acceptance of that recommendation they favoured a rewording of the defence (still applicable only to murder) so that psychiatrists would have a firmer medical basis upon which to testify; pp. 244–248, paras. 19.8–19.21. It was this latter view that was adopted by the Criminal Law Revision Committee.

[22] The defence of diminished responsibility is, in any event, likely to become less important in practice if the draft Code proposals on insanity are implemented.

[23] [1970] 1 Q.B. 152.

[24] (1977) S.L.T. 151.

doing, it is irrelevant that he would not have committed the crime, but for the drinks he has consumed. It was stressed in *Sheehan and Moore* that "a drunken intent is nevertheless an intent."[25] The law is thus only concerned with the more extreme states of drunkenness that might prevent a defendant from having *mens rea*.

Glanville Williams, Textbook of Criminal Law (2nd ed., 1983) p. 464:

"*The Effect of Intoxicants.*
The effect of alcohol on the brain is depressant from the beginning. Its apparently stimulating effect is due solely to the fact that it deadens the higher control centres (and progressively the other centres as well), so weakening or removing the inhibitions that normally keep us within the bounds of civilised behaviour. It also impairs perception, reasoning, and the ability to foresee consequences. . . .
Alcohol is generally distinguished from drugs as a matter of speech, though scientifically speaking it is a drug. Nearly all the cases concern alcohol, but other toxic drugs have come to present similar legal problems which are answered on the same principles as those established for alcohol. Cocaine, which is frequently injected with heroin, is an intense stimulant which in large doses causes acute paranoia . . . [L]arge overdoses (of amphetamines and barbiturates) can issue in violence, sometimes, apparently, as the result of producing a psychosis (insanity) . . .
The hallucinogens, including L.S.D., produce hallucinations, as their name implies; under their influence repressions and learned patterns of behaviour are dissolved away . . .
Drugs or mental illness may bring about a narrowing of the field of consciousness, so that, while attention is directed to some items, there is total unawareness of other items of which a normal person would have been aware."

2. Meaning of voluntary intoxication

Report of the Committee on Mentally Abnormal Offenders (Butler Committee) Cmnd. 6244 (1975), para. 18.56:

" 'Voluntary intoxication' would be defined to mean intoxication resulting from the intentional taking of drink or a drug knowing that it is capable in sufficient quantity of having an intoxicating effect; provided that intoxication is not voluntary if it results in part from a fact unknown to the defendant that increases his sensitivity to the drink or drug. The concluding words would provide a defence to a person who suffers from hypoglycaemia, for example, who does not know that in that condition the ingestions of a small amount of alcohol can produce a state of altered consciousness, as well as to a person who has been prescribed a drug on medical grounds without warning of the effect it may produce."

The present law does not appear to go quite as far as the above proposal. In *Allen*[26] the defendant claimed that he had not realised that

---

[25] [1975] 1 W.L.R. 739; in *Stubbs* (1989) 88 Cr.App.R. 53 it was stated that the intoxication needed to be "very extreme;" this is so even in cases of involuntary intoxication as in *Davies* [1983] Crim.L.R. 741 where the defendant's drink had been "spiked" with a tablet.
[26] [1988] Crim.L.R. 698.

wine he had drunk had a high alcohol content. It was held that where an accused knows he is drinking alcohol it is irrelevant whether he knows the precise nature or strength of the alcohol. It was a clear case of voluntary intoxication.

R. v. Hardie (1984) 80 Cr.App.R. 157 (Court of Appeal, Criminal Division)

Parker L.J.:
"The problem is whether . . . [the taking of] valium . . . should properly be regarded as self-inducted intoxication . . .

There can be no doubt that the same rule applies both to self-intoxication by alcohol and intoxication by hallucinatory drugs, but this is because the effects of both are well-known and there is therefore an element of recklessness in the self-administration of the drug . . .

In the present instance the defence was that the valium was taken for the purpose of calming the nerves only, that it was old stock and that the appellant was told it would do him no harm. There was no evidence that it was known to the appellant or even generally known that the taking of valium in the quanity taken would be liable to render a person aggressive or incapable of appreciating risks to others or have other side effects such that its self-administration would itself have an element of recklessness. It is true that valium is a drug and it is true that it was taken deliberately and not taken on medical prescription, but the drug is, in our view, wholly different in kind from drugs which are liable to cause unpredictability or aggressiveness. It may will be that the taking of a sedative or soporific drug will, in certain circumstances, be no answer, for example in a case of reckless driving, but if the effect of a drug is merely soporific or sedative the taking of it, even in some excessive quantity, cannot in the ordinary way raise a *conclusive* presumption against the admission of proof of intoxication for the purpose of disproving *mens rea* in ordinary crimes, such as would be the case with aloholic intoxication or incapacity or automatism resulting from the self-administration of dangerous drugs."

Draft Criminal Code Bill 1989 (Law Com. No. 177) clause 22:

"(5) 'Voluntary intoxication' means the intoxication of a person by an intoxicant which he takes, otherwise than properly for a medicinal purpose, knowing that it is or may be an intoxicant.

(6) An intoxicant, although taken for a medicinal purpose, is not properly so taken if—
(a) —
  (i) it is not taken on medical advice; or
  (ii) it is taken on medical advice but the taker fails then or thereafter to comply with any condition forming part of the advice; and
(b) the taker is aware that the taking, or the failure, as the case may be, may result in his doing an act capable of constituting an offence of the kind in question;

and accordingly intoxication resulting from such taking or failure is voluntary intoxication."

3. Law on voluntary intoxication

What is the law's response to a defendant's plea that he lacked *mens rea* because of his voluntary intoxication?

R. v. Caldwell [1982] A.C. 341 (House of Lords)

(The facts are set out *ante* p. 178)

(Criminal Damage Act 1971, s.1(2):
"A person who without lawful excuse destroys or damages any property, whether belonging to himself or another—(a) intending to destroy or damage any property or being reckless as to whether any property would be destroyed or damaged; and (b) intending by the destruction or damage to endanger the life of another or being reckless as to whether the life of another would be thereby endangered; shall be guilty of an offence.")

Lord Diplock:
"As respects the charge under section 1(2) the prosecution did not rely upon an actual intent of the respondent to endanger the lives of the residents but relied on his having been reckless whether the lives of any of them would be endangered. His act of setting fire to it was one which the jury were entitled to think created an obvious risk that the lives of the residents would be endangered; and the only defence with which your Lordships are concerned is that the respondent had made himself so drunk as to render him oblivious of that risk. If the only mental state capable of constituting the necessary mens rea for an offence under section 1(2) were that expressed in the words 'intending by the destruction or damage to endanger the life of another,' it would have been necessary to consider whether the offence was to be classified as one of 'specific' intent for the purposes of the rule of law which this House affirmed and applied in *Reg.* v. *Majewski* [1977] A.C. 443; and this it plainly is. But this is not, in my view, a relevant inquiry where 'being reckless as to whether the life of another would be thereby endangered' is an alternative mental state that is capable of constituting the necessary mens rea of the offence with which he is charged.

The speech of Lord Elwyn-Jones L.C. in *Reg* v. *Majewski* . . . with which Lord Simon of Glaisdale, Lord Kilbrandon and I agreed, is authority that self-induced intoxication is no defence to a crime in which recklessness is enough to constitute the necessary mens rea. The charge in Majewski was of assault occasioning actual bodily harm and it was held by the majority of the House, approving *Reg* v. *Venna* [1976] Q.B. 421, 428, that recklessness in the use of force was sufficient to satisfy the mental element in the offence of assault. Reducing oneself by drink or drugs to a condition in which the restraints of reason and conscience are cast off was held to be a reckless course of conduct and an integral part of the crime. The Lord Chancellor accepted at p. 475 as correctly stating English law the provision in section 2.08(2) of the American Model Penal Code:
'When recklessness establishes an element of the offence, if the actor, due to self-induced intoxication, is unaware of a risk of which he would have been aware had he been sober, such unawareness is immaterial.'
So in the instant case, the fact that the respondent was unaware of the risk of endangering the lives of residents in the hotel owing to his self-induced intoxication would be no defence if that risk would have been obvious to him had he been sober.

My Lords, the Court of Appeal in the instant case regarded the case as turning on whether the offence under section 1(2) was one of 'specific' intent or 'basic' intent. Following a recent decision of the Court of Appeal by which they were bound, *Reg.* v. *Orpin* [1980] 1 W.L.R. 1050, they held that the offence under section 1(2) was one of 'specific' intent in contrast to the offence under section 1(1) which was of basic intent. This would be right if the only mens rea capable of constituting the offence were an actual intention to endanger the life of another. For the reasons I have given, however, classification into offences of 'specific' and 'basic' intent is irrelevant where being reckless as to whether a particular harmful consequence will result from one's act is a sufficient alternative mens rea."

Lord Edmund-Davies (dissenting):
"Something more must be said . . . having regard to the view expressed by my noble and learned friend, Lord Diplock, . . . that the speech of Lord Elwyn-Jones L.C. in *Reg.* v. *Majewski* 'is authority that self-induced intoxication is no defence to a crime in which recklessness is enough to constitute the necessary mens rea.' It is a view which, with respect, I do not share. In common with all the noble and learned Lords hearing that appeal, Lord Elwyn-Jones L.C. adopted the well-established (though not universally favoured) distinction between basic and specific intents. *Reg.* v. *Majewski* . . . related solely to charges of assault, undoubtedly an offence of basic intent, and the Lord Chancellor made it clear that his observations were confined to offences of that nature. . . . My respectful view is that *Majewski* accordingly supplies no support for the proposition that, in relation to crimes of specific intent (such as section 1(2)(b) of the Act of 1971) incapacity to appreciate the degree and nature of the risk created by his action which is attributable to the defendant's self-intoxication is an irrelevance. The Lord Chancellor was dealing simply with crimes of basic intent, and in my judgment it was strictly within that framework that he adopted the view expressed in the American Penal Code . . . and recklessness as an element in crimes of specific intent was, I am convinced, never within his contemplation.
For the foregoing reasons, the Court of Appeal were in my judgment right in quashing the conviction under section 1(2)(b) and substituting a finding of guilty of arson contrary to section 1(1) and (3) of the Act of 1971. It follows, therefore, that I agree with learned counsel for the respondent that the certified point of law should be answered in the following manner:
   Yes, evidence of self-induced intoxication can be relevant both to (a) whether the defendant *intended* to endanger the life of another, and to (b) whether the defendant *was reckless* as to whether the life of another would be endangered, within the meaning of section 1(2)(b) of the Criminal Damage Act 1971.
My Lords, it was recently predicted that 'There can hardly be any doubt that *all* crimes of recklessness except murder will now be held to be crimes of basic intent within *Majewski*': see *Glanville Williams, Textbook of Criminal Law,* p. 431. That prophecy has been promptly fulfilled by the majority of your Lordships, for, with the progressive displacement of 'maliciously' by 'intentionally' or 'recklessly' in statutory crimes, that will surely be the effect of the majority decision in this appeal. That I regret, for the consequence is that, however grave the crime charged, if recklessness can constitute its mens rea the fact that it was committed in drink can afford no defence. It is a very long time since we had so harsh a law in this country."

Appeal dismissed

Two propositions thus appear clear:
   (i) If the crime can be committed recklessly, then the defendant's intoxication at the time of the crime cannot be a defence. Given the objective test of recklessness laid down in *Caldwell*, the defendant is liable if the reasonable man would have foreseen

the risk as "obvious"; it is irrelevant whether the defendant, because of his intoxication, foresaw the risk himself. As most crimes can now be committed recklessly, it follows that intoxication is no defence to the majority of crimes in English law.[27]

(ii) If the crime can only be committed intentionally, then it is necessary to decide whether it is a crime of basic intent or one of specific intent. Intoxication is only a defence to the latter—and, as we shall see, it is seldom a *complete* defence to such crimes.

The meaning and rationale of each of these propositions must be examined.

(i) *Intoxication is no defence to crimes that can be committed recklessly*

The notion that intoxication is no defence to crimes that can be committed recklessly is not new,[28] but before *Caldwell* the principle was articulated somewhat differently as can be seen from the following words of Lord Elwyn-Jones L.C. in *Majewski*:

"If a man of his own volition takes a substance which causes him to cast off the restraints of reason and conscience, no wrong is done to him by holding him answerable criminally for any injury he may do while in that condition. His course of conduct in reducing himself by drugs and drink to that condition in my view supplies the evidence of mens rea, of guilty mind certainly sufficient for crimes of basic intent. It is a reckless course of conduct and recklessness is enough to constitute the necessary mens rea in assault cases: see *Reg.* v. *Venna* [1976] Q.B. 421, . . . The drunkenness is itself an intrinsic, an integral part of the crime, the other part being the evidence of the unlawful use of force against the victim. Together they add up to criminal recklessness."[29]

There were two problems with this approach. Suppose a defendant starts drinking at 8.00 p.m. and by 10.00 p.m. is no longer aware of his actions. At 11.00 p.m. he commits the *actus reus* of the crime. The *mens rea* of the crime (getting so drunk which is a reckless thing to do) precedes the *actus reus*. There is no coincidence of *actus reus* and *mens rea*, and as Dashwood points out:

"It might be argued that the carry-over of *mens rea* in the present situation would correspond to that in the famous cases of *Thabo-Meli* and *Church* [*ante*, p. 247] where the immediate cause of death was not the

---

[27] What is the position of those offences which can be committed "maliciously"? In *Dolbey* (1989) 88 Cr.App.R. 1 it was held that this term is not synonymous with recklessness and still bears its old subjective meaning (see *ante*, p. 197). Accordingly, it might be necessary to subject such crimes to the test in (ii)—*viz.* is it a crime of specific or basic intent? However, it does seem odd to ask of a crime that does *not require intention* whether it is a crime of specific or basic *intention*! This point is probably not of great practical importance because it is well-established law that intoxication is no defence to most such offences, for example, section 20 of the Offences against the Person Act 1861.

[28] See Model Penal Code, Art. 2, s.2.08(2).

[29] [1977] A.C. 443 at 474–475.

attack upon the victim but the measures taken to dispose of what was believed to be a dead body. However, an important distinction is that in these cases the attack and the disposal of the supposed corpse represented successive steps in a single criminal transaction, the later act being consciously linked in the mind of the accused with the earlier act; such an analysis would not apply to the case of misconduct following reckless intoxication."[30]

The second problem with Lord Elwyn-Jones' approach is that recklessness does not exist in the abstract. One has to be reckless as to a particular consequence. Thus under the old subjective test of recklessness it should have been necessary to establish that when the defendant was getting drunk (the recklessness) he foresaw the possibility of his committing the crime.

It is quite clear that the courts were less concerned with fine arguments such as these than with ensuring that a fair and just solution (in terms of balancing the competing interests of protection of society and the rights of the defendant) was achieved. As Lord Simon said:

"One of the prime purposes of the criminal law, with its penal sanctions, is the protection from certain proscribed conduct of persons who are pursuing their lawful lives. Unprovoked violence has, from time immemorial, been a significant part of such proscribed violence. To accede to the argument on behalf of the appellant would leave the citizen legally unprotected from unprovoked violence where such violence was the consequence of drink or drugs having obliterated the capacity of the perpetrator to know what he was doing or what were its consequences."[31]

If the doctrine of *mens rea* were to be put in its old strait-jacket of subjective intention and recklessness, strict logic would clearly demand the acquittal of those incapacitated by drink or drugs. But, if a broader view of *mens rea* was taken, that it indicates fault or blameworthiness, then one can attribute blame to the person who renders himself insensible through drink and commits a crime. As Lord Russell in *Majewski* said:

"*Mens rea* has many aspects. If asked to define it in such a case as the present I would say that *the element of guilt or moral turpitude* is supplied by the act of self-intoxication reckless of possible consequences."[32]

Such views were endorsed by Lord Simon in *Majewski*:

"*Mens rea* is therefore on ultimate analysis the state of mind stigmatised as wrongful by the criminal law which, when compounded with the relevant prohibited conduct, constitutes a particular offence. There is no juristic reason why mental incapacity brought about by self-induced intoxication, to realise what one is doing or its probable

---

[30] A. Dashwood, "Logic and the Lords in Majewski" [1977] Crim.L.R. 532, 591 at 540.

[31] *Majewski* [1977] A.C. 442 at 476.

[32] *Ibid.* at p. 498 (Emphasis added).

consequences should not be such a state of mind stigmatised as wrongful by the criminal law."[33]

The whole case of *Majewski* provides a striking instance of how the attack upon subjective *mens rea* had commenced many years[34] before *Caldwell*. When subjective *mens rea* correllated with ordinary people's notions of fault or blameworthiness, it could be left well alone; when it did not the concept of subjective *mens rea* had to be jettisoned; the true (though until *Caldwell*, unarticulated) basis of *mens rea* was the attribution of blame, which might, or might not, coincide with a defendant's subjective state of mind. These points were taken by Lord Diplock in *Caldwell*. By redefining recklessness to make it an objective test, he was able to avoid such criticisms as "recklessness does not exist in the abstract." Under the new test, if the particular risk would have been obvious to ordinary people, then the defendant *is* reckless *as to the particular consequence*.

As if in anticipation of *Caldwell*, the Criminal Law Revision Committee recommended in 1980 that the rules on voluntary intoxication be placed on a statutory basis:

> "267(1): . . . evidence of voluntary intoxication should be capable of negating the mental element in murder and the intention required for the commission of any other offence; and
>
> (2) in offences in which recklessness constitutes an element of the offence, if the defendant owing to voluntary intoxication had no appreciation of a risk which he would have appreciated had he been sober, such lack of appreciation is immaterial . . .
>
> 270. The test in (2) above is formulated in such a way as to require the court to take into consideration any particular knowledge or any other personal characteristics of the defendant, as for example backwardness. Thus in a case where a gun is discharged killing or injuring another a jury might consider that many people could have made a mistake about the risk. But if the defendant was familiar with firearms the jury may find that he would have appreciated the risk if he had been sober. For similar reasons it would be unjust that a subnormal person should be judged on the same basis as one of average intelligence."[35]

Is this the same as the test that Lord Diplock put forward in *Caldwell*?

(ii) *If the crime can only be committed intentionally, intoxication is only a defence to those crimes of "specific" intent*

Until *Caldwell* when the "recklessness test" was firmly laid down, the law was that intoxication was a defence to crimes of "specific intent"

---

[33] P. 153.
[34] *Majewski* was the culmination of a long line of cases. See notes 36–38.
[35] 14th Report, Offences Against the Person, Cmnd. 7844 (1980).

but not to crimes of "basic intent." This rule is now only applicable to those crimes that cannot be committed recklessly.

The rule has a long and eminent progeny dating back to *Beard*[36] and being endorsed by the House of Lords in *Gallagher*,[37] *Bratty*[38] and *Majewski*.[39]

The distinction was a purely functional one aimed at achieving a "compromise between the rigors of denying the relevance of intoxication and allowing it to undercut all liability."[40] Thus crimes such as murder and section 18[41] could be deemed crimes of specific intent and the defendant could be convicted of the lesser-included offences of manslaughter or section 20.[42] Thus intoxication was, in effect, taken into account as a mitigating factor, but the defendant was still being held responsible (to a lesser extent) for his drunken acts. Problems started arising however when the courts tried "to employ these terms as though they had a meaning beyond their function."[43] What actually do these terms "specific" and "basic" intent mean? The true answer is—nothing. They are like elephants—the courts know them when they see them (*i.e.* they know when a defendant's liability can be reduced without his escaping all liability), but they cannot be defined.

But over the last decade, several attempts have been made to define "specific" and "basic" intent. While there has not been complete unanimity on the subject,[44] the cumulative effect of *Majewski* and *Caldwell* would appear to be the following[45]: crimes of specific intent are crimes where the *mens rea* of the offence extends beyond the *actus reus* (sometimes called crimes of ulterior intent), while in crimes of basic intent the *mens rea* goes no further than extending to the elements of the *actus reus* itself. An example will illustrate this distinction. Assault is a crime of basic intent—the *actus reus* is causing apprehension of immediate force; the *mens rea* is an intention (or recklessness) to cause such apprehen-

---

[36] [1920] A.C. 479.

[37] [1963] A.C. 349.

[38] [1963] A.C. 386.

[39] [1977] A.C. 443.

[40] Fletcher, p. 849.

[41] Offences against the Person Act 1861 (wounding or causing grievous bodily harm with intent to cause grievous bodily harm). See *post*, p. 555.

[42] Offences against the Person Act 1861 (maliciously inflicting grievous bodily harm). See *post*, p. 550.

[43] Fletcher, p. 850.

[44] Lord Simon in *Majewski* equated specific intent with "direct" intent (*i.e.* aim, purpose): "the prosecution must in general prove that the purpose for the commission of the act extends to the intent expressed or implied in the definition of the crime" (p. 479). This view is supported in Alan R. Ward, "Making Some Sense of Self-Induced Intoxication" (1986) 45 C.L.J. 247. Lord Elwyn-Jones L.C. in *Majewski* employed the "recklessness test" to determine whether a crime was one of specific intent (see *ante*, p. 381). Note the difference between this approach and that of Lord Diplock in *Caldwell*. Lord Elwyn-Jones L.C. uses the "recklessness test" to identify crimes of basic and specific intent. To Lord Diplock the basic/specific intent distinction is only of relevance to those crimes that cannot be committed recklessly.

[45] This was the view of Lord Diplock and the majority in *Caldwell*; it also appears to be the view of the dissenting judges (Lord Edmund-Davies and Lord Wilberforce) in that case. A clear majority in *Majewski* can also be found to support this view (Lords Elwyn-Jones, Diplock, Kilbrandon and Edmund-Davies).

sion—no *mens rea* extending beyond the *actus reus* is required. But assault with intent to resist arrest,[46] is a crime of specific intent—the *actus reus* is the same as that of common assault, namely, causing apprehension of immediate force; the *mens rea* is two-fold—there must be the *mens rea* of the assault *and in addition* there must be an intent to resist arrest. This additional intention does not relate to anything in the *actus reus* of the crime; it extends beyond the *actus reus*; the crime is thus one of specific intent.

Whether the courts will apply this principle with any degree of consistency remains to be seen, but on the basis of principle and pre-existing authority it would appear that the following cannot be committed recklessly, and are crimes of specific intent, thus allowing drunkenness to operate as a defence thereto: wounding with intent contrary to section 18, Offences Against the Person Act 1861[47]; theft[48]; robbery[49]; burglary[50]; attempt[51]; forgery[52]; assault with intent to resist arrest[53]—and murder. It must be emphasised that this list does not purport to be exhaustive.

(iii) *The special position of murder*

There is abundant authority for the proposition that intoxication is a defence to the crime of murder; the defendant will instead be found guilty of the lesser included offence of manslaughter.[54] This proposition is however difficult to square with the rules outlined above. Since *Moloney* and *Hancock*, murder is now a crime of intention; it cannot be committed recklessly and so the first hurdle has been overcome. However, in the years preceding *Moloney* and *Hancock* when murder was a crime that probably could have been committed recklessly,[55] it was never doubted that drunkenness was a defence to murder. But further, irrespective of this argument, the second hurdle is not overcome; it is not a crime of specific intent as the *mens rea* does not extend beyond the *actus reus*. As already suggested, the only explanation for this approach is in terms of policy.

---

[46] Offences against the Person Act 1861, s.38, as amended.

[47] *Bratty* [1963] A.C. 386; *Pordage* [1975] Crim.L.R. 575; *Majewski* [1977] A.C. 443; *Bailey* [1983] 1 W.L.R. 760. While *wounding* with intent to cause grievous bodily harm is clearly a crime of specific intent under this test, *causing grievous bodily harm* with intent to cause grievous bodily harm is equally clearly *not* a crime of specific intent. However, the courts in the past have not distinguished between these two and it is doubted whether they will do so in future as there is no harm in allowing intoxication as a defence to a charge of s.18 as the defendant can still be convicted of the lesser included offence, s.20, a crime to which drunkenness is no defence.

[48] Theft Act 1968, s.1. *Ruse* v. *Reed* [1949] 1 K.B. 377; Lord Salmon in *Majewski* at 482.

[49] *Ibid.*, s.8.

[50] *Ibid.*, s.9.

[51] The *actus reus* is doing an act more than merely preparatory to the proposed offence; the *mens rea* goes beyond this—there must be an intention actually to commit the crime. *Cf.* Lord Salmon in *Majewski* indicating that attempted suicide was a crime of specific intent (p. 483).

[52] Forgery and Counterfeiting Act 1981, s.1. See *Durante* [1972] 3 All E.R. 962 on s.7(*a*) of the now repealed Forgery Act 1913. In *Durante* it was also held that handling stolen goods contrary to the Theft Act 1968, s.22 was a crime of specific intent—this is not however a crime of "ulterior" intent.

[53] *Ante*, n. 46.

[54] *Beard* [1920] A.C. 479; *Gallagher* [1963] A.C. 349; *Majewski* [1977] A.C. 443.

[55] This was certainly a plausible interpretation of *Hyam* [1975] A.C. 55.

John Sellers, "Mens Rea and the Judicial Approach to 'Bad Excuses' in the Criminal Law" (1978) 41 M.L.R. 245, 261:

"For two distinct reasons murder is in a special position. First, it is distinct in that the penalty on conviction is mandatory. Though it may be felt inappropriate to acquit the intoxicated defendant of an offence of 'basic intent,' this does not mean that it may not be appropriate to differentiate between the punishment of such a defendant and the truly deliberate wrongdoer. The fact that the penalty for murder affords no scope for such differentiation may be a good reason for allowing a conviction for manslaughter where the court does have a discretion about sentence. . . . Secondly . . . murder is distinct in that it is a rare example of an offence of 'basic intent' which has, in manslaughter, a counterpart designed to punish those who accidentally as opposed to deliberately bring about the actus reus. The choice in homicide therefore, has never been simply between acquittal or conviction for an offence of 'basic intent' . . . there is, as an alternative, the possibility of conviction for an offence which is designed to punish a certain kind of culpable accident. Murder, therefore, is an offence of 'basic intent,' but there are special reasons, in the shape of an alternative conviction for manslaughter, which make it appropriate to allow evidence of intoxication its factual relevance to malice aforethought."[56]

(iv) A partial defence?

As we have seen, the courts have been loath to admit intoxication as a complete defence to a criminal charge as the defendant was clearly at fault in reducing himself to such a level of intoxication. But as such a defendant was not aware of his actions at the time of the crime, his position was analogous to that of a negligent wrongdoer—who deserved punishment but possibly not to the same extent as the intentional wrongdoer. Thus the compromise was developed that intoxication would be a defence to those crimes of intention where there was a lesser included offence for which the defendant could be convicted. Thus intoxication has the practical effect of reducing murder to manslaughter[57] and of reducing section 18 to section 20. The Californian Penal Code expressly incorporates this compromise that intoxication can only reduce liability to an offence of a lower species or degree.[58]

However, despite this underlying rationale of the defence of drunkenness, it is clear that intoxication can sometimes operate as a complete defence in English law. As Lord Russell stated in *Majewski*:

"special intent cases are not restricted to those crimes in which the absence of a special intent leaves available a lesser crime embodying no special intent, but embraces all cases of special intent even though no alternative lesser criminal charge is available."[59]

The crime of theft is just such a case. Intoxication is a defence to a

---

[56] Such an approach was endorsed by the Criminal Law Revision Committee, 14th Report. See *ante*, n. 35.
[57] See C. M. V. Clarkson, "Drunkenness, Constructive Manslaughter and Specific Intent" (1978) 41 M.L.R. 478.
[58] Cal. Penal Code, Art. 22; Fletcher, pp. 848–849.
[59] At p. 499.

charge of theft,[60] although there is no lesser included offence of which the defendant can be convicted.

Is it satisfactory that intoxication is sometimes a complete defence and sometimes only a partial defence?

(v) *Drunken mistake*

In most cases a drunken defendant will claim that a mistake has been made with the result that *mens rea* is missing. For example, there will be a claim that there was no intention to kill; the drunken defendant thought he was shooting at a tree stump. Such a plea will be dealt with under the rules canvassed above.

But, what is the position where a drunken defendant makes a mistakes as to a "defence"? For instance, in his drunken stupor he thinks he is being attacked or being subjected to duress. The position now taken by the English courts is that such a drunken mistake, however genuinely believed, is no defence to a criminal charge—not even to crimes of specific intent.

R. v. O'Grady [1987] 1 Q.B. 995 (Court of Appeal, Criminal Division)

The appellant woke from a drunken stupor to find his equally drunken friend hitting him. In order to defend himself he retaliated with several blows and then returned to sleep. He awoke to find his friend dead. He was convicted of manslaughter and appealed on the ground that the judge had misdirected the jury as to the law of mistake.

Lord Lane C.J.:
"We have come to the conclusion that where the jury are satisfied that the defendant was mistaken in his belief that any force or the force which he in fact used was necessary to defend himself and are further satisfied that the mistake was caused by voluntarily induced intoxication, the defence must fail. We do not consider that any distinction should be drawn on this aspect of the matter between offences involving what is called specific intent, such as murder, and offences of so called basic intent, such as manslaughter. Quite apart from the problem of directing a jury in a case such as the present where manslaughter is an alternative verdict to murder, the question of mistake can and ought to be considered separately from the question of intent. . . .

This brings us to the question of public order. There are two competing interests. On the one hand the interest of the defendant who has only acted according to what he believed to be necessary to protect himself, and on the other hand that of the public in general and the victim in particular who, probably through no fault of his own, has been injured or perhaps killed because of the defendant's drunken mistake. Reason recoils from the conclusion that in such circumstances a defendant is entitled to leave the Court without a stain on his character. . . .

We have therefore come to the conclusion that a defendant is not entitled to rely, so far as self-defence is concerned, upon a mistake of fact which has been induced by voluntary intoxication."

Appeal dismissed

---

[60] *Ante*, n. 48.

R. v. Fotheringham (1989) 88 Cr.App.R. 206 (Court of Appeal, Criminal Division)

The appellant and his wife went out for the evening leaving a fourteen year-old girl to babysit. The wife (probably in the appellant's absence) told the girl to sleep in the matrimonial bed. On returnng home the appellant got into the matrimonial bed and had sexual intercourse with the girl without her consent. The wife appeared and the intercourse ceased. The appellant was charged with rape but claimed that because of drunkenness, he had mistaken the girl for his wife. He admitted that he would not have made this mistake if he had been sober. The judge directed the jury to disregard the appellant's self-induced intoxication in considering whether there were reasonable grounds for his believing that he was having sexual intercouse with a consenting woman, namely, his wife. The appellant was convicted and appealed.

Watkins L.J.:
"The point of law . . . [is] whether it is a defence to a charge of rape . . . that a defendant, as a result of self-induced intoxication, has an honest but mistaken belief that he was having conjugal relations . . .

Counsel had to recognise, as in fact he did, that where the issue in rape is consent, a defendant's self-induced intoxication is not a relevant matter which a jury are entitled to take into account in deciding whether there were reasonable grounds for the defendant's belief that the woman consented—see *Woods* (1982) 74 Cr.App.R. 312. Likewise he had to face the law, which is that 'self-induced intoxication is no defence to a crime in which recklessness is enough to constitute the necessary *mens rea*'—see . . . [*Caldwell* where Lord Diplock refers to *Majewski*] where it was held that rape is a crime of basic intent to which self-induced intoxication is no defence . . .

[The appellant'argument] clearly runs counter to authority, which is that in rape self-induced intoxication is no defence, whether the issue be intention, consent or, as here, mistake as to the identity of the victim. We do not doubt that the public would be outraged if the law were to be declared to be otherwise . . . "

Appeal dismissed

There are severe problems with the approach adopted in these cases. Intoxication is a partial defence to offences of specific intent where the defendant has made a mistake regarding one of the *actus reus* elements, for example, thinking he is shooting a tree-stump. But it is no defence to a mistake affecting the existence of a "defence" element. However, we saw that in *Williams (Gladstone)* and *Beckford* the court achieved their desired consequence of allowing an honest mistake to exculpate by classifying the requirement of "unlawfulness" as part of the *actus reus*. It does seem distinctly odd that criminal liability should depend on whether one classifies the requirement of "unlawfulness" as relating to *actus reus* or to a defence. It further seems odd that the criminal law should devise the whole artificial construct of specific intent but then refuse to apply it in such cases. It is difficult to see any material distinction in culpability between a defendant who makes a drunken mistake about the *actus reus* and one who makes a similar mistake concerning a defence element. If policy dictates that intoxication should be a defence to crimes of specific intent, this should be true irrespective of the nature of the mistake made.

There are certain statutes that expressly provide that a defendant has a defence if he holds a particular belief. For example, the Criminal Damage Act 1971, section 5(2) provides that a person has a defence (or a 'lawful excuse' as per section 1(1)) to a charge of criminal damage if he believed that he had the consent of the person entitled to give consent and section 5(3) provides that "it is immaterial whether a belief is justified or not if it is honestly held." What is the position where a defendant only holds such a belief because of his drunkenness?

Jaggard v. Dickinson [1981] Q.B. 527 (Queen's Bench Divisional Court)

The appellant while drunk broke two windows and damaged a curtain in another person's house. She honestly believed that the house belonged to a friend who would have consented to her breaking in and causing the damage.

Mustill J.:

"Her defence is founded on the state of belief called for by section 5(2). True, the fact of the appellant's intoxication was relevant to the defence under section 5(2), for it helped to explain what would otherwise have been inexplicable, and hence lent colour to her evidence about the state of her belief. This is not the same as using drunkenness to rebut an inference of intention or recklessness. Belief, like intention or recklessness, is a state of mind: but they are not the same states of mind.

Can it nevertheless be said that, even if the context is different, the principles established by *Reg v. Majewski* . . . ought to be applied to this new situation? If the basis of the decision in *Reg. v. Majewski* had been that drunkenness does not prevent a person from having an intent or being reckless, then there would be grounds for saying that it should equally be left out of account when deciding on his state of belief. But this is not in our view what *Reg. v. Majewski* decided. The House of Lords did not conclude that intoxication was irrelevant to the fact of the defendant's state of mind, but rather that, whatever might have been his actual state of mind, he should for reasons of policy be precluded from relying on any alteration in that state brought about by self-induced intoxication. . . . But these considerations do not apply to a case where Parliament has specifically required the court to consider the defendant's actual state of belief, not the state of belief which ought to have existed. It seems to us that the court is required by section 5(3) to focus on the existence of the belief, not its intellectual soundness; and a belief can be just as much honestly held if it is induced by intoxication as if it stems from stupidity, forgetfulness or inattention. . . .

Parliament has specifically isolated one subjective element, in the shape of honest belief, and has given it separate treatment, and its own special gloss in section 5(3). This being so, there is nothing objectionable in giving it special treatment as regards drunkenness, in accordance with the natural meaning of the words."

Appeal allowed

Should this decision be regarded as "anomalous"[61] or as "an occasion

---

[61] Smith and Hogan, p. 215.

for rejoicing"[62] as a triumph for subjectivism? It does seem distinctly odd that the whole test of recklessness was made objective in *Caldwell* so that evidence of drunkenness would be irrelevant—and yet the test of "belief" in section 5(3) remains subjective so that drunkenness is highly relevant. Where a defendant causing criminal damage makes a drunken mistake, his entire criminal liability depends on the precise form of his mistake. For instance, if he makes a mistake and thinks the property is his own, he will be liable as drunkenness is no defence to a charge of criminal damage. If, however, because of his drunkenness he believes that the owner would consent to the damage to the property, then section 5(3) applies and, as in *Jaggard* v. *Dickinson*, the defendant will escape liability.

It is interesting to compare section 5(3) with section 8 of the Criminal Justice Act 1967. In *Majewski* Lord Elwyn-Jones held that drunkenness could not be taken into account under section 8:

"It's purpose and effect [section 8] was to alter the law of evidence about the presumption of intention to produce the reasonable and probable consequences of one's acts. It was not intended to change the common law rule. In referring to 'all the evidence' it meant all the *relevant* evidence. But if there is a substantive rule of law that in crimes of basic intent, the factor of intoxication is irrelevant (and such I hold to be the substantive law), evidence with regard to it is quite irrelevant."[63]

It has been commented that it "is difficult to see that section 5(3) performs any different function in relation to lawful excuse than section 8 of the Criminal Justice Act 1967 performs in relation to intention and recklessness."[64] If evidence of drunkenness is irrelevant to an ascertainment of intention or foresight, it is difficult to understand why it is relevant to determining whether one believes another had consented to their property being damaged.[65]

(vi) *Reform of the law*

George P. Fletcher, Rethinking Criminal Law (1978), pp. 847–8:

"His fault in rendering himself non-responsible at the time of the violent act is constant, whether he commits a burglary, a rape, or a murder. To bring the scope of his liability into line with his culpability in getting drunk, the law seeks a compromise. There has to be some accommodation between (1) the principle that if someone gets drunk, he is liable for the violent consequences, and (2) the principle that liability and punishment should be graded in proportion to actual culpability.

German law and American law reveal two different approaches to reconciling

---

[62] Glanville Williams, *Textbook*, p. 479.
[63] At p. 475–476.
[64] Celia Wells, "Swatting the Subjectivist Bug" [1982] Crim.L.R. 209.
[65] See also *Woods* (1982) Cr.App.R. 312. *Cf. Young* [1984] 2 All E.R. 164. These cases were discussed in the first edition of this book at pp. 308–309.

these conflicting principles. German law includes intoxication along with mental illness as a basis for denying the capacity to be held accountable for a wrongful act. Deference to the conflicting principle of liability for the risk implicit in getting drunk is found in a special section of the Code, which is here translated in full:

§323a (1) Whoever intentionally or negligently becomes intoxicated through the use of alcohol or other intoxicating substances is punishable up to five years in prison, if while in that intoxicated condition he commits a wrongful act and if by virtue of the intoxication is not responsible for that act (or his non-responsibility is a possibility).

(2) In no event may the punishment be greater than that for the wrongful act committed in the state of intoxication.

The concept of negligence underlying this provision is negligence as to the risk of committing a crime while intoxicated. If the suspect takes adequate precautions against committing a crime while intoxicated, there is no negligence. If, for example, he hires someone to supervise his conduct while he is intoxicated and the hired person unexpectedly fails to restrain him, there would be a good case against liability. If he gets drunk in a bar and while in a state of non-responsibility he throws a bottle at a valuable mirror, he is not punished for the wrongful act of intentionally destroying the property of another; rather he is punished for the wrongful act of creating a risk that he would behave non-responsibly and intentionally destroy property. . . .

[T]he theory of the provision is not simply that he negligently take the risk that he might do some harm. The requirement of a wrongful act while intoxicated is an important limitation.

Indeed the limitation suggests that the theory underlying the provision is not simply one of negligently endangering other persons. If risk-taking were the essence of the crime, there would be no concern about the wrongfulness of the intoxicated act and indeed it would be hard to explain why the subsequent act should be required at all."

Criminal Law Revision Committee, 14th Report, Offences Against the Person, Cmnd. 7844 (1980) paras. 259–264:

"259. . . . What calls for punishment is getting intoxicated and when in that condition behaving in a way which society cannot, and should not, tolerate. An offence which covers this situation must make some reference to the harm caused, and cannot be expressed simply in terms of getting dangerously intoxicated, however gross the intoxication may have been. Furthermore, the harm needs to be identified to some extent: the drunken man who on arrest punches a police officer should not be labelled with the same offence as the alcoholic who kills a child when trying to interfere with her sexually. It is doubtful whether any solution to the problem based solely upon legal principle would be generally acceptable. Policy has to be taken into account. . . .

260. The Butler Committee considered offences committed while voluntarily intoxicated (paragraphs 18.51—18.59 of their report), and they proposed the creation of a strict liability offence where a person while voluntarily intoxicated does an act (or makes an omission) that would amount to a dangerous offence if it were done or made with the requisite state of mind for that offence. Their proposal is that the offence should not be charged in the first instance. On indictment the jury would be directed to find on this offence in the event of intoxication being successfully raised as a defence to the offence originally charged. A bench of magistrates dealing summarily with an offence would have

to direct themselves. For convenience in the rest of this section of the report we have referred only to juries. On this proposal the jury would have no option but to convict of the dangerous intoxication offence. On conviction of the offence on indictment the maximum penalty suggested is one year's imprisonment for a first offence or three years' imprisonment for a second or subsequent one; on summary trial the maximum sentence of imprisonment would be six months.

261. One of the defects in the Butler Committee proposal is, in our opinion, the problem of the nomenclature of the offence. A conviction of the Butler Committee offence would merely record a conviction of an offence of committing a dangerous act while intoxicated. This is insufficient. The record must indicate the nature of the act committed, for example whether it was an assault or a killing. It would be unfair for a defendant who has committed a relatively minor offence while voluntarily intoxicated to be labelled as having committed the same offence as a defendant who has killed. The penalty suggested is also in our opinion insufficient to deal with serious offences such as killings or rapes while voluntarily intoxicated by drink or drugs.

262. Professors Smith and Glanville Williams support the proposal of a separate offence because in the first place they consider it to be a fundamental principle that a person should not be convicted of an offence requiring recklessness when he was not in fact reckless. In such a case the verdict of the jury and the record of the court do not represent the truth. Secondly, they think it important that the verdict of the jury should distinguish between an offender who was reckless and one who was not because that is relevant to the question of sentence. . . .

263. For these reasons Professors Smith and Glanville Williams provided an improved version of the Butler Committee proposal for the consideration of the Committee. In the interests of conciseness and clarity their proposal is set out in the following propositions: it is not intended to be a final legislative draft.

1. Intoxication shall be taken into account for the purpose of determining whether the person charged had formed an intention, specific or otherwise, in the absence of which he would not be guilty of the offence.

2. Where a person is charged with an offence and he relies on evidence of voluntary intoxication, whether introduced by himself or by any other party to the case, for the purpose of showing that he was not aware of a risk where awareness of that risk is, or is part of, the mental element required for conviction of the offence, then, if:

    (a) the jury are not satisfied that he was aware of the risk, but
    (b) the jury are satisfied
       (i) that all the elements of the offence other than any mental element have been proved, and
       (ii) that the defendant would, in all the circumstances of the case, have been aware of the risk if he had not been voluntarily intoxicated,

the jury shall find him not guilty of the offence charged but guilty of doing the act while in a state of voluntary intoxication. . . .

5. A person convicted under (2) . . . above shall, where the charge was of murder, be liable to the same punishment as for manslaughter; and in any other case shall be liable to the same punishment as that provided by the law for the offence charged.

264. If there is to be a separate offence of doing the *actus reus* of an offence while voluntarily intoxicated we are all agreed that the proposal set out above is to be preferred to that of the Butler Committee. The majority of us feel, however, that that proposal would also create problems. The separate offence would add to the already considerable number of matters which a jury often has to consider when deciding whether the offences charged have been proved, and some of us feel that the separate offence would make the jury's task even more diffi-

cult than it is at present in some cases. . . . It seems likely moreover, that if the separate offence is created there would be many more trials in which defendants would raise the issue of drunkenness, . . . [M]any defendants might seek to plead to the special offence rather than the offence charged, either because they might prefer to be convicted of the special offence rather than the offence charged (as for example rape), or because the special offence might tend to be regarded as a less serious offence. . . . We also consider that it is artificial and undesirable to have a separate offence for which conviction is automatic but which carries the same maximum penalty as the offence for which a defendant would have been convicted but for the lack of proof of the required mental element due to intoxication. It is also important to consider the public reaction to the creation of a separate offence: we are of the opinion that they would be confused by it."

Andrew Ashworth, "Intoxication and General Defences" [1980] Crim.L.R. 556 at 558–560:

"[M]any people drive whilst intoxicated without infringing any other rules of the road, and yet the criminal law does not hesitate to strike at the risk-creation involved in drunken driving, without waiting for the risk to materialise. Indeed, for that offence complete intoxication is not required and a certain blood/alcohol concentration suffices, and for controlled drugs mere possession attracts criminal liability. A prohibition on alcohol would be unworkable; yet, since drinking oneself into a state of intoxication involves voluntarily casting off 'the restraints of reason and conscience,' should the law not go further than the summary offences of public drunkenness and make intoxication itself a serious crime, as a kind of inchoate offence? The Committee might well use the following arguments against this. First, it might be possible to construct a statistical argument that only a minority of totally intoxicated persons actually cause harm whilst in that condition. Secondly, the social effects of criminalising intoxication would be more widely resented than the prohibition on driving with excess alcohol. But thirdly, when an intoxicated person does cause harm, the balance is tilted in favour of criminal liability. Whilst it might be oppressive to punish all intoxicated persons (even though no harm is caused) on the basis that they have voluntarily created a risk, a law which reserves that punishment for those intoxicated persons who do cause harm cannot be reproached with sacrificing individual liberty to a statistical possibility. If he has caused harm, the risk has materialised. Thus a higher value is set upon popular conceptions of liberty (perhaps because alcohol fulfils a social want, and because wider criminalisation might bring a style of law enforcement which would unduly infringe other liberties) than upon the benefits to society in general and to victims in particular of a peremptory requirement that citizens should not so intoxicate themselves as to lose control over their behaviour.

The Appropriate Label for the Offence

The Committee agree that a principal defect of the Butler recommendation was the proposed label: a single offence of being dangerously intoxicated would lump together the intoxicated child killer and the drunken brawler (paras. 259, 261). Why exactly do the Committee object to this? . . .

What is the nature of "the offender's fault" in intoxicated harm-doing? His fault lies in rendering himself insensible and uncontrolled. . . . "

What do the above arguments tell us about the importance (or otherwise) of the harm done in the ascertainment of criminal liability?

Draft Criminal Code Bill 1989 (Law Com. No. 177, 1989):

22.—(1) Where an offence requires a fault element of recklessness (however described), a person who was voluntarily intoxicated shall be treated—
  (a) as having been aware of any risk of which he would have been aware had he been sober;
  (b) as not having believed in the existence of an exempting circumstance (where the existence of such a belief is in issue) if he would not have so believed had he been sober.
  (2) Where an offence requires a fault element of failure to comply with a standard of care, or requires no fault, a person who was voluntarily intoxicated shall be treated as not having believed in the existence of an exempting circumstance (where the existence of such a belief is in issue) if a reasonable sober person would not have so believed.
  (3) Where the definition of a fault element or of a defence refers, or requires references, to the state of mind or conduct to be expected of a reasonable person, such person shall be understood to be one who is not intoxicated.
  (4) Subsection (1) does not apply—
  (a) to murder (to which section 55 applies); or
  (b) to the case (to which section 36 applies) where a person's unawareness or belief arises from a combination of mental disorder and voluntary intoxication.
  55. A person is guilty of manslaughter if—
  (b) he is not guilty of murder by reason only of the fact that, because of voluntary intoxication, he is not aware that death may be caused or believes that an exempting circumstance exists;
  36. A mental disorder verdict shall be returned if—
  (a) the defendant is acquitted of an offence only because, by reason of evidence of mental disorder or a combination of mental disorder and intoxication, it is found that he acted or may have acted in a state of automatism, or without the fault required for the offence, or believing that an exempting circumstance existed; and
  56.—(3) Where a person suffering from mental abnormality is also intoxicated, this section (diminished responsibility) applies only where it would apply if he were not intoxicated."

4. Involuntary intoxication

Where a defendant is reduced to a state of intoxication through no fault of his own (because, for example, his drinks were "laced")[66] he cannot be "blamed" for his actions and will accordingly have a defence to any criminal charge. This is consistent with the now prevailing view that unless some "blame" (but not necessarily subjective *mens rea*) can be laid at the defendant's door, he ought not to be held responsible for his actions.

5. "Dutch courage" intoxication

Where a person deliberately reduces himself to a state of intoxication to give himself "Dutch Courage" to commit a crime, his intoxication

---

[66] See *ante*, p. 377 for the definition of "voluntary" intoxication; see also *ante*, n. 25.

will not be a defence even to crimes that can only be committed with a specific intention. He is to be "blamed" to the same extent as the person who intentionally commits a crime. As Lord Denning stated in *Gallagher*:

"If a man, whilst sane and sober, forms an intention to kill . . . and then gets himself drunk so as to give himself Dutch courage to do the killing . . . he cannot rely on this self-induced drunkenness as a defence to a charge of murder, nor even as reducing it to manslaughter . . . the wickedness of his mind before he got drunk is enough to condemn him, coupled with the act which he intended to do and did do."[67]

6. Intoxication can cause insanity

Drunkenness can cause a disease of the mind sufficient to bring the defendant within the insanity rules.[68] It can cause, for example, a *delirium tremens*. However, the defence is rarely successful in England. In *Burns*[69] a psychiatrist testified that Burns had a disease of the mind because his brain was damaged by alcohol with the result that on the occasion of the alleged crime he was suffering from "amnesia in the sense that the thing does not register at the time because the brain function is impaired" which meant that Burns did not know what he was doing, or that it was wrong. It was accepted that this defence could result in an insanity verdict, but the jury rejected the psychiatric evidence and concluded that Burns knew what he was doing.

English law does not accept the view that chronic alcoholism in itself is a disease of the mind. Contrast this approach with the following views.

Salzman v. United States, 405 F.2d 358 (1968) (United States Court of Appeals, District of Columbia Circuit)

Skelly Wright, Circuit Judge:
"Appellant Salzman raises questions regarding the relationship of chronic alcoholism to criminal responsibility. Specifically, he argues that the jury should have been allowed to consider, and to acquit if it so found, whether the act with which he is charged—robbery—was the product of a disease from which he claims to be suffering—chronic alcoholism. Because the record is inadequate to present this claim, his conviction is affirmed. However, . . . because the problems are important, I set forth my own view.

---

[67] [1963] A.C. 349.
[68] *Davis* (1881) 14 Cox C.C. 563; *Beard* [1920] A.C. 479; *Gallagher* [1963] A.C. 349. It is doubtful whether the transient effect of drink or drugs could amount to an "injury" causing an "abnormality of mind," as specified by the Homicide Act 1957, s.2(1) (*Di Duca* (1959) 43 Cr.App.R. 167; *Fenton* (1975) 119 S.J. 695.), but it is likely that a permanent injury to the brain caused by drink or drugs would amount to an "injury." This point does not have much practical significance however, as the effect of a defence of voluntary intoxication is to reduce murder to manslaughter—exactly the same effect as a defence of diminished responsibility.
[69] (1974) 58 Cr.App.R. 364.

I

The question is whether a person claiming to be a chronic alcoholic should be acquitted of any crime if the jury finds that he was suffering from a disease and that his actions were a product of that disease; whether, therefore, the proper disposition of such a person is to a treatment facility rather than to a penal institution. I think the question should be answered in the affirmative.

In the long-standing debate over criminal responsibility there has always been a strong conviction in our jurisprudence that to hold a man criminally responsible his actions must have been voluntary, the product of a 'free will'. Accordingly, when there has been a consensus that in a certain type of case free will is lacking, the defendant in such a case may raise involuntariness as a defense to criminal prosecution. This has been true where various forms of automatism have been claimed, where a person has acted under external threat of compulsion and where a person has been involuntarily made intoxicated by the actions of others. And, of course, there has been the long tradition in the area of mental illness that:

'[A] person may commit a criminal act and yet not be responsible. If some controlling disease was, in truth, the acting power within him which he could not resist, then he will not be responsible . . . '

In deciding responsibility for crime, therefore, the law postulates a 'free will' and then recognizes known deviations. Thus the postulates can be undermined in certain areas where there is a broad consensus that free will does not exist. Once there is such a consensus, as in the mental illness area today, the jury is allowed to inquire whether the particular person claiming to be within that class lacked the free will necessary for criminal responsibility. No reason appears why this concept should not be applied to any disease. The question is whether society recognizes that the behaviour pattern in question is caused by the diseased determinants and not free will. (This approach is a recognition that notions of criminal responsibility, free will, disease, and moral culpability are community beliefs, subject to evolution and change in light of scientific advances or exposure to particular problems). If so, there should be no criminal responsibility. In determining societal recognition, four areas should be explored: (1) medical opinion, (2) the existence of treatment methods and facilities, (3) legal opinion, and (4) governmental recognition (legislative, executive and judicial). On exploration, I find sufficient consensus to hold, as a matter of law, that chronic alcoholism is a disease which in some instances may control behaviour and that in those instances where it does, criminal sanctions may not be imposed.

II

Medical Opinion
. . . That there is no clear definition of alcoholism and no complete agreement as to its causes is not a ground for denying it disease status. The same might be said of cancer or epilepsy; certainly the same can be said for mental illness. . . .

The point is not whether the medical profession has come up with an exact label. Rather, the approach is functional—does the medical profession, or a substantial part of it, view alcoholism as a disease, properly the subject of medical treatment? It seems clear that, measured by this test alcoholism does qualify as a disease.

Treatment Methods and Facilities
Since alcoholism has only recently received the medical attention the medical profession now feels it deserves, it is not surprising that the availability of treatment methods, and especially treatment facilities, lags behind the need. However, in recent years there has been a burgeoning of methods and a rapid

increase in facilities for alcoholics. While recognising how much farther we have to go, I feel that we have now progressed sufficiently to route alcoholics out of the criminal process and into a treatment process.

Various methods have been, and are being, used with alcoholics. Psychotherapy, group therapy, drug therapy, and a host of special programmes such as aversive conditioning, hypnotherapy and group psychodrama have received discussion in the literature. And every authority recognises that a very important aid to any treatment program exists—Alcoholics Anonymous. . . .

Legal Opinion

It is instructive that the President's Commission on Law Enforcement and Administration of Justice, Task Force on Drunkenness, singled out an article by Hutt to include in its appendix. Hutt concluded:

'Judges and lawyers are trained in the law. We are not competent to decide exactly what type of noncriminal public health procedures are most likely to result in rehabilitation of chronic inebriates. But we are competent, and we do have the duty, to make certain that the present criminal procedures are not continued. The public cannot be expected to respect a system of criminal justice that condemns sick people to jail because they are sick. . . .'

Governmental Recognition

. . . I think that the dialogue over alcoholism among the medical profession, the government and the legal profession has reached a point where the disease should be recognised as a basis for denying criminal responsibility for any actions produced by the disease. The rule I would fashion for alcoholism parallels this court's rule in the area of insanity. The jury would be instructed that if it finds that the defendant was suffering from a disease, and that his actions were a product of that disease, it should find the defendant not guilty. Using civil commitment procedures, the defendant should then be committed to an appropriate treatment facility. As with insanity, labels should be avoided."

Glanville Williams, Textbook of Criminal Law (2nd ed., 1983), p. 466:

"From the social point of view an insanity verdict is not the preferred outcome. It is unlikely that either a special hospital or an NHS hospital would willingly accept an alcoholic as an in-patient for any length of time, if at all. Such methods of treatment as exist require the active desire of the patient for treatment, and the problem is one of motivation. The desirable solution is some legal mechanism by which the alcoholic or drug-addict can be held to be legally responsible, and therefore punishable—not by way of retribution, but in order to induce him to accept treatment or otherwise to discontinue his habit, or in the last resort to contain him for some time for the protection of the public."

J. Lack of Age

1. Introduction

The condition of childhood exempts young children from accountability for their actions; they are deemed not to be responsible actors and are thus excused from punishment. Where this state ends and responsibility begins is, in reality, a gradual process with the child becoming more and more aware of his place in the order of things. The law does not reflect this reality,[70] however, but sets an arbitrary age of responsibility for the purposes of the criminal law. This currently stands at 10.[71] The Children and Young Persons Act 1969, s.4, raised the age at which punishment becomes acceptable to 14 but this has never been implemented; nor is it likely to be. The spirit of keeping children away from the courts which pervaded that Act has been replaced by one which seeks to hold them liable for their actions. The new dogma is influenced in part by a general change in governmental attitudes towards punishment but also by the high levels of offending by very young persons; research indicates, for example that the peak age of offending is 15 for males and 14 for females.[72] However, as has been pointed out "it is one of the many paradoxes of current thought that troublesome children should be made more responsible for their actions without giving them any additional rights."[73]

2. Below the age of 10[74]

The child who commits what would be a criminal offence had he been older may be made the subject of care proceedings[75] in the juvenile court (staffed by magistrates thought to have special expertise with children). These are civil proceedings instituted by the police, N.S.P.C.C. (as "authorised persons") or local authority if they feel that the child is in need of care and control, which he is unlikely to receive unless the court makes an order,[76] and provided that one of a number of conditions is satisfied.[77] The child may, as a result of the hearing, be passed into the care of the local authority and placed in a residential home or fostered. Alternatively, he may be allowed to remain with natural parents or relatives under the supervision of the local authority.

3. Above the age of 10

Care proceedings are still available for juveniles up to the age of 17 but do not tend to be used when a child or young person has committed

---

[70] Except in one sense: between the ages of 10 and 14 there is a presumption of *doli incapax*, which can only be rebutted by evidence (direct or inferred) that the child knew what he was doing was "seriously or gravely wrong" and not just "naughty or mischievous." See *J. M. (A Minor)* v. *Runeckles* (1984) 79 Cr.App.R. 255, *J. B. H. and J. H. (Minors)* v. *O'Connell* [1981] Crim.L.R. 632, *I. P. H.* v. *Chief Constable of South Wales* [1987] Crim.L.R. 42 and *T.* v. *D.P.P.* [1989] Crim.L.R. 498. Although entirely sound in relation to the underlying principles of the criminal law, it is usually ignored by the juvenile courts in practice and is subject to the criticism that it is the child who does not know the difference between right and wrong who is in most need of control, and that it may well be the child from what is perceived to be a "good" home who is actually caught by the test.
[71] Children and Young Persons Act 1933, s.50 as amended by Children and Young Persons Act 1963, s.16. At common law the age of responsibility was 7.
[72] K. Pease and K. Bottomley, *Crime and Punishment: Interpreting the Data,* (1986) p. 14.
[73] Such as those rights of natural justice which surround the trial of an adult. See M.D.A. Freeman, "The Rights of Children when they do Wrong" (1981) 21 Brit.J. Criminol 210.
[74] Although the age of responsibility stands at 10, the term "child" in statutory language refers to anyone up to the age of 14, and "young person" to those between 14–17.
[75] Children and Young Persons Act 1969, s.1
[76] *Ibid.,* s.1(2).
[77] *Ibid.* For example, under s.1(2)(c) that the child is exposed to moral danger, and under s.1(2)(f) that he is guilty of an offence, excluding homicide. In relation to the offence condition, see also the Children and Young Persons Act 1969, s.3.

an offence. It is felt that care proceedings would come to be perceived as punitive, even though that is not their purpose, if used regularly in such cases.

Criminal proceedings must be brought in the juvenile court.[78] The court is to "have regard to the welfare of the child or young person"[79] but as this is not the only consideration, the court may find persuasive, for example, the need to deter certain kinds of criminal activity, such as football hooliganism.[80]

K. Sundry Defences

1. Introduction

Further to the general defences discussed in this chapter are numerous other defences which it is beyond the scope of this book to discuss. Such defences are more specific: it is, for example, a defence to a charge of unlawful possession of a firearm to show reasonable excuse or lawful authority.[81] Likewise it is a defence to the offence of failing to provide a specimen of breath or blood or urine (for the purposes of the offence of driving or being in charge of a vehicle with a blood/alcohol concentration above the prescribed limit) to show a reasonable excuse.[82] Another example of a specific defence is that a police officer may use such force as is reasonable in effecting a lawful arrest.[83]

2. Entrapment

But apart from specific statutory defences such as the above, there appear to be no other general defences developed by the common law in England. In the United States the courts have recognised and developed the defence of entrapment.[84] This applies when the police, acting under cover, positively promote a crime that would not otherwise have taken place. It would not apply (and the defendant would thus bear responsibility) if the police merely joined an existing illegal enterprise. So in the United States entrapment might operate to relieve someone of liability who was suspected without futher evidence of pushing drugs, if the police agent were to ask him to supply him with say, cannabis or heroin. But it would not be available if the police were to join others who were being supplied by the pusher. Similarly, entrapment may

---

[78] Unless the offence is homicide (see, for example, *Darren Coulburn* (1988) 87 Cr.App.R. 309, where a 13 year old boy who fatally stabbed a fellow schoolboy was found guilty of murder by Manchester Crown Court), or he is between the ages of 14–17 and the offence is punishable with imprisonment for 14 years or more in the case of an adult: Magistrates' Courts Act 1980, s.24, Children and Young Persons Act 1933, s.53 and Criminal Justice Act 1988, s.126.

[79] Children and Young Persons Act 1933, s.44(1) as amended.

[80] The range of sentences available to the court is considerable but is dependent upon the age of the offender, the facilities available locally and the policy of the particular government in power. See further Criminal Justice Act 1988.

[81] Firearms Act 1968, s.17.

[82] Road Traffic Act 1988, s.7(6).

[83] Criminal Law Act 1967, s.3(1).

[84] *Sorrells* v. *United States* 287 U.S. 435, 53 S.Ct. 210, 77 L.Ed. 413 (1932); *Sherman* v. *United States*, 356 U.S. 369, 78 S.Ct. 819, 2 L.Ed. 2d 848 (1958).

arise if the police agent were to "invite" the attentions of someone thought to be a homosexual and then charge him with soliciting.[85]

In England the defence of entrapment has now been firmly rejected by the House of Lords in *Sang*[86] on the ground that the "fact that the counsellor and procurer is a policeman or a police informer, cannot affect the guilt of the principal offender; both the physical element (*actus reus*) and the mental element (*mens rea*) of the offence with which he is charged are present."[87] The House of Lords further held that any evidence so obtained by such police activity was admissible evidence against the defendant; the court has no discretion to refuse to admit such evidence—as an exclusionary rule to this effect would amount to admitting the defence of entrapment via the back-door. The Law Commission, too, has rejected proposals for the introduction of a defence of entrapment into English law.[88]

In *Sang* the House of Lords indicated that entrapment could be taken into consideration in mitigation of sentence. This seems to suggest that there *is* a moral distinction between the actions of a defendant entrapped by the police and one induced by another criminal. The defendant has an excuse, or at least a partial excuse. Whether such excuses, or partial excuses, should be dealt with at the substantive or at the sentencing stage is a matter to be considered in the final chapter of this book.[89]

---

[85] Contrary to the Sexual Offences Act 1956, s.32.
[86] [1980] A.C. 402.
[87] *Ibid.* at 432.
[88] Report on Defences of General Application, Law Com. No. 83.
[89] On entrapment generally, see Heydon, "The Problems of Entrapment" [1973] C.L.J. 268; Barlow, "Entrapment and the Common Law: Is there a Place for the American Doctrine of Entrapment?" (1978) 41 M.L.R. 266; Ashworth, "Defences of General Application, The Law Commission's Report, No. 83, (3) Entrapment" [1978] Crim.L.R. 137.

CHAPTER 4

CAUSATION

I Introduction

The Herald of Free Enterprise

On the evening of March 6, 1987 the *Herald of Free Enterprise*, a ferry owned by Townsend Thoresen (now P. & O. European Ferries) and travelling from Zeebrugge to Dover capsized off Zeebrugge because the bow doors had not been properly closed.[1] At least 188 people were drowned. Who caused the death of these people? There were several candidates for blame:

The Assistant Bosun

According to regulations issued to the crew it was the responsibility of the Assistant-Bosun, Mr. Marc Stanley, to ensure that the bow doors were closed. However, in practice he was not the only one responsible. On many voyages Mr. Stanley was engaged on maintenance work and on those occasions not shut the bow doors.

On the day in question Mr. Stanley had been primarily engaged on such maintenance duties. Before the ferry sailed Mr. Stanley spoke to the Bosun, Mr. Terry Ayling and was told "That will do." Stanley interpreted this to mean that he could go off-duty and so he went back to his cabin to sleep without ensuring that the bow doors were closed (although there was some dispute later as to whether he believed he had been relieved from his duties on the door).

The Loading Officer/Officer of the Watch

On the day in question Mr. Leslie Sable was doubling up as loading officer and officer of the watch—despite such doubling up involving a complete conflict of duty. It was the responsibility of the loading officer to check that the bow doors had been closed. According to the ship's standing orders it was the duty of the Officer of the Watch to be on the bridge 15 minutes before the ferry sailed.

Sable, who had been supervising the loading of vehicles, did not remain on the loading deck until the doors were shut. Knowing he was required on the bridge he only waited until he saw someone whom he thought, mistakenly, was Stanley going to shut the doors. However, he later admitted in evidence that even if he had not been Officer of the Watch he would only have remained on the loading deck until Stanley got there. He would not have waited until the doors were shut. "Mr Sable failed to carry out his duty to ensure that the bow doors were closed. He was seriously negligent by reason of that failure. Of all

---

[1] The facts and quotations here, unless otherwise stated, are from the Sheen Report (*M.V. Herald of Free Enterprise*, Report of Court, No. 8074, Department of Transport (1987)).

the many faults which combined to lead directly or indirectly to this tragic disaster that of Mr. Leslie Sable was the most immediate."

The Captain

As master of the ship Captain Lewry was responsible for the safety of everyone on the ship. He "took the Herald to sea with the bow doors fully open. It
follows that Captain Lewry must accept personal responsibility for the loss of
his ship. . . . [His] negligence was one of the causes contributing to the
casualty." Further, because the ship was running late he did not follow the practice of restricting speed so that water did not come above the spade (at the
ship's bow). The ship was approaching its maximum speed with water at two
metres above the spade.

The Senior Master

"One of the functions . . . [of Captain John Kirby] was to act as a co-ordinator
between all the masters and officers of the ship in order to achieve uniformity in
the practice operated by the different crews . . . But not only did Captain Kirby
fail to enforce such orders as had been promulgated, he also failed to issue clear
and concise orders about the closing of the most important doors on G deck. He
should have introduced a fail-safe system. Furthermore, he was content to
accept without demur the Ship's Standing Orders issued by the Company . . .
[He] must bear his share of the responsibility for the disaster."

The ship owners

The system operated by the ship owners, Townsend Thoresen, was criticised
as "a very sloppy system" and "inherently dangerous" (Mr. David Steel Q.C.
for the Department of Transport). They had told the Captain to assume that
everything was in order unless he was told otherwise. The closing of the doors
being a mundane task was liable to be forgotten. Accordingly three ferry cap-
tains had written to suggest that warning lights should be installed on the
bridge to indicate if the doors were open. The ship owners' response to this was
"dilatory" and "penny-pinching' (Mr. Charles Haddon-Cave, representing the
passengers and their families). There should have been four officers on the ferry
instead of three so that Mr. Sable would not have had to double up. The ship
owners later "accepted full responsibility"; there ought to have been an express
rule that the captain check the doors were closed.

Findings of inquiry

Captain Lewry's certificate of competency was suspended for one year. Mr.
Sable's certificate was suspended for two years as he bore the "most immediate" responsibility. Mr. Stanley was found to have been "seriously negligent"
but no sanction was imposed. As to the role of the Townsend Thoresen management, Mr. Justice Sheen said:

"A full investigation into the circumstances of the disaster leads inexorably
to the conclusion that the underlying or cardinal faults lay higher up in the
company. The Board of Directors did not appreciate their responsibility for
the safe management of their ships. . . . All concerned in management,
from the members of the Board of Directors down to the junior superin-
tendents, were guilty of fault in that all must be regarded as sharing
responsibility for the failure of management. From top to bottom the body
corporate was infected with the disease of sloppiness. . . . The failure on
the part of shore management to give proper and clear directions was a contributory cause of the disaster."

He nevertheless ruled that no statutory offence had been committed by the operators—a conclusion which led to "outrage" in the Commons and accusations that the three men had been made "scapegoats" for the "appalling negligence" of the company.[2]

Ex parte Spooner, The Times, October 10, 1987 (Divisional Court)

In the course of the inquest into the deaths resulting from the capsize of *The Herald of Free Enterprise* the Coroner ruled that as a matter of law a corporate body could not be guilty of manslaughter. An application for judicial review of this decision was made.

Lord Justice Bingham:
"The Coroner decided as a matter of law that:
1. A corporate body could not be guilty of manslaughter. . . .
3. The acts and omissions of the company, Townsend Car Ferries Ltd., were not the direct cause of the deaths. . . .
The company had failed to consider seriously a proposal to fit a warning light system on the ferry; five or six previous incidents of ferry doors being left open had not been properly reported and collated by the company and it lacked any proper system to ensure that the highest standards of safety were observed.
His Lordship was prepared tentatively to accept that a corporate body was capable of being found guilty of manslaughter; however, no sustainable case had been made against the named directors of the company. . . . The court was reluctant to intervene especially because it was an inquest. A coroner acted as an inquisitor and as such was the master of his own procedure."

Application refused

The prosecution
At the inquest the coroner directed the jury not to return a verdict of unlawful homicide. The coroner's jury rejected this instruction and returned verdicts of unlawful death.
All papers were sent to the D.P.P. for consideration as to whether a criminal prosecution be brought. By September 1988 it was being reported in the Press that families of the victims were considering a private prosecution against the Board of Directors of the Ship Owners.
In July 1989 it was decided that prosecutions for manslaughter would be brought against three directors of P. & O.; the assistant bonsun, Mr. Marc Stanley; the loading officer/officer of the watch, Mr. Leslie Sable; the captain, Capt. David Lewry; and the Senior Master, Capt. John Kirby. Committal proceedings were held in December 1989.

Commonwealth v. Welansky, 316 Mass. 383, 55 N.E. 2d 902 (1944) (Supreme Judicial Court of Massachusetts)

On the evening of November 28, 1942 a fire broke out at the New Cocoanut Grove, a nightclub in Boston. The fire quickly spread throughout the crowded premises. Panic resulted and nearly 500 people died of burns, smoke inhalation,

[2] *The Times*, July 25, 1987.

or injuries suffered in the attempt to escape. Who caused the death of these people?[3] There were several candidates for blame:

1. *The waiter, Stanley Tomaszewski*

A prankster had turned off a light bulb set in a decorative palm tree. A bartender ordered Stanley, a sixteen year old boy, to light the bulb. He got a stool, lit a match in order to see the bulb and turned the bulb in its socket. The flame of his match ignited the artificial palm tree which in turn speedily ignited a low cloth ceiling near it. Did Stanley cause the death of the 500 victims? Initially he was blamed by the local press, but as other "scapegoats" were found, he was exonerated from blame and treated with "near adulation" and started receiving "fan letters." But for the next 28 years Stanley received abusive telephone calls in the middle of the night and his life was threatened "hundreds of times by people who blame me for the fire."[4]

2. *The prankster*

The prankster who turned off the light bulb was also blamed initially in the press, but as his identity was never discovered, his condemnation was short-lived. Can he be said to have caused the death of the victims?

3. *Public officials*

The week before, the Fire Department had inspected the Cocoanut Grove and approved it as safe, despite the fact that there was a lack of adequate fire-exits and that highly inflammable materials were used throughout the nightclub and, in particular, in the decorative palm tree and in the low cloth ceiling. Did the particular fire inspector cause the deaths?

The local Press also blamed other public officials. They condemned the Fire Commissioner on the basis that he was responsible for his subordinate's performance of duty. They castigated a Captain in the Police Department who was inside the club at the time of the fire on inspection duties for not enforcing the law against over-crowding. Even the mayor was blamed for appointing such "negligent" and "lax" heads of departments and because he had taken no action to adopt a new building code that had been in the hands of the City Council for the previous four years. Did any of these public officials cause the deaths?

4. *The owners*

The nightclub was owned and run by Barnett Welansky. In decorating and equipping the club he had used defective wiring and installed the inflammable decorations. There were insufficient exit doors and some of these doors were kept locked. At the time of the fire Barnett Welansky was confined in hospital with a serious illness—his brother James Welansky and an employee, Jacob Goldfine, "assumed some of [his] duties at the night club, but made no change in methods."[5] To what extent can it be said that the death of the victims was caused by Barnett Welansky or by his two delegates?

---

[3] The ensuing discussion of *Welansky* is drawn from the report of the case itself, from Veltford and Lee, "The Cocoanut Grove Fire: A Study in Scapegoating," Journal of Abnormal and Social Psychology, XXXVIII (No. 2 clinical supp.; 1943) 138, pp. 141–154, and from Goldstein, Dershowitz and Schwartz, *Criminal Law: Theory and Process* (1974), pp. 833–837. Our thanks are due to Prof. Joe Goldstein for drawing attention to the Veltford and Lee article which is extracted in his book cited above.

[4] *The Boston Globe*, December 28, 1970, p. 10 col. 3. See Goldstein, p. 836.

[5] *Welansky*, 55 N.E. 2d 902 at 905.

The result

Barnett Welansky and his two delegates were charged with the crime of manslaughter. The two delegates were acquitted by the jury, but Barnett Welansky was convicted of manslaughter and sentenced to a term of imprisonment of not less than twelve years and not more than fifteen years. Welansky's appeal was dismissed. Thus both the trial court and the Supreme Judicial Court of Massachusetts clearly found that Barnett Welansky caused the death of the victims of the fire. After serving three years of his sentence, Welansky, who was suffering from terminal cancer and was not expected to live for more than another year, was granted a full and complete pardon by the Governor of Massachusetts.

It is interesting to contrast the views expressed in two of the many letters addressed to the Governor prior to his granting a pardon.

(i) "If Welansky was guilty of manslaughter in connection with the terrible deaths resulting from the Cocoanut Grove fire, then it was a technical guilt and nothing more. Certainly, in those circumstances, the sentence that was imposed upon him by the court was much too severe . . . It may well be true that in appropriate cases, such as criminals whom the public would have a right to fear if they were released, that the criminal's health should not be taken into consideration, but in this particular case where there was no intention to do harm in the first place, but through a succession of misfortunes a man has been found guilty of manslaughter only from a technical point of view and not otherwise, [he is deserving of a pardon.]"[6]

(ii) "I vehemently oppose any pardon for Barnett Welansky whose criminal re-construction of the Cocoanut Grove building sacrificed 492 human beings. I am a close relative of one of the victims. This horrible holocaust was a civic disgrace. It would become even more unspeakable were this man to be freed. In his petition for premature freedom, Welansky claims illness—says he wants to spend the rest of his days with his family. I recall 492 persons (one in particular) who wanted to live out their lives with their families. *They are dead.* He also disclaims guilt because he was at home the night of the fire.

Guiltless? He *accepted guilt* when he criminally flouted the building laws in callously renovating his nightclub and did *not* have the work done according to the plans which he had had okayed.

He evaded the law when he employed a young fellow to do some electrical wiring and *knew* that this worker did not have the proper license to do this work. Has it been *absolutely proven* that faulty wiring *did not* cause this fire? Although he was not present he *knew* that his illegally reconstructed club was open for public attendance the night of the fire.

Governor Tobin, consider the fact of locked exits in a place of public patronage. Hundreds died because a locked exit barred their way to the street's safety. These facts are on public record. They also are hideous facts burning deeply into the hearts of hundreds of heartbroken families."[7]

Veltford and Lee, "The Cocoanut Grove Fire: A Study in Scapegoating." Journal of Abnormal and Social Psychology, XXXVIII (No. 2 clinical supp; 1943) 138:

"The people [of Boston] felt some person or persons must be held responsible; attaching responsibility to mere laws or to the *panic* provided neither sufficient outlet for their emotions nor opportunity for punishment . . .

Significantly, newspapers and public alike overlooked the fact that the panic created by the fire must have been largely responsible for the great loss of life. In

---

[6] Letter by Frank G. Lichtenstein, cited in Goldstein (*ante*, n. 3) p. 835.
[7] Letter by Katherine F. Denehy, cited in Goldstein (*ante*, n. 3) p. 835–6.

spite of statements by officials immediately after the fire, the people were not ready to accept the fact that 'the Boston tragedy was due in part to a psychological collapse.' To the extent that they ignored this fact, the blame that the newspapers and public placed on various persons involved in the fire was disproportionate to their responsibility."

Sally Lloyd-Bostock, "The Ordinary Man, and the Psychology of Attributing Causes and Responsibility" (1979) 42 M.L.R. 143 at 155–156:

"Walster ("Assignment of Responsibility for an Accident" (1963) 3, 1 Journal of Personality and Social Psychology, 73–79) . . . found that people attributed more responsibility for an accident (in which a car parked unbraked ran down a hill) as the severity of the consequence increased. She formulated a version of what has become known as 'the defensive attribution hypothesis.' Chance happenings over which the individual has no control (and, hence, no responsibility) are threatening. Therefore, when faced with an accident with serious consequences, an individual will seek to attribute responsibility to somebody in order to protect himself from acknowledging that the accident could happen to anyone, including himself. The need to protect himself in this way will increase with increasing severity of outcome . . .

Often more than one kind of responsibility may be attributed in relation to the same event. For example, a *Sunday Times* article (April 13, 1977) after describing at some length the circumstances surrounding the collision between two jumbo jets at Santa Cruz airport in Tenerife, concluded by attributing responsibility—'Blame for the world's worst aviation tragedy will no doubt be apportioned in time. One name will certainly not feature in any official inquest however: Antonio Cubillo. It is he who, no matter how indirectly, must shoulder responsibility for what happened at Santa Cruz.' (Cubillo was leader of the movement which claimed responsibility for a bomb at Las Palmas airport. As a result of the bomb, aircraft, including those in the accident, were diverted to Santa Cruz, overloading the airport.) This illustrates a number of interesting things about reactions to disasters and attributing responsibility for them in newspapers. The writers recognise that it will differ from other attributions, and that Antonio Cubillo's causal contribution will in other contexts be insufficient grounds. It is a non-legal attribution of responsibility, but even if nobody quarrelled with it in this context, it is clearly not *the* everyday answer to the question 'who is responsible for the crash?,' nor does it exemplify *the* common-sense principles on which questions about remoteness of causes, etc. are decided.

The fact that everyday judgments are related to everyday purposes and consequences must be a major limitation on the usefulness of comparisons between legal and ordinary common-sense notions of cause and fault."

II APPROACHES TO CAUSATION

How does the law determine which of several candidates in such cases actually caused the result? And how far does the chain of causation extend? Welansky did not start the fire. Why was he liable for the resultant deaths? If the waiter had deliberately started the fire, would

Welansky still have been liable or would the chain of causation have then been broken?

There are three approaches that can be adopted in relation to the problem of causation.

A. "Policy" Approach

There are no underlying general *principles* of causation. Judges simply resort to considerations of "policy" to determine whether a particular defendant caused the specified harm.

H. L. A. Hart and A. M. Honoré, Causation in the Law (2nd ed., 1985) pp. 103–104:

"For writers of the first school 'policy' is just a name for an immense variety of considerations which do weigh and should weigh with courts considering the question of the existence or extent of responsibility. No exhaustive enumeration can be given of such factors and no general principles can be laid down as to how a balance should be struck between them. Policy, on this interpretation, is atomized: the courts must focus attention on the precise way in which harm has eventuated in a particular case, and then ask and answer, in a more or less intuitive fashion, whether or not on these particular facts a defendant should be held responsible. The court's function is to pass judgments acceptable to society for their time and place on these matters, and general policies can never take the place of judgment. Edgerton says, 'It neither is nor should be possible to extract rules which cover the subject (of legal cause) and are definite enough to solve cases . . . The solution . . . depends upon a balancing of considerations which tend to show that it is or is not reasonable or just to treat the act as the cause of the harm . . . these considerations are indefinite in number and in value and incommensurable' ("Legal Cause," (1924) U.Pa. L.R. 211)."

In holding that Welansky caused the death of the victims of the Cocoanut Grove fire, were the judges (and jury) simply giving effect to their conceptions of justice, expediency, or "policy"? In deciding who to prosecute, are prosecutors to be guided by the same considerations of "policy"? Is such an *ad hoc* approach acceptable? It must be remembered that, apart from crimes of strict liability, criminal liability does not necessarily follow from a finding that causation is established. Some *mens rea* or culpability must also be found to exist. If policy considerations are to affect legal decisions, should they not be reserved for the *mens rea* assessment, or is it unrealistic to divorce policy considerations from any one aspect of a crime?

B. Mens Rea Approach

Because of the doctrine of *mens rea* and the test of responsibility, principles of causation are unnecessary in the criminal law. *Any* factual cause can be held to be *the legal* cause, but actual liability will be limited to those who have *mens rea*. "Under the modern conception of *mens rea* no hardship can result from any fine drawn investigation of causes, since the more remote the cause the greater the difficulty of proving that the accused person intended or realised what the effect of it would be."[8] Thus in *Welansky* the prankster's action of switching the light bulb off was *a* cause of the fire and subsequent deaths, but as *mens rea* could never be attributed to the prankster, there was no point in prosecuting him. On the other hand, because recklessness (or gross negligence) could be attributed to Welansky he was prosecuted and convicted. Under this view all the "real work" is done by the doctrine of *mens rea*. No rules on causation are necessary other than the simple primary proposition that the defendant's act must have been *a* cause in the sense that without it, the ultimate harm would not have occurred (known as the *sine qua non* rule or "but for" causation: *but for* the prankster turning the bulb off, the fire would never have started and the patrons would not have died).

There are problems with this approach. How could it be adopted when dealing with crimes of strict liability? In *Southern Water Authority v. Pegrum and Pegrum*[9] it was expressly stated that causation may be established even though the defendant did not intend the harm and was not even negligent; any other approach would defeat the object of strict liability legislation.[10] As there would be no *mens rea* operating as a limiting factor, it would mean that causation would be established on a "but for" basis in all such cases regardless of how far removed the act was from the result. Also, even in some cases where *mens rea* was established, there would be problems. Thus under this approach, Welansky, because he had *mens rea* (as defined in that case) would still have been liable even if the waiter, Stanley, had deliberately started the fire with the intention of killing everyone in the nightclub. Would such a result be acceptable? *If* this view is correct, is it right that *all* liability should turn on such a nebulous and elusive concept as *mens rea*? Might it not be better to tighten up, and clarify, the rules on causation which could lead to a diminution of the importance of the doctrine of *mens rea*, and perhaps even the eventual elimination of the doctrine from the criminal law?

C. Quest for General Principles

Not satisfied with the above approaches, attempts have been made to formulate general principles of causation that could be applicable in all cases. Three of these attempted formulations will be presented:
  (1) Hart and Honoré's principles derived from our commonsense
      notions of causation; and

---

[8] J. W. C. Turner, *Kenny's Outlines of Criminal Law*, p. 16.
[9] [1989] Crim.L.R. 442.
[10] See also, *Wrothwell Ltd. v. Yorkshire Water Authority* [1984] Crim.L.R. 43.

(2) The Model Penal Code's attempt to structure legal thought on this matter.

(3) The Draft Criminal Code Bill's "restatement" of the present law.

1. Hart and Honoré's principles of causation

Events do not have single "causes," but only occur when there is a combination of a complex set of conditions. Thus we might identify the dropping of a lighted cigarette in a waste-paper basket as the cause of a fire but in reality this leads to a fire only if certain other conditions are satisfied: there must be oxygen in the air; there must be combustible material in the waste-paper basket, and so on. Each of these conditions is equally necessary if a fire is to be started.[11] How are we to select one of this complex set of conditions as the cause?

H. L. A. Hart and A. M. Honoré, Causation in the Law (2nd ed., 1985) pp. 29, 33–34, 42, 77–80, 326, 340–341:

"Human action in the simple cases, where we produce some desired effect by the manipulation of an object in our environment, is an interference in the natural course of events which *makes a difference* in the way these develop . . . Common experience teaches us that, left to themselves, the things we manipulate, since they have a 'nature' or characteristic way of behaving, would persist in states or exhibit changes different from those which we have learnt to bring about in them by our manipulation. The notion that a cause is essentially something which interferes with or intervenes in the course of events which would normally take place, is central to our commonsense concept of cause. . . .

[I]n distinguishing between causes and conditions two contrasts are of prime importance. These are the contrasts between what is abnormal and what is normal in relation to any given thing or subject-matter, and between a free deliberate human action and all other conditions. . . .

(a) *Abnormal and normal conditions*
 . . . In the case of a building destroyed by fire 'mere conditions' will be factors such as the oxygen in the air, the presence of combustible material or the dryness of the building. . . . These factors are, of course, just those which are present alike both in the case where such accidents occur and in the normal cases where they do not; and it is this consideration that leads us to reject them as the cause of the accident, even though it is true that without them the accident would not have occurred . . . : such factors do not 'make the difference' between disaster and normal functioning, as . . . the dropping of a lighted cigarette [does] . . .

(b) *Voluntary action*
 . . . [A] voluntary human action intended to bring about what in fact happens, and in the manner in which it happens, has a special place in causal inquiries; not so much because this, if present among a set of conditions required for the production of the effect, is often treated as the cause (though this is true), but because, when the question is how far back a cause shall be traced through a number of intervening causes, such a voluntary action very

[11] Hart and Honoré, *Causation in the Law*, p. 17.

often is regarded both as a limit and also as still the cause even though other later abnormal occurrences are recognized as causes . . .

[However in certain cases even when an actor intends to achieve a result (and that result occurs), the chain of causation between the actor's conduct and the result might be broken.]

Tracing consequences

. . . A hits B who falls to the ground stunned and bruised by the blow; at that moment a tree crashes to the ground and kills B. A has certainly caused B's bruises but not his death . . .

The connexion between A's action and B's death . . . would naturally be described in the language of *coincidence*. 'It was a coincidence: it just happened that, at the very moment when A knocked B down, a tree crashed at the very place where he fell and killed him.' . . . We speak of a coincidence whenever the conjunction of two or more events in certain spatial or temporal relations (1) is very unlikely by ordinary standards and (2) is for some reason significant or important, provided (3) that they occur without human contrivance and (4) are independent of each other. . . .

In the present case the fall of the tree just as B was struck down within its range satisfies the four criteria for a coincidence which we have enumerated. First, though neither event was of a very rare or exceptional kind, their conjunction would be rated very unlikely judged by the standards of ordinary experience. Secondly, this conjunction was causally significant for it was a necessary part of the process terminating in B's death. Thirdly, this conjunction was not consciously designed by A; had he known of the impending fall of the tree and hit B with the intention that he should fall within its range B's death would not have been the result of any coincidence. A would certainly have caused it. The common-sense principle that a contrived conjunction cannot be a coincidence is the element of truth in the legal maxim (too broadly stated even for legal purposes) that an intended consequence cannot be too 'remote.' Fourthly, each member of the conjunction in this case was independent of the other; whereas if B had fallen against the tree with an impact sufficient to bring it down on him, this sequence of physical events, though freakish in its way, would not be a coincidence and in most contexts of ordinary life, as in the law, the course of events would be summarized by saying that in this case, unlike that of the coincidence, A's act was the cause of B's death, since each stage is the effect of the preceding stage. Thus, the blow forced the victim against the tree, the effect of this was to make the tree fall and the fall of the tree killed the victim.

One further criterion in addition to these four must be satisfied if a conjunction of events is to rank as a coincidence and as a limit when the consequences of the action are traced . . . An abnormal *condition* existing at the time of a human intervention is distinguished both by ordinary thought and, with a striking consistency, by most legal systems from an abnormal event or conjunction of events subsequent to that intervention; the former, unlike the latter, are not ranked as coincidences or 'extraneous' causes when the consequences of the intervention come to be traced. Thus A innocently gives B a tap over the head of a normally quite harmless character, but because B is then suffering from some rare disease the tap has, as we say, 'fatal results.' In this case A has caused B's death though unintentionally. The scope of the principle which thus distinguishes contemporaneous abnormal conditions from subsequent events is unclear; but at least where a human being initiates some physical change in a thing, animal, or person, abnormal physical states of the object affected, existing at the time, are ranked as part of the circumstances in which the cause 'operates.' In the familiar controlling imagery these are part of 'the stage already set' before the 'intervention.'

. . . Just how unlikely must a conjunction be to rank as a coincidence, and in the light of what knowledge is likelihood to be assessed? The only answer is: 'very unlikely in the light of the knowledge available to ordinary men.'

. . . [S]o in criminal law courts have often limited responsibility by appealing to the causal distinctions embedded in ordinary thought, with their emphasis on voluntary interventions and abnormal or coincidental events as factors negativing responsibility.

Voluntary conduct

The free, deliberate, and informed intervention of a second person, not acting in concert with the first, and intending to bring about the harm which in fact occurs or recklessly courting it, is normally held to relieve the first actor of criminal responsibility. One must distinguish, however, the situation where the first actor's conduct was sufficient in the existing circumstances to bring about the harm (. . . the case for holding the first actor responsible despite the voluntary intervention of the second is naturally much stronger) . . . from that where it was not sufficient without the intervention of the second actor (. . . here most decisions relieve the first actor of responsibility) . . .

Abnormality

The basic principle here is that a physical state or event, even if subsequent to the act of the defendant, does not negative causal connection if it is normal or usual in the context.

In criminal as in civil law a conjunction of events amounting to a coincidence is held to negative causal connection."

2. The Model Penal Code

American Law Institute, The Model Penal Code, Proposed Official Draft (1962):

"*Section 2.03. Causal Relationship Between Conduct and Result: Divergence Between Result Designed or Contemplated and Actual Result or Between Probable and Actual Result*

(1) Conduct is the cause of a result when:
 (a) it is an antecedent *but for* which the result in question would not have occurred; and
 (b) the relationship between the conduct and result satisfies any additional causal requirements imposed by the Code or by the law defining the offense.

(2) When purposely or knowingly causing a particular result is an element of an offence, the element is not established if the actual result is not within the purpose or the contemplation of the actor unless:
 (a) the actual result differs from that designed or contemplated, as the case may be, only in the respect that a different person or different property is injured or affected or that the injury or harm designed or contemplated would have been more serious or more extensive than that caused; or
 (b) the actual result involves the same kind of injury or harm as that designed or contemplated and is not too remote or accidental in its occurrence to have a (just) bearing on the actor's liability or on the gravity of his offense.

(3) When recklessly or negligently causing a particular result is an element of an offense, the element is not established if the actual result is not within the risk of which the actor is aware or, in case of negligence, of which he should be aware unless:

(a) the actual result differs from the probable result only in the respect that a different person or different property is injured or affected or that the probable injury or harm would have been more serious or more extensive than that caused; or

(b) the actual result involves the same kind of injury or harm as the probable result and is not too remote or accidental in its occurrence to have a (just) bearing on the actor's liability or on the gravity of his offense.

(4) When causing a particular result is a material element of an offense for which absolute liability is imposed by law, the element is not established unless the actual result is a probable consequence of the actor's conduct."

American Law Institute, Model Penal Code, Tent Draft No. 4. (1955)— Comments to s.2.03:

"Sub-paragraph (b) (of paragraph (2)) deals with the situation where the actual result involved the same kind of injury or harm as that designed or contemplated but the precise injury inflicted was different or occurred in a different way. Here the draft makes no attempt to catalogue the possibilities, *e.g.* to deal with the intervening or concurrent causes, natural or human; unexpected physical conditions; distinctions between the infliction of mortal or non-mortal wounds. It deals only with the ultimate criterion by which the significance of such possibilities ought to be judged . . . [*viz.*] whether the actual result is 'too accidental in its occurrence to have a just bearing on the actor's liability or on the gravity of his offense.' . . .

It may be useful in appraising [the] treatment of the problem to note that what will usually turn on the determination will not be the criminality of a defendant's conduct but rather the gravity of his offense. Since the actor, by hypothesis, has sought to cause a criminal result or has been reckless or negligent with respect to such a result, he will be guilty of some crime under a well-considered penal code even if he is not held for the actual result, *i.e.* he will be guilty of attempt, assault or some offense involving risk creation, such as reckless driving. Thus the issue in penal law is very different than in torts. Only in form is it, in penal law, a question of the actor's liability. In substance, it is a question of the severity of sentence which the Court is authorized or obliged to impose. Its practical importance thus depends on the disparity in sentence for the various offenses that may be involved, *e.g.* the sentences for an attempted and completed crime.

How far a Model Code ought to attribute importance in the grading of offenses to the actual result of conduct, as distinguished from results attempted or threatened, presents an issue of some difficulty which is of general importance in the Code. It may be said, however, that distinctions of this order are to some extent essential, at least when the severest sanctions are involved. For juries will not lightly find convictions that will lead to the severest types of sentences unless the resentments caused by the infliction of important injuries have been aroused. . . .

Thus, if the defendant . . . had shot his wife and in the hospital she had contracted a disease which was medically unrelated to the wound (though related to her presence in the hospital) her death from the disease may well be thought to have been rendered substantially more probable by the defendant's conduct, as presumably he should have known. Yet juries might regard it as a too unusual result to justify convicting him of murder. The advantage of putting the issue squarely to the jury's sense of justice is that it does not attempt to force a result which the jury may resist. It also leaves the principle flexible for application to the infinite variety of cases likely to arise."

Draft Criminal Code Bill 1989 (Law Com. No. 177), clause 17:

"(1) Subject to subsections (2) and (3), a person causes a result which is an element of an offence when—
  (a) he does an act which makes a more than negligible contribution to its occurrence; or
  (b) he omits to do an act which might prevent its occurrence and which he is under a duty to do according to the law relating to the offence.
(2) A person does not cause a result where, after he does such an act or makes such an omission, an act or event occurs—
  (a) which is the immediate and sufficient cause of the result;
  (b) which he did not foresee, and
  (c) which could not in the circumstances reasonably have been foreseen.
(Clause 17(3) states that subject to exceptions 'a person who procures, assists or encourages another to cause a result that is an element of an offence does not himself cause that result so as to be guilty of the offence as a principal.')"

III The Law's Response

We are now in a position to examine some of the leading cases on causation in order to assess whether they are consistent with any of the above views on the subject. These cases will be grouped under broad headings that fairly represent the present English law.

A. Operative Cause

1. Positive aspect

The causal connection between the defendant's act and the prohibited result must not be too remote. It is not enough that the defendant's act be a *sine qua non* (or a "but for" cause) of the result (although this is of course an essential pre-requisite).[12] To attribute causal responsibility, the defendant's acts must be the "operative,"[13] "substantial,"[14] "beyond the *de minimis* range,"[15] or "proximate"[16] cause of the prohibited consequence; it must "contribute significantly" to the result.[17] This does not imply that the result must be a direct consequence of the accused's physical actions. One can, for example, cause death by fright or shock without touching one's victim.[18]

But how great must the defendant's contribution be for his acts to

---

[12] Glanville Williams, *Textbook*, pp. 379–381.
[13] *Malcherek & Steel* (1981) 73 Cr.App.R. 173.
[14] *Smith* [1959] 2 Q.B. 35; *Mitchell* [1983] 2 W.L.R. 938.
[15] *Cato* [1976] 1 W.L.R. 110.
[16] Hart and Honoré, p. 4.
[17] *Pagett* (1983) 75 Cr.App.R. 279.
[18] *Towers* (1874) 12 Cox C.C. 530; *Hayward* (1908) 21 Cox C.C. 692.

constitute an "operative," etc., cause, sufficient to amount to a legal cause?

R. v. Smith [1959] 2 Q.B. 35 (Courts Martial Appeal Court)

During a fight in a barracks the appellant twice stabbed the victim, Private Creed, with a bayonet. He appealed against his conviction for murder on the ground *inter alia* that the summing up by the judge-advocate on the question of causation was defective.

Lord Parker C.J. (delivering the judgment of the Court):
"The second ground concerns a question of causation. The deceased man in fact received two bayonet wounds, one in the arm and one in the back. The one in the back, unknown to anybody, had pierced the lung and caused haemorrhage. There followed a series of unfortunate occurrences. A fellow-member of his company tried to carry him to the medical reception station. On the way he tripped over a wire and dropped the deceased man. He picked him up again, went a little further, and fell apparently a second time, causing the deceased man to be dropped on to the ground. Thereafter he did not try a third time but went for help, and ultimately the deceased man was brought into the reception station. There, the medical officer, Captain Millward, and his orderly were trying to cope with a number of other cases, two serious stabbings and some minor injuries, and it is clear that they did not appreciate the seriousness of the deceased man's condition or exactly what had happened. A transfusion of saline solution was attempted and failed. When his breathing seemed impaired, he was given oxygen and artificial respiration was applied, and, in fact, he died after he had been in the station about an hour, which was about two hours after the original stabbing. It is now known that, having regard to the injuries which the man had in fact suffered, his lung being pierced, the treatment that he was given was thoroughly bad and might well have affected his chances of recovery. There was evidence that there is a tendency for a wound of this sort to heal and for the haemorrhage to stop. No doubt his being dropped on the ground and having artificial respiration applied would halt or at any rate impede the chances of healing. Further, there were no facilities whatsoever for blood transfusion, which would have been the best possible treatment. There was evidence that, if he had received immediate and different treatment, he might not have died. Indeed, had facilities for blood transfusion been available and been administered, Dr. Camps, who gave evidence for the defence, said that his chances of recovery were as high as 75 per cent.
In these circumstances Mr. Bowen [counsel for the appellant] urges that not only was a careful summing-up required but that a correct direction to the court would have been that they must be satisfied that the death of Private Creed was a natural consequence and the sole consequence of the wound sustained by him and flowed directly from it. If there was, says Mr. Bowen, any other cause, whether resulting from negligence or not, if, as he contends here, something happened which impeded the chance of the deceased recovering, then the death did not result from the wound. The court is quite unable to accept that contention. It seems to the court that if at the time of death the original wound is still an operating cause and a substantial cause, then the death can properly be said to be the result of the wound, albeit that some other cause of death is also operating. Only if it can be said that the original wounding is merely the setting in which another cause operates can it be said that the death does not result from the wound. Putting it in another way, only if the second cause is so

overwhelming as to make the original wound merely part of the history can it be said that the death does not flow from the wound. . . .

Mr. Bowen placed great reliance on . . . *Jordan* . . . The court is satisfied that *Jordan's* case was a very particular case depending on its exact facts. . . .

In the present case . . . : a man is stabbed in the back, his lung is pierced and haemorrhage results; two hours later he dies of haemorrhage from that wound; in the interval there is no time for a careful examination, and the treatment given turns out in the light of subsequent knowledge to have been inappropriate and, indeed, harmful. In those circumstances no reasonable jury or court could, properly directed, in our view possibly come to any other conclusion than that the death resulted from the original wound. Accordingly, the court dismisses this appeal."

Appeal dismissed

R. v. Jordan (1956) 40 Cr.App.R. 152 (Court of Criminal Appeal)

The appellant stabbed the deceased who died some days later in hospital. Jordan, who had been convicted of murder, sought to adduce further medical evidence on appeal to the effect that the wound was not the cause of death.

Hallet J.:
"There were two things other than the wound which were stated by these two medical witnesses to have brought about death. The stab wound had penetrated the intestine in two places, but it was mainly healed at the time of death. With a view to preventing infection it was thought right to administer an antibiotic, terramycin.

It was agreed by the two additional witnesses that that was the proper course to take, and a proper dose was administered. Some people, however, are intolerant to terramycin, and Beaumont was one of those people. After the initial doses he developed diarrhoea, which was only properly attributable, in the opinion of those doctors, to the fact that the patient was intolerant to terramycin. Thereupon the administration of terramycin was stopped, but unfortunately the very next day the resumption of such administration was ordered by another doctor and it was recommenced the following day. The two doctors both take the same view about it. Dr. Simpson said that to introduce a poisonous substance after the intolerance of the patient was shown was palpably wrong. Mr. Blackburn agreed.

Other steps were taken which were also regarded by the doctors as wrong—namely, the intravenous introduction of wholly abnormal quantities of liquid far exceeding the output. As a result the lungs became waterlogged and pulmonary oedema was discovered. Mr. Blackburn said that he was not surprised to see that condition after the introduction of so much liquid, and that pulmonary oedema leads to broncho-pneumonia as an inevitable sequel, and it was from broncho-pneumonia that Beaumont died.

We are disposed to accept it as the law that death resulting from any normal treatment employed to deal with a felonious injury may be regarded as caused by the felonious injury . . . It is sufficient to point out here that this was not normal treatment. Not only one feature, but two separate and independent features, of treatment were, in the opinion of the doctors, palpably wrong and these produced the symptoms discovered at the post-mortem examination which were the direct and immediate cause of death, namely, the pneumonia resulting from the condition of oedema which was found . . .

We feel no uncertainty at all that, whatever direction had been given to the jury and however correct it had been, the jury would have felt precluded from saying that they were satisfied that death was caused by the stab wound."

Conviction quashed

R. v. Malcherek; R. v. Steel (1981) 73 Cr.App.R. 173 (Court of Appeal, Criminal Division)

Both cases raised the same question. M. stabbed his wife with a kitchen knife causing a deep abdominal wound. S. attacked a girl causing grave head injuries. Both victims were put on life support machines during normal courses of treatment. In each case the machines were switched off after a number of tests indicated that brain death had occurred. Both M. and S. were convicted at their trials of murder. They appealed alleging that the judge should not have withdrawn the question of causation from the jury. S. also sought leave to adduce further medical evidence that the doctors in each case had not complied with all the Royal Medical College's suggested criteria for establishing brain death.

Lord Lane C.J.:
"This is not the occasion for any decision as to what constitutes death . . .

We have had placed before us, and have been asked to admit, evidence that in each of these two cases the medical men concerned did not comply with all the suggested criteria for establishing such brain death. Indeed, further evidence has been suggested and placed before us that those criteria or tests are not themselves stringent enough . . .

The question posed for answer to this Court is simply whether the judge in each case was right in withdrawing from the jury the question of causation. Was he right to rule that there was no evidence on which the jury could come to the conclusion that the assailant did not cause the death of the victim?

The way in which the submissions are put is as follows; the doctors, by switching off the ventilator and the life support machine were the cause of death or, to put it more accurately, there was evidence which the jury should have been allowed to consider that the doctors, and not the assailant, in each case may have been the cause of death. . . .

In the view of this Court, if a choice has to be made between the decision in *Jordan* and that in *Smith*, which we do not believe it does (*Jordan* being a very exceptional case), then the decision in *Smith* is to be preferred. . . .

There is no evidence in the present case here that at the time of conventional death, after the life support machinery was disconnected, the original wound or injury was other than a continuing, operating and indeed substantial cause of the death of the victim, although it need hardly be added that it need not be substantial to render the assailant guilty. There may be occasions, although they will be rare, when the original injury has ceased to operate as a cause at all, but in the ordinary case if treatment is given bona fide by competent and careful medical practitioners, then evidence will not be admissible to show that the treatment would not have been administered in the same way by other medical practitioners. In other words, the fact that the victim has died, despite or because of medical treatment for the initial injury given by careful and skilled medical practitioners, will not exonerate the original assailant from responsibility for the death. It follows that so far as the ground of appeal in each of these cases relates to the direction given on causation, that ground fails . . .

Where a medical practitioner adopting methods which are generally accepted comes bona fide and conscientiously to the conclusion that the patient is for practical purposes dead, and that such vital functions as exist—for example, circulation—are being maintained solely by mechanical means, and therefore discontinues treatment, that does not prevent the person who inflicted the initial injury from being responsible for the victim's death. Putting it in another way, the discontinuance of treatment in those circumstances does not break the chain of causation between the initial injury and the death."

Appeal dismissed

2. Negative aspect

This same requirement (that the defendant's act be the "operative," etc., cause of the prohibited consequence) may be stated negatively: a *novus actus interveniens* will break the chain of causation. This intervening event will take over as the "operative," etc., cause of the consequence,[19] relegating the defendant's actions to the realms of the "history"[20] of the case.

Glanville Williams, *"Finis for Novus Actus?"* [1989] C.L.J. 391, 397:

"Policy arguments in favour of novus actus . . .
(1) The law should not saddle a person with liability for consequences that not only he but also the general public would blame on someone else. The intervention of the responsible actor diverts our retributive wrath from the first actor, who may, in the event, appear to be so much less culpable than the later actor; and this switching of retributive feeling from the first actor to the later actor is expressed in casual language.
(2) Sometimes we may feel that making people responsible for the subsequent behaviour of others, merely because they foresaw or could have foreseen that behaviour, would be too great a restriction upon liberty. . . .
(3) The rule has the beneficial effect of restricting the number of persons made liable for a particular occurrence. Part of the object of the criminal trial is to dramatise society's rejection of the deed, and, generally speaking, this is adequately done by prosecuting the immediate author and his accomplices."

But in what circumstances will such an intervening event be sufficient to constitute a *novus actus interveniens*?
In all of the above cases there was an intervening act. In *Smith* it was the dropping from the stretcher and the "thoroughly bad" medical treatment; in *Malcherek* it was the switching off of the life support machines; In neither of these cases was the intervening act sufficiently overwhelming to break the chain of causation. Yet in *Jordan* the "palpably wrong" medical treatment *did* constitute a *novus actus interveniens*. Can any principles be extracted from these cases to indicate *when* an

---

[19] There need not necessarily be any criminal responsibility attaching to the causer of this intervening event—*cf. Malcherek (ante* p. 416).
[20] *Smith (ante* p. 414).

intervening event will be sufficient to relieve the original actor from responsibility?

People v. Kibbe and Krall, 35 N.Y. 2d 407 (1974) (New York Court of Appeals)

The defendants robbed the victim who was an inebriated passenger in their car and then thrust him from the car on a cold winter's evening. They drove off leaving their "thoroughly intoxicated" victim where he had fallen on the shoulder of a rural two-lane highway. His trousers were down around his ankles; his shirt was rolled up towards his chest; he was shoeless and had been stripped of his outer clothing (his shoes and jacket had been tossed on to the shoulder of the highway near him); his glasses were still in the defendant's vehicle; the temperature was near zero and there was snow on both sides of the road; visibility was "occasionally obscured" by heavy winds blowing the snow across the road; there was no lighting on this section of the road; the nearest building was a gasoline service station nearly half a mile away on the other side of the highway. In an inebriated state the victim crawled to the middle of the road where he was struck by an oncoming truck and killed. The defendants were convicted of murder and appealed alleging that the actions of the driver of the truck constituted an intervening and superseding cause which relieved them of criminal responsibility.

Gabrielli J.:

"[T]o be a sufficiently direct cause of death so as to warrant the imposition of a criminal penalty therefor, it is not necessary that the ultimate harm be intended by the actor. It will suffice if it can be said beyond a reasonable doubt, as indeed it can be here said, that the ultimate harm is something which should have been foreseen as being reasonably related to the acts of the accused. . . .

We subscribe to the requirement that the defendants' actions must be a sufficiently direct cause of the ensuing death before there can be any imposition of criminal liability, and recognise, of course, that this standard is greater than that required to serve as a basis for tort liability. Applying these criteria to the defendants' actions, we conclude that their activities on the evening of December 30, 1970 were a sufficiently direct cause of the death of George Stafford so as to warrant the imposition of criminal sanctions. In engaging in what may properly be described as a despicable course of action, Kibbe and Krall left a helplessly intoxicated man without his eyeglasses in a position from which, because of these attending circumstances, he could not extricate himself and whose condition was such that he could not even protect himself from the elements. The defendants . . . argue that it was just as likely that Stafford would be miraculously rescued by a good samaritan. We cannot accept such an argument. There can be little doubt but that Stafford would have frozen to death in his state of undress had he remained on the shoulder of the road. The only alternative left to him was the highway, which in his condition, for one reason or another, clearly foreboded the probability of his resulting death.

Under the conditions surrounding Blake's operation of his truck (*i.e.* the fact that he had his low beams on as the two cars approached; that there was no artificial lighting on the highway; and that there was insufficient time in which to react to Stafford's presence in his lane), we do not think it may be said that any supervening wrongful act occurred to relieve the defendants from the directly foreseeable consequences of their actions."

Orders affirmed

R. v. Roberts (1972) 56 Cr.App.R. 95 (Court of Appeal, Criminal Division)

A girl who was a passenger in the appellant's car injured herself by jumping out of the car while it was in motion. Her explanation was that the appellant had made sexual advances to her and was trying to pull her coat off. The appellant was convicted of an assault occasioning actual bodily harm. He appealed on the ground *inter alia* that causation had not been established.

Stephenson L.J.:
"The test is: Was it the natural result of what the alleged assailant said and did, in the sense that it was something that could reasonably have been foreseen as the consequence of what he was saying or doing? As it was put in one of the old cases, it had got to be shown to be his act, and if of course the victim does something so 'daft,' in the words of the appellant in this case, or so unexpected, not that this particular assailant did not actually foresee it but that no reasonable man could be expected to foresee it, then it is only in a very remote and unreal sense a consequence of his assault, it is really occasioned by a voluntary act on the part of the victim which could not reasonably be foreseen and which breaks the chain of causation between the assault and the harm or injury."

Appeal dismissed

D.P.P. v. Daley [1979] 2 W.L.R. 239 (Privy Council)

The defendants threw stones at the deceased. He ran away from them, tripped, fell and was killed. Lord Keith held that causation (for manslaughter) would be established if the following essential ingredients were made out:
"(1) that the victim immediately before he sustained the injuries was in fear of being hurt physically; (2) that this fear was such that it caused him to try to escape; (3) that whilst he was trying to escape, and because he was trying to escape he met his death; (4) that his fear of being hurt there and then was reasonable and was caused by the conduct of the defendant."

R. v. Mackie (1973) 57 Cr.App.R. 453 (Court of Appeal, Criminal Division)

A three year old boy whom the appellant was looking after fell downstairs while running away in fear of being ill-treated by the appellant. The boy died. The appellant appealed against conviction for manslaughter.

Stephenson L.J.:
"In this case there were two complications: (1) the victim was a child of three and regard must be had to his age in considering whether his reaction was well-founded or well-grounded on an apprehension of immediate violence (in the language of the old cases appropriate to adults) and therefore reasonably to be expected. (2) This defendant was in the position of a parent, which may have entitled him to 'assault' the child by smacking or threatening him without breaking the law . . . How far was it reasonable, and therefore lawful, for the appellant to go on punishing this child was one of the questions the jury had to decide. Whether the boy 'over-reacted' (as Mr. Back put it) in a way which the appellant could not reasonably be expected to have foreseen was another. . . .

At the end of the summing-up the judge came back to these questions in suggesting what the vital points might be: 'First, was the boy in fear of Mackie? Secondly, did that cause him to try to escape? Thirdly, if he was in fear, was that fear well-founded? If it was well-founded, was it caused by the unlawful conduct of the accused, that is, by conduct for which there was no lawful excuse even on the part of a man in the position of a father?' "

Appeal dismissed

R. v. Pagett (1983) 76 Cr.App.R. 279 (Court of Appeal, Criminal Division)

The appellant shot at police officers who were attempting to arrest him for various serious offences. He had a girl with him, and against her will used her body to shield him from any retaliation by the officers. The officers returned the appellant's fire; three of their bullets hit the girl; she died from these wounds. The appellant was convicted of manslaughter and appealed to the Court of Appeal.

Goff L.J.:
"[One of the] specific points raised on behalf of the appellant . . . [was that] the learned judge . . . ought to have held that the appellant had not in the circumstances of this case caused the death of the deceased. The learned judge, in directing himself upon the law, ought to have held that where the act which immediately resulted in a fatal injury was the act of another party, albeit in legitimate self-defence, then the ensuing death was too remote or indirect to be imputed to the original aggressor . . .

[I]t was pressed upon us by Lord Gifford [counsel for the appellant] that there either was, or should be, a . . . rule of English law, whereby, as a matter of policy, no man should be convicted of homicide (or, we imagine, any crime of violence to another person) unless he himself, or another person acting in concert with him, fired the shot (or, we imagine, struck the blow) which was the immediate cause of the victim's death (or injury).

No English authority was cited to us in support of any such proposition, and we know of none. So far as we are aware, there is no such rule in English law; and . . . we can see no basis in principle for any such rule in English law. . . .

In our judgment, the question whether an accused person can be held guilty of homicide, either murder or manslaughter, of a victim the immediate cause of whose death is the act of another person must be determined on the ordinary principles of causation, uninhibited by any such rule of policy as that for which Lord Gifford has contended. . . .

In cases of homicide, it is rarely necessary to give the jury any direction on causation as such . . . Even where it is necessary to direct the jury's minds to the question of causation, it is usually enough to direct them simply that in law the accused's act need not be the sole cause, or even the main cause, of the victim's death, it being enough that his act contributed significantly to that result. Occasionally, however, a specific issue of causation may arise. One such case is where although an act of the accused constitutes a *causa sine qua non* of (or necessary condition for) the death of the victim, nevertheless the intervention of a third person may be regarded as the sole cause of the victim's death, thereby relieving the accused of criminal responsibility. Such intervention, if it has such an effect, has often been described by lawyers as a *novus actus interveniens*. . . .

Professors Hart and Honoré, *Causation in the Law* . . . consider the circumstances in which the intervention of a third person, not acting in concert with the accused, may have the effect of relieving the accused of criminal responsibility. The criterion which they suggest should be applied in such circumstances is whether the intervention is voluntary, *i.e.* whether it is 'free, deliberate and informed.' We resist the temptation of expressing the judicial opinion whether we find ourselves in complete agreement with that definition; though we certainly consider it to be broadly correct and supported by authority. Among the examples which the authors give of non-voluntary conduct, which is not effective to relieve the accused of reponsibility, are two which are germane to the present case, *viz.* a reasonable act performed for the purpose of self-preservation, and an act done in performance of a legal duty.

There can, we consider, be no doubt that a reasonable act performed for the purpose of self-preservation, being of course itself an act caused by the accused's own act, does not operate as a *novus actus interveniens*. If authority is needed for this almost self-evident proposition, it is to be found in such cases as *Pitts* (1842) C & M 284, and *Curley* (1909) 2 Cr.App.R. 96. In both these cases, the act performed for the purpose of self-preservation consisted of an act by the victim in attempting to escape from the violence of the accused, which in fact resulted in the victim's death. In each case it was held as a matter of law that, if the victim acted in a reasonable attempt to escape the violence of the accused the death of the victim was caused by the act of the accused. Now one form of self-preservation is self-defence; for present purposes, we can see no distinction in principle between an attempt to escape the consequences of the accused's act, and a response which takes the form of self-defence. Furthermore, in our judgment, if a reasonable act of self-defence, against the act of the accused causes the death of a third party we can see no reason in principle why the act of self-defence, being an involuntary act caused by the act of the accused, should relieve the accused from criminal responsibility for the death of the third party. . . .

The principles which we have stated are principles of law. . . . It follows that where, in any particular case, there is an issue concerned with what we have for convenience called *novus actus interveniens*, it will be appropriate for the judge to direct the jury in accordance with these principles. It does not however follow that it is accurate to state broadly that causation is a question of law. On the contrary, generally speaking causation is a question of fact for the jury. . . . But that does not mean that there are no principles of law relating to causation, so that no directions on law are ever to be given to a jury on the question of causation. . . . [Goff L.J. then cited the principle in *Blaue* (*post*), as an illustration of a legal principle of causation].

. . . [I]t is for the judge to direct the jury with reference to the relevant principles of law relating to causation, and then to leave it to the jury to decide, in the light of those principles, whether or not the relevant causal link has been established."

Appeal dismissed

Southern Water Authority v. Pegrum and Pegrum [1989] Crim.L.R. 442 (Queen's Bench Divisional Court)

"The respondents were charged with an offence contrary to section 31(1) of the Control of Pollution Act 1974, causing polluting matter (pig effluent) to enter a stream. The respondents reared pigs; effluent produced by the pigs was held initially in tanks and then transferred by gravity into a lagoon constructed for the purpose. The lagoon itself was emptied of liquid content for use as manure several times a year and of sediment annually. In the winter of 1987, after heavy rain, a blocked drain resulted in rain water flowing into the lagoon. A fissure developed at the top of one side of the lagoon and polluting liquid escaped, finding its way into a stream and eventually into a river. The magistrates found that the overflow from the lagoon was caused by an act of God—the ingress of rainwater— . . .

They further found that the blocked drain causing the ingress of rainwater was an intervening event 'breaking the chain of causation.' They dismissed the information and the prosecutor appealed by way of case stated.

Held, allowing the appeal and remitting the case with a direction to convict, the following principles applied: (i) where the defendant conducts some active operation involving the storage, use or creation of material capable of polluting a river should it escape, then if it does escape and pollute, the defendant is liable if he 'caused' that escape; (ii) the question of causation is to be decided in a commonsense way; (iii) a defendant may be found to have caused that escape even though he did not intend that escape and even though the escape happened without his negligence; (iv) it is a defence to show that the cause of the escape was the intervening act of a third party or act of God or vis major which are the '*novus actus interveniens*' defences to strict civil liability; (v) in deciding whether the intervening cause affords a defence the test is whether it was of so powerful nature that the conduct of the defendant was not a cause at all but was merely part of the surrounding circumstances. On the facts of the present case, the active operations or positive acts of the respondents were the storage and re-use of the effluent which resulted in the formation of the toxic sediment which polluted the stream. The magistrates erred in finding that the ingress of rainwater was an act of God; an act of God is an operation of natural forces so unpredictable as to excuse a defendant all liability for its consequences. The quantity of rain could not properly be regarded in itself as an act of God and in any event the ingress of rainwater into the lagoon was the result of the overflow from the blocked drain. Although unpredictable and unforeseeable operation of animate forces can amount to an act of God (see *Carstairs* v. *Taylor* (1870) L.R. 6 Exch. 217), there was no factual basis for such a finding in the present case."

Appeal allowed

Commonwealth v. Atencio and Marshall, 345 Mass. 627, 189 N.E. 2d. 223 (1963) (Supreme Judicial Court of Massachusetts)

The two defendants and the deceased played a "game" of "Russian roulette" with a gun containing one cartridge. Marshall spun the gun, pointed it at his head and pulled the trigger. Nothing happened. He handed the gun to Atencio, who repeated the process, again without result. Atencio passed the gun to the deceased, who spun it, put it to his head, then pulled the trigger. The cartridge exploded, and he was killed. The defendants' conviction for manslaughter was affirmed.

Wilkins, Chief Justice:

"That the defendants participated could be found to be a cause and not a mere condition of Stewart Britch's death. It is not correct to say that his act could not be found to have been caused by anything which Marshall and Atencio did, nor that he would have died when the gun went off in his hand no matter whether they had done the same. The testimony does not require a ruling that when the deceased took the gun from Atencio it was an independent or intervening act not standing in any relation to the defendants' acts which would render what he did imputable to them. It is an oversimplification to contend that each participated in something that only one could do at a time. There could be found to be mutual encouragement in a joint enterprise . . . . . . Nor, if the facts presented such a case, would we have to agree that if the deceased and not the defendants, had played first that they could not have been found guilty of manslaughter. The defendants were much more than merely present at a crime. It would not be necessary that the defendants force the deceased to play or suggest that he play."

Two recent English cases are similar to *Atencio* except that it was drugs instead of a gun being handed over to the victim. In both cases the victim injected himself with the drugs and died. The defendant escaped liability in both with the court in *Dalby* arguably,[21] and the judge in *Armstrong*[22] expressly, ruling that the victim injecting himself was a *novus actus interveniens*.

Att.-Gen. of Hong Kong v. Tse Hung-lit [1986] 3 All E.R. 173 (Privy Council)

The defendants loaded a speed boat with video recorders for which there was no export licence and no cargo manifest. They were to carry the recorders to a meeting place within Hong Kong waters and there transfer them to a fishing boat which would take the recorders to China. The fishing boat never arrived but the defendants were arrested and subsequently convicted of attempting to commit offences of causing unmanifested cargo to be taken out of Hong Kong and of causing articles without an export licence to be removed from Hong Kong.

Lord Bridge:
"[The argument here is that it is immaterial] whether or not the independent action of a third party may intervene between the action of the person alleged to have exported goods by causing them to be taken out of Hong Kong and the event of the goods crossing the Hong Kong border. So here, it is said, the respondents, if the fishing boat had kept the appointment and taken the video cassette recorders out of Hong Kong, would have been a necessary link in the chain of causation between Ah Fai, who planned and initiated the operation, and the crew of the fishing boat, who brought it to fruition. The respondents knew that the goods were to be taken out of Hong Kong, they played their allotted part in attempting to effect that result and, if the plan had not miscarried, they could properly be said to have caused the goods to be taken out of Hong Kong.
This is a formidable argument which perhaps gains in attraction from the consideration that its application to the circumstances of the instant case would cause no injustice whatever. The respondents have no merit and were fully alive to the criminality of the enterprise in which they were prepared to participate. . . .
In the High Court of Australia in *O'Sullivan* v. *Truth and Sportsman Ltd.* (1957) 96 C.L.R. 220. . . . the judgment of Dixon C.J., Williams, . . . contains the following statement . . .
'This appears to mean that when it is made an offence by or under statute for one man to "cause" the doing of a prohibited act by another the provision is not to be understood as referring to any description of antecedent event or con-

[21] (1982) 74 Cr.App.R. 348; see *post*, p. 619.
[22] [1989] Crim.L.R. 149 (this case is only a Crown Court report).

dition produced by the first man which contributed to the determination of the will of the second man to do the prohibited act. Nor is it enough that in producing the antecedent event or condition the first man was actuated by the desire that the second should be led to do the prohibited act. The provision should be understood as opening up a less indefinite inquiry into the sequence of anterior events to which the forbidden result may be ascribed. It should be interpreted as confined to cases where the prohibited act is done on the actual authority, express or implied, of the party said to have caused it or in consequence of his exerting some capacity which he possesses in fact or law to control or influence the acts of the other. He must moreover contemplate or desire that the prohibited act will ensue.'. . .

Their Lordships gratefully adopt . . . [this] passage. If the general principle is here applicable, it appears to their Lordships to afford to the respondents a complete defence. Had the fishing boat kept the appointment with the respondents and taken the video cassette recorders out of Hong Kong, there would have been a plain inference that the crew of that boat were acting on the authority of Ah Fai, the organiser of the forbidden exportation, and expecting no doubt, like the respondents, to be rewarded by Ah Fai. But there was nothing in the evidence led by the prosecution which could have justified the inference that the respondents were in any position, in fact or in law, to control or influence the crew of the fishing boat, or that, if the plan had been carried through, the crew of the fishing boat would have been acting on the express or implied authority of the respondents."

Appeal dismissed

B. Condition of Victim

The defendant must take his victim as he finds him.

1. Physical condition

In *Hayward*[23] the defendant chased his wife into the street. She fell down and he kicked her arm. She died. Medical evidence established that she had a persistent thyrus gland and such persons could die from a combination of fright or strong emotion and physical exertion. The defendant was convicted of manslaughter.

2. Religious condition

R. v. Blaue (1975) 61 Cr.App.R. 271 (Court of Appeal, Criminal Division)

The appellant stabbed a woman piercing her lung. She refused to have a blood transfusion as it was contrary to her religious beliefs as a Jehovah's Witness. The surgeon advised her that without the transfusion she would die. Medical evidence established that with the transfusion she would have survived. She died and the appellant was convicted of manslaughter (on grounds of diminished responsibility). He appealed on the ground that causation was not established.

[23] (1908) 21 Cox C.C. 692.

Lawton L.J.:

"Maule J.'s direction to the jury reflected the common law's answer to the problem. He who inflicted an injury which resulted in death could not excuse himself by pleading that his victim could have avoided death by taking greater care of himself. See Hale, *Pleas of the Crown* (1800 ed.) pp. 427–428. The common law in Sir Matthew Hale's time probably was in line with contemporary concepts of ethics. A man who did a wrongful act was deemed *morally* responsible for the natural and probable consequences of that act. [Counsel for the appellant] . . . asked us to remember that since Sir Matthew Hale's day the rigour of the law relating to homicide has been eased in favour of the accused. It has been—but this has come about through the development of the concept of intent, not by reason of a different view of causation . . .

The physical cause of death in this case was the bleeding into the pleural cavity arising from the penetration of the lung. This had not been brought about by any decision made by the deceased girl but by the stab wound.

[Counsel for the appellant] . . . tried to overcome this line of reasoning by submitting that the jury should have been directed that, if they thought the girl's decision not to have a blood transfusion was an unreasonable one, then the chain of causation would have been broken. At once the question arises—reasonable by whose standards? Those of Jehovah's Witnesses? Humanists? Roman Catholics? Protestants of Anglo-Saxon descent? The man on the Clapham omnibus? But he might well be an admirer of Eleazar who suffered death rather than eat the flesh of swine . . . or of Sir Thomas More who, unlike nearly all his contemporaries, was unwilling to accept Henry VIII as Head of the Church in England. Those brought up in the Hebraic and Christian traditions would probably be reluctant to accept that these martyrs caused their own deaths.

As was pointed out to . . . [counsel for the appellant] in the course of argument, two cases, each raising the same issue of reasonableness because of religious beliefs, could produce different verdicts depending on where the cases were tried. . . . It has long been the policy of the law that those who use violence on other people must take their victims as they find them. This in our judgment means the whole man, not just the physical man. It does not lie in the mouth of the assailant to say that his victim's religious beliefs which inhibited him from accepting certain kinds of treatment were unreasonable. The question for decision is what caused her death. The answer is the stab wound. The fact that the victim refused to stop this end coming about did not break the causal connection between the act and death."[24]

Appeal dismissed

3. Psychological condition

In *Lewis*[25] the defendant shot the deceased in the abdomen—a wound that would have caused death in an hour. The deceased however cut his own throat and died within five minutes. The court conceded that the defendant would nevertheless be liable if the self-inflicted knife wound could be causally connected to the defendant's gunshot wound, *i.e.*, if it was self-inflicted because of grief or pain or through a desire to shield the defendant. Temple J. stated:

"But, if the deceased did die from the effect of the knife wound alone,

---

[24] See also *Holland* (1841) 2 Mood. & R. 351 where a victim who could have recovered, ignored medical advice and died two weeks later; the original assailant was held to have caused the death.
[25] 124 Cal. 551, 57 Pac. 470 (1889).

no doubt the defendant would be responsible, if it was made to appear . . . that the knife wound was caused by the wound inflicted by the defendant, in the natural course of events. If the relation was causal, and the wounded condition of the deceased was not merely the occasion upon which another cause intervened, not produced by the first wound, or related to it in other than in a causal way, then defendant is guilty of a homicide. But, if the wounded condition only afforded an opportunity for another unconnected person to kill, the defendant would not be guilty."

In *Jones*[26] the defendant raped a girl who then jumped or fell into a river and drowned. The court concluded that the suicide attempt was the natural result of the defendant's acts; he could thus be held to have caused her death.

Lewis and *Jones* are both decisions from the U.S.A. Would they be followed here? The position is uncertain. In *Bunn*[27] the defendant hit the victim on the head with a snooker cue. This allegedly led to mental illness and three and a half months later the victim committed suicide. The defendant was charged with murder but the prosecution abandoned its case on the ground that "no jury could be sure beyond a reasonable doubt that the death . . . was caused by the blow." In *Prudom*[28] an intensive armed search was mounted in Yorkshire against Prudom who had killed two policemen. After a search lasting several days Prudom was cornered by police who warned that they were about to open fire. Prudom shot himself in the head. At the coroner's inquest a verdict was returned that Prudom had taken his own life; the actions of the police had not caused his death.

IV Evaluation

Are these above cases consistent with any of the "theories" of causation explored earlier in this chapter?

A. The "Policy" View

Many of the cases examined appear to satisfy a policy-orientated analysis. Was it not for "policy" reasons that the police were held not to have caused Prudom's death, while the opposite result was reached in *Lewis* and *Jones* where the victims similarly committed suicide? But again it must be emphasised that a finding of causation, without more, entails

---

[26] Ind. 384, 43 N.E. 2d 1017 (1942).
[27] *The Times*, May 11, 1989.
[28] *The Times*, October 8, 1982, p. 2.

no criminal liability. Thus the police *could* have been held to have caused Prudom's death, but to have been justified in doing so or to have lacked the *mens rea*, or culpability required for murder or manslaughter. "Policy" can clearly explain why defendants such as *Pegrum, Kibbe* and *Malcherek* were found liable. In *Kibbe*, for instance, the defendants were engaged in "a despicable course of action" whereas the driver of the truck that actually struck the victim was a "college student" behaving, as the court was at pains to point out, in an exemplary manner. Could there be any doubt as to the result in that case? But what of *Jordan* where the medical treatment was "palpably wrong" and broke the chain of causation? Surely there were no policy considerations at stake in exempting the defendant, who had brutally stabbed his victim, from liability for the death of the victim? The same must be true of the defendants in *Dalby, Armstrong* and *Tse Hung-lit*. If policy was the guiding criterion, liability would surely have ensued.

It must be remembered that many of the above defendants could have been charged with, or found guilty of, lesser offences which would have raised no causation problems. *Pagett* was convicted of possession of a firearm, kidnapping and attempted murder; *Hayward* was clearly guilty of an assault, *Blaue* of attempted murder, *Jones* of rape, and so on. *Welansky* could have been found guilty of a violation of safety regulations. Policy considerations clearly dictate that they all be blamed and punished for something, but it is not at all clear what the policy considerations were that dictated they be found liable for homicide offences, as opposed to these lesser offences.

B. Mens Rea Limits the Chain of Causation

Cases such as *Smith, Malcherek, Atencio* and *Blaue* are clearly consistent with this view. These defendants had *mens rea*: their actions were *a* cause of the result; they could fairly be blamed for the results that occurred. But this view cannot explain the different approaches adopted in *Smith* and *Jordan*. Jordan had the *mens rea* of murder: his acts were *a* cause of death; why was he not found liable? Can the different approaches in *Jones* and *Prudom* be explained in this way? *Roberts* was held to have caused the girl's injuries when she jumped from his moving car despite his having no *mens rea* in relation to those injuries. In *Southern Water* the defendant was held to have caused the result despite no *mens rea* or even negligence on his part being established.

C. Principles of Causation

1. Hart and Honoré
In all the above cases the defendant's actions "made a difference" in the way in which the natural course of events occurred. But in all these

cases there was an intervening act. Hart and Honoré argue that the chain of causation is broken by a "coincidence" but this does not include "abnormal conditions."[29] Further, the chain will be broken by the voluntary conduct on the part of another person.

Smith and *Jordan* can be reconciled within such a framework. In *Jordan* "palpably wrong" treatment of such a nature was so unlikely as rightly to qualify as a coincidence. In *Smith*, on the other hand, while the intervening treatment was perhaps unlikely, it would have failed to qualify under Hart and Honoré's other test of a coincidence, namely, that it was not significant or important. The victim did not die from medical treatment as in *Jordan*; he died from loss of blood caused by the stab wound inflicted by the defendant. Similarly in *Southern Water* the flooding of the lagoon was not sufficiently unlikely to constitute a *novus actus interveniens*.

The real problem arises in that in most of the discussed cases the consequence only occurred because of some action by the victim or a third person. In *Daley* it was the victim running away. In *Kibbe and Krall* it was the truck driver who actually ran the victim over. How are such cases to be resolved?

The "victim escape" cases such as *Roberts*, *Daley* and *Mackie* are easily explicable. The actions of the victim were not very unlikely (a synonym for reasonably foreseeable) and, in the circumstances, were hardly the result of voluntary action. Their fear was such that they had no real choice but to act as they did—their actions were "morally involuntary."[30] The same can be said of cases such as *Pagett* and *Kibbe and Krall*. The actions of the third party were not "free, deliberate and informed" and thus did not break the chain of causation. Finally, some of the "victim condition" cases such as *Blaue* and *Hayward*, although involving some action (or deliberate inaction) on the part of the victim, are in fact straightforward applications of Hart and Honoré's "abnormal condition" exception. The "abnormality" of the victim does not break the causal chain.

This still leaves problems. What of *Atencio*, *Dalby* and *Armstrong*? In *Atencio* the defendant handed the victim a gun; the victim shot himself. The court (albeit in the United States) had no hesitation in finding causation established. Following this decision it seems hard to see that injecting oneself with drugs provided by the defendant constitutes a *novus actus interveniens*—even if, under Hart and Honoré's thesis they are "voluntary actions." Where one party supplies another with drugs to enable the other to inject himself it is surely not difficult to say the parties are "acting in concert." Hart and Honoré exclude the actions of persons acting in concert from the ambit of "voluntary conduct." Using the more familiar language of the law it is surely reasonably foreseeable

---

[29] *Ante*, p. 409.
[30] Fletcher, p. 803.

that the other will indeed inject himself—in fact, highly predictable. It seems an odd principle that allows the expected actions of the victim to break the causal chain.

However, this approach ought not to be adopted with regard to the voluntary "in concert" actions (albeit predictable) of a third person other than the victim—as in *Tse Hung-lit*. Were the position otherwise there would be a complete breakdown of any distinction between principal offenders and counsellors and procurers. The latter would be held *themselves* to have caused the ultimate harm. It is important, for sentencing reasons at least, that these distinctions not be collapsed.

What of *Malcherek and Steel*? Were the actions of the doctors a "coincidence"? While they might not have been that unlikely, there is surely a case that they constituted "free, deliberate and informed" intervention by another party, thus breaking the chain of causation. Perhaps, however, the better argument here is that doctors acting in accordance with their proper medical procedures are akin to police acting in accordance with their proper procedures—which include defending themselves when under attack as in *Pagett*. Such proper and predictable actions do not constitute a *novus actus interveniens*.

A final problem exists with regard to those cases where the defendant is held to take his victim as he finds him. In *Hayward, Blaue*, etc., the victim's physical or mental condition is counted as an "abnormal condition" and thus unable to rank as a coincidence. But in *Roberts, Daley* and *Mackie* the victim's psychological make-up that induced him to flee from the defendant is disregarded and insistence is placed on his actions being reasonable, likely or foreseeable. How can this divergence of approach be explained? It has been suggested that the issue in all such cases be determined by whether the victim's act was "voluntary."[31] If the victim's suicide or leaping from a moving car was voluntary it breaks the chain of causation as "[i]n the view of many theorists, the attribution of a harm cannot be traced past a voluntary intentional act that brings it about."[32] This was the solution adopted in *Pagett* for determining whether the actions of a third person constituted a *novus actus interveniens*. It is submitted that a better (and certainly simpler) approach is to allow the central principle of reasonable foresight or expectation to prevail. However, in ascertaining whether the victim's response is reasonable, account should be taken of any particular idiosyncrasies of the victim. Thus in *Roberts* the girl was "normal." The question is simply whether her response was reasonable. In *Blaue* the issue is whether it is reasonably foreseeable that a Jehovah's Witness would refuse a blood transfusion. In this way we do take account of the victim's condition or characteristics but are able to impose some limit to the chain of causation.

[31] Hart and Honoré, p. 326; Fletcher, p. 365; *Pagett, ante*, p. 420.
[32] Fletcher, *ibid*.

2. Model Penal Code's principles of causation

Can the above cases be explained in terms of the Model Penal Code's principles? It will be recalled that under those principles an actor will not be treated as having caused a harm if it occurred in a manner different from that contemplated[33] unless the actual manner of occurrence was not too "remote or accidental" to have a just bearing on the actor's liability or on the gravity of his offence. Does "remote or accidental" mean the same as Hart and Honoré's "coincidence" or the law's *"novus actus interveniens"*?

Cases such as *Atencio* pose no problems here as the harm occurred in exactly the same manner as that contemplated. Similarly cases such as *Kibbe, Daley* and *Pagett* pose little problem as the harm was either "within the risk" or was not too "remote or accidental." Possibly even *Smith* and *Jordan* are reconcilable with these principles—the medical treatment in the former not being too "remote or accidental," but in the latter being so "palpably wrong" as to become too "remote or accidental." And what of the "condition of the victim" cases? Again, where causation is established in cases such as *Lewis* or *Blaue*, the conclusions can be rationalised on the basis that the result was not too "remote or accidental," whereas in *Prudom* it was.

But as this analysis demonstrates, every case can be rationalised in this manner as ultimately the test is one of the "jury's sense of justice." But does this not mean that different juries will reach different results on the same facts? Are these really "principles" of causation? Do they provide any guidance to a prosecutor as to when or whom to prosecute?

3. Draft Criminal Code Bill

This purports to "restate satisfactorily"[34] the law on causation, and, it is submitted, it has for the most part achieved this objective and would greatly clarify some of the ambiguities presently bedevilling the law.[35] Under this test causation would clearly be established in *Dalby* and *Armstrong* as the victim's injecting himself would clearly be reasonably foreseeable. Equally, there would be no liability in a case such as *Bunn*[36] as it is hardly foreseeable that someone who has been struck over the head with a snooker cue will subsequently commit suicide. One problem with this approach is the failure to address the problem of third party voluntary intervention—although under clause 17(3) it would appear that causation would not be established in *Tse Hung-lit*—which must surely be the better approach.

---

[33] Or in crimes of recklessness or negligence, if the harm was "not within the risk."

[34] Law Com. No. 177 Vol. 2, *Commentary on Draft Criminal Code Bill*, para. 7.17.

[35] This view is not shared by Glanville Williams, "Finis for *Novus Actus?*" [1989] C.L.J. 391 who argues that the clause is both too wide in that it allows events as well as human actions to break the causal chain—and too narrow in that causation is never excluded when a consequence is foreseen or could have been foreseen by the defendant: e.g., a tobacco company could be held to have caused the death of smokers because their acts of smoking would clearly have been foreseen and thus could not constitute a *novus actus interveniens*.

[36] *Ante*, n. 27.

It has been written that there are "no principles" governing causation in this context.[37] While it is true that ultimately it is a question of fact for the jury to decide, such limited principles as provided by the Draft Criminal Code will be of immense utility in enhancing certainty and predictability in the law.

---

[37] Glanville Williams, *Textbook*, (1st ed., 1978), p. 329.

CHAPTER 5

INCHOATE OFFENCES

I INTRODUCTION

An inchoate crime is one that is "committed by doing an act with the purpose of effecting some other offence."[1] It is committed when the defendant takes certain steps towards the commission of a crime. There are three main inchoate offences in English law—attempt, conspiracy and incitement—and the nature of the requisite steps that need be taken varies with each. With attempt the defendant must have tried to commit the offence and have got relatively close to achieving his objective. With conspiracy at least two defendants must have agreed to commit a crime. And with incitement the defendant must have tried to persuade another to commit a crime.

An inchoate offence is one that is "relative to the offense-in-chief."[2] It consists of actions falling short of the consummated crime. It is thus not a crime existing in the abstract. One cannot be indicted for "conspiracy" or "attempt." The indictment must be drafted with reference to the complete offence, for example, conspiracy to murder or attempt to steal.

There are many other offences in English law that might be thought of as inchoate in the sense that they penalise conduct that might be preparatory to the commission of other offences—for example, possession of firearms.[3] These offences are however "crimes in themselves" as they are indictable as such without any reference to any further offence. While there is no magic in the terminology, for the sake of convenience of exposition we shall describe these offences as "precursor offences."

Both inchoate and precursor offences share a common element. No harm is caused, in the ordinary sense of the word; no person need be injured; no proprietary interest is damaged. A crucial question, therefore, running through our analysis of such offences will be: how can we justify the existence of such offences and how should they be punished in comparison with the completed offence?

---

[1] Glanville Williams, *Textbook*, p. 402.
[2] Fletcher, p. 132.
[3] Firearms Act 1968, ss.16–22. See *post* pp. 497–500.

II ATTEMPT

A. Criminology of Attempts

Editorial "The Criminology of Attempts" [1986] Crim.L.R. 769:

"In recent years the law of criminal attempts has been one of the most discussed areas of the criminal law . . . . Over the same period there has also been an increasing criminological interest in the prevention of crime, which has manifested itself in the publication of various Home Office Research Studies on crime prevention, with many of the studies based on experiments undertaken in different areas of the country. Both the Home Office and the police have been placing more emphasis on the taking of measures to prevent crime, and few would argue with the general proposition that successful prevention is preferable to *post hoc* efforts to reform or deter offenders. If the crime prevention movement has had any success, then one might expect that more criminal endeavours are ending in failure—to be precise, that the proportion of offences which are mere attempts rather than completed crimes is increasing. Has this happened?

The present structure of the annual criminal statistics does not permit such inferences, since the statistical categories are not apt, but there is now some interesting material from the two sweeps of the British Crime Survey . . . . [S]ome 11,000 households were asked about offences which had been committed against them or their members in the previous year, and it has thus been possible to obtain a realistic estimate of how many crimes are actually committed each year rather than relying on police figures of the offences recorded by them. Home Office Research Bulletin no. 21 (1986), at pages 10–13, discusses the British Crime Survey findings on attempted burglaries, an area in which crime prevention has received considerable publicity. The general finding is that only about half of all burglaries or attempts are reported to the police, but when the figures were examined further it was found that two-fifths of all burglaries are unsuccessful attempts to gain entry. Only about 20 per cent. of attempts are ever reported to the police, and therefore the proportion coming through the courts is much smaller. It is speculated that about half of the attempts failed because of the level of security, and that the proportion of attempts has increased in recent years."

B. Should There be a Law of Attempt?

It was argued earlier that the imposition of criminal liability ought to be (and can be) analysed in terms of the following equation:

Blame + Harm = Criminal Liability.[4]

We have seen that an important (and often decisive) indicator of blame is the existence of *mens rea*. With attempts, this element is clearly satisfied. The man who attempts to commit an offence clearly has the *mens rea* of that full offence.[5] But he has caused no harm, in the usual

---

[4] *Ante* p. 277, and see *post* Chap 10.
[5] Indeed, his *mens rea* will often have to be of a *greater* degree than that required for the completed offence; see *post* p. 445.

sense of the word: for instance, the victim has not died or has not lost any property. Are we justified in imposing criminal liability upon an actor who has caused no such harm?

There are two quite distinct ways of answering this question—both leading to the conclusion that criminal liability *should* be imposed for attempts:

1. Where a crime is attempted, there *is* a harm, namely, a threat to security. In our society we all have rights to bodily and proprietary security. An attempt to commit a crime represents a danger to these rights. Our right to security has been infringed. This infringement of our rights constitutes, in itself, a harm that the criminal law seeks to punish. Gross expresses the point well:

"When there is only attempt liability, the conduct itself may usefully be regarded as a second order harm: in itself it is the sort of conduct that normally presents a threat of harm; and that, by itself, is a violation of an interest that concerns the law. The interest is one in security from harm and merely presenting a threat of harm violates that security interest."[6]

2. In utilitarian terms, criminal liability for attempts may be justified in the absence of any harm. A person who attempts to commit a crime is dangerous; he needs restraining. Such a person is also in need of rehabilitation and punishment for individual deterrence, otherwise he might try to commit the crime again being more careful the next time. It is however, doubtful whether punishment for general deterrence purposes will suffice here: people who attempt crimes, by definition, aim at success; if punishment for the complete crime is an ineffective deterrent, nothing is gained by punishment for an attempt to commit the crime. There is also a final important utilitarian justification here: the police should be given every encouragement to prevent crime, not simply to detect it. On this basis the police should be empowered to arrest, and prosecute, for attempts to commit crimes.

Of course, whenever utilitarian arguments such as these are raised, we find ourselves faced with the same central question posed earlier[7]: while utilitarian considerations might explain the *purpose* of punishment, are we ever justified in punishing exclusively for such reasons? Or may we only punish offenders who *deserve* punishment? If the latter, then we are back to our starting point that generally, punishment is only deserved where there is a combination of blame and harm. However this is not a cast-iron rule. With crimes of strict liability, the law is prepared to dispense with the element of blame in imposing liability. It could be that with crimes of attempt, the utilitarian arguments for punishment are so strong that we are prepared to dispense with the element

---

[6] Gross, *A Theory of Criminal Justice* (1979), p. 125.
[7] *Ante* p. 43.

of harm, and assert that punishment is justified (*i.e.* deserved) on the basis of the blame element alone.

Thus under either of these explanations it is possible to justify the existence of a law of attempt. The contours of such a law will vary however, depending on which of the two views is accepted. This is because the first view focuses on attempts that threaten people's interests in security from interference. Thus unless the attempter gets near to completing the crime (and generally unless the crime is possible), no interests are threatened and criminal liability is not justified. But the emphasis in the second view is on the *mens rea* of the attempter: if he has the requisite *mens rea*, he need not get near to committing the complete offence (and generally it will be irrelevant whether the crime is possible). The tensions between these two approaches and their impact upon the law will be explored further when we examine the *actus reus* of attempt.

Can there be an attempt to commit all crimes? Whatever the position at common law might have been,[8] section 1(4) of the Criminal Attempts Act 1981 now provides that there can only be criminal liability for attempts to commit "any offence which, if it were completed, would be triable . . . as an indictable offence."[9] Criminal liability for attempts to commit summary offences was excluded because there is "no social need to extend the punishment of attempt outside the class of serious crime. The amount of time spent considering complicated questions would be out of all proportion to the advantage accruing from allowing the law to intervene at an early stage."[10] It is submitted that such an approach is justifiable.[11] With attempts, criminal liability is imposed in the absence of any direct harm (other than a threat to security). When dealing with serious offences we are arguably justified in dispensing with the requirement of harm. But when dealing with the lesser summary offences which pose less of a threat to society, we should insist on harm actually occurring as a prerequisite to any criminal liability.

It has been suggested that we do not need a *general* law of attempt. Each substantive offence could be defined, or redefined, so as to include attempts to commit that offence.[12] Thus, for instance, the crime of handling stolen goods is defined by section 22 of the Theft Act 1968 in the following terms:

"(1) A person handles stolen goods if . . . he . . . receives the goods, or . . . undertakes or assists in their retention, removal, disposal or realisation . . . , *or if he arranges to do so.*"

---

[8] See "Attempts to Commit Summary Offences" (1922) 86 J.P.N. 550.
[9] Section 1(4) also excludes liability for attempted (a) conspiracy; (b) aiding, abetting, counselling, procuring or suborning an offence; and (c) offences under section 4(1) (assisting offenders) or section 5(1) (accepting or agreeing to accept consideration for not disclosing information about an arrestable offence) of the Criminal Law Act 1967.
[10] H.C.Deb., Vol. 2, ser. 6, cols. 214 (1981).
[11] *Contra*, Law Commission Working Paper No. 50, para. 109.
[12] Glazebrook, "Should we have a law of Attempted Crime?" (1969) 85 L.Q.R. 28.

Arranging to receive stolen goods is part of the substantive offence. Without this provision many such arrangements would have constituted attempts to commit the offence. If all offences were defined in a comparable manner, a general law of attempt would be unnecessary. Such an approach, however, poses immense problems. First, is it realistic to expect that *all* criminal offences could be defined (and all existing offences redefined) so as to include attempts within their definition? Secondly, and most importantly, if, as will be suggested in the next section, attempts are to be regarded as less serious than completed offences, we surely do not wish to collapse the distinction between the two. For punishment reasons, if for no other, it is important that the attempt to commit a crime, and the completed crime itself, be retained distinct from each other.

C. Punishment of Attempts

Criminal Attempts Act 1981, s.4(1)

"A person guilty . . . of attempting to commit an offence shall—
(a) if the offence attempted is murder or any other offence the sentence for which is fixed by law, be liable on conviction on indictment to imprisonment for life; and
(b) if the offence attempted is indictable but does not fall within paragraph (a) above, be liable on conviction on indictment to any penalty to which he would have been liable on conviction on indictment of that offence; and
(c) if the offence attempted is triable either way, be liable on summary conviction to any penalty to which he would have been liable on summary conviction of that offence."

California Penal Code, s.664. Attempts; punishment

"Every person who attempts to commit any crime, but fails, or is prevented or intercepted in the perpetration thereof, is punishable, where no provision is made by law for the punishment of such attempts as follows:
1. Offenses punishable by imprisonment in the state prison
1. If the offense so attempted is punishable by imprisonment in the state prison, the person guilty of such attempt is punishable by imprisonment in the state prison for one-half the term of imprisonment prescribed upon a conviction of the offense so attempted; provided, however, that if the crime attempted is one in which the maximum sentence is life imprisonment or death the person guilty of such attempt shall be punishable by imprisonment in the state prison for a term of five, seven, or nine years.
2. Offenses punishable by imprisonment in a county jail
2. If the offense so attempted is punishable by imprisonment in a county jail, the person guilty of such attempt is punishable by imprisonment in a county jail for a term not exceeding one-half the term of imprisonment prescribed upon a conviction of the offense so attempted.
3. Offenses punishable by fine
3. If the offense so attempted is punishable by a fine, the offender convicted of

such attempt is punishable by a fine not exceeding one-half the largest fine which may be imposed upon a conviction of the offense so attempted."

Thus the completed crime of theft carries a maximum of 10 years imprisonment in England[13] and attempted theft can similarly be punished up to this maximum of 10 years. But in California, if theft there carried a presumptive penalty of 10 years imprisonment in the state prison, attempted theft would carry a presumptive penalty of five years imprisonment. This divergence of approach raises the fundamental question: should attempts be punished to the same, or to a lesser, extent as the completed crime? On what basis can either of these approaches be rationalised?

James Brady, "Punishing Attempts" (1980) 63 The Monist 246 at 247–250:

"*2. Equal harm*
    . . . According to Becker ('Criminal Attempt and the Law of Crimes,' Philosophy and Public Affairs, Vol. 3 (Spring, 1974): pp. 262–94), we need to distinguish between the private harm done to the individual, which, of course, is different in the case of attempts and completions, and the 'social' harm to which the criminal law is mainly addressed. The harm which is the concern of the criminal law is that which disrupts social stability and arouses self-defensive reactions within persons in the society. One's assurance that one will not be interfered with is perceived to be threatened equally by an attempt on others and by completed crimes. Thus, in general, attempts and completed crimes are equal in what Becker calls their 'social volatility'; the *criminal* harm is the same. . . .
    However . . . his claim . . . is unfounded. The fear, resentment, and apprehension occasioned when harm, in its ordinary sense, occurs does appear to be different than when, even by accident, no harm occurs. These attitudes seem to be what Becker has in mind when he talks of the 'social volatility' of conduct. Therefore, on Becker's own theory we should, *contra* his position, treat attempts differently . . .

3. Equal dangerousness
    A more plausible claim than the argument that attempts and the completed crime do not differ in the harm done, is the claim that, in general, attempts pose no less danger to the legally protected interest than does the completed crime. If the general purpose in punishing is to prevent harm, the law should identify, at the earliest feasible moment, the dangerous individual who is likely to cause harm. In such a theory, conduct might be required before such intervention is justifiable, but the primary function of the conduct requirement would be evidentiary, serving as proof of the intent which is an index to the dangerousness of the offender.
    If the dangerousness of the offender is the key element in grading offenses, then it follows that two equally dangerous offenders should be treated the same.

---

[13] Theft Act 1968, s.7.

If there is no difference in dangerousness between the successful offender and the person who fails to cause harm because he is prevented by some external circumstance, the law should treat them equally. Being equally dangerous, they are equally in need of treatment and reform.

There is, of course, the chance that the person who attempts a crime might be deterred from completing it if he were to receive a more severe penalty for the successful crime than if the penalty for attempts and the completed crime are the same. If he is already liable to the full penalty for the attempt, then he has no motive to desist from completing the crime. But this does not provide an argument, under an equal dangerousness theory, for punishing attempts, in general, less than the completed crime. To take care of these special, and probably rare cases, it would seem to be better to provide, as the Model Penal Code does, an affirmative defense of abandonment or, renunciation of purpose. Such a defense is a defense to the crime of attempt.[14] If the defendant is successful in proving the defense, he receives no punishment at all. Thus, the offender has an even greater motive for not carrying out his purpose than if the law merely provided an across-the-board reduction in punishment for attempts.

[But if this] equal dangerousness argument were to be followed consistently, crimes of unequal culpability should also be treated the same. The focus of a dangerousness approach is on the characteristics of a person which identify him as presenting a threat of harm to society. Negligent or reckless offenders may pose as much of a continuing threat of harm and may require as much treatment and reform to 'neutralize' their dangerousness as the intentional offender. Thus, if we accept the equal dangerousness rationale for punishing attempts, it would appear that we should also accept the premise that offenses should not be ranked according to culpability elements such as intention, recklessness, and negligence. We could, of course, simply accept this conclusion that intentional offenses should be classified as being of the same criminal 'degree' as reckless or negligent offenses where there is reason to believe that there is no difference in the dangerousness of the offender. But this would entail a radical reform of the criminal law; indeed, to follow a dangerousness rationale consistently would be, in effect, to abolish the system of control now known as the criminal law and substitute a system of treatment and prevention. . . .

4. *Equal culpability*

. . . [This] assumes that the sole determining factor in assessing the degree of blame in attempts is the person's intention. If the offender has done everything in his power to carry out his intention to cause harm and fails through some fortuity, then he should be considered as culpable as if he had succeeded. The first version holds, moreover, that cases of attempts other than the extreme case should also be ranked equally with the extreme case and with the completed offense. After all, what difference in intent is discernible between a person who is apprehended before he has taken the last step toward the commission of the offense, if we are convinced that he had the intention or the 'fixed' intention to commit the offense, and one who has taken that step in furtherance of his intent? On this view, how can there be any difference in culpability between the person apprehended while 'lying in wait,' or at an even earlier stage of preparation, and the person who shoots but misses? Under this version, punishment for attempts should be the same whenever we are satisfied that intent or 'fixed' intent is present, the conduct requirement serving as evidence of that intent."

---

[14] This is the position in the United States. Whether such a defence exists in English law is discussed *post* at p. 465.

Andrew Ashworth, "Criminal Attempts and the Role of Resulting Harm under the Code, and in the Common Law" 19 (1988) Rutgers Law Journal 725:

"An intent-based form of retributivism would start with the proposition that the technique of the criminal law is to impose on individuals in society various duties of self-restraint, in order to provide a basic security of person, property, amenity, and so on. A person who voluntarily casts off this burden of self-restraint deserves punishment, in that he or she has used unfair means to gain an advantage over law-abiding citizens. Th purpose of criminal punishment then is to counter-balance, at least symbolically, a voluntary breaking of the rules. Since fairness is an integral element in this 'just deserts' approach, it would be wrong to allow random or chance factors to determine the threshold of criminal liability or the quantum of punishment . . . According to this fully subjective view, the quantum of punishment should be determined by what the defendant tried to do or thought she was doing, and not according to how things turned out. The principle draws a straight line through the vicissitudes of life and the vagaries of fortune, minimising the influence of chance and keeping as close as possible to the defendants's choice and to what lay within her control. On this principle, complete attempts should attract the same quantum of punishment as substantive offences."

Andrew Ashworth, "Belief, Intent and Criminal Liability" in J. Eekelaar and J. Bell, Oxford Essays in Jurisprudence (1987), p. 2 at pp. 16–17:

"Is A, who shoots at X intending to kill him but misses because X unexpectedly moves, any less culpable than B, who shoots at Y intending to kill him and does so? An external description of both sets of events would probably not suggest that they have 'done' the same thing, whereas an account which paid more attention to the actor's point of view and to matters which lay within the actor's control would suggest that they both intended and tried, to the same extent, to do the same thing. The argument here is that, because of the element of uncertainty in the outcome of things which we try to do, it would be wrong for assessments of culpability to depend on the occurrence or non-occurrence of the intended consequences. 'Success or failure . . . makes no difference at all to [an agent's] moral status in relation to his original act. His original act, strictly considered, was simply his trying and *that* is what moral assessment must concern itself with' (P. Winch, *Ethics and Action*, 1972, p. 139) . . . Moral blame and criminal liability should be based so far as possible on choice and control, on the trying and not on what actually happened thereafter.

What are the reasons for wishing to reduce the influence of chance upon criminal liability? It cannot be doubted that luck plays a considerable part in everyday events. Actual results also play a considerable part in judgments of others, and tend to dominate assessments in such fields as business, sport, and education. Those who try hard but are unsuccessful often receive less recognition than those who achieve goals (no matter how little effort they put into it). But these are not moral assessments of the individuals or their characters. If one turns to moral and social judgements, it is doubtful whether outcomes should be proper criteria. It may be desirable overall to have fewer bad outcomes and more good outcomes in society, but that does not lead to the conclusion that moral praise and blame should be allocated solely according to result. Indeed, a bad outcome stemming from a good intent may be a better predictor of good outcomes than a good outcome born of a bad intent. From time to time we may praise someone for producing a good result, even though it was not what he was trying to do, but this is more a reflection of our pleasure at the outcome than an assessment of his conduct and character. If we turn to blaming, is it not unacceptable to blame people for causing results irrespective of whether they were caused intentionally, negligently, or purely accidentally? Blaming is a moral activity which is surely only appropriate where the individual had some choice or control over the matter. For this reason the criminal law should seek to minimize the effect of luck upon the incidence and scale of criminal liability."

A relatively common view is that punishment for attempts should depend upon the dangerousness of the defendant's actions; this is measured by determining how imminent the threatened harm is and by examining the reason for failure.

Cross and Ashworth, Cross: The English Sentencing System (3rd ed., 1981), pp. 154–155:

"[T]he question whether an attempt should be punished less severely than the completed crime is largely dependent on the reason why the attempt failed. If it failed because the attempter voluntarily abandoned the attempt, he should be punished less because he is less wicked or needs less deterring. If it failed because of his incompetence, either in executing his design clumsily or in choosing a method which, owing to his failure to appreciate the true facts, proved to be impossible, he may be punished less on the ground that he represents less of a social danger than successful criminals. If it failed because of someone's intervention before he had done all he set out to do, he may be treated more leniently than the successful criminal: his wickedness may be less, since (as Blackstone said) it takes more wickedness to carry through a plan than to conceive it, and it may be desirable (on a utilitarian view) to mark each stage of an attempt by a portion of punishment in order to deter the attempter from pursuing his criminal design to its conclusion. There remain difficulties, however, with cases . . . where the attempter has done all the acts he intended and has failed to produce the planned result. . . . On principle . . . there is no distinction in point of either wickedness or social danger between the successful criminal and the unsuccessful attempter in this last class. Chance may well be the only explanation of why one attempt succeeded and the other failed, and a sound sentencing policy should take little notice of a factor which lies outside the offender's control. He should be judged on the basis of what he intended to do, believed he was doing or knowingly risked."

Gross, in a complex variation of this theme, pushes the argument to its logical conclusion by asserting:

"In some cases, then, attempt liability will be as extensive as liability for the completed crime, and may even be greater, for sometimes, even though harm does not occur, the conduct of the accused was more dangerous than in a case in which harm does occur. In other cases of attempt the conduct is less dangerous and so liability is less extensive."[15]

It is our submission that it can *never* be justifiable to impose greater

---

[15] *Theory of Criminal Justice*, pp. 423–436 at p. 425. For a criticism of Gross's views, see Brady, "Punishing Attempts" (1980) 63 *The Monist* 246, at 251–255.

punishment for an attempt than for the completed crime. Indeed, it is our submission that attempts should *always* be punished to a lesser extent than the completed crime. The obvious thrust of our argument is that the basic equation of blame plus harm equals criminal liability can only be "balanced" in the field of attempt by reading it as blame plus no harm (or at most, "second-order harm"[16]) equals *less* criminal liability. But why should this be so? Why should the causing of harm be regarded as so significant?

Michael Davis, "Why Attempts Deserve Less Punishment than Complete Crimes" 5 Law & Phil. (1986) 1 at pp. 28–29:

"Someone who attempts a crime but fails to do the harm characteristic of success still (ordinarily) risks doing that harm. He deserves punishment for risking that harm because even risking such harm is an advantage the law abiding do not take. He deserves less punishment for the attempt than he would for the complete crime because being able to risk doing harm is not as great an advantage as being able to do it. To attempt murder is, for example, not worth as much as to succeed. The successful murderer has the advantage of having done what he set out to do. The would-be murderer whose attempt failed has only had the *chance* to do what he set out to do. The difference is substantial."

J. C. Smith, "The Element of Chance in Criminal Liability" [1971] Crim.L.R. 63 at 69–72:

"Ought we then to get rid of the element of harm and base liability purely on fault?. . . .

Even the most ardent advocate for the re-introduction of capital punishment did not—so far as I know—want it for *attempted* murder as well as murder. Yet the only difference between the attempt and the full offence is that in the latter the harm which it is the object of the law to prevent is caused, in the former it is not; but it seems to be generally accepted that this justifies a difference in the gravity of the offence and the punishment which may be imposed. . . .

[This] suggests that great significance is still attached to the harm done, as distinct from the harm intended or foreseen. Perhaps the significance of the harm done derives from our emotional reaction to the acts of others. If one of my small boys, not looking what he is doing, throws a stone which just misses the dining room window, I shall be very cross with him; but if the stone breaks the dining room window, I shall be absolutely furious. His behaviour is just as bad and just as dangerous in the one case as in the other; but my indignation is much greater in the case where he has caused the harm than in that where he has not. . . .

Stephen J., the great criminal law judge of the nineteenth century, thought . . . there was nothing irrational in basing liability on the harm done:

'If two persons are guilty of the very same act of negligence, and one of them causes thereby a railway accident, involving the death and mutilation of many persons, whereas the other does no injury to anyone, it seems to me that it would be rather pedantic than rational to say that each had committed the same offence, and should be subjected to the same punishment. In one sense, each has committed an offence, but the one has had the *bad*

[16] Gross, *ante*, n. 6.

luck to cause a horrible misfortune, and to attract public attention to it, and the other the *good fortune* to do no harm. Both certainly deserve punishment, but it gratifies a natural public feeling to choose out for punishment the one who actually has caused great harm, and the effect in the way of preventing a repetition of the offence is much the same as if both were punished.'

(*History of the Criminal Law*, Vol. III, pp. 311 *et seq.*; italics supplied by writer)."

H. L. A. Hart, Punishment and Responsibility (Essays in the Philosophy of Law) (1968), p. 131:

"It is pointed out that in some cases the successful completion of a crime may be a source of gratification, and, in the case of theft, of actual gain, and in such cases to punish the successful criminal more severely may be one way of depriving him of these illicit satisfactions which the unsuccessful have never had . . .

My own belief is that this form of retributive theory appeals to something with deeper instinctive roots than the last mentioned principle. Certainly the resentment felt by a victim actually injured is normally much greater than that felt by the intended victim who has escaped harm because an attempted crime has failed."

James Brady, "Punishing Attempts" (1980) 63 The Monist, 246 at 255:

"[F]eelings of guilt and remorse are significantly different in the case where one has actually caused harm than in the case where, acting with the same intent, one has not been the cause of harm. Feelings of guilt and remorse do vary in degree when one has, for example, through reckless driving caused a death and where one has acted with equal recklessness but there has been no victim. In this case, as with the unsuccessful attempt, there is a kind of 'space' in which the person is allowed to express relief that he has not been the cause of harm."

Thus the occurrence of harm plays a crucial role in the shaping and assessing of moral responsibility. As Silber puts it:

"The man who has attempted murder . . . is as guilty *volitionally* as he can possibly be. But he lacks the *being* or *status* of a murderer. It would be a *reductio ad absurdum* of the theory of voluntary responsibility to assume that he would not be far more blameworthy had he acted in an ontological matrix that supported his intent and brought about its full realization. . . . Fortunately he is not a murderer with regrets and remorse but only a man who has come very close to being one. He is protected from or relieved of some moral blame by the collapse of the ontological matrix required for the completion of his murderous intent."[17]

Related arguments as to why the causing of harm should be regarded as significant are to be found in the concluding chapter of this book.[18]

---

[17] John R. Silber, "Being and Doing: A study of Status Responsibility and Voluntary Responsibility" (1967) 35 University of Chicago Law Review 47, at 78–79. For a critique of Silber's thesis that the theory of voluntary responsibility be replaced by a notion of "status" responsibility, see James B. Brady, "Status Responsibility" (1973) 33 *Philosophy and Phenomenological Research* 408.

[18] See *post* pp. 801–805.

However, before concluding this section it is perhaps worth pausing to consider briefly the concept of "blame" as applied in the field of attempts—and to question the assumption that the blameworthiness of those who attempt and those who succeed is necessarily the same. It is a prerequisite of criminal liability for attempts that the attempter intends to commit the criminal offence—in the sense that he *means* to commit the crime. But while many attempters *appear for legal purposes* to possess this necessary intention, closer examination reveals that this might not necessarily be so. As Menninger has written:

"[T]he failure to achieve success . . . is apt to express accurately the mathematical resultant of component wishes—conscious and unconscious—acting as vectors."[19]

And Freud wrote that:

"Errors . . . are not accidents; they are serious mental acts; they have their meaning; they arise through the concurrence—perhaps better, the mutual interference—of two different intentions.[20]

Note: Why Do Criminal Attempts Fail? A New Defense (1960) 70 Yale L.J. 160 at 166–167:

"Courts and commentators have long realized that many 'attempters' are different from 'completers.' The much lower degree of punishment meted out to attempters represents, in part, an unarticulated recognition that the person who tries and fails is often less dangerous than the person who succeeds in his criminal purpose. Recently these judicial hunches have been to some degree empirically verified. The past five years have witnessed a systematic and thorough study of one type of attempted crime—suicide. The notion that only a fortuitous and unexpected event distinguishes the attempted suicide from the successful suicide has been replaced by the finding that the great majority of attempted suicides fail as the result of conscious or unconscious control exercised by the actor himself. These studies indicate the existence and influence of a great variety of internal control mechanisms, ranging from conscious repentance and abandonment, to deliberate but unconscious omission to perform an act necessary for success, and finally to the commencement of the attempt under circumstances where the probability of success is low.

Since suicide is often an 'internalization' of aggressive drives, the results of these specialized studies appear to be at least partially applicable to all types of attempted crimes. They tend to substantiate the suspicion that some foiled attempts reflect internal control, and thus they supply an empirical foundation for a defense based upon internal control—at the unconscious as well as the conscious level."

However, while many attempts might have failed as a result of the attempter exercising internal control at the unconscious level (and thus surely deserving less punishment), it is clear that in some cases the attempt only fails as a result of factors lying outside the attempter's con-

---

[19] *Man against Himself* (1938), p. 22.
[20] *A General Introduction to Psychoanalysis* (1958), p. 48.

trol, namely, chance. In that respect it has already been argued that attempts ought *on principle* to be punished to a lesser extent than the completed crime.[21] Indeed this is the practice in the English courts.

R. v. Carmichael (1930) 22 Cr.App.R. 142 (Court of Criminal Appeal)

The defendant threw corrosive fluid at a girl with intent to burn her. He was sentenced to six years imprisonment and appealed against sentence.

Humphreys J.:

"There are in my opinion no mitigating circumstances in this case. You did it deliberately; you wrote a letter to her threatening her that unless she did what you wanted you would do this thing and that you had bought the vitriol for the purpose. After you had thrown the bottle of vitriol at her and had been arrested your only statement to the police officer was one of regret that you had not done all you had intended to do. In search of mitigating circumstances the only thing I can find is something which in truth does not redound to your credit and that is that in fact you did her no harm . . . But I do take it into consideration and I substantially lessen your sentence on account of that fact because it does, in my view, reduce your crime rather to the category of attempts than the category of completed crimes and you are entitled, fortunately for yourself, to have it remembered that you really only attempted to burn and disfigure this poor girl."[22]

In *Jones*[23] a father attempted to murder his two daughters by giving them drugged ice-cream. If his attempt had been successful, he would have received mandatory life imprisonment. As it was, he was sentenced to two years imprisonment, suspended. While this is an admittedly extreme example (the usual range of sentence for attempted murder is between five and seven years imprisonment[24]), it nevertheless serves as a dramatic illustration of judicial attitudes to the crime of attempt.

A final question remains: should it be left to the judiciary to exercise a broad discretion and impose lesser sentences for attempts? Surely it is incumbent upon the law to perform its symbolic function of indicating *how seriously* it regards offences, by grading them (with appropriate penalties) in terms of their gravity. If this latter solution is adopted, there would have to be a clear articulation of the exact bases upon which attempts are punished, and a rational assessment of just how seriously attempts are regarded in comparison with completed crimes.

---

[21] For further extracts supporting this view that the occurrence of harm is decisive in determining the level of criminal responsibility, see *post* pp. 801–805.

[22] See Cross, *The English Sentencing System*, pp. 151 *et seq*. It ought perhaps to be added that despite Humphreys J. stating that there were "no mitigating circumstances," the girl had provoked the defendant; she had also subsequently forgiven him and wished to marry him.

[23] *The Times*, March 3, 1976.

[24] But sentences up to 14 years in aggravating circumstances are not uncommon (D.A. Thomas, *Current Sentencing Practice*, p. 2087).

D. The Law

1. Mens rea

Section 1(1) of the Criminal Attempts Act 1981 provides that the defendant must act "with intent to commit an offence."

Merrit v. Commonwealth, 164 Va. 653, 180 S.E. 395 (1935) (Supreme Court of Appeals of Virginia)

"[W]hile a person may be guilty of murder though there was no actual intent to kill, he cannot be guilty of an attempt to commit murder unless he has a specific intent to kill . . . . A common example, illustrating this principle is: 'If one from a house-top recklessly throw a billet of wood upon the sidewalk where persons are constantly passing, and it fall upon a person passing by and kill him, this would be by the common law murder. But if, instead of killing, it inflicts only a slight injury, the party could not be convicted of an assault with intent to commit murder.' (*Moore* v. *State*, 18 Ala. 532) . . .

When we say that a man attempted to do a given wrong, we mean that he intended to do it specifically; and proceeded a certain way in the doing. The intent in the mind covers the thing in full; the act covers it only in part.

. . . To commit murder, one need not intend to take life; but to be guilty of an attempt to murder, he must so intend. It is not sufficient that his act, had it proved fatal, would have been murder."

In *Whybrow*[25] the defendant constructed a device and administered an electric shock to his wife while she was taking a bath. The Court of Appeal held that while an intention to kill *or to cause grievous bodily harm* would suffice for the completed crime of murder, for attempted murder an intention to kill was necessary. This was because for attempted murder "the intent becomes the principal ingredient of the crime."

In *O'Toole*[26] the defendant was charged with attempted arson (causing criminal damage by fire). It was held that while recklessness would suffice for the completed offence,[27] there had to be intention for the attempted offence.

If the complete crime can be committed recklessly or negligently, why does this same *mens rea* not suffice for an attempt to commit the crime?

R. v. Mohan [1976] Q.B. 1 (Court of Appeal, Criminal Division)

James L.J.:

"In our judgment it is well established law that intent (*mens rea*) is an essential ingredient of the offence of attempt . . .

An attempt to commit crime is itself an offence. Often it is a grave offence. Often it is as morally culpable as the completed offence which is attempted but not in fact committed. Nevertheless it falls within the class of conduct which is preparatory to the commission of a crime and is one step removed from the

---

[25] (1951) 35 Cr.App.R. 141. See also *Pond* [1984] Crim.L.R. 164.
[26] [1987] Crim.L.R. 759.
[27] Criminal Damage Act 1971, s.1(2).

offence which is attempted. The court must not strain to bring within the offence of attempt, conduct which does not fall within the well-established bounds of the offence. On the contrary, the court must safeguard against extension of those bounds save by the authority of Parliament."

Donald Stuart, "Mens Rea, Negligence and Attempts" [1968] Crim.L.R. 647 at 656, 658–659, 661–662:

"Many writers rely heavily on the fact that the word 'attempt' refers to an endeavour or an effort to commit a crime. It is argued that there cannot be an attempt unless the defendant was trying to commit the crime and that, in legal terms, this necessarily means that there must have been an intention of the 'purpose' type to commit the crime. Even Howard (*Australian Criminal Law* (1965) 253) says:

'Attempt implies purpose. To say that D is attempting to do something means that he is acting with the purpose of accomplishing that which he is said to be attempting. There is no disagreement that purpose must be proved for conviction of attempts but different views have been expressed on the scope of the purpose.'

It is, however, difficult to see why there is such magic in the popular meaning of the word 'attempt' but not in the words 'murder,' 'assault' or 'rape'—crimes for which recklessness is now sufficient *mens rea*. . . .

Do any of the theories of punishment offer an explanation of why it is that only direct intention will suffice in these cases of attempt? . . . It is difficult to challenge Professor Hart's (*Punishment and Responsibility*, p. 127) assertion that

'No calculation of the efficacy of deterrence or reforming measures, and nothing that would ordinarily be called retribution seems to justify this distinction. In the attempt case, for example, the variant where the intention is indirect seems equally wicked, equally harmful, and equally in need of discouragement by the law.'

If these instances of . . . an intent to commit a crime in the case of attempts could rightfully be regarded as cases of bare intention—an intention 'to do something in the future without doing anything to execute this intent now'—it would be possible to argue that they should connote direct intention in the sense of hope, desire or aim, both for conceptual reasons and on the policy ground of the need to narrow an anomalous extension of the rule that the law does not punish bare intention. But this is not so as there cannot be an attempt without the commission of some type of act. . . .

There seems, furthermore, to be every reason to apply the full notion of *mens rea* (embracing intention and recklessness) . . . to attempts. . . .

. . . If a fanatical punter contrives to half-sever the stirrup on the saddle of the favourite horse before a race he would be guilty of recklessly assaulting the jockey if the stirrup broke during the race and the jockey fell and was trampled. If, however, the mischief was unearthed before the race was run the punter should surely be guilty of recklessly attempting an assault even though he was aiming, not to injure the jockey, but merely to stop the horse from winning. . . .

Further there is much to be said for . . . [the] suggestion that a negligent attempt to commit a crime of negligence should be punished. Negligence is a failure to measure up to a standard and if this failure occurs or is stopped short of the completed offence there seems to be no reason of policy why it should escape punishment. This would lead to the view, at present widely rejected, that it is possible to attempt to commit the crime of involuntary manslaughter. If a pharmacist is grossly negligent in making up a prescription and the patient dies as a result of taking the dosage on the bottle the pharmacist is clearly guilty of manslaughter. Surely the policy considerations which dictate such a conviction apply equally if, through chance, the negligent error is discovered before any damage is done. There seems to be every reason for a verdict of attempted manslaughter.

If, in the Code of the Brave New World, the codifiers are prepared to cast off the traditional misplaced fear of liability based on negligence, there is, then, a strong case for declaring that the mental element for an attempt may consist in the mental element—here including negligence—required for the completed crime."

Such an approach is surely unacceptable. Apart from the semantic argument that it is linguistic nonsense to speak of someone attempting to commit a crime unless he is trying to commit that crime, there is a more important argument of principle. With attempts we are punishing in the absence of any harm (or "first order harm"). While such an approach can be justified (just), it is surely only permissible when dealing with the highest degree of blame. Exceptions to the basic equation of criminal liability involve huge extensions of liability and should be rigidly controlled. As attempt is essentially a crime of *mens rea*, with the *actus reus* performing only a secondary or subsidiary role, only the clearest form of *mens rea* should suffice, namely, intention.

This latter reasoning was given statutory force by section 1(1) of the Criminal Attempts Act 1981. It is thus now clear that even for attempting a crime of strict liability, the defendant must intend to produce the prohibited consequence.[28]

What meaning is to be attributed to the word "intention" in section 1(1)?

R. v. Mohan [1976] Q.B. 1 (Court of Appeal, Criminal Division)

James L.J.:
" . . . The first question we have to answer is: what is the meaning of 'intention' when that word is used to describe the *mens rea* in attempt? It is to be distinguished from 'motive' in the sense of an emotion leading to action: it has never been suggested that such a meaning is appropriate to 'intention' in this context. It is equally clear that the word means what is often referred to as 'specific intent' and can be defined as 'a decision to bring about a certain consequence' or as the 'aim.' . . .

The bounds are presently set requiring proof of specific intent, a decision to bring about, in so far as it lies within the accused's power, the commission of the offence which it is alleged the accused attempted to commit, no matter whether the accused desired that consequence of his act or not."

What has been the approach of the cases since the Criminal Attempts Act 1981? In *Millard and Vernon* the court cited *Mohan* with approval, interpreting it as requiring a direct or purposive intention: it had to bear its "ordinary meaning", namely, that the defendant must have

---

[28] This was probably the position at common law: *Gardner* v. *Akeroyd* [1952] 2 Q.B. 743; *cf. Collier* [1960] Crim.L.R. 204. It should however be borne in mind that most strict liability offences are summary offences which cannot be attempted. See *ante* n. 9, 10.

"decided, so far as in him lay, to bring about" the result.[29] It would of course be possible (albeit messy) for intention to bear different meanings in different contexts and for direct intent to be required here as the concept of an "attempt" connotes trying or intending to achieve a result. However, the courts seem now to have rejected such an approach holding that "intention" bears the same meaning, whether for a completed crime or an attempt.

R. v. Pearman (1984) 80 Cr.App.R. 259 (Court of Appeal, Criminal Division)

Stuart-Smith J:
"We see no reason why the passing of the 1981 Act should have altered the law as to what is meant by the word 'intent.' The purpose of the Act was to deal with other matters rather than the content of the word 'intent.' We can see no reason why the judgment of the court in that case [*Mohan*] should not still be binding upon this court.

The words of James L.J. [in *Mohan*] which he used at the end of that passage, namely 'no matter whether the accused desired that consequence of his act or not,' are probably designed to deal with a case where the accused has, as a primary purpose, some other object, for example, a man who plants a bomb in an aeroplane, which he knows is going to take off, it being his primary intention that he should claim the insurance on the aeroplane when the freight goes down into the sea. The jury would not be put off from saying that he intended to murder the crew simply by saying that he did not want or desire to kill the crew, but that was something that he inevitably intended to do. Similarly, for example, a man who is cornered by the police when he is in a car may have the primary purpose of simply escaping from that situation. If he drives straight at the police officers at high speed, a jury is likely to conclude that he intended to injure a police officer and maybe cause him serious grievous bodily harm."

R v. Walker and Hayles (1990) 90 Cr.App.R. 266 (Court of Appeal, Criminal Division)

The defendants threw the victim from a third floor balcony. At their trial for attempted murder the judge directed the jury that they had to be sure that the defendant intended and tried to kill. The jury asked for clarification and the judge directed them in *Moloney/Hancock* terms that if
(1) there was a very high degree of probability that the victim would be killed, and
(2) the defendant knew there was such a high risk, then
(3) they were entitled to draw the inference that the defendants intended to kill.
The defendant appealed against this direction.

Lloyd L.J.:
"By the use of the word 'entitled' [the recorder] was making it sufficiently clear to the jury that the question whether they drew the inference or not was a question for them . . . [He was not] equating foresight with intent . . . He was perfectly properly saying that foresight was something from which the jury could infer intent. He was treating the question as part of the law of evidence, not as part of the substantive law of attempted murder . . .

[29] [1987] Crim.L.R. 393.

[I]n the great majority of cases of attempted murder, as in murder, the simple direction will suffice, without any reference to foresight. In the rare case where an expanded direction is required in terms of foresight, courts should continue to use virtual certainty as the test, rather than high probability."

[*For further extract, see ante* p. 158]

Appeals dismissed

It has been suggested that this decision is consistent with the view that only a direct intention will suffice for an attempt: "The further direction was not a direction on oblique intention because all that the Recorder told the jury was that the defendant's foresight of high probability was evidence that he was trying to kill. He did not suggest that anything less than a purpose of killing would do."[30] But could not the same be said of all cases of intention? Foresight of high probability or virtual certainty is evidence from which juries can infer intent. It thus seems tolerably clear now that the concept "intention" bears its same meaning throughout the criminal law.

What *mens rea* is required with regard to relevant surrounding circumstances? The position at common law appears to have been that the consequence had to be intended; recklessness with regard to circumstances would suffice for attempt, provided such recklessness would suffice for the completed offence.[31] Thus if a defendant, being reckless as to whether his first wife was alive, was about to go through a second marriage ceremony, he could be convicted of attempted bigamy. The 1981 Act draws no distinction between consequences and circumstances,[32] but simply states that the defendant must act "with intent to commit an offence."Despite the wording of this statute, the common law approach has now been confirmed.

R v. Khan, The Independent, January 31, 1990 (Court of Appeal, Criminal Division)

The appellant attempted to have sexual intercourse with a non-consenting girl, but failed. The trial judge directed the jury that recklessness as to whether the girl consented was sufficient for attempted rape. The appellant appealed on this point.

Russell L.J.:
"The only difference between the two offences was that in rape, sexual intercourse took place whereas in attempted rape it did not, although there had to be some act which was more than preparatory to sexual intercourse. Considered in this way the intent of the defendant was precisely the same in rape and in attempted rape, and the *mens rea* was identical, namely an intention to have

---

[30] J.C. Smith, [1990] Crim.L.R. 47.

[31] *Pigg* (1982) 74 Cr.App.R. 352; Smith and Hogan, p. 289; Glanville Williams, *Textbook*, p. 409; Buxton, "Inchoate Offences: Incitement and Attempt" [1973] Crim.L.R. 656 at 661–664.

[32] Such a distinction was drawn by the Law Commission Working Paper, No. 50 and by the original Government Bill, but not by the Law Commission's Final Report, No. 102.

intercourse plus a knowledge of or recklessness as to the woman's absence of consent. No question of attempting to achieve a reckless state of mind arose; the attempt related to the physical activity; the mental state of the defendant was the same. Recklessness in rape and attempted rape arose not in relation to the physical act of the accused but only in his state of mind when engaged in the activity of having or attempting to have sexual intercourse. If that was the true analysis, the attempt did not require any different intention from that for the full offence of rape. The words 'with intent to commit an offence' in section 1 of the Criminal Attempts Act 1981 meant, when applied to rape, 'with intent to have sexual intercourse with a woman in circumstances where she does not consent and the defendant knows or could not care less about her absence of consent'. The only 'intent' of the rapist was to have sexual intercourse. He committed the offence because of the circumstances in which he manifested that intent—when the woman was not consenting and he either knew it or could not care less about the absence of consent."

Appeal dismissed

It is possible to support such an approach. If recklessness as to surrounding circumstances suffices for the complete offence it should also suffice for an attempt, as "the *mens rea* of the complete crime should be modified only in so far as it is necessary in order to accommodate the concept of attempt."[33] This view is adopted by the Criminal Code Bill:

"[A]n intention to commit an offence is an intention with respect to all the elements of the offence other than fault elements, except that recklessness with respect to a circumstance suffices where it suffices for the offence itself."[34]

However, it is submitted that the better view is that such recklessness should not suffice. It would surely be absurd, and involve a totally unjustifiable extension of liability, to punish an attempt where the defendant is only reckless as to the circumstances and where the crime is impossible. If a defendant goes through a marriage ceremony believing his first wife is dead, and she is dead, what possible objective can be achieved in convicting him of attempted bigamy on the basis that there was an obvious, serious risk that she might still be alive (the *Caldwell* test of recklessness)? Further, it is often extremely difficult to draw a clear distinction between consequences and circumstances and it seems inappropriate to make criminal liability hinge upon such difficult distinctions. Also, the same argument applied above to recklessness as to consequences, applies here. Attempt is essentially a crime of *mens rea*. Only the strictest form of *mens rea*, intention, should suffice— for all the elements of the offence. Finally, the plain wording of the Act hardly supports the view that recklessness as to anything could suf-

---

[33] Smith and Hogan p. 289. These learned authors however effectively resile from this position by asserting that it would "be going altogether too far" to allow *Caldwell* recklessness to apply. As it now seems tolerably clear that *Caldwell* recklessness does apply throughout the criminal law, their position is somewhat weakened.

[34] Law Com. No. 177, clause 49(2).

fice.[35] The Law Commission clearly states that an intention as to every element of the offence is required (even though in practice knowledge of surrounding circumstances will suffice to establish the necessary intent):

"And to take an instance where the completed offence is one of strict liability, where a defendant is charged with an attempt to have intercourse with a girl under the age of 13, it will be necessary to show that he intended to have intercourse with a girl under that age. The mental elements for the completed offences in these examples require varying degrees of knowledge of circumstances and intent to do the proscribed acts, stretching from strict liability to full knowledge and intent; but the mental element for the attempt to commit them may in each case be described as an intent that the offence shall be brought about. This intention will in practice be established by proof of the defendant's intention to bring about the consequences, and of his knowledge of the factual circumstances, expressly or implicitly required by the definition of the substantive offence."[36]

A final problem remains: will a so-called "conditional intention" suffice for attempt? If a defendant opens a suitcase intending to steal its contents "on condition they are of some value," can he be convicted of attempted theft?

The Law Commission (Law Com. No. 102) Attempt . . . , 1980, Appendix E, " 'Conditional Intent' and R. v. Husseyn":

"2. Theft-related offences, such as attempted theft, burglary, attempted burglary, assault with intent to rob, going equipped for burglary or theft, (all under the Theft Act 1968) . . . form a large part of the cases being tried every day in the magistrates' courts and Crown Court.

3. They all have two features in common—
   (i) each requires proof that the accused 'intended to steal' at the time when he committed the *actus reus* of the offence;
   (ii) none requires proof that anything has in fact been stolen.

4. In delivering the judgment of the Court of Appeal in the attempted theft case of *R. v. Husseyn*, Lord Scarman stated ((1978) 67 Cr.App.R. 131, at p. 132) 'it cannot be said that one who has it in mind to steal only if what he finds is worth stealing has a present intention to steal.'

5. This simple statement, taken by itself and out of context, was the origin of the difficulties. It gave rise to the doctrine that 'conditional intent' in the sense of 'intending to steal whatever one might find of value or worth stealing' was not a sufficient mental element in these theft-related offences; the prosecution must aver and prove that at the time of attempting, entering as a trespasser, etc.,

---

[35] This problem was considered in *Millard and Vernon (ante,* n. 29) but deliberately left open. The court did however state that "a partial answer is supplied by *R. v. Mohan.*" While it is tempting to argue that this supports our view, it is conceded that *Mohan* was not dealing with this problem at all— and, with respect, does not attempt to answer this question.

[36] Law Com. No. 102, para. 2.15. This raises the problem that most people will not *know* that the girl is under 13 or that their first wife is alive no matter how strongly they might believe it. It is possible however that section 1(3) of the Criminal Attempts Act 1981 (see *post,* p. 472), although primarily inserted to deal with the problem of impossible attempts, could be utilised here and the defendant's belief deemed to be an intention.

the accused had a settled intention to steal some particular and specified object existing or believed by him to exist in his target area.

6. In such a form, the doctrine was obviously capable of mischievous results. In particular, it excluded from criminal liability the large majority of sneak thieves and burglars who conduct their operations 'on spec.' Without knowing what a handbag, a package left in a car, or a house contains, they nevertheless proceed in the hope or expectation that they will find something of value or worth stealing there, and intend, in that event, to steal it. As Geoffrey Lane L.J. pungently remarked (*R.* v. *Walkington* [1979] 1 W.L.R. 1169, 1179), after setting out the reasoning that led to the acquittal of one burglar, 'a reading of that would make the layman wonder if the law had taken leave of its senses. . . . Nearly every prospective burglar could no doubt truthfully say that he only intended to steal if he found something in the building worth stealing.'

7. Unfortunately, several factors obscured the clarity of the issue. As reported, *R.* v. *Husseyn* gave no indication that the charge of attempted theft in that case had related to specific identifiable objects, and although Lawton L.J. did stress that the indictment in the subsequent case of *R.* v. *Hector* ((1978) 67 Cr.App.R. 224) also charged attempted theft of particular objects, the report was headed 'Whether conditional intention enough,' a phrase not used in the judgment. So it was not realised that Lord Scarman's statement related only to the facts of the case before him or that the decision in both cases rested on the basic rule of criminal pleading that an allegation that the accused attempted to steal a particular item involves proof that that item was what he intended to steal; in such a case it is not enough to show that he intended to steal whatever he found worth stealing. . . .

8. Whatever the reasons, within a few months of the decision in *R.* v. *Husseyn*, submissions that 'conditional intent is not enough' were being accepted by magistrates and Crown Court judges in all these theft-related offences, causing frustration and perplexity to prosecuting authorities and bringing the criminal law into disrepute.

9. Study of the relevant indictments and transcripts convinced us that, once the complications mentioned in paragraph 7 had been cleared out of the way, the matter could be put right without recourse to legislation and that the appropriate way to proceed was by way of Attorney General's References to the Court of Appeal under section 36 of the Criminal Justice Act 1972. . . .

10. The two References were decided by the Court of Appeal as *Attorney General's References* (*Nos. 1 and 2 of 1979*) ([1979] 3 W.L.R. 577) on June 18, 1979 and together with the ancillary judgments of the same judges sitting as a Divisional Court in *Scudder* v. *Barrett* and *Miles* v. *Clovis* ([1979] 3 W.L.R. 591), restore clarity and common sense to the law. Where the accused's state of mind is that of intending to steal whatever he may find worth stealing in his target area, there is no need to charge him with attempting to steal specific objects. In appropriate cases of attempted theft a charge of attempting to steal some or all of the contents of (for example) a car or a handbag will suffice. In cases where the substantive offence does not require anything to be stolen, it is not necessary to allege more than 'with intent to steal.' The important point is that the indictment should correctly reflect that which it is alleged the accused did and that the accused should know with adequate detail what he is alleged to have done.' (at 590). The result, in the Commission's view, is that it is now possible to state with confidence that in cases where an intention to steal anything of value or worth stealing accurately reflects the accused's state of mind at the time of the actus reus, this is sufficient to constitute 'an intention to steal' and applies equally to all the theft-related offences."

The law on this point is unaffected by the Criminal Attempts Act

1981, which abolishes "the offence of attempt at common law" (s.6(1)). These developments on "conditional intention" are best regarded as part of the "common law of intention"; some of the important decisions on this point were not delivered in the context of attempted crime at all.[37] It is simply that the point is of particular importance when dealing with attempts.

2. Actus reus

(i) *Act must be more than merely preparatory*

Criminal Attempts Act 1981, s.1(1):

"If, with intent to commit an offence to which this section applies, a person does an act which is more than merely preparatory to the commission of the offence, he is guilty of attempting to commit the offence."

This is similar to the common law rule as laid down by Baron Parke in *Eagleton* that:

"[S]ome act is required . . . Acts remotely leading towards the commission of the offence are not to be considered as attempts to commit it; but acts immediately connected with it are . . ."[38]

Suppose a defendant wakes up one morning and decides to kill his wife by poisoning her. He walks to a shop where he purchases some rat poison. He returns home and adds the poison to the whisky in his whisky decanter. That evening he offers his wife a drink of whisky; she accepts. He pours the poisoned whisky into a glass and hands it to her. She starts drinking the whisky. At what point in this chain of actions could he be said to have done an act which was "more than merely preparatory to the commission of the offence?" When he handed her the whisky? When he put the poison in the decanter? When he purchased the poison?

Questions such as these cannot be answered in a jurisprudential vacuum; they, and all the contours of the law of attempt, can only be determined by reference to the underlying justification (and policy) of the law of attempt. Thus if attempts are viewed as being threats to people's interests in security from interference (the "second order harm" discussed above[39]), one ought to insist on the attempter getting near to completing the crime. Until he has got near to committing the complete crime, the wife's interests in security from interference are not threatened, but if the law of attempt is justified on the utilitarian bases canvassed above, then the emphasis is on the *mens rea* of the attempter and liability can be imposed at a much earlier stage in the chain of

---

[37] *Greenhof* [1979] Crim.L.R. 108, *Bozickovic* [1978] Crim.L.R. 686 and *Walkington* [1979] 1 W.L.R. 1169 were all decisions on burglary.

[38] (1855) Dears C.C. 515 at 538.

[39] *Ante* p. 434.

actions. Of course, such an approach still does not tell us exactly when the husband has done enough to threaten the wife's interests; or when his *mens rea* is sufficiently manifest to justify the imposition of criminal liability for attempt, but adoption of one or other of these views does provide an important indication of *how* to try and answer the question.

Fletcher suggests another approach, not dissimilar in its effect.

George P. Fletcher, Rethinking Criminal Law (1978), pp. 138–139:

"The critical question . . . is the elementary issue whether the act of attempting is a distinct and discernible element of the crime of attempting. To say that the act is a distinct element is to require that the act conform to objective criteria defined in advance. The act must evidence attributes subject to determination independently of the actor's intent. In short, there must be features of the attempt as palpable as the death of the victim in homicide or a trespassory taking in larceny. We shall refer to the set of arguments favoring this approach as the 'objectivist' theory of attempts. Though the term 'objective' may have a different connotation in some contexts, we shall use the term to mean a legal standard for assessing conduct that does not presuppose a prior determination of the actor's intent.

The opposing school is appropriately called 'subjectivist,' for it dispenses with the objective criteria of attempting. The act of execution is important so far as it verifies the firmness of the intent. No act of specific contours is necessary to constitute the attempt, for any act will suffice to demonstrate the actor's commitment to carry out his criminal plan.

As we delve more deeply into objectivist and subjectivist theories of liability for criminal attempts, we shall discover that objectivists tend to favor a minimalist approach, and subjectivists, a maximalist approach to liability. . . . [T]his means that objectivists tend to draw the line of liability as close as possible to consummation of the offense and tend, further, to be sympathetic to claims of impossibility as a bar to liability. This combination of views generates a minimalist approach to liability. Subjectivists, in contrast, tend to push back the threshold of attempting and reject the relevance of impossibility—a stance that yields a maximalist net of liability. In turning to a more detailed study of objectivist and subjectivist theories, we should keep in mind that the watershed between them is the question whether the act of attempting is a distinct element of liability."

Thus there are two competing theories underlying the law of attempt. First, there is Fletcher's "objectivist" theory which requires the defendant to have come sufficiently close to committing the crime for his conduct to generate apprehension and thus amount to a "second order harm." Secondly, there is Fletcher's "subjectivist" theory which stresses the mental element of the defendant: if he has *mens rea* he is dangerous and needs restraining. Liability can accordingly be imposed at a much earlier stage (which will facilitate the task of the police and other law enforcement agencies). The only conduct required would be some action that would be corroborative of this intention. The tensions between these two theories is demonstrated by a consideration of the various "tests" flirted with by English law in its effort to demarcate how much action is required for the *actus reus* of attempt. Whether it is still permissible to refer to these tests and the cases decided before the 1981 Act will be discussed later.[40]

(a) The equivocality test

Under this test a defendant only commits the *actus reus* of attempt when he has taken sufficient steps towards the crime that his actions clearly and unequivocally indicate that his purpose is to commit the crime. Other evidence of *mens rea*, such as confessions, is discarded as irrelevant. The defendant's objective actions must be such that they "cannot reasonably be regarded as having any other purpose than the commission of the specific crime."[41] The following is a helpful illustration of this test:

"If the example may be permitted, it is as though a cinematograph film, which had so far depicted merely the accused person's acts without stating what was his intention, had been suddenly stopped, and the audience were asked to say to what end those acts were directed. If there is only one reasonable answer to this question then the accused has done what amounts to an 'attempt' to attain that end. If there is more than one reasonably possible answer, then the accused has not yet done enough."[42]

This test is clearly in accord with the "second order harm" theory. As Fletcher states:

"Conduct can generate apprehension only if it is manifestly criminal. Reasoning from the harm of apprehension to the type of conduct that can induce it, we are led to the standard that is conventionally called the requirement of 'unequivocally' criminal conduct. . . .

That criminal conduct is unnerving to the community is sufficient to justify either private or official intervention. Private intervention takes the form of defensive force; public intervention, of prosecution for a criminal offense. If the public feels 'apprehension' at the suspect's manifestly criminal conduct, that is a sufficient social interest to warrant suppression. The corollary is that if an act is so equivocal that it does not generate apprehension, then it should not be subject to either private or public suppression."[43]

This equivocality test has however been firmly rejected by English law.[44] The difficulties with the test were insurmountable. In *Jones* v. *Brooks and Brooks*[45] the defendant was observed trying to unlock a car door. Here he was very close to the complete crime (taking and driving away a motor vehicle without consent), yet his actions were still equi-

---

[40] *Post,* p. 461.

[41] *Davey* v. *Lee* [1968] 1 Q.B. 366, 371.

[42] L. Radzinowicz and J. W. C. Turner (eds.), *The Modern Approach to Criminal Law,* (1948), p. 280.

[43] Pp. 142, 144.

[44] *Jones* v. *Brooks and Brooks* (1968) 52 Cr.App.R. 614. It is interesting to note that this test has been revived by Indian law (*State of Maharashtra* v. *Mohd Yakub* (1980) S.C.C. (Cri) 513). See further, K. L. Koh, C. M. V. Clarkson and N. A. Morgan, *Criminal Law in Singapore and Malaysia: Text and Materials* (1989).

[45] *Ibid.*

vocal: he could have been going to borrow the car, steal the car, steal the contents of the car, vandalise the car, sleep in the car and so on. Equally, a defendant may have been a hundred miles from the scene of his planned crime that was only to be committed the following week, yet his actions could unequivocally have indicated his purpose. A final objection to the equivocality test was that it was impossible for a jury to decide whether the defendant's actions objectively indicated his purpose because they would know what the charge was and this would colour their interpretation of those actions. If a jury faced with facts similar to those of *Jones* v. *Brooks and Brooks* were simply asked in the abstract "what was the defendant going to do?," it is clear that they might respond with more than one answer. But, if the jury were asked this same question in a case where they knew the charge was one of attempted theft, they might clearly reply, "his actions unequivocally indicate that he was trying to steal a car." The equivocality test was thus clearly defective.

(b) The substantial step test

Law Commission Working Paper No. 50, Inchoate Offences, 1973:

"74. The approach favoured by the majority is the 'substantial step' theory . . .

75. It may be that certain criticisms can be levelled at the substantial step test. First, the words 'substantial step' are not words of much precision in themselves, nor do they relate the closeness of the step to the commission of the crime. . . . Secondly, the adoption of the test would cast very much wider the net by which acts preceding the commission of an offence would be brought within the operation of the criminal law. . . . It may be thought that this is penalising conduct which is too remote from a contemplated offence, and comes very near to making an offence out of mere formulation of an intent. On the other hand, the majority of us feel that these possible disadvantages are outweighed by the advantage the test would bring of enabling unsatisfactory cases such as *Robinson* and *Comer* v. *Bloomfield* [see *post* p. 458] to be considered afresh; and the provision of examples as guides would assist in ensuring that preliminary steps only, which are not substantial, are not held to be attempts.

[The Law Commission suggested the following illustrations of a substantial step.]

(a) Committing an assault for the purpose of the intended offence. . . .
(b) Lying in wait for, searching out or following the contemplated victim or object of the intended offence. . . .
(c) Enticing or seeking to entice the contemplated victim of the intended offence to go to the place contemplated for its commission.
(d) Reconnoitring the place contemplated for the commission of the intended offence. . . .
(e) Unlawful entry upon a structure, vehicle or enclosure, or remaining thereon unlawfully for the purpose of committing or preparing to commit the intended offence. . . .
(f) Acquiring, preparing or equipping oneself with materials to be employed in the commission of the offence, which are specially designed

for such unlawful use or which serve no lawful purpose in the circumstances. . . .
(g) Preparing or acting a falsehood for the purpose of an offence of fraud or deception. . . .
(h) Soliciting any person, whether innocent or not, to engage in conduct constituting an external element of the offence."

This proposed test is similar to the United States Model Penal Code's test of attempt and this is clearly consistent with Fletcher's "subjectivist" theory of attempts. The primary objective of the substantial step is to provide evidence of the defendant's intention. The substantial step must be "strongly corroborative of the actor's criminal purpose."[46]

This substantial step test was however firmly rejected.

The Law Commission (Law Com. No. 102), Attempt . . . (1980):

"2.32. . . . The Law Society thought that the danger of the substantial step approach was that 'its imprecision may increase the ambit of the criminal law so far back from what has hitherto been understood to be punishable as an attempt, as to involve serious danger to the liberty of the subject and the possibility of abuse by the authorities.' The late Lord Reid, in his comments to us, was 'wholly against the "substantial step." It is far too vague and goes much too far in making guilty intention overshadow guilty conduct.' . . .
2.34. . . . Inclusion by means of examples of what are at present regarded as acts of preparation within the concept of substantial step would have the effect of stretching the legal meaning of attempt far beyond what is ordinarily understood by that term. . . .
2.37. . . . In our view the disadvantages of the approach discussed in the preceding paragraphs greatly outweigh any advantage to be gained from it, and we do not recommend its adoption."

(c) Stephen's "Series of Acts" test

Stephen, Digest of Criminal Law, 9th edn. (1950) p. 24, art. 29:

"An attempt to commit a crime is an act done with intent to commit that crime, and forming part of a series of acts which would constitute its actual commission if it were not interrupted."

This is not helpful as it gives no indication of when the "series of acts" starts: it could be at an intolerably early stage—perhaps even earlier than under the substantial step test rejected above.

(d) The Proximity Test

The King v. Barker [1924] N.Z.L.R. 865 (New Zealand Court of Appeal)

Salmond J.:
" . . . The rule so suggested in *R. v. Eagleton* was that in order to constitute a criminal attempt, as opposed to mere preparation, the accused must have taken

[46] American Law Institute, Model Penal Code, Proposed Official Draft, s.5.01 (1962).

the last step which he was able to take along the road of his criminal intent. He must have done all that he intended to do and was able to do for the purpose of effectuating his criminal purpose. . . . Until he has done his best to complete his guilty purpose, he has not attempted to complete it. On this principle the act of firing a pistol at a man would be attempted murder, although the bullet missed him. So would the act of pulling the trigger, although the pistol missed fire. But the prior and preliminary acts of procuring and loading the pistol, and of going with it to look for his enemy, and of lying in wait for him, and even of presenting the pistol at him, would not constitute criminal attempts, none of these being the proximate and final step towards the fulfilment of his criminal purpose. . . .

Subsequent authorities make it clear that the test so suggested and adopted is not the true one. It is now settled law that to constitute an attempt, it is not necessary that the accused should have done his best or taken the last or proximate step towards the completed offence. The suggested rule was definitely rejected by the Court of Criminal Appeal in *R.* v. *White* [1910] 2 K.B. 124; 4 Cr.App.R. 257. It was held that the first administration of poison in a case of intended slow poisoning by repeated doses amounted in itself to attempted murder. It is said by the Court: 'The completion (or attempted completion) of one of a series of acts intended by a man to result in killing is an attempt to murder, even though the completed act would not, unless followed by other acts, result in killing. It might be the beginning of an attempt but would none the less be an attempt.'

Although the test adopted by Parke B. has been rejected, no definite substitute for it has been formulated. All that can be definitely gathered from the authorities is that to constitute a criminal attempt, the first step along the way of criminal intent is not necessarily sufficient and the final step is not necessarily required. The dividing line between preparation and attempt is to be found somewhere between these two extremes; but as to the method by which it is to be determined the authorities give no clear guidance."

R. v. Robinson [1915] 2 K.B. 342 (Court of Criminal Appeal)

The appellant, a jeweller, who had insured his stock against burglary, hid the jewellery, tied himself up, called for help and represented to the police that his premises had been burgled. His object was to obtain policy money from his insurance company. He was convicted of attempting to obtain money from the insurers by false pretences. He appealed against conviction.

Lord Reading C.J.:
"[T]he only question was whether, the police having intervened and prevented its execution, the offence of attempting to obtain the money had been committed. If he had made a claim of the money from the underwriters, or had communicated to them the facts of the pretended burglary upon which a claim was to be subsequently based, he clearly could have been convicted of an attempt to obtain the money. . . .

The difficulty lies in the application of [the *Eagleton*] principle to the facts of the particular case. In some cases it is a difficult matter to determine whether an act is immediately or remotely connected with the offence of which it is alleged to be an attempt. . . . In the present case the real difficulty lies in the fact that there is no evidence of any act done by the appellant in the nature of a false pretence which ever reached the minds of the underwriters, though they were the persons who were to be induced to part with the money. The evidence falls short of any communication of such a pretence to the underwriters or to any agent of theirs. The police were not acting on behalf of the underwriters. In truth what the appellant did was preparation for the commission of a crime, not a step in the commission of it. It consisted in the preparation of evidence which might indirectly induce the underwriters to pay; . . . But there must be some act beyond mere preparation if a person is to be charged with an attempt. Applying the rule laid down by Parke B., we think that the appellant's act was only remotely connected with the commission of the full offence, and not immediately connected with it. . . . We think the conviction must be quashed, . . . upon the broad ground that no communication of any kind of the false pretence was made to [the underwriters]."

Appeal allowed

Comer v. Bloomfield (1971) 55 Cr.App.R. 305 (Queen's Bench Divisional Court)

The defendant hid his badly damaged van in a wood, reported to the police that it had been stolen and told them a number of lies. He then wrote a letter to his insurance company, asking if he could make a claim for the stolen van and, if so, to furnish him with particulars. An information preferred against the defendant for attempting to obtain money by deception was dismissed by a magistrates' court on the ground that the letter written by the defendant to the insurance company amounted only to an inquiry and was not sufficiently proximate to the commission of the offence of obtaining money by deception to constitute an attempt. The prosecutor appealed by case stated.

Shaw J.:
"The justices took the view that the letter of November 29 was no more than a preliminary inquiry in order to sound the position and see if a claim could effectively be put forward at all. The respondent might then have desisted from the course on which he had embarked and proceeded no further. Upon that view they were right in saying that the writing of that letter following the lies which the respondent had told the police did not of itself constitute an act sufficiently proximate to the obtaining of compensation under the policy to amount to an attempt to obtain it. It cannot be said they were not entitled on the facts to come to that conclusion and I would dismiss the appeal."

Appeal dismissed

A similar approach was adopted in *Ilyas*[47] where a defendant abandoned his car outside a scrap-yard, reported it stolen to the police and his insurance brokers, obtained a claim form—but never completed the form. It was held that his actions were "merely preparatory and remote from the contemplated offence." In *Komaroni*[48] the defendants trailed a lorry for some 130 miles, waiting for a chance to steal it and its load. They were not liable for attempt; again this conduct was merely preparatory.

While these cases tend to support the view that the defendant will only be liable for attempt if he has done the last act, dependent on himself, necessary for the commission of the crime, it is important to

[47] (1984) 78 Cr.App.R. 17.
[48] (1953) 103 L.J. 97.

remember Salmond J.'s statement in *Barker* that the line can be drawn at an earlier stage. Thus in *Harris*[49] the defendant checked into a hotel for a four night stay, providing a false name, address and vehicle registration number. He intended not to pay the bill. He went to his room but was arrested before spending even the first night in the hotel. His conviction for attempting to obtain a pecuniary advantage contrary to section 16 of the Theft Act 1968[50] was upheld on the ground that the whole series of steps taken together were sufficiently proximate to the completed offence to amount to an attempt to commit it.

This proximity test is clearly in accord with Fletcher's "objectivist" theory.[51] Glanville Williams, however, prefers to rationalise it in terms of the dangerousness of the defendant:

"[A]nother reason for the proximity rule is the comparative non-dangerousness of the mere preparer. If the defendant is still at the stage of remote preparation, we are not sure that he would have the ability or constancy of purpose to go on with his plan. A man who takes only the first step in preparation, as when he studies a book on engraving with a view to becoming a forger, may be barely distinguishable from a person who merely has criminal fantasies. Since most of us have inhibitions against criminality, there is no telling that such a person will get much further, though the further he proceeds the less likely it becomes that he will repent. It is not reasonable to punish a person for an attempt until he has gone far enough to show that he has broken through the psychological barrier to crime."[52]

It seems odd to say that the defendant in *Harris* had broken through the "psychological barrier," but that the defendants in *Robinson, Comer* v. *Bloomfield* and *Komorani* had not!

The proximity test was endorsed twice by the House of Lords.

Haughton v. Smith [1975] A.C. 476 (House of Lords)

Lord Hailsham:
"The act relied on as constituting the attempt must not be an act merely preparatory to commit the completed offence, but must bear a relationship to the completion of the offence referred to in *R.* v. *Eagleton* . . . as being 'proximate' to the completion of the offence and in *Davey* v. *Lee* . . . as being 'immediately and not merely remotely connected' with the completed offence."

D.P.P. v. Stonehouse [1978] A.C. 55 (House of Lords)

The defendant, having insured his life in England for the benefit of his wife, faked his death and disappeared. His plan was that when his "death" was discovered, his wife would be paid the insurance moneys. Before the wife had made any claim, the defendant was discovered alive and well in Australia. He

---

[49] (1976) 62 Cr.App.R. 28.
[50] Section 16(1)(*a*) has since been replaced by the Theft Act 1978.
[51] *Ante* p. 454. See Fletcher, pp. 138–141.
[52] Glanville Williams, *Textbook*, (1st ed., 1978), pp. 379–380.

was convicted of attempting to obtain property (*viz.* the money for his wife) by deception contrary to section 15 of the Theft Act 1968. His appeal against conviction to the Court of Appeal was dismissed; he appealed to the House of Lords.

Lord Diplock:
"The constituent elements of the inchoate crime of an attempt are a physical act by the offender sufficiently proximate to the complete offence and an intention on the part of the offender to commit the complete offence. Acts that are merely preparatory to the commission of the offence such as, in the instant case, the taking out of the insurance policies are not sufficiently proximate to constitute an attempt. They do not indicate a fixed irrevocable intention to go on to commit the complete offence unless involuntarily prevented from doing so. . . .
[He then cited the famous *Eagleton* dictum]
In other words the offender must have crossed the Rubicon and burnt his boats.
In the instant case I have pointed out, the accused by November 20, 1974, had done all the physical acts lying within his power that were needed to enable Mrs. Stonehouse to obtain the policy moneys if all had gone as he had intended. There was nothing left for him to do thereafter except to avoid detection of his real identity. That was the day on which he crossed his Rubicon and burnt his boats.
[The House of Lords also settled the point that while it was for the judge to rule whether there was any evidence capable of constituting an attempt, it was for the jury actually to determine whether the defendant's actions had gone far enough to amount to an attempt.]"

(e) Criminal Attempts Act 1981

Section 6(1) abolished the common law of attempt and accordingly none of the above cases can be regarded as precedent any longer. Indeed, in *Jones*[52a] it was held that such references were impermissible; the Act was to be construed according to its natural meaning. The better view however is the one adopted in *Boyle and Boyle* that courts are still permitted to examine the pre-1981 cases and the tests there applied, although it is uncertain what use this reference will be. Section 1(1) states that it is necessary that the defendant do "an act which is more than merely preparatory to the commission of the offence." The question that arises is whether this is in any way different from the proximity test developed by the common law.

R. v. Boyle and Boyle (1987) 84 Cr.App.R. 270 (Court of Appeal, Criminal Division)

The appellants were apprehended standing by the door of a house. They had damaged the door and were about to enter the house as trespassers and steal therefrom.

Kenneth Jones J.:
"The full offence here was that of entering a building as trespassers with intent to steal therein, and the appellants were charged with attempting to commit that offence, in other words, attempting to enter this building with that alleged intent. The *actus reus* relied upon here was the breaking of the door . . .
Mr. Cowan has cited to us the case of *Ilyas* (1984) 78 Cr.App.R. 17, in which . . . Tudor Evans J. set out the two tests which had been applied in the

---

[52a] [1990] *The Times,* April 4.

past in different cases to decide whether the facts constituted an attempt to commit the offence. . . .

[His Lordship then cited the proximity test approved in *Stonehouse* and Stephen's 'series of acts' test]

The Court [in *Ilyas*] was therefore not deciding which test it was appropriate to apply there.

In the judgment of this Court, in deciding whether an act is more than merely preparatory to the commission of the offence the court is entitled to look back to the law as it existed before 1981 and to see the tests that were then applied. This Court expresses some doubt whether the first of the tests referred to by Tudor Evans J., that set out in *Eagleton* (*supra*), is now the test that should be applied. It seems to be inconsistent with the Act, which requires only an act "more than merely preparatory to the commission of the offence," to apply the test of looking to see whether the defendant has done all the physical acts towards the commission of the offence that lay within his power so that there was nothing more left for him to do.

However, as in *Ilyas* (*supra*), this Court has to say that, whichever of the two tests is applied here, the answer must be the same. Even applying the first test referred to by Tudor Evans J., quoted above, which the learned assistant recorder invited the jury to apply in this case, it would seem that there was no more for the appellants to do in the commission of the attempt charged. They had broken down the door. All that remained was for at least one of them to enter the premises, and once that had been done both would have been guilty of the full offence.

Be all of that as it may, this Court has no hesitation whatever in coming to the conclusion that there was ample evidence for the jury to find that the appellants intended to enter the flat and steal and so to commit an offence of burglary, and that in breaking down the door they did more than a merely preparatory act to the commission of the offence."

Appeal dismissed

R. v. Gullefer [1987] Crim.L.R. 195 (Court of Appeal, Criminal Division)

"The appellant was convicted of attempted theft. During a race at a greyhound racing stadium the appellant had climbed on to the track in front of the dogs and in an attempt to distract them had waved his arms. His efforts were only marginally successful and the stewards decided it was unnecessary to declare 'no race.' Had they done so the bookmakers would have had to repay the amount of his stake to any punter, but would not have been liable to pay any winnings to those punters who would have been successful had the race been valid. The appellant told the police he had attempted to stop the race because the dog on which he had staked £18 was losing. He had hoped for a 'no race' declaration and the recovery of his stake. The appellant's main ground of appeal was that the acts proved to have been carried out by the appellant were not 'sufficiently proximate to the completed offence of theft to be capable of comprising an attempt to commit theft.'

Held, allowing the appeal and quashing the conviction, the appellant was not guilty of attempted theft. The judge's task was to decide whether there was evidence on which a jury could reasonably conclude that the defendant had gone beyond mere preparation and had embarked on the actual commission of the offence. If not, the judge had to withdraw the case from the jury. If there was such evidence, it was then for the jury to decide whether the defendant did in fact go beyond mere preparation. That was how the judge had approached the case and he had ruled there was sufficient evidence. Counsel for the appellant submitted his ruling had been wrong. The Court's first task was to apply the words of the Criminal Attempts Act 1981, s.1, to the facts. Was the appellant still in the stage of preparation to commit the substantive offence, or was there a basis of fact which would have entitled the jury to say that he had embarked on the theft itself? Might it properly be said that when he jumped onto the track he was trying to steal £18? In the view of the Court it could not be said that at that stage he was in the process of committing theft. What he was doing was jumping onto the track in an effort to distract the dogs, which in its turn, he hoped, would force the stewards to declare 'no race,' which would in its turn give him the opportunity to demand his £18 stake from the bookmaker. There was insufficient evidence that the appellant had, when he jumped on the track, gone beyond mere preparation.

Sections 1(1) and 4(3) of the 1981 Act seemed to be a blend of decisions some of which were not easy to reconcile with others. As appeared from *Ilyas* (1984) 78 Cr.App.R. 17 there seemed to have been two lines of authority. The first was exemplified by *Eagleton* (1854) Dears C.C. 515, 538. The other was based on a passage in *Stephen's Digest of the Criminal Law* that an attempt to commit a crime was an act done with intent to commit that crime and forming part of a series of acts which would constitute its actual commission if it were not interrupted. However, Stephen's definition did not define the exact point of time at which the series of acts could be said to begin. The words of the 1981 Act sought to steer a midway course. They did not provide that the *Eagleton* test was to be followed or (as Lord Diplock had suggested in *D.P.P.* v. *Stonehouse* (1977) 65 Cr.App.R. 192, 208) that the defendant must have reached a point from which it was impossible for him to retreat before the *actus reus* of an attempt was proved. On the other hand the words gave as clear a guidance as was possible in the circumstances on the point of time at which Stephen's "series of acts" began. It began when the merely preparatory acts came to an end and the defendant embarked on the crime proper. When that was would depend, of course, on the facts in any particular case."

It seems likely that no real change in the law was intended by the enactment of section 1(1). The government in the course of the parliamentary proceedings, took the view that the law on this matter was not being altered.[53] The Law Commission, whose Report led to the legislation, felt that it was "undesirable to recommend anything more complex than a rationalisation of the present law."[54] However, they did recommend abandoning the phrase "proximate" as its literal meaning was "nearest, next before or after . . . [and] thus would clearly be capable of being interpreted to exclude all but the 'final act.' "[55] The Law Commission disapproved of such an approach and clearly felt that their new terminology could open the door to conviction in cases such as *Robinson* and *Comer* v. *Bloomfield*. Glanville Williams comments on this: "the abandonment of the language of proximity appears to be only a matter of words. The Act preserves the rule that the act of attempt must go beyond mere preparation, which in the past was only another way of saying that it must be 'proximate.' If this interpretation is true,

[53] Ian Dennis, "The Criminal Attempts Act 1981" [1982] Crim.L.R. 379.
[54] Law Com. No. 102 (1980), para. 2.47.
[55] *Id.* para. 2.48.

the 'reform' effected by the Act in this part of the law is almost entirely vacuous."[56]

Nevertheless, it emerges from the above cases that the judges are trying to push back the boundaries of the law of attempt. Three related points seems to emerge:

(i) The courts are striving at some sort of half-way house between the old proximity test and Stephen's "series of acts" test. The problem with this is that it is impossible to find a "midway" point between proximity (which was reasonably well ascertainable) and something completely unascertainable (which is all that can be said for Stephen's test).

(ii) This pushing back of the boundaries has meant abandoning the "Rubicon test." A defendant need not have reached the point of no return. Similarly, the fact that he has reached such a point will not necessarily indicate that his actions are more than merely preparatory. When a defendant climbs on to a race track in front of racing dogs and waves his arms at the animals it would surely be permissible to assert that he has "crossed the Rubicon and burnt his boats." This is what the defendant did in *Gullefer* and it was insufficient for liability.

(iii) In *Gullefer* it was stated that the test for pinpointing the "midway" point was whether the defendant had "embarked on the crime proper." This means, in effect, that the defendant must have started committing the crime. He must be "on the job."[57] Such a test works well when applied to some cases. In *White*[58] the defendant had given his mother the first dose of poison; he had effectively started killing her and ought clearly to be liable for an attempt. In *Boyle and Boyle* the defendants had broken down a door. Burglary requires an *entry* as a trespasser. To break down a door means that you have embarked on the process of securing entry to the building—and again to someone on such a threshold of committing the complete crime, liability seems justified.

But beyond such obvious cases this "test" is problematic. When can a defendant be said to have embarked on the commission of the offence? A narrow view would be that one only embarks on, say, theft, when one starts appropriating property. But at this point the full crime will have been committed.[59] At what point will one have embarked on the "crime proper" of rape? Surely one only starts committing rape on penetration—at which point, again, the full crime is committed. It would thus appear that under this view the law of attempt would become so narrow that many crimes would simply be impossible to attempt.

It is extremely difficult to predict how this new "test" will be devel-

---

[56] *Textbook of Criminal Law*, (1983) 2nd ed., p. 417.
[57] Smith and Hogan, p. 294.
[58] *Ante*, p. 458.
[59] See *post*, p. 686.

oped. The courts appear to be saying that they want to expand the ambit of the *actus reus* of attempt—but it is difficult to see any actual change in result. The defendants in *Boyle and Boyle* would have been guilty under any of the tests so far discussed. The defendant in *Gullefer* had gone a very substantial way towards the commission of his offence (as far as the defendants in *Robinson* and *Comer* v. *Bloomfield*) and yet was not liable.[60] It follows that it is extremely unlikely that these notorious pre-1981 cases would be decided any differently today.

It is important to stress that the ultimate decision here is one for the jury. Section 4(3) of the Criminal Attempts Act 1981 provides:

"Where . . . there is evidence sufficient in law to support a finding that he did an act falling within [section 1(1)] . . . , the question whether or not his act fell within that subsection is a question of fact."

Applying this to the facts of *Gullefer*, it would be for the judge, using the law outlined above, to decide whether there was sufficient evidence that the defendant *could* come within the law of attempt—and, if so, it must be left to the jury to decide whether the acts did or did not constitute an attempt. It thus follows that inconsistency of jury verdict is inevitable.

(ii) *Abandonment*

What is the position if a defendant, with intention to commit the complete offence, does an act which is more than merely preparatory, but then decides to abandon his criminal enterprise? Is he still liable for an attempt to commit the crime?

Le Barron v. State, 32 Wis. 2d 294; 145 N.W. 2d 79 (1966) (Supreme Court of Wisconsin)

Currie C.J.:

"Was the evidence adduced sufficient to prove the finding of defendant guilty beyond a reasonable doubt of the crime of attempted rape? . . .

[The defendant accosted a woman and took her to a deserted coal shack.] He then forced her into the shack and up against the wall. As she struggled for her breath he said, 'You know what else I want,' unzipped his pants and started pulling up her skirt. She finally succeeded in removing his hand from her mouth, and after reassuring him that she would not scream, told him she was pregnant and pleaded with him to desist or he would hurt her baby. He then felt of her stomach and took her over to the door of the shack, where in the better light he was able to ascertain that, under her coat, she was wearing maternity clothes. He thereafter let her alone and left after warning her not to scream or call the police, or he would kill her."

Conviction affirmed

Should such a defendant be guilty of attempted rape? Would it make

---

[60] See also *Widdowson* (1986) 130 S.J. 88, a case not dissimilar to *Robinson* in which the conviction was quashed.

any difference if, instead of discovering the woman was pregnant, the defendant had simply been struck by remorse and had desisted saying: "I won't do it; God has stayed my hand"?[61]

It is clear that there is no "defence" of abandonment in English law.

Haughton v. Smith [1975] A.C. 476 (House of Lords)

Lord Hailsham:
"First [the defendant] may simply change his mind before committing any act sufficiently overt to amount to an attempt. Second, he may change his mind, but too late to deny that he had got so far as an attempt. . . . In the first case no criminal attempt is committed. At the relevant time there was no *mens rea* since there had been a change of intention, and the only overt acts relied upon would be preparatory and not immediately connected with the completed offence. In the second case there is both *mens rea* and an act immediately connected with the completed offence. . . . It follows that there is a criminal attempt."

The Law Commission (Law Com. No. 102), Attempt . . . (1980):

"2.132. There is no authority to suggest that withdrawal from an attempt to commit an offence may at present be raised as a defence. Any interruption of the defendant's acts, whether or not due to his voluntary desistance, is not material to whether there has been an attempt, although it might show that there was not the *mens rea* necessary for liability. As the Working Party pointed out, an attempt is committed as soon as there are proximate acts accompanied by the necessary intent; thus even though withdrawal might result in the completed offence not being committed, it could not undo the fact that at some stage the defendant would have committed the inchoate offence. . . . In favour of the defence was the suggestion that it could operate as an inducement to one who had embarked upon criminal conduct to desist from the completion of the offence by enabling him to raise a complete defence to criminal charges. On the other hand, it was suggested that, since the principal justification for provision of inchoate offences lay in the opportunity they gave for intervention by the police at an early stage in criminal activity, there would be an inherent contradiction in providing a defence when that activity had already reached a stage sufficiently advanced to warrant such intervention. The social danger already manifested by the defendant's conduct made it appropriate that any effort he might make to nullify its effects should instead be reflected by mitigation of penalty.
2.133. . . . We believe that provision of a defence could only be justified if there were decisive arguments in its favour; particularly in the context of attempt, the defence could raise difficulties for law enforcement authorities still greater than those which already exist in deciding where the law may impose criminal sanctions. . . .
For these reasons we do not recommend any defence of withdrawal in relation to attempt."

Such a defence is however widely accepted in the United States.

---

[61] See *People* v. *Graham*, 176 App.Div. 38, 162 N.Y.S., 334 (1916).

American Law Institute, Model Penal Code, Proposed Official Draft, s.5.01(4):

"Renunciation of criminal purpose. When the actor's conduct would otherwise constitute an attempt . . . it is an affirmative defense that he abandoned his effort to commit the crime or otherwise prevented its commission, under circumstances manifesting complete and voluntary renunciation of his criminal purpose. . . .

Within the meaning of this Article, renunciation of criminal purpose is not voluntary if it is motivated, in whole or in part, by circumstances, not present or apparent at the inception of the actor's course of conduct, which increase the probability of detection or apprehension or which make more difficult the accomplishment of the criminal purpose. Renunciation is not complete if it is motivated by a decision to postpone the criminal conduct until a more advantageous time or to transfer the criminal effort to another but similar objective or victim."

Should English law follow this lead and allow for such a defence?

Martin Wasik, "Abandoning Criminal Intent" [1980] Crim.L.R. 785, at 787–788, 790–794:

"It is clear that the *voluntary* nature of the abandonment is an essential requirement for the success of any excuse in this area. . . . [T]wo reasons [are] put forward] for the central importance of the requirement of voluntariness. Sometimes it is argued that voluntary desistance provides clear evidence that the actor lacked the resolve to carry out the crime, and hence was not truly dangerous, and sometimes it is said that voluntary desistance is a 'good act' which somehow compensates for or erases the initial criminal act, thus making an acquittal appropriate.[62]

. . . One argument in favour of excusing the defendant who renounces a criminal purpose is in terms of negation of *mens rea*. According to Glanville Williams (*Criminal Law: The General Part* (1961), pp. 620–621) ' . . . where the accused has changed his mind, it would only be just to interpret his previous intention where possible as only half-formed or provisional, and hold it to be an insufficient *mens rea* . . . ' . . . Any [such] suggestion . . . would greatly undermine the law of attempt. There must be few cases where the defendant would not accept the need to give up the attempt in certain circumstances . . . [Also] the problems of proof would be considerable. . . . In the leading Australian case on this topic, *Page* ([1933] V.L.R. 351), Mann A.C.J. emphasised the problems of proof involved in accepting such an excuse to crime. It

> ' . . . would seem to involve the necessity, in almost every case of an unsuccessful attempt to commit a crime, of determining whether the accused desisted from sudden alarm, from a sense of wrongdoing, from failure of resolution, or from any other cause. In the great majority of attempts to commit a crime the persons concerned desist because of causes affecting their volition . . . '

. . . [W]hat other reasons exist for allowing [the excuse] to relieve the defendant of responsibility? First, it is argued that any dangerousness of character is negatived by clear evidence of abandonment . . . It *may* follow from the fact that the course of conduct can no longer be regarded as dangerous that the defendant can be regarded as being no longer dangerous, but this is surely not a

---

[62] If this latter view is adopted, must the abandonment be prompted by a commendable motive? *Cf.* Fletcher, pp. 193–194.

necessary inference from the abandonment of one attempt. The dangerousness of the conduct and the dangerousness of the actor are closely related concepts, but they are not identical. It might be that the defendant could experience profound remorse from coming very close to the commission of a criminal offence, and thus never seek to commit one again. . . . An acceptance of abandonment as an excuse would support . . . [Glanville Williams' theory of the "psychological barrier" (*ante* p. 460)], however, since voluntary abandonment, no matter how late it came, presumably would show that the psychological barrier had not been crossed. Under English law, as we have seen, such late abandonment could not amount to an excuse because a proximate act has already been committed. On the other hand such questions of individual psychology and relative dangerousness are the very stuff of mitigation and sentencing policy. . . .

The second reason often advanced for allowing a defence of withdrawal is one of legal policy. It is claimed that since it is a prime purpose of the criminal law to prevent the occurrence of harm, it makes sense to provide a reasonable inducement for the attempter to desist before any real harm is done. . . . The importance of the argument turns upon how realistic it is. How likely is it that a man who is sufficiently far along the path towards committing a criminal offence, that he would be guilty of an attempt if stopped, and who then decides not to commit it, would change his mind again and decide to carry on, since he realises he is guilty of the attempt anyway? The argument is far-fetched.[63] . . .

It has been strongly argued, then, that mitigation is not enough in cases of voluntary abandonment and that 'No argument of deterrence, reformation or prevention seems to require the punishment of one who is truly repentant and has done no harm.' It may be conceded that in a case of 'perfect' voluntary and complete abandonment, this argument is irrefutable. On a retributive view, punishment would be in accordance with bad intent, so on withdrawal the reason for punishment is removed. D's own change of heart perhaps rules out the need for preventative or reformative measures. Individual or general deterrence may also be out of place on the 'economy of threats' argument that punishing a man who has a good moral excuse will not serve to deter him or anyone else. In such a clear case punishment, and perhaps even the stigma of a conviction, seems inappropriate. . . .

[Wasik, nevertheless, concludes that abandonment should only be relevant in mitigation of sentence.]"

Is this excuse of abandonment more in accord with Fletcher's "objectivist" or his "subjectivist" theory of attempts? Ought such important matters of principle be left simply to judicial discretion at the sentencing stage?

(iii) *Impossibility*

(a) Introduction

Can there be criminal liability for attempting the impossible? If a defendant shoots at his victim trying to kill him, but unknown to him

---

[63] *Cf.* H. Wechsler, "The Treatment of Inchoate Crimes in the Model Penal Code . . ." (1961) 61 Col.L.R. 571, at pp. 617–618. "It is possible, of course, that the defense of renunciation of criminal purpose may add to the incentives to take the first steps toward crime. Knowledge that criminal endeavours can be undone with impunity may encourage preliminary steps that would not be undertaken if liability inevitably attached to every abortive criminal undertaking that proceeded beyond preparation. But this is not a serious problem. . . . [A]ny consolation the actor might draw from the abandonment defense would have to be tempered with the knowledge that the defence would be unavailable if the actor's purposes were frustrated by external forces before he had an opportunity to abandon his effort."

the victim has had a heart attack and is already dead, can the defendant be liable for attempted murder? If a defendant is trying to commit rape, but at the last moment discovers that the victim is a transvestite whom it is impossible to rape,[64] can he nevertheless be convicted of attempted rape?

In order to understand the present law (and because it still applies in other areas to be considered shortly[65]), it is necessary briefly to outline the position at common law before the enactment of the Criminal Attempts Act 1981.

(b) The common law

The common law utilised a three-fold classification:

1. Legal impossibility:

This is where the defendant performs all the physical actions he intends to perform, but, unknown to him, what he has done does not amount to a crime. For example, he intends to steal an umbrella but unknown to him, the umbrella turns out to be his own.

In *Haughton* v. *Smith*[66] the defendant was charged with attempting to handle stolen goods contrary to section 22 of the Theft Act 1968. The defendant had actually handled the goods but unknown to him, they were not stolen goods.[67] The House of Lords unanimously held that there could be no liability for attempt in such circumstances. Lord Hailsham stated:

" . . . there must be an overt act of such a kind that it is intended to form and does form part of a series of acts which would constitute the actual commission of the offence if it were not interrupted. In the present case the series of acts would never have constituted and in fact did not constitute an actual commission of the offence, because at the time of the handling the goods were no longer stolen goods."[68]

Lord Reid:

"The crime is impossible in the circumstances, so no acts could be proximate to it . . . [H]e took no step towards the commission of a crime because there was no crime to commit."[69]

Lord Morris:

"His belief that the goods were stolen did not make them stolen goods. . . . To convict him of attempting to handle stolen goods would be to convict him not for what he did but simply because he had had a guilty intention."[70]

---

[64] Rape requires vaginal intercourse (see, *post* p. 567). Non-consensual buggery with a man is often referred to as "rape" by the press—but this is an incorrect use of English legal language.

[65] Common law conspiracy and incitement. See *post*, pp. 491–492, 495–497.

[66] [1975] A.C. 476.

[67] The goods had been stolen, but when the police commandeered the van in which the goods were travelling, the goods ceased to be "stolen" by virtue of section 24(3) of the Theft Act 1968 as they had been "restored to lawful custody."

[68] At p. 492.

[69] At pp. 499–500.

[70] At p. 501.

2. Physical impossibility:

This is where it is physically impossible for the defendant to commit the complete crime, whatever means he adopts. For example, he intends to pick a pocket; he places his hand in the victim's pocket, but it is empty; there is nothing to steal. In *Partington* v. *Williams* it was held that there could be no liability[71] in such cases because the commission of the substantive offence was, in the circumstances impossible.

The House of Lords in *D.P.P.* v. *Nock*,[72] a conspiracy case, considered *obiter* "the proper limits" of *Haughton* v. *Smith* and attempts to commit the impossible, and held that liability depended on the manner in which the particular indictment was framed. If, in an attempted theft case, the indictment was limited to an attempt to steal specific property or property from a specific place, then if the property was not there, the *actus reus* of the complete crime, namely, the appropriation of the *specific* property belonging to another, would be incapable of proof. The defendant would escape liability. But if the indictment alleged an attempt to steal from the person generally, then the pickpocket who put his hand in an empty pocket could be liable for attempted theft. This would be a mere "transient frustration." The crime would still be possible; the pickpocket, if undetected, would continue his attempts until successful.

This purported limitation of the *Haughton* v. *Smith* principle does not stand up to close analysis. First, it ignores the immense difficulties involved in proving the requisite general intent to continue until the crime is eventually completed successfully, and secondly, it overlooks the necessity to prove that the defendant's actions were proximate to the complete offence. As Smith states:

" . . . the theft attempted is from some unascertainable pocket containing money carried by some unascertainable person at some unascertainable place and time in the future. What has become of the doctrine of proximity?"[73]

This whole approach on attempts to commit the physically impossible caused other problems. What was meant by an empty pocket or an empty box? What if the pocket contained only a dirty handkerchief or a broken match? Was the test of emptiness a purely objective one, or was it relative to the defendant, namely, was there something there that he would (or might) have stolen? For instance, the Law Commission[74] cite an unreported case in which a suitcase full of luggage was effectively held to be "empty" because it contained nothing the defendant wanted. In *Bayley and Easterbrook*[75] the defendants opened a box hoping to steal

---

[71] (1975) 62 Cr.App.R. 220. The Divisional Court considered itself bound by *Haughton* v. *Smith* which is not technically correct as the cases were dealing with different categories of impossibility.
[72] [1978] A.C. 979.
[73] [1978] Crim.L.R. 486. For a general analysis and criticism of *Nock*, see C. M. V. Clarkson, "Impossibility: Transient Frustrations and other Confusions" (1979) 9 *Kingston Law Review* 88.
[74] Law Com. No. 102, para. 2.62.
[75] [1980] Crim.L.R. 503.

from it; the box contained "a Pammex Model 60 rail and flange lubricator"—a valuable article, but useless to the defendants so they returned the box and its contents. Their conviction for "attempting to steal the contents of a box belonging to the British Railways Board" was upheld, but as Smith points out:

"It is clear then that the defendants were convicted of attempting to steal not the actual contents but something, unidentified, that was not in the box. . . . Apart from the Pammex Model 60 rail and flange lubricator, this was an empty box. The presence of those articles was clearly totally irrelevant. They were of no more significance than, say, pieces of straw in which they had been packed."[76]

3. *Impossibility through ineptitude*

This is where the crime is impossible in the circumstances because of the defendant's ineptitude, inefficiency or his adoption of insufficient means. For example, he tries to force open a door with a jemmy, but the jemmy is too weak ever to open the door. Here the common law took a different approach from that adopted in relation to the above two categories of impossibility and held that here there would be criminal liability for attempt. The reasoning was that such crimes were not really "impossible" because the crime *was* possible with different means. The defendant could open the door; he simply needed to fetch and use a stronger jemmy.

In *White*[77] the defendant tried to kill his mother with poison but used an insufficient quantity of poison for the purpose. His conviction for attempted murder was upheld. In *Haughton* v. *Smith*, Lord Reid said:

"A man may set out to commit a crime with inadequate tools. He finds that he cannot break in because the door is too strong for him. Or he uses poison which is not strong enough. He is certainly guilty of attempt: with better equipment or greater skill he could have committed the full crime."[78]

In *Farrance*[79] the defendant had been convicted of attempting to drive with a blood alcohol concentration above the prescribed limit contrary to section 6(1) of the Road Traffic Act 1972. The clutch of his car had burnt out so that he could not drive the car. The Court of Appeal upheld his conviction on the ground that a burnt out clutch was only an impediment to the commission of a crime similar to the inadequate burglar's tool or the poisoner's insufficient dose. In the Brunei case of *Zainal Abidin b Ismail*[80] the defendant's impotence prevented him from

---

[76] [1980] Crim.L.R. 504. On this problem, see generally, Glanville Williams, "Three Rogues' Charters" [1980] Crim.L.R. 263.

[77] [1910] 2 K.B. 124.

[78] At p. 500.

[79] (1977) 67 Cr.App.R. 136.

[80] [1987] 2 M.L.J. 741. For a discussion of this case see C. M. V. Clarkson, "Rape: Emasculation of the Penal Code" [1988] 1 M.L.J. cxiii.

raping a woman. This was regarded as an instance of impossibility by ineptitude and the defendant was convicted of attempted rape.

Holding that there could be liability in these cases, but not in cases of attempting the physically impossible, posed immense problems. Suppose a defendant fired his gun at a victim who was out of range. Was this ineptitude or physical impossibility? Did it matter whether the victim was only just out of range or miles out of range? Or suppose that a defendant tried to kill his victim with a weak solution of poison; this was presumably ineptitude, but what if the solution was so weak that it could cause no harm at all? Or if the solution was entirely innocent, as where water was administered in mistake for cyanide? At what point did ineptitude become transformed into impossibility?

(c) Criminal Attempts Act 1981

Criminal Attempts Act 1981, section 1:

"(2) A person may be guilty of attempting to commit an offence to which this section applies even though the facts are such that the commission of the offence is impossible.
(3) In any case where—
(a) apart from this subsection a person's intention would not be regarded as having amounted to an intent to commit an offence; but
(b) if the facts of the case had been as he believed them to be, his intention would be so regarded,
then, for the purposes of subsection (1) above, he shall be regarded as having had an intent to commit that offence.
(4) This section applies to any offence which, if it were completed, would be triable in England and Wales as an indictable offence. . . . "

Section 1(2) provides that there can be liability for attempting the impossible—irrespective of the category of impossibility. Section 1(3) purports to confirm the self-evident proposition that where a person believes the facts to be such that he would be committing a crime, he is to be regarded as having the necessary intention to commit the offence. This means that a defendant who intends to handle a particular radio believing it to be stolen, when in fact it is not stolen cannot argue that he intended to handle a "non-stolen radio." Section 1(3) makes it plain that if he believed the radio was stolen, he intended to handle a "stolen radio." This provision is actually completely redundant. Intention relates purely to a defendant's subjective state of mind. An intention to handle a stolen radio is just that: an intention to handle a radio believed to be stolen. The objective status of the goods (stolen or not stolen) has no bearing upon the defendant's intention.[81]

These provisions represented a clear and emphatic victory for the

---

[81] S.1(3) can possibly be utilised in a different situation where it is not totally redundant. See *ante*, n. 36.

"subjectivist" theory of attempts where emphasis is placed on the intention of the defendant and the firmness of that intention. However, the House of Lords was not prepared to accept such blatant subjectivism, and in an extraordinary judgment, declared that the statute would lead to "asinine" results and proceeded to subvert the legislation from its original purpose.

Anderton v. Ryan [1985] A.C. 560 (House of Lords)

The defendant was charged with dishonestly attempting to handle a stolen video recorder. She had purchased the recorder believing it was stolen and had confessed this to police investigating a burglary at her home. There was however no evidence that the recorder had been stolen and it therefore had to be treated as if it were not stolen.

Lord Bridge:
"Does section 1 of the Act of 1981 create a new offence of attempt where a person embarks on and completes a course of conduct which is objectively innocent, solely on the ground that the person mistakenly believes facts which, if true, would make that course of conduct a complete crime? If the question must be answered affirmatively it requires convictions in a number of surprising cases: the classic case, put by Bramwell B. in *Reg.* v. *Collins* (1864) 9 Cox C.C. 497, of the man who takes away his own umbrella from a stand, believing it not to be his own and with intent to steal it; the case of the man who has consensual intercourse with a girl over 16 believing her to be under that age; the case of the art dealer who sells a picture which he represents to be and which is in fact a genuine Picasso, but which the dealer mistakenly believes to be a fake.

The common feature of all these cases, including that under appeal, is that the mind alone is guilty, the act is innocent. I should find it surprising that Parliament, if intending to make this purely subjective guilt criminally punishable, should have done so by anything less than the clearest express language, and, in particular, should have done so in a section aimed specifically at inchoate offences.

. . . [S]ection 1(1) and (4) of the Act of 1981 provide a statutory substitute for the common law offence of attempt . . .

It is sufficient to say of subsection (2) that it is plainly intended to reverse the law, . . . that the pickpocket who puts his hand in an empty pocket commits no offence. Putting the hand in the pocket is the guilty act, the intent to steal is the guilty mind, the offence is appropriately dealt with as an attempt, and the impossibility of committing the full offence for want of anything in the pocket to steal is declared by the subsection to be no obstacle to conviction . . .

It seems to me that subsections (2) and (3) are in a sense complementary to each other. Subsection (2) covers the case of a person acting in a criminal way with a general intent to commit a crime in circumstances where no crime is possible. Subsection (3) covers the case of a person acting in a criminal way with a specific intent to commit a particular crime which he erroneously believes to be, but which is not in fact, possible. Given the criminal action, the appropriate subsection allows the actor's guilty intention to be supplied by his subjective but mistaken state of mind, notwithstanding that on the true facts that intention is incapable of fulfilment. But if the action is throughout innocent and the actor has done everything he intended to do, I can find nothing in either subsection which requires me to hold that his erroneous belief in facts which, if true, would have made the action a crime makes him guilty of an attempt to commit that crime."

Appeal allowed

C. M. V. Clarkson, Understanding Criminal Law (1987) pp. 111–112:

"This distinction between 'objectively innocent' acts on the one hand and 'criminal' or 'guilty' acts on the other is particularly interesting. It would appear that a 'criminal' or 'guilty' act is one that looks *manifestly criminal*. (This cannot refer to actual crimes. The defendant stabbing the pillow believing he is stabbing his victim commits no offence if it is his own bedding and pillow that he is damaging. Yet Lord Roskill clearly held that there would be liability for attempt in such a situation.) Fletcher (1978) states that 'manifestly criminal' activities must exhibit at least the following essential features. First, the criminal act must manifest, on its face, the actor's criminal purpose. And secondly, the conduct should be 'of a type that is unnerving and disturbing to the community as a whole.' These requirements are clearly satisfied in the pickpocket and defendant stabbing the pillow cases. The actions manifest the defendant's unlawful purpose and are 'unnerving and disturbing' to the community. This requirement of manifest criminality is, of course, one that lays emphasis on *harm*, albeit of a second-order nature. It insists that actions infringe another's security interests; they must seemingly pose real and objective threats of harm.

On the other hand, 'objectively innocent' activities such as those of Mrs. Ryan or the defendant having sexual intercourse with the 16-year-old girl believing her to be under 16 pose no threat of harm to anyone. Nobody's security interests are being violated thereby. If criminal liability were to be imposed in such cases it would be in the complete absence of any degree of harm, however defined. On this basis it can be suggested that the House of Lords in *Anderton* v. *Ryan* (1985), despite blatantly ignoring Parliament's intentions and creating confused distinctions, did lend its weight to the view here advanced that the causing of harm is an essential prerequisite in the general formula for the construction of criminal liability."

In one of the most dramatic about-turns in English law, the House of Lords one year later overruled itself and held that there could be criminal liability in all cases of attempting the impossible.

R. v. Shivpuri [1987] A.C. 1 (House of Lords)

The defendant thought he was dealing in prohibited drugs but it transpired that the substance in his possession was only snuff or similarly harmless vegetable matter. He was charged with attempting to be knowingly concerned in dealing with prohibited drugs, contrary to section 1(1) of the Criminal Attempts Act 1981 and section 170(1)(*b*) of the Customs and Excise Management Act 1979.

Lord Bridge:
[T]he first question to be asked is whether the appellant intended to commit the offences of being knowingly concerned in dealing with and harbouring drugs of Class A or Class B with intent to evade the prohibition on their importation. Translated into more homely language the question may be rephrased, without in any way altering its legal significance, in the following terms: did the appellant intend to receive and store (harbour) and in due course pass on to

third parties (deal with) packages of heroin or cannabis which he knew had been smuggled into England from India? The answer is plainly yes, he did. Next, did he in relation to each offence, do an act which was more than merely preparatory to the commission of the offence? The act relied on in relation to harbouring was the receipt and retention of the packages found in the lining of the suitcase. The act relied on in relation to dealing was the meeting at Southall station with the intended recipient of one of the packages. In each case the act was clearly more than preparatory to the commission of the *intended* offence; it was not and could not be more than merely preparatory to the commission of the *actual* offence, because the facts were such that the commission of the actual offence was impossible. Here then is the nub of the matter. Does the 'act which is more than merely preparatory to the commission of the offence' in section 1(1) of the Act of 1981 (the *actus reus* of the statutory offence of attempt) require any more than an act which is more than merely preparatory to the commission of the offence which the defendant intended to commit? Section 1(2) must surely indicate a negative answer; if it were otherwise, whenever the facts were such that the commission of the actual offence was impossible, it would be impossible to prove an act more than merely preparatory to the commission of that offence and subsections (1) and (2) would contradict each other.

This very simple, perhaps over simple, analysis leads me to the provisional conclusion that the appellant was rightly convicted of the two offences of attempt with which he was charged. But can this conclusion stand with *Anderton* v. *Ryan*? . . .

Running through Lord Roskill's speech and my own in *Anderton* v. *Ryan* is the concept of 'objectively innocent' acts which, in my speech certainly, are contrasted with 'guilty acts.'

I am satisfied on further consideration that the concept of 'objective innocence' is incapable of sensible application in relation to the law of criminal attempts. The reason for this is that any attempt to commit an offence which involves 'an act which is more than merely preparatory to the commission of the offence' but for any reason fails, so that in the event no offence is committed, must ex hypothesi, from the point of view of the criminal law, be 'objectively innocent.' What turns what would otherwise, from the point of view of the criminal law, be an innocent act into a crime is the intent of the actor to commit an offence. . . . A puts his hand into B's pocket. Whether or not there is anything in the pocket capable of being stolen, if A intends to steal, his act is a criminal attempt; if he does not so intend, his act is innocent. A plunges a knife into a bolster in a bed. To avoid the complication of an offence of criminal damage, assume it to be A's bolster. If A believes the bolster to be his enemy B and intends to kill him, his act is an attempt to murder B; if he knows the bolster is only a bolster, his act is innocent. These considerations lead me to the conclusion that the distinction sought to be drawn in *Anderton* v. *Ryan* between innocent and guilty acts considered 'objectively' and independently of the state of mind of the actor cannot be sensibly maintained.

Another conceivable ground of distinction which was to some extent canvassed in argument, both in *Anderton* v. *Ryan* and in the instant case, though no trace of it appears in the speeches in *Anderton* v. *Ryan*, is a distinction which would make guilt or innocence of the crime of attempt in a case of mistaken belief dependent on what, for want of a better phrase, I will call the defendant's dominant intention. According to the theory necessary to sustain this distinction, the appellant's dominant intention in *Anderton* v. *Ryan* was to buy a cheap video recorder; her belief that it was stolen was merely incidental. Likewise in the hypothetical case of attempted unlawful sexual intercourse, the young man's dominant intention was to have intercourse with the particular girl; his mistaken belief that she was under 16 was merely incidental. By contrast, in the instant case, the appellant's dominant intention was to receive and distribute illegally imported heroin or cannabis.

Whilst I see the superficial attraction of this suggested ground of distinction, I also see formidable practical difficulties in its application. By what test is a jury to be told that a defendant's dominant intention is to be recognised and distinguished from his incidental but mistaken belief? But there is perhaps a more formidable theoretical difficulty. If this ground of distinction is relied on to support the acquittal of the appellant in *Anderton* v. *Ryan*, it can only do so on the basis that her mistaken belief that the video recorder was stolen played no significant part in her decision to buy it and therefore she may be acquitted of the intent to handle stolen goods. But this line of reasoning runs into head-on collision with section 1(3) of the Act of 1981. The theory produces a situation where, apart from the subsection, her intention would not be regarded as having amounted to any intent to commit an offence. Section 1(3)(*b*) then requires one to ask whether, if the video recorder had in fact been stolen, her intention would have been regarded as an intent to handle stolen goods. The answer must clearly be yes, it would. If she had bought the video recorder knowing it to be stolen, when in fact it was, it would have availed her nothing to say that her dominant intention was to buy a video recorder because it was cheap and that her knowledge that it was stolen was merely incidental. This seems to me fatal to the dominant intention theory.

I am thus led to the conclusion that there is no valid ground on which *Anderton* v. *Ryan* can be distinguished. I have made clear my own conviction . . . that the decision was wrong."

Appeal dismissed

H. L. A. Hart, "The House of Lords on Attempting the Impossible" in Crime Proof and Punishment (Essays in Memory of Sir Rupert Cross) (1981), pp. 18–19:

"[I]f the punishment of unsuccessful attempts to commit crimes is morally justifiable at all, exactly the same deterrent and retributive justifications are available in the cases of impossibility as in the ordinary cases of attempt. The accused in the impossibility case having done his best to implement his intention to commit a crime is just as much deserving of punishment as the accused in the ordinary case; and the same considerations of general and individual deterrence apply with equal force, whether or not at the relevant time and place the object on which the accused intends to operate exists and has the properties required for the commission of the intended offence."

The Law Commission (Law Com. No. 102), Attempt . . . (1980):

"2.96. We think it would be generally accepted that if a man possesses the appropriate *mens rea* and commits acts which are sufficiently proximate to the *actus reus* of a criminal offence, he is guilty of attempting to commit that offence. Where, with that intention, he commits acts which, if the facts were as he believed them to be, would have amounted to the *actus reus* of the full crime or would have been sufficiently proximate to amount to an attempt, we cannot see why his failure to appreciate the true facts should, in principle, relieve him of liability for the attempt. We stress that this solution to the problem does not punish people simply for their intentions. The necessity for proof of proximate acts remains. The fact that the impossibility of committing the full crime reduces the social danger is adequately reflected in the generally milder penalty which an attempt attracts instead of that for the full offence. And even if it is conceded that there may be some reduction in the social danger in cases of impossibility, it has to be borne in mind that a certain social danger undoubtedly remains. Defendants in cases such as *Haughton* v. *Smith* and *Nock and Alsford* are prepared to do all they can to break the criminal law even though in the circumstances their attempts are doomed to failure; and if they go unpunished, they may be encouraged to do better at the next opportunity. Finally, if the solution under consideration is accepted, it makes it possible to dispense with the doctrine of 'inadequate means' and with strained efforts to catch those who might otherwise escape by resort to broadly drawn indictments and an 'inferred general intention.'

2.97. If it is right in principle that an attempt should be chargeable even though the crime which it is sought to commit could not possibly be committed, we do not think that we should be deterred by the consideration that such a change in our law would also cover some extreme and exceptional cases in which a prosecution would be theoretically possible. An example would be where a person is offered goods at such a low price that he believes that they are stolen, when in fact they are not; if he actually purchases them, upon the principles which we have discussed he would be liable for an attempt to handle stolen goods. Another case which has been much debated is that raised in argument by Bramwell B. in *R.* v. *Collins* (1864) 9 Cox C.C. 497. If A takes his own umbrella, mistaking it for one belonging to B and intending to steal B's umbrella, is he guilty of attempted theft? Again, on the principles which we have discussed he would in theory be guilty but in neither case would it be realistic to suppose that a complaint would be made or that a prosecution would ensue. On the other hand, if our recommendations were formulated so as to exclude such cases, then it might well be impossible to obtain convictions in cases such as *Haughton* v. *Smith*, where a defendant handles goods which were originally stolen, intending to handle stolen goods, but where, unknown to him, the goods had meanwhile been restored to lawful custody. Another example of possible difficulty which has been suggested is where a person in the erroneous belief that he can kill by witchcraft or magic takes action such as sticking pins into a model of his enemy—intending thereby to bring about his enemy's death. Could that person be charged with attempted murder? It may be that such conduct could be more than an act of mere preparation on the facts as the defendant believes them to be; and in theory, therefore, it is possible that such a defendant could be found guilty. In the ordinary course, we think that discretion in bringing a prosecution will be sufficient answer to any problems raised by such unusual cases; but even if a prosecution ensued, it may be doubted whether a jury would regard the acts in question as sufficient to amount to an attempt.

2.98. A possible difficulty of another kind which we have considered is the distinction which it will be necessary to draw between impossibility arising from misapprehension as to the facts and impossibility arising from a misapprehension of the law in situations which at first sight appear to be similar. As we have seen, if the defendant believes, because of a mistake of law, that certain conduct constitutes an offence when it is not, he should not be liable for attempt if he acts in accordance with his intent. For example, the defendant intends to smuggle certain goods through the customs in the belief that they are dutiable; under the relevant law those goods are in fact not dutiable. He has made no mistake as to the nature of the goods; his error is solely one of law, and if he imports them he should not be liable for an attempt improperly to import goods without paying duty, since he had no intent to commit an offence known to the law.[82] The position is different if the defendant is asked while abroad to smuggle into the country goods which he is assured by the person making the request are goods which are actually dutiable, but which are not in fact dutiable because they are not what he believes them to be. Here the defendant's error arises solely from his misapprehension as to the nature of the goods; it is a pure error of fact. He has every intention of committing an offence on the facts as he believes them to be, and if he succeeds in importing the goods or in getting sufficiently close to his objective, he must be liable for an attempt upon the principles which we have been considering. Fine as the distinction appears to be in these cases it is one which is in our view vital to make."

Supporters of the objective theory of attempts tend to reject such reasoning and assert that such "subjectivism" amounts to little more than punishing people for their guilty intentions. The Law Commission themselves conceded the absurdity of there being liability in situations where a person buys legitimate goods but at such a low price that he thinks (wrongly) that they are stolen. Their solution to this problem was to conclude that prosecutions would never be brought in such cases. Yet it was exactly on such facts that a prosecution was brought in *Anderton* v. *Ryan* forcing the House of Lords to adopt some highly innovative techniques to ensure an acquittal.

However, even the hardened "objectivist" concedes the necessity for liability in certain obvious cases. The problem is in isolating such situations.

George P. Fletcher, Rethinking Criminal Law (1978), pp. 149–150, 152–154, 161–163, 165–166:

"It is agreed by all supporters of an objectivist approach to attempts that there should be no liability in the case of shooting at a tree stump with the intent to kill. Yet the courts have found liability in closely related situations. . . . [A] Missouri court convicted on a charge of attempted murder for shooting at the bed where the intended victim usually slept. (*State* v. *Mitchell*, 170 Mo. 633, 71 S.W. 175 (1902)). . . . Shooting at the intended victim's bed and aiming a gun manifest the intent to kill. In shooting at a tree stump, in contrast, there is nothing in the facts to indicate that an attempt is under way. According to objectivist theory, attempting is not just an event of inner experience. It is an effort in the real world to accomplish one's objective. Therefore, when the act is aptly related to the actor's objective, the courts perceive a manifest attempt to commit an offense. Yet when the act is objectively unrelated to the intent, as in the case of shooting at a tree stump, judges and theorists properly balk at positing an act of attempting. The notion of aptness here is obviously closely related to the principle of manifest criminality. . . .

[T]he problem of aptness is one of assessing whether in the long run the type of conduct involved is likely to produce harm. If the type of conduct would pro-

---

[82] This is illustrated by *Taaffe* [1984] 1 A.C. 539, where the defendant, believing that the importation of currency was prohibited, tried to smuggle several packages of what he (wrongly) believed was currency into the country. Although this made his actions "morally reprehensible," he could not be guilty of an attempt to commit any crime—there is no such crime. He had made a classic mistake of law, which was "irrelevant." See *ante*, p. 268.

duce harm in the long run, then the defendant's act is apt and a punishable attempt, even though it is impossible under the circumstances. . . .

The principle that inapt efforts should be exempt from liability readily explains why the courts do not discern an act of attempting in the giving of an innocuous substance as an intended poison or abortifacient.

The difficult problem in these cases is drawing the distinction between giving the intended victim an innocuous substance and giving him too small a dosage of a noxious poison. It is the distinction between trying to kill by putting sugar in his coffee and trying to kill by administering a harmless dosage of cyanide. In the latter cases, the courts have been willing to convict, and as a result we are put to the challenge to explain why sugar makes the attempt inapt but a harmless dosage of cyanide makes it apt. As we discovered in our analysis of the shooting cases, the standard of aptness does not apply to isolated events, but rather to types or classes of acts. Apt attempts belong to a class of acts that are likely to generate harm. If the class is defined as administering a dosage of cyanide or other deadly poison, there is no doubt that the class of acts is likely to generate harm, and therefore we can regard every instance of the class as an apt attempt. . . .

[Dealing with the empty pocket cases] there is nothing inapt about these efforts. They are well calculated to provide a thief's income, even if it turns out that in the particular situation the bounty is not there. . . .

[However for other cases, for example, cases such as *Haughton* v. *Smith*, Fletcher suggests an alternative theory—'the test of rational motivation.'] The thesis is this: mistaken beliefs are relevant to what the actor is trying to do if they affect his incentive in acting. They affect his incentive if knowing of the mistake would give him a good reason for changing his course of conduct. . . . Suppose the accused engages in sexual intercourse with a girl he takes to be under the age of consent; in fact, she is overage. Is he guilty of attempted statutory rape? In the normal case it would not be part of the actor's incentive that the girl be underage (again, one could imagine a variation in which the youth of the girl did bear upon the actor's motivation). If he is just as happy to have intercourse with a girl over age, then his mistake would not bear on his incentive and it would be incorrect to describe his act as trying to have intercourse with a girl under the age of consent. . . . The thesis is that there should be liability in a case of impossibility only if the actor fails in his purpose. . . . The only way to determine whether the actor is attempting an act that includes a particular circumstance, X, is to inquire: what would the actor do if he knew that X was not so? If he would behave in precisely the same way, we cannot say that his mistaken belief in X bears on his motivation; and if it does not, we cannot say that he is attempting to act with reference to X. . . .

If applied to the cases of shooting at stumps and 'poisoning' with sugar, the test of rational motivation leads to convictions where the standard of aptness would favor an acquittal. It is obviously part of the actor's system of incentives that he believe the stump to be a person, or the dosage to be sufficient to kill. If told of the truth, he would presumably change his plans. So far as the standard of incentive is controlling, the person shooting at the stump is undoubtedly attempting to kill. The problem is whether the test of aptness should prevail over the theory of rational motivation in cases involving assaults on the core interests protected by the criminal law. . . .

One reason to believe that the principle of aptness is indispensable in a comprehensive theory of attempt liability is that there is no other way to solve one case in which virtually everyone agrees that there should be no liability. That is the case of nominal efforts to inflict harm by superstitious means, say by black magic or witchcraft. The consensus of Western legal systems is that there should be no liability, regardless of the wickedness of intent, for sticking pins in a doll or chanting an incantation to banish one's enemy to the nether world.[83] Against the background of the fears and taboos prevailing in modern Western society, objectivist theorists take these cases to be inapt attempts, therefore exempt from punishment. Yet the theory of rational motivation points in the direction of liability. If the intending party knows the truth about black magic (namely, that it does not work), he would have a good reason to change his plan of attack. To account for the consensus favoring an exemption in this type of case, we need the principle of aptness to offset the implications of the competing theory of rational motivation.

The problem that remains to be resolved is determining the relative scope of these two competing theories."

If this last extract seems familiar, the reader is to be congratulated for such perception. A broadly similar analysis to Fletcher's theory of aptness was adopted in *Anderton* v. *Ryan.* An extra problem here however is the failure to spell out the exact circumstances in which the theory of aptness is applicable and those in which it is appropriate to apply Fletcher's theory of rational motivation. Prior to the enactment of the Criminal Attempts Act 1981 there were countless attempts to discover some such appropriate half-way house for imposing liability for attempting the impossible—all of which endeavours failed. Perhaps there is no compromise here. One either returns to *Haughton* v. *Smith* or accepts the present law as it is *in toto.*

III Conspiracy

A. Introduction

D.P.P. v. Nock [1978] A.C. 979 (House of Lords)

Lord Salmon:
"Lord Tucker . . . [in *B.O.T.* v. *Owen* [1957] A.C. 602] by stressing the 'auxiliary' nature of the crime of conspiracy, and by explaining its justification as being to prevent the commission of substantive offences, has placed the crime firmly in the same class and category as attempts to commit a crime. Both are criminal because they are steps towards the commission of a substantive offence. The distinction between the two is that, whereas a 'proximate' act is that which constitutes the crime of attempt, agreement is the necessary ingredient in conspiracy. The importance of the distinction is that agreement may, and usually will, occur well before the first step which can be said to be an attempt. The law of conspiracy thus makes possible an earlier intervention by the law to prevent the commission of the substantive offence."

---

[83] *Cf. The Times,* October 12, 1983: "Aborigines in the West Australian town of Roebourne say they will use traditional methods to punish a local policeman who, they say, was responsible for the death of an Aboriginal youth in police custody more than a week ago. They say they will 'sing' him to death.

The ceremony, equivalent to a execution is carried out only rarely. Anthropologists have documented many Aboriginal deaths after such ceremonies.

Mr. Mick Lee, the stepfather of the boy, said 'When someone is sung to death by Aboriginal lawmen, he dies in two days. Black or white, all the same.' "

B. Should there be a Law of Conspiracy?

Richard Card, "Reform of the Law of Conspiracy" [1973] Crim.L.R. 674 at 675–676:

"It may be asked whether it is desirable that criminal liability should attach to persons who, albeit at the time of the agreement intend to carry it out, never get beyond the stage of agreement. To take an extreme case, suppose that there is a bare agreement, the details remaining to be agreed, and that the next day the parties withdraw from their agreement; is this really conduct deserving of punishment?

It must be admitted that in practice a conviction for conspiracy in such a case will not generally be possible because of the difficulty of proving the agreement. Convictions for conspiracy usually depend on inferences from overt acts said by the prosecution to have been performed in pursuance of the agreement. In practical terms liability often arises by virtue of overt acts done in pursuance of the agreement . . . In such cases, . . . the offence of conspiracy would seem to be in part redundant. If these further acts constitute an attempt the conspirators who commit them can be convicted of attempt (to which any other conspirator would be an accomplice). On the other hand, if the further acts are insufficient to constitute an attempt, the punishment of the conspirators, both those who committed the overt acts and those who did no more than enter the agreement, can only be justified on the basis that it is the combination of persons which aggravates their conduct and produces liability. . . .

It is merely suggested that criminal liability should not attach to those who merely agree, . . . where no further steps are taken to effect it. Such a rule has been adopted in part in the Model Penal Code of the American Law Institute. Article 5.03 provides:

'*Overt Act.* No person may be convicted of conspiracy to commit a crime, other than a felony of the first or second degree, unless an overt act in pursuance of such conspiracy is alleged and proved to have been done by him or by a person with whom he conspired.'

Conspiracy has another rationale besides that of 'nipping crime in the bud.' This is that it is an appropriate offence to charge where a series of crimes have been committed at different times by different people pursuant to a prior agreement. The series of crimes may be so large that there would be great difficulty in indicting for all of them. In addition, each offence taken on its own may be relatively trivial but the gravity of the conduct of those involved greatly increased by viewing their acts as part of a larger criminal enterprise. These matters can be dealt with at present by the use of a conspiracy charge. Such situations may well warrant the creation of a crime which specifically deals with such completed criminal enterprises but, it is submitted, they do not justify the continued existence of a crime where liability is based on agreement and no more.

If it was accepted that there should no longer be a crime of conspiracy based on mere agreement to commit a crime, it is submitted that the criminality of acts done pursuant to that agreement (which did not result in the commission of a substantive offence) should be dealt with by the law of attempt."

Phillip Johnson, "The Unnecessary Crime of Conspiracy" (1973) 61 Cal.L.Rev. 1137 at 1157–1158:

"Conspiracy is also an inchoate or preparatory crime, permitting the punishment of persons who agree to commit a crime even if they never carry out their scheme or are apprehended before achieving their objective. . . .

The Model Penal Code commentary offers perhaps the most carefully stated justification for a doctrine of conspiracy that 'reaches further back into preparatory conduct than attempt':

First: The act of agreeing with another to commit a crime, like the act of soliciting, is concrete and unambiguous; it does not present the infinite degrees and variations possible in the general category of attempts. The danger that truly equivocal behaviour may be misinterpreted as preparation to commit a crime is minimized; purpose must be relatively firm before the commitment involved in agreement is assumed.

Second: If the agreement was to aid another to commit a crime or it otherwise encouraged its commission, it would establish complicity in the commission of the substantive offense. . . . It would be anomalous to hold that conduct which would suffice to establish criminality, if something else is done by someone else is insufficient if the crime is never consummated. This is a reason, to be sure, which covers less than all the cases of conspiracy, but that it covers many is the point.

Third: In the course of preparation to commit a crime, the act of combining with another is significant both psychologically and practically, the former since it crosses a clear threshold in arousing expectations, the latter since it increases the likelihood that the offense will be committed. Sharing lends fortitude to purpose. The actor knows, moreover, that the future is no longer governed by his will alone; others may complete what he has had a hand in starting, even if he has a change of heart."

Abraham Goldstein, "Conspiracy to Defraud the United States" (1959) 68 Yale L.J. 405 at 414:

"More likely, empirical investigation would disclose that there is as much reason to believe that a large number of participants will increase the prospect that the plan will be leaked as that it will be kept secret; or that the persons involved will share their uncertainties and dissuade each other as that each will stiffen the other's determination."

Note, "The Conspiracy Dilemma: Prosecution of Group Crimes or Protection of Individual Defendants," (1948) 62 Harv.L.Rev. 276 at 283–284:

"Several factors, seldom articulated by the courts, seem to underlie this concept of the unique criminality of group action. Basic is the increased danger to the public welfare and safety that exists in the combination of united wills to effect a harmful object, as contrasted with the menace of the criminal purpose of a single individual. Reliance on the co-operation of co-conspirators and the intent to support and aid them in the future increases the likelihood of criminal conduct on the part of individual conspirators. And it is more difficult to guard against the antisocial designs of a group of persons than those of an individual. Thus, the crucial importance of the conspiracy weapon stems from its effectiveness in reaching organized crime. The advantages of division of labor and complex organization characteristic of modern economic society have their counterparts in many forms of criminal activity. Manufacture or importation and distribution of contraband goods, for example, often demands a complicated organization. The interrelations of the parties in schemes to defraud may be highly complex. Except for the conspiracy device, society would be without protection until the criminal object is actually executed or at least sufficiently approached to become indictable as an attempt; and even then often only the actual perpetrator and perhaps his immediate accessories could be reached. Through the conspiracy dragnet, all participants in gang operations, the catspaw and his principal, those who contribute from afar as well as the immediate actors can be punished often before the evil design has fully matured into the criminal act."

Johnson[84] makes the point that if one adopts the proximity test for attempts, an independent inchoate crime of conspiracy makes sense, but if one were adopting the substantial step test, this could easily cover agreements to commit crimes, rendering the law of conspiracy redundant.

As with attempts, a conspiracy, in itself, causes no actual harm. Bearing in mind our discussion of the rationale of the law of attempt, the following questions present themselves:

(1) Do conspiracies pose a "second order" harm—in the sense of posing a threat to security? or

(2) Is the blameworthiness of a conspirator so great as to justify dispensing with the requirement of harm from the basic equation of criminal liability? Or are there (and can there ever be) sufficient utilitarian arguments to justify dispensing with the requirement of harm?

C. Punishment of Conspiracies

Section 3 of the Criminal Law Act 1977 limits the punishment for conspiracy, contrary to section 1 of that Act, to the maximum sentence for the complete crime which the defendants conspired to commit.[85]

R. Cross & A. Ashworth, Cross; The English Sentencing System (3rd ed., 1981), p. 156:

"Conspiracies might, however, be regarded as more serious crimes than attempts. Indeed, at common law it was held in *Verrier* v. *Director of Public Prosecutions* ([1967] 2 A.C. 195) that some conspiracies might call for a greater punishment than could be imposed for the completed offence. Although s.3 of the Criminal Law Act now prohibits courts from exceeding the statutory maximum for the completed offence in conspiracy cases, a court still might wish to visit conspirators with more severe punishment than it would mete out to an individual committing the completed offence, whilst keeping within the statutory maximum. The argument is that the nature of the offence is exceptionally changed by the co-operation of large numbers in its commission, because of the greater chance of the occasioning of alarm and of the use of force. In fraud cases, the co-operation of different people in different places may facilitate both the execution and the concealment of the design. These considerations go to show that any offence, whether inchoate or completed, which is committed by a number of people acting in concert may be viewed as presenting a greater social danger than the same offence committed by an individual. On general deterrent

[84] *Ante* p. 481.
[85] The maximum penalty for a conspiracy to defraud is 10 years imprisonment (Criminal Justice Act 1987, s.12).

grounds the sentence for 'group' offences may therefore be longer. Sentences for rape by gangs are on this account higher than those for rape by an individual."

Callanan v. United States, 364 U.S. 587 (1961) (Supreme Court of the United States):

Frankfurter J.:
"This settled principle derives from the reason of things in dealing with socially reprehensible conduct: collective criminal agreement—partnership in crime—presents a greater potential threat to the public than individual delicts. Concerted action both increases the likelihood that the criminal object will be successfully attained and decreases the probability that the individuals involved will depart from their path of criminality. Group association for criminal purposes often, if not normally, makes possible the attainment of ends more complex than those which one criminal could accomplish. Nor is the danger of a conspiratorial group limited to the particular end towards which it has embarked. Combination in crime makes more likely the commission of crimes unrelated to the original purpose for which the group was formed. In sum, the danger which a conspiracy generates is not confined to the substantive offense which is the immediate aim of the enterprise."

Consider, again, the discussion on the punishment of attempts and the significance of the absence of harm. Are those considerations not equally applicable here? Are they not perhaps even stronger here, as with conspiracy the defendants are further removed from the crime and have not yet crossed the threshold of preparation? Is the so-called "dangerousness of collaboration" sufficient to outweigh all these considerations?

D. The Law

1. Types of conspiracy

At common law a conspiracy was an agreement between two or more persons "to do an unlawful act, or to do a lawful act by unlawful means."[86] Thus it was not necessary to prove that there was an agreement to commit a crime; agreements to commit other "unlawful acts," such as fraud, some torts or corruption of public morals, clearly sufficed. For instance, in *Kamara* v. *D.P.P.*[87] an agreement to commit the tort of trespass to land, if accompanied by an intention to inflict more than merely nominal damage, was held to be a criminal conspiracy. Of course, it was virtually impossible to justify making it a crime to agree to do something that if actually done by one person acting alone would not have been criminal. Accordingly the Criminal Law Act 1977 sought to limit conspiracy primarily to agreements to commit crimes. However, fearing that gaps might be created, and pending a comprehensive review of the law of fraud, obscenity and indecency, section 5 preserved certain common law conspiracies. We are thus left with the rather

---

[86] *Mulcahy* (1868) L.R. 3 H.L. 306.
[87] [1974] A.C. 104.

unsatisfactory situation (hopefully only temporarily) of having two types of conspiracies:

(1) There are agreements to commit a crime. These are termed statutory conspiracies and are governed by the provisions of section 1 of the Criminal Law Act 1977;

(2) There are common law conspiracies governed by the old common law rules. Under section 5 of the Criminal Law Act 1977, two species of common law conspiracy have been preserved:

   (a) *conspiracy to defraud.* Section 5(2) provides that the common law rules continue to apply "so far as relates to conspiracy to defraud."[88] Now many agreements to pursue a dishonest course of conduct will amount to both a crime and a defrauding. Many headaches were caused by the courts trying to work out which type of conspiracy defendants should be charged with in such cases. Fortunately, these problems need not detain us as section 12 of the Criminal Justice Act 1987 now provides that defendants may be charged with either offence in such cases.

   (b) *Conspiracy to corrupt public morals or outrage public decency.* Section 5(3) provides that the common law rules continue to apply to such conspiracies providing the object of the agreement does not amount to a crime.[89] (If it does, the statutory rules of section 1 are applicable). The Law Commission has argued that corrupting public morals and outraging public decency are probably substantive offences at common law.[90] If that view is correct, then agreements to commit such offences are statutory conspiracies.

As the life-expectancy of these common law conspiracies is hopefully short, the ensuing analysis of the law will concentrate on statutory conspiracies, that is, conspiracies to commit a crime.

2. Definition of statutory conspiracy

Criminal Law Act 1977 (as amended by the Criminal Attempts Act 1981)

"s.1(1) Subject to the following provisions of this Part of this Act, if a person agrees with any other person or persons that a course of conduct shall be pursued which, if the agreement is carried out in accordance with their intentions, either—

---

[88] As amended by the Criminal Justice Act 1987.

[89] Section 5(3)(*b*).

[90] Law Com. No. 76, paras. 3.21–3.24 (1976). This was confirmed in a recent case where the defendants, who had displayed earrings made from freeze-dried human foetuses, were convicted of the common law offence of outraging public decency. ([1989] New L.J. 210). See also dicta in *Knuller* v. *D.P.P.* [1973] A.C. 435 to the same effect. This however still leaves open the question whether corrupting public morals is different—and, if so, whether it is an offence.

(a) will necessarily amount to or involve the commission of any offence or offences by one or more of the parties to the agreement, or

(b) would do so but for the existence of facts which render the commission of the offence or any of the offences impossible,

he is guilty of conspiracy to commit the offence or offences in question. [Substituted, as to conspiracies entered into or continuing to exist after August 31, 1981, by Section 5(1) Criminal Attempts Act 1981].

(2) Where liability for any offence may be incurred without knowledge on the part of the person committing it of any particular fact or circumstance necessary for the commission of the offence, a person shall nevertheless not be guilty of conspiracy to commit that offence by virtue of subsection (1) above unless he and at least one other party to the agreement intend or know that that fact or circumstance shall or will exist at the time when the conduct constituting the offence is to take place."

(a) Agreement

There must be an agreement between at least two persons. There must have been a meeting of minds; decisions must have been communicated between the parties.[91]

There must, of course, be at least two parties to the agreement. However, section 2(2)(*a*) provides that a husband and wife cannot be liable for conspiracy, if they are the only parties to the agreement[92]; this is a policy provision aimed at exempting marital confidences from the ambit of the criminal law. The Act also provides that a person cannot be liable for conspiracy if the only other party to the "agreement" is a person under the age of criminal responsibility (section 2(2)(*b*)) or is the intended victim of the offence (section 2(2)(*c*)). It would thus appear that there *can* be liability if the defendant conspired with any other person having a defence (say insanity) other than the above, provided of course, that such person was capable of reaching an *agreement* with the defendant.[93] Where a defendant and others are charged with conspiracy and those others are acquitted, section 5(8) provides that the defendant may nevertheless be convicted "unless under all the circumstances of the case his conviction is inconsistent with the acquittal of the other person or persons in question."[94] This is sensible. There may be evidence admissible against the defendant that he conspired with A and B, but that evidence might not be admissible against A or B. Or it might be clear that he conspired with either A or B, but it is not certain which one it was. A and B must be given the benefit of the doubt and acquitted, but there is no reason why the defendant, whose guilt is beyond doubt, should be offered the same indulgence.[95]

---

[91] *Scott* (1979) 68 Cr.App.R. 164. See generally, Orchard, "Agreement in Criminal Conspiracy" [1974] Crim.L.R. 297 at 335.

[92] This confirms the common law decision of *Mawji* [1957] A.C. 126.

[93] This confirms the common law decision of *Duguid* (1906) 75 L.J. K.B. 470.

[94] This was already the position at common law in relation to separate trials (*D.P.P.* v. *Shannon* [1975] A.C. 717), but reverses the common law position in relation to joint trials (*Thompson* (1851) 16 Q.B. 832; *Coughlan* (1977) 64 Cr.App.R. 11).

[95] See, *Longman and Cribben* (1980) 72 Cr.App.R. 121; *Roberts* [1985] Crim.L.R. 218.

(b) Object of agreement

There must be an agreement that:
   (i)   a course of conduct be pursued
   (ii) which if carried out in accordance with their intentions
   (iii) will necessarily amount to (or involve) a crime.

(i) *Course of conduct be pursued:*

The phrase "course of conduct" here does not refer purely to physical actions, but must be taken to include intended consequences—in short, the plan. This point is best illustrated with an example. Suppose two persons agree to place a bomb under another's car and detonate the bomb so as to kill the owner. The physical course of conduct agreed to, namely, the physical actions of planting the bomb, will not necessarily amount to the crime because the bomb may never go off. But if the *plan* is carried out according to their intentions, the bomb will explode and the owner of the car will be killed. This necessarily amounts to a crime; killing someone in such circumstances is murder.

To say that the agreed course of conduct includes the planned consequences is also a limiting qualification. Only planned consequences can be included within the agreed course of conduct. Thus, as stated in *Siracusa*,[96] an agreement to cause grievous bodily harm is not sufficient to support a charge of conspiracy to murder even though it is sufficient to support a charge of murder itself. The planned course of conduct only extends as far as causing grievous bodily harm. It is further submitted that planned consequences means striven-for consequences. Thus if arson is planned between conspirators who are reckless as to whether anyone is killed during their fire, the death of those persons is not part of their plan. One does not plan for and work towards an event possibly happening. One plans and works towards consequences which one wants. And what of consequences foreseen as virtually certain—so called "oblique intention"? This point remains unresolved but it is submitted that the agreed course of conduct should be interpreted to include such "intended" (albeit not purposively so) consequences. Section 1(1) is ambiguous so it is perhaps better to rest one's case on grounds of principle (the minimal moral difference between the person who hopes for a consequence and the one who foresees it as certain) and expedience (the desirability of having the term "intention" bearing the same meaning throughout the criminal law).

The planned course of conduct also includes (and only includes) *intended or known* surrounding circumstances.[97] Although section 1(2)

---

[96] (1990) 90 Cr.App.R. 340. This case held that although a person smuggling heroin could be convicted of a substantive offence if he thought he was smuggling cannabis, the same was not true on a conspiracy charge: "the essence of the crime of conspiracy was the agreement and, in simple terms, one did not prove an agreement to import heroin by proving an agreement to import cannabis."

[97] Section 1(2). On its actual wording section 1(2) appears to be limited to crimes of strict liability. It must, however, *a fortiori* apply to crimes of full *mens rea*. It would be truly paradoxical if greater *mens rea* were required for conspiracies to commit crimes of strict liability than for other conspiracies.

uses the term "intend or know" it is submitted that "know" here must be interpreted to mean "believe." If parties conspire to handle stolen goods, they can never *know* those goods are stolen—but it should suffice that they *believe* that they are stolen.[98]

(ii) *If carried out in accordance with their intentions*:

What is the position if the parties' intentions are equivocal? For example, they might agree to burgle a house if a window has been left open. The better view here is that the "plan" is a plan to burgle a house (albeit subject to a condition) and if that plan is carried out it will necessarily amount to a crime.

R. v. Reed [1982] Crim.L.R. 819 (Court of Appeal, Criminal Division)

"In the first, A and B agree to drive from London to Edinburgh in a time which can be achieved without exceeding the speed limits, but only if the traffic which they encounter is exceptionally light. Their agreement will not necessarily involve the commission of any offence, even if it is carried out in accordance with their intentions, and they do arrive from London to Edinburgh within the agreed time. Accordingly the agreement does not constitute the offence of statutory conspiracy or indeed of any offence. In the second example, A and B agree to rob a bank, if when they arrive at the bank it seems safe to do so. Their agreement will necessarily involve the commission of the offence of robbery if it is carried out in accordance with their intentions. Accordingly, they are guilty of the statutory offence of conspiracy."

R. v. Jackson [1985] Crim.L.R. 442 (Court of Appeal, Criminal Division)

The appellants agreed to shoot their friend, W, in the leg if he was convicted of a burglary for which he was being tried. They thought this would provide mitigation! W was shot and permanently disabled. The appellants appealed against their conviction for conspiracy to pervert the course of justice on the ground that their agreement did not necessarily involve the commission of a crime, as everything depended on a contingency (W's conviction for burglary) which might not have taken place.

Held, "[P]lanning was taking place for a contingency and if that contingency occurred the conspiracy would necessarily involve the commission of an offence. 'Necessarily' is not to be held to mean that there must inevitably be the carrying out of an offence. It means, if the agreement is carried out in accordance with the plan, there must be the commission of the offence referred to in the conspiracy count."

Appeal dismissed

The plan must be carried out "in accordance with their intentions."

---

[98] Smith and Hogan (4th ed.) p. 221: "One cannot *know* a thing to be so, unless it *is* so. One cannot *know* that a thing will be so, unless it *will be so*. To think one knows is not the same as to know." Thus no matter how much the defendants believe that goods are stolen, they *cannot know* they are stolen, unless they are in fact stolen.

What does this mean? What is the position of a person who agrees to the commission of a crime and agrees perhaps to supply tools for the crime but who thereafter has no interest in what happens and indeed thinks the planned crime is over-ambitious and will never be committed? Or what is the position of a plain-clothes police officer who, with a view to entrapping the others, "agrees" to a plan to commit a crime, but he actually intends to prevent the crime at the last moment? In short, must each conspirator intend that the crime actually be carried out?

R. v. Anderson [1986] A.C. 27 (House of Lords)

The defendant agreed for a fee to supply diamond wire to cut through bars in order to enable another to escape from prison. He claimed that he only intended to supply the wire and then go abroad. He believed the plan could never succeed. He appealed against his conviction for conspiring with others to effect the release of one of them from prison claiming that as he did not intend or expect the plan to be carried out, he lacked the necessary *mens rea* for the offence of conspiracy.

Lord Bridge:
"[I]t is not necessary that more than one of the participants in the agreed course of conduct shall commit a substantive offence. It is, of course, necessary that any party to the agreement shall have assented to play his part in the agreed course of conduct, however innocent in itself, knowing that the part to be played by one or more of the others will amount to or involve the commission of an offence.
. . . The heart of the submission for the appellant is that in order to be convicted of conspiracy to commit a given offence . . . the party charged should not only have agreed that a course of conduct shall be pursued which will necessarily amount to or involve the commission of that offence by himself or one or more other parties to the agreement, but must also be proved himself to have intended that that offence should be committed. Thus, it is submitted here that the appellant's case that he never intended that Andaloussi should be enabled to escape from prison raised an issue to be left to the jury, who should have been directed to convict him only if satisfied that he did so intend. . . .
I am clearly driven by consideration of the diversity of roles which parties may agree to play in criminal conspiracies to reject any construction of the statutory language which would require the prosecution to prove an intention on the part of each conspirator that the criminal offence or offences which will necessarily be committed by one or more of the conspirators if the agreed course of conduct is fully carried out should in fact be committed. A simple example will illustrate the absurdity to which this construction would lead. The proprietor of a car hire firm agrees for a substantial payment to make available a hire car to a gang for use in a robbery and to make false entries in his books relating to the hiring to which he can point if the number of the car is traced back to him in connection with the robbery. Being fully aware of the circumstances of the robbery in which the car is proposed to be used he is plainly a party to the conspiracy to rob. Making his car available for use in the robbery is as much a part of the relevant agreed course of conduct as the robbery itself. Yet, once he has been paid, it will be a matter of complete indifference to him whether the robbery is in fact committed or not. In these days of highly organised crime the most serious statutory conspiracies will frequently involve an elaborate and complex agreed course of conduct in which many will consent to

play necessary but subordinate roles, not involving them in any direct participation in the commission of the offence or offences at the centre of the conspiracy. Parliament cannot have intended that such parties should escape
conviction of conspiracy on the basis that it cannot be proved against them that
they intended that the relevant offence or offences should be committed.

There remains the important question whether a person who has agreed that
a course of conduct will be pursued which, if pursued as agreed, will necessarily
amount to or involve the commission of an offence is guilty of statutory conspiracy irrespective of his intention, and, if not, what is the *mens rea* of the offence. I
have no hesitation in answering the first part of the question in the negative.
There may be many situations in which perfectly respectable citizens, more particularly those concerned with law enforcement, may enter into agreements that
a course of conduct shall be pursued which will involve commission of a crime
without the least intention of playing any part in furtherance of the ostensibly
agreed criminal objective, but rather with the purpose of exposing and frustrating the criminal purpose of the other parties to the agreement. To say this is in
no way to encourage schemes by which police act, directly or through the
agency of informers, as agents provocateurs for the purpose of entrapment. That
is conduct of which the courts have always strongly disapproved. But it may
sometimes happen, as most of us with experience in criminal trials well know,
that a criminal enterprise is well advanced in the course of preparation when it
comes to the notice either of the police or of some honest citizen in such circumstances that the only prospect of exposing and frustrating the criminals is that
some innocent person should play the part of an intending collaborator in the
course of criminal conduct proposed to be pursued. The *mens rea* implicit in the
offence of statutory conspiracy must clearly be such as to recognise the innocence of such a person, notwithstanding that he will, in literal terms, be obliged
to agree that a course of conduct be pursued involving the commission of an
offence.

I have said already, but I repeat to emphasise its importance, that an essential
ingredient in the crime of conspiring to commit a specific offence or offences
under section 1(1) of the Act of 1977 is that the accused should agree that a
course of conduct be pursued which he knows must involve the commission by
one or more of the parties to the agreement of that offence or those offences. But,
beyond the mere fact of agreement, the necessary *mens rea* of the crime is, in my
opinion, established if, and only if, it is shown that the accused, when he
entered into the agreement, intended to play some part in the agreed course of
conduct in furtherance of the criminal purpose which the agreed course of conduct was intended to achieve. Nothing less will suffice; nothing more is
required.

Applying this test to the facts which, for the purposes of the appeal, we must
assume, the appellant, in agreeing that a course of conduct be pursued that
would, if successful, necessarily involve the offence of effecting Andaloussi's
escape from lawful custody, clearly intended, by providing diamond wire to be
smuggled into the prison, to play a part in the agreed course of conduct in furtherance of that criminal objective. Neither the fact that he intended to play no
further part in attempting to effect the escape, nor that he believed the escape to
be impossible, would, if the jury had supposed they might be true, have
afforded him any defence."

Appeal dismissed

One of the major reservations underlying all the inchoate offences is
that no harm (first order) has been caused. How do we justify the invo-

cation of the criminal law? We saw that (apart from arguments of there being a second order harm) the main case for criminalisation was on grounds of blameworthiness. A person who attempts or conspires to commit a crime is just as blameworthy (and, as has been seen, for attempts needs the highest degree of blameworthiness, namely, intention) as the one who commits the full offence. In the light of this it is interesting to note the implications of *Anderson*. A defendant can be guilty of a serious criminal offence when there has been no conduct beyond a bare agreement and where the defendant never intended that the offence be carried out. This seems to be pushing back the threshold of criminal liability rather too far.

(iii) *Necessarily amount to (or involve) a crime:*

We have already examined the meaning of "necessarily." It does not matter whether the actual conduct will in fact amount to a crime. What matters is whether the plan, if successfully carried out, will do so. It therefore follows that it is irrelevant whether the crime is even possible.[99]

What is meant by "amount to or involve the commission of any offence or offences by one or more of the parties to the agreement?" In *Hollinshead*[1] the Court of Appeal held that this meant that one of the parties had to commit the offence as a principal offender. This means that there cannot be a conspiracy to aid and abet an offence.[2]

(b) Draft Criminal Code Bill 1989, (Law Com. No. 177), clause 48:

"(1) A person is guilty of conspiracy to commit an offence or offences if—
- (a) he agrees with another or others that an act or acts shall be done which, if done, will involve the commission of the offence or offences by one or more of the parties to the agreement; and
- (b) he and at least one other party to the agreement intend that the offence or offences shall be committed.

(2) For the purposes of subsection (1) an intention that an offence shall be committed is an intention with respect to all the elements of the offence (other than fault elements), except that recklessness with respect to a circumstance suffices where it suffices for the offence itself."

(c) Impossibility

At common law the House of Lords in *Nock*[3] followed *Haughton* v. *Smith*[4] and held there could be no liability for a conspiracy to commit the impossible. This decision has now been reversed by the amendment to section 1(1) which clearly states that there can be liability even though there exist facts which render the commission of the offence

---

[99] This is confirmed by section 1(1)(*b*) of the Criminal Law Act 1977, as amended by the Criminal Attempts Act (1981). See *post*, pp. 491–492.

[1] [1985] 1 All E.R. 850.

[2] The House of Lords in *Hollinshead* left this point open. See Smith and Hogan (pp. 265–266) for an argument that the House of Lords did effectively hold that there can be no agreement to aid and abet an offence.

[3] [1978] A.C. 979. See C. M. V. Clarkson, (1979) 9 Kingston Law Review 88.

[4] [1975] A.C. 476.

impossible. Thus if two defendants agree to kill X, but unknown to them X is already dead, they can nevertheless still be liable for criminal conspiracy. This provision is, however, limited to statutory conspiracies. The result is somewhat anomalous: there can be liability for a statutory conspiracy to commit the impossible, but no liability for similar common law conspiracies. And again, in relation to statutory conspiracies, the question must be asked: when defendants have done no more than *agree* to commit a crime, and when it is quite impossible in any event for that crime to be committed, are we justified in imposing criminal liability?

(d) Repentance

If a conspirator repents and withdraws immediately after the agreement has been reached, it would appear that he is still guilty of conspiracy.[5] In the light of the material on repentance in the law of attempt,[6] should not a defendant who never gets further than agreeing to commit a crime, and who never does anything in pursuance of that agreement—indeed, who positively disassociates himself from it—be entitled to a defence? Or is the "dangerousness of collaboration" argument sufficient to justify liability in such cases?

(e) Complete offence committed

Even when the substantive offence is actually committed, the parties can nevertheless be charged additionally with conspiracy. However, the courts tend to discourage such a practice unless the prosecution can justify both charges as being in the interests of justice.[7]

IV INCITEMENT

A. Introduction

The crime of incitement[8] is a common law inchoate offence[9] whereby the defendant persuades or encourages another to commit a crime. When tried on indictment[10] it is an offence punishable with a fine and imprisonment at the discretion of the court—thus a greater penalty

---

[5] Martin Wasik, *ante* p. 467 at p. 788; *Barnard* [1980] Crim.L.R. 235.
[6] *Ante*, p. 465.
[7] *Practice Direction (Crime: Conspiracy)* [1977] 1 W.L.R. 537.
[8] Sometimes known as "solicitation," particularly in the United States.
[9] Statute sometimes prohibits certain specific incitements—for example, incitement to racial hatred contrary to section 18(1) of the Public Order Act 1986. These are generally not true inchoate offences in the sense of being steps on the way to the commission of a crime: there is no substantive crime of "racial hatred." See also Incitement to Mutiny Act 1797, s.1; incitement to sedition contrary to section 3 of the Aliens Restriction (Amendment) Act 1919; Incitement to Disaffection Act 1934, ss.1, 2 (T. Young, *Incitement to Disaffection*, 1976); causing disaffection (inciting disaffection amongst members of the police force) contrary to section 53 of the Police Act 1964.
[10] An incitement to commit a summary offence is only triable summarily (Magistrates' Courts Act 1980, s.45(1)) and the defendant cannot be punished to a greater extent than he would have been liable to on summary conviction of the completed offence (Magistrates' Courts Act 1980, s.45(3)).

could be imposed for incitement than for the actual commission of the substantive offence.

B. Rationale and Punishment of Incitement

Wayne R. LaFave and Austin W. Scott, Criminal Law, 2nd ed. (1986) pp. 488–489:

"One view is that a mere solicitation to commit a crime, not accompanied by agreement or action by the person solicited, presents no significant social danger. It is argued, for example, that solicitation is not dangerous because the resisting will of an independent agent is interposed between the solicitor and commission of the crime which is his object. Similarly, it is claimed that the solicitor does not constitute a menace in view of the fact that he has manifested an unwillingness to carry out the criminal scheme himself. There is not the dangerous proximity to success which exists when the crime is actually attempted, for, 'despite the earnestness of the solicitation, the actor is merely engaging in talk which may never be taken seriously.' (1 National Commission of Reform of Federal Criminal Laws, Working Papers 370 (1970)).

On the other hand, it is argued 'that a solicitation is, if anything, more dangerous than a direct attempt, because it may give rise to that cooperation among criminals which is a special hazard. Solicitation may, indeed, be thought of as an attempt to conspire. Moreover, the solicitor, working his will through one or more agents, manifests an approach to crime more intelligent and masterful than the effort of his hireling.' (Wechsler, Jones and Korn, . . . 61 Colum.L.Rev. 571 (1961)). It is noted, for example, that the imposition of liability for criminal solicitation has proved to be an important means by which the leadership of criminal movements may be suppressed.

Without regard to whether it is correct to say that solicitations are more dangerous than attempts, it is fair to conclude that the purposes of the criminal law are well served by inclusion of the crime of solicitation within the substantive criminal law. Providing punishment for solicitation aids in the prevention of the harm which would result should the inducements prove successful, and also aids in protecting the public from being exposed to inducements to commit or join in the commission of crimes. As is true of the law of attempts, the crime of solicitation (a) provides a basis for timely law enforcement intervention to prevent the intended crime, (b) permits the criminal justice process to deal with individuals who have indicated their dangerousness, and (c) avoids inequality of treatment based upon a fortuity (here, withholding of the desired response by the person solicited) beyond the control of the actor.

Objections to making solicitation a crime . . . are sometimes based upon the fear that false charges may readily be brought either out of a misunderstanding as to what the defendant said or for purposes of harassment. This risk is inherent in the punishment of almost all inchoate crimes, although it is perhaps somewhat greater as to the crime of solicitation in that the crime may be committed merely by speaking."

Consider again our earlier discussion of the rationale and punishment of attempts and conspiracies.[11] Bearing in mind that if the person incited agrees to commit the crime there will be a criminal conspiracy and thus incitement amounts to no more than an attempted conspiracy

[11] *Ante* pp. 433–444, 481–484.

(an offence abolished by section 1(4) of the Criminal Attempts Act 1981), can one really justify the existence of the offence of incitement? Such persons clearly have indicated some degree of dangerousness and it is obviously desirable to deter people from encouraging others to commit crime—but unlike attempt, incitors are far removed from the complete crime; their actions are not *manifestly* dangerous; they constitute no "second order" harm—and unlike conspiracy, there is no "dangerousness of combination" argument that can possibly justify the existence of the offence. In short, bearing in mind why the law does not punish guilty intentions alone but insists upon a manifestation of those intentions,[12] is not the crime of incitement pushing back the threshold of criminal liability too far? And even if the crime could be justified, surely for the same reasons, it could *never* be justifiable to impose even the same sentence (let alone a greater one) as for the completed crime.

C. The Law

1. Actus reus

The *actus reus* of the crime of incitement is the act of persuading, encouraging or commanding another to commit a crime. In *Fitzmaurice*[13] it was held that the necessary "element of persuasion" was satisfied by a "suggestion, proposal or request [that] was accompanied by an implied promise of reward." And in *R.R.B.* v. *Applin*[14] Lord Denning stated that: "a person may 'incite' another to do an act by threatening or by pressure, as well as by persuasion." The incitement can take any form (words or deeds). It may be addressed to a particular person or group of persons or to the public at large. Thus in *Most*[15] it was held that publishing an article in a newspaper urging revolutionaries throughout the world to assassinate their Heads of State would be incitement to commit murder. The solicitation must be communicated to the person being incited, but if the communication fails (*e.g.* letter failing to reach incitee) there can be liability for attempted incitement.[16]

If the person incited agrees to commit the crime, both are liable for conspiracy. If the incitee actually commits the crime, the incitor will be liable as an accessory to the complete offence.

2. Mens Rea

The incitor must intend that as a result of his persuasion, the incitee will bring about the crime. But if the incitor knows that the incitee has no *mens rea* (assuming the complete crime requires *mens rea*) there can be no incitement; he is not inciting a crime.[17] If the incitee actually com-

---

[12] *Ante* pp. 103–104.
[13] [1983] 1 All E.R. 189, 192.
[14] [1973] 1 Q.B. 815, 825; *Evans* [1986] Crim.L.R. 470.
[15] (1881) 7 Q.B.D. 244. *Cf. Invicta Plastics* v. *Clare* [1976] R.T.R. 251.
[16] *Chelmsford Justices, Exp. Amos* [1973] Crim.L.R. 437.
[17] *Curr* [1968] 2 Q.B. 944. *Cf. Whitehouse* [1977] Q.B. 868.

mitted the crime, the incitor could be liable as a principal offender acting through an innocent agent.[18]

3. Draft Criminal Code

Draft Criminal Code Bill 1989 (Law Com. No. 177), clause 47:

(1) A person is guilty of incitement to commit an offence or offences if—
  (a) he incites another to do or cause to be done an act or acts which, if done, will involve the commission of the offence or offences by the other; and
  (b) he intends or believes that the other, if he acts as incited, shall or will do so with the fault required for the offence or offences.

4. Impossibility

In *McDonough*[19] it was held that there could be liability for an incitement to commit the impossible. This was approved *obiter* by the House of Lords in *Nock*.[20] However, doubt has now been cast on the correctness of this proposition.

R. v. Fitzmaurice [1983] Q.B. 1083 (Court of Appeal, Criminal Division)

The appellant was asked by his father to find someone to rob a woman on her way to a bank by snatching wages from her. The appellant, believing the robbery was to take place, approached B, who was unemployed and in need of money, and encouraged him to take part in the proposed robbery. In fact the proposed robbery was a fiction invented by the father to enable him to collect reward money from the police for providing false information about a false robbery. The appellant was convicted of inciting B to commit robbery by robbing a woman near the bank. He appealed against the conviction, contending that at common law incitement to commit an offence could not be committed where it was impossible to commit the offence incited, and that, since the proposed robbery of the woman was fictitious, it was impossible to commit that robbery.

Neill J.:
"It is to be observed that the omission of the crime of incitement from the Criminal Attempts Act 1981, followed the recommendations of the Law Commission in their Report published in 1980 (Law Com no. 102). . . . The Law Commission explained the omission of incitement from the draft bill on the basis that in their view the House of Lords in *DPP* v. *Nock* was prepared to distinguish the law relating to incitement from that relating to attempts: see paras 4.2 to 4.4 We have had to give careful attention to these paragraphs in the Law Commission's Report. . . .
We have come to the conclusion that, . . . Lord Scarman's speech [in *Nock*] does not support the proposition that cases of incitement are to be treated quite differently at common law from cases of attempt or conspiracy. . . . The explanation of *McDonough's* case, as it seems to us, is that though there may have been no stolen goods or no goods at all which were available to be received at

---

[18] *Post* p. 502.
[19] (1962) 47 Cr.App.R. 37.
[20] [1978] A.C. 979.

the time of the incitement, the offence of incitement to receive stolen goods could nevertheless be proved because it was not impossible that at the relevant time in the future the necessary goods would be there.

In our view, therefore, the right approach in a case of incitement is the same as that which was underlined by Lord Scarman in *DPP* v. *Nock* when he considered the offence of conspiracy. In every case it is necessary to analyse the evidence with care to decide the precise offence which the defendant is alleged to have incited . . .

In our view . . . [this is] the correct approach at common law to any inchoate offence. It is necessary in every case to decide on the evidence what was the course of conduct which was (as the case may be) incited or agreed or attempted. In some cases the evidence may establish that the persuasion by the inciter was in quite general terms whereas the subsequent agreement of the conspirators was directed to a specific crime and a specific target. In such cases where the committal of the specific offence is shown to be impossible it may be quite logical for the inciter to be convicted even though the alleged conspirators (if not caught by s.5 of the Criminal Attempts Act 1981) may be acquitted. On the other hand, if B and C agree to kill D, and A standing beside B and C, though not intending to take any active part whatever in the crime, encourages them to do so, we can see no satisfactory reason, if it turns out later that D was already dead, why A should be convicted of incitement to murder whereas B and C at common law would be entitled to an acquittal on a charge of conspiracy. The crucial question is to establish on the evidence the course of conduct which the alleged inciter was encouraging.

We return to the facts of the instant case. Counsel for the appellant submitted that the 'crime' which Bonham and the two Browns were being encouraged to commit was a mere charade. The appellant's father was not planning a real robbery at all and therefore the appellant could not be found guilty of inciting the three men to commit it. In our judgment, however, the answer to counsel's argument is to be found in the facts which the Crown proved against the appellant. As was made clear by counsel on behalf of the Crown, the case against the appellant was based on the steps he took to recruit Bonham. At that stage the appellant believed that there was to be a wage snatch and he was encouraging Bonham to take part in it. As counsel put it: 'The appellant thought he was recruiting for a robbery not for a charade.' It is to be remembered that the particulars of offence in the indictment included the words 'by robbing a woman at Bow.' By no stretch of the imagination was that an impossible offence to carry out and it was that offence which the appellant was inciting Bonham to commit.

For these reasons, therefore, we are satisfied that the appellant was rightly convicted. The appeal is dismissed."

Appeal dismissed

It is ironic (to put it mildly) that so soon after the Criminal Attempts Act 1981 declared that there could be liability for attempt or conspiracy to commit the impossible, this decision should hold that in some cases there would be no liability for incitement to commit the impossible. The irony is heightened by recalling that the reason incitement was not included in the Criminal Attempts Act 1981 was because it was assumed that *McDonough* (as approved in *Nock*) had already clearly established that there could be liability in such cases.

We are thus left in the appalling situation that there can be liability for attempting the impossible and for statutory conspiracies to commit the impossible—but there can be no liability in such situations[21] for common law conspiracies or incitement. Such diversity of approach is indefensible.

V. PRECURSOR OFFENCES

R. A. Duff, "Intentions Legal and Philosophical" (1989) Oxford J. of L.S. 76, at p. 86:

"What harms should the criminal law aim to prevent? Death, bodily injury and the loss of property may seem to be three obvious 'primary harms' (each primary harm will generate a range of 'secondary harms,' which take their character as harms from their relation to a primary harm; if death is a primary harm, then being subjected to the threat, risk or fear of death is a secondary and derivative harm); . . .

Though these harms are initially identified without reference to human actions as their causes, the criminal law, as a set of sanction-backed prohibitions, can help to prevent them by prohibiting and thus preventing actions which cause them. It can do this in various ways: by directly prohibiting actions which cause such harms ('killing,' 'wounding and causing greivous bodily harm,' 'damaging or destroying property' or 'depriving another of his property'); by prohibiting actions which are likely to cause such harms, under descriptions which refer directly to those harms ('attempting to kill'; 'reckless driving,' defined in terms of the creation of an 'obvious and serious risk of causing physical injury'; or 'causing danger to the lieges by culpable recklessness'); by prohibiting conduct which is likely to cause such harms, but under descriptions which make no *direct* reference to those harms ('driving with excess alcohol in the blood,' or offences under s.19 and s.20 of the Firearms Act 1968). For our present purposes, however, we may focus on prohibitions which refer directly to some primary harm, and take homicide as our main example."

The term "precursor offence" is used here to describe the latter type of criminal offence. They are offences that are complete in themselves and not dependent upon proof that any further offence was intended. Yet the main rationale for penalising such conduct is similar to that for the inchoate offences. They are usually conceived of as being steps to the commission of further offences. People who carry offensive weapons in public places could well use those weapons. As Bazelon J. reasoned in *Benton* v. *United States*,[22] such possession gives "rise to sinister implications."

English law abounds with a wide variety of such offences. There are many offences of possessing prohibited articles, such as possessing explosives,[23] firearms,[24] or counterfeiting tools.[25] The object of the legislation prohibiting such possession is "frequently to prevent the articles

---

[21] As explained in *Nock* and *Fitzmaurice*, which only apply to "the most complete impossibility" (Glanville Williams, *Textbook*, p. 440).

[22] 232 F.2d 341 at 344–345 (D.C Cir. 1956).

[23] Explosive Substances Act 1883, s.4(1).

[24] Firearms Act 1968, ss.16–22.

[25] Forgery and Counterfeiting Act 1981, s.17.

being used for criminal purposes."[26] Possession of such goods *may* be totally innocent in reality but it nevertheless gives rise to "sinister implications." The Criminal Attempts Act 1981, s.9, creates the new offence of interfering with vehicles; such conduct again has "sinister implications" as being indicative that theft or a similar offence is likely to be committed.

In the United States many states have general offences of "reckless endangerment." Section 211.2 of the Model Penal Code provides the following definition of such an offence:

"A person commits a misdemeanour if he recklessly engages in conduct which places or may place another person in danger of death or serious bodily injury. Recklessness and danger shall be presumed where a person knowingly points a firearm at or in the direction of another, whether or not the actor believed the firearm to be loaded."

English law has no such general counterpart, preferring to focus instead on specific areas of risk-creation, such as reckless driving[27] or criminal damage "intending . . . or being reckless as to whether the life of another would be thereby endangered."[28] Further, acts of reckless endangerment can often be punished for what they are in reality; the defendant can be convicted for a precursor offence such as unlawful possession of a firearm. For instance, in *Pennifold and Naylor*[29] the defendants toured a residential area with a ·22 rifle, shooting into lighted rooms; no-one was injured. They were convicted of a number of offences, mainly relating to possession of a firearm. The trial judge imposed a sentence of 10 years imprisonment on one of the defendants. The Court of Appeal confirmed that this was "a reckless and disgraceful episode and someone might have been killed," but for other reasons reduced the sentence to three years.[30]

In evaluating these precursor offences it is important to remember that, unlike the inchoate offences, they are all complete crimes in themselves, each carrying their own penalty. Indeed, if they are indictable offences, there may be liability for attempting to commit them—or for conspiracy or incitement. Can one ever justify liability for an inchoate offence, when the offence-in-chief is itself only a precursor offence?

Precursor offences are too varied to be susceptible to any generalised justification and analysis. Basically whether such conduct ought to be

---

[26] Glanville Williams, *Textbook*, p. 446.

[27] Road Traffic Act 1988, s.2.

[28] Criminal Damage Act 1971, s.1(2). See also Explosive Substances Act 1883, s.2 (offence to cause an explosion likely to endanger life or property). For a list of offences under the Offences Against the Person Act 1861 involving danger to life or bodily harm, see Criminal Law Revision Committee, 14th Report, *Offences Against the Person*, Cmnd. 7844, (1980) paras. 192–214. See generally, K. J. M. Smith, [1983] Crim.L.R. 127.

[29] [1974] Crim.L.R. 130.

[30] It is interesting, in the light of our analysis of the importance of harm being caused, that the Court of Appeal added that "if someone had been killed a sentence approaching 10 years might have had to be considered." Presumably in such a case the defendant would have been facing charges of, at least, manslaughter.

criminal falls to be determined by the criteria already discussed.[31] However, for the sake of completeness, let us consider one such precursor offence, namely, possession of a firearm.

Under section 1 of the Firearms Act 1968 it is an offence to purchase, acquire or possess any firearm or ammunition without a firearms certificate. This offence is punishable by a maximum of three years imprisonment.[32] Bearing in mind the basic equation of blame plus harm equals criminal liability, how do we justify the existence of such an offence? It is worth recalling that "harm" does not necessarily bear its lay-meaning of injury to person or property. At its broadest, a harm is a violation of some interest of a person or society. Now what interest is being violated by a defendant who unlawfully possesses a firearm, but does not use it? It could be argued that such possession violates others' interests in security and freedom from alarm similar to the "second order" harms caused by attempts. But, the sceptic might retort: surely social disruption and alarm only occur when the defendant threatens or plans to use that firearm in an unauthorised manner? However, as Gross states:

> "[S]ome impairment of collective welfare [may constitute a harm].
> Social life, particularly in the complex form of civilised societies,
> creates many dependencies among members of a community. The
> welfare of each member depends upon the exercise of restraint and
> precaution by others in the pursuit of their legitimate activities, as
> well as upon co-operation toward certain common objectives. These
> matters of collective welfare involve many kinds of interests that may
> be said to be possessed by the community."[33]

On this basis in our society today, and given the great dangerousness of firearms, we all owe a duty of "restraint and precaution" not to possess firearms unlawfully. Society has a vested interest in controlling such possession. Unauthorised possession therefore infringes society's interests and constitutes "a harm." Further, it is a harm deserving the sanctions of the criminal law on grounds similar to those enunciated by Packer that "we make it an offense to possess tools specially adapted for burglary so that we may reduce the incidence of burglary, and thereby reduce the incidence of further offenses, such as larceny, robbery, rape, and even murder."[34] By prohibiting the unlawful possession of firearms, we hope to reduce the incidence of their unlawful use. Of course, such possession is a lesser harm than the actual unauthorised *use* of such weapons or the infliction of injury thereby; it therefore deserves a lesser punishment. But such possession is in itself a harm, and one for which the imposition of criminal liability can be justified.

---

[31] *Ante*, pp. 77–95.

[32] Firearms Act 1968, Sched. 6, Pt. I. If the offence is committed in an aggravated form (s.4(4)) it is punishable by a maximum of five years imprisonment.

[33] *A Theory of Criminal Justice*, p. 120.

[34] *Ante*, p. 90.

But what about the blameworthiness element in the equation of criminal liability?

R. v. Hussain (1981) 47 Cr.App.R. 143 (Court of Appeal, Criminal Division)

The defendant possessed an eight inch metal tube with a striker pin activated by a spring, capable of firing ·32 cartridges. He was charged with contravening section 1(1) of the Firearms Act 1968, in that he did not have a firearm certificate in respect of the article. He claimed that it was a toy used by his son. At the Crown Court the judge directed the jury that if the article was proved by the prosecution to be a firearm then that was sufficient for the defendant to be guilty of the offence, regardless of his state of mind. The defendant was convicted and was fined £100. He appealed against conviction on the ground that the prosecution were required to prove that a person knew the nature of an article in order for there to be a successful prosecution under section 1 of the Firearms Act 1968.

Everleigh L.J.:
"Section 1(1) . . . makes no reference to the state of knowledge of the accused. It is drafted in absolute terms and can be contrasted with other sections of the Act where the accused's state of mind is specifically referred to . . .
. . . In the present case the prosecution proved that the appellant knowingly had in his possession an article which was in fact a lethal weapon, in other words a firearm."

Appeal dismissed[35]

Whether punishment in such a case can ever be justified raises the arguments for and against strict liability—arguments already considered.[36] But surely, quite apart from such views (which would tend to support the conclusion that there ought to be no liability in such a case in the absence of blame), does not the fact that the possession of the firearm was "innocent" indicate that such possession does not give rise to "sinister implications" and that therefore no societal interest is being infringed? Precursor offences are commonly justified on the basis that they "facilitate early intervention to prevent the occurrence of substantive harm; and . . . [they] offer weighty evidence of the socially dangerous disposition of the actor."[37] Such arguments are surely inapplicable to defendants such as Hussain.

---

[35] See also *Howells* [1977] Q.B. 614 where the defendant was convicted of possessing a firearm despite his honest and reasonable belief that the firearm was an antique (s.58(2) exempts antique firearms possessed as a curiosity or ornament from the operation of the Act).
[36] *Ante*, pp. 215–223.
[37] K. J. M. Smith, *ante* n. 28.

CHAPTER 6

PARTIES TO CRIME

I. INTRODUCTION

So far in our analysis of the criminal law we have been able to assume that only one defendant is involved—and we have considered his liability for acting alone. This may well be the case but it is also very likely that at some stage either in the planning or commission of the crime that other persons have become involved.[1] They may have supplied tools, information, advice, kept a look-out or perhaps, say, held the bank staff at bay with a shot-gun. We will consider what the responsibility (if any) of such "helpers" is at law. We will then examine the question of whether the law has adopted the right approach towards their liability and punishment.

II. THE TYPES OF ACCOMPLICES

The term accomplices covers all parties to crime, from the defendant who fires a gun, to the shopkeeper who sold it to him.[2] In order to assess the relative responsibility of these accomplices, however, a distinction needs to be drawn between such defendants.[3] It is customary to speak of the defendant who fires the gun as the principal. Others who help in some way towards the commission of the crime may be termed secondary parties, or accessories.[4]

---

[1] Official statistics, however, do not break down participation in crime in this way, so accurate figures are impossible. Criminological studies, however, support the view that many offenders do act in concert. See for example, J. Baldwin, A. E. Bottoms, *The Urban Criminal* (1976) pp. 140–142, and Frances Heidensohn, *Crime and Society* (1989) for a useful review of sub-cultural/gang studies.

[2] Subject, of course, to *mens rea* considerations.

[3] Whilst, as we shall see, the distinction is not necessary from the point of view of punishment, other reasons for distinguishing between parties remain: see *post* p. 502.

[4] Until 1967 principals were known as principals in the first degree and secondary parties as principals in the second degree if they were present at the crime and accessories if they were not. The Criminal Law Act of that year effectively abolished the need for that distinction to be drawn.

A. Principal Offenders

Wayne R. LaFave and Austin W. Scott, Criminal Law (2nd Ed.), p. 569:

"A principal . . . may simply be defined as the criminal actor. He is the one who, with the requisite mental state, engages in the act or omission . . . which causes the criminal result. . . . One who uses an intermediary to commit a crime is not ordinarily a principal . . . it is otherwise, however, when the crime is accomplished by the use of an innocent or irresponsible agent, as where the defendant causes a child, or mentally incompetent or one without a criminal state of mind (most likely because the defendant has misled or withheld facts from him) to engage in conduct. In such a case the intermediary is regarded as a mere instrument and the originating actor is the principal. . . . The principal is accountable for the acts or omissions of the innocent agent or irresponsible person, and the principal's liability is determined on the basis of that conduct and the principal's own mental state. Thus, if A with intent to bring about B's death, causes C (a child) to take B's life, A is guilty of . . . murder. . . . There can be more than one principal. . . . This occurs when more than one actor participates in the criminal offence. Thus, when one man beats a victim and another shoots him, both may be principals . . . to murder. . . .

Although it has been said that a principal. . . . must be present at the commission of the offence, this is not literally so. He may be 'constructively' present when some instrument which he left or guided caused the criminal result. Thus, when an actor leaves poison for another who later drinks it, he is a . . . principal, as is the person whose unwitting agent acts for him in his absence."

B. Secondary Parties

The liability of such parties is governed by section 8 of the Accessories and Abettors Act 1861:

"whosoever shall aid, abet, counsel or procure the commission of any indictable offence . . . shall be liable to be tried, indicted and punished as a principal offender."[5]

English law, therefore, proceeds on the basis that secondary parties may be as blameworthy as the principal offender. We will discuss the rationale and implications of this approach later but, for the moment, we may consider whether the drawing of any distinction between principal and secondary parties is necessary, given that the judicial process increasingly treats them similarly and that they may be punished to a similar extent.

The main remaining distinction is that strict liability does not extend to accessories; even if the principal can be convicted without proof of *mens rea*, this does not extend to those who assist him.[6] Moreover, there does have to be a principal (even though he may be

---

[5] As amended by the Criminal Law Act 1977, Sched. 12.
[6] *Callow* v. *Tillstone* (1900) 8 L.T. 411.

acquitted for some reason special to himself) in order for there to be an accessory.[7]

Given then that the Accessories and Abettors Act does not abolish the need for the distinction between principals and secondary parties, we must examine the meaning of the terms "aid, abet, counsel or procure" used in section 8. To facilitate this examination some preliminary points may be made.

(i) Judges have made it clear that whenever possible the words of section 8 must be given their "ordinary" meaning.[8]
(ii) The prosecution in any case may charge the secondary party in language which embraces all four terms.[9]
(iii) The terms aiding and abetting tend to be applied when the defendant is present at the scene of the crime, and counselling or procuring when he is absent.

It must be stressed, however, that confusion exists as to whether any real distinction can be drawn between the terms in section 8. Nevertheless, for clarity of exposition and because some judges do defend the distinction, we shall briefly examine separately aiding and abetting, counselling and procuring.

1. Aiding and abetting

There is judicial and academic disagreement as to whether these terms are to be given different meanings or whether they are to be treated as indistinguishable. There is some strength to the former view—that "aiding" more naturally relates to the activity of someone who assists the principal to commit the offence and that "abet" describes activities such as incitement and encouragement. However, sheer weight of repetition of these words in tandem (if nothing more meritorious) lends support to the view that there is nothing to choose between them.[10]

(i) *Presence at crime*

The minimum condition for liability is presence (broadly interpreted so as to include, for instance, the look-out man standing outside[11]) at the scene of the crime, but further conditions must be satisfied before the defendant can be held responsible for the crime.

---

[7] But *post* n. 9 if there *is* evidence against both of them, it is immaterial that it is not possible to identify which was the principal and which the secondary party. It has been made clear in *Dunnington* [1984] Q.B. 472 that one further possible basis of distinction does not exist; just as a principal can attempt to commit a crime, so too can accessories be charged with the crime of attempt. There is, however, no such crime as attempting to aid, abet, counsel or procure: Criminal Attempts Act 1981, s.1(4)(*b*). See also *Hampshire* v. *Mace* [1988] Crim.L.R. 752.

[8] *Attorney-General's Reference (No. 1 of 1975)* [1975] Q.B. 773; *post* p. 507.

[9] He may even in appropriate cases be charged with committing the crime rather than aiding, etc. This avoids prosecution problems where uncertainty exists as to who the principal is. *R.* v. *Forman and Ford* [1988] Crim.L.R. 677.

[10] This is the view also of Lords Morris of Borth-y-Gest and Simon of Glaisdale in *D.P.P.* v. *Lynch* [1975] A.C. 653 and Devlin J. in *N.C.B.* v. *Gamble* [1959] 1 Q.B. 11. It contradicts the view expressed by Lord Widgery C.J. in *Att.-Gen.'s Ref. (No. 1 of 1975)* [1975] Q.B. 773, *post* p. 507.

[11] *Betts and Ridley* (1930) 22 Cr.App.R. 148.

R. v. Clarkson (1971) 55 Cr.App.R. 445 (Courts-Martial Appeal Court)

The defendant was convicted of aiding and abetting the rape of a woman in an army barracks. He and another defendant, Carroll, appealed.

Megaw L.J.:
"[T]he presence of those two appellants in the room where the offence was taking place was not accidental in any sense and it was not by chance, unconnected with the crime, that they were there. Let it be accepted that they entered the room when the crime was committed because of what they had heard, which indicated that a woman was being raped, and they remained there.

R. v. *Coney* (1882) 8 Q.B.D. 534 decides that non-accidental presence at the scene of the crime is not conclusive of aiding and abetting. . . .

What has to be proved is stated by Hawkins J. in a well-known passage in his judgment in *Coney* at p. 557 of the report. What he said was this:

' . . . In my opinion, to constitute an aider and abettor some active steps must be taken by word, or action with the intent to instigate the principal, or principals. Encouragement does not of necessity amount to aiding and abetting, it may be intentional or unintentional, a man may unwittingly encourage another in fact by his presence, by misinterpreted words, or gestures, or by his silence, or non-interference or he may encourage intentionally by expressions, or gestures, or actions intended to signify approval. In the latter case he aids and abets, in the former he does not. It is no criminal offence to stand by, a mere passive spectator of a crime, even of a murder. Non-interference to prevent a crime is not itself a crime. But the fact that a person was voluntarily and purposely present witnessing the commission of a crime, and offered no opposition to it, though he might reasonably be expected to prevent and had the power so to do, or at least to express his dissent, might under some circumstances, afford cogent evidence upon which a jury would be justified in finding that he wilfully encouraged and so aided and abetted. But it would be purely a question for the jury whether he did so or not.'

It is not enough, then, that the presence of the accused person has, in fact, given encouragement. It must be proved that he intended to give encouragement; that he *wilfully* encouraged. In a case such as the present, more than in many other cases where aiding and abetting is alleged, it was essential that that element should be stressed; for there was here at least the possibility that a drunken man with his self-discipline loosened by drink, being aware that a woman was being raped, might be attracted to the scene and might stay on the scene in the capacity of what is known as a voyeur; and, while his presence and the presence of others might in fact encourage the rapers or discourage the victim, he, himself, enjoying the scene or at least standing by assenting, might not intend that his presence should offer encouragement to rapers and would-be rapers or discouragement to the victim; he might not realise that he was giving encouragement; so that, while encouragement there might be, it would not be a case in which, to use the words of Hawkins J., the accused person 'wilfully encouraged.'

A further point is emphasized in passages in the judgment of the Court of Criminal Appeal in *Allan* [1965] 1 Q.B. 130, at 135 and 138. That was a case concerned with participation in an affray. On . . . page 135 . . . the Court said this:

'In effect, it amounts to this: that the judge thereby directed the jury that they were duty bound to convict an accused who was proved to have been present and witnessing an affray, if it was also proved that he nursed an intention to join in if help was needed by the side he favoured and this notwithstanding that he did nothing by words or deeds to evince his intention and outwardly played the role of a purely passive spectator. It was said that, if that direction is right, where A and B behave themselves to all outward appearances in an exactly similar manner, but it be proved that A had the intention to participate if needs be, whereas B had no such intention, then A must be convicted of being a principal in the second degree to the affray, whereas B should be acquitted. To do that, it is objected, would be to convict A on his thoughts, even though they found no reflection in his action.' . . .

From that it follows that mere intention is not in itself enough. There must be an intention to encourage; and there must also be encouragement in fact in cases such as the present case. . . . "

Appeal allowed[12]

George P. Fletcher, Rethinking Criminal Law (1978), pp. 678–679:

"The difficult problem is whether intended encouragement at the scene of the crime must actually have a psychological effect on the perpetrator. If the perpetrator does not know the intended encouragement, can the would-be accessory still be liable on a theory of attempted aid? . . .

The Model Penal Code declares that 'attempted aid' is sufficient for liability as an accomplice. . . . It is not difficult to reconstruct the reasoning that led to the Model Penal Code's recommendation. The premise is that actually aiding the perpetrator is a harmful consequence of the 'accessory's' act. . . . As the Code endorses liability for all impossible attempts . . . there is no reason why it should not dispense with the element of harm in cases of aiding and abetting. After all, whether the aid is actually rendered is fortuitous; the actor is equally culpable and his dangerousness is equally great if the perpetrator never receives the aid."

In such cases is there a violation of an interest that merits punishment?

Exceptionally, presence without intended and actual encouragement may give rise to liability if the defendant has a right to control the actions of the principal offender: if, for instance, the owner of a vehicle sits in the passenger seat and does nothing whilst the defendant behind the wheel drives recklessly, his omission may inculpate him.[13] Perhaps because visions of owners grabbing the steering wheel from the reckless driver (and exacerbating the situation) arose before the judges' eyes, the rule of control being the legal equivalent of actual encouragement is now regarded as *evidence* only that the owner may have encouraged the commission of the crime.[14] This principle is retained in the Draft Criminal Code: "Assistance or encouragement includes assistance or encouragement arising from a failure by a person to take reasonable steps to exercise any authority or to discharge any duty he has to control the relevant acts of the principal in order to prevent the commission of the offence."[15]

---

[12] See also R. v. *Bland* [1988] Crim.L.R. 41.

[13] *Du Cros* v. *Lambourne* [1907] 1 K.B. 40; *cf. Harris* [1964] Crim.L.R. 54 where the supervisor of a learner-driver was convicted as accessory to the learner-driver's traffic offences, for knowingly failing to take steps to stop them.

[14] *Cassady* v. *Reg. Morris* [1975] R.T.R. 470. *R.* v. *Forman and Ford* [1988] Crim.L.R. 677.

[15] Clause 27(3), (Law Com. No. 177), (1989).

(ii) *Participation pursuant to a joint unlawful enterprise*

Where there is a shared joint enterprise, each member of the group assumes responsibility for the actions of other members in that group. However, one is only a "member of a group" if one is acting in accordance with some joint "plan" or joint common enterprise. If one of the parties departs completely from the concerted action of the common design, the other parties are no longer responsible for his actions. It is as if some enthusiastic (and foolhardy) reporter were to stop the defendants as they were about to put their plan into action and question them as to what they intended to do and what they thought might happen in the course of the crime. For example, in *Davies* v. *D.P.P.*[16] a gang of boys went to Clapham Common to engage in a fist fight. It was held that if one of them produced a gun and shot another, the remaining boys would not be liable as the action of shooting was beyond the scope of the joint unlawful enterprise. If our journalist had asked the boys what their plan was they would have replied that they were going to have a fist fight. They would of course be responsible for all consequences flowing from actions within the scope of the joint unlawful enterprise. Thus, for example, if the victim had died from a fist blow, the others would all be liable.[17] But there can be no liability for the actions of another totally removed from the plan. To produce a gun in these circumstances is effectively the act of a "stranger"—and we cannot be held responsible for the unagreed acts of strangers. This was confirmed in *Anderson and Morris*:

"Where two persons embark on a joint enterprise, each is liable for the acts done in pursuance of that joint enterprise, that that includes liability for unusual consequences if they arise from the execution of the agreed joint enterprise but (and this is the crux of the matter) that, if one of the adventurers goes beyond what has been tacitly agreed as part of the common enterprise, his co-adventurer is not liable for the consequences of that unauthorised act. Finally . . . it is for the jury in every case to decide whether what was done was part of the joint enterprise, or went beyond it and was in fact an act unauthorised by that joint enterprise. . . . "

2. Counselling

Unlike aiding and abetting, the terms counselling and procuring may have distinct and separate meanings. Counselling normally refers to help given before the commission of a crime that may take the form of advice, information, encouragement or the supply of equipment etc. The form of help given is not crucial and may, in fact, be fairly minimal. The question that does arise in this context is whether there has to be any causal connection between the help given and the principal offence.

---

[16] [1954] A.C. 378.
[17] The exact extent of their liability depends on their *mens rea*. See *post*, p. 510.

R. v. Calhaem [1985] 1 Q.B. 808 (Court of Appeal, Criminal Division)

The defendant, Mrs. Calhaem, was infatuated with her solicitor. She was charged with the murder of a woman who was having an affair with her solicitor. She had instructed one Zajac to commit the murder. He pleaded guilty to the murder but said in evidence that up to the point when he went berserk and killed the woman, he had come to a decision not to go through with the plan. The defendant appealed against her conviction for murder on the basis that counselling required a substantial causal connection between the acts of the counsellor and the commission of the offence and that none existed on the facts.

Parker L.J.:
"We must therefore approach the question raised on the basis that we should give to the word 'counsel' its ordinary meaning, which is as the judge said, 'advise,' 'solicit,' or something of that sort. There is no implication in the word itself that there should be any causal connection between the counselling and the offence. It is true that, unlike the offence of incitement at common law, the actual offence must have been committed and by the person counselled. To this extent there must clearly be, first, contact between the parties, and secondly, a connection between the counselling and the murder. Equally, the act done must, we think, be done within the scope of the authority or advice, and not, for example, accidentally when the mind of the final murderer did not go with his actions. For example, if the principal offender happened to be involved in a football riot in the course of which he laid about him with a weapon of some sort and killed someone, who, unknown to him, was the person whom he had been counselled to kill, he would not, in our view, have been acting within the scope of his authority; he would have been acting entirely outside it, albeit what he had done was what he had been counselled to do.

We see, however, no need to import anything further into the meaning of the word. . . . "

Appeal dismissed

3. Procuring

Attorney-General's Reference (No. 1 of 1975) [1975] Q.B. 773 (Court of Appeal, Criminal Division)

The defendant surreptitiously laced a friend's drinks with double measures of spirits when he knew his friend would be driving home. He was charged with aiding, abetting, counselling and procuring the offence of driving with an excess quantity of alcohol in the blood under section 6(1) of the Road Traffic Act 1972. The reference concerned the question of whether there had to be a shared intention between the parties or encouragement of the offence.

Lord Widgery C.J.:
"Of course it is the fact in the great majority of instances where a secondary party is sought to be convicted of an offence there has been a contact between the principal offender and the secondary party. Aiding and abetting almost inevitably involves a situation in which the secondary party and the main offender are together at some stage discussing the plans which they may be making in respect of the alleged offence, and are in contact so that each knows what is passing through the mind of the other.

In the same way it seems to us that a person, who counsels the commission of a crime by another, almost inevitably comes to a moment when he is in contact with that other, when he is discussing the offence with that other and when, to use the words of the statute, he counsels the other to commit the offence.

The fact that so often the relationship between the secondary party and the principal will be such that there is a meeting of minds between them caused the trial judge in the case from which this reference is derived to think that this was really an essential feature of proving or establishing the guilt of the secondary party and, as we understand his judgment, he took the view that in the absence of some sort of meeting of minds, some sort of mental link between the secondary party and the principal, there could be no aiding, abetting or counselling of the offence within the meaning of the section.

So far as aiding, abetting and counselling is concerned we would go a long way with that conclusion. It may very well be, as I said a moment ago, difficult to think of a case of aiding, abetting or counselling when the parties have not met and have not discussed in some respects the terms of the offence which they have in mind. But we do not see why a similar principle should apply to procuring. We approach section 8 of the Act of 1861 on the basis that the words should be given their ordinary meaning, if possible. We approach the section on the basis also that if four words are employed here, 'aid, abet, counsel or procure,' the probability is that there is a difference between each of those four words and the other three, because, if there were no such difference, then Parliament would be wasting time in using four words where two or three would do. Thus, in deciding whether that which is assumed to be done under our reference was a criminal offence we approach the section on the footing that each word must be given its ordinary meaning.

To procure means to produce by endeavour. You procure a thing by setting out to see that it happens and taking the appropriate steps to produce that happening. We think that there are plenty of instances in which a person may be said to procure the commission of a crime by another even though there is no sort of conspiracy between the two, even though there is no attempt at agreement or discussion as to the form which the offence should take. In our judgment the offence described in this reference is such a case.

If one looks back at the facts of the reference: the accused surreptitiously laced his friend's drink. This is an important element and, although we are not going to decide today anything other than the problem posed to us, it may well be that, in similar cases where the lacing of the drink or the introduction of the extra alcohol is known to the driver, quite different considerations may apply. We say that because, where the driver has no knowledge of what is happening, in most instances he would have no means of preventing the offence from being committed. If the driver is unaware of what has happened, he will not be taking precautions. He will get into his car seat, switch on the ignition and drive home and, consequently, the conception of another procuring the commission of the offence by the driver is very much stronger where the driver is innocent of all knowledge of what is happening, as in the present case where the lacing of the drink was surreptitious.

The second thing which is important in the facts set out in our reference is that, following and in consequence of the introduction of the extra alcohol, the friend drove with an excess quantity of alcohol in his blood. Causation here is important. You cannot procure an offence unless there is a causal link between what you do and the commission of the offence, and here we are told that in consequence of the addition of this alcohol the driver, when he drove home, drove with an excess quantity of alcohol in his body.

Giving the words their ordinary meaning in English, and asking oneself whether in those circumstances the offence has been procured, we are in no doubt that the answer is that it has. It has been procured because, unknown to the driver and without his collaboration, he has been put in a position in which in fact he has committed an offence which he never would have committed otherwise."

Opinion accordingly

Lord Widgery C.J. goes on in his speech to deal with the issue of the "generous host"—the host who provides his friends with drink. His suggested answer to the issue of whether such a person should be liable for offences his friends subsequently commit is "that the basis on which the case will be put against the host is, we think, bound to be on the footing that he has supplied the tool with which the offence is committed. This, of course, is a reference back to such cases as those where oxy-acetylene equipment was bought by a man knowing it was to be used by another for a criminal offence."[18] However, rather than dealing with such defendants as counsellors, it is suggested that the truly blameworthy host is better identified by means of the test of procuring itself. To procure, as Lord Widgery said, means to "produce by endeavour." "The generous host who aims at procuring the drunkenness of his friends knowing they are going to drive is liable and there is every reason why such a person should be liable. Generous hosts without such objectives escape liability."[19]

4. The Draft Criminal Code

Under the Draft Criminal Code these outmoded terms will all be jettisoned. They will be replaced by phrases that certainly have more relevance to late twentieth century life. Clause 27 uses the terms assist, encourage and procure to describe the forms of accessorial liability. None of these are dependent upon presence at the crime and all are to be used in their ordinary, everyday sense.[20] However, it has been suggested that the advance is not as great as it might have been:

Glanville Williams, "Complicity, Purpose and the Draft Code" [1990] Crim.L.R. 4 at pp.6–7:

"The three verbs used in the Draft Code for the acts of accessories are 'procure,' 'assist' and 'encourage,' and all three are open to some objection. The worst is the first. [Williams then points out that the modern meaning of this term is 'acquiring' or 'getting' something for someone—rather than the archaic meaning of 'produce by endeavour'] . . . I would suggest that the code should use the word 'influencing' instead of 'procuring.' 'Influencing' says what it means; 'procuring' perpetuates mysticism. Why use an unhelpful and misleading term when an apt one is ready to hand?
    This solution leads to a further thought. The notion of influencing in this

---

[18] *R.* v. *Bainbridge* [1960] 1 Q.B. 129; *post* p. 512.
[19] C. M. V. Clarkson, "Direct and Oblique Intention: Two Recent Cases" (1976) 6 Kingston Law Review 63 at 64. The same issue also relates to the publican who supplies alcohol to his customers.
[20] Draft Criminal Code 1989, (Law Com. No. 177).

sense is so wide that it includes encouraging . . . we do not need encouragement as a separate category. For the purposes of the code, 'influencing' can be
defined as the use of words or conduct for the purpose of encouraging or otherwise inducing the perpetrator to commit the criminal act or omission.

The insight that the forms of accessorship reduce to two was reached some
years ago by Professor Kadish.

'Two kinds of actions render the secondary party liable for the criminal
actions of the primary party: intentionally influencing the decision of the
primary party to commit the crime, and intentionally helping the primary
actor to commit the crime, where the helping actions themselves constitute
no part of the actions prohibited by the definition of the crime.' (*Blame and
Punishment*, (1987))

As to the word 'assist,' the codifiers had the choice of 'help,' 'aid,' and assist,
and they chose the worst. . . . Why? If the code says 'assist' the judge is likely to
translate it for the benefit of the jury as 'help,' a much commoner word. . . . The
reason given by the academic team for their choice was that 'assist' is 'more formal' than 'help.' A rotten reason."

5. The mens rea of secondary parties

The law in this area is in a state of considerable confusion, partly due
to a recent surge in the number of appellate decisions being decided,
with, it has to be said, less than perfect consistency and partly due to an
underlying and long-standing lack of attention to principle. In an
attempt to bring some rationality to this area and because, as Glanville
Williams states, such a distinction is "broadly the result of the present
authorities"[21] we shall adopt the suggested distinction between forms
of accessorial liability of helping and influencing.

(i) *Helping—knowledge required*

The issue here is how much must the secondary party who helps in
the commission of a crime know about what the principal intends to do,
in order to render him liable for the acts of assistance he performs. It
used to be regarded as settled law that all that was required on the part
of the secondary party was an act of voluntary assistance with knowledge of the circumstances that rendered the act criminal.[22] So the person who acted in total ignorance of the plan would not be implicated,
but a crime would be committed by the secondary party if, as on the
facts of *Gamble* he, in the course of his job as a weigh-bridge operator,
knowingly permitted an over-loaded lorry to leave the colliery premises. The defendant in *Gamble* was said to have "intended to aid" the
commission of the offence, but this was taken to mean nothing more
than that there was a voluntary act with knowledge of the circumstances
(*i.e.* that the lorry was over-loaded).

There have always been difficulties with the case of *Gamble*; there is
some equivocality in the speech of Devlin J. and no evidence was heard
from the weigh-bridge operator himself. More importantly, there were

---

[21] "Complicity, Purpose and the Draft Criminal Code" [1990] Crim. L.R.4 at p.9.
[22] *N.C.B.* v. *Gamble* [1959] 1 Q.B. 11; *D.P.P.* v. *Lynch* [1975] A.C. 653.

difficulties with the entire approach: "It seems a strong thing to hold that a man who is simply pursuing his ordinary and lawful vocation and takes no special steps to assist illegalities, becomes involved as a party to a crime committed by another . . . , merely because he realises that his customer will be enabled by what he himself does to commit such a crime."[23]

It may be, however, that the words "intent to aid" have now taken on a stronger meaning. The reason for thinking this lies with the following House of Lords case and the way in which it ties in with other complicity cases.

Gillick v. West Norfolk and Wisbech Area Health Authority [1986] 1 A.C. 112 (House of Lords)

The plaintiff, a mother of five girls under the age of 16, sought an assurance from her local area health authority that contraceptive advice or treatment would not be given to her daughters without her consent, as was possible under D.H.S.S. guidance on family planning if the doctor was satisfied as to certain matters. When the area health authority refused to comply, she sought a declaration in the courts that the guidance gave advice that was unlawful and wrong and adversely affected parental rights and duties. The trial judge decided that this would only be the case if the doctor would necessarily be committing the offence of aiding and abetting under-age sexual intercourse if he prescribed contraceptives. He concluded that the probabilities were that he would not be committing an offence and thus refused to give the plaintiff the declaration. The Court of Appeal gave judgment for the plaintiff.

Lord Scarman:
"So far as criminality is concerned, I am happy to rest on the judgment of Woolf J. whose approach to the problem I believe to be correct. Clearly a doctor who gives a girl contraceptive advice or treatment not because in his clinical judgment the treatment is medically indicated for the maintenance or restoration of her health but with the intention of facilitating her having unlawful sexual intercourse may well be guilty of a criminal offence. It would depend . . . upon the doctor's intention. . . . The department's guidance avoids the trap of declaring that the decision to prescribe the treatment is wholly a matter of the doctor's discretion. He may prescribe only if she has the capacity to consent or if exceptional circumstances exist which justify him in exercising his clinical judgment without parental consent. The adjective 'clinical' emphasises that it must be a medical judgment based upon what he honestly believes to be necessary for the physical, mental and emotional health of his patient. The bona fide exercise by a doctor of his clinical judgment must be a complete negation of the guilty mind which is an essential ingredient of the criminal offence of aiding and abetting the commission of unlawful sexual intercourse."

Appeal allowed

The interpretation put on this case by Ian Dennis is that their Lordships were using "intention" in its ordinary, everyday sense of "purpose": "(t)he 'innocent' doctor does not prescribe contraceptives in

---

[23] Glanville Williams, *Textbook*, p. 342.

order that intercourse shall take place, but in order that health shall be preserved and unwanted outcomes avoided."[24] It is in this sense that the phrase "intent to aid" should be understood.[25] However, this does not mark as dramatic a change as might appear at first sight. "This is not purpose in the sense of giving assistance 'with the motive of endorsing the commission of the offence' . . . 'an indifference to the result of the crime does not of itself negative abetting.' Rather it is purpose in the sense of the defendant's reason for acting; the outcome or state of affairs that he had decided to achieve by his act. If it can fairly be said that the outcome the defendant had decided to achieve was assistance or encouragement of the principal's intended act, then the intention to aid is established. Proof only of a voluntary act of assistance or encouragement with the requisite knowledge is *evidence* of such a purpose, but does not constitute its equivalent."[26] If Devlin J. in *Gamble* was making an inference of intention from the available evidence, then the case is consistent with this approach; if, on the other hand, he equated knowledge with intention, then, according to Dennis, the case has been impliedly overruled.[27]

One of the merits of this approach would be that it would bring the law in this area into line with that of intention generally. If intention is to be given its ordinary meaning in, for example, the context of murder, then the case for similar treatment here is a strong one. However, other commentators have rejected any idea that *Gillick* should be regarded in this way suggesting that it is a wholly exceptional case. A defendant who acts knowing that his conduct will aid the principal must be taken to intend to aid the principal—no other inference is possible—and his motive, which may be admirable, does not avail him. According to this analysis of *Gillick*, the criminality of the doctor is avoided by "a hidden defence of necessity."[28]

(ii) *The specificity of knowledge required*

How detailed must the knowledge of the helping party be of the principal's intended offence? Is it enough that he knows that some sort of property offence is being planned or would he have to have a fair idea of when or how or where? In the case of *Bainbridge*[29] it was held that as long as the defendant was aware that the type of offence which was in fact committed was intended, that would be enough to incriminate him. The "type of offence" formula was not without difficulties (establish-

---

[24] "The Mental Element For Accessories" in *Essays in Honour of J. C. Smith*, (1986), p. 40, at p. 54.

[25] Support for this view can be found in the case of *Att.-Gen.* v. *Able* [1984] Q.B. 795. Dennis also cites the case of *Clarke* (1984) 80 Cr.App.R. 344.

[26] Dennis, *ante* n. 24 at p. 52.

[27] "Intention and Complicity: A Reply," [1988] Crim.L.R. 649 at p. 657.

[28] J. C. Smith, Commentary to *Gillick* [1986] Crim.L.R. at p. 117. Under the Draft Criminal Code the actions of the doctor would not be criminal if done "with the purpose of avoiding or limiting any harmful consequences of the offence and without the purpose of furthering its commission: clause 27(6), (Law Com. No. 177), (1989).

[29] [1960] 1 Q.B. 129.

ing, for example, whether one offence was of a similar type to another) and so the issue was re-examined by the House of Lords in the following case.

Maxwell v. D.P.P. for Northern Ireland (1979) 68 Cr.App.R. 128 (House of Lords)

Lord Scarman:
"I think *Bainbridge* . . . was correctly decided. But I agree with counsel for the appellant that in the instant case the Court of Criminal Appeal in Northern Ireland has gone further than the Court of Criminal Appeal for England and Wales found it necessary to go in *Bainbridge*. It is not possible in the present case to declare that it is proved, beyond reasonable doubt, that the appellant knew a bomb attack upon the Inn was intended by those whom he was assisting. It is not established, therefore, that he knew the particular type of crime intended. The Court, however, refused to limit criminal responsibility by reference to knowledge by the accused of the type or class of crime intended by those whom he assisted. Instead, the Court has formulated a principle which avoids the uncertainties and ambiguities of classification. The guilt of an accessory springs, according to the Court's formulation, 'from the fact that he contemplates the commission of one (or more) of a number of crimes by the principal and he intentionally lends his assistance in order that such a crime will be committed': *per* Sir Robert Lowry C.J. 'The relevant crime,' the Lord Chief Justice continues, 'must be within the contemplation of the accomplice and only exceptionally would evidence be found to support the allegation that the accomplice had given the principal a completely blank cheque.'
The principle thus formulated has great merit. It directs attention to the state of mind of the accused—not what he ought to have in contemplation, but what he did have: it avoids definition and classification, while ensuring that a man will not be convicted of aiding and abetting any offence his principal may commit, but only one which is within his contemplation. He may have in contemplation only one offence, or several: and the several which he contemplates he may see as alternatives. An accessory who leaves it to his principal to choose is liable, provided always the choice is made from the range of offences from which the accessory contemplates the choice will be made. Although the court's formulation of the principle goes further than the earlier cases, it is a sound development of the law and in no way inconsistent with them. I accept it as good judge-made law in a field where there is no statute to offer guidance."[30]

Maxwell leaves unresolved one further question. Does the counsellor continue to be liable for the crimes of the principal so long as they continue to be on his "shopping list" of crimes? One could imagine the well-worn and well-used jemmy being the source of endless liability for the supplier of it. There is nothing in the law as it presently stands, which prevents (in theory at least) the counsellor being implicated every time the tool is used for one of the "shopping list" crimes. We may consider two proposals for reform, the one far-reaching, the other, put forward by the Law Commission being much more limited in scope.

[30] Under the Draft Criminal Code a person may be guilty of an offence as an accessory although he did not foresee, or is not aware of, a circumstance of the offence which is not an element of it, such as the identity of the victim or time or place of its commission: clause 27(4), (Law Com. No. 177), (1989).

Richard Buxton, "Complicity and the Law Commission" [1973] Crim.L.R. 223 at 227–228:

"It has been suggested that the way out of these difficulties would be to create a general offence of aiding or encouraging crime, committed by one who does acts which are known to be likely to be of assistance or encouragement to another in committing a crime, whether or not that principal crime is in fact committed. . . .

It is submitted that the accessory's fault, and his danger to society, lies in his taking steps to produce or assist criminal acts by others, and the mere fact that those principal crimes are not, or have not yet been, carried out by those aided or incited does not of itself lessen the accessory's culpability or the need to restrain him. Indeed, if the actual occurrence of a completed crime were a necessary condition for the imposition of criminal liability it would not be possible to justify the existence of the law of attempt. Some may see the removal of the requirement that the crime abetted must be actually committed as a dangerous widening of the law, or at least as the introduction of a dangerous degree of vagueness. In fact, the reverse might well be the case. Under *Bainbridge*, and the expansion of that case envisaged by the Working Paper [No. 43, *Parties, Complicity and Liability for the Acts of Another*, (1972)], instead of the prosecution having to be precise about the criminal acts that the accused foresaw and encouraged, culpability is based on the accused's assistance or advice having *in fact* been used by the principal in committing another, possibly considerably different, crime. In theory, the Working Paper's test could be operated by asking, first, precisely what the accused intended to happen when providing the assistance and, second, whether what in fact occurred was sufficiently like what was foreseen to be thought similar to it in kind. But one suspects that most juries would find this demanding exercise in fact-classification beyond them much preferring a direction, in the words of illustration (a) on page 53 of the Working Paper, in terms of whether the accessory knew that the principal had some dishonest purpose in mind.

To oblige the prosecution to specify the course of conduct which the accessory anticipated on the part of the principal at least with more precision than is required by the extensions of *Bainbridge* would add certainty to the law of complicity. The other advantage of dropping the requirement that the principal crime should actually have been committed is that, in suitable cases, the police can then move against accessories (or gangland bosses) without having to wait for the mischief that they have encouraged actually to be put into operation. . . .

But we can in fact go further than this in support of abandoning the requirement that the principal crime should actually be committed, and say that the improved possibility of preventive action would not only assist the law enforcement agencies, but also would hold out the hope of introducing greater precision, and therefore greater fairness, into the law of secondary offences as a whole."

Whilst the Buxton proposal would sweep away problems relating to the specificity of knowledge required and that of infinite liability, it may well create some new ones in the process. How, for instance, is the judge to sentence the defendant convicted of the crime of assistance? Whilst sentencing could be based on what the defendant thought was going to happen, it seems very likely that judges would wish to refer to the crime that actually took place. If that were to happen, would the result be any different from that achieved today?

The Law Commission contented themselves with the more modest step of proposing that "where a principal is helped in the commission of more than one offence by a single act of help, the accessory who afforded that help shall not, after having been convicted of one or more of such offences, be convicted of another of such offences of equal or lesser gravity."[31]

(iii) *Mens rea of "influencers"*

Must the secondary party himself have *mens rea* with regard to the principal offence or even here will knowledge of what the principal intends suffice? It is on this point that the law is most opaque. The problem has tended to manifest itself mainly in the joint unlawful enterprise cases. Some situations present no problem. If the defendant and the principal are *ad idem* about their plan and if all goes according to that plan, both are fully liable for the consequences. At the other extreme, as we have seen,[32] if the defendant knows nothing about the real plan or change of plan by the principal, he will not be liable for any consequences flowing from the principal's independent actions.

The real problem, however, arises in those cases where the result is within the scope of the joint unlawful enterprise but perhaps goes further than the secondary party wants or expected. For example, in *Reid*[33] the defendant was a party to a joint unlawful enterprise of joint possession of offensive weapons with intent of "causing fright by threats to use them." The defendant went with two other men to the victim's house, but instead of simply frightening the victim, one of the other men (subsequently convicted of murder) shot and killed the victim. The question is whether the defendant is guilty of murder because he was a party to a joint unlawful enterprise, or guilty of manslaughter because that would be his own individual *"mens rea"* under constructive manslaughter,[34] or guilty of nothing (other than those offences such as assault that he committed in his own right) because he did not possess the same *mens rea* as the principal offender.

The answer to this question used to be relatively clear but recent cases have adopted all three views.

(a) *Liability dependent on accessory's own mens rea*:

This used to be the law's clear response to the problem. The defendant in *Reid* was a party to a joint unlawful enterprise. This involvement amounted to his *actus reus* of the alleged homicide offence. His precise liability depended on his *mens rea*. He could not be convicted of murder because while his associates possessed such *mens rea* he did not. He did however, have the *mens rea* of constructive manslaughter and was therefore convicted of that offence.

---

[31] *Ibid.* proposition 10. This proposition has been dropped from the Draft Criminal Code.
[32] *Davies* v. *D.P.P.*; *Anderson and Morris, ante* p. 506.
[33] (1975) 62 Cr.App.R. 109.
[34] *Post*, p. 613.

(b) *Accessory must possess same mens rea as principal*:

R. v. Dunbar [1988] Crim.L.R. 693 (Court of Appeal, Criminal Division)

"[The appellant] suspected that the co-defendants planned to burgle the victim's flat and that in the course of the burglary some violence might be done to her former lover. [The appellant was convicted of manslaughter and appealed.]

Held, allowing the appeal and quashing the conviction, the jury's verdict must have been reached upon the basis that while the appellant contemplated the use of some unlawful violence, short of the infliction of grievous bodily harm, one or other or both of her co-defendants must have gone beyond the scope of that design and used the extreme violence which was intended to cause grievous bodily harm or death. The judge's direction in the appellant's case did not deal with that situation and the appropriate verdict of not guilty should the jury find that the second and/or third defendant went beyond what was contemplated by the appellant. On the facts of the case there were only two verdicts open to the jury, guilty or not guilty of murder. If, as the Crown contended, she was a party to an agreement to kill, she was guilty of murder. If she was a party to an agreement to inflict some harm, short of grievous bodily harm, then she was guilty of neither murder nor manslaughter. The victim's killing and the manner of the killing could not be within the ambit of the agreement to which the appellant was a party, if the ambit was confined on her part to an intention that only some harm should befall the deceased, albeit not death or really serious injury. The issues involved could not be distinguished from those adumbrated by Widgery L.J. in *Lovesey and Peterson* (1969) 53 Cr.App.R. 461. The judge failed to remind the jury of the law as laid down in *Anderson and Morris* (1966) 50 Cr.App.R. 216 and followed in *Lovesey and Peterson* (1969) 53 Cr.App.R. 461. The result of that non-direction was that the jury returned a verdict which was not open to them."

Appeal allowed

R. v. Smith [1988] Crim.L.R. 616 (Court of Appeal, Criminal Division)

"The appellant was convicted of causing grievous bodily harm with intent. The victim and his friend were attacked because the appellant and his co-defendants believed them to be rival football club supporters. The defendants attacked the victim and his friend twice. During the second attack they were kicked as they lay on the ground; the victim died after the appellant's trial. The appellant admitted to the police that he had kicked a man lying on the ground; his description of that man matched the victim. At the trial the prosecution relied upon the appellant's involvement in a joint enterprise with his co-defendants rather than upon direct evidence of physical violence by the appellant. The judge directed the jury that if two persons agree to do some harm but it was no part of the agreement to do really serious bodily harm and one person attacks the victim intending and causing really serious bodily harm, the second person is guilty of causing grievous bodily harm with intent even though he did not himself intend that his partner should cause the victim really serious bodily harm, if he could and did foresee that in the course of the agreed attack there was a real risk that his partner might attack one of the victims viciously with the intention of causing him really serious bodily harm. The appellant appealed against conviction on the ground that the judge's directions erred in that (1) it was left open to the jury to convict even if the co-defendant acted outside the scope of the agreement; (2) the concept of foresight was equated with the concept of intent; (3) the jury could have convicted even though there was no intent demonstrated on the part of the appellant; (4) the case was regarded as one which could be equated with the Privy Council decision in *Chan Wing-Siu and others* [1984] All E.R. 877.

Held, allowing the appeal and quashing the conviction, the Court bore in mind the decisions in *Anderson* v. *Morris* [1966] 50 Cr.App.R. 216; *Moloney* (1985) 81 Cr.App.R. 93 and *Hancock and Shankland* (1986) 82 Cr.App.R. 264. The present case concerned a specific intent and it was incumbent upon the judge to direct in the plainest terms that the appellant could only be convicted if the jury were sure that he had the requisite intent to cause grievous bodily harm and that the foresight the judge referred to was not of itself to be regarded as an intent, though it could properly be regarded as evidence supporting the existence of the intent necessary to establish the offence. The Court agreed that the present case was not to be equated with *Chan Wing-Siu and others* (*supra*). The Court regarded it as impossible to substitute a verdict on the lesser count of inflicting grievous bodily harm because of the judge's direction that the appellant could be convicted of that offence even though he did not personally intend that the victim should suffer any physical injury whatsoever, provided that he foresaw a real risk of the co-defendant causing some physical harm in the course of carrying out their agreement to attack the victim."

If this approach is followed, it raises the problem of what is meant by "intention" in those cases, such as the ones above, where intention is required on the part of the principal offender. Presumably, if the same *mens rea* as the principal offender is required, then the *Moloney* and *Hancock* test must be adopted.[35] It would hardly be plausible to assert that the "same" *mens rea* is required and then to argue that intention bears any special meaning (such as "purpose") here.

According to the approach adopted in these two cases, the defendant in *Reid* would have escaped all liability as an accessory because he lacked the *mens rea* for murder. (He could of course be liable for any offence, such as assault, committed by him as a principal). Such an approach seems unduly favourable to the defendant. If he was a party to a joint unlawful enterprise and had the *mens rea* of manslaughter and the victim has been killed, it is difficult to see why he is not convicted of manslaughter.

(c) *Secondary party must be aware of risk of consequence occurring:*

Chan Wing-Siu v. The Queen [1985] 1 A.C. 168 (Privy Council)

Sir Robin Cooke:
"Where a man lends himself to a criminal enterprise knowing that potentially murderous weapons are to be carried, and in the event they are in fact carried, and in the event they are in fact used by his partner with an intent sufficient for murder, he should not escape the consequences by reliance upon a nuance of prior assessment, only too likely to have been optimistic. . . .
On the other hand, if it was not even contemplated by the particular accused

---

[35] *C.f.* G. R. Sullivan, "Intent, Purpose and Complicity" [1988] Crim.L.R. 641; Ian Dennis, "Intent and Purpose" [1988] Crim.L.R. 649 and [1989] Crim.L.R. 166–170.

that serious bodily harm would be intentionally inflicted, he is not a party to murder . . .

The test of *mens rea* here is subjective. It is what the individual accused in fact contemplated that matters. As in other cases where the state of a person's mind has to be ascertained, this may be inferred from his conduct and any other evidence throwing light on what he foresaw at the material time, including of course any explanation that he gives in evidence or in a statement put in evidence by the prosecution. It is no less elementary that all questions of weight are for the jury. . . . If, at the end of the day and whether as a result of hearing evidence from the accused or for some other reason, the jury conclude that there is a reasonable possibility that the accused did not even contemplate the risk, he is in this type of case not guilty of murder or wounding with intent to cause serious bodily harm.

In some cases in this field it is enough to direct the jury . . . [thus], did the accused contemplate that in carrying out a common unlawful purpose one of his partners in the enterprise might use a knife or a loaded gun with the intention of causing really serious bodily harm."

R. v. Slack [1989] 3 W.L.R. 513 (Court of Appeal, Criminal Division)

The appellant agreed with A to burgle a flat, intending to rob the occupant. While they were in the flat, A, in the absence of the appellant, murdered the occupant. The trial judge directed the jury that they could convict the appellant of murder if they found that he contemplated and foresaw that A might kill or cause grievous bodily harm to the occupant as part of the joint unlawful enterprise.

Lord Lane C.J.:

"The Judicial Committee [in *Chan Wing-Siu*] seems primarily to have been concerned with the problem posed by a conditional agreement e.g., 'We do not want to kill or seriously injure, but if necessary we will.'

Chan Wing-Siu v. *The Queen* was considered and approved by this court in *Reg.* v. *Ward* (1986) 85 Cr.App.R. 71. The appellant's submission in that case was that the decisions of the House of Lords in *Reg.* v. *Moloney* and *Reg.* v. *Hancock* had the effect of completely altering the law relating to joint enterprise; that no man can be convicted of murder unless it is specifically decided against him that he had a murderous intent; since intent had to be read against the decisions in *Reg.* v. *Moloney* and *Reg.* v. *Hancock* the jury ought to be directed on the basis of those cases.

This court in *Reg.* v. *Ward* reiterated the passage from *Reg.* v. *Anderson* [1966] 2 Q.B. 110, 118–119, cited above and went on to hold that *Reg.* v. *Moloney* and *Reg.* v. *Hancock* had had no effect on the well known and well established principles of joint enterprise. . . .

A must be proved to have intended to kill or do serious harm at the time he killed. B may not be present at the killing: he may be a distance away, for example, waiting in the getaway car; he may be in another part of the house; he may not know that A has killed; he may have hoped, and probably did hope, that A would not kill or do serious injury. If however as part of their joint plan it was understood between them expressly or tacitly that if necessary one of them would kill or do serious harm as part of their common enterprise, then B is guilty of murder.

As appears from the cases we have cited, the direction may be in a variety of different forms. Provided that it is made clear to the jury that B to be guilty must be proved to have lent himself to a criminal enterprise involving the infliction, if necessary, of serious harm or death or to have had an express or tacit understanding with A that such harm or death should, if necessary, be inflicted, the precise form of words in which the jury are directed is not important.

In our judgment the second question posed by the judge in the instant case [did the accused contemplate and foresee that Buick *might* kill or cause grievous bodily harm to Mrs. Crowder as part of their joint enterprise . . . ?] was in accordance with the principles we have endeavoured to express."

Appeal dismissed

This view appears to be emerging as the dominant one and has been endorsed in other cases such as *Ward*[36] and the New Zealand case of *Tomkins*.[37] According to this then, if the defendant in *Reid* had foreseen that there was a *risk* of his associates causing death or grievous bodily harm, he would have been liable for *murder*. This is surely ludicrous. The actual killer is only guilty of murder if he intended (in the *Moloney* and *Hancock* sense of that word) to kill or cause grievous bodily harm— but the secondary party, who might not even be present at the scene of the crime, is guilty of the murder on the basis of recklessness alone. How can it possibly be justifiable for an accessory to be guilty of the same offence as the principal on the basis of a lesser *mens rea*. As has been said: "Since the act and cause requirements of accomplice liability are so minimal, and since . . . an accomplice [can be punished] the same as the perpetrator of the substantive offense, the *mens rea* requirement becomes more significant. Accomplice liability hinges upon the *mens rea* element."[38] It is accordingly strongly submitted, for the reasons given above,[39] that the best approach to the question of the *mens rea* of influencers and encouragers is the old *Davies* v. *D.P.P.* and *Reid* one of assessing liability on the basis of each party's blameworthiness.

III. THE LIMITS OF ACCESSORIAL LIABILITY

A. No Principal Offender

Accessorial liability is a form of derivative liability. It presupposes the existence of a crime; "[a] man cannot be guilty of having abetted a crime, or counselled it, unless the crime has actually been committed by the principal offender."[40]

This simple proposition requires qualification:

(a) The principal may be acquitted through lack of evidence or because of some procedural defect that applies to him. Secondary

---

[36] (1987) 85 Cr.App.R. 71. See also *Wakely* [1990] Crim.L.R. 119.
[37] [1985] 2 N.Z.L.R. 253. It is also the view adopted in the Draft Criminal Code (1989). Clause 27(1)(c) says all that is necessary is that the accessory must intend that the principal will act or is aware that the principal may act with the fault required for the offence, (Law Com. No. 177), (1989).
[38] Grace Mueller, "The Mens Rea of Accomplice Liability" (1988) 61 South. Calif. L.R. 2169 at p. 2172.
[39] *Ante*, p. 515.
[40] Smith and Hogan, p. 152.

parties may nevertheless be convicted if the evidence shows clearly that there was a crime.

(b) The principal may be acquitted and the court apply the doctrine of innocent agency to justify the conviction of the secondary party. In such a case the secondary party is in fact deemed to be the principal offender.[41]

(c) The principal may be acquitted because he has a defence, or because either the *mens rea* or the *actus reus* of his "crime" has been negated. In certain circumstances the secondary party may nevertheless be convicted.

Three cases, *Thornton* v. *Mitchell, Bourne* and *Cogan and Leak* will be used to explore the relationship between these last two propositions ((a) needs no further explanation) and to determine the "certain circumstances" in (c) when liability may nevertheless attach to the secondary party.

Thornton v. Mitchell [1940] 1 All E.R. 339 (King's Bench Divisional Court)

A bus driver relied upon the signalling and guidance of his conductor to reverse his bus. The conductor failed to see two pedestrians standing behind the bus. When they were injured the driver was charged with careless driving and the conductor was charged with abetting that offence. The charge against the driver was dismissed. He had not been careless; it had been reasonable for him to rely upon the conductor's advice. However, the conductor was convicted. He appealed.

Lord Hewart C.J.:
"In my opinion, this case is *a fortiori* upon *Morris* v. *Tolman* [1923] 1 K.B. 166 . . . [that] 'a person cannot aid another in doing something which that other has not done.'

That I think is the very thing which these justices have decided that the bus conductor did. In one breath they say that the principal did nothing which he should not have done and in the next breath they hold that the bus conductor aided and abetted the driver in doing something which had not been done or in not doing something which he ought to have done."

Appeal allowed

R. v. Bourne (1952) 36 Cr.App.R. 1251 (Court of Criminal Appeal)

The defendant terrorised his wife into committing buggery with a dog. He was convicted of aiding and abetting his wife to commit buggery with a dog. He appealed.

Lord Goddard C.J.:
"I am willing to assume for the purpose of this case . . . that if this woman had been charged herself with committing the offence, she could have set up

---

[41] See *ante*, p. 502.

the plea of duress, not as showing that no offence had been committed, but as showing that she had no *mens rea* because her will was overborne by threats of imprisonment or violence so that she would be excused from punishment. . . . [T]he offence of buggery . . . depends on the act, and if an act of buggery is committed, the felony is committed.

. . . The evidence was . . . that he caused his wife to have connection with a dog, and . . . he is guilty, whether you call him an aider and abettor or an accessory, as a principal in the second degree."

Appeal dismissed

R. v. Cogan and Leak [1976] Q.B. 217 (Court of Appeal, Criminal Division)

Leak compelled his wife to have sexual intercourse with Cogan, who believed that she consented. As Cogan's conviction was quashed on the strength of his belief, it became necessary to decide whether Leak's conviction as aider and abettor could stand.

Lawton L.J.:

"Leak's appeal against conviction was based on the proposition that he could not be found guilty of aiding and abetting Cogan to rape his wife if Cogan was acquitted of that offence as he was deemed in law to have been when his conviction was quashed. . . . Counsel for Leak conceded, however, that his proposition had some limitations. The law on this topic lacks clarity as a perusal of some of the text-books shows: . . . We do not consider it appropriate to review the law generally because, as was said by this court in *Reg.* v. *Quick* [1973] Q.B. 910, 923, when considering this kind of problem:

'The facts of each case . . . have to be considered and in particular what is alleged to have been done by way of aiding and abetting.'

The only case which counsel for Leak submitted had a direct bearing on the problem of Leak's guilt was *Walters* v. *Lunt* [1951] 2 All E.R. 645. In that case the respondents had been charged under the Larceny Act 1916, s.33(1), with receiving from a child aged seven years, certain articles knowing them to have been stolen. In 1951 a child under eight years was deemed in law to be incapable of committing a crime: it followed that at the time of receipt by the respondents the articles had not been stolen and that the charges had not been proved. That case is very different from this because here one fact is clear—the wife had been raped.

Cogan had had sexual intercourse with her without her consent. The fact that Cogan was innocent of rape because he believed that she was consenting does not affect the position that she was raped.

Her ravishment had come about because Leak had wanted it to happen and had taken action to see that it did by persuading Cogan to use his body as the instrument for the necessary physical act. In the language of the law the act of sexual intercourse without the wife's consent was the *actus reus*; it had been procured by Leak who had the appropriate *mens rea*, namely his intention that Cogan should have sexual intercourse with her without her consent. In our judgment it is irrelevant that the man whom Leak had procured to do the physical act himself did not intend to have sexual intercourse with the wife without her consent. Leak was using him as a means to procure a criminal purpose.

Before 1861 a case such as this, pleaded as it was in the indictment, might have presented a court with problems arising from the old distinctions between principals and accessories in felony. Most of the old law was swept away by s.8

of the Accessories and Abettors Act 1861 and what remained, by s.1 of the Criminal Law Act 1967. The modern law allowed Leak to be tried and punished as a principal offender. In our judgment he could have been indicted as a principal offender. It would have been no defence for him to submit that if Cogan was an 'innocent' agent, he was necessarily in the old terminology of the law a principal in the first degree, which was a legal impossibility as a man cannot rape his own wife during co-habitation. The law no longer concerns itself with niceties of degrees in participation of crime; but even if it did, Leak would still be guilty. The reason a man cannot by his own physical act rape his wife during co-habitation is because the law presumes consent from the marriage ceremony: see *Hale, Pleas of the Crown*, (1778) vol. 1, p. 629. There is no such presumption when a man procures a drunken friend to do the physical act for him. Hale C.J. put this case in one sentence; at p. 629:

> 'tho in marriage she hath given up her body to her husband, she is not to be by him prostituted to another.'

Had Leak been indicted as a principal offender, the case against him would have been clear beyond argument. Should he be allowed to go free because he was charged with 'being aider and abettor to the same offence'? If we are right in our opinion that the wife had been raped (and no one outside a court of law would say that she had not been), then the particulars of offence accurately stated what Leak had done, namely he had procured Cogan to commit the offence. This would suffice to uphold the conviction. We would prefer, however, to uphold it on a wider basis. In our judgment convictions should not be upset because of mere technicalities of pleading in an indictment. Leak knew what the case against him was and the facts in support of that case were proved. But for the fact that the jury thought that Cogan in his intoxicated condition might have mistaken the wife's sobs and distress for expressions of her consent, no question of any kind would have arisen about the form of pleading. By his written statement Leak virtually admitted what he had done. As Judge Chapman said in *R. v. Humphreys* [1965] 3 All.E.R. 689, 692:

> 'It would be anomolous if a person who admitted to a substantial part in the perpetration of a misdemeanour as aider and abettor could not be convicted on his own admission merely because the person alleged to have been aided and abetted was not or could not be convicted.'

In the circumstances of this case it would be more than anomalous: it would be an affront to justice and to the common sense of ordinary folk. It was for these reasons that we dismissed the appeal against conviction.

The sentence passed on Leak for his part in the rape was severe; but the circumstances were horrible. We can see nothing wrong with that sentence. The assault on the wife the previous day had been brutal. The doctor found no less than 13 bruises in the middle and lower region on the left hand side of her spine. There were other bruises on her back and multiple bruises on her left hip. These bruises were consistent with punching and kicking. Men who use violence of this kind on their wives must expect severe sentences. The sentence of three years was not too severe."

Appeal dismissed

Can any principles be extracted from these cases?

(i) *Doctrine of innocent agency*:

Cogan and Leak has clearly stretched this doctrine beyond acceptable limits.

G. R. Sullivan, "Aiding and Abetting the Commission of a Non-Existent Offence," (1976) 39 M.L.R. 350 at 351–352:

"The lack of regard given to the difficulty of convicting L as a secondary offender may stem from the fact that the conviction was also affirmed on an alternative ground. According to Lawton L.J., if L had been indicted as a principal offender, 'the case against him would have been clear beyond argument' and a conviction should not be upset because of 'mere technicalities in the form of the indictment.' One can only agree with this if such a verdict had been open to the jury. But was this so? As the principal offender must be the immediate author of the *actus reus*, how can it be said that L had sexual intercourse? Even if such a finding could be made how can the anachronistic but still valid rule that a man cannot rape his own wife during co-habitation be circumvented?

The first difficulty could be overcome by the doctrine of 'innocent agency' which operates to convict as a principal offender one who has procured physical performance of the *actus reus*, by a person who lacks *mens rea* or who has a defence. The act of the 'innocent agent' is, in law, as much the act of the procurer as if he had performed the act himself. Lawton L.J. adopts this doctrine, referring to C as 'the instrument for the necessary physical act.' The second difficulty is dismissed: . . . [by Lawton L.J. citing Hale that there is no presumed consent when a husband procures another to have intercourse with his wife].

But the quotation from Hale does not carry the point. Hale was approving *Audley* where the husband was convicted as an *aider and abettor*. Also it is difficult to see how at one and the same time the doctrine of 'innocent agency' can be used to attribute C's actions to L and the consequences of such an attribution denied to avoid the rule that a husband cannot rape his wife. The conviction of C as a principal would hardly have been 'beyond argument.' "

Even if one accepts, further, the abuse of language necessitated in order to say that Leak raped Y (his wife) when he committed no such act against her, Glanville Williams points to one final flaw with the application of the innocent agency doctrine: "The decision was rendered possible by the fact that the defendant happened to be a man. Rape can only be perpetrated by a man; the statute says so . . . if the duress is applied by a woman it would need an even greater degree of hawkishness than that displayed by the court in Cogan to call her a constructive man. Yet it is highly illogical that a man can commit rape through an innocent agent when a woman cannot."[42]

Fletcher adds that cases of innocent agency or "perpetrator-by-means" ought to be restricted to situations where "the party behind the scenes in fact dominates and controls his agent."[43] Was there any evidence of such control in *Cogan and Leak*?

Could the doctrine of innocent agency have been applied in *Thornton v. Mitchell* and *Bourne*?

(ii) *"Certain circumstances"*:

We saw above that in "certain circumstances" the secondary party could be convicted, despite the acquittal of the principal offender. Thus Leak was convicted but Cogan acquitted. Bourne was convicted

---

[42] Glanville Williams, *Textbook*, p. 371.
[43] Fletcher, pp. 665–667.

although his wife had a defence. How are these cases to be explained if not by the doctrine of innocent agency? Any such explanation would have to make clear why the conductor in *Thornton* v. *Mitchell* was not convicted.

It is submitted that there is an explanation of these cases, and one that accords with the actual reasoning adopted therein. According to this view, there was indeed a "crime" (in the sense of a wrongful act) in both *Cogan and Leak* and *Bourne* but Cogan and Mrs. Bourne had an excuse. As seen earlier, "excuses admit that the deed may be wrong, but excuse the actor because conditions suggest that the actor is not responsible for his deed. . . . Acts are justified; actors are excused."[44] As Fletcher says: "If Mrs Leak was 'raped' by Cogan's penetration . . . then, in this sense, Cogan committed the offence. His act was wrongful, but excused."[45]

According to this reasoning, if a principal offender has a *justificatory defence*, the secondary party must escape liability as no "crime" (wrongful act) has been committed. But if the principal offender only escapes liability because of an *excuse*, a "crime" (wrongful act) has been committed and the secondary party can still be liable according to his *mens rea*. This analysis also explains *Thornton* v. *Mitchell*.

R. D. Taylor, "Complicity and Excuses" [1983] Crim.L.R. 656 at 657–658:

"*Thornton* v. *Mitchell* is not a case of excuse at all. The notion of excuse presupposes a wrongful act, even given the existence of the facts of the excuse. There must be something wrongful to excuse. If an alleged excuse means that there is no wrongful act, then the excuse is really a justification (or denial of wrongfulness). . . . Now in *Thornton* v. *Mitchell*, the driver's defence denies the objective wrongness of his act, in that given due care and attention, he is merely driving. The denial of negligence in relation to this offence dissolves the harm rather than excuses it. One can hardly say that merely driving is the wrongful act prohibited by the offence of driving without due care and attention. [Taylor goes on to argue that there is a practical difference between this view and the '*actus reus* view' in that while in many cases 'the *actus reus* coincides with the notion of a wrongful act, there are cases where an act can only be said to be wrongful if accompanied by a certain mental element or degree of fault']."

B. Accessory can be Guilty of Graver Offence than the One Committed

Until the decision of *Howe*[46] the law was that if the principal had the *mens rea* of one offence, such as manslaughter, it was not possible for a counsellor to be guilty of the graver offence of murder.[47] The reason for this rule was "that one could [not] say that that which was done can be

---

[44] *Ante*, p. 274.
[45] At p. 667.
[46] [1987] 1 A.C. 417.
[47] *Richards* [1974] Q.B. 776.

said to be done with the intention of the defendant who was not present at the time."[48] Without, it must be said, much discussion of the merits or demerits of this approach, the law has now changed.

R. v. Howe [1987] 1 A.C. 417 (House of Lords).

(The facts and a fuller extract appear, *ante* p. 325)

Lord Mackay of Clashfern:
"I turn now to the second certified question [whether a secondary party can be convicted of murder despite the conviction of the principal for manslaughter] . . . I am of the opinion that the Court of Appeal reached the correct conclusion upon it as a matter of principle.

Giving the judgment of the Court of Appeal Lord Lane C.J. said [1986] Q.B. 626, 641–642:

'The judge based himself on a decision of this court in *Reg. v. Richards* [1974] Q.B. 776. The facts in that case were that Mrs. Richards paid two men to inflict injuries on her husband which she intended should "put him in hospital for a month." The two men wounded the husband but not seriously. They were acquitted of wounding with intent but convicted of unlawful wounding. Mrs. Richards herself was convicted of wounding with intent, the jury plainly, and not surprisingly, believing that she had the necessary intent, though the two men had not. She appealed against her conviction on the ground that she could not properly be convicted as accessory before the fact to a crime more serious than that committed by the principals in the first degree. The appeal was allowed and the conviction for unlawful wounding was substituted. The court followed a passage from *Hawkins' Pleas of the Crown*, vol. 2. c. 29, para. 15: "I take it to be an uncontroverted rule that [the offence of the accessory can never rise higher than that of the principal]; it seeming incongruous and absurd that he who is punished only as a partaker of the guilt of another, should be adjudged guilty of a higher crime than the other."

James L.J. delivering the judgment in *Reg. v. Richards* said: "If there is only one offence committed, and that is the offence of unlawful wounding, then the person who has requested that offence to be committed, or advised that that offence be committed, cannot be guilty of a graver offence than that in fact which was committed." The decision in *Reg. v. Richards* has been the subject of some criticism—see for example *Smith & Hogan, Criminal Law*, 5th ed. (1983), p. 140. Counsel before us posed the situation where A hands a gun to D informing him that it is loaded with blank ammunition only and telling him to go and scare X by discharging it. The ammunition is in fact live, as A knows, and X is killed. D is convicted only of manslaughter, as he might be on those facts. It would seem absurd that A should thereby escape conviction for murder. We take the view that *Reg. v. Richards* was incorrectly decided, but it seems to us that it cannot properly be distinguished from the instant case.'

I consider that the reasoning of Lord Lane C.J. is entirely correct and I would affirm his view that where a person has been killed and that result is the result intended by another participant, the mere fact that the actual killer may be convicted only of the reduced charge of manslaughter for some reason special to himself does not, in my opinion in any way, result in a compulsory reduction for the other participant."

---

[48] *Ibid. per* James L.J.

If, as some cases considered earlier suggest, all parties are going to be judged by reference to the full offence and on the basis of their own *mens rea*, then at least this approach is consistent. However, despite all the criticism of *Richards* there may have been a sound principle underlying it: that of control. Mrs. Richards lacked control over the principal offender and should not have been guilty of a more serious offence despite her greater *mens rea*. This, we will return to in the final section of this chapter.

C. Repentance of Accessories

R. v. Becerra and Cooper (1975) 62 Cr.App.R. 212 (Court of Appeal, Criminal Division)

Becerra broke into a house with Cooper and another. They intended to steal but Becerra gave a knife to Cooper which he was to use if anyone interrupted them. Lewis, an upstairs tenant, came to investigate the noise, at which Becerra said "There's a bloke coming. Let's go," and jumped out of a window. As he ran away Cooper stabbed and killed Lewis with the knife. Becerra was convicted with Cooper of murder, but appealed.

Roskill L.J.:
"The second ground of appeal requires more elaborate treatment. It was argued in the alternative on behalf of Becerra, that even if there were this common design, . . . nonetheless Becerra had open to him a second line of defence, namely that . . . —whatever Cooper did immediately before and at the time of the killing of Lewis, Becerra had by then withdrawn from that common design and so should not be convicted of the murder of Lewis, even though the common design had previously been that which I have stated.

Mr. Owen [counsel for the appellant] says, . . . the learned judge in effect, though perhaps not in so many words, withdrew the defence of 'withdrawal' from the jury, because the learned judge was saying to the jury that the only evidence of Becerra's suggested 'withdrawal' was the remark, if it were made, 'come on let's go,' coupled with the fact of course that Becerra then went out through the window and ran away and that that could not in those circumstances amount to 'withdrawal' and therefore was not available as a defence, even if they decided the issue of common design against Becerra. It is upon that passage in the summing-up that Mr. Owen has principally focused his criticism.

It is necessary, before dealing with that argument in more detail, to say a word or two about the relevant law. [Roskill L.J. then cited a decision of the Court of Appeal of British Columbia in *Whitehouse (alias Savage)* (1941) 1 W.W.R. 112, at pp. 115 and 116]. 'Can it be said on the facts of this case that a mere change of mental intention and a quitting of the scene of the crime just immediately prior to the striking of the fatal blow will absolve those who participate in the commission of the crime by overt acts up to that moment from all the consequences of its accomplishment by the one who strikes in ignorance of his companion's change of heart? I think not. After a crime has been committed and before a prior abandonment of the common enterprise may be found by a jury there must be, in my view, in the absence of exceptional circumstances, something more than a mere mental change of intention and physical change of place by those associates who wish to dissociate themselves from the consequences attendant upon their willing assistance up to the moment of the actual commission of that crime. I would not attempt to define too closely what must be done in criminal matters involving participation in a common unlawful purpose to break the chain of causation and responsibility. That must depend upon the circumstances of each case but it seems to me that one essential element ought to be established in a case of this kind. Where practicable and reasonable there must be timely communication of the intention to abandon the common purpose from those who wish to dissociate themselves from the contemplated crime to those who desire to continue in it. What is "timely communication" must be determined by the facts of each case but where practicable and reasonable it ought to be such communication, verbal or otherwise, that will serve unequivocal notice upon the other party to the common unlawful cause that if he proceeds upon it he does so without the further aid and assistance of those who withdraw. The unlawful purpose of him who continues alone is then his own and not one in common with those who are no longer parties to it nor liable to its full and final consequences.' . . .

In the view of each member of this Court, that passage, if we may respectfully say so, could not be improved upon and we venture to adopt it in its entirety as a correct statement of the law which is to be applied in this case. . . .

We therefore turn back to consider the direction which the learned judge gave in the present case to the jury and what was the suggested evidence that Becerra had withdrawn from the common agreement. The suggested evidence is the use by Becerra of the words 'Come on let's go,' coupled, as I said a few moments ago, with his act in going out through the window. The evidence, as the judge pointed out, was that Cooper never heard that nor did the third man. But let it be supposed that that was said and the jury took the view that it was said.

On the facts of this case, in the circumstances then prevailing, the knife having already been used and being contemplated for further use when it was handed over by Becerra to Cooper for the purpose of avoiding (if necessary) by violent means the hazards of identification, if Becerra wanted to withdraw at that stage, he would have to 'countermand,' to use the word that is used in some of the cases or 'repent' to use another word so used, in some manner vastly different and vastly more effective than merely to say 'Come on, let's go' and go out through the window.

It is not necessary, on this application, to decide whether the point of time had arrived at which the only way in which he could effectively withdraw, so as to free himself from joint responsibility for any act Cooper thereafter did in furtherance of the common design, would be physically to intervene so as to stop Cooper attacking Lewis, as the judge suggested, by interposing his own body between them or somehow getting in between them or whether some other action might suffice. That does not arise for decision here. Nor is it necessary to decide whether or not the learned judge was right or wrong, on the facts of this case, in that passage which appears at the bottom of p. 206, which Mr. Owen criticised: 'and at least take all reasonable steps to prevent the commission of the crime which he had agreed the others should commit.' It is enough for the purposes of deciding this application to say that under the law of this country as it stands, and on the facts (taking them at their highest in favour of Becerra), that which was urged as amounting to withdrawal from the common design was not capable of amounting to such withdrawal. Accordingly Becerra remains responsible, in the eyes of the law, for everything that Cooper did and continued to do after Becerra's disappearance through the window as much as if he had done them himself."

Appeal dismissed

Is repentance or withdrawal a practical possibility once the criminal enterprise has commenced?[49]

Under the Draft Criminal Code 1989 an accessory who has previously encouraged (but not procured or assisted) the commission of an offence, can avoid liability if

"(a) he countermanded his encouragement with a view to preventing its commission; or

(b) he took all reasonable steps to prevent its commission."[50]

D. Victims Cannot Be Accessories

R. v. Whitehouse [1977] Q.B. 868 (Court of Appeal, Criminal Division)

The defendant pleaded guilty to two charges of inciting his 15 year old daughter to commit incest with him and was sentenced to two years' imprisonment. He appealed against the sentence but the Court of Appeal granted leave to appeal against conviction on the basis that he might have pleaded guilty to an offence unknown to the law.

Scarman L.J.:
"Is there such an offence known to the law? The difficulty arises from two features of the law. . . . First, at common law the crime of incitement consists of inciting another person to commit a crime . . . [secondly] . . . a woman under the age of 16 cannot commit the crime of incest. But, says the Crown, a man can commit incest, and so they go on to make their submission that a girl of 15 can aid and abet him to do so.

There is no doubt of the general principle, namely that a person, provided always he or she is of the age of criminal responsibility, can be guilty of aiding or abetting a crime even though it be a crime which he or she cannot commit as a principal in the first degree. . . .

But what if the person alleged to be aiding and abetting the crime is herself the victim of the crime? This poses the short question with which this appeal is concerned. . . .

The important matters in our judgment are these. First this girl, aged 15, belongs to a class which is protected, but not punished, by sections 10 and 11 of the Sexual Offences Act 1956, and secondly the girl is alleged to be the victim of this notional crime. The whole question has an air of artificiality because nobody is suggesting either that the father has committed incest with her or that she has aided and abetted him to commit incest upon her. What is suggested is that the father has committed the crime of incitement because by his words and conduct he has incited her to do that which, of course, she never has done.

The question in our judgment is determined by authority. It is, strictly speaking, persuasive authority only because it deals with a different Act of Parliament, but it is a decision by a strong court which has declared a principle which is as applicable to the statutory provision with which we are concerned as to that with which that case was concerned. The case is *Reg.* v. *Tyrrell* [1894] 1 Q.B. 710. . . .

---

[49] See *Grundy* [1977] Crim.L.R. 543, where the party also sought (successfully) to withdraw before the commission of the crime (some two weeks hence); see also *Croft* (1944) 29 Cr.App.R. 169 and *Whitefield* (1984) 79 Cr.App.R. 36.

[50] Clause 27(8), (Law Com. No. 177), (1989).

Lord Coleridge C.J. in giving judgment said, at p. 712:
'The . . . Act was passed for the purpose of protecting women and girls against themselves. At the time it was passed there was a discussion as to what point should be fixed as the age of consent. That discussion ended in a compromise, and the age of consent was fixed at 16. With the object of protecting women and girls against themselves the Act of Parliament has made illicit connection with a girl under that age unlawful; if a man wishes to have such illicit connection he must wait until the girl is 16, otherwise he breaks the law; but it is impossible to say that the Act, which is absolutely silent about aiding or abetting, or soliciting or inciting, can have intended that the girls for whose protection it was passed should be punishable under it for the offences committed upon themselves.' . . .

In our judgment it is impossible, as a matter of principle, to distinguish *Reg.* v. *Tyrrell* from the present case. Clearly the relevant provisions of the Sexual Offences Act 1956 are intended to protect women and girls. Most certainly, section 11 is intended to protect girls under the age of 16 from criminal liability, and the Act as a whole exists, in so far as it deals with women and girls exposed to sexual threat, to protect them. The very fact that girls under the age of 16 are protected from criminal liability for what would otherwise be incest demonstrates that this girl who is said to have been the subject of incitement was being incited to do something which, if she did it, could not be a crime by her. . . .

We have therefore come to the conclusion, with regret, that the indictment does not disclose an offence known to the law because it cannot be a crime on the part of this girl aged 15 to have sexual intercourse with her father, though it is of course a crime, and a very serious crime, on the part of the father. There is here incitement to a course of conduct, but that course of conduct cannot be treated as a crime by the girl. Plainly a gap or lacuna in the protection of girls under the age of 16 is exposed by this decision."

Appeal allowed

Under the Draft Criminal Code Bill 1989 the common law rule is retained but not extended.[51]

E. Accomplices and Transferred Malice

David Lanham, "Accomplices and Transferred Malice" (1980) 96 L.Q.R. 110 at 110–111:

"An accomplice (A) instigates a principal offender (PO) to commit a specific crime. PO commits a crime of the same description but against a different victim or subject-matter or in a different manner. In what circumstances is A criminally liable for the crime committed by PO? The law in this area has become incoherent for two reasons. First, opinions differ on the nature of the link required between A and the crime actually committed. There are four theories running through the authorities. First, the direct consequences theory. Under this theory it is enough that the crime committed by PO flows directly from PO's attempt to commit the crime suggested. The second theory is the probable

---

[51] The Law Commission Working Paper (No. 43) proposition 8 had recommended extension of the protection from liability to those whose actions are "inevitably incidental" to the commission of an offence. The Code team concluded, however, that this would be too wide a protection: clause 27(7) and comments thereto (pp. 210–211).

consequence theory. A is liable only if the crime actually committed is a probable consequence of the crime suggested by A. This has been held to mean that A is liable if he ought to have foreseen the likelihood of the crime actually committed by PO. The third theory is that of recklessness. A will be liable only if he actually foresees the possibility that the crime actually committed will occur. Finally, there is the express authority theory. A will be liable only if he has expressly authorised the crime which is actually committed.

These four approaches would be enough in themselves to lead to confusion but the law is complicated still further by the fact that some authorities appear to apply different principles to different aspects of the problem. While the problem is basically one of transferred malice, the situations requiring the transfer can arise in various different ways. First, PO may attempt to harm the right victim (X) but harm another (V) by accident. Secondly, he may believe that V is X and so harm the wrong victim by mistake. Thirdly, he may do more harm that A ordered, *e.g.* injuring V (an unintended victim) as well as X (the intended victim). Fourthly, he may deliberately depart from A's orders and injure V even though he knows that V is not X. Fifthly, he may commit the crime ordered by A against the correct victim but at a different time, place or in a different manner from that ordered or advised by A. Finally, he may commit the crime ordered but against the wrong subject-matter.''

Authority on this problem is scarce with most of the controversy revolving around the following case.

R. v. Saunders and Archer (1573) 2 Plowden 473; 75 E.R. 706 (Warwick Assizes)

Saunders wished to kill his wife so that he could marry another woman. He explained his plans to Archer who advised him to kill her by poison. Archer bought the poison and gave it to Saunders to give to his wife. Saunders mixed the poison with two pieces of roasted apple and gave it to his wife. After tasting it the wife handed the rest of the apple to Eleanor, their three year old daughter. Saunders, on seeing this, merely said that "apples were not good for such infants" but when his wife persisted he simply watched his daughter eat the apple and did nothing "lest he be suspected." The daughter died of the poison. Saunders was found guilty of murder but the question remained as to the liability of Archer.

Lord Dyer C.J.:
"But the most difficult point in this case . . . was, whether or no Archer should be adjudged accessory to the murder. For the offence which Archer committed was the aid and advice which he gave to Saunders, and that was only to kill his wife, and no other, for there was no parol communication between them concerning the daughter, and although by the consequences which followed from the giving of the poison by Saunders the principal, it so happened that the daughter was killed, yet Archer did not precisely procure her death, nor advise him to kill her, and therefore whether or not he should be accessory to this murder which happened by a thing consequential to the first act, seemed to them to be doubtful. For which reason they thought proper to advise and consider of it until the next goal delivery, and in the meantime to consult with the justices in the term. . . . [It was finally agreed] that they ought not to give judgment against the said Alexander Archer, because they took the law to be that he could not be adjudged accessory to the said offence of murder, for that he did not assent that the daughter should be poisoned, but only that the wife should be poisoned,

which assent cannot be drawn further than he gave it, for the poisoning of the daughter is a distinct thing from that to which he was privy, and therefore he shall not be adjudged accessory to it; and so they were resolved before this time."

The judges took two years to decide that Archer was not liable as accessory to the crime of murder.[52] Many times that number of years have been spent interpreting this decision. A narrow interpretation of the case suggests that secondary parties will not be liable if the principal *deliberately* chooses another victim; effectively this is what Saunders did. He chose to let a different victim die, rather than step in to prevent it. On the other hand, if Saunders had not been present when his daughter ate the apple, he would not have deliberately changed the plan and the doctrine of transferred malice could apply and Archer would have been liable. The first case to arise on similar facts in recent times is *Leahy*.[53] In this case, where a deliberate wounding of a different victim took place, the defendant was held not to have aided and abetted the principal's offence. The Draft Criminal Code Bill 1989 echoes this interpretation with their proposition that the accessory will be liable where the intended offence takes place on an unintended victim or property, but not liable for "an offence intentionally committed by the principal in respect of some other person or thing."[54]

A broader, more positive, interpretation of *Saunders and Archer* is that the accomplice will only be liable if he expressly authorises or foresees the harm which occurs.[55]

How would the principle of direct consequences suggested by Lanham resolve the problem of Archer's liability? Does it achieve a just solution?

IV. A New Approach

We have seen that the underlying assumption of the present law is that secondary parties are as blameworthy as principal offenders. They are liable to the same extent and deserve comparable punishment. The Accessories and Abettors Act 1861, s.8 expressly endorses this approach. But is this premise a sound one? If not, what are the implications for the present law?

It is striking that in England there is still little discussion of the underlying rationale for holding accessories liable to the same extent as

---

[52] Even then, his release was not immediately ordered; he was kept in prison until he could purchase his pardon.
[53] [1985] Crim.L.R. 99.
[54] Clause 27(5), (Law Com. No. 177), (1989).
[55] See *ante* p. 517 for recent cases on this point.

principal offenders.[56] Even the Law Commission[57] feel the rationale to be so self-evident as not to warrant mention. Indeed, at a superficial level, the rationale is obvious: the accessory's role may have greatly facilitated the commission of the crime; he may in fact have master-minded the whole crime—he "may sometimes be more guilty than the perpetrator. Lady Macbeth was worse than Macbeth."[58] The liability of the accessory should be equal to that of the principal offender. Where it was the accessory who master-minded the crime, he may receive greater punishment than the principal offender. Where his contribution to the crime is relatively minor, he may receive less punishment.

It is our submission that this approach is ill-conceived. The primary question is to determine whether, *in principle*, accessories should be punished to the same, or to a lesser, extent than principal offenders. This question can only be answered by reference to some coherent theory of criminal liability. If the answer is that accessories ought, *in principle*, to be punished to a lesser extent, then this ought to be reflected by the *substantive law*; this would involve accessories being liable for *lesser criminal offences* than principal offenders.

By now it should be apparent (particularly from a reading of the chapters on general defences and inchoate offences) that a basic theme of this book is that criminal liability ought generally to be imposed only when a blameworthy actor has caused a specified harm.[59]

This is only a general proposition, not a necessary rule. Thus as we have seen, one *might* be justified in imposing criminal liability in the absence of blameworthiness (as in crimes of strict liability) or in the absence of obvious harm, or "first order harm" (as with inchoate offences). But where one of these elements is missing and liability is nevertheless justified, the equation ought only to be balanced by imposing *less* criminal liability. We shall also argue that this model provides the key for the structuring of all criminal offences and ascertaining their appropriate levels of punishment. Thus there can be degrees of blameworthiness (for instance, intentionally causing harm being regarded as worse than recklessly causing harm), and of course there are degrees of harm (for instance, killing one's victim is worse than injuring him). The correlation of the degree of blameworthiness with the degree of harm ought to provide a fairly precise level of criminal liability with appropriate level(s) of punishment.[60]

How does accessorial liability fit into such a model of criminal liability and punishment? The answer is clear. If an accessory is less blame-

---

[56] But see, as an exception to this: Helen Beynon, "Causation, Omissions and Complicity" [1987] Crim.L.R. 539.

[57] Law Commission, Working Paper No. 43, *Parties, Complicity and Liability for the Acts of Another.*

[58] Glanville Williams, *Textbook* (1st ed.) p. 287; see also J. C. Smith, "A Note on Duress" [1974] Crim.L.R. 349 at 351, cited with approval by Lord Edmund-Davies in *Lynch* v. *D.P.P.* [1975] A.C. 653 at p. 709. Lord Simon in *Lynch* and Lords Wilberforce and Edmund-Davies in *Abbott* [1977] A.C. 755, all opined that no distinction could be based on the degree of participation in a crime.

[59] For a fuller discussion of these terms, see *ante*, pp. 83–88, 277–278, 433–434 and *post*, pp. 795–799.

[60] *Ibid.*

worthy or causes less harm than the principal offender, then he deserves less criminal liability. If he is *both* less blameworthy *and* causes less harm, then he deserves *even less* criminal liability and punishment. So the central questions become:

1. Is the accessory less blameworthy, and/or
2. Does he cause less harm than the principal offender?

1. Blameworthiness

We have seen that an important indicator of blame is the *mens rea* of the defendant.[61]

The liability of the accessory, is derivative; it stems from the offence committed by the principal. "Since the source of culpability as an accessory is not the offence definition, there is no logical imperative that the mental element for an accessory should be the same as that required for a principal."[62] As we have seen, it is this question that has embroiled the courts recently. But if it is accepted[63] that the concept of *mens rea* presupposes a capacity to control one's actions and to choose between alternative courses of conduct, then the answer to this problem becomes clear. An accessory lacks control over the principal offender; he cannot make choices for that principal. (If he could we should classify him as a principal acting through an innocent agent, or as a co-principal.) The principal is "always the dominant party in the transaction. In criminal schemes, the principal is the actor-on-stage, who makes the final determination whether to commit the discrete criminal act."[64] The principal can have the *mens rea* of the actual offence because of his hegemony and control. The accessory at most has choice and control over his *own actions, namely, his acts of assistance or encouragement.* Once it is realised that this *mens rea* of the accessory is not the *mens rea* of the offence itself, that it is, in a sense, a step removed from the offence, we can then focus on the real question: is this *mens rea* of assisting as reprehensible as the *mens rea* of the principal who actually commits the offence? The answer to this question must be delayed until we have considered the next problem.

2. Causing harm

Again, an accessory, by definition, does not cause the ultimate harm. He contributes to the crime by his assistance or encouragement, but he does not actually cause the ultimate harm if it is inflicted by a responsible principal. So, in *Lynch* v. *D.P.P.*,[65] for example, Lynch drove some I.R.A. gunmen to a place where they killed a policeman. By his driving,

---

[61] For present purposes, it will be assumed that there are no other indicators of blame involved, or that these are constant as between principal offender and accessory.

[62] Ian Dennis, "The Mental Element For Accessories" in *Essays in Honour of J. C. Smith* (1986) p. 40.

[63] *Ante*, Chap. 2.

[64] Fletcher, p. 656.

[65] [1975] A.C. 653.

Lynch assisted in the commission of the crime, but his actions clearly did not "cause" the death of the policeman. Indeed, the rules of accessorial liability only exist because such an accessory does not cause the prohibited harm; if he did, he would be a principal offender (or co-principal) and such rules would be unnecessary.

David Lanham, "Accomplices, Principals and Causation" (1980) 12 Melbourne University Law Review, 490 at 510–511:

"*Assistance or permission*: neither assistance nor permission should be sufficient to amount to cause. If this is all that can be proved against A, it seems plain that the main motivation for the deed has come from B or elsewhere. Assistance or permission may be enough to make A liable as a secondary party where the other conditions for such liability have been met but they should not be sufficient to make A a principal on the basis of causation. . . .
Advice or counselling: These should arguably be enough where A knows the facts which make B's conduct criminal and B does not. They should not amount to causation where B knows that his conduct is criminal. In this latter situation it is reasonable to regard B, the immediate actor as the principal offender and to relegate A's position to that of secondary party."

So causation is not established in such cases. But why is this so? Mrs. Richard's actions were clearly *a* cause of her husband's ultimate injuries. Why can they not be regarded as the *legal* cause? Unless one adopts the "policy approach" or the "*mens rea* approach" to causation the answer would appear to be as follows: an accessory cannot cause that over which he has no control[66] and the causal link cannot be traced through the actions of a responsible actor.[67] Mrs. Richards caused the principal to act,[68] but by being a responsible actor not subject to the control or dominance of Mrs. Richards, the principal's actions broke the chain of causation between Mrs. Richards' actions and the injuries sustained by her husband. The principal caused the injuries.

In some cases, particularly those of aiding and abetting, it might be difficult even to establish that the accessory's actions were *a* cause of the ultimate harm. Thus in *State* v. *Tally*[69] it was stated:

"The assistance given, however, need not contribute to the criminal result in the sense that, but for it, the result would not have ensued. It is quite sufficient if it facilitated a result that would have transpired without it. It is quite enough if the aid merely renders it easier for the principal actor to accomplish the end intended by him and the aider

---

[66] Fletcher, p. 656; Lanham, at p. 506.

[67] *Ante*, pp. 410–411.

[68] Hart and Honoré would dispute even this. Where the actions of the principal offender are fully voluntary "it will not strictly be correct to say that the instigator has caused the principal to act as he does." They argue however that the actions of the principal "may, in a sense, be described as the *consequence* of the instigator"—this they describe as a different variety of causal connexion. (*Causation in the Law*, (1959) p. 340.)

[69] (1894) 102 Ala. 25.

and abettor, though in all human probability the end would have been attained without it."[70]

However, even though the accessory does not cause the ultimate harm, it is clear that he does cause a harm, namely, the harm of assisting or encouraging the principal offender. The harm involved in assisting or encouraging other criminals is quite different from the ultimate harm actually inflicted and does not necessarily deserve the same level of criminal liability and punishment.

3. Lesser liability and punishment

An accessory causes a different harm from the principal (the harm of assisting or encouraging a criminal act); he has a different *mens rea* from the principal (the *mens rea* of assisting or encouraging). We can now face the central question: is this different *mens rea* and harm less reprehensible than the *mens rea* and harm caused by the principal? If so, then this lesser blameworthiness and/or lesser harm caused should result in a lesser level of criminal liability and punishment.

There is one context in which the courts have had to face questions similar to these and that is in relation to whether the defence of duress should be made available to an accessory to murder, but withheld from the principal. In the case of *Lynch* v. *D.P.P.*[71] the House of Lords held that duress was a defence to an accessory to murder. In *Abbott*[72] the Privy Council held that duress was no defence to a principal offender to murder. Lord Morris in *Lynch* v. *D.P.P.* felt there was a material difference between the role of the principal and that of the accessory. An accessory "may cling to the hope that perhaps X will not be found at the place or that there will be a change of intention before the purpose is carried out or that in some unforeseen way the dire event of a killing will be averted. *The final and fatal moment of decision has not arrived.* He saves his own life at a time when the loss of another life *is not a certainty.* . . . [But the principal offender] must personally there and then take an innocent life. It is for him to pull the trigger or otherwise personally to do the act of killing."[73]

Lynch has now been overruled by the decision of *Howe*,[74] partly on the basis of finding the weight of previous authority to have been against extending the defence of duress to any party to murder, but also partly as a disavowal of there necessarily being a distinction between the killer and his side-kick:

"I can, of course see that as a matter of commonsense one partici-

---

[70] Hart and Honoré; *ante* n. 68: "When the participant merely assists he neither 'causes' the principal to act nor does the latter act 'in consequence' of his assistance. Probably the assistance need not even be a *sine qua non* of success." (p. 347).

[71] [1975] A.C. 653.

[72] [1977] A.C. 755.

[73] Emphasis added; the opposite view to this was expressed by Lords Wilberforce and Edmund-Davies dissenting in *Abbott*.

[74] [1987] 1 A.C. 417.

pant in a murder may be considered less morally at fault than another. The youth who hero-worships the gang-leader and acts as a look-out man whilst the gang enter a jeweller's shop and kill the owner in order to steal is an obvious example. In the eyes of the law they are all guilty of murder, but justice will be served by requiring those who did the killing to serve a longer period in prison before being released on licence than the youth who acted as look-out. However, it is not difficult to give examples where more moral fault may be thought to attach to a participant in murder who was not the actual killer; I have already mentioned the example of a contract killing, when the murder would never have taken place if a contract had not been placed to take the life of the victim. Another example would be an intelligent man goading a weakminded individual into a killing he would not otherwise commit."[75]

Are these arguments convincing? Or do the views of Lord Morris reflect the way most people think? The accessory who provides assistance or encouragement is clearly blameworthy, but not as blameworthy as the principal who actually pulls the trigger, stabs with the knife or takes the property. It is the principal who is the dominant party who has to make the final decision to commit the crime. It is the principal who is in control and has the power to choose whether to commit the crime or not.[76] In moral terms this surely makes his actions "worse" than those of the accessory. The principal is "tainted,"[77] contaminated by being the direct instrument of the crime; he is the one with the "blood on his hands." The accessory is likewise tainted or contaminated—but for what he has done, namely his lesser role of assistance or encouragement.

These ideas are recognised by German law which provides that punishment for an accessory be reduced as follows:

"1. Instead of life imprisonment, the punishment is imprisonment for not less than three years.
2. In cases of prescribed terms of imprisonment, the maximum term may be reduced to three-fourths of the prescribed maximum. The same reduction applies to monetary penalties.
3. The minimum term of imprisonment is mitigated as follows:
    A. From a minimum of ten or five years to a minimum of two years.
    B. From a minimum of three or two years to a minimum of six months.
    C. From a minimum of one year to a minimum of three months.
    D. In other cases the statutory minimum is retained."[78]

---

[75] *Per* Lord Griffiths at pp. 444–445.

[76] The "weak-willed individual" cited by Lord Griffiths (above), either has this ability to choose, or if not should have a partial defence available to him, or even be able to plead lack of *mens rea*.

[77] See Fletcher, pp. 345–347.

Punishment and substantive criminal law are the two sides of the same coin. Once it is accepted that accessories deserve lesser punishment, this is tantamount to creating a lesser level of criminal liability.[79] Accessories would no longer be liable "as a principal offender,"[80] but would be liable "as an accessory." Such an approach would permit attention to be focused on the real issue of the true bases of accessorial liability which would hopefully result in the emergence of a more coherent set of rules.

There would be several consequences to such an approach. There would need to be a clearer (not less clear, as is the current trend) distinction drawn between principals and accessories than was previously necessary—the principal being the one with control and hegemony over the execution of the crime.[81] One might also wish to distinguish between different classes of accessories in terms of their liability and punishment. The actions of the instigator or master-mind behind the crime are arguably more reprehensible than those of an accessory simply assisting the principal at the scene of the crime; the causal contribution of such an instigator towards the ultimate crime is certainly greater; he may thus deserve greater punishment.

Even if not all the substantive ideas expressed in this section are fully accepted, it is nevertheless hoped that one fact has clearly emerged. Rules of criminal liability cannot be rationalised or reformed in a vacuum. This can only be done by reference to a coherent theory of criminal liability, and such a theory can only be constructed by ultimate reference to the punishment to be meted out to offenders.

[78] StGB Art. 49(1); See Fletcher, p. 650.
[79] See *post*, pp. 807–810.
[80] The Accessories and Abettors Act 1861, s.8.
[81] See Fletcher, pp. 657–673; David Lanham, "Accomplices, Principals and Causation" (1980) 12 Melbourne University Law Review 490.

CHAPTER 7

NON-FATAL OFFENCES AGAINST THE PERSON

I. Offences Against the Person (Non-Sexual)

A. Introduction

1. The level of offending

Offences of violence (both those which result in fatalities and those which involve lesser harms), comprise only a small proportion of recorded crime in this country. In 1988, for example, violence against the person accounted for 4.3 per cent. of offences recorded by the police (with sexual offences accounting for another 0.6 per cent.).[1] The following diagram shows the breakdown of such offences.

Criminal Justice: Key Statistics, England and Wales 1988

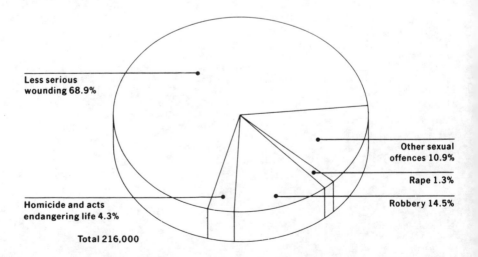

Violence against the person, sexual offences, and robbery, 1988

Less serious wounding 68.9%

Other sexual offences 10.9%

Rape 1.3%

Homicide and acts endangering life 4.3%

Robbery 14.5%

Total 216,000

---

[1] Criminal Justice: Key Statistics, England and Wales 1988. See *post*, p. 562.

There is no doubt, of course, that the total figure of 216,000 does not reveal the true picture of violence. This is true in at least two senses. Firstly, it hides the large regional variations in the level of personal violence offences: generally speaking, the highest levels are recorded in large urban police areas,[2] although recent research indicates a growth in violent crime in "mixed town and country areas" and "high status growth areas."[3] More significantly, perhaps, it under-represents the total level of offending in this area, particularly, as we shall see, in the context of sexual offences.[4] Even for non-sexual offences, the picture is far from complete. The Second British Crime Survey uncovered "a great many incidents which according to the letter of the law are assaults—family fights, fights at school and scuffles in pubs, clubs and football matches. Some are serious by any standard, but most involve little or no injury, and few are reported to the police."[5] Thus, most of the unreported offences occur at the least serious end of the spectrum of violence; the survey reveals a 60 per cent. reporting rate for wounding but only a 31 per cent. rate for common assault.[6] The commonest reasons given for not reporting were factors such as triviality, the inability of the police to do anything about the incident and being able to deal with the matter themselves.[7]

Seriousness is not the only determining factor, however, in the question of whether an offence is reported and then recorded. It is clear that domestic violence is under-represented in the official statistics. A recent Home Office review of domestic violence has estimated that only 25 per cent. of such incidents are reported to the police.[8] The picture is made even more confused because even if the assault is made known to the police they may not record it, claiming that is is not their responsibility or may record it under a different classification, such as drunk and disorderly or criminal damage.[9] Even if it is recorded, in 80 per cent. of cases it will be "no-crimed" later on the ground of the victim's reluctance to have the case pursued.[10]

Another form of assault about which knowledge is limited because it is not categorised by the police in this way, is racial assault. The Islington Crime Survey estimated that 7 per cent. of all assaults within the survey were racist. "(T)his figure is probably an underestimate for two reasons. First, not all the descriptions provided by the respondents give sufficient detail to classify their assault as racist, if in fact it was. Secondly, there was a number of instances in which the victim tended

[2] R. Walmsley, *Personal Violence*, (H.O.R.S. No. 89), (1986), p. 4.
[3] Mary Tuck, *Drinking and Disorder: a Study of Non-Metropolitan Violence*, (H.O.R.S. No. 108), (1989).
[4] *Post* p. 563.
[5] M. Hough and P. Mayhew, *Taking Account of Crime: Key Findings from the Second British Crime Survey*, (H.O.R.S. No. 85), 1985, p. 5. First findings from the 1988 British Crime Survey tend to suggest that no real change in this picture has taken place in the interim: P. Mayhew, D. Elliott and L. Dowds, *The 1988 British Crime Survey*, (H.O.R.S. No. 111), (1989).
[6] *Ibid.* p. 21.
[7] *Ibid.* p. 19.
[8] Lorna Smith, *Domestic Violence: an overview of the literature*, (H.O.R.S. No. 107), (1989).
[9] T. Jones, B. Maclean and J. Young, *The Islington Crime Survey*, (1986), p. 61.
[10] Lorna Smith, *Domestic Violence: an overview of literature*, (H.O.R.S. No. 107), (1989).

to ignore minor racist assault."[11] The latest British Crime Survey has, for the first time, sought to tackle the issues of racially motivated crime. In relation to assaults, a third of Afro-Caribbean and 44 per cent. of Asian respondents felt that there was a racial motive to the attack.[12]

2. Violence in context

Stephen Box, Power, Crime and Mystification, (1983), p. 145:

"To be a 'real' man in our culture is to realize that 'a man's gotta do what a man's gotta do.' He has to be strong, powerful, and independent; he should be prepared to be tough in overcoming adversity, to be forceful and never flinch or show cowardness, to be dominant by fair means or foul, to be constantly striving for achievement and success, even at the expense of others if necessary, to be competitive and determined to win although prepared to take defeat 'like a man' and above all, never, never to be seen acting or talking like a girl. In a man's world, to be a 'sissy,' or 'mother's boy' is the stigmatized fate that awaits those who lack the manly qualities of ambitious striving, shrewdness in outsmarting others, and moral flexibility to secure a desired end."

Violence is seen as part of the male culture and the antithesis of femininity and this is reflected in the criminal statistics: male offenders make up over 90 per cent. of those convicted, for example, of wounding or assault.[13] Whether women are less violent by "nature," by socialisation and lack of opportunity, or by mistaken chivalry on the part of men[14] is the subject of a fierce debate that has continued since Lombroso first "discovered" that women committed less crime than men. He did add, as a rider, the "fact" that what she lacked in numbers, she made up for by the excessive vileness of her crime, without, it must be said, much evidence to support his assertion.[15]

What victim research does show (official statistics only give information on this point for homicide) is that women are much more likely to be the victim of personal violence than the offender. Are they more likely to be the victim of violence than men? Latest figures from the 1988 British Crime Survey[16] lend support to the accepted view that men are the most likely victims of violence just as they are most likely to be the offender.[17] However, this picture of violence has not gone unchal-

---

[11] *Ante*, n. 9, p. 63. This finding, that for some ethnic groups the general level of racist abuse is so high that it becomes part of their every day reality and "background noise" has been echoed elsewhere: Malcolm Hibberd, "Violent Crime and Trouble in Small Shops," paper presented to the Second British Criminology Conference, July 1989. See also, R. Walmsley, *Personal Violence* (1986) p. 25, where the estimate of 3 per cent. of all crimes of violence against the person and robbery being racially motivated is given.

[12] *Ante*, n. 5, p. 48.

[13] R. Walmsley, *Personal Violence*, (H.O.R.S. No. 89), 1986, p. 5.

[14] The argument is that women commit as many (if not more) offences than men but that male protectiveness all along the line from victim to judge prevents these offences being dealt with in the same way they would be had the offender been male: O. Pollak, *The Criminality of Women*, (1961).

[15] Thus originating one of the many myths about female criminals. *The Female Offender*, (1895).

[16] *Ante* n. 5, pp. 33–34.

[17] R. Walmsley, *Personal Violence*, p. 8.

lenged; in Islington, for example, women were one and a half times as likely to be the victim of assault as men.[18] One major reason given by the authors of the survey for this apparent discrepancy is the absence of domestic violence from official statistics. This does seem to be the most plausible explanation and the reason it does not appear to have been picked up by the larger British Crime Survey is that that survey was concerned with "street crime."

Both surveys reveal that younger people are far more likely to be the victim of violence than people in the over 45 years of age category (they are, of course, far more likely to be the offenders as well), and the Islington survey suggests that black people are almost twice as likely to be victims of assault than other people. The picture that emerges from this localised survey, at least, is at odds both with the official statistics (where crime is apparently mainly inter-male) and the picture presented by the media (where crimes against the elderly or very young make better headlines).

The final point to be considered is the often stated view that society is becoming more violent. It is a question that is almost impossible to answer. Certainly, if one takes one's lead from the official statistics, it can be seen that crimes of personal violence rose by 72 per cent. between 1974 and 1984 (although this was more or less in line with the overall rate); more significantly, armed robbery[19] almost trebled during the same period.[20] So concerned was the government about this trend that maximum penalties for firearm offences have been raised.[21] However, whilst the debate about the influence of the media,[22] and lack of "discipline" on the part of parents and teachers alike rumbles on, there is some evidence that rises may be due, in part at least, to changes in police recording practices.[23] Society has always been violent, and even if, as seems to be the case, violent crime is increasing, a solution is unlikely to be found in increases to the maxima available to the courts. Sentencing in this area is traditionally tough,[24] and so, rather than attributing any rise to the failure of courts to reflect society's disapproval, much more searching and unpalatable questions have to be asked about the structure of the society in which we live.

---

[18] T. Jones, B. Maclean and J. Young, *The Islington Crime Survey*, (1986) p. 65. The effect fear of crime has on women will be explored in the context of sexual offences, *post*, p. 563.

[19] Dealt with by us in the context of property offences, but self-evidently a violent crime as well. *Post* pp. 776–780.

[20] R. Walmsley, *Personal Violence*, (H.O.R.S No. 89) 1986, p. 4.

[21] Criminal Justice Act 1988, s.44 raises the maximum penalty, *e.g.* for carrying a firearm or imitation firearm with intent to commit an indictable offence from 14 years to life.

[22] For a critique of the evidence, see J. Wilson and R. Herrnstein, *Crime and Human Nature*, (1985), pp. 337–354, where the results of research to date are described as equivocal: "even giving to existing research the most generous interpretation, viewing televised violence cannot explain more than a very small proportion of the variation in aggressive acts among young persons.".

[23] Findings from the 1988 British Crime Survey suggest that whereas police statistics indicate a 44 per cent. rise in woundings and robbery between 1981 and 1987, the survey found an 11 per cent. rise (*ante* n. 5, p. 16).

[24] See C. Emmins, *A Practical Approach to Sentencing*, (1985), pp. 285–289.

B. The Law

1. Introduction

There is a plethora of offences involving personal violence, from "mainstream" offences such as causing grievous bodily harm through kidnapping and administering poison to those such as assaulting a clergyman in the execution of his duties. The main offences, which are mostly statutory,[25] will be considered as these represent an ideal forum for considering how the law deals with the various configurations of degrees of harm and degrees of *mens rea*. The offences are ranked in some sort of hierarchy of seriousness: the extent to which this ordering is based on principle will emerge as the offences are examined in turn. As we shall see, they range from "the merest touching of another in anger,"[26] to injuries which fall only just short of death. Because many of the offences contain the basic element of assault, and as it constitutes the lowest rung in the hierarchy of seriousness of offences, this will be examined first.

2. Common Assault (Assault and Battery)

The terms "common assault," "assault" and "battery" are often used interchangeably by laymen and even lawyers. However it is clear that at common law there are two quite separate offences of assault and battery. An assault is putting someone in fear of immediate force; a battery is the actual infliction of force on that person. But confusion has arisen because the term "assault" or "common assault" was also used in a broad generic sense to cover both these separate offences. Thus section 47 of the Offences against the Person Act 1861 used to specify the penalties for a "common assault"; this was actually specifying the penalty for both an assault and a battery. The penalties for these two common law offences are now contained in section 39 of the Criminal Justice Act 1988 which refers to "common assault and battery;" this suggests that a battery is not a sub-species of a common assault. However, to avoid confusion in this book we will use the term "assault" in its broad generic sense as encompassing either an assault or a battery. When referring to either of these specific crimes, we shall speak of a technical assault or a battery.

(i) *Technical Assault*

This offence is committed when the defendant intentionally or recklessly causes the victim to apprehend immediate force.

(a) **Actus Reus**

The defendant must do something to make the victim apprehend immediate force. It is often stated that the victim must fear an immedi-

---

[25] Offences Against the Person Act 1861.
[26] *Cole v. Turner* (1705) 6 Mod. 149, 87 E.R. 907, *post*, p. 545.

ate attack. This latter formulation, while actually describing most situations of technical assault, is deceptive for two reasons. First, the victim need not be placed in "fear" in the sense of being frightened; he might be confident of his ability to repel the attack. He is nevertheless assaulted as he is made to apprehend the force. Secondly, he need not apprehend an "attack" in the sense of a severe measure of aggressive or destructive force; he need only apprehend that degree of physical force necessary to constitute a battery, which, as we shall see, in some circumstances need amount to little more than an unlawful touching.

Can the threat to use force be of any nature or form? Clearly physical gestures such as shaking fists, raising a knife or pointing a gun at a victim will suffice if the victim apprehends these being used against him. But what if there have been no physical gestures? Can mere words constitute an assault? Can there be an assault if the defendant merely utters verbal threats of violence or if the threats occur in, say, a dark alleyway where the victim is unable to see any physical gestures?

The case of *Meade and Belt*,[27] where Holroyd J. stated that "no words or singing are equivalent to an assault", is often cited as authority for the proposition that words alone, unaccompanied by physical gestures, cannot amount to an assault. Such an approach would be absurd and would mean there was no assault if a defendant came up behind his victim and threatened to shoot him. Clearly in many instances, threatening words can be far more frightening than physical actions. Perhaps what is meant is that in many situations verbal threats do not arouse apprehension of *immediate* violence; the fact that there is no physical action indicates that the threatened force is not yet imminent. But this will, of course, not be true of all situations.

The better view is that words alone can constitute an assault, provided they threaten a sufficiently immediate use of force. In *Wilson*[28] Lord Goddard C.J. stated *obiter*: "He called out 'Get out the knives,' which itself would be an assault." This view is supported by civil law cases holding that a conditional threat will suffice for an assault. In *Ansell* v. *Thomas*[29] the defendant threatened forcibly to eject the victim from a meeting if he did not leave voluntarily; this was held to be an assault. In *Read* v. *Coker*[30] the defendant and others surrounded the victim and rolling up their shirt sleeves, threatened to "break his neck" if he did not leave the premises. The victim sued successfully for assault. As Glanville Williams says:

"In essence the assault was by words. There was, in a sense, some conduct in addition on the part of D and his men, for they tucked up their sleeves. But when a number of men propose to eject a single person from premises, it is not at all necessary that they should first tuck

[27] (1823) 1 Lew CC 184.
[28] [1955] 1 All E.R. 744 at 745; see also, *Tennant* [1976] Crim.L.R. 133.
[29] [1974] Crim.L.R. 31.
[30] (1853) 13 C.B. 850.

up their sleeves. This is merely a conventional way of conveying a threat . . . [s]ymbolic gestures of this kind are logically the same as the utterance of words, for words are symbols. There would be no sense in attaching legal significance to the one that is not attached to the other."[31]

Thus it seems that words may constitute an assault. Another rule is, however, beyond doubt: words may negate an assault. In *Tuberville* v. *Savage*[32] the defendant placed his hand on his sword hilt and told the victim: "If it were not assize-time, I would not take such language from you." This was held not to be an assault. The words accompanying the action (of placing the hand on the sword) clearly demonstrated that because the assize judge was in town, the defendant was *not* going to use his sword. There could thus be no apprehension of immediate force. This case must be carefully distinguished from the conditional threat cases, such as *Read* v. *Coker*[33] where there *is* a threat to use immediate force; the victim *does* apprehend immediate force and the onus is on him to do something to avert that force. If the rule were otherwise it would mean there could be no assault where a robber says "Your money or your life"; such a position would be intolerable.

One final point to be considered is the stance the law takes in relation to empty threats. It may be, for example, that although the gun used to frighten gives every impression of being real, that it is in fact a toy, or, although real, is unloaded. Understandably, the law regards this fact as immaterial as long as the victim is made to fear an attack[34]; after all, the victim cannot be expected to know whether the threat is real or not.

The threat, however, may be empty in another sense; it may lack immediacy. Because in such circumstances there is no threat of present harm, there can be no assault. It is a serious gap in the law that it is no offence whatsoever to tell someone that you intend to break both their legs the next day rather than there and then. Because of this the courts have developed a rather generous interpretation of "immediacy"[35] and one of the recommendations in the Draft Criminal Code is that the existing offence of threatening to kill should be extended to include non-immediate threats to cause serious injury.[36]

(b) Mens Rea

The defendant must intentionally or recklessly cause his victim to apprehend the infliction of immediate force.[37] Thus if he intends (or is

---

[31] *Textbook*, p. 176.
[32] (1669) 1 Mod.Rep. 3; 86 E.R. 684.
[33] *Ante*, n. 30.
[34] *Lodgen* v. *D.P.P.* [1976] Crim.L.R. 121, *St. George* (1840) 9 C & P 483; 173 E.R. 921.
[35] *e.g.* In *Lodgen*, *ibid*, the threat consisted of showing a pistol lying in a drawer; this apparently was immediate enough. See also, *Smith* v. *Chief Sup. Woking Police Station* (1983) 76 Cr.App.R. 234 and *Pratt* [1984] Crim.L.R. 41.
[36] This would only encompass threats to cause serious harm as well as death; *Codification of the Criminal Law*, (Law.Com. No. 177), (1989), clause 65.
[37] *Venna* [1976] Q.B. 421, *post*, p. 548.

reckless) to alarm his victim the *mens rea* requirement is satisfied, even if he never intended to carry out the threat. There is some doubt as to the meaning of recklessness here. While *D.P.P.* v. *K*.[38] held that the *Caldwell* meaning applied, the Court of Appeal recently disapproved this in *Spratt*[38a] holding that the old subjective *Cunningham* test applied.

(ii) *Battery*

A battery is the intentional or reckless infliction of unlawful personal force by one person upon another. Thus while a technical assault is the *threatening* of such force, a battery is the actual infliction of the force.

(a) **Actus Reus**

The defendant must inflict unlawful personal force. What is meant by "force" in this context?

Wilson v. Pringle [1986] 2 All E.R. 440 (Court of Appeal, Civil Division)

Croom-Johnson L.J.:
"In our view the authorities lead to the conclusion that in a battery there must be an intentional touching or contact in one form or another of the plaintiff by the defendant. That touching must be proved to be a hostile touching. That still leaves unanswered the question, when is a touching to be called hostile? Hostility cannot be equated with ill-will or malevolence. It cannot be governed by the obvious intention shown in acts like punching, stabbing or shooting. It cannot be solely governed by an expressed intention, although that may be strong evidence. But the element of hostility, in the sense in which it is now to be considered, must be a question of fact for the tribunal of fact. . . .
Although we are all entitled to protection from physical molestation, we live in a crowded world in which people must be considered as taking on themselves some risk of injury (where it occurs) from the acts of others which are not in themselves unlawful."

This interpretation of the meaning of a battery was given in the context of a civil action for trespass to the person; nevertheless, it is accurate in relation to a criminal battery as well.[39] However, because the passage concentrates on what is not a battery, two matters demand some further consideration. Firstly, the passage is silent on the point of whether a battery can take place by omission. We have already seen in relation to this that although courts are reluctant to base liability in this area on omissions alone they are prepared to use devices that achieve substantially similar results.[40]

The remaining point of issue is whether the force need be applied directly in order for there to be an assault. Is it necessary, for example, that the defendant actually physically come into contact with the victim

---

[38] [1990] 1 All E.R. 331, *post* p. 546.
[38a] *The Times*, May 14, 1990.
[39] See also *Cole* v. *Turner* (1705) 6 Mod, 149, 87 E.R. 907; *Collins* v. *Wilcock* [1984] 1 W.L.R. 1172; *Faulkner* v. *Talbot*, [1981] 1 W.L.R. 1528. On the issue of the amount of every day contact to which we are deemed to consent see also, *Sutton* [1977] 3 All E.R. 476, *ante*, p. 286.
[40] See *Fagan* v. *Metropolitan Police Commissioner* [1969] 1 Q.B. 439, *ante*, p. 248.

with his fist or some weapon? A line of older authorities[41] suggests that such was indeed the case (although "direct" was interpreted with a certain amount of flexibility). However, the case of *Martin*[42] can be read as dispensing with the requirement of direct force.[43] In this case the defendant barred the exits to a theatre with an iron bar, turned off the lights and shouted "fire." A number of people were subsequently injured as they were crushed against the exit in the panic to escape. The defendant was convicted under section 20 of the Offences Against the Person Act 1861 of *inflicting* grievous bodily harm (an offence thought to require proof of an assault).

The decision of *Wilson*,[44] however, interpreted *Martin* somewhat differently as supporting the view that "to inflict" grievous bodily harm under section 20 does not necessitate an assault taking place. On the issue of whether an assault itself necessitates direct force, Lord Roskill in *Wilson* approved a passage from the Australian decision of *Salisbury*[45] where a distinction was drawn between "directly and violently" inflicting a harm (an assault) and inflicting harm that was "not itself a direct application of force to the body of the victim, [but] does directly result in force being applied violently to the body of the victim" (not an assault). However, the recent case of *D.P.P.* v. *K*,[46] suggests than an assault may still take place even if the force is applied indirectly.

D.P.P. v. K (a minor) [1990] 1 All E.R. 331 (Queen's Bench Divisional Court)

The defendant, a 15 year old schoolboy, was carrying out an experiment using concentrated sulphuric acid in a chemistry class at school when he splashed some of the acid on his hand. He was given permission to go to the toilet to wash it off and without his teacher's knowledge, took a test-tube of the acid with him to test its reaction on some toilet paper. While he was in the toilet he heard footsteps in the corridor and in a panic poured the acid into a hot air drier to conceal it. He returned to his class intending to return later to remove it and wash out the drier. Before he could do so another pupil used the drier. Acid squirted onto his face causing a permanent scar. The defendant was charged with assault occasioning actual bodily harm but was acquitted because he had not intended to harm anyone. The prosecution appealed by way of case stated.

Parker L.J.:
"[I]n my judgment there can be no doubt that if a defendant places acid into a machine with the intent that it shall, when the next user switches the machine on, be ejected onto him and do him harm there is an assault when the harm is done. The position was correctly and simply stated by Stephen J in *R v Clarence* (1888) 22 QBD 23 at 45, where he said:
> 'If a man laid a trap for another into which he fell after an interval, the man who laid it would during the interval be guilty of an attempt to assault, and of an actual assault as soon as the man fell in.'

[41] See Glanville Williams, *Textbook*, p. 179 where he cites authorities such as *Scott* v. *Sheppherd* (1773) W. Black 892.
[42] (1881) 8 Q.B.D. 54.
[43] See, for example, Smith and Hogan, *Criminal Law*, (5th. ed.) p. 356.
[44] [1984] A.C. 242.
[45] [1976] V.R. 452 at 461.
[46] [1990] 1 All E.R. 331.

This illustration was also referred to by Wills J in the same case in relation to s.20 of the 1861 Act. Wills J there also referred to *R* v *Martin* (1881) 8 QBD 54, saying:

'The prisoner in that case did what was certain to make people crush one another, perhaps to death, and the grievious bodily harm was as truly inflicted by him as if he had hurled a stone at somebody's head.'

In the same way a defendant who pours a dangerous substance into a machine just as truly assaults the next user of the machine as if he had himself switched the machine on.

So, too, in my judgment would he be guilty of an assault if he was guilty of relevant recklessness.

The real question raised on this appeal is whether, on the facts found, the respondent was so guilty in law.

For the Director of Public Prosecutions it was contended that, on the basis of Lord Diplock's speeches in [*Caldwell* and *Lawrence*], the respondent was plainly so guilty. The Director of Public Prosecutions also referred us to the speech of Lord Roskill in *R* v. *Seymour* [1983] 2 All ER 1058 at 1064, [1983] 2 AC 493 at 506, where he said:

' "Reckless" should today be given the same meaning in relation to all offences which involve "recklessness" as one of the elements unless Parliament has otherwise ordained.'

For the respondent it was submitted that the above-mentioned cases could all be distinguished from the present case in that in none of them was there any gap between the act of the defendant and the resultant harm to the victim during which the defendant had an opportunity to disarm or neutralise the risk, whereas in the present case there was such a gap. In the case of a mantrap it was submitted that the relevant recklessness did not occur until the setter of the trap abandoned the opportunity to disarm. If such abandonment was for good reason then there could be no offence. Good reason might be constituted, for example, if the defendant had left a dangerous situation such as a mantrap unattended in an emergency in order to go to the rescue of someone being assaulted or to answer a scream for help. In the present case, the respondent had left the drier in a dangerous condition through mindless panic and accordingly, it was submitted, the *Caldwell/Lawrence* test was inapplicable.

In my judgment those submissions cannot avail the respondent in the light of the authorities, even if panic was the cause of abandoning the machine in the dangerous condition which he had created. The appeal should in my judgment be allowed and the case sent back to the magistrates with a direction to convict on the s 47 charge and proceed to sentence.

I should add this. In *Elliott* v. *C* (*a minor*) [1983] 2 All ER 1005, [1983] 1 WLR 939 Robert Goff L.J. would have decided the other way had he not felt bound by the decisions mentioned above to take the course he did. As appears from his judgment in that case, criticisms of and misgivings about the scope of the *Caldwell/Lawrence* test have also been voiced by academic writers of distinction.

In the present case, whilst I respectfully share the misgivings so clearly expressed by Robert Goff L.J., I have no reluctance about concluding that the appeal should be allowed. The magistrates' findings make it abundantly clear that the respondent knew full well that he had created a dangerous situation and the inescapable inference appears to me to be that he decided to take the risk of someone using the machine before he could get back and render it harmless or gave no thought to that risk. Moreover, although it was, on the findings, panic which led him to pour the acid into the machine, the panic had been engendered by the footsteps which had disappeared before he left the machine.

There is no finding that panic caused him to abandon the machine in its dangerous condition."

Appeal allowed

(b) Mens Rea

R. v. Venna [1976] Q.B. 421 (Court of Appeal, Criminal Division)

James L.J.:
"In *Fagan* v. *Metropolitan Police Commissioner* [1969] 1 Q.B. 439, 444, it was said:

'An assault is any act which intentionally—or possibly recklessly—causes another person to apprehend immediate and unlawful person violence.'

In *Fagan* it was not necessary to decide the question whether proof of recklessness is sufficient to establish the *mens rea* ingredient of assault. That question falls for decision in the present case. . . .

In so far as the editors of textbooks commit themselves to an opinion on this branch of the law they are favourable to the view that recklessness is or should logically be sufficient to support the charge of assault or battery. . . .

In our view the element of mens rea in the offence of battery is satisfied by proof that the defendant intentionally or recklessly applied force to the person of another. . . .

We see no reason in logic or in law why a person who recklessly applies physical force to the person of another should be outside the criminal law of assault. In many cases the dividing line between intention and recklessness is barely distinguishable. This is such a case. In our judgement . . . this ground of appeal fails."

Given the decision of *Spratt*,[47] recklessness here appears to bear its old subjective meaning.

(iii) *Punishment*

A common assault is punishable upon summary conviction by a fine of up to (currently) £2,000 and/or six months imprisonment. The offence is no longer triable upon indictment.[48]

3. The Statutory Offences

(i) *Assault occasioning actual bodily harm*

Offences Against the Person Act, 1861, s.47:

"Whosoever shall be convicted on indictment[49] of any assault occasioning actual bodily harm shall be liable . . . to be imprisoned for any term not exceeding five years. . . ."

---

[47] *The Times*, May 14, 1990, disapproving *D.P.P.* v. *K.* [1990] 1 All E.R. 331. See *ante*, p. 546.

[48] Section 39 Criminal Justice Act 1988. Exceptionally, common assault can still be tried on indictment if it is founded on the same facts as an indictable offence which is charged, or if it forms part of a series of offences of a similar character to an indictable offence charged.

[49] The offence is also triable summarily by virtue of the Magistrates' Court Act 1952, s.19, Sched. 1 and punishable by a maximum of six months imprisonment or £2,000 fine, or both.

(a) Actus Reus

There must be an "assault." This is broadly accepted to mean that there must be either a technical assault or a battery. This assault must cause "actual bodily harm."

R. v. Miller [1954] 2 Q.B. 282 (Hampshire Assizes)

The defendant was charged with raping his wife and also with assault occasioning actual bodily harm. The first count of rape was dismissed on the basis of the wife's deemed consent to intercourse.

Lynskey J.:
"The point has been taken that there is no evidence of bodily harm. The bodily harm alleged is said to be the result of the prisoner's actions, and that is, if the jury accept the evidence, that he threw the wife down three times. There is evidence that afterwards she was in a hysterical and nervous condition, but it is said by counsel that that is not actual bodily harm. Actual bodily harm, according to Archbold, 32nd ed., p. 959, includes 'any hurt or injury calculated to interfere with the health or comfort of the prosecutor.' There was a time when shock was not regarded as bodily hurt, but the day has gone by when that could be said. It seems to me now that if a person is caused hurt or injury resulting, not in any physical injury, but in an injury to her state of mind for the time being, that is within the definition of actual bodily harm, and on that point I would leave the case to the jury."

Not Guilty of rape;
Guilty of common assault

Is the harm which occurred in *Miller* really describable as actual bodily harm?

Harm of this nature may be inferred from the facts as in *Taylor* v. *Granville*.[50] The evidence established that the defendant had struck the victim in the face and it was held that bruising must at the least, have been thereby caused. Such a finding clearly fell within the definition of actual bodily harm, and demonstrates the ease with which a common assault (punishable by a maximum of 6 months imprisonment) can be transformed into an offence punishable by up to five year's imprisonment.

(b) Mens Rea

Section 47 makes no express reference to any *mens rea* requirement, but it seems settled that liability is established if the defendant has the *mens rea* of common assault.[51] The defendant must, in other words, act intentionally or recklessly in relation to the victim being made to apprehend force. There is no requirement that the defendant have any *mens rea* in relation to the actual use of force. The effect, as Glanville Williams points out, is that section 47 is at best a crime of "half *mens rea*"[52]

[50] [1978] Crim.L.R. 482. *Cf. Reigate Justices, ex p. Counsell,* (1984) 148 J.P. 193.
[51] *Roberts, ante,* p. 419; *Smith (David George)* [1985] Crim.L.R. 42.
[52] *Textbook* p. 192.

where the *mens rea* requirement does not in any way "match" the *actus reus*. The case of *Spratt*[53] confirms that recklessness here bears its old subjective meaning.

(c) Punishment

In view of the above, it is alarming that the crime under section 47 is punishable by up to five years imprisonment. The issue of punishment is made more vexed, as we shall see, when section 47 is compared with the requirements under section 20.

(ii) *Malicious wounding and inflicting grievous bodily harm*

Offences Against the Person Act 1861, s.20

"Whosoever shall unlawfully and maliciously wound or inflict any grievous bodily harm upon any other person, either with or without any weapon or instrument, shall be guilty of [an offence punishable up to a term not exceeding five years imprisonment]."

(a) Actus Reus

In order for liability to arise under section 20 there must be a wounding or infliction of grievous bodily harm. As we shall see, the *actus reus* of the offence under section 18 is defined as wounding or causing grievous bodily harm. The common elements of wounding and grievous bodily harm are interpreted in precisely the same way under both sections.

(a) To *wound* necessitates that the continuity of the whole skin be broken.[54] It probably used to be the case that "wound" necessitated a battery to have taken place. Even if this is still so, it is unlikely to cause problems in practice. However, although the House of Lords in *Wilson*[55] leave the matter unclear, it is our view that no such requirement should be read in; moreover the need for the presence of the term "wound" at all must be questionable; given medical advances it is surely unnecessary that a wound, by itself, without grievous bodily harm, be the basis of a charge under section 20 or 18.

(b) *Grievous bodily harm* means nothing more technical than really serious bodily harm.[56] It has been held that it is not even necessary to include the word "really" in the summing up to the jury.[57]

What is meant by "inflict"?

---

[53] [1990] *The Times*, May 14; *contra D.P.P.* v. *K.* [1990] 1 All E.R. 331. *Ante* p. 546.

[54] Both the dermis and the epidermis must be broken. (*Moriarty* v. *Brooks* (1834) 6 C. & P. 684). Thus a scratch or break to the outer skin is not sufficient if the inner skin remains intact (*M'Loughlin* (1838) 8 C. & P. 635), nor is an internal rupture of blood vessels (*J.C.C.C.* (*A minor*) v. *Eisenhower* (1984) 78 Cr.App.R. 48); see Smith & Hogan pp. 372–373.

[55] *Post* p. 551.

[56] *D.P.P.* v. *Smith* [1961] A.C. 290. This issue is left very much to juries; some commentators have felt that there is a real danger that different juries will have different notions of what constitutes grievous bodily harm.

[57] *Saunders* [1985] Crim.L.R. 230.

The use of this word is peculiar to section 20[58] and has been the subject of considerable interpretation. Until recently, grievous bodily harm was said to have been "inflicted" when there had been a common assault.[59]

This understanding of the meaning of the term "inflict" has never gone without criticism and was reconsidered by the House of Lords in *Wilson.*

R. v. Wilson [1984] A.C. 242 (House of Lords)

The appellant, a motorist, misunderstood a pedestrian's signals and nearly ran him down. He then got out of his car and punched the pedestrian in the face, injuring him quite seriously. He was charged on one count only of inflicting grievous bodily harm contrary to section 20. He was found not guilty of inflicting grievous bodily harm but guilty of assault occasioning actual bodily harm. He appealed against conviction on the basis that assault occasioning actual bodily harm was not a lesser included charge within section 20. His conviction was quashed by the Court of Appeal but a certificate granted for appeal to the House of Lords in the following terms:

"Whether on a charge of inflicting grievous bodily harm contrary to section 20 of the Offences Against the Person Act 1861 it is open to a jury to return a verdict of not guilty as charged but guilty of assault occasioning actual bodily harm."

Lord Roskill:
"Stated briefly, the reason [for the Court of Appeal quashing the conviction of Wilson] was that the decision of the Court of Appeal (Criminal Division) in *Reg* v. *Springfield* (1969) 53 Cr.App.R. 608 made it impossible to justify a conviction for assault occasioning actual bodily harm, contrary to section 47 of the Offences Against the Person Act 1861, since the offence charged of '*inflicting* grievous bodily harm' did not, upon the authorities, *necessarily* include the offence of *assault* occasioning actual bodily harm. The emphasis added to these three words is mine.

. . . In the present case, the issue to my mind is not whether the allegations in the section 20 charge, expressly or impliedly, *amount* to an allegation of a section 47 charge, for they plainly do not. The issue is whether they either expressly or impliedly *include* such an allegation. The answer to that question must depend upon what is expressly or impliedly *included* in a charge of 'inflicting any grievous bodily harm'. . . .

What then, are the allegations expressly or impliedly included in a charge of 'inflicting grievous bodily harm.' Plainly that allegation must, so far as physical injuries are concerned, at least impliedly if not indeed expressly, include the infliction of 'actual harm' because infliction of the more serious injuries must include the infliction of the less serious injuries. But does the allegation of 'inflicting' include an allegation of 'assault'? The problem arises by reason of the fact that the relevant English case law has proceeded along two different paths. In one group it has, as has already been pointed out, been held that a verdict of assault was a possible alternative verdict of a charge of inflicting grievous bodily harm contrary to section 20. In the other group grievous bodily harm was

---

[58] S.18 refers instead to "cause," *post*, p. 555.
[59] *R.* v. *Clarence* (1888) 22 Q.B.D. 23; *R.* v. *Halliday* (1889) 61 L.T. 701; *Lewis* [1970] Crim.L.R. 647 and *Cartledge* v. *Allen* [1973] Crim.L.R. 530.

said to have been inflicted without any assault having taken place, unless of course the offence of assault were to be given a much wider significance than is usually attached to it. This problem has been the subject of recent detailed analysis in the Supreme Court of Victoria in *Reg.* v. *Salisbury* [1976] V.R. 452. In a most valuable judgment—I most gratefully acknowledge the assistance I have derived from that judgment in preparing this speech—the full court drew attention, in relation to comparable legislation in Victoria, to the problems which arose from this divergence in the main stream of English authority. The problem with which your Lordships' House is now faced arose in *Salisbury* in a different way from the present appeals. There, the appellant was convicted of an offence against the Victoria equivalent of section 20. He appealed on the ground that the trial judge had refused to leave to the jury the possibility of convicting him on that single charge of assault occasioning actual bodily harm or of common assault. The full court dismissed the appeal on the ground that at common law these latter offences were not 'necessarily included' in the offence of 'inflicting grievous bodily harm.' The reasoning leading to this conclusion is plain:

'It may be that the somewhat different wording of section 20 of the English Act has played a part in bringing about the existence of the two lines of authority in England, but, be that as it may, we have come to the conclusion that, although the word "inflicts" . . . does not have as wide a meaning as the word "causes" . . . the word "inflicts" does have a wider meaning than it would have if it were construed so that inflicting grievous bodily harm always involved assaulting the victim. In our opinion, grievous bodily harm may be inflicted . . . either where the accused has directly and violently "inflicted" it by assaulting the victim, or where the accused has "inflicted" it by doing something, intentionally, which, though it is not itself a direct application of force to the body of the victim, does directly result in force being applied violently to the body of the victim, so that he suffers grievous bodily harm. Hence, the lesser misdemeanours of assault occasioning actual bodily harm and common assault . . . are not necessarily included in the misdemeanour of inflicting grievous bodily harm . . . ' (see p. 461).

This conclusion was reached after careful consideration of English authorities such as *Reg.* v. *Taylor*, L.R. 1 C.C.R. 194; *Reg.* v. *Martin* (1881) 8 Q.B.D. 54; *Reg.* v. *Clarence* (1888) 22 Q.B.D. 23 and *Reg.* v. *Halliday* (1889) 6 T.L.R. 109. My Lords, it would be idle to pretend that these cases are wholly consistent with each other. . . .

My Lords, I doubt any useful purpose would be served by further detailed analysis of these and other cases, since to do so would only be to repeat less felicitously what has already been done by the full court of Victoria in *Salisbury* [1976] V.R. 452. I am content to accept, as did the full court, that there can be an infliction of grievous bodily harm contrary to section 20 without an assault being committed. The critical question is, therefore, whether it being accepted that a charge of inflicting grievous bodily harm contrary to section 20 may not necessarily involve an allegation of assault, but may nonetheless do so, and in very many cases will involve such an allegation, the allegations in a section 20 charge 'include either expressly or by implication' allegations of assault occasioning actual bodily harm. If 'inflicting' can, as the cases show, include 'inflicting by assault,' then even though such a charge may not necessarily do so, I do not for myself see why these allegations do not at least impliedly *include* 'inflicting by assault.' That is sufficient for present purposes though I also regard it as also a possible view that those former allegations *expressly* include the other allegations."

Appeal allowed

Apart from the difficulties in relation to assault and directness already discussed,[60] *Wilson* marks a welcome simplification of the law in this area. It has the fortunate effect of removing the anomaly that for the more serious offence, section 18, no assault needed to be established but for the *lesser* offence, section 20, as assault was always necessary. Such anomalies, based on the historic development of the offences, are best consigned to the history books.

(b) Mens Rea

The *mens rea* element of section 20 is supplied by the inclusion of the word "maliciously" within the section.[61] In the case of *Cunningham*[62] where the charge concerned the malicious administrating of a noxious thing under section 23 of the Act, the Court of Criminal Appeal interpreted "malicious" to mean that the defendant had to foresee the particular kind of harm that might be done and that he nevertheless went on to take the risk of it occurring. They clearly, within the context of the facts of the case, felt that the defendant had to foresee that the victim might inhale gas which the defendant knew was, or might be, noxious. In other words, the crime was one of "full *mens rea*," where the *mens rea* "matched" the *actus reus*.

Since then, however, this principle has been so whittled away that as Glanville Williams puts it, "*Cunningham* is well on the way to becoming so 'distinguished' that it never applies."[63]

R. v. Mowatt [1967] 1 Q.B. 421 (Court of Appeal, Criminal Division)

The defendant, D1, with another man, D2, accosted their victim. D2 took £5 from him and ran off. In the following argument between D1 and the victim, D1 struck the other several times. He was convicted under section 20 but appealed on the basis that the trial judge had given no instructions to the jury on the meaning of "malicious."

Diplock L.J.:

"The facts [of *Cunningham*] were very special. The appellant went to the cellar of a house and wrenched the gas meter from a gas pipe and stole it together with its contents, and gas seeped through the wall. The cellar was under a divided house, one part of which an elderly couple occupied, and one of them inhaled some gas and her life was endangered. He was indicted under section 23 of the Act of 1861. No doubt upon these facts the jury should be instructed that they must be satisfied before convicting the accused that he was aware that physical harm to some human being was a possible consequence of his unlawful act in wrenching off the gas meter. In the words of the court, 'maliciously in a statutory crime postulates foresight of consequence,' and upon this proposition we do not wish to cast any doubt. But the court in that case also expressed approval obiter of a more general statement by Professor Kenny, (Kenny's Outlines of Criminal Law, 18th ed. (1962) p. 202) which runs as follows:

---

[60] *Ante*, pp. 545–548.
[61] The term also appears in s.18; *post*, p. 555.
[62] [1957] 2 Q.B. 396.
[63] Glanville Williams, *Textbook*, (lst ed., 1978) p. 175.

'in any statutory definition of a crime, 'malice' must be taken not in the old vague sense of wickedness in general, but as requiring either (1) an actual intention to do the particular kind of harm that in fact was done, or (2) recklessness as to whether such harm should occur or not (*i.e.* the accused has foreseen that the particular kind of harm might be done, and yet has gone on to take the risk of it). It is neither limited to, nor does it indeed require, any ill will towards the person injured.'

This generalisation is not, in our view, appropriate. . . .

In the offence under section 20 . . . the word 'maliciously' does import upon the part of the person who unlawfully inflicts the wound or other grievous bodily harm an awareness that his act may have the consequence of causing some physical harm to some other person. That is what is meant by 'the particular kind of harm' in the citation from Professor Kenny. It is quite unnecessary that the accused should have foreseen that his unlawful act might cause physical harm of the gravity described in the section, *i.e.* a wound or serious physical injury. It is enough that he should have foreseen that some physical harm to some person, albeit of a minor character, might result.

In many cases in instructing a jury upon a charge under section 20 . . . it may be unnecessary to refer specifically to the word 'maliciously.' . . . Where the evidence for the prosecution, if accepted, shows that the physical act of the accused which caused the injury to another person was a direct assault which any ordinary person would be bound to realise was likely to cause some physical harm to the other person (as, for instance, an assault with a weapon or the boot or violence with the hands) and the defence put forward on behalf of the accused is not that the assault was accidental or that he did not realise that it might cause some physical harm to the victim, but is some other defence such as that he did not do the alleged act or that he did it in self-defence, it is unnecessary to deal specifically in the summing-up with what is meant by the word 'maliciously' in the section. It can only confuse the jury."

Appeal dismissed

Is it satisfactory that if the defendant pleads that he did not do the act and it is found that he did, that no evidence need be heard about his *mens rea*? What effect, if any, has section 8 of the Criminal Justice Act 1967 had upon this aspect of *Mowatt*?

Mowatt decided firstly, that actual foresight is required[64] and secondly, that all that is required is foresight of *some* harm, even (as in the instant case) where the charge was unlawful wounding and not inflicting grievous bodily harm. It was true to say, therefore, that the *mens rea* was quite out of step with the *actus reus* of the crime.

Mowatt was, of course, decided before the case of *Caldwell*,[65] and it has, therefore, to be considered whether that case has had any effect upon the meaning of malice within section 20. A number of cases have now made it clear that this term should continue to bear its subjective pre-*Caldwell* meaning. In *W(A Minor)* v. *Dolbey*,[66] the court refused to interpret the term "maliciously" within section 20 in the same way as "recklessly." In other words, *Caldwell* has been held not to apply to sec-

---

[64] See also *Flack* v. *Hunt* (1979) 70 Cr.App.R. 51, and *Sullivan* [1981] Crim.L.R. 46.
[65] [1982] A.C. 341; *ante* p. 178.
[66] (1989) 88 Cr.App.R. 1.

tion 20, and it will be necessary to prove that the defendant actually foresaw harm in order to hold him liable. In *Morrison*,[67] the Lord Chief Justice said: "Unhappily there are now in the law of this country two types of recklessness according to the nature of the crime which is charged. The first is that defined by Lord Diplock in *R.* v. *Caldwell*. . . . The other type of recklessness is that defined by Byrne J. in the Court of Criminal Appeal in *Cunningham*. . . . (This) decision . . . still stands and is binding upon this court."[68]

This reference to *Cunningham* is unfortunate in one sense. It conveys the impression that *the particular kind of harm* test is being resurrected. This would seem to be most unlikely and has been rejected in one case explicitly. In *Grimshaw*[69] the court not only firmly endorsed the subjective meaning of "maliciously" adopted in *Mowatt*, but also indicated that foresight of even *minor physical harm* would suffice for liability.

(c) Punishment

As with section 47, upon conviction under section 20, the defendant is liable to imprisonment for up to a maximum of five years. Not only does this cast the notion of the relative severity of offences into confusion[70] but until recently, as a matter of practical significance, there was little incentive for the prosecution to charge under section 20, when a conviction under section 47 was more easily secured bearing a similar penalty. The paradoxical situation now exists, that as a result of *Wilson*[71] it may be harder to prove at least one of the elements (assault) under section 47 than under section 20.

(iii) *Wounding and causing grievous bodily harm with intent*

Offences Against the Person Act 1861, s.18

"Whosoever shall unlawfully and maliciously by any means whatsoever wound or cause any grievous bodily harm to any person, with intent . . . to do some grievous bodily harm to any person, or with intent to resist or prevent the lawful apprehension or detainer of any person, shall be guilty of [an offence and shall be liable . . . to imprisonment for life]."

(a) Actus reus

The terms "wound" and "grievous bodily harm" bear the same meaning as that under section 20. "Cause" however, has never been held to imply that the injury need be the result of a common assault.

---

[67] (1989) 89 Cr.App.R. 17. This case involved a secton 18 charge of wounding with intent to resist arrest; nevertheless, the meaning of maliciously fell to be determined in relation to this charge as there was no intent to cause grievous bodily harm, but only an intent to resist arrest.

[68] See also *Jones* (1986) 83 Cr.App.R. 375. In this case the trial judge was not faulted for his *Mowatt* type directions but for his failure to leave the defence of consent to the jury; see *ante*, p. 291. See also, *Farrell* [1989] Crim.L.R. 376 and *Rainbird* [1989] Crim.L.R. 505.

[69] [1984] Crim.L.R. 108.

[70] *Post*, p. 558.

[71] *Ante*, p. 551.

Until the decision of *Wilson*[72] it was, therefore, true to say that "cause" was wider than "inflict" with the paradoxical result that it was easier to prove the *actus reus* of the supposedly more serious offence, section 18, than that of section 20. *Wilson* has, at least, remedied that defect in the structure of these offences.

(b) **Mens rea**

Two *mens rea* elements are contained within section 18; the offence must be committed "maliciously" and "with intent."

1. *Maliciously*. In order to appreciate the significance of this term in section 18, it is worthwhile dismantling the section—to find the possible charges contained within it. If one is charged with maliciously causing grievous bodily harm with intent to cause grievous bodily harm, then *Mowatt*[73] is right in suggesting that the word maliciously adds nothing that is not already present in the requirement of intent.

On the other hand, if the defendant is charged with maliciously causing grievous bodily harm with intent to resist or prevent arrest, the inclusion of the term malicious may be crucial. If, for example, the defendant intends only to resist arrest and has no state of mind at all in relation to the possibility of harm, he cannot be convicted because he is not malicious. He must, at least, foresee the possibility of some harm.[74]

2. *With intent*. The defendant must either intend grievous bodily harm or intend to resist arrest. What is the meaning of "intent"?

R. v. Belfon [1976] 1 W.L.R. 741 (Court of Appeal, Criminal Division)

The defendant slashed another man with an open razor, causing severe injuries to forehead and wounds to chin and chest. He appealed against his conviction under section 18 on the basis that the trail judge had misdirected the jury on the meaning of intent within the section.

Wein J.:
"Counsel for the appellant submitted that the direction was plainly wrong. 'Recklessness' will not suffice to establish the specific intent required to cause grievous bodily harm though it might be sufficient to establish malice aforethought in a case of murder. In this respect he says that the law is accurately and succinctly stated by the learned editors of Smith and Hogan's *Criminal Law* 3rd ed., 1973, at p. 47, where it is stated ' . . . attention should be drawn to the fact that, where an ulterior intent is required, recklessness is not enough. On a charge of wounding with intent to cause grievous bodily harm, proof that D was reckless whether he caused grievous bodily harm will not suffice. Yet, para-

---

[72] [1984] A.C. 242.
[73] [1967] 1 Q.B. 421 (*ante*, p. 553).
[74] *Morrison* (1989) 89 Cr.App.R. 17, *ante*, p. 555.

doxically, if death resulted from the wound, D's recklessness would probably be enough to found liability for murder.'

We agree that recklessness cannot amount to the specific intent required by the section, for the reasons shortly to be stated. Counsel for the appellant further submitted that whilst foreseeability of serious physical injury that will probably flow from a deliberate act is a relevant factor in cases of murder, it has no application to a case of wounding with intent because the nature of the particular intent is defined in section 18 and no further definition is permissible, let alone desirable. . . .

[Wein J. then examined the judgments in *Hyam* (*ante*, p. 153)]

. . . It may be anomalous that to establish the crime of murder it need be necessary only to show that the accused foresaw that his deliberate acts were likely to expose his victim to the risk of grievous bodily harm whereas to establish an offence under section 18 of the Act of 1861 it must be proved that there was an intent to cause grievous bodily harm. It is not the first time that this Court has been faced with an anomalous situation. Such a situation can arise where the offence charged is an attempt to commit a crime. To prove attempted murder nothing less than an intent to kill will do. To prove an attempt to commit any crime the prosecution has to prove a specific intent. It is not sufficient to establish that the accused knew or foresaw that the consequences of his act would be likely to result in the commission of the complete offence. In *Mohan* (1975) 60 Cr. App. R. 272, 277; [1976] 1 Q.B. 1, 10, James L.J. in giving the judgment of the Court said 'We do not find in the speeches of their Lordships in *Hyam* v. *D.P.P.* anything which binds us to hold that *mens rea* in the offence of attempt is proved by establishing beyond reasonable doubt that the accused knew or correctly foresaw that the consequences of his act unless interrupted would "as a high degree of probability," or would be "likely" to, be, the commission of the complete offence.' . . . At any rate we do not find . . . in any of the speeches of their Lordships in *Hyam's* case . . . anything which obliges us to hold that the 'intent' in wounding with intent is proved by foresight that serious injury is likely to result from a deliberate act. There is certainly no authority that recklessness can constitute an intent to do grievous bodily harm. Adding the concept of recklessness to foresight not only does not assist but will inevitably confuse a jury. Foresight and recklessness are evidence from which intent may be inferred but they cannot be equated either separately or in conjunction with intent to do grievous bodily harm.

We consider that the directions given by the judge in this case were wrong in law. Had he refrained from elaborating on the meaning of intent he would have given a quite adequate direction. It is unnecessary in such a case as this to do anything different from what has been done for many years."

Appeal allowed

The refusal of the Court of Appeal to follow *Hyam* now looks inspired in the light of subsequent developments in the law of intention. In 1976 they were saying in relation to section 18 what it took the House of Lords another nine years to say in relation to murder.[75] Foresight is evidence from which intent may be inferred but it is not intention. It thus appears clear now that "intent" in section 18 bears the same meaning as in *Moloney* and *Hancock*.[76]

---

[75] *Ante*, pp. 153–156.
[76] *Purcell* (1986) 83 Cr.App.R. 45.

(c) **Punishment**

Section 18 carries a maximum sentence of life imprisonment. In practice the vast majority of sentences fall well below this maximum.[77]

C. Evaluation

It is obvious that something needs to be done about the present structure of non-fatal offences against the person. What precisely, however, is needed?

The present structure of these offences, both in terms of substance and penalty structure, is little short of chaotic. Given the large difference in penalty, it is highly anomalous that the same *mens rea* suffices for both common assault and section 47 and that the difference in harm caused in these two offences need only be slight. Section 20 is supposed to be a far more serious offence than section 47—yet both carry the same maximum penalty. Both section 18 and section 20 cover the same harm—grievous bodily harm; can the difference in their maximum penalties (life imprisonment and five years respectively) be justified exclusively in terms of their differing *mens rea* requirements?

It is clear that both the substance of these offences and their scale of punishments must be restructured so as to represent a true hierarchy of seriousness. Failure to do this "might either confuse moral judgments or bring the law into disrepute, or both."[78] Further, "principles of justice or fairness between different offenders require morally distinguishable offences to be treated differently and morally similar offences to be treated alike."[79]

But how should this relative seriousness of the offences be determined? The present unhappy distinction between offences rests on a confused combination of *mens rea* and harm done. Law reform efforts in England have been mainly aimed at achieving a more rational combination of these two elements.

Criminal Law Revision Committee, Fourteenth Report, Offences Against the Person, Cmnd. 7844, (1980), para. 152:

"It was suggested by some commentators (to the Working Paper) that our proposed offences of causing serious injury with intent to cause serious injury and causing serious injury recklessly should be merged into one offence, and similarly the offences of causing injury with intent to cause injury and causing injury recklessly. This was at first sight attractive, but, on considering the types of cases which might fall into each category of offence, we decided that just as there is a need to separate death caused by an intentional act (murder) from death caused recklessly (manslaughter), in order to distinguish the gravest from

---

[77] The Advisory Council on Penal Reform: Sentences of Imprisonment, A Review of Maximum Penalties (1978) found that 90 per cent. of those sentenced under section 18 get sentences of five years imprisonment or less.

[78] H. L. A. Hart, *Law, Liberty and Morality* (1963), p. 36.

[79] *Ibid.* p. 37.

the less grave forms of homicide, there is similarly a need to separate the intentional causing of serious injury from the reckless causing of serious injury. There is, in our opinion, a definite moral and psychological difference between the two offences which it is appropriate for the criminal law to reflect. We are also of opinion that the merging of the mental element in such cases would cause difficult problems in the matter of penalty. All of us share the view that causing serious injury with intent to cause serious injury should carry a maximum penalty of life imprisonment to deal with those who repeatedly commit this grave offence of violence or who commit it on one occasion in circumstances just short of murder, but there is no justification in our opinion for increasing to life imprisonment the penalty for causing serious injury recklessly, the offence intended to replace section 20, and which now carries a maximum penalty of 5 years. . . . "

Draft Criminal Code Bill 1989, (Law Com. No.177) Clauses 70–72, 75:

"70.—(1) A person is guilty of an offence if he intentionally causes serious personal harm to another.

71. A person is guilty of an offence if he recklessly causes serious personal harm to another.

72. A person is guilty of an offence if he intentionally or recklessly causes personal harm to another. . . .

75. A person is guilty of assault if he intentionally or recklessly—

(a) applies force to or causes an impact on the body of another; or

(b) causes another to believe that any such force or impact is imminent,

without the consent of the other or, where the act is likely or intended to cause personal harm, with or without his consent."

Heather Keating, "Fatal and Non–Fatal Offences against the Person under the Draft Criminal Code" in Criminal Law and Justice, (1987) ed. I. Dennis, pp. 132–134:

"[W]hat has been attempted is a more rational structuring of the combination of *mens rea* and harm done. If one accepts the limits of this orthodoxy, then an advance has certainly been made. A clearer distinction is drawn between intentionally causing serious . . . [personal harm] and recklessly causing serious . . . [personal harm]. . . . Furthermore, we have a definition of assault in the Draft Code Bill; this is not a legacy from the Criminal Law Revision Committee who recommended that its definition be left to the common law. This was a somewhat strange omission and it is obviously right that assault should be brought within the Code. The proposed definition, however, to borrow Brian Hogan's phrase does little more than incorporate 'the potting shed' and 'outside privy' in the new 'properly insulated, double-glazed semi' ('Non-Fatal Offences, the Fourteenth Report of the Criminal Law Revision Committee" [1980] Crim.L.R. 542). It incorporates the ambiguity that lawyers have become inured to: a threat of, and the use of violence both being an assault. . . .

As for *mens rea*, the two forms of blameworthiness codified are intention and recklessness. . . . There are no offences of 'heedlessly' (the Code's term for Caldwell recklessness) causing [harm]. But is such a defendant not blameworthy at all?

'The fact that D consciously and without justification decided to run a risk indicates his indifference or thoughtlessness. But thoughtlessness and indifference can equally well exist without advertance. Thus when a man lights his garden bonfire, he does not generally advert to the inevitable risk that he will kill many insects who will perish in the flames. Such inadvertance is not culpable. But what are we to say of the man who, as in *Caldwell*, sets a hotel on fire without adverting to the risk that the guests may be burned? Such inadvertance indicates a shocking state of mind—one that cares as little for human beings as for insects.' (J. Stannard, 'Subjectivism, Objectivism and the Draft Criminal Code' (1985) 100 L.Q.R. 540 at p.551.)

This is not *mere* inadvertance, not *mere* negligence. This, if qualified by something like Hart's second limb to his test of negligence, of *capacity* to advert, (*ante* p. 203) is a culpable state of mind. . . . One might wish to create new offences, possibly based upon the Code's definition of 'heedlessness' which enabled such defendants to be punished albeit to a lesser extent than those deemed to be reckless.

One final point needs to be made at this stage, about the proposed Code on non-fatal offences. The sentence of life imprisonment would be retained for intentionally causing serious . . . [personal harm], allowing for the maximum to be given in cases, for example, of persistent re-offending of this nature. The proposed sentence for recklessly causing serious . . . [personal harm] is that of five years and for intentionally or recklessly causing . . . [harm] one year. This does, at least, introduce a gradation that makes some sense, but . . . this still leaves the difference between life and five years dependent solely upon a difference in the mental element required."

The Draft Bill, in addition, simply distinguishes between personal harm and serious personal harm. "Harm," the term that is preferred to "injury" by the Code team, is defined as "harm to body or mind and includes pain and unconsciousness."[80] This answers one of the criticisms, not only of the existing law, where, as we have seen, "actual bodily harm" means virtually nothing, but remedies the failure of the Criminal Law Revision Committee to provide a definition. Serious personal harm is, however, left undefined. In the United States the Model Penal Code has defined "serious injury" as "bodily injury which creates a substantial risk of death or which causes serious, permanent disfigurement, or protracted loss or impairment of the function of any bodily member or organ."[81]

Is there not a case for drawing more precise distinctions in the hierarchy of offences between different levels of injury? For instance, should we not distinguish between serious injury which is of a temporary nature (such as a broken limb) and that which is permanently crippling or disfiguring?

A final, and more fundamental question needs to be asked: must the restructuring of these offences be based *entirely* on new combinations of *mens rea* and harm? Could not other factors also be utilised in enforcing our moral assessments (to be translated into legal judgments) of the relative seriousness of offences. One such factor could be the use of a deadly weapon.

---

[80] Clause 3, Draft Criminal Code.
[81] Proposed Official Draft, s.210.0(3).

American Law Institute, Model Penal Code (Proposed Official Draft) 1962:

"211.1 *Assault*

1. Simple assault
   A person is guilty of assault if he:
   (a) attempts to cause or purposely, knowingly or recklessly causes bodily injury to another; or
   (b) negligently causes bodily injury to another with a deadly weapon; or
   (c) attempts by physical menace to put another in fear of imminent serious bodily injury.
Simple assault is a misdemeanor unless committed in a fight or scuffle entered into by mutual consent, in which case it is a petty misdemeanor.

2. *Aggravated assault*
   A person is guilty of aggravated assault if he:
   (a) attempts to cause serious bodily injury to another, or causes such injury purposely, knowing or recklessly under circumstances manifesting extreme indifference to the value of human life; or
   (b) attempts to cause or purposely or knowingly causes bodily injury to another with a deadly weapon.
Aggravated assault under paragraph (a) is a felony of the second degree; aggravated assault under paragraph (b) is a felony of the third degree.[82]

[The penalties range in severity from a petty misdemeanor, which carries a maximum term of only 30 days, to a felony of the second degree, which is punishable by a maximum of 10 years.]

211.2. *Recklessly Endangering Another Person*
   A person commits a misdemeanor if he recklessly engages in conduct which places or may place another person in danger of death or serious bodily injury. Recklessness and danger shall be presumed where a person knowingly points a firearm at or in the direction of another, whether or not the actor believed the firearm to be loaded."[83]

Why has the Model Penal Code chosen to utilise such a factor as the means adopted (deadly weapon) in its structuring of offences against the person? Dealing in particular with firearms, Ashworth has stated:

"In general it is fair to say that firearms can be more lethal than other weapons or methods, that they put the victim at a greater disadvantage, and that often their use (where this is forearmament) is evidence of premeditation . . . Firearms tend to put victims in a terrible state of fear."[84]

The relative seriousness of offences must be judged in moral (and if necessary, utilitarian) terms. Surely our moral assessments are not so blinkered as to exclude any considerations other than *mens rea* and harm? We have seen that the true criterion for assessing appropriate levels of criminal liability should be a combination of blame and harm. *Mens rea* is an important (and often the only) indicator of blame—we may rightly choose to blame the intentional actor more than the reckless

---

[82] The Model Penal Code provision has been substantially adopted by a number of states—*e.g.* N.H. §§ 631: 1, 2; N.J. § 2C: 12–1; Pa. tit. 18 §§ 2701, 2702; S.D. §§ 22–18–1. –1.1; Vt.tit.13 §§ 1023 to 1024.

[83] For a discussion of s.211.2, see *ante*, p. 498.

[84] *Sentencing and Penal Policy*, (1983) p. 166.

one. But the concept of blame is broader than that of *mens rea*. We have seen that it can include the absence of a valid defence—for instance, we can blame a defendant for reducing himself to an unacceptable level of intoxication.[85] But going even further than this, if two actors with the same *mens rea* cause the same harm,[86] we *might* nevertheless blame one of them more if he used a deadly weapon or if he inflicted the injuries in a particularly cruel manner. And if we do blame such a person more, he clearly deserves greater punishment—which, in turn, arguably at any rate, means that there should be a more precise *substantive* level of criminal liability to reflect his degree of blame.[87]

Indeed there could be many other indicators of blame, such as the circumstances of the crime, and the identity of the victim and defendant, that could aggravate the seriousness of a crime. It is interesting that in English law the method by which the crime was committed is crucial in many property offences (for example, whether property has been obtained by theft or by deception), yet is generally irrelevant in crimes of violence. One crime where the identity of the victim aggravates the seriousness of an offence is assault on a police constable contrary to section 51 of the Police Act 1964.[88] As Ashworth states:

"Submission of citizens to lawful authority is an important part of social order: assaulting a law enforcement officer is therefore morally worse than assaulting a private citizen, *ceteris paribus*, because of the implied rejection of the authority of the law itself."[89]

While there are probably more obvious deterrent reasons underlying the existence of this offence, it nevertheless serves as a useful illustration of the point. We shall return in more depth to the matter in the following chapter.[90] Suffice it to conclude here that, in our opinion, a careful consideration of these broader issues should precede any restructuring of the present non-fatal offences against the person.

II. Rape

Both the crime and phenomenon of rape are highly controversial and emotive issues. In seeking to explore the crime of rape one cannot

---

[85] *Ante*, p. 390; *post*, p. 796.

[86] The argument here presupposes that the harm *is* regarded as equal in both cases. It could of course be argued that the use of a weapon, etc., itself involves a greater harm as in addition to physical injuries the victim's interests will have been further violated by the extra fear he will probably suffer. However even this approach will lead to the same result—the offence is rendered more serious, whether by virtue of the greater blame, greater harm, or both together.

[87] As to why this should be reflected at the substantive level, as opposed to the sentencing stage, see *post*, pp. 807–810.

[88] See also: assaulting a clergyman in the discharge of his duties (Offences against the Person Act 1861, s.36); assaulting a magistrate in the exercise of his duty concerning the preservation of a vessel in distress or a wreck (s.37). These offences would go under the Draft Criminal Code, in line with the thinking of the Criminal Law Revision Committee that the victim's identity should generally be relevant to sentencing only and not to the definition of the offence (14th. Report, para. 162).

[89] *Ante*, n. 84, pp. 158–159.

[90] *Post*, p. 795.

ignore its social context, not least because of the implications such a study have for the crime itself.

A. Sociological Context

1. The level of offending

Few would deny that rape is one of the most under-reported of crimes. What is disputed is the extent to which official statistics are inaccurate. It is only comparatively recently that research has been done in this country to shed some light on the dark figures of offending. The second British Crime Survey revealed only a very small number of sexual offences (the authors accept that they may not have been able to overcome the reticence of victims to talk to them) but even here the reporting rate was only 11 per cent.[91] Other studies have revealed a much higher level of rape in society; for example, in one study, 17 per cent. of respondents to a questionnaire said they had been raped and a further 20 per cent. said they had been the victim of attempted rape. If one excludes those women who had been raped by their husbands (which, as we shall see, for the purposes of the law is not rape), then the reporting rate amongst victims was 8 per cent. only.[92] In another study the level of reporting was estimated to be around 25 per cent.[93] In 1987, the number of rapes recorded by the police was 2,471: this is clearly a gross under-representation of the level of rape in society.

Victim surveys, as well as providing us with insight into the amount of crime, also enable a picture to be built up about the way crime, and the fear of crime, affects people's lives. All the evidence supports the view that women's lives and freedom of movement are curtailed by the fear of violence and, in particular, the fear of rape. The latest British Crime Survey reveals that one in five women felt "very unsafe" when walking outside at night,[94] and in the earlier, 1984 survey half of the respondents said they would always be accompanied if they went out at night.[95] So real are women's fears that some taxi firms now guarantee women drivers to their customers. For many, in other words, there is a self-imposed curfew—an interesting concept given that they are not the criminals! It is sometimes said that these fears are exaggerated out of all proportion; indeed, the newspaper report which gave details of the latest British Crime Survey was headed "Women too wary of violent attack."[96] Given the low level of offending revealed by the survey, per-

---

[91] M. Hough and P. Mayhew, *Taking Account of Crime: Key Findings From the 1984 British Crime Survey*, (H.O.R.S. No. 85), (1985). pp. 9–11. Preliminary findings from the 1988 British Crime Survey (*ante* n. 5) indicate similar findings.

[92] R.E. Hall, *Ask Any Woman: A London Inquiry into Rape and Sexual Assault*, (1985).

[93] London Rape Crisis Centre, *Annual Report 1982*, p. 37. See further, Jennifer Tempkin, *Rape and the Legal Process*, (1987) pp. 8–11 for details of studies in this country and abroad.

[94] *The Sunday Correspondent*, September 17, 1989. (See also *ante* n. 5.)

[95] M. Hough and P. Mayhew, *ante*, n. 91 p. 40.

[96] *The Sunday Correspondent*, September 17, 1989.

haps this is none too surprising, but as the other studies above show, women's fears may be based on fairly solid ground.

There is one last insight provided by victim studies that needs to be considered: why is it that rape is so under-reported? The reason given most frequently is that of having to deal with unsympathetic police at a time when they are most vulnerable,[97] but the real dynamics of the decision to report can only be truly understood against the backdrop of societal attitudes to women and rape generally, and it is to this that we will now turn.

2. Rape in context

Allison Morris, Women, Crime and Criminal Justice, (1987), pp. 165–181:

"Most of us believe we know what rape is, but our knowledge is derived from social not legal definitions. 'True' rape in popular imagination involves the use of weapons, the infliction of serious injury and occurs in a lonely place late at night. The 'true' rapist is over-sexed, sexually frustrated or mentally ill, and is a stranger. The 'true' rape victim is a virgin (or has had no extra-marital affairs), was not voluntarily in the place where the act took place, fought to the end and has bruises to show for it. . . . (T)he reason (other) kinds of situations are not seen as rape is the strength of the assumptions we hold about rape. . . . I will now examine some of these assumptions. . . .

'Rape is impossible'
. . . [Some] criminologists have argued that to force a woman into intercourse is an impossible task in most cases if the woman is conscious and extreme pain is not inflicted. These beliefs have become part of rape folklore (. . . 'a woman with her skirt up can run faster than a man with his trousers down' and the like) and embedded in the practice of criminal justice professionals. . . .

'Women want to be raped'
This assumption has its roots in Freudian beliefs about the masochistic nature of female sexuality . . . rape is believed to dominate women's sexual fantasies. . . .

' "No" means "Yes" '
Nineteenth-century women—or, at least, ladies—were seen as asexual and presumed not to enjoy sex. Whereas they were passive and submitted (rather than consented) to the sex act, men were viewed as the aggressors and the initiators, and as having sexual needs. These beliefs have resonances today. . . . Men are expected to make advances (otherwise the woman thinks she is unattractive) and women are expected to be sexually attractive and, at the same time, both coy and flirtatious. They are expected to play hard to get, to need to be seduced. . . . A judge in a recent rape trial in Cambridge told the jury that women sometimes say 'no' when they mean 'yes' and to remember the expression 'stop it. I like it'. . . .

[97] See Jennifer Tempkin, *Rape and the Legal Process*, (1987), pp. 2–3, 11–13; the police would argue that as the victim will be put through an ordeal by the defence counsel, they need to assess the strength of her case, but that they would not be unsympathetic. Increasingly, women police officers may be made responsible for preliminary questioning.

' *"Yes" to one, then "yes" to all'.*[98]

'The victim was asking for it'

In essence this assumption implies that the victim should not have dressed like that, (*e.g.* with no bra), behaved like that, (*e.g.* hitch-hiked), gone to places like that, (*e.g.* singles' bars). . . . Amir, in his study of rape, developed the notion of victim precipitation. His definition is both extremely broad and stresses the offender's interpretation of the victim's behaviour, not the victim's. 'The victim actually—or so it was interpreted by the offender—agreed to sexual relations but retracted . . . or did not resist strongly enough when the suggestion was made by the offender.' The term applies also to cases in which the victim enters vulnerable situations charged sexually. (*Patterns in Forcible Rape*, (1971) p. 266.) Earlier, he seems to define any form of female behaviour as rape-precipitating. . . . Despite this, only 19 per cent. of the rapes in Amir's sample could be so 'explained'. . . .

'Rape is a cry for vengeance'

. . . Standard legal texts on evidence and procedure . . . warn of the danger of women contriving false charges of sexual offences. And as recently as 1984, the Criminal Law Revision Committee prefaced its report on sex offences with the words that 'by no means every accusation of rape is true' (15th. Report, Sexual Offences, Cmnd. 9213, p. 5). . . . [99]

'Rape is a sexual act'

. . . The popular conception now is that rape is sexually motivated: this is most apparent in accounts offered to excuse rape. Smart and Smart (*Women, Sexuality and Social Control* (1978) pp. 98–9) provide examples of this from media coverage of rape:'

The pregnancy of B's wife may have been 'one of the reasons for his committing the offence.'

R attacked her five days before his wife gave birth to their first child. . . . "

Sexual gratification however, may not be the major reason for rape. As Brownmiller says "the penis is deployed as a weapon,"[1] and research . . . conducted amongst convicted rapists suggests that the desire to dominate and humiliate the rape victim (often coupled with revenge motives) features most commonly.[2] In furtherance of this motive, the attractiveness of the victim is not a vital ingredient, although it is a paradox in a society that demands its females to make themselves attractive, that if the rape victim has done so, she may well be condemned for it. Whilst most rape victims are young,[3] what matters more than physical appearance is vulnerability. As one rape victim

---

[98] For discussion of the extent to which evidence of past sexual experience can be introduced, see *post*, p. 572.

[99] See also, D. Elliot, "Rape Complainants' Sexual Experience with Third Parties" [1984] Crim.L.R. 4 as representative of this view. See *post*, p. 572, for rules of corroboration that have developed because of this distrust of complainants.

[1] S. Brownmiller, *Against Our Will*, (1975), p. 11.

[2] Queen's Bench Foundation, *Rape—Prevention and Resistance* (1976), p. 80; *contra* M. Amir, *Patterns in Forcible Rape* (1971), p. 131 who concluded without much supportive evidence that strong sexual emotion was the dominant motive.

[3] The ages most at risk are those between 15–19 (Amir, pp. 50–52). But studies do report ranges between 1–82 years, S. Brownmiller, *Against Our Will*, p. 272.

said, "what I exuded that night was not sexuality . . . but vulnerability . . . I, by virtue of my size and gender . . . was recognisable to the
rapist as easy game and an exemplary target for his generalised mis-
ogyny."[4]

It has often been asserted that rapists are pathological individuals;
they are "victims of a disease from which many of them suffer more
than their victims"[5]; they are "sexual psychopaths." Whilst there are
undoubtedly rapists who are psychologically disturbed, more recent
research has shown how rare this is.[6] The better view, it is submitted, is
that rape is the result of a structure of society that generally sets men up
as powerful, and women as victims: "When the sex roles of both men
and women are defined by individual needs and talents rather than by
stereotypic expectations based on sex and power motives, only then
will there be an end to rape."[7]

3. Sentencing

Rape is punishable by a maximum sentence of life imprisonment and
it is now almost axiomatic that if the defendant is convicted,[8] he will
serve a period of immediate imprisonment. The guideline case of
Billam,[9] makes it clear that custodial sentences of five years will be the
normal sentence for rape without aggravating features and that only in
the most exceptional circumstances will a non-custodial sentence be
imposed.[10] There is already evidence that the guidelines are having the
effect of lengthening sentences for rape.[11] If these guidelines continue
to be followed then there should be an end to the judicial *faux pas* that
litter this area. It is not a reason for reducing the sentence that the victim was hitch-hiking,[12] or that she had prior sexual experience, and it is
of only minor significance that the defendant was of previous good
character. Given the poor record of sentencing in this area, however, it
is likely that some judges will continue to pass idiosyncratic sentences;
it is, perhaps, fortunate that there is now a right of appeal against too
lenient sentences.[13]

---

[4] Anon. letter to *The Observer* (January 10, 1982).

[5] B. Karpman, *The Sexual Offender and His Offenses* (1954), p. 482.

[6] For example, S. Smithyman in *Perspectives on Victimology*, ed. W. Parsonage (1979), pp. 99–120. See also Howard League Working Party, *Unlawful Sex* (1985), pp. 47 *et seq.*.

[7] E. Hilberman, *The Rape Victim* (1976), p. 62.

[8] It should be said that the conviction rate for rape is lower than for other serious offences: see J. Tempkin, "Towards a Modern Law of Rape" (1982) 45 M.L.R. 399; Z. Adler, "Rape—The Intention of Parliament and The Practice of the Courts" (1982) 45 M.L.R. 664; Soothill, "Rape Acquittals" (1980) 43 M.L.R. 159 and *Sexual Offences, Consent and Sentencing*, H.O.R.S. No. 54 (1979).

[9] (1986) Vol. no. Cr.App.R. 347; *ante*, p. 61.

[10] As, for example, in the case of *Taylor* (1983) 5 Cr.App.R.(S) 241, where the defendant was a mentally retarded man who raped a girl with Downs Syndrome.

[11] *Crime, Justice and Protecting the Public* (1990) p. 14.

[12] The statement by Judge Bernard Russell that such action constituted contributory negligence (*The Guardian*, January 8, 12 and 16, 1982), was one of the reasons for the tightening up of sentencing by means of a guideline judgment—*Roberts* (1982) 4 Cr.App.R.(S.) 8, which has now been superseded by *Billam*.

[13] *Ante*, p. 71.

B. The Law

Sexual Offences Act 1956, s.1(1)

"It is [an offence] for a man to rape a woman.
[and shall be liable to a maximum of life imprisonment]."

Sexual Offences (Amendment) Act 1976, s.1(1)

"For the purposes of section 1 of the Sexual Offences Act 1956 . . . a man commits rape if:—
(a) he has unlawful sexual intercourse with a woman who at the time of the intercourse does not consent to it; and
(b) at that time he knows that she does not consent to the intercourse or he is reckless as to whether she consents to it."

1. Actus reus

The *actus reus* of the crime of rape is unlawful sexual intercourse with a woman without consent. Three issues thus need to be considered; the requirement of sexual intercourse, the element of unlawfulness, and lack of consent.

(i) *Sexual intercourse*

It is clear that full sexual intercourse need not take place for rape to occur; the slightest degree of penetration of the vagina with the penis suffices.[14] Thus, the rubbing of the entrance to the vagina with the penis causing ejaculation is not rape, nor is anal or oral sex (buggery and fellatio). So too, penetration of the vagina or anus with inanimate objects is not rape, although all of these may be criminal offences.[15] The Criminal Law Revision Committee have recommended that the definition of rape should not be extended to cover any of these acts. In their view, "the concept of rape, as a distinct form of criminal misconduct, is well established in popular thought and corresponds to a distinctive form of wrongdoing" and that "the risk of pregnancy is a further and important distinguishing characteristic of rape."[16] Whether these reasons are persuasive will be examined later.[17]

(ii) *The unlawful element*

This is always taken to refer to intercourse outside the bonds of marriage. A woman is deemed to consent to the act of intercourse by the marriage ceremony and, therefore, during the lifetime of the marriage a husband cannot be found guilty of rape even though *in fact* his wife did not consent.[18] Those who defend this rule feel as a matter of policy that

---

[14] *People (Att.-Gen.)* v. *Dermody* [1956] I.R. at 32; Sexual Offences (Amendment) Act 1976, s.7(2).

[15] Either the offence of buggery or indecent assault: Sexual Offences Act 1956, ss.12(1) and 14(1) respectively.

[16] 15th. Report, *Sexual Offences*, (1984), para. 45.

[17] *Post*, p. 579.

[18] He may, of course, be charged with assault, etc., if force is used in the act—*Miller* [1954] 2 Q.B. 282. Or he may also be guilty of rape if he aids and abets another to have non-consensual sexual intercourse: *Cogan and Leek* [1976] Q.B. 217, *ante*, p. 521.

the police and courts ought not to become involved in domestic disputes of this nature. However, inroads have been made into the operation of this rule.

R. v. Steele (1977) 66 Cr.App.R. 22 (Court of Appeal, Criminal Division)

The appellant was convicted of raping his wife from whom he was living apart, after he had entered the nurses' home in which she was living, and had sexual intercourse with her without her consent, being in breach of a non-molestation agreement. He appealed.

Lane L.J.:
"As a general principle, there is no doubt that a husband cannot be guilty of rape upon his wife. The reason in Sir Matthew Hale's *Pleas of the Crown*, Vol. 1 at p. 629 is stated in this way: ' . . . by their mutual matrimonial consent and contract the wife hath given up herself in this kind unto her husband, which she cannot retract.' No doubt in times gone by there were no circumstances in which the wife could be held to have retracted the overall consent which, by the marriage ceremony, she gave to sexual intercourse with her husband. Researches have failed to reveal any exception to the general rule until 1949: that was the case of *Clarke* (1949) 33 Cr.App.R. 216 decided by Byrne J. In *Clarke*, there was in existence at the time of the alleged rape, a separation order on the grounds of the prisoner's persistent cruelty towards his wife. That separation order was in force and it contained a clause that the wife was no longer bound to co-habit with the prisoner. . . . [Clarke was accordingly convicted of rape.]
    The next case in point of time was the decision by Lynskey J. in *Miller* [1954] 38 Cr.App.R. 1. In that case, the only relevant action which the wife had taken was to file a petition for divorce on the grounds of adultery. . . . [The husband] was indicted for rape and also for assault occasioning actual bodily harm. Lynskey J. . . . held that the mere filing of a petition for a divorce, even though there had been a partial hearing of that petition, without any order from the Court at all, was not sufficient to revoke the wife's consent and consequently the husband was entitled to have intercourse, albeit by force, with his wife without being guilty of rape although, in certain circumstances, he might be guilty of inflicting harm and violence upon her.
    The third decision is that of *O'Brien (Edward)*, a decision of Park J. reported in [1974] 3 All E.R. 663. In that case, the wife was granted a decree nisi and it was after that decree that the husband had intercourse with her by force. It was held by the learned judge that the decree nisi effectively terminated the wife's consent to marital intercourse. Therefore, the husband was liable to be convicted of rape.
    In this case, the circumstances are of course different from any of those in the three cases to which I have referred. Here there has been no decree of the Court, here there has been no direct order of the Court compelling the husband to stay away from his wife. There has been an undertaking by the husband not to molest his wife. The question which the Court has to decide is this. Have the parties made it clear, by agreement between themselves, or has the Court made it clear by an order or something equivalent to an order, that the wife's consent to sexual intercourse with her husband implicit in the act of marriage, no longer exists? A separation agreement with a non-co-habitation clause, a decree of divorce, a decree of judicial separation, a separation order in the justices' court containing a non-co-habitation clause and an injunction restraining the husband from molesting the wife or having sexual intercourse with her are all obvious

cases in which the wife's consent would be successfully revoked.[19] On the other hand, the mere filing of a petition for divorce would clearly not be enough, the mere issue of proceedings leading up to a magistrates' separation order or the mere issue of proceedings as a preliminary to apply for an *ex parte* injunction to restrain the husband would not be enough but the granting of an injunction to restrain the husband would be enough because the Court is making an order wholly inconsistent with the wife's consent and an order, breach of which would or might result in the husband being punished by imprisonment.

What then of the undertaking in lieu of an injunction? It is, in the judgment of this Court, the equivalent of an injunction. It is given to avoid, amongst other things, the stigma of an injunction. Breach of it is enforceable by the Court and may result in imprisonment. It is, in effect equivalent to the granting of an injunction. Indeed, whether one considers this as equivalent to the order of the Court or the equivalent of an agreement between the parties, it does not matter. It may indeed have aspects of both. The effect is to eliminate the wife's matrimonial consent to intercourse. That is the judgment of the Court on that first point. Therefore, there is no bar to this man being found guilty of rape if the other ingredients of the offence are successfully proved by the prosecution."

Appeal allowed on another point

R. v. Caswell [1984] Crim.L.R. 111 (Wakefield Crown Court)

"C was charged with indecent assault upon his estranged wife. On the night in question they had met and argued, and he had attacked her in a park, kicking her in the face and ribs. This formed the subject of a charge of assault occasioning actual bodily harm, to which he pleaded guilty. Thereafter the prosecution allegation was that he pulled her by the arm into a nearby public lavatory, ordered her to remove her knickers, pulled her head down on to his erect penis to make her suck him (which activity they had performed consensually during cohabitation), and made her have intercourse; he then made her go into a cubicle and repeat the procedures; all against her will. She submitted to the acts of intercourse out of fear of further violence.

On a defence submission that neither indecent nor common assault should be allowed to go to the jury, it was held that:

1. It was still the law that the issue and service of a divorce petition, without more (*e.g.* an injunction), did not terminate the wife's deemed consent to intercourse during marriage: *cf. Steele* [1977] Crim.L.R. 290.

2. Following *Miller* [1954] 2 All E.R. 529 and the case there cited of *Jackson* [1891] 1 Q.B. 671, a husband who uses force to exercise his marital right does so at his peril; the acts of pulling her to the lavatory, and pulling her head down on to his penis, were capable in law of being assaults, going beyond any lawful persuasion open to a husband whose wife was unwilling.

3. As to whether a husband using such force could be guilty of an indecent, as opposed to a common, assault, indecency (*cf. Leeson* (1968) 52 Cr.App.R. 185) means that which is sexually repugnant, either to the public generally or to the complainant.

But if the law implies her consent to the act of sexual intercourse, whether she wills it in fact or not, then a lesser sexual act cannot in law be indecent or repugnant to her. Further or alternatively, if her deemed consent were limited to the

---

[19] In the case of *Roberts* [1986] Crim.L.R. 188 consent was held to have been terminated where there was a formal deed of separation, even though this lacked a non-cohabitation clause or a non-molestation clause. But see *Sharples* [1990] Crim.L.R. 198 where a restrictive interpretation was placed upon *Steele*.

act of intercourse, it would mean that any other act preliminary to or during intercourse would be capable of being an indecent assault (*e.g.* the husband stroking his wife's breasts), and it is not practicable to draw a dividing line between 'acceptable' acts and those which could be treated as indecent.

4. Although only common assault would be left to the jury, it would (as both prosecution and defence agreed) be proper to direct the jury as to the need for corroboration."

This decision emphasised the important point that a husband who uses force "to exercise his marital rights" runs the risk of being convicted of common assault or other related offences. However, according to *Caswell*, it would not be possible to convict the husband of indecent assault; this looks as if the law has taken leave of its senses. Pulling one's wife's head down to one's penis would be an assault but forcing her to commit fellatio would be no offence at all! Yet the decision was an understandable one; the court did not want to become involved in difficult discussions about what constituted "normal" preliminaries to intercourse (to which her deemed consent would apply) and those which were not. However, the more recent case of *Kowalski*[20] has opened the door to just such discussions. It decided that marital consent does not extend to oral intercourse—the question of whether preliminary acts to intercourse fell within the marital consent protection was left open. This ruling about oral intercourse must be the right one, but one is left to wonder how the courts are going to resolve the dilemma they have now set themselves.

The central issue, of course, is whether the rule that a husband cannot rape his wife (other than in the situations outlined in *Steele*) should be retained. The Criminal Law Revision Committee have recommended that the present law be retained for cohabiting spouses, but that "if a satisfactory definition could be achieved, the offence of rape should be extended to all cases where husband and wife are no longer cohabiting."[21]

Criminal Law Revision Committee, 15th Report, Sexual Offences, Cmnd. 9213 (1984):

"Arguments for retaining the present law . . .
2.64 . . . They may well have had sexual intercourse regularly before the act in question and, because a sexual relationship may involve a degree of compromise, she may sometimes have agreed only with some reluctance to such intercourse. Should he go further and force her to have sexual intercourse without her consent, this may evidence a failure of the marital relationship. But it is far from being the 'unique' and 'grave' offence described earlier (paragraph 2.3). Where the husband goes so far as to cause injury, there are available a number of offences against the person with which he may be charged, but the gravamen of the husband's conduct is the injury he has caused not the sexual intercourse he has forced.

---

[20] (1988) 86 Cr.App.R. 339.
[21] Para. 2.81. The Draft Criminal Code, clause 87(vi) talks in terms of the husband and wife "not living with each other in the same household," (Law Com. No. 177), (1989).

2.65 . . . For rape between cohabiting spouses, however, immediate imprisonment might not be appropriate; where no physical injury was caused to the wife, imprisonment would be most unlikely. A category of rape that was dealt with leniently might lead to all rape cases being regarded less seriously . . .

2.66 . . . The effect of the intervention of the police might well be to drive couples further apart in cases where a reconciliation might have occurred . . .

2.68 . . . Nor would the actual investigation of the offence be easy . . .

2.69 . . . [A]n allegation of the serious and emotive offence of rape might be used by a wife as a bargaining counter in negotiations for maintenance or custody, or as the basis of a charge of unreasonable behaviour in a divorce petition . . . Moreover, a prosecution for rape might necessitate a complicated and unedifying investigation of the marital history. . . . Some of us consider that the criminal law should keep out of marital relationships between cohabiting partners—especially the marriage bed—except where injury arises, when there are other offences which can be charged. . . .

Arguments for extending the offence to all married couples cohabiting at the time of the act of sexual intercourse

2.71 Those of us who consider that the offence of rape should be extended to all marriages argue that it is wrong for a married woman to remain excluded from the protection afforded to women generally by the criminal law against sexual intercourse without their consent just because the man committing the act is her husband. . . .

2.72 Those Members who are not content with the present position see an extension of the law of rape as a further development in the removal of discrimination against women. . . . They say that a woman, like a man, is entitled on any particular occasion to decide whether or not to have sexual intercourse, outside or inside marriage; the woman should be protected by the law of rape in both situations (though repeated refusal may be grounds for divorce). . . .

2.74 [With regard to] the difficulties in investigating allegations of rape . . . [T]hese difficulties already exist in relation to other offences that can arise between husband and wife . . .

2.76 They are aware too that extending the offence to all married couples cohabiting at the time of the act of sexual intercourse would pose evidential difficulties. It would not, however, be impossible to obtain convictions, and there are many other offences already in existence where similar problems of evidence occur. Without complaint, there can be no charge. Without proof there can be no conviction. But it is wrong that the law should turn a blind eye to criminal acts merely because they are difficult to prove. Some of these Members are of the view that there should be a restriction on prosecutions, namely that no prosecution should be brought without the consent of the Director of Public Prosecutions in any case where at the time of the act the defendant and the woman were married to each other."

(iii) *Lack of consent*

It is the element of lack of consent that transforms sexual intercourse into rape. What needs to be established? The answer in theory is clear; lack of consent is required and not positive dissent.[22] The woman who submits to an act of intercourse through fear of physical violence, ought

---

[22] *Lang* (1975) 62 Cr.App.R. 50; *Olugboja* (1981) 73 Cr.App.R. 344.

not, it is felt, to be precluded from complaining of rape.[23] After all, the statute no longer defines rape as sexual intercourse by force. Whilst, therefore, any consent that she gives through fear of force[24] is not regarded in law as real consent, there are substantial problems with the operation of this rule in practice. In the absence of any marks resulting from resistance, the rape victim may not be believed. Evidentially then, there is real pressure upon the rape victim to struggle and further endanger herself. Further, the courts tend to treat uncorroborated evidence with great caution.[25] They are obliged to warn the jury of the dangers of accepting the victim's uncorroborated story. As in no other crime, the victim's veracity is doubted: "It is truly extraordinary to say that all female victims of sex crimes are presumed to be perjurers or fantasists unless the jury is convinced otherwise."[26] The myth of the revengeful woman or, frightened, pregnant girl is what really underpins the corroboration requirement.[27]

One further related question bears examination at this point. The prosecution in seeking to show that the woman did, in fact, consent to sexual intercourse, may wish to adduce evidence of prior relationships with the defendant or with other men. This question assumes great importance particularly in cases where the victim claims to have been a virgin. May evidence of this type be introduced at the trial?

Z. Adler, "Rape—the Intention of Parliament and the Practice of the Courts" (1982) 45 M.L.R. 664 at 666–667:

"Before 1976, the defence in a rape trial were free to cross-examine about any prior sexual behaviour, whether with the defendant or anyone else. Her experience with a third party was thought to be relevant to her credibility: the law of evidence seemed to reflect an assumption that women involved in rape cases were likely to be untruthful as a direct result of their sexual 'immorality' . . . [It] gave the defence a virtually unconstrained licence to sling sexual mud . . .

The Advisory Group on the law of Rape . . . expressed particular anxiety about the humiliation and distress suffered by complainants during cross-examination and argued that the procedure was in need of urgent reform. 'We have reached the conclusion that the previous sexual history of the alleged victim with third parties is of no significance so far as credibility is concerned, and

---

[23] In the New Zealand case of *Daniels* [1986] 2 N.Z.L.R. 106, this protection extended to the victim who through fear of harm, helped the defendant insert his penis into her vagina.

[24] Lesser threats are unlikely to vitiate consent. See *Olugboja* (1981) 73 Cr.App.R. 344 at 347–348 but *contra*, *Wellard* (1978) 67 Cr.App.R. 364 at 368 where the defendant had a previous conviction of rape resulting from threatening to tell his victim's parents and police that she had been seen having intercourse in a public place.

[25] Jennifer Tempkin, *Rape and the Legal Process* (1987) pp. 133–143 and Jennifer Tempkin, "Towards a Modern Law of Rape" (1982) 45 M.L.R. 399 at 417–418.

[26] Ian Dennis, "Corroboration Requirements Reconsidered" [1984] Crim.L.R. 316 at p. 326. See also Celia Well's attack of the thinking of the Criminal Law Revision Committee on this point in "Law Reform, Rape and Ideology" (1985) 12 J.L.S. 63.

[27] In the United States there is commonly a requirement that the victim resist up to, but not including, the point at which she is exposed to serious danger: P. Oretsky, "Forcible Rape and Statutory Rape: The Delicate Balance between the Rights of Victim and Defendant" (1978) 11 J.M.J.P.P. 481 and M. Amir, *Patterns of Forcible Rape* (1971).

is only rarely likely to be relevant to the issues directly before the jury.' (Report of the Advisory Council on the Law of Rape, 1975, para. 131.)"

As a result of this report and subsequent debate in Parliament (which watered down the group's recommendations) section 2 of the Sexual Offences (Amendment) Act 1976 gives the trial judge complete discretion as to whether general or specific past history and reputation of the victim may be introduced.[28]

Just as consent induced by fear of violence is not regarded as real consent, neither is consent which is given under certain fundamental mistakes brought about by the deceit of the defendant, regarded as real. In *Clarence*[29] Stephen J. identified two such kinds of fundamental mistake, the first as to the identity of the actor and the second as to the nature of the act. As far as the first kind of mistake is concerned, the Sexual Offences Act 1956, s.1(2) states that "A man who induces a married woman to have sexual intercourse with him by impersonating her husband commits rape."

The limitations of such a provision are all too obvious; a man who impersonates an unmarried girl's boyfriend, for example, does not, it seems, commit rape if she consents because of the deception.

The second type of fundamental mistake induced by fraud goes to the very nature of the act. In *Flattery*[30] the defendant induced a woman to submit to intercourse by maintaining the deception that he was performing a surgical operation. He was convicted of rape. This was followed by the not dissimilar case of *Williams*[31] where the defendant, who was a singing-master, had intercourse with one of his pupils aged 16. She made no resistance as she believed his claim that he was merely improving her breathing. He too was convicted. The principle upon which both cases were decided was made clear by the trial judge in *Williams* and approved by Lord Hewart C.J. on appeal.

"Branson J. stated the law in the course of the summing-up in the present case in accurate terms. He said, 'The law has laid it down that where a girl's consent is procured by the means which the girl says the prisoner adopted, that is to say, where she is persuaded that what is being done to her is not the ordinary act of sexual intercourse but is some medical or surgical operation in order to give her relief from some disability from which she is suffering, then it is rape although the actual thing that was done was done with her consent, because she never consented to the act of sexual intercourse. She was persuaded to consent to what he did because she thought it was not sex-

---

[28] In Z. Adler's study, the defence applied for leave in 40 per cent. of cases and were successful (in part or wholly) in some 75 per cent. of applications. Adler believes that any scheme based on judicial discretion controlling sexual history evidence is doomed to fail, because judges will have no fall back on their own beliefs and attitudes (*Rape on Trial*, (1987) p. 154).

[29] (1888) 22 Q.B.D. 23.

[30] (1877) 2 Q.B.D. 410.

[31] [1923] 1 K.B. 340.

ual intercourse and because she thought it was a surgical operation.' "[32]

Richard Card, "The Criminal Law Revision Committee's Working Paper on Sexual Offences" [1981] Crim.L.R. 361 at 363:

" . . . [I]t is not easy to see why [the] above two types of mistake should be
marked out from any other situation where the accused has had intercourse,
knowing that the women would not have consented to it but for his deception.
It is arguable that all (or most) cases of fraudulently induced consent to intercourse should amount to rape, or none . . .
A majority of the Criminal Law Revision Committee thinks that the offence of
rape should not apply when a woman has knowingly consented to the defendant putting his penis into her vagina: mistake as to his identity or the purpose
of the penetration should be irrelevant."

In their Final Report, however, the Criminal Law Revision Committee have recommended a retention of the present law on this point,
with one extension—namely, that it should be rape where consent is
obtained by impersonating "another man."[33] Other examples of fraud
should be dealt with under section 3 of the Sexual Offences Act 1956.[34]

Does a defendant in such cases deserve to be labelled a rapist? When
a woman has "knowingly consented to the defendant putting his penis
into her vagina," will she suffer the same degree of emotional and psychological trauma as in other rape cases? Should not the crime, and
label, "rape" be reserved for those cases where penetration was not
consented to?[35]

2. Mens rea

The *mens rea* of the crime of rape is defined by section 1(1)(*b*) of the
Sexual Offences (Amendment) Act 1976. In addition to intending to
have sexual intercourse the defendant must *know* that the woman is not
consenting, or be *reckless* as to whether she is consenting. This is a
statutory endorsement of the law as laid down by the House of Lords in
Morgan.[36] Prior to *Morgan* a defendant's belief that the woman was consenting had to be based on reasonable grounds. The House of Lords
dispensed with this requirement—if the defendant honestly believed
the woman was consenting, he lacked *mens rea*.[37]

---

[32] *Ibid.* at p. 347.
[33] *Sexual Offences*, 15th Report, 1984, Cmnd. 9213 (1984), paras. 2.24—2.25.
[34] Section 3(1):"It is an offence for a person to procure a woman, by false pretences or false representations, to have unlawful sexual intercourse in any part of the world.".
[35] In *Kaitamaki* (1985) 79 Cr.App.R. 251 the Privy Council held that a man could be guilty of rape,
despite having penetrated the woman with her consent, if he continued sexual intercourse after a stage
when he realised that she was no longer consenting. Sexual intercourse was held to be a continuing act
which only ended with withdrawal of the penis. Clearly a woman must have a right to terminate sexual
intercourse—but should the man who fails to desist be guilty of rape? Might not a lesser level of criminal liability be more appropriate in such cases?.
[36] [1976] A.C. 182. This case is fully discussed, *ante*, pp. 254 *et seq.*
[37] In *Taylor* (1985) 80 Cr.App.R. 327, and *Haughian* (1985) 80 Cr.App.R. 334, the courts held that it was
unnecessary to give detailed guidance in every case on mistaken belief. Where the conflict of evidence
is acute, once the jury decides that the victim's account is truthful, there is no room for such a belief on
the part of the defendant.

The House of Lords did, however, emphasise that the reasonableness of the defendant's belief would be taken into account by the jury when deciding whether he could possibly have entertained such a belief. This evidential proposition was also enshrined by the Sexual Offences (Amendment) Act 1976, s.1(2):

"It is hereby declared that if at a trial for a rape offence the jury has to consider whether a man believed that a woman was consenting to sexual intercourse, the presence or absence of reasonable grounds for such a belief is a matter to which the jury is to have regard, in conjunction with any other relevant matters, in considering whether he so believed."

It is important to remember that *Morgan* was decided, and the Sexual Offences (Amendment) Act 1976 enacted, at a time when recklessness bore its old "subjective" meaning—the defendant had actually to be aware that there was a risk the woman was not consenting. Since then, however, the House of Lords in *Caldwell* and *Lawrence* have redefined the concept of recklessness so as to encompass a failure to consider an obvious risk. Does this new test of recklessness apply to rape?

R. v. Pigg [1982] 1 W.L.R. 762 (Court of Appeal, Criminal Division)

The defendant appealed against conviction of the attempted rape of two girls, both of whom had been "subjected to a catalogue of almost every sexual indignity of which one can think."

Lord Lane C.J.:
"The next ground of appeal advanced by Mr. Worsley on behalf of this appellant is that the judge misdirected the jury on the question of recklessness as it applies to the crime of rape. . . .
The way in which Mr. Worsley puts it is this. He concedes that the direction given by the judge, . . . was favourable to the defendant in the sense that it sought to inquire as to the defendant's own frame of mind. But, he suggests it was not put strongly enough. The judge he submits, should have made it clear to the jury that the defendant must have been aware of a serious and obvious risk that the girl was not consenting before they could come to the conclusion that the word "reckless" was made out. He invited us to define rape in the following terms: where a man has sexual intercourse with a woman who does not consent to it when he appreciates from the situation that a real risk exists that she is not consenting and nonetheless carries on with the act. That is rape, he submits, and nothing short of that will do. . . .
On any view of the word 'reckless' it seems to us that it clearly includes a case where the man appreciates the possibility that the woman may not be consenting and, nevertheless, goes on to have sexual intercourse with her. That is the direction in the present case. We take the view that the judge's directions are at least as favourable to the appellant as they should be.
What is of concern, and what has exercised the court in this case, is the theoretically possible case where the man never addresses his mind at all to the possibility of the woman not consenting, even though she is not consenting in fact. Can it be said that in those circumstances he is reckless as to whether she consents? That is the problem, stated broadly, with which this court has been dealing today.

It is perhaps fair to say that the word 'reckless' is a somewhat strange word for the Act of 1976 to employ in these circumstances. As already indicated, reckless as to consequences or as to the foresight of them is a common enough expression, but recklessness on the part of A as to what is going on in the mind of B is a concept which has its difficulties. However that may be, the word is in the Act of 1976. . . . (I)t seems to us that in the light of (the) decision of *Caldwell* [1982] A.C.341, so far as rape is concerned, a man is reckless if either he was indifferent and gave no thought to the possibility that the woman might not be consenting in circumstances where if any thought had been given to the matter it would have been obvious that there was a risk she was not, or, that he was aware of the possibility that she might not be consenting but nevertheless persisted regardless of whether she consented or not.

That being the case, it is plain that the judge's direction was, if anything, too favourable to the defendant. Accordingly, this aspect of the appeal must fail."

Appeal allowed on another ground

R. v. Satnam and Kewal (1984) 78 Cr.App.R. 149 (Court of Appeal, Criminal Division)

The appellants were convicted of raping a young girl. They appealed on the ground that there had been a misdirection as to the meaning of recklessness for the purposes of rape.

Bristow J.:

"The question of law is whether, in directing the jury as to the state of mind of the appellants in 'reckless' rape, the judge should have left to the jury the question whether they genuinely though mistakenly believed that the victim was consenting to sexual intercourse; and whether the judge was right to direct them that it was sufficient, in order to prove recklessness, if it was obvious to an ordinary observer that she was not consenting. . . .

Any direction as to the definition of rape should therefore be based upon section 1 of the 1976 Act and upon *R. v. Morgan*, without regard to *R. v. Caldwell* or *R. v. Lawrence* which were concerned with recklessness in a different context and under a different statute.

The word 'reckless' in relation to rape involves a different concept to its use in relation to malicious damage or, indeed, in relation to offences against the person. In the latter cases the foreseeability, or possible foreseeability, is as to the consequences of the criminal act. In the case of rape the foreseeability is as to the state of mind of the victim.

A practical definition of recklessness in sexual offences was given in *R. v. Kimber* [1983] 1 W.L.R. 1118, where [Lawton L.J. said] . . . ' . . . his attitude to her was one of indifference to her feelings and wishes. This state of mind is aptly described in the colloquial expression, "couldn't care less." In law this is recklessness.'

In summing-up a case of rape which involves the issue of consent, the judge should, in dealing with the state of mind of the defendant, first of all direct the jury that before they could convict of rape the Crown had to prove either that the defendant knew the woman did not want to have sexual intercourse, or was reckless as to whether she wanted to or not. If they were sure he knew she did not want to they should find him guilty of rape knowing there to be no consent. If they were not sure about that, then they would find him not guilty of such rape and should go on to consider reckless rape. If they thought he might genuinely have believed that she did want to, even though he was mistaken in his belief, they would find him not guilty. In considering whether his belief was genuine, they should take into account all the relevant circumstances (which could at that point be summarised) and ask themselves whether, in the light of those circumstances, he had reasonable grounds for such a belief. If, after considering those circumstances, they were sure he had no genuine belief that she wanted to, they would find him guilty. If they came to the conclusion that he could not care less whether she wanted to or not, but pressed on regardless, then he would have been reckless and could not have believed that she wanted to, and they would find him guilty of reckless rape."

Appeals allowed

There are now a number of decisions that have endorsed the subjective approach taken in *Satnam and Kewal*. Some of them, it must be said, appear to do so whilst actually offering up an objective test,[38] but the overall trend is clear.[39] The implications of *Satnam and Kewal* have been explored elsewhere,[40] suffice it to repeat the central point. Section 1(2) of the Sexual Offences (Amendment) Act clearly endorsed a subjective approach. The issue then has to be what the defendant actually believed—the reasonableness of this belief is only of evidential importance. This definition of belief is being taken to apply to both *knowledge* and *recklessness* in section 1(1)(*b*), and, thus there is clearly no room for the *Caldwell* test of recklessness in rape. The alternative interpretation, that this provision applies only to *knowledge* in section 1(1)(*b*), (on the basis that "know" in criminal law is often interpreted to mean "believe"), would have left the door open for *recklessness* to be defined in *Caldwell* terms.

This interpretation appears to have fallen by the wayside, but raises the broader issues of the exact bases upon which criminal liability ought to be based—again, an issue explored earlier.[41] This issue translates itself here into the simple question: *should* the law require that any belief as to the woman's consent be based on reasonable grounds?

J. C. Smith, "Comment" [1975] Crim.L.R. 719:

"As Lord Hailsham said, [in *Morgan*] the question for the House was one of great academic importance in English law. The question of principle received a

[38] See *Thomas* (1983) 77 Cr.App.R. 63, *Bashir* (1983) 77 Cr.App.R. 59. In both these cases a definition of recklessness similar to that in *Pigg* was approved, yet the Court seemed to feel it was endorsing a subjective approach. In *Bashir* Watkins L.J. cited *Pigg* and *Thomas* in relation to a defendant who was "indifferent and gave no thought to the possibility that the woman might not be consenting," and stated that "that definition allows of none other than a subjective approach to the state of mind of a person of whom it is said he acted recklessly in committing a crime." This seems extraordinary. How can someone be indifferent to something he has not considered as a possibility? How can a failure to think be "subjective" in other than a rather unreal sense of the word (see *ante*, p. 201). See also *Breckenridge* (1984) 79 Cr.App.R. 244 where it was stated that the "central" issue in "reckless rape" was whether the defendant "could not care less" whether the woman was consenting.
[39] See also *Taylor* (1985) 80 Cr.App.R. 327 and *Haughlian* (1985) 80 Cr.App.R. 334. Both appeals failed because it was held that the trial judges had made it quite clear that the defendant's state of mind was the crucial factor.
[40] *Ante*, pp. 195, 263–264.
[41] *Ante*, pp. 77–95.

very satisfactory answer. The case may be taken to establish that, once it is settled that the definition of a crime requires intention or recklessness with respect to particular elements of an offence, a mistake of fact whether reasonable or not, which is inconsistent with that intention or recklessness is also incompatible with the guilt of the accused and must lead to his acquittal. In the present case the trial judge had stressed to the jury that the *mens rea* of rape was an intention not merely to have intercourse with a woman, but an intention to have intercourse with a woman *without her consent*. Yet he went on to tell the jury that they could convict if the accused believed, without reasonable grounds, that the woman was consenting. This, as Lord Cross pointed out, was to present the jury with two incompatible alternatives. Lord Hailsham said, 'Once one has accepted, what seems to me abundantly clear, that the prohibited act in rape is non-consensual sexual intercourse, and that the guilty state of mind is an intention to commit it, it seems to me to follow as a matter of inexorable logic that there is no room either for a "defence" of honest belief or mistake, or of a defence of honest and reasonable mistake. Either the prosecution proves its case or it does not.' Lord Fraser also recognised that it would be illogical to uphold the direction of the trial judge and he held that there was no authority which compelled him to do so.

The first question, in every case, is, of course, what *mens rea* does the definition of the crime in question require? The present case decides that in rape the *mens rea* is an intention to have intercourse with a woman without her consent or an intention to have intercourse with a woman being indifferent (reckless) whether she consents or not. (The House favours a broad definition of 'intention' which would encompass both of these states of mind but it is thought preferable, and it is certainly safer, to spell both out.) The present case decides nothing about the *mens rea* of any other crime. It does decide, it is submitted, that, as a matter of general principle, once it is settled that the crime in question requires an element of intention or recklessness any mistake, whether reasonable or not, which is inconsistent with that intention or recklessness requires an acquittal. This conclusion appears, perhaps, to be so obvious that it is absurd to make a fuss about it. It is, as Lord Hailsham says, a 'matter of inexorable logic.' But in the present case, not only were the jury directed in defiance of 'inexorable logic' but the direction was upheld by the Court of Appeal and by two dissenting members of the House of Lords; which surely shows that this is no mere Aunt Sally set up by academic writers, with nothing better to do with their time, so that they can knock it down again."

Criminal Law Revision Committee, 15th Report, Sexual Offences, Cmnd. 9213 (1984):

"2.37 . . . Sexual intercourse on the part of a man is in general a deliberate course of conduct (although drugs or drink may affect his awareness of his actions). As the Policy Advisory Committee said . . . sexual intercourse is 'an act which can be a fundamental means of expressing love for another; and to which as a society we attach considerable value.' Sexual intercourse is an intimate act between man and woman, and a man is expected to have regard to the question whether the woman is consenting to the act or not.

2.38 Where the man knows that the woman is not consenting he should clearly be guilty of rape. The mental element in rape must, however, go wider than that. It should also be rape if he is aware of a possibility, however slight, that she may not be consenting but he persists regardless. . . .

2.40 If however, the defendant was mistaken in his belief that the woman was consenting, he should not be liable to conviction for rape, even if he had no reasonable grounds for his belief. None of us would wish to extend the offence of rape to such a case. This would in effect turn rape into a crime of negligence, an approach which was rejected by the majority of their Lordships in *Morgan*, a decision endorsed by Parliament in 1976. . . .

　2.41 We recommend, therefore, that the mental element in rape should cover:
　(a) the man who knew that the woman was not consenting, and
　(b) the man who either was aware that she might not be consenting or did not believe that she was consenting."

T. Pickard, "Culpable Mistakes and Rape: Relating Mens Rea to the Crime" (1980) 30 University of Toronto Law J. 75 at 77, 83:

"There can be no doubt that it is a major harm for a woman to be subjected to non-consensual intercourse notwithstanding that the man may believe he has her consent. There can be little doubt that the cost of taking reasonable care is insignificant compared with the harm which can be avoided through its exercise: indeed, the only cost I can identify is the general one of creating some pressure towards greater explicitness in sexual contexts. To accept an honest but unreasonable belief in consent as a sufficient answer in these circumstances is to countenance the doing of a major harm that could have been avoided at no appreciable cost. Therefore, in terms of simple balancing of interest, it is sound policy to require reasonable care, given the capabilities of the actor. It is true, of course, that not all sound policies can be appropriately pursued through the use of criminal law. But considering the disparate weights of the interests involved, a failure to inquire carefully into consent constitutes, in my view, such a lack of minimal concern for the bodily integrity of others that it is good criminal policy to ground liability on it. . . . I accept that in many instances, particularly where inadvertence is involved, mistaken wrongdoing may not be bad enough to deserve criminal sanction. But a major part of my effort is to show that there are different kinds of mistakes. In rape, we are dealing not with the kind of mistake that results from the complexity of our endeavours and inevitable human frailty, but with an easily avoided and self-serving mistake produced by the actor's indifference to the separate existence of another. When the harm caused is so great, it seems clear to me that making such a mistake is sufficiently culpable to warrant criminal sanction."

C. Evaluation

Almost every aspect of the law of rape evokes controversy. There is much to cause concern in the attitude of judges to both corroboration and to the sentencing of rapists. In relation to the substantive law, there are overwhelming arguments in favour of change to much of the existing law.

　It is offensive that in the late twentieth century, the wife should still be regarded as so much the plaything of her husband, that the husband may have intercourse with her whenever he likes, irrespective of whether she consents or not. The marital rape exception has been described as "an outrage to human conscience and reason in an enlightened country in our time."[42] The arguments of the Criminal Law Revision Committee above, are not only weak in comparison with the opposition to the rule, but reflect a very narrow view of the crime of

---

[42] *Jerusalem Post*, International Edition, September 28, 1980, quoting an Israeli Supreme Court judge.

rape. Perhaps at long last this is being realized. An "urgent review" of the marital bar has now been requested by the government.[43]

The rule that the defendant need only make an honest mistake about the victim's consent—and that reasonableness is evidentially important only—is highly questionable, to say the least. If personal property is protected to the extent that the unthinking risk taker is punished, then the person should be entitled to the same protection—most people, after all, would rate harm to the person more highly than harm to property. Moreover, the moral judgement that holds such defendants not blameworthy, is, as we have seen, suspect.

Lastly, we turn to the question of what acts should be included within the *actus reus* of rape. This opens up the broader issue of whether the current division of sexual offences is the most appropriate. As we have seen, rape is so defined so that only penetration of the vagina by the penis constitutes the offence. Other acts such as oral intercourse or the insertion of objects into the vagina are indecent assaults and are punishable by up to 10 years' imprisonment.[44] There can be no doubt, hearing evidence from victims, that the trauma and harm involved in these assaults can be every bit as bad as that involved in rape. Other jurisdictions have widened the definition of rape to include, for example, penile penetration of the anus or mouth as well.[45] This possibility was rejected by the Criminal Law Revision Committee, but is it really the case that the British public would not regard these as rape? Can the risk of pregnancy really be that significant when it is still rape, for example, to have intercourse with a pre-pubertal child and emission of semen is not required for the offence?[46] Might there not be the remnants of a tradition which sees rape as a property offence against the husband lingering on here; penetration of the vagina by the penis goes more fundamentally, perhaps, to the woman's "virtue" than other sex acts.

If it is decided that the term "rape" does have a special significance that ought not to be diluted by the inclusion of other forms of assault, then another possibility ought to be seriously considered. It would be possible to distinguish between degrees of indecent assault, the former having a penalty as grave as that, possibly, for rape, the less serious having some lesser penalty. This course has been rejected too by the Criminal Law Revision Committee.[47] But the difficulties involved in

---

[43] See [1990] New L.J. 233. See further Jennifer Tempkin, *Rape and the Legal Process*, (1987), pp. 40–60. Tempkin gives details of many jurisdictions that have no such exemption. Further, the view taken by the Criminal Law Revision Committee is very different from that pertaining in Scotland. For recent developments see, Ian D. Brownlie, "Marital Rape—lessons from Scotland?" [1989] New L.J. 1275.

[44] S.15 Sexual Offences Act 1985. Under the previous legislation (Sexual Offences Act 1956), an indecent assault upon a man was punishable to this extent but indecent assault upon a woman was punishable by up to two years only.

[45] South Australian Criminal Law Consolidation Amendment Act 1976 s.3. The Law Commission of Ireland have gone even further, recommending that in addition to the above, penetration by inanimate objects should also be rape: L.R.C. 24, (1988).

[46] Jennifer Tempkin, *Rape and the Legal Process*, (1987) p. 30.

[47] 15th. Report, *Sexual Offences*, (1984), paras. 4.20–4.27.

making a distinction between more and less serious assaults are not incapable of resolution. The idea has considerable merit and deserves a reappraisal, not least, because it would convey a much sharper moral message to society than does the broad category of indecent assault.

CHAPTER 8

HOMICIDE

I. Introduction

A. The Level of Offending

We have already seen that violent crime generally only accounts for about 5 per cent of offences recorded by the police[1]; within that, homicide, that is, murder, manslaughter and infanticide, accounts for a very small proportion of offences committed. In 1988, for example, of the 12,772 *serious* offences of violence, 624 were homicide.[2] Whereas official statistics only reveal part of the picture of offending for many offences, for homicide, by virtue of the very nature of the offence, the data is likely to be almost entirely accurate. Not only that, but official statistics for this area of offending are so detailed that an insight is provided into the characteristics of homicide in this country.

As with other offences, more homicide appears to be taking place: the total number of such offences recorded during 1979–1988 was one-quarter higher than the total for the period 1969–1978.[3] However, two points have to be borne in mind when interpreting these figures. First, because there are so few offences, the large variations that occur look very large in percentage terms. For example, in 1987, one incident, the Hungerford killings, accounted for 16 homicides alone. Secondly, there is evidence that despite the current trend, historically, there are now less killings recorded as homicides than in earlier centuries: "homicide rates were three times higher in the thirteenth century than the seventeenth, three times higher in the seventeenth than the nineteenth, and in London they were twice as high in the early nineteenth century as they are now."[4]

B. Homicide in Context

Looking at the official statistics, the picture that emerges is that homicide is still predominantly "domestic" in nature. The victim is likely to have known his killer, (and in about a third of cases will be a member of

---

[1] *Ante* p. 538.
[2] *Criminal Statistics, England and Wales*, (1988), (Cm. 847).
[3] *Ibid.*
[4] T. R. Gurr, "On the History of Violent Crime in Europe and America" in H. Graham and T. R. Gurr (eds.) *Violence in America* (1979) p. 356.

his family); in about half the cases the killing will take place during a quarrel or loss of temper (in only about 10 per cent. will the killing be in furtherance of theft or gain); the most common weapon is a sharp instrument, that may be just a kitchen knife; the offender is most likely to be a young male, who may well have a previous criminal record (this is especially true where the killing is of a stranger). This all adds up to one particular pattern of homicide, but if another fact is added, the picture changes dramatically. The most likely victim of homicide is under one year old.[5] What this means, of course is that generalisations are only of limited usefulness and care must be taken in their interpretation. One more example: if the under five age group and the over seventies are excluded from the picture, then males are almost twice as likely to be victims as females. All of these factors are important and all have a bearing on the way in which the law responds—with the partial defence of provocation, with self-defence and, of course, with the "special" offence of infanticide.

What is it that makes a human being resort to the extremes of violence? For some the answer lies at the level of the individual: "if one wishes to understand the act of killing, the individual psychology of the murderer is the single most important area of study."[6] This approach is characterised by regarding most killings as irrational and the product of a disturbed personality. Obviously some homicides can only be viewed in this way—the Hungerford killings, and the killings by Sutcliffe for example—but other writers have been critical of the psychiatric approach as a general explanation. Some have turned to theories of socialisation. "While some individuals learn to manage interpersonal conflict in nonviolent ways, others learn to use force."[7] Both of these explanations may be attached to accounts which look at the interaction between the victim and offender. "Murder and assault are not one-sided, mechanical activities, with offenders simply acting out aggressive dispositions and victims serving as mere instigators or passive foils. Rather, they are products of a dynamic interchange. The opponents establish and escalate conflict, reject peaceful or mildly aggressive means for resolving it, and turn to massive force as an effective, perhaps mutually agreed-upon method."[8] The official statistics lend considerable support to this interpretation.[9]

Homicide is regarded as the most serious of offences. Our revulsion against it is embedded deep within us and our reactions to killings such

---

[5] *Official Statistics, England and Wales,* (1988) (Cm. 847). See also, R. Walmsley, *Personal Violence* (H.O.R.S. No. 89) (1986).

[6] D. Lunde, *Murder and Madness,* (1975) p. 83.

[7] D. Luckenbill, "Murder and Assault" in Robert Meier, *Major Forms of Crime,* (1984) p. 29.

[8] *Ibid.* p. 32.

[9] There are many other influential attempts to explain violence in general, and homicide in particular. Some of these look to the structure of the society in which the offender is placed, claiming to be able to identify sub-cultures of violence, where a system of values supports the use of violence (for example, M. Wolfgang and F. Ferracuti, *The Sub-culture of Violence,* (1967)), or to inequalities in the structure of society (for example, A. Henry and J. Short, *Suicide and Homicide,* (1954)).

as those at Hungerford may be extreme. The following extract attempts to explain the underlying significance of homicide.

George P. Fletcher, Rethinking Criminal Law (1978), pp. 235–236, 341:

"What makes homicide unique is, among other things, the uniqueness of causing death. While all personal injuries and destruction of property are irreversible harms, causing death is a harm of a different order. Killing another human being is not only a worldly deprivation; in the Western conception of homicide, killing is an assault on the sacred, natural order. In the Biblical view, the person who slays another was thought to acquire control over the blood— the life force—of the victim . . .

Though we are inclined today to think of homicide as merely the deprivation of a secular interest, the historical background of desecration is essential to an adequate understanding . . . of the current survival of many historic assumptions. For example, consent is not a defense to homicide, as it is in cases of battery and destruction of property. The reason is that the religious conception of human life still prevails against the modern view that life is an interest that the bearer can dispose of at will . . .

There are three prominent starting places for thinking about criminal liability. In the pattern of manifest criminality, the point of departure is an act that threatens the peace and order of community life. In the theory of subjective criminality, the starting place is the actor's intent to violate a protected legal interest. In the law of homicide, the focal point is neither the act nor the intent, but the fact of death. This overpowering fact is the point at which the law begins to draw the radius of liability. From this central point, the perspective is: who can be held accountable, and in what way, for the desecration of the human and divine realms? The question is never where to place the point of the legal compass, but how far the arc should sweep in bringing in persons to stand responsible for the death that has already occurred."

The task of this chapter is to determine who should be swept within this arc of liability for homicide—and to assess the bases upon which we grade the liability of such persons. This necessarily raises the question of why we grade homicide offences, and whether we should continue to do so.

In England there are three categories of homicide: murder, manslaughter (of which there are several species) and infanticide. We shall examine each in turn before asking whether such categorisation serves any useful purpose.

II. Actus Reus of Murder and Manslaughter

Both these forms of homicide share a common *actus reus*, namely,
"unlawfully killing a reasonable person who is in being and under the King's Peace, the death following within a year and a day"[10]:
1. *"unlawfully"*: some killings, such as those in self-defence, may be justified and therefore lawful[11];

---

[10] Coke, 3 Inst. 47.
[11] *Ante*, p. 292.

2. *"killing"*: the act (or omission) of the defendant must have killed the victim; it must have been the legal cause of the death of the victim. Causation must be established[12];

3. *"a reasonable person who is in being"*: the victim must be a human being who was alive at the time of the defendant's actions. This raises problems outside the scope of this book as to the precise moment when life begins and ends. In view of developments with heart transplant operations and life support machines the problem of determining the exact moment of death has assumed some importance in recent years.[13]

According to English law a foetus is not a human being for the purposes of the law of homicide. However if a miscarriage is intentionally procured, and is not a lawful abortion within the terms of the Abortion Act 1967, s.1, the procurer will be guilty of the offence of criminal abortion.[14] There is also a separate offence of child destruction covering cases of destroying a foetus that is capable of being born alive.[15] A pregnancy that has lasted 28 weeks provides *prima facie* proof that the foetus is capable of being born alive.[16] Both these offences—criminal abortion and child destruction carry the same maximum penalty as manslaughter, namely, life imprisonment.

4. *"under the King's Peace"*: all human beings are under the "Queen's" peace except an alien enemy "in the heat of war, and in the actual exercise thereof."[17]

5. *"death following within a year and a day"*: this rule developed at a time when medical science was relatively primitive and there was great difficulty in establishing causation where a long interval elapsed between the infliction of the injury and the death.[18] However, medical science has now developed to a point where it is possible to establish the cause of death even though death only occurred several years after the injury thus raising the question whether the year-and-a-day rule should be abolished.

Criminal Law Revision Committee, 14th Report, Offences Against the Person, Cmnd. 7844 (1980), para. 39:

"[I]t would be wrong for a person to remain almost indefinitely at risk of prosecution for murder. A line has to be drawn somewhere and in our opinion the present law operates satisfactorily. When death follows over a year after the

---

[12] *Ante*, Chap. 4.

[13] See *Malcherek, ante*, p. 416; and see generally, Atkinson "Life, Birth and Live Birth" (1904) L.Q.R. 134; Glanville Williams, *The Sanctity of Life and the Criminal Law* (1958), pp. 17–22; "When is the Moment of Death?" (1964) 4 Med.Sc. & L. 11; "Diagnosis of Death" [1976] B.M.J. 1187–8, [1979] B.M.J. 332; Skegg, "Irreversibly Comatose Individuals: Alive or Dead" [1974] C.L.J. 130; C. Pallis, *ABC of Brain Stem Death*, 1983; I. Kennedy & A. Grubb, *Medical Law: Text and Materials*, 1989, Ch. 15.

[14] Offences Against the Person Act 1861, s.58.

[15] Infant Life (Preservation) Act 1929, s.1.

[16] *Ibid.* s.1(2). Recent cases have however been very willing to hold a foetus to be capable of being born alive at less than 28 weeks (see *Rance* v. *Mid-Downs Health Authority, The Times*, February 15, 1990; see also *C. v S.* [1987] 2 W.L.R. 1108). *At the time of writing, the Human Fertilisation and Embryology Bill 1990, which reduces the period to 24 weeks, is passing through Parliament.*

[17] Hale, 1 P.C. 433.

[18] *Dyson* [1908] 2 K.B. 454.

infliction of injury the killer does not necessarily escape justice. He may be charged with attempted murder or causing grievous bodily harm with intent . . . Accordingly, we recommend that a killing should not amount to murder unless death follows before the expiration of a year after the day on which the injury was inflicted."

III. MURDER

Murder is committed when a defendant commits the *actus reus* of homicide with *malice aforethought*. Murder is the most heinous form of homicide carrying the severest penalty in English law—mandatory life imprisonment. The law reserves this category of homicide for those who kill with the most blameworthy state of mind, known technically as "malice aforethought."[19] Defining the parameters of murder is thus primarily[20] a task of defining malice aforethought, the *mens rea* of murder.

A. History

The term "malice aforethought" originally[21] bore its literal meaning and it would only be murder if the defendant had thought out, planned or premeditated the killing. In the fifteenth and sixteenth centuries an intentional homicide "on the sudden" was not murder but manslaughter. However it soon became clear that this was too narrow a definition for murder. Other types of homicide were just as reprehensible and deserving of the ultimate penalty. Accordingly the judges started expanding the concept "malice aforethought" and dispensing with the requirement of a premeditated intent, until by the mid-seventeenth century it was clear that malice aforethought could be established in any of the following ways.

1. Intent to kill. The development that an intent to kill, without premeditation, sufficed for murder was initially achieved by resorting to the fiction that where there was a sudden killing without provocation, the defendant must have planned the killing and thus the requisite "aforethought" was inferred. Before long, however, judges had abandoned this fictitious reasoning and were clearly stating that malice aforethought was present whenever there was an intent to kill.[22]

---

[19] This phrase was described in *Moloney* [1985] A.C. 905, 920 as "anachronistic and now wholly inappropriate."

[20] In certain cases, such as where there is adequate provocation, a killing can be committed with malice aforethought, but nevertheless because of the circumstances of the killing, the crime is reduced to voluntary manslaughter. See *post*, p. 638.

[21] For a full discussion of the earliest development of the term "malice aforethought," and of the separation of murder from manslaughter in the late fifteenth century, see Sayre, "Mens Rea" (1932) 45 Harv.L. Rev. 974; R. Moreland, *The Law of Homicide* (1952), pp. 1–16, and references cited therein.

[22] Moreland, *ibid.* Chap. 1; Perkins "A Re-examination of Malice Aforethought" (1934) 43 Yale L.J. 537.

2. Intent to cause grievous bodily harm. This has long been established as a form of malice aforethought.[23] In *Vickers*[24] the Court of Appeal confirmed that this was an independent species of malice aforethought and not merely a particular example of the felony-murder rule[25] (intentionally causing grievous bodily harm was a felony and thus if death resulted would have been murder under the felony-murder rule). In *D.P.P.* v. *Smith*[26] the House of Lords held that the words "grievous bodily harm" must bear their ordinary natural meaning: "Bodily harm needs no explanation, and 'grievous' means no more and no less than 'really serious.' " This species of malice aforethought is often called "implied malice."

3. Constructive malice. This covered two situations:

(i) *killing a police officer while resisting arrest.* Initially this extension to the law was rationalised as being an intentional killing. By strained reasoning it was inferred that the killer must have thought the matter over and determined to kill rather than be taken into custody. However, as the term malice aforethought began to lose its natural meaning and became a technical phrase with several meanings, efforts to rationalise this extension ceased and it became clearly accepted as a separate species of malice aforethought. The only intention that had to be proved was an intention to resist arrest by force.

(ii) *killing in the course of committing a felony—the felony-murder rule.* Until 1967 crimes were classified as either felonies or misdemeanours,[27] the former being the more serious offences.

The extension of the concept of malice aforethought to cover felony-murders was again originally rationalised on the basis that the killer must have intended to kill rather than be unsuccessful in the commission of the felony. Again such attempted rationalisations soon ceased; it became necessary only to establish an intention to commit the felony; the defendant had shown himself to be a "bad person"—he could fairly be blamed for the resulting death. However, the scope of the felony-murder rule was greatly restricted by Sir James Stephen in *Serné*[28] when he held that the doctrine only applied if the felony was "known to be dangerous to life, and likely in itself to cause death."

The felony-murder rule still flourishes today in the United States[29] where one of its main rationales is that it is a deterrent to the commission of felonies that create a risk of death. Accordingly it is generally limited to felonies that are "inherently dangerous." This is sometimes

---

[23] For a full historical discussion, see *Hyam* [1975] A.C. 55 and *Cunningham* [1982] A.C. 566.
[24] [1957] 2 Q.B. 664.
[25] *Post*, pp. 587–588.
[26] [1961] A.C. 290 at 334.
[27] Or as treason. The Criminal Law Act 1967, s.1 abolished this distinction and substituted the present classification of crimes as being either arrestable offences or non-arrestable offences (s.2).
[28] (1887) 16 Cox C.C. 311.
[29] It has only been abolished in Hawaii and Kentucky.

achieved by a statutory limitation of the doctrine to those felonies perceived (normally) to involve danger to human life. Thus in Colorado, for example, the only felonies that qualify for an application of the felony-murder rule are arson, robbery, burglary, kidnapping and sexual assaults.[30] In other states it is left to the courts to determine whether a particular felony is "inherently dangerous."[31]

Other restrictions have been placed on the felony-murder rule in the United States. Thus in many cases a strict causation requirement is imposed that the felon's act must "directly" cause the death of the victim.[32] Also the underlying felony must be "independent" of the killing, *i.e.* it must include an element which is not an element of murder.[33] Thus assault and battery is not independent of the killing since all the elements of this crime are included in murder. But robbery is independent of the killing because it includes an element (theft) which is not an element of murder.[34] A final restriction on the felony-murder rule has been achieved by placing a restrictive interpretation on the time period surrounding the felony upon which liability for murder can be based.[35]

The result of all these limitations is that most persons convicted under the felony-murder rule could be regarded as grossly reckless as to the causing of death. The Model Penal Code in the United States recognised this by proposing the abolition of the felony-murder rule *per se*, but providing instead that the commission of a listed dangerous felony should raise a presumption of the requisite "recklessness . . . [and] extreme indifference to the value of human life" required for murder.[36]

Such persons would almost certainly have been liable for murder in England under the loose *Hyam* test of murder.[37] However, English law has now attempted to limit the crime of murder to intentional killings and to classify killings by excessive risk-taking as manslaughter (subject to the preservation of the grievous bodily harm rule). Thus the felony-murder rule and the other species of constructive malice, killing an officer while resisting arrest, were abolished by the Homicide Act 1957, section 1, and *Hyam* has been judicially laid to rest by the House of Lords in *Moloney*[38] and *Hancock*.[39]

D.P.P. v. Smith. Before turning to the present law of murder and the meaning of malice aforethought today, it is necessary to mention one

---

[30] Colo.Rev.Stat.Ann. s.18–3–102(1)(*b*).
[31] Some courts make this determination on an abstract basis without reference to the particular facts of the case (*e.g. Morales* 49 Cal.App. 3d 134, 122 Cal.Rptr. 157 (1975)). Other courts prefer to consider whether the particular defendant's commission of the felony was inherently dangerous (*e.g. State* v. *Chambers* 524 S.W. 2d 826 (Mo. 1975)).
[32] *Commonwealth* v. *Redline*, 391 Pa. 486, 137 A.2d 472 (1958).
[33] *People* v. *Ireland*, 70 Cal. 2d 522, 450 P.2d 580, 75 Cal.Rptr. 188 (1969).
[34] *People* v. *Burton* 491 P.2d 793 (Cal. 1971).
[35] *People* v. *Walsh*, 186 N.E. 422 (N.Y. 1933); *Parson* v. *State* 222 A.2d 326 (Del. 1966).
[36] s.210.2(1)(*b*), see *post*, p. 597.
[37] See *post*, p. 589.
[38] [1985] A.C. 905.
[39] [1986] A.C. 455.

final development already discussed in a different context.[40] The House of Lords in *D.P.P.* v. *Smith*[41] in 1960 effectively laid down an objective test of malice aforethought in holding that a defendant would be guilty of murder if he intended to do an act where death or grievous bodily harm was the natural and probable result. Condemnation of this decision resulted in the enactment of section 8 of the Criminal Justice Act 1967.[42] The House of Lords in *Hyam* has confirmed that as a result of section 8, the test of malice aforethought is clearly the subjective one of determining the actual state of mind of the defendant. Further, the Privy Council in *Frankland*[43] has held that the objective test never accurately represented English law and that *D.P.P.* v. *Smith* was wrong.

B. Present Law

The *mens rea* of murder can now be simply stated.

The defendant must either:
1. intend to cause death, or
2. intend to cause grievous bodily harm.

This of course does not solve the central problem, namely the meaning of intention. The leading decisions on intention are *Moloney*, *Hancock* and *Nedrick* which are extracted earlier[44] and to which reference should be made.

These cases have however removed one problem. In *Hyam*[45] it was held that foresight of death or grievous bodily harm as a (highly) probable consequence of one's actions was sufficient to constitute the mental element for murder. It was uncertain whether this amounted to separate head of malice aforethought apart from intention—or whether this was an alternative and broad way of defining intention itself. It is now clear that there is no head of malice aforethought apart from the two intention tests listed above—and it is also clear that the concept intention cannot be given such a broad meaning.

The validity of the grievous bodily harm rule would appear to be beyond doubt as a result of the House of Lords decision of *Cunningham*. Prior to that it had been argued that the grievous bodily harm rule was simply a sub-species of the felony-murder rule and was thus also abolished by the Homicide Act 1957. This view, endorsed by a minority in *Hyam*, was rejected in *Cunningham*. It had further been argued in *Hyam* that the reason for the grievous bodily harm rule was that in the last century because of the poor state of medical knowledge and experience persons sustaining such injuries were likely to die; such a rationale was unacceptable today with the advances in medical knowledge. If trans-

---

[40] *Ante*, p. 235.
[41] [1961] A.C. 290.
[42] See *ante*, pp. 236–237.
[43] [1988] Crim.L.R. 117.
[44] *Ante*, pp. 153–158.
[45] [1975] A.C. 55.

planting the grievous bodily harm rule into the 1980s it would need qualifying so that only grievous bodily harm which endangered life should come within the *mens rea* of murder. This argument was similarly rejected.

R. v. Cunningham [1982] A.C. 566 (House of Lords)

Lord Hailsham:
"I . . . genuflect before the miracles of modern surgery and medicine, though I express some doubt whether these may not have been offset to some extent by the increased lethal characteristics of modern weaponry (particularly in the fields of automatic weaponry, explosives and poisons), and the assistance to criminality afforded by the automobile, the motorway and international air transport. I also take leave to doubt whether in the case of injuries to the skull in particular or indeed really serious bodily harm in general these advances have made the difference between inflicting serious bodily harm and endangering life sufficiently striking as to justify judicial legislation on the scale proposed. But, more important than all this, I confess that I view with a certain degree of scepticism the opinion expressed in *Reg* v. *Hyam* . . . that the age of our ancestors was so much more violent than our own that we can afford to take a different view of 'concepts of what is right and what is wrong that command general acceptance in contemporary society'. . . ."

Lord Edmund-Davies:
"[T]he view I presently favour is . . . that there should be no conviction for murder unless an intent to kill is established, the wide range of punishment for manslaughter being fully adequate to deal with all less heinous forms of homicide. I find it passing strange that a person can be convicted of murder if death results from, say, his intentional breaking of another's arm, an action which, while undoubtedly involving the infliction of 'really serious harm' and, as such, calling for severe punishment, would in most cases be unlikely to kill. And yet, for the lesser offence of attempted murder, nothing less than an intent to kill will suffice. But I recognise the force of the contrary view that the outcome of intentionally inflicting serious harm can be so unpredictable that anyone prepared to act so wickedly has little ground for complaint if, where death results, he is convicted and punished as severely as one who intended to kill.
So there are forceful arguments both ways. And they are arguments of the greatest public consequence, particularly in these turbulent days when, as the Lord Chancellor has vividly reminded us, violent crimes have become commonplace. Resolution of that conflict cannot, in my judgment, be a matter for your Lordships' House alone. It is a task for none other than Parliament. . . ."

C. Penalty for Murder

The Murder (Abolition of the Death Penalty) Act 1965 abolished capital punishment for murder and substituted a mandatory life sentence. Thus the judge has no discretion as to sentence. A convicted murderer must be sentenced to imprisonment for life. However the length of time he actually spends in custody will be determined by the Parole Board (subject to the Home Secretary's acceptance of the Board's recommendations). Section 1(2) of the Act empowers the judge to recommend a minimum period which in his view should elapse before the offender can be released. Such recommendations are made in about one out of every 12 murder cases.[46] In *Flemming*[47] it was held that such recommendations should not be for less than 12 years.

A release from custody is on "licence." This means that the offender does not regain absolute liberty. The licence is subject to conditions: for example, requiring supervision by a probation officer. All such persons released on licence are liable to be recalled to prison at any time during the rest of their lives should there be a breach of the conditions of the licence or should their conduct indicate that there is a risk of a further serious offence being committed.

House of Lords, Report of the Select Committee on Murder and Life Imprisonment (Session 1988–89, H.L. Paper 78), 1989, paras. 127–140:

"127. Following the judgment in the case of *Handscomb* [(1987) 86 Cr.App.R. 59] in the Divisional Court, the present procedure, followed in all life sentence cases in England and Wales, is that the trial judge now writes to the Home Secretary, through the Lord Chief Justice, immediately after the trial, to inform the Home Secretary of the conviction and to give his views on the necessary period of detention to meet the requirements of retribution and deterrence. The Lord Chief Justice adds his own view. Taking these views into account, a junior Minister, on behalf of the Home Secretary, decides upon the period of imprisonment necessary to meet the requirements of retribution and deterrence. This period of imprisonment is widely referred to as the 'tariff,' and is so referred to in this Report. Following *Handscomb*, in the case of a discretionary life sentence (but not a mandatory life sentence), the tariff is fixed strictly in accordance with the judicial recommendation:

'In determining how long such a person should be detained for punitive purposes the Secretary of State should fix the date of the first review . . . strictly in accordance with a period of detention (that is to say, the notional determinate sentence less one-third remission) recommended by the judiciary as necessary, to meet the requirements of retribution and deterrence.'

128. If and when the Parole Board recommend release, the trial judge and the Lord Chief Justice are again consulted before the papers are referred to the Minister.

129. In murder cases, which at present attract a mandatory life sentence, the Home Secretary is not bound by the views of the judiciary when setting the tariff . . .

130. The 'tariff' date determines the date when the prioner's suitability for release will first be reviewed by the Local Review Committee (LRC) at his prison ('the LRC date'). In the case of tariffs of up to and including 20 years, the LRC date will be three years before the expiry of the tariff period. In the case of prisoners with tariffs longer than 20 years, the LRC date will be fixed at 17 years into the sentence. The prisoner is told his LRC date, not the tariff wich has been set. It follows that a prisoner who is told that his LRC date is 16 or less years away can calculate the 'tariff' by adding three years onto the LRC date. A prisoner

---

[46] R. Cross, *The English Sentencing System* (3rd ed., 1981), p. 48.
[47] [1973] 2 All E.R. 401.

told that his LRC date is set at 17 years will not be able to calculate his tariff date with any certainty . . .

139. Following the consideration of the case by the LRC, P2 Division will refer the case to a 'lifer panel' of the Parole Board. The panel must include a judicial member, a psychiatrist, and preferably a probation member of the Board . . .

The panel informs the Home Office of the results of their consideration of the case, and makes a recommendation. The most usual recommendations are either that a provisional release date be given, or that a further review be held at a future date after a prisoner's transfer to another closed prison or to an open prison, or that a further review be held at a later date at the same prison.

140. No prisoner serving a life sentence can go to an open prison or be released without the Home Secretary's approval. If the Parole Board recommend that a prisoner should be released, the Home Secretary is not bound to accept their recommendation. However, if the Board do not recommend release, the Home Secretary may not release the prisoner."

Report of the Parole Board for 1970, para. 47:

"In determinate sentences consideration by the Board is not a sentencing operation because the sentence has been fixed by the court. With life sentences, however, the sentence is indeterminate and our function assumes a sentencing character, because there is no fixed term. The question is not simply whether the conditions, bearing in mind the nature of the offence, are such as to justify granting parole. The primary question is whether the time served is appropriate to the crime."

Is it appropriate for the Parole Board to be exercising such a sentencing function?

Should the mandatory life sentence for murder be retained?[48]

Report of the Advisory Council on the Penal System, Sentences of Imprisonment (A Review of Maximum Penalties), (1978):

"235. . . . [If] life imprisonment should remain the penalty for murder and manslaughter . . . [t]here remains the specific question whether life imprisonment should continue to be the *mandatory* penalty for murder, or whether it should become the *maximum* penalty, thus permitting the imposition of determinate sentences of any length for the offence. . . .

236. The mandatory penalty of life imprisonment was substituted for the death penalty by the Murder (Abolition of Death Penalty) Act 1965. The Government at that time supported the new penalty essentially on two grounds: that murder was a unique offence and should be marked by a unique penalty; and that to permit determinate sentencing for the offence could be risky, since there might be cases in which the Home Secretary would have to release a prisoner who had served a determinate sentence, less remission, even though he might feel that it was unsafe to do so.

---

[48] See also Criminal Law Revision Committee, 14th Report, Offences Against the Person, Cmnd. 7844, paras. 42–74; Criminal Law Revision Committee, 12th Report, Penalty for Murder, Cmnd. 5184 and the Report of the Committee on the Penalties for Homicide (Scottish Home and Health Department), Cmnd. 5137.

237. One of the arguments of those who believe that murder merits a unique penalty is that the mandatory life sentence reflects the retributive view that anyone who murders another must place his life at the disposal of the State to the extent that both his release and his liberty to remain at large will always be subject to executive decision. This view is usually associated with the argument that to sentence murderers in the same way as other offenders would be to devalue murder as an offence and to reduce the deterrent effect of the existing penalty.

238. Another argument in favour of the mandatory element is that acts of murder can arouse a good deal of public passion and indignation which would attract more than usual interest to apparent discrepancies in sentencing decisions and tend to bring the administration of justice into undesirable public controversy. This, it is argued, would be likely to cause particular difficulty in what are considered the less culpable types of homicide, where a judge might think it appropriate to pass a shorter sentence than in a bad case of, for instance, robbery, but would immediately become susceptible to the accusation that the courts care more for property than for lives.

239. It is also argued that the absence of the mandatory element in the penalty for murder might actually lead (as the result of public attitudes to the crime of murder) to a situation in which the least dangerous of murderers might remain in custody longer as a result of relative determinate sentencing than they would have done if sentenced to life imprisonment. A related objection to the abolition of the mandatory sentence is that it would lead to over-long sentences in very serious cases. . . .

243. . . . [W]e see a number of positive arguments to justify the abolition of the mandatory element in the penalty for murder. The Criminal Law Revision Committee rightly recognised that the main advantage to be derived from the mandatory life sentence is its flexibility in providing the releasing authorities with the freedom to gauge the public interest and the needs of the offender throughout the period of his imprisonment and after release. The prison service and the Parole Board can take account of continuing observation of the prisoner's development in prison and the Board can monitor his behaviour while on licence and, if necessary, recall him without recourse to the courts. These are powerful considerations in favour of the indeterminacy implicit in the life sentence. We do not, however, consider that they necessarily imply that the life sentence must be imposed indiscriminately on every person convicted of murder. Where the nature of the offence connotes dangerousness and there is evidence of a likely continued threat that it will be repeated, the life sentence may be the appropriate, indeed the only wise, sentence to pass. But for some murderers we think that there are strong reasons for giving courts the power to pass fixed terms of imprisonment.

244. Although murder has been traditionally and distinctively considered the most serious crime, it is not a homogeneous offence but a crime of considerable variety. It ranges from deliberate cold-blooded killing in pursuit of purely selfish ends to what is commonly referred to as 'mercy killing.' Instead of automatically applying a single sentence to such an offence, . . . sentences for murder should reflect this variety with correspondingly variable terms of imprisonment or, in the exceptional case, even with a non-custodial penalty . . . [We] cannot believe that the problems of predicting future behaviour at the time of conviction are inherently more difficult in a murder case than in any other case where there is a measure of instability, or that judges are any less able to make predictions or to assess degrees of culpability in murder cases than in any others. . . . [Further] efforts to alleviate the harshness of the mandatory penalty, [provocation and diminished responsibility] have led to complications in legal proceedings for which we believe there can be no proper justification."

House of Lords, Report of the Select Committee on Murder and Life Imprisonment (Session 1988–89, H.L. Paper 78), 1989, paras. 108B–118:

"108B. The counter-arguments [against retention of the mandatory sentence] are as follows:

(i) Not all murders are 'uniquely serious' . . . Some cases of murder will be less grave than some cases of attempted murder, or of manslaughter, or of causing grievous bodily harm with intent. The organisation JUSTICE has examined in some detail over 200 cases over the last 30 years and concluded that the circumstances giving rise to murder vary infinitely so that the relative heinousness of the crime covers the whole spectrum from the tragic mercy killing to the most sadistic type of sex murder of young children.

(ii) The defintion of murder is not and, if the Committee's recommendations are accepted, will not be confined to intentional killings . . . All murderers receive the same sentence whether they are intentional killers or not. If the intentional and unprovoked killings are to be regarded as 'uniquely serious' the definition of murder ought to be limited to such killings . . .

(iv) The alleged 'unique' quality of a life sentence for murder is undermined by the availability of that sentence for other offences. . . .

111B(i) Many murderers are not generally dangerous. This was asserted by Dr Thomas who pointed out that, during a ten-year period when 6,000 persons convicted of homicide (including manslaughter) were at large, only six persons previously convicted of murder committed a second murder—and several of these were committed in prison . . .

(ii) The opinion of the Lord Chief Justice is that the problem of dangerousness arises in a more acute form in relation to offences other than murder. Rapists and arsonists may be much more likely to commit the same sort of offences than a murderer; and they are dealt with by passing a life sentence or a sentence which is somewhat longer than would have been necessary without the element of risk . . .

113A. The abolition of the mandatory sentence would present peculiarly difficult sentencing problems for the trial judge. Because the sentence has always been fixed in law there are no precedents to guide the judge in imposing a determinate sentence for murder: . . .

113B. The counter argument is that the Court of Appeal would soon establish appropriate principles of sentencing for murder as it has for other offences . . .

114A. The mandatory life sentence is, or may be, a valuable deterrent . . .

114B. The counter argument is that the fact that the life sentence is mandatory actually reduces any deterrent value a life sentence may have. It dilutes what should be the awe-inspiring nature of the life sentence. Because many murderers receive unnecessary life sentences, the average time served is reduced, giving credence to the common belief that 'life' means nine years [see post p. 670] . . .

117. Finally, the Committee were impressed by the argument put forward by Victim Support, that the existence of the mandatory life sentence led to inappropriate verdicts of manslaughter. Many families of murder victims felt that 'somebody being charged and found guilty of murder does imply and represent an appropriate recognition of the crime that has actually happened' . . .

Opinion of the Committee
118. The Committee agree with the majority of their witnesses that the mandatory life sentence for murder should be abolished."

D. Evaluation

Apart from criticism of the fixed mandatory penalty of life imprisonment for murder, there are two further criticisms of the present law[49]:

(1) Criticism of the grievous bodily harm rule.

(2) Criticism of the *Moloney/Hancock* test of intention.

1. The grievous bodily harm rule

There are arguments in favour of the retention of the grievous bodily harm rule as a species of malice aforethought. If a defendant intends *really* serious bodily harm to another there is always a probability that death may result from such injuries. Most defendants would know this; in any event, following *Caldwell*, it would be just as reprehensible not to consider such an obvious risk. Thus he who intends to cause grievous bodily harm has chosen to run a risk of endangering life. He is as dangerous and as blameworthy as one who actually intends to kill. His excessive risk-taking as to the death should render him liable for murder.

Criminal Law Revision Committee, Working Paper on Offences Against the Person, 1976, para. 29:

"It is argued that a person who inflicts serious injury on another intentionally must know that by so doing there is a real chance that his victim will die and if death results it is right that he should be convicted of murder. There is force also in the argument that a person who is minded to use violence in achieving an unlawful purpose may take more care to refrain from inflicting serious injury if he knows that he may be convicted of murder if his victim dies. A few of our members are in favour of an intent to cause serious injury, simpliciter, remaining a sufficient intent in murder."

The Law Commission, Imputed Criminal Intent (Director of Public Prosecutions v. Smith), 1965, para. 13:

"13. The main arguments in favour of retaining the intent to inflict grievous bodily harm as an alternative to the intent to kill in murder are as follows:

(a) It is in accord with the general sense of justice of the community that a man who causes death by the intentional infliction of grievous bodily harm, although not actually intending to kill, should not only be punished as severely as a murderer, but should be treated in law as a murderer.

(b) Grievous bodily harm is a relatively simple concept which can be readily explained to a jury. Any attempt to define 'grievous bodily harm' as, for example, 'harm likely to endanger life,' or further to require that the accused should *know* that the harm inflicted is likely to endanger life, would make the judge's direction more difficult for the jury to follow.

(c) It is true that, with the suspension of the death sentence, a person who kills while intending to inflict grievous bodily harm could, if such an

[49] For more fundamental criticisms of the relationship of murder to manslaughter, see *post*, pp. 660–673.

offence were only manslaughter, receive as a maximum the same sentence, namely life imprisonment, as that which would remain obligatory for murder. But the judge might face practical difficulties in such a case of manslaughter in ascertaining the intent to inflict grievous bodily harm, which he would require to know in order to fix the appropriate sentence. These difficulties would be most acute if the prosecution had accepted pleas of not guilty of murder but guilty of manslaughter, when the judge would have to rely on depositions; but they would also exist to some extent where the accused had been tried on a count of murder but had been found guilty of manslaughter, in which event the judge would have heard the evidence in the case, but would have no verdict of the jury on the question whether the killing followed an act intended to inflict grievous bodily harm."

How convincing is the argument that there is always a probability of death resulting in such cases? Is this harping back to the old thinking behind the felony-murder rule that the felony had to be dangerous and likely to endanger life? Is it reviving the objective approach of *D.P.P.* v. *Smith* that if grievous bodily harm is intended, death must be reasonably foreseeable? Or is this reasoning in fact in tune with the modern approach of *Caldwell*—death has occurred; it ought to have been foreseen; the defendant has acted in a reprehensible manner; he is to be blamed to the same extent as he who kills intending death?

Despite the approval of the grievous bodily harm rule in *Hyam* and *Cunningham*, the majority of commentators reject it in its present form.

The Law Commission, Imputed Criminal Intent (Director of Public Prosecutions v. Smith), 1965, paras. 15, 18:

"15. The main arguments for changing the present law, which prescribes intent to inflict grievous bodily harm as an alternative to the intent to kill in murder, are as follows:
  (a) Murder is commonly understood to mean the intentional killing of another human being; and, unless there are strong reasons which justify a contrary course, it is generally desirable that legal terms should correspond with their popular meaning.
  (b) To limit intent in murder to the intent to kill is not to disregard the very serious nature of causing death by the infliction of grievous bodily harm, but, since the suspension of the death sentence, if such an offence were to be treated as manslaughter only, it could nevertheless be punished by a maximum penalty as severe as the penalty prescribed for murder, namely, imprisonment for life. . . .
  (d) Furthermore, a man should not be regarded as a murderer if he does not *know* that the bodily harm which he intends to inflict is likely to kill. . . . If there is any special deterrent effect in the label 'murder' as distinguished from manslaughter, it should be attached to an act done with intent to inflict bodily harm which the accused knows is likely to kill. . . .
18. . . .
  (a) So long as a distinction between murder and manslaughter is to be maintained, there must be a defensible criterion for distinguishing between them. In our view the essential element in murder should be willingness to kill, thereby evincing a total lack of respect for human life."

**Criminal Law Revision Committee, Working Paper on Offences
Against the Person, 1976, paras. 29, 32:**

"29. . . . The majority of us . . . think that if an intent to cause serious injury
is to remain part of the mens rea of murder, it should be limited in some way so
that it is related more closely to the fact of death. Some of us take the view that
the law should distinguish between a person who, although intending to cause
serious injury, inflicts it in such a way that death is not likely to result and the
person who intentionally causes serious injury in such a way that death is likely
to be caused. These members hope that such a distinction might deter a person
from causing serious injury with the likelihood of death resulting. Other members think that the distinction should depend on whether or not the offender
realised at the time that he might well cause death. . . .

32. We have given careful consideration to the Law Commission's recommendation that the intent in murder should be limited to intent to kill but that this
should be defined to include willingness to kill. They say that an intent to inflict
bodily harm, even knowing that life would be endangered, does not necessarily
show willingness to kill. We find it difficult to envisage a situation in which a
person intentionally inflicts serious harm on another, knowing that the death of
the other is a likely result, and yet can be said to be not willing to kill. Similarly,
if a person hopes that he may not kill or does not care whether he kills or not but
inflicts serious harm intentionally on another knowing that death is a likely
result we find it difficult to understand why it is said that such a person is not
willing to kill. We think that the meaning of willing to kill is uncertain and
ambiguous and that the test is likely to be too difficult and subtle for a jury to
understand. We do not think, however, that the jury will find it too difficult to
determine whether there was a likelihood that life would be endangered."

In the United States the Model Penal Code recommended that no
express significance be accorded to an intent to cause grievous bodily
harm, but that such cases be subsumed under the standards of extreme
recklessness (murder)[50] or recklessness (manslaughter).[51] Thus the fact
that the defendant intended to cause serious injury would simply
become a relevant consideration in determining whether he acted with
"extreme indifference to the value of human life" (murder) or "recklessly" with respect to the death of another (manslaughter). While many
states have given effect to this recommendation,[52] others continue to
specify "intent to cause serious injury" as sufficing for murder (generally murder in the second degree). Many of these latter states however
define "serious bodily injury" in a manner relating it to the death. Thus
in Texas, for instance, it is murder if one "intends to cause serious
bodily injury and commits an act clearly dangerous to human life that
causes the death of an individual."[53]

On the other hand, four states (Connecticut, Delaware, Kentucky and
New York) have taken the significant step of declaring that killing "with
intent to cause serious physical injury" only constitutes manslaughter—and the serious physical injury must "to a reasonable man in the

[50] Section 210.2(1)(*b*).
[51] Section 210.3(1)(*a*).
[52] *E.g.* North Dakota (N.D. Cent. Code ss.12.1–16–01–02).
[53] Tex. Penal Code Ann. s.19.02(a)(2).

defendant's situation, knowing the facts known to him, seem likely to cause death"[54] or, as in the other three states, " 'serious physical injury' means physical injury which creates a substantial risk of death, or which causes serious disfigurement, serious impairment of health or serious loss or impairment of the function of any bodily organ."[55]

Is a defendant who takes such a clear risk as to death that much less culpable or blameworthy as to be liable only for manslaughter? Perhaps this question cannot be fully answered until the *Moloney/Hancock* test of intention has been considered.

2. Moloney/Hancock test of intention

As we have seen, the House of Lords in *Moloney* and *Hancock* has ruled that there must be an *intention* to kill or cause grievous bodily harm. While intention has specifically not been defined it would appear that most people who foresee a consequence as virtually certain will be held to intend that consequence.[56] To put this in the terminology used in Chapter 2, an "oblique" intention will suffice for murder. These decisions overruled *Hyam* in which it had been held that the *mens rea* of murder could be satisfied by proof that the defendant foresaw death or grievous bodily harm as a likely consequence.

It ought perhaps to be emphasised that in overruling *Hyam* the House was overruling what had in reality been the law for at least a hundred years. It is true that there had long been a tendency before *Hyam* to assert that, because murder was the most serious crime in the land, it could only be committed intentionally. This however was "really a sort of hypocrisy stemming from the days of capital punishment: a desire to pretend to the public that the law only hanged people for intentional killing, while at the same time hanging people who were felt to deserve hanging whether they killed intentionally or not."[57] Some of their Lordships in *Hyam* were prepared to admit openly that murder was not a crime of intention alone—alternative states of mind could suffice. But the others, desirous of clinging to the false notion that murder was a crime of intention, were forced to place expansive interpretations on the concept of intention so as to encompass the alternative state of mind approved by the others.[58]

Indeed, it could be argued that the House of Lords, by refusing to define "intention," are continuing the same hypocrisy. Murder is a "crime of intention," but maximum flexibility is retained by not defining intention to ensure that juries can still legitimately convict of murder those felt to be deserving of that label, even if such persons did not

---

[54] Del. Code Ann. tit. 11, s.11–632(2).
[55] Conn.Gen.Stat.Annot. s.53a–3(4); Kentucky (Ky.Rev.Stat., s.500.080(15)) and New York (N.Y. Penal Law, s.10.00(10)) have similar definitions.
[56] *Ante*, p. 163.
[57] G. H. Gordon, "The Mental Element in Crime," 16 J.L.S.S. 282, 285.
[58] This point is elaborated in the first edition of this book, pp. 506–507.

actually mean to kill or cause grievous bodily harm.[59] Two questions present themselves for consideration. Was the House of Lords in *Moloney* and *Hancock* justified in overruling *Hyam* and so narrowing the *mens rea* of murder? If so, did they go far enough? Should not the crime of murder have been restricted to those who *directly*[60] intend to kill (or cause grievous bodily harm)?

The argument for limiting the *mens rea* of murder to a *direct* intention is a two-fold one. Murder is the most serious crime in the land carrying the most severe penalty. It should be reserved for the worst cases which are directly intended killings. In such cases the defendant has acted with a degree of control and deliberation that enhances his responsibility for the outcome of his actions and affects our judgment of him as a moral agent. He is not simply showing indifference to the value of human life; he is actually taking positive and purposeful steps towards the ending of the life of another. This evil aim marks him out as more blameworthy. Also, a person who is trying to achieve a result is usually more likely to succeed than someone who merely foresees that result as a by-product of his actions, and can thus perhaps be regarded as more blameworthy than one who engages in conduct with a lesser chance of harm.[61]

Secondly, such an approach avoids all problems of having to draw fine lines on the continuum of risk-taking—for example, distinguishing between foresight of the virtually certain (murder) and foresight of the extremely probable (manslaughter). The argument against such a strict limitation is that it would unduly narrow the crime of murder and many persons, such as the bomber on the aeroplane wanting the insurance money,[62] deserve to be brought within the murder category. This raises the question as to whether there is a moral distinction between one who wants death to result and one who foresees death as virtually certain—or one who merely foresees death as likely.[63]

Criminal Law Revision Committee, 14th Report, Offences Against the Person, Cmnd. 7844 (1980), paras. 19–31:

"19. It is the mental element in murder which distinguishes it from involuntary manslaughter. . . . [W]e need to define the mental element which will distinguish the gravest from the less grave homicides. . . . It is important that the definition of murder should, so far as possible, ensure that those convicted of murder will be deserving of the stigma. Too wide a law of murder would not only be unjust but would also tend to diminish the stigma to which we . . . attach value.

20. In our opinion the mental element of murder is too broadly stated in

---

[59] C. M. V. Clarkson, *Understanding Criminal Law*, 1987, pp. 137–138.

[60] *Ante*, p. 153.

[61] *Ante*, p. 212. See also C. M. V. Clarkson and H. M. Keating, "Codification: Offences against the Person under the Draft Criminal Code" (1986) 50 J.C.L. 405.

[62] *Ante*, pp. 169, 173.

[63] See *ante*, pp. 167–175, for argument as to moral distinctions between the various types of "intention."

Hyam. . . . . [The C.L.R.C. then went on to reject the grievous bodily harm rule as it stands at present.]

Should all reckless killings be murder?

23. We considered whether to propose a definition of murder in terms of intentional or reckless killing, but it seems to us such a wide offence that it could not be called murder. It would include many killings that are now man-slaughter and would not be generally thought to be murder. A builder who uses a method of construction which he knows might, in some circumstances, be dangerous to life, might be guilty of an unlawful homicide if a fatal accident results; but it would be wrong to hold him guilty of the same offence as the deliberate killer and for him to be subject to a mandatory sentence of life imprisonment. . . .

Should killing with a high degree of recklessness be murder?

24. If reckless conduct causing death is not enough to make a man guilty of murder, why should there not be a conviction for that offence if the defendant knows that there is a high probability or even a mere probability or a serious risk that death will be caused? . . . What is a high probability? Or a mere prob-ability? Or a serious risk? Some may think that there is a probability if death is more likely than not to result—the 3 to 2 odds on chance—and that there is a high probability if the odds are shorter (but how much shorter?). Others may think that there is a probability when the odds are much longer. Should a man who kills another while playing an adaptation of 'Russian roulette' be guilty of murder if he knows there is a bullet in one of the six chambers of the revolver? Or in two, three, four or five chambers? It has been suggested that, since the outcome of death is so serious, knowledge of a statistically small risk of causing death could be held to be knowledge of probability and even high probability. We do not accept that suggestion, but the fact that it can be made confirms our opinion as to the unsatisfactory nature of the formula.

25. We appreciate that it is difficult to draw the line between what we recom-mend should be the meaning of intention and the high probability test men-tioned in *Hyam.* To confine intention to wanting a particular result to happen would be too rigid . . .

Should killing ever be murder when death is not intended?

28. We think that murder should be extended beyond intentional killing in one respect. There is one category of reckless killing where we believe there would be general agreement that the stigma of murder is well merited. That is where the killer intended unlawfully to cause serious bodily injury and knew that there was a risk of causing death. The intention to cause serious bodily injury puts this killing into a different class from that of a person who is merely reckless, even gravely reckless. The offender has shot, stabbed or otherwise seriously injured the victim, and the circumstances are so grave that the jury can find that he must have realised that there was a risk of causing death. . . . To classify this particular type of risk-taking as murder does not involve the danger of escalation to cases of recklessness in general, since it is tied specifically to cir-cumstances in which the defendant intended to inflict serious injury.

Recommendations

31. We therefore conclude that it should be murder:
   (a) if a person, with intent to kill, causes death and
   (b) if a person causes death by an unlawful act intended to cause serious injury and known to him to involve a risk of causing death.
   In addition, if Parliament favours . . . [a further] provision . . . we recom-mend that it should be on the following lines: that it should be murder if a per-

son causes death by an unlawful act intended to cause fear (of death or serious injury) and known to the defendant to involve a risk of causing death."

Draft Criminal Code Bill 1989, (Law Com. No. 177), clause 54(1):

"A person is guilty of murder if he causes the death of another—
(a) intending to cause death; or
(b) intending to cause serious personal harm and being aware that he may cause death."

Commonwealth v. Ashburn, 459 Pa. 625, 331 A. 2d 167 (1975) (Supreme Court of Pennsylvania)

The victim suggested playing "Russian roulette." The defendant loaded one chamber of a pistol, pointed it at the victim, and pulled the trigger twice. On the second pull, the gun discharged, killing the victim. The defendant was convicted of murder in the second degree and appealed.

Pomeroy J:
"Lastly, appellant contends that the court's discussion of *Commonwealth* v. *Malone*, 354 Pa. 180, 47 A.2d 445, . . . in its charge to the jury was tantamount to a direction to return a verdict of guilty of murder in the second degree. There is no merit to this contention.

The *Malone* case bears certain striking factual similarities to the case at bar. Malone and Long, two adolescents on friendly terms with each other, procured a five chamber pistol and one cartridge, and decided to play 'Russian poker.' Malone then placed the muzzle of the pistol against Long's body and pulled the trigger three times, fatally discharging the pistol on the third pull. Malone was convicted of murder in the second degree. On appeal, this Court affirmed his conviction, remarking:

'The killing of William H. Long by this defendant resulted from an act intentionally done by the latter, in reckless and wanton disregard of the consequences which were at least sixty per cent certain from his thrice attempted discharge of a gun known to contain one bullet and aimed at a vital part of Long's body. This killing was, therefore, murder for malice in the sense of a wicked disposition is evidenced by the intentional doing of an uncalled-for act in callous disregard of its likely harmful effects on others.' 354 Pa. at 188, 47 A.2d at 449.

It was Ashburn's counsel who first broached the subject of the *Malone* case to the jury. Seizing on the passage quoted above, he argued that the odds that Ashburn's second pull of the trigger would result in Santagada's death were significantly less than three in five. In making this argument, counsel suggested that this Court in *Malone* had defined murder in the second degree as any act at least sixty per cent certain to result in the death of another.

This was a misstatement of the law which the court was duty-bound to correct. This the court did in a fair and judicious manner. After defining the elements of murder in the second degree, the court delivered the standard charge, based on *Malone*, relative to acts of gross recklessness resulting in death. The court then briefly described the *Malone* case, and pointed out that the application of the general principles of law announced therein does not depend on any precise mathematical calculation of the probable consequences of the defendant's acts. This was an accurate statement of the law. Taken as a whole, the court's instructions clearly indicated that the task of applying the law to the facts of Ashburn's case was the jury's and the jury's alone. We find no error in it."

Judgment of sentence affirmed

It seems clear that tests of foresight of consequences cannot be defined exclusively by reference to mathematical probabilities.

W. LaFave & Austin W. Scott, Criminal Law (2nd ed., 1986) p. 619:

"Since the amount of risk which will do for depraved-heart murder varies with . . . two variable factors—the extent of the defendant's knowledge of the surrounding circumstances and the social utility of his conduct—the mathematical chances of producing death required for murder cannot be measured in terms of percentages. . . . Thus it would be nice, but not possible, to create a table of homicidal risk for purposes of distinguishing among homicidal crimes along some such lines as these:
Below 1% chance of death—no homicide crime
1%–5% chance of death—manslaughter
Over 5% chance of death—murder. . . .
When defendant fired two bullets into the caboose of a passing train, thereby killing a brakeman, the chances were doubtless much greater that he would not kill than that he would kill. Perhaps the chances of killing were no more than 5%, taking into account the area of the side of the caboose in relationship to the space taken up by the vital parts of its occupants. In view of the lack of social utility in shooting into the side of the caboose, the risk of 5% was held enough for murder in that case. *Banks* v. *State*, 85 Tex.Crim. 165, 211 S.W. 217 (1919)."

There are serious problems with any approach based on foresight of probability of a consequence occurring. In this respect the demise of *Hyam* is to be welcomed—but the Draft Criminal Code Bill, in that it endorses a concept of "oblique intention"[64] and links the grievous bodily harm rule to an awareness that death "may" result, is to be treated with caution. This is preserving one species of risk-taking. It is difficult however to see why the other forms of risk-taking are not regarded as equally reprehensible. Surely, being grossly reckless as to *death* is at least on a par morally with intending serious injury and being aware that one "may" cause death—especially if "may" covers knowledge that there is a *chance*, albeit a minute one, of death resulting.[65] Alternative approaches are possible and deserve consideraton.

American Law Institute, Model Penal Code, Proposed Official Draft, 1962:

"Section 210.3 *Murder*
(1) . . . [C]riminal homicide constitutes murder when:
 (a) it is committed purposely or knowingly; or
 (b) it is committed recklessly under circumstances manifesting extreme

---

64 *Ante*, p. 171.
65 C. M. V. Clarkson & H. M. Keating, *ante*, n. 61.

indifference to the value of human life. Such recklessness and indifference are presumed if the actor is engaged or is an accomplice in the commission of, or an attempt to commit, or flight after committing or attempting to commit robbery, rape or deviate sexual intercourse by force or threat of force, arson, burglary, kidnapping or felonious escape.
[Under s.210.3 it is manslaughter when a criminal homicide is 'committed recklessly.']"

Thus under the Mode Penal Code formulation the distinction between murder and manslaughter is a distinction between extreme recklessness and recklessness.

Critics of this formulation ask: When does "reckless" become "extremely reckless"? "It is like drawing the weight line between a 'big bear' and an 'extremely big bear,' "[66] and the Criminal Law Revision Committee have stated:

"It seems to us that, apart from the adjective 'extreme,' this formula merely restates a requirement of recklessness as to causing death in somewhat emotive terms. Everyone who recklessly causes death must by definition manifest indifference to the value of human life; at least, he is indifferent to the extent of being willing to run the risk of extinguishing life in the particular circumstances. . . . [W]e do not think that an adjective like 'extreme' is a satisfactory way of excluding from the law of murder cases of risk-taking that ought not to be included. We conclude that recklessness alone, of whatever degree, should not be a sufficient mental element for murder. Murder should be limited, insofar as a definition can do so, to the worst cases, and, other things being equal, to kill a person by taking an unreasonable risk of doing so, wicked though it is, is not as bad as intentionally to kill another."[67]

The commentary to the Model Penal Code argues, on the other hand, that some reckless homicides are as reprehensible as deliberate homicides and thus need to be classed as murder:

"Since risk, however, is a matter of degree and the motives for risk creation may be infinite in variation, some formula is needed to identify the case where recklessness should be assimilated to purpose or knowledge. The conception that the draft employs is that of extreme indifference to the value of human life. The significance of purpose or knowledge is that, cases of provocation apart, it demonstrates precisely such indifference. Whether recklessness is so extreme that it demonstrates similar indifference is not a question that, in our view, can be further clarified; it must be left directly to the trier of the facts. If recklessness exists but is not so extreme, the homicide is manslaughter."[68]

Such a test is not dissimilar to one commonly employed in the United

---

[66] Moreland, "A Re-examination of the Law of Homicide in 1971: The Model Penal Code," 59 Ky.L.J. 788, 828 at 798.
[67] 14th Report, Offences Against the Person, Cmnd. 7844, para. 26.
[68] Commentary to 9th Tent. Draft, p. 29.

States that it is murder "when the circumstances attending the killing show an abandoned and malignant heart,"[69] or if the killing is "by conduct imminently dangerous to another and evincing a depraved mind, regardless of human life."[70]

Lord Goff, "The Mental Element in the Crime of Murder" (1988) 104 L.Q.R. 30, 54–58:

"It is on the element commonly known as 'wicked recklessness' that I now wish to concentrate. Sheriff Gordon comments:

'Recklessness is . . . not so much a question of gross negligence as of wickedness. Wicked recklessness is recklessness so gross that it indicates a state of mind which is as wicked and depraved as the state of mind of a deliberate killer.' (*The Criminal Law of Scotland* (2nd ed., 1978) at pp. 735–736) . . .

Now we may not be too happy about the use of the word 'wicked,' which is perhaps rather emotive; but the concept is clear enough—it is the fact that the accused did not care whether the victim lived or died—which can be epitomised as indifference to death.

I think it important to observe that the principle so stated does not necessarily involve a conscious appreciation of the risk of death at the relevant time. This is of importance, because we can think of many cases in which it can be said that the accused acted regardless of the consequences, not caring whether the victim lived or died, and yet did not consciously appreciate the risk of death in his mind at the time—for example, when a man acts in the heat of the moment, as when he lashes out with a knife in the heat of a fight; or when a man acts in panic, or in blind rage. These circumstances may explain why the man has gone to the extent of acting as he did, not caring whether the victim lived or died; but I cannot see that the fact that, in consequence, he did not have the risk of death in his mind at the time should prevent him from being held guilty of murder, and this indeed appears to be the position in Scots law . . .

Cases of intention to cause grievous bodily harm. As I see it, adoption of the concept of 'wicked recklessness' provides a far more just solution than does this form of intent, and indeed renders it surplus to requirements . . .

So it looks as though the concept of 'wicked recklessness' work well in practice. Moreover, having regard to the reactions of judges and juries in some of the decided cases, it appears to produce results which conform to their feelings. It has another advantage, because, with this as an alternative, intention to kill can be confined to its ordinary meaning—did the defendant mean to kill the victim? We do not have to try to expand intention by artificial concepts such as oblique intention. Furthermore, in directing juries on intention to kill, judges should not have to embark on complicated dissertations about foresight of consequences and such like. With the alternative of 'wicked recklessness' open to them, the jury in *Hancock* (the case of the striking miners) should not have been puzzled if they had been told to ask themselves the simple questions—did the defendants mean to kill? Or did they act totally regardless of the consequences, indifferent whether anybody in the convoy died or not?"

The advantage of such a proposal is that it attempts to emphasise the essential or substantive difference between murder and manslaughter, rather than concentrating on the form of the distinction.

---

[69] Cal. Penal Code, s.188.
[70] Wis. Stat. Ann. s 940.02(1).

The distinction between murder and manslaughter should be based on a policy of discrimination between "ethically extremely blameworthy attitudes on the part of the offender toward the life he took on the one hand and attitudes which are considerably less blameworthy on the other."[71] The distinction depends on an ethical-legal value judgment of the defendant's actions. Such judgment must reflect community values which can be reflected by the jury. Again, a problem with this approach is the inherent uncertainty and unpredictability involved— although in the United States a certain jurisprudence has grown up around the concept of "a depraved and malignant heart." For example, use of a dangerous weapon can be indicative of such "depravity"— whereas use of a motor car with its greater social utility can be a pointer in the opposite direction.[72]

There are however problems with such an approach.

People v. Phillips, 64 C.2d 574; 51 Cal.Rptr. 225, 414 P.2d 353 (Supreme Court of California)

Tobriner J.:
"The [direction to the jury] of the 'abandoned and malignant heart' could lead the jury to equate the malignant heart with an evil disposition or a despicable character; the jury, then, in a close case, may convict because it believes the defendant a 'bad man.' We should not turn the focus of the jury's task from close analysis of the facts to loose evaluation of defendant's character. . . .

The instruction in terms of 'abandoned and malignant heart' contains a further vice. It may encourage the jury to apply an objective rather than a subjective standard in determining whether the defendant acted with conscious disregard of life, thereby entirely obliterating the line which separates murder from involuntary manslaughter."

3. Conclusion

As long as murder is retained as a separate crime, it must be reserved for the "worst," the "most reprehensible" killings. Emotive tests such as those involving criteria of depravity or wantonness must be rejected—judgments must relate to a man's actions, not to the man himself. It is further submitted that the Draft Criminal Code's proposed test is inadequate in that *only* the mental state of the defendant is considered—whether it be intention or a requisite degree of foresight. It is our submission that the test of "worst" or "most reprehensible" can only be determined by reference to current community values as to which killings are ethically the most blameworthy. In assessing this, the mental element of the defendant will usually be of primary importance—but not of exclusive importance. There must be room for a consideration of important factors such as the circumstances or method of the killing[73] and the social utility, if any, of the actions causing death.

---

[71] Mueller, "Where Murder Begins." (1960) 2 N.H.B.J. 214, 217. *Contra,* Glanville Williams,"The *mens rea* for Murder" (1989) 105 L.Q.R. 387.

[72] *People* v. *Phillips,* 64 C.2d 574; 51 Cal.Rptr. 225; 414 P.2d 353.

[73] See *post,* p. 666.

Such factors are excluded from consideration under the Draft Criminal Code's tests, but, as we have seen, the concept of recklessness does allow, to some extent, for a consideration of such factors.[74] It is clear that recklessness *simpliciter* is too broad a concept to isolate the "worst" killings. What is needed is a test that can isolate killings by *gross* recklessness. Perhaps this standard could be left undefined on the basis that a jury "might not be able to define an elephant but they will know one when they see it." Or, alternatively, of the formulations considered in this chapter, perhaps the Model Penal Code's definition of murder comes closest to allowing room for a wide-ranging assessment of the ethical-legal value of the deed.

Or, perhaps, distinguishing murder from manslaughter is so impossible a task that we ought to abandon the effort and simply merge the two crimes into one offence of unlawful homicide. We shall return to consider this possibility after the remaining categories of homicide have been investigated.

IV. MANSLAUGHTER

The crime of manslaughter is committed when a defendant commits the *actus reus* of homicide but the killing is not sufficiently blameworthy to warrant liability for murder. This will be so in two situations:

1. where the defendant does not have the necessary mental element for murder (malice aforethought), but his actions can nevertheless be regarded as blameworthy to some extent (involuntary manslaughter); or

2. where the defendant does possess the necessary malice aforethought for murder, but has killed under certain specified circumstances which the law regards as mitigating the seriousness of his offence (voluntary manslaughter).

This lesser blameworthiness is reflected by an avoidance of the label and stigma of murder, and by an avoidance of the mandatory penalty of life imprisonment imposed for murder. The maximum penalty for the crime of manslaughter is life imprisonment, enabling the judge to impose any sentence up to that maximum to reflect the appropriate degree of culpability of the defendant.[75]

A. Involuntary Manslaughter

"[O]f all crimes manslaughter appears to afford most difficulties of definition, for it concerns homicide in so many and so varying conditions."[76]

---

[74] See *ante*, p. 178.
[75] Offences against the Person Act 1861, s.5.
[76] *Andrews* v. *D.P.P.* [1937] A.C. 576, *per* Lord Atkin.

This is because manslaughters range from killings just short of murder to killings only just above the accidental. This can be represented diagramatically[77]:

	A		B	
MURDER		MANSLAUGHTER		ACCIDENTAL KILLINGS

In assessing the parameters of the crime of manslaughter, attention must be focussed on two questions:

(a) How is manslaughter distinguished from murder (A)? The two crimes are separated by a most narrow line on the continuum of risk-taking. "Somewhere in the ascending or descending scale of seriousness, recklessness, wantonness and disregard for human life ceases to be manslaughter and becomes equivalent malice sufficient for . . . murder. The precise line or distinction between them [the jury] have to draw."[78] Despite the minimal discussion of manslaughter in *Hyam*, *Moloney* and *Hancock*, the House of Lords, in defining the parameters of the crime of murder, in each or these cases was, in essence, focussing on the distinction between murder and manslaughter. The point at which they drew this line was considered above.[79]

(b) How is manslaughter distinguished from accidental or non-culpable killings (B)? What factors make a killing sufficiently blameworthy to justify liability for manslaughter as opposed to liability for some lesser offence or no liability at all? It is this question that requires close consideration in this section.

There are two species of involuntary manslaughter in English law:

(1) Reckless manslaughter; and

(2) Constructive manslaughter.

1. Reckless Manslaughter

Until the House of Lords decision in *Seymour*[80] it was clear that manslaughter could be committed by *gross negligence*. For the criminal law mere negligence could not suffice; there had to be gross negligence reflecting the blameworthiness of the defendant. The classic statement on gross negligence was that of Lord Hewart C.J. in *Bateman* that:

"in order to establish criminal liability the facts must be such that, in the opinion of the jury, the negligence of the accused went beyond a mere matter of compensation between subjects and showed such disregard for the life and safety of others as to amount to a crime against the state and conduct deserving punishment."[81]

---

[77] Justifiable killings have not been included in this diagram, see *ante*, pp. 275, 584.
[78] *Blackwell* v. *State*, 34 Md.App. 547 at 551 (1977).
[79] *Ante*, p. 598.
[80] [1983] 2 A.C. 493.
[81] (1925) 19 Cr.App.R. 8.

H. Wechsler & J. Michael, "A Rationale of the Law of Homicide" (1937) 37 Col. Law Rev. 701 at 721–722:

"The jury must . . . determine, first, whether the danger created was unduly great, *i.e.* whether the risk should be regarded as a normal and desirable, or as an abnormal, undesirable and, therefore, unjustifiable incident of an otherwise lawful activity; and, second, whether the unjustifiable risk was slight, great or very great. Since human beings can make only rough estimates of degrees of danger, the jury may be expected in many cases to do no more than ask itself whether the particular behaviour should be punished. . . . The question is left to the jury subject to a limited and uncertain censorship by the court."

This gross negligence test was often loosely described as reckless-ness[82] which was, of course, incorrect as long as recklessness bore a subjective meaning. However, as we saw earlier, the House of Lords in *Caldwell* and *Lawrence* redefined recklessness in objective terms making it essentially indistinguishable from gross negligence. Accordingly, the House of Lords in *Government of U.S.A.* v. *Jennings*[83] and in *Seymour* collapsed the distinction and chose to adopt the new *Lawrence* test of recklessness as the appropriate one for this species of manslaughter.

R. v. Seymour [1983] 2 A.C. 493 (House of Lords)

The appellant, who was driving an 11-ton lorry, was involved in a slight accident with a car being driven by his mistress. He put his lorry into gear and drove it into the car, pushing it out of the way. The woman was crushed between the two vehicles and died. The appellant was charged and convicted of manslaughter and appealed.
(The "statutory offence" referred to in the judgment is that of causing death by reckless driving punishable by a maximum of five years' imprisonment—see *post*, p. 626.)

Lord Roskill:
"It was an extremely grave case of 'motor-manslaughter' to use the popular phrase, a view which the learned trial judge clearly took since he passed a sentence of five years' imprisonment upon the appellant . . .
[S]ince the enactment of . . . [the offence] of causing death by reckless or dangerous driving . . . , charges of 'motor-manslaughter' have been comparatively rare. It is common knowledge that the statutory offence was created carrying a maximum penalty of five years' imprisonment because of the extreme reluctance of juries to convict motorists of manslaughter . . .
The learned judge . . . gave the '*Lawrence* direction' subject only to the omission of any reference to the 'obvious and serious risk . . . of doing substantial damage to property' . . . In my view, he was entirely right not to refer to damage to property, a reference to which was irrelevant in this case and might well have confused the jury. . . .
[O]nce it is shown that the two offences [manslaughter and causing death by reckless driving] co-exist it would be quite wrong to give the adjective 'reckless' or the adverb 'recklessly' a different meaning according to whether the statutory or the common law offence is charged. 'Reckless' should today be given the

---

[82] *Andrews* v. *D.P.P.* [1937] A.C. 576; *Cato* (1976) 62 Cr.App.R. 41; *Stone and Dobinson* [1977] 1 Q.B. 354.
[83] [1983] 1 A.C. 624.

same meaning in relation to all offences which involve 'recklessness' as one of the elements unless Parliament has otherwise ordained . . .

The very difficulty which Mr. Connell encountered in trying to distinguish between a defendant who gave no thought to a risk to which he was indifferent and who even if he had thought of that risk would have acted in precisely the same way and a defendant who gave no thought to a risk because it never crossed his mind that the risk existed, is eloquent of the need to prescribe a simple and single meaning of the adjective 'reckless' and the adverb 'recklessly' throughout the criminal law unless Parliament has otherwise ordained in a particular case. That simple and single meaning should be the ordinary meaning of those words as stated in this House in *Caldwell* [1982] A.C. 341 and in *Lawrence* [1982] A.C. 510.

Parliament must however be taken to have intended that 'motor-manslaughter' should be a more grave offence than the statutory offence. While the former still carries a maximum penalty of imprisonment for life, Parliament has thought fit to limit the maximum penalty for the statutory offence to five years' imprisonment, the sentence in fact passed by the learned trial judge upon the appellant upon his conviction for manslaughter. This difference recognises that there are degrees of turpitude which will vary according to the gravity of the risk created by the manner of a defendant's driving. In these circumstances your Lordships may think that in future it will only be very rarely that it will be appropriate to charge 'motor-manslaughter': that is where, as in the instant case, the risk of death from a defendant's driving was very high . . .

In the instant case the prosecution properly charged manslaughter and manslaughter alone. In doing so the prosecution took the risk that a jury might have refused to convict the appellant of that crime though on the evidence it is difficult to see how any reasonable jury could have acquitted him of that offence . . .

I would therefore answer the certified question as follows: 'Where manslaughter is charged and the circumstances are that the victim was killed as a result of the reckless driving of the defendant on a public highway, the trial judge should give the jury the direction suggested in *Reg.* v. *Lawrence* but it is appropriate also to point out that in order to constitute the offence of manslaughter the risk of death being caused by the manner of the defendant's driving must be very high.' "

Appeal dismissed

Kong Cheuk Kwan v. R. (1985) 82 Cr.App.R. 18 (Privy Council)

In perfect weather conditions in Hong Kong two hydrofoils collided with resultant loss of life. The appellant, captain of one of the vessels, was convicted of manslaughter and appealed.

Lord Roskill:
"The trial judge directed the jury that, *inter alia*, there must be 'something in the circumstances whch would have drawn the attention of an ordinary prudent individual . . . to the possibility that his conduct was capable of causing some injury albeit not necessarily serious to the deceased including injury to health, which does not apply here, and that the risk was not so slight that the ordinary prudent individual would feel justified in treating it as negligible . . .'

It thus becomes necessary for their Lordships to restate the current position . . .

Their Lordships emphasise that . . . Lord Diplock [in *Lawrence*] was speaking of an obvious and serious risk of causing physical injury created by the defendant. He was *not* there concerned to deal with cases where the conduct complained of was of a defendant's reaction or lack or reaction to such a risk created by another person . . .

Finally in *Seymour (supra)* the House of Lords held that the appropriate direction in motor-manslaughter cases was the same as had been suggested in *Lawrence (supra)* in cases where only the statutory offence had been charged. Their Lordships think it right to add that the word added at the end of the answer to the certified question regarding the very high degree of the risk of death were added not to alter the pre-existing law as to manslaughter by recklessness but only to point to those cases in which it still might be thought appropriate to charge the common law rather than the statutory offence . . .

Their Lordships are of the view that the present state of the relevant law in England and Wales and thus in Hong Kong is clear. The model direction suggested in *Lawrence (supra)* and held in *Seymour (supra)* equally applicable to cases of motor-manslaughter requires first, proof that the vehicle was in fact being driven in such as manner as to create an obvious and serious risk of causing physical injury to another and second, that the defendant so drove either without having given any thought to the possibility of there being such a risk or having recognised that there was such a risk nevertheless took it. Once that direction is given, it is for the jury to decide whether or not on their view of the evidence the relevant charge has been proved.

In principle their Lordships see no reason why a comparable direction should not have been given in the present case . . . Did their respective acts of navigation create an obvious and serious risk of causing physical damage to some other ship and thus to other persons who might have been travelling in the area of the collision at the material time? If so did any of the defendants by their respective acts of navigation so navigate either without having given any thought to the possibility of that risk or, while recognising that the risk existed, take that risk . . .

Though Lord Atkin in his speech in *Andrews* v. *Director of Public Prosecutions* (1937) 26 Cr.App.R. 34; [1937] A.C. 576 did not disapprove of what was there said, he clearly thought, (at p. 47 and p. 583), that it was better to use the word 'reckless' rather than to add to the word 'negligence' various possible vituperative epithets. Their Lordships respectfully agree. Indeed they further respectfully agree with the comment made by Watkins L.J. in delivering the judgment of the Court of Appeal (Criminal Division) in *Seymour*.

[W]e are of the view that it is no longer necessary or helpful to make reference to compensation and negligence. The *Lawrence* directon on recklessness is comprehensive and of general application to all offences, including manslaughter involving the driving of motor vehicles recklessly and should be given to juries without in any way being diluted. Whether a driver at the material time was conscious of the risk he was running or gave no thought to its existence, is a matter which affects punishment for which purposes the judge will have to decide, if he can, giving the benefit of doubt to the convicted person, in which state of mind that person had driven at the material time."

Appeal allowed

R. v. Goodfellow (1986) 83 Cr.App.R. 23 (Court of Appeal, Criminal Division)

The appellant, who wished to be rehoused, set fire to his council house in such a way as to try and create the impression that a petrol bomb had been thrown through the window. His wife, son and girl-friend were killed.

Lane L.C.J.:

"Lord Roskill pointed out in *Kong Cheuk Kwan* v. *The Queen* . . . that the question for the jury was whether or not the defendants had been guilty of recklessness (or gross negligence) . . .

Mr. Stewart [counsel for the appellant] submits that the judge failed to direct the jury specifically that they must be satisfied that the appellant was reckless as to whether the lives of the people upstairs were in danger.

What he said on this point was as follows: ' . . . Goodfellow would have acted recklessly if the prosecution had proved either that first, when he set fire to the house he gave no thought at all to the possibility that the inmates might be injured in circumstances where, if he had given any thought to the matter, it would have been obvious that there was some risk. Or secondly, that he appreciated the risk of injury but nonetheless went on to take it.'

We consider that in the circumstances of this case if there was risk of injury at all to the people upstairs then it must follow that there was risk of death."

Appeal dismissed

It has been suggested that perhaps there still exists a gross negligence test quite separate from the *Lawrence* test of recklessness.[84] Such a suggestion is quite untenable. The two concepts are so close as to be virtually indistinguishable. Further, there is nothing in the above cases to lend credence to such a view; all indications are to the contrary.[85]

There are references in the above cases, particularly *Seymour*, to "motor-manslaughter" which could give the misleading impression that this is a separate species of manslaughter. This is clearly not the position. There is no special crime of "motor-manslaughter." The law is the same whether the implement used in the manslaughter was a gun, a knife or a car. This point is confirmed by the fact that the same test was used in *Kong Cheuk Kwan* where the instrument of death was a hydrofoil and in *Goodfellow* where it was arson.

The only real outstanding problem (but a critical one) relates to the nature of the consequence that must be foreseeable or actually foreseen. Must there be an obvious risk of injury or of death or even of damage to property? Recklessness, as with negligence, must exist in relation to some particular consequence. If a defendant tosses a book out of a window on to the pavement below, this might be recklessness as to causing a *minor injury* (depending on the number of people normally walking on the pavement); but if a defendant, as in *Green*[86] threw a 11lb. lump of concrete from a bridge on to a busy motorway, he could be held to be reckless (or grossly negligent) as to causing death or really serious injury. It is widely argued that for a crime as serious as manslaughter there should be recklessness (or gross negligence) as to death or (at the very least) grievous bodily harm.[87] The Draft Criminal Code Bill pro-

[84] Smith & Hogan, p. 353.
[85] In *Ball* [1989] Crim.L.R. 730 the court spoke in terms of the old gross negligence test. This was however purely *obiter* and no reference was made to the leading House of Lords and Privy Council decisions.
[86] Unreported. No. 4475/C2/79 (Court of Appeal, Criminal Division) 1980.
[87] Glanville Williams, *Textbook*, p. 266; Smith & Hogan, 5th ed. p. 323.

poses that it should be manslaughter when the defendant causes death being reckless whether death or serious personal harm will be caused.[88]

The cases however suggest otherwise—but quite what they conclude is far from clear. The *Lawrence* test (which subsequent cases purport to apply) is satisfied by proof of "an obvious and serious risk of causing physical injury to some other person . . . or of doing substantial damage to property." This was followed in *Griffiths*.[89] In *Seymour* Lord Roskill emphasised that the test for manslaughter (with which he was dealing) was "identical" with that of causing death by reckless driving (with which *Lawrence* was dealing). Yet, despite the test being the same, he proceeded to drop all references to "serious risk of doing substantial damage to property"—and twice stated that there must be a very high risk of *death*! Lord Fraser in *Seymour* was explicit that in manslaughter cases (as opposed to causing death by reckless driving) there must be a high risk of *death*. In *Kong Cheuk Kwan* Lord Roskill explained that his reference (in *Seymour*) to a risk of death was not meant to alter the law; this was advice to prosecutors as to when to charge with manslaughter as opposed to causing death by reckless driving! The test adopted in this latter case is that there must be a serious risk of causing *physical injury* to another. However, it would be perfectly permissible to give a direction that the creation of "an obvious and serious risk of causing physical damage to some other ship *and thus to other persons*" would suffice (emphasis added). In *Goodfellow* Lane L.C.J. held that a direction in terms of a risk of injury was not deficient because on the facts of the case "if there was risk of injury at all to the people upstairs then it must follow that there was risk of death."

Quite what conclusion is to be drawn from this is little less than speculation. Nevertheless, the following is tentatively submitted:
1. A risk of substantial damage to property will never suffice for manslaughter (but will for causing death by reckless driving).[90]
2. There must be a risk of causing physical injury. It is probably not necessary that there be a risk of death for manslaughter (and certainly not necessary for causing death by reckless driving).

It must however be remembered, although the point seems almost too obvious to warrant stating, that in all manslaughter cases the defendant is being charged with having *killed a victim*. In all homicide trials the metaphysical presence of the deceased looms large. If a jury are directed that they can only convict if they find gross negligence or recklessness (in its post-*Caldwell* sense) they are hardly likely to convict of manslaughter our earlier hypothetical defendant who tossed a book (say, as slim as the present one) out of a window into a (crowded) street. The circumstances and the extent of the risk are crucial and in a *man-*

---

[88] Cl. 55(*c*)(ii). Under this proposal it is also manslaughter if there is an intention to cause serious personal harm (Cl. 55(*c*)(i), Law Com. No. 177).

[89] [1984] Crim L.R. 628. This was a case on causing death by reckless driving.

[90] *Post*, pp. 628–629.

slaughter case a conviction is most unlikely unless the *extent of the risk* to the victim was severe. After all, as Stephen said, "in order that negligence may be culpable it must be of such a nature that the jury think that a person who caused death by it ought to be punished."[91]

2. Constructive manslaughter

As a correlative to the felony-murder rule,[92] the law developed a misdemeanour-manslaughter rule whereby it was manslaughter to kill in the course of committing a misdemeanour. The obvious rigours of such a rule were soon mitigated, but this species of manslaughter survived the abolition of the felony-murder rule and abolition of the distinction between felonies and misdemeanours. The present law may be stated in the following terms:

(i) The defendant must commit an unlawful act; and

(ii) The unlawful act must be dangerous, namely, it must expose the victim to the risk of some bodily harm resulting therefrom.

(i) *The unlawful act*

Not all unlawful acts will suffice for constructive manslaughter. Three limitations upon the earlier rule have been developed:

(a) The unlawful act must constitute a crime. A mere tort or other civil wrong will not suffice. In *Franklin*,[93] Field J. ruled that "the mere fact of a civil wrong committed by one person against another ought not to be used as an incident which is a necessary step in a criminal case. I have a great abhorrence of constructive crime."

(b) The act must be criminal for some other reason than that it has been negligently performed. For example, driving a car is a lawful act; driving that car negligently is a criminal offence. Such a crime will not suffice for constructive manslaughter. In *Andrews* v. *D.P.P.* Lord Atkin held:

"There is an obvious difference in the law of manslaughter between doing an unlawful act and doing a lawful act with a degree of carelessness which the legislature makes criminal. If it were otherwise a man who killed another while driving without due care and attention would *ex necessitate* commit manslaughter."[94]

(c) It is doubtful whether an omission will suffice for constructive manslaughter. In *Lowe* it was held that the mere fact that a parent was guilty of the statutory offence of wilful neglect of a child, did not make that parent liable for manslaughter if the child died in consequence of the neglect. Phillimore L.J. said:

"Now in the present case the jury negatived recklessness. How then can mere neglect amount to manslaughter? The court feels that there is something inherently unattractive in a theory of constructive man-

[91] Stephen, 2 *History of the Criminal Law of England* (1883) at 123.
[92] *Ante*, p. 587.
[93] (1883) 15 Cox 163.
[94] [1937] A.C. 576.

slaughter. It seems strange that an omission which is wilful solely in the sense that it is not inadvertent and the consequences of which are not in fact foreseen by the person who is neglectful should, if death results, automatically give rise to an indeterminate sentence instead of the maximum of two years which would otherwise be the limit imposed.

We think that there is a clear distinction between an act of omission and an act of commission likely to cause harm. Whatever may be the position with regard to the latter it does not follow that the same is true of the former. In other words, if I strike a child in a manner likely to cause harm it is right that, if the child dies, I may be charged with manslaughter. If, however, I omit to do something with the result that it suffers injury to health which results in its death, we think that a charge of manslaughter should not be the inevitable consequence, even if the omission is deliberate."[95]

Apart from these three limitations it would appear that any unlawful act will suffice. It is irrelevant whether that act previously constituted a felony or a misdemeanour. In practice however, the vast majority of constructive manslaughter cases are based on some form of assault as the unlawful act.[96]

R. v. Lamb [1967] 2 Q.B. 981 (Court of Appeal, Criminal Division)

Lamb, in jest, with no intention of doing any harm, pointed a revolver at his best friend who was similarly treating the incident as a joke. He knew there were two bullets in the chambers but as neither bullet was in the chamber opposite the barrel he did not foresee any danger. He pulled the trigger; this rotated the cylinder and placed a bullet opposite the barrel so that it was struck by the striking pin. The bullet was fired and the friend killed. Three experts agreed that Lamb's mistake was natural for somebody unfamiliar with the way the revolver mechanism worked. Lamb was convicted of manslaughter and appealed.

Sacks J.:
"The trial judge took the view that the pointing of the revolver and pulling of the trigger was something which could of itself be unlawful even if there was no attempt to alarm or intent to injure.

It was no doubt on that basis that he had before commencing his summing-up stated that he was not going to 'involve the jury in any consideration of the niceties of the question whether or not the' action of the 'accused did constitute or did not constitute an assault': and thus he did not refer to the defence of accident or the need for the prosecution to disprove accident before coming to a conclusion that the act was unlawful.

---

[95] [1973] Q.B. 702. In stating that manslaughter should not be the *inevitable* consequence, Phillimore L.J. need not necessarily be read as excluding all possibilities of an omission sufficing for constructive manslaughter. Presumably, then, an omission where "the consequences of which *are* . . . in fact foreseen" could suffice.

[96] But *cf. Cato* (1976) 62 Cr.App.R. 41, *post* p. 616 and *Dalby* (*post*, p. 619). There is some doubt as to the exact nature of the unlawful act in *Newbury* (*post* p. 617); was it a common assault or criminal damage—or "endangering the safety of any person conveyed upon a railway" contrary to the Offences against the Person Act 1861, s. 34? (This last possibility was pointed out by J.E. Hall Williams in a review of the first edition of this book—(1985) 15 Kingston Law Review 89, 93).

Mr. Mathew, [counsel for the Crown] however, had at all times put forward the correct view that for the act to be unlawful it must constitute at least what he then termed 'a technical assault.' In this court moreover he rightly conceded that there was no evidence to go to the jury of any assault of any kind. Nor did he feel able to submit that the acts of the defendant were on any other ground unlawful in the criminal sense of that word. Indeed no such submission could in law be made: if, for instance, the pulling of the trigger had had no effect because the striking mechanism or the ammunition had been defective no offence would have been committed by the defendant.

Another way of putting it is that *mens rea*, being now an essential ingredient in manslaughter (compare *Andrews* v. *Director of Public Prosecutions* and *Reg.* v. *Church*) that could not in the present case be established in relation to the first ground except by proving that element of intent without which there can be no assault.

It is perhaps as well to mention that when using the phrase 'unlawful in the criminal sense of that word' the court has in mind that it is long settled that it is not in point to consider whether an act is unlawful merely from the angle of civil liabilities. That was first made clear in *R.* v. *Franklin* . . .

The whole of that part of the summing-up which concerned the first ground was thus vitiated by misdirections based on an erroneous concept of the law . . .

[As to whether Lamb was liable for manslaughter by gross negligence Sacks J. continued] . . . When the gravamen of a charge is criminal negligence—often referred to as recklessness—of an accused, the jury have to consider among other matters the state of his mind, and that includes the question of whether or not he thought that that which he was doing was safe. In the present case it would, of course, have been fully open to a jury, if properly directed, to find the defendant guilty because they considered his view as to there being no danger was formed in a criminally negligent way. But he was entitled to a direction that the jury should take into account the fact that he had undisputedly formed that view and that there was expert evidence as to this being an understandable view.

Strong though the evidence of criminal negligence was, the defendant was entitled as of right to have his defence considered, but he was not accorded this right and the jury was left without a direction on an essential matter. Those defects of themselves are such that the verdict cannot stand."

Appeal allowed

This case can be contrasted with that of *Larkin*[97] where the defendant brandished a razor at a man in order to terrify him. His mistress fell against the razor, cut her throat and died. Larkin's conviction for manslaughter was upheld. In this case, unlike *Lamb*, there was clearly an unlawful act, namely, an assault by intentionally terrifying the man.[98]

However, despite this clear insistence upon the need to establish an unlawful act for the purposes of constructive manslaughter, the courts are not beyond simply manufacturing an unlawful act as and when the need arises.

[97] (1942) 29 Cr.App.R. 18.
[98] *Cf. Arobieke* [1988] Crim.L.R. 314 where a conviction for manslaughter was quashed on the basis of lack of unlawful act. The victim, terrified of the defendant, had run away and electrocuted himself. The defendant had, however, done no more than look for the victim which was insufficient to amount to an assault.

R. v. Cato (1976) 62 Cr.App.R. 41 (Court of Appeal, Criminal Division)

The defendant, Cato, injected his friend, at the friend's request with a mixture of heroin and water. The friend died. Cato was convicted of administering a noxious thing contrary to section 23 of the Offences against the Person Act 1861, and of manslaughter. He appealed against conviction on both counts.

Lord Widgery C.J.:
"The next matter, I think, is the unlawful act. Of course, on the first approach to manslaughter in this case it was necessary for the prosecution to prove that Farmer had been killed in the course of an unlawful act. Strangely enough, or it may seem strange to most of us, although the possession or supply of heroin is an offence, it is not an offence to take it, and although supplying it is an offence, it is not an offence to administer it. At least it is not made to be an offence, and so Mr. Blom-Cooper [counsel for the defendant] says there was no unlawful act here. That which Cato did—taking Farmer's syringe already charged and injecting the mixture into Farmer as directed—is not an unlawful act, says Mr. Blom-Cooper, because there is nothing there which is an offence against the Misuse of Drugs Act 1971, and when he shows us the terms of the section it seems that that is absolutely right.

Of course if the conviction on count 2 remains (that is the charge under section 23 of administering a noxious thing), then that in itself would be an unlawful act. The prohibition in that statute would be enough in itself, and it is probably right to say that, as we are going to uphold the conviction on count 2, as will appear presently, that really answers the problem and destroys the basis of Mr. Blom-Cooper's argument.

But since he went to such trouble with the argument, and in respect for it, we think we ought to say that had it not been possible to rely on the charge under section 23 of the Offences against the Person Act 1861, we think there would have been an unlawful act here, and we think the unlawful act would be described as injecting the deceased Farmer with a mixture of heroin and water which at the time of the injection and for the purposes of the injection the accused had unlawfully taken into his possession."

Appeal dismissed

(ii) *The unlawful act must be dangerous*

It is now clear that constructive manslaughter requires more than simply an unlawful act which causes death. The unlawful act must be a dangerous one, in the sense that it must expose the victim to the risk of some bodily harm resulting therefrom.

R. v. Church [1966] 1 Q.B. 59 (Court of Criminal Appeal)

The appellant knocked a woman unconscious. On failing to revive her he threw her into a river where she drowned. He appealed against his conviction for manslaughter on the ground of a misdirection by the trial judge.

Edmund-Davies L.J.:
"In the judgment of this court [the trial judge's direction on unlawful act manslaughter] . . . was a misdirection. It amounted to telling the jury that, whenever any unlawful act is committed in relation to a human being which resulted in death there must be, at least, a conviction for manslaughter. This

might at one time have been regarded as good law: . . . But it appears to this court that the passage of years has achieved a transformation in this branch of the law and, even in relation to manslaughter, a degree of *mens rea* has become recognised as essential. . . . [T]he conclusion of this court is that an unlawful act causing the death of another cannot, simply because it is an unlawful act, render a manslaughter verdict inevitable. For such a verdict inexorably to follow, the unlawful act must be such as all sober and reasonable people would inevitably recognise must subject the other person to, at least, the risk of some harm resulting therefrom, albeit not serious harm. . . .

[However the trial judge's direction was not sufficiently defective to warrant quashing the conviction; further, the defendant might have been convicted on grounds of criminal negligence.]"

Appeal dismissed

D.P.P. v. Newbury [1977] A.C. 500 (House of Lords)

The appellants, two boys aged 15, pushed part of a paving stone off the parapet of a railway bridge. The stone struck an oncoming train, went through the glass window of the driver's cab and killed a guard who was sitting next to the driver. The boys were convicted of manslaughter. The Court of Appeal dismissed their appeal but certified the following point of law: "Can a defendant be properly convicted of manslaughter, when his mind is not affected by drink or drugs, if he did not foresee that his act might cause harm to another?"

Lord Salmon (with whom Lords Diplock, Simon and Kilbrandon agreed):
"In *R. v. Larkin*, Humphreys J. said:
'Where the act which a person is engaged in performing is unlawful, then if at the same time it is a dangerous act, that is, an act which is likely to injure another person, and quite inadvertently the doer of the act causes the death of that other person by that act, then he is guilty of manslaughter.'
I agree entirely . . . that that is an admirably clear statement of the law which has been applied many times. It makes it plain (a) that an accused is guilty of manslaughter if it is proved that he intentionally did an act which was unlawful and dangerous and that that act inadvertently caused death and (b) that it is unnecessary to prove that the accused knew that the act was unlawful or dangerous. This is one of the reasons why cases of manslaughter vary so infinitely in their gravity. They may amount to little more than pure inadvertence and sometimes to little less than murder. . . .
The test is still the objective test. In judging whether the act was dangerous the test is not did the accused recognise that it was dangerous but would all sober and reasonable people recognise its danger. . . . "

Lord Edmund-Davies:
"My Lords, for the reasons developed in the speech of my noble and learned friend, Lord Salmon, I concur in holding that these appeals against conviction should be dismissed.
Reg. v. Church, which the learned trial judge adopted for the purpose of his direction to the jury, marked no new departure in relation to the offence of involuntary manslaughter. In so far as the charge was based on the commission of an unlawful act causing death, the Court of Criminal Appeal was there concerned to demolish the old notion (which the direction to the jury in that case was thought to have resurrected) that, whenever *any* unlawful act is committed in relation to a human being which causes his death, there must at least be a

conviction for manslaughter. In delivering the judgment of the court, I therefore said, at p. 70:

'Stressing that we are here leaving entirely out of account those ingredients of homicide which might justify a verdict of manslaughter on the grounds of (a) criminal negligence, or (b) provocation or (c) diminished responsibility, the conclusion of this court is that an unlawful act causing the death of another *cannot*, simply because it is an unlawful act, render a manslaughter verdict inevitable.'

The key sentence which followed has often been quoted. I would respectfully say that Widgery L.J. (who was a member of the court in *Reg.* v. *Church*) was perfectly correct in observing in *Reg.* v. *Lipman* [1970] 1 Q.B. 152, 159 that, 'The development recognised by *Reg.* v. *Church* relates to the *type* of act from which a charge of manslaughter may result, not in the intention (real or assumed) of the prisoner.'

But, in so far as *Reg.* v. *Church* has been regarded as laying down that for the proof of manslaughter in such circumstances what is required is no more than the *intentional* committing of an unlawful act of the designated type or nature, it followed a long line of authorities which the court there cited. . . . Accordingly, if *Reg.* v. *Church* was wrong, so was its long ancestry.

I believe that *Reg.* v. *Church* accurately applied the law as it then existed. I believe, further, that, since it was decided, nothing has happened to change the law in relation to the constituents of involuntary manslaughter caused by an unlawful act. The Criminal Justice Act 1967 has certainly effected no such change, for, as I sought to show in *Reg.* v. *Majewski* [1977] A.C. 443, section 8 thereof has nothing to do with *when* intent or foresight or any other mental state has to be established, but simply *how* it is to be determined where such determination is called for.

That is not to say that a change in the law may not be opportune. If I may be permitted to introduce a personal note into a judgment, I have the best reason to know that the forthcoming working paper of the Criminal Law Revision Committee on offences against the person will afford those concerned in such important matters an opportunity to assess the cogency of the argument for a drastic change in the law applicable to such cases as the present. But, unless and until such argument prevails and so leads on to legislation, the existing law has to be applied. I hold that the direction of the learned trial judge, Watkins J., was in strict accordance with the settled law and that these appeals should therefore be refused."

Appeal dismissed

The unlawful act in *Newbury* was presumably the crime of criminal damage. It does however seem somewhat odd that at no point did the House of Lords bother to state this fact. As one is here dealing with what is often referred to as "unlawful act manslaughter," surely it is incumbent upon our judiciary to pinpoint the unlawful act before upholding convictions on this basis.[99]

In *Watson*[1] it was held that the "sober and reasonable" bystander was to be endowed with whatever knowledge the defendant possessed. In this case the defendant and another burgled an elderly man's house and verbally abused him. The victim was suffering from a serious heart con-

---

[99] See Glanville Williams, *Textbook*, p. 275. See also *ante*, n. 96.
[1] [1989] 1 W.L.R. 684.

dition and died an hour and a half later. It was held that the unlawful act, the burglary, lasted throughout the time the appellant was on the premises and during that time the defendant must have become aware of the victim's frailty and age. The question then was whether a sober and reasonable bystander, armed with this knowledge, would have recognised that the burglary was likely to expose that elderly man to the risk of some harm. In *Ball*[2] however, it was emphasised that the sober and reasonable bystander could *not* be endowed with any mistaken belief held by the defendant. In this case the defendant fired at his victim thinking his gun contained blanks (he kept live and blank cartridges together and had grabbed a handful when picking up his gun). Such an act was unquestionably dangerous from the required objective point of view.

In *Dawson*[3] it was held that the unlawful act must expose the victim to the risk of some physical harm. Shock or pure emotional disturbance produced by terror would not suffice. However, there could be liability for manslaughter if it was likely that the shock would cause a physical injury—for example, cause a heart attack.[4]

(iii) *Must the unlawful act be directed at the victim?*

It has been suggested that because the unlawful act must expose the victim to the risk of some bodily harm, it must be aimed at that victim.

R. v. Dalby (1982) 74 Cr.App.R. 348 (Court of Appeal, Criminal Division)

The appellant who had obtained Diconal tablets upon prescription unlawfully supplied his friend, O'Such, with some of the tablets (this was the unlawful act, namely, an offence contrary to section 4(1) of the Misuse of Drugs Act 1971). The friend injected himself intravenously with the tablets and later died. He appealed against his conviction for manslaughter.

Waller L.J.:
"The difficulty in the present case is that the act of supplying a scheduled drug was not an act which caused direct harm. It was an act which made it possible, or even likely, that harm would occur subsequently, particularly if the drug was supplied to somebody who was on drugs. In all the reported cases, the physical act has been one which inevitably would subject the other person to the risk of some harm from the act itself. In this case, the supply of drugs would itself have caused no harm unless the deceased had subsequently used the drugs in a form and quantity which was dangerous . . .

In the judgment of this Court, the unlawful act of supplying drugs was not an act directed against the person of O'Such and the supply did not cause any direct injury to him. The kind of harm envisaged in all the reported cases of involuntary manslaughter was physical injury of some kind as an immediate

---

[2] [1989] Crim.L.R. 730.
[3] (1985) 149 J.P. 513.
[4] See Mark Stallworthy, "Can Death by Shock be Manslaughter?" (1976) 135 New L.J. 51.

and inevitable result of the unlawful act, *e.g.*, a blow on the chin which knocks the victim against a wall causing a fractured skull and death, or threatening with a loaded gun which accidentally fires, or dropping a large stone on a train (*D.P.P.* v. *Newbury*) or threatening another with an open razor and stumbling with death resulting (*Larkin*).

In the judgment of this Court, where the charge of manslaughter is based on an unlawful and dangerous act, it must be directed at the victim and likely to cause immediate injury, however slight."

Appeal allowed

R. v. Mitchell (1983) 76 Cr.App.R. 293, (Court of Appeal, Criminal Division)

The appellant hit a man who fell against an 89-year-old woman causing her to fall to the ground; she sustained injuries and later died. He appealed against his conviction for manslaughter.

Staughton J.:

"Counsel for Mitchell . . . argued that the act must have been directed at the victim in the sense . . . that it must have had some immediate impact upon the victim. . . .

We can well understand, if we may say so, why the Court [*in Dalby*] held that there was no sufficient link between Dalby's wrongful act (supplying the drug) and his friend's death. As Waller L.J. said: 'the supply of drugs would itself have caused no harm unless the deceased had subsequently used the drugs in a form and quantity which was dangerous . . . the supply did not cause any direct injury to him.'

Here however the facts were very different. Although there was no direct contact between Mitchell and Mrs Crafts, she was injured as a direct and immediate result of his act. Thereafter her death occurred. The only question was one of causation: whether her death was caused by Mitchell's act. It was open to the jury to conclude that it was so caused; and they evidently reached that conclusion.

Since the conclusion of the argument we have seen a transcript of the judgment of this Court in *Pagett* [*ante*, p. 420]. This supports the views we have expressed in two respects. . . . Robert Goff L.J., delivering the judgment of the Court, said: 'If, as the jury must have found occurred in the present case, the appellant used Gail Kinchen by force and against her will as a shield to protect him from any shots fired by the police, the effect is that he committed not one but two unlawful acts, both of which were dangerous—the act of firing at the police, and the act of holding Gail Kinchen as a shield in front of him when the police might well fire shots in his direction in self-defence. Either act could, in our judgment . . . constitute the *actus reus* of the manslaughter.'

In the case of the first act mentioned—firing at the police—it could scarcely be said to have been *aimed* at the ultimate victim, Gail Kinchen; nor could it be said by itself to have caused harm to the victim by direct physical contact. We agree that neither requirement exists for manslaughter. Granted an unlawful and dangerous act, the test is one of causation. . . . "

Appeal dismissed

R. v. Goodfellow (1986) 83 Cr.App.R. 23 (Court of Appeal, Criminal Division)

(The facts are given above, p. 610.)

Lane L.C.J.:
"It is submitted . . . that this was not a case of "unlawful act" manslaughter, because the actions of the appellant were not directed at the victim . . .
[W]e do not think that . . . [Waller L.J. in *Dalby*] was suggesting that there must be an intention on the part of the defendant to harm or frighten or a realisation that his acts were likely to harm or frighten . . . what he was, we believe, intending to say was that must be no fresh intervening cause between the act and the death."

The issue cannot however be regarded as resolved. In *Ball*[5] the court, in passing, approved *Dalby* stating: "His act in firing at G was 'an act directed at the victim' . . . with 'no fresh intervening cause between the act and the death' . . . He had used his own cartridges and loaded the gun himself; no other agency was involved."

If one accepts that the only question "is one of causation," these cases become easily reconcilable. In *Mitchell* and *Goodfellow* (and *Pagett*) causation was easily established. In *Dalby* the drugs were taken voluntarily by the victim thus breaking the chain of causation.[6] The supply of the drugs "did not cause any direct injury" to the victim. Thus arguably, where causation cannot be established, the unlawful act will not be one *likely* to cause bodily harm to the victim. However, such a purported reconciliation is questionable in view of the clear dicta in *Dalby* that the unlawful act *must* be directed at the victim which is clearly not a prerequisite for establishing causation. Further, counsel for the appellant in *Dalby* indeed argued that the voluntary act of the victim broke the chain of causation. The Court however chose not to comment on this contention and in fact seemed to assume that causation *was* established when they certified that their decision involved the following point of law of general public importance, *i.e.* "whether in order to constitute the offence of manslaughter an unlawful, dangerous and intentional act by the defendant, *which act is a substantial cause of the death of another*, must be an act directed at the victim and likely, in itself, to cause some injury, however slight" (our italics). Thus according to *Dalby* the "only question" is *not* one of causation, but whether the act must be directed at the victim.

Smith welcomes the decision of *Dalby* on the ground that it "at least introduces a subjective element. . . . An act can only be 'directed at the victim' if there is an intention so to direct it" and because the "second

---

[5] [1989] Crim.L.R. 730; *ante.* p. 611.
[6] *Ante,* Chap. 4.

qualification stated, that the act must be likely to cause immediate injury also seems to be new, significant and appropriate."[7] On the other hand, it could equally be argued, apart from *Dalby* being inconsistent with the objective approach endorsed by the House of Lords in *Newbury*, that assuming causation is established and assuming that the unlawful act is dangerous in itself and likely to cause some injury, there is no particular reason to require it to be directed at the victim. On this basis *Mitchell* and *Goodfellow* are the preferable decisions which ought to be followed. The relative strengths of these two arguments will become apparent once the rationale of the law of manslaughter has been examined.

3. Rationale and reform

The law of involuntary manslaughter raises, yet again, the fundamental question of what importance should be attached to the actual harm done in the criminal law. If a defendant has acted recklessly, or has committed an unlawful act, why should he not simply be punished for that recklessness or for that unlawful act? Why should he be punished for the more serious crime of manslaughter merely because his actions cause death—if that death was not within his range of contemplation? Take *Larkin*[8] for example. He committed an unlawful act, an assault. Why was he not simply punished for that unlawful act? Why should he be guilty of the much more serious offence of manslaughter merely because his drunk mistress happened to fall against his razor? Was not his blameworthiness the same, whether she fell against the razor or whether she fell to the ground, missing his razor and not injuring herself?

H. Wechsler, "The Challenge of a Model Penal Code" (1952) 65 Harv.L.Rev. 1097 at 1106–1107:

"From the preventive point of view, the harmfulness of conduct rests upon its tendency to cause the injuries to be prevented far more than on its actual results; results, indeed, have meaning only insofar as they may indicate or dramatize the tendencies involved. Reckless driving is no more than reckless driving if there is a casualty and no less if by good fortune nothing should occur. Actual consequences may, of course, arouse resentments that have bearing on the proper sanction. But if the criminality of conduct is to turn on the result, it rests upon fortuitous considerations unrelated to the major purpose to be served by declaration that behaviour is a crime. . . .
A major issue to be faced, therefore, is whether penal law ought to be shaped to deal more comprehensively with risk creation, without reference to actual results."

---

[7] [1982] Crim.L.R. 440.
[8] *Ante*, p. 615.

Glanville Williams, Textbook of Criminal Law (1st ed., 1978) pp. 245–247:

"Judges who compiled a memorandum on punishment as long ago as 1901 agreed that in manslaughter cases where death results from an assault the punishment should pay no regard to the death. The logical conclusion is that there is no point in charging manslaughter: the prosecution might just as well charge the assault. Some decisions seem to accept the principle, especially where the death is accounted 'nearly accidental,' or the result of an act done in self-defence that falls just outside the strict rules of self-defence. Here the offender may be given a nominal sentence, a discharge or a suspended sentence, or the Crown may accept a plea of guilty to assault. But in other cases, even of near accident, the punishment is sometimes severe, apparently because different judges take different views. . . .

The figures of [homicide] convictions for 1975 are as follows:

Convicted of murder	86
manslaughter (s. 2)	74
other manslaughter	185
infanticide	35

The cases of 'other manslaughter' included not only killing upon provocation but near-murders where there was an attack with a weapon, and cases of the latter type were probably the large majority. Judging from newspaper reading, cases of manslaughter by negligence like *Pike* and *Lamb* are exceptional. They may come before the court in other ways, but not as manslaughter.

No one has studied how people become selected for the privilege of being prosecuted for manslaughter. Here are some more grisly figures. In 1975 there were 582,825 deaths in England and Wales from all causes, including the following (provisional figures).[9]

Motor vehicle accidents	5,834
Accidents in factories	427
Accidents in the construction industries	182
Other accidents (home, rail, air, etc)	8,817

Some of these fatalities must have been caused by the negligence of other persons, often (one may imagine) criminal in degree. If the culprits are charged at all, it is almost invariably with some more specific offence than manslaughter. Negligent drivers are proceeded against for a driving offence, and the outcome is generally lenient, even where death has been caused. Fatal 'accidents' at work are charged as summary offences under the relevant legislation, if a breach has occurred. The average fine for all infractions (fatal or not) in factories and the construction industries in 1975 was £75; and the usual fine in fatal cases was not much higher: say about £200. Since the proceedings are almost invariably against companies, the individuals at fault are in effect shielded from liability. Inspectors regard it as their sole duty to bring a charge under the relevant legislation, not the more serious and cumbrous charge at common law. Similarly, when a man is killed at a poisonous waste tip, those responsible are likely to be brought to court under the Deposit of Poisonous Waste Act 1972 rather than for manslaughter. When a child is killed, by neglect or even by assault, the charge brought by the local authority or by the National Society for the Prevention of

---

[9] The 1987 statistics reveal a similar pattern. There were 17,823 deaths by violence or accident. Of these only 568 were classified as "homicide and injury purposely inflicted by others" *Mortality Statistics—Accidents and Violence* (1987).

Cruelty to Children is a minor one under the Children and Young Persons Act, or other legislation, though very occasionally the police intervene to make it manslaughter.[10]

Can it be, therefore, that the few people who are indicted for negligent manslaughter each year generally suffer this fate only because there happens to be no other offence covering the case? It is noticeable that this was so with both Pike and Lamb (unless Lamb happened not to possess a certificate for his gun).

Evidently thinking little of the law of manslaughter as an effective schoolmaster for clots, Parliament has proliferated offences aimed at preventing accidents. An astonishing example is the Children and Young Persons Act 1933, s.11 as amended.

> 'If any person who has attained the age of 16 years, having the custody, charge or care of any child under the age of 12 years, allows the child to be in any room containing an open fire grate or any heating appliance liable to cause injury to a person by contact therewith not sufficiently protected to guard against the risk of his being burnt or scalded without taking precautions against that risk, and by reason thereof the child is killed or suffers serious injury, he shall on summary conviction be liable to a fine not exceeding £10.'

This is a perfect example of the simple belief that any social ill can be cured, or anyway alleviated, by passing a law against it."

Criminal Law Revision Committee, 14th Report, Offences against the Person, 1980, Cmnd. 7844, paras. 120–121, 124:

"120 . . . Suppose that A strikes B and gives him a bleeding nose; B, unknown to A, is a haemophiliac and bleeds to death. Or, A strikes B who falls and unluckily hits his head against a sharp projection and dies. Or A chases B with the object of chastising him; B runs away, trips and falls into a river in which he drowns. In each of these cases, although A is at fault and is guilty of an assault or of causing injury, his fault does not extend to the causing of death or to the causing of serious injury which he did not foresee and in some cases could not reasonably have foreseen. In our opinion, they should not be treated as manslaughter because the offender's fault falls too far short of the unlucky result. So serious an offence as manslaughter should not be a lottery. There seems to be no reason for calling it manslaughter. Indeed, the name is positively objectionable for several reasons, among which are the fact that it gives a false idea of the gravity of the defendant's moral offence and that there is always the possibility that it may receive a punishment going beyond that appropriate to the assault.

121 . . . The second instance is causing death by an act of gross negligence. Evidence of this will often be sufficient to enable the jury to draw an inference of recklessness as to the causing of death or serious injury, in which case the act will amount to manslaughter under our recommendation. . . . But sometimes the jury may not be able to find more than that the defendant was extremely foolish; and although the foolishness may amount to gross negligence we do not think that it should be sufficient for manslaughter in the absence of advertence to the risk of death or serious injury. It seems that in fact prosecutions falling exclusively under this heading of manslaughter are very rare, and bear no relation to the number of accidental deaths on the road, in factories, in construc-

---

[10] E.g., in one case a butcher allowed a 14-year-old schoolboy to cut meat unsupervised with a very sharp knife. The boy fatally stabbed himself while boning a piece of beef. At the inquest the coroner described the butcher's activities as "extremely dangerous for youngsters," "appalling" and "quite extraordinary." But the inquest was told that the D.P.P. had ruled that the butcher should not be prosecuted for manslaughter; he was to be prosecuted under the Health and Safety at Work Act 1974. (*The Guardian*, October 29, 1982).

tion industries, in the home, and so on. If the law of manslaughter by gross negligence were strictly enforced, many drivers, employees, workmen and parents would be in the dock on this charge. It seems to us that here again the accident of death should be ignored for the purpose of the criminal law.

124 . . . We recommend that it should be manslaughter if a person causes death with intent to cause serious injury, or being reckless as to death or serious injury. All other forms of the existing offence of involuntary manslaughter, for example manslaughter by gross negligence, should be abolished."

This proposal has been accepted in clause 55(*c*) of the Draft Criminal Code Bill.[11] There is, however, another view and that is that the harm done is crucial in assessing the extent of criminal liability. The fact of death is seen as crucial in justifying increased liability and punishment. This is much the same argument as that considered earlier, namely, that attempts should be punished to a lesser extent than completed crimes.[12]

C. M. V. Clarkson and H. M. Keating, "Codification: Offences against the Person under the Draft Criminal Code" (1986) 50 J.C.L. 405, pp. 422–423:

"It is submitted that this proposal is based on a mistaken premise. Criminal liability cannot and should not be based exclusively on mental elements. The significance of the harm caused, in this case, death, is critical in the construction of criminal liability. We do not judge people solely on the basis of the quality of their actions and their exertions, but also by the *results* of those actions. The fact that a person's negligent or unlawful actions have resulted in the death of a human being totally alters our moral judgment; it arouses resentment in society (quite apart from the bitterness and pain caused to the relatives and friends of the deceased). Imagine a workman high on a building who negligently tosses a brick to the street below where it strikes and kills a passer-by. The response of the C.L.R.C. and the Code Team is that this death is "pure chance." It is simply "bad luck." The workman's actions must be judged *totally* on the basis of his *subjective mens rea*.

It is strongly submitted that this view is unacceptable. Those observing the above incidents would respond with horror. The workman has *killed* the passer-by. His actions were not just dangerous, that is, likely to cause danger. The danger has materialised and someone lies dead. This resultant harm makes its mark and leaves a lasting impression. If the workman tried to run away, we would chase him and attempt his detention . . .

Following these arguments it is possible to mount a strong argument for the retention of both constructive manslaughter and manslaughter by gross negligence/recklessness. The harm (death) has occurred; the defendant is blameworthy; criminal liability is appropriate. However, such a defendant is clearly *less* blameworthy than a defendant coming within clause(*c*) and should be liable for a lesser offence than manslaughter with its stigmatic associations and severe penalty (maximum of life imprisonment). What is thus needed is the creation of a lesser offence such as criminally negligent homicide. Such an offence exists in seventeen states in the U.S.A. and carries a lesser penalty than that carried by manslaughter."

---

[11] Law Com. No. 177 (1989).
[12] *Ante*, p. 441.

George Fletcher, Rethinking Criminal Law (1978) pp. 474, 476, 478, 481–482:

"It is important to see that the problem arises in cases of negligent as well as intentional wrongdoing. If negligent risk-taking issues in death, the actor might be liable for manslaughter; but if nothing happens, the negligent risk-taker is not liable at all. If she were reckless in creating the risk, she might be liable in some jurisdictions for the newly framed offence of 'reckless endangerment.' Again we confront the question why, if the risk-creating act is the same, the fortuitous accrual of harm should matter in the assessment of punishment. . . .

One argument is that the purpose of the criminal law is to prevent external harm; wrongdoing should consist, therefore, in the causing of external harm. . . .

A good defense of the objective theory requires a return to the harm-oriented theory of homicide. If one sees an act causing death as an evil, then it follows that wrongdoing—at least in homicide cases—consists in causing harm. . . . [W]e should recall that causing death was treated as an evil by virtue of the taint implicit in taking human life. . . .

It is often argued that the occurence of harm fulfils an important evidentiary function. If the actor has succeeded in killing, he is more likely to have actually intended the death. If a reckless driver causes harm, he is more likely to have been truly reckless . . .

A totally different approach begins with the observation that persons who inadvertently cause harm feel greater remorse than those who have 'close calls.' If a reckless driver goes into a skid and collides with another car, he is likely to feel different from another driver, equally reckless, whose car merely slides into an embankment. If an assassin aims, shoots and hits her intended victim, she is likely to feel different about her act than she would if the bullet had gone astray. Feelings of guilt, and remorse are appropriate where harm is done, but if all is the same after as before the act, there would be nothing to be remorseful about, and the actor's feelings of guilt would make us wonder why he wanted to suffer inappropriate anguish. Feelings of remorse and guilt are closely connected with causing harm, for these feelings are part of a broader pattern of human interaction. The notions of causing harm, injuring others, feeling guilt and making amends are all part of the patterns by which human relationships are disturbed and then restored. The notion of guilt cannot be lifted out of context and fitted to cases where there is merely a risk of harm, but no concrete impact on the lives of others."

B. Causing Death by Reckless Driving

1. Introduction

Section 1 of the Road Traffic Act 1988 (previously the Road Traffic Act 1972) provides as follows:

"A person who causes the death of another person by driving a motor vehicle on a road recklessly shall be guilty of an offence."

The offence is triable only on indictment and is punishable by a maximum penalty of five years imprisonment. Before 1977 (section 50(1) of the Criminal Law Act 1977) the offence was broader in that it covered causing death by reckless or dangerous driving. Now only reckless driving will suffice. The incidence of this offence as recorded by the police is surprisingly low given the enormous number of road traffic accidents. In 1986 there were over 321,000 road casualties including 5,382 deaths[13] yet only 232 were classified by the police as causing death by reckless driving.[14]

Despite the fact that the offence is not classified as a homicide offence by the Criminal Statistics, the House of Lords has clearly held that it is no more than a particular species of manslaughter.

Government of U.S.A. v. Jennings [1983] 1 A.C. 624 (House of Lords)

Lord Roskill:
"If Parliament had in the 1977 Act intended to abolish the relevant part of the common law offence of manslaughter I should have expected to find an . . . [express reference to that effect] somewhere in the legislation between 1956 and 1977. My Lords there is none. On the contrary there are . . . plenty of indications of an intention that that common law offence [of manslaughter] should remain intact after 1956 and after 1977. . . . The fact that Parliament made it possible in those years for prosecuting authorities to choose to prosecute for a lesser offence (causing death by reckless driving) carrying a lesser penalty does not seem to me to militate against the correctness of the view I have formed. No doubt the prosecuting authorities today would only prosecute for manslaughter in the case of death caused by the reckless driving of a motor vehicle on a road in a very grave case.
. . . [T]he wide spectrum of cases embraced by the offence of manslaughter at common law makes it desirable that that offence with its infinite flexibility should remain and should not be fragmented . . .
I must therefore . . . hold without doubt that the offence of causing death by reckless driving of a motor vehicle on a road is still manslaughter by the law of England even though since 1977 it is also a statutory offence."

Three questions need to be considered:
   (1) What is meant by "reckless driving" for the purposes of section 1 of the Road Traffic Act 1988?
   (2) What would be a "very grave case" in which a prosecution and conviction for manslaughter would be appropriate?
   (3) Why was this special statutory offence introduced and should it be retained?

2. Reckless Driving

R. v. Lawrence [1982] A.C. 510 (House of Lords)

(The facts and a fuller extract from this case are set out *ante* at p. 183).

Lord Diplock:
"One does not speak of a person acting 'recklessly,' even though he has given no thought at all to the consequences of his act, unless the act is one that presents a real risk of harmful consequences which anyone acting with reasonable

---

[13] The North Report, see *post*, p. 636, para. 2.5.
[14] Criminal Statistics, Cmnd. 8668 (1986). It is interesting that the incidence of this offence has more than halved since the crime was limited to causing death by reckless driving. This should be seen in the context that the number of deaths on the road has in fact *decreased* by 33 per cent. since 1966 (North Report, para. 2.6).

prudence would recognise and give heed to. So the *actus reus* of the offence under sections 1 and 2[15] is not simply driving a motor vehicle on a road, but driving it in a manner which in fact creates a real risk of harmful consequences resulting from it. Since driving in such a manner as to do no worse than create a risk of causing inconvenience or annoyance to other road users constitutes the lesser offence under section 3 (driving without due care and attention, and driving without reasonable consideration for other persons using the road), the manner of driving that constitutes the *actus reus* of an offence under sections 1 and 2 must be worse than that; it must be such as to create a real risk of causing physical injury to someone else who happens to be using the road or damage to property more substantial than the kind of minor damage that may be caused by an error of judgment in the course of parking one's car . . .

I turn now to the *mens rea*. . . . Recklessness on the part of the doer of an act does presuppose that there is something in the circumstances that would have drawn the attention of an ordinary prudent individual to the possibility that his act was capable of causing the kind of serious harmful consequences that the section which creates the offence was intended to prevent, and that the risk of those harmful consequences occurring was not so slight that an ordinary prudent individual would feel justified in treating them as negligible . . .

In my view, an appropriate instruction to the jury on what is meant by driving recklessly would be that they must be satisfied of two things:

First, that the defendant was in fact driving the vehicle in such a manner as to create an obvious and serious risk of causing physical injury to some other person who might happen to be using the road or of doing substantial damage to property; and

Second, that in driving in that manner the defendant did so without having given any thought to the possibility of there being any such risk or, having recognised that there was some risk involved, had nonetheless gone on to take it.

It is for the jury to decide whether the risk created by the manner in which the vehicle was being driven was both obvious and serious and, in deciding this, they may apply the standard of the ordinary prudent motorist as represented by themselves.

If satisfied that an obvious and serious risk was created by the manner of the defendant's driving, the jury are entitled to infer that he was in one or other of the states of mind required to constitute the offence and will probably do so; but regard must be given to any explanation he gives as to his state of mind which may displace the inference."

In *Madigan*[16] it was held that the above direction "should be given *ipsissima verba* to juries from the speech in the House of Lords."

The North Report observes that the direction is treated and interpreted by the courts as though it was a statute.[17]

It will be recalled from the analysis of the reckless manslaughter cases[18] that there was much uncertainty as to what consequence the defendant had to be reckless about. It would appear that for the offence of causing death by reckless driving, the "pure" *Lawrence* test still applies[19] and accordingly all that is necessary is that there be reckless-

[15] *Post* p. 634.
[16] (1982) 75 Cr.App.R. 145.
[17] *Ibid.*, para. 5.12.
[18] *Ante*, p. 608.
[19] *Griffiths* [1984] Crim.L.R. 628.

ness as to some "substantial damage to property" or to "some physical injury." It also seems established now that recklessness need not be established purely from the manner of driving. It could arise from the state of the vehicle (for example, no brakes or badly loaded)[20] or from the state of the driver (for example, that he was drunk).[21]

3. When manslaughter?

In *Jennings*[22] the House of Lords indicated that a prosecution for manslaughter would be appropriate in "a very grave case" of causing death by reckless driving. There is no difference in substance between the two offences; the "very grave case" test is simply one to help inform prosecutorial discretion. This view was reiterated in the following case.

R. v. Seymour [1983] 1 A.C. 493 (House of Lords)

(The facts and further extracts appear *ante* at p. 608)

Lord Roskill:
"In his able submissions on behalf of the appellant, Mr. Connell accepted, as he was indeed bound to accept, that the common law and statutory offences co-existed but he challenged that it necessarily followed that the same direction was appropriate in both cases. He founded upon the phrase 'aggravating circumstances'—a phrase used by Mr. Littman, counsel for the respondent in *Jennings* [1983] 1 A.C. 624 and adopted in the last paragraph but two of my speech.

Mr. Connell urged that the reference to 'aggravating circumstances' showed that there might be different degrees of recklessness in the different cases. He also urged that what I had said regarding the ingredients of the two offences being identical was obiter and should not be followed, especially as there had been no argument that knowledge of the risk involved was a prerequisite to conviction for manslaughter though not for the statutory offence. . . .

My Lords, I have carefully considered these criticisms but I am unable to accept any of them as valid . . .

Since for the reasons given the two offences co-existed and the ingredients were thus the same, there was no room for Mr. Littman's argument on 'aggravating circumstances.' . . .

Mr. Connell also submitted that if the '*Lawrence* direction' were given in manslaughter cases and a conviction followed, the trial judge when considering sentence would not know whether the jury took the view that the defendant had deliberately taken a risk of which he was aware or not. My Lords juries do not and should not be asked to explain their verdicts. It is by no means unusual for a guilty verdict to be properly founded for a number of reasons and it is for the judge, who is the person best placed to assess the degree of turpitude involved in the light of the evidence and the jury's verdict, to pass such sentence as he thinks right in all the circumstances. That sentence is of course always open to review if necessary.

My Lords, I would accept the submission of Mr. Hamilton for the Crown that once it is shown that the two offences co-exist it would be quite wrong to give the adjective 'reckless' or the adverb 'recklessly' a different meaning according to whether the statutory or the common law offence is charged. 'Reckless'

---

[20] *Crossman* (1986) 130 S.J. 89.
[21] *Griffiths* [1984] Crim.L.R. 628.
[22] *Ante*, p. 627.

should today be given the same meaning in relation to all offences which involve 'recklessness' as one of the elements unless Parliament has otherwise ordained. . . .

That simple and single meaning should be the ordinary meaning of those words as stated in this House in *Caldwell* . . . and in *Lawrence* . . .

Parliament must however be taken to have intended that 'motor manslaughter' should be a more grave offence than the statutory offence. While the former still carries a maximum penalty of imprisonment for life, Parliament has thought fit to limit the maximum penalty for the statutory offence to five years' imprisonment, the sentence in fact passed by the learned trial judge upon the appellant upon his conviction for manslaughter. This difference recognises that there are degrees of turpitude which will vary according to the gravity of the risk created by the manner of a defendant's driving. In these circumstances your Lordships may think that in future it will only be very rarely that it will be appropriate to charge 'motor manslaughter': that is where, as in the instant case, the risk of death from a defendant's driving was very high.

My Lords, there was some debate before your Lordships whether in England and Wales it should, since the decision in *Jennings* [1983] 1 A.C. 624, be permissible to join in the same indictment one count alleging manslaughter and another alleging the statutory offence, it now being clear that these offences co-existed and their ingredients were identical in point of law.

In England and Wales it is for the prosecution and not for the court to decide what charge or charges should be made against a particular defendant. The prosecution is entitled to consider all the circumstances of the case before so deciding. In the instant case the prosecution properly charged manslaughter and manslaughter alone . . .

In future if in any case in England and Wales any such joinder should occur I think it must behove the trial judge to require the prosecution to elect upon which of the two counts in the indictment they wish to proceed and not to allow the trial to proceed upon both counts. . . .

I would therefore answer the certified question as follows: 'Where manslaughter is charged and the circumstances are that the victim was killed as a result of the reckless driving of the defendant on a public highway, the trial judge should give the jury the direction suggested in *Reg.* v. *Lawrence* but it is appropriate also to point out that in order to constitute the offence of manslaughter the risk of death being caused by the manner of the defendant's driving must be very high.'

I would dismiss this appeal."

Appeal dismissed

In *Kong Cheuk Kwan*[23] Lord Roskill explained that this reference to a risk of death in *Seymour* was not meant to change the law. It was advice to prosecutors. When there was a high risk of death a manslaughter charge was appropriate. When the risk was of physical injury (or substantial damage to property[24]) it would be better to charge with causing death by reckless driving.

In some ways this approach makes sense. If manslaughter is, as Lord Roskill asserts, a "more grave offence" involving greater "turpitude" than causing death by reckless driving, then it is appropriate that the

---

[23] (1985) 82 Cr.App.R. 18; *ante*, p. 609.
[24] *Ante*, p. 612.

gravity of the risk be the distinguishing feature between the two offences. But it is far from satisfactory that this distinction not be incorporated into the substantive law but be left entirely to prosecutorial discretion.

Nevertheless, the overall effect of *Seymour* is plain. Prosecutions for manslaughter should be reserved for the most grave cases of causing death by reckless driving—cases where one might reasonably anticipate a sentence of longer than five years imprisonment. Yet until recently it seemed that courts would not impose a custodial sentence at all unless the case was a "bad" one.[25] Spencer cites an array of alarming cases of persons effectively using their motor vehicles as offensive weapons to run people down and receiving very mild sentences—almost all well below the five year maximum available for causing death by reckless driving.[26]

Sentencing for this offence is now "controlled" by the following leading sentencing guideline judgment.

R. v. Boswell (1984) 79 Cr.App.R. 277 (Court of Appeal, Criminal Division)

Lord Lane C.J.:
"It is not possible—it needs hardly to be said—to say in advance what the proper sentence should be in any particular case . . .

The criminal statistics on the subject of causing death by reckless driving in the light of proceedings in Crown Courts in the years 1982, 1981 and 1980, produce some interesting, and to some extent unexpected, results . . .

First of all it is an offence almost exclusively committed by males. The number of female defendants convicted its minimal. Roughly speaking there are 200 people per year over these three years falling to be sentenced for this particular offence, and the majority of those did not receive a custodial sentence at all. Of those who did, the large majority received sentences of six months or under and almost all of them received sentences of 12 months or under.

Those figures seem us to show that the offence is regarded by the Courts as less serious than in fact it is: less serious than Parliament intended it to be and less serious than the public in general regard it. It is a trite observation, and I make no apologies for making it, that the motor car is a potentially lethal instrument. Any driver who fails to realise that what he is doing at the wheel is creating a risk when to any ordinary person such risk would be obvious, or, even worse, sees the risk and nevertheless takes a chance on avoiding disaster and so kills, is prima facie deserving of severe punishment. In our view such punishment should in many cases involve immediate loss of liberty.

One may perhaps pause for a moment to consider what factors in the driving may tend to aggravate the offence, and what factors tend to mitigate it. The following, amongst others, may be regarded as aggravating features; first of all, the consumption of alcohol or drugs, and that may range from a couple of drinks to what was described by the Court in *Wheatley* (1982) 4 Cr.App.R.(S.) 371, as a 'motorised pub crawl.' Secondly, the driver who races: competitive driving

---

[25] *Guilfoyle* (1973) 57 Cr.App.R. 549. See, for example, *Hudson* (1979) 1 Cr.App.R.(S.) 65 where it was held that the fact that five people were killed did not necessarily mean that the case was one which required a sentence of imprisonment.
[26] J. R. Spencer, "Motor Vehicles as Weapons of Offence" [1985] Crim.L.R. 29.

against another vehicle on the public highway; grossly excessive speed; showing off. Thirdly, the driver who disregards warnings from his passengers, a
feature which occurs quite frequently in this type of offence. Fourthly, prolonged, persistent and deliberate course of very bad driving—one of the cases
today illustrates that—a person who over a lengthy stretch of road ignores traffic signals, jumps red lights, passing other vehicles on the wrong side, driving
with excessive speed, driving on the pavement and so on. Next, other offences
committed at the same time and related offences, that is to say, driving without
ever having had any licence, driving whilst disqualified, driving whilst a
learner driver without a supervising driver and so on. Next, previous convictions for motoring offences, particularly offences which involve bad driving or
offences involving the consumption of excessive alcohol before driving. In other
words the man who demonstrates that he is determined to continue driving
badly despite past experience. Next, where several people have been killed as a
result of the particular incident of reckless driving. Then, behaviour at the time
of the offence, for example, failure to stop, or, even more reprehensible, the
driver who tries to throw off the victim from the bonnet of the car by swerving
in order that he may escape. Finally causing death in the course of reckless driving carried out in an an attempt to avoid detection or apprehension, and again
in one of the cases today we find an illustration of that.

On the other hand the mitigating features may be numbered as follows
amongst others. First of all the piece of reckless driving which might be described in the vernacular as a 'one-off,' a momentary reckless error of judgment:
briefly dozing off at the wheel (*Beeby* (1983) 5 Cr.App.R.(S.) 56, to which reference was made in the course of argument); sometimes failing to notice a pedestrian on a crossing. Next, a good driving record will serve the defendant on
good stead. Good character generally will serve him in good stead. A plea of
guilty will always be taken into account by the sentencing court in favour of the
defendant. Sometimes the effect on the defendant, if he is genuinely remorseful,
if he is genuinely shocked. That is sometimes coupled with the final matter
which we wish to mention as being a possible mitigating factor, namely where
the victim was either a close relative of the defendant or a close friend and the
consequent emotional shock was likely to be great.

The situation where there are no aggravating features present is that, so far as
sentencing is concerned, a non-custodial penalty may well be appropriate, but
where aggravating features, or an aggravating feature is present then a custodial
sentence is generally necessary. At present, as already indicated, the statistics
seem to show that the general maximum term is about 12 to 18 months as
imposed by the courts. It is not easy to see why this should be so. Drivers who
for example indulge in racing on the highway and/or driving with reckless disregard for the safety of others after taking alcohol, should understand that in
bad cases they will lose their liberty for two years or more. It will seldom be that
a community service order, or a suspended or partly suspended sentence will be
appropriate in a serious case. By the same token that type of driver should be
removed from the road by a long period of disqualification.

It should be noted that there is a distinction to be drawn so far as disqualification is concerned between cases of driving whilst disqualified and such like
offence where there is no question of bad driving, and cases such as the present
list on the other, where the essence of the crime is the actual manner of the driving on the occasion in question. In the latter case, where the driver has shown
himself to be a menace to others using the highway, he should be debarred
from driving for a substantial length of time. In bad cases, seven to 10 years will
not be too long.''

While such an approach is certainly to be welcomed in attempting to achieve consistency and in articulating some sort of sentencing policy, it still leaves one baffled as to when a sentence of more than five years would ever be appropriate, thus justifying a manslaughter prosecution. To take one random recent example: in *Turner*[27] the driver was described as an "absolute menace on the road" and sentenced to two years imprisonment in what was "undoubtedly a very bad case." It would thus appear that the only cases where a manslaughter prosecution would be appropriate would be those cases, as in *Seymour* itself, where the defendant basically uses his motor vehicle as an offensive weapon—in much the same way as he might use a gun. But, again, one is left wondering why such persons are not more often charged with murder.[28] What is it about society's moral values that such tolerance is shown to those who recklessly kill with their cars? As Spencer concludes:

"But unless we agree with Peter Simple's mythical J. Bonnington Jagworth that it is part of the British motorist's birthright to wipe out any more primitive road user who offends him, there is no case whatever for lenity towards those who run pedestrians and cyclists over on purpose. They deliberately attack defenceless people with an lethal weapons, and they deserve to be punished accordingly. If a car is a lethal weapon which several million inhabitants of this country normally take around with them for lawful purposes, much as the Tudor Englishman used to carry his sword, and attack other people with an impulse rather than with premeditation, that is no reason for treating these cases the less seriously."[29]

4. Rationale and reform of the law

Why was this special statutory offence introduced? Is it less blameworthy to kill another with a motor vehicle than with some other instrument?

Sir Brian MacKenna, "Causing Death by Reckless or Dangerous Driving: a Suggestion" [1970] Crim.L.R. 67:

"By 1955–56 it was clear to all that prosecutions for motor manslaughter were a failure: juries just would not convict. Different reasons were assigned for their perversity . . . 'The very word "manslaughter" is ugly and is associated in the minds of most people with brawls and sordid offences of various kinds. A jury is therefore reluctant to convict of this offence a person who is obviously very decent, and about whom the jury may think "there but for the grace of God, go I" ' (Mr. Molson, *Hansard*, H.C. Vol. 534, Cols. 782–783). For those who favoured this diagnosis the remedy seemed obvious: a new offence of causing death by reckless driving . . . punishable by a maximum of five years imprisonment."

---

[27] (1988) 10 Cr.App.R.(S.) 234.
[28] See Spencer, *ante*, n. 26.
[29] *Ante*, n. 26. at p. 40–41.

Sally Lloyd-Bostock, "The Ordinary Man, and the Psychology of Attributing Causes and Responsibility" (1979) 42 M.L.R. 143 at 156–157:

"[It has been pointed out] that the more relevant a particular type of accident becomes to the perceiver, the more he is forced to find ways of avoiding acknowledging that he could be blamed for, as distinct from just injured in, such an accident. He may therefore be expected to attribute less blame in accidents which are situationally relevant to himself. For example, a motorist may be more lenient in his judgment about someone involved in a road accident. As well as situational relevance, a misfortune may be personally relevant, *i.e.* the actor or victim may be similar to the perceiver. Similarity to oneself has often been found to relate to empathy and liking and to a tendency to judge another's actions more leniently . . . [Another possibility is that where] the judger can identify with an actor and his act, he is more likely to perceive the situation as if he were himself the actor and hence assign less personal responsibility."

We have seen how few cases of causing death by reckless driving are actually prosecuted and the relatively low level of punishment imposed. This has led to calls for the abolition of the offence. Prosecutions should simply be brought under section 2 of the Road Traffic Act 1988 which provides:
"A person who drives a motor vehicle on a road recklessly shall be guilty of an offence."
On indictment this offence is punishable by a maximum of two years imprisonment. Prosecutors would be more willing to charge with this offence, juries more willing to convict; judges generally do not impose sentences of more than two years imprisonment in any event; and in the very worst cases a manslaughter prosecution could be brought.

Criminal Law Revision Committee, 14th Report, Offences Against the Person, Cmnd. 7844 (1980), para. 142:

"We consider that the fact that death occurs in motoring cases should not enable a graver charge than reckless driving to be preferred unless the facts are that the full mental element appropriate to manslaughter can be proved. The real mischief where that mental element cannot be proved is the very bad driving, and the fact that it causes death should be treated as no more than an aggravating factor of that road traffic offence for sentencing purposes in appropriate cases."

This is the simple view that it is the bad driving that is the reprehensible thing and the defendant should be blamed for that. The fact that death has been caused is "chance" and thus should be irrelevant in terms of substantive criminal liability.[30] This approach is not adopted by the following leading proposal for a major reform of the law.

---

[30] Such an approach was adopted in *Krawec* [1985] 149 J.P. 709 and is criticised in C. M. V. Clarkson, *Understanding Criminal Law* (1987), pp. 106–108. See also *Ruby* (1988) 86 Cr.App.R. 186.

Department of Transport and Home Office, Road Traffic Law Review Report (The North Report) (1988), paras. 5.8

"5.8 . . . There is a general . . . view that, . . . the test in *Lawrence* is too subjective. It is said that the more subjective the test, and the further removed from an objective assessment of the standard of driving, the harder it is to provide cogent evidence of the commission of the offence and that this deters the bringing of prosecutions for reckless driving in serious instances of bad driving . . .

There is criticism that the test in *Lawrence* allows a defendant to exculpate himself by admitting that, in retrospect, his driving created an obvious risk but by showing also that he did at the time apply his mind to the question of the existence of the risk and (foolishly perhaps) concluded that there was none . . .

The *Lawrence* test can also be interpreted as being too wide in scope . . . [as including cases] when the behaviour involved was no more than mere thoughtless incompetence . . . "

[The Report recommended abolition of the offence of reckless driving and its substitution with an offence of "very bad driving."]

This proposal appears to have been accepted by the Government.

The Road User and The Law (The Government's Proposals for Reform of Road Traffic Law) Cm. 576, (1989) 2.5–2.10:

"2.5 The Government agrees with the North Report that the present reckless driving offences do not operate satisfactorily in England and Wales. It is proposed to replace the present offences with ones based more firmly on the actual standard of driving.

2.6 There are already helpful precedents in Scottish case law which it is intended to dollow in formulating the new section 2 offence. It will have two ingredients:

  (a) a standard of driving which falls far below that expected of a competent and careful driver; and

  (b) the driving must carry a potential or actual danger of physical injury or serious damage to property.

2.7 *The standard of driving* will be judged in absolute terms, taking no account of factors such as inexperience, age or disability (though such factors are relevant in sentencing). It is not intended that the driver who merely makes a careless mistake of a kind which any driver might make from time to time should be regarded as falling *far* below the standard expected of a competent and careful driver.

2.8 The *danger* must be one which a competent and careful driver would have appreciated or observed. It means any danger of injury (however minor) to a person, or of serious damage to property. It will not be necessary to establish that any person or property was actually endangered. It will be sufficient for the prosecution to establish that a competent and careful driver would have appreciated that some person or property might be endangered by the accused's manner of driving.

2.9 The requirements will be met if the state of the vehicle driven is such that a competent and careful driver would not drive at all. They will not be met simply by the physical condition of the driver, which will be dealt with by the proposed amendment to the offence of driving while unfit. However, if an unfit driver drives dangerously as defined above he will be guilty of the reformulated reckless driving offence, and his unfitness will not be an excuse.

2.10 In view of these elements the new offence might appropriately be known as 'dangerous driving.' "

Department of Transport and Home Office, Road Traffic Law Review Report (The North Report) (1988), paras. 6.5–6.9, 6.23–6.27:

6.5 . . . The detailed arguments for abolishing the offence [causing death by reckless driving] (excluding the argument that all such cases should be charged as manslaughter) included the following:

there is a danger that the existence of the offence would be seen as downgrading cases where there is *no* death or injury;

it is improper to create greater liability based on consequences which may to a degree be fortuitous, resulting for example from the non-availability at the time of medical help or the presence of a pedestrian who happens to be struck;

although the offence is not unique in the fact that its seriousness depends on the results of unintended conduct (the whole of involuntary manslaughter being so based), it is desirable to limit the number of such instances;

why should the road user continue to be singled out as the only kind of person whose act causing death constitutes a separate offence?

it is wrong, in England and Wales, to have a complete overlap with the offence of manslaughter;

the law takes no account of injury short of death as a constituent element of an offence;

the maximum sentence of 2 years imprisonment for reckless driving is adequate in the vast majority of reckless driving cases involving death; and if the case is very bad, then manslaughter or culpable homicide should be charged.

6.6 The arguments in favour of retaining a causing death offence concentrated more on practicality and on public expectations of the law. They included the following:

it is generally accepted in the law that consequences can affect the nature of an offence, as may be illustrated by the different offences of murder and attempted murder, and murder where there is no intent to kill but where there is intent to cause grievous bodily harm which has resulted in death;

the public sense of justice requires that the very bad driver who has killed should be guilty of a more serious offence;

the seriousness of the offence (and penalty) is desirable in order to have a deterrent effect;

juries are reluctant to convict of manslaughter in most causing death cases.

Death should be singled out for special treatment because it is the most serious consequence of a criminal act, and so doing would exemplify the concern of the law for the sancity of life;

though logic might suggest that consequences should be irrelevant, public opinion is strongly in favour of the retention of such an offence;

the case for the retention of an offence of causing death by bad driving is strong if there is no longer a complete overlap with the offence of manslaughter or culpable homicide;

outside the motoring sphere, reckless acts may amount either to no offence at all or, if death happens to result, to manslaughter or culpable homicide; so consequences should be no less relevant in the road traffic context;

if someone drives so badly as to be reckless, the consequences are not 'fortuitous,' for the driver has created a real risk of death or injury;

if there continues to be some overlap between causing death by reckless driving and manslaughter, it would be strange to be able to take consequences into account in the latter but not in the former . . .

6.9 Taking all these arguments into consideration, we have concluded that, on balance, an offence of causing death by very bad driving, however defined, should be retained. Two main factors have influenced our thinking. To abolish the offence in the absence of compelling reasons for doing so would mean that some cases of very bad driving were nor dealt with with appropriate seriousness. Repeal of section 1 would be seen as a down-grading of bad driving as a criminal activity. This is not a message which we wish to convey. Secondly, though logic might pull us towards arguments in favour of abolition, neither English nor Scots law in fact relies entirely on intent as the basis for offences. There seems to be a strong public acceptance that, if the consequence of a culpable act is death, then this consequence should lead to a more serious charge being brought than if death had not been the result. We concur with this view. We recommend that a separate causing death offence be retained, but that it be reformulated in terms consistent with our recommended very bad driving offence.

[The report considered the relationship between their new proposed offence and manslaughter and concluded that the distinction between the offences would be clearer than at present—but that, in any event, it should be possible to bring alternative charges of manslaughter and the new offence so that the jury (rather than purely the prosecution) could determine the appropriate level of seriousness in a particular case.

The Report also recommended the creation of a new special offence, in addition to causing death by very bad driving.]

6.23 [W]e recommend that there should be a new offence the elements of which would be:

(i) that the driver was over the legal limit for alcohol consumption or was unfit to drive through drink or drugs; and

(ii) that there had been bad driving amounting at least to driving without due care and attention or without reasonable consideration for other road users; and

(iii) that the bad driving had caused a death.

We see this offence as being equivalent in seriousness to the section 1 causing death offence . . .

6.27 We have considered carefully the merits of recommending the introduction of injury related offences, taking account of the disquiet expressed over conduct which maims but does not kill. We recognise that some very serious injuries are caused by bad drivers, and that these can in many respects be considered to be as bad as causing a death. We have, however, concluded that the arguments in favour of the injury offences . . . are not sufficiently compelling to outweigh the disadvantages of extending consequence linked offences to injuries as well as to death. The special emphasis which society places on the wrong created by causing a death justifies the retention of an offence from which death results, but we do not recommend the introduction of new offences based on the causing of injury."

At the time of writing the Government plans to implement these proposals.[31]

C. Voluntary Manslaughter

A defendant who possesses malice aforethought may, when charged with murder, be convicted of the lesser crime of manslaughter if he satisfies one of three mitigating criteria. At common law there was one such mitigating criterion only; killing under provocation. Two further partial defences have been added by statute: diminished responsibility[32] and killing in pursuance of a suicide pact.[33] The term voluntary manslaughter is nothing more than a convenient label for these forms of killing.

1. Provocation

(i) *Introduction*

In *Duffy*[34] a young woman killed her husband after having been savagely beaten by him; in *Camplin*[35] a 15 year old boy who had been buggered killed his assailant; in *Bedder*[36] a man who knew himself to be impotent, stabbed to death a prostitute who had jeered at him and kicked him in the groin after he had unsuccessfully tried to have intercourse with her. All claimed that they had been provoked into losing their self-control and killing their "victims."[37]

Do we wish to blame such persons for their actions and hold them criminally responsible? If we can envisage situations in which violence of this sort would be a natural response to their suffering, how is our understanding of their plight to be reflected in the law? By no punishment? By less punishment?

---

[31] *The Road User and the Law (The Government's Proposals for Reform of Road Traffic Law)* (1989), Cm. 576.
[32] Homicide Act 1957, s.2.
[33] *Ibid*, s.4.
[34] [1949] 1 All E.R. 932.
[35] [1978] A.C. 705.
[36] (1954) 38 Cr.App.R. 133.
[37] The classic example of a provoking incident is that of the adulterous spouse being killed by the other spouse.

The law has traditionally accepted claims of provocation affecting liability in one area only. Provocation may reduce murder to manslaughter because it is felt unjust to subject the defendant to the full rigour of a conviction for murder[38]—in other words the courts wish to avoid the mandatory life sentence. A conviction for manslaughter, on the other hand, gives the courts the necessary flexibility to impose whatever sentence is deemed appropriate.[39] Provocation is not a defence to any other crime as no other serious offence in England carries a fixed penalty. For other crimes provocation can be taken into account as a mitigating factor, lessening the severity of the sentence.

(ii) *The Rationale of the Law's Response*

It seems, therefore, that the law regards the actions of the provoked defendant as less blameworthy, but not free from blame. What is the basis of this approach?

(a) One possible rationale of the law's response is that in weighing the competing interests of the eventual victim against those of the defendant it decides that the victim, by participating in the chain of events is to *some* extent responsible for his own demise. The victim, therefore, loses some of his claim to be protected by the law. Viewed in this manner, the defence of provocation can be seen as a partial justification.

This interplay of victim and offender witnessed in cases of provocation raises fundamental legal issues of responsibility.

M. E. Wolfgang: "Victim-Precipitated Criminal Homicide," Journal of Criminal Law, Criminology and Police Science, (1957) Vol. 48, pp. 2–3:

"Primary demonstration of physical force by the victim, supplemented by scurrilous language, characterizes the most common victim-precipitated homicides. All of [the] . . . slayings (below) that were listed by the Philadelphia Police as criminal homicides, none of the offenders was exonerated by a coroner's inquest, and all of the offenders were tried in criminal court.

A husband accused his wife of giving money to another man, and while she was making breakfast, he attacked her with a milk bottle, then a brick and finally a piece of concrete. Having had a butcher knife in hand, she stabbed him during the fight. . . .

During a lover's quarrel, the male (victim) hit his mistress and threw a can of kerosene at her. She retaliated by throwing the liquid on him, and then tossed a lighted match in his direction. He died from the burns.

A drunken husband, beating his wife in their kitchen, gave a butcher's knife to her and dared her to use it on him. She claimed that if he should strike her once more, she would use the knife, whereupon he slapped her in the face and she fatally stabbed him."

---

[38] It is sometimes claimed (*Holmes* [1946] A.C. 588) that provocation negates malice aforethought. Both *Lee Chun-Chuen* [1963] A.C. 220 and the Royal Commission on Capital Punishment, Cmd. 8932 (1953), at p. 51, point out that this is wrong if it means that the prosecution do not have to establish *mens rea*. If it did, one would not need a special defence of provocation.

[39] See J. Horder, "Sex, Violence and Sentencing in Domestic Provocation Cases" [1989] Crim.L.R. 546. Reviewing domestic provocation killings, Horder concludes that, despite judicial statements that a custodial sentence will almost always be necessary, for such killings they are almost unusual.

J. E. Conklin, Criminology (1981), pp. 302–304:

"Victim precipitation of a crime means that the person who suffers eventual harm from a crime may play a direct role in causing the crime to be perpetrated. For example, the homicide victim may be the first to use force. . . . About one murder in four is victim precipitated, although one study found that 38% of a sample of murders were caused in part by the victim. . . . There is a continuum from deliberate provocation by the victim, to some involvement by the victim, to little or no victim contribution. . . . One study has examined the social inter-action between offender and victim prior to the commission of murder. In about half of the seventy murders there was a prior history of hostility or even physi-cal violence between the parties to the crime. This study found that homicides were not one-sided events in which a passive victim was attacked by the mur-derer. In fact, in nearly two thirds of the murders the victim initiated the inter-change, the offender stated his intent to harm the victim and the offender killed the victim."

Victimological studies bring an awareness of how close in reality may be the plea of self-defence and the plea of provocation. With a plea of self-defence, however, the claims of the defendant totally supersede those of the apparent victim (if the actions taken in defence are reason-able[40])—he is acquitted of any crime. But with a plea of provocation, even if the response to that provocation is reasonable[41] the defendant is still held to be blameworthy to some extent and thus guilty of man-slaughter. Yet he may, in some 25 per cent. of cases[42] be the true victim of the whole affair. Could one not argue that in such cases the apparent victim has no claim at all to the law's protection and that the defendant ought to be regarded as blameless? And in cases where the victim has played a part and non-fatal injuries have been sustained, should the law reflect the shades of grey (rather than the black and white colours) of *responsibility* rather than merely mitigate the severity of the sentence?

(b) However, while it may well be that the common law defence of provocation was a partial justification,[43] the law, especially since the Homicide Act 1957, s.3, now seems to regard the defence as a "partial excuse." The law is no longer solely concerned with the victim-offender relationship. Provocation may now be pleaded even if the victim was not the provoking agent[44] (in other words, was entirely innocent in the affair). The victim need no longer commit an "unlawful act"[45]; indeed, the victim may be far too young to appreciate the quality of his actions at all.[46] In short, the thrust of the inquiry has shifted from the victim (and his provocative acts) to the defendant (and his loss of self-

---

[40] *Ante* p. 292.
[41] *Post* p. 643.
[42] Wolfgang: "Victim Precipitated Criminal Homicide . . ."; *ante* p. 639.
[43] See A. Ashworth, "The Doctrine of Provocation" [1976] C.L.J. 292; P. Alldridge, "The Coherence of Defences" [1983] Crim.L.R. 665.
[44] *e.g. Davies* [1975] Q.B. 691.
[45] See Alldridge, *ante*, n. 43.
[46] As in the recent case of *Doughty* (1986) 83 Cr.App.R. 319, *post* p. 641.

control).[47] We may now simply say that the rationale is "compassion for human infirmity."[48] Much as in the cases of diminished responsibility and duress, the law recognises that man is not in perfect control of his emotions and actions, particularly when subject to great pressure.

George P. Fletcher, Rethinking Criminal Law (1978), pp. 246–247:

"The primary source of difficulty in the analysis of provocation derives from the failure of the courts and commentators to face the underlying normative issue whether the accused may be fairly expected to control an impulse to kill under the circumstances. Obviously there are some impulses such as anger and even mercy . . . that we do expect people to control. If they fail to control these impulses and they kill another intentionally, they are liable for unmitigated homicide or murder. The basic moral question in the law of homicide is distinguishing between those impulses to kill as to which we as a society demand self-control, and those as to which we relax our inhibitions."

(iii) *The Law*

Homicide Act 1957, s.3

"Where on a charge of murder there is evidence on which the jury can find that the person charged was provoked (whether by things done or by things said or by both together) to lose his self-control, the question whether the provocation was enough to make a reasonable man do as he did shall be left to be determined by the jury; and in determining that question the jury shall take into account everything both done and said according to the effect which, in their opinion, it would have on a reasonable man."

It has been held that the words "provoked" and "provocation" are to be given their plain, ordinary meaning, unaffected by any technical legacies from the pre-1957 common law as to what may or may not constitute provocation.

R. v. Doughty (1986) 83 Cr.App.R. 319 (Court of Appeal, Criminal Divison):

The defendant was charged with the murder of his 17 day old son. He had had to look after both his wife (who had had a caesarian operation) and the baby since their return from the hospital. The baby was extremely restless and cried persistently. The defendant, agreed to have been a conscientious father who had done his best, finally tried to stop the crying by placing a cushion over the baby's head and then kneeling on it. The trial judge refused to allow the baby's crying immediately prior to the killing to go to the jury as evidence of provocation.

Stocker L.J.:
"The learned [trial] judge said: . . . 'In my judgment the perfectly natural episodes or events of crying and restlessness by a 17 day old baby does not constitute evidence of provocation in relation to the first subjective question. Put

---

[47] See, generally, on this transmutation of provocation from a partial justification to a partial excuse, P. Alldridge, at pp. 669–672.
[48] *Hayward* (1908) 21 Cox C.C. 692 at 694 *per* Lord Tindal C.J.

another way, the crying and restlessness of a 17 day old baby cannot be utilised as being provocative to enable the defendant to raise the defence of provocation. Though provocation can be constituted by conduct or words which are not unlawful, provocation cannot be founded, in my judgment, on the perfectly natural episodes or events arising in the life of a 17 day old baby. It is notorious that every baby born cries, that every baby can at times be burdensome. It is notorious that a baby of 17 days is incapable of sustaining his own life, that he is defenceless and harmless. These notorious facts are common to every baby who is only days old. I think that the episodes or events in the life of the baby of 17 days old could not have been in the mind of Parliament when section 3 became the law. The words of section 3, I quote: 'Whether by things done or words said or by both together'—are not, in my judgment, apposite to embrace the perfectly ordinary, certain, and natural episodes or events in the life of a 17 day old baby. Further, common law directions cannot be construed as including these natural and certain episodes that occur in the life of every baby of days old. Finally, I think civilised society dictates that the natural episodes occurring in the life of a baby only days old have to be endured and cannot be utilised as the foundation of subjective provocation to enable his killer to escape a conviction for murder.'

We appreciate the reasons which the learned judge gave for reaching the conclusion that he did, but we are unable to construe section 3 in such a light. The first sentence of section 3 reads: 'Where on a charge of murder there is evidence on which the jury can find that the person charged was provoked . . . to lose his self-control.' There is no doubt, and it is not in dispute, that there was here evidence upon which the appellant was—I use the word loosely 'provoked' to lose his self-control. Part of that evidence has been cited earlier in this judgment.

The reasoning in which the learned judge gave, understandable though it was, involves, in our view, adding in to section 3 words which are not there, presumably by way of restriction. It is accepted by Mr. Klevan [for the Crown] that there was evidence which linked causally the crying of the baby with the response of the appellant. Accordingly, in our view, it seem inevitable that that being so the section is mandatory and requires the learned judge to leave the issue of the objective test to the jury.

Mr. Klevan also referred us to what might, in shorthand, be called the 'floodgates proposition,' that if the learned judge's direction was wrong it opens up the possibility that in any case in which there is a battered baby allegation and the baby dies, the argument based on provocation may be raised. We feel that even if that submission was right it could not be allowed to dissuade us from putting a construction on section 3 which, in our view, its wording plainly constrains. We also feel that reliance can be placed upon the common sense of juries upon whom the task of deciding the issue is imposed by section 3 and that common sense will ensure that only in cases where the facts fully justified it would their verdict be likely to be that they would hold that a defendant's act in killing a crying child would be the response of a reasonable man within the section. That matter is, in our view, imposed by Parliament upon the jury, not upon a judge, and the common sense of juries can be relied upon not to bring in perverse verdicts where the facts do not justify the conclusion.

In our view, therefore, though fully understanding his reasons, we are of the view that the learned judge was wrong in not leaving the issue of provocation to the jury. . . . ''

Appeal allowed in part
Conviction for murder quashed
Conviction of manslaughter substituted
Sentence varied

As this case makes clear, once there is evidence of provocation in a "loose" sense, the issue must be put to the jury.[49]

The jury then have to satisfy themselves as to two questions:

(a) Subjective loss of self-control

The defendant must actually have lost his self-control. He must have been "subjectively provoked." No matter how severe the provocation, if the defendant was in control at the time of the killing, there is no evidence upon which the defence can be based.[50] So if, for example, the defendant has had sufficient time between the provoking incident and his response to collect his thoughts, a so-called "cooling-time," the defence may be denied him. Generally, unless the time span is considerable, it will be for the jury to decide whether he can still be said to be acting under provocation.[51] *A fortiori*, if the defendant deliberately plans and takes revenge for what may be years of provocation and suffering, the defence of provocation cannot be available to him. He has not killed under a loss of self-control. Here, however, there is some evidence that the courts will find the slightest "new" act on the part of the "victim" sufficient to enable the entire history of events to be included. If the courts refuse to do so, there is every chance that the jury will refuse, out of sympathy with the defendant, to follow the judge's directions to convict of murder.[52]

The second and crucial question, is the evaluative one:

(b) The reasonable man test

State v. Hoyt, 128 N.W. 2d 645, 21 Wis. 2d 284 (1964) (Supreme Court of Wisconsin)

Wilkie J.:

"The 'reasonable man' concept in the law generally has two distinct meanings. There is the statistical concept under which the reasonable man does what most people do in fact under the circumstances. Yet if this is the meaning of the test, it is clear that as a matter of fact a great majority of people will never com-

---

[49] For criticism of this case, see J. Horder, "The Problem of Provocative Children" [1987] Crim.L.R. 655. He argues that cases where children are the provokers "pose difficulties that go to the root of the rationale for the doctrine of provocation" (p. 661), because the courts seem to concentrate exclusively on provocation as partial excuse. His view is that provocation is still a partial justification; the victim was to some extent asking for it. But as he rightly argues, a baby cannot be said to have enough responsibility to be "asking for it". See also, *Johnson* [1989] Crim.L.R. 738 where it was held that the evidence must be put to the jury even where provocation had not been raised specifically as a defence and even where there was evidence that it was self-induced.

[50] As, *e.g.*, in *Cocker* [1989] Crim.L.R. 740 where the undeniably provocative behaviour of his terminally ill wife did *not* cause the defendant to lose control (as it could have done) but lead him *calmly* to accede to her requests to die.

[51] In *Ibrams, Gregory* (1982) 74 Cr.App.R. 154 the Court of Appeal upheld the withdrawal of the defence of provocation from the jury in the case of two appellants who had delayed several days before retaliating. See *post* p. 654 for a discussion of the physiology of "cooling-time."

[52] For a detailed discussion of cumulative provocation see M. Wasik, "Cumulative Provocation and Domestic Killing" [1982] Crim.L.R. 29.

mit murder no matter how violently provoked by another. A consistent application of this test, viewing the reasonable man as the statistical factual norm would, in effect read . . . [the defence] . . . out of existence.

However, in other contexts there is the ethical concept under which the reasonable man functions as the person the law *expects* everyone to be, regardless of whether a majority, in fact, fall short of the *moral* normal in actual conduct. To take this view of the reasonable man for the purposes of the provocation test would propel courts and juries into the strange task of deciding when a person, taken as the ethical ideal, would commit murder. This may well result in reading . . . [the partial defence] out of existence. The person we expect people to be like would not solve his problems by murder. If we conclude that an ethical ideal—that person whom all others aspire to emulate—would be driven to kill under the circumstances of a given case, logically the verdict should be not guilty, not morally blameworthy to any degree. . . .

The basic question is whether [the defendant] . . . is as culpable as a person who kills solely for self-aggrandizement or out of sheer malevolence. To answer this question, we must place ourselves emphatically in the actual situation in which the defendant was placed, a situation which may be relatively unique. Therefore, an inquiry into what most people would do in such circumstances cannot be completely determinative of the issue. The test cannot be wholly objective or wholly subjective. . . . The victim's conduct must be such that we conclude that the feeling and conduct of the defendant can be understood sympathetically, albeit not condoned. The trier-of-fact must be able to say: although I would have acted differently, and I believe most people would have acted differently, I can understand why this person gave way to the impulse to kill."

The question of what the reasonable man looks like—what characteristics of the defendant he may be said to possess—has long perplexed the judiciary. Fletcher[53] argues that the concern over individuation of the standard is part of the decline in moral thinking generally in the analysis of liability for homicide. The courts have sought to evade the real question (a moral question) of whether the defendant could be expected to control the impulse to kill, by constructing the reasonable man test. This test has in itself become so concretised and glorified that the real question has been lost from sight. Instead, the courts have become bogged down with questions such as whether the reasonable man can be impotent,[54] mentally deficient,[55] excitable,[56] young,[57] pregnant,[58] etc. Traditionally, the courts have been loathe to include any unusual physical characteristic for fear of "not knowing where to draw the line."[59] How much of a departure from such thinking are the following decisions?

[53] Fletcher, p. 249.
[54] *Bedder* v. *D.P.P.* [1954] 1 W.L.R. 1119.
[55] *Alexander* (1913) 9 Cr.App.R. 139.
[56] *Lesbini* [1914] 3 K.B. 1116; *Bedder* [1954] 1 W.L.R. 1119.
[57] *Camplin* [1978] A.C. 705.
[58] *Smith* (1914) 11 Cr.App.R. 36.
[59] Fletcher, p. 249; see also *Holmes* [1946] A.C. 588 and Royal Commission on Capital Punishment, Cmd. 8932, paras. 139–145 where some reluctance to close the door completely was expressed before agreeing with judicial evidence that this should be done.

D.P.P. v. Camplin [1978] A.C. 705 (House of Lords)

(The facts appear from the judgment of Lord Diplock)

Lord Diplock:
"The respondent, Camplin, who was 15 years of age, killed a middle-aged Pakistani, Mohammed Lal Khan, by splitting his skull with a chapati pan, a heavy kitchen utensil like a rimless frying pan. At the time the two of them were alone together in Khan's flat. At Camplin's trial for murder before Boreham J. his only defence was that of provocation so as to reduce the offence to manslaughter. According to the story that he told in the witness box but which differed materially from that which he had told to the police, Khan had buggered him in spite of his resistance and had then laughed at him. Whereupon Camplin had lost his self-control and attacked Khan fatally with the chapati pan. . . .
The point of law of general public importance involved in the case has been certified as being:
'Whether, on the prosecution for murder of a boy of 15, where the issue of provocation arises, the jury should be directed to consider the question, under section 3 of the Homicide Act 1957 whether the provocation was enough to make a reasonable man do as he did by reference to a "reasonable adult" or by reference to a "reasonable boy of 15." ' . . .
. . . [U]ntil the 1957 Act was passed there was a condition precedent which had to be satisfied before any question of applying this dual test could arise. The conduct of the deceased had to be of such a kind as was capable in law of constituting provocation; and whether it was or not was a question for the judge, not for the jury. The House so held in *Mancini* v. *D.P.P.* ((1942) A.C. 1). . . .
My Lords, this was the state of law when *Bedder* v. *D.P.P.* ((1959) 1 W.L.R. 1119) fell to be considered by this House. The accused had killed a prostitute. He was sexually impotent. According to his evidence he had tried to have sexual intercourse with her and failed. She taunted him with his failure and tried to get away from his grasp. In the course of her attempts to do so she slapped him in the face, punched him in the stomach and kicked him in the groin, whereupon he took a knife out of his pocket and stabbed her twice and caused her death. The struggle that led to her death thus started because the deceased taunted the accused with his physical infirmity; but in the state of the law as it then was, taunts unaccompanied by any physical violence did not constitute provocation. The taunts were followed by violence on the part of the deceased in the course of her attempt to get away from the accused, and it may be that this subsequent violence would have a greater effect on the self-control of an impotent man already enraged by the taunts than it would have had upon a person conscious of possessing normal physical attributes. So there might have been some justification for the judge to instruct the jury to ignore the fact that the accused was impotent when they were considering whether the deceased's conduct amounted to such provocation as would cause a reasonable or ordinary person to lose his self-control. This indeed appears to have been the ground on which the Court of Criminal Appeal had approved the summing-up when they said at p. 1121:
' . . . no distinction is to be made in the case of a person who, though it may not be a matter of temperament is physically impotent, is conscious of that impotence, *and therefore mentally liable to be more excited unduly* if he is "twitted" or attacked on the subject of that particular infirmity.'
This statement, for which I have myself supplied the emphasis, was approved by Lord Simonds L.C. speaking on behalf of all the members of this House who sat on the appeal; but he also went on to lay down the broader proposition at 1123, that:

'It would be plainly illogical not to recognise an unusually excitable or pugnacious temperament in the accused as a matter to be taken into account
but yet to recognise for that purpose some unusual physical characteristic,
be it impotence or another.'

. . . My Lords, . . . section [3] . . . was intended to mitigate in some degree
the harshness of the common law of provocation as it had been developed by
recent decisions in this House. It recognises and retains the dual test: the provocation must not only have caused the accused to lose his self-control but also be
such as might cause a reasonable man to react to it as the accused did. Nevertheless it brings about two important changes in the law. The first is it abolishes all
previous rules of law as to what can or cannot amount to provocation and in
particular the rule of law that, save in the two exceptional cases I have mentioned, words unaccompanied by violence could not do so. Secondly it makes
clear that if there was any evidence that the accused himself at the time of the
act which caused the death in fact lost his self-control in consequence of some
provocation however slight it might appear to the judge, he was bound to leave
to the jury the question, which is one of opinion not of law, whether a reasonable man might have reacted to that provocation as the accused did. . . .

Although it is now for the jury to apply the 'reasonable man' test, it still remains
for the judge to direct them what, in the new context of the section, is the meaning
of this apparently inapt expression, since powers of ratiocination bear no obvious
relationships to powers of self-control. Apart from this the judge is entitled, if he
thinks it helpful, to suggest considerations which may influence the jury in forming their own opinions as to whether the test is satisfied; but he should make it
clear that these are not instructions which they are required to follow: it is for them
and no one else to decide what weight, if any, ought to be given to them.

As I have already pointed out, for the purposes of the law of provocation the
'reasonable man' has never been confined to the adult male. It means an ordinary person of either sex, not exceptionally excitable or pugnacious, but possessed of such powers of self-control as everyone is entitled to expect that his
fellow citizens will exercise in society as it is today. A crucial factor in the
defence of provocation from earliest times has been the relationship between
the gravity of provocation and the way in which the accused retaliated, both
being judged by the social standards of the day. When Hale was writing in the
seventeenth century, pulling a man's nose was thought to justify retaliation
with a sword; when *Mancini* v. *D.P.P.* . . . . was decided by this House, a blow
with a fist would not justify retaliation with a deadly weapon. But so long as
words unaccompanied by violence could not in common law amount to provocation the relevant proportionality between provocation and retaliation was
primarily one of degrees of violence. Words spoken to the accused before the
violence started were not normally to be included in the proportion sum. But
now that the law has been changed so as to permit of words being treated as
provocation, even though unaccompanied by any other acts, the gravity of verbal provocation may well depend on the particular characteristics or circumstances of the person to whom a taunt or insult is addressed. To taunt a person
because of his race, his physical infirmities or some shameful incident in his
past may well be considered by the jury to be more offensive to the person
addressed, however equable his temperament, if the facts on which the taunt is
founded are true than it would be if they were not. It would stultify much of the
mitigation of the previous harshness of the common law in ruling out verbal
provocation as capable of reducing murder to manslaughter if the jury could not
take into consideration all those factors which in their opinion would effect the
gravity of taunts and insults when applied to the person to whom they are
addressed. So to this extent at any rate the unqualified proposition accepted by·
this House in *Bedder* v. *D.P.P.* . . . . that for the purposes of the 'reasonable man'

test any unusual physical characteristics of the accused must be ignored requires revision as a result of the passing of the Act of 1957.

That he was only 15 years of age at the time of the killing is the relevant characteristic of the accused in the instant case. It is a characteristic which may have its effects on temperament as well as physique. If the jury think that the same power of self-control is not to be expected in an ordinary, average or normal boy of 15 as in an older person, are they to treat the lesser powers of self-control possessed by an ordinary, average or normal boy of 15 as the standard of self-control with which the conduct of the accused is to be compared?

It may be conceded that in strict logic there is a transition between treating age as a characteristic that may be taken into account in assessing the gravity of the provocation addressed to the accused and treating it as a characteristic to be taken into account in determining what is the degree of self-control to be expected of the ordinary person with whom the accused's conduct is to be compared. But to require old heads on young shoulders is inconsistent with the law's compassion of human infirmity to which Sir Michael Foster ascribed the doctrine of provocation more than two centuries ago. The distinction as to the purposes for which it is legitimate to take the age of the accused into account involves considerations of too great nicety to warrant a place in deciding a matter of opinion, which is no longer one to be decided by a judge trained in logical reasoning but by a jury drawing on their experience of how ordinary human beings behave in real life.

There is no direct authority prior to the Act of 1957 that expressly states that the age of the accused could not be taken into account in determining the standard of self-control for the purposes of the reasonable man test—unless this is implicit in the reasoning of Lord Simonds L.C. in *Bedder.* . . . The Court of Appeal distinguished the instant case from that of *Bedder* on the ground that what it was there said must be ignored was an unusual characteristic that distinguished the accused from ordinary normal persons, whereas nothing could be more ordinary or normal than to be aged 15. The reasoning in *Bedder* would, I think, permit of this distinction between normal and abnormal characteristics, which may affect the powers of self-control of the accused; but for reasons that I have already mentioned the proposition stated in *Bedder* requires qualification as a consequence of changes in the law affected by the Act of 1957. To try to salve what can remain of it without conflict with the Act could in my view only lead to unnecessary and unsatisfactory complexity in a question which has now become a question for the jury alone. In my view *Bedder*, like *Mancini* . . . and *Holmes*, . . . ought no longer to be treated as an authority on the law of provocation.

In my opinion a proper direction to a jury on the question left to their exclusive determination by section 3 of the Act of 1957 would be on the following lines. The judge should state what the question is using the very terms of the section. He should then explain to them that the reasonable man referred to in the question is a person having the power of self-control to be expected of an ordinary person of the sex and age of the accused, but in other respects sharing such of the accused's characteristics as they think would affect the gravity of the provocation to him; and that the question is not merely whether such a person would in like circumstances be provoked to lose his self-control but also whether he would react to the provocation as the accused did. . . . "[60]

Appeal dismissed

---

[60] In *Burke* [1987] Crim.L.R. 336, it was held unnecessary for the judge to use the *exact* words of this direction but that the *full substance* of them must be made clear. In this case it was held that being a church-goer was a relevant characteristic to be put to the jury in determining reaction to sexual harassment.

As is made clear in the model direction, not all characteristics of the defendant have to be taken into account by the court. Only those characteristics that affect the gravity of the provocation are relevant. So in *Newell* where the defendant killed someone who had made disparaging remarks about his ex-girlfriend and had issued a homosexual invitation to him, his alcoholism, his depression at the defection of his girlfriend, and his confused state following a drug overdose were all ignored for the purposes of provocation.[61] The court interpreted *Camplin* as laying down a requirement that there be a direct connection between the characteristic and the provocative remark or incident. Not only were the characteristics of the defendant in *Newell* held not to be sufficiently connected to the provocative remarks (but on that basis, were they in *Camplin* itself?) but they were "not of sufficient significance or . . . of sufficient permanency to be regarded as 'characteristics' which enable(d) the offender to be distinguished from the ordinary man."[62]

Newell also suggested that it would not be enough that the defendant was in "some general way" mentally deficient. Presumably, however, their view would be different if the provocation went directly to that issue. In *Raven*,[63] the jury were directed to consider whether the reasonable man with the characteristics of the defendant who had a mental age of nine (he was 22) would have responded as the defendant had. The authority of this Crown Court decision must be in some doubt given the gloss put upon *Camplin* in *Newell*. It might well have been the case that there was no direct connection between the provoking incident and this characteristic but it undoubtedly affected the gravity of the provocation. The justice of the decision in *Raven* is beyond question; how could such a defendant be expected to exercise self-control? But it must be admitted that it makes the task of the jury very difficult and that it makes substantial inroads into the notion of the reasonable man. The reasonable man may be 15, but can he really be mentally deficient? As will be argued later, this illustrates the inherent defects in the reasonable man test in this area of law.

As a result of *Camplin* and *Newell*, it is difficult to state with any degree of certainty the limits of the "reasonable man" test. Despite the difficulties in showing a direct connecton between age and the provoking incident in *Camplin*, age is obviously one characteristic with which the reasonable man can be endowed. So too it seems is the sex of the defendant, and Lord Simon in *Camplin* also considers that factors such

---

[61] (1980) 71 Cr.App.R. 331. It would seem that this defendant would have fared better to have pleaded diminished responsibility or provocation and diminished responsibility together. There is some evidence that juries tend to be more generous in their approach when this is done, possibly because they find it difficult to untangle the issues: R. D. Mackay, "Pleading Provocation and Diminished Responsibility Together" [1988] Crim.L.R. 411.

[62] *R. v. Newell* (1980) 71 Cr.App.R. 331 *per* Lord Lane C.J. See also *Ali* [1989] Crim.L.R. 736, where the age of the defendant (who was 20) was held not to be a factor that would have affected the gravity of the provocation in that case.

[63] [1982] Crim.L.R. 51. See also *R v. Roberts* [1990] Crim.L.R. 122.

as pregnancy could be built in as well.[64] But what of the race of the defendant? Consider the following case:

R. v. Muddarubba (Aboriginal) 1956 (Unreported) (Northern Territory of Australia in the Supreme Court, Alice Springs Sittings)

The case concerned the killing of an aborigine woman by an aborigine man for having used the word "karlu" (male genitalia) to him.

Kriewaldt J.:
"[T]he law takes notice of human temper and human frailty and decrees that in some cases the unlawful killing of one person by another is not murder but manslaughter. In the eyes of the law, if something happens which would make the ordinary reasonable person react with violence and death ensues as a result of that violence, the crime is not murder but manslaughter . . . and is called killing under provocation. . . . The rules relating to provocation have given me some worry in native trials. After much thought I have when summing up to a jury in a case where a native is on trial perhaps departed somewhat from the strict rule applied in trials of white persons. Perhaps my view is not correct . . . [but] I believe the law to be as I shall put it to you.

In my opinion, in any discussion of provocation, the general principle of law is to create a standard which would be observed by the average person in the community in which the accused person lives. It is clear from the cases decided by courts whose decisions bind me that in white communities matters regarded as sufficient provocation a century ago would not be regarded as sufficient today. This suggests that the standard is not a fixed and unchanging standard, it leaves it open, and I think properly so, to regard the Pitjintara tribe as a separate community for purposes of considering the reaction of the average man. I tell you that if you think that the average member of the Pitjintara tribe . . . would have retaliated to the words and actions of the woman, by spearing her, then the act of spearing is not murder but manslaughter. If provocation sufficient for the average reasonable person in his community to lose his self-control exists, then the unlawful killing is manslaughter and not murder . . .

Now let us consider the nature of the provocation in this case. For a white person, it has been laid down that mere words are not provocation under any circumstances. In this case, if the aboriginal word 'karlu' was used by the woman, I have no doubt that you will regard the use of this word as a serious insult. But whether or not it was sufficiently serious to cause a person to whom it was used to retaliate by throwing a spear (and remember that you must consider how the average member of the Pitjintara tribe would react) is a matter for you to decide."[65]

Verdict: Guilty of manslaughter

This case shows clearly that some insults will be meaningless unless the racial and cultural background is taken into account. Now that

---

[64] At p. 724. He also considers menstruation and menopause.

[65] The judge made it clear after the case that he believed that members of the tribe would have approved of the punishment inflicted on the woman. Similar approaches towards racial and cultural characteristics can be found in both African and Asian cases: *Kwaku Mensah* v. *The King* [1946] A.C. 83 (P.C.). *C.f.* N. Morris and C. Howard, *Studies in Criminal Law* (1964), pp. 93–99; B. Brown, "The 'Ordinary Man' in Provocation: Anglo-Saxon Attitudes and 'Unreasonable Non-Englishmen' " (1964) 13 I.C.L.Q. 203.

words alone are capable of amounting to provocation there is a very strong case for including racial characteristics in the analysis of the reasonable man test.

English courts have expressed reluctance to admit race as a relevant characteristic where the only mitigating factor is the excitability of the defendant's racial group.[66] It is thought to be unjust to judge the racially excitable man by a more generous standard than that pertaining to a more phlegmatic race: if the characteristic of racial excitability is taken into account a verdict of manslaughter may have to follow, whereas the racially phlegmatic individual may be found guilty of murder. Glanville Williams describes the issue of the inclusion of racial characteristics as "an insoluble problem of criminal justice,"[67] for, on the one hand there are the arguments of injustice to the racially phlegmatic and the potentially "socially divisive"[68] effect of distinguishing between races, and on the other, the undeniable injustice involved in ignoring the racial background of insults.

What if the excitability or irascibility is merely idiosyncratic rather than cultural? Should this characteristic be included? The courts have so far declined to do so and we may identify two reasons for their refusal. First, as above, they feel it penalises unfairly the man who is phlegmatic. He is made to pay a higher price for his restraint. But that is already the case: the first requirement in the defence of provocation is that the defendant must have lost his self-control; if this has not taken place, say because the person provoked is exceptionally phlegmatic, the issue of reasonableness does not arise. It is, therefore, fallacious to exclude excitability to protect the phlegmatic individual; as has been pointed out, it has never been suggested that the loss of self-control rule is unjust.[69]

The second reason is a survivor from the days when the courts refused to take any personal characteristics into account. If one were to take characteristics such as excitability into consideration it is feared that the standard of judgment would become so individualised as to be meaningless. Because we would know everything about the defendant we would have to excuse him. Moreover, one cannot endow the reasonable man with characteristics that would make him unreasonable; a bad-tempered reasonable man is a contradiction in terms as the reasonable man is not bad-tempered.[70] To avoid the destruction of the reasonable man test, therefore, the objective standard has to be maintained,[71] and with it comes problems: for example, is the man who is bad-tempered because he is impotent to be protected by the defence or not?

What these reasons and preceding problems add up to is the failure of

---

[66] *Newell* (1980) 71 Cr.App.R. 331, *per* Lord Lane C.J.
[67] *Textbook*, (1st ed., 1978) p. 490.
[68] *Textbook* p. 542.
[69] Glanville Williams "Provocation and the Reasonable Man" [1954] Crim.L.R. 740 at 751–752.
[70] *Camplin*, p. 726.
[71] Fletcher, p. 513.

the reasonable man test to determine who ought to be punished and who ought in part, at least, to be excused. As both Fletcher[72] and Glanville Williams[73] point out, the reasonable man test is inappropriate to this area of law.

Before we examine what, if anything, ought to take its place, one final issue of judicial debate needs to be considered. So far, in our analysis, we have concentrated on the question of what characteristics the reasonable man may be said to possess. But in judging provocation we may well wish to include another dimension; we may consider that it was reasonable to retaliate, but question the particular mode of retaliation chosen by the defendant. Dealing with this problem in pre-1957 days was relatively straightforward.

Mancini v. D.P.P. [1942] A.C. 1 (House of Lords)

The appellant had stabbed a member of a club of which he was manager with a sharp dagger-knife.

Viscount Simon L.C.:
"It is not all provocation that will reduce the crime of murder to manslaughter. Provocation, to have that result, must be such as temporarily deprives the person provoked of the powers of self-control, as the result of which he commits the unlawful act which causes death. . . . The test to be applied is that of the provocation of the reasonable man . . . it is of particular importance . . . to take into account the instrument with which the homicide was effected, for to retort, in the heat of passion induced by provocation, by a simple blow, is a very different thing from risking use of a deadly instrument like a concealed dagger. In short, the mode of resentment must bear a reasonable relationship to the provocation if the offence is to be reduced to manslaughter."

Is there anything contradictory in requiring both loss of control and reasonable retaliation?

The status of this rule of law is now in some doubt as a result of section 3. It is not at all clear whether the words "whether the provocation was enough to make a reasonable man do as he did" mean, simply, "make a reasonable man kill" or "make a reasonable man kill in the manner used by the defendant." "The Homicide Act is ambiguous, but it can be read as affirming a rule of reasonable relationship to the mode of killing (what we may call a modal reasonable relationship rule)."[74] The better view, however, is that the reasonable relationship test is no longer a rule of law—but it is still evidence for the jury to take into account in their task of determining what a reasonable man would have done in the situation; the more excessive the response, the more the

---

[72] At 247.
[73] At 536.
[74] Glanville Williams, *Textbook* p. 543.

jury will be inclined to decide that the reasonable man would not have responded similarly.[75]

(c) Reform of the reasonable man test

Given that the present law is unsatisfactory, does the formulation adopted by the Model Penal Code or the recommendations of the Criminal Law Revision Committee provide a more satisfactory basis for judging provocation?

American Law Institute, Model Penal Code, Proposed Official Draft (1962):

"Section 210.3.
(1) Criminal homicide constitutes manslaughter when: . . . b) a homicide which would otherwise be murder is committed under the influence of extreme mental or emotional disturbance for which there is reasonable explanation or excuse. The reasonableness of such explanation or excuse shall be determined from the viewpoint of a person in the actor's situation under the circumstances as he believed them to be."

American Law Institute, Model Penal Code, Tentative Draft No. 9 (1959) Comments pp. 47–48:

"Though it is difficult to state a middle ground between a standard which ignores all individual peculiarities and one which makes emotional distress decisive regardless of the nature of its cause, we think that such a statement is essential. . . . We submit that the formulation in the draft affords sufficient flexibility to differentiate between those special features in the actor's situation which should be deemed material for purposes of sentence and those which properly should be ignored . . .

There will be room, of course, for interpretation of the breadth of meaning carried by the word 'situation,' precisely the room needed in our view. There will be room for argument as to the reasonableness of the explanations or excuses offered; we think again that argument is needed in these terms. The question in the end will be whether the actor's loss of self-control can be understood in terms that arouse sympathy enough to call for mitigation in the sentence. That seems to us the issue to be faced."

The Criminal Law Revision Committee have recommended changes in the light of *Camplin*[76] and *Newell*[77] that will bring the English law on provocation much closer to that adopted by the Model Penal Code.

---

[75] *Walker* [1969] 1 W.L.R. 311; *Phillips* [1969] 2 A.C. 130; *Brown* [1972] 2 Q.B. 229; *Davies* [1975] Q.B. 691. It is, of course, difficult to understand how a jury can even begin to take this factor into consideration when a defendant is killed in response to a purely verbal provocation. Such a retaliation is clearly grossly excessive—yet section 3 plainly states that provocation may be by words alone.
[76] *Ante* p. 645.
[77] *Ante* p. 648.

Criminal Law Revision Committee, Offences Against the Person, 14th Report Cmnd. 7844 (1980):

"81. Our principle recommendation is that the law of provocation should be reformulated and in place of the reasonable man test the test should be that provocation is a defence to a charge of murder if, on the facts as they appeared to the defendant, it can reasonably be regarded as a sufficient ground for the loss of self-control leading the defendant to react against the victim with a murderous intent. This formulation has some advantage over the present law in that it avoids reference to the entirely notional 'reasonable man' directing the jury's attention instead to what they themselves consider reasonable—which has always been the real question.

82. A number of commentators queried one detail of the suggestions made in the Working Paper, namely that provocation would be sufficient if, on the facts as they appeared to the accused, it constituted a reasonable excuse for the loss of self-control on his part. They did not like the phrase 'a reasonable excuse': they preferred 'a reasonable explanation' because there could never be a reasonable excuse for taking another's life. We found this rather difficult to resolve. We accepted the criticisms made of the word 'excuse' but remained of the opinion that 'explanation' was not a suitable word either. We finally decided that 'a sufficient ground for the loss of self-control' would be an easier phrase for juries to understand and apply.

83. . . . [We] recommend that the defendant should be judged with due regard to all the circumstances, including any disability, physical or mental, from which he suffered . . . "[78]

May racial characteristics be included within "the circumstances?" Is any guidance provided as to whether temper, excitability and pugnacity are to be considered "circumstances"?[79] Does either the law since *Camplin* and *Newell* or the proposals above, tackle the moral issue highlighted by Fletcher[80] that the question is whether the defendant could be expected to control his impulse to kill?

George P. Fletcher, Rethinking the Criminal Law (1978), pp. 513–514:

"The obvious difference between the irascible man and the impotent man is that, absent a documentable psychological impediment, we properly expect people to control their anger as we expect them to control greed and jealousy. Therefore persons who are irascible, greedy or given to jealousy hardly warrant preferential treatment in the assessment of their conduct. These are character traits for which people are properly held accountable, not excused. Yet no one is to be blamed for impotence, and therefore it is a feature of the defendant that must be considered in assessing whether he was adequately provoked by taunting or teasing related to his impotence."

Do you agree with this assessment of the moral task? Do *Camplin* and *Newell* and the reforms suggested provide at the end of the day, as good

---

[78] The Draft Criminal Code (Law Com. No. 177 (1989)) reformulates this in clause 58(b): "the provocation is, in all the circumstances (including any of his personal characteristics that affect its gravity), sufficient ground for the loss of self-control."

[79] S. Prevezer, "Criminal Homicides other than Murder" [1980] Crim.L.R. 530 at 535–539.

[80] *Ante* p. 641.

a working rule as any that might have been found by adhering more closely to the moral issue? Even if one decides that the present law or the reforms suggested satisfy, in practice, these moral demands, a further problem arises with the reasonable man test, however modified.

P. Brett, "The Physiology of Provocation" [1970] Crim.L.R. 634 at 635, 637:

" 'The reasonable man' rules quite plainly assume a particular view of human behaviour. They treat a human being as basically a rational being who can control his activities and determine by an act of the mind whether he will respond to a hostile or provocative act, and who, if he does respond, can control the duration of his anger and the extent of his response.[81]

[Brett then goes on to dispute, with physiological evidence (A. Storr, *Human Aggression* (1968), pp. 12–15), this view of man. He claims that the 'fight-or-flight' reaction induced by anger (causing an increased flow of oxygen into the bloodstream to prepare the body for fighting or fleeing) does not dissipate as quickly as the law suggests it does unless there is a physical outlet for the reaction. Neither does the reaction vary in direct proportion to the provocation.] The changes have something of an all-or-none quality. [Moreover] . . . the degree of response to a stress situation varies considerably from one individual to another. Some men are highly vulnerable to stress, others are strikingly resistant to it. . . .

. . . it would be perverse for the law to ignore these teachings of science, and absurd for it to doubt their validity. But if we pay attention to them it at once becomes clear that the reasonable man of provocation law is a figment of the imagination."

If indeed it were the case that there was irrefutable medical evidence all pointing towards this view of man, Brett's claim would be substantiated. The reasonable man would be a figment of the imagination. But the medical evidence is by no means as clear-cut as that: Glanville Williams, for example, produces evidence that supports, rather than destroys the judicial view of the reasonable response: "In humans, the emotion of fear is mainly associated with the increased release of adrenaline from the adrenal glands, while that of anger causes noradrenaline to be liberated. The hormones fall to normal within 20 minutes after the end of the stressful situation . . . [thus providing] some support for the common-sense attitude of the judges towards the 'heat of blood.' "[82]

(iv) *Conclusion*

If, in the absence of incontrovertible medical evidence, there is, therefore, a case for a defence of provocation based on an amended reasonable man test that does address itself to the essential moral issue (however unconsciously), the crime of murder with its mandatory life sentence is obviously one area where it can be usefully employed. But

---

[81] This requirement would be abolished if the recommendations of the C.L.R.C. are implemented. *Ante*, p. 653.
[82] *Textbook*, (1st ed., 1978) p. 483.

this raises two further questions. First, would the defence still be desirable if the mandatory life sentence were abolished? The Criminal Law Revision Committee, although evenly divided on the question of whether the fixed penalty ought to be abolished, thought that there would still be a good case for the partial defence even if it were.[83] If that is the case, is there, secondly, any justification for restricting the operation of the defence to the crime of murder? There will obviously be instances in lesser crimes where men will act as they do because of severe stress and provocation. Should the law give formal recognition to this? The Criminal Law Revision Committee have recommended that the partial defence be extended to attempted killings[84]; they backed away from their preliminary proposal that it should also operate to reduce "causing serious injury with intent to cause serious injury"[85] to a lesser crime. The only justification for this refusal in the light of their attitude towards the fixed penalty must be that murder "is a crime standing out from all others."[86] Is this sufficient justification to warrant the denial of the partial defence to other defendants who act under stress?

2. Diminished responsibility

Where a defendant is suffering from "diminished responsibility" he will have a partial defence to murder and will instead be convicted of manslaughter—again giving the court the necessary flexibility as to sentence.

Although it is only a defence to murder and is thus not a general defence, because of its close nexus to the defence of insanity, the partial defence of diminished responsibility has been discussed in the chapter on general defences.[87]

3. Killing in pursuance of a suicide pact

Homicide Act 1957, s.4

"(1) It shall be manslaughter, and shall not be murder, for a person acting in pursuance of a suicide pact between him and another to kill the other or be a party to the other being killed by a third person . . .
(3) For the purposes of this section 'suicide pact' means a common agreement

---

[83] This was endorsed by House of Lords, *Report of the Select Committee on Murder and Life Imprisonment*. (Session 1988–89, H.L. Paper 78), 1989, para. 83. M. Wasik "Partial Excuse in the Criminal Law" (1982) 45 M.L.R. 516 argues from this that there is now room for partial defences to develop a life of their own in the criminal law, overcoming the traditional reluctance to find a place for them in the orthodox division of excusing conditions (such as infancy) and mitigating circumstances (those taken into account in sentencing only). The Law Commission in evidence to the C.L.R.C. proposed a general defence of extenuating circumstances to a charge of murder (including provocation), dependent on the abolition of the fixed penalty; the C.L.R.C. rejected the proposal: para. 80. See also C. Wells "The Death Penalty for Provocation" [1978] Crim.L.R. 662.
[84] Para. 98. Clause 61, Draft Criminal Code, Law. Com. No. 177 (1989).
[85] C.L.R.C. Working Paper (1976) para. 109.
[86] 14th Report, para. 84.
[87] *Ante* p. 370.

between two or more persons having for its object the death of all of them, whether or not each is to take his own life, but nothing done by a person who enters into a suicide pact shall be treated as done by him in pursuance of the pact unless it is done while he has the settled intention of dying in pursuance of the pact."

The law acts, therefore, with some clemency towards a defendant who survives a suicide pact when he had intended to die himself. Such clemency does not, however, extend to other situations. If the agreement to "kill and then die" is merely a front for murder where the defendant has no intention of killing himself, then he will be convicted of murder. This will be the case, even if the deceased consented to die, and even if, furthermore, it can be described as a mercy-killing. It is, therefore, thought to be more blameworthy to kill in such situations than where a suicide pact exists. The basis of this distinction in blameworthiness must lie in the "settled intention" of the defendant to die himself. Perhaps it is felt that the person killed would not have consented had he not been aware of the intention of the other; more probably, however, the consent of the "victim" is still irrelevant and the partial defence represents "a concession to human frailty." It recognises with compassion the state of despair of one who would kill and then die himself. Or could it be that this is a remnant of the Biblical historical origins of the law of homicide—that he who kills intending to die himself immediately thereafter does not "acquire the [same] control over the blood—the life force—of the victim"[88]—and therefore deserves lesser punishment?

This distinction in blameworthiness will be further enhanced if the Draft Criminal Code is brought into effect. This states that suicide pact killing is a separate offence, punishable by a maximum of seven years imprisonment.[89]

Killing in pursuance of a suicide pact is distinguished from the separate crime of aiding and abetting suicide.

Suicide Act 1961, s.2

"A person who aids, abets, counsels or procures the suicide of another or an attempt by another to commit suicide, shall be liable on conviction on indictment to imprisonment for a term not exceeding 14 years."

J. C. Smith and B. Hogan, Criminal Law (1988), p. 361:

"The distinction between . . . [complicity in suicide and manslaughter by suicide pact] . . . will frequently be very fine. If D and P agree to gas themselves and D alone survives, it appears that he will be liable under the Homicide Act if he turned on the tap and under the Suicide Act if P did."

---

[88] Fletcher, p. 236.
[89] Clause 62, Law Com. No. 177, (1989) implementing the proposals of the Criminal Law Revision Committee.

The distinction is currently of importance in terms of punishment. Killing in pursuance of a suicide pact is punishable as manslaughter by up to life imprisonment, whilst aiding and abetting suicide is punishable by up to 14 years. The Draft Criminal Code recognises the strength of the point made above by proposing to make both offences subject to a seven year maximum sentence.[90]

V. INFANTICIDE

Infanticide Act 1938, s.1

"(1) Where a woman by any wilful act or omission causes the death of her child being a child under the age of twelve months, but at the time of the act or omission the balance of her mind was disturbed by reason of her not having fully recovered from the effect of giving birth to the child or by reason of the effect of lactation consequent upon the birth of the child, then, notwithstanding that the circumstances were such that but for this Act the offence would have amounted to murder, she shall be guilty of . . . infanticide, and may for such offence be dealt with and punished as if she had been guilty of the offence of manslaughter of the child."

Infanticide is thus similar to voluntary manslaughter in that it is effectively a partial defence to murder. It has especially close links with the partial defence of diminished responsibility and indeed, as we shall see, there is some question whether infanticide is not now redundant given the existence of this wider defence. When introduced, in this form,[91] however, infanticide was seen by many as a welcome solution to juries' reluctance to convict distressed women of the murder of their babies—and, of course, at that time, sentence them to death. One of the reasons for the welcome the crime of infanticide received was that it avoided the hypocrisy of passing a death sentence that all in authority (at least) knew would not be carried out; the sentence of death would invariably be commuted to one of life imprisonment by the Royal Prerogative of Mercy. Since 1849 no mother had been executed for the murder of her own child under the age of one year.[92]

Whilst useful therefore, in giving effect to both judicial and societal desire to express their understanding for and sympathy with the defendant's plight, the medical basis upon which infanticide has rested in the twentieth century[93] has never been beyond doubt. Increasingly

---

[90] *Ibid*, Clause 63.

[91] The Infanticide Act 1922, s.5(1) first made a finding of manslaughter instead of murder possible if "at the time of the act or omission [in killing her *newly-born* child] she had not fully recovered from the effect of giving birth to such child." For an account of the history of infanticide before that date, see, W. L. Langer "Infanticide: A Historical Survey," (1974) 1 Hist. of Childhood Quarterly 353.

[92] Royal Commission on Capital Punishment (1953), Cmd. 8932, p. 11.

[93] It was not until 1922 that infanticide was framed with reference to the medical effects of childbirth; previously it had been more concerned with social conditions and moral values. Originally, for example, infanticide applied only to the killing of illegitimate children and was more concerned with the concealment of death (which acted as a presumption of guilt to murder) rather than the death itself (21 Jac. 1, c. 27, 1623).

(and especially since the advent of diminished responsibility) the statutes' references to the effects of both childbirth and lactation have been criticised as not reflecting the reality of the woman's condition.

The Report of the Committee on Mentally Abnormal Offenders (Butler Committee), Evidence of the Governor and Staff of Holloway Prison, Cmnd. 6244, (1975), para. 19.24:

"The disturbance of the 'balance of mind' that the Act requires can rarely be said to arise directly from incomplete recovery from the effects of childbirth and even less so from the effects of lactation.[94]

Infanticide due to puerperal psychotic illness is rare. The type of killing where the child is killed immediately after birth and which is usually associated with illegitimate concealed pregnancies is also very uncommon. Most cases of child murder dealt with by the courts as infanticide are examples of the battered child syndrome in which the assault has had fatal consequences and the child is aged under 12 months. A combination of environmental stress and personality disorder with low frustration tolerance are the usual aetiological factors in such cases and the relationship to 'incomplete recovery from the effects of childbirth or lactation' specified in the Infanticide Act is often somewhat remote. The Act is nevertheless nearly always invoked in cases of maternal filicide when the victim is aged under 12 months, in order to reduce the charge from murder to manslaughter. The illogical operation of the Act is illustrated by the fact that an exactly similar type of case where the victim happened to be over the age of 12 months can no longer be dealt with as infanticide."

This illogicality is reinforced by the lack of any mitigating provision to protect the woman who does not succeed in killing her child. She may be charged with attempted murder or wounding with intent. The Criminal Law Revision Committee have stated that the particular drafting of section 1 of the Infanticide Act 1938 makes the charging of *attempted infanticide* impossible.[95] Despite this, in the case of *R. v. K. A. Smith*,[96] the trial judge accepted a plea of guilty of attempted infanticide. Whilst the means by which this was done are suspect—the section seems much more like a partial defence to murder than anything else— the result is admirable. Such a woman in these circumstances is trying to commit infanticide and the law should recognise this. Further, if found guilty of attempted murder she may be sentenced to imprisonment.[97] The woman who is convicted of infanticide (which, like attempted murder and wounding with intent, carries a maximum sentence of life imprisonment) is almost never sent to prison—and presumably this would also be true of attempted infanticide. The sentence is normally one of probation for the five or six convictions of infanticide

---

[94] As the Butler Committee noted, (para. 19.23), D. J. West in "*Murder followed by Suicide* (1955) found no significant connection between women who killed their children and this period.
[95] 14th Report, Offences Against the Person, Cmnd. 7844 (1980), para. 113.
[96] [1983] Crim.L.R. 739.
[97] See N. Walker *Crime and Insanity in England* (1968).

annually.[98] In more serious cases of imbalance the woman may be made subject to a hospital order to her local hospital.

The Draft Criminal Code recognises the present anomaly: attempted infanticide will become the appropriate charge where a woman in such circumstances fails to kill her child.[99]

One might also wish to add that if the current medical basis rests much more on the effects of child-rearing than on childbirth, then is it not also illogical that the defence is open to mothers only? May not fathers be subject to similar pressures?[1]

Is infanticide redundant?

Given the inaccurate medical understanding reflected in the statute and the illogical limitations it imposes, the Butler Committee on Mentally Abnormal Offenders[2] decided that infanticide could be subsumed in the partial defence of diminished responsibility. Not only would the limitations to 12 months and to the mother be abolished, but they concluded that there would be little difficulty in establishing the necessary medical evidence for a finding of diminished responsibility. In view of the ease with which the "imbalance of mind" for the purposes of infanticide is established one feels that there might be some truth in the Butler Committee's conclusion.

However, the Criminal Law Revision Committee are opposed to any such reform.

Criminal Law Revision Committee, 14th Report, Offences against the Person, Cmnd. 7844 (1980):

"102. . . . we are not, with respect to the Butler Committee, satisfied that the offence of manslaughter by diminished responsibility could cover all such cases as does infanticide at present. Nor are we satisfied that the kinds of disturbances of mind which now lead to an infanticide verdict would in all cases be regarded as a mental disorder within section 4 of the Mental Health Act 1959. There would be the possibility, if the offence of infanticide were abolished, that in a case where a conviction for infanticide would today result, the defendant would be convicted of murder. Naturally in such a case counsel and medical witnesses would strain the interpretation of the law on diminished responsibility to ensure that a verdict of manslaughter was returned, but we would not wish to make a recommendation that puts too great a strain upon the professional consciences of expert witnesses.

104. A second reason why infanticide should not be merged with manslaughter but should continue to be a separate offence is that it is an offence for which imprisonment is rarely an appropriate sentence and for which a life sentence, the maximum for manslaughter, is never likely to be imposed. We are satisfied that the maximum penalty for infanticide should be no more than 5 years' imprisonment."

[98] Criminal Law Revision Committee, 14th Report, Offences Against the Person, Cmnd. 7844 (1980), para. 108.
[99] Clause 64(2), Law Com. No. 177, (1989). The incorporates the recommendation of the Criminal Law Revision Committee, *ante* n. 98, para. 113.
[1] He would have to plead diminished responsibility and/or provocation. See *ante* p. 370 and p. 638.
[2] Cmnd. 6244, paras. 19.22, 19.26.

How persuasive do you find the Criminal Law Revision Committee's arguments in view of the fact that they accept the psychological stress (rather than the effects of childbirth or lactation) basis of infanticide but do not propose extension of protection to the killing of children over the age of 12 months?[3]

Consensus exists that although the present basis of the offence is outmoded, that protection ought to be afforded to the unbalanced woman who kills her baby. If the Draft Criminal Code is brought into effect, this protection will be substantially extended, as we have seen. It will also bring about a very welcome reduction in the maximum sentence from life to five years.[4]

VI. The Structure of Homicide Offences

In England there are several categories of homicide. The main distinction is between murder and involuntary manslaughter, a distinction resting on the presence or absence of a mental element, malice aforethought. However, murder is also distinguished from voluntary manslaughter, this distinction being based either on the mental condition of the defendant (diminished responsibility), or on the circumstances of the killing (provocation and suicide pacts). There are two other main species of homicide: infanticide, which refers specifically to the death of a particular type of victim (child under one year of age); and causing death by reckless driving[5] which refers to death being caused in a particular manner.

In this section we shall be concerned with four questions:
1. Why do we distinguish between different categories of homicide?
2. Do we distinguish between these categories with sufficient particularity?
3. On what basis ought such distinctions to be made?
4. Should we abolish these categories and replace them with a single offence of unlawful homicide?

A. Rationale of Distinction between Different Categories of Homicide

Homicides range from cold-blooded, malicious killings to killings not far removed from accidents or killings where there are severe mitigating circumstances, such as provocation. It was felt necessary to differentiate between these homicides in terms of their perceived seriousness. This differentiation is useful for two purposes:

[3] Criminal Law Revision Committee, 14th Report, para. 106.
[4] Implementing the recommendations of the Criminal Law Revision Committee, para. 108.
[5] Technically, a species of manslaughter (*Jennings, ante*, p. 627).

(a) Different penalties can be attached for the different categories of homicide. Thus the fact that murder is perceived as being far more serious than manslaughter is clearly reflected in the sentence—capital punishment before 1965 and mandatory life imprisonment since then, as opposed to a *maximum* of life imprisonment for manslaughter. Thus the fact that the crime of causing death by reckless driving is perceived as being so much less serious than other unlawful homicides can be reflected by its sentence of a maximum of five years' imprisonment.

(b) Differentiating between homicide offences emphasises the different stigma attached to each and enables us to differentiate between different kinds of moral wrong. It is "to express the moral distinctions and categories which inform our considered moral beliefs."[6] Thus, for example, the label "murder" emphasises the special stigma attached to that crime. One of the main purposes of the criminal law and punishment is its symbolic value in communicating messages to the public as to what is permissible or not. Different labels are used for different crimes to communicate the degree of rejection of the specific crime. The label "murder" is used to emphasise the "dreadfulness"[7] and the "uniquely horrible [nature of the] crime."[8] Also it may have a significant deterrent value.[9] Abolishing the label "may appear to have the effect of lessening the seriousness of taking life."[10] Similar arguments may be put forward to explain why we retain the label "manslaughter" and treat separately the offences of infanticide and the causing death by reckless driving.

T. Morris and L. Blom-Cooper, A Calendar of Murder (Criminal Homicide in England since 1957) (1964), pp. 271–272:

"[W]anton murder is dramatically defined as the most dreadful of crimes, a view which has been upheld by the laws and customs of civilised societies down the ages. The act of murder occupies a unique place in the feelings of men in that it falls into a class of actions the results of which are irreversible. . . . Around the notion of death a whole series of institutional beliefs and practices have arisen creating a sense of social balance in which the realisation of mortality is incorporated into the fabric of human experience; only thus is death made tolerable.

The act of murder disturbs this balance. It accelerates the inevitable in a way which profoundly unsettles the delicate equilibrium which social institutional devices have achieved, and arouses in individuals the most deep-seated unconscious fears and anxieties . . .

Murder produces a sense of profound social shock—heightened in our own society by dissemination of the details through modern mass media. It can nor-

---

[6] R. A. Duff "Implied and Constructive Malice in Murder" (1979) 95 L.Q.R. 418 at 427.
[7] *La Fontaine* 11 A.L.R. 507, 535, *per* Jacobs J.
[8] R. Cross "Penal Reform in 1965 . . ." [1966] Crim.L.R. 184 at 189.
[9] C.L.R.C., Working Paper on Offences against the Person, 1976, para. 7.
[10] *Ibid.*

mally be relieved only by some highly dramatic act on the part of the community towards the offender. In days gone by this act was the public imposition of capital punishment; latterly . . . the criminal trial and the dramatisation of its preliminaries may be gradually taking its place. . . . Clearly, it is the special character of murder, the attendant sensationalism of the re-enactment of the killing with its actual risk of imitation, which wide advertisement brings in its trail, that gives murder its quintessential quality—a crime apart."

B. Greater Specificity

Given the above views, another question presents itself. Does English law distinguish with sufficient precision between different homicides? Many would assert that it does not. Murder and manslaughter, in particular, are far too broad, each encompassing too many different types of conduct, circumstances and offenders—in short, too many different degrees of "heinousness." Murders, for example, vary widely: they cover planned, cold-blooded killings, deliberate killings with torture all the way down to killings only marginally qualifying as intentional under *Moloney* and *Hancock*. They cover people who coldly kill for no reason, down through all the different motivations and explanations to mercy killings, where an anguished defendant kills a loved one to end their suffering. Manslaughters, too, cover a vast field: they range from conduct just short of murder to just above the non-criminal category of justifiable or accidental death. Is not each crime, each label, covering too vast a field?

When the English common law was introduced into the United States, these points were taken. The English categories of murder and manslaughter were each seen to be too broad to serve any useful purpose. In particular, it was felt to be wrong for the death penalty to apply to all murders. The crime of murder should, be divided into categories with the death penalty only applying to the "worst." In 1794 the pioneering Pennsylvania Code divided murder into two degrees, with the death penalty only applying to first degree murder. Similarly manslaughters were divided into different degrees, each degree carrying a separate penalty. This approach has been widely adopted with the result that murder is now divided into degrees or categories in 42 states and manslaughter is similarly divided into degrees or categories in 26 states. In addition, the majority of States have yet further homicide offences, apart from murder and manslaughter, such as reckless homicide, negligent homicide and vehicular homicide.

Arizona Rev.Stat.Ann. (Amended 1983)

"13–1102 Negligent Homicide
A person commits negligent homicide if with criminal negligence such person causes the death of another person. [4 years]
13–1103 Manslaughter

A person commits manslaughter by:

1. Recklessly causing the death of another person; or

2. Committing second degree murder (13–1104) upon a sudden quarrel or heat of passion resulting from adequate provocation by the victim; or

3. Intentionally aiding another to commit suicide; or

4. Committing second degree murder (13–1104) while being coerced to do so by the use or threatened immediate use of unlawful deadly physical force upon such person or a third person which a reasonable person in his situation would have been unable to resist. [5 years]; or

5. Knowing or recklessly causing the death of an unborn child at any stage of its development by any physical injury to the mother of such child which would be murder if the death of the mother had occurred. [5 years]

13–1104 Second Degree Murder

A person commits second degree murder if without premeditation:

1. Such person intentionally causes the death of another person; or

2. Knowing that his conduct will cause death or serious physical injury, such person causes the death of another person; or

3. Under circumstances manifesting extreme indifference to human life, such person recklessly engages in conduct which creates a grave risk of death and thereby causes the death of another person. [15 years]

13–1105 First Degree Murder

(a) A person commits first degree murder if:

1. Knowing that his conduct will cause death, such person causes the death of another with premeditation; or

2. Acting either alone or with one or more other persons such person commits or attempts to commit sexual assault . . . , child molestation . . . , [specified] narcotics offences . . . , kidnapping . . . , burglary . . . , arson of an occupied structure . . . , robbery . . . , escape . . . , and in the course of and in furtherance of such offence or immediate flight from such offence, such person or another person causes the death of any person.[11]

(b) Homicide, as defined in paragraph 2 (above) requires no specific mental state other than what is required for the commission of any of the enumerated felonies. [Death or life imprisonment depending on presence or absence of specified aggravating and mitigating circumstances.]

[Note: All the above penalties are presumptive penalties that a defendant will receive in the absence of aggravating or mitigating circumstances. Thus, for example, 15 years is the presumptive penalty for second degree murder, but this may be increased or reduced by five years depending on aggravating or mitigating circumstances.[12]]"

Vehicular homicide is a separate offence in 28 states. In some states, for example Colorado, criminally negligent homicide and vehicular homicide co-exist as separate offences (in addition to manslaughter and two degrees of murder.[13])

There is a major problem with such precise gradations of homicide offences. It assumes that one can isolate those factors or criteria that *always* make a homicide more or less reprehensible. Let us take the deliberation/premeditation formula as an example. In most states in the United States the "worst" murders, first degree murder, are reserved for

---

[11] Details of each of these felonies have been omitted.

[12] Ariz.Rev.Stat.Ann. s.13–1104 (B).

[13] Colo.Rev.Stat.Ann. ss.18–3–101—18–3–106.

deliberate and premeditated killings. One can perhaps understand the rationale behind such provisions, namely that it "reflect[s] a belief that one who meditates an intent to kill and then deliberately executes it is more dangerous, more culpable or less capable of reformation than one who kills on sudden impulse; or that the prospect of the death penalty is more likely to deter men from deliberate than from impulsive murder."[14] There are, however, severe problems involved with such an approach:

(a) It is almost impossible to distinguish between a "premeditated" and a "merely intentional" killing. In the United States most statutes have defined "intention" in terms of "conscious objective." If something is your objective, that, of necessity, means you have made a decision to bring that objective about. The making of that decision must, by definition, involve premeditation and deliberation. As Cardozo J. put it:

" . . . an intent to kill is always deliberate and premeditated. . . . There can be no intent unless there is a choice, yet by the hypothesis, the choice without more is enough to justify the inference that the intent was deliberate and premeditated . . . [such statutes are] framed along the lines of a defective and unreal psychology."[15]

(b) A "purely impulsive" murder may be just as, if not more, reprehensible than the cold-blooded, premeditated killing. The American Law Institute have recently written:

"Prior reflection may reveal the uncertainties of a tortured conscience rather than exceptional depravity. The very fact of a long internal struggle may be evidence that the homicidal impulse was deeply aberational and far more the product of extraordinary circumstances than a true reflection of the actor's normal character."[16]

And as Stephen put it:

"As much cruelty, as much indifference to the life of others, a disposition at least as dangerous to society, probably even more dangerous, is shown by sudden as by premeditated murders. The following cases appear to me to set this in a clear light. A, passing along the road, sees a boy sitting on a bridge over a deep river and, out of mere wanton barbarity, pushes him into it and so drowns him. A man makes advances to a girl who repels him. He deliberately but instantly cuts her throat. A man civilly asked to pay a just debt pretends to get the money, loads a rifle and blows out his creditor's brains. In none of these cases is there premeditation unless the word is used in a sense as unnatural as 'aforethought,' in 'malice aforethought'; but each represents even more diabolical cruelty and fero-

---

[14] *Bullock* v. *U.S..*, 122 F. 2d 213 (D.C. Cir. 1941).
[15] Cardozo, "What Medicine Can Do for Law," in *Law and Literature and other Essays and Addresses* (1930) pp. 99–100.
[16] American Law Institute, Model Penal Code and Commentaries, Part II (1980) p. 127.

city than that which is involved in murders premeditated in the natural sense of the word."[17]

(c) Many premeditated killings are clearly not the most reprehensible killings. Thus mercy killings, for example, are invariably premeditated killings, yet they are generally regarded as far less blameworthy than most other types of killings. A good example of this is to be found in the United States case of *Repouille* v. *United States*.[18] In this case the defendant's son was aged 13, had been bedridden since infancy and was described as an incurable imbecile who could not walk or talk; he had been blind for five years. The defendant had spent all his savings on an operation for the child but his condition had not improved. The defendant began to talk of putting the boy out of his misery and one day soaked a rag with chloroform and applied it to the boy's face, while he lay in his crib, until he died. This was a clear case of a planned premeditated killing which would be first degree murder. Yet the jury convicted the defendant of second degree manslaughter and requested sentencing leniency. The judge suspended execution of a five year sentence and placed the defendant on probation. Commenting on this, Learned Hand J. stated:

" . . . the jury . . . did not feel any moral repulsion at his crime. Although it was inescapably murder in the first degree, not only did they bring in a verdict that was flatly in the face of the facts and utterly absurd—for manslaughter in the second degree presupposes that the killing was not deliberate—but they coupled even that with a recommendation which showed that in substance they wished to exculpate the offender. Moreover, it is also plain, from the sentence which he imposed, that the judge could not have seriously disagreed with their recommendation."

A case such as this highlights the total inadequacy of the premeditation/deliberation formula in that it has not succeeded in isolating the worst killings. Categories of homicide become meaningless if they do not reflect common views of reprehensibility.

C. Basis of Distinctions

Given the inadequacy of the deliberation/premeditation formula, what of the other bases utilised to distinguish between homicide offences? Can such offences be graded exclusively in terms of different mental elements?

Kentucky Revised Statutes 1974

"507–020 Murder
(1) A person is guilty of murder when:
(a) With intent to cause the death of another person, he causes the death of

---

[17] Stephen, 3 *History of the Criminal Law*, (1883) p. 94.
[18] 165 F. 2d 152 (2d Cir. 1947).

such person or of a third person . . . [unless defendant acted under extreme . . . emotional disturbance].

(b) [U]nder circumstances manifesting extreme indifference to human life, he wantonly[19] engages in conduct which creates a grave risk of death to another person and thereby causes the death of another person.

507–030 Manslaughter in the First Degree

(1) A person is guilty of manslaughter in the first degree when:

(a) With intent to cause serious physical injury to another person, he causes the death of such person or of a third person; or

(b) [extreme emotional disturbance].

507–040 Manslaughter in the Second Degree

(1) A person is guilty of manslaughter in the second degree when he wantonly causes the death of another person . . .

507–050 Reckless Homicide

(1) A person is guilty of reckless homicide when, with recklessness, he causes the death of another person."

Such fine distinctions are surely impracticable. Even if they could be justified philosophically they would not be meaningful to a jury. In England the Criminal Law Revision Committee has proposed important reforms in the law of homicide which have been adopted by the Draft Criminal Code (Law Com. No. 177, 1989). Their proposals proceed on an assumption, apparently felt to be so obvious as not even to need articulation, that the only way to distinguish murder from manslaughter is to specify different mental elements for each.

In the previous chapter on non-fatal offences against the person it was argued that appropriate levels of criminal liability and punishment ought to be fixed by reference to a combination of *blame* and harm—and that "blame" could involve a consideration of many factors in addition to *mens rea*. Thus, as we saw, we might blame someone more because of the method or circumstances of the crime—*e.g.* torturing his victim. In homicide the harm is, of course, constant—the victim is dead, but there is no particular reason why the blame element giving rise to different offence categories, *must* be limited to a consideration of the mental element of the defendant.

Indeed, a glance at other jurisdictions reveals that classifications of homicide offences could be made to depend on a variety of other factors. The identity of the victim, for instance, could be regarded as the key factor distinguishing two homicides with identical mental states.[20] In Arizona dangerous crimes against children carry greater penalties than when committed against adults: for example, the presumptive penalty for second degree murder against an adult is 15 years imprisonment but against a child it is 20 years imprisonment.[21] In France there has long been a separate crime of parricide where a parent or grandpar-

---

[19] Section 501.020 defines "wantonly": " . . . consciously disregards a substantial and unjustifiable risk. . . . The risk must be of such a nature and degree that disregard thereof constitutes a gross deviation from the standard of conduct that a reasonable person would observe in the situation . . .".

[20] Such a proposal was considered and rejected by the Criminal Law Revision Committee in relation to assaults (14th Report, para. 162).

[21] Ariz.Rev.Stat. Ann., s.13–604.01 (A).

ent is killed.[22] In Louisiana it is first degree murder to kill intentionally a fireman or a police officer engaged in the performance of his duties.[23] Or it could be the identity of the killer that was regarded as decisive as in New York where it is first degree murder if the murderer was confined in prison.[24]

Alternatively, the categorisation could be made to depend on the method and circumstances of the killing. Thus in Louisiana it is first degree murder to kill after being offered anything of value for the killing,[25] and in Idaho it is first degree murder to kill by torturing a victim to death.[26] In many states in the United States it is a first degree murder to kill by using poison.[27]

Such an approach would not be totally alien to English law where the identity of the victim and the killer are highly relevant for the crime of infanticide, and the method and circumstances of the killing are equally relevant for the crime of causing death by reckless driving.

And moving away from homicide offences, we have already seen that assaulting a police constable contrary to section 51 of the Police Act 1964 is regarded as "worse" than assaulting other persons—and the method of committing a crime is crucial in distinguishing between many property offences, for example, whether the property was obtained by theft or deception.

An objection to such an approach might be that it would be impossible to achieve agreement as to what factors rendered a killing more or less reprehensible. Yet in the United States there is a surprising measure of uniformity among the 50 states as to this. Typical of the factors widely regarded there as aggravating a murder are: killing with poison; killing with explosives; killing while in prison or escaping from prison; killing after being paid to kill; intentionally killing while committing certain crimes such as robbery, kidnapping or rape; killing a prospective witness in a criminal trial; killing a police officer, fireman or judge; if the defendant has previously been convicted of murder; killing a hostage or kidnap victim; if the circumstances of the killing are particularly heinous, atrocious or cruel. And factors widely regarded as mitigating the seriousness of a homicide are: adequate provocation; diminished responsibility; if the victim consented or participated in his own killing; duress; if the defendant was an accessory and his participation was relatively minor.

In England there have been proposals in the House of Commons that the death penalty be restored for certain aggravated classes of murder. These were murder resulting from an act of terrorism; murder of a police office in the course of his duties; murder of a prison officer in the

---

[22] Code Penal, Art. 299.
[23] La.Rev.Stat., s.14.30(2).
[24] N.Y. Penal Law, s.125.27(1)(a)(iii).
[25] La.Rev.Stat., s.14.30(4).
[26] Idaho Code, s.18–4003(a).
[27] For example, California (Cal. Penal Code, s.189), Pennsylvania (Pa.Stat.Ann. tit.18, s.2502(a), (d)).

course of his duties; murder by shooting or causing an explosion; and murder in the course or furtherance of theft.[28] All these proposals were rejected. It is important to emphasise that what was rejected was capital punishment; the possibility of distinguishing between murders is still open. Indeed the Home Secretary has indicated that certain categories of murderers (those who have killed police or prison officers, terrorist killings, murder during robbery or the sadistic or sexual murder of children) will not be released on parole until the expiry of at least 20 years.[29]

It is not being suggested here that English law should adopt wholesale any such bases for distinguishing homicides. For instance, it is submitted that it would generally be inappropriate to assess the level of criminal liability on the basis of the identity of the victim. All human life is equally valuable and the law should reflect this. But what *is* being urged here is that English law adopt a less blinkered approach and at least consider such alternative bases for distinguishing between homicide offences; such new bases need not involve a complete elimination of our notion of utilising mental elements for this purpose; they could be used in addition thereto.

D. Unlawful Homicide—A Single Offence

Should English law abandon any such thoughts of further categorisation, indeed abandon its existing categories of homicide offences, and replace them with a single offence of unlawful homicide?

In *Hyam* v. *D.P.P.* Lord Kilbrandon said:

"There does not appear to be any good reason why the crimes of murder and manslaughter should not both be abolished, and the single crime of unlawful homicide substituted; one case will differ from another in gravity, and that can be taken care of by variation of sentences downwards from life imprisonment."[30]

The following arguments can be adduced in favour of the introduction of a single offence of unlawful homicide:

1. Murder varies so widely both in character and in culpability that the judge ought to have a discretion as to sentence.

Royal Commission on Capital Punishment, Report, Cmd. 8932, (1953) para. 21:

"The crime [of murder] may be human and understandable, calling more for pity than for censure, or brutal and callous to an almost unbelievable degree. It may have occurred so much in the heat of passion as to rule out the possibility of premeditation, or it may have been well prepared and carried out in cold

---

[28] *The Times*, July 14, 1983.

[29] This new parole policy has been held to be lawful, even though it involves the Home Secretary binding himself in advance to exercise his discretion according to a set policy. (*Findlay* v. *Secretary of State for the Home Department* [1985] A.C. 318).

[30] [1975] A.C. 55 at 98. A similar proposal was made by the New Zealand Law Reform Committee but has not been implemented (*Report on Culpable Homicide*, 1976, pp. 3–4).

blood. . . . The motives, springing from weakness as often as from wickedness, show some of the basest and some of the better emotions of mankind, cupidity, revenge, lust, jealousy, anger, fear, pity, despair, duty, self-righteousness, political fanaticism; or there may be no intelligible motive at all."

The argument is that not all these persons deserve the label "murder" with its mandatory life sentence.

2. Since the abolition of the death penalty, there is no longer the same need to draw a distinction between murder and manslaughter. One can receive the same penalty now for manslaughter as for murder. With the sentencing justification for the distinction largely gone, one is forced to ask: is the labelling justification (that one needs to retain the special label "murder" for the "worst" killings) sufficient to outweigh all the problems involved in drawing the distinction?

M. D. Farrier, "The Distinction between Murder and Manslaughter in its Procedural Context" (1976) 39 M.L.R. 414 at 428:

"[T]here is an undeveloped hypothesis that criminal labelling in general is functional for society in that it lays down the limits of tolerable behaviour by revealing in a stark form the type of behaviour which is not to be tolerated. Thus Erikson ("Notes on the Sociology of Deviance" in Scheff, T.J., ed., *Mental Illness and Social Processes*, pp. 299–303) regards the transactions taking place between deviant persons and agencies of control as boundary maintaining mechanisms which mark the outer limits of acceptable conduct and assert how much diversity can be contained within the system before it begins to lose its distinctive structure. It would be extremely difficult to justify the distinction drawn in *Hyam* on this basis, given its nebulous nature and its probable lack of meaning to those not versed in the mysteries of the law. Indeed, although it might be true that this kind of argument would justify the existence of a distinct homicide label as compared merely with one encompassing the broad area of conduct relating to violence to the person, any further division within the sub-category of homicide would have to be a very sharp one if it was going to have any meaning for the social audience and be capable of implementation by a jury."

3. Since the abolition of the death penalty and because of the difficulty in defining the "intention" necessary for murder, the distinction between murder and manslaughter appears to be dying a natural death. In many cases where a murder conviction could probably have been obtained, prosecutors are content to charge with manslaughter, or accept pleas of guilty to manslaughter. This saves much time and expense and indicates that prosecutors, at least, are often willing to rely on judges exercising their sentencing discretion reasonably. Thus, for example, in the Iranian Embassy siege case[31] the prosecution accepted a plea of guilty to manslaughter in a fairly clearly-cut case of murder; the defendant was promptly sentenced to life imprisonment, the same sentence he would have received after a long, expensive trial resulting in a

---

[31] *The Times*, May 8, 1981, p. 1, Col. 2.

murder conviction. Similar considerations, coupled with a desire to shield the relatives of victims from hitherto unrevealed details, prompted the prosecution in *Sutcliffe* (the so-called Yorkshire Ripper case)[32] to agree to a plea for manslaughter (the judge declined to accept such a plea).[33] If there were a single offence of unlawful homicide, one would avoid the present anomalous situation of some prosecutors accepting lesser pleas, while other prosecutors insist on pursuing a murder charge.

Further, juries appear unwilling to convict of murder except in the clearest, "worst" cases as this is tying the judge's hands as to sentence. By returning verdicts of manslaughter in many cases, they are allowing the judge to take all the circumstances into account before imposing an appropriate sentence. Thus of all those indicted for murder in 1986, only 39 per cent. were actually convicted of murder.[34] Lord Denning has said that "in many cases which are in law plainly murder, juries return verdicts of manslaughter, because they do not think the death sentence is appropriate."[35] Such a practice seems to have survived the abolition of the death penalty. In *Repouille* v. *U.S.*,[36] a case described as "inescapably first degree murder," the jury, quite perversely, returned a verdict of second degree murder enabling the judge to impose a suspended sentence. If the law is in a strait-jacket, judges, prosecutors and juries will start ignoring the law. If this starts happening too extensively, should not the law be changed?

4. A single offence of unlawful homicide would mean that life imprisonment would be restricted to the worst cases. Such persons would actually remain in prison for a substantial period of time. This would increase public confidence in the life sentence. At the moment many people receive the mandatory life sentence for murder who arguably do not deserve it. Justice is achieved by the Parole Board releasing such persons on licence after a relatively short period of time. The message communicated to the public is "Murderer Released After One Year in Prison" or the over-simplistic "Life Means Nine Years." Any utility in the special label "murder" is soon devalued by such practices.

Report of the Advisory Council on the Penal System, Sentences of Imprisonment: A Review of Maximum Penalties, 1978, para. 255:

"[L]ife imprisonment would be reserved for those cases where both the gravity of the offence and the instability of the offender suggested that an indeterminate sentence was necessary for the protection of the public. The effect of this would probably be a presumption that any murderer given a life sentence should remain in custody longer than most of those given fixed sentences; the

[32] *The Times*, April 30, 1981, p. 1, Col. 1.
[33] See also, *Walsh, The Times*, July 5, 1974; *O'Brien, Noonan* and *Wilkinson, The Times*, July 11, 1974.
[34] Criminal Statistics, Cm. 498 (1987).
[35] Royal Commission on Capital Punishment, Cmd. 8932 (1953), para. 27.
[36] *Ante*, n. 18.

Parole Board and the Home Secretary would be bound to take account of the length of determinate sentences when deciding on release from life imprisonment and this, because life imprisonment would be restricted to the worst cases, would mean that the period served would be substantially longer than the average period at present. This, in our opinion, would increase, rather than diminish, public confidence in the life sentence."

5. Partial defences, such as provocation and diminished responsibility—and the special offence of infanticide—exist mainly to alleviate the harshness of the mandatory penalty for murder and give the judge a discretion to take all the circumstances into account in fixing sentence.

Baroness Wootton, Crime and Penal Policy: Reflections on Fifty Years Experience, (1978), p. 143:

"[D]iminished responsibility seems to come perilously near to merely providing a means of escape from the life sentence for murder, in circumstances where, if this sentence was not mandatory, it might be held that there were grounds for mitigation. In other instances, however, the terms of Section 2 are stretched to a point at which (again clearly as a method of mitigation) the offender, far from suffering from any diminution of responsibility, appears to have acted from excessively responsibile motives. Thus, in 1960 a retired Army officer became increasingly worried as he realised that his baby son was a mongol. He therefore read up all that he could find about mongolism and came to the conclusion that the kindest course would be to do away with the child. So he smothered it, and immediately informed the police. Although it might be thought that this action was morally wrong, it would be difficult to argue that it was not responsibly motivated. Nevertheless, in a successful Section 2 defence, a sentence of 12 months' imprisonment was imposed."

The creation of a single offence would mean that the somewhat artificial rules on provocation, diminished responsibility, infanticide and suicide pacts could be abandoned. These matters could be relegated to their proper place—as mitigating factors relevant to sentencing.

What are the arguments against the introduction of a single offence of unlawful homicide?

Criminal Law Revision Committee, Working Paper on Offences against the Person, 1976:

"5. To have a single offence of homicide, combining murder with a lesser offence of manslaughter, would mean that the jury's verdict would leave the judge with no guidance as to the gravity of the offence. In the absence of any new provision introducing a system of special verdicts, the judge would have to assess, in deciding what penalty to impose, whether intent to kill or a less serious degree of criminality amounting to what is now manslaughter had been proved. If the accused pleaded not guilty, the facts of the case would come out in the evidence, but the verdict of the jury would be confined to the issue of guilt or innocence of the offence of homicide. The judge would be left to decide, for example, whether the provocation alleged in mitigation (with the merger of murder and manslaughter, provocation would be a matter of mitigation only) existed in fact. If the accused pleaded guilty to homicide, the judge would have even less material on which to decide such questions since he would not have had the benefit of hearing detailed evidence. Thus the offence of homicide would apply to a very wide range of circumstances, varying in their degree of gravity, and the judge would be left to determine the true nature of the offence without the assistance of the jury. The majority of us think that the argument discussed in this paragraph is a very strong one; a minority of members, however, consider that it is overstated.

6. To have a single offence of homicide covering such a wide range of acts would make a conviction of the offence relatively uninformative in that it would be used to describe the most heinous case of murder and the least serious case of manslaughter. Although the Committee's proposals about the existing offence of manslaughter would reduce the scope of the single offence of homicide (combining murder and manslaughter), it would still be a wide-ranging offence classifying under the same head both a person who killed under provocation or while suffering from diminished responsibility and a person who killed deliberately without any provocation and not suffering from any mental disorder.

7. To abolish the offence of murder as such, although retaining it as part of a wider offence of homicide, may appear to have the effect of lessening the seriousness of taking life. We think that, in the public's mind, there is a stigma attaching to a conviction of murder and that this rightly emphasises the seriousness of the offence and may have a significant deterrent value . . .

8. . . . . [T]he majority of us see advantages in the mandatory sentence and think that there is a need for a special penalty for the most serious cases of homicide in order to reassure the public and also for the purposes of prevention and deterrence."[37]

There is a further major objection to the suggested new offence of unlawful homicide. Such a proposal would result in a substantial increase of judicial discretion in sentencing. In Chapter 1 the dangers of such discretion were considered. In the United States where there has been a strong movement away from judicial discretion in sentencing, there has been a corresponding swing towards more precise classifications of homicide offences over the last decade. Even if we, in England, do not wish to follow the United States lead on sentencing reform, it is doubtful whether we should actually step backwards and propose reforms to the substantive law that would involve an *increase* in judicial discretion in sentencing.

A final possibility remains and deserves brief mention. Could one not introduce a single offence of unlawful homicide together with a "guideline model" of sentencing for such an offence? This would involve a separate sentencing hearing after the primary ascertainment of criminal liability. The various aggravating and mitigating factors could then be properly taken into account. The weight to be given to each factor would have been determined in advance and reflected in the "offence score" and "offender score," thus largely eliminating judicial discretion in sentencing. Ultimately, different categories of offence exist to enable

---

[37] Similar views were expressed by Lord Hailsham in *Cunningham* [1982] A.C. 566 at 580.

different ranges of penalties to be imposed. This proposal would involve the break-down of existing hairsplitting substantive categories and would permit attention to be focussed on the true issue: given the mental element of this defendant, given the position of this defendant (in terms of criminal history and other matters relevant to the "offender score"), given the circumstances of this crime, what penalty should this defendant receive for committing this crime?

CHAPTER 9

OFFENCES AGAINST PROPERTY

I. INTRODUCTION

There is a wide variety of offences against property in English law, for example, theft, robbery, burglary, offences involving deception and fraud, taking a motor vehicle or other conveyance without authority, abstracting electricity, blackmail, handling stolen goods, forgery, criminal damage—and many more.

A. *The level of offending*

So widespread are these offences that people are more likely to be the victim of a property offence than any other kind,[1] whether it be by taking, damage or destruction. As the following figure indicates, official statistics state that property offences constitute 94 per cent. of the known picture of criminality in England and Wales.

[1] Pat Mayhew, David Elliott and Lizanne Dowds, *The 1988 British Crime Survey* (1989) p. 9.

Criminal Justice, Key statistics, England and Wales, 1988

Notifiable offences recorded by the police, 1988

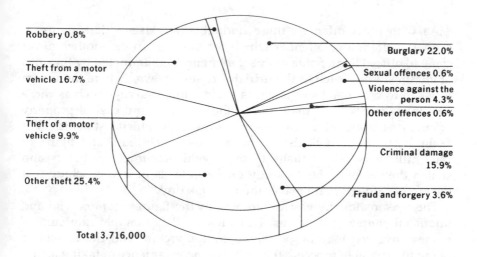

Robbery 0.8%

Theft from a motor vehicle 16.7%

Theft of a motor vehicle 9.9%

Other theft 25.4%

Burglary 22.0%

Sexual offences 0.6%

Violence against the person 4.3%

Other offences 0.6%

Criminal damage 15.9%

Fraud and forgery 3.6%

Total 3,716,000

The annual cost of such property offences to victims is vast. For instance, the official statistics put the annual cost of recorded offences of theft, robbery and burglary alone at £1600 million.[2] There is no attempt made to measure the losses involved with other offences such as fraud.[3]

M. Hough and P. Mayhew, Taking Account of Crime: Key findings from the 1984 British Crime Surveys, (1985), (H.O.R.S. No. 85) p. 27:

"The BCS obtained information from victims on their own assessment of the value of any property which they had had stolen. In terms of the initial 'take' for different crimes, stolen vehicles had—as one might expect—the highest value: the majority of losses were valued at more than £100; in contrast, only half of burglary victims and 15 per cent. of victims of thefts from cars had losses of this order. Three-quarters of victims of robbery and snatch thefts had property worth less than £25 stolen. . . .

As well as losses from theft, victims can sustain damage to their property,

---

[2] *Criminal Statistics, England and Wales*, 1988, (Cm. 847).
[3] *Post* p. 741.

committed either in the furtherance of theft or for its own sake. Victims' assessments of their losses through damage were generally smaller than losses through theft, though 14 per cent. of vehicle thefts and 8 per cent. of burglaries involved more than £100 worth of damage ... ... Despite public concern about the prevalence of 'soiling'—where a burglar defecates or urinates on the furniture or floor—there were only three such instances in over 300 burglaries.

Those who had property stolen did not usually get it back. 87 per cent. of burglary victims, and 94 per cent. of those who had items taken from their vehicles did not recover their property. The exception was vehicle theft where there was a 70 per cent. recovery rate."

As with other offences, there undoubtedly exists a dark figure of property offending; offences which for one reason or another never come to official light. Some of this dark figure is illuminated by findings of victim studies, such as the British Crime Surveys,[4] where the victim is asked to give details of offences against him. Surveys such as these enable estimates to be made about the real level and cost of property offences as opposed to the picture drawn by official statistics. For example, the second British Crime Survey suggested that a figure of £400 million is lost annually through vehicular theft, robberies and snatch thefts alone.[5] Levi's study on fraud leads him to conclude that the losses through fraud makes the rest look tiny.[6]

The reasons for the vast differences in the figures from official and unofficial sources are not hard to identify. For example, the sum of money involved may be perceived by the victim (and the police) as being too trivial to proceed, the cost and inconvenience of taking action may make some victims reluctant to proceed, it may be impossible to identify offenders (as will be the case with much shoplifting), the behaviour may not be seen by even the victim as truly criminal (as may be the case with the problem of bad cheques). Finally, by way of example, the victim may never even learn of his loss.

All of these examples illustrate the diversity of offences thrown together under the umbrella of property offences. The harm done may vary from damage that endangers life, through "professional" theft[7] and robbery to behaviour that lies at the very fringes of criminality. There is no highly typical offender (although the chances of his being young are even higher than for other types of offence). The public imagination may conjure up images of Fagin, Bill Sykes or Ronald Biggs, and those large scale professional crimes that capture the news headlines[8] but, although professional criminals do exist there also exists a vast army of occasional criminals[9]: the opportunist burglar, the shop-

---

[4] *Ante* n. 1.

[5] Mike Hough and Pat Mayhew, *Taking Account of Crime: Key Findings from the Second British Crime Survey*, (1985) (H.O.R.S. No. 85), p. 29).

[6] M. Levi, *Regulating Fraud, post* p. 741.

[7] This phrase was first coined by Sutherland in *The Professional Thief* (1937): it conveys the idea of someone who makes a calculated living out of crime.

[8] *E.g.* the Brinks-Mat bullion raid in 1983 in which £26.5 million was taken: the largest ever robbery in this country.

[9] *Cf.* J. Hepburn, "Occasional Property Crime" in *Major Forms of Crime* (1984) ed. R. Meier.

lifter, the juvenile joy-rider, the naive passer of bad cheques, the respectable employee who takes advantage of his employers' trust to embezzle funds. In short, the property offender may be 10 and showing off, 14 and a committed member of a gang, 21, a mugger, involved in a life of crime or 28 and an apparent pillar of society. Property offences encompass crime that could be described as violent[10] to crime that could be labelled as white-collar crime.[11]

B. *The sociological background*

1. Why do people commit property offences?

Given the diversity of property offenders and their offences, it is not surprising that there exists a multiplicity of theories attempting to account for such criminality. Some attempts have tried to establish links between economic conditions and the rate of property offending. However, on the whole the expected relationship between economic downturns and increased offending has not been substantiated.[12]

Other theories are dependent upon the drawing of a distinction between utilitarian and non-utilitarian crime. Merton, for example, in his theory of anomie,[13] saw crime as an unorthodox route to achieving the American Dream of monetary wealth, in a society that held out this goal to all as achievable but at the same time savagely restricted legitimate means of obtaining the goal. In such a society where the emphasis was all upon success and not on the means of achieving success, there was pressure upon individuals to take whatever route would transform them from plough-boys to presidents. Crime was strictly utilitarian. Cohen, on the other hand, emphasised the non-utilitarian nature of much juvenile property crime.[14] He believed that as a result of school failure in a system that was inherently middle-class and, therefore, stacked against them, working-class boys would respond by inverting the norms of their parent culture. They would reject the values of working hard and having respect for other people's property, for example, and behave in a way that showed their commitment to opposite values. By doing this they would thereby set standards that they were capable of achieving. Delinquency was thus an attempt to disassociate themselves from a culture that had doomed them to fail; the characteristic crimes engaged in would be stealing and then throwing away or acts of small scale vandalism.

---

[10] Robbery and burglary, although violent offences, are properly described as property offences because the violence is incidental to the main aim, the acquisition of property.

[11] The term was invented by Sutherland in *White-collar Crime* (1949) to illuminate that crime committed not by young working-class males but by persons of apparent respectability in the course of their employment. There now exists a wealth of literature on this area; for a useful introduction to it, see D. C. Gibbons *Society, Crime and Criminal Behaviour* (1982). See also Geis and Stotland, *White-collar Crime* (1980), and Levi, *Regulating Fraud* (1987) and bibliography cited therein.

[12] J. Wilson and R. Herrnstein, *Crime and Human Nature*, (1985), pp. 423–424.

[13] *Society Theory and Social Structure*, (1949).

[14] *Delinquent Boys: The Culture of the Gang*, (1955).

Other theorists have concentrated not so much on the delinquent act itself, but on the way in which society responds to it. This argument runs counter to deterrence reasoning already discussed,[15] in that here it is claimed that by "dramatising the evil"[16] and acting repressively against it by legal sanctions, criminality is exacerbated. By society acting to prevent further crime, it actually creates a criminal. Evidence exists on both sides of this evergreen debate but it must be admitted that the labelling perspective is of particular significance in shaping penal policy towards young offenders. Many commentators regard some juvenile delinquency as quite a normal feature of growing up. It is in the best interests of everyone, therefore, not to be too heavy handed in the treatment of such offenders, to avoid as much as possible the stigmatising effect of court appearances and the like. The risk of ignoring this is, that what is only a phase in the juvenile's life may become a permanent feature.

Despite this criticism of the way in which delinquency can be amplified, most such theories do not attack the framework of the criminal law or the criminal justice system in any fundamental sense. Both mainstream criminologists[17] and labelling theorists accept the existence of laws protecting property. This represents a consensus view of society; there is a shared sense of right and wrong. Conflict criminology attacks this view and suggests that whilst the notion of consensus might be appropriate for simple societies, complex, industrial, multi-racial and cultural societies such as those as Great Britain and the U.S.A. are dominated by conflict instead. The important task for such theorists is, therefore, to describe the process by which some members of society consistently have their interests protected at the expense of others.

S. Box, Power, Crime and Mystification, (1983) p. 10:

"The criminal law sees only some types of property deprivation as robbery or theft; it excludes, for example, the separation of consumers and part of their money that follows manufacturers' malpractices or advertisers' misrepresentations; it excludes shareholders losing their money because managers behaved in ways which they thought would be to the advantage of shareholders even though the only tangible benefits accrued to the managers . . . it excludes the *extra* tax citizens, in this or other countries, have to pay because: (i) corporations and the very wealthy are able to employ financial experts at discovering legal loopholes through which money can be safely transported to tax havens; (ii) Defence Department officials have been bribed to order more expensive weaponry systems or missiles in 'excess' of those 'needed'; (iii) multinational drug companies charge our National Health Services prices which are estimated to be at least £50 millions in excess of alternative supplies. If an employee's hand slips into the governor's pocket and removes any spare cash, that is theft;

---

[15] *Ante* p. 14.
[16] F. Tannenbaum's term for societal reaction: *Crime and the Community*, (1938), laid the foundations from which developed modern day labelling theory. For a detailed criticism of such theories cf. D. Downes and P. Rock, *Understanding Deviance* (1988).
[17] Merton, for example, *ante* p. 677.

if the governor puts his hand into the employees' pockets and takes their spare cash, *i.e.* reduces wages, even below the legal minimum, that is the labour market operating reasonably. To end the list prematurely and clarify the point, the law of theft includes, in the words of that anonymous poet particularly loved by teachers of 'A' level economic history, 'the man or woman who steals the goose from off the common, but leaves the greater villian loose who steals the common from the goose.' "

From this beginning came the development of radical criminology where crime was seen as the inevitable by-product of a society divided into classes by capitalism. Offenders might be forced into committing crime by the laws designed to protect the ruling classes, either as a means of survival or as part of the struggle to be free from repression. Emphasis was placed on crime committed by the powerful and their relative immunity from prosecution. The resolution of the conflict was seen in terms of the elimination of capitalism; with this would come the end of all crime not based on biological or psychological factors.[18]

Despite the insight offered into modern society, radical criminology has fared very badly at the hands of its critics. Cross-cultural studies, for example, have shown that high working-class crime rates are not necessarily a feature of capitalist societies.[19] Crime surveys in this country have made it clear that typically it is the working-class who are the victims of crime; that the laws are protective of them as well as the despised bourgeoisie.[20] Moreover, and overwhelmingly, radical criminology ignores the fact that most crime is intra-group rather than inter-group: crimes by the powerful against the powerful and crimes by the working-classes against the working-classes. The notion of classes at war cannot be sustained by the empirical evidence.

Because of crime surveys much more is known about the picture of property crime in this country. This has implications not only for etiological theories as we have seen, but for policing and sentencing and at a substantive level as well. If it transpires that much property crime is being dealt with non-legally then there may be a case[21] for the decriminalisation of some offences at the fringes of criminality.

2. Societal attitudes towards property offences

J. Hepburn, Occasional Property Crime, from Major Forms of Crime, (1984), p. 73 at pp. 88–89:

"Among the earliest criminal laws were those pertaining to property. In a highly stratified society, especially one with a capitalistic economy, power and

---

[18] See, *e.g.* Taylor, Walton and Young, *The New Criminology* (1973).

[19] *E.g.* Clinard, *Cities with little Crime: The case of Switzerland* (1978).

[20] As well as the British Crime Surveys (*ante* n. 1 and 5), see also more localised surveys: *e.g.* Jones, Maclean, Young, *The Islington Crime Survey* (1986) and generally, Sparks *et al*, *Surveying Victims* (1977). For similar findings in other countries, see *e.g.* the President's Commission on Law Enforcement and the Administration of Justice, *Crime and its Impact: an Assessment*, (1967).

[21] *Post* p. 791.

status depend to a large degree on the economic resources a person accumulates. Consequently, there generally is a strong, negative public reaction to property offenses in the United States. The reaction is particularly strong against armed robbery, mugging, and arson, because these offenses combine loss of property with a potential for physical harm to the victim. Residential burglary, which violates the sanctity of the home, also generates a strong condemnation. In contrast, the public outcry against shoplifting, vandalism, and other 'petty' forms of property crime is least vocal.

The magnitude of the public's reaction to property offenses does not seem to be associated with the amount of financial loss involved. Compared to the multimillion-dollar losses which result from corporate crime and organized crime, the losses incurred by occasional property crimes are quite small . . .

Armed robbery netted a total of $339 million in property loss, for example, while the total loss due to burglary was $3 billion. According to the FBI, the total cost of all Part I property offenses was slightly over $10 billion. In comparison, the annual cost to the public of faulty goods, monopolistic practices, and other corporate crimes has been estimated at between $174 and $231 billion . . . Furthermore, the financial losses due to the criminal activities of organized crime are estimated to be upwards of $50 billion annually . . . Despite the greater loss due to corporate and organized crime, these crimes receive less public condemnation than the more traditional property crimes.

The public's reaction to property crimes is reflected in the legal reaction taken by law enforcement agencies. Police agencies are largely reactive; they respond to the crimes that are brought to their attention by citizens. Legislators also are responsive to their constituency's concern with property crimes. As a result, a significant amount of the time, money, and energy of law enforcement agencies is directed toward ordinary property crimes. Increased police patrols are justified on the (false) assumption that they reduce the opportunity for crime and increase the risk of arrest. Merchants and residents are advised by the police of various 'target-hardening' tactics, such as exterior lighting and barred windows, designed to reduce the opportunity for crime. Prosecutors and legislators champion the view that more severe legal penalties are needed to deter crime.

Although the public and legal reaction to property crimes in general is rather severe, the reaction to those who are occasional offenders tends to be more restrained. Compared to other offenders processed routinely by the courts, the occasional offender is (1) less likely to have a criminal record of prior arrests and convictions, (2) more likely to have been charged with a minor offense, (3) more respectable, as defined in terms of employment history, residential stability, and family relationships, and (4) more repentant. As a result of these characteristics of the offender and the offense, the occasional offender is treated less harshly by the criminal justice system. The prosecutor's office is less likely to file initial charges against the offender. If it does, there is a strong probability that the offender will be diverted from prosecution to some special restitution-oriented program or that the charges will be dismissed before trial. Should the offender be convicted, a prison sentence is most unlikely. . . . "

The second British Crime survey is also a useful source of information about public attitudes towards property offences, in two main contexts. First, such surveys have a great deal to say about the sorts of crime that people are most anxious about and the steps they take to reduce their vulnerability. Fear of being "mugged" is a commonly expressed concern; for some people this may cause them to avoid going out at night at all if it can be avoided, for others it might (especially in the case of women) mean never going out alone.[22] Fear of burglary might cause some to support neighbourhood watch schemes. Fear of having their computers used for fraud might cause executives to spend large amounts of money on security systems and security experts.[23]

Secondly, such surveys are of use in finding out what the public think about sentencing practice in the area of property offences. Generally, opinion polls of the public reveal a punitive approach to sentencing[24] but it may well be that for some crimes at least "people overestimate the leniency of the courts."[25] This was certainly true of burglary in the case of the second British crime survey and "it seems quite likely that people may overestimate the leniency of sentences for other offences as well."[26]

The attitudes expressed in such surveys are not always in favour of stiffer penalties. Where the offence is perceived as less serious, there may be considerable support for non-custodial alternatives to imprisonment. One in 12 of the respondents in the second British Crime Survey favoured the use of informal police warnings for shop-lifters over the age of 25 with previous convictions.[27] This raises once again the issue of whether some offences are properly the concern of the criminal law.

C. *The Legal Background*

Discussion so far makes it clear that the structure of property offences is very different from the offences against the person already covered. With the latter, the seriousness of the harm was critical in the structuring of offences and concomitant levels of punishment: for example, causing death is more serious than causing grievous harm, which in turn is worse than causing actual bodily harm—and so on. Offences against property, however, are not structured in such a clear manner. It is not possible to follow the same pattern in structuring liability because of the difficulty in measuring the "harm" done. One possible method here is by assessing the value of the property involved. English law, however, has eschewed such an approach at least at a substantive level[28] and instead has chosen to distinguish its property offences by the method of taking or dealing with the property. According to this approach, deceiving someone into agreeing to part with his property (obtaining property by deception) is treated differently from coercing

---

[22] *Post* p. 777.

[23] *Post* p. 740.

[24] *Second British Crime Survey*, (*ante* n. 5) p. 43. *Cf.* Walker and Hough, *Public Attitudes to Sentencing*, (1988), particularly pp. 203–217.

[25] *Ibid.*, p. 43. This finding was confirmed by a study conducted for the Home Office by Walker, Hough and Lewis: *Public Attitudes to Sentencing*, (1988), pp. 185–202.

[26] *Ibid.*, p. 44 and Walker and Hough (p. 208) confirmed this in relation to both burglary and causing death by reckless driving at least.

[27] *Ibid.*, p. 44.

[28] See further, *post*, pp. 786 *et seq.*

someone with threats into parting with his property (blackmail). Whether each grouping is sufficiently precise and/or meaningful is a matter to be returned to after an examination of the offences themselves.

Another distinctive feature of the offences against property is that they are statutory and largely found in modern statutes, in particular, the Theft Act 1968, the Theft Act 1978, the Criminal Damage Act 1971 and the Forgery and Counterfeiting Act 1981. Such statutes are somewhat distinctive in that they approximate to a code. Most English statutes consolidate, amend or add to the pre-existing law. The approach here is different. Take, for instance, the Theft Act 1968. This Act swept away all the previous law on the subject, creating entirely new law dealing with most forms of dishonest dealings with property. As English law enters an era possibly culminating in a codification of the whole of the criminal law,[29] it becomes particularly important and interesting to see how our courts have handled these areas of law.

Before examining the property offences themselves two important preliminary points must be made.

The Criminal Law Revision Committee, in putting forward its proposals[30] which largely became the Theft Act 1968, wished to avoid the technicality and complexity of the old law under the Larceny Acts and accordingly tried deliberately to frame as much of the legislation as possible in ordinary "simple" language capable of being easily understood by the layman. Accordingly, many key concepts (for example, "dishonesty") were inserted in the legislation without definition. The courts could of course have developed their own legal definitions of such concepts but have instead preferred to leave the meaning of such words to the jury, as questions of fact. The jury are ordinary people; they know what ordinary words mean—and don't need judges to explain their meaning to them. This approach, leading to a lack of fixed standards and inconsistency, has proved highly controversial, as will be seen in this chapter.

The second preliminary issue in some ways completely contradicts the above point. Offences against property deal with interference with other persons' rights or interests in property. One is free to do as one likes with one's own property. It is therefore always necessary to ascertain that there is some other person who has some right or interest in the property. For instance, in *Corcoran* v. *Whent*[31] a defendant ate a meal in a hotel restaurant and left without paying. In order to determine his liability for theft it becomes necessary to determine whether at the time he decided not to pay, (after he had eaten the food) the food (in his stomach) belonged to anyone else! If it belonged to himself he could com-

---

[29] Law Commission Working Paper, No. 143, *Codification of the Criminal Law* (1985).
[30] Criminal Law Revision Committee, Eighth Report, *Theft and Related Offences*, Cmnd. 2977.
[31] [1977] Crim.L.R. 52.

mit no crime as he would not be interfering with any one else's rights or interests in property.[32]

But how is one to determine whether anyone else has such proprietary right or interest in the property? There is a whole body of law— the law of property, contract and quasi-contract—devoted to answering such questions. The Theft Act 1968, for example, uses many technical legal terms such as "trespasser,"[33] "proprietary right or interest,"[34] "trust,"[35] etc. As these terms are undefined it would appear reasonable that they be assigned their established civil law meaning. Such an approach would however fly in the face of the philosophy that words in such legislation be assigned their ordinary meaning by ordinary people, the jury. There is indeed force in such an approach. Civil law meanings of words need adaptation to the purposes of the criminal law, for instance, to accommodate the normal requirement of *mens rea*. Further, the criminal law ought to reflect everyday values and "the way we live." Who better to reflect such values than those everyday folk, the jury? This appears to be the prevailing articulated view. In *Morris*,[36] the leading House of Lords decision on theft, Lord Roskill was highly critical of the approach that relied on the civil law meaning of concepts. For instance, whether a contract was void or voidable, was "so far as possible" not a relevant question in relation to the law of theft.

As will be seen, however, courts are not always prepared to jettison established legal meanings and replace them with "ordinary meanings." (What is the ordinary meaning of those ordinary words, "trust" or "equitable interest"?)[37] Accordingly, one of the fascinations of this area of law is to observe the lurchings from the tightrope as the English courts try to achieve an impossible balance between these two competing and irreconcilable interests.

A thorough consideration of all property offences is not possible, even in a book of this size. Accordingly, the enquiry will be limited to those offences that tell us most about the purposes and structures of this area of law. The main offences to be considered will thus be theft and the various deception offences. Brief consideration will also be given to the offences of robbery, burglary, handling stolen goods and making off without payment.

---

[32] The defendant's conviction for theft was quashed. Once he had eaten the food he could not "deal with it" and it was no longer property "belonging to another."
[33] s.9.
[34] s.5(1).
[35] s.5(2).
[36] [1984] A.C. 320
[37] Theft Act 1968, s.5(1).

II. Theft

A. *The Sociological Background*

As can be seen from the figure on offence rates above,[38] theft offences account for 52·7 per cent. of all reported crime in England and Wales. Even that, however, fails to reflect the true significance and extent of theft in this country. As suggested earlier, theft, or at least certain categories thereof, may be considerably under-reported. Whereas it would appear that almost all thefts of motor vehicles are reported (because of the value of the article and for insurance purposes) the picture for theft *from* motor vehicles and shoplifting is rather different. In relation to thefts from motor vehicles, the 1988 British Crime Survey estimate is that about 40 per cent. of such offences are reported.[39] In relation to shoplifting (a particularly difficult crime to observe) the percentage is certainly lower than that. Astor's research concluded, for example, that one in 15 people stole goods from stores with store detectives noticing only about one per cent. of those.[40] Such research renders almost meaningless the official figure of recorded thefts from shops of 216,242 in 1988.[41] It also means that despite the fact that the average value of goods taken tends to be small in shoplifting offences, official statistics on losses through theft are likely to be wildly inaccurate. The figure of about £1000 million for the year 1988 is just the tip of the iceberg— although unlike icebergs it is impossible to gauge how much remains hidden!

Under-reporting occurs, as we have seen, for a variety of reasons, but it does reflect to some extent the degree of seriousness with which the offence is regarded. Vehicle thefts, for instance, were viewed seriously in the latest British Crime Survey and are almost always reported.[42] This survey also enables assessments of seriousness to be made on the basis of the penalties chosen by respondents for a variety of offences. In relation to car thefts, 23 per cent. of the respondents thought that prison was the appropriate penalty for 25 year old offenders with previous convictions, in comparison with 12 per cent. who felt it to be the appropriate penalty for shoplifting. One might be tempted to conclude from this, and the lower rate of reporting of theft from shops, that this crime is regarded less seriously than other forms of theft. The development of the term "shoplifting" may even be seen as evidence of this, separating as it does this form of activity from "theft." But any such conclusions would have to be highly qualified. The relationship between reporting and seriousness is by no means a perfect one. Sexual crimes, for example, are rated highly seriously, yet are grossly under-reported. In

---

[38] *Ante*, p. 674.
[39] *Ante* n. 1, p. 11.
[40] Astor, S.D., "Shoplifting Survey," Security World, Vol. 8, Part 3 (1971), pp. 3–4.
[41] *Criminal Statistics, England and Wales*, 1988 (Cm. 847) p. 41.
[42] *Ante* n.1, p. 11. (This is consistent with earlier surveys).

other words, there are other reasons for not reporting an offence other than an attitude as to its seriousness. Despite this, it is probably the case that shoplifting is regarded as a comparatively minor offence: the amount involved will generally be small; the victim of the offence may be perceived as being a large, impersonal organisation able to absorb the loss; and there may even be at times a "there but for the grace of God . . . " sentiment. All this does not of course amount to an argument for the decriminalisation of "shoplifting"—but it may well be an argument for the creation of a separate lesser offence.[43]

B. *The Legal Background*

Prior to the Theft Act 1968, what is now the crime of theft was dealt with by three separate offences: larceny, embezzlement and fraudulent conversion. Each of these offences and the distinction between them was technical and highly complex. Further, the offences were felt to be defective in that certain conduct that would ordinarily be regarded as stealing did not come within the definitions of the offences.

Criminal Law Revision Committee, Eighth Report, Theft and Related Offences, Cmnd. 2977 (1966), paras. 33, 60:

"33. The committee generally are strongly of opinion that larceny, embezzlement and fraudulent conversion should be replaced by a single new offence of theft. The important element of them all is undoubtedly the dishonest appropriation of another's property—the treating of 'tuum' as 'meum'; and we think it not only logical, but right in principle, to make this the central element of the offence. In doing so the law would concentrate on what the accused dishonestly achieved or attempted to achieve and not on the means—taking or otherwise—which he used in order to do so. This would avoid multiplicity of offences . . .

60. We recommend that the maximum penalty for stealing should be 10 years' imprisonment in all cases. It may seem drastic to double the present penalty for simple larceny. But this seems right to us for several reasons.

(i) Ten years does not seem too high for the most serious cases . . .

(ii) . . . It seems very unlikely that a single offence of stealing would ever be punished with more than 10 years' imprisonment under the present law.

(iii) . . . The introduction of a single penalty would greatly simplify the law . . . "

This proposal was accepted by section 7 of the Theft Act 1968 which lays down the maximum penalty of 10 years imprisonment. It is interesting to compare this with the sentencing reality of today where, in 1988 there were 164,000 offenders sentenced for theft and handling stolen goods (nearly half of all offenders). Of these 42 per cent. were fined and 47 per cent. given other non-custodial sentences. Of the 11 per cent. given cus-

---

[43] *Post*, pp. 791–794.

todial sentences, the average length of such sentence was 2·5 months (magistrates' court) and 10·5 months (Crown Court).[44]

C. *The Law*

1. Definition

Theft Act 1968, s.1(1)

"A person is guilty of theft if he dishonestly appropriates property belonging to another with the intention of permanently depriving the other of it; and 'thief' and 'steal' shall be construed accordingly."

In *Lawrence*[45] it was stressed by the House of Lords that this definition involved several elements, all of which must be proved to coincide before liability can be imposed. Each of these elements is defined, wholly or partially, in the ensuing sections of the Theft Act 1968 as follows:

section 2: dishonesty
section 3: appropriation
section 4: property
section 5: belonging to another
section 6: intention of permanent deprivation.

We shall deal first with the *actus reus* elements, namely, appropriation of property belonging to another—before turning to the *mens rea* elements, dishonesty and intention of permanent deprivation.

2. Appropriation

Theft Act 1968, s.3

"(1) Any assumption by a person of the rights of an owner amounts to an appropriation, and this includes, where he has come by the property (innocently or not) without stealing it, any later assumption of a right to it by keeping or dealing with it as owner.

(2) Where property or a right or interest in property is or purports to be transferred for value to a person acting in good faith, no later assumption by him of rights which he believed himself to be acquiring shall, by reason of any defect in the transferor's title, amount to theft of the property."

---

[44] *Criminal Statistics, England and Wales* 1988, (Cm. 847). For a discussion of the factors influencing the sentence for some of the different species of theft, namely, shoplifting, pickpocketing, theft in breach of trust, theft in the course of employment and theft of a motor vehicle, see C. Emmins, *A Practical Approach to Sentencing* (1985), pp. 294–297. The recent White Paper proposes reducing the maximum penalty to 7 years imprisonment (Govt White Paper, *Crime, Justice and Protecting the Public*, Cm. 965, 1990).

[45] v. *Metropolitan Police Commissioner* [1972] A.C. 626.

Criminal Law Revision Committee, Eighth Report, Theft and Related Offences, 1966, Cmnd. 2977, paras. 34–35:

"34. We hope, and believe, that the concept of 'dishonest appropriation' will be easily understood even without the aid of further definition. But there is a partial definition of 'appropriates' in . . . (section) 3(1) . . . It seems to us natural to refer to the act of stealing in ordinary cases as 'appropriation.' We see no reason why the word should seem strange for more than a short time . . .

35. There is an argument for keeping the word 'converts' because it is well understood. But it is a lawyers' word, and those not used to legal language might naturally think that it meant changing something or exchanging property for other property. 'Appropriates' seems altogether a better word."

An appropriation is thus the *assumption of the rights of an owner*. But what are the rights of an owner?

F. H. Lawson and Bernard Rudden, The Law of Property (1982) Clarendon Law Series, pp. 8–9:

"The main elements (of ownership) are (a) the right to make physical use of a thing; (b) the right to the income from it, in money, in kind, or in services; and (c) the power of management, including that of alienation. Thus the owner of a car may drive it, hire it out, or sell it. And of course within these areas he may do the same things more generously: take the children for a drive, lend it to a friend, give it away."

In short, as Roman law used to put it, an owner has the right to "use, enjoy and abuse" his property as he sees fit.[46] An owner of a book may keep it, sell it, give it away or destroy it. *Assuming* the rights of owner is laying claim to be in such a position. If a defendant, with the consent of the owner, removes a book from another's room in order to read and then return it, he is not asserting any of the rights of ownership; he is accepting that another, the real owner, is the only one with these powers. But if he surreptitiously took the book with a view to keeping, selling or destroying it he would be "laying claim," or "treating as his own" and thus "assuming . . . the rights of an owner" as specified in the first part of section 3(1).

The method of acquiring the property is not important. There does not have to be a taking or removal although this is of course what occurs in the paradigmatic theft. The second part of section 3(1) makes this clear. If the owner accidentally left his book in the defendant's room there could be an appropriation the moment the defendant decided to keep the book. At this point he would be assuming a right to the book by keeping or dealing with it as owner, despite the fact he originally came by the property quite innocently.

This last point leads directly to the central problem in the interpretation of an "appropriation." When the book has been accidentally left

---

[46] This is subject of course to numerous restrictions aimed at protecting the interests of others.

in the defendant's room he assumes the right of an owner the moment he *decides* to keep it. At this point he is exercising one of the rights of ownership. But if it were held that this amounted to an appropriation this would mean that there could be a theft by a defendant who had done nothing *wrong*—other than have a blameworthy state of mind. Following this logic, a defendant in a supermarket who placed goods in a wire basket as provided but who had a secret intention of stealing them would be guilty of theft. He had decided not to pay for the goods and to make off with them as and when he saw fit. The argument runs that this is treating the goods as one's own and is thus an appropriation.

There is of course a fallacy in this argument. A person can only fully "lay claim" to the rights of owner if he is representing to others that the property is his to dispose of as he sees fit. As long as the goods are in the trolley the defendant is recognising and respecting the rights of the owner by doing exactly what he is expected to do. On the other hand, the moment he slips the goods into his pocket he is "laying claim" to them. He is treating the goods as owner, to use and abuse without any recognition of the rights of another. This conduct, which amounts to objective wrongdoing, is the essence of an appropriation.

R. v. Morris, Anderton v. Burnside [1984] A.C. 320 (House of Lords)

Two defendants took goods from a shelf in a supermarket and removed the proper price labels and replaced them with labels from cheaper goods. The goods, bearing their incorrect price labels were presented at the check-out counter. One defendant was arrested before, and the other after, paying for the goods. The appeals were heard together.

Lord Roskill (with whom Lords Fraser of Tullybelton, Edmund-Davies, Brandon of Oakbrook and Brightman concurred):
"[Counsel for the defendants argued that Morris] was not guilty of theft because there was no appropriation by him before payment at the checkpoint sufficient to support a charge of theft, however dishonest his actions may have been in previously switching the labels . . .
It is to be observed that the definition of 'appropriation' in section 3(1) is not exhaustive . . .
The starting point . . . must, I think, be the decision of this House in *Reg.* v. *Lawrence (Alan)* [*post*, p. 692] . . . [in which] Viscount Dilhorne also rejected the argument that even if [the] four elements were all present there could not be theft within the section if the owner of the property in question had consented to the acts which were done by the defendant. That there was in that case a dishonest appropriation was beyond question and the House did not have to consider the precise meaning of that word in section 3(1).
Mr. Denison submitted that the phrase in section 3(1) 'any assumption by a person of *the rights*' (my emphasis) 'of an owner amounts to an appropriation' must mean any assumption of '*all* the rights of an owner.' Since neither respondent had at the time of the removal of the goods from the shelves and of the label switching assumed *all* the rights of the owner, there was no appropriation and therefore no theft. Mr. Jeffreys for the prosecution, on the other hand, contended that *the* rights in this context only meant *any* of the rights. An owner of

goods has many rights—they have been described as 'a bundle or package of rights.' Mr. Jeffreys contended that on a fair reading of the subsection it cannot have been the intention that every one of an owner's rights had to be assumed by the alleged thief before an appropriation was proved and that essential ingredient of the offence of theft established.

My Lords, if one reads the words 'the rights' at the opening of section 3(1) literally and in isolation from the rest of the section, Mr. Denison's submission undoubtedly has force. But the later words 'any later assumption of a right' in subsection (1) and the words in subsection (2) 'no later assumption by him of rights' seem to be to militate strongly against the correctness of the submission. Moreover the provisions of section 2(1)(*a*) also seem to point in the same direction. It follows therefore that it is enough for the prosecution if they have proved in these cases the assumption by the respondents of *any* of the rights of the owner of the goods in question, that is to say, the supermarket concerned, it being common ground in these cases that the other three of the four elements . . . [of theft] had been fully established.

My Lords, Mr. Jeffreys sought to argue that any removal from the shelves of the supermarket, even if unaccompanied by label switching, was without more an appropriation. In one passage in his judgment in Morris's case, the learned Lord Chief Justice appears to have accepted the submission, for he said [1983] Q.B. 587, 596:

> 'it seems to us that in taking the article from the shelf the customer is indeed assuming one of the rights of the owner—the right to move the article from its position on the shelf to carry it to the check-out.'

With the utmost respect, I cannot accept this statement as correct. If one postulates an honest customer taking goods from a shelf to put in his or her trolley to take to the checkpoint there to pay the proper price, I am unable to see that any of these actions involves any assumption by the shopper of the rights of the supermarket. In the context of section 3(1), the concept of appropriation in my view involves not an act expressly or impliedly authorised by the owner but an act by way of adverse interference with or usurpation of those rights. When the honest shopper acts as I have just described, he or she is acting with the implied authority of the owner of the supermarket to take the goods from the shelf, put them in the trolley, take them to the checkpoint and there pay the correct price, at which moment the property in the goods will pass to the shopper for the first time. It is with the consent of the owners of the supermarket, be that consent express or implied, that the shopper does these acts and thus obtains at least control if not actual possession of the goods preparatory, at a later stage, to obtaining the property in them upon payment of the proper amount at the checkpoint. I do not think that section 3(1) envisages any such act as an 'appropriation,' whatever may be the meaning of that word in other fields such as contract or sale of goods law.

If, as I understand all your Lordships to agree, the concept of appropriation in section 3(1) involves an element of adverse interference with or usurpation of some right of the owner, it is necessary next to consider whether that requirement is satisfied in either of these cases. As I have already said, in my view mere removal from the shelves without more is not an appropriation. Further, if a shopper with some perverted sense of humour, intending only to create confusion and nothing more both for the supermarket and for other shoppers, switches labels, I do not think that that act of label switching alone is without more an appropriation, though it is not difficult to envisage some cases of dishonest label-switching which could be. In cases such as the present, it is in truth a combination of these actions, the removal from the shelf and the switching of the labels, which evidences adverse interference with or usurpation of the right of the owner. Those acts, therefore, amount to an appropriation and if they are accompanied by proof of the other three elements to which I have referred, the offence of theft is established. Further, if they are accompanied by other acts such as putting the goods so removed and re-labelled into a receptacle, whether a trolley or the shopper's own bag or basket, proof of appropriation within section 3(1) becomes overwhelming. It is the doing of one or more acts which individually or collectively amount to such adverse interference with or usurpation of the owner's rights which constitute appropriation under section 3(1) and I do not think it matters where there is more than one such act in which order the successive acts take place, or whether there is any interval of time between them. To suggest that it matters whether the mislabelling precedes or succeeds removal from the shelves is to reduce this branch of the law to an absurdity . . .

I would answer the certified questions in this way:

'There is a dishonest appropriation for the purposes of the Theft Act 1968 where by the substitution of a price label showing a lesser price on goods for one showing a greater price, a defendant either by that act alone or by that act in conjunction with another act or other acts (whether done before or after the substitution of the labels) adversely interferes with or usurps the right of the owner to ensure that the goods concerned are sold and paid for at that greater price.'

I would dismiss these appeals."

Appeals dismissed

This requirement that the defendant must do acts objectively inconsistent with the rights of the owner is consistent with what Fletcher calls the "theory of manifest criminality."[47] We saw when examining the law of attempts how this theory led to an "objectivist orientation," with insistence that the acts must come close to the completed crime so as to be manifestly dangerous and a threat to security. This was the theory endorsed by the House of Lords in *Anderton* v. *Ryan*[48] where a distinction was drawn between "objectively innocent" acts on the one hand and "criminal" or "guilty" acts on the other.

Fletcher states that "manifestly criminal" activities must exhibit at least the following essential features. First, the criminal act must manifest, on its face, the actor's criminal purpose. And secondly, the conduct should be "of a type that is unnerving and disturbing to the community as a whole."

George P. Fletcher, Rethinking Criminal Law (1978), pp. 82–89:

"The principle of manifest criminality supported the expansion of the law to include all acts of taking that conformed to the shared paradigms of stealthful and forcible taking. A guest sneaking out with his host's dining utensils looked as much like a thief as any then punished. So, too, the customer that runs from the store with the shopkeeper chasing after him . . . The purpose of raising an issue of *animus* was to challenge the authenticity of appearances. Someone who looked like a thief in the act of taking might not have been one in fact . . . The primary inquiry was the act of larceny (theft), and only in extraordinary cases

---

[47] See below and *ante* pp. 454–464.
[48] [1985] A.C. 567.

might there have been a dispute about whether someone who acted like a thief had the 'spirit' or *animus* of a thief. Thus the law was structured so as to render intent a subsidiary issue. It was a basis for defeating the implications of the primary element of acting manifestly like a thief . . . [49] Routine business transactions, deliveries and takings by consent do not bear this imprint of larceny, and therefore . . . lack the features of manifest thievery . . . The value implicitly protected in the pattern of manifest criminality is the privacy of criminal suspects. Judges may not enquire about the accused's mental state, self-control and culpability unless they find preliminarily that the accused's conduct meets an objective standard of liability. The objective standard is the manifestly criminal act."

This whole approach adopted in *Morris* can be seen as consistent with the thrust in criminal law towards limiting criminal liability to those who *deserve* punishment, and that the causing of harm, albeit of a "second order" nature,[50] is important in the determination of the just imposition of criminal liability. The defendant by doing something manifestly observable as wrong, for example switching price labels, is doing something that is a threat to the security of the store; the interests of the store have been violated and they have sustained a "second-order harm." This approach stands in sharp contrast to "protectionalist criminology"[51] sustained by the utilitarian philosophies of punishment. Where the main interest is the protection of the property of others, then whatever measures are necessary to effect such protection become acceptable, even if this means imposing liability at an early stage when a defendant has done nothing observably wrong. Under this latter philosophy if he has a blameworthy state of mind, then for deterrent, incapacitative and rehabilitative reasons he needs punishment.

The operation of the *Morris* principle can best be seen by applying it to the facts of several of the leading cases on theft:

In *Eddy* v. *Niman* the defendant, intending to steal goods from a store, took them from a shelf and placed them in the provided receptacle. He was not liable for theft because he had done nothing manifestly wrong. He was doing precisely what the store expected all its customers to do, namely, place goods in a receptacle provided by the store.[52]

R. v. Meech [1974] Q.B. 549 (Court of Appeal, Criminal Division)

The defendant agreed to cash a cheque for P. He then planned a fake robbery with two friends whereby he would draw P's money out of the bank and take it to a prearranged destination where the fake robbery would be staged. The plan was carried out, with the defendant, Meech left as the apparent victim of a robbery.

---

[49] Ed.: This secondary role of *mens rea* is particularly important in those cases where the defendant's conduct is neutral or prima facie wrongful but he lacks the intention to assume the rights of owner. Thus the finder of "lost" property who picks it up and places it in his pocket can only be regarded as appropriating the property if he intended to assume the rights of owner, as opposed to pocketing the goods with a view to handing them in at the police station.

[50] *Ante*, p. 434.

[51] Fletcher, p. 101.

[52] (1981) 73 Cr.App.R. 237.

Roskill L.J.:

" . . . it was argued . . . that there was a misdirection in relation to appropriation. The judge said:

'As I direct you in law, the time of the appropriation was the time of the fake robbery. Up to that moment, although Meech had drawn the money from the bank, it was still open to him to honour the agreement which he had made with (P) . . . but once the fake robbery had taken place, that was no longer possible.'

It was argued that Meech alone had dishonestly misappropriated the proceeds of the cheque when he drew the money from the bank . . . We think that the judge's direction when he said that the time of the appropriation was the time of the fake robbery was right. A dishonest intention had been formed before the money was withdrawn but the misappropriation only took place when the three men divided up the money at the scene of the fake robbery. It was then that the performance of the obligation by Meech finally became impossible by the dishonest act of these three men acting in concert together."

Appeals dismissed

What would have been the position if the police had had prior notice of the fake robbery and had intervened during the robbery, but before the money was split up? It is possible here to argue that Meech, in participating in the fake robbery, was acting in a manner quite inconsistent with the owner's rights. The owner did not and would not have authorised Meech to be a willing victim to a mugging—he was therefore acting inconsistently with and in usurpation of the owner's rights. On the other hand, it is possible to contend that at this stage the defendant had not yet done anything manifestly criminal. He had drawn the money out and was dealing with it precisely as the owner would have expected. The fact that he had not pocketed it but had gone to such extraordinary lengths, objectively demonstrated his deference to, and thus non-assumption of, the owner's rights. He was not representing to others that the money was his to deal with as he liked. The fact that he was secretly a willing victim is analogous to the defendant in *Eddy* v. *Niman* who had a secret intention to steal the goods. The House of Lords in *Morris* approved the decision of *Meech* (as it did that of *Eddy* v. *Niman*) but as the trial judge in *Meech* spoke of the appropriation occurring at the time of the fake robbery, and as the Court of Appeal both approved this and then stated that the appropriation occurred at the time *when the money was divided up* at the scene of the fake robbery, it is impossible to know quite what was decided.

This last controversy leads us directly to the central outstanding problem in this area of law. The House of Lords in *Morris* approved their earlier famous decision of *Lawrence*. To some these two cases are not easy to reconcile.

Lawrence v. M.P.C. [1972] A.C. 626 (House of Lords)

Occhi, an Italian visitor who spoke little English, arrived in England at Victoria station and asked the defendant, Lawrence, a taxi driver, to take him to an address in Ladbroke Grove. The defendant informed Occhi that it was a long way and would be expensive. (In reality the correct fare would have been about 10s. 6d.) Occhi got into the taxi and offered a £1 note. Lawrence said that this was not enough and with Occhi holding out his wallet for him, helped himself to a further £6 from the wallet. He then drove Occhi to his destination. The defendant was convicted of the theft of the approximate sum of £6 contrary to section 1(1) of the Theft Act 1968 and appealed against his conviction.

Viscount Dilhorne:
"Mr. Occhi, when asked whether he had consented to the money being taken, said that he had 'permitted' . . . It may well be that when he used the word 'permitted,' he meant no more than that he had allowed the money to be taken. It certainly was not established at the trial that he had agreed to pay to the appellant a sum far in excess of the legal fare for the journey and so had consented to the acquisition by the appellant of the £6.

The main contention of the appellant in this House and in the Court of Appeal was that Mr. Occhi had consented to the taking of the £6 and that, consequently, his conviction could not stand. In my opinion, the facts of this case to which I have referred fall far short of establishing that Mr. Occhi had so consented.

Prior to the passage of the Theft Act 1968, which made radical changes in and greatly simplified the law relating to theft and some other offences, it was necessary to prove that the property alleged to have been stolen was taken 'without the consent of the owner' (Larceny Act 1916, section 1(1)).

These words are not included in section 1(1) of the Theft Act, . . .

I see no ground for concluding that the omission of the words 'without the consent of the owner' was inadvertent and not deliberate, and to read the subsection as if they were included is, in my opinion, wholly unwarranted. Parliament by the omission of these words has relieved the prosecution of the burden of establishing that the taking was without the owner's consent. That is no longer an ingredient of the offence . . .

That there was an appropriation in this case is clear. Section 3(1) states that any assumption by a person of the rights of an owner amounts to an appropriation. Here there was clearly such an assumption. . . .

Belief or the absence of belief that the owner had with such knowledge consented to the appropriation is relevant to the issue of dishonesty, not to the question whether or not there has been an appropriation. That may occur even though the owner has permitted or consented to the property being taken. So proof that Mr. Occhi had consented to the appropriation of £6 from his wallet without agreeing to paying a sum in excess of the legal fare does not suffice to show that there was not dishonesty in this case. There was ample evidence that there was."

Appeal dismissed

At one level this looks inconsistent with *Morris*. This was a routine business transaction. Occhi was consenting to Lawrence taking his property so how can it be said that the latter was doing anything inconsistent with the former's rights? The defendant was not doing anything that he had not been authorised to do and was acting with full deference to the rights of Occhi. (Of course the defendant was practising a deception and thereby obtaining money, but there is a special offence, section 15, which covers such conduct). On the other hand, however, it can be argued that Occhi in offering his wallet was only authorising the defendant to take the correct fare. In taking more he was doing what he was not authorised to do.[53] He was taking £6 that he was not entitled to take and to the taking of which Occhi, because of the fraud, had not in reality consented. It ought to be pointed out that if this latter view is to be accepted, the consequence will be that the boundaries of "objectively inconsistent acts" and "manifest criminality" will have been subtly but materially shifted. Such tests hypothesise a reasonable observer who would look at the defendant in *Eddy* v. *Niman* and say that nothing wrong had been done, but that in *Morris* there had been wrongdoing. Such an observer in *Lawrence* would not perceive anything wrong *unless he knew the correct fare to Ladbroke Grove.* In other words, for the conduct in *Lawrence* to be viewed as manifestly criminal it is necessary to endow the observer with a degree of knowledge about the transaction. But with how much knowledge should he be endowed? It cannot be full knowledge because the observer would then know of the secret intentions of all defendants, and liability could be imposed in cases such as *Eddy v. Niman,* which would bring us back full circle to imposing liability on the basis of "secret intentions."

R. v. Skipp [1975] Crim.L.R. 114 (Court of Appeal, Criminal Division)

The defendant, posing as a genuine haulage contractor, obtained instructions and collected two loads of oranges and onions to be delivered from London to Leicester. He had the intention of stealing the goods from the outset but only after loading them did he actually make off with them. An issue arose as to when the oranges and onions had been appropriated.

Held
"An assumption of the rights of an owner over property did not necessarily take place at the same time as an intent permanently to deprive the owner of it. There might be many cases in which a person having formed the intent was lawfully in possession of the goods and could not be said to have assumed the rights of an owner because he had not done something inconsistent with those rights. In the present case it was proper to take the view that up to the point when all the goods were loaded, and probably up to the point when the goods were diverted from their true destination, there had been no assumption of rights, and so there was only one appropriation."

Appeal dismissed

This case was also approved in *Morris.*[54] Prima facie it also looks difficult to reconcile with *Lawrence.* If the taxi driver in *Lawrence* was liable when he took the money from the "consenting" Italian, why was the defendant in *Skipp* not liable when he loaded the oranges and onions on

---

[53] Smith and Hogan, p. 502, fn. 1. Bingham L.J. in *Dobson* v. *General Accident Fire and Life Assurance Corp. PLC* [1989] 3 W.L.R. 1066—See *post* p. 696.

[54] See also *Fritschy* [1985] Crim.L.R. 744 where a "secret intention" to steal Krugerrands was insufficient for an appropriation; there had to be physically observable evidence of adverse interference with the rights of the owner.

to his lorry? The suppliers of the oranges and onions were no more consenting to what Skipp had in mind than was the Italian in *Lawrence* consenting to paying 12 times the proper fare. However, the cases become reconcilable if one applies a test of manifest criminality, whereby the reasonable observer is endowed with knowledge of all the surrounding circumstances and facts, but not with any knowledge of the defendant's intentions. The fare from Victoria station to Ladbroke Grove is an objective fact, knowledge of which can be attributed to the reasonable observer. The secret intentions of the haulage contractor in *Skipp* cannot be so attributed. Accordingly the court was right in *Skipp* in holding that the appropriation only occurred when the defendant did something observably wrong and inconsistent with the owner's rights by diverting the goods from their proper destination.

Two recent cases have however moved away from this whole approach and have sought to discredit the standing of *Morris*—and to the extent that they might be incompatible, have preferred *Lawrence*.

R. v. Philippou [1989] Crim.L.R. 585 (Court of Appeal, Criminal Division) (Lexis Report)

The appellant and another were sole directors of a company. They drew money from the company's bank account and purchased a block of flats in Spain for their own benefit. The appellant was convicted of theft of a debt owed by the bank to the company. On appeal it was submitted that the appellant and the other director were the sole will and mind of the company; the company was bound to consent to all that they consented to and accordingly they were not doing anything adverse to the rights of the company.

O'Connor L.J.
"It will be seen that although Lord Roskill [in *Morris*] begins by pointing out that the definition of 'appropriation' in section 3(1) of the Theft Act 1968 is not exhaustive, the rest of the passage which we have cited at length treats it as if it were exhaustive and no reference is made to the use of the word 'appropriates' in section 1(1) of the Theft Act 1968 or to the dictionary definition: the Shorter Oxford Dictionary defines it as 'to take for one's own, or to oneself.' We do not have to consider the large number of difficulties and problems created by Lord Roskill's speech. . . . We can find nothing in *R v. Morris* that persuades us that Lord Roskill considered that he was saying anything contrary to what Viscount Dilhorne had said in *Lawrence v. Metropolitan Police Commissioner* . . .
It follows that when he says: 'The concept of appropriation, in my view, involves not an act expressly or impliedly authorised by the owner, but an act by way of adverse interference with or usurpation of those rights', he cannot be understood as saying that the prosecution must prove that the appropriation alleged was without the authority of the owner, for that would be directly contrary to what was said in *Lawrence v. Metropolitan Police Commissioner* . . . We think it obvious that the House of Lords in *R v. Morris*, . . . was not inserting into the definition of theft in section 1(1) of the Theft Act 1968 after the word 'appropriates' the words 'without the authority of the owner'. The express approval by Lord Roskill of *R v. McPherson* [1973] Crim.L.R 191, and *Anderton v. Wish* 72 Cr App Rep 23, [1980], (a case in which he himself gave the judgment of the Court of Appeal) shows that the fact from which dishonesty is established

can operate to make the act relied upon as constituting appropriation adverse. That this is what Lord Roskill was saying is, we think, shown by the passage in his judgment already cited: 'It is the doing of one or more acts which individually or collectively amount to such adverse interference . . .'

Mr Thomas submitted that the appellant and Panayides, as sole shareholders and directors, were the mind and will of Sunny Tours. When they gave instructions to the bank to transfer money to Spain, the instructions were the instructions of the company, so that the company had consented to the transfer in the sense that the transfer could not be said to be adverse to any right of the company. But the order to the bank is only one part of a composite transaction. The other component is the fact that the money was being used to put the block of flats into the pockets of the appellant and Panayides through the Spanish company. That component was the fact from which the jury could infer not only that the transaction was dishonest, but was intended to deprive Sunny Tours permanently of its money . . . [T]here was no 'consent' by the company on which the appellant can rely. His position is not improved by substituting 'authority' for consent. Once the two components are put together, the drawing of the money from the bank is shown to be adverse to the rights of the company and there was an appropriation."

Appeal dismissed

Dobson v. General Accident Fire and Life Assurance Corp. PLC [1989] 3 W.L.R. 1066 (Court of Appeal, Civil Division)

The plaintiff had a home insurance policy with the defendant which covered him against loss by "theft." He advertised a Rolex watch and diamond ring for sale for £5,950. The goods were purchased by a rogue using a stolen building society cheque which was worthless. The plaintiff claimed under his insurance policy and the question was whether there had been a "theft."

Parker L.J.:
"On the basis of *Reg.* v. *Lawrence* . . . the facts of the present case appear to establish that the rogue assumed all the rights of an owner when he took or received the watch and ring from the plaintiff. That he did so dishonestly and with the intention of permanently depriving the plaintiff of it are matters beyond doubt . . .

[O]n general principles, it would in my judgment be a plain interference with or usurpation of an owner's rights by the customer if he were to remove a label which the owner had placed on goods or put another label on. It would be a trespass to goods and it would be usurping the owner's rights, for only he would have any right to do such an act and no one could contend that there was any implied consent or authority to a customer to do any such thing. There would thus be an appropriation. In the case of the customer with a perverted sense of humour there would however be no theft for there would probably be no dishonesty and certainly no intent permanently to deprive the owner of the goods themselves.

The case of the customer who simply removes goods from the shelves is of course different because the basis on which a supermarket is run is that customers certainly have the consent of the owner to take goods from the shelves and take them to the checkout point there to pay the proper price for them. Suppose, however, that there were no such consent—in, for example, a shop where goods on display were to be taken from the shelves only by the attendant. In such a case a customer who took from the shelves would clearly be usurping the right of the owner. Indeed he would be doing so if he did no more than move an item from one place on a shelf to another. The only difference appears to be that in the one case there is a consent and in the other there is not. Since, however, it was held in *Reg.* v. *Lawrence* that consent is not relevant to appropriaton there must, one would have supposed, be no difference between the two cases on that aspect of the offence . . .

After anxious consideration I have reached the conclusion that whatever *Reg.* v. *Morris* did decide it cannot be regarded as having overruled the very plain decision in *Reg.* v. *Lawrence* that appropriation can occur even if the owner consents and that *Reg.* v. *Morris* itself makes it plain that it is no defence to say that the property passed under a voidable contract . . .

[*Reg.* v. *Skipp* (*ante*, p. 694)] can in my view only be reconciled with *Reg.* v. *Lawrence* (*Alan*) [1972] A.C. 626 on the basis that there was much more than mere consent of the owner. There was express authority, indeed instruction to collect the goods. It could not therefore be said that the defendant was assuming any rights. Whatever his secret intentions he was, until he diverted, exercising the owner's right on his instructions and on his behalf. *Reg.* v. *Fritschy* was a somewhat similar case . . .

Here, as in *Reg.* v. *Skipp*, what the defendant did was expressly authorised, i.e. there was more than mere consent. On this basis the decision can be reconciled with both *Reg.* v. *Lawrence* and *Reg.* v. *Morris*.

Returning now to the present case the insurers' contention that there was no theft is based on consent and the fact that there was a clear section 15(1) offence, both of which are negatived as answers to appropriation by *Reg.* v. *Lawrence*, and the fact that the contract of sale between the plaintiff and the rogue was voidable only and not void which is not relevant according to *Reg.* v. *Morris*.

If consent and the existence of a voidable contract under which property passes are irrelevant, there was in my judgment a plain interference with or usurpation of the plaintiff's rights.

I am fully conscious of the fact that in so concluding I may be said not to be applying *Reg.* v. *Morris*. This may be so, but in the light of the difficulties inherent in the decision, the very clear decision in *Reg.* v. *Lawrence* (*Alan*) [1972] A.C. 626 and the equally clear statement in *Reg.* v. *Morris* (*David*) [1984] A.C. 320 that the question whether a contract is void or only voidable is irrlevant, I have been unable to reach any other conclusion. I would therefore dismiss the appeal.

Bingham L.J.

" . . . It therefore appears that A commits theft if he dishonestly assumes any of the rights of an owner over B's property intending to deprive B of that property permanently.

This simple analysis may be applied to the everyday example of a customer selecting goods from a supermarket shelf and putting them in the wire basket or trolley provided. The goods on the shelves belong to the supermarket. They continue to belong to the supermarket until paid for by a customer: *Lacis* v. *Cashmarts* [1969] 2 Q.B. 400. The customer assumes some of the rights of an owner when he takes them into his (or her) possession and exercises control over them by putting them in a basket or trolley. The customer, not intending to return the goods to the supermarket, intends to deprive the supermarket of the goods permanently. In the ordinary case the customer will honestly intend to pay the marked price for the goods at the cash desk, so no offence of theft will be committed. But a customer who dishonestly intends not to pay the marked price will be guilty of theft, at the time of dishonest appropriation. On this analysis it is irrelevant that the supermarket displays the goods for sale and invites, perhaps even tempts, customers to put them in their basket or trolleys. The acid test is whether when doing so the customer acts honestly or dishonestly . . .

I do not find it easy to reconcile this ruling of Viscount Dilhorne, which was

as I understand central to the answer which the House of Lords gave to the certified question, with the reasoning of the House in *R* v. *Morris*. Since, however,
the House in *R* v. *Morris* considered that there had plainly been an appropriation in *Lawrence's* case, this must (I think) have been because the Italian student, although he had permitted or allowed his money to be taken, had not in
truth consented to the taxi driver taking anything in excess of the correct fare.
This is not a wholly satisfactory reconciliation, since it might be said that a
supermarket consents to customers taking goods from it shelves only when they
honestly intend to pay and not otherwise. On the facts of the present case, however, it can be said, by analogy with *Lawrence's* case, that although the plaintiff
permitted and allowed his property to be taken by the rogue, he had not in truth
consented to the rogue becoming owner without giving a valid draft drawn by
the building society for the price. On this basis I conclude that the plaintiff is
able to show an appropriation sufficient to satisfy s 1(1) of the 1968 Act when
the rogue accepted delivery of the articles."

Appeal dismissed

It is submitted that both these decisions are unfortunate. In *Philippou*
the defendant and his co-director were the sole shareholders of the
company and so in withdrawing the money for their own purposes they
were not doing any unauthorised act. The only thing they were doing
wrong was presumably defrauding their creditors and the only dishonesty that existed was in relation to such creditors. But they were not
charged with any offence in relation to their creditors—say, an offence
under the company law legislation such as fraudulent trading contrary
to section 458 of the Companies Act 1985 (or, perhaps, with conspiracy
to defraud). Instead, they were charged with theft from their own company. If the criminal law is to perform its symbolic and expressive function of condemning certain activities as wrong, it is important that
labels borne by crimes bear some approximation to their content and
that persons be charged with offences that describe what they did
wrong. What is happening in cases such as *Philippou* is that the law of
theft is being used as a rubbish bin into which too many diverse cases
of dishonesty are being swept.

   Dobson is a further sorry step away from *Morris*. It confirms, following
Lawrence, that there is now an almost complete overlap between theft
and section 15. Virtually every time a defendant obtains property by
deception there can be a charge of theft.[55] In addition, Parker L.J. has
muddied the waters by introducing a distinction between cases where
there is "mere consent" (can be an appropriation) and those where
there is "express authorisation" (cannot be an appropriation). It hardly
seems appropriate to introduce such illusory distinctions that will pose
immense interpretive problems to the courts in the years ahead (when
does consent become authorisation?), and which appear to have no
sound rationalisation and, in fact, serve no useful purpose whatsoever.

---

[55] The overlap is probably not complete. Presumably there could be an offence of obtaining by
deception contrary to s. 15 where there was no appropriation because there had been "express authorisation."

The main objection however lies in the ruling in *Dobson* that an appropriation can take place where the defendant does nothing *manifestly* inconsistent with the other's rights. It was argued earlier in this chapter that such a requirement ought to be necessary in all theft cases. This has always been the position, even before the Theft Act 1968.[56] The bulk of judicial authority, including the leading House of Lords decision, *Morris*, still supports this view—and it is to be hoped that this view will ultimately prevail.

Another problem that has arisen is whether there can be an appropriation by a defendant who acts inconsistently with an owner's rights, but is not in a position to exercise power or control over the property. Can a defendant sitting in a pub in Leicester appropriate the crown jewels (situated in the Tower of London) by "selling" them to the mythical, ever-gullible foreign tourist?

R. v. Pitham and Hehl (1976) 65 Cr.App.R. 45 (Court of Appeal, Criminal Division)

A man called Millman, knowing that his friend McGregor was in prison, decided to take advantage of his friend's hapless plight and steal his furniture from his house. He took round the two appellants and sold them some furniture. Millman was convicted of stealing[57] the furniture and the two appellants of handling stolen goods. They argued that their handling was still "in the course of stealing"; the goods were not yet stolen and therefore they were not handling stolen goods.

Lawton L.J.:
"What was the appropriation in this case? The jury found that the two appellants had handled the property *after* Millman had stolen it . . . What had Millman done? He had assumed the rights of the owner. He had done that when he took the two appellants to 20 Parry Road, showed them the property and invited them to buy what they wanted. He was then acting as the owner. He was then, in the words of the statute, 'assuming the rights of the owner.' The moment he did that he appropriated McGregor's goods to himself. The appropriation was complete. After this appropriation had been completed there was no question of these two appellants taking part, in the words of the section 22, in dealing with the goods 'in the course of the stealing.' "

Appeal dismissed

Smith and Hogan, Criminal Law, 6th ed. (1988), pp. 497–499:

"D may appropriate property where he is not in possession of it and does not seek to take possession of it . . . Suppose, then, that D sells the crown jewels, securely guarded in the Tower of London, to a gullible tourist. A clear case of deception but has D appropriated the crown jewels? . . . P's (the victim in *Pitham*) rights (are not) usurped in the sense that P's title to the furniture is lost

---

[56] J.C. Smith [1989] Crim.L.R. 587, 588.
[57] In fact the conviction was for burglary. This offence is committed in several ways but in this case it was by entering a building as a trespasser and committing theft therein. (s.9(1)(*b*): see *post*, p. 780.)

but his rights are clearly interfered with and that interference arises because E (the rogue, Millman) has purported to assume P's rights as owner . . . s.3(1) says that any assumption of the rights of an owner (and to purport to sell another's property would appear to be such an assumption) 'amounts to' an appropriation. 'Amounts to' here seems to mean 'is.' There would seem to be no warrant for qualifying the wording by some such requirement that the assumption must in fact threaten P's title to, or enjoyment of, the property.

If it is the case, as it is argued here that it is, that D may appropriate property without ever having or acquiring possession then some strange results ensue. D intends to hijack a lorry containing video-recorders if he can find a buyer for the goods. E agrees to buy them. D has now appropriated the goods though the lorry is in Nottingham and he is in Leeds and much needs to be done before he can get his hands on the goods."

Glanville Williams, Textbook of Criminal Law, 2nd ed. (1983), p. 765:

"But to say that X would be guilty of theft merely by making the offer is jurisprudentially preposterous. How could X's offer, made in respect of something not in his possession, not operating to transfer the ownership of the thing and not followed by a taking of possession, intelligibly be called an appropriation? . . . But whereas the owner has a right against others that they shall not deliver his thing to a third person (because that involves a physical interference with it, which is a tort), he has no general right in the strict sense that they shall not contract to sell it, or to purport to pass ownership in it. He does not need such a right, because other people generally do him no harm in offering his goods for sale, and *cannot* pass ownership in them except by his authority. Their purported exercise of the power is not an infringement of the rights of an owner; it is merely an unsuccessful and wholly nugatory effort to usurp one of the powers of the owner. The purported offer of sale by X was, so far as the rights of the owner were concerned, so much wind. A stranger who thus uses empty words of sale does not commit a tort against the owner, unless he causes possession of the thing to be taken; and there is no reason why he should be convicted of stealing it."

The latter view does seem the more persuasive. Under the Smith and Hogan proposal, persons would be guilty of the full crime of theft when, viewed from another perspective, they appear not even to have done enough to be liable for an attempt!

Indeed, it is difficult to see how there can be any scope at all for the crime of attempted theft under their proposal. Doing any act that was "more than merely preparatory" to theft would itself amount to an appropriation.

It is submitted that there can be no manifestly criminal act or act by way of objective interference with the owner's rights unless the actor is in a position to threaten the owner's rights. Sitting in a pub offering to sell the crown jewels poses no threat whatsoever and therefore does not amount to an assumption of the rights of the owner. The law of incitement, conspiracy and attempt exists to cover such cases (assuming the parties have done enough to come within the scope of any of these offences). On the other hand, the rogue Millman in *Pitham* was in a position to threaten his friend's rights. His was an act of adverse interference with the rights of owner and was an assumption of the rights of owner.[58]

Bank accounts

Many of the more recent reported cases concern theft and other property offences where the victim is a bank, or a person who has had money wrongfully transferred from a bank account. Accordingly, a brief separate word needs to be added concerning appropriation from bank accounts.

The first point to be noted is that when a customer places money in a bank account, the bank owns that money, but owes the customer a debt.

Accordingly, two situations need to be distinguished. First, what is the position if a customer with no funds in his account and no overdraft facility, writes a cheque, backed by a cheque card, on that account? The bank, because of the use of the cheque card, is forced to honour the cheque. Has the customer appropriated property?

R. v. Navvabi [1986] 3 All E.R. 102 (Court of Appeal, Criminal Division)

Lord Lane C.J.:

"[T]he matter . . . turns essentially on the construction of s.3(1): was use of the cheque cards to guarantee payment of a cheque delivered to the casino and drawn on an account with inadequate funds an assumption of the rights of the bank and thus appropriation? In our judgment it was not. That use of the cheque card and delivery of the cheque did no more than give the casino a contractual right as against the bank to be paid a specified sum from the bank's funds on presentation of the guaranteed cheque. That was not in itself an assumption of the rights of the bank to that part of the bank's funds to which the sum specified in the cheque corresponded: there was therefore no appropriation by the drawer either on delivery of the cheque to the casino or when the funds were ultimately transferred to the casino."

Secondly, what is the position if a defendant writes a forged cheque, or in some other way gets money transferred from another person's bank account into his own? This is theft of the debt, or part of it, owed by the bank to the other person—and as we shall see, debts are "property" capable of being stolen. But when would the appropriation occur in such a case? In *Chan Man-sin* the Privy Council held that "one who draws, presents and negotiates a cheque on a particular bank account is assuming the rights of the owner of the credit in the account or (as the case may be) of the pre-negotiated right to draw on the account up to the agreed figure."[59] This was qualified in the following case.

---

[58] It ought to be pointed out that Glanville Williams not only dismisses the Smith and Hogan "crown jewels argument," but rejects the decision in *Pitham* on the ground that "appellate judges will always be subject to an irresistible impulse to lay down wrong law in cases like this." (*Textbook*, p. 764).

[59] v. *Att.-Gen. of Hong Kong* (1988) 86 Cr.App.R. 303, 306.

R v. Governor of Pentonville Prison, ex parte Osman (1990) 90 Cr.App.R. 281 (Queen's Bench Divisional Court)

The applicant sought *habeas corpus* pursuant to section 8 of the Fugitive Offenders Act 1967. It was alleged that he, as chairman of X company, had been bribed in Hong Kong to make loans above authorised amounts to the Carrian group of companies. One alleged method was the sending of a telex to a New York bank instructing payment from X's account to the account of one of the Carrian companies. This was theft of the debt owed by the New York bank to X company. The applicant however argued that the Hong Kong courts would have no jurisdiction to hear the case as the theft, if committed, took place in New York.

Lloyd L.J.:
"[Counsel for Osman] argued that the theft of the chose in action took place in the United States when BMFL's account was debited, and not before. That was the moment of appropriation. The dealing ticket, confirmation slip and telex were the means whereby the theft was carried out. The theft was not completed until the account was debited . . .
In *R. v. Morris* . . . the House of Lords made it clear that it is not necessary for an appropriation that the defendant assume all rights of an owner. It is enough that he should assume any of the owner's rights . . . If so, then one of the plainest rights possessed by the owner of the chose in action in the present case must surely have been the right to draw on the account in question . . . So far as the customer is concerned, he has a right as against the bank to have his cheques met. It is that right which the defendant assumes by presenting a cheque, or by sending a telex instruction without authority. The act of sending the telex is therefore the act of theft itself, and not a mere attempt. It is the last act which the defendant has to perform and not a preparatory act. It would not matter if the account were never in fact debited . . .
[Following *Morris*] we would hold that a defendant 'usurps' the customer's rights when he, without the customer's authority, dishonestly issues the cheque drawn on the customer's account. If 'adverse interference' adds anything to usurpation, then he also thereby adversely interferes with the customer's rights. The theft is complete in law, even though it may be said that it is not complete in fact until the account is debited . . . [W]e would hold that Hong Kong was the place of appropriation."

Bona fide purchasers

Section 3(2) provides a special exemption for the bona fide purchaser for value of stolen goods. If a person bought goods at a reasonable price not knowing they were stolen and then later discovered they were, but decided to keep them, this would (without section 3(2)) come within the latter half of section 3(1), namely, he would have come by the property innocently without stealing it but would be appropriating it when he decided to keep it. The Criminal Law Revision Committee specifically proposed this exception on the ground that while there was a case for the imposition of criminal liability in such cases, "on the whole it seems to us that, whatever view is taken of the buyer's moral duty, the law would be too strict if it made him guilty of theft."[60]

---

[60] C.L.R.C., 8th Report, *Theft and Related Offences* (1966) Cmnd. 2977, para. 37.

3. Property

Theft Act 1968, section 4

"4.—(1) 'Property' includes money and all other property, real or personal, including things in action and other intangible property.

(2) A person cannot steal land, or things forming part of land and severed from it by him or by his directions, except in the following cases, that is to say—

(a) when he is a trustee or personal representative, or is authorised by power of attorney, or as liquidator of a company, or otherwise, to sell or dispose of land belonging to another, and he appropriates the land or anything forming part of it by dealing with it in breach of the confidence reposed in him; or

(b) when he is not in possession of the land and appropriates anything forming part of the land by severing it or causing it to be severed or after it has been severed; or

(c) when, being in possession of the land under a tenancy, he appropriates the whole or part of any fixture or structure let to be used with the land.

For purposes of this subsection 'land' does not include incorporeal hereditaments; 'tenancy' means a tenancy for years or any less period and includes an agreement for such a tenancy, but a person who after the end of a tenancy remains in possession as statutory tenant or otherwise is to be treated as having possession under the tenancy, and 'let' shall be construed accordingly.

(3) A person who picks mushrooms growing wild on any land, or who picks flowers, fruit or foliage from a plant growing wild on any land does not (although not in possession of the land) steal what he picks, unless he does it for reward or for sale or other commercial purpose.

For purposes of this subsection 'mushroom' includes any fungus, and 'plant' includes any shrub or tree.

(4) Wild creatures, tamed or untamed, shall be regarded as property; but a person cannot steal a wild creature not tamed nor ordinarily kept in captivity, or the carcase of any such creature, unless either it has been reduced into possession by or on behalf of another person and possession of it has not since been lost or abandoned, or another person is in course of reducing it into possession."

Theft is an offence against property and inevitably the question arises as to the meaning of "property." Section 4(1) provides an extremely wide definition that property includes:

1. money
2. all real property: *i.e.*, land and things attached to the land such as houses. However, the breadth of this provision is greatly limited by sections 4(2), (3) and (4). Section 4(2) isolates the only circumstances in which land and the things attached to the land may be stolen. Section 4(3) deals with the circumstances in which things growing wild on land may be stolen. Section 4(4) deals similarly with wild animals.[61]

---

[61] For detail on these provisions, see Smith and Hogan, pp. 506–509; Smith, *The Law of Theft*, 5th ed. (1984), pp. 47–54; Griew, *The Theft Acts 1968 and 1978*, 5th ed. (1986) 13–17.

3. all personal property: *i.e.* moveable property.[62] These concepts include:

4. things in action: a thing in action is non-physical property; one's rights in it can only be enforced by a legal action. The best example of such a "thing in action" is a debt. We saw above that a bank owns the money in an account but owes a debt to the account holder. This debt is a thing in action; it is property and can be stolen.[63] Other examples of things in action are copyright, trademark and shares in a company.

5. other intangible property: this is also non-physical property in which one can have a legal interest: for example, statute has declared that a patent is intangible property but not a thing in action.[64]

Three areas of dispute are of interest and deserve consideration.

Electricity

In *Low* v. *Blease*[65] it was held that electricity is not property for the purposes of theft. Section 13 of the Theft Act creates a special offence of abstracting electricity, carrying a maximum of five years' imprisonment.

Trade secrets

In *Oxford* v. *Moss*[66] a University student acquired a proof of one of his examination papers. He read the questions; he never intended to deprive the University of the piece of paper on which the questions were printed. He was charged with theft of intangible property, namely, the confidential information contained in the examination questions. On appeal it was held that this was not intangible property within the meaning of section 4.

Edward Griew, The Theft Acts 1968 and 1978, 5th ed. (1986), p. 22:

"It is probably a good guess that few of the people responsible for the Act contemplated trade secrets (secret industrial processes, for example) as 'property' within the meaning of section 4(1) or as capable of being stolen. During the debates on the Bill, however, Lord Wilberforce took a wide view of the word 'property' as including 'things like business secrets.' He did not pursue in detail the analysis required to demonstrate that the law of theft has become an effective weapon against modern forms of industrial espionage. Probably it has not. One can in popular parlance describe a person who 'bugs' a private conversation or photocopies a confidential document as 'stealing' a secret. But to

---

[62] Gray, *Law of Personal Property*: "Personal property, of course, includes both tangible chattels and choses in action . . . To this must be added growing annual crops . . . (and) leasehold interests in land." (p. 2).

[63] *Attorney General's Reference (No. 1 of 1983)* [1985] Q.B. 182.

[64] Patents Act 1977, s.30.

[65] (1975) 119 S.J. 695.

[66] (1978) 68 Cr.App.R. 183.

achieve that result in law would involve reading the Act in a very robust way for the purpose of producing a dramatic new offence not hinted at by the Committee. The Act is not in fact the appropriate instrument to deal with this specialised kind of mischief. The short way of disposing of an argument to the contrary is to deny that trade secrets are 'property' within the Act."

Following this, information stored on a computer is similarly not property and therefore cannot be stolen, although here a charge of abstracting electricity contrary to section 13 may be possible. It has been said that "the traditional lawyer will feel that to speak of a secret as though it were a thing is too metaphysical."[67] It will however seem even more odd and metaphysical to a jury that copyright is intangible property but trade secrets are not!

The human body and its parts

Can one steal bits of the human body? To answer this one needs to distinguish live from dead persons.

Dealing first with live persons it has been held that blood,[68] urine[69] and hair[70] are property capable of being stolen from a person. Clearly, once these samples have been removed from the body and stored in, say, a sperm or blood bank, they possess all the attributes of personal property falling within section 4(1). Perhaps it is academic to discuss whether the severing of limbs from the body (for example, when the kidnappers of Paul Getty's grandson severed his ear) can be theft—as it would amount to a far more serious offence against the person, probably section 18 of the Offences against the Person Act 1861—and it is simply ludicrous to think of this as an offence against property.

Theft from corpses also raises problems, as a commonly accepted view is that a corpse is not property and nobody can have a proprietary right or interest in it. For the purposes of the criminal law this is clearly outmoded. Take for instance, a cadaver "owned" by a University Medical Faculty. If the University does not "own" the cadaver under the property law, it does have a bailment of the corpse,[71] or, at least, "control" over it (which, as we shall see, suffices for the purposes of theft) and it does possess all the other necessary attributes to be classified as personal property capable of being stolen.

A. T. H. Smith, "Stealing the Body and its Parts" [1976] Crim.L.R. 622, p. 626:

"Perhaps the strongest argument against a reappraisal of the no-property rule at this stage is that the medical profession is in practice the group most likely to

---

[67] Glanville Williams, *Textbook of Criminal Law*, 2nd ed. (1983), p. 717.
[68] *Rothery* [1976] R.T.R. 550.
[69] *Welsh* [1974] R.T.R. 478.
[70] *Herbert* (1960) 25 J. Cr.L. 163.
[71] D. Brahams, "Bailment and Donation of Parts of the Human Body" (1989) 139 New L.J. 803.

fall foul of it. It has recently been held that it is an offence under section 1(4) of the Human Tissue Act 1961, punishable by unlimited fine or imprisonment, for a person other than a full registered medical practitioner to remove part of a dead body. It could be argued that this provides ample protection against unauthorised tampering with therapeutically useful corpses without at the same time jeopardising the medical profession. Indeed doctors might be forgiven for thinking that the law has already proved itself hopelessly slow in responding to urgent medical problems. That a fresh obstacle should be raised at this stage is but a further example of an unnecessarily legalistic and obstructive approach.

In reply, the following points could be made. It is precisely the advance in medical knowledge, which has added a new dimension to the usefulness of the deceased human body, that necessitates a fresh look at the law. A rule premised on medical knowledge not much more advanced than that of Harvey scarcely commands much respect. As has been pointed out, the rule is in any case an anomaly of uncertain ambit, and although a prosecution for theft is unlikely, it cannot be ruled out altogether. It is in just such emotively charged areas that a private prosecution is an ever present possibility."

4. Belonging to Another

Theft is an interference with the proprietary rights of another. One of the central problems here has been identifying who has sufficient "rights" in property to be afforded protection by the criminal law. The owner clearly needs protection—but ownership is only one form of proprietary right and others, particularly those with possession of property, need similar protection. Accordingly, section 5 of the Theft Act 1968 spells out the situations in which property is regarded as "belonging to another." It must be stressed that in some of these situations the property does not *really* (under the civil law) belong to anyone else— but someone else has an interest thought to be worth protecting and therefore the property is artificially *deemed* to belong to that person. Section 5 lays down five rather different situations where property "belongs to another" and it is convenient to deal with each of these separately.

(1) Theft Act 1968, section 5(1)

"Property shall be regarded as belonging to any person having possession or control of it, or having in it any proprietary right or interest (not being an equitable interest arising only from an agreement to transfer or grant an interest)."

(a) *Possession or control*

"Possession" is a complex legal concept which involves both physical control and an intention to possess. "Control," on the other hand, signifies no more than its literal meaning, namely, physical control—and therefore covers many of the cases that could be described as possession, making it unnecessary to draw any distinction between the two concepts. Thus a customer in a shop examining a book has control of the book; a diner in a restaurant has control over the cutlery with which he is eating; a golf club has either possession or control (it does not matter which) over balls lost on its golf course[72]; a person has possession or control over any articles in his house or on his land even if he has forgotten or does not know they are there.[73]

Theft by owner

The law of theft is designed to protect a variety of interests in property. The result is that theft can be committed by a person with an interest in the property against another with an interest (even a lesser interest) in the same property. In particular, this means that the real owner may be guilty of stealing his own property from another who has possession or control of that property. For instance, if a defendant pawns his watch as security for a loan and then surreptitiously takes his watch back, he would be appropriating property (the watch) belonging to another (the pawnbroker, who at a minimum has possession or control over the watch).

R. v. Turner (No. 2) [1971] 1 W.L.R. 901 (Court of Appeal, Criminal Division)

The defendant took his car to a garage to be repaired. The repairs were almost completed and the car parked outside in the road. The defendant, without telling the garage or offering to pay for the repairs, drove his car away. He was convicted of theft and appealed against his conviction.

Lord Parker C.J.:
"[T]he judge directed the jury that they were not concerned in any way with lien and the sole question was whether Mr. Brown [the garage proprietor] had possession or control. This court is quite satisfied that there is no ground whatever for qualifying the words 'possession or control' in any way. It is sufficient if it is found that the person from whom the property is taken . . . was at the time in fact in possession or control. At the trial there was a long argument whether that possession or control must be lawful, it being said that by reason of the fact that this car was subject to a hire-purchase agreement, Mr. Brown could never even as against the appellant obtain lawful possession or control . . . As I have said, this court is quite satisfied that the judge was quite correct in telling the jury that they need not bother about lien, and that they need not bother about hire-purchase agreements. The only question was: was Mr. Brown in fact in possession or control?"

Appeal dismissed

Glanville Williams describes this case as "one of the most extraordinary cases decided under the Theft Act" and states that "it is hard to believe that the decision represents the law."[74] The gist of his argument is that if one ignores the lien, which the jury were instructed to do, the defendant had a right to repossess his car whenever he liked and one should

[72] *Hibbert* v. *McKiernan* [1948] 2 K.B. 142.
[73] *Woodman* [1974] Q.B. 754.
[74] *Textbook of Criminal Law* 2nd ed. (1983), 749, 750.

not be held guilty of theft for doing what one has a right to do. It is submitted that this criticism is misplaced. The Theft Act has chosen to protect a wide range of proprietary interests, including possession and control—irrespective of the rights or interests of the defendant. In this case there can be little doubt that the defendant appropriated (acted inconsistently with the rights of Mr. Brown) property (the car) belonging to another (to Mr. Brown by virtue of his possession or control). In most cases defendants with greater property rights than their victims, such as rights to repossession of their property, will not be acting dishonestly. Generally, the owner who takes back his own property would not be condemned by ordinary community standards as dishonest[75] and would thus not be convicted of theft. But the defendant in *Turner* (*No. 2*) surreptitiously removed his car without paying for the repairs and without the garage proprietor knowing his name or address so as to be able to send him his bill. In such a case a conviction for theft, based on the ordinary meaning of the words "possession or control," does seem more appropriate than an acquittal based on a technical analysis of the meaning of a "bailment at will," which is what Mr. Brown had at civil law if he did not have a lien. The short point is surely that whatever else he might have had at civil law, Mr. Brown clearly had possession or control of the car and the defendant acted dishonestly and satisfied the remaining elements of the offence of theft. A conviction was inevitable.[76]

(b) *Proprietary Right or Interest*

The most obvious instance of a proprietary right or interest is that of ownership. Ownership is a proprietary right and thus property belongs to an owner. With co-owners of property, each owner has a proprietary right and therefore one co-owner can steal from another.[77]

However, there are interests in property less than ownership that qualify as "proprietary rights or interests" and the interests may be either legal or equitable. For instance, the garage proprietor in *Turner* (*No. 2*) had a lien on the car which is a legal right. (As seen above, however, the case was not decided on that basis.) The beneficiary of a trust has an equitable interest in the trust property. However, section 5(1) specifically excludes "equitable interests arising only from an agreement to transfer or grant an interest." With some contracts, for example, contracts to buy land or shares, the person contracting to purchase acquires an equitable interest, while the other party retains legal ownership. If that legal owner then sells to a third party he does not

---

[75] *Post*, p. 725.
[76] Cf. *Meredith* [1973] Crim.L.R. 253 where a defendant who had had his car towed away to a police yard took his car back without paying any fee. It was held that a charge of theft was improper as "The police had no right, as against the owner to retain it." This Crown Court decision cannot be accepted. The police had possession or control of the car; it therefore "belonged" to them for the purposes of theft. The only proper route to an acquittal on these facts should have been lack of dishonesty.
[77] *Bonner* [1970] 1 W.L.R. 838.

commit theft as the original contracting party only has an "equitable interest arising from an agreement . . . " which is not sufficient for the property to be regarded as belonging to him.

It is here that we see the sharpest tensions because the criminal law, with its traditional emphasis on blame and harm, is having to define part of the harm component in terms of the civil law. We saw in the introduction to this chapter[78] that there is a conflict between two views. On the one hand, there is the view that criminal liability should only be imposed on the blameworthy who cause harm and that this determination should be divorced from technical analyses of the civil law. This view tends to maintain that words in the Theft Acts be given their "ordinary meanings" by ordinary folk, the jury. This was the view adopted in *Turner* (*No. 2*) where the judge refused to direct the jury in terms of liens. On the other hand, it is difficult to exclude the civil law, as theft is a property offence and some other person must have a legally recognised interest in the property. It seems ludicrous to convict a defendant of theft if nobody else has any such interest in the property because as we saw, an owner is generally free to use, enjoy and abuse his own property to his heart's content. When adopting this latter view judges tend to turn to the civil law, particularly the law of property, contract and quasi-contract in order to determine whether there is any other person with a proprietary right or interest in the property.

Powell v. McRae [1977] Crim.L.R. 571: (Queen's Bench Divisional Court)

The defendant, a turnstile operator at Wembley Stadium when admission was by ticket only, accepted a £2 bribe from a member of the public and allowed him to enter the ground without a ticket. The defendant was charged with theft of the £2, the property of his employers. The justices ruled that as the money had been received in the course of employment, it belonged to the employers. The defendant was convicted.

Held,
"The defendant was no more than the recipient of a bribe; that by no stretch of language could it be said that the money 'belonged to' the employers; that, therefore, the definition of theft in section 1 of the Theft Act 1968 was not satisfied."

Appeal allowed

The defendant's criminal liability thus depended on whether money accepted as a bribe during the course of employment vested in the employer or not.

The passing of property

Even greater problems have arisen with regard to the passing of property. The legal phrase "passing of property" is used to signify

---

[78] *Ante*, p. 682.

ownership passing from one person to another. When goods are bought
and paid for in a shop "property passes" from the shop to the purchaser. The basic rule at civil law is that property passes when the parties intend it to pass. For example, in a supermarket parties are deemed
normally to intend that property should pass only on payment of the
goods.

In some cases however the transaction might be defective because
one of the parties might have made a mistake. Such a mistake might
prevent property passing.

The basic rule here is simple:

(a) if one of the parties has made a *fundamental mistake*, the transaction
    is rendered *void* and property does *not* pass pursuant to a void
    transaction. A void transaction is a nullity. It is as though it never
    happened and obviously ownership cannot be transferred pur-
    suant to nothing. A mistake as to identity is an example of a funda-
    mental mistake.

(b) Lesser of *non-fundamental mistakes*, however, can render contracts
    merely *voidable* and property *does* pass pursuant to a voidable
    transaction. A voidable transaction is one that is valid until one of
    the parties "avoids" the transaction. An example here would be a
    mistake as to the quality of the goods being sold.

The requirement that at the time of the appropriation the property
must "belong to another" means that the imposition of criminal liability and punishment could depend entirely on whether property
passed pursuant to a transaction.

Kaur v. Chief Constable of Hampshire [1981] 1 W.L.R. 578 (Queen's Bench Divisional Court)

The defendant chose a pair of shoes from a rack of shoes marked at £6.99 per
pair. One shoe was marked at £6.99 and the other at £4·99. Without concealing
either label she took the shoes to the cashier hoping to be charged the lower
price—which she was. She paid £4·99, placed the shoes in her shopping bag and
left the store. She was convicted of theft and appealed.

Lord Lane C.J.:
"She certainly assumed the rights of an owner when, having paid, she took
the shoes in the paper bag from the cashier in order to go home. I do not pause
to inquire at the moment whether 'appropriation' is an accurate description of
what she did. There is no doubt that she intended permanently to deprive the
owner of the shoes. So the only matter in issue in this case is whether the prosecution had proved that at the moment she took the shoes out of the shop the
ownership of the shoes was still in the shop. If so, the offence was proved; if
not, it was not proved.

There is ample authority for the proposition that, so far as supermarkets, at
any rate, are concerned, and in so far as an ordinary transaction in a supermarket is concerned, the intention of the parties, under section 18 of the Sale of
Goods Act 1979, is that the ownership of the goods should pass on payment by
the customer of the price to the cashier . . .

Prima facie, then, when the defendant picked up the shoes to take them home, she was already the owner of the shoes. They did not then belong to somebody else, and she was not intending to deprive the owner of them.

But the prosecutor contends that the apparent contract between the shop and the defendant was no contract at all, was void, and that therefore, despite the payment made by the defendant, the ownership of the shoes never passed to the defendant, and the offence was accordingly made out . . .

The mistake here was the cashier's, induced by the wrong marking on the goods as to the proper price of these goods. It was not to the nature of the goods or the identity of the buyer. Speaking for myself, I find it very difficult to see how this could be described as the sort of mistake which was so fundamental as to destroy the validity of the contract. It was in essence, as Lloyd J. pointed out in argument, very little, if at all, different from a mistake as to quality. A mistake as to quality has never been held sufficiently fundamental so as to avoid a contract. The cashier was in effect thinking that these were £4·99 quality shoes, when in fact they were £6·99 quality shoes. Consequently in my judgment the prosecution failed to prove that this alleged contract was void. If it was merely voidable it had certainly not been avoided when the time came for the defendant to pick up the shoes and go."

Appeal allowed

R. v. Williams [1980] Crim.L.R. 589 (Court of Appeal, Criminal Division)

The defendant, a schoolboy, went to Stanley Gibbons and purchased some obsolete Yugoslav dinar for £7.00. He then went to the *bureau de change* at a department store and cashed them in for some £107. He was convicted of theft and appealed.

Held, " . . . As to theft . . . The notes were not still valid. That was a fundamental mistake operating on the mind of the cashier handing over the money. The contract was void ab initio. When the money was handed over it was the property of the store throughout and was appropriated by the appellant when he put it in his pocket. The dishonest intention was plainly to deprive the owner permanently of the money, given the chance. The offence of theft was made out."

Appeal dismissed

The imposition of criminal liability thus depends on fine points of civil law. However, it is far from clear that the courts are even applying the civil law principles correctly. For example, Smith has argued that the decision in *Williams* is wrong because the contract was voidable and not void and thus ownership in the money did pass to the schoolboy and he was, therefore, appropriating property belonging to himself.[79] Similar criticism has been levelled at the famous case of *Gilks*[80] where a punter at the races was mistakenly paid out £106 even though his horse came nowhere. It was held that the bookmaker in paying out the money in the mistaken belief that a certain horse had won was making a fundamental mistake. Accordingly, property did not pass and so when the

---

[79] Commentary to *Williams* [1980] Crim.L.R. 590.
[80] [1972] 1 W.L.R. 1341.

punter decided to keep the money he was appropriating property that did still belong to another. This case has been roundly castigated for getting the civil law wrong.[81] It is a controversial matter that the imposition of criminal liability should depend on fine points of civil law—but when the courts misapply that civil law, it becomes a matter of utmost concern.

R. v. Morris, Anderton v. Burnside [1984] A.C. 320 (House of Lords)

(The facts are given above, *ante* p. 688)

Lord Roskill:

"*Kaur* . . . is a difficult case. I am disposed to agree . . . that it was wrongly decided but without going into further detail I respectfully suggest that it is on any view wrong to introduce into this branch of the criminal law questions whether particular contracts are void or voidable on the ground of mistake or fraud or whether any mistake is sufficiently fundamental to vitiate a contract. These difficult questions should so far as possible be confined to those fields of law to which they are immediately relevant and I do not regard them as relevant questions under the Theft Act 1968."

R. v. Walker [1984] Crim.L.R. 112 (Court of Appeal, Criminal Division)

The appellant sold an unsatisfactory video recorder which was returned to him for repair. After some time the purchaser issued a summons claiming the price of the video as the "return of money paid for defective goods." Two days after the summons was served on him the appellant sold the video to another. The judge directed the jury that it was for them to decide on the evidence whether the property belonged to the original purchaser when it was sold by the appellant to another. The appellant was convicted of theft and appealed.

Held,

"[T]he onus was on the prosecution to prove as a matter of law that the video did not belong to the appellant when he sold it to another. In effect the trial judge had withdrawn the issue of law from the jury. The relevant law, which was contained in the Sale of Goods Act 1979 was complicated but the judge had made no attempt to explain it. For centuries juries had decided civil actions on points arising under the law of sale of goods. There was no reason why this jury should not have had the relevant law explained to them and in the absence of such an explanation it was impossible for them to do justice in the case."

Appeal allowed

J. C. Smith, Commentary to R. v. Walker [1984] Crim.L.R. 113

"As the present case shows, when a question arises whether property belongs to another, recourse to the civil law is inevitable and it must be the whole of the civil law, including that part which determines whether contracts are void or merely voidable when that is relevant . . . to ~~determine~~ whether property belongs to another.

[81] Smith and Hogan, p. 520; R. Heaton, "Belonging to Another" [1973] Crim.L.R. 736, 738–739.

In the present case, it is clear that, after the sale, the video belonged to the purchaser and that it continued to do so when it was returned to the appellant for repair. The purchaser was at that stage a bailee of the recorder. It may well be, however, that the service of the summons claiming the return of the price amounted to a rescission of the contract of sale. In that case, the parties would be restored to the position they were in before the contract. Ownership in the recorder would be re-vested in the appellant. If that were so, since the appellant was already in possession he would hold the entire proprietary interest, the property would no longer belong to the purchaser, and theft would be an impossibility."

Dobson v. General Accident Fire and Life Assurance Corp. PLC [1989] 3 W.L.R. 1066 (Court of Appeal, Civil Division)

(The facts are given above, *ante,* p. 696)

Parker L.J.:
"[At the time of the appropriation] the property had, it was submitted, already passed to the rogue . . .
This agrument is put in two ways. First it is said that there was an agreement of sale over the telephone and accordingly the property passed [then]. Alternatively it is said that an agreement of sale took place [the following day] prior to the rogue receiving the articles in exchange for the cheque, and accordingly the property again passed to him, before delivery and receipt of the articles.
The agrument is founded upon sections 17 and 18 of the Sale of Goods 1979 . . .
[His Lordship then cited the two sections]
Having regard to the terms of the contract, the conduct of the parties and the circumstances of the case, I have no doubt that the property was not intended to pass in this case on contract but only in exchange for a valid building society cheque . . . "

Davies v. Leighton [1978] Crim.L.R. 575 (Queen's Bench Divisional Court)

The defendant, a customer in a supermarket, had a quantity of apples and tomatoes weighed, bagged, priced and handed to her by a store assistant. She was expected to pay at the exit of the store but left with the goods and without paying. She submitted that the ownership of the goods passed to her under the Sale of Goods Act 1893 when she received them from the assistant, and as there was no evidence that she then intended to avoid payment, she could not be convicted of theft as she had not appropriated property belonging to another. The justices acceded to this submission and dismissed the information. The prosecutor appealed by way of case stated.

Held,
"[T]hat the law which was well settled in relation to goods in a supermarket store, was that the property in them did not pass to a customer until he had paid the price. The fact that the goods had not been merely bagged but had been weighed accordingly to the quantity required by the defendant did take the case out of the general rule . . . [A] counter assistant who had wrapped up and handed over meat to a customer had not had authority to deal with the transfer

of property . . . A different situation might have arisen if the assistant in the present case had been in a managerial or other special category."

Appeal allowed

So the defendant's liability to punishment, stigma and societal condemnation depends in such a case on whether the person weighing and bagging the goods was of a managerial status or a mere shop assistant!

Much of course depends on when the moment of appropriation occurs. If, as in *Kaur*, it only occurs when the goods are placed in the shopper's bag after payment, there is the very real problem as property has indisputably passed at civil law. In *Lawrence*[82] a similar problem arose. As the defendant took each note from the hapless Mr. Occhi, property in the note passed and it was, therefore, argued by the defence that there was no appropriation of property belonging to another. However, the House of Lords held that the appropriation of each note occurred when the defendant took it from the wallet and at that time (or at any rate, the split second before) "the money in the wallet which he appropriated belonged to another, Mr. Occhi."

This same dilemma can be seen in a group of formerly problematic cases relating to theft of petrol from self-service stations. In *Edwards* v. *Ddin*[83] the defendant filled his car with petrol and drove away without paying. It was held that the appropriation occurred when he drove away, but as property passed when the petrol was put in his tank, he could not be liable; at the time of appropriation the property belonged to him. On the other hand, in *McHugh*[84] it was held that the appropriation occurred when the petrol was put in the tank and at that time (or the split second before, as in *Lawrence*) the petrol still belonged to another.[85]

(2) Theft Act 1968, section 5(2)

"Where property is subject to a trust, the persons to whom it belongs shall be regarded as including any person having a right to enforce the trust, and an intention to defeat the trust shall be regarded accordingly as an intention to deprive of the property any person having that right."

With most trusts the beneficiary already has a "proprietary right or interest," making section 5(2) unnecessary.

However, with charitable trusts there are no beneficiaries having beneficial interests in the trust property—but such trusts are enforced

---

[82] [1972] A.C. 626 at 632. This approach was approved by Parker L.J. in *Dobson, ante,* p. 696.
[83] [1976] 1 W.L.R. 942.
[84] (1976) 64 Cr.App.R. 92.
[85] These cases would now be charged as making off without payment contrary to s.3 of the Theft Act 1978. See *post* pp. 772–776.

by the Attorney-General.[86] Under section 5(2) the trust property is deemed to belong to the Attorney-General.

(3) Theft Act 1968, section 5(3)

"Where a person receives property from or on account of another, and is under an obligation to the other to retain and deal with that property or its proceeds in a particular way, the property or proceeds shall be regarded (as against him) as belonging to the other."

If a person receives property and ownership passes to him he is generally free to do as he likes with the property. Sometimes, however, the recipient of the property is obliged to deal with it in a particular way. For instance, a person collecting with a tin can for charity is obliged to hand over the money to the appropriate charity. When the donor placed his coin in the tin can this was the clear understanding between donor and collector. Accordingly section 5(3) deems that money still to belong to the donor and if the collector makes off with the money he is appropriating money "belonging to" the donor.

Several conditions need to be satisfied for section 5(3) to apply.

(i) *The money must have been received from or on account of another to whom the obligation is owed*

Reference by the Attorney-General under Section 36 of the Criminal Justice Act 1972 (No. 1 of 1985) (1986) 83 Cr.App.R. 70. (Court of Appeal, Criminal Division)

The defendant, a salaried manager of a tied public house, was only allowed to sell his employer's beer and was under a duty to pay all his takings into his employer's account. However, he sold other beer and kept the profit for himself. He was charged with theft from his employers on the basis that the money he received from his customers belonged to his employers by virtue of section 5(3).

The Lord Chief Justice:
"We were told at the outset of this hearing that this sort of behaviour by managers of 'tied' houses is becoming more prevalent. They do not, it seems, appear to be deterred by the prospect of losing their job or of being compelled by civil action to disgorge their illicit profit. An additional deterrent, it is suggested, in the shape of a conviction for theft would not be inappropriate.

That is not a matter which concerns us. We have to decide whether Parliament intended to bring such behaviour within the ambit of the criminal law . . .

[Liability] depends on whether A can properly be said to have received property, (*i.e.* the payment over the counter for the beer he has sold to the customer) 'on account of the employers.' We do not think he can. He received the money on his own account as a result of his private venture. No doubt he is in breach of his contract with the employers; no doubt he is under an obligation to account

---

[86] Charities Act 1960, s.28.

to the employers at least for the profit he has made out of his venture, but that is a different matter . . . As this court pointed out in *Kaur* v. *Chief Constable of Hampshire* (*ante*, p. 710), ' . . . the court should not be astute to find that a theft has taken place where it would be straining the language so to hold, or where the ordinary person would not regard the defendant's acts, though possibly morally reprehensible, as theft.' "

It is perhaps worth considering the point made in this case, that the defendant was undoubtedly in breach of contract and liable to his employers at civil law for the profit he had made—but was not criminally responsible. Breach of contract is not a crime. But, if accompanied by dishonesty, why not? A dishonest breach of contract could have as disastrous an impact upon the innocent party as stealing from him.

It could be asserted that there is the entire structure of the civil law to provide remedies for breach of contract. Criminalisation is unnecessary. This argument, however, collapses when one recalls that there are similar civil remedies provided for those who "lose" their property wrongfully. The existence of civil remedies is no argument for the decriminalisation of theft. So the question remains: why is theft a crime but *dishonest* breach of contract not a crime?

Apart from historical explanations relating to the evolution of the law of larceny and its metamorphosis into theft, an explanation of principle is not easy. It is perhaps best to focus on the paradigmatic instances of theft and breach of contract. A typical theft involves a surreptitious or forceful taking. The victim is helpless against such a taking. If the thief is interrupted there is a risk of violence. Because of his anonymity there is extra difficulty in identifying and apprehending the thief. With the typical breach of contract, however, one is dealing with two parties, both "free" and "equal" who have both chosen to enter into a contractual nexus. The risk of one party breaching his contract was always there and, in a free market economy, a factor to be assessed at the time of entering into the contract—taking account of the civil remedies available. Bearing in mind the basic proposition that conduct should not be made criminal merely because it is immoral, but that additionally criminalisation should be "necessary" and "profitable",[87] one should only expand the reaches of the criminal law with the utmost caution. Certain instances of dishonest breach of contract have already been made criminal, particularly where the contract is breached by deception, or the defendant is attempting unilaterally to avoid his liability in circumstances where it would be difficult to trace him.[88] Beyond such cases the criminal law should not go. Section 5(3) does extend the tentacles of the law of theft beyond the paradigmatic instances. Great caution must be exercised to keep some rein over the section so that it does not stray too far from ordinary understanding of the crime of theft.

[87] *Ante*, p. 88.
[88] *Post*, pp. 767, 773.

(ii) *There has to be an obligation to deal with that property or its proceeds in a particular way*

Lewis v. Lethbridge [1987] Crim.L.R. 59 (Queen's Bench Divisional Court)

The appellant obtained sponsorship for a colleague who had entered the London Marathon. He also completed sponsorship forms in false names. He received £54 which he did not hand over to the charity. The appellant was convicted of theft from the charity on the ground that while he did not have to hand over the actual notes and coins collected, he had dishonestly appropriated the *proceeds* of the money received. The appellant appealed by way of case stated.

Held,
"[T]he justices erred in finding that the debt owed by the appellant could be described as proceeds of the property received. In any event he could not be said to have appropriated a debt which he himself owed simply by not paying it . . . The court approved of the summary set out by Professor J. C. Smith in *The Law of Theft* (5th ed.): 'the obligation is to deal with that property or its proceeds in a particular way.' The words 'or its proceeds' make it clear that D need not be under an obligation to keep in existence a fund equivalent to that which he has received. If the arrangement permits D to do what he likes with the money, his only obligation being to account in due course for an equivalent sum, section 5(3) does not apply."

Appeal allowed

The court here held that the defendant could do as he liked with the money. He was not obliged to "earmark" it, or money exchanged for it, for the charity. He simply owed a debt to the charity. Not paying one's debts or breaching a contract is, as seen above, not theft. The court pointed out that the result might have been very different if the defendant had been collecting money in a collecting box as this might have imported a duty to deliver the contents.[89] As examined above, section 5(3) pushes the law of theft to its extremities, but that the difference between criminal and civil liability should hinge on the method of collecting the money for charity is stretching credulity.

R. v. Hall [1973] 1 Q.B. 496 (Court of Appeal, Criminal Division)

The defendant was a travel agent who accepted deposits for air trips to the United States. The flights never materialised and the money was not refunded. The appellant paid all the monies into the firm's general trading account. He was convicted of theft and appealed on the ground that the monies paid to him became his and therefore did not "belong to another."

Edmund-Davies L.J.:
"Counsel for the appellant . . . concedes that [by receiving the monies] the travel agent undertakes a contractual obligation in relation to arranging flights . . . But what counsel for the appellant resists is that in such circum-

[89] [1987] Crim.L.R. 60.

stances the travel agent 'is under an obligation' to the client 'to retain and deal with . . . in a particular way' sums paid to him in such circumstances.

What cannot of itself be decisive of the matter is the fact that the appellant paid the money into the firm's general trading account . . .

Nevertheless, when a client goes to a firm carrying on the business of travel agents and pays them money, he expects that in return he will, in due course, receive the tickets and other documents necessary for him to accomplish the trip for which he is paying, and the firm are 'under an obligation' to perform their part to fulfil his expectation and are liable to pay him damages if they do not. But, in our judgment, what was not here established was that these clients expected them 'to retain and deal with that property or its proceeds in a particular way,' and that an 'obligation' to do so was undertaken by the appellant. We must make clear, however, that each case turns on its own facts. Cases could, we suppose, conceivably arise where by some special arrangement (preferably evidenced by documents), the client could impose on the travel agent an 'obligation' falling within s.5(3). But no such special arrangement was made in any of the seven cases here being considered. It follows from this that, despite what on any view must be condemned as scandalous conduct by the appellant, in our judgment on this ground alone this appeal must be allowed and the convictions quashed."

Appeal allowed

The jury at first instance in this case convicted the defendant, being satisfied, *inter alia*, of his dishonesty. Edmund-Davies L.J. described the defendant's conduct as scandalous. But again, for the reasons outlined above, the courts resisted the temptation to expand the role of the criminal law into the arena of "free business enterprise," albeit a totally unacceptable facet thereof.

L. H. Leigh (with assistance of Susannah Brown), "Crimes in Bankruptcy" in L. H. Leigh (ed.), Economic Crime in Europe (1980), pp. 194–195:

"We appear, indeed, to be witnessing a transition from the employment, in corporate matters, of criminal sanctions, to the employment of administrative disabilities. The emphasis is less upon fraud than upon the fitness of individuals to conduct enterprises. Whether loss is caused to investors and the public by ineptitude or by fraud is no doubt an important distinction, but it is not all-important . . . [R]ecent legislation provides for the disqualification from acting as directors . . . [Such measures are] intended to prevent incompetents from managing companies; it also can be used to strike at persons who loot companies, or who arrange insolvencies as part of a scheme of fraud . . .

In effect, governments necessarily become more flexible in their search for measures to combat forms of economic criminality; less imbued with the desirability of employing the criminal model purely; and more respectful, perhaps, of some of the traditional limitations attaching to the use of the criminal law. Problems posed by difficulties of proof do not stand alone, of course: there is also the problem of defining standards in such a way as to leave scope for what are thought to be desirable entrepreneurial practices while protecting the public from imposition or worse. Thus, it becomes difficult to define offences."

As stressed in *Hall*, whether one is under an obligation to keep a separate fund in existence depends entirely on the facts of each case.

Davidge v. Bunnett [1984] Crim.L.R. 297 (Queen's Bench Divisional Court)

The defendant shared a flat with three other women. There was an oral agreement to share the costs of gas, electricity and telephone. The gas account was in one of the others' names. When the gas bill arrived the others all gave the defendant their shares in cheques made payable to the defendant's employer. They expected her to pay the bill, either by cashing the cheques with her employer and adding her own share, or, alternatively, that her employer, on receipt of all the monies, would write out a cheque for the Gas Board. They did not expect the defendant to use any actual banknotes received from her employer to pay the bill. Instead, the defendant spent most of the money on her Christmas shopping; the gas bill went unpaid; the defendant left the flat without giving notice or leaving a forwarding address. She was convicted of theft and appealed.

Held,
"D was under an obligation to use the cheques or their proceeds in whatever way she saw fit so long as they were applied *pro tanto* to the discharge of the gas bill. This could have been achieved by one cheque from her employer, or a banker's draft, or her own cheque . . . Hence the magistrates' finding that she was not obliged to use the actual banknotes. Using the proceeds of the cheques on presents amounted to a very negation of her obligation to discharge the bill. She was under an obligation to deal with the proceeds in a particular way. As against D, the proceeds of the cheques were properly belonging to another within section 5(3) of the Act."

Appeal dismissed

D.P.P. v. Huskinson [1988] Crim.L.R. 620 (Queen's Bench Divisional Court)

The defendant fell into arrears with his rent. He applied for housing benefit and was sent a cheque for £479 to pay off some of the arrears which then amounted to £800. He gave his landlord £200 and spent the remainder on himself. He was acquitted of theft and the prosecutor appealed by way of case stated.

Held,
"The decision turned on section 5(3) . . . and whether the respondent was under an obligation to the Housing Services Department to deal with the cheque or its proceeds in a particular way . . . (The obligation had to be a legal one.) Any such obligation would have to be found in the statutory provisions which gave rise to the payment of housing benefit. The court had examined the relevant statute and regulations, (*i.e.* the Social Security and Housing Benefit Act 1982, s.28 and regulations made thereunder which had since been replaced by the Social Security Act, s.26 . . .) It was quite clear that the regulations did not impose an express obligation on the tenant to pay the sum received directly to the landlord and it was impossible to imply any such obligation. Housing benefit provided a fund from which the tenant was expected to pay his rent. He

had a legal obligation to the landlord to pay the rent. However there was no obligation to apply the cheque or proceeds directly in satisfaction of any rent. For example, if the tenant obtained the money from some other source before he received the housing benefit he would be quite entitled to use the cheque or its proceeds for his own purposes. The justices had been right to dismiss the charges."

Appeal dismissed

J. C. Smith, Commentary on D.P.P. v. Huskinson [1988] Crim.L.R. 621:

"Housing benefit, it appears, is the tenant's money to do as he likes with. There is no reason in law why he should not take it to a betting shop and put it straight on a horse. That, perhaps, is a matter which those responsible for the administration of housing benefit may wish to reconsider. No doubt there is a number of considerations which must be taken into account; but the fact that the money is paid to meet a specific need suggests that there ought to be an obligation to apply it for that purpose . . .

The court points out that, if the tenant finds the money for his rent from some other source and pays it before he receives the housing benefit from the local authority, he can do as he likes with it. This is obviously so, but it does not follow that, where he has not paid his rent, he is not under an obligation to the local authority to do so and to retain the money paid, until he pays the rent, either with that or other money. Any obligation to retain and deal with money is extinguished when the purpose for which the obligation to retain and deal was imposed is satisfied."

(iii) *The obligation must be a legal* one

It is not enough that the defendant is under a social or moral obligation to deal with the property in a particular way. He must be under a legal obligation which means that the party imposing the obligation must be able to commence legal proceedings against the defendant at civil law for a failure to perform his obligations. One must be careful here to distinguish a legal obligation to do something (for example, pay one's rent as in *Huskinson*) from a legal obligation to use particular property or its proceeds in the performance of that thing (for example, using the housing benefit to pay one's rent). It is only when there is a legal obligation of the latter kind, that property is deemed to belong to another for the purposes of the law of theft.

Whether the obligation for the purposes of section 5(3) had to be a "legal" one or not used to be controversial. One school of thought was that "obligation" was an ordinary word—like many of the other "ordinary words" used in the Theft Act. Whether there was an obligation or not was simply a matter fact to be left to the jury. As the jury know no law, this means that they can only decide on the basis of whether they think the defendant ought to be under an obligation, *i.e.* whether a moral obligation exists.[90]

---

[90] *Hayes* (1977) 64 Cr.App.R. 82.

However, it is the opposing school of thought that has won the day here in the continuing see-saw battle of: ordinary meaning versus civil law meaning. In *Mainwaring*[91] it was held that there must be a legal obligation at civil law for the purposes of section 5(3). Glanville Williams applauds this outcome on the grounds that:

"Parliament is not in the habit of legislating about moral obligations as such; and that Parliament should do so without making its meaning plain is inconceivable."[92]

This criticism applies throughout the criminal law, particularly to property offences, when established civil law meanings of words are ignored and replaced by "ordinary meanings" given by juries. There is however an opposing case that this approach can be justifiable. This case is canvassed below.[93]

(4) Theft Act 1968, section 5(4)

"Where a person gets property by another's mistake, and is under an obligation to make restoration (in whole or in part) of the property or its proceeds or of the value thereof, then to the extent of that obligation the property or proceeds shall be regarded (as against him) as belonging to the person entitled to restoration, and an intention not to make restoration shall be regarded accordingly as an intention to deprive that person of the property or proceeds."

This subsection was specifically enacted to combat the mischief revealed in the case of *Moynes* v. *Cooper*[94] where an employee was given a pay packet which, owing to a mistake, contained too much money. When he opened the packet and saw the excess he dishonestly kept the whole. He was acquitted of larceny. If these facts were to reoccur, the case could be brought within section 5(4) and, therefore, even though property in the excess money might have passed to the employee when his wages were handed over, he could be liable in the following manner: on discovering and keeping the excess money there was an appropriation of property (the money) which was deemed to belong to the employer by virtue of section 5(4) because he had got the money by mistake and was under an obligation to make restoration of the excess—or its proceeds or value.

Section 5(4) is in fact of limited use. Where a person receives property by another's mistake, the mistake may be fundamental, in which case property does not pass at all and the property will still belong to the other by virtue of section 5(1) (proprietary right or interest). Section 5(4) is not needed in such cases. On the other hand, where the mistake is not so fundamental as to prevent property passing, the receiver of the property will not necessarily be under an obligation to make restoration of

---

[91] (1982) 74 Cr.App.R. 99.
[92] *Textbook of Criminal Law*, 2nd ed. (1983), p. 752.
[93] *Post*, p. 732.
[94] [1956] 1 Q.B. 439. See C.L.R.C., *ante*, n. 30, para. 24.

the property. Whether there is an obligation to make restoration is a complex matter governed by the law of restitution.

Accordingly, the following points can be made about section 5(4):

1. The obligation must be a legal one—*i.e.* under the civil law of restitution.[95]
2. The obligation must be to return *the* property or *its* proceeds or the *value* thereof. (Under section 5(3) only the property or its proceeds is specified).
3. The section says "is" under an obligation. The use of the present tense is significant here. If in a supermarket a cashier makes a mistake as a result of which the contract is *voidable*, property does pass, but the recipient of the property *is* not *there and then* under an obligation to make restitution. The obligation to make restitution only comes into existence when the person who made the mistake "avoids" the contract. At that point the recipient will become under an obligation to make restitution and only then does the present tense "is" become applicable. But in most cases, by the time the mistake is discovered and the contract avoided, the appropriation will already have occurred—and thus liability ought not to ensue.

It ought to be pointed out, however, that courts have not been rigorous in their application of these civil law principles, and while insisting with one breath that the obligation be a legal one, they have at the same time tended to adopt a more cavalier approach.

Attorney-General's Reference (No. 1 of 1983) [1985] Q.B. 182 (Court of Appeal, Criminal Division)

The defendant, a policewoman, was overpaid her wages. The money was paid by direct debit straight into her bank account. When she realised the mistake she decided to keep the excess. The judge directed an acquittal and the Attorney General referred a question on a point of law for the court's opinion under section 36 of the Criminal Justice Act 1972.

Lord Lane C.J.:

"In order to determine the effect of that subsection upon this case one has to take it piece by piece to see what the result is read against the circumstances of this particular prosecution. First of all: 'Did the respondent get property?' The word 'get' is about as wide a word as could possibly have been adopted by the draftsman of the Act. The answer is 'Yes,' the respondent in this case did get her chose in action, that is, her right to sue the bank for the debt which they owed her—money which they held in their hands to which she was entitled by virtue of the contract between bank and customer.

Secondly: 'Did she get it by another's mistake?' The answer to that is plainly 'Yes.' The Receiver of the Metropolitan Police made the mistake of thinking she was entitled to £74·74 when she was not entitled to that at all.

'Was she under an obligation to make restoration of either the property or its proceeds or its value?' We take each of those in turn. 'Was she under an obligation to make restoration of the property?'—the chose in action. The answer to

---

[95] *Gilks* [1972] 1 W.L.R. 1341.

that is 'No.' It was something which could not be restored in the ordinary meaning of the word. 'Was she under an obligation to make restoration of its proceeds?' The answer to that is 'No.' There were no proceeds of the chose in action to restore. 'Was she under an obligation to make restoration of the value thereof?'—the value of the chose in action. The answer to that seems to us to be 'Yes.'

I should say here, in parenthesis, that a question was raised during the argument this morning as to whether 'restoration' is the same as 'making restitution.' We think that on the wording of section 5(4) as a whole, the answer to that question is 'Yes.' One therefore turns to see whether, under the general principles of restitution, this respondent was obliged to restore or pay for the benefit which she received. Generally speaking, the respondent, in these circumstances, is obliged to pay for a benefit received when the benefit has been given under a mistake on the part of the giver as to a material fact. The mistake must be as to a fundamental or essential fact and the payment must have been due to that fundamental or essential fact. The mistake here was that this police officer had been working on a day when she had been at home and not working at all. . . .

As a result of the provisions of section 5(4) the debt of £74·74 due from the respondent's bank to the respondent notionally belonged to the Receiver of the Metropolitan Police; therefore the prosecution, up to this point, have succeeded in proving—remarkable though it may seem—that the 'property' in this case belonged to another within the meaning of section 1 in the Theft Act 1968 from the moment when the respondent became aware that this mistake had been made and that her account had been credited with the £74·74 and she consequently became obliged to restore the value. . . .

Before parting with the case we would like to say that it should often be possible to resolve this type of situation without resorting to the criminal law. We do, however, accept that there may be occasions—of which this may have been one—where a prosecution is necessary."

Opinion accordingly

The defendant here owed a debt and dishonestly tried to avoid paying that debt. This is yet another instance of the grey area of criminality discussed above: when, if ever, should not paying one's debts or in other ways breaching one's contract be a crime? In one sense the defendant in this case was even more blameless than most debtors because she did not choose to incur the debt. It was thrust upon her by the mistake of another. And again, there were civil remedies available. The money could have been recovered. The court rightly stressed at the end that such cases could usually be dealt with without resort to the criminal law. In *A.-G.'s Ref. (No. 1 of 1983)* the amount of the overpayment was some £74. In *Shadrokh-Cigari*[96] a bank account was credited $286,000 instead of $286. English law does not formally take account of the value of property in assessing criminality,[97] or levels thereof. Yet this is surely an instance where the sums involved are so huge that perhaps criminal liability is appropriate. Or is it that the value of the property affects our assessment as to dishonesty? We can conceive of perhaps "turning a

[96] [1988] Crim.L.R. 465.
[97] *Post*, pp. 786–794.

blind eye" to an extra £74 credited to our bank account, but when the excess amount is some $286,000, an assessment of dishonesty becomes inevitable.

R. v. Davis [1988] Crim.L.R. 762 (Court of Appeal, Criminal Division)

The defendant was entitled to housing benefit from the local authority. By mistake the authority's computer issued duplicate issues of a number of cheques. When he ceased to be eligible for housing benefit only one of the computer entries was deleted and he continued to be sent one cheque. He kept the proceeds of the cheques and appealed against his conviction for theft.

Held,
"[T]he language of the first part of section 5(4) of the Theft Act 1968 was framed to cater for the ordinary tangible article and to recognise that by the time the defendant comes to commit his dishonest appropriation, the article may be in one of three conditions: it may still exist, so that it can and should be returned; it may have been exchanged for money or goods, in which case the defendant may be under an obligation to account for the fruits of the exchange, at least if they are traceable; and it may have ceased to exist altogether or to have gone out of reach of recovery, in which event the defendant may be obliged to 'restore' the value. In those cases where the defendant is indeed under a duty to 'make restoration' the second part of the subsection will put him in peril of conviction for stealing the article or its proceeds, although not its value, since there is no reference to value in this part of the subsection. The deceptively plain words of section 5(4) give rise to problems, *e.g.* when is the defendant obliged to 'make restoration'; where the property received by the defendant by mistake is exchanged for something else? The Court did not need to answer those questions in the circumstances of the present case. It was plain that if an article is sold for cash, the sum represents the 'proceeds' of the article; there is no reason why this should be any the less so where the transaction involves not simply the piece of paper but also the rights which it conveys. On the assumption that the appellant was paid cash for the cheque, the offences were made out subject to the proof of dishonesty.
In relation to the count concerning a duplicate cheque, . . . It was not material that the appellant had received two cheques; there was no true difference between an overpayment effected by an excessive number of coins inserted in the same pay packet and an excessive number of cheques transferred separately. When the 'property' was turned into 'proceeds,' in circumstances where these proceeds formed an undifferentiated whole, it is in accordance with the words as well as the spirit of the statute to regard the surplus as the subject matter of the theft, without engaging on the task of ascertaining the exact source of that surplus."

Appeal allowed in part

(5) Theft Act 1968, section 5(5)

"Property of a corporation sole shall be regarded as belonging to the corporation notwithstanding a vacancy in the corporation."

Normally there is no problem whether property belongs to an individual or a company, as the latter is a legal person and property belongs to it irrespective of the membership of the company. However, there could be a problem with a "corporation sole" (such as a bishop or the Treasury Solicitor). If, say, a bishop were to die, it could be argued that the property of the bishopric belonged to nobody and therefore could not be stolen. Section 5(5) however makes it clear that in such a situation the property is regarded as belonging to the corporation notwithstanding the vacancy in the corporation.

5. Dishonesty

The *mens rea* of theft is twofold: dishonesty and intention of permanent deprivation. It is a theme of this book that blameworthiness is generally a pre-requisite to the imposition of criminal liability and that *mens rea* is an important indicator of blame. *Mens rea* is generally taken to refer to a state of mind in relation to consequences or circumstances of a defendant's actions—for example, did he intend, foresee or know of something happening? But apart from the requirement of intending permanent deprivation, this traditional concept of *mens rea* fits ill with property offences where, in essence, a judgment is being made about behaviour and standards of acting. As was said in one of the leading cases, *Feely*,[98] the taking of property must be one to which "moral obloquy can reasonably" be attached.

The interference with property rights must be such that we can blame the defendant for disregarding the value system inherent in the law of theft. The requirement of "dishonesty" is introduced as a mechanism by which moral judgments can be made and blame attributed.

Dishonesty is only partially defined by the Theft Act 1968. Where defined, the meaning of dishonesty is a question of law. Where undefined, it is a question of fact.

A. *Question of law*

Theft Act 1968, section 2

"2.—(1) A person's appropriation of property belonging to another is not to be regarded as dishonest—
  (a) if he appropriates the property in the belief that he has in law the right to deprive the other of it, on behalf of himself or of a third person; or
  (b) if he appropriates the property in the belief that he would have the other's consent if the other knew of the appropriation and the circumstances of it; or
  (c) (except where the property came to him as trustee or personal representative) if he appropriates the property in the belief that the person to whom the property belongs cannot be discovered by taking reasonable steps.
  (2) A person's appropriation of property belonging to another may be dishonest notwithstanding that he is willing to pay for the property."

[98] [1973] 1 Q.B. 530.

Theft Act 1968, section 1(2)

"It is immaterial whether the appropriation is made with a view to gain, or is made for the thief's own benefit."

(a) *Belief in legal right*

Section 2(1)(*a*) allows a person who genuinely believes he has a legal right to the property to be regarded as honest—irrespective of the reasonableness or otherwise of the belief.[99] There is a well known maxim that "ignorance of the law is no defence." This however relates to ignorance of the criminal law, for instance to a defendant who claims he did not know theft was a crime. Section 2(1)(*a*) only applies to persons who have made a mistake as to the *civil law*—believing they have legal rights to property when, perhaps, they have no such rights.

(b) *Belief in consent*

We have seen that the essence of theft is the doing of an *unauthorised* act, inconsistent with and in usurpation of the owner's rights. It follows that if the defendant genuinely believes he has the other's consent to deal with the property he cannot be condemned as dishonest. Again, the reasonableness of his belief is irrelevant except in evidential terms.

(c) *Belief that property lost*

Lost property continues to belong to the owner therefore the finder of lost property is appropriating property belonging to another. However, if he genuinely (again, a subjective test) believes that the owner "*cannot be discovered by taking reasonable steps*" he is not to be condemned for deciding to keep the property. Obviously, factors such as the type and value of the property and the location where it was found will be important evidential factors in assessing the defendant's belief.

(d) *Willingness to pay*

Section 2(2) makes it clear that a willingness to pay will not necessarily exempt one from a finding of dishonesty. The owner might not wish to sell at whatever price, and it would be unthinkable to allow the unscrupulous to help themselves to other people's property and escape liability, simply by being able to pay.

(e) *Not for thief's benefit*

Despite dishonesty being a moral concept, section 1(2) makes it clear that even though the theft is for the good of others, with the thief himself gaining nothing, he can still be found dishonest.[1]

---

[99] *Small* (1988) 86 Cr.App.R. 170.

[1] The Criminal Law Revision Committee gave two more limited instances of arguments that section 1(2) was designed to meet, *viz.*, taking property that is either useless to the taker or which he intends to destroy. (8th Report, *Theft and Related Offences*, (1966) Cmnd. 2977, p. 125).

B. *Question of fact*

Apart from the above specific instances, the concept of dishonesty was left undefined in the Theft Act 1968 although judges soon began to give the concept a legal meaning.[2] However, in 1973 the Court of Appeal embarked on a new course.

R. v. Feely [1973] 1 Q.B. 530 (Court of Appeal, Criminal Division)

The defendant was employed by a firm of bookmakers as manager of one of their branches. The employer sent round a circular to all managers stating that the practice of borrowing from tills was to stop. The defendant knowing this "borrowed" £30. When the deficiency was discovered (but not yet attributed to him) he immediately offered an IOU. He was owed more than twice that sum by his employers. The trial judge directed the jury that this was dishonest, and he was convicted of theft and appealed, on the ground that this question should have been left to the jury.

Lawton L.J.:
"The design of the new Act is clear . . . Words in everyday use have replaced legal jargon in many parts of the Act . . .
In section 1(1) of the Theft Act 1968 the word 'dishonesty' can only relate to the state of mind of the person who does the act which amounts to appropriation. Whether an accused person has a particular state of mind is a question of fact which has to be decided by the jury . . . We do not agree that judges should define what 'dishonesty' means.
This word is in common use . . . Jurors, when deciding whether an appropriation was dishonest can be reasonably expected to, and should, apply the current standards of ordinary decent people. In their own lives they have to decide what is and what is not dishonest. We can see no reason why, when in a jury box, they should require the help of a judge to tell them what amounts to dishonesty."

Appeal allowed

Dishonesty describes a state of mind and is often described as "subjective." How does this square with the above statement that dishonesty is a moral concept to be determined by the jury applying community values?

R. v. Lewis (1975) 62 Cr.App.R. 206 (Court of Appeal, Criminal Division)

The appellant, a Canadian, cashed two cheques in England which were dishonoured. His defence was that he expected a relative to pay money into his account when he arrived in England—but he had made no enquiries to find out if that money had actually been paid into his account. The jury were directed that a genuine belief by the appellant that the money had been paid into his account was not enough. The belief had to be based on reasonable grounds. The appellant was convicted and appealed.

[2] *Rao* [1972] Crim.L.R. 451.

Lawton L.J.:

"[*Feely*] decided that for the purposes of the Theft Act 1968 the concept of dishonesty was a subjective one which had nothing to do with reasonable belief. That decision followed . . . *Waterfall* (1969) 53 Cr.App.R. 596. At p. 599 Lord Parker C.J. said this: 'The test here is a subjective test, whether the particular defendant had an honest belief, and of course whereas the absence of reasonable ground may point strongly to the fact that that belief is not genuine, it is at the end of the day for the jury to say whether or not in the case of this particular defendant he did have that genuine belief.' . . .

The reference to reasonable grounds was a mistake: the jury should not have been directed on that basis."

Appeal dismissed by application of proviso to section 2(1) of the Criminal Appeal Act 1968

From this it is clear that the jury first have to establish what is in the defendant's mind, for example, whether he believed that he would be able to repay the money, and then they have to judge that behaviour committed with that state of mind, applying their own moral standards. Thus using the facts of *Feely*, the jury might find that first, the defendant did believe he could, and did intend to, repay the money. The jury, now armed with this knowledge, must make a moral assessment as to whether such conduct, in the circumstances, was dishonest.

But what of the defendant whose actions might be regarded as dishonest by the jury applying their standards, but who insists (and is believed) that according to *his* systems of values, he was acting honestly? For example, in *Gilks*[3] the defendant claimed that he thought he was honest in keeping money mistakenly paid to him by a bookmaker because he thought bookmakers were "a race apart" and thus fair game.

R. v. Ghosh [1982] Q.B. 1053 (Court of Appeal, Criminal Division)

The defendant was a consultant who acted as a locum at a hospital. He falsely claimed fees in respect of an operation that he had not carried out. He claimed that he thought he was not dishonest by his standards because the same amount of money was legitimately payable to him for consultation fees. The judge directed the jury that they must simply apply their own standards. He was convicted of an offence contrary to section 15 of the Theft Act 1968 (which uses the same concept "dishonesty" and appealed against his conviction).

Lord Lane C.J.:

"The sentence [in *Feely*] requiring the jury to apply current standards leads up to the prohibition on judges from applying *their* standards. That is the context in which the sentence appears. It seems to be reading too much into that sentence to treat it as authority for the view that 'dishonesty can be established

---

[3] (1972) 56 Cr.App.R. 734.

independently of the knowledge or belief of the defendant.' If it could, then any reference to the state of mind of the defendant would be beside the point.

This brings us to the heart of the problem. Is 'dishonestly' in section 1 of the Theft Act 1968 intended to characterise a course of conduct? Or is it intended to describe a state of mind? If the former, then we can well understand that it could be established independently of the knowledge or belief of the accused. But if, as we think, it is the latter, then the knowledge and belief of the accused are at the root of the problem.

Take for example a man who comes from a country where public transport is free. On his first day here he travels on a bus. He gets off without paying. He never had any intention of paying. His mind is clearly honest; but his conduct, judged objectively by what he has done, is dishonest. It seems to us that in using the word 'dishonestly' in the Theft Act 1968, Parliament cannot have intended to catch dishonest conduct in that sense, that is to say conduct to which no moral obloquy could possibly attach. This is sufficiently established by the partial definition in section 2 of the Theft Act itself. All the matters covered by section 2(1) relate to the belief of the accused. Section 2(2) relates to his willingness to pay. A man's belief and his willingness to pay are things which can only be established subjectively. It is difficult to see how a partially subjective definition can be made to work in harness with the test which in all other respects is wholly objective.

If we are right that dishonesty is something in the mind of the accused (what Professor Glanville Williams calls 'a special mental state'), then if the mind of the accused is honest, it cannot be deemed dishonest merely because members of the jury would have regarded it as dishonest to embark on that course of conduct.

So we would reject the simple uncomplicated approach that the test is purely objective, however attractive from the practical point of view that solution may be.

There remains the objection that to adopt a subjective test is to abandon all standards but that of the accused himself, and to bring about a state of affairs in which 'Robin Hood would be no robber': *Reg.* v. *Greenstein* [1975] 1 W.L.R. 1353. This objection misunderstands the nature of the subjective test. It is no defence for a man to say 'I knew that what I was doing is generally regarded as dishonest; but I do not regard it as dishonest myself. Therefore I am not guilty.' What he is however entitled to say is 'I did not know that anybody would regard what I was doing as dishonest.' He may not be believed; just as he may not be believed if he sets up 'a claim of right' under section 2(1) of the Theft Act 1968, or asserts that he believed in the truth of a misrepresentation under section 15 of the Act of 1968. But if he *is* believed, or raises a real doubt about the matter, the jury cannot be sure that he was dishonest.

In determining whether the prosecution has proved that the defendant was acting dishonestly, a jury must first of all decide whether according to the ordinary standards of reasonable and honest people what was done was dishonest. If it was not dishonest by those standards, that is the end of the matter and the prosecution fails.

If it was dishonest by those standards, then the jury must consider whether the defendant himself must have realised that what he was doing was by those standards dishonest. In most cases, where the actions are obviously dishonest by ordinary standards, there will be no doubt about it. It will be obvious that the defendant himself knew that he was acting dishonestly. It is dishonest for a defendant to act in a way which he knows ordinary people consider to be dishonest, even if he asserts or genuinely believes that he is morally justified in acting as he did. For example, Robin Hood or those ardent anti-vivisectionists who remove animals from vivisection laboratories are acting dishonestly, even though they may consider themselves to be morally justified in doing what they do, because they know that ordinary people would consider these actions to be dishonest."

Appeal dismissed

The enquiry is thus threefold:

1. The defendant's subjective state of mind, (*i.e.* his beliefs and expectations) must be established; and then
2. The jury, applying their own standards, must judge the defendant's actions committed with that state of mind; was he honest or dishonest?
3. If the jury find that according to their standards he was dishonest, they must then establish whether the defendant knew that ordinary people would regard such conduct as dishonest.

In *Roberts*[4] it was held that this third limb of the *Ghosh* direction need only be put to the jury in those cases where the defendant raised the special plea that he did not think he was being dishonest by his own standards.

Edward Griew, "Dishonesty: The Objections to Feely and Ghosh" [1985] Crim.L.R. 341:

"The question tends to increase the number of trials. Whereas a different approach to the dishonesty issue might make it clear that given conduct was dishonest as a matter of law and therefore constituted an offence, the *Feely* question leaves the issue open. It may be worth a defendant's while to take his chance with the jury . . . [B]efore *Feely* defendants might have felt constrained to plead guilty.

The question tends to complicate and lengthen contested cases . . . [I]t may be in the interests of some defendants to extend and complicate trials in order to obfuscate the issue . . .

The *Feely* question carries an unacceptable risk of inconsistency of decision . . .

[It] implies the existence of a relevant community norm. In doing so it glosses over differences of age, class and cultural background . . . It is simply naive to suppose . . . that there is, in respect of the dishonesty question, any such single thing as 'the standards of ordinary decent folk . . .'

[It is] unsuitable where the context of the case is a specialised one, involving intricate financial activities or dealings in a specialised market. It is neither reasonable nor rational to expect ordinary people to judge as 'dishonest' or 'not dishonest' conduct of which, for want of relevant experience, they cannot appreciate the contextual flavour . . . [O]rdinary people (might) have no standards in relation to the conduct in question . . .

A person may defend his attack on another's property by reference to a moral or political conviction so passionately held that he believed (so he claims) that

---

[4] (1987) 84 Cr.App.R. 117. Professor Smith ([1988] Crim.L.R. 123) regards this case as important in being a retreat from *Feely* because, he argues, the court decided as a matter of law whether the defendant was dishonest. With respect, the decision does not go that far. O'Connor L.J. did no more than hold that on the facts it was simply not plausible for anyone to assert that they thought they were acting honestly. The third limb of *Ghosh* therefore did not arise.

'ordinary decent' members of society would regard his conduct as proper, even laudable. If the asserted belief is treated as a claim to have been ignorant that the conduct was 'dishonest' by ordinary standards . . . and if the jury think (as exceptionally they might) that the belief may have been held, *Ghosh* produces an acquittal. The result is remarkable. Robin Hood must be a thief even if he thinks the whole of the right-thinking world is on his side.

A person reared or moving in an environment in which it is generally regarded as legitimate to take advantage of certain classes of people—perhaps bookmakers or employers—may plausibly claim that he did not realise that his conduct, of which a member of such a class was a victim, was generally regarded as dishonest. It is not acceptable that a claim of that sort should be capable even of being advanced."

Glanville Williams, Textbook of Criminal Law, 2nd ed. (1983) pp. 726–730:

"The practice of leaving the whole matter to the jury might be workable if our society were culturally homogeneous, with known and shared values, at it once very largely was. But the object of the law of theft is to protect property rights; and disrespect for these rights is now widespread. Since the jury are chosen at random, we have no reason to suppose that they will be any more honest and 'decent' in their standards than the average person . . .

Evidence of the poor level of self-discipline now prevailing abounds—and this without taking any account of tax defaults. Observers agree upon a very large scale of theft: not merely shoplifting and fare bilking but stealing from employers by employees and an assortment of frauds perpetrated upon customers by employees. Great numbers of employed people of all classes believe, or affect to believe, that systematic dishonesty of various kinds is a 'perk.' It is tolerated by many employers, provided that it does not exceed some ill-defined limit; and some employers even encourage fiddles when they are at the expense of customers, since this is a way of increasing employees' remuneration without cost to the employers. For the employee, illicit remuneration has the advantage of being untaxed. Fiddling also brings non-material rewards: it is a pleasant departure from routine, a game of chance against the risk of detection, all the better since the consequences of detection are now rarely serious. So highly do some workers value the practice that a change in the system of work threatening to interfere with it, or an attempt by employers to prosecute offenders, is met by strikes. Notable examples were the strike at Heathrow Airport when baggage loaders were arrested for pilferage in 1973 . . . If ordinary people in steady employment develop these lax notions about the right of property, it seems from the judgment in *Feely* that the law of theft is to be automatically adjusted to suit . . .

[Commenting on *Gilks* Professor Williams continues] Subjectivism of this degree gives subjectivism a bad name. The subjective approach to criminal liability, properly understood, looks to the defendant's intention and to the facts as he believed them to be, not to his system of values . . .

What must be found is a definition of dishonesty . . . I would suggest that the definition should be that dishonesty involves a disregard for rights of property. Professor Smith's suggestion, however, is that a judicial definition of dishonesty might be . . . : a person appropriates dishonestly 'where he knows that it will or may be detrimental to the interests of the other in a significant practical way.' ([1982] Crim.L.R. 609) We can at least be certain that almost any definition making the position independent of current social attitudes would be better than the rule in *Ghosh*."

Professor Williams assumes that because large numbers of employees "fiddle" from their employers, for example, that such employees have lost all standards of knowing right from wrong and therefore, being in a moral vacuum would be unable to assess "dishonesty" if sitting in a jury box. But surely a plausible explanation is that most such employees know perfectly well their conduct is dishonest, but have chosen nevertheless to go ahead and do it. Such persons are perfectly capable of sitting on a jury and judging standards of dishonesty. And charges of hypocrisy will not do, otherwise any juror who had ever committed a (relevant) offence would have to be disqualified—an impossible task given the vast unknown figure of unrecorded property crime.

The above extract also challenges the view that the defendant's system of values are relevant in an assessment of culpability.

C.M.V.Clarkson, Understanding Criminal Law, (1987), pp. 153–155:

"The courts were faced with a quandary here. Acceptance of such pleas (*viz.*, that the defendant did not think he was dishonest by his own standards) would undercut the moral imperative laid down by the criminal law. The criminal law largely reflects (and attempts to uphold) community values. The *Feely* test allows these community values to be enunciated by a so-called representative section of the community, namely, the jury. If the values of the jury and the community are to be ignored and replaced by the values of the defendant, (who, for example, might endorse the political ideology that 'property is theft'), the result would be a complete absence of any objective standard. The door would be open to the 'Robin Hood defence.' The defendant would effectively become his own judge and jury.

On the other hand, the courts were reluctant to dismiss such pleas totally. The criminal law is based largely on the premise of moral responsibility. We blame those who are morally at fault. If a defendant openly rejects the value system inherent in the law of theft, he can be blamed even if, according to his own values, he thinks his actions are honest. He has knowingly 'declared war' on the values of society and can be blamed therefor. It can never be an excuse in the criminal law that one does not agree with any given law. But what of the defendant who genuinely thinks he is acting honestly according to his values—*and* who really believes that most other people would agree with him as to the morality of his conduct—and can convince a jury of these beliefs? Such a defendant is not openly defying the law; he believes he is upholding the value system inherent in the law of theft. The case for exempting such a defendant from blame becomes strong.

This latter thinking was endorsed in the leading decision of *Ghosh* which lays down that a defendant acts 'dishonestly' if what he does is dishonest according to the ordinary standards of reasonable and honest people (the *Feely*, test), *and* if he realised that what he was doing was dishonest according to those standards. Thus using the examples given in *Ghosh* itself: Robin Hood or anti-vivisectionists who remove animals from vivisection laboratories are acting dishonestly, even though they may consider themselves to be morally justified in so acting *provided that they know* that ordinary people would consider such actions to be dishonest . . .

The quest throughout the criminal law is for the isolation of the blameworthy. If the jury, reflecting community standards, can attach 'moral obloquy' to the defendant's actions and are satisfied that the defendant knows he is acting contrary to the moral standards of ordinary people, a judgment of blameworthiness is truly appropriate. The test has tried to combine the need to preserve objective standards within the criminal law with the need to maintain the importance of moral fault."

6. Intention of permanent deprivation

Theft Act 1968, section 6

(1) A person appropriating property belonging to another without meaning the other permanently to lose the thing itself is nevertheless to be regarded as having the intention of permanently depriving the other of it if his intention is to treat the thing as his own to dispose of regardless of the other's rights; and a borrowing or lending of it may amount to so treating it if, but only if, the borrowing or lending is for a period and in circumstances making it equivalent to an outright taking or disposal.

(2) Without prejudice to the generality of subsection (1) above, where a person, having possession or control (lawfully or not) of property belonging to another, parts with the property under a condition as to its return which he may not be able to perform, this (if done for purposes of his own and without the other's authority) amounts to treating the property as his own to dispose of regardless of the other's rights."

This not a definition of "intention of permanent deprivation." Rather, it *extends* the natural meaning of the phrase and provides that in certain circumstances even though the defendant did not "mean" the other to lose the thing permanently he is "to be regarded" as having an intention of permanent deprivation. In *Lloyd*[5] it was made clear that section 6 should only be referred to in exceptional cases; for most purposes it would be unnecessary to go beyond section 1(1).[6]

(a) Section 6(1)

This deals with two separate situations where a defendant is deemed to intend to deprive the other permanently of the property.

[i] *if his intention is to treat the thing as his own to dispose of regardless of the other's rights:*

R. v. Coffey [1987] Crim.L.R. 498 (Court of Appeal, Criminal Division)

The defendant obtained machinery from another with whom he was having a dispute. He decided to exert pressure on the victim by keeping the machinery as "ransom" until the victim gave in, at which point he would return the property. He appealed against conviction on the ground, *inter alia*, that the judge's direction did not accurately state the law as to intention.

Held,
"The culpability of the appellant's act depended upon the quality of the intended detention, considered in all its aspects, including in particular the

---

[5] [1985] Q.B. 829.
[6] *Warner* (1970) 55 Cr.App.R. 93; *Cocks* (1976) 63 Cr.App.R. 79.

appellant's own assessment at the time as to the likelihood of the victim coming to terms and of the time for which the machinery would have to be retained. The Court preferred this view.

This was one of the rare cases where it was right for the judge to bring section 6(1) before the jury. The judge could usefully have illustrated the first part of section 6(1) by the expression 'equivalent to an outright taking or disposal.' If they thought that the appellant might have intended to return the goods even if the victim did not do what he wanted, they would not convict unless they were sure that he intended that the period of detention should be so long as to amount to an outright taking. Even if they did conclude that the appellant had in mind not to return the goods if the victim failed to do what he wanted, they would still have to consider whether the appellant had regarded the likelihood of this happening as being such that his intended conduct could be regarded as equivalent to an outright taking."

Appeal allowed

[ii] *Borrowing or lending for a period and in circumstances making it equivalent to an outright taking or disposal:*

This makes it clear that certain borrowings are to be treated the same as outright takings. The classic example here is borrowing another's football season ticket and then returning the piece of paper at the end of the season after watching all the matches. At that stage the ticket has no value and is useless—or as Smith has described it: the "virtue" has gone out of the thing.[7]

R v. Lloyd [1985] Q.B. 829 (Court of Appeal, Criminal Division)

Films were removed from a cinema for a few hours and "pirate" copies made of them; the originals were then returned. The defendant appealed against his conviction for conspiracy to steal.

Lord Lane C.J.:
"[T]he intention of the appellants could more accurately be described as an intention temporarily to deprive the owner of the film and was indeed the opposite of an intention permanently to deprive.

What then was the basis of the prosecution case and the basis of the judge's direction to the jury? It is said that section 6(1) of the Theft Act 1968 brings such actions as the appellants performed here within the provisions of section 1 . . . [T]he first part of section 6(1) seems to us to be aimed at the sort of case where a defendant takes things and then offers them back to the owner for the owner to buy if he wishes. If the taker intends to return them to the owner only upon such payment, then, on the wording of section 6(1), that is deemed to amount to the necessary intention permanently to deprive: . . .

Borrowing is ex hypothesi not something which is done with an intention permanently to deprive. This half of the subsection, we believe, is intended to make it clear that a mere borrowing is never enough to constitute the necessary guilty mind unless the intention is to return the 'thing' in such a changed state that it can truly be said that all its goodness or virtue has gone: for example *Reg. v. Beecham* (1851) 5 Cox C.C. 181, where the defendant stole railway tickets intending that they should be returned to the railway company in the usual way only after the journeys had been completed. He was convicted of larceny. . . .

---

[7] J. C. Smith, *The Law of Theft*, 5th ed., (1984), p. 71.

That being the case, we turn to inquire whether the feature films in this case can fall within that category. Our view is that they cannot. The goodness, the virtue, the practical value of the films to the owners has not gone out of the article. The film could still be projected to paying audiences. . . .

Our view is that those particular films which were the subject of this alleged conspiracy had not themselves diminished in value at all. What had happened was that the borrowed film had been used or was going to be used to perpetrate a copyright swindle on the owners whereby their commercial interests were grossly and adversely affected in the way that we have endeavoured to describe at the outset of this judgment. That borrowing, it seems to us, was not for a period, or in such circumstances, as made it equivalent to an outright taking or disposal. There was still virtue in the film."

Appeals allowed

Difficult questions of fact will of course remain. In *Lloyd* Lord Lane spoke in terms of "all" the virtue or goodness being gone. This raises the problem of the football season ticket which is returned after it has been used for 19 matches, but is still valid for one final match. The ticket clearly has *some* value or virtue left. Presumably, questions such as these, were they to arise, would be left to the jury as questions of fact.

(b) Section 6(2)

This is dealing with the specific situation of a person who pawns the property of another. In such a case he is taking what is regarded as an unacceptable risk with the property of another and, if dishonest, is felt to deserve to come within the ambit of the law of theft. It is uncertain whether the defendant must himself realise that he may be unable to redeem his security or whether it suffices that he "may" objectively be so unable. As Griew says: "The former view is doctrinally the purer; the latter is more readily suggested by the terms of the poorly drafted section."[8]

Dishonest borrowings

Apart from these specific situations where section 6 has deemed dishonest borrowings to be the equivalent of permanent deprivation, the Theft Act 1968 has generally chosen not to punish dishonest borrowings. Why?

Criminal Law Revision Committee, 8th Report, Theft and Related Offences (1966) Cmnd. 2977, para. 56:

"[A]n intention to return the property, even after a long time makes the conduct essentially different from stealing. Apart from this . . . [criminalising tem-

---

[8] Griew, *The Theft Acts 1968 and 1978*, 5th ed., (1986), p. 63.

porary deprivations] would be a considerable extension of the criminal law, which does not seem to be called for by any existing serious evil. It might moreover have undesirable social consequences. Quarrelling neighbours and families would be able to threaten one another with prosecution. Students and young people sharing accommodation who might be tempted to borrow one another's property in disregard of a prohibition by the owner would be in danger of acquiring a criminal record. Further, it would be difficult for the police to avoid being involved in wasteful and undesirable investigations into alleged offences which had no social importance."

Glanville Williams, "Temporary Appropriation should be Theft" [1981] Crim.L.R. 129, 131–132, 135:

"Suppose that a person removes a small piece of sculpture from a private exhibition, or a valuable book from a University library, and returns it after a year. During that time it has of course been lost to its owner; and both the owner and the police have been put to trouble . . . The taker of the article may use it in such a way as to put it at risk, or he may make a profit from it, or he may return it in an impaired condition; and if he is a person of no substance the owner's civil remedy against him will be insufficient penalty . . .

If a person has gone off with the property of another, and upon being apprehended and charged with theft swears that he meant to return it, is his statement to be accepted or not? To accept it too readily gives guilty defendants an easy line of escape; to reject it carries the risk of convicting people who are technically innocent, even though they are morally guilty because they have taken the article dishonestly . . . Why should not the dishonest taking be sufficient to constitute the offence of theft, thus relieving the prosecution of a very difficult burden of proof? . . .

When an article is unlawfully taken, even if only for a temporary purpose and without substantial risk of permanent loss of the article, the owner suffers an immediate loss, namely in respect of the use of it . . . Sometimes the economic loss resulting from the loss of use of an article that is essential to an undertaking can be considerable.

One of the principal arguments for changing the law is that the value of articles lies in their use. More and more things are used by way of hiring . . . Many articles of use have comparatively short useful 'lives'. In a few years they wear out or become unfashionable or technically obsolete . . . Besides, the owner is in a dilemma of either being without the article for that time or putting himself to the expense of buying another—an expense that may turn out to have been unnecessary if the article is returned."

There are two well-known exceptions[9] to the intention of permanent deprivation rule (apart from the exceptions within section 6 itself). Section 11 creates the offence of removing articles from places open to the public, for example removing works of art from museums or galleries albeit intending to return them at some time. Section 12 of the Theft Act 1968 creates the second exceptional offence of taking a motor vehicle or other conveyance without authority. This is designed to prevent "joy-

---

[9] For further exceptions, *e.g.* Post Office Act, s.53; see Glanville Williams, "Temporary Appropriation should be Theft" [1981] Crim.L.R. 129, 130.

riding," where a car is taken and after being driven around, abandoned. In such cases an intention of permanent deprivation would be difficult to establish.

It is interesting to contrast this last activity of joyriding with the conduct of a person who walks into a bookshop and dishonestly removes a book which he takes home and reads before returning it to the shop. It appears that the only reasons for the criminalisation of the former but not the latter activity are, first, the prevalence of joyriding[10] and secondly, the difficulty of proving the necessary intent with taking cars (with the book example, a finding of intent of permanent deprivation would be almost irresistible and thus a conviction for theft would result in fact).

It is worth pausing on this point for a little further reflection, as perhaps some insight can here be gleaned into the real harm that is sought to be prevented by the crime of theft. When the book is dishonestly taken from the store, the store clearly suffers a harm. First, there is economic harm. The book is removed from their shelves, meaning it cannot be sold to another. The used book that is returned is not the same thing that was taken, which was a new book. The store sustains an economic loss of the difference in value between the new book and the second-hand book.[11] Secondly, there is all the non-economic harm associated with most thefts. The shop has had its rights of ownership assaulted. It has lost control of its property, lost the power to make choices and decisions about it. The identity of the borrower is probably unknown and therefore there can be no certainty as to when and if the property will be returned. For instance, the Criminal Law Revision Committee considered the striking example of someone who "borrowed" Goya's portrait of the Duke of Wellington from the National Gallery for four years![12]

It is worth stressing at this stage that it is not necessary for a victim to lose his property permanently. What matters is that the defendant, at the time of the appropriation, *intends* that he shall lose it permanently. Thus the result may be the same as with the borrowing. In our example, the book is ultimately returned. It is the intention of the taker that distinguishes the cases. Why? Is this approach justifiable?

O. W. Holmes, The Common Law (1882), pp. 70–72:

"[In theft] acts are punished which of themselves would not be sufficient to accomplish the evil which the law seeks to prevent, and which are treated as equally criminal, whether the evil has been accomplished or not . . .

In larceny the consequences immediately flowing from the act are generally

---

[10] C.L.R.C., *ante* n. 30. The offence was first created by s.28 of the Road Traffic Act 1930 "to deal with a mischief which had even then become common." (para. 82).

[11] Fletcher, p. 48.

[12] *Ante*, n. 30.

exhausted with little or no harm to the owner. Goods are removed from his possession by trespass, and that is all, when the crime is complete. But they must be permanently kept from him before the harm is done which the law seeks to prevent. A momentary loss of possession is not what has been guarded against with such severe penalties. What the law means to prevent is the loss of it wholly and forever . . .

The reason is plain enough. The law cannot wait until the property has been used up or destroyed in other hands than the owner's, or until the owner has died, in order to make sure that the harm which it seeks to prevent has been done . . .

There must be an intent to deprive such owner of his ownership . . . But why? . . . The true answer is, that the intent is an index to the external event which probably would have happened, and that, if the law is to punish at all, it must, in this case, go on probabilities, not on accomplished facts. The analogy to the manner of dealing with attempts is plain. Theft may be called an attempt to permanently deprive a man of his property, which is punished with the same severity whether successful or not. If theft can rightly be considered in this way, intent must play the same part as in other attempts. An act which does not fully accomplish the prohibited result may be made wrongful by evidence that but for some interference it would have been followed by other acts co-ordinated with it to produce that result. This can only be shown by showing intent. In theft the intent to deprive the owner of his property establishes that the thief would have retained, or would not have taken steps to restore, the stolen goods."

The real harm in theft is thus, that when a defendant intends permanent deprivation there is a greater risk to the victim that he will lose his property permanently. (In most cases he will in fact have already lost the property.) As with the law of attempt, the threat to the property amounts to a "second order harm." This, however, only explains why the actual loss of property need not occur—but still does not explain why there must be an intention of permanent deprivation as opposed to an intention to borrow dishonestly.

What is being punished is disapproved-of behaviour which poses an unacceptable risk to the property of another. It is fairly obvious that where there is an intention of permanent deprivation there is a greater risk of actual permanent deprivation occurring (for much the same reason that there is greater danger when a defendant is intending a consequence than when he is being reckless as to it: he is trying to achieve the objective and must, in general, stand more chance of success than if not so trying). So the question reduces itself to whether permanent deprivation is sufficiently "worse" than temporary deprivation to justify criminalisation of the former but not the latter. Most people would surely agree that, in general, a permanent loss is qualitatively worse than a temporary loss. The owner has been deprived completely and irrevocably of his property. Insurance, if obtainable, will not compensate for such loss of power and control over the property. Whether it is *so much* worse as to justify the criminalisation line being drawn between the two is uncertain. Perhaps, it is best at this stage to conclude that while a temporary loss caused by dishonest conduct is unfortunate and deserves moral condemnation, one should refrain from expanding the role of the criminal law without clear and strong reasons.

Particular property

There must be an intention permanently to deprive the other of the *particular* property alleged to be appropriated. It is no defence that similar property was to be returned. This rule is most often applied to coins and banknotes. It is clear law that if one "borrows" money, intending to repay it the next day, one is not intending to return the same notes or coins; one therefore does have an intention of permanently depriving the other of the particular property alleged to be stolen.[13] Of course, actual liability still depends on a finding of dishonesty which, in such cases, may be difficult to establish.

Cheques

There is a particular problem with cheques in that if a defendant wrongfully obtains and cashes another's cheque, that cheque will ultimately be returned to that other and so the defendant could assert he had no intention of permanently depriving the other of that piece of paper. In *Duru* however it was stressed that in such a case the defendant would have an intention of depriving the other permanently of a thing in action: the right to receive payment for the amount specified on the cheque.

R. v. Duru (1973) 58 Cr.App.R. 151 (Court of Appeal, Criminal Division)

Megaw L.J.:
"The charge as laid was the charge of obtaining property, namely, a cheque. That cheque must be treated either as being the piece of paper, or as being the money which was represented by the cheque—the money that would be paid by the Greater London Council's bank on the due presentation to it of the cheque. In the view of this Court, there can be no doubt that the intention of both of these appellants, . . . was permanently to deprive the Greater London Council of that thing in action, that cheque; that piece of paper, in the sense of a piece of paper carrying with it the right to receive payment of the sum of £6,002·50, which is the amount concerned in count 3.
So far as the cheque itself is concerned, true it is a piece of paper. But it is a piece of paper which changes its character completely once it is paid, because then it receives a rubber stamp on it saying it has been paid and it ceased to be a thing in action, or at any rate it ceases to be, in its substance, the same thing as it was before: that is, an instrument on which payment falls to be made. It was the intention of the appellants, dishonestly and by deception, not only that the cheques should be made out and handed over, but also that they should be presented and paid, thereby permanently depriving the Greater London Council of the cheque in its substance as a thing in action . . .
If it were necessary to look to section 6(1) of the Theft Act, this Court would have no hesitation in saying that that subsection, would also be relevant, since

---

[13] *Williams* [1953] 1 Q.B. 660; *Velumyl* [1989] Crim.L.R. 299.

it is plain that the appellants each had the intention of causing the cheque to be treated as the property of the person by whom it was to be obtained, to dispose of, regardless of the rights of the true owner."

III. Offences Involving Deception

A. *The Sociological Background*

The terms 'theft,' 'robbery,' and 'burglary' evoke immediate under-standing in the hearer (even if that understanding is less than perfect); the same is less true of offences involving deception. The behaviour emcompassed by this group of offences may, however, be just as devas-tating to the victim as any of that in the other categories, or just as close to the fringes of criminality. It may be the classic con-man who tricks an elderly lady into parting with her valuable antique for vastly less than it is worth; it may be the individual passing bad cheques or falsely claim-ing social security; it may be the employee who abuses his position of trust to defraud his employers or it may be a company perpetrating a fraud against the public or the state. An increasing threat is perceived in the rise in the use of computers to commit crime. Large amounts of money[14] may be stolen through "salami" methods, where by rounding up, or down, small amounts are diverted from accounts into the offenders account or, for example, by "trojan horse" methods where secret codes are hidden in somebody else's computer programme. Such offending may go on for years without detection and then only come to light through accident.[15] To try to prevent or detect computer crime, companies may be told by security specialists to watch for staff living beyond their means, staff having drug or alcohol problems, staff being unwilling to take holidays, change jobs, be promoted, etc. . . . [16]

Certainly, such advice ties in with classic studies on embezzle-ment such as that by Donald Cressey. He found the motivation for embezzle-ment to be where a trusted person conceived of themselves as having a financial problem which was non-shareable, when that problem could be secretly resolved by violating that position of trust and when the offender was able to justify by rationalisations his behaviour to him-self.[17]

The examples given should indicate two other features of offences involving deception; that the amount of money involved, as with theft, may vary from small to huge and that it is inevitable that much of the offending will remain hidden and thus not appear in the official stat-

---

[14] In the United States, *e.g.* official data suggest that computer thieves steal more than $100 million every year; this may be only the tip of the iceberg however. Unofficial estimates put the figure closer to $40 billion a year; A. Bequi, *Computer Crime* (1978).
[15] For further discussion of computer related fraud see M. Levi, *Regulating Fraud* (1987) pp. 37–41 and D. Parker, "Computer-related white-collar Crime" in *White-collar Crime* ed. Geis and Stotland (1980).
[16] R. Doswell and G. L. Simons, *Fraud and Abuse of IT Systems* (1986).
[17] D. Cressey, *Other People's Money* (1953).

istics. According to such statistics there is far less offending of this nature than there is of theft; over two million offences of theft were recorded in 1987 whereas the number of recorded offences involving fraud (including deception offences) amounted to just over 120,000.[18]

Given the secretive nature of deception offences (the victim may never learn of his loss!), reliable estimates about the level of offending are impossible to come by, although it would seem reasonable to conclude that more is left hidden than is the case with other property offences. But work has been done to estimate the financial losses involved in fraud.[19] Levi's major study on fraud gathers together statistics from a variety of sources to conclude that "those data that are available show that in purely financial terms losses from fraud dwarf all other types of property crime."[20] For instance, in 1985, the cost of all recorded theft, burglary and robbery combined was £1084 million. The cost of Fraud Squad recorded fraud alone was £2113 million.[21] In the same year, a British study of companies by means of a telephone survey, asked how much money the companies thought they lost through fraud of any kind in any year (fraud being defined more widely than under the criminal law). The figure that resulted from the survey was £3 billion and not surprisingly this resulted in considerably raised media concern (at least) about losses from fraud.[22]

Whilst more research is obviously necessary in this area, one thing is clear: it is fundamentally flawed to conceive of the "crime problem" in terms of traditional street activities—it does contain within it the stereo-typical working-class villain and his species of fraud, but it also contains the sophisticated frauds of "respectable," powerful members of society.

B. *The Legal Background*

Whilst the protection of property by means of a law of theft (or larceny) has very early origins in the common law, the emergence of laws protecting those who parted with their property because of fraud or deceit was rather slower. The ruling spirit of "caveat emptor" made it inappropriate to use the criminal law in such instances. "(W)e are not to indict one for making a fool of another,"[23] and similarly, "(It is) needless to provide severe laws for such mischiefs, against which common prudence and caution may be a sufficient security."[24]

---

[18] *Criminal Statistics, England and Wales*, 1988, (Cm. 847), p. 43. The criminal statistics, unfortunately, do not distinguish deception offences from other types of fraud, but for instance 16,660 proceedings were brought under s.15 in 1987.
[19] The official statistics are completely silent on the question of losses from fraud although figures are given for theft, robbery and burglary.
[20] M. Levi, *Regulating Fraud* (hereinafter referred to as Levi) (1987) p. 23.
[21] *Ibid.*, p. 22.
[22] As Levi points out, it would, however, be unwise to place too much reliance upon this figure, *ibid.* pp. 26–27.
[23] *Per* Holt C.J. in *R. v. Jones* (1703) 91 Eng.Rep. 330.
[24] 1 Hawkins, Pleas of the Crown 344, (6th. ed. 1788).

Just as elsewhere in the law, however, the principle of "caveat emptor" was gradually eroded, so that by the time of the Theft Act 1968 distinct offences existed dependent upon the type of title obtained; if *ownership* passed by means of deception the offence was obtaining by false pretences. If only *possession* were obtained then it was larceny by a trick. Not only did this cause difficulties in distinguishing the two but there were other separate offences as well, such as larceny by a servant, fraudulent conversion and embezzlement.

All of these were swept away by the reforms of 1968.

Criminal Law Revision Committee, Theft and Related Offences, Eighth Report (1966) Cmnd. 2977:

"§ 38 The sub-committee for a considerable time proposed that the general offence of theft should be made to cover the present offence of obtaining by false pretences under 1916, s.32(1). It might seem appropriate to extend theft in this way in order to make it cover as many ways as possible of getting property dishonestly. But in the end the sub-committee gave up the idea (to the regret of some members), and the full committee agreed. In spite of its attractions, it seemed to the majority of the committee that the scheme would be unsatisfactory. Obtaining by false pretences is ordinarily thought of as different from theft, because in the former the owner in fact consents to part with his ownership; a bogus beggar is regarded as a rogue but not as a thief, and so are his less petty counterparts. To create a new offence of theft to include conduct which ordinary people would find difficult to regard as theft would be a mistake. The unnaturalness of including obtaining by false pretences in theft is emphasised by the difficulty of drafting a satisfactory definition to cover both kinds of conduct. . . . "

Under the Theft Acts of 1968 and 1978 there now exist the following deception offences.

1968 Act: s.15 Obtaining property by deception
        s.16 Obtaining pecuniary advantage by deception
1978 Act: s.1 Obtaining services by deception
        s.2 Evading liability by deception.

From a starting point of not being regarded as warranting criminal status, it now seems that cases involving deception may well be regarded more seriously by the courts than those involving theft, (perhaps because of the element of rational execution or betrayal of trust), although not as seriously as robbery or burglary. Section 15, for example, bears the same legal maximum penalty as theft, *i.e.* 10 years, but those found guilty of deception offences tend to be given immediate sentences of imprisonment, rather more frequently and for longer periods than those found guilty of theft.[25] Generalisations are, however, difficult to draw in this area: the sentencing task is more than ordinarily complicated. The problem has been described as paradoxically having

[25] C. Emmins, *A Practical Approach to Sentencing* (1985) pp. 298–299.

to sentence *offences* of high gravity but *offenders* of low "essential" bad-ness and light prior records.[26]

This problem consists of two main factors; the first of which is the strong positive relationship between the scale of the offence and the status of the offender.[27] The second issue is that of public attitudes towards "white-collar" offences: what these are and the extent to which these should be and are reflected in sentencing. Accepted wisdom sug-gests ignorance of and indifference to "white-collar" crime on the part of the public. However, recent studies suggest that the picture is rather more complex than that. Not only does it depend on the sector of the "public" to which one addresses enquiries (top executives, for example, rating fraud more seriously and police rating it less seriously than the "public") but upon the type and amount of harm caused. For example, in one survey members of the public rated fraud offences involving respectively, sums of £1,000 and £2,000 more seriously than a domestic burglary in which £20 was taken. Members of the public also dis-tinguished between, for example, income tax frauds and social security frauds, more people regarding the latter as morally wrong than the former.[28]

Surveys such as these suggest an intolerance towards commercial fraud at the very least whilst those that result in physical harm will be regarded very seriously indeed.[29] Public opinion can, of course, be ignored or heeded as suits the interests of the user, but generally it ought to play a part in the formulation of sentences. To that extent it would appear that sentencing patterns do broadly reflect the views of the public, although it may be that too much credit is given to the pre-vious good character of the defendant for the public's liking.

It is not proposed to deal with all the offences involving deception in great detail; instead, they will be used to illustrate the principles that have emerged in this area of law.[30]

C. *The Law*

1. Common Elements
There are certain elements shared by most of these offences; they are:
    (i) There must be a deception.
    (ii) The deception must cause the prohibited result.
    (iii) There must be dishonesty on the part of the defendant.

---

[26] Levi, p. 234. See also *Barrick* (1985) 7 Cr.App.R.(S.) 142 and *Aspin* (1987) 9 Cr.App.R.(S.) 288 as examples of this.

[27] S. Wheeler and M. Rothman, "The Organisation as Weapon in White-collar Crime" (1982) 80 Mich.L.R. 1403–26.

[28] Levi, pp. 57–75 and 136–144.

[29] *Cf.* L. Schrager and J. Short, "How Serious a Crime?" in *White-collar Crime* ed. Geis and Stotland (1980).

[30] For a fuller discussion see the specialist texts; J. C. Smith, *The Law of Theft* (6th. ed. 1988) and E. Griew, *The Theft Acts 1968 and 1978* (5th ed. 1986).

(i) *Deception*

Theft Act 1968 s.15(4)

"For purposes of this section 'deception' means any deception (whether deliberate or reckless) by words or conduct as to fact or as to law, including a deception as to the present intentions of the person using the deception or any other person."[31]

A. T. H. Smith, "The Idea of Criminal Deception" (1982) Crim.L.R. 721 at pp. 722–723:

"Deception could have been explained by the legislators in the Theft Act, but it was not. The Act confines itself to the somewhat unhelpful observation that ' "deception" means any deception,' the remainder of the section being devoted to reversing certain of the old common law rules surrounding the former 'false pretences.' To some extent this left the courts free to apply their own gloss to the word as the need to do so arose. But 'deception' already had, by the time the Theft Act became law in 1968, acquired a reasonably settled meaning, classically that stated by Buckley J. in *Re London and Globe Finance Corporation* ([1903] 1 Ch. 728 at p. 732) 'to deceive is, I apprehend, to induce a man to believe that a thing is true which is false . . . to deceive is by falsehood to induce a state of mind.' The Criminal Law Revision Committee explained its use of 'deception' by saying:
    'The substitution of "deception" for "false pretence" is chiefly a matter of language. The word "deception" seems to us (as to the framers of the American Law Institute's Model Penal Code) to have the advantage of directing attention to the effect that the offender deliberately produced on the mind of the person deceived, whereas "false pretence" makes one think of what exactly the offender did in order to deceive. "Deception" seems also more apt in relation to deception by conduct.' (8th Report, Cmnd. 2977, para. 187).
This reinforces the suggestion in Buckley J.'s definition that it is essential that the representation must operate on the conscious mind of the victim and cause him to believe that the facts are otherwise than they really are."

The essence of a deception is two-fold: first, the defendant must make an untrue representation, and second, as a result of this, the victim must believe that the untrue representation is true.

Section 15(4) specifies the circumstances and/or conditions in which the untrue representation must be made:

(a) words.

This is generally the most obvious way of practising a deception—for example, telling a victim one is selling a diamond when it is in fact glass.

---

[31] ss.16(3) Theft Act 1968 and 5(1) Theft Act 1978 import the same meaning into the other offences.

(b) conduct.

More difficulties are raised here in that it is necessary to determine what may be implied by the conduct of the defendant. The following are important instances of such implied representations.

[i] hotels

If one books into a hotel one is taken to be representing that one intends to pay one's bill at the end of one's stay.[32]

[ii] restaurants

Ordering and eating a meal in a restaurant is a representation that one intends to pay for that meal. If during or after the meal one decides not to pay, then remaining at the table thereafter is a false representation that one still intends to pay.[33]

[iii] quotations

R. v. Silverman (1988) 86 Cr.App.R. 213 (Court of Appeal, Criminal Division):

The appellant charged two elderly sisters grossly excessive prices for work done to the central heating and wiring of their flat. They had trusted him to charge a fair price because of previous work done by him for their family. The appellant placed no pressure on them to accept his quotation and there was nothing wrong with the work done. He was charged and convicted under section 15. He appealed on the grounds, *inter alia*, that an excessively high quotation did not amount to a false representation and that the trial judge had erred in not putting his defence (that the sisters seemed happy with his work) to the jury in express terms.

Watkins L.J.:

"Mr. Hopmeier, who appears here for the appellant, has argued, first, that the appellant made no representations to the complainants. He has not shrunk from conceding that the appellant was dishonest. He has submitted that the appellant quoted the sisters for the work to be done but that it was open to them either to accept or reject the quotation upon such advice as they might seek and perhaps in the light of tenders by others, and that the appellant was in much the same position as anyone else who is asked to quote for work to be done. He has argued that it is a dangerous concept to introduce into the criminal law that an excessively high quotation amounts to a false representation under section 15(1) of the Theft Act 1968. In certain circumstances that submission may we think be well founded. But whether a quotation amounts to false representation must depend upon the circumstances.

It seems clear to us that the complainants, far from being worldly wise, were unquestionably gullible. Having left their former home, they relied implicitly upon the word of the appellant about their requirements in their maisonette. In such circumstances of mutual trust, one party depending upon the other for fair and reasonable conduct, the criminal law may apply if one party takes dishonest advantage of the other by representing as a fair charge that which he but not the other knows is dishonestly excessive. . . .

---

[32] *Harris* (1975) 62 Cr.App.R. 28.
[33] *D.P.P.* v. *Ray* [1974] A.C. 370, *Post* p. 750.

. . . As to directing the jury upon what the prosecution had to prove and the circumstances in which they might succeed, we find no fault whatever in the way in which the judge directed them. There was material for a finding that there had been a false representation although it is true that the appellant had said nothing at the time he made his representations to encourage the sisters to accept the quotations. He applied no pressure upon them, and apart from mentioning the actual prices to be charged was silent as to other matters that may have arisen for question in their minds.

On the matter of representation we have been referred to *D.P.P.* v. *Ray* [1974] A.C. 370, which concerned someone leaving a restaurant without paying for a meal. At p. 379 Lord Reid said: 'So the accused, after he changed his mind, must have done something intended to induce the waiter to believe that he still intended to pay before he left. Deception, to my mind, implies something positive.'

Mr. Hopmeier submits that nothing positive was done in this case. Lord Reid continued (*ibid.*): 'It is quite true that a man intending to deceive can build up a situation in which his silence is as eloquent as an express statement.'

Here the situation had been built up over a long period of time. It was a situation of mutual trust and the appellant's silence on any matter other than the sums to be charged were, we think as eloquent as if he had said: 'What is more, I can say to you that we are going to get no more than a modest profit out of this.'

There is, we think, no foundation for the criticism of the judge in the first ground of appeal nor any substance in this ground in law. . . . ' [However, it was decided that the judge should have included D's defence 'worthless though it might have been in the minds of the jury' in the summing up]."

Appeal allowed

The implications of this decision are immense. In a free market economy it is regarded as acceptable to maximise one's profits—in short, to make as big a profit as possible. Those making grossly inflated quotations had, in the past, only to contend with the risk of their quotation being rejected. Now the risk of criminal prosecution is a possibility. Again, we are dealing with dubious business practice being criminalised. Rather than continually extending the reaches of the criminal law, it would surely be better here for the victim to resort to civil remedies.

To prevent any such expansion of the law it is important to stress two features of the above decision that would need to be satisfied in any case before an inflated quotation could give rise to liability. First, there was the rather special circumstance of a relationship of mutual trust that had been built up over a long time. Such special circumstances will seldom exist. Second, for all the deception offences it is necessary to prove dishonesty. It is highly unlikely that any jury would convict in cases of excessive quotations unless there were some very special circumstances as in *Silverman*.

[iv] Cheques

Handing over a signed cheque is an implied representation that when the cheque is presented to the bank it will be honoured.[34]

---

[34] *M.P.C.* v. *Charles* [1977] A.C. 177 *per, e.g.*, Lord Diplock at p. 182.

[v] Cheque cards

The nature of the representation changes when one uses a cheque card to support a cheque. This is because the cheque is bound to be honoured by the bank if certain conditions have been fulfilled and, therefore, the representation made with respect to the cheque is in fact true.

The representation thus is not about the cheque but about the cheque card itself. Issuing a cheque supported by a cheque card is an implied representation by conduct that one has actual authority from the bank to use the card and to contract on behalf of the bank that it will honour the cheque. If this representation is untrue (because, say, the bank has withdrawn its authority) it becomes a deception.[35]

[vi] Credit cards

Acceptance of a credit card gives rise to a contract between the acceptor and the credit card company under which the latter must honour the relevant voucher on presentation. Use of a credit card is thus an implied representation that one has actual authority from the credit card company:

1. to use the card to make contracts on behalf of that company, and
2. to bind the credit card company to honour the relevant voucher on presentation.

If these representations are untrue, then use of the credit card amounts to a deception.

[vii] Silence

What will be the law's response, therefore, where there is no "conduct" at all? What if, for example, the defendant silently acquiesces in the self-deception of another? Here there is nothing to which the intent of the defendant to profit by the misapprehension of another, can be attached—he has produced no change of mind in another—and there can be no liability.[36] However, the rule that silence is no deception is a limited one, as is illustrated by the case of *D.P.P.* v. *Ray*.[37] Here the defendant ordered a meal in a restaurant with the intention of paying for it. He subsequently formed an intention not to pay, thus falsifying the continuing representation made by his eating the meal. This, in effect, coupled with his failure to speak out to "undeceive" the waiter, made his actions culpable.

It is interesting to contrast the behaviour in all these cases with that required for theft. We saw earlier that for theft the actions of the defendant must be objectively inconsistent with the rights of the owner—a

---

[35] *Ibid.* For discussion of this case see *post* p. 758. The case of *Lambie* [1982] A.C. 449 established that the same representation is made when paying by credit-card, *cf.* Glanville Williams, *Textbook* pp. 778–780 who argues that these two cases take the notion of implied representation too far into mere non-disclosure.

[36] See further, J. C. Smith, *The Law of Theft* p. 85 and A. T. H. Smith, "The Idea of Criminal Deception" [1982] Crim.L.R. 721 at pp. 729–731.

[37] [1974] A.C. 370, *Post* p. 750.

view which accords with Fletcher's theory of manifest criminality.[38] In the above instances of deception the behaviour appears objectively innocent. Indeed, such overt innocence is necessary because one can hardly *deceive* a victim by acting in a manifestly criminal manner. However, it will be recalled that the notorious case of *Lawrence* can, it was suggested, be brought within the ambit of the definition of theft if one applied a test of manifest criminality, whereby the reasonable observer is endowed with knowledge of the surrounding circumstances and facts, but not with any knowledge of the defendant's intentions. Applying this reasoning to the above deception cases the reasonable observer could be endowed with knowledge of the fact that a credit card company had revoked a right to use a credit card. Use of such card is, as was the taxi-driver's conduct in *Lawrence*, a manifestly criminal act. There is thus a huge overlap between theft and the deception offences (particularly obtaining property by deception) leading to the possible conclusion that all such latter cases could be charged as theft.

This view is the one taken in the case of *Dobson*, where as discussed earlier[39] the court found liability for theft (for insurance purposes) in what was clearly a case of obtaining by deception. A purported distinction was drawn between acts which are merely consented to and those which are expressly authorised. In the former case the overlap between the two offences is total, in the latter only section 15 can be charged. It is to be regretted that such an unworkable distinction is being sought to be made. It was suggested earlier that the paradigmatic theft was illustrative of a theory of manifest criminality. Deception offences, on the other hand, are more indicative of a theory of *subjective* liability where the defendant's state of mind and intentions colour his otherwise innocent actions, rendering them criminal.[40] It is unfortunate that such a distinction appears to be in the process of collapsing.

(c) Deception as to fact or law or present intentions.

Section 15(4) talks of a deception as to fact or law and statements of present intention. This latter inclusion must be right: the implied representation of the restaurant customer that he intends to pay, is, for example, just as much a fact as the "fact" that he has sufficient money on him to pay. The Act is, however, silent as to whether statements of opinion are capable of being deceptions although they were not under the pre-1968 law.[41] Given that there are difficulties distinguishing fact from opinion, and given that mere advertising puffs would be excluded by potential victims not being gulled by them, there seems to be some force to the argument that opinions ought to be included. "Deliberate mis-statements of opinion would today be generally condemned as dishonest, no less dishonest, indeed, than mis-statements of other facts—

---

[38] *Ante* p. 690.
[39] [1989] 3 All E.R. 927 *Ante* p. 696.
[40] Fletcher p. 118.
[41] Larceny Act 1916, See *Bryan* (1857) Deers & B. 265.

for whether an opinion is held or not is a fact."[42] Moreover, such an inclusion would be in line with the subjectivist pattern of liability discernible elsewhere in deception offences.

(d) Deliberate or reckless.

Section 15(4) requires the deception to be "deliberate or reckless." A deception will be deliberate where the defendant is aware of the falsity of his statement and knows that the victim will (or may) believe in its truth. But what is meant by reckless? One view is that reckless must here be given its pre-*Caldwell* meaning: the defendant must have adverted to the possibility of his representation being false and have gone ahead and taken the risk. The argument here is that the additional requirement of dishonesty dictates such a result; the defendant who does not realise the possibility of his representation being false cannot be described as dishonest.[43]

On the other hand, it could be argued that the *Caldwell* test of recklessness is meant to be of general application and there is no reason in principle (not that juries need to operate according to any principles!) why a jury should not regard as dishonest someone who failed to consider the possibility of the falsity of his representations, particularly when the truth thereof could be easily ascertained and the risk of falsity was gross and obvious. The *Feely/Ghosh* test of dishonesty requires the jury first to ascertain the state of mind of the defendant and then to assess it as dishonest or not. There is nothing there to prevent a jury concluding that a defendant did believe a representation to be true but that this was such a grossly negligent representation that it is appropriate to adjudge the defendant dishonest.

However, on balance it is submitted that the first view is preferable and perhaps here an exception could be made to the normal *Caldwell* meaning of "reckless." Another way of saying that a person really believes his representation is true is to say that the belief is "*honestly and genuinely held.*" To allow a jury to deem an "honest" belief to be dishonest would be to push the criminal law into the realms of legal fiction, and away from the soil of everyday values in which it should be rooted.

(ii) *The deception must cause the prohibited result*

The deception must be operative, that is, it has to be established that the representation deceived the victim, for example, into providing a meal or a hotel room or accepting a cheque. Therefore, if the victim does not rely on the representation for whatever reason (say, for example, he is aware of its falsity), the offence has not been committed. It may, of course, be possible to charge the defendant with attempting to obtain by deception.

---

[42] Smith, *The Law of Theft* p. 92.
[43] Smith and Hogan p. 545, fn. 8.

D.P.P. v. Ray [1974] A.C. 370 (House of Lords)

The defendant and four other young men went to a Chinese restaurant for a meal, intending at that stage to pay for it. After eating the meal they decided not to pay but only left when the waiter left the room. The defendant's conviction under s.16(2)(a) Theft Act 1968 (now repealed) was quashed by the Divisional Court for lack of deception. The prosecution appealed to the House of Lords.

Lord Reid:
"It is, I think apparent from the case stated that the magistrates accepted the prosecution contention that
' . . . as soon as the intent to evade payment was formed and the appellant still posed as an ordinary customer the deception had been made.'
The magistrates stated that they were of opinion that
' . . . having changed his mind as regards payment, by remaining in the restaurant for a further 10 minutes as an ordinary customer who was likely to order a sweet or coffee, the appellant practised a deception.'
I cannot read that as a finding that after he changed his mind he intended to deceive the waiter into believing that he still intended to pay. And there is no finding that the waiter was in fact induced to believe that by anything the accused did after he changed his mind. I would infer from the case that all that he intended to do was to take advantage of the first opportunity to escape and evade his obligation to pay.

Deception is an essential ingredient of the offence. Dishonest evasion of an obligation to pay is not enough. I cannot see that there was, in fact, any more than that in this case.

I agree with the Divisional Court [1973] 1 W.L.R. 317, 323:
'His plan was totally lacking in the subtlety of deception and to argue that his remaining in the room until the coast was clear amounted to a representation to the waiter is to introduce an artificiality which should have no place in the Act.'
I would therefore dismiss this appeal."

Lord Morris of Borth-y-Gest:
"In the present case it is found as a fact that when the respondent ordered his meal he believed that he would be able to pay. One of his companions had agreed to lend him money. He therefore intended to pay. So far as the waiter was concerned the original implied representation made to him by the respondent must have been a continuing representation so long as he (the respondent) remained in the restaurant. There was nothing to alter the representation. Just as the waiter was led at the start to believe that he was dealing with a customer who by all that he did in the restaurant was indicating his intention to pay in the ordinary way, so the waiter was led to believe that that state of affairs continued. But the moment came when the respondent decided and therefore knew that he was not going to pay: but he also knew that the waiter still thought that he was going to pay. By ordering his meal and by his conduct in assuming the role of an ordinary customer the respondent had previously shown that it was his intention to pay. By continuing in the same role and behaving just as before he was representing that his previous intention continued. That was a deception because his intention, unknown to the waiter, had become quite otherwise. The dishonest change of intention was not likely to produce the result that the waiter would be told of it. The essence of the deception was that the waiter should not know of it or be given any sort of clue that it (the change of intention) had come about. Had the waiter suspected that by a change of intention a

secret exodus was being planned, it is obvious that he would have taken action to prevent its being achieved.

It was said in the Divisional Court that a deception under section 16 should not be found unless an accused has actively made a representation by words or conduct which representation is found to be false. But if there was an original representation (as, in my view, there was when the meal was ordered) it was a representation that was intended to be and was a continuing representation. It continued to operate on the mind of the waiter. It became false and it became a deliberate deception. The prosecution do not say that the deception consisted in not informing the waiter of the change of mind; they say that the deception consisted in continuing to represent to the waiter that there was an intention to pay before leaving.

On behalf of the respondent it was contended that no deception had been practised. It was accepted that when the meal was ordered there was a representation by the respondent that he would pay but it was contended that once the meal was served there was no longer any representation but that there was merely an obligation to pay a debt: it was further argued that thereafter there was no deception because there was no obligation in the debtor to inform his creditor that payment was not to be made. I cannot accept these contentions. They ignore the circumstance that the representation that was made was a continuing one: its essence was that an intention to pay would continue until payment was made: by its very nature it could not cease to operate as a representation unless some new arrangement was made. . . .

The final question which arises is whether, if there was deception and if there was pecuniary advantage, it was by the deception that the respondent obtained the pecuniary advantage. In my view, this must be a question of fact and the magistrates have found that it was by his deception that the respondent dishonestly evaded payment. It would seem to be clear that if the waiter had thought that if he left the restaurant to go to the kitchen the respondent would at once run out, he (the waiter) would not have left the restaurant and would have taken suitable action. The waiter proceeded on the basis that the implied representation made to him (*i.e.* of an honest intention to pay) was effective. The waiter was caused to refrain from taking certain courses of action which but for the representation he would have taken. In my view, the respondent during the whole time that he was in the restaurant made and by his continuing conduct continued to make a representation of his intention to pay before leaving. When in place of his original intention he substituted the dishonest intention of running away as soon as the waiter's back was turned, he was continuing to lead the waiter to believe that he intended to pay. He practised a deception on the waiter and by so doing he obtained for himself the pecuniary advantage of evading his obligation to pay before leaving. That he did so dishonestly was found by the magistrates who, in my opinion, rightly convicted him.

I would allow the appeal."

Appeal allowed

R. v. Laverty [1970] 3 All E.R. 432 (Court of Appeal, Criminal Division)

(The facts appear from the judgment)

Lord Parker C.J.

" . . . [T]he appellant was convicted of obtaining property by deception, the property being £65 in cash and a cheque for £165, and was sentenced to six months' imprisonment suspended for two years. He now appeals against his conviction.

The facts are in a very short compass. The car bearing number plates DUV 111C, a Hillman Imp, was bought by a Mr. Bedborough from the appellant, and a cheque was given as part of the price. In fact that a car bearing those number plates was a car originally bearing number plates JPA 945C which had been stolen. According to the appellant when he got the car, and there was no question of his having stolen it, it was in a bad condition, he repaired it and he put on to it the chassis and rear number plates of DUV 111C, those plates having been obtained from another source relating of course to another car.

The charge made in the indictment in count 3 took the form of alleging a false representation which here was by conduct. It was not a false representation that the appellant was the owner and had a good title to sell but the false representation was by purporting that a Hillman Imp motor car which the appellant sold to Roy Clinton Bedborough was the original Hillman Imp motor car, index number DUV 111C.

Although it was contested at the trial, it was conceded in this court that there was a representation by conduct that the car being sold to Mr. Bedborough was the original Hillman Imp to which the chassis plate and rear plate which it bore had been assigned. It is conceded that such a representation was made by conduct; it is clear that that was false, and false to the knowledge of the appellant. The sole question was whether this false representation operated on Mr. Bedborough's mind so as to cause him to hand over this cheque.

As sometimes happens, in this case Mr. Bedborough did not give the answers which were helpful to the prosecution, and no leading questions could be put. The nearest answer was 'I bought this because I thought the appellant was the owner.' In other words Mr. Bedborough was saying: 'What induced me to part with my money was the representation by conduct that the appellant had a title to sell. . . .'

The proper way of proving these matters is through the mouth of the person to whom the false representation is conveyed, and further it seems to the court in the present case that no jury could say that the only inference here was that Mr. Bedborough parted with his money by reason of this false representation. Mr. Bedborough may well have been of the mind as he stated he was, namely that what operated on his mind was the belief that the appellant was the owner. Provided the appellant was the owner it may well be that Mr. Bedborough did not mind that the car did not bear its original number plates. At any rate as it seems to the court it cannot be said that the only possible inference here is that it actuated on Mr. Bedborough's mind.

In those circumstances, although with some reluctance, this court feels that the proper course here is to allow the appeal and quash the conviction."

Appeal allowed. Conviction quashed

R. v. King (1987) 84 Cr.App.R. 357 (Court of Appeal, Criminal Division)

The appellants went to the house of a 68-year-old widow, falsely representing themselves as from a firm of tree surgeons, of whom she had heard. They purported to examine the trees in her garden and told her that four trees needed to be removed urgently to prevent damage to a gas main and the house foundations. They offered to do it if paid £470 in cash. The widow withdrew £100 from one account and was in the process of withdrawing £200 from the second account when the cashier noticed she seemed very distressed. Following a conversation between the widow and the cashier the police were informed and the appellants were arrested and charged with attempting to obtain property by deception contrary to section 1(1) of the Criminal Attempts Act 1981. They were convicted and appealed on the ground that their conduct did not constitute the criminal offence of obtaining property by false pretences or by deception because as a matter of causation, the relevant property would have been obtained by reason of the work carried out (the felling of the trees) rather than by reason of any deception.

Neill L.J.:
" . . . The argument advanced on behalf of the appellants on causation or remoteness was founded on the decision in *Lewis*. . . .
In that case (which was decision at Somerset Assizes in January, 1922) a schoolmistress obtained her appointment by falsely stating that she possessed a teacher's certificate. She was held to be not guilty of obtaining her salary by false pretences, on the ground that she was paid because of the services she rendered, and not because of the false representation.
It was submitted on behalf of the appellants that the principle underlying the decision in *Lewis* could be applied in the present case. . . .
It is to be observed, however, that Professor Glanville Williams in his *Textbook on Criminal Law* at p. 751 has this to say of the decision in *Lewis* (*supra*):
'Yet *Lewis* would not have got the job and consequently her salary, if it had not been for the pretence. Her object in making the pretence was to get the salary. Assuming, as is likely, that the employer would not have made her any payment of salary if a lie had not been operating on his mind, there was certainly a factual causal connection between the lie and the obtaining of salary. Why should it not be a causal connection in law? We have seen that when the defendant produces a consequence intentionally, it is generally regarded as imputable to him. Why should it not be so here?' . . .
We have given careful consideration to the argument based on causation or remoteness, and have taken account of the fact that some support for the argument may be provided by the writings of a number of distinguished academic lawyers. Nevertheless, we have come to the conclusion that on the facts of the present case the argument is fallacious.
In our view, the question in each case is: was the deception an operative cause of the obtaining of the property? This question falls to be answered as a question of fact by the jury applying their commonsense. . . .
In the present case there was, in our judgment, ample evidence upon which the jury could come to the conclusion that had the attempt succeeded the money would have been paid over by the victim as a result of the lies told to her by the appellants. We consider that the judge was correct to reject both the motion to quash the indictment and the submission that there was no case to answer.
For the reasons which we have set out, we consider that the appellants were rightly convicted in this case, and the appeals must therefore be dismissed.[44]

Appeals dismissed

The decision of *Ray* lies somewhere between *Laverty* (where it would have been improper for causal inferences to be drawn) and *King* (where any other inference would have been absurd). Whilst it is true in *Ray* that the waiter would not have left the room had he known of the

[44] The law of remoteness applies to criminal deception just as it applies in civil law. Here the court decided that the causal connection was not too remote. *Contra, Clucas* [1949] 2 K.B. 226. In this case decided under the old law of false pretences (similar in relation to remoteness), the defendant induced a book-maker to accept bets on credit by falsely representing that the bets came from a number of persons. When the bet was successful, it was held that the winnings had not been obtained by the false pretences but by the horse winning the race, *cf. Levene* v. *Pearcey* [1976] Crim.L.R. 63.

defendant's change of mind, it does not automatically follow that he left the room *because* of the defendant's continuing representation; not having the evidence of the crucial witness—the waiter, himself—the majority still felt, however, that there was enough evidence to enable the justices to have inferred the causal link. This rather cavalier approach to the question of causation has been taken much further in other cases.

R. v. Lambie [1982] A.C. 449 (House of Lords)

A bank issued a credit card to the defendant, with a credit limit of £200. She used the card for a number of transactions that exceeded her credit limit. The bank sought to recover the card, and the defendant agreed to return it on December 7, 1977, but she did not do so. By December 15, she had used the card for further transactions, incurring a total debt to the bank of £1,005·26. On that date she selected goods in a shop to the value of £10·35 and produced the credit card to a departmental manager of the shop. The departmental manager completed the voucher and checked that the card was correct in date, that it was not on the current stop list and that the defendant's signature on the voucher corresponded with that on the card. The defendant then took away the goods. She was charged in respect of that transaction with obtaining a pecuniary advantage by deception, contrary to section 16(1) of the Theft Act 1968, (now repealed) in that she dishonestly obtained for herself a pecuniary advantage, namely the evasion of a debt for which she then made herself liable by deception, namely by false representations that she was authorised to use a credit card to obtain goods. She was convicted, but the Court of Appeal (Criminal Division) allowed her appeal against conviction.

Lord Roskill:
" . . . [In *Charles* [1977] A.C. 177] this house was concerned with the dishonest use, not as in the present appeal of a credit card, but of a cheque card. The appellant defendant was charged and convicted on two counts of obtaining a pecuniary advantage by deception, contrary to section 16 of the Act of 1968. The Court of Appeal (Criminal Division) and your Lordships' House both upheld those convictions. Your Lordships unanimously held that where a drawer of a cheque which is accepted in return for goods, services or cash uses a cheque card he represents to the payee that he has the actual authority of the bank to enter on its behalf into the contract expressed on the card that it would honour the cheque on presentation for payment.

My Lords, I quote in their entirety three paragraphs from the speech of my noble and learned friend, Lord Diplock [1977] A.C. 177, 182–183, which, as I venture to think, encapsulate the reasoning of all those members of your Lordships' House who delivered speeches:

'When a cheque card is brought into the transaction, it still remains the fact that all the payee is concerned with is that the cheque should be honoured by the bank. I do not think that the fact that a cheque card is used necessarily displaces the representation to be implied from the act of drawing the cheque which has just been mentioned. It is, however, likely to displace that representation at any rate as the main inducement to the payee to take the cheque, since the use of the cheque card in connection with the transaction gives to the payee a direct contractual right against the bank itself to payment on presentment, provided that the use of the card by the drawer to bind the bank to pay the cheque was within the actual or ostensible authority conferred upon him by the bank.

By exhibiting to the payee a cheque card containing the undertaking by the bank to honour cheques drawn in compliance with the conditions indorsed on the back, and drawing the cheque accordingly, the drawer represents to the payee that he has actual authority from the bank to make a contract with the payee on the bank's behalf that it will honour the cheque on presentment for payment.

It was submitted on behalf of the accused that there is no need to imply a representation that the drawer's authority to bind the bank was actual and not merely ostensible, since ostensible authority alone would suffice to create a contract with the payee that was binding on the bank; and the drawer's possession of the cheque card and the cheque book with the bank's consent would be enough to constitute his ostensible authority. So, the submission goes, the only representation needed to give business efficacy to the transaction would be true. This argument stands the doctrine of ostensible authority on its head. What creates ostensible authority in a person who purports to enter into a contract as agent for a principal is a representation made to the other party that he has the actual authority of the principal for whom he claims to be acting to enter into the contract on that person's behalf. If (1) the other party has believed the representation and on the faith of that belief has acted upon it and (2) the person represented to be his principal has so conducted himself towards that other party as to be estopped from denying the truth of the representation, then, and only then, is he bound by the contract purportedly made on his behalf. The whole foundation of liability under the doctrine of ostensible authority is a representation, believed by the person to whom it is made, that the person claiming to contract as agent for a principal has the actual authority of the principal to enter into the contract on his behalf.'

If one substitutes . . . the words 'to honour the voucher' for the words 'to pay the cheque,' it is not easy to see why mutatis mutandis the entire passages are not equally applicable to the dishonest misuse of credit cards as to the dishonest misuse of cheque cards. . . .

My Lords, as the appellant says in paragraph 9 of his printed case, the Court of Appeal (Criminal Division) laid too much emphasis upon the undoubted, but to my mind irrelevant, fact that Miss Rounding said she made no assumption about the respondent's credit standing with the bank. They reasoned from the absence of assumption that there was no evidence from which the jury could conclude that she was 'induced by a false representation that the defendant's credit standing at the bank gave her authority to use the card.' But, my Lords, with profound respect to the learned Lord Justice, that is not the relevant question. Following the decision of this House in *Reg.* v. *Charles*, it is in my view clear that the representation arising from the presentation of a credit card has nothing to do with the respondent's credit standing at the bank but is a representation of actual authority to make the contract with, in this case, Mothercare on the bank's behalf that the bank will honour the voucher upon presentation. Upon that view, the existence and terms of the agreement between the bank and Mothercare are irrelevant, as is the fact that Mothercare, because of that agreement, would look to the bank for payment. That being the representation to be implied from the respondent's actions and use of the credit card, the only remaining question is whether Miss Rounding was induced by that representation to complete the transaction and allow the respondent to take away the goods. My Lords, if she had been asked whether, had she known the respondent was acting dishonestly and, in truth, had no authority whatever from the bank to use the credit card in this way, she (Miss Rounding) would have completed the transaction, only one answer is possible—no. Had an affirmative answer been given to this question, Miss Rounding would, of course, have become a participant in furtherance of the respondent's fraud and a conspirator with her to defraud both Mothercare and the bank. Leading counsel for the respondent was ultimately constrained, rightly as I think, to admit that had that question been asked of Miss Rounding and answered, as it must have been, in the negative, this appeal must succeed. But both he and his learned junior strenuously argued that, as my noble and learned friend, Lord Edmund-Davies, pointed out in his speech in *Reg.* v. *Charles* [1977] A.C. 177, 192–193, the question whether a person is or is not induced to act in a particular way by a dishonest representation is a question of fact, and since what they claimed to be the crucial question had not been asked of Miss Rounding, there was no adequate proof of the requisite inducement. In her deposition, Miss Rounding stated, no doubt with complete truth, that she only remembered this particular transaction with the respondent because some one subsequently came and asked her about it after it had taken place. My Lords, credit card frauds are all too frequently perpetrated, and if conviction of offenders for offences against sections 15 or 16 of the Act of 1968 can only be obtained if the prosecution are able in each case to call the person upon whom the fraud was immediately perpetrated to say that he or she positively remembered the particular transaction and, had the truth been known, would never have entered into that supposedly well-remembered transaction, the guilty would often escape conviction. In some cases, of course,it may be possible to adduce such evidence if the particular transaction is well remembered. But where as in the present case no one could reasonably be expected to remember a particular transaction in detail, and the inference of inducement may well be in all the circumstances quite irresistible, I see no reason in principle why it should not be left to the jury to decide, upon the evidence in the case as a whole, whether that inference is in truth irresistible as to my mind it is in the present case.In this connection it is to be noted that the respondent did not go into the witness box to give evidence from which that inference might conceivably have been rebutted. . . .

My Lords, I would answer the certified question in the negative and would allow the appeal and restore the conviction of the respondent upon the second count in the indictment which she faced at Bedford Crown Court."

Appeal allowed

R. v. Doukas [1978] 1 W.L.R. 372 (Court of Appeal, Criminal Division)

The defendant, a hotel waiter, was found in the hotel with six bottles of wine on him of a kind not stocked by the hotel. He was charged and convicted under section 25 of the Theft Act 1968 with going equipped to cheat having admitted that he intended to sell the wine to the hotel customers for his own profit.

Geoffrey Lane L.J.:
"There must be proof that the obtaining would have been, wholly or partially, by virtue of the deception. The prosecution must prove that nexus between the deception and obtaining. It is this last and final ingredient which, as we see it in the present case, is the only point which raises any difficulty. Assuming, as we must, and as was obviously the case, that the jury accepted the version of the police interviews and accepted that the defendant had made the confession to which I have referred, then the only question was, would this obtaining have in fact been caused by the deception practised by the defendant.

We have, as in the notice of appeal, been referred to the decision in *Rashid* [1977] 1 W.L.R. 298, which was a decision by another division of this court. That case concerned not a waiter in a hotel, but a British Rail waiter who substituted not bottles of wine for the railway wine but his own tomato sandwiches for the railway tomato sandwiches; and it is to be observed that the basis of the decision in that case was that the summing up of the judge to the jury was inadequate. On that basis the appeal was allowed. But the court went on to express its views obiter on the question whether in those circumstances it could be said that the obtaining was by virtue of deception, and it came to the conclusion, as I say obiter, that the answer was probably no.

Of course each case of this type may produce different results according to the circumstances of the case and according, in particular, to the commodity which is being proffered. But, as we see it, the question has to be asked of the hypothetical customer, 'Why did you buy this wine; or, if you had been told the truth, would you or would you not have bought the commodity?' It is, at least in theory, for the jury in the end to decide that question.

Here, as the ground of appeal is simply the judge's action in allowing the case to go to the jury, we are answering that question, so to speak, on behalf of the judge rather than the jury. Was there evidence of the necessary nexus fit to go to the jury? Certainly so far as the wine is concerned, we have no doubt at all that the hypothetical customer, faced with the waiter saying to him: 'This of course is not hotel wine, this is stuff which I imported into the hotel myself and I am going to put the proceeds of the wine, if you pay, into my own pocket,' would certainly answer, so far as we can see, 'I do not want your wine, kindly bring me the hotel carafe wine.' Indeed it would be a strange jury that came to any other conclusion, and a stranger guest who gave any other answer, for several reasons. First of all, the guest would not know what was in the bottle which the waiter was proffering. True, he may not know what was in the carafe which the hotel was proffering, but he would at least be able to have recourse to the hotel if something was wrong with the carafe wine, but he would have no such recourse with the waiter; if he did, it would be worthless.

It seems to us the matter can be answered on a much simpler basis. The hypothetical customer must be reasonably honest as well as being reasonably intelligent and it seems to us incredible that any customer, to whom the true situation was made clear, would willingly make himself a party to what was obviously a fraud by the waiter upon his employers. If that conclusion is contrary to the obiter dicta in *Rashid* [1977] 1 W.L.R. 298, then we must respectfully disagree with those dicta.

It is not necessary to examine the question any further as to whether we are differing from *Rashid* or not. But it seems to us beyond argument that the judge was right in the conclusion he reached and was right to allow the matter to go to the jury on the basis which he did."

Application refused

R. v. Cooke [1986] A.C. 909 (House of Lords)

Lord Bridge of Harwich:
" . . . Upright citizens as the ordinary run of British Rail passengers may be presumed to be, I am not prepared to assume that they would necessarily refuse to take and pay for refreshments even if they knew perfectly well that the buffet staff were practising the kind of 'fiddle' here involved."

Lord Mackay of Clashfern:
" . . . I respectfully agree that the elements necessary to establish the offence are correctly described . . . in *Doukas* . . .
In my opinion the question whether the necessary ingredients for the offence have been established in any particular case is one for the jury, and whether

they have been will depend on the detail of the evidence, particularly that relating to the attitude and understanding of those receiving the supplies."

The decisions of *Charles*, *Lambie*, *Rashid* and *Doukas* have generated much debate. A. T. H. Smith argues that their combined effect is to extend "the concept of deception beyond what it meant when the Theft Act was framed in 1968, to mean something much more like fraud. . . . [W]hereas elsewhere in the criminal law the conduct objected to must be an 'operating and substantial cause' the courts are now saying that a man has been deceived when he has been told an untruth (verbally or by conduct) and where it may be assumed that he would have done otherwise had he known the truth."[45] In other words, causation is reduced to the *sine qua non* level. Smith and Hogan, however, see *Charles* and *Lambie* as exceptions to the rule requiring a causal link[46] prompted by the opportunities for fraud in the area of cheques and credit-cards. *Doukas* is not seen as part of that exception:

J.C. Smith and B. Hogan, Criminal Law (6th ed. 1988) pp. 553–554:

"It is possible to argue that a buyer who purchases goods without consciously adverting to their origin has not been deceived though he has been defrauded. It may be said that to be deceived a man must be induced into an affirmative belief that something is true which is false. Against this it can be argued that people enter into many routine transactions on certain implicit assumptions whether they are consciously adverted to or not. One who buys goods assumes that the buyer is either the owner or is authorised to sell whether he consciously thinks about it or not. It must follow that if he deals with British Rail or with an hotelier he must assume that the goods emanate from British Rail or the hotelier. And it cannot be a matter of indifference to him whether the goods supplied belong to British Rail or the hotelier. Quite apart from the fact that he would not lend himself to a fraud in purchasing goods supplied by an employee, he would not willingly forgo his legal remedies against British Rail or the hotelier should the goods prove to be defective. So too a tenant or lodger will assume that a person letting premises is authorised to let since his own position is precarious if that person is a trespasser who is not authorised to let."

But it may be that these cases reveal much more than just the ambit of the concept "deception" (important though that is). They also have much to say about the interests being protected by the deception offences. In none of these cases did it matter whether the "victim" lost out, in fact, by the defendant's action. ("Victim" meaning for these purposes the customer who was deceived for the purposes of s.25(5) although the *real* victim was, of course, the person cheated: *i.e.* British Rail or the hotel). It was irrelevant in *Rashid*, for example, to determine whether the sandwiches would have been better, fresher or cheaper! No attention was paid to the fact that the wine in *Doukas* may have been of

---

[45] "The Idea of Criminal Deception" [1982] Crim.L.R. 721 at p. 721.

[46] *Criminal Law* pp. 552–3. Glanville Williams argues that these cases were not meant to and do not change the requirement of causation, but, proceeded on highly questionable findings of fact about the victims' states of mind: *Textbook* p. 791.

superior quality to that offered by the restaurant. It was described as "irrelevant" in *Lambie*[47] that the shop assistant was unconcerned about the credit-worthiness of the defendant. Liability centred not on whether the victims had suffered harm to their "net wealth" but on whether their autonomy to direct their assets without being deceived by another's fraud had been infringed.[48] This is seen as the interest the law is seeking to protect—commercial freedom—and not the knotty issue of whether the victim got value for money.[49] As such, liability can be seen as centred around what the defendant did by way of threatening this interest.

One final question remains to be considered in relation to the *Charles* and *Lambie* type of situation. Whilst the concern of the appellate courts to convict and punish rogues such as those who may engage in such activities, dominated their reasoning, the problem of bad cheques etc., is wider than this. The person who passes a bad cheque may be part of a large-scale organisational fraud, a lone "professional" criminal making his living out of it, or someone whose actions fall into a grey area of both "deception" and "dishonesty." It is probably the case that more fraud offences involve cheques and credit-cards than anything else, [50] but it is also true that many cases are dealt with through non-legal means, and that many losses will be written off altogether. If, as we have seen,[51] the criminal law should only be invoked when no other means is appropriate, then perhaps the courts ought not to strain too hard to bring such actions within the ambit of the deception offences.

J. C. Smith, Commentary to Lambie [1981] Crim.L.R. 716–717:

" . . . Such straining of language and of concepts has been all too common a feature of the law of stealing and related offences for at least 150 years but it has usually been directed to procuring the conviction of a rogue who clearly ought to be guilty of a crime. In the present case it is not so clear. One view is that it is the responsibility of the banks and credit companies to ensure that these cards are given only to creditworthy and responsible people and that they should not look to the criminal law to protect them from dishonest breaches of contract by their clients. They put great temptation in the way of ordinary people, often young and inexperienced, some of whom take too literally the slogan that the card 'takes the waiting out of wanting.' Views of this nature have recently been expressed from the bench by His Honour, Judge Sir Harold Cassel. *The Times*, July 28, 1981. The Council of Europe Committee on Crime Problems considered this problem recently: Report on Decriminalisation (1980) Chapter XIII. They found that the law of most member states covered cases where there is a false declaration, forgery or falsification of identity but, they said (p. 201)—'it is not appropriate to criminalise other forms of credit cards abuse (*e.g.* exceeding the

---

[47] *Per* Lord Roskill at p. 459.

[48] *Cf.* Fletcher pp. 51–57.

[49] As Fletcher points out, Anglo-Amercian systems are very reluctant to assess this, as, for example, in relation to the doctrine of consideration in contract, p. 54.

[50] The official statistics are unhelpful in this respect because offences are not broken down in this way, but Levi's research supports this view and indicates that generally the sum of money involved with such frauds is low. Levi, pp. 42–3 and 103–4.

[51] *Ante* pp. 77–95.

credit allowed) since there is a civil law contract freely entered into between the credit institution and its customer for which the guarantee of civil damages seems adequate. It is up to the banks and credit institutions to look to the "morality" of their credit policy by making all necessary checks beforehand on the reliability of their customers and their financial standing, applying the necessary safeguards, moderating their advertising policy, etc.

Criminalisation in this field might have the contrary effect of encouraging banks and credit institutions to be irresponsible and hence increase credit card abuse.'

As for cheques, the committee would decriminalise the use of guaranteed cheques in countries where their use is an offence.

If we followed these recommendations, neither *Charles* nor *Lambie* would be guilty of an offence.

There is a good deal of force in these observations though it may be a bit unrealistic to suggest a civil remedy as a solution in the United Kingdom. The offending party would usually not be worth suing and, if he were, the cost involved would probably be uneconomic. Furthermore, while these modern methods of credit and of trading are certainly of benefit to the banks and to the traders, they are also of benefit to the public, as is apparent from the readiness of the public to take advantage of them. Most people, it is thought, would regard the conduct of *Charles* and of *Lambie* as fraudulent. The Law Commission is now reviewing the law relating to fraud, with a view to the abolition of the common law conspiracy to defraud. If they should succeed in defining a single general offence of fraud, it is very likely that this conduct would be embraced by it; but it is doubtful whether it is possible to frame a satisfactory definition of a single offence—it is likely to be too vague, to embrace all the great variety of carefully defined offences of dishonesty which exist in the law and to lack the precision which our traditions demand. If that is right, the question will be whether we should have a simple offence penalising the dishonest use of a cheque card or credit card. There is, a case for doing so; but there is also a case for reversing *Charles* and *Lambie* as the European Committee would suggest. The arguments deserve, and will no doubt receive, careful consideration by the Law Commission."

(iii) *Dishonesty*

The partial definition of dishonesty contained in section 2 of the Theft Act 1968 does not apply to the deception offences.[52] However, in other respects, the same meaning is to be given to dishonesty in this context as under section 1.[53]

Criminal Law Revision Committee, Eighth Report, Theft and Related Offences, 1966, Cmnd. 2977, para. 88:

"§ 88 The provision in (section 15(1)) making a person guilty of criminal deception if he 'dishonestly obtains' the property replaces the provision in 1916, s.32(1), making a person guilty of obtaining by false pretences if he 'with intent to defraud, obtains' the things there mentioned. The change will correspond to the change from 'fraudulently' to 'dishonestly' in the definition of stealing which is discussed in § 39. . . . . 'Dishonestly' seems the right word to use in relation to criminal deception also. Owing to the words 'dishonestly obtains' a person who uses deception in order to obtain property to which he

---

[52] The Theft Act 1968, s.1(3).
[53] *Ante* p. 725. See also *Melwani* [1989] Crim.L.R. 565.

believes himself entitled will not be guilty; for though the deception may be dishonest, the obtaining is not. In this respect also the offence will be in line with theft because a belief in a legal right to deprive an owner of property is for the purpose of theft inconsistent with dishonesty and is specifically made a defence by the partial definition of 'dishonesty' in (section) 2(1)."

R. v. Woolven (1983) 73 Cr.App.R. 231 (Court of Appeal, Criminal Division)

The defendant opened a bank account in a false name knowing that money would be transferred to it from an account belonging to his former employer, who could not withdraw money in the ordinary way because his account was in overdraft. Acting on the instructions of the other and with a false letter of identification he attempted to cash a cheque. He was charged with attempting to obtain property by deception contrary to s.15 of the Theft Act 1968. He admitted that ordinary people would have found his behaviour dishonest but that he had not thought it so because he thought the money belonged to his employer. He was convicted and appealed.

Leonard J.:
"The question which arises for our decision is whether the learned judge's direction as to the element of dishonesty was adequate to do justice in the present case. At an early stage in the summing up he directed the jury in accordance with the judgment of this Court in *Ghosh* [1982] Q.B. 1053. In giving the judgment of the Court the Lord Chief Justice said at p. 1064: 'In determining whether the prosecution has proved that the defendant was acting dishonestly, a jury must first of all decide whether according to the ordinary standards of reasonable and honest people what was done was dishonest. If it was not dishonest by those standards, that is the end of the matter and the prosecution fails. If it was dishonest by those standards, then the jury must consider whether the defendant himself must have realised that what he was doing was by those standards dishonest.'

The learned judge in the present case said to the jury: 'So the final . . . and the determining question . . . is whether on the evidence you are satisfied that [the appellant] was acting dishonestly.' He told them to ask themselves first what the appellant had done. Then they were to consider whether his actions were dishonest, measured by the standards of any ordinary honest man. Finally they had to decide whether they were satisfied that the appellant must have realised his conduct would be condemned as dishonest by any other ordinary person. He added the following words: 'If, having heard all the evidence in the case, your final conclusion is that notwithstanding what he did he may not have regarded it as dishonest, that is an answer to this charge.' . . . .

In the judgment of this Court any direction based on the concept of claim of right as set out in section 2(1)(a), or otherwise, would have added nothing to what the learned judge in fact said. Indeed a direction based on *Ghosh (supra)* seems likely to us to cover all occasions when a section 2(1)(a) type direction might otherwise have been desirable. . . .

[T]he summing up in the present case clearly brought home to the jury that they must consider the appellant's own account of events and what he said about his state of knowledge and if, on that basis, they thought he might have regarded his actions as honest, they must acquit. . . . .

The jury in the present case had the facts before them. The appellant eventually conceded that ordinary people would, on the basis of his own version, have found his behaviour to be dishonest. He maintained that he himself had not thought it to be dishonest at the time. In the view of this Court it was inevitable that the jury would disbelieve the last proposition, even if they believed the appellant's account otherwise.

There is in our view nothing unsafe or unsatisfactory about this conviction. Accordingly, for the reasons stated, the appeal is dismissed."

Appeal dismissed

2. The Offences

(i) *Obtaining property by deception*

Theft Act 1968, section 15(1)

"A person who by any deception dishonestly obtains property belonging to another, with the intention of permanently depriving the other of it, shall on conviction on indictment be liable to imprisonment for a term not exceeding 10 years."

(a) *Actus reus*

The *actus reus* of this offence is complete if the defendant:

1. by deception
2. obtains
3. property
4. belonging to another

1. Deception. This is discussed above.

2. Obtains.

Theft Act 1968, section 15(2)

"For purposes of this section a person is to be treated as obtaining property if he obtains ownership, possession or control of it, and 'obtain' includes obtaining for another or enabling another to obtain or to retain."

By virtue of this sub-section, section 15 covers cases that would previously have been dealt with by both larceny by a trick and obtaining by false pretences. It is sufficient to establish liability that the defendant obtain any of the titles; typically the offence will be committed, however, when the defendant obtains ownership by deception for himself. It will not be committed where the defendant by deception is allowed to "retain" property for himself; the section affixes "retaining" to another only.[54]

---

[54] The defendant could probably be convicted of theft if, lawfully in possession, he deceives the rightful owner of the property into allowing him to retain it if he has an intention to permanently deprive.

3. Property.

Section 34(1) of the 1968 Act makes it clear that the definition of property given in section 4(1) applies here.[55] The only distinction to be drawn is that the limitations to what can be stolen for the purposes of theft found in ss.4(2)–4(4) do not apply to section 15. Land and things in action (such as copyright, etc.) may be at the basis of a deception charge.

4. Belonging to another.

By virtue of section 34(1), section 5(1) applies to section 15. Thus the artificial definitions of "belonging to another" contained in sections 5(2), (3) and (4) do not apply here.

(b) *Mens rea*

The *mens rea* requirement for section 15 is:
1. Dishonestly
2. With intent permanently to deprive
3. Deliberately or recklessly makes a false statement.

All of these terms have been discussed elsewhere.[56] It should be noted that section 15(3) specifically makes section 6 applicable to section 15.

(c) *Punishment*

Section 15(1) states that a person convicted of obtaining property by deception shall be liable to a term of imprisonment not exceeding 10 years. This offence would appear, therefore, to be regarded more seriously than the other deception offences although it is not immediately clear why obtaining *property* by deception should be so much more serious than obtaining *services* by deception (punishable by a maximum of five years).

(ii) *Obtaining pecuniary advantage by deception*

Theft Act 1968, section 16

"(1) A person who by any deception dishonestly obtains for himself or another any pecuniary advantage shall on conviction on indictment be liable to imprisonment for a term not exceeding five years.

(2) The cases in which a pecuniary advantage within the meaning of this section is to be regarded as obtained for a person are cases where—
   (a) [Repealed]
   (b) he is allowed to borrow by way of overdraft, or to take out any policy of insurance or annuity contract, or obtains an improvement of the terms on which he is allowed to do so; or
   (c) he is given the opportunity to earn remuneration or greater remuneration in an office or employment, or to win money by betting.

(3) For purposes of this section 'deception' has the same meaning as in section 15 of this Act."

---

[55] *Ante* p. 703.
[56] *Ante* pp. 743–762.

(a) *Background*

The history behind this section is a most unhappy one. In their draft Bill the Criminal Law Revision Committee had proposed two offences (obtaining credit by deception and inducing an act by deception with a view to gain), but these had foundered in the House of Lords. Instead, section 16 was passed containing within section 16(2)(*a*) references to the reduction, evasion or deferment of a debt or charge. This quickly proved to be the sort of section likely to keep lawyers in work for the rest of their days! Following intense academic and judicial criticism the Criminal Law Revision Committee were invited to resolve the difficulties; their report became the basis for the 1978 Act and section 16(2)(*a*) was repealed.[57]

What is left is *one* offence which can be committed in two different ways (subsections (*b*) and (*c*)).[58] Fletcher suggests that the language of section 16 indicates some movement towards the protection of economic interests[59] (a movement which would presumably pay more heed to the actual value of the property "lost"), rather than, as suggested above, being more concerned with the protection of commercial autonomy. However, the movement is only linguistic. In neither situation is it necessary for any *actual* advantage to be obtained. For example, under subsection (*c*) the offence will be made out if the defendant secures the opportunity to earn, even though he may not actually have earned anything. In such situations the defendant is deemed to have obtained a pecuniary advantage.[60] As Fletcher points out, "the basic principle is still the protection of commercial autonomy."[61]

(b) *Actus reus*

The *actus reus* of section 16 is:

1. deception
2. obtains for himself or another
3. pecuniary advantage.

"Pecuniary advantage" is given a precise definition in section 16(2)(*b*) and (*c*).

It covers four situations:

(a) allowed to borrow by way of overdraft:

The word "allow" here has presented some problems in that *prima facie* it implies a consensual act with the bank agreeing to the overdraft facility. However, in *Charles*[62] the court accepted without question that the defendant had been "allowed" to borrow when his account had become overdrawn without per-

---

[57] Thirteenth Report, 1977 (Cmnd. 6733.).
[58] The indictment should, however, specify under which sub-section the case is being brought, *Aston and Hadley* [1970] 3 All E.R. 1045.
[59] At p. 56.
[60] *D.P.P.* v. *Turner* [1974] A.C. 357.
[61] At p. 57.
[62] [1977] A.C. 177, *ante* p. 754.

mission. The point was faced more squarely in *Waites*[63]: by issuing a cheque card to the defendant (which was then used to borrow by way of overdraft) the bank was giving the card-holder the power to use that card; by binding themselves to honour cheques drawn in excess of the amount in the defendant's account they were in effect "allowing" him to overdraw his account. And in *Bevan*[64] it was held that "the overdraft was consensual, since the appellant impliedly requested it and the bank had, albeit reluctantly, agreed."

(b) allowed to take out an insurance policy etc. or obtain improved terms thereon.

(c) given an opportunity to earn remuneration in an office or employment:

There is some doubt about the ambit of the words "office or employment." As Smith suggests, it will be unfortunate if the provision is limited to the master and servant type of situation.[65] The independent contractor who by deception obtains work should be caught by it as well.

(d) opportunity to win by betting.

(c) *Mens rea*

The *mens rea* requirement under section 16 is:
1. Dishonestly
2. Deliberately or recklessly makes a deception.

(d) *Punishment*

Section 16(1) lays down the maximum penalty for obtaining pecuniary advantage by deception as five years upon conviction on indictment.

(iii) *Obtaining Services by Deception*

Theft Act 1978, section 1

"(1) A person who by any deception dishonestly obtains services from another shall be guilty of an offence.

(2) It is an obtaining of services where the other is induced to confer a benefit by doing some act, or causing or permitting some act to be done, on the understanding that the benefit has been or will be paid for."

This section remedies an obvious defect of section 15; namely, that it does not cover the situation where someone is deceived into providing a service rather than parting with property. When someone provides, for example, a meal or a hair-cut, it really makes a mockery of the law to

---

[63] [1982] Crim.L.R. 369.
[64] [1987] Crim.L.R. 129.
[65] *The Law of Theft* at p. 109.

have to resort to descriptions of the food or shampoo as property (although, of course they are) in order to render the defendant liable for an offence. The real loss here is the "labour" that has been expended; the only surprising thing is that it took so long to recognise the need for a separate offence.[66]

(a) Actus reus

The elements of the *actus reus* are that the defendant

1. By any deception
2. Obtains
3. Services.

1. By any deception.

The only points to note in addition to the discussion elsewhere[67] are that, first the obtaining can be by any deception and not just a deception as to payment. So if, for example, the defendant induces a friend to drive him to work by falsely representing that he was still over the legal limit because of alcohol drunk the previous night, he will have committed the offence if the friend was to be paid for his acts. However, whilst this is the case it is also true that the deception must cause the victim to provide the services on the understanding that he will be paid. The Act thus excludes deceptions which induce gratuitous services.

One final point in relation to deception and payment: technically under the section the victim need not have lost out economically by the defendant's deception. In the above example the defendant may have paid the victim as agreed. Whilst it may well be that a jury would be reluctant to convict in such circumstances,[68] it falls very much into line with the view expressed earlier that deception offences are primarily concerned with the protection of commercial autonomy, and not with the protection of economic interests.

2. Obtains.

Causation must be established. It must be proved that the deception causes the services to be obtained.

3. Services.

The term "services" in subsection (1) has to be understood in the light of subsection (2) where a very wide definition is laid down. Glanville Williams refers to "services" as a "joker word, standing only for the notion defined in subsection (2). It is narrower than the usual meaning of 'services' because it does not cover gratuitous services. It is wider because it covers much conduct that would not ordinarily be described as performing a service."[69] In other words, *any* act, so long as it confers

---

[66] The defendant in such circumstances might have been liable under (the now repealed) s.16(2)(*a*) of the Theft Act 1968 of obtaining a pecuniary advantage by deception through deferment of the debt.

[67] *Ante* pp. 744–749.

[68] Smith, *The Law of Theft* p. 111.

[69] *Textbook*, p. 798.

a "benefit" and is done on the understanding that it will be paid for, will amount to a service. This raises two issues, the first of which is illustrated by the case of *Widdowson*.[70] In this case it was held that obtaining a van on hire-purchase was obtaining services. If this view is correct then surely every section 15 case could come under section 1(2). Such an overlap cannot have been intended by the legislators. The second issue is the question of what is meant by the term "benefit." There is some disagreement amongst commentators about this. Griew thinks that it is nothing more than convenient shorthand for "the thing (service) that has or will be paid for,"[71] whilst others suggest that it implies some sort of qualitative test to services. Smith suggests that where, for example, someone is induced to perform an illegal abortion by deception, that could hardly be described in law as the conferring of a benefit. The limitation to "benefit," therefore, would be where the relevant act was one from which the law sought to protect the defendant.[72]

Finally, it is worth reiterating that the section only applies to those services induced on the understanding that they will be paid for. Thus the more effective one's lies, the less the chance of liability here. If one's deception is so convincing that a service is provided free, there is no liability. Deceiving someone into the provision of a gratuitous service may, however, fall within section 2(1)(c) of the 1978 Act.[73]

(b) Mens rea.

The *mens rea* requirement of section 1 is:
1. Dishonestly
2. Deliberately or recklessly making the deception.

(c) Punishment.

Section 4 lays down the maximum penalties for offences under the 1978 Act. Section 1 is punishable on indictment by up to five years' imprisonment. On summary conviction the maximum is six months and/or a fine of (currently) a maximum of £1000.

(iv) Evasion of liability by deception

(a) Introduction

We saw earlier[74] that the criminal law does not generally punish those who breach their contracts—even those who dishonestly and blatantly refuse to pay their debts. Such matters are more appropriately dealt with by the civil law. The extension of the reaches of the criminal law should always be limited by the criteria of necessity and effectiveness.[75] However, when the breach of contract is secured by deception,

---

[70] [1986] Crim.L.R. 233.
[71] *The Theft Acts 1968 and 1978* p. 150.
[72] Smith, *The Law of Theft* p. 115 and Spencer, "The Theft Act 1978" [1979] Crim.L.R. 24 at pp. 27–28.
[73] *Post* p. 768.
[74] *Ante* p. 716.
[75] *Ante* pp. 88–95.

in addition to dishonesty, then even though there is no greater harm, the law feels that this added blameworthiness now pushes the case into territory where criminalisation is appropriate. Whether this approach is appropriate is a controversial matter.[76]

(b) *The Law*

Theft Act 1978, section 2

"(1) Subject to subsection (2) below, where a person by any deception—
(a) dishonestly secures the remission of the whole or part of any existing liability to make a payment, whether his own liability or another's; or
(b) with intent to make permanent default in whole or in part on any existing liability to make a payment, or with intent to let another do so, dishonestly induces the creditor or any person claiming payment on behalf of the creditor to wait for payment (whether or not the due date for payment is deferred) or to forgo payment; or
(c) dishonestly obtains any exemption from or abatement of liability to make a payment;
he shall be guilty of an offence.
(2) For purposes of this section 'liability' means legally enforceable liability; and subsection (1) shall not apply in relation to a liability that has not been accepted or established to pay compensation for a wrongful act or omission.
(3) For purposes of subsection (1)(b) a person induced to take in payment a cheque or other security for money by way of conditional satisfaction of a pre-existing liability is to be treated not as being paid but as being induced to wait for payment.
(4) For purposes of subsection (1)(c) 'obtains' includes obtaining for another or enabling another to obtain."

It would appear that section 2 creates three *separate* offences unlike section 16.[77] This is because there are material differences between the subsections, although it is also the case that there is considerable overlap, all of them dealing in one way or another with the dishonest debtor.

J. R. Spencer, "The Theft Act 1978" [1979] Crim.L.R. 24 at pp. 34–35:

"There seems little practical need for 2(1)(a). Where it applies, D has been fraudulent and dishonest, but his conduct is unlikely to have done P any harm. In theory harm has been caused: P used to own a debt against D; by deceiving P into waiving it, D has deprived him of it. So, it may be said, D ought to be punished just as if he had deprived P of any other item of his property—his car, for example—by deception. But the analogy is false. Where D obtains P's car by deception, P once had a car, and is left with a civil remedy against D which usually is worthless. Where D secures the remission of a debt by deception, P is also left with a probably worthless civil remedy. He can rescind the remission for fraud, and then enforce the debt—but D probably has no assets with which

---

[76] See, for example, J. R. Spencer, *The Theft Act 1978* [1979] Crim.L.R. 24.
[77] Although in *Holt* [1981] 1 W.L.R. 1000, Lawson J. was unsure whether one or three offences had been created, the latter would appear to be the better view.

to pay it. However, in this case what did P have *before* D deprived him of it by deception? Merely a debt—a right to sue D for the money. It is possible that D had the money to pay at the time of the deception, and spent it on beer after the debt was remitted; but this is most unlikely. Usually, the reason why D deceived P will be that D had no money but lacked the effrontery to say so. Therefore, as a result of D's deception, P is unlikely to be any the worse off. The only result of fining and imprisoning D if he is caught will be to make P's civil remedy against D worthless in the rare case where D was, before the prosecution, worth powder and shot.

Section 2(1)(b) seems to have little more rhyme or reason to it. It is said to be aimed mainly at those who knowingly write dud cheques in purported settlement of existing liability—conduct which frequently does the creditor good rather than harm [giving the creditor the right to sue on the cheque as well as the debt]. It is harmful in only two ways. First, the payee may unsuspectingly draw against the cheque and so overdraw his own bank account. If this is the mischief aimed at, however, 2(1)(b) is too narrow, because the offence is only committed where D intends never to pay, and P is equally likely to overdraw whatever D's intentions. Secondly, tendering the cheque may enable D to disappear without trace. However, the mischief here is only the same as that involved in 'making off without payment.' Why should running away after telling lies carry a sentence of five years' imprisonment under 2(1)(b), when running away without telling lies—which is more harmful, because D is likely to be harder to trace—only carries a sentence of two years under section 3? Furthermore, as against any dubious benefits to society which 2(1)(b) may provide, there is the uncomfortable fact that because of it, anyone who, however innocently, tenders a cheque which is dishonoured, can be threatened with a prosecution which is likely to get past the committal stage.

The only part of section 2 which seems to strike accurately at an evil worthy of criminal sanction is 2(1)(c), which applies to the evasion of future liability by deception. Although originally intended partly to cover obtaining services cheap or free by deception, and now in that respect redundant, [because section 1 is wider in scope than intended by the C.L.R.C.] it still covers conduct which is really harmful to the victim and amounts to no other criminal offence. Take for example the case of the council-house tenant who by deception has his rent halved by way of rent rebate. The council will thereafter fail to collect half his rent as it would otherwise have fallen due. If the fraud is not discovered for several years, the council may lose thousands of pounds. On discovery of the fraud, the council will have in theory a right to sue the tenant for the money, but whereas he could have paid it in instalments over the years, the chance of his ever finding it now—in addition to future rent at the proper rate—is remote. This sort of conduct surely does deserve a prosecution.

A final criticism of section 2 is that it is complicated. Long, expensive hours will be spent in the courts discussing arid procedural questions resulting from a failure to specify what the relationship between the three main clauses is, and whether they are three offences or one. It is an ill wind of legal change which blows no barrister any good."

(1) Securing the remission of liability.

This subsection deals with the defendant who has an *existing* debt and who persuades his creditor to let him off the whole or part of the debt. An example, given by the Criminal Law Revision Committee,[78]

---

[78] Thirteenth Report, 1977, (Cmnd. 6733), para. 13.

would be where the defendant who has borrowed £100 from a neighbour tells a false hard luck story of family tragedy at the time of repayment and is thus let off the loan. This offence would seem to take place whether or not the creditor's promise is binding because it is secured by deception.[79] But it would not be appropriate to charge under this subsection where the defendant deceives the creditor into thinking that the debt has already been paid or that it is less than the true figure. In this situation the proper charge is under subsection (b).

(2) Inducing a creditor to wait for or forgo payment.

Two situations are covered by this subsection: inducing a creditor to wait for payment and inducing a creditor to forgo payment. In neither case, unlike subsection (a), is the *agreement* of the creditor necessary. Whilst the creditor may be deceived into waiting for payment or into forgoing the debt completely, it is important to note that the defendant must intend to make permanent default to be caught by this offence. "Waiting" would seem to be appropriate when the debtor stalls by, for example, sending a child to the door when the creditor comes and making the child say "Daddy's out." Importantly, by virtue of subsection (3) a person who accepts a cheque as payment is deemed to be made to wait for payment.[80]

To "forgo" would appear to apply to situations such as those in *Holt*[81]; here the defendant, having dined in a restaurant, told the waiter that another waiter had already taken payment.

(3) Obtaining exemption from or abatement of liability.

Whilst the previous two offences were limited to existing debts by the express wording of the provisions, such is not the case with subsection (c). However, like subsection (a) it does seem to require agreement on the part of the person who is to be owed the debt. An example of conduct falling within this subsection would be the woman who falsely claims to be an old-age pensioner and thus obtains a reduction in the price of her hair cut. The offence would not be made out if she only made the claim after her hair had been cut; in this case the appropriate charge would be under subsection (a).

Many of the factual circumstances falling within subsection (c) will also fall within section 1—obtaining services by deception—and should be charged as such. The overlap is not total, however; if the defendant induces another to provide him with a free service, section 1 is inapplicable because there is no understanding that the service will be paid for; it would, however, fall within section 2(1)(c).

---

[79] But see Smith, *The Law of Theft*, pp. 118–121.

[80] The Crown court case of *Andrews* v. *Hedges* [1981] Crim.L.R. 106 decided that this will only be the case where the creditor is induced to accept a cheque instead of cash.

[81] [1981] 1 W.L.R. 1000.

R. v. Sibartie [1983] Crim.L.R. 470 (Court of Appeal, Criminal Division) and commentary:

"The appellant, a law student who lived in Acton and attended college in Hendon, bought two season tickets on the Underground, one ticket covering the beginning of his journey on one line for two stations and the other ticket covering the end of his journey on another line for two stations; in between were 14 stations including an interchange station between the two lines. At the interchange station, on passing a ticket inspector, the appellant held aloft a wallet containing the season ticket—according to the inspector, 'flashing it' so that she could not see what was on it—and on being challenged said that he was going to the first of the two stations at the end of his journey. The appellant's version was that he was going out at the interchange station and was intending to pay. He was charged on counts 1 and 2 with evasion of a liability by deception, contrary to section 2(1)(c) of the Theft Act 1978 and on count 3 of an attempted evasion of a liability by deception. The jury acquitted him on counts 1 and 2 but convicted on count 3. He appealed against conviction.

Held, dismissing the appeal, that the correct method of approach was to ask whether, taking the words of section 2(1)(c) in their ordinary meaning, one would say that what the appellant was attempting to do fell within the ambit of the words. The jury by their verdict must have been satisfied that the appellant dishonestly used his season tickets, which did not in fact cover the journey he was making, in an attempt to persuade the ticket inspector that they did cover the journey. Did that amount to an attempt to obtain exemption from liability to make a payment for the journey he was making or had made? He was saying, albeit tacitly, by waving the supposed season ticket in the air that he was the holder of a ticket authorising him to be making the journey without further payment and consequently he was not under any liability to pay any more. In the ordinary meaning of words that was dishonestly obtaining an exemption from the liability to pay the excess which, had he been honest, he would have had to pay. There might be a degree of overlap between section 2(1)(a), (b) and (c), and the fact that what the appellant did might also have been an attempt to commit an offence under section 2(1)(b) was neither here nor there.

Commentary. When the defendant 'flashed' his wallet he was, it appears, attempting to avoid having to pay the proper fare for the journey which he was in fact undertaking. Payment was due at the outset of the journey and he was trying to deceive the inspector into believing that the fare had been paid by the purchase of a season ticket covering the whole journey. Section 2(1) of the Theft Act probably creates three offences and a case may be made for saying that he was guilty of an attempt to commit all of them.

Assuming he had succeeded—
  (a) Did he secure the remission of part of an existing liability to make a payment? (s.2(1)(a))
  (b) Did he induce the creditor to forgo payment of part of an existing liability, with intent to make permanent default? (s.2(1)(b))
  (c) Did he obtain an exemption from liability to make a payment? (s.2(1)(c))

If he was guilty of three offences, does not this look like a case of overkill on the part of the legislator? Some overlap of offences is reasonable and to be expected; but it must surely be assumed that Parliament intended each offence to have some function. If the broadest construction is put upon each offence there seems to be nothing for paragraph (b), in so far as it relates to forgoing payment, to do.

Paragraphs (a) and (c) do not require proof of an intent to make permanent default and, if they cover cases of forgoing payment, Parliament's evident intention, that one who merely induces a creditor to forgo payment should not be guilty unless he has an intent to make permanent default, is defeated. It is no answer to this argument that there was evidence of an intent to make permanent default in the present case. Such an intent was no part of the offence of which the appellant was convicted.

There is, however, an interpretation of the section which avoids this result, and which requires nothing more extravagant than a literal reading of the words of the section. Offence (a) is not committed unless the defendant 'secures the remission' of a liability. Offence (c) is not committed unless the defendant obtains an 'exemption from . . . liability to make a payment.' Assuming again that the defendant had succeeded in deceiving the inspector in the present case, the inspector would have had no intention to 'remit' an existing liability because he would have been persuaded that there was no liability to remit, nor would he in law have remitted any liability. The defendant's liability to pay the proper fare would unquestionably have continued unimpaired. Similarly, the inspector would not have intended to exempt the defendant from any liability to make a payment, existing or otherwise, being persuaded that there was no liability, and the defendant would not have been exempted from any liability.

What the defendant would have succeeded in doing if he had deceived the inspector was to induce him to forgo payment of an unremitted, still existing liability to pay the full fare, from which no one intended to exempt him and from which he was not exempted.

Though lip-service is from time to time paid to the principle that a penal statute must be construed strictly in favour of the accused, in practice that approach is out of fashion. . . . "

One cannot conclude a discussion of section 2 without echoing the sentiments expressed by Spencer earlier. The criminal law's resources are finite and should be concentrated upon those who are blameworthy and cause harm. Most of section 2 could be repealed without any major threat being thereby occasioned.[82]

(c) Punishment.

By virtue of section 4 the offences contained within section 2 are punishable to the same extent as obtaining services by deception under section 1: *i.e.* the maximum penalty for conviction on indictment is five years' imprisonment and six months on summary conviction.

IV. MAKING OFF WITHOUT PAYMENT

A. Introduction

We have already examined the general rule that the criminal law does not punish non-payment of debt even when dishonest, unless there has been a deception. It is the element of deception in securing such non-payment that marks conduct out as deserving of criminal liability.[83]

---

[82] It is perhaps unfortunate that the drafters of the Draft Criminal Code were not at times more ambitious in their proposals. All these provisions are retained in substance (The Law Commission (Law Com. No. 177), *A Criminal Code for England and Wales* (1989), cl. 158).
[83] *Ante* p. 767.

However, in certain situations where debts have been incurred, such as at restaurants, hotels and self-service petrol stations, it has been felt necessary to criminalise dishonest avoidance of payment even in the absence of a deception. This is because of problems of law enforcement. Normally in contractual situations the identity of the other person is known (or where it is not, as in contracts in shops, a charge of theft will often be possible) and, therefore, it is appropriate to leave remedies to the civil law. However, in restaurants or self-service petrol stations, for example, debts are incurred by anonymous debtors in circumstances where a charge of theft is not possible because property might have passed prior to the appropriation.[84] Accordingly, as civil remedies are useless against the unknown, a special criminal offence has been created to deal with such situations and, to secure its effectiveness, a power of arrest has been given to "any person." Thus, a restaurateur or petrol station attendant has the power to arrest any person whom he reasonably suspects to be committing the offence.[85]

B. The Law

Theft Act 1978, section 3

"(1) Subject to subsection (3) below, a person who, knowing that payment on the spot for any goods supplied or service done is required or expected from him, dishonestly makes off without having paid as required or expected and with intent to avoid payment of the amount due shall be guilty of an offence.

(2) For purposes of this section 'payment on the spot' includes payment at the time of collecting goods on which work has been done or in respect of which service has been provided.

(3) Subsection (1) above shall not apply where the supply of the goods or the doing of the service is contrary to law, or where the service done is such that payment is not legally enforceable.

(4) Any person may arrest without warrant anyone who is, or whom he, with reasonable cause, suspects to be, committing or attempting to commit an offence under this section."

Strange though it may seem to start with a list of what one does not have to prove under this section, it is, nevertheless a useful way of proceeding. Thus, one does not need to determine whether or not property has passed as one would have to for a charge of theft; one does not need to establish deception at any stage of the conduct and finally, one does not have to show dishonesty any earlier than at the time of making off.

However, useful and necessary as this section is, it is not without its own difficulties. Some of the terms employed in the section require closer consideration.

---

[84] *Ante* p. 714.
[85] Normally a warrant is required for an offence carrying such a low maximum penalty. See section 24, Police and Criminal Evidence Act 1984.

1. Makes off.

In the case of *Brooks and Brooks*[86] the court said that making off "may be an exercise accompanied by the sound of trumpets or a silent stealing away after the folding of tents." In other, more prosaic words, there is no need for the leaving to be done by stealth. All that making off requires is that the defendant leave the place where payment is required for another place. Neither does it appear to matter that the defendant has the victim's consent to his leaving, as, for example, will be the case where the defendant has deceived the creditor into thinking that payment has already been made.

2. The spot.

What constitutes the "spot" is a matter of some importance: it will determine whether the defendant can be charged with the full offence or only with an attempt. If the spot is deemed to be the premises, as is likely, then the offence is only committed when the defendant has left. So in *MacDavitt*,[87] where the spot was held to be the restaurant, the defendant, who was apprehended as he made for the door, could only be convicted of attempting to make off without payment.

3. Goods supplied or service done.

The classic instance that this provision is designed to cover is the defendant who fills up the petrol tank of his car and drives off without paying; this would fall within the category of "goods supplied." The creditor has made the goods available to the defendant. So too would be the case in a self-service shop. However, in the case of a non self-service shop, the shoplifter who runs off without paying cannot be dealt with under section 3; no goods have been *supplied* to him. It may, of course, be theft.

Neither the term "goods" nor "service" is defined by section 3, but it seems unlikely that this omission will lead to practical difficulties. Service may well bear a similar meaning to "services" under section 1 although there are suggestions that it is narrower.[88] Just as the goods must be "supplied," so the service must be "done." Clearest examples of this will be the meal provided in a restaurant or the accommodation provided by a hotel, but it would also seem broad enough to cover the defendant who parks his car in someone's car park, thereby taking up the offer to do so.

4. Without having paid.

In practice, the only area likely to cause difficulties here is in relation to payment by dud cheques. The issue is whether such cheques are to be regarded as payment or not. Various views have been expressed

---

[86] (1983) 76 Cr.App.R. 66 at p. 69.
[87] [1981] Crim.L.R. 843.
[88] See Smith, *The Law of Theft* pp. 125–127 and Glanville Williams, *Textbook* p. 878.

about this. On the one hand it is argued that such payment is not "as required or expected"[89] and should not, therefore, be regarded as payment. The other view is that such cheques should be regarded as payment because they conditionally discharge the defendant's liability to pay (although this does not apply to forged cheques because they do not amount to such a conditional discharge of liability).[90] If the problem of dud cheques (as opposed to forged cheques) is still to be dealt with under the criminal law, then the best legal way to proceed in such instances is to use section 2(1)(*b*) and not section 3 at all. Paradoxically, however, this would have the effect of bringing the defendant within a more serious offence.

5. As required or expected.

One final point to be noted, is that making off without payment will not be an offence where the payment is legally unenforceable or the supply of goods or services is contrary to law. The defendant who leaves a prostitute without paying commits no offence under section 3.

Troughton v. The Metropolitan Police [1987] Crim.L.R. 138 (Queen's Bench Divisional Court)

"The appellant was convicted before the magistrates of making-off without payment of a taxi-fare contrary to section 3 of the Theft Act 1978. His appeal against conviction was dismissed by the Crown Court. The findings of fact were as follows. A taxi driver agreed to take the appellant to his home somewhere in Highbury. The appellant, having had a great deal to drink, had not told the driver his address. The driver had to stop to obtain directions from the appellant at some point. There was an argument, the appellant accusing the driver of making an unnecessary diversion. The taxi driver, being unable to get an address from the appellant, drove to the nearest police station to see if someone else could help. The evidence concerning what occurred there was unclear. The Crown Court left unresolved the conflicting evidence as to whether or not the appellant left the police station to go to the taxi and steal from the driver's pouch. There was also difficulty in resolving the appellant's allegation that he had tendered money to the driver at the police station. The Crown Court having dismissed the appeal the appellant appealed by case stated to the High Court.

Held,
allowing the appeal and quashing the conviction (the prosecutor not contesting the appeal), that *R. v. Brooks and Brooks* (1983) 76 Cr.App.R. would have shed some light on this case but not necessarily determined it. It was not referred to in the Magistrates' or Crown Court. The basis for allowing this appeal was that the journey had not been completed and the consequence of that was a breach of contract by the taxi driver. Instead of resolving the argument about further instructions during the journey the driver broke away from the route which would have taken the appellant home and in order to go to the police station. The driver being in breach of contract was not lawfully able to demand the fare at any time thereafter. For that reason, among others, the

---

[89] Smith, p. 128.
[90] See Syrota, "Are Cheque Frauds covered by Section 3 of the Theft Act 1978?" [1981] Crim.L.R. 412 and *Hammond* [1982] Crim.L.R. 611.

appellant was never in a situation in which he was bound to pay or even tender the money for the journey, and thus it could not be contended that he made off without payment."

6. Mens rea.

The *mens rea* required under section 3 is:
knowing that payment on the spot is required the defendant makes off *dishonestly with intent to avoid payment.*

It is clear that there has to be an intent to make permanent default.[91]

7. Punishment.

The maximum penalty for an offence under section 3 is two years.[92]

V. OTHER PROPERTY OFFENCES

There are a large number of other property offences, some serious like blackmail, robbery, burglary and handling stolen goods and some not so serious, like taking a conveyance. Whilst it is beyond the scope of this book to deal with all these offences in detail, the chief provisions of some of these offences must be sketched.

A. *Sociological Background*

The incidence and gravity of the conduct encompassed by these offences varies enormously. If we use robbery, taken to be the most serious offence of dishonesty because of the combination of violence (or threats of violence) and theft, as an example, it may be seen that the crime may consist of well-planned, professional raids on banks, post-offices and the like and may well be accompanied by the carrying or use of weapons. It may consist of a "mugging," the phrase being used by the media in particular (it has no place in law) to mean street robberies where there is at least a threat of force against the victim.[93] Finally, by way of example, it may be the robbery that takes place during a burglary; where the victim is tied up and forced by violence to reveal where valuables are. Despite the seriousness of all these offences, robbery accounts for less than 1 per cent. of recorded offences.[94]

At the other end of the scale will be the actions of the juvenile joy-rider, dealt with in this country by means of section 12 of the 1968 Theft Act (and liable to a maximum penalty of three years imprisonment[95])

---

[91] *Allen* [1985] A.C. 1029.
[92] S.4, Theft Act 1978.
[93] For an account of the importation of this term from the U.S.A with the consequential "moral panic" generated (where official and media reaction was out of all proportion to the threat posed) see Stuart Hall, *Policing the Crisis* (1978).
[94] *Criminal Statistics, England and Wales* 1988, (Cm. 847), p. 24.
[95] Sentences of imprisonment appear to be imposed in a surprisingly high number of cases; see C. Emmins, *A Practical Approach to Sentencing* (1985), p. 297.

but in some other jurisdictions seen to be so much a part of growing up that, despite the unquestionable inconvenience caused to the owner of the vehicle, courts may go to considerable lengths to avoid invoking the full rigour of the criminal law.[96] Theft of and unauthorised taking (the official statistics do not distinguish between the two) typically represent 10 per cent. of recorded crime in this country.[97]

Victim surveys have considered in some detail crimes such as burglary and robbery. The second British Crime Survey, for example, asked people how worried they were about particular types of crimes. Burglary was a source of anxiety for all ages although more women than men admitted to this. Men were more worried about being mugged than burglary; women were equally concerned about both. The findings of the more local Islington Crime Survey also stressed the general concern of people about being the victim of robbery or burglary and reinforced the idea that women generally feel most at risk of crime.[98] This survey also looked at the question of how people from different ethnic origins perceived the risk of crime. On the whole there was little difference in the views expressed by members of the community on this basis, but, for example, blacks tended to regard street robberies as more common five years earlier than either whites or Asians, and both blacks and whites thought there was more risk of burglary five years earlier than did Asians.[99]

This fear of crime (including for women the fear of rape) has led people to adjust their behaviour in a variety of ways, including, for example, the taking of security precautions such as extra locks and burglar alarms. 10 per cent. of those questioned for the second British Crime Survey who said they never went out of doors after dark for leisure purposes, gave fear of crime as the reason or part of the reason. Almost a third of the entire sample said they avoided certain areas after dark as a precaution against crime. Half the women in the survey said they always or usually had someone with them when they went out after dark. Whilst younger women's fears tended to focus more on the risk of being raped, anxiety was also expressed by women about other dangers, some specific, like the fear of being robbed and others unspecified and unfocused.[1]

Fear, of course, has to be judged against risk. The second British Crime Survey indicates that whilst people have a fair grasp of the relative degrees of risk (those living in high risk areas being more worried than those living in low risk areas), generally people over-estimated the likelihood of victimisation. "If 'mugging' is counted as robbery and theft from the person, four per cent. of respondents in the high-risk

[96] *Cf.* J. Hall, *Theft, Law and Society*, (1952), pp. 262–275.
[97] *Criminal Statistics, England and Wales 1988*, (Cm. 847), p. 24.
[98] T. Jones, B. Maclean, J. Young, *The Islington Crime Survey* (1986).
[99] *Ibid.*, pp. 15 and 20.
[1] M. Hough and P. Mayhew, *Taking Account of Crime: Key Findings from the 1984 British Crime Survey* (H.O.R.S. No. 85) pp. 34 and 39–40.

areas . . . were victimised in 1983. Risks were uniformly low outside these areas: in each of the remaining . . . areas, one per cent. or less of the respondents were victims. If mugging is taken to comprise robbery and snatch theft but not pickpocketing and other surreptitious thefts from the person, the risks are very much lower in all areas."[2] Against this picture of risk nearly one in six people felt themselves likely to be a victim of mugging.[3] In relation to burglary, people overestimated the likelihood of such crime in their area; across the sample their estimate was almost five times the real risk.[4] The higher the perceived risk, of course, the higher the anxiety will be. Whilst people are not worrying for no good reason, it may be that more information about the real risks of crime would help to allay fear and enable more appropriate preventative measures to be taken. For example, theft from and of cars is far more prevalent a crime than burglary.[5]

B. *The Legal Background*

Some of the offences incorporated in the Theft Act of 1968 were already statutory, such as burglary and handling stolen goods under the Larceny Act of 1916, others were common law offences, such as robbery. There can be no doubt, however, that the reforms introduced were very timely. Burglary had become a particularly complex offence, with distinctions having to be drawn between "breaking in the night" and "breaking in the day." Fletcher makes the point that the insistence upon the requirement of "breaking" in the development of this offence marks an adherence to a manifest theory of liability, where the actions of the defendant had to be manifestly criminal for an offence to be committed.[6] What has happened since has been a retreat from that position; the new law not only does away with the archaic distinction between breaking by day or night but does away with the requirement of breaking altogether. The replacement, trespass, however, "retains at least a trace of the traditional rule that the entry must be manifestly suspicious."[7]

The severity with which most of these offences are regarded is indicated not only by the legal maxima for the offences: robbery and aggravated burglary are punishable by up to life imprisonment and burglary and handling stolen goods by up to 14 years' imprisonment[8] but by the sentences actually handed down by the courts: 75 per cent. of those convicted of robbery in 1988, for example, were sentenced to immediate terms of custody, as opposed to 11 per cent. for theft and handling

---

[2] *Ibid.*, at p. 38.
[3] *Ibid.*, at p. 38.
[4] *Ibid.*, at p. 38.
[5] *Ibid.*, at pp. 61–63.
[6] Fletcher, pp. 124–128; *ante* p. 690.
[7] *Ibid.* at p. 128.
[8] Theft Act 1968 ss.8(2), 9(4), 10(2) and 22(2).

stolen goods and 34 per cent. for burglary.[9] The length of sentences is also of interest. The Court of Appeal takes a particularly strong line in relation to robbery and burglary sentences because of the elements of violence and trespass and associated trauma involved. For instance, the Court of Appeal has indicated that a sentence of 15 years' imprisonment would be an appropriate starting point for a well-planned, large-scale robbery.[10]

As discussed in the introduction to this chapter, public attitudes towards these offences are generally to ask for stiffer sentencing. However, this appears to be based upon a misapprehension about the type and levels of sentences actually being passed. On the whole then, actual sentencing practice in this area may well concur with what the public would like to see happening.[11]

C. *The Law*

It is proposed to highlight the main features only of these offences.

1. **Robbery**

Theft Act 1968, section 8

"(1) A person is guilty of robbery if he steals, and immediately before or at the time of doing so, and in order to do so, he uses force on any person or puts or seeks to put any person in fear of being then and there subjected to force.

(2) A person guilty of robbery, or of an assault with intent to rob, shall on conviction on indictment be liable to imprisonment for life."

Robbery is theft aggravated by the threat of or use of force. Therefore, the elements of theft must be established if a conviction for robbery is to be obtained. If the defendant believes he has a legal right to the property he takes (even if not to the way he takes it) then there can be no theft and, therefore, no robbery.[12]

The element additional to theft is that of force and a number of points need to be made about this. First, force is a question of fact to be determined by a jury, although it would seem that very little force is actually required.[13] Secondly, the force must take place immediately before or at the time of the theft.[14] Lastly, the threat or force must be used in order to steal and not for any other purpose such as rape.[15] While the *mens rea* of theft is not spelt out in section 8, it is clear that there must be the *mens*

---

[9] *Criminal Statistics, England and Wales,* 1988, (Cm. 847) p. 149..

[10] *R.* v. *Turner* (1975) 61 Cr.App.R. 67 *per* Lawton L.J; *cf.* C. Emmins, *A Practical Approach to Sentencing* (1985) pp. 289–294.

[11] *Ante* p. 681.

[12] *R.* v. *Robinson* [1977] Crim.L.R. 173.

[13] *Dawson and James* (1976) 64 Cr.App.R. 170; *Clouden* [1987] Crim.L.R. 56.

[14] In *Hale* (1978) 68 Cr.App.R. 415 it was held that it was for the jury to decide at what point the theft finished and thus whether the force was used at the time of the theft.

[15] In a situation such as this the defendant may be convicted of theft or possibly attempted rape.

rea of theft, and the force or threatened force must be *in order to steal*; an accidental, negligent or even reckless use of force will not suffice.

2. Burglary and Aggravated Burglary

Theft Act 1968, sections 9 and 10

"9. (1) A person is guilty of burglary if—

(a) he enters any building or part of a building as a trespasser and with intent to commit any such offence as is mentioned in subsection (2) below; or

(b) having entered any building or part of a building as a trespasser he steals or attempts to steal anything in the building or that part of it or inflicts or attempts to inflict on any person therein any grievous bodily harm.

(2) The offences referred to in subsection (1)(a) above are offences of stealing anything in the building or part of a building in question, of inflicting on any person therein any grievous bodily harm or raping any woman therein, and of doing unlawful damage to the building or anything therein. . . .

(4) A person guilty of burglary shall on conviction on indictment be liable to imprisonment for a term not exceeding fourteen years.

10. (1) A person is guilty of aggravated burglary if he commits any burglary and at the time has with him any firearm or imitation firearm, any weapon of offence, or any explosive; and for this purpose—

(a) 'firearm' includes an airgun or air pistol, and 'imitation firearm' means anything which has the appearance of being a firearm, whether capable of being discharged or not; and

(b) 'weapon of offence' means any article made or adapted for use for causing injury to or incapacitating a person, or intended by the person having it with him for such use; and

(c) 'explosive' means any article manufactured for the purpose of producing a practical effect by explosion, or intended by the person having it with him for that purpose.

(2) A person guilty of aggravated burglary shall on conviction on indictment be liable to imprisonment for life."

There are two offences of burglary within section 9. The first is where the defendant enters a building as a trespasser with the intention of stealing, inflicting grievous bodily harm, raping any woman or of doing unlawful damage. The second offence is committed where the defendant, having entered as a trespasser steals (or attempts to steal) or inflicts (or attempts to inflict) grievous bodily harm on any person therein. Section 10 creates a more serious offence: burglary aggravated by the presence of weapons.

R. v. Collins [1973] Q.B. 100 (Court of Appeal, Criminal Division)

(The facts appear in the judgment)

Edmund-Davies L.J.:
" . . . Let me relate the facts. Were they put into a novel or portrayed on the stage, they would be regarded as being so improbable as to be unworthy of

serious consideration and as verging at times on farce. At about 2 o'clock in the early morning of Saturday, July 24, 1971, a young lady of 18 went to bed at her mother's home in Colchester. She had spent the evening with her boyfriend. She had taken a certain amount of drink, and it may be that this fact affords some explanation of her inability to answer satisfactorily certain crucial questions put to her at the trial.

She has the habit of sleeping without wearing night apparel in a bed which is very near the lattice-type window of her room. At one stage in her evidence she seemed to be saying that the bed was close up against the window which, in accordance with her practice, was wide open. In the photographs which we have before us, however, there appears to be a gap of some sort between the two, but the bed was clearly quite near the window.

At about 3.30 or 4 o'clock she awoke and she then saw in the moonlight a vague form crouched in the open window. She was unable to remember, and this is important, whether the form was on the outside of the window sill or on that part of the sill which was inside the room, and for reasons which will later become clear, that seemingly narrow point is of crucial importance.

The young lady then realised several things: first of all that the form in the window was that of a male; secondly, that he was a naked male; and thirdly, that he was a naked male with an erect penis. She also saw in the moonlight that his hair was blond. She thereupon leapt to the conclusion that her boyfriend, with whom for some time she had been on terms of regular and frequent sexual intimacy, was paying her an ardent nocturnal visit. She promptly sat up in bed, and the man descended from the sill and joined her in bed and they had full sexual intercourse. But there was something about him which made her think that things were not as they usually were between her and her boyfriend. The length of his hair, his voice as they had exchanged what what was described as 'love talk,' and other features led her to the conclusion that somehow there was something different. So she turned on the bed-side light, saw that her companion was not her boyfriend and slapped the face of the intruder, who was none other than the defendant. He said to her, 'Give me a good time tonight,' and got hold of her arm, but she bit him and told him to go. She then went into the bathroom and he promptly vanished.

The complainant said that she would not have agreed to intercourse if she had known that the person entering her room was not her boyfriend. But there was no suggestion of any force having been used upon her, and the intercourse which took place was undoubtedly effected with no resistance on her part.

The defendant was seen by the police at about 10.30 later that same morning. According to the police, the conversation which took place then elicited these points: He was very lustful the previous night. He had taken a lot of drink. . . . He went on to say that he knew the complainant because he had worked around her house. On this occasion, desiring sexual intercourse—and according to the police evidence he added that he was determined to have a girl, by force if necessary, although that part of the police evidence he challenged—he went on to say that he walked around the house, saw a light in an upstairs bedroom, and he knew that this was the girl's bedroom. He found a step ladder, leaned it against the wall and climbed up and looked into the bedroom. He could see through the wide-open window a girl who was naked and asleep. So he descended the ladder and stripped off all his clothes, with the exception of his socks, because apparently he took the view that if the girl's mother entered the bedroom it would be easier to effect a rapid escape if he had his socks on than if he was in his bare feet. That is a matter about which we are not called upon to express any view, and would in any event find ourselves unable to express one.

Having undressed, he then climbed the ladder and pulled himself up on to the window sill. His version of the matter is that he was pulling himself in when she awoke. She then got up and knelt on the bed, she put her arms around his neck and body, and she seemed to pull him into the bed. He went on: 'I was rather dazed because I didn't think she would want to know me. We kissed and cuddled for about 10 or 15 minutes and then I had it away with her but found it hard because I had had so much to drink.' . . .

Now, one feature of the case which remained at the conclusion of the evidence in great obscurity is where exactly Collins was at the moment when, according to him, the girl manifested that she was welcoming him. Was he kneeling on the sill outside the window or was he already inside the room, having climbed through the window frame, and kneeling upon the inner sill? It was a crucial matter, for there were certainly three ingredients that it was incumbent upon the Crown to establish. Under section 9 of the Theft Act, 1968, which renders a person guilty of burglary if he enters any building or part of a building as a trespasser and with the intention of committing rape, the entry of the accused into the building must first be proved. Well, there is no doubt about that, for it is common ground that he did enter this girl's bedroom. Secondly, it must be proved that he entered as a trespasser. We will develop that point a little later. Thirdly, it must be proved that he entered as a trespasser with intent at the time of entry to commit rape therein.

The second ingredient of the offence—the entry must be as a trespasser—is one which has not, to the best of our knowledge, been previously canvassed in the courts. . . .

What does that involve? . . . .' . . .

The matter has been dealt with by Professor Griew, who in paragraph 4–05 of his work *The Theft Act* 1968 has this passage: 'What if D wrongly believes that he is not trespassing? His belief may rest on facts which, if true, would mean that he was not trespassing: for instance, he may enter a building by mistake, thinking that it is the one he has been invited to enter. Or his belief may be based on a false view of the legal effect of the known facts: for instance, he may misunderstand the effect of a contract granting him a right of passage through a building. Neither kind of mistake will protect him from tort liability for trespass. In either case, then, D satisfies the literal terms of section 9(1): he "enters . . . as a trespasser." But for the purposes of criminal liability a man should be judged on the basis of the facts as he believed them to be, and this should include making allowance for a mistake as to rights under the civil law. This is another way of saying that a serious offence like burglary should be held to require *mens rea* in the fullest sense of the phrase: D should be liable for burglary only if he knowingly trespasses or is reckless as to whether he trespasses or not. Unhappily it is common for Parliament to omit to make clear whether *mens rea* is intended to be an element in a statutory offence. It is also, though not equally, common for the courts to supply the mental element by construction of the statute.'

We prefer the view expressed by Professor Griew. . . . In the judgment of this court there cannot be a conviction for entering premises 'as a trespasser' within the meaning of section 9 of the Theft Act unless the person entering does so knowing that he is a trespasser and nevertheless deliberately enters, or, at the very least, is reckless as to whether or not he is entering the premises of another without the other party's consent.

Having so held, the pivotal point of this appeal is whether the Crown established that this defendant at the moment that he entered the bedroom knew perfectly well that he was not welcome there or, being reckless as to whether he was welcome or not, was nevertheless determined to enter. That in turn involves consideration as to where he was at the time that the complainant indicated that she was welcoming him into her bedroom. If, to take an example that was put in the course of argument, her bed had not been near the window but was on the other side of the bedroom, and he (being determined to have her sexually even against her will) climbed through the window and crossed the bedroom to reach her bed, then the offence charged would have been established. But in this case, as we have related, the layout of the room was different, and it became a point of nicety which had to be conclusively established by the Crown as to where he was when the girl made welcoming signs, as she unquestionably at some stage did . . .

Unless the jury were entirely satisfied that the defendant made an effective and substantial entry into the bedroom without the complainant doing or saying anything to cause him to believe that she was consenting to his entering it, he ought not to be convicted of the offence charged. The point is a narrow one, as narrow maybe as the window sill which is crucial to this case. But this is a criminal charge of gravity and, even though one may suspect that his intention was to commit the offence charged, unless the facts show with clarity that he in fact committed it he ought not to remain convicted . . .

We have to say that this appeal must be allowed on the basis that the jury were never invited to consider the vital question whether this young man did enter the premises as a trespasser, that is to say knowing perfectly well that he had no invitation to enter or reckless of whether or not his entry was with permission. . . . "

Appeal allowed

(i) Actus Reus

From this case it can be seen that the offence of burglary contrary to section 9(1)(*a*) involves the following elements[16]:

(a) Enters.

Whether there has been an entry is a question of fact for the jury. In giving them guidance the court in *Collins* held that there had to be an effective and substantial entry. In *Brown*[17] the court generally followed this approach although the test was reduced to that of effective entry. Thus it is unnecessary for the entire body of the defendant to be inside the building but minimal intrusions such as a few fingers would be insufficient.

(b) As a trespasser.

Reference must be made to the civil law in order to understand the term "trespass." Under civil law, trespass is entry without the consent of the lawful possessor. No conviction for burglary can be obtained without a finding of civil trespass but as *Collins* makes clear, more than this is required, the defendant must enter "knowing that he is a trespasser . . . or, at the very least, is reckless whether or not he is entering the premises of another without the other party's consent."[18]

---

[16] The same elements are required under s.9(1)(*b*) subject to the necessary modifications.
[17] [1985] Crim.L.R. 212.
[18] *Ante* p. 782.

Even if there is consent, if the defendant acts in a way that goes beyond what the possessor would have consented to, he may be deemed to enter as a trespasser. Thus in *Jones and Smith*[19] the defendant had left his parents' home but was a frequent, welcome visitor. One night he entered their home and stole two television sets. Despite the father's loyal statement that his son was welcome at *any* time, the court held that they were entitled to infer that he would not have consented to entry for the purposes of theft. The son was thus held to have entered as a trespasser.

(c) Any building or part of a building.

Two issues are raised here. First, what constitutes a "building?" Section 9(3) gives an extended meaning to the term by including within it inhabited vehicles and vessels such as caravans and houseboats. The occupant does not have to be present at the time in order to render it "inhabited" but it would seem that it would have to be lived in.

Little other statutory guidance is given as to the ambit of "building"; generally it would seem appropriate to take a commonsense view of it. It would be too restrictive to think in terms of just houses, flats, offices and the like. Outbuildings such as garages and sheds must also be included. The courts have tended to regard both a degree of permanence and considerable size as appropriate criteria to determine whether something constitutes a "building."[20] As Smith points out, for example, tents and telephone kiosks are, therefore, probably not buildings for the purposes of burglary.[21]

The second issue relates to "part of a building." This does not necessarily mean a separate room. It includes areas such as those behind counters in shops from which the defendant is excluded.[22]

(ii) *Mens Rea*

The *mens rea* requirement for burglary under section 9 is:

(i) Intention or recklessness as to trespass.
(ii) Intention to commit one of the offences in section 9(2).

(iii) *Punishment*

A person found guilty of burglary is liable to imprisonment for up to 14 years. If the burglary is aggravated the maximum is life imprisonment.

3. Handling Stolen Goods

(i) *Introduction*

The offence of handling stolen goods should be seen very much as the partner of the offence of theft. This is so for a number of reasons. First,

---

[19] [1976] 1 W.L.R. 672.
[20] *Stevens* v. *Gorley* (1859) 7 CBNS 99.
[21] Smith, p. 171.
[22] Either expressly or impliedly: *Walkington* [1979] 1 W.L.R. 1169.

there is considerable overlap between the two offences. Someone who commits theft may, by subsequent actions, find himself guilty of handling as well and the defendant whose actions are primarily those of handling may also satisfy the definition of theft.[23] The Criminal Law Revision Committee were fully aware of this overlap and saw "no reason in principle or convenience" against it, although circumstances and evidentiary requirements may dictate the more natural charge.[24] Secondly, and very much related to the first point, handling is regarded very seriously indeed. It is thought that without professional handlers of stolen goods, so-called "fences" and "placers," that there would be a lot less theft. Handling thus has a higher maximum sentence (of 14 years) than theft to deal with large-scale handling operations. However, whilst handlers are generally more likely than thieves to get a custodial sentence, even here the ordinary, run-of-the-mill case is unlikely to attract an immediate term of imprisonment. In 1987, for example, of the 7,032 offenders found guilty at Crown courts under section 22, 2479 received immediate sentences of imprisonment. Thus 35 per cent. of handlers received such sentences as opposed to 11 per cent. of those found guilty of either handling or theft.[25]

(ii) *The law*

Theft Act 1968, section 22

"(1) A person handles stolen goods if (otherwise than in the course of the stealing) knowing or believing them to be stolen goods he dishonestly receives the goods, or dishonestly undertakes or assists in their retention, removal, disposal or realisation by or for the benefit of another person, or if he arranges to do so.
(2) A person guilty of handling stolen goods shall on conviction on indictment be liable to imprisonment for a term not exceeding 14 years."

It should be noted initially that section 22 creates only *one* offence, although there are a large number of ways in which this offence can be committed. In fact, it renders culpable almost any way of dealing with stolen goods as long as there is *mens rea*. So, for example, the person who arranges to handle stolen goods commits the offence under section 22 despite the fact that, but for this provision, he would not even have done enough to constitute an attempt.

(a) Actus reus
The elements of the *actus reus* are:
1. The goods must be stolen at the time of handling.
2. There must be a handling of the goods.

---

[23] He appropriates property belonging to another by his act of handling and may well have the necessary intent.
[24] Criminal Law Revision Committee, Eighth Report, (1966), Cmnd. 2977, para. 132.
[25] The Criminal Statistics do not distinguish between theft and handling. This information was obtained with the help of the Home Office.

1. The goods must be stolen at the time of handling.

Section 34(2)(*b*) defines "goods" as including money and every other description of property, except land. In addition, section 24 defines stolen goods as those obtained by theft under section 1, those obtained by deception under section 15 and those obtained by blackmail under section 21. Importantly, the goods must remain stolen at the time the handling occurs; so, for example where the goods have been reduced to police custody and used to bait a trap to catch handlers there can be no conviction under section 22.[26]

2. There must be handling.

Although the preferred view as indicated above is that there is only one offence, there are 18 ways in which the property may be handled![27] The stereo-typical case of handling will involve receiving the goods but it will also encompass disposal (even by way of destruction) and assisting another to deal with the stolen goods. A brief look at the interpretation of this latter form of handling reinforces how very wide this offence is. In *Kanwar*,[28] the Court of Appeal held that "assistance" requires that something be done to aid the retention, removal, disposal or realisation of the goods but that this was not limited to physical acts. On the facts of the case, lying to protect one's husband who had brought stolen goods into the house was held to be sufficient.

(b) Mens rea

The *mens rea* requirement for handling under section 22 is:

1. The defendant must know or believe the goods to be stolen.[29]
2. There must be dishonesty.[30]

(c) Punishment

As indicated above, the maximum penalty for handling stolen goods is 14 years.

VI. Conclusion

An evaluation of these property offences cannot be undertaken until the underlying elements and rationale of such offences have been exposed. Only then can comment about structure and sentencing levels be made.

---

[26] See s.24(4) and *Re Att.-Gen. Ref. (No. 1 of 1974)* [1974] 2 All E.R. 899. The exception will be where it is possible to establish arranging to handle at some earlier time. Alternatively, a charge of attempting to handle stolen goods may be possible; *ante* p. 453.

[27] *Nicklin* [1977] 1 W.L.R. 403.

[28] [1982] 1 W.L.R. 845.

[29] There seems to be hardly any difference in the meaning of these words in this context. Belief, if anything, falls only just short of knowledge: where no other reasonable conclusion can be drawn by the defendant but that the goods were stolen. Mere suspicion is not enough, *Hall* (1985) 81 Cr.App.R. 260.

[30] It would seem that the same test for dishonesty applies in this context as under s.1, *ante* p. 725.

A. *Underlying Rationale*

What do all the different property offences have in common? Clearly, the common denominator in such offences is that they all involve an interference with the property interests of the victim. But what degree of interference is necessary?

We have already seen that the emphasis is *not* on actual loss of property. Indeed, there need not be any loss of property. In theft, for example, there need only be an *intention* of permanent deprivation; there need be no actual deprivation. In burglary, there need only be an entry to a building with one of the specified intents. Again, no property need be taken. This same point emerged strongly when dealing with the non-criminalisation of breach of contract.[31] Losses from theft can be minimal or non-existent, in comparison with losses from breach of contract and many losses from theft, and other property offences can be made good—either by actions for recovery of the goods or by insurance.

It thus seems clear that the emphasis is not on the loss of the property (which could be described as the direct or "first order" harm), but on the quality of the defendant's actions. The focus is on *wrongdoing*. This manifests itself in many ways—for example, the requirement that the defendant's actions be objectively inconsistent with the owner's rights. The requirement of dishonesty for most property offences underlines this. The defendant's actions must be such that the community as a whole can reject them as "wrong." The defendant's actions pose a threat to the value system inherent in our whole concept of property. This threat, which raises the risk that there will be actual loss to property, can be seen as the real harm in the property offences. It is not the only harm. Many of the offences have their own special and distinctive harms—but it is the harm common to all of them and can be seen as a "second-order" harm analogous to the "second-order" harms encountered in the law of attempt.[32]

Acceptance of the idea that the focus in property offences is on the wrongdoing of the defendant and not on the direct harm caused, has important implications for the structuring of such offences. If it is not necessary that *any* direct harm be caused, it follows that the *extent* of direct harm is not important—and this explains why English law pays no attention (at the substantive level) to the *value* of the property interfered with. Thus in England the same crime of theft is committed whether it is a magazine or a million pounds that is stolen. The position elsewhere is different. For instance, many states in the United States grade theft offences according to the value of the property stolen. The Model Penal Code there states that theft of property worth less than $50 constitutes a petty misdemeanour; theft of property valued at between $50 and $500 constitutes a misdemeanour; theft of property with a value

---

[31] *Ante*, pp. 716, 767, 773.
[32] *Ante*, p. 434, and p. 691.

exceeding $500 constitutes a felony of the third degree.[33] Each offence category carries its own range of penalties. The question presents itself whether English law should follow this approach.

Criminal Law Revision Committee, Eighth Report, Theft and Related Offences, Cmnd. 2977 (1966) para. 62:

"We considered whether instead of a general maximum of 10 years there should be different maximum penalties depending on the value of the property stolen. But although there is a case for specially high penalties for stealing large sums, we are not in favour of such a provision. Apart from the difficulty of laying down a satisfactory scale, the value of the property is only one of the possible aggravating features of theft, and it seems to us wrong to single this out. Besides, the property may be far more or far less valuable than the thief imagined."

The value of property is at present taken into account procedurally[34] and in sentencing.[35] Accordingly, the real debate is not as to *whether* the value of the property should be taken into consideration, but *how* this should be achieved: whether at the substantive level or the sentencing stage.

The present approach of English law is consistent with its general view that the causing of harm (and the extent thereof) is irrelevant. The argument is that it can be "chance" whether a large or small sum is stolen. The criminal law is not a "lottery"[36] with criminal liability being governed by "the invisible hand of Fate."[37] It is also argued that the value of property in abstract terms is irrelevant. What matters is the value of the property relative to the particular victim. Stealing £20 from a pensioner is worse than stealing £20 worth of goods from a large supermarket. Further, it is argued that the value of the property is only one way of assessing the extent of the harm and should not be made decisive. Other factors are equally important: the characteristics of the offender, (*e.g.* theft by persons in positions of trust); the characteristics of the victim, (*e.g.* theft from the old or disabled); and the circumstances of the offence, (*e.g.* pickpocketing, thefts committed jointly with others).

On the other hand, it is submitted that these above factors (not related to the value of the property) cannot be treated as having the same significance as the causing of harm. They are relevant and are rightly taken into account at the sentencing stage. However, they have

---

[33] M.P.C. s.223.1(2).

[34] S.22 of the Magistrates' Courts Act 1980 (as amended by the Criminal Justice Act 1988) provides that various offences under the Criminal Damage Act 1971 shall be triable summarily if the value of the property does not exceed £2000. A consultative document published prior to the Criminal Justice Act 1988 proposed that offences of dishonesty where the value involved was less than £50 should be triable only summarily. This proposal was however not included in the legislation. See further, C. J. Emmins & G. Scanlan, *Blackstone's Guide to the Criminal Justice Act 1988* (1988), p. 87.

[35] Home Office Research Study No. 103, *Sentencing Practice in the Crown Court* by David Moxon; C. J. Emmins, *A Practical Approach to Sentencing* (1985), pp. 295–297.

[36] J. C. Smith, "The Element of Chance in Criminal Liability" [1971] Crim L.R. 63.

[37] S. J. Schulhofer, "Harm and Punishment: A Critique of Emphasis on Results of Conduct in the Criminal Law" (1974), 122 U.Penn.L.R. 1497, 1516.

no special relevance here and are no more important than in the field of offences against the person where they are retained at the sentencing level—while the level of harm, say, actual bodily harm as opposed to grievous bodily harm is crucial in distinguishing offences of different gravity. The same is true of the wealth or otherwise of the victim. The impact of the loss of the property on the particular victim is something that could only be taken into account at the sentencing stage. The full argument in favour of allowing the causing of harm to inform the structure of criminal offences generally has been explored elsewhere in this book.[38] Suffice it to conclude here that *if* that view is accepted then that must translate itself in the property offences to according greater weight to the value of property. Such value, like the level of personal injury or success or failure in the law of attempt, is critical in our moral assessment of the defendant's actions[39] and accordingly ought to be introduced at the substantive level.

This could be achieved in one of two ways: there could be different levels of property offences based purely on the economic value of the goods interfered with (as suggested by the Model Penal Code), or certain property offences where the economic value of the goods is *generally* small, such as shoplifting, could be made the subject of separate treatment. It is to this and other ideas relating to the general structure of all the property offences that we now turn.

B. *Structure of Property Offences*

Many of the property offences are so similar that perhaps one ought to consider, if not one single broad property offence, then at least collapsing the distinctions between some of the offences. For example, the various offences of deception, particularly section 15, overlap heavily with theft. The defendants in many of the leading theft cases such as *Lawrence* and *Morris* could all have been charged with obtaining property by deception contrary to section 15 of the Theft Act 1968. We also saw earlier that there is a view under which every case of section 15 could be theft—a view largely confirmed by the recent decision of *Dobson*.[40] Accordingly, either section 15 could be abolished with all such cases being simply charged with theft, or a new broad offence embracing all "involuntary" transfers of property could be introduced. Similarly, theft and handling stolen goods are closely related offences with a considerable overlap between them. In most cases a person who handles stolen goods is "assuming the rights of owner" over property and is thereby appropriating it, becoming guilty of theft. The official Criminal Statistics do not even distinguish between these two offences.

It is submitted, however, that such an approach would be misguided

---

[38] *Ante*, pp. 277, 433 and *post* p. 798.
[39] The arguments in support of this view are to be found at pp. 558–562 and pp. 436–444.
[40] *Ante*, p. 696.

and that there should be no merging of present offences. Criminal offences should describe as accurately as possible the conduct which is prohibited. The moral messages sought to be communicated by the criminal law and the punishment of offenders become confused if offence categorisations are not clearly understood by the public. And there are important moral distinctions between these offences which the public, albeit only intuitively, recognise and which needs protecting. The typical theft, for instance, is very different from the typical obtaining by deception: it involves a surreptitious taking against which the owner is helpless; there is a risk of violence if the thief is interrupted; because of the thief's anonymity there are extra difficulties in identifying and apprehending the thief. On the other hand, with the typical obtaining by deception the victim handed over the property "voluntarily": he had an opportunity to resist; he could have avoided being deceived (or at least more easily than the general theft can be avoided); the deceiver has had to face the victim openly, thereby increasing the chances of subsequent identification and apprehension. The differences between the paradigmatic instances of the two offences suggest their retention as separate offences. Similarly, there are important differences between theft and handling—apart from the fact that the overlap is not complete, with not all cases of handling amounting to theft. Handling is a very different offence in terms of public perception, (see below) and in terms of the need to be able to impose high deterrent sentences (hence the 14 years maximum). Handlers of stolen goods provide much of the market for theft; their activities are a significant source of the economic motivation behind much theft. If the law could stamp out professional handlers much of the incentive to commit theft would be reduced.

Finally, one must ask the opposite of the above question. Are perhaps each of the present offences too broadly drawn? Should there be some further subdivision of the offences—perhaps along the lines of the distinction between burglary and aggravated burglary. With burglary there is a special harm, namely, the violation of the security and sanctity of the home. This can cause special psychological harm: distress, alarm, and the fear of knowing one is not safe even in one's own home.[41] With aggravated burglary there is, in addition, the extra harm of possession of a weapon of offence at the scene of the burglary, which is not only more frightening but increases the risk of violence actually being used, in that the burglar might be "tempted to use it if challenged."[42] The recent Government White Paper has recommended a further distinction: burglaries of dwellings should continue to be subject to the present maximum of 14 years imprisonment, but the maximum penalty for

---

[41] The lives of a large majority of victims of burglary are affected for some weeks after a burglary, and over a quarter of such victims suffer serious shock (M. Maguire, "The Impact of Burglary upon Victims" (1980) Brit. J. Criminol. 261).

[42] *Stones* [1989] 1 W.L.R. 156.

burglaries which are not in dwellings should be reduced from 14 to 10 years.[43]

C. M. V. Clarkson, Understanding Criminal Law (1987) pp. 162–163:

"[M]ost people today regard handling as a lesser offence in terms of moral stigma; defendants will often plead guilty to handling on condition that all charges of theft are dropped. This attitude has come about because of a growing view that handlers and purchasers of stolen goods are 'only slightly dishonest people' (Spencer, 1985) who are not as blameworthy as those who actually steal or burgle. Theft and burglary create an immediate sense of danger in the community; there must often be a risk of violence with such activities; the thief or burglar is the primary cause of harm, directly invading the rights of the owner of property. In contrast, the criminal receiver, the 'fence,' is regarded only as a shady, somewhat disreputable character—and the secondary purchaser as simply someone who has succumbed to the 'natural temptation' of buying something very cheap.

The law is accordingly faced with a dilemma. On the one hand, it recognises that the punishment of handlers is crucial if theft and burglary is to be reduced but, on the other hand, it is faced by an apathetic public almost prepared to 'turn a blind eye' to handling. A possible way out of this dilemma could be to divide the offence of handling stolen goods into degrees. The more serious offence could be reserved for the professional 'fence,' the lesser offence covering secondary purchasers. Such a division might be a fairer reflection of the moral stigma felt by most to attach to the two categories of handlers and could have the advantage of underwriting the necessity of enforcement against, and harm caused by, the professional handler. The danger with such an approach, however, could be that even less moral stigma would be attached to secondary purchasers than at present and, after all, it is these purchasers who buy stolen goods from fences who are the 'key element in the incentive structure that supports property crime.' "

In Denmark the authorities refuse to prosecute in cases of shoplifting of items worth less than 500 Kr. (£36).[44] A case can be made for the decriminalisation of some of the activities presently covered by the Theft Acts—particularly in those areas where civil remedies such as breach of contract seem more appropriate. However, it is highly questionable whether such thinking can or should be applied to shoplifting.

Daniel J. I. Murphy, Customers and Thieves—an Ethnography of Shoplifting (1986) p. 240:

"[T]here are essentially two methods for controlling shoplifters on the shopfloor: 'law-enforcement' and 'peace-keeping.' It is obvious that the numbers of suspects who are handed to the police differ dramatically according to which model is being pursued. The peace-keeping model is the preferred one of a few retailers who acknowledge the temptation to steal which modern marketing techniques create and they accept the responsibility to convert ordinary shoppers who have succumbed to this temptation. Retailers who pursue the law-

---

[43] *Crime, Justice and Protecting the Public*, Cm. 965, 1990.
[44] C. Fitzmaurice and K. Pease, *The Psychology of Judicial Sentencing* (1968); *cf.* Daniel J. I. Murphy, *Customers and Thieves* (1986) p. 239.

enforcement model would criticise the peace-keeping model for being an insufficient deterrent to shoplifters, and the Home Office Standing Committee supports their position: 'A reminder to pay without fear of penalty is no deterrent, and in effect would mean that the thief could not lose.' However, the research clearly demonstrates that all stores on occasions use this method to control shoplifting. . . . The point made here is that there are methods of controlling shoplifting which do not involve the criminal justice system and these should be given more public discussion."

The real point is surely that there are indeed ways of dealing with many offences outside the criminal justice system—but that these alternatives presuppose the existence of criminal laws as an ultimate threat or moral backdrop.

Perhaps an easier case can be made for treating shoplifting as a separate and lesser offence.

Andrew Ashworth, Sentencing and Penal Policy (1983), pp. 186–187:

"[T]here are three major reasons for regarding offences against larger companies, such as Woolworth and Marks and Spencer, as less serious than an offence involving the same amount of property but committed against an individual victim. First, an individual's possessions are more likely to have a personal ('sentimental') value to him which is additional to, and may indeed be more important to him than, the economic value . . . Secondly, thefts from individuals are more likely to cause fear and alarm than thefts from companies . . . Thirdly, companies would generally be better able than individuals to afford and to off-set any loss through theft."

The case for a separate lesser offence is strengthened when one considers that the value of the property stolen in shops is generally small, such thefts are regarded by the public as the least serious of the various types of theft that can be committed,[45] and even when shoplifters are detected[46] prosecutions are often not brought[47] "in order to avoid 'image' problems, because of the claimed risk of false arrest tort actions by innocent customers, and because of the claimed cost of time away from work when security personnel have to testify."[48]

On the other hand, there is the clear view expressed by Lawton L.J. in *Wood*[49] that "Shoplifting is stealing and stealing is a serious offence." A Home Office Working Party Report on internal shop security was to similar effect:

"We also noted the suggestion . . . that shoplifting should be made an administrative offence. This would do nothing to reduce the number of shoplifting offences. Indeed, it might increase it. We see

[45] R. Sparks, H. Genn and D. J. Dodd, *Surveying Victims* (1977); and see *ante*, pp. 684–685.
[46] *Ante*, p. 684.
[47] In 1971 prosecution followed in only 39.9 per cent. of cases reported to the police (Home Office, *Shoplifting, and Thefts by Shop Staff* (1973), para. 6.11.
[48] C. Foote & R. J. Levy, *Criminal Law: Cases and Materials* (1981), p. 757.
[49] (1979) 1 Cr.App.R.(S.) 34.

no reason why shoplifting should be treated differently from any other type of crime."[50]

A central problem with this approach, as with all attempts to divide offences into narrower subcategories, is that the subdivision has to be rational and must not miss any important moral distinctions. This raises the question: What is so special about shoplifting? Why not make pickpocketing or employee theft a separate offence?

L.R. Zeitlin, "A Little Larceny can do a Lot for Employee Morale" *Psychology Today* (June 1974), 22–26, 64:

"Thefts of merchandise alone amount to approximately five per cent. of the yearly sales of American retail establishments, and internal losses outweigh external losses by about three to one. That is, the stores' own employees steal three times as much as do shoplifters . . . [W]ell over 75 per cent. of all employees participate to some extent in merchandise shrinkage . . . [I]n retail establishments internal theft averages out to an unevenly distributed five per cent. to eight per cent. of the typical employee's salary . . .

When the average retail employee becomes dissatisfied with his job, if he doesn't quit, he starts stealing from his employer. He gets back at the system. In a sense, the intellectual and physical challenges provided by opportunities to steal represent a significant enrichment of the individual's job. He can take matters into his own hands, assume responsibility, make decisions and face challenges . . . He is in business for himself . . .

The dishonest worker is enriching his own job in a manner that is very satisfactory (for him) . . . [and] management gets a bargain. By permitting a controlled amount of theft, management can avoid reorganising jobs and raising wages . . .

[M]anagement may decide that the monetary cost of enforcing honesty is too great . . . [M]anagement would have to maintain a figurehead security system. After all, the major benefit of employee theft is the job enrichment provided by the indiviual's attempt to beat the system. If all need for precaution is eliminated, then the employee gets no satisfaction from theft. All he gets is a slight addition to his income in merchandise instead of cash . . .

Uncontrolled theft can be disastrous for any business concern but *controlled* theft can be useful. Employee theft, used as a motivational tool, can be an economic benefit to an organisation, if management finds it too costly to meet its traditional responsibilities to make jobs rewarding and to pay a living wage."

In the United States an examination was made into several substantive offences to ascertain whether subcategorisation was feasible.[51] The bulk of the examination was devoted to the crime of armed robbery with the conclusion that armed robbery be divided into six degrees. Yet these six divisions only take account of two variables: the type of weapon used and the extent of physical violence threatened. No account is taken of the numerous other variables that would normally affect the type and length of sentence imposed. Accordingly, it has been pointed out that:

---

[50] *Ibid.* n. 47, para. 6.16.
[51] Report of the Twentieth Century Fund Task Force on Criminal Sentencing, *Fair and Certain Punishment* (1976), p. 18.

"if the legislature actually *tried* to anticipate every conceivable offence
and offender variation, the result would be a penal law of enormous
length and complexity, replete with hair-splitting distinctions. We
doubt whether any legislative would be willing or able to spend all its
time hammering out a definition of robbery in the 68th degree (and
deciding upon the appropriate penalty); but even if it were, it is
doubtful whether all offence variations could really be anticipated."[52]
It thus seems clear that little can be gained from subdividing the property offences into smaller separate offences such as shoplifting. No area
of law can be adequately, and with sufficient specificity, subcategorised
to reflect the nuances of situation, blameworthiness and harm that condition the seriousness of particular criminal acts. Accordingly, the only
options left are a broad simple subcategorisation based purely on the
value of the property involved, as suggested by the Model Penal Code—
or retention of the existing offences in their present broad form. In this
latter situation one would still need to face the central problem[53]
whether the various factors aggravating or mitigating the seriousness of
the offence should be taken into account at the sentencing level on a
discretionary basis or be enshrined in some form of sentencing guidelines. These issues have already been raised. Indeed, the whole question of the structure of property offences raises similar issues to those
already canvassed with regard to the structure of offences against the
person. Answers to all such questions depend on the basic philosophy
underlying the construction of criminal liability and the criminal justice
system—to which, in conclusion, we now turn.

---

[52] Executive Advisory Committee on Sentencing in New York, *Crime and Punishment in New York*
(1979) p. 220.
[53] *Post*, p. 807.

CHAPTER 10

TOWARDS A GENERAL THEORY OF CRIMINAL LAW

Throughout this book we have been concerned with many specific questions such as: why is attempting to commit a crime an offence? Why is an intentional killing regarded as worse than a negligent one? Why is causing death by reckless driving regarded as worse than reckless driving *simpliciter*? Such questions cannot be answered in a jurisprudential vacuum. Accordingly, we have suggested answers in the context of the overall purposes of the criminal law and punishment. We have tried to suggest some general principles to determine the bases of criminal liability and the bases upon which the relative seriousness of that conduct is fixed. In short, we have been concerned to introduce the beginnings of an overall theory of the criminal law. In this concluding chapter we shall draw together some of these threads and attempt to state this theory more completely.

We have already developed a thesis[1] that there is (and ought to be) a general basic equation of criminal liability, namely:

when a *blameworthy* actor causes a prohibited *harm*, criminal liability ensues.

Let us now examine each of these concepts, blame and harm, and then explore the effect of their conjunction.

I. BLAME

We do not blame people for what they are. We blame them for what they have done, namely, their conduct (which can include appropriate failures to act). Thus, for instance, we do not blame someone for being six years old or for being insane. Sometimes it *appears* as though we are blaming people for what they are as when we punish people for being members of the I.R.A. or for being drunk in a public place. But, as has been argued,[2] the reality in such cases is that we are blaming those persons for their *actions* in joining the I.R.A. or for becoming so drunk in the first place.

So, when we talk of blame, we mean *conduct* that can be regarded as

---

[1] *Ante*, pp. 206–212, 277–279, 434–435, 533, 501–562, 666.
[2] *Ante*, pp. 119–126, 277–280, 390–394.

blameworthy. In many, if not most, cases, this conduct will coincide with elements of the *actus reus* of the crime—for example, we blame a person for firing his gun at another. But we can equally blame a person for conduct prior to the crime—if it was his fault that he got himself into a situation that later caused, or contributed to, his committing the crime. Thus in addition to the above so-called situational offences, we blame people for joining terrorist organisations knowing that they might be compelled to commit crimes—accordingly we deny the defence of duress to such persons.

Blame, then, involves a moral assessment of conduct (again, which can include certain failures to act). On what basis is this moral assessment to be made?

Clearly, there can be several indicators of blame. We have already suggested that the defendant's state of mind or failure to take precautions is an important factor indicating blame. We blame people for their intentional, reckless and "negligent" conduct in relation to the harmful consequence. By "negligent" here, we follow the view[3] that one cannot blame someone simply for failing to foresee something or consider a possibility; he might not be capable of such foresight. But one *can* blame those who are capable of such foresight if they fail to consider possibilities. Such a failure to consider the possible consequences of one's actions expresses a certain attitude towards those consequences[4]—an attitude deserving of blame.

Secondly, a moral assessment of "blame" can, as we have already seen, involve factors beyond the particular conduct and accompanying mental state of the defendant. Thus, as in the examples already taken of situational crimes and the denial of the defence of duress to one who joins a terrorist organisation, an assessment of blame can include considerations of *how* and *why* the defendant got himself into the situation wherein he acted as he did. We clearly blame the defendant in *Lipman*[5] for getting himself so "intoxicated" that he killed his lady-friend. When we try and analyse Lipman's liability in terms of *actus reus* and *mens rea*, we are faced with immense difficulties: Lipman clearly did not have *mens rea* as that term is commonly understood. But when we analyse *Lipman* in terms of blame and harm, there are no such problems: he caused the harm; his conduct was blameworthy—criminal liability can be attached.

Thirdly, looking at the matter negatively: we do not blame a defendant if he has a valid justification or excuse for his actions[6] (or we blame him less[7]). This point has already been argued. Suffice it to repeat that,

---

[3] *Ante*, pp. 203–206.
[4] *Ante*, pp. 206–212.
[5] *Ante*, p. 376.
[6] It can be argued (see *ante*, pp. 277) that our first indicator of blame—*mens rea*, including negligence, properly belongs to this category, *i.e.* lack of *mens rea* is an excuse. There is no magic in the classification, but we have here separated the two for clarity of exposition.
[7] *Ante*, pp. 273–280, *post*, pp. 797–798.

in our view, an excuse destroys, or lessens, blame.[8] We do not blame someone for being insane, for being nine years old, for making a reasonable mistake, for acting in a morally involuntary manner when subjected to duress, etc. Adopting this view helps define the parameters of all such defences. Take duress for example: all questions relating to this defence, such as—must the threat be imminent, must the threat be of death or grievous bodily harm, will the defence avail a defendant who placed himself in a position wherein he was likely to be subjected to such threats?—are essentially asking one thing; in what circumstances is the defendant, who has been subjected to threats, free from, or deserving less, blame?

Turning to justifications, such as necessary defence, discipline or consent, one could adopt one of two views. First, one could assert that no blame attaches to an actor who acts with justification. Thus, for instance, we do not blame a defendant who inflicts injury on an aggressor in order to save his own life. Or, alternatively, one could assert that because a justification "denies the objective wrongness of the act,"[9] no "harm" is caused. "Acts are justified; actors are excused."[10] A "harm" thus becomes, by definition, an *unjustified* infringement of the interests of another. Such a view is indeed plausable, but, without re-entering the dispute over the distinction between justification and excuse, one can here clearly assert that, whether or not a justification negates the harm requirement, we certainly do not blame an actor who acts with justification.

Before continuing with the indicia of blame, it is worth pausing to re-emphasise an important point. Blame is not an "all or nothing" concept.[11] Some conduct is more blameworthy than other. Thus it was argued earlier[12] that intentionally killing is more blameworthy than negligently killing a person. We blame the provoked killer less than the unprovoked one. We blame the intoxicated killer less than the sober one, and so on. There are, in effect, degrees of blameworthiness which can (or, at least, ought to) have an important effect on the way in which we structure our offences in terms of their perceived seriousness.

This brings us to yet another possible constituent of the notion of blame—or, at least, to assessing the appropriate level of blame. In the chapter on homicide[13] we canvassed the possibility of allowing the circumstances and method of the killing, and the identity of the killer or victim, to be a factor in assessing the gravity of a killing. It was there argued that we might (although there are counter-arguments[14]) wish to blame the premeditated killer more than the impulsive one; we might

---

[8] *Ante*, pp. 277–280.
[9] *Ante*, p. 275.
[10] *Robinson, ante*, p. 275.
[11] *Ante*, pp. 278–279.
[12] *Ante*, pp. 212–215.
[13] *Ante*, pp. 665–668.
[14] *Ante*, p. 667.

blame the "hit-man" who kills for reward more than the anguished husband who suddenly (but with no adequate provocation) kills his wife. There are arguments for asserting that we attach more blame to the killer who uses a gun or poison, than to one who picks up a nearby chapati-pan and beats his victim to death.[15] With regard to the identity of the killer (or any person committing another crime), his conduct might be regarded as more blameworthy if he was abusing a position of trust, or if he was one of a group committing a crime (such as gang-rape), or if he was a member of an organised crime group.[16] And as to the identity of the victim, we might blame a defendant who mugs or rapes an old lady or child more than if these crimes had been committed on other persons.[17]

It is clear then that there are many indicia, and degrees, of blame. The question of how this is to be translated into appropriate levels of criminal liability and punishment will be considered after the other ingredient of the criminal liability equation, harm, has been investigated.

II. HARM

By "harm" we mean the unjustified violation of an interest perceived to be sufficiently important to warrant protection via the criminal law and punishment of violators. We have seen that, defined in this manner, harm embraces "first order" harms such as death or deprivation of property, and "second order" harms such as the violation of one's right to security in the law of attempt.[18] The term "harm" is thus broad enough to encompass offences to sensibility (such as indecent exposure), the protection of morality (such as the obscenity laws), the impairment of collective welfare (such as mislabelling food products or possession of firearms) and the violation of some governmental interest (such as filing a fraudulent tax return).[19] Whether all these activities *ought* to be criminal—for example, whether morality, as such, is an interest deserving protection via the criminal law—is another, admittedly crucial, matter already covered.[20] For the purposes of this analysis we shall assume that this logically anterior question of whether such conduct should be criminalised has been answered affirmatively.

Again, it is clear that some harms are worse than others. It is worse to kill another than to injure him. It was argued earlier that it is worse to

---

[15] *Camplin* [1978] A.C. 705.

[16] A. Ashworth, *Sentencing and Penal Policy*, pp. 194–199.

[17] Arguably, the identity of the victim does not affect the degree of blame, but rather the degree of harm. The apprehension caused and the psychological (as well as, possibly, physical) damage done to the elderly and young by such crimes is greater than that suffered by adults of reasonable firmness.

[18] *Ante*, p. 434.

[19] Gross, pp. 119–121. See *ante*, pp. 83–89.

[20] *Ante*, pp. 77–95.

maim a victim permanently than to cause him grievous bodily harm from which he can fully recover.[21] The harm involved in causing grievous bodily harm is clearly worse than the "second-order" harm involved in attempted grievous bodily harm. So, as with the notion "blame," there are plainly degrees of harm which must be utilised in any categorisation of criminal offences.

In assessing appropriate degrees of harm it might be necessary to consider again the circumstances and method of the crime, and the identity of the victim. Thus in the chapter on homicide[22] it was argued that torturing a victim slowly to death was worse than killing him outright. While it might be that we regard a defendant as more blameworthy for acting in this manner, it is clear that in the former case the harm is greater in that the victim is being made to suffer to a greater extent. With regard to the identity of the victim, it was argued,[23] for example, that the harm involved in assaulting a police officer could be construed as worse than in other assaults because it involves "so direct a challenge to the social order"[24] *in addition* to the actual or threatened physical harm.

III. CAUSATION

The equation, blame plus harm equals criminal liability, presupposes, of course, that it is the blameworthy actor who has caused the prohibited harm. Indeed, this is a prerequisite. However, one possible view must be mentioned. It is generally assumed that there is only one level of causal responsibility. But arguably this need not necessarily be true. It could be asserted that there are degrees of causal responsibility. For instance, it was earlier argued; that an accessory bore less causal responsibility for the resultant harm than a principal offender.[25] If this is so, and there are in effect, degrees of causation, then this would need reflection in the basic equation. Possibly, an accessory causes less harm than a principal. Using murder as an example, the principal *kills* his victim. The accessory *helps* the principal, or at most *contributes* to the death of the victim.

However, for the sake of simplicity in developing our thesis, it will be assumed in the remainder of this chapter that we are dealing with "primary causers"—bearing in mind that appropriate adjustment might be necessary to accommodate "secondary causers."

---

[21] *Ante*, p. 560.
[22] *Ante*, p. 667.
[23] *Ante*, p. 562.
[24] A. Ashworth, *ante*, n. 16, at p. 161.
[25] *Ante*, pp. 533–535. See also the discussion on causation and omissions, *ante*, pp. 139–145.

IV. A NECESSARY EQUATION?

Is the basic equation, blame plus harm equals criminal liability, a general proposition capable of admitting exceptions, or is it a necessary pre-requisite in *all* cases?

A. Blame

It is arguable that the requirement of a blameworthy actor is only a *general* proposition and that criminal liability *might in some cases* be justifiable in the absence of blame. The problem reduces itself roughly[26] to the one already canvassed: are we justified in having crimes of strict liability?[27]

Without rehearsing all the arguments, our view is that again this question must *generally* be answered in the negative. In the absence of blame there can only be utilitarian justifications for the imposition of criminal liability in such cases. The prevention of many of the harms involved in offences of strict liability could be best achieved by the civil law—particularly the law of tort or administrative law.

We do however recognise that for certain regulatory crimes, such as parking offences (and others perceived by many not to be "truly criminal"), the imposition of criminal liability without blame might be necessary. Utilitarian and purely practical considerations become so overwhelming as to demand such a conclusion. Further, the absence of stigma associated with such offences makes the bitter pill easier to swallow.

But even in such cases, caution is necessary. If a defendant committed such an offence of strict liability while in a state of automatism (assuming he was not to be blamed for being in such a state), the imposition of strict liability would surely be an affront to justice.[28] But if automatism merely negates blame, and blame is being dispensed with in such cases, how are we to avoid imposing criminal liability? The answer must clearly be that even in such crimes of strict liability, it must be established that the defendant's actions caused the prohibited harm, or that his actions placed him in the situation constituting the prohibited harm: if the defendant is in a true state of automatism "there is not 'really' a human action at all."[29] An automaton cannot "cause" a harm, or cause himself to be in a situation constituting the harm. The harm has occurred, but without volitional action it cannot be attributed to the defendant—and criminal liability cannot be justified.[30]

---

[26] In some situations, presently regarded as strict liability, we might seek to blame the actor if it was his fault that he was in a particular situation.

[27] *Ante*, pp. 216–223.

[28] H. L. A. Hart, *Punishment and Responsibility*, p. 107.

[29] *Ibid.*

[30] On defences to strict liability offences, see *ante*, pp. 229–231.

This approach then would necessitate a re-examination of all present offences of strict liability (assuming they were to remain criminalised[31]) to determine which are justifiable as such, and for which there should be an insistence upon some blame, say negligence at the least, as a prerequisite of criminal liability.

B. Harm

It is clear that our definition of harm[32] is sufficiently expansive to cover virtually all proscribed activities. There is always a harm even in crimes such as obscenity or mislabelling a tin of beans. The true focus with regard to such crimes must be on the logically anterior question of whether such conduct ought to be criminal in the first place.[33] The main utility of our concept "harm" is in terms of structuring offences according to different *degrees* of harm. The direct harm of killing someone is clearly different to the second order harm of threatening interests involved in attempted murder.

But what significance does the criminal law attach to this difference? Assuming equal blameworthiness, is it necessarily worse to kill than to come close to killing?

We have already seen that there is a strong view expressed by many criminal law jurists that criminal liability and the degree thereof ought to be based on blameworthiness or culpability alone.[34] The occurrence or non-occurrence of harm is seen as sheer chance; the view taken is that the criminal law should not be reduced to a "lottery,"[35] with liability being based on the "invisible hand of Fate."[36] This view is reflected in several areas of the present law particularly with regard to the law of attempt: both with respect to attempting the impossible and the punishment of attempts.[37] The same is true with respect to all conduct crimes. Their definition is such that the causing of any further harm, such as death or injury, is irrelevant. For example, the offence of careless driving[38] is unaffected by the fact that the driving might cause the death of another. The gravity of theft and the other property offences is not dependent on the extent of direct harm caused. With theft, for example, the victim need not suffer any loss. All that matters is that the defendant *intended* permanently to deprive the victim of property. The only harm that need be suffered by the victim is that the property be "interfered with."

[31] In many cases this assumption could be questioned. See *ante*, n. 27.

[32] *Ante*, pp. 83–89.

[33] *Ante*, pp. 77–95.

[34] *Ante*, p. 436. See also J. C. Smith, "The Element of Chance in Criminal Liability" [1971] Crim.L.R. 63; A. Ashworth, "Belief, Intent and Criminal Liability" in J. Eekelaar and J. Bell (eds.) *Oxford Essays in Jurisprudence* (1987), p. 2.

[35] C.L.R.C., 14th Report, Offences against the Person, 1980, Cmnd. 7844, para. 120.

[36] Stephen J. Schulhofer, "Harm and Punishment: A Critique of Emphasis on the Results of Conduct in the Criminal Law" (1974) 122 U. Pen.L.R. 1497 at 1516.

[37] *Ante*, pp. 436–444, 468, 480.

[38] Road Traffic Act 1988, s.3. See Krawec [1985] R.T.R.1.

In other situations, however, English law regards the causing of harm as critical to the existence or extent of criminal liability. The best example here is common assault. If the only harm is that the victim is made to apprehend immediate physical force or is subjected to unlawful force, the defendant is liable for a common assault (carrying a maximum penalty of six months imprisonment). If, however, the defendant with the same *mens rea* commits the same assault but this time some injury flows from the actions, there will be liability for assault occasioning actual bodily harm contrary to section 47 of the Offences against the Person Act 1861 (maximum penalty five years imprisonment). But finally, if death were to result from that same assault committed with the same *mens rea*, the defendant becomes liable for manslaughter (maximum penalty life imprisonment). In these cases the degree of direct harm caused is critical in determining the defendant's level of criminal liability.

Many of the arguments for and against attributing importance to the causing of direct harm have been canvassed throughout this book[39] and will not be repeated here. Suffice it to provide a few extracts encapsulating the central case for attaching significance to the causing of harm.[40]

Tony Honóre, "Responsibility and Luck" (1988) 104 L.Q.R. 530, 539–540, 545:

"Outcome-responsibility means being responsible for the good and the harm we bring about by what we do. By allocating credit for the good outcomes of actions and discredit for bad ones, society imposes outcome-responsibility. Under a system of outcome-responsibility we are forced, if we want to keep our social account in balance, to make what amounts to a series of bets on our choices and their outcomes. Provided we have a minimum capacity for choosing and acting, we win the bets and get credit for good outcomes more than we lose them and incur discredit for bad ones. We have to take the risk of harmful outcomes which may be sheer bad luck and not our fault; but that does not make the system unfair to people who are likely to be winners overall . . .
Imagine that when we reach a decision to do X rather than Y—let us say to attempt a U-turn rather than to go on to the next roundabout,—we are choosing to put our money on X and its outcome rather than Y and its outcome. When we opt for the U-turn rather than the roundabout, we implicitly bet that we will get to our destination quicker by making the U-turn. Our decision for U-turn rather than roundabout will be like a decision to put money on L'Escargot rather than Red Rum to win the Grand National. But we will not be like ordinary punters but rather jockeys who, contrary to existing practice, are allowed to back a horse and ride on it so that they can influence the result of their bet. Thus, when we choose X (say the U-turn), the bet we make is to be analysed as follows. We bet we can do X (the U-turn) and that X will have the more favourable outcome (getting there quicker). In calculating the odds for achieving the favourable outcome we have to discount the chance that we may not be able to do X or that the outcome of X, if we do it, will not be what we predict. Thus, we may not manage

[39] Pp. 433–444, 558–562, 660–668. See especially Fletcher extract at p. 626.
[40] For a further discussion of the arguments, including the utilitarian ones, see C. M. V. Clarkson, *Understanding Criminal Law* (1987) pp. 106–108. See also Schulhofer, *ante*, n. 36.

the U-turn; we may instead cause an accident. Or, we may manage it but find we were misinformed about the route, so that it would have been quicker to go on to the roundabout anyhow.

One difference between an implicit bet on outcomes and an ordinary wager concerns the stake and the winnings. In an ordinary bet we know the amount of the stake and often the potential winnings in advance. In implicit bets on the outcome of our actions, on the other hand, we do not precisely know the stake and winnings in advance; only that they will be proportionate to the outcome. The terms of the bets we make with other members of our community (and indirectly with ourselves) when we choose X rather than Y is that if we succeed and have guessed the outcome right we receive credit for it. If we manage the U-turn and get to our destination quicker we get credit for that success. But if we botch it, have an accident, or mistake the route, that is chalked up against us. This remains true even if the botch or miscalculation is not our fault, though of course it generally is. How much responsibility in terms of credit or debit accrues to us—how big the stake and winnings are—depends on how important the successful or botched outcome is in the eyes of others. . . . To choose and execute a course of conduct is to bet on your skill and judgment of the probabilities. Choosing is inescapably betting.

If this suggestion is correct, we live under a system by which a community allocates responsibility according to outcomes, and we are consequently forced to make bets on those outcomes.

The person concerned, though he cannot be sure what the outcome of his action will be, has chosen to act in the knowledge that he will be credited or debited with whatever it turns out to be. Moreover we cannot opt out of the system by which we obtain credit for favourable outcomes; and so we cannot slough off the burden of discredit either. Finally, it is outcomes that in the long run make us what we are."

Daniel M. Mandil, "Chance, Freedom and Criminal Liability" (1987) 87 Col.L.R. 125, 137, 139, 140:

"The paradigmatic crime involves an intentional act causing harm for a certain defined class of harms. . . . Certain crimes, however, depart from the paradigm—some by reason of the absence of harm, some by the absence of intent. . . .

Since both the elements of an intentional act and resulting harm are present in a paradigmatic crime, both subjectivists and objectivists agree that the imposition of criminal liability is appropriate. Imposing liability vindicates the legal interests that the intentional act offended. Moreover, an infringement on the actor's freedom is justified because the act, in causing harm, infringed another's freedom. In nonparadigmatic crimes, however, the value of freedom and other social values do not align. . . .

[I]n cases of criminal negligence, the criminal law generally preserves the supremacy of freedom over other social values—only the existence of isolated reckless endangerment statutes disturbs the congruence. In the case of intentional acts that do not cause harm but are accompanied by an intent to cause harm, however, the value of freedom of action yields to an array of competing values that militate in favour of liability and punishment. While a liberal criminal theory can never disregard the value of freedom of action, the criminal law must provide a means of signalling the importance of other competing social values by criminalizing these acts intended to cause harm. Although precluding liability entirely would displace those social values that rationally militate in favor of liability and punishment, to impose a degree of liability equal to the liability attaching to paradigmatic crimes—as objectivism and subjectivism do—would displace the value of freedom from the criminal law. To avoid both extremes and still to resolve this conflict of values, the criminal law attaches a lesser degree of liability to these acts. This difference in liability serves to signal the preservation of the value of freedom in a liberal theory of criminal law on one hand, and the importance of other competing social values, on the other. Criminal law resolves this conflict by balancing these social values against one another. Such balancing determines the appropriate degree of liability and thereby accounts for the difference in liability between paradigmatic and non-paradigmatic crimes. The habitual appearance of luck in human affairs and the legal effects that luck's appearance entails provide an occasion to consider the weight and importance law accords to the value of freedom."

Michael Davis, "Why Attempts Deserve Less Punishment than Complete Crimes" (1986) 5 Law and Philosophy 1, 28–29:

"Someone who attempts a crime but fails to do the harm characteristic of success still (ordinarily) risks doing that harm. He deserves punishment for risking that harm because even risking such harm is an advantage the law abiding do not take. He deserves less punishment for the attempt than he would for the comlete crime because being able to risk doing harm is not as great an advantage as being able to do it. To attempt murder is, for example, not worth as much as to succeed. The successful murderer has the advantage of having done what he set out to do. The would-be murderer whose attempt failed has only had the *chance* to do what he set out to do. The difference is substantial."

Andrew Ashworth, "Belief, Intent and Criminal Liability" in J. Eekelaar and J. Bell (eds.) *Oxford Essays in Jurisprudence* (1987), p. 18:

"One counter-argument is that this reasoning (that no account be taken of the causing of harm) is too simplistic. Not only does it conflict with widely held assumptions that the occurrence of consequences should be relevant to blame and punishment, but it also overlooks the difference in moral status between B, who committed murder, and A, who committed attempted murder. According to Winch, (*Ethics and Action*, 1972, 149–150) the key to the distinction is what a person becomes afterwards: a simple equiparation of the cases of A and B fails to take account of the complexities of moral judgment.

'In *doing* something evil one *becomes* something evil. . . . What one thus becomes is inseparable from the complex network of relations one enters into with other people which imposes limits on what can and what cannot be intelligibly said of one's subsequent life by way of moral assessment. If a man tries to do something evil and fails, then he does not become what his success would have made him and thereby the possibilities of moral assessment of him are different. It is not that the man who fails has nothing to condemn himself for or to be condemned for; but he does not have that to condemn himself for which he would have had if successful.' "

It seems clear that the causing of harm is widely accepted as critical in the assessment of moral responsibility. Such harm arouses resentment in society (quite apart from the bitterness, pain and anxiety caused to the victim or his family and friends). The causing of harm makes an impression in the way that "close calls" do not. Such causers of harm are regarded as "tainted"[41] and deserving of condemnation. Further,

[41] George P. Fletcher, *ante* p. 626.

those who have caused harm feel guilt and remorse knowing that their actions have had a concrete impact on the lives of others. Such feelings can be regarded as a barometer of moral judgements in this field. If the criminal law is to mirror society and reflect the way we live, it follows that the causing of harm ought to be regarded as critical in the creation and structuring of criminal liability.

V. THE BASIC EQUATION

We have seen that there are degrees of blame and degrees of harm. In order to develop a coherent structure of criminal offences, these degrees need to be broken down with some precision. Using offences against the person (fatal and non-fatal) as a model, these degrees can be expressed, for the sake of simplicity, in symbols.

1. Levels of blame

B1 *intentionally* bringing about the harm *in aggravated circumstances*—(these aggravating circumstances would need to be clearly defined; they would include the matters discussed above relating to the method and circumstances of the crime, and, where appropriate, the identity of the offender and/or victim).

B2 *intentionally* bringing about the harm

B3 *recklessly* bringing about the harm

B4 *negligently* bringing about the harm.[42]

The other indicators of blame could be incorporated within this structure. Thus the defendant who is at fault in getting himself into a situation, such as in *Quick*,[43] when the diabetic brought on his own state of automatism, is being punished, in reality, for his negligence. His level of blame would be B4. If that preceding fault is adjudged to be recklessness, as is the present approach of the English courts to intoxication, then the appropriate level of blame would be B3. The other partial excuses can similarly be incorporated. We might, for instance, wish to excuse the killer who kills in provocation or excessive self-defence or imperfect duress *more* than the killer who kills when intoxicated. If so, B4 would appear to best represent the appropriate degree of blame.

2. Levels of harm

H1 death[44]

H2 "permanent" grievous bodily harm

H3 "temporary" grievous bodily harm[45]

---

[42] It can, of course, be argued quite plausibly that there is no moral distinction between B3 and B4 (see *ante*, p. 179). If such a view were accepted, these two levels could be collapsed into one.

[43] [1973] Q.B. 910—or the defendants in situational crimes (*ante*, p. 119).

[44] An extra category—"death plus aggravation" might be needed to cover cases such as where the victim is made to suffer excessively prior to his death. (*ante*, p. 666). However, it might be more convenient simply to treat such a killer as being in the blame category, B1.

[45] *Ante*, p. 560.

H4 attempted homicide
H5 actual bodily harm; attempted grievous bodily harm
H6 battery; attempted actual bodily harm
H7 technical assault[46]

The precise classification of the nature of the harm involved in an attempt is obviously open to dispute, but it is suggested that the harm involved in attempted homicide would be perceived as worse than actual bodily harm, but not as serious as grievous bodily harm.

This basis of classifying harms is based on the present approach adopted by the law. If the importance of causing harm were to be fully recognised it would open the door to more sophisticated methods of classifying harms.

Andrew von Hirsch, "Guiding Principles for Sentencing: The Proposed Swedish Law" [1987] Crim.L.R. 746, 751–752:

"A simple criterion would be that of violence: crimes are to be deemed more injurious, as the extent of physical injury they visit or threaten increases. But this would not suffice: a variety of seemingly quite serious offences, such as major economic crimes, are not crimes of violence. Recently, I have suggested a broader standard: harms may be graded according to the degree to which they characteristically restrict people's ability to direct the course of their own lives. The gravest harms are those which interfere with almost any choice a person might make. This accounts for our sense of the gravity of violence, for violence restricts victim's choices so drastically. (The person who is murdered has no choices left at all.) The theory also accounts for the harmfulness of certain economic crimes, such as those involving swindling people of their savings. A person cannot order his life if deprived of his means of subsistence. Such a conception addresses harms with individual victims, and needs to be supplemented by a theory for dealing with crimes primarily injurious to state or collective interests, such as treason or tax fraud."

3. Conjunction of elements

What is the relative importance of the two key elements, blame and harm? Is either controlling or to have more weight attached to it in assessing appropriate levels of criminal liability and sentencing ranges? In our view it is the conjunction of these two elements that provides the key for the structuring of all criminal offences; both elements must be equally weighted. This is demonstrated in the following Table. The appropriate levels of criminal liability and/or punishment have been assigned alphabetical symbols ranging in order of seriousness from A, the most serious, downwards.[47]

---

[46] Technical assault and battery are now only summary offences (Criminal Justice Act 1988, s.39). As there can be no attempts to commit summary offences (Criminal Attempts Act 1981, s.1(4)) it follows that there can no longer be such an offence as attempted battery.

[47] This approach has the obvious advantage of objectivity over other attempts to construct an index of crime, which have tended to be based on what was likely to be transitory, atypical samples of public opinion about the relative gravity of offences. See, for example, T. Sellin and M. Wolfgang, *The Measurement of Delinquency* (1964), and R. Sparks, H. Genn and D. Dodd, *Surveying Victims* (1977). See also N. Walker & M. Hough, *Public Attitudes to Sentencing* (1988).

Offences against the Person (including Homicide)

$$B1 + H1 = A$$
$$B2 + H1 = B$$
$$B3 + H1 = C$$
$$B4 + H1 = D$$
$$B1 + H2 = C$$
$$B2 + H2 = D$$
$$B3 + H2 = E$$
$$B4 + H2 = F$$
$$B1 + H3 = E$$
$$B2 + H3 = F$$
$$B3 + H3 = G$$
$$B4 + H3 = H$$
$$B1 + H4 = G^{48}$$
$$B2 + H4 = H$$
$$B1 + H5 = I$$
$$B2 + H5 = J$$
$$B3 + H5 = K^{49}$$
$$B4 + H5 = L^{49}$$
$$B1 + H6 = K$$
$$B2 + H6 = L$$
$$B3 + H6 = M$$
$$B4 + H6 = N$$
$$B1 + H7 = M$$
$$B2 + H7 = N$$

We have not attempted to assign precise penalties to these alphabetical symbols. Suffice it to say that the penalty structure could embrace the whole range of present penalties from life imprisonment down to the non-custodial sentences.

VI. SUBSTANTIVE LAW OR SENTENCING?

The criminal trial is divided into two stages:
1. There is the fact-establishing process before jury or magistrate. At this stage the rules of substantive law are applied to the facts and a determination of guilt or innocence, or degree of guilt, made.
2. The sentencing stage. Here the judge, unassisted by the jury, or the magistrate, determines the appropriate sentence.

The practice of the present English law is "to define offences in fairly broad bands, leaving matters of 'fine tuning' on individual culpability to the sentencer's discretion."[50] Thus *some* of our suggested indicators of blame and harm (such as presence of *mens rea*) are utilised by the present law at the substantive level in fixing offence levels. But others (such as factors aggravating blame or imperfect defences, *e.g.* excessive

[48] With attempted crimes, only levels of blame involving intention will suffice for criminal liability.
[49] This only applies to causing actual bodily harm, not to attempted grievous bodily harm.
[50] M. Wasik, "Excuses at the Sentencing Stage" [1983] Crim. L.R. 450.

self-defence) are only taken into account at the sentencing stage. The judge will take these factors into consideration in exercising his discretion as to the appropriate sentence to be imposed.

The clear implication of our proposals is that some matters currently dealt with at the sentencing stage would be transferred into the substantive law and would help determine the precise offence category. We offer two simple reasons for this proposal:

1. It is the function of the law to draw moral distinctions between offences of differing severity. This serves as notice to the public of the differing degrees of rejection of the prohibited conduct. This is the reason why most people support the retention of the separate crimes of murder and manslaughter, and reject proposals for the creation of a single offence of unlawful homicide.[51] But, at present, offences such as murder, manslaughter, section 18 and section 20 are too broad to be morally informative. Greater specificity is needed. This does not mean that murder need be broken down into numerous degrees—the above Table has only four categories of homicide. But this limited breakdown would enable the law to make the sorts of distinctions we all make in our everyday life—and to better perform its expressive function.

2. The suggested indicators of blame and harm cannot be satisfactorily established at the sentencing stage under the present English sentencing system. Given the broad nature of most present offences, the jury's verdict provides the judge with insufficient guidance as to these various indicators. While it is possible for a judge to hold a "Newton-hearing"[52] in certain cases to attempt to establish some relevant facts before sentencing, it is plainly inappropriate that the judge should be left to decide these matters on his own and sentence offenders on the basis of allegations which have not been proved according to the normal standard of proof "beyond reasonable doubt."[53] This problem is exacerbated when a defendant pleads guilty or when no evidence is adduced on a particular point because it is irrelevant at the substantive stage. As Lord Wilberforce said in *Lynch* in relation to the significance of duress at the sentencing stage:

"If the defence is excluded in law, much of the evidence which would prove the duress would be inadmissible at the trial, not brought out in court, and not tested in cross-examination."[54]

Further, while there is an increasing tendency to cite previous sentencing decisions, these are not binding precedents and have been described as "no more than examples."[55] Even "guideline judgements" are

[51] *Ante*, pp. 668–673.

[52] (1982) 4 Cr.App.R.(S) 388.

[53] This was one of the main reasons why the Criminal Law Revision Committee felt it necessary to maintain the distinction between murder and manslaughter, rather than introducing a single offence of unlawful homicide (Working Paper on Offences against the Person, 1976, para.5).

[54] [1975] A.C. 653, 685; Lord Edmund-Davies was of the same view (p. 707), but Lord Morris was "not greatly impressed" by this argument (pp. 670–671).

[55] *de Havilland* (1983) 5 Cr.App.R.(S.) 109.

not binding precedent to be applied rigidly in every case but merely provide "assistance" to the sentencer.[56] Given this lack of coherent "common law of sentencing," it would be extremely difficult to achieve consistency if the indicators of blame and harm were left to the sentencing stage. Such matters are thus best dealt with at the substantive stage:

"In short, the sentencing process is a disgrace to the common law tradition. Indeed, the absence of a requirement upon sentencers to give reasons and the resistance of certain judges to such a requirement seem to ensure that English sentencing falls below the standards which a court of law should properly attain."[57]

This whole objection could possibly be met by greatly improving the procedures at the post-conviction stage to ensure that matters relevant to sentence are adequately proved.[58] However, unless these matters are to be established by a standard less than "proof beyond reasonable doubt," this proposal seems no different in substance from the one suggested by us, but suffers from the possible defect that distinctions drawn at the sentencing stage might not be perceived as being as morally informative as distinctions drawn at the substantive stage.

It must be emphasised that our proposals only involve shifting our suggested indicators of blame and harm to the substantive level. Many other matters currently relevant at the sentencing stage could continue to be dealt with there. Thus matters such as the defendant's age and record, pleading guilty or not guilty, remorse, assistance to the police, and so on, would all still be dealt with at the post-conviction stage. The point is that while these matters can be construed as relevant to sentence (depending on the basis of one's sentencing system), they are *not* matters relating to our moral assessment of the crime. They have no bearing on blame or harm and therefore are irrelevant to establishing appropriate levels of criminal liability.

It follows that our suggested model is capable of adaptation to almost any sentencing structure. Under the present English sentencing system the alphabetical symbols in the above table could indicate offence levels, each bearing its own maximum penalty, the judge having discretion to impose any sentence up to that maximum. Or, under a guideline model of sentencing, the alphabetical symbols would again indicate the maximum permissible sentence, but a more detailed breakdown would be necessary to indicate the various possible ranges of sentence up to that maximum. Under such a scheme certain "senten-

---

[56] *Temple* (1986) 8 Cr.App.R. (S.) 305; *Nicholas The Times*, April 23, 1986.
[57] A. Ashworth, *Sentencing and Penal Policy*, p. 450.
[58] This is the solution favoured by Ashworth (*ibid.* p. 97) and Wasik "Excuses at the Sentencing Stage" [1983] Crim. L.R. 450. Guidance could certainly be gained here from those U.S. states retaining the death penalty who have devised elaborate sentencing hearings before a jury to determine whether listed aggravating or mitigating circumstances are proved to exist. The death penalty can generally only be imposed if aggravating circumstances are found to exist, and no mitigating circumstances are established. See, for example, Cal. Penal Code, ss.190.1—190.4; Wash. Rev. Code Ann. ss.9A.32.045–046.

cing matters," such as the defendant's prior record, would need to be incorporated into the guidelines.

VII. Conclusion

We openly admit that the above represents no more than the beginnings of a search for a more rational way of constructing criminal liability. Clearly there are rough edges to some of our proposals. But it was felt necessary to be fairly specific if the full implications of our thesis are to be properly assessed. We do fully concede, however, that there can be great disagreement about many of our specific proposals, particularly the final offence levels in the Table. Such specificity and the Table is simply used to demonstrate how a new *method* of constructing criminal liability could operate. In a book of this nature one cannot possibly hope to develop a fully rounded, complete theory of the criminal law. But if our ideas do no more than provoke discussion, then, hopefully, some of the seeds we have tried to plant (or those of our critics) might finally germinate and develop one day into a general theory of the criminal law.

INDEX